Cabinetmaking
and
Millwork

Cabinetmaking

and Millwork

John L. Feirer

Chas. A. Bennett Co., Inc., Peoria, Ill.

Distributed by Charles Scribner's Sons

Popular Science Book Club Edition

Library of Congress Catalogue No. 67-10060

PRINTED IN THE UNITED STATES OF AMERICA

SBN-87002-075-7

VH   10   9   8

LIST OF COLOR ILLUSTRATIONS

Page

Colonial or Early American
furniture 48A
Traditional furniture 48B
Modern furniture 48C
Contemporary furniture 48D, 48E
Italian furniture 48F
Spanish or Mediterranean furniture.... 48G
French furniture 48H
Fine Hardwood Samples
   Ebony, Macassar .... 96^1
   Oak, Red .... 96^2
   Birch .... 96^3
   Teak .... 96^4
   Pecan .... 96^5
   Maple, Hard .... 96^6
   Oak, White .... 96^7
   Rosewood .... 96^8
   Lauan, Red .... 96^9
   Limba .... 96^{10}
   Mahogany, Honduras .... 96^{11}
   Zebrawood .... 96^{12}
   Cherry, American .... 96^{13}
   Mahogany, African .... 96^{14}
   Primavera .... 96^{15}
   Walnut, American .... 96^{16}
Classic style furniture. Illustrates
the use of a wide variety of
materials 144A
Contemporary furniture of this den
blends with materials used to
furnish the room 144B
A family room and its furnishings...... 144C
Interior walls of a home showing
plank-and-beam construction 144D
A family room of Philippine
mahogany 144D
Plastic laminates add beauty and
ease of maintenance to built-ins
of a bathroom 592A
Kitchen showing how plastic
laminates add beauty and utility..... 592A
Modular cabinets; an attractive
study area 592B
Table for a den; dressing table unit.... 592C

Page

Combination studio and kitchen
with exposed beam ceiling and
translucent roof 592D
Early American kitchen 752A
Simple kitchen paneled with
honey-tone oak 752B
Snack bar built of knotty
incense cedar 752B
Elegant kitchen, traditional in
flavor 752C
Modern kitchen, spacious and
beautiful 752D
Handsome all-wood home, com-
bining beauty and warmth of
wood and the skills of the
cabinetmaker's art 784A
Interior of a living room paneled
in pre-finished walnut V-plank
plywood 784B
Walls of a living room paneled
with pre-finished pecan plywood
of V-plank design, grooved
vertically 784C
Built-in wall of cabinets and
bookcase 784D
Living room paneled in solid
redwood 784D
Early American or Colonial
furniture, with dark, English-
tavern finish 816A
Color used in a bedroom to make
it bright and gay 816B
Kitchen playroom, gaily decorated..... 816C
Red oak kitchen cabinets 816D
Furniture for schools and
institutions ....
Dormitory rooms, functional and
attractive 912A
Restaurant showing use of plastic
laminates 912B
Clothing-store counter unit 912C
Plastic laminates used for walls
and counter tops of restaurant........ 912D

ACKNOWLEDGMENT LIST

Adjustable Clamp Company
Ajax Hardware Corporation
Allis-Chalmers Manufacturing Company
American Forest Products Industries
American Hardboard Association
American Plywood Association
Andersen Corporation
Architectural Woodworking Institute
Armstrong Machine Works
Atlas Press Company
Auto-Nailer Company
Baker Furniture Company
Barton Wood Products, Incorporated
G. M. Basford Company
Bassett Furniture Industries
Baumritter Corporation
Behr-Manning Division of Norton Company
Bell Machine Company
Robert Benjamin Incorporated
Better Homes and Gardens
The Black Brothers' Company
The Black and Decker Manufacturing Company
Boice-Crane Company
Bostitch Incorporated
The Brandt Cabinet Works, Incorporated
Brett-Guard Corporation
British Columbia Industrial Design Committee
Buck Brothers Company
Buss Machine Works, Incorporated
California Redwood Association
Caterpillar Tractor Company
Clamp Nail Company
Cleveland Twist Drill Company
Columbia Fastener Company
The Columbus Show Case Company
Comet Industries Corporation
The Conde' Nast Publications Incorporated
Curtis Companies, Incorporated
H. T. Cushman Manufacturing Company
Dansk Designs, Incorporated
Davis and Wells Company
Dependable Machine Company, Incorporated
The DeVilbiss Company
Diehl Machines, Incorporated
Disston Saw Company
Dodds Machinery Company
Drexel Furniture Company
Dunbar Furniture Corporation
Duro Metal Products Company
Dux, Incorporated
L. G. Edelen Company, Incorporated
Ekstrom, Carlson and Company

Fine Hardwoods Association
Foley Saw Company
Ford Motor Company (Educational Affairs)
Formica Corporation
Francher Furniture Company
The Franklin Glue Company
Frederick Post Company
Furniture Design and Manufacturing
Gamble Brothers
General Electric Company
Georgia-Pacific Corporation
The Otto Gerdau Company
Gizco
Greenlee Bros. and Company
Grant Pulley and Hardware Corporation
Hamilton Manufacturing Company
Handy Manufacturing Company
Hardwood Dimension Manufacturers
   Association
Hardwood Plywood Institute
Hekman Furniture Company
Heritage Furniture Company
Hillyer Deutsch Edwards, Incorporated
Holub Industries, Incorporated
Huther Brothers, Incorporated
Imperial Furniture Company
Independent Nail and Packing Company
International Paper Company
Arvids Iraids Multi-purpose Spring Clamps
I-XL Furniture
Janet Rosenblum
Jansen Furniture Company
Jens Risom Design, Incorporated
B. P. John Furniture Company
Johnson Furniture Company
Jones Sheet Metal, Incorporated
Keller Products Incorporated
Kewaunee Manufacturing Company
Knape and Vogt Manufacturing Company
Knoll Associates, Incorporated
Kreamer Snyder Company
The Lane Company, Incorporated
Mahogany Association, Incorporated
B. L. Marble Furniture, Incorporated
Martin Senour Paints
Masonite Corporation
Mattison Machine Works, Incorporated
Mereen-Johnson Machine Company
Howard Miller Clock Co.
Millers Falls Company
Minnesota Mining and Manufacturing Company
Minnesota Woodworkers Supply Company

5

Misener Manufacturing Company, Incorporated
Module Grille Company
Mohawk Furniture Finishing Products, Incorporated
Molly Corporation
Benjamin Moore and Company
Mutschler Brothers Company
Myrtle Desk Company
Nash-Bell-Dyken-Challoner Machine Companies
National Lock Company
National Lumber Manufacturers Association
National Particleboard Association
National Safety Council
National Woodwork Manufacturers Association
Newman Machine Company, Incorporated
Noblecraft Industries, Incorporated
Nordson Corporation
Northfield Foundry and Machine Company
Ohio Blow Pipe Company
Oliver Machinery Company
Onsrud Machine Works, Incorporated
Panelyte Division, St. Regis Paper Company
Frank Paxton Lumber Company
Perkins Glue Company
Philippine Mahogany Association, Incorporated
Pittsburgh Plate Glass Company
Ply-Curves Incorporated
C. A. Porter Machinery Company
H. K. Porter Company, Incorporated
Powermatic Incorporated
Red Devil Tools
Rockwell Manufacturing Company
Rolscreen Company
Ronthor Reiss Corporation
B. M. Root Company
Saranac Machine Company
Scandiline Furniture Incorporated
Scandinavian Design, Incorporated
Sears Roebuck and Company
Shakeproof—Division of Illinois Tool Works Incorporated
Sherwin-Williams Company
Simonds Saw and Steel Company
Skil Corporation
Snap-on Tools Corporation
Solem Machine Company
Southern Hardwood Lumber Manufacturers Association
Southern Pine Association
Sprague and Carleton Incorporated
Stanley Tools
Star Chemical Company, Incorporated
John Stuart Incorporated
George Tanier, Incorporated
The Tannewitz Works
James L. Taylor Manufacturing Company
Thomas Industries Incorporated
Thonet Industries, Incorporated

Tomlinson Furniture Company
Torit Manufacturing Company
Union-National, Incorporated
United States Department of Agriculture
United States Forest Service, Forest Products Laboratory
United States Plywood Corporation
Watco-Dennis Corporation
Weldotron Corporation
West Coast Lumbermen's Association
Western Electric Company
Western Pine Association
Western Wood Products Association
Westinghouse Electric Corporation
Weyerhaeuser Company
Baxter D. Whitney and Sons, Incorporated
The Widdicomb Furniture Company
Wilkenson Manufacturing Company
Winchendon Furniture Company
Winzeler Stamping Company
Wisconsin Knife Works
Wood-Mode Kitchens
WorkRite Products Company
Wysong and Miles Company
Xacto Company
Yates-American Machine Company

The completion of this book was brought about through the cooperation of many persons in the organizations listed above. Also of much value was the research carried out by the Forest Products Laboratory. To all who assisted, the author is grateful.

A special note of thanks goes to two individuals and their companies for unusual help in supplying illustrations for this book. Mr. William F. Kinderwater, Manager of Public Information Services of The Black and Decker Manufacturing Company, was of great help in making available all the illustrations for Unit 27 and many others showing the radial-arm saw throughout the book. Mr. Kinderwater also gave permission to use certain project ideas that were formerly the property of the Atlas Press Company but are now owned by his company. Mr. John E. Greguric, editor of *Rockwell Power Tool Instructor*, a publication of Rockwell Manufacturing Company, supplied many of the illustrations that appear in Units 26 through 37.

▼ PREFACE...

THIS BOOK has been designed for an advanced course in woodworking. It will also aid anyone interested in the fundamentals of materials, tools, machines, and processes that are used in the building of cabinets and interiors, the production of furniture, and the other work of the finish carpenter, cabinetmaker, and millman.

The book can be used in the upper levels of the senior high school, in vocational and technical schools, and in colleges. It will be useful for studying not only cabinetmaking but also building construction and related activities. It includes coverage of which woods to use, and why and how to use them, in the interiors of homes and commercial buildings. Fixed installations such as paneling, built-ins, and cabinets are discussed, as well as movable wood products such as furniture and fixtures.

In the present industrial world, the cabinetmaker, finish carpenter, and millman require knowledge and skills that are very similar; any of these people can profit by the use of this textbook. So can those entering any area of the business and professional world which relates to furniture, building construction, or other wood industries. The prospective interior designer, the furniture designer, the industrial-education teacher, the architect, and those who sell lumber and lumber products will all find valuable information in these pages. Finally, the book should have great appeal to anyone who likes to work with woods, tools, and machines as a hobby.

The reader should note that the title of the book is CABINETMAKING, not THE CABINETMAKER. This emphasizes that the field of cabinetmaking is important to many workers besides those who are formally known as cabinetmakers. Essen-

tially, cabinetmaking is the fundamental base on which all other occupations relating to woodworking must rest. The term "cabinetmaking" denotes skill in the use of tools and machines, an appreciation of good design, and a feeling for beauty in wood *wherever it is used*. The skillful use of hand and machine tools is not in itself sufficient for the person interested in cabinetmaking. He must understand the nature of the material with which he works. He must also have an appreciation of what modern science and technology have accomplished in his field.

There are those who think of cabinetmaking as an old field that has not changed much since the days of Chippendale, Duncan Phyfe, or the Adams Brothers. One only has to look at the synthetic finishes, abrasives, and the applications of electronics and fluid power in cabinetmaking to realize that this area has been changed as much by modern science and technology as any other field. The good things that should remain from the great cabinetmakers of a century or more ago are attention to good design, the use of fine woods, and an appreciation of excellent craftsmanship. These are the elements that tie the cabinetmaker of old to modern cabinetmaking.

In keeping with the modern content, a special attempt has been made to design this book with great visual appeal. Two-color printing has been used throughout to emphasize the important points of each process or procedure. In addition, four-color illustrations have been included to show the true beauty of wood in furniture and interiors. The importance of cabinetmaking to the woodworking field has been stressed.

JOHN L. FEIRER

7

Table of Contents

List of Color Illustrations 4

Acknowledgment List 5

Preface 7

Table of Contents 8

Section I. Introduction 15

    1. CABINETMAKING—THE KEY TO ALL WOODWORKING 16
    History of Cabinetmaking, Millwork, 20; Survey of Occupations, 23; Training Requirements for Cabinetmaking, 24; Cabinetmaking for Pleasure, 25; Occupations Associated with Wood, 27.

    2. FURNITURE DESIGNS 29
    Early American or Colonial, 29; Traditional, 30; Contemporary, including Modern, Scandinavian, Transitional, and Oriental, 35; French Provincial, 37; Italian Provincial, 39; Spanish or Mediterranean, 40.

    3. DESIGNING FURNITURE AND CABINETS 41
    Fundamentals of Good Design, 41; Average Furniture Sizes, 42; Construction, 44; Elements of Design, 45; Principles of Design, 50; Common Errors in Furniture and Cabinet Design, 53; Steps in Designing Furniture, 54; Simplified Style Changes, 56; Making a Working Drawing from a Picture or Sketch, 57.

    4. SAFETY AND HOUSEKEEPING 57
    Dress, 58; Housekeeping, Courtesy to Other Workers, Hand Tools, 60; Portable Power Tools, Woodworking Machines, 61; Always Plan Your Work Before Starting, 62; Fire Control, Treatment of Accidents, 63.
    Questions and Discussion Topics, 63; Problems and Activities, 64.

Section II. Materials and Layouts 65

    5. WOOD—ITS NATURE AND PROPERTIES 66
    Parts of a Tree, 66; Specific Gravity of Lumber, 67; Cell Structure, Growth Rings, 69; Springwood and Summerwood, Sapwood and Heartwood, Other Characteristics, 70; Cutting Methods, 71; Hardwoods and Softwoods, Seasoning, 72; Shrinkage of Lumber, 75; Lumber Defects, 76.

    6. KINDS OF WOODS 80
    Softwoods: Douglas-Fir, Western Larch, 82; Ponderosa Pine, 83; Shortleaf Pine, 84; Sugar Pine, 85; Western White Pine, Redwood, 86; Sitka Spruce, 87; Hardwoods: White Ash, 88; American Basswood, American Beech, 89; Yellow Birch, 90; Black Cherry, Cottonwood, 91; Rock Elm, 92; American Elm, 93; Hickory, Mahogany, 94; Mahogany, Philippine, 95; Sugar Maple, White

Oak, 96; Red Oak, 97; Pecan, Sweetgum, 98; Black Walnut, 99; Yellow-Poplar, 100.

7. FINE FURNITURE WOODS **101**
Walnut, 101; Mahogany, 103; Cherry, 105; Maple and Birch, 108; Oak, 110; The Exotics, 112.

8. PLYWOOD **116**
Advantages of Plywood, 117; Kinds of Plywood Construction, Balanced Construction, 118; Manufacture of Plywood, 120; Hardwood Plywood Grading, 123; Softwood Plywoods, Plywood Products with Special Properties, 125; Working with Plywood, 127.

9. HARDBOARD AND PARTICLE BOARD **129**
Hardboard, 129; Typical Working Characteristics, Typical End Uses, 135; Particle Board, 136.

10. MILLWORK INCLUDING MOLDING **139**
Millwork, 142; Moldings, 145.

11. FASTENERS **147**
Nails, 148; Other Types of Nails and Staples, Nailing Tools, 149; Nailing Techniques, 150; Screws, 151; Chart of Screw Sizes, 153; Kinds of Screwdrivers, 154; Installing Screws, 156; Hollow-Wall Fastening Devices, 158; Fasteners for Masonry Walls, 160; Miter-Joint Fasteners, 161; Other Fasteners for Furniture, Repair Plates, 162.

12. HARDWARE **162**

13. GLASS AND MIRRORS **166**
Production of Glass, 166; Kinds of Glass, 167; Cutting Glass, Steps in Cutting Glass, 169; Installing Glass, Plate or Crystal Glass for Furniture, 172.

14. MACHINE-MADE CANE WEBBING **172**
Kinds of Cane, 172; Installing Cane, 173.

15. ORDERING LUMBER AND OTHER MATERIALS **174**
Solid Lumber, 174; Other Materials, Lumber Sizes, 175; Common Lumber Abbreviations, 176; Lumber Grading, 177; Standard Hardwood Grades, 180; Writing Lumber Specifications, 181; Measuring the Amount of Lumber, 183.

16. READING PRINTS AND MAKING SKETCHES **185**
Elements of Drawing, Scale, 189; Kinds of Drawings, 191; Pictorial Drawings, 192; Multiview Drawings, 193; Architectural Drawings, 201; Making a Sketch, 204.

17. MATERIAL NEEDS, PLANNING, AND ESTIMATING **205**
Points to Remember in Stock Billing, Making a Lumber and Materials Order, 206; Supplies, Fasteners and Hardware List, 208; Developing a Plan of Procedure, Estimating, 210; Materials, Labor, Overhead and Profit, 213.

18. MAKING A LAYOUT -- 213
Steel Square, 214; Geometric Construction, 216; Enlarging and
Transferring an Irregular Design, Layout on the Rod, 220.
*Questions and Discussion Topics, 224; Problems and Activities,
226.*

Section III. Tools and Machines ------------------------------------ 227

19. LAYOUT, MEASURING, AND CHECKING DEVICES --------------------- 228

20. SAWING TOOLS --- 230

21. EDGE-CUTTING TOOLS --- 231

22. DRILLING AND BORING TOOLS -------------------------------------- 234

23. METALWORKING TOOLS -- 235

24. TOOL AND MACHINE MAINTENANCE --------------------------------- 237
Equipment for Sharpening, 237; Sharpening Hand Tools, 239;
Sharpening a Hand Saw, 245; Machine Tools, 250.

25. PLANER OR SURFACER -- 260
Parts and Controls, 261; Operating Procedure, 263; Squaring Up
Legs, Planing Thin Stock, 264; Surfacer Planer, Planer Hints, 265;
Abrasive Planing, 266.

26. CIRCULAR OR VARIETY SAW --- 267
Common Adjustments, 268; Guards and Other Protective Devices,
269; Circular Saw, Commercial Accessories, 270; Selecting the
Saw Blades, 273; Replacing a Blade, 274; Crosscutting Operations,
277; Ripping Operations, 282; Cutting Wedges or Triangular
Pieces, 289; Taper Cutting with a Fixed Jig, with an Adjustable
Jig, 290; Using the Dado Head, 292; Cutting Joints, 294; Cutting
Coves, Saw-Cut Moldings, Molding Head, 303.

27. RADIAL-ARM SAW --- 306
Radial-Arm Saw, 307; Accessories, 308; Saw Blades, Replacing a
Saw Blade, Common Adjustments, 309; Crosscutting Operations,
310; Ripping, 316; Horizontal Cutting, 320; Using a Dado Head,
321; Joinery, Cutting Joints, 325; Special Cutting Operations, 333;
Molding Operations, 335.

28. BAND SAW -- 337
Sizes and Parts, 337; Band-Saw Blades, Replacing a Blade, 339;
Band Saw, 340; Basic Operating Techniques, 342; Cutting Curves,
346; Compound Sawing, 347; Cutting Circles, 348; Sawing with a
Pattern Guide, 350; Multiple Sawing, 351.

29. JIG OR SCROLL SAW --- 351
Parts and Size, 351; Jig or Scroll Saw, Blade Selection, 353; In-
stalling a Blade, External Curve Cutting, 355; Internal Curve
Cutting, Straight Cutting, 356; Bevel Cuts or Angle Sawing,

Making Identical Parts, Cutting Thin Metal, Making a Simple Inlay, 358; Making a Coped Joint, Filing Attachments, 359.

30. PORTABLE SAWS AND PLANES 360
Portable Power Saw, 360; Panel Saw, 362; Portable Saws and Planes, Bayonet Saw, 363; Jig Saw Blades for Cutting Different Materials, 364; Reciprocating Saw, 367; Portable Planes, 368.

31. JOINTER 370
Parts and Sizes, 370; Adjusting the Rear Table or Cutter Head, 371; Adjusting for Depth of Cut, 372; Jointer, Adjusting the Fence, 373; Methods of Holding Stock for Feeding, 374; Facing or Surfacing, 375; Edge Jointing, 376; End Jointing, Squaring Up Stock, 377; Rabbeting, Beveling and Chamfering, Stop Chamfering, Cutting a Long Taper, 378; Cutting a Stop Taper, 379; Cutting a Short Taper, Honing, 380.

32. SHAPER 381
Parts, 381; Kinds of Cutters, 383; Shaper, 384; Installing the Cutters, 385; Adjusting the Shaper, Methods of Shaping, 386; Shaping on the Radial-Arm Saw, 391; Shaping on the Drill Press, 393.

33. ROUTERS 394
Portable Router, Router, 395; Common Shapes of Router Bits, 397; Controlling the Cutting, 398; Floor-Type Router, 408; Routing on the Radial-Arm Saw, 411.

34. DRILLING AND BORING MACHINES 412
Stationary Equipment, 412; Portable Equipment, 414; Drilling and Boring Machines, 416; Cutting Tools, 417; Using the Drill Press, 418; Using Portable Electric Drills, Using a Single-Spindle Boring Machine, 430; Drilling and Boring on a Radial-Arm Saw, 431.

35. MORTISER AND TENONER 433
Mortiser, Parts, 433; Using the Mortiser, 435; Mortising Attachment, 437; Single-End Tenoner, Tenoner, 439.

36. SANDING MACHINES AND COATED ABRASIVES............................ 441
Coated Abrasives, 441; Sanding Machines, Crushing and Grading, 442; Kinds of Backings, Adhesives or Bonds, Manufacturing, 443; Forms of Coated Abrasives, 445; Kinds of Sanding, Sanding Machines, 446; Radial-Arm Saw as a Sander, 457; Band Saw as a Sander, 458; Drill Press as a Sander, Jigsaw with Sanding Attachment, Hand Sanding, 459.

37. WOOD LATHE 461
Parts and Sizes, 461; Wood Lathe, 462; Tools, Kinds of Turning, 465; Spindle Turning, 466; Duplicator Attachment, 477; Faceplate Turning, 480; Finishing, 484.
Questions and Discussion Topics, 484; Problems and Activities, 486.

Section IV. Construction ----------------------------------- 487

38. BASIC CONSTRUCTION PROBLEMS ----------------------------- 488
Kinds of Construction, 488; Selection and Treatment of Woods, 494; Determining Moisture Content of Lumber, Peg-Treated Woods, 495; Working with Hardwoods, Characteristics That Affect Machining, 496; Sawing, Planing, 500; Shaping, 503; Wood Turning, Boring, 504; Mortising, Sanding, Compatibility of Grain and Color, 505.

39. C ____NETMAKING JOINTS -------------------------------- 507
Elements of Joinery, 507; Fastening and Strengthening Joints, 509; Kinds of Joints, 517.

40. GLUING AND CLAMPING --------------------------------- 533
Problems in Gluing, 534; Kinds of Adhesives, 535; Clamping Devices, 538; Gluing Procedure, 543; Assembling Cabinets and Furniture, 548; Gluing Problems, 549.

41. BENDING AND LAMINATING ------------------------------- 551
Procedure for Laminating and Bending, 558.

42. VENEERING AND INLAYING ------------------------------- 561
Method of Cutting, 562; Kinds of Veneers, 565; Matching Veneers, Tools and Materials for Veneering, 566; Cutting Veneers, 567; Applying Fine Veneer to a Panel Core, 568; Making Lumber-Core Plywood, 572; Marquetry and Built-Up Patterns, Inlaying, 573.

43. PLASTIC LAMINATES ----------------------------------- 575
Grades of Laminates, 576; Sheet Sizes, 577; Core Materials, Adhesives, 578; Clamping and Pressure for Bonding, Methods of Cutting, 579; Drilling and Boring, 580; Edge Treatment and Banding, 582; Metal Moldings, Applying Laminate to a Table Top, 586; Applying Laminate to Counter Tops, 588; Applying Laminate to Kitchen-Cabinet Fronts, 589; Other Uses for Plastic Laminates in the Home, 592.

44. FRAME-AND-PANEL CONSTRUCTION ------------------------- 593
Interior Cabinet Parts, 593; Exterior Furniture Parts and Architectural Woodwork, 596; Cutting the Molded Edges (Sticking), 600; Cutting a Raised Panel, 603; Making a Frame and Panel, 605.

45. CABINET AND FURNITURE DOORS -------------------------- 606
Material for Furniture and Case Doors, 607; Hanging Doors, 612; Catches, Pulls and Knobs, 624.

46. DRAWERS AND DRAWER GUIDES ---------------------------- 626
Types of Drawers, 627; Parts of a Drawer, 628; Drawer Joinery, 632; Kinds of Drawer Supports, 637; Drawer Guides, 639; Drawer Opening Devices, 645; Drawer Dividers, Planning for Drawer Construction, 646; Constructing a Drawer, 647; Quality of Drawer Construction, 648; Trays, 649.

47. SHELVES AND CABINET INTERIORS ----------------------------------- **650**
Designing the Shelving, 650; Stationary or Fixed Shelving, 651;
Adjustable Shelving, 652; Closet Shelving and Fixtures, 658.

48. LEGS AND POSTS --- **659**
Common Leg Shapes, 661; Reeding and Fluting, 666; Joining
Tripod Table Legs, 671; Commercial Legs, 674.

49. LEG-AND-RAIL CONSTRUCTION --------------------------------------- **674**
Kinds of Leg-and-Rail Joinery, 674; Installing a Drawer, 678;
Installing the Lower Shelf, Chair Construction, 679.

50. TABLE AND CABINET TOPS -- **682**
Kinds of Table and Cabinet Tops, 682; Edge Treatment, Drop-
Leaf Tables, 687; Dining Table Tops with Removable Leaves,
690; Fastening Tops to Furniture, 693; Fastening Tops to Casework, Drop-Leaf Table, 694.

51. BASIC CASEWORK --- **697**
Materials, 697; Interior Construction, Base or Legs, 698; Construction of Corners and Backs, 701; Installing Drawers and
Doors, 702; Faceplate and Trim, 703; Assembly, Finish, 705; Examples of Simple Casework, 706.

52. FINE FURNITURE CABINETWORK ------------------------------------- **714**
Types of Cabinet Corner Construction, 718; Typical Chests,
Larger Cabinet Pieces, 719.

53. KITCHEN CABINETS --- **728**
Methods of Producing Kitchen Cabinetry, 731; Kinds of Cabinets,
735; Planning the Kitchen Layout and Cabinets, 737; Kitchen
Arrangements, 738; Installing Mill or Factory-Built Cabinets,
742; Building Kitchen Cabinets on the Job, 746; Sample Kitchen
Cabinets, 748.

54. PANELING --- **761**
Kinds of Paneling, 761; Installing Solid Wood Paneling, 763;
Installing Plywood Panels, 768.

55. BUILT-INS, INCLUDING ROOM DIVIDERS ----------------------------- **770**
Kinds of Built-Ins, 773; General Procedure for Constructing
Built-Ins, 776; Building a Storage Wall, 777; Room Dividers, 781.
*Questions and Discussion Topics, 782; Problems and Activities,
784.*

Section V. Finishing --- **785**

56. PREPARATION FOR FINISHING -------------------------------------- **786**
Removing Excess Glue, Repairing Wood Surfaces, 786; Bleaching,
788; Removing Hardware, Final Sanding of Casework and Built-
Ins, 791; Final Sanding of Furniture, 792.

57. FINISHING EQUIPMENT AND SUPPLIES ------------------------------- **793**
Portable Spraying, Using a Spray Gun in a Booth, 797; Spraying

Techniques, 798; Common Spraying Problems, 800; Cleaning a Suction-Feed Gun, Finishing Supplies, 801; Brushes, 803; Rollers, 804.

58. FINISHING PROCEDURES 804
A Standard Finishing System, 805; Finishing Open-Grained Wood, Commercial Synthetic Finishes, 807; Watco Natural Wood or Danish Oil Finish, 808; Synthetic Sealer Finishes, 809; Simplified Shop Finishes, 810.

59. STAINING 811
Sap Staining, Ingredients in Stains, Kinds of Stains, 812; Common Colors in Oil, Using Colors in Oil for Finishing, Oil Stains, 814; Non-Grain-Raising Stains (NGR), 815; Sealer Stains, 816.

60. FILLING 816
Kinds of Fillers, 816; Applying Paste Fillers, 817; Applying Liquid Fillers, Filling Defects, 819; Applying a Sealer, 820.

61. DISTRESSING, GLAZING, AND OTHER OVERTONE TREATMENTS 820
Distressing, 820; Glazing, 821; Other Treatments, 822.

62. PROTECTIVE COATINGS 822
Lacquer, 822; Varnish, 825; Synthetics, Rubbing, Polishing, and Cleaning, 826; Commercial Finishing Methods, 827; Shop Methods, 828.

63. INTERIOR FINISHING 829
Finishing Solid Wood Paneling and Interiors, 829; Finishing Hardwood Plywood, Finishing Softwood Plywood, 832.
Questions and Discussion Topics, 833; Problems and Activities, 834.

Section VI. Industrial Production 835

64. PRODUCTION EQUIPMENT 836
Cutting Room or Rough Mill, 836; Gluing Equipment, 840; Veneering, Laminating, and Bending Department, 842; Machining Department, 848; Carving Department, Sanding Department, 862; Assembly Department, 868; Spraying Department, 872.

65. WOODWORKING MANUFACTURING 875
Furniture Manufacturing, 875; Kitchen-Cabinet Manufacturing, 888; Engineering and Drafting Equipment Manufacturing, 890.

66. STORE, OFFICE, AND INSTITUTIONAL FIXTURES 895
Materials, 896; Wall Cases, 898; Show or Display Cases, Counters, Central Shelving and Gondolas, 903; Fixture for Dining Establishments, Office and Bank Fixtures, Health, Research, and Other Institutional Fixtures, 905; Installing Plastic-Laminate Paneling, 907; Installing Fixtures, 911.
Questions and Discussion Topics, Problems and Activities, 913.

Index 914

A high degree of cabinetmaking skill and knowledge is represented in this combination kitchen and family room. Note the attractive cabinets, the serving bar with plastic-laminate top, the casework under the bar, the special millwork, and the furniture.

Section I

Introduction

1 Cabinetmaking—The Key To All Woodworking

Cabinetmaking is the key to all woodworking. Its basic skills and knowledge are needed by everyone who works in wood, whether or not he carries the title of cabinetmaker. Fig. 1-1.

Look at the description of what a cabinetmaker must be able to do: He performs hand and machine operations necessary to lay out, cut, shape, and assemble prepared parts of high-quality products for furniture, cabinets, store fixtures, office equipment, and home furniture. He studies drawings of products to be made, and lays out an outline or dimension of the parts on the stock to certain specifications. He also operates such woodworking machines as the radial-arm saw, circular saw, band saw, jointer, mortiser, and others, to cut and shape parts. Fig. 1-2. He bores holes for installing screws or dowels by hand or machine. He adds glue to parts and clamps them together. He inserts nails, dowels, and screws through joints to reinforce them. He glues and fits sub-assemblies and other parts together to form completed units. He smooths surfaces with scrapers and sandpaper. He must also install hardware such as hinges, catches, and drawer pulls.

There are some who still think of the cabinetmaker as a specialized woodworker who laboriously builds a piece of furniture using hand tools and hand con-

1-1. To build this beautiful cabinetwork and install the paneling above the fireplace, the woodworker needs much the same skills as those for making furniture.

1-2. This young man is learning the correct use of machine tools. Notice the sensible way he is dressed.

1-3. Very little furniture is produced piece by piece as this old-time cabinetmaker is doing. These people are both rare and highly skilled.

1-4. This *finish carpenter* has opened his tool kit and is ready to install the interior paneling in a home.

1-5. Constructing and installing store fixtures like these require the skills of cabinetmaking.

1-6. Building and installing kitchen cabinets of this quality can be done only by the skilled workman. compare the quality of construction with some of the furniture illustrated in this book.

trolled machine tools. Fig. 1-3. This occupation has been adversely affected by mass production. Yet the "know-how" of cabinetmaking is becoming increasingly important to the finish carpenter, millman, patternmaker, and even the boat builder. Today a little fewer than 100,000 persons are employed strictly as *cabinetmakers.* The closely associated field of *carpentry,* however, is the largest skilled trade in the United States, employing over one million people. In carpentry there are two types of work: rough carpentry and finish carpentry. Let's look at the work of the *finish carpenter.* He cuts, fits, and installs moldings, baseboards, door frames, doors, hardwood floors, windows, paneling, kitchen and bathroom cabinets and built-ins, and performs a wide variety of other work requiring the skillful use of many different tools and machines. Fig. 1-4. His work is classified as finish or trim work, as distinguished from rough work. He is the woodworker who installs the visible items in a building—such as listed above.

18

1-7. The design for a piece of furniture such as this movable chest is the responsibility of the furniture designer.

His work must be done accurately and carefully.

Note the similarity between the two occupational groups of finish carpenter and cabinetmaker. Many of the same skills and knowledge are required by both. The need for cabinetmaking skills is increasing. With more production-type homes being built, there is great need for woodworkers who can do the details of finish carpentry. Skilled men are also needed to specialize in remodeling and installing office, store, and bank fixtures. Fig. 1-5. Today more than ever before the finish carpenter must know excellent cabinetmaking. In better-quality homes, a large part of the total cost is involved in the labor and materials that go into paneling, cabinetwork, and built-ins. Many of today's kitchen cabinets are equal in quality—as far as woods used, workmanship, and finish are concerned —to some of our finest furniture. Fig. 1-6.

Built-ins for bedrooms, dens, bathrooms, and family rooms are made of both solid wood and plywood. Many architects include designs for movable cases and other special furniture that must be custom-built by the skilled carpenter or cabinetmaker. Fig. 1-7. Hotels, motels, and apartments built of steel and concrete have wood interior units that require high-grade cabinetmaking. Modelmakers who work for automobile companies or aircraft manufacturers must be

1-8. The great cabinetmakers of 18th-century England achieved such stately, balanced beauty in furniture design that their creations have survived the fads of many succeeding generations.

1-9. Furniture manufacturers make use of automated equipment and assembly-line techniques the same as do all other major manufacturers. In spite of this, there is much more hand work than in automotive manufacturing.

skilled cabinetmakers. As mentioned earlier, even the wood patternmaker and boat builder must know the essentials of cabinetmaking. So, too, must the mill-man in production plants who grinds knives and saws and sets up production equipment. Some cabinetmakers continue to be needed in custom cabinet shops where furniture is made to order.

HISTORY OF CABINETMAKING

Since earliest times, two of mankind's basic requirements have been shelter and furniture. People began to use wood wherever it was available for their homes and furnishings. During and shortly after the Renaissance, from the 14th to the 17th centuries, there was an increased interest in fine woodworking for both interiors and home furnishings. Cabinetmaking reached the height of individual achievement during the 18th century. This period was known as the Golden Age of furniture design. Fig. 1-8. The designs of the "Big Four" of the

18th century set the standards. These designers included Thomas Chippendale, George Hepplewhite, Thomas Sheraton, and the Adams Brothers. Many of their apprentices came to America and established shops of their own. Then, as production machines began to produce furniture less expensively, most of such cabinetmakers closed up shop. Duncan Phyfe, who was an immigrant from Scotland, was the only American designer-cabinetmaker for whom a style of furniture was named. At one time he employed as many as 100 cabinetmakers, turning out some of the finest furniture then available. Even he was forced to close his shop when the machine began to take over the manufacture of furniture.

HISTORY OF MILLWORK

In the early history of the United States, homes were built almost entirely by hand on the site. These early homes, some of which can still be seen, included excellent examples of cabinetmaking created by the early carpenter who made his own doors, shutters, moldings, and trim. In many cases, the skills and knowledge of early carpenter-cabinetmakers were acquired in the Old World. Some of these men excelled in fabricating more complicated wood items such as windows, doors, and cabinets. They emerged as the *millmen* who set up wood shops to fill the needs of local communities. The millman's counterpart is still found in custom shops, mills, and furniture plants throughout this nation. As production equipment became available, the need for large numbers of skilled cabinetmakers who could make an entire piece by hand began to decrease. Today, mass-produced furniture of the large plants requires only a limited number of skilled cabinetmakers and millmen. They create the experimental models, grind the knives, set up machines, and make other

1-10(a). This manufacturer specializes in kitchen cabinets. Such plants also have assembly lines.

contributions to fine millwork and furniture making.

Production Furniture Plants

Production furniture plants utilize high-volume, semi-automated and automated equipment to produce completed furniture. Fig. 1-9. Many furniture factories specialize in certain types or styles of furniture, while others have a general line. In the furniture factory, assembly-line techniques produce large numbers of identical pieces. In all plants, the great majority of the work can be done by semi-skilled workers with need for only a few skilled cabinetmakers and millmen to handle the highly skilled jobs. The professional people in furniture manufacturing must know many wood species, which ones to use for various furniture parts and types, how the parts can be fabricated, and how to finish each for best results.

Custom Furniture Plants

Custom furniture plants are small establishments which employ anywhere from 2 to 20 people to produce furniture

of unusual design to specification, and to reproduce antique styles. Others work in conjunction with interior designers to create special pieces of furniture. Still others specialize in traditional designs as well as in the reproduction of antiques.

Millwork Plants

Millwork plants produce a large volume of units required by the building industry for doors, sash frames, moldings, panels, and many other items. Fig. 1-10. There are two types of millwork: stock millwork and special millwork. Stock millwork is manufactured in large quantities featuring standardized designs, sizes, grades, and types. A good example is found in the kitchen-cabinet industry which annually produces well over 1/4 billion dollars worth of millmade kitchen cabinets. Specialized millwork is that which is produced from architectural or detailed plans rather than from stock plans. This kind of millwork is usually done under a contract plan. An example of this is the special millwork needed for churches and commercial interiors.

Fixture Manufacturers

Some companies specialize in the manufacture of fixtures for stores, offices,

1-10(b). Compare this method of construction with units built individually by the skilled carpenter.

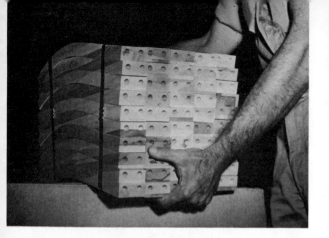

1-11. These are frame parts for chairs made by a hardwood dimension manufacturer. They are ready for shipment to a furniture plant.

1-13. This *cabinetmaker* is a specialist in sanding operations. He builds jigs for production work.

banks, and other commercial buildings. If fixtures are produced for chain stores, much of the work is standardized as to design. However, for other kinds of establishments, the fixtures are custom designed.

Hardwood Dimension Plants

These are wood-production plants that specialize in the manufacture of quality furniture parts rather than the completed product. They are usually located near a good source of hardwood lumber and have their own kiln-drying and production equipment. These plants will produce any part or all of the parts in great quantity for the furniture or other wood-product manufacturer. Fig. 1-11. However, they *do not* assemble and finish complete items.

Specialized Woodworking Manufacturers

Many other manufacturers use wood either in limited amounts or almost com-

1-12. This set of chalkboard drawing instruments is typical of the product of the specialized wood manufacturer.

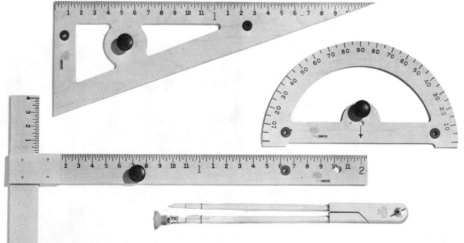

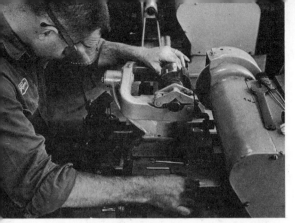

1-14(a). Sharpening, adjusting and setting knives require specialized skills of a *millman*.

pletely in the production of items such as scientific instruments, musical instruments, and sports equipment. Fig. 1-12. Others specialize in wood toys, novelties, and industrial and school equipment.

SURVEY OF OCCUPATIONS

Following is a survey of the major occupational areas that either require skill in cabinetmaking or are associated with the trade:

Vocational and Skilled Occupations

• The CABINETMAKER may be an all-around woodworker or he may be a specialist such as an assembly man, a bench workman, a cabinet-frame assembler, a detailer, or a layout man. Fig. 1-13.

• The MILLMAN may be an all-around machine woodworker or simply a machine operator. In the furniture industry, some of the common jobs include set-up man, furniture assembler, bed maker, case framer, chair assembler, or furniture finisher. Fig. 1-14.

• The FINISH CARPENTER may be an all-around skilled carpenter or he may specialize in some type of work such as installing plastic laminates, building kitchen cabinets, or installing paneling and trim.

• The WOOD PATTERNMAKER must understand foundry blueprints and be able to construct a pattern. He must select the correct kind of wood, make the layout, design the parts, and fabricate them. Fig. 1-15.

Professional and Semi-Professional Occupations

The wood industry offers thousands of opportunities to enter one of the professional or semi-professional occupations in which a knowledge of cabinetmaking is required. While most of these careers

1-14(b). By contrast, *machine operators* need only limited skills.

23

do not demand that you actually use tools and machines to fabricate wood products, this "know how" will make you much more successful in your field or specialty. For example, an interior designer who knows woods, finishing, and construction can be far more creative than one who knows only the aesthetics of decorating. The businessman in the building-construction industry or in furniture manufacturing can do a much better job if he has a background in cabinetmaking. For best advantage in one of the many professional careers, you must plan to complete a college degree in a program such as Industrial Education, General Forestry, Wood Technology, Furniture Manufacturing, Wood Products Engineering, or Architecture. More than 250 colleges and universities offer one or more of these programs. Following are some of the major careers:

• A MODELMAKER is a workman who uses wood and clay to make models for production. Some modelmakers work in the automotive and aircraft industries while others specialize in making architectural models. Fig. 1-16. Modelmakers also work in the theater, television, and motion-picture industries making set models.

• INTERIOR DESIGNERS must know furnishings and woods in order to select correct styles of furniture, design custom furniture, and specify the specialized cabinetmaking necessary to interior decorating. Fig. 1-17.

• The INDUSTRIAL EDUCATION TEACHER is responsible for teaching students the fundamentals of tools, materials, and processes relating to the use of wood products in our industrial democracy. Fig. 1-18.

• The FORESTER is responsible for supervising the growth and harvest of timber crops and for other activities that keep the forest-products industries supplied with suitable raw materials. Fig 1-19.

• The WOOD TECHNOLOGIST, WOOD PRODUCTS ENGINEER, or SCIENTIST may work at any one of a wide variety of jobs in research and development, production, and sales. Fig. 1-20. In the forest-products industry there are thousands of chemists, physicists, engineers, and technologists who continually search for new and better ways to use wood as well as its fibers and extractives. Fig. 1-21. Thousands of others, working as professional managers and supervisors, are responsible for the technical operations in construction and wood-products manufacturing. Fig. 1-22. The construction industry alone, for example, annually uses 20 billion dollars worth of wood products in producing 60 billion dollars worth of homes and other structures.

Many other professional people are needed for work in lumbering, plywood and furniture manufacture, and in other types of production plants. Those who work in product sales must have a firsthand knowledge of their products, from the raw lumber to finished items. Those who sell equipment and materials in the woodworking fields need to know everything they can learn about what they are selling. Fig. 1-23.

• The ARCHITECT designs all kinds of homes and other structures. He must know materials. Fig. 1-24.

• The FURNITURE DESIGNER must have creative ability as well as drafting skills and knowledge of cabinetmaking. Fig. 1-25.

TRAINING REQUIREMENTS FOR CABINETMAKING

Well over a million people are employed in the woodworking craft trades which require the skills and knowledge of cabinetmaking. The requirements for all of these occupations are very similar. If you wish to enter the woodworking field as a skilled craftsman, you must be able to use hand and machine tools for cutting, shaping, fitting, and assembling parts made of wood and related materials. You must also have a good general education which includes the ability to read technical literature and prints, and do mathematics through algebra. After this general education, you must complete a specialized educational training program of at least two to four years. This may include vocational or technical education as well as an apprenticeship.

To do cabinetmaking, you must have the temperament to enjoy variety or change of work since jobs tend to be somewhat different from each other. You must be able to set limits, tolerances, and standards of accuracy. Fig. 1-26. You should be interested in things and objects showing tangible results. You should find satisfaction from building and producing something with your own hands.

All woodworking crafts require only medium strength, but they also include a great deal of kneeling, stooping, reaching, and handling. Most jobs are inside, although there may be some outside work. You must be willing to work in an area that is relatively noisy and vibrant. Most jobs involve some hazard, since the work includes handling materials and working with sharp cutting tools, both hand- and power-operated.

1-15. A wood *patternmaker* using precision instruments to check the accuracy of a pattern being built.

CABINETMAKING FOR PLEASURE

Many of you may not want to enter one of the woodworking occupations as a lifework. There are few men, however, who do not enjoy working with wood. As a matter of fact, woodworking is the most popular creative hobby in this country. Fig. 1-27. You may want to build a piece of furniture, install a cabinet, or design and build a wood model. There is genuine joy of accomplishment in working with woods as you cut, shape, fit, and assemble something of your own design or selection. Woodworking skills and knowledge will be of value to you all of your life, both on the job and as an avocation or hobby.

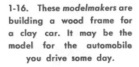

1-16. These *modelmakers* are building a wood frame for a clay car. It may be the model for the automobile you drive some day.

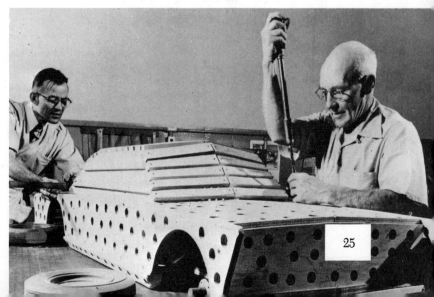

1-17. The *interior designer* must not only understand furniture design and construction but must also have artistic talent. Both men and women work as interior designers for themselves or for a decorator with a showroom like this one.

1-18. An *industrial education teacher* has an interesting occupation. He works with people, but demonstrates use of tools and materials.

Occupations Associated with Wood

1-19. Forest insects can ruin the quality of a vigorous, fast-growing tree. *Foresters* must guard against this danger to trees.

Fig. 1-21. These wood *chemists* are making a laboratory test of material used to preserve telephone poles.

1-20. This wood *engineer* is checking the results of an abrasive machining method of surfacing lumber. This is a recent development in furniture production. He would have been well advised to wear safety glasses for this work.

1-22. This *plant foreman* is checking the quality of the furniture for which he is responsible.

27

1-23. A *sales representative* for a telephone company inspects the poles tagged for purchase.

1-25. This *furniture designer* is making a full-size or scale drawing of a new furniture product.

1-24. The *architect* has an interesting job. Each structure he designs must have a distinct character.

1-26. Accuracy is extremely important in all cabinetmaking. Much of the work must be done to fittings and clearances of $\frac{1}{64}$" or less.

1-27. Maybe you "just like to build things of wood" for the joy and satisfaction you get from working with your hands as well as with your mind.

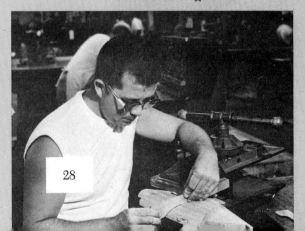

② Furniture Designs

Ever since people began to use household furnishings, there have been trends in furniture design. Fig. 2-1. The history of furniture includes hundreds of different styles. Furniture encyclopedias are a good source for detailed descriptions, although it is difficult to describe and place in neat compartments all the styles that are in common use today. Not many years ago there were only three main classifications: Early American, Traditional, and Modern. However, now there are a great many mixtures which combine the good features of former styles with other features that impart a style all their own. Nevertheless, popular furniture styles in this country fall generally into six major groups: Early American or Colonial, Traditional, Contemporary (including Modern, Transitional, Oriental, and Scandinavian), French Provincial, Italian Provincial, and Spanish or Mediterranean.

EARLY AMERICAN OR COLONIAL

Any furniture made in the American colonies from 1608 to 1830 is called Early American or Colonial. Early settlers in this country found wood plentiful for both houses and furnishings. With the simple hand tools of their day, they developed sturdy, utilitarian pieces that met their needs for storage, seating, sleeping, and eating. Fig. 2-2. These pieces were made of the available native woods,

2-1(a). This Contemporary dining-room set illustrates one trend towards the design motifs of the Asian and Middle Eastern countries. The handsome chairs are slightly curved for comfort and the cane panels are accented at the top with beautifully shaped openings.

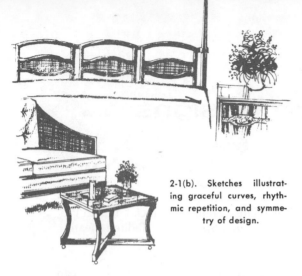

2-1(b). Sketches illustrating graceful curves, rhythmic repetition, and symmetry of design.

2-2. Early American designs have a distinctly hand-made appearance because much furniture in Colonial America was actually made not by professional craftsmen but by the pioneers themselves. Hardware is used sparingly. Trim parts such as moldings are purposely machined and sanded to produce a rather uneven surface or edge, thus reflecting the simple tools with which the colonists worked. The drawer cedar chest shown in this drawing and photograph is made of maple. It measures 41″ W x 19″ D x 25¾″ H.

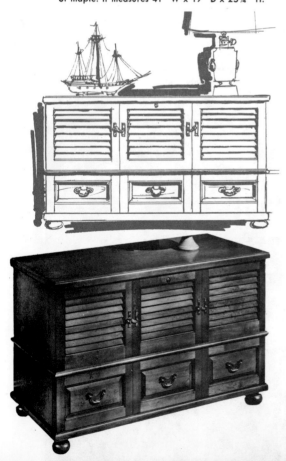

such as oak, pine, and maple. Fig. 2-3. Often, the parts were assembled with wood pegs instead of metal nails. Frequently these early pieces had whittled legs instead of turned parts. The chest was all-important because it served the need for storage even more than it does today. It was also a table, chair, desk, or cupboard as sheer necessity demanded. Even those families with the most furniture had pitifully little. Later settlers who came from all parts of Europe brought with them some of their best furniture pieces. Colonial furniture became more ornate as it was influenced by the designers of France, England, and other European countries. Fig. 2-4.

In the transitional period from Early to Middle Colonial, the chest was naturally the first piece to "grow." First it became a chest of drawers for greater convenience; then it grew to be a chest-on-chest, forerunner of today's stacking chests. It was at this time that a desk with drawers and slanting top was developed.

The heavier pieces of English and French furniture soon gave way to a lighter, more practical style that is popular even today. Fig. 2-3. The Windsor chair, with its fine turned legs, is still prized. Fig. 2-5. To the cabinetmaker of early America, the wood lathe was a real friend. He developed beautiful turnings for posts and legs, as shown. Other characteristic pieces of Early American or Colonial were the hutch cabinet, the cobbler's bench, the butterfly table, and the long trestle table. Figs. 2-6, 2-7 and 2-8. Today, Early American or Colonial is made primarily from maple and birch, with some use of pine. Fig. 2-9. The common finishes are russet browns or light honey-tone maple.

TRADITIONAL

Traditional furniture traces its history to the 18th century, the age of Chipendale, Hepplewhite, Sheraton, and the

2-3. An apothecary chest made of maple which shows the simplest design so common in earlier furniture of this period. 30"W x 18½"D x 30"H.

2-5. Good examples of the Windsor chair with solid wood seats. Note the simple balusters and fine turnings.

2-4. This Colonial furniture, including the George Washington desk and tier tables, represents the more ornate Colonial furniture of later years and its wide use of turned parts.

2-6. The simple trestle harvest table requires no turnings. Closed: 26″ x 72″. Open: 45″ x 72″. Height: 30″

2-7. **This American Colonial desk has the Dutch Colonial or spoonfoot legs that give it an appearance distinctly different from the turned legs of Early American.**

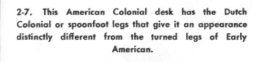

2-8. The hutch cabinet, with a lower chest and upper shelf sections for displaying fine china and accessories, has always been a favorite piece.

2-9. This chest-on-chest made of maple is one of the basic furniture pieces in the Colonial group. Compare the short, thick legs, which curve on both the inside and outside, with those in Fig. 2-2. 38″ W x 20″ D x 52″ H.

Adams Brothers. Fig. 2-10. Thomas Chippendale, one of the great English cabinetmakers who worked in London, was the first to bring out a book on furniture designs, which he called "Gentlemen and Cabinetmakers Directory." This became the cabinetmaker's "bible" both in Europe and America. Chippendale's furniture had great versatility in design. He made use of the handsomely carved cabriole leg in addition to simple, straight legs. Fig. 2-11. He applied much delicate fretwork inspired by Chinese artisans. Fig. 2-12. Chippendale also made wide use of the ball-and-claw foot. His chair sizes were generous and many of them had open or ladder backs.

Two other English furniture designers and cabinetmakers who also published books of designs were George Hepplewhite and Thomas Sheraton. Their designs were often very similar. They both featured simple straight-lined legs, square-back chairs, and table tops with or without drop leaves. Many of their pieces were beautiful, graceful, and well proportioned. Both Sheraton and Hepplewhite made wide use of mahogany with fine moldings and carvings.

While the Adams Brothers, Robert and James, were primarily architects, they also greatly influenced furniture styles. They developed a classic style adapted from ancient Rome.

As mentioned in Unit 1, the only American for whom a style of furniture was named is the great cabinetmaker-designer, Duncan Phyfe. He understood the designs of the great English craftsmen, and his pieces followed the Sheraton lines somewhat. He developed a characteristic style of his own, however. His earlier pieces featured fine carving and considerable reeding. One of his best known designs is his table with pedestal and three or four legs. Fig. 2-13. He introduced the lyre-back chair and the

2-10. The great cabinetmakers of 18th century England designed furniture so beautiful that their creations are as popular as ever today. Most of their furniture was mahogany. Although not overly ornate, it featured enough carved details along edges of tops, pilasters, and legs to lend great warmth and richness.

2-11. Cabriole (cab-ree-ol) is a style of leg shaped in a double curve, the top a convex line and the lower part a concave form ending with various styles of feet.

2-12. Fretwork and lattice work are interchangeable terms for wood that is cut into decorative designs or patterns.

33

2-15. A free-form coffee table with an interesting combination of form and materials. 64"W x 36"D x 15"H.

2-13. This drum table has a top of selected mahogany veneer and underparts of genuine mahogany. It is a typical Duncan Phyfe design. Top: 32". Height: 27".

2-14. This dining-room group reflects the work of three great masters—Sheraton, Hepplewhite, and the Adams Brothers. It was Sheraton who began to design elegant "functional" furniture inspired by the Adams Brothers' concern for architectural "built-ins" which would not disturb the beauty of the interior.

2-16. This handsome double-door walnut hi-fi cabinet has interior space for a tuner, phonograph or tape recorder, and storage for record albums. Any kind of components can be installed in this cabinet. 44"W x 19"D x 55"H.

2-17. Many pieces of furniture can be "made" by combining units.

bronze claw at the ends of legs. Duncan Phyfe's favorite wood was mahogany, since it was so adaptable to fine carving. During the height of his career his designs were known for their fine workmanship.

Today, Traditional styles combine many of the best features of all of these designers. Fig. 2-14. The wood most commonly used for Traditional is mahogany, and the finish is usually dark red or brown.

CONTEMPORARY, INCLUDING MODERN, SCANDINAVIAN, TRANSITIONAL, AND ORIENTAL

As machines took over from the fine hand tools of the early craftsman, quality of furniture fast deteriorated. Earliest forms of Modern had harsh, square lines and sharp angles that seem cheap and ugly today. The fronts of chests and beds often featured a "waterfall" design that was thought of as "modernistic." Early designers of Modern furniture turned their backs on Traditional styles in order to develop an entirely new variety. Unlike the styles of period furniture that developed one after another, quietly and with only slight changes, Modern came on the market as a distinct shock. Since the early grotesque and garish Modern, however, designers have slowly evolved a style with distinctive qualities, using many materials, including wood, metal, glass, plastics, ceramics, and cane. Fig. 2-15. Much Contemporary furniture is designed to be adaptable to many different uses. Storage pieces are equally at home in the living room, dining room, bedroom, or family room. Contemporary is also relatively compact, to suit the smaller homes of today. Contemporary, which is characterized by its flexibility,

2-18. This Contemporary lamp table shows the simplicity, warmth, and richness that are in such contrast to earlier Modern pieces. 24"W x 28"D x 19"H.

2-19. Chair arm detail. The overall feeling of airiness, free-flowing line, and unusual grace are characteristics of the Danish influence.

2-20. A desk and chair of teak with an oil finish. These are good examples of the Scandinavian style. Desk: 61"W x 32"D x 29"H.

2-22(a). This walnut lamp table has a slightly Oriental feeling, brought about by bold hardware accents and the striking shape of the legs. 28"W x 28"D x 22"H.

2-21. Transitional designs represent a bridge between Modern and Traditional. These designs combine the function and scale of Modern with the soft lines and elegant detail of more Traditional styling.

usefulness, and informality, is an attempt to combine the best elements of previous designs, successfully adapted to present-day needs and tastes. Fig. 2-16. It must be functional and truly serve the needs of present-day life. In addition to saving space, many pieces are built as units which can be combined in various ways. Fig. 2-17. Simplicity and informality are characteristics of Contemporary. There is little or no display of carving or other elaborate details. Fig. 2-18. Generally, this furniture is finished in a color more natural to the wood itself, in lighter to medium-warm hues.

The Scandinavian style (mostly Danish and Swedish) which is part of the Contemporary group is characterized by sculptured forms, usually in wood such as mahogany, walnut, teak, and smoked oak. Graceful lines flow into each other smoothly. Figs. 2-19 and 2-20. Finishes are usually natural, with much use of oil, producing the deeper shades of rich brown.

Many people still prefer the appearance of Traditional styling but like the flexibility and informality of Contemporary. As a result, designers have combined desirable features from many periods and called the style Transitional. Fig. 2-21. The influence of the Orient may be found coupled with characteristic Traditional features. Fig. 2-22.

French Provincial

French Provincial is the most popular of the fine lines of furniture which take their inspiration from the Old World. This style appeals to women particularly because of its dainty size and graceful curves. Fig. 2-23. The style came, as you might imagine, from the French provinces during the latter part of the 18th century when the reigning French monarchs Louis XIV and XV favored very elaborate furniture designs. Fig. 2-24.

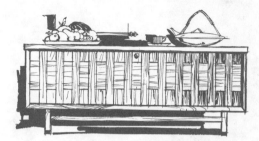

2-22(b). Oriental furniture is sometimes characterized by rather intricate geometric patterns. Often it is finished in red, black, or gold enamel.

2-23. French Provincial styling has a pronounced feminine character due to its many graceful curves which achieve softness and a feeling of luxury.

2-24. A small French Provincial chest of very ornate design which displays superb brass hardware.

2-25. This lamp table with its graceful cabriole legs and bold deep carving is less ornate than some French Provincial designs. 28″W x 28″D x 22″H.

2-27. This French-styled desk in brushed black with gold striping would be a handsome addition to any home.

2-26. This large china cabinet is a typical dining-room piece. It features short cabriole legs with deeply carved panels and a graceful hooded top with a shaped valance.

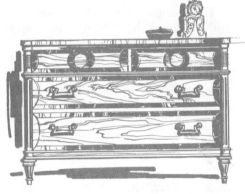

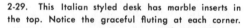

2-28. Italian Provincial has rich, formal elegance. Its stately, fluted pilaster and legs are suggestive of the classic architecture of ancient Rome.

2-29. This Italian styled desk has marble inserts in the top. Notice the graceful fluting at each corner.

2-30. A coffee table of cherry in a fruitwood finish, with elegant brass hardware. 50"W x 20"D x 16"H.

The people of the rural areas of France preferred a simpler style more adaptable to their way of life. Fig. 2-25. Using the woods at hand, primarily fruitwood and walnut, craftsmen worked out simple imitations of the more elaborate court designs. The cabriole leg was almost universally used, with some scrollwork, carving, and fluting. Fig. 2-26. Today, French Provincial is made primarily of cherry with some use of mahogany. The finishes are russet tan, fruitwood, or a light tan fruitwood. Another popular finish is white or black paint, trimmed in gold. Fig. 2-27. One characteristic of French Provincial is the small black scratches in the wood surface, called a *distressed* finish. These are purposely added to imitate wear marks of the original furniture.

ITALIAN PROVINCIAL

Italian Provincial gets its inspiration from furniture developed by craftsmen of the Italian provinces in the 18th and

2-31. Carvings, ceramics, metalwork, and fine fabrics are all part of the Spanish tradition.

2-32. These deeply carved panels of geometric figures are typical of the Moorish influence in Spanish architecture and furniture.

19th centuries. Fig. 2-28. These men copied the ornate furniture fashionable in Rome and other large cities of Italy and, in the process, simplified the designs and eliminated some of the ornament. A characteristic of much Italian Provincial is the use of straight lines. Fig. 2-29. Many chairs, tables, and cabinets have straight, tapered legs on four sides, often with a graceful recess just below the rails. Fine inlay, overlay, and fluting are found on legs to enhance the design quality. The style also makes use of cornices and fluted bands. In an Italian Provincial piece you find well proportioned paneling framed with molding to create interesting patterns. In appearance, Italian Provincial has more in common with Traditional than with French Provincial. Fig. 2-30. The wood normally used is cherry or walnut, frequently finished in a light tan fruitwood.

SPANISH OR MEDITERRANEAN

The Spanish influence in furniture and architecture that was so prevalent several decades ago has had a notable return to popularity. Spanish style is a mixture of Moorish and Gothic architectural influences. Fig. 2-31. Contemporary Spanish or Mediterranean designs make use of many different materials including fine woods, ceramics, wrought-iron metalwork, and glass. Featured are both the classic forms of Spanish-Roman conquerors and the beautiful, simple geometric forms reflecting the influence of the Moors who once ruled Spain. The horseshoe shape of the Moorish arch is seen in many furniture pieces. The woods most commonly used are pecan and oak, with the common finishes being bleached tan walnut or antique brown oak. Fig. 2-32.

3 Designing Furniture And Cabinets

Good furniture and cabinet design should be determined by man's need to live with things that are comfortable, convenient, pleasing in appearance, sturdy, and easy to maintain. Fig. 3-1. If a piece of furniture meets most of these requirements, the chances are that it is well designed.

It is almost impossible to make a list of specific rules that will produce a well designed piece. Taste and a feeling for good design can be acquired by observing quality furniture in homes, stores, magazines, and books. Many of the designs that appear on the following pages are the work of the finest furniture designers in America today. All illustrate better than average design. While certain styles may not appeal to you or suit your needs, still they represent quality furniture and cabinets.

FUNDAMENTALS OF GOOD DESIGN

The fundamentals of good design include purpose or function, appearance, materials, and construction.

Function

A product is well designed only if it meets the need for which it is intended. For example, a table must be the right height for its particular use, and a chair must be comfortable. Specifically, chairs are made in different heights and seat depths. The angle between seat and chair back also varies. These and other dimensions must be designed so that a person can sit in the chair comfortably.

3-1. Both of these rooms show furniture of good design. (a). The more Traditional design is ornate with its fancy carving, shaping and fluting. Does this style appeal to you?

41

3-1(b). Perhaps you prefer the simpler Contemporary design.

3-2. Average furniture sizes.

AVERAGE FURNITURE SIZES

ITEM	HEIGHT	DEPTH	LENGTH-WIDTH
Tables			
Coffee or Cocktail	14″ to 18″	18″ to 24″	36″ to 60″
Card	29″	30″	30″
Game	30″	30″	30″
Writing	30″	24″	36″ to 40″
Kitchen	32″	30″	42″
End	30″	15″	24″
Dining	29″ to 32″	42″	60″
Chairs			
Desk	16½″	15″ to 18″	15″ to 18″
Dining	16″ to 18″	15″ to 18″	15″ to 18″
Cabinets			
Sectional	30″	12″ to 14″	Any
China Storage	54″ to 60″	20″ to 22″	Any
Kitchen	32″ to 36″	12″ to 24″	Any
Chests	32″ to 54″	24″	Any
Bookcases	32″ to 82″	18″	Any
Desks	30″	24″ to 30″	40″ to 60″

Thus you see that furniture sizes are influenced by the sizes of human beings. Fig. 3-2. The designer makes a careful study of the human body to determine man's furniture needs.

Equally important, the designer must know the answer to the question, "What will the piece be used for?" A chest, for example, must be designed for storage, but what kind of things: books, clothing, utensils, or others? Only when this is known can many other points be decided, such as height of the chest and size of drawers.

Appearance

The furniture piece or cabinet must be pleasing to the user. It must be "in tune" with his personality. Even though two chests may be equally efficient for storage, one may have greater appeal simply because of its appearance. Fig. 3-3. People have strong preferences for dif-

ferent styles of furniture, which is why so many are on the market. For some, the informality of Contemporary seems best. To others, furniture in the classic Traditional fashion is more appealing. Still others prefer the elegance of French Provincial. Furniture and cabinets that are true to their own particular style are attractive and, in most cases, represent the principles of good design. When established styles are disregarded, poor design usually results. All too often, furniture made in the school shop is poorly designed simply because it represents no particular style. In furniture that you construct, why not try to express your tastes by making your own development of some established style? You will find this a true test of originality. Fig. 3-4.

Materials

Materials selected for furniture must

3-3. These two chests are almost identical in size and usefulness. Which one would you choose?

3-4. One of these tables was designed and built by a student. The other is an excellent commercial product. Can you tell which one was built in a school shop?

3-5. This high-quality chest couldn't be built without using solid wood for the posts and other structural parts. Usually veneers make up the door fronts and other large surfaces.

be right for both use and style. It is possible to imitate a more expensive hardwood with one of lesser quality. For example, gumwood is sometimes stained to imitate mahogany. However, this practice would never deceive anyone who knows fine furniture woods. Certainly the fine hardwoods possess great beauty and durability, but it must be remembered that well designed furniture also makes use of plywoods. Fig. 3-5. There are still people who consider the term "veneer" to mean something of inferior quality. The truth is that fine hardwood plywoods are ideal for the large flat surfaces of chests, tables, and cabinets. Quality furniture today also makes use of many non-wood materials such as plastic laminates, ceramics, tile, metal, glass, cane, and textiles.

CONSTRUCTION

The construction of furniture and cabinets must be basically sound. Fig. 3-6. Good joinery should be the rule throughout the product. Flimsy construction in itself is poor design. A table that is wobbly or a chair that tips is useless. If the glue joints don't hold, the product is worthless.

Quality furniture construction means building to last a long time with minimum maintenance. It also means that if two construction methods provide equal durability and sturdiness, the less expensive method should be followed. In chairs and tables, for example, modern adhesives with dowels and corner blocks on legs and rails are just as effective as mortise-and-tenon joints. Furniture intended for hard use, as in motels or in homes with small children, is often made with plastic laminates for the tops of chests, desks, and tables. Frequently these materials closely match the grain of fine wood veneer. The resulting product is just as attractive, lasts longer, and is easier to maintain than one made entirely of wood.

ELEMENTS OF DESIGN

The elements of design include *line, shape, mass, color, tone,* and *texture.* These "building blocks" of all design are found to varying degree in all furniture and cabinets.

Line

Lines may be straight, curved, S-shaped, circular, or spiral. They reveal a great deal about a product. Fig. 3-7. Much Contemporary and Modern furniture is largely made up of straight lines, whereas Traditional, Early American, and French Provincial styles have many curves. Fig. 3-8. Lines can be used to give a certain feeling to an object. The graceful curves of French Provincial seem somewhat feminine, while the straight, businesslike lines of Modern office furniture impart a masculine quality.

3-6. Fine construction in a cabinet or chest: 1. Exposed panels are of five-ply veneer construction for maximum strength, durability, and uniformity of grain character and color. 2. Drawers are dovetailed and made of carefully finished, solid hardwood. 3. Double-dowel construction of case goods provides a close, strong joint. 4. Drawers are fitted with solid hardwood guides and wood, metal, or plastic runners to insure smooth operation. 5. All drawers are dust-proofed.

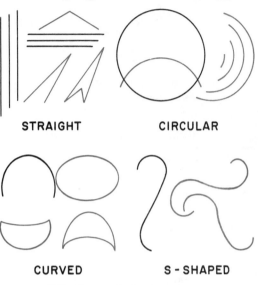

STRAIGHT **CIRCULAR**

CURVED **S - SHAPED**

3-7. Common kinds of lines.

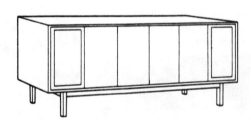

3-8(a). Compare the straight lines of this modern chest with the very different style shown in Fig 3-8(b).

3-8(b). This Early American table has many curved lines.

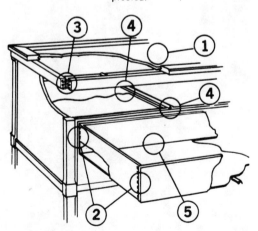

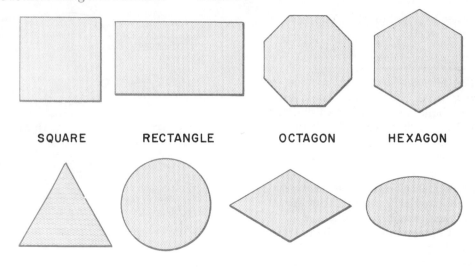

SQUARE   **RECTANGLE**   **OCTAGON**   **HEXAGON**

TRIANGLE   **ROUND**   **DIAMOND**   **ELLIPSE**

3-9. Common shapes used as design elements in furniture.

3-10. How many of the common shapes can you recognize in these unusual accessories made of rare woods?

46   3-11. Two common solid shapes: (a). A round table that is 48"D x 15"H. (b). An octagonal table that measures 18½"W x 18½"D x 22"H.

Shape

Lines make up the shape of a product. The most common shapes are square, rectangular, round, triangular, diamond, elliptical, hexagonal, and octagonal. Fig. 3-9. We see these shapes in all kinds of furniture. For example, table tops can take almost any shape, from the common rectangle to the unusual hexagon. Many drawer pulls are circular, while a table leg commonly has a triangular shape. As you look through the illustrations of furniture and cabinetry in this book, see how many common shapes you can identify. Fig. 3-10.

Mass

Line and shape make up mass, or the three-dimensional appearance of an object. Fig. 3-11. All furniture has height, depth, and width or length to form mass. Basic construction materials come in many shapes. Some examples are the rectangular pieces of wood, round dowel rod, and oval or triangular drawer pulls.

In planning the mass of a furniture piece, the designer thinks more in terms of form than of a solid shape. The form may be open, as for a table or chair, or closed as for a chest, cabinet, or storage unit. Fig. 3-12.

Color

Color is a most important element in furniture and interior design. The appearance of a room will not be pleasing unless there is a close relationship between the colors of the furniture and those of the background and accessories. In this book you will see many excellent illustrations of the use of color. Nature has given each species of wood a color all its own. Color can be enhanced or changed by using stains, fillers, and other finishing materials. Upholstering also adds color to furniture.

All colors or hues are blends of the primary and secondary colors. In Fig. 3-13 primaries are marked No. 1, secondaries No. 2. Pairs of adjoining colors on the color wheel are known as *har-*

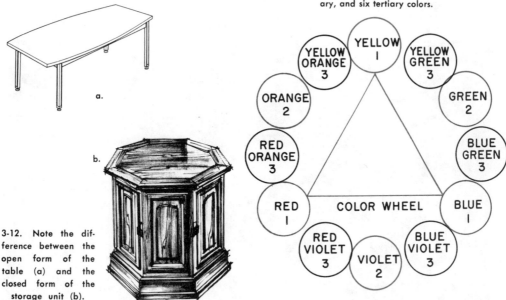

3-13. Color wheel with three primary, three secondary, and six tertiary colors.

3-12. Note the difference between the open form of the table (a) and the closed form of the storage unit (b).

3-14. Frequently French Provincial furniture is painted white and trimmed in gold. The white reflects light and gives the furniture piece a feeling of lightness.

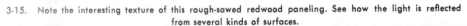

3-15. Note the interesting texture of this rough-sawed redwood paneling. See how the light is reflected from several kinds of surfaces.

Colonial or Early American. A look of comfortable formality is captured in this room of Early American or Colonial design. Light and dark finishes are combined for interesting contrast. The secretary not only offers adequate writing and desk space but has a file drawer built in the cabinet below. The Windsor chair with its finely turned legs and rungs is distinctively Early American. *Drexel*

Traditional. The furniture in this Traditional bedroom is made of fine mahogany, a proud and respected wood that was used to perfection by skilled cabinetmakers of the eighteenth century. Inlays of boxwood and bandings of yew wood are used as accents on several pieces. *Heritage*

Modern. This furniture is designed to reflect today's taste for a warm look with modern styling. It brings together a variety of themes which emphasize the simplicity of form so desirable for beauty in the Modern style. In addition, the furniture has these special features: beautiful walnut veneers, rich highlights in grain patterns, a sable finish of warm brown, elegant accent woods including rosewood, teak, and oak, and distinctive bold hardware. The upholstery would be equally striking if red or gold were substituted for the green shown here. *Drexel*

Contemporary. This Contemporary furniture of Appalachian oak is comfortable, functional and up-to-date in styling. Like all good Contemporary design, this boy's room offers a variety of pieces that could fit equally well into a den, living room, or family room. Plastic tops are used on all casework. Recessed drawer pulls are complemented by brass installed at corners and parting rails.

Heritage

Contemporary. This furniture is truly modern in materials and design. While acknowledging the heritage of fine furniture, modern designers do not limit themselves to the materials of the past. For instance, note the chrome in the handsome love seat, teak and cork in the group of occasional tables, beads imbedded in plastic in the cube table, leather and cane on the chair, and split bamboo laminated in plastic in the base of the cabinet. Except in the tables, the wood is beautiful walnut veneer with a 'dark, translucent, highly polished finish, accented with slim moldings. *Drexel*

Italian. The elegance of Italian styling is exemplified by these unusual and versatile pieces. Note the beautiful, straight lines of the tapered legs on the desk. The woods are beautifully matched cherry veneers, accented with elm burl. The light lustrous finish blends well with Contemporary furnishings. *Drexel*

Spanish or Mediterranean. Spanish or Mediterranean designs feature carvings, ceramics, metalwork, and fabrics that are typical of Spain's rich and varied past. The style emphasizes the classic forms left by Spain's Roman conquerors and the beautiful, simple shapes introduced to Spain by the Moors. *Heritage*

French. This furniture illustrates the spirit of the original, old designs native to the country regions of France. The distinctive cabriole legs of the chairs and desk show the graceful curve so common to this style. The fruitwood finish gives the surface a waxy sheen and glow. To many people, French Provincial represents true elegance. *Drexel*

3-16. This room has a variety of textures. How many can you identify? Do you think too many different materials were used?

monious hues. Those opposite each other are *complementaries*.

The furniture designer considers color as important as line or form. Sometimes it is added to furniture by using rich bright plastic laminates, ceramic tile, cane, or fabrics. Some interior designers like to relate all of the colors in a room to one major color. One-color interiors can be monotonous; therefore, accent colors from another part of the wheel are effective. Other designers prefer lavish use of colors from all parts of the wheel. Fig. 3-14.

Tone and Texture

Tone is the contrast between light and dark or shadow and brightness on a surface. The values of reflected light range from pure white through gray to black. Fig. 3-13. All surfaces, except black, reflect light, thus producing tone.

Texture is the way a surface feels to the touch. Each wood has its own texture. Fig. 3-15. Further variations in texture can be achieved by combining the

3-17. How many rectangular shapes can you identify in this hutch cabinet?

49

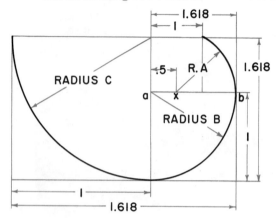

3-18. The "golden mean" rectangle and how to use it. Start with a square of one unit. Then find the center of the lower side (ab) and, with x as the radius, strike an arc that will intersect a continuation of line ab. This will give you the golden rectangle. Continue to enlarge the rectangle as shown to obtain a number of proportionate rectangles. These can then be used for the overall dimensions and for parts within the total product.

wood with different kinds of materials, by cutting and finishing the wood in various ways, by machining, and by installing hardware. Fig. 3-16.

PRINCIPLES OF DESIGN

Proportion

Proportion is the relationship of the parts of an object to each other and to the total product. A rectangle often has better proportion than a square because the exact relationship between its height and width or width and depth is not easy to see. This creates interest. Fig. 3-17. Many designers consider the *golden mean rectangle* to have perfect proportion. The ratio between its shorter and longer dimensions is 1 to 1.618, or approximately 5 to 8. Fig. 3-18. Many picture frames, chests and cabinets show this proportion. Fig. 3-19. A relationship of 1 to 3 or 2 to 3 is also superior to a perfect square in many instances.

3-19. This beautiful china cabinet is a perfect "golden mean" rectangle in its overall width and height.

3-20. Do you like this tier end table? It is a perfect cube of 22" in all directions.

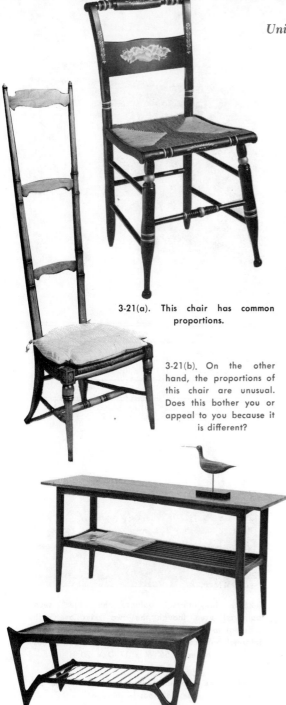

3-21(a). This chair has common proportions.

3-21(b). On the other hand, the proportions of this chair are unusual. Does this bother you or appeal to you because it is different?

3-22. Do either or both of these tables have the school-made look? One is a commercial design while the other is student-designed and student-built.

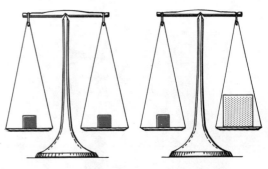

3-23. These balance scales illustrate formal and informal balance. The one on the left has units of equal size and shape. The scale on the right is balanced by units of different size but the same weight.

However, much modern furniture of excellent design does make use of the perfect square and the cube. Fig. 3-20. As stated, proportion is greatly concerned with the relationship of one part to another. Fig. 3-21. A large chair with spindly legs or a dainty coffee table with bulky ones has poor proportion. Slight variation in the sizes of parts will frequently influence proportion to a great extent. Often the "school-made" look in furniture is due to the use of parts that are either too bulky and heavy or too light and flimsy in appearance. Figs. 3-21 and 3-22.

Balance

An object that appears stable or at rest is said to have balance. Fig. 3-23. Nature provides many examples of this. The body of a cat, for instance, is excellently balanced by the symmetrical arrangement of the legs. When a designer arranges the parts of an object symmetrically, this produces *formal* balance. Fig. 3-24. Another kind of balance, called *informal*, results when dissimilar parts are arranged to make an object appear stable. Fig. 3-25. This, of course, is not symmetrical.

51

3-24(a). This sideboard illustrates perfect balance that is always pleasing to the eye and not too difficult to achieve.

3-24(b). In formal balance the design is symmetrical around a center point (equal on both sides).

Harmony

Harmony is concerned with the way materials and parts of a product "get along" with one another. Even when many different materials are to be used, the combination must blend. Fig. 3-26. You do not have harmony, for example, if you combine a French Provincial leg with a Modern style table top, if you combine too many different materials, or if you use too many colors.

Rhythm

Rhythm in design is marked by the occurrence of certain distinct features or elements at regular intervals. This causes eye movements much the same as musical rhythm often causes foot movement. Rhythm can be achieved by repetition of shape, color, line, or design details. Fig. 3-27.

52

3-25(a). In informal balance the object seems balanced even though the two sides are really different in size, shape, color, or design details. The informal balance of this window chest is rather easy to observe. 56"W x 17"D x 20"H.

3-25(b). The informal balance of this storage unit is less obvious to the eye.

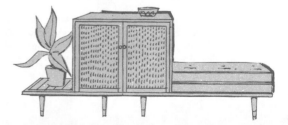

Emphasis

Emphasis means focusing attention on a point of attraction or special interest. Fig. 3-28. It might be obtained by skillful use of carving, by placement of hardware, or by choice of fabric.

COMMON ERRORS IN FURNITURE AND CABINET DESIGN

If you design a piece of furniture, do not slavishly follow the elements and principles of design. It is much better to work with materials in a creative and experimental fashion. As you develop a feeling for good design, you will instinctively know when the principles and elements have been successfully applied. The common mistakes in furniture and cabinet design which impart an undesirable appearance are these:

• A definite style of furniture has not evolved. As stated earlier, too often a piece represents no particular style but rather a combination of many, resulting in a complete *lack of style*. Much inexpensive, commercial furniture is of this type.

• Basic principles of design have been ignored. The appearance of a school-made object is often too heavy and clumsy, rather than light and attractive.

3-26. Here wood, metal, and ceramics are combined in a striking coffee table. Notice that different shapes (rectangular, round, and irregular) are combined. The designer had a strong feeling for good appearance achieved through harmony.

3-27. This storage lamp table repeats an unusual design motif which gives character to the furniture piece. 30"W x 30"D x 19"H.

53

3-28. The square, "twisted" legs of this sideboard are certainly a point of emphasis.

3-29. A sketch will help you to picture the final product in your mind.

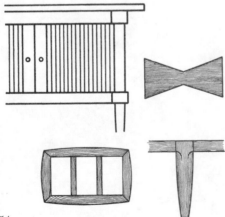

• A poor selection of materials has been made. It is impossible to produce quality furniture from cheap woods. Likewise, it is usually faddish and garish to combine woods of highly contrasting color, texture, or quality.

• A product has been over decorated. Surface decoration should be applied sparingly and only as is fitting to the particular furniture style. Texture is more pronounced in Contemporary furniture than in most other styles, and such furniture includes surface decoration such as reeding, fluting, and inlaying, but here also the designer must use discretion.

• Workmanship is poor. The quality of workmanship is extremely important in furniture construction. If there are large cracks in the joinery or rough edges, the final product certainly will not be attractive.

• The finish is bad. Poor finish will ruin an otherwise fine piece of furniture. Quality furniture has a smooth, even, attractive finish. Most furniture manufacturers use lacquer or a synthetic finish. School-made furniture too often suffers from a varnish finish that dries too slowly, becomes tacky, and picks up dust, making the finish quite uneven. In selecting or designing furniture or cabinetry, keep the finish in mind.

STEPS IN DESIGNING FURNITURE

1. Determine your own need and the exact use of the piece. Remember, a sound product has an attractive appearance and fits into the space available. It also has a distinctive style.

DESIGN DETAILS

3-30. The total effect of a product is greatly influenced by such details as surface decoration, hardware, and finish. Keep these in mind when preparing your sketches.

2. Develop several sketches of the product. Fig. 3-29. When you have decided on a particular furniture style, become thoroughly familiar with its characteristics. Fig. 3-30.

3. Develop a model and do some experimentation. For example, if you are designing a hi-fi cabinet, you may want to study the sound-reproduction qualities of various woods. You may also want to investigate which kinds of construction in the speaker cabinet will produce the best sound. The sizes of the components will also affect your design.

3-31(a). An attractive night stand of Early American or Colonial design.

3-31(b). A few external changes can greatly influence the visual effect of a product. The function and size of this night stand are the same regardless of changes in outward appearance.

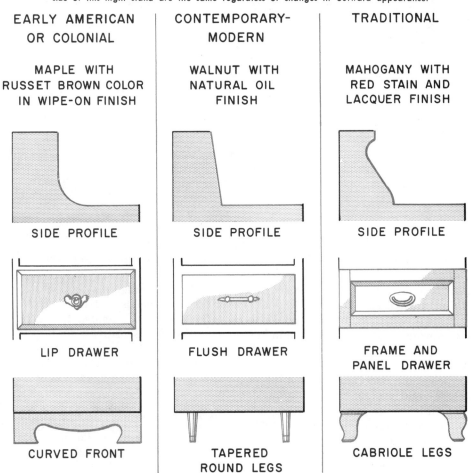

EARLY AMERICAN OR COLONIAL	CONTEMPORARY- MODERN	TRADITIONAL
MAPLE WITH RUSSET BROWN COLOR IN WIPE-ON FINISH	WALNUT WITH NATURAL OIL FINISH	MAHOGANY WITH RED STAIN AND LACQUER FINISH
SIDE PROFILE	SIDE PROFILE	SIDE PROFILE
LIP DRAWER	FLUSH DRAWER	FRAME AND PANEL DRAWER
CURVED FRONT	TAPERED ROUND LEGS	CABRIOLE LEGS

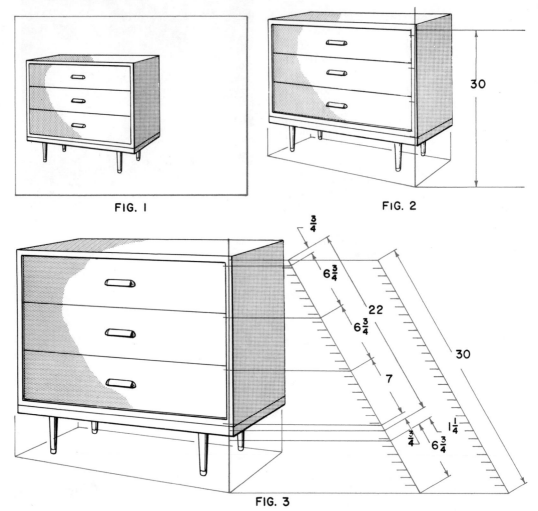

FIG. 1

FIG. 2

FIG. 3

3-32. Determining the dimension of the parts of this chest. The overall size is 30″W x 15″D x 30″H.

Balsa wood is often a good choice for building a small model of the product.

4. Develop the sketch and model into final drawings. These should be complete furniture drawings such as appear in this book.

5. Select the materials. Make a bill of materials and a plan of procedure.

6. Construct the piece, using the correct woods and applying good workmanship, as explained in this book.

7. Apply a good finish, preferably by spraying.

8. Finally, judge the product to see if it fits your needs and is satisfactory in every respect. Remember that good design involves sensitivity to beauty. As you learn more about design, you will become more sensitive to it and will reject products that reflect poor design.

SIMPLIFIED STYLE CHANGES

Some large automobile manufacturers use only two or three basic body shells for all the different-model cars they produce. Variety in appearance is achieved by changing the grills, fenders, trim, and other exterior parts. This keeps down the cost and simplifies production. To a limited extent the same technique is applied by some furniture manufacturers. An identical chest may be used for several different furniture styles. Only the kind of wood, the finish, the hardware, and certain other exterior items are changed to give one chest Colonial, another Contemporary, and still another Traditional style. An example of this is illustrated in Fig. 3-31.

MAKING A WORKING DRAWING FROM A PICTURE OR SKETCH

You may see a picture or sketch of a furniture piece that you would like to make. In many cases the three major dimensions of height, depth, and width are given. With careful planning you can design a product that is very similar by following this procedure:

1. Fasten the picture or sketch to the left edge of a piece of paper. Fig. 3-32.

2. Use a T square or drafting machine to project straight lines from the edges of the furniture piece.

3. Suppose that the overall height is 30″. Select a scale in which 30 units equal in length will fit diagonally between the two horizontal lines. Place the first division point on the scale on the top line and the last on the bottom line.

4. Now project lines until they intersect the diagonal line for each dimension needed. It is then easy to count the number of units or inches for this part. The same method can be used to find other dimensions.

4 Safety And Housekeeping

An accident can cause injury to you, other persons, machinery, or the product you are making. A serious accident could ruin your life. Though you are safer working with good woodworking machines and tools than in certain other school activities, the wood shop does have its dangers. The accident rate for industrial wood working is about twice as high as the national average for all industries. This must be expected since wood working is done with sharp cutting tools and high-speed machines.

To avoid accidents, safety must be foremost in your mind at all times. Though damage to a piece of wood or a machine can be serious, it is not a tragedy like the loss of a finger. Remember at all times that you must guarantee safety for two: *the tool and you.* The machine can't think, *but you can.* Make safety a habit. Some people are "accident prone." If you are one of these, you probably shouldn't be working with power tools.

To achieve maximum safety in the wood shop, the equipment must be kept in top condition. Fig. 4-1. Still more important, you—the operator of the machine—must know what you are doing and how to do it. You will find this information throughout the book; there are special safety suggestions for each machine.

You must realize that each woodworking machine and tool has its own special hazards. When working with the circular saw, keep your fingers away from the revolving blade and make sure that the stock does not kick back and injure you.

4-1. Tools must be kept sharp and in good condition if you are to work safely with woods and related materials. If the tool you plan to use isn't sharp, take time to recondition it.

On the jointer, the problem is to keep your fingers away from the revolving cutter. The shaper is particularly dangerous because it operates at such extremely high speeds and because it is difficult to guard the cutters. The major hazard of the surfacer is the danger of kickback. Machines such as the band saw and the jig saw are relatively safe to use.

A cabinetmaker works in various kinds of places. He may work with hand tools and stationary machines in a well equipped shop; or he may work in a new house installing kitchen cabinets or built-ins. Perhaps he will remodel the interior of a store or office, which requires tearing out old fixtures and installing new ones. In each of these cases there are special things to remember. The following discussion includes safety practices for all jobs as well as for specific situations.

DRESS

Wear tight-fitting clothes with sleeves buttoned. If it is not too inconvenient, roll up your sleeves. Tuck in your tie and, when necessary, wear a shop coat, apron, or other protective garment.

4-2. This student is properly dressed for work.

4-3(a) and (b). Contrast the housekeeping and working conditions in these two industrial plants. Both specialize in the same kind of work, namely, rough cutting stock to size.

4-4. A clean, well organized wood shop.

4-5. A great deal of cabinetmaking is done with hand tools. Use them with care.

4-6. A test of the fiber-glass housing on this portable drill shows that it will not conduct electricity; it is virtually shockproof.

4-7. What good and bad safety practices do you find in the use of this circular saw?

4-8. Eye protection is especially important for grinding, turning, and certain sanding operations.

Fig. 4-2. When operating machines, avoid wearing jewelry including rings, wrist watches, and similar items. Though it is not always convenient to remove such items, they do present a hazard. Wear a good, sturdy pair of shoes, especially when working out of doors.

HOUSEKEEPING

Many accidents are caused by poor housekeeping in regard to tools, machines, and materials. Make sure all materials are neatly stacked where they will not interfere with the use of tools and machines. Fig. 4-3. Keep the areas around each machine and where you are working free of lumber scraps, workpieces, excessive sawdust, and oil. Always take nails and screws out of boards that have been removed for remodeling. Arrange tools neatly in a case or cabinet. Keep tables of machines and other work surfaces free of nails, tools, wrenches and materials. Fig. 4-4.

COURTESY TO OTHER WORKERS

Do not try to move materials or equipment past a person who is using a power tool or machine. Also, do not come up behind a person who is doing such work. Startling him could easily cause a serious accident. Wait until a worker has finished using a machine before moving into his area. When you are through using a machine, remove the special set-ups. Leave the machine in its normal operating condition for the next person. Clean up waste stock and place it in a scrap box. Never start or stop a machine for someone else. If you are working with someone else on a machine—for example, as the tail-off man on a circular saw or surfacer—always follow the operator's directions. Never try to pull stock through the machine.

HAND TOOLS

While hand tools are relatively safe,

they are the cause of many small injuries. Make sure that all tools are sharp and in good condition. That way they will do their job better and are safer to use. Fig. 4-5. Always carry sharp-pointed tools away from your body. Never hold a small piece of wood in your fingers as you cut it. It is always better to clamp it in a vise. If it is necessary to hold the stock, make sure that the cutting edge moves away from your hand, not toward it.

PORTABLE POWER TOOLS

Portable power tools are widely used for on-the-job construction. In using these tools, the cutting edge is fed into the stock. For safe operation, make sure that the stock is fixed so it will not move. Keep your hands away from the cutting edge and, whenever possible, keep both hands on the portable tool. Never use electrical equipment on a wet or damp floor. Make sure that the tool is properly grounded and that the extension cord wire is large enough. There are, of course, many cordless power tools that are relatively safe to use, especially on cabinetwork around water and in damp buildings. Also, some portable tools have a housing of fiber glass which eliminates much danger of shock. Fig. 4-6.

WOODWORKING MACHINES

Detailed instructions for safe use of stationary machines are given in each unit. However, there are some general practices that should be observed. Make sure you know how to use the machine properly before you attempt to operate it. Keep guards in place for all cutting and shaping operations. Fig. 4-7. Guards should always be used unless it makes cutting impossible. If a standard guard cannot be used, make use of holding and clamping devices, and push sticks.

4-9(a). This is what happens when there is no dust-collection system. Not only is this a fire hazard but also a threat to health and safety in other ways.

4-9(b). A good dust-collection system will keep a shop clean with minimum effort. On a few machines, such as the wood lathe, it is difficult to attach such a system. Machines like the jig saw, radial-arm saw, and drill press, that aren't connected directly to the system, should have a floor-sweep suction outlet near them for easy, dust-free removal of the sweepings.

ALWAYS PLAN YOUR WORK
BEFORE STARTING

Planning your work before you begin can eliminate much potential danger. If large stock is to be cut, get help before you begin, not after you are in difficulty. Keep your mind on your work. Guard against becoming distracted by noise or anything that is going on around you. Make sure that all clamping devices are secured before turning on the power. Wait until the machine is at full speed before using it. Then feed the stock into the machine with a firm, even touch.

Never hurry when working on a machine. Accidents often happen when someone tries to do things too fast or fails to follow instructions. Never attempt to stop the machine with a stick of wood or anything else after the power is off. Make sure that the machine has come to a dead stop before adjusting, oiling, or changing a blade.

Always wear goggles or a face mask when there is danger of flying chips. This especially applies to wood turning, grinding, and most sanding operations. Fig. 4-8. Keep your fingers away from the path of the cutting tool.

4-10. Kinds of fire extinguishers needed in a wood shop.

FOR CLASS "A" FIRES   SODA-ACID   WATER PUMP   FOAM

FOR CLASS "B" FIRES   CARBON DIOXIDE   DRY CHEMICAL   FOAM   VAPORIZING LIQUID

FOR CLASS "C" FIRES   CARBON DIOXIDE   DRY CHEMICAL   VAPORIZING LIQUID

FIRE CONTROL

There is special danger of fire in the cabinet shop due to sawdust and inflammable materials. A good dust-collection system for stationary tools is necessary for fire control and health reasons. Fig. 4-9. Store finishing materials in metal containers and cabinets. Keep oily rags in metal waste cans.

Fires must be extinguished differently, depending upon what is burning. Three classes of fires are a threat to the woodshop; consequently, three kinds of fire extinguishers should be available. Fig. 4-10.

A *class A* fire involves only ordinary combustible material such as wood chips, paper, or rubbish. The cooling and quenching effect of water or a watery solution works well against such fires.

A *class B* fire involves inflammable liquids such as alcohol, paint, or lacquer thinner, or other chemicals. Use an extinguisher that will cover the burning area with a chemical blanket.

A *class C* fire is one involving electrical equipment. It is very important to use an extinguishing agent that will not conduct electricity.

TREATMENT OF ACCIDENTS

Most accidents can be avoided. However, there is always the possibility that one may happen. Make sure that you get first aid and medical treatment promptly for even the slightest scratch. Only a person with medical training should remove something from your eye. If you get a small sliver in the skin, remove it and then treat against infection.

SECTION I

QUESTIONS AND DISCUSSION TOPICS

1. Why is cabinetmaking the key to all industrial woodworking?
2. Describe the difference between cabinetmaking and the cabinetmaker.
3. Compare the work of the finish carpenter and the cabinetmaker.
4. Who were the Big Four of the Eighteenth Century, described as the Golden Age of furniture design?
5. What do millmen do?
6. Are a large number of skilled cabinetmakers and millmen needed in production plants? Why?
7. What kinds of products does a millwork plant produce?
8. Identify the kind of company that specializes in making interior items for offices, banks, and other businesses.
9. How do the operations of a hardwood-dimension plant differ from those of furniture production?
10. Name four skilled occupations in which a knowledge of cabinetmaking is important.
11. In what professional and semi-professional occupations would a knowledge of cabinetmaking be valuable?
12. Describe the training requirements for a skilled craftsman in woodworking.
13. Name the six major groups of furniture styles used in this country.
14. What was the most important single piece of furniture in colonial times?
15. Who was Duncan Phyfe? What was his contribution to the development of furniture?
16. Describe the cabriole leg.
17. What is a distressed finish?
18. How do the leg shapes of Italian Provincial and French Provincial pieces differ?
19. In what style of furniture do you find the simple geometric forms introduced by the Moors?

20. What question must always be answered when considering the purpose or function of a furniture piece?

21. Why is the appearance of a furniture piece important?

22. Is veneer furniture of inferior quality?

23. Name some elements of good design.

24. What is the golden mean rectangle? Tell how it can be applied to furniture design.

25. Give examples of the two kinds of balance.

26. List some common errors in designing a furniture piece.

27. Describe the steps in designing furniture.

28. Tell how a working drawing can be made from a picture or sketch.

29. Describe the correct way to dress in the woodworking shop.

30. What is meant by good housekeeping in a shop?

31. What are some dangers involved in using hand tools?

32. Discuss fire hazards in a wood shop.

33. List woodworking operations that require eye protection.

PROBLEMS AND ACTIVITIES

1. Make a detailed study of one occupation in which a knowledge of cabinetmaking is essential. Use the *Occupational Outlook Handbook* and other publications to get this information; also interview someone working in the occupation.

2. Study the life of a great cabinetmaker (Chippendale, Sheraton, Duncan Phyfe, or other). Pay special attention to his contributions to the field.

3. Review the life and work of a current designer of wood products.

4. Design and sketch a wood product that you would like to build.

5. Visit a furniture store or showroom and evaluate a piece of furniture displayed. Discuss its design, construction, and finish.

6. As a group, develop a cleanup schedule for your shop.

Section II

Materials and Layouts

The major raw materials needed for cabinetmaking come from forests which are one of America's richest natural resources. Wood is used for such basic building materials as solid lumber, plywood, particle board, and hardboard. These materials in turn are made into cabinets, furniture, millwork, paneling and all the other products of the cabinetmaker. A skilled woodworker must know how to select and order these basic materials.

Wood—Its Nature And Properties

Wood is a remarkable raw material with thousands of uses, many of them in cabinetmaking. While wood may seem to be a relatively simple substance, a study reveals that in some ways it is one of the most unusual and complicated natural materials. Fig. 5-1. The more you know about the characteristics of wood and its properties, the more valuable wood becomes to you.

Wood is made up of countless tiny tubular cells cemented solidly together by wood's own adhesive, *lignin*. Fig. 5-2. These tubes or cells form a sort of plumbing system, supplying chemical ma-

5-1. Here is the raw material for all wood products.

terials which nourish the life processes of the tree. The walls of these tubes also provide strength for the tree trunk. In general, these tubes run up and down the trunk. They produce the grain that you see on cut surfaces and edges of lumber.

PARTS OF A TREE

The tree is the largest plant found in nature. Fig. 5-3. Roots anchor it to the ground and absorb water, dissolving minerals and nitrogen necessary for the life of the cells which transport the food. Roots also help to hold the soil against erosion. The tree trunk produces the bulk of useful wood. It supports the *crown*, the bushy part of the tree, which includes the twigs and leaves. A cross section of a log cut from a tree trunk is shown in Fig. 5-4. Its parts function as follows:

The *outer bark* is a shield that protects the tree from fire, insects, and disease. Fig. 5-5. This dead, corky part varies in thickness with the kind of tree and its age. The inner part of the bark, called *bast* or *phloem*, is living material. Its cells carry the food (sap) made in the leaves downward to feed the branches, trunk, and roots. The *cambium* is a living two-celled layer between the bark and the wood. This is where the tree grows in width. New wood forms on the inside of the cambium, and new bark on the outside. This is called *annular* growth because it is ring-shaped.

The wood itself is the part of the tree used to make lumber. It consists of *sapwood* and *heartwood*. *Sapwood* is the newer, lighter-colored, growing part of the tree. It carries sap from the roots to the leaves. The *heartwood,* which at one time was sapwood, has become inactive. It is the darker part and is dead as far as growth is concerned. The *pith* is the small growth center of the tree. This is the first growth, formed when the woody stem or branch grows longer. Radiating out from the center of the tree are the *medullary ray cells.* As mentioned earlier, these structures form passageways for the food which nourishes the tree. Energy carried through these cells starts the tree growing in the spring, until the leaves are formed and the tree makes its own food.

SPECIFIC GRAVITY OF LUMBER

The composition of cell walls is about the same for all species of wood. Differences in density between various kinds of woods and between individual pieces of lumber are principally due to the open spaces in the cells. Specific gravity is a scientific way to measure the relative density of a substance. This measure-

ment is expressed as a ratio. The weight of a wood compared with the weight of an equal amount of water at 4 degrees Centigrade determines the specific gravity of the wood. For instance, the specific gravity of *ash* is .50, which means that it weighs exactly half as much as an equal amount of water. *Basswood,* a light wood, has a specific gravity of .35, while that of *hickory* is .61, which is relatively heavy.

Because it is based upon the amount of actual wood substance in a piece of wood, specific gravity is an excellent indication of strength and hardness. In general, the higher the specific gravity, the stronger the wood.

5-3. How a tree grows. A tree grows by forming new layers of wood between the bark and sapwood in the cambium. The actual growth is due to the chemical combination of water and salts from the earth with carbon dioxide from the air. The change takes place in the leaves where chlorophyll uses the energy of the sun to make food called carbohydrate. The process by which the leaves give off moisture is called transpiration.

5-2. An enlarged view of a very small part of a log. The top represents end grain. As you can see, the cells have been cut open. About half the volume of the wood is made up of these hollow spaces.

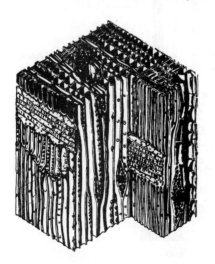

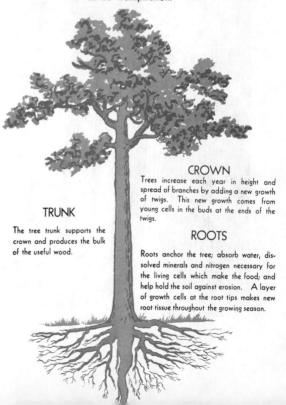

CROWN

Trees increase each year in height and spread of branches by adding a new growth of twigs. This new growth comes from young cells in the buds at the ends of the twigs.

TRUNK

The tree trunk supports the crown and produces the bulk of the useful wood.

ROOTS

Roots anchor the tree; absorb water, dissolved minerals and nitrogen necessary for the living cells which make the food; and help hold the soil against erosion. A layer of growth cells at the root tips makes new root tissue throughout the growing season.

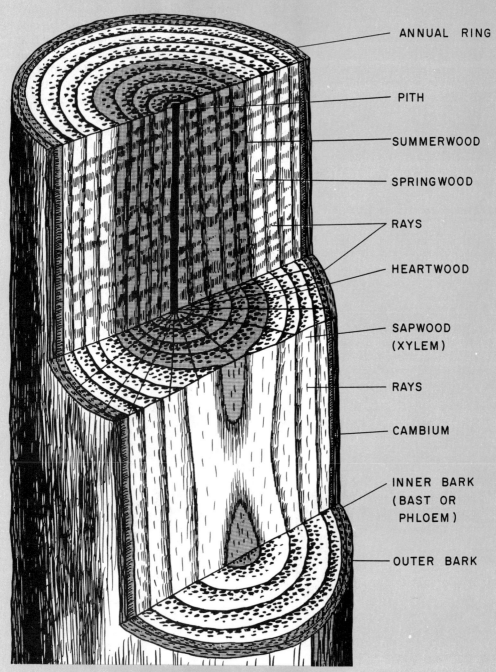

ANNUAL RING

PITH

SUMMERWOOD

SPRINGWOOD

RAYS

HEARTWOOD

SAPWOOD
(XYLEM)

RAYS

CAMBIUM

INNER BARK
(BAST OR
PHLOEM)

OUTER BARK

5-4.   Cross section of a tree trunk.

CELL STRUCTURE

As stated earlier, wood contains countless cells or vessels through which moisture moves to the leaves and branches. These cells are very narrow but may be rather long. Within the cells of living sapwood is a liquid called protoplasm, which is the physical basis of life. It is the living substance of cells, not only in plants but also in animals. Heartwood cells, however, do not contain protoplasm. You will recall that heartwood does not contribute to the growth of the tree and is, in a sense, dead.

Pores are cross sections of cells. When wood is sawed, the open spaces in the cells are exposed, forming openings in the wood surface. To give you some idea of how porous wood is, one cubic inch of wood, having an average specific gravity of .40, will have about 15 square feet of internal surface area at the first level of cells. Even more astonishing, if this internal surface area could be laid out flat in its green condition, it would equal 21,780 square feet, approximately the size of a football field.

This interesting structure of open space and cell walls gives wood its tremendous strength and unusual properties.

GROWTH RINGS

The term *growth ring* is often used in reference to the annual growth of a tree. However, the rings are not always as easy to see as in Fig. 5-6. In certain warm climates, as well as cold ones, there is no sharp division between seasons of growth and non-growth; therefore some tropical woods do not display definite annular indications of growth. Also, some species of woods have distinct growth rings, while others are quite indistinct.

Hardwoods are classified in three groups, based on the pattern of growth rings:

Ring porous has springwood cells that

5-5. When the bark is damaged, the tree must be cut soon or insects and disease will kill it.

5-6. Growth rings. Each ring represents the growth of the tree during one year. If you would count the growth rings on this pine tree, you'd find that there are 43 which is the age of the tree. In counting growth rings, the end of the log towards the ground should be examined. The upper part of the tree shows fewer rings because it is more recent growth.

69

are large and distinct, usually several tiers of cells wide. The summerwood cells are small, indistinct, and thick-walled. The rings are very distinct. Good examples are oak and ash.

Semi-ring porous has fairly distinct springwood cells but not as wide a band of them as in ring-porous wood. Summerwood, which comprises most of the growth ring, is composed of indistinct, thick-walled cells. This is found in hickory and elm. *Diffuse porous* has no distinct demarcation between springwood and summerwood. This absence results in lack of distinct grain pattern. Examples are birch, poplar, walnut, maple, basswood, and cherry.

SPRINGWOOD AND SUMMERWOOD

As indicated earlier, growth rings in trees are made up of springwood and summerwood. The portion formed early in the growing season is called springwood, or early wood, and that which forms later is summerwood, or late wood. In general, springwood has larger cell cavities and thinner walls.

SAPWOOD AND HEARTWOOD

Sapwood is the part of the tree just inside the cambium; it helps to carry sap and to store food for tree growth. Heartwood is made up of inactive cells that have already performed their function for sap conductivity and other life processes of the tree. Heartwood is usually darker than sapwood, as the next paragraph explains.

OTHER CHARACTERISTICS

Color in lumber is determined by chemical substances that are part of the cell walls. Because heartwood contains these materials in greater amounts, it is the darker portion of most woods. Wood colors are often quite variable, particularly in highly pigmented woods such as walnut. Most woods darken with expo-

sure as the coloring matter in the cell walls combines with oxygen. This process is called *oxidation*.

Texture is defined according to the relative porousness or uniformity of the wood tissues. Wood made up entirely of small cells has *fine* texture. When many of the cells are relatively large, the texture is *coarse*.

Grain is determined by the arrangement of cells when the wood is cut longitudinally or from end to end. When most cells are parallel to the center of the tree, the result is called *straight grain*. Frequently, the presence of knots or other defects will cause wood tissues to grow in an unusual manner. This is called *irregular grain*. *Curly grain* is found in wood in which the fibers of the cells are distorted, giving them a curly appearance. A good example is bird's-eye maple. *Spiral grain* results when wood cell fibers take a spiral course around the trunk of the tree instead of the normal vertical course. The spiral may extend in a righthand or lefthand direction. *Interlocked grain* develops when the elements of the growth ring twist in alternate directions as they go up the tree.

Figure is the pattern produced in the wood surface by growth rings, rays, knots, irregular colorations, and deviations from regular grain such as interlocked or curly grain. Fig. 5-7.

Density, you recall, was discussed in

5-7. The wood used in this tray has a very distinct figure.

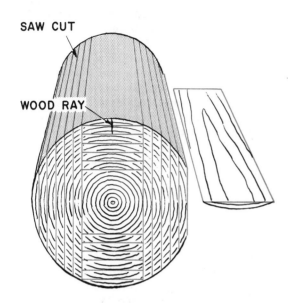

SAW CUT

WOOD RAY

PLAIN-SAWED OR FLAT-GRAINED
(CUT TANGENT TO ANNUAL RINGS)

5-8. This is the least expensive way to cut lumber because it involves less labor and waste. The surface of the lumber shows a U-shaped figure pattern due primarily to the growth rings.

5-9. This flat-grained redwood shows how growth rings form the grain pattern.

connection with specific gravity, page 69. To repeat an important rule, the higher the density, the stronger and harder the wood.

Hardness is the ability of wood to resist indentation. It depends largely upon the thickness of the cell walls and the narrowness of the cell cavities. Hardness is an extremely important quality in selecting woods for furniture.

CUTTING METHODS

The methods of cutting wood are determined by the intended use, appearance, and stability of the wood. We shall consider three cutting methods, of which the first two are the most common. Fig. 5-8.

Wood sawed by the simplest method is called *plain sawed* when it is hardwood, or *flat grained* when softwood. Such wood is sawed at a tangent to the annual rings. The log is squared and sawed lengthwise. Knots that occur are round or oval-shaped and have relatively little weakening effect on the lumber. The annual rings appear as approximately straight lines running across grain. The lines join at the bottom, forming a U-shape; however, this part is sometimes cut off. Fig. 5-9. Rays appear as short lines. Wood cut this way shrinks and swells very little in thickness.

Wood cut by the second method is called *quarter sawed,* if hardwood; it is called *edge grained* or *vertical grained,* if softwood. The log is sawed into quarters, then into boards. Fig. 5-10 shows a common method of cutting the boards. The angle between the cut and the growth rings varies from 90 degrees to about 65 degrees. In such wood the lines formed by the rings run with the grain. Again they will appear as relatively straight or as U-shaped, depending upon how much is cut off. Fig. 5-11. Rays, which are more pronounced than in plain-sawed lumber, are seen as flakes

71

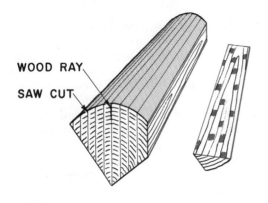

WOOD RAY

SAW CUT

QUARTER-SAWED OR EDGE-GRAINED

5-10. Lumber cut like this is somewhat more expensive to produce but has the advantages of less shrinkage across grain and a better-wearing surface.

5-11. This vertical-grain redwood shows clearly how the annual rings appear as straight lines.

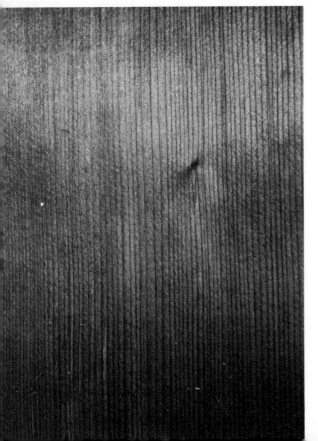

across the board. Such lumber shrinks and swells less in width and warps less than plain-sawed lumber.

The third method is called *rift sawing*. Fig. 5-12. The logs are sawed at not less than 35 or more than 65 degrees to the annual rings, usually about 45 degrees. In wood sawed this way, the rings appear as longitudinal lines. Rays also run longitudinally and are longer than in lumber cut by the other methods.

Hardwoods and Softwoods

The terms hardwood and softwood as used to identify woods are botanical terms and do not indicate actual softness or hardness. Some hardwoods are actually softer than certain of the softwood species. Softwoods are those that come from evergreens (conifers) which are cone-bearing or needle-bearing trees. Common examples are pine, fir, cedar, and redwood. Hardwoods are cut from the broad-leaf, *deciduous* trees. A deciduous tree is one that sheds its leaves annually. Some common hardwoods are walnut, mahogany, maple, birch, cherry, and oak.

Seasoning

When a tree is cut down, the wood may contain from 30 to 300 per cent more moisture than it will after drying.

5-12. This method of cutting is sometimes called comb grain.

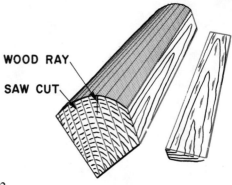

WOOD RAY

SAW CUT

RIFT-SAWED

For example, a piece of wood 2″ x 4″ x 8′ may contain as much as three gallons of water! Fig. 5-13.

There are two methods of seasoning or drying wood: *air drying* and *kiln drying*. Air drying, or seasoning, is done out of doors. The rough lumber is stacked either on edge at an angle or in layers separated by cross pieces called *stickers*. Fig. 5-14. The wood is allowed to remain stacked usually from one to three months and sometimes longer. After correct air drying, the wood should have a minimum moisture content of about 12 to 15 per

cent, but no more than an average of 19 per cent.

In kiln drying, the lumber is stacked in piles with stickers between the boards and then placed in a kiln or oven in which moisture, air, and temperature are carefully controlled. Fig. 5-15. Steam is applied to the wood at low heat; then the steam is reduced and the heat increased. Fig. 5-16. As the heat increases, moisture is taken out of the wood. Properly kiln-dried lumber should have less than 10 per cent moisture content. Moreover, if it is intended for cabinet and furniture

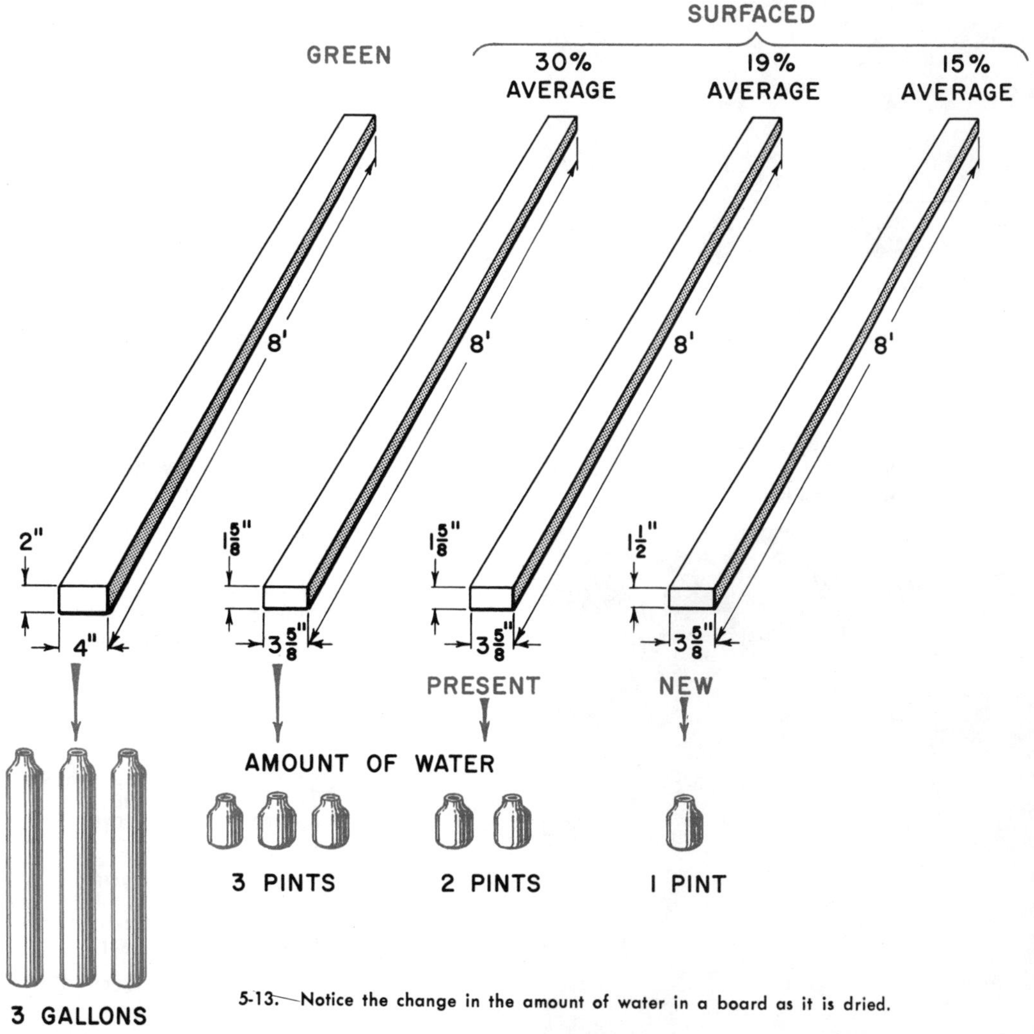

5-13. Notice the change in the amount of water in a board as it is dried.

STEP 1

HIGH STEAM

LOW HEAT

GREEN WOOD

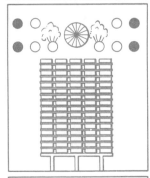

STEP 2

STEAM REDUCED

HEAT INCREASED

WOOD DRYING

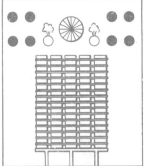

STEP 3

LITTLE STEAM

HIGH HEAT

WOOD SEASONED

5-14. Stacks of lumber being air dried in a sawmill yard. Softwood is stacked at the right while hardwoods are in the distance.

5-15. Loading lumber into a kiln.

5-16. Steps in kiln drying lumber. The heat and humidity of the air are carefully controlled.

5-17. How a cell changes in size as the water is removed.

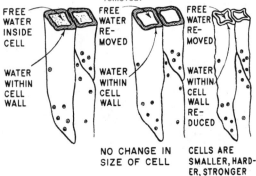

FREE WATER INSIDE CELL

WATER WITHIN CELL WALL

FREE WATER REMOVED

WATER WITHIN CELL WALL

FREE WATER REMOVED

WATER WITHIN CELL WALL REDUCED

NO CHANGE IN SIZE OF CELL

CELLS ARE SMALLER, HARDER, STRONGER

74

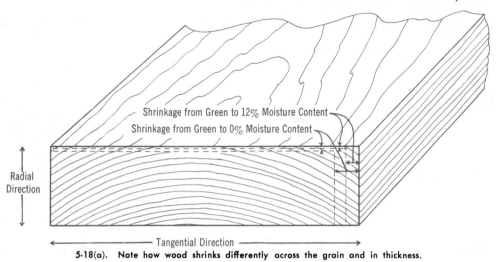

Radial Direction

Tangential Direction

5-18(a). Note how wood shrinks differently across the grain and in thickness.

construction, it should have 7 to 8 per cent, or even slightly less.

SHRINKAGE OF LUMBER

In the drying process lumber tends to shrink, both in width and in length. However, shrinkage in length is normally so small that in almost all species it is not considered a problem. The United States Forest Products Laboratory has conducted many tests which bear this out. Following is an explanation of why wood shrinks.

Water exists in green wood in two conditions: *free* in the cell cavities, and *absorbed* in the cell walls. When the cell walls have absorbed all the water they can hold, but there is no water in the cavities, the wood is at the *fiber-saturation point*. Water in excess of this amount cannot be absorbed by the cell walls and, therefore, fills the cell cavities. Removal of this free water has no apparent effect upon the properties of wood except to reduce its weight. However, as soon as any water in the cell walls is removed, wood begins to shrink. Since the free water is the first to be removed, shrinkage does not begin until after the fiber-saturation point is reached.

Fiber-saturation point for woods varies from about 23 to 30 per cent moisture content but, for practical purposes, it can be taken as approximately 28 per cent for most woods. Reductions in moisture from natural or green condition down to roughly 28 per cent, therefore, do not result in shrinkage. Fig. 5-17.

After the fiber-saturation point has been passed and the cell walls begin to give up their moisture, they shrink in all directions and not uniformly. The cause of shrinkage is contraction of the cell walls. The cells are reduced in diameter and drawn closer together. This is traceable to the peculiar structure of the cell walls. The theory is that most vegetable-cell walls are composed of minute, elongated fibrils which have an affinity for water. The water is held around each particle of fibril and holds the group of fibrils apart. As the cell walls dry out, the space between the fibrils becomes narrower and the fibrils themselves draw together, causing shrinkage of the cell walls. Combined shrinkage of all cell walls decreases the size of the whole piece. This process causes a certain amount of shrinkage across the face of wood that is edge-grained (vertical) or

75

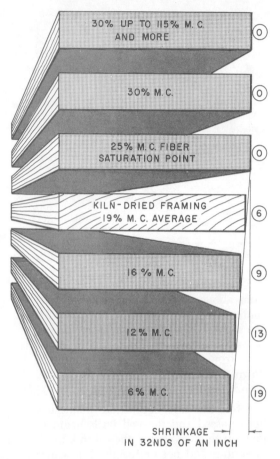

30% UP TO 115% M.C. AND MORE — 0

30% M.C. — 0

25% M.C. FIBER SATURATION POINT — 0

KILN-DRIED FRAMING 19% M.C. AVERAGE — 6

16% M.C. — 9

12% M.C. — 13

6% M.C. — 19

SHRINKAGE
IN 32NDS OF AN INCH

5-18(b). Here you see how much shrinkage there is in the width of a plain-sawed piece of 2″ x 10″ softwood lumber.

5-19. Check defect.

quarter-sawed, and about twice as much in plain-sawed or flat-grained wood. Fig. 5-18(a).

Rays are groups of cells which run perpendicular to the trunk. Thus they are also perpendicular to the regular bundles of cells, which are parallel to the trunk. These rays radiate from the center of the tree, passing between cell bundles, through the cambium layer, to almost the outer part of the bark. The stiffening effect of these rays helps prevent vertical-grained or quarter-sawed wood from shrinking as much as plain-sawed or flat-grained. Fig. 5-18(b).

Another factor which influences the extent to which wood shrinks is its density, that is, the actual amount of wood substance is a unit of volume, as indicated by the dry weight of the wood. Heavier woods shrink and swell more than lighter ones with a given change in moisture content.

In carefully dried wood there is little difference between sapwood and heartwood in respect to shrinking and swelling. Sapwood, however, may be more susceptible to changes in atmospheric humidity and, therefore, its dimensions may change more quickly than those of heartwood.

As a rule, the manufacturer of wood products is more interested in how to keep his lumber from "working" while it is run through the shop and after it is in place in the finished article than he is in the extent of shrinkage from the green to the dry condition. Except for the PEG (polyethylene glycol) treatment described in Unit 38, nothing practical has been devised for keeping wood products absolutely free from shrinking and swelling when in use.

LUMBER DEFECTS

Defects in lumber are faults which detract from its quality, either in appearance or utility. Defining various defects is difficult. A light or small defect in one piece would often be a medium or large defect in another. In better grades of lumber the defects are light, small, or serious depending upon the size of the piece and the way they come in combination with other defects. Some common defects may be defined as follows:

A *bark pocket* is a patch of bark partially or wholly enclosed in wood. A *check* is a crack in the wood structure of a piece, usually running lengthwise. Fig. 5-19. A *peck* consists of a channeled or pitted area or pocket. Wood tissues between pecky areas remain unaffected in appearance and strength. Peckiness occurs only while the tree is still alive. *Decay* is disintegration of wood fiber. It shows in various stages from barely perceptible to soft and very evident. Fig. 5-20. *Rot* and *dote* mean the same as decay. *Heart pith* is the spongy center of the tree which appears on the surface of a piece of lumber. *Shake* is a crack between and parallel to the rings of annual growth. It produces a defect in the lumber noticeably different from heart pith. *Stain* is a discoloration that penetrates the wood fiber. It can be any color other than the natural color of the piece in which it is found. It is classed as light, medium, or heavy and is generally blue or brown. Light stain is often barely perceptible. Fig. 5-21. *Wormholes* are caused by insects and beetles. A *pin wormhole* is not over 1/4″ in diameter. Wormholes bigger than 1/4″ are classed as large. Fig. 5-22.

A *knot* in a piece of sawed lumber is a portion of a branch or limb of the tree. Fig. 5-23. If a board has more than one knot, the average diameter of the largest and smallest knots determines the measurement, unless otherwise stated. A *branch knot* is one that has been sawed at an angle parallel, or nearly parallel, to the direction of limb growth. A *spike*

5-20. Decay.

5-21. Heavy blue stain which developed in lumber that was piled solid outdoors in wet, warm weather.

5-22. Insect damage. The upper piece has large grub holes probably caused by round-headed borers. The lower piece has small pin holes probably caused by beetles.

knot is a branch knot that runs to the edge of a piece of lumber, growing larger as it nears the edge. A *pin knot* is one not over 1/2″ in diameter. A *small knot* is one between 1/2″ and 3/4″ in diameter. A *medium knot* is one larger than 3/4″, but not over 1½″ in diameter. A *large knot* is one over 1½″ in diameter. A *red knot* results from live branch growth in the tree; it is firmly grown into the wood structure. An *intergrown knot* is partly or wholly grown together with the fiber of the surrounding wood. A *black knot* results from a dead branch which the wood growth of the tree has surrounded. A *sound knot* is free from decay. An *unsound knot* has some decay; it may vary in degree from incipient (just the first traces) to pronounced. An *encased* or *tight* knot is one so fixed by growth or position in the wood structure that it firmly retains its place in the piece. A *not-firm knot*, under ordinary conditions, will hold its place in a dry board. Under pressure it can be started but not easily pushed out of the piece. A *loose knot* is one that cannot be relied upon to remain in place in the piece.

Pitch is an accumulation of resinous material. It may be light, medium, or heavy, as shown by its color and consistency. *Massed pitch* is a clearly defined accumulation of solid pitch. A *pitch pocket* is a well defined opening in the wood fiber which holds, or has held, pitch. A *very small pitch pocket* is one not over 1/8″ wide and not over 2″ long. A *small pitch pocket* is one not over 1/8″ in width and not over 4″ in length, or not more than 1/4″ in width nor over 2″ in length. A *medium pitch pocket* is one not wider than 1/8″ nor longer than 8″, or not over 3/8″ in width nor over 4″ in length. In a *large pitch pocket* the width or length exceeds the maximum for a medium pitch pocket.

Wane is the presence of bark or absence of wood on corners of a piece of

5-23. Common kinds of knots: (a). Intergrown. (b). Encased. (c). Spike. (d). Decayed. (e). Knot hole.

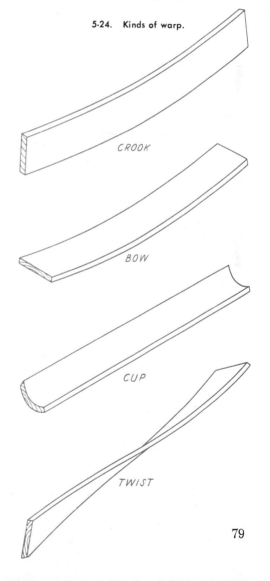

5-24. Kinds of warp.

CROOK

BOW

CUP

TWIST

lumber. *Warp* is any variation from a true or plane surface including crook, bow, cup, twist, or any combination of these. Fig. 5-24. *Bow* and *crook* are similar. Both are deviations from a straight line drawn from one end of the piece of lumber to the other. If you were to place a slender board on its thin edge and draw the corners back toward you, this would give you an idea of *bow*. By placing the thin board on its flat side and bending the corners toward you, you get the effect of *crook*.

Manufacturing imperfections are those defects that develop during the processing of lumber. A *roller check* is caused when a piece of cupped lumber is flattened as it passes between the machine rollers. *Torn grain* is a roughened area. This sometimes happens during the surfacing of lumber when the machine tears out bits of wood. A *skip* is an area that the planer failed to surface. In a *slight skip* the area was not surfaced smooth. In a *heavy skip* the planer knife did not touch the area at all. A *machine burn* is a darkening of the wood due to sticking and overheating of the knives.

⑥ Kinds Of Woods*

Over 100,000 different varieties of woods, from several hundred species, are used commercially. However, many are used in rather limited amounts for specialized purposes. Even among the more common woods there is great difference in demand, partly depending on the availability of the particular wood in various sections of the country. Fig. 6-1. Except for the fine cabinet woods described in the next unit, cabinetmakers tend to use those woods that are in good supply in their areas.

Identifying most of the common wood species is relatively simple. However, identification of each kind of wood is more difficult because there are so many kinds and because pieces of the same kind vary more or less in appearance and properties. Mahogany, for example, is sometimes light-colored and sometimes dark. One piece of mahogany can be twice as heavy as another of the same size. Sometimes there is also a superficial resemblance between entirely unrelated woods. Birch and maple or cherry and mahogany can, at times, look very much alike. For these reasons it is necessary to be precise when describing woods.

You can learn to recognize the more common woods by general appearance. However, precise exact identification requires careful study of such details as pores, growth rings, rays, color, odor, weight, and hardness. If you ever have difficulty identifying a particular wood, the safest practice is to send a sample to the official wood identification agency of the United States Government, which is the Forest Products Laboratory at Madison, Wisconsin. This organization receives thousands of requests annually for identification. The service is free.

Most woods for furniture must have good appearance, be comparatively free from warp, excessive shrinking, and swelling, and have sufficient hardness to resist indentation. For this reason, most furniture woods are hardwoods. The

---

*Adapted from material by courtesy of Forest Products Laboratory, U. S. Forest Service.

Forest Regions of the United States

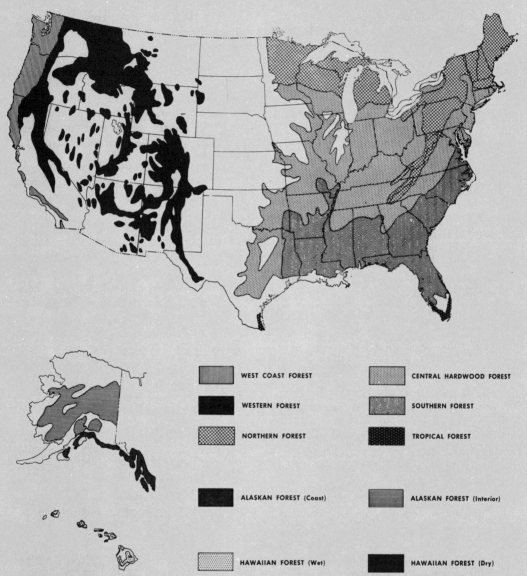

WEST COAST FOREST	CENTRAL HARDWOOD FOREST
WESTERN FOREST	SOUTHERN FOREST
NORTHERN FOREST	TROPICAL FOREST
ALASKAN FOREST (Coast)	ALASKAN FOREST (Interior)
HAWAIIAN FOREST (Wet)	HAWAIIAN FOREST (Dry)

6-1. This map shows areas of renewable natural wealth. The West Coast or Pacific forests are primarily Douglas fir. However, they also have western red cedar, spruce, and hemlock. The western forests include much of our softwood timber, primarily pine, although there are some hardwoods. The northern forests have such trees as hemlock, red spruce, white pine, and several kinds of hardwoods. The central hardwood forests include oak, cherry, birch, and many other kinds of hardwoods. In the southern forests are such softwoods as pine and cypress, and many kinds of hardwoods. The tropical forests have ebony and palm trees. The coast regions of Alaska have primarily western hemlock and spruce while the interior forests are heavy with white spruce and white birch. The Hawaiian forests have many softwoods and some unusual trees such as monkey pod and koa. The forest areas of the United States comprise over three quarters of a billion acres, or more land than in all the states east of the Mississippi.

term "hardwood" here applies to the wood of any broadleaf (deciduous) tree. The term "softwood" is used to describe cone-bearing trees regardless of whether their wood is hard or soft. Softwoods as a group are rarely used for furniture but more generally for interior cabinets, paneling, built-ins, and trim. Following are descriptions of some woods in common use.

SOFTWOODS *(Cone-Bearing Species)*

DOUGLAS-FIR

(Pseudotsuga menziesii) Fig. 6-2.

Range.—In the United States, Douglas-fir grows in most forests from the Rocky Mountains to the Pacific coast and from the Mexican to Canadian borders. Botanically it is not a true fir. It reaches its largest size and fastest rate of growth in Washington and Oregon, where large trees form very dense forests that sometimes yield as much as 100,000 board-feet of lumber per acre.

Properties.—Most old-growth Douglas-fir from the Pacific coast and northern Rocky Mountain states is moderately heavy, very stiff, moderately strong, and moderately shock resistant. It averages about 33 pounds a cubic foot. The wood is also moderately hard, with an average specific gravity ranging from 0.40 to 0.48. Wide-ringed second-growth Douglas-fir from the coastal states and material grown in the southern Rocky Mountain states tends to be lighter in weight and to have lower strength properties.

The wood of Douglas-fir can be readily kiln-dried if proper methods are used. Although it is more difficult to work with handtools than the soft pines, it holds fastenings well and can be glued satisfactorily. Dense heartwood has moderate decay resistance.

Uses.—The principal uses of Douglas-fir are for lumber, timbers, piling, and plywood. Remanufactured lumber goes mostly into sash, doors, general millwork, railroad car construction and repair, and boxes and crates. Plywood is now in wide use for sheathing, concrete forms, prefabricated house panels, millwork, ships and boats, and other structural forms.

Description.—Heartwood is orange red to red or sometimes yellowish. Resin canals, which are seen as brownish streaks in the summerwood, appear to be more abundant and more readily detectable than in western larch. Transition from springwood to summerwood is similar to that in western larch. The heartwood of Douglas-fir may be confused with that of the southern yellow pines, but resin canals are larger and much more abundant in southern pines. Most Douglas-fir has a distinctive odor.

WESTERN LARCH

(Larix occidentalis) Fig. 6-3.

Range.—Western larch grows in mountain valleys and on slopes at elevations of 2,000 to 7,000 feet in Washington, Oregon, western Montana, and northern Idaho. It reaches its best development and greatest commercial importance in northern Idaho and western Montana, where it is generally associated with other species, although sometimes forming pure forests of limited extent.

6-2. Douglas-fir grain pattern and other characteristics. (For all softwoods, Figs. 6-2 through 6-9, top view shows end surface. Middle view shows edge-grained surface. Bottom view shows flat-grained surface.)*

*All photos of wood surfaces in this unit are courtesy of U. S. Forest Service. Forest Products Laboratory Photos.

Properties.—A heavy wood, western larch has an average weight of 38 pounds per cubic foot. Also, it is moderately hard, with a specific gravity of 0.51, stiff, strong, and moderately high in shock resistance.

Western larch and Douglas-fir are frequently logged together and sold in mixture under the commercial name of "larch-fir." Heartwood of both species is moderately decay resistant. Western larch has large shrinkage in drying and presents seasoning problems because of the slowness with which it gives up its moisture. Although it ranks high in nail-withdrawal resistance, small or blunt-pointed nails are preferred to reduce splitting.

Uses.—Western larch is used principally in building construction as rough dimension, small timbers, planks, and boards. Considerable amounts also are made into crossties and mine timbers. Probably three-fourths of the lumber produced is used for structural purposes as it comes from the sawmill. Some of the high-grade lumber is remanufactured into interior finish, flooring, sash, doors, blinds, and other products.

Description.—Heartwood is russet brown and the color is best seen in summerwood bands on flat-grained surfaces. Resin canals are present, but are very small and difficult to find unless the resin has stained the wood surfaces or the exudation actually appears as very small droplets. Transition from springwood to summerwood is abrupt and there is little difference in color between the two zones. The heartwood lacks a distinctive odor.

PONDEROSA PINE

(Pinus ponderosa) Fig. 6-4.

Range.—Ponderosa pine grows in every state west of the Great Plains, with the largest stands and greatest commercial production in California, Oregon, and Washington. The tree is found on a wide variety of soils, sites, and elevations and occurs both in pure stands and in mixture with other species. Because it can

6-2. Douglas-fir.   6-3. Western larch.   6-4. Ponderosa pine.

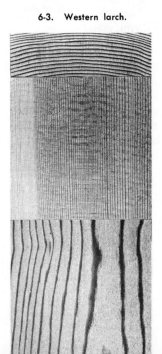

maintain itself on dry sites, this tree is the principal species on areas of low rainfall.

Properties.—The wood of ponderosa pine varies considerably in its properties. However, in the outer portions of trees of sawtimber size, it generally is moderately light in weight, averaging 28 pounds per cubic foot, and moderately soft, with a specific gravity of 0.38. This wood also ranks as moderately weak, moderately limber, and moderately low in shock resistance. It has moderately small shrinkage and little tendency to warp.

Ponderosa pine compares favorably with woods of similar density in nail-withdrawal resistance, is not easily split by nails, and glues easily. The heartwood has low to moderate decay resistance.

Uses.—Ponderosa pine is used principally for lumber and, to a lesser extent, for piling, poles, posts, mine timbers, veneer, and hewn ties. The lumber has a variety of uses ranging from high-grade millwork to boxes and crates. For cabinets and millwork, the clearer, softer material is used, while the manufacture of boxes and crates consumes the lower grade lumber. Knotty ponderosa pine has come into wide use as paneling for interior.

Description.—Heartwood is yellowish to light reddish or orange brown. Transition from springwood to summerwood is abrupt as in the southern pines, but the summerwood bands are narrow. Growth rings are generally most prominent on the flat-grained surfaces, which also frequently exhibit a dimpled appearance. This appearance is common in lodgepole pine too, but in lodgepole the dimples are smaller and more abundant. The resin canals of ponderosa pine are abundant and easily found in all annual rings. They are larger than those in lodgepole pine, and the heartwood of lodgepole pine is lighter colored than that of ponderosa.

SHORTLEAF PINE

(Pinus echinata) Fig. 6-5.

Range.—Shortleaf pine, which has the widest distribution of the southern pines, grows throughout most of the southeastern United States. It is generally a tree of the uplands and foothills, but its range extends into the lower levels. Stands of shortleaf pine are concentrated in Arkansas, but Texas, Georgia, Alabama, and Mississippi also contain large stands.

Properties.—Shortleaf pine, a moderately heavy wood but ranking with the lightest of the important southern pines, has an average weight of 36 pounds a cubic foot. Typically, the wood is moderately hard, with a specific gravity of 0.46, moderately strong, stiff, and moderately shock resistant. The heartwood is moderately decay resistant.

Like all southern pines, shortleaf has moderately large shrinkage but tends to stay in place well after seasoning. In nail-withdrawal resistance, it ranks above hemlock, spruce, and Douglas-fir. And, like other southern pines, it produces a resinous substance from which turpentine and rosin can be made.

Uses.—Shortleaf pine lumber is used principally for building material such as interior finish, ceiling, frames, sash, sheathing, subflooring, and joists, and for boxes and crates, caskets, furniture, woodenware, and novelties. Considerable use is also made of shortleaf pine for crossties, telephone and telegraph poles, and mine timbers. In addition, the resin-rich heartwood is distilled to make wood turpentine, tar, and tar oils.

Description.—Heartwood r a n g e s from shades of yellow and orange to reddish brown or light brown. Transition from springwood to summerwood is abrupt, with the annual rings prominent on all surfaces. Resin canals are large and abundant and are easily found in all annual rings. Summerwood bands are generally wider than those of ponderosa pine. In appearance, the wood of shortleaf pine closely resembles that of longleaf, loblolly, and slash, the other principal southern pines.

SUGAR PINE

(Pinus lambertiana) Fig. 6-6

Range.—Sugar pine grows from the Coast and Cascade Mountain Ranges of southern Oregon, along the Coast range and the Sierra Nevada of California, through southern California in scattered stands, and into Mexico. The heaviest stands and largest trees are found in California from Tulare to Eldorado Counties, in cool, moist sites on the west slope of the Sierra Nevada at elevations of 4,000 to 7,000 feet.

Properties.—Sugar pine is lightweight, averaging 25 pounds a cubic foot. The wood is moderately soft, with a specific gravity of 0.35, moderately limber, moderately weak, and low in shock resistance.

In decay resistance, sugar pine heartwood is rated low to moderate. The wood has very small shrinkage, seasons readily without checking or warping, and stays in place well. It is easy to work with tools, does not split easily in nailing, and has moderate nail-withdrawal resistance.

Uses.—Sugar pine is used almost entirely for lumber in buildings, boxes and crates, sash, doors, frames, general millwork, and foundry patterns. It is suitable for all phases of house construction, with the high-grade material going into interior and exterior trim, siding, and paneling, while the lower grade material is used for sheathing, subflooring, and roof boards.

The wood also has proved very satisfactory for containers because of its light weight and color, nailing properties, and freedom from taste and odor. Sugar pine is widely used for foundry patterns because it meets the exacting requirements

6-5. Shortleaf pine.

6-6. Sugar pine.

6-7. Western white pine.

and is readily available in wide, thick pieces practically free from defects.

Description.—Heartwood is light brown to pale reddish brown. Resin canals are abundant and commonly stain the surface of the wood with resin. Transition from springwood to summerwood is gradual; making the growth rings appear less prominent on flat-grained surfaces.

WESTERN WHITE PINE

(Pinus monticola) Fig. 6-7.

Range.—Western white pine grows from the Canadian border southward into western Montana and northern Idaho, and along the Cascade and Sierra Nevada Mountains through Washington and Oregon to central California. The heaviest stands occur in northern Idaho and in adjacent parts of Montana and Washington. The trees usually grow in mixture with western hemlock, western redcedar, western larch, grand fir, and Douglas-fir, but occasionally occur in pure stands on limited areas.

Properties.—Moderately light in weight, western white pine averages 27 pounds a cubic foot. The wood is moderately soft, with a specific gravity of 0.36, weak, moderately stiff, and moderately low in ability to resist shock.

Although the wood has moderately large shrinkage, it is easy to kiln-dry and stays in place well after seasoning. In decay resistance, it is ranked as low to moderate. Western white pine works easily with tools and glues readily. It does not split easily in nailing and occupies an intermediate position in nail-withdrawal resistance.

Uses.—Practically all of the western white pine cut is sawed into lumber. About three-fourths of this lumber is used in building construction. The lower grades are used for subflooring and wall and roof sheathing, while the high-grade material

is made into siding of various kinds, exterior and interior trim, partition, casing, base, and paneling. Other uses of western white pine include match planks, boxes, and millwork products.

Description.—Heartwood is cream colored to light brown or reddish brown. Resin canals are abundant and transition from springwood to summerwood is like that in sugar pine. Separation of western white pine and sugar pine is generally accomplished on the basis of the resin canals, which are larger in sugar pine than in the other white pines. Microscopic characteristics, however, offer a more reliable means of differentiation than gross features.

REDWOOD

(Sequoia sempervirens) Fig. 6-8.

Range.—Redwood grows along or near the coast of California in a narrow, irregular strip not more than 35 miles wide and about 500 miles long, extending from 100 miles south of San Francisco to a little above the Oregon border. This massive tree does not grow naturally outside this area, which is characterized by frequent fogs and considerable soil moisture. Single acres of redwood have been found that contained over 1 million board-feet of lumber.

Properties.—Typical virgin-growth redwood is moderately light in weight, averaging 28 pounds a cubic foot. The wood is moderately hard, with a specific gravity of 0.38, moderately strong, and moderately stiff. Except for shock resistance, it has somewhat higher strength properties for its weight than would be expected.

Redwood is thought to owe its outstanding decay resistance to the reddish extractive in the tree, which colors the wood and accounts for its name. The wood has very small shrinkage, is comparatively easy to season, and holds its shape well after seasoning. Redwood has only intermediate nail-withdrawal resistance but takes and holds paint exceptionally well. Redwood, the cedars, and baldcypress make up the group of woods with the highest resistance to termites.

Uses.—Probably from one-half to two-thirds of the redwood lumber produced is used in the form of planks, dimension, boards, joists, and posts. A large part of this material goes into framing for houses and industrial buildings, and into bridges, trestles, and other heavy construction. Much of the remaining lumber is remanufactured into house siding, sash, blinds, doors, general millwork, outdoor furniture, and tanks. Richly colored redwood paneling provides pleasing interior effects.

Description.—Heartwood is usually a uniform deep reddish brown. The wood is without resin canals and has no distinctive odor, taste, or feel. Western redcedar may approach redwood in color, but the distinctive odor of western redcedar separates the two woods.

SITKA SPRUCE

(Picea sitchensis) Fig. 6-9.

Range.—Sitka spruce grows along the Pacific coast from Alaska to northern California. It is rarely found over 40 miles from the coast and generally grows in mixture with Douglas-fir, grand fir, western hemlock, and western redcedar. It occasionally forms pure stands.

Properties.—Sitka spruce is a moderately lightweight wood, averaging 28 pounds a cubic foot. The wood also is moderately soft, with a specific gravity of 0.37, moderately weak in bending and compressive strength, moderately stiff, and moderately low in resistance to shock. On the basis of weight, however, it ranks high in strength properties.

Although the wood has moderately large shrinkage, it is not difficult to kiln-dry. It works easily, holds fastenings well, and can be obtained in clear, straight-grained pieces of large size and uniform texture with hardly any hidden defects. Its decay resistance is low. Although planed surfaces of Sitka spruce lumber

For hardwoods, Figs. 6-10 through 6-27, top view shows end surface, middle view shows quarter-sawed surface, bottom view shows plain-sawed surfaces, except as noted on Figs. 6-19 and 6-20.

6-8. Redwood.   6-9. Sitka spruce.   6-10. White ash.

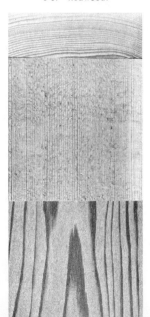
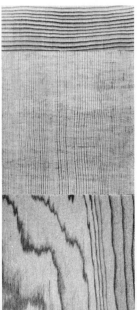

may show a silky sheen, the wood has a tendency to produce woolly or fuzzy grain under the action of planer knives. As a pulpwood, Sitka spruce ranks high because of its long, strong fibers and the ease with which it can be pulped by any of the pulping processes.

Uses.—Sitka spruce is used principally for lumber, cooperage, and paper pulp. Some of the lumber is used for construction just as it comes from the sawmill, but the greater part is remanufactured into various products. At least half of the remanufactured lumber goes into boxes and crates. The other major uses of the lumber are for furniture, planing-mill products, sash, doors, blinds, and gen-eral millwork. Specialty uses include air-craft, ladder rails, and piano sounding boards.

Description.—Heartwood is light pinkish yellow to pale brown. Transition from springwood to summerwood is gradual, making the annual rings appear rather inconspicuous on flat-grained surfaces. Resin canals are usually more prominent than in the other spruces. On end-grain surfaces, the canals appear as small dots or very short lines that run parallel to the growth ring. Flat-grained surfaces are lustrous and frequently exhibit dim-pling. The pinkish color of the heart-wood distinguishes this species from all other spruces.

HARDWOODS *(Broad-Leafed Species)*

WHITE ASH

(Fraxinus americana) Fig. 6-10.

Range.—White ash grows throughout the entire eastern half of the United States except along the Atlantic Coastal Plain, the gulf coast, and Florida. It is cut com-mercially everywhere except in the ex-treme outer limits of this range and the lower Mississippi Valley.

Properties.—White ash is a heavy wood with an average weight of 42 pounds a cubic foot. Ranked as a hard wood, it has a specific gravity of 0.55. It also is classified as strong and stiff, and has good shock resistance.

The wood of white ash is noted for its excellent bending qualities. In ease of working, tendency to split, and ability to hold nails and screws, it has moderately high rank. White ash lumber can be rap-idly and satisfactorily kiln-dried, and it holds its shape well even under the ac-tion of water. The wood remains smooth under continual rubbing but is low in decay resistance.

Uses.—The use of white ash that dwarfs all others is its utilization for handles. It is the standard wood for D-handles for shovels and spades and for long handles for forks, hoes, rakes, and shovels. The wood is used too in the manufacture of furniture, where it is especially valuable for the bent parts of chairs. White ash is used almost exclusively for many types of sports and athletic equipment, such as long oars and baseball bats.

Description.—Heartwood is b r o w n to dark brown, sometimes with a reddish tint. As in black ash, the zone of large pores is visible and usually sharply de-fined. The white dots or lines that indi-cate summerwood pores are usually more prominent in white than in black ash. The small wood rays are generally visible only on quartersawed surfaces.

White ash is sometimes confused with hickory, but the two species are readily distinguishable. The zone of large pores is more distinctive in ash than in hickory. Also, the summerwood zone in ash shows white dots or lines that are visible to the unaided eye, but in hickory these dots or lines are visible only upon mag-nification.

AMERICAN BASSWOOD

(Tilia americana) Fig. 6-11.

Range.—Basswood grows throughout the eastern half of the United States from Maine westward to North Dakota and southward to Florida and eastern Texas. More than half of the total stand is located in the Lake States, and another quarter is in the east central part of the range.

Properties.—Basswood is a lightweight hardwood with an average weight of 26 pounds a cubic foot. The wood is weak, moderately stiff, and low in resistance to shock. Its specific gravity of 0.32 classes it as soft.

Although it has large shrinkage, basswood is fairly easy to air-dry or kiln-dry and stays in place well after seasoning. It has low nail-withdrawal resistance, but well resists splitting while being nailed. In decay resistance it is low. The wood is easy to work with tools, takes and holds paint well, and is easily glued. When pulped by the soda process, basswood yields a soft, short-fibered, easily bleached pulp.

Uses.—Most of the basswood cut in this country is first made into lumber for a variety of items. The largest amounts are used for crates and boxes. The manufacture of sash, doors, and general millwork also accounts for much of the basswood lumber produced each year. In addition considerable lumber and veneer is used in the furniture industry, especially as core material overlaid with high-grade furniture veneers, such as walnut and mahogany.

Description. — Heartwood is creamy white to creamy brown or sometimes reddish. Pores are very small, as in aspen, and growth rings on plainsawed surfaces are generally faint. Wood rays are broader and higher than in aspen, and the two species can be readily distinguished by comparing their quarter-sawed faces. While the rays of aspen are low and uniform in height, some of those in basswood are distinctly higher than others and frequently darker than the background wood.

AMERICAN BEECH

(Fagus grandifolia) Fig. 6-12.

Range. —The natural range of beech in the United States extends from Maine to northern Florida and westward from the Atlantic coast into Wisconsin, Missouri, and Texas. It usually grows in mixture with other species, although pure stands of considerable extent occur in the Blue Ridge Mountains, especially in North Carolina.

Properties.—One of the heavy woods, American beech has an average weight of 45 pounds a cubic foot and, with a specific gravity of 0.56, is classified as hard. It is rated high in strength and shock resistance and is readily bent when steamed.

Beech is subject to very large shrinkage and requires considerable care during seasoning if checks, warp, and discoloration are to be avoided. Heartwood ranks low in resistance to decay. The wood wears well and stays smooth when subjected to friction, even under water. Although ranking high in nail-withdrawal resistance, it has a tendency to split when nails are driven into it. When pulped by the soda process, beech yields a short-fibered pulp that can be mixed with longer fibered pulps to obtain paper of satisfactory strength.

Uses.—American beech is used for lumber, distilled products, veneer, railroad ties, pulpwood, cooperage, and fuel. The lumber is used largely in the manufacture of boxes, crates, baskets, furniture, handles, flooring, woodenware, general millwork, and novelties. Beech is especially suitable for food containers, since it does not impart taste or odor.

Description.—Heartwood is white with a reddish tinge to reddish brown. Pores are not visible but wood rays can be seen on all surfaces. On the end grain, the rays appear to be irregularly spaced, while on quartersawed surfaces they appear to be of different heights along the grain. On the plainsawed surfaces, the rays also appear to be of different height, but they look much narrower in this view. Beech is readily distinguishable from other native species by its weight, conspicuous rays, and tiny pores.

YELLOW BIRCH

(Betula alleghaniensis) Fig. 6-13.

Range.—Yellow birch grows in the Lake States, New England, New York, New Jersey, Pennsylvania, and along the Appalachian Mountains into southern Georgia. It reaches its best development near the Canadian border, and more than half of the stand is located in Michigan. The largest amounts of lumber are produced in Michigan and Wisconsin.

Properties.—Yellow birch is heavy, averaging 43 pounds a cubic foot, and hard, with specific gravity averaging 0.55. The wood is strong, stiff, and has very high shock resistance.

Yellow birch has very large shrinkage and must be seasoned carefully to prevent checking and warping. Like all commercial birches, it is low in decay resistance. Although the wood is difficult to work with handtools, it can be readily shaped by machine and ranks high in nail-withdrawal resistance.

Uses.—Yellow birch is used principally for lumber, veneer, distilled products, and crossties. The lumber and veneer go mostly into furniture, boxes, baskets, crates, woodenware, interior finish, and general millwork. It is because of its pleasing grain pattern and ability to take a high polish that yellow birch is widely used in the furniture industry Spools, bobbins, and other turned articles are also important products.

6-11. American basswood.

6-12. American beech.

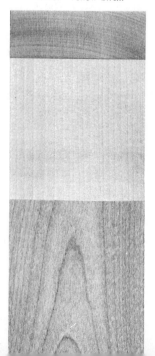

6-13. Yellow birch.

Description.—Yellow birch heartwood is light reddish brown. Pores are very small, sometimes just barely visible on smoothly cut end-grain surfaces, and are uniformly distributed through the annual ring cross section. Pore lines are visible on longitudinal surfaces as very fine grooves that may even be seen through natural finishes. Wood rays may be seen only on quartersawed surfaces, where they appear to be of one size and of uniform height along the grain. Growth rings are moderately distinct on plainsawed surfaces.

BLACK CHERRY

(Prunus serotina) Fig. 6-14.

Range.—Black cherry's natural growth range is throughout Maine westward to eastern North Dakota and southward to central areas of Florida and Texas. It also occurs in the mountain ranges of western Texas. The largest supplies of black cherry are believed to be located in the Appalachian Mountains in New York, Pennsylvania, and West Virginia.

Properties.—Black cherry is a moderately heavy wood with an average weight of 35 pounds a cubic foot. The wood is also moderately hard, with a specific gravity of 0.47. Stiff and strong, it ranks high in resistance to shock.

Although it has moderately large shrinkage, black cherry stays in place well after seasoning and is comparatively free from checking and warping. It has moderate resistance to decay. The wood is difficult to work with handtools but ranks high in bending strength. It can be glued satisfactorily with moderate care.

Uses.—Nearly all the black cherry cut is sawed into lumber for various products. Much goes into furniture and considerable amounts are used for backing blocks on which electrotype plates, used in printing, are mounted. Other uses include burial caskets, woodenware and novelties, patterns and flasks for metalworking, plumbers' woodwork, and finish in buildings and railway coaches.

Description.—Black cherry, which is not easily confused with other native species because of its distinctive color, has light to dark reddish brown heartwood. Although individual pores are not visible to the naked eye, their pattern is sometimes distinctive. On end-grain surfaces, the pores may appear to form lines that parallel the growth rings, while on plainsawed surfaces, they may follow the outline of the growth-ring boundary.

The wood rays of cherry are barely visible on end-grain surfaces and tend to produce a distinctive flake pattern on true quartersawed surfaces. They are higher along the grain than those of walnut and hence show more prominently on quartersawed surfaces.

COTTONWOOD

(Populus) Fig. 6-15.

Species names. — Eastern cottonwood *(Populus deltoides)*, swamp cottonwood *(P. heterophylla)*, and black cottonwood *(P. trichocarpa)*.

Range.—Eastern and swamp cottonwood grow in small scattered stands or in mixture with other species. They range from southern New England westward to the southern part of the Lake States and southward to northern Florida and eastern Texas, except in the Appalachian highlands from New York to Georgia and in the Ozark Mountains of Arkansas and Missouri. Black cottonwood grows in the Pacific coast states and in western Montana, northern Idaho, and western Nevada.

Properties.—The cottonwoods are moderately light in weight, ranging from 24 to 28 pounds a cubic foot. With a specific gravity of 0.37, eastern cottonwood is classified as moderately soft, while black cottonwood's specific gravity of 0.32 classifies it as soft. The cottonwoods are moderately weak in bending and compression, moderately limber, and moderately low in shock resistance.

Moderately large shrinkage is a characteristic of cottonwood and it requires careful seasoning if warp is to be avoided. The heartwood has low decay resistance and the wood is rather difficult to work with tools without producing chipped or fuzzy grain. Cottonwood is low in nail-withdrawal resistance but does not split easily when nailed. The wood is classed among those that glue satisfactorily with moderate care. It has a good reputation for holding paint.

Uses.—A large proportion of the annual output of cottonwood is cut into lumber and veneer and then remanufactured into containers and furniture. Both lumber and veneer are used in the furniture industry for core material, which is overlaid with high-grade furniture veneers.

Description.—Heartwood of all three cottonwood species is grayish white to light grayish brown with occasional streaks of light brown. The annual rings are rather wide. Pores are barely visible on smooth cut, end-grain surfaces. Aside from the color of the heartwood, cottonwood is extremely similar to black willow. Separation of the two species is based mainly on heartwood color, which is light brown or reddish brown in willow, or on microscopic examination if only sapwood material is available.

ROCK ELM

(Ulmus thomasii) Fig. 6-16.

Range. — Rock elm grows from New Hampshire to Nebraska and as far south as Tennessee. Much of the commercially important rock elm is located in Wisconsin and Michigan and more than 80 per cent of rock elm lumber and veneer comes from these two states.

Properties.—Rock elm is a heavy wood,

6-14. Black cherry.

6-15. Cottonwood.

6-16. Rock elm.

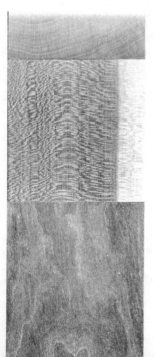

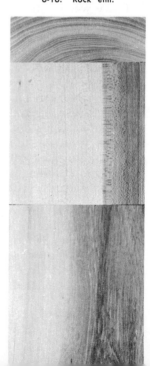

averaging 44 pounds a cubic foot. The wood is classified as hard, with a specific gravity of 0.57. It is stronger, harder, and stiffer than any of the other commercial elms. With the exception of hickory and dogwood, rock elm has higher stock resistance than any other American hardwood.

Although rock elm undergoes large shrinkage when drying, it tends to shrink somewhat less than the other commercial elms. As with all the elms, care must be taken to prevent warp during seasoning. Rock elm is somewhat difficult to work with hand or machine tools, and the heartwood has low to moderate resistance to decay. However, all the commercial elms have excellent bending qualities.

Uses.—Elm lumber is used principally for containers and furniture. In some cases, the different species of elm are employed indiscriminately, but when hardness or shock resistance is required to a high degree, rock elm is preferred. Rock elm veneer is used in considerable quantities in manufacturing various types of containers, especially fruit and vegetable boxes and baskets.

Large quantities of rock elm also go into crating for heavy articles, such as furniture, glass, and porcelain. The strength and toughness of this wood make it very serviceable for certain types of containers that must stand rough usage, such as market baskets and bushel baskets for home use. Considerable quantities are used in the manufacture of furniture, especially the bent parts of chairs.

Description.— Heartwood is brown to dark brown, sometimes with shades of red. Summerwood pores are arranged in concentric wavy lines that appear lighter than the background wood. The springwood pores in rock elm are visible only upon magnification.

AMERICAN ELM

(Ulmus americana) Fig. 6-17.

Range.—American elm grows throughout the eastern United States except in the Appalachian highlands and southern Florida. About three-fourths of the stand of sawtimber size is located in the Lake States and the Mississippi Delta region. Wisconsin, Michigan, Louisiana, Arkansas, Ohio, and Indiana have large volumes of elm.

Properties.—American elm is moderately heavy, averaging 35 pounds a cubic foot, and moderately hard, with a specific gravity of 0.46. It rates as moderately weak, but is moderately stiff and has good shock resistance.

The wood of American elm has large shrinkage and care must be taken to prevent warping as it seasons. Like all of the commercial elms, it has excellent bending qualities. Its heartwood has low to moderate resistance to decay. The wood is slightly below average in woodworking properties, but is among the top woods in ease of gluing. In nail-withdrawal resistance, it has an intermediate rank.

Uses. — American elm lumber is used principally in the manufacture of containers, furniture, and dairy and poultry supplies. Because of its excellent bending properties, the wood has been much used for barrels and kegs. Considerable quantities of veneer go into the manufacture of fruit and vegetables boxes and baskets. American elm also is used a great deal for crating heavy articles, such as furniture, glass, and porcelain products. It is used in sizable quantities in the furniture industry, particularly for the bent parts of chairs.

Description. — Heartwood is brown to dark brown, sometimes containing shades of red. Although the summerwood pores are not visible as individuals, they are arranged in concentric wavy lines within the boundaries of the growth rings. The wavy lines appear lighter than the background wood. American elm shows a springwood pore zone with a single row of large and easily visible pores.

HICKORY

(Carya) Fig. 6-18.

Species names. — True hickories: shagbark hickory *(Carya ovata)*, shellbark hickory *(C. laciniosa)*, pignut hickory *(C. glabra)*, and mockernut hickory *(C. tomentosa)*.

Range. — The true hickories grow throughout most of the eastern United States except in northern New England, the northern portions of Michigan and Wisconsin, and southern Florida. Close to 40 percent of the total stand of true hickory is located in the lower Mississippi Valley region.

Properties.—The wood of the true hickories is very heavy, averaging from 42 to 52 pounds per cubic foot, and very hard, with a specific gravity ranging from 0.56 to 0.66. It also is very strong as a post or beam, very stiff, and exceedingly high in shock resistance. Some woods are stronger than hickory and others are harder, but the combination of strength, toughness, hardness, and stiffness possessed by hickory has not been found to the same degree in any other commercial wood.

Hickory has very large shrinkage and must be carefully dried to avoid checking, warping, and other seasoning defects. It has low decay resistance but can be glued satisfactorily.

Uses. — Nearly 80 percent of the true hickory used in the manufacture of wood products goes into tool handles, for which its hardness, toughness, stiffness, and strength make it especially suitable. Other uses include agricultural implements, athletic goods, and lawn furniture.

Description. — Heartwood is brown to reddish brown. Pores are visible, but the zone of large pores is not sharply outlined as in oak and ash. Pores grade in size from one side of the annual ring to the other. Wood rays are very small and seen without magnification only on quartersawed surfaces. Tyloses frequently plug the pores, making their outlines indistinct. Under magnification, the end grain shows numerous white lines paralleling the growth ring.

MAHOGANY

(Authentic or True) Fig. 6-19.

Species names. — African *(Khaya ivorensis)*, West Indies *(Swietenia mahogoni)*, and Tropical American *(Swietenia macrophylla)*.

Range.—African mahogany comes from the Gold, Ivory, and Nigerian coasts of West Africa. West Indies mahogany comes primarily from British Honduras, Bermuda, and the keys of southern Florida. Tropical American mahogany comes from Mexico, Central America, Venezuela, and parts of Peru.

Properties. — Mahogany is of moderate density and hardness. It weighs about 36 pounds per cubic foot with a specific gravity of 0.46. The wood has excellent working and finishing characteristics. The wood is diffuse porous with open pores that require filling during finishing. It has high resistance to decay, pleasing figure, slight shrinkage, and is relatively easy to work.

Uses.—Mahogany is one of the principal woods used in quality furniture of all styles. It is used both as solid wood and fine veneer plywood. It is one of the best of all woods for boat construction. Another practical use is for patterns.

Description.—The heartwood of mahogany varies in color from a pale to a deep reddish brown, becoming darker on exposure to light. The narrow sapwood is from white to light brown in color. The figure in mahogany is due to differences in the reflection of light from different portions of the surface. Since mahogany usually has interlocked grain, quartersawed surfaces usually have a ribbon or stripe figure. Plainsawed mahogany has a figure of soft outlines and low contrast. The flat-cut surfaces have small grooves, often partly filled with dark gum. The distinctness and abundance of "ripple marks" help to distinguish the true mahogany from other woods that are used to imitate this wood.

Mahogany, Philippine

Fig. 6-20.

Species names.—Red Lauan (*Shorea negrosensis*), Tanguile (*Shorea polysperma*), Almon (*Shorea exima*), and Bagtican (*P. Malaanonan*).

Range.—Woods of this group are all grown primarily in the Philippine Islands; therefore they are sold in this country without distinction as Philippine mahogany.

Properties.—Woods from these trees are often mixed as to species but are sold as either dark-red or light-red mahogany. These woods are very similar to genuine mahogany in general properties although they are somewhat coarser in texture and general appearance. They are a little more difficult to finish than the true mahogany. However, they are easy to work and finish, easy to glue, and relatively inexpensive.

Uses. — These woods are used as both lumber and veneer plywood for furniture, built-ins, and paneling. Even though they resemble true mahogany, they have an individuality which is distinguished easily in many furniture pieces.

Description. — There are two basic kinds of Philippine mahogany as distinguished by color. The Red Lauan and Tanguile are of the dark-red variety in which the

6-17. American elm.

6-18. Hickory.

6-19. Authentic, or true, mahogany.

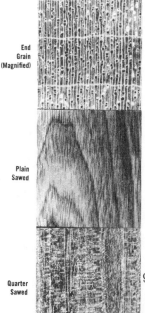

End Grain (Magnified)

Plain Sawed

Quarter Sawed

heartwood varies in color from pale to dark reddish-brown. They often have a slight purplish tinge, especially the Tanguile. The Almon and Bagtican are light-red in color with some pieces even straw-colored. The sapwood of these pieces is a very pale grayish or reddish-brown. The pores are plainly visible on the end grain. In the lengthwise section the pores are visible as fine grooves which, on quartersawed surfaces, may be very short in places due to interlocking grain. On quartersawed surfaces the rays, though not large, are very conspicuous because of their reddish color.

Sugar maple

(Acer saccharum) Fig. 6-21.

Range. –Sugar maple grows from Maine to Minnesota and southward to eastern Texas and northern Mississippi, Alabama, and Georgia. The largest stands are in the Lake States and the Northeast. The tree grows singly or in groups in mixed stands of hardwoods.

Properties.–Sugar maple is heavy, averaging 44 pounds a cubic foot, and hard, with a specific gravity of 0.56. Strong and stiff, it has high resistance to shock. Although it has large shrinkage and presents some difficulties in drying, the wood can be satisfactorily seasoned. Its resistance to decay is low to moderate.

Sugar maple ranks high in nail-withdrawal resistance and intermediate in ease of gluing. The wood takes stain satisfactorily and is capable of a high polish. Although generally straight-grained, sugar maple occasionally occurs with curly, wavy, or bird's-eye grain. The wood turns well on a lathe, is markedly resistant to abrasive wear, and is without characteristic taste or odor.

Uses.–Sugar maple is used principally for lumber, distilled products, veneer, crossties, and paper pulp. Probably 90 percent of the lumber is manufactured into such products as flooring, furniture, boxes and crates, handles, woodenware, and novelties. It is especially suitable for bowling alleys, dance floors, and other flooring that is subjected to hard use.

Description.–Heartwood is light reddish brown and sometimes shows greenish-black streaks near injuries. Pores are extremely small and not visible on any surface. Wood rays may be seen on the end grain and especially on quartersawed faces, where the higher rays are distinctive because of their color and size and smaller rays appear as fine lines between them. The wood rays may also be seen on plainsawed surfaces as very small darker colored flecks that are parallel to the grain of the wood.

White oak

(Quercus) Fig. 6-22.

Species names.–The white oak group includes white oak (*Quercus alba*), chestnut oak (*Q. prinus*), post oak (*Q. stellata*), overcup oak (*Q. lyrata*), swamp chestnut oak (*Q. michauxii*), bur oak (*Q. macrocarpa*), chinkapin oak (*Q. muehlenbergii*), swamp white oak (*Q. bicolor*), and live oak (*Q. virginiana*).

Range.–White oaks grow mainly in the eastern half of the United States, although some species are found as far west as eastern Oregon, Washington, and California. Commercial white oaks grow east of a line from western Minnesota to western Texas.

Properties.–The white oaks are heavy woods, averaging 47 pounds a cubic foot, and are very hard, with a specific gravity ranging from 0.57 in chestnut oak to 0.81 in live oak. Led by live oak, they rank high in strength properties.

The wood of the white oaks is subject to large shrinkage and seasoning must be done carefully to avoid checking and

Fine Hardwood Samples

The hardwoods shown in this 16-page section range from widely used varieties to some of the most exotic species in the world. The illustrations are highly accurate reproductions of actual wood samples. Not only are the colors faithfully represented, but the grain patterns are shown in their full striking beauty, without reduction in size. The original wood samples were provided by the Fine Hardwoods Association. Following is a list of these illustrations and the pages on which they appear:

Ebony, Macassar _____ 96¹
Oak, Red _____ 96²
Birch _____ 96³
Teak _____ 96⁴
Pecan _____ 96⁵
Maple, Hard _____ 96⁶
Oak, White _____ 96⁷
Rosewood _____ 96⁸
Lauan, Red _____ 96⁹
Limba _____ 96¹⁰
Mahogany, Honduras _____ 96¹¹
Zebrawood _____ 96¹²
Cherry, American _____ 96¹³
Mahogany, African _____ 96¹⁴
Primavera _____ 96¹⁵
Walnut, American _____ 96¹⁶

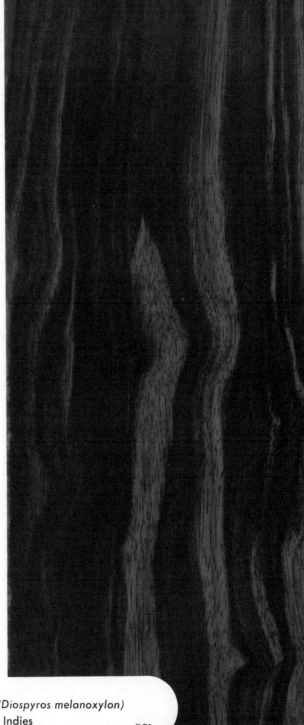

EBONY, MACASSAR *(Diospyros melanoxylon)*
East Indies

96¹

OAK, RED, flat cut *(Quercus borealis)*
Eastern United States

96²

BIRCH, flat cut *(Betula alleghaniensis)*
U. S. and Canada

96³

TEAK, flat cut *(Tectona grandis)*
96⁴ Burma, Java, East India, French Indo-China

PECAN *(Carya illinoensis)*
So. U.S., East of Mississippi

96[5]

MAPLE, HARD, flat cut (*Acer saccharum*)
96⁶ Lake States, No. West U. S. and Canada

OAK, WHITE, rift cut *(Quercus alba)*
Eastern United States

96[7]

ROSEWOOD, flat cut *(Dalbergia nigra)*
Brazil

96[8]

LAUAN, RED, flat cut *(Shorea negrosensis)*
Philippine Islands

96[9]

LIMBA, quartered *(Terminalia superba)*
West Africa

96^{10}

MAHOGANY, HONDURAS, flat cut *(Swietenia macrophylla)*
Mexico, Brazil, Peru and Central America 96[11]

ZEBRAWOOD, quartered *(Microberlinia brazzavillanensia)*
West Africa

96¹²

CHERRY, AMERICAN, flat cut *(Prunus serotina)*
East Central United States
96¹³

MAHOGANY, AFRICAN *(Khaya ivorensis)*
Africa

96¹⁴

PRIMAVERA, quartered *(Cybistax donnell-smithii)*
Central Mexico to Salvador
96¹⁵

WALNUT, AMERICAN, flat cut *(Juglans nigra)*
96[16]
Central United States

warping. Pores of the heartwood, with the exception of chestnut oak, are usually plugged with tyloses, a frothlike growth that makes the wood impervious to liquids. The heartwood itself is comparatively decay resistant, generally more so than that of the red oaks. White oaks are above average in all machining operations except shaping.

Uses.—Most white oak is made into lumber for flooring, furniture, general millwork, and boxes and crates. Large amounts are used for flooring and furniture and it is the outstanding wood for tight barrels, kegs, and casks because of the nonporous heartwood. It has long been the leading wood for the construction of ships and boats.

Description.—Heartwood is grayish brown. The outlines of the larger pores are indistinct except in chestnut oak, which has open pores with distinct outlines. On smooth-cut, end-grain surfaces, the summerwood pores are not distinct as individuals. Wood rays are generally higher than in red oak, the larger ones

ranging from 1/2 to 5 inches in height along the grain. As in red oak, rays appear lighter in color than the background wood on end-grain surfaces and darker than the background wood on side-grain surfaces.

RED OAK

(Quercus) Fig. 6-23.

Species names.—The red oak group includes northern red oak *(Quercus rubra)*, black oak *(Q. velutina)*, scarlet oak *(Q. coccinea)*, shumard oak *(Q. shumardii)*, pin oak *(Q. palustris)*, Nuttall oak *(Q. nuttallii)*, southern red oak *(Q. falcata)*, water oak *(Q. nigra)*, laurel oak *(Q. laurifolia)*, and willow oak *(Q. phellos)*.

Range.—Red oaks grow quite generally east of the Great Plains except for a narrow coastal strip along the Gulf of Mexico and in Florida. The largest amounts of commercial timber are cut in Tennessee, Arkansas, Kentucky, and Missouri.

6-20. Philippine mahogany.

6-21. Sugar maple.

6-22. White oak.

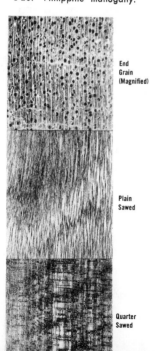

End Grain (Magnified)

Plain Sawed

Quarter Sawed

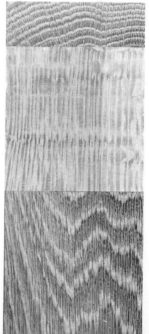

Properties.—The red oaks are similar in many properties to the white oaks. A major difference is that red oak, because it lacks tyloses in its pores, is extremely porous. A heavy wood, it averages 44 pounds a cubic foot and the average specific gravity of the more important species ranges from 0.52 to 0.60. The wood is hard, stiff, and has high shock resistance.

Red oak undergoes large shrinkage while drying, and seasoning must be done carefully to avoid checking and warping. It is considerably above average in all machining operations except shaping, and the heartwood ranks low to moderate in decay resistance.

Uses.—Most of the red oak cut in this country is converted into flooring, furniture, millwork, boxes and crates, caskets and coffins, agricultural implements, boats, and woodenware. Considerable lumber is also used in building construction, and some is exported. The hardness and wearing qualities of red oak have made it an important flooring wood for residences. Preservative-treated red oak is used extensively for crossties, mine timbers, and fence posts.

Description.—Heartwood is grayish brown with a more or less distinctive reddish tint. Pores are commonly open, and the outlines of the larger pores are distinct. On smoothly cut end-grain surfaces, the summerwood pores can be seen as individuals and readily counted when examined with a hand lens. Wood rays are commonly 1/4 to 1 inch high along the grain. On end-grain surfaces, rays appear as lines crossing the growth rings.

PECAN

(Carya illinoiensis) Fig. 6-24.

Species names.—Bitternut Hickory *(Cardiformis)*, water hickory *(Hicoria aquatica)*, and nutmeg hickory *(Myristicaformis)*.

Range.—Even though the range of bitternut hickory includes most of eastern United States, pecan is primarily a southern wood. It grows naturally in states bordering on the Mississippi River from northern Illinois south to central Louisiana and the Delta region. It also ranges through the gulf states to Florida.

Properties.—Pecan is a heavy wood although not quite as heavy as hickory. It averages about 48 pounds per cubic foot with a specific gravity of 0.58. It is hard, elastic, and strong. Next to true hickory, it is the toughest and strongest of American woods in common use. Although pecan is a member of the hickory family of woods, the species is usually referred to simply as pecan. The wood machines and turns well and also steam-bends well.

Uses.—Pecan is used for furniture in combination with or in place of walnut. The wood is good for this purpose since it satisfies all the requirements of strength, hardness, and rigidity. While the wood is not as highly figured, it can be stained and finished to resemble walnut so that only an expert can tell the difference. It also makes very attractive paneling.

Description.—The heartwood is reddish-brown in color, often with darker streaks. The sapwood is from one to several inches wide and is white. The pores are plainly visible on the end grain. The rays are not distinctly visible without a magnifying glass. On flat surfaces the pores are visible as distinct grooves and lines. The medullary rays on quarter-sawed surfaces are distinct but not conspicuous, while on plainsawed surfaces they are invisible.

SWEETGUM

(Liquidambar styraciflua) Fig. 6-25.

Range.—Sweetgum grows from southwestern Connecticut westward almost to

Kansas and southward to eastern Texas and central Florida. The commercial range in the United States is confined largely to the moist lands of the lower Ohio and Mississippi basins and to the lowlands of the southeastern coast.

Properties.—Sweetgum is a moderately heavy wood with an average weight of 36 pounds per cubic foot. The wood is hard, with a specific gravity of 0.46, moderately strong when used as a beam or post, moderately stiff, and has moderately high shock resistance.

Sweetgum has very large shrinkage in drying, and the sapwood and heartwood require different drying processes. The heartwood has low to moderate decay resistance. In nail-holding ability and in ability to resist splitting by nails and screws, sweetgum is rated intermediate. The heartwood requires special treatment before gluing can be done with best results.

Sweetgum ranks above average in turning, boring, and steam-bending properties but somewhat below average in the other machining properties. Its heartwood can be finished in a wide variety of color effects and the sapwood can be readily stained if a darker color is desired.

Uses.—The principal uses of sweetgum are for lumber, veneer, plywood, and slack cooperage. The lumber goes principally into boxes and crates, furniture, interior trim, and millwork. Veneer is used mainly for boxes, crates, baskets, furniture, and interior woodwork. Some sweetgum is used for crossties and fuel, and comparatively small amounts go into fencing, excelsior, and pulpwood.

Description.—Heartwood is reddish brown and occasionally variegated with streaks of darker color. Pores are so small that they are not visible except upon magnification. Growth rings are usually indistinct or inconspicuous. Rays are visible on quartersawed faces.

BLACK WALNUT

(*Juglans nigra*) Fig. 6-26.

Range.—Black walnut grows naturally

6-23. Red oak.

6-24. Pecan.

6-25. Sweetgum.

over a large area extending from Vermont westward to Nebraska and southward to southern Georgia and southern Texas. The area of greatest commercial production is limited to the central part of this natural range.

Properties.—Black walnut is classified as a heavy wood, averaging 38 pounds a cubic foot. The wood is hard, with a specific gravity of 0.51, is strong and stiff, and has good shock resistance.

Even under conditions favorable to decay, black walnut heartwood is one of our most durable woods. It can be satisfactorily kiln-dried or air-dried, and holds its shape well after seasoning. Black walnut works easily with handtools and has excellent machining properties. The wood finishes beautifully with a handsome grain pattern. It takes and holds paints and stains exceptionally well, can be readily polished, and can be satisfactorily glued.

Uses.—The outstanding use of black walnut is for furniture. Large amounts are also used for gunstocks and interior fin-ish, while smaller quantities go into railroad ties, fence posts, and fuelwood. In the furniture industry, it is used either as solid wood cut from lumber or as veneer and plywood. It also is extremely popular for interior finish wherever striking effects are desired. The wood of black walnut is particularly suitable for gunstocks because of its ability to stay in shape after seasoning, its fine machining properties, and its uniformity of texture.

Description.—Heartwood is chocolate brown and occasionally has darker, sometimes purplish, streaks. Unless bleached or otherwise modified, black walnut is not easily confused with any other native species. Pores are barely visible on the end grain but are quite easily seen as darker streaks or grooves on longitudinal surfaces. Arrangement of pores is similar to that in the hickories and persimmon, but the pores are smaller in size.

YELLOW-POPLAR

(Liriodendron tulipifera) Fig. 6-27.

Range.—Yellow-poplar grows in all the states east of the Mississippi River except Maine, New Hampshire, Vermont, and Wisconsin, and in parts of Oklahoma and Missouri. Virginia, North Carolina, South Carolina, Georgia, and Alabama contain more than half of the yellow-poplar sawtimber in the United States.

Properties.—Moderately light in weight, yellow-poplar averages 30 pounds a cubic foot. The wood is classed as moderately soft, with a specific gravity of 0.40, and is moderately low in bending and compressive strength, moderately stiff, and moderately low in shock resistance. Although it undergoes moderately large shrinkage when dried from a green condition, it is not difficult to season and stays in place well when seasoned. The

6-26. Black walnut.   6-27. Yellow poplar.

100

heartwood is low to moderate in resistance to decay.

Yellow-poplar ranks intermediate in machining properties. Although low in nail-withdrawal resistance, it has little tendency to split when nailed. Also, the wood has an excellent reputation for taking and holding paint, enamel, and stain and can be glued satisfactorily. Yellow-poplar containers do not impart taste or odor to foodstuffs, and the wood can be easily pulped by the chemical and semi-chemical processes.

Uses.—The principal uses of yellow poplar are for lumber, veneer, and pulpwood. The lumber goes mostly into furniture, boxes and crates, interior finish, siding, fixtures, and musical instruments. The veneer is used extensively for finish, furniture, and various forms of cabinetwork.

Description.—Heartwood is brownish yellow, usually with a definite greenish tinge. The wood rays, as seen on a smoothly cut end-grain surface, are somewhat more prominent than in cucumber tree. Positive identification of yellow-poplar and cucumber tree is best accomplished microscopically, but it is possible to separate them on the basis of gross features when both woods are at hand.

7 Fine Furniture Woods*

Most fine furniture is made from hardwoods although a few softwoods, particularly pine, are chosen for some Early American furniture. There are about 250 commercial varieties of hardwoods, but only about a half dozen are universally popular for furniture. Many of the better hardwoods, particularly fine walnut, are in rather limited supply. For this reason more plentiful woods are often substituted in furniture manufacturing. A good example is *pecan* which is a member of the hickory family. Fig. 7-1. Following are the most popular and important hardwoods for fine furniture.

WALNUT

Furniture woods have their ups and downs in popularity, like the furniture styles for which they are used. However, one which seems to have kept its

7-1. This table with flower-petal legs is a good example of a pleasing combination of woods. The base is solid *pecan* while the top features a sunburst pattern of *walnut* veneers.

*Adapted from material by courtesy the Conde' Nast Publications, Inc.

walnut

7-2(a). Walnut tree. (Copyright 1960 by the Conde' Nast Publications, Inc.)

7-2(b). Because its great strength permits slender, tapered legs, *walnut* is a favored choice for sculptured designs. Note the beautiful crotch veneers on the drawer fronts.

popularity is walnut. Fig. 7-2(a). Today it is used more than any other wood for American furniture. One reason for this is that walnut grain has an almost endless variety of figures.

Persian walnut, the original species, is quite rare today and is reserved for fine detail work such as inlays because of its dramatic figuring. The walnut crotch produces the most remarkable patterns. Crotches are cut from the trunk of the tree just below the branches. Here the growing fibers swirl as they twist their way toward first one branch, then another. Walnut burls are often interesting enough to hang on your walls. The prized burl is actually cut from a wartlike growth, sometimes several feet in diameter. When the burl is cut crosswise, tiny circular mottled areas can be seen. Stumpwood provides grain with another pattern. Walnut veneers sawed from the base or stump of the tree have a great variety of dark and light tones providing a rich, dramatic appearance.

Walnut varies considerably in color, depending on where it is grown. The American variety is called *black walnut*, but only because of the color of the nut shells. Actually the wood ranges from light gray-brown to darker, purplish-brown. It is often treated to remove the purplish cast.

In addition to its beauty, walnut has many practical advantages. Though not as hard as oak, it is harder than mahogany and, as such, an ideal wood for the sculptured forms so popular in Contemporary furniture. Fig. 7-2(b). It shrinks less than most woods so it can withstand varying climatic conditions.

Walnut has been given almost every known finish. No other wood so readily takes oiled finishes. Another reason for its popularity in Contemporary pieces.

The History of Walnut

Walnut has a long ancestry. Some 500

102

years before the beginning of the Christian era, seeds of the great tree were carried from Persia to eastern Europe. By the time of the Renaissance, walnut had become a dominant wood for fine furniture and interior architecture. Earlier settlers in America found walnut trees in great supply, including some of great height and with diameters of eight or nine feet. The trees were cut down indiscriminately to make way for the first farms and roads and later for cities and highways. Only in the last 40 or 50 years has any attempt been made to restore this loss. These recent plantings comprise our present source for cabinet woods.

Walnut has always been popular for American furniture. It was commonly used in this country before mahogany, and still today it is at a peak of popularity because of its use in Contemporary furniture. Fig. 7-3. It is used in much the same way that the Scandinavians use teak: in very simple designs that let the fine grain speak for itself.

Buying Walnut

The wise buyer looks for proof of authenticity when he buys a piece of walnut furniture. Many trade names for walnut apply to cheaper woods or are actually plastic laminates printed with walnut grain and color. Sometimes walnut comprises only a small part of the wood used in a furniture piece. While this is not necessarily a disadvantage, you should know what you are buying. Walnut veneers are widely used on cabinets and table tops to provide distinctive decorative interest, but the legs and structural parts should be solid walnut rather than veneered.

The Care and Upkeep Of Walnut Furniture

Walnut furniture takes about the same care and attention as other hardwood furniture. For conventional finishes, mild

7-3. This lamp table shows a typical use of *walnut* for Contemporary furniture. 22"W x 28"D x 22"H.

soap and water and good paste wax will preserve the original appearance. The oil finish you find on so much Contemporary walnut furniture needs only a light application of boiled linseed oil about twice a year. Buy the oil already boiled and warm it up in a double boiler. For regular care, wipe off an oil finish occasionally with a damp cloth and a little linseed-oil soap.

MAHOGANY

The word "mahogany" has become almost synonymous with fine furniture. Fig. 7-4(a). Its popularity results from many excellent qualities such as handsome, varying grain, adaptability to finishes, and texture that is firm, yet easy to cut and carve. It is softer than many hardwoods, yet has excellent strength compared to its weight. Mahogany boards have fewer defects than most other hardwoods. Fig. 7-4(b). This makes for economy in production. Also, some of the broadest boards come from the huge mahogany tree.

The great variety of distinctive mahogany figures lends itself to practically

mahogany

7-4(a). Mahogany tree. (Copyright 1960 by the Conde' Nast Publications, Inc.)

7-4(b). Mahogany is an excellent wood for turning, carving, fluting, and other machining. It also has great tensional strength.

any design. This wood can be finished in red, yellow, or bleached tones, high-gloss or dull, and many others. Natural mahogany, when given only a protective covering of colorless beeswax, will mellow to light brown.

In the 18th century, Thomas Chippendale introduced and popularized the familiar red finishes also used by Sheraton, Hepplewhite, and the Adams Brothers. There was no major change until bleached mahogany became the favorite for the garish Modern of the 1920's. The "bleached look" remained popular until recently when the trend to Contemporary design called for more natural finishes. Fig. 7-5. It is to mahogany's credit that it takes flat, rubbed oil finishes as readily as it takes hard, glossy lacquer finishes.

Note that certain other woods are sometimes finished to look like mahogany. Also, some woods commonly called mahogany are not of the true variety. It should not be assumed that all products resembling mahogany, or even those advertised as mahogany, will have the excellent qualities of the true species.

Mahogany's Rise to Popularity

Mahogany grows only in the tropical

regions of the West Indies, Central America, South America, and along the Gold Coast of Nigeria. No one in England knew of its existence until the 16th century era of exploration. Cortez is said to have built ships with mahogany planking during the first half of the 16th century. In America, early craftsmen were more interested in woods that were serviceable and plentiful. They turned to native woods such as maple, cherry, birch, and walnut. However, colonial land-owners and traders soon began to improve their homes, bringing delicate mahogany furniture into fashion. From these early days mahogany has enjoyed continuing popularity.

What to Expect in Mahogany Furniture

From true mahogany you can expect furniture and veneers of high quality. Mahogany furniture is available in every price bracket, but on the average it tends to cost a little less than other hardwood pieces. This is because the lumber has little waste and can be sawed into wide planks requiring fewer joints. For veneers, the fine quality and even grain of mahogany make thin slicing possible, and its open pores help glues to hold firm.

Care and Upkeep

Care of mahogany was once a problem. Early methods of finishing gave the wood surface little protection from scratches or discoloration. However, improved finishes now give mahogany the same resistance to stains, burns, watering marks, and scratches as any other fine hardwood. Periodic application of a furniture paste or spray wax will clean and preserve the wood.

CHERRY

Cherry furniture is an undeniable part of the American tradition. Fig. 7-6(a). However, this wood was used in

7-5. Much Traditional furniture, such as this beautiful breakfront, is made of mahogany. This piece has a more natural finish than the dark red of the 18th century.

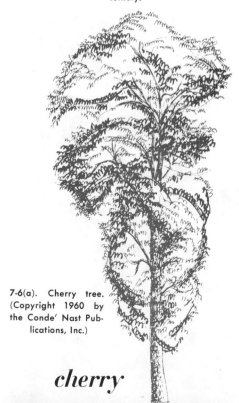

7-6(a). Cherry tree. (Copyright 1960 by the Conde' Nast Publications, Inc.)

cherry

furniture making at least as early as 400 B.C. Greek and Roman artisans, highly skilled in the decorative arts, used cherry wood for inlays. At that time furniture consisted mainly of benches, tables, and a few accessory pieces. By the 16th and 17th centuries, when oak and walnut were the most popular cabinet woods in Italy and France, cherry was still used widely for furniture inlay. In 19th century Europe, cherry was one of the leading furniture woods.

Early American Cherry

Cherry was introduced into American furniture in the 17th century when it caught the fancy of colonial cabinetmakers because of its good qualities and abundance. White pine and maple were used for most of the practical household furniture we usually think of as Early American, while cherry was reserved for the more elegant adaptations of European designs. Fig. 7-6(b). By the 19th century, cherry was sharing favor with walnut and mahogany.

Characteristics and Grain

Wild black cherry is the species that provides furniture hardwood. It is strong, stiff, and moderately hard. Though considered close-grained, there is enough character in the grain to interest many designers. The markings of cherry are less distinct than walnut and mahogany.

People often associate cherry with a reddish-brown color seen most frequently in cherry furniture. However, cherry logs often have a distinct grayish cast, while others are light straw-colored. The freshly cut heartwood is usually of a light amber hue which darkens with age. Heartwood may eventually show alternate light and dark streaks. Sapwood is even lighter, varying from white to yellow-brown. Fig. 7-7.

Forests of cherry are found principally in the Appalachian region of Pennsylvania, West Virginia, and Ohio. There are also some growths in Michigan and upper New York State. In Europe this wood grows in France, Italy, Germany, Spain, and Portugal.

The Range of Finishes

Cherry takes a variety of finishes. Many furniture manufacturers prefer to treat it with a clear, natural lacquer-and-wax finish. However, because of its close grain this wood may also be given a sleek, painted finish, and you may see very dark, almost black finishes on some of the more expensive cherry furniture.

The finish most often associated with cherry is the so-called "fruitwood." Orig-

7-6(b). A plentiful supply of cherry in the New England colonies made it a logical choice of early American cabinetmakers. This portable cabinet is a fine Colonial design. 24½″W x 14¾″D x 40″H.

inally the term referred to the delicate, natural color of furniture made of any of the fruitwoods, such as cherry, apple, or pear. Although many of these woods are no longer popular, a version of the original fruitwood finish is now commonly applied to maple and birch as well as to cherry. It features the *distressed* appearance popularized by early French Provincial furniture.

Cherry is not too difficult to distinguish. You can tell it by its strong annual growth rings and by numerous character markings such as pitch pockets and tiny pin knots.

Cherry is a relatively expensive wood. While the price of logs is not great, the percentage of waste is high. This means that the quality standards of the manufacturer are an important element in the price of the furniture. The manufacturer who insists on the finest wood and maintains the best quality of construction must put a higher price tag on his cherry furniture.

If a piece of furniture is advertised as wild black cherry, you can be reasonably certain that it is made of this wood. However, there is quite a bit of inexpensive furniture on the market in which cherry is combined with less expensive maple.

Care and Upkeep

Black cherry furniture requires no special care beyond the usual fine treatment any hardwood deserves. An occasional washing with mild soap and water followed by a gentle rubdown with a soft cloth will maintain the original beauty of the wood. An application of furniture wax three or four times a year will highlight cherry's lovely color and graining.

7-7. Cherry is also the choice for such French Provincial pieces as this handsome clock.

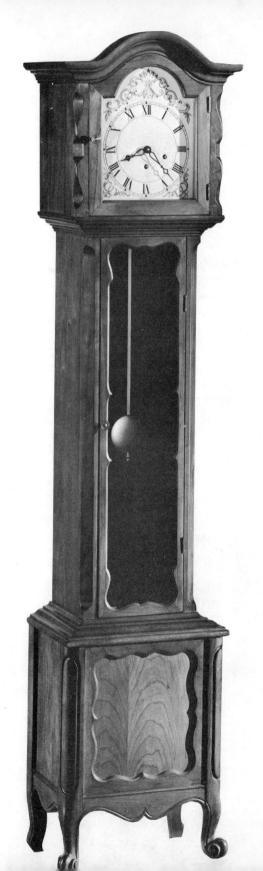

maple

birch

7-8(a). Maple and birch trees. (Copyright 1960 by the Conde' Nast Publications, Inc.)

7-8(b). This clock-barometer has been built into a cabinet of selected *maple* with polished brass trim. 10"W x 18"H.

MAPLE AND BIRCH

Maple trees that give us maple sugar and syrup for pancakes also supply us with fine hardwood for furniture. Fig. 7-8(a). Birch trees that once gave bark for Indian canoes—as in the poem *Hiawatha*—now provide hardwood for chairs, tables, and chests. Maple and birch have been twin favorites of American furniture makers since early colonial days. Fig. 7-8(b).

Both trees grow all across the northern part of our country. The ready supply of both woods has had much to do with their long and enduring popularity.

Color and Grain

Two species of birch are used in furniture production: yellow birch and sweet birch. Yellow birch is far more abundant today. Sweet birch, which is found in the Appalachian region, was more popular in colonial days and was called "mountain mahogany" because of its dark reddish-brown color. In its natural state yellow birch is actually a warm, light brown. It is dense and hard, and ranges from a very straight, fine grain when the logs are quartersawed to a swirl figure when they are flat-sliced or rotary-cut. Stumps, crotches, and trees which have been subjected to unusual growing conditions produce intricate curls and swirl patterns that are used in furniture veneers and wall paneling.

The species of maple most commonly used in furniture is usually known as sugar maple. It is a hard, heavy wood of fine and even texture. While the grain is normally straight, lumber with a bird's-eye figure or with wavy, curly grain is also available. Fig. 7-9. Maple sapwood is white to pinkish-white in color. There is an abrupt change from sapwood to the pinkish-brown heartwood. The dark pink to reddish-brown growth rings can be easily seen, but the pores are almost invisible. Maple is not as easily glued as

7-9. The simple, sturdy furniture of the Early American period was often made of *maple*. The dropleaf table was popular because of its practicality.

some of the softer, more porous woods, but modern production techniques have overcome this problem to some extent. The fine, even texture of maple makes it highly suitable for painted and enameled finishes, since the surface needs no filling and paint adheres to it well.

Birch has a similar close, compact grain which makes it ideal for spool beds and turned posts and legs of tables, chairs, and desks. Birch is used in combination with maple because of their similarity in color and grain. Fig. 7-10.

Range of Finishes

Maple is often used for the reproduction of Early American furniture pieces. At one time such pieces were stained or glazed to a red-brown shade but in recent years a more mellow yellow-brown finish has become popular. The natural light tone of birch brought it to the attention of 18th and 19th century designers. In the present century birch again

7-10. A six-drawer chest of maple and birch. 38"W x 20"D x 47"H.

109

had a surge of popularity for Modern Scandinavian style pieces. Smooth-glazed, light-yellow birch was almost synonymous with the Modern look of the 1920's and early 1930's. Then teak assumed the first-place position it enjoys today among such styles. For a short time maple had a similar popularity in this country for Modern furniture but, as designers of Contemporary pieces began to employ darker finishes, maple returned to its former prominence for Early American designs.

Multitude of Uses

In volume of production of lumber and other wood products, maple ranks fourth among hardwoods. It is found in a remarkable range of everyday items. Because of its hardness, superior strength, and fine grain, it makes excellent flooring and is often used in combination with walnut for parquet floors (inlaid floors made up of geometric designs). Because of its acoustical properties, maple is used in the manufacture of pianos and stringed instruments. Maple bread boards, meat servers, and similar kitchen wooden-ware are in countless American homes. For recreation we use croquet mallets and balls, Indian clubs and dumbbells, bowling pins, and billiard cues, all commonly of maple.

Birch in its many different tones and grain patterns is widely used for doors, floors, and wall paneling. Kitchen-cabinet manufacturers are very partial to both birch and maple. Both woods have the strength to take daily wear, and both have a clear, smooth grain that takes natural or painted finishes well. Maple and birch furniture is available from the very lowest-priced, painted pieces to quite high-priced designs. As with other furniture, the cost is not affected as much by the wood itself as by the craftsmanship, construction standards, and finishing techniques.

Durability and Maintenance

Both maple and birch stand up well under ordinary household use. Because gluing in maple and birch cabinetwork is more difficult than with softer, more porous woods, they may not survive high humidity. On the other hand, these solid woods can be relied upon to keep their shape in humid climates where solid doors and table tops of softer woods are likely to warp.

Birch and maple furniture presents no problems of care or upkeep. Today's tough, sturdy finishes protect the wood from wear and tear. Periodic wiping with a damp, soaped cloth along with monthly treatments with a good paste or spray wax will keep the luster bright.

OAK

It would be difficult to name a wood with a longer and more illustrious history in furniture design than oak. Fig. 7-11(a). Oak furniture has been found in excavations of Greek and Roman homes. History shows that oak has remained in constant use in many countries, and during the Middle Ages in England it took on singular importance. Lords and ladies sat around great oak tables in medieval halls while jesters squatted on oak stools. Bishops and cardinals mounted oak pulpits. English kings ruled from carved oak thrones. The "Golden Age of Oak" continued from the 14th through the 17th centuries when it merged with the "Age of Walnut."

As more elegant, refined furniture styles came into fashion, oak was replaced by walnut and mahogany. The return of oak in the Victorian period was unfortunate in that the designs of that period—the late 19th century—were grotesque. Similarly, a great deal of the early Modern oak furniture of the 1920's showed remarkably poor design. Of course, these failures of design do not reflect discredit upon oak.

The historical popularity of this wood was not confined to England. Oak was also dominant in carved and ornamented Spanish furniture, and in our country it is most commonly associated with the furniture of the early Spanish missions. "Mission oak" or "ranch oak" furniture was a part of life in the Old West.

Kinds of Oak

Of the more than 200 species of oak distributed over the world, about 50 are native to the United States. Among the best-known is white oak, a stately tree which reaches heights of 70 to 100 feet. Red oak is perhaps the most beautiful of the American species. Its wood is an attractive amber color with a reddish tinge, and is coarse-textured, hard, and durable. Oak is extremely well adapted

oak

7-11(a). Oak tree. (Copyright 1960 by Conde' Nast Publications, Inc.)

7-11(b).   The rugged character of oak paneling makes it a happy choice for a room that will get hard usage.

111

7-12. Deeply carved and overscaled rosette pulls highlight the door panels of this handsome *oak* cabinet.

to woodworking. Depending upon the way the wood is sliced, the figures vary from a straight, pencil-striped, open-pored surface to a leaf-and-lacewood effect. Oak is often used today in furniture and paneling for which a bold texture is desired. Fig. 7-11(b). Oak is heavier than most cabinet woods, at least as strong as most, and exceptionally durable. Oak works well by machine. The craftsman can utilize its strong, interesting figure and open-pore grain without having to worry about the splintering or fuzzing of hickory, ash, and other similar woods. Fig. 7-12.

Historically, oak was almost always used in its solid form, but since the advent of modern veneer and plywood it has been used more for its decorative figures. Often it is combined with close-grained woods such as walnut, cherry, and ebony.

Oak Finishes

Oak takes many distinctive finishes. Because of its open grain, unique coloring effects can be obtained by varying the material used to fill the pores before applying lacquer or varnish finish. Water stains can also be used to achieve a variety of color effects ranging from dark brown to gray, amber, and red-brown.

112

With the use of bleach and a white filler, oak can be given a light platinum tint. Often a light gray filler is used, then a paint is applied and wiped off, revealing the wood's distinctive figure in flaky white outlines.

Oak furniture, flooring, and paneling are unusually resistant to changes in climate and to general use. White oak's close cell structure makes it practically impervious to liquids. Red oak cells are not so close and the wood, therefore, is less resistant to stains. Because of its sturdy character, oak furniture needs less care and attention than most. Occasional wiping with a soft cloth or washing with mild soap and water will keep oak looking as good as new. If oak has not been properly dried, you may have a warpage problem.

THE EXOTICS

Most furniture hardwoods come from rather familiar trees but there is one group, the exotics, that is largely unfamiliar to North Americans. Fig. 7-13(a). These woods and their names, such as paldao, teak limba, zebrawood,

7-13(a). A huge teak tree. (Copyright 1960 by Conde' Nast Publications, Inc.)

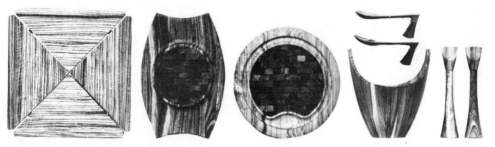

7-13(b). These accessories were made of some of the world's most exotic woods from the jungles of Nicaragua, Brazil, British Honduras, and East Africa.

ebony, and rosewood, suggest the jungles of Africa, the mountains of Japan and India, and other faraway, romantic lands from which they come. Fig. 7-13(b). Teak has gained prominence for its use in Contemporary design, and occasionally you will find a chest or table made of some other exotic wood. However, with these exceptions, the vivid colors and dramatic textures of the exotics are used almost exclusively for decorative accent. Fig. 7-14.

Teak

Teak comes from the rugged regions of the Indian Peninsula, Burma, and Thailand. Because of its extraordinary weight and density, it will not float. The logs have to be hauled down from the mountains by elephant. A single log may weigh as much as seven tons and require seven elephants to move it! The wood ranges in color from honey tone to warm brown, and tends to darken on exposure. Some logs are richly grained. Today teak is popular for furniture of both Scandinavian and Oriental styles. Fig. 7-15. The world-wide reputation of teak is based on its high resistance to decay, its ability to hold its shape under varying moisture conditions, and the relative ease with which it can be worked with car-

bide tools. The wood feels oily to the touch. It is hard, and comparable in strength to our native white oak.

Satinwood

Satinwood comes from Ceylon and India. Furniture made of this wood has been uncovered in the ruins of Pompeii, buried by a volcano in 79 A.D. A French nobleman, Count de Caylus, during the 18th century created the elegant, carved and gilded satinwood designs with which we are most familiar today. The wood has a deep luster and is often highly figured. It is extremely hard and brittle, which makes it subject to surface checking. Satinwood is so expensive that you will find it used in only the finest furniture, usually in the form of banding.

7-14. This *teak* chest is typical of Contemporary furniture which often features rare woods. 23"W x 18"D x 34"H.

113

7-15. This antelope chair of solid wood, coffee table, and accessories are all made of *teak* wood. The chair is upholstered with suede leather.

7-16. *Elm* burl is used as an accent in the drawer fronts and top of this cherry chest.

7-17. This octagonal table with black plastic-laminate top is made from *rosewood*. 20"W x 20"D x 20"H.

114

Myrtle

Southern Oregon and northern California have myrtle trees which are widely known for their interesting burls. Myrtle bowls, plates, and other accessories are popular tourist items. The wood varies from golden-brown to yellow-green, splotched with purple. Because of this unusual coloring, the wood is used in furniture as an accent.

Paldao

Paldao is often described as "the wood afire." While many woods appear somewhat flat when a finish is applied, paldao becomes even brighter. The wood varies in color from gray-brown to red-brown with sharp, black markings. Paldao trees grow in small clusters deep in the jungles of southeastern Asia and the Philippines. Loggers have to brave poisonous insects, the ferocious black panther, the boa constrictor, and even head hunters to bring the wood to shipping ports. The wood is therefore exceedingly expensive. Recently paldao was chosen by three prominant designers for new groups of Contemporary furniture.

Zebrawood

One of the most dramatic of the exotic woods, zebrawood comes from a gigantic tree that grows on the west coast of Africa. It gets its name because of its basic markings which consist of black or dark-brown stripes on a light background. The wood can assume a variety of patterns depending on the way it is cut. When cut on the bias, the stripes make a shell design. By matching several pieces, any number of figures can be obtained. As a rule, zebrawood is used sparingly, principally in inlay. Too much of it would appear garish.

Limba

In this country, limba is sometimes

7-18. This sleek, slim, and elegant clock of *rosewood* veneer has a face of *ebony*, one of the exotic woods.

known as *korina*. It comes from west Africa. Because of its natural pale-blond color, it was important in the early days of Modern style furniture. After a decline in popularity, new finishes are again creating interest in limba.

Elm

Though not strange or scarce, the uses of elm are similar to those of truly exotic woods. Elm makes a warm, elegant accent for other woods, although it is sometimes used alone. Whether from France, England, or the United States, elm has a prized burl with a small-to-medium pattern. Fig. 7-16. The color varies from light-brown to tan or reddish brown tones.

Rosewood

Rosewood comes from Brazil and India, and has a long and romantic history in furniture design. The wood varies in color: a light tan in the younger trees, purple tones in mature growth, and almost black in the older trees. The pattern is streaked with dark-brown or black pigment. A heavy residue of oil in the wood makes possible high-luster finishes. Rosewood is used in fine furniture today for both inlay and cabinetwork. Fig. 7-17.

Yew

Yew wood from England often has a wild but graceful pattern which varies in color from pale red to cedar. Yew is popular for small, occasional furniture such as desks and commodes.

Ebony

Ebony from Africa and Asia, which is used for the black keys of a piano, is perhaps the best-known of the exotic woods. Actually, ebony used in furniture is not solid black but is striped with bands of dark brown or salmon pink. Ebony furniture has been traced as far back as the 17th century B.C. when the Egyptians and the Babylonians used it in combination with gold, silver, and ivory for court furniture. The wood was highly prized by the Greeks and Romans and was again popular in Europe in the 15th century. Ebony is exceptionally hard and heavy. At present it is used mostly for decorative inlay. Fig. 7-18.

Primavera

Primavera comes from Mexico and Central America. It is sometimes misnamed "white mahogany" because both woods have a medium-to-coarse texture and a straight or slightly wavy grain. The color of primavera is lighter than mahogany, varying from yellow-white to yellow-brown. The wood is most commonly used for cabinetwork, although highly figured boards are good for inlay.

8   Plywood

Plywood is a man-made wood product used extensively in furniture, built-ins, kitchen cabinets, and paneling. Figs. 8-1, 8-2, and 8-3. There is a common, but mistaken, belief that quality furniture is made entirely of solid wood. The fact is that the greatest part of the wood used in fine furniture today, over 90 per cent, is plywood.

Most furniture pieces are a combination of plywood and solid wood. Fig. 8-4. Large, flat areas, such as the tops of

8-1. This Contemporary sideboard is made largely of *lumber-core* plywood with only limited use of solid wood for the base, handles, and certain drawer parts. 57½"W x 17½"D x 28½"H.

and across the panel. While solid wood is relatively strong with the grain, it is weaker across the grain. In plywood, the grain direction of adjoining plies is at right angles, giving strength in both directions.
• Checking, splitting, and warpage are greatly reduced.
• Dimensional stability is high. In plywood there is little change in dimensions due to moisture.
• The natural beauty of the wood (color, figure, grain, and texture) can be shown to best advantage because of the various methods of cutting the veneers.
• A wide range of sizes and thicknesses is possible. Special sizes and types of panels can be produced for specific purposes. Fig. 8-5.
• Plywood conserves our wood supply by making maximum use of natural raw materials.
• Ease of construction and finishing with large plywood panels saves time and money.

tables, cabinets, and chests, are usually of plywood construction, and this technique can also be used for simple and compound curves.

ADVANTAGES OF PLYWOOD

Plywood has many advantages over solid wood. Some of these include:
• Plywood has equal strength both along

8-2. This built-in is made entirely of softwood *veneer-core* plywood.

8-3. Kitchen cabinets are usually constructed either of veneer-core or lumber-core plywood with some use of solid wood.

8-4. A piece of quality furniture with just the right combination of plywood and solid wood. The posts, frame parts, drawer sides, and back are made of solid wood while the remainder of the chest is lumber-core plywood processed by the manufacturer in his own plant. In this way the consumer is assured of the best possible construction.

KINDS OF PLYWOOD CONSTRUCTION

There are two major methods of producing plywood. *Veneer-core* plywood is made by gluing together three, five, seven or nine plies of thin veneer to make up a sort of "wood sandwich." Fig. 8-6. *Lumber-core* plywood contains a core of narrow, sawed-lumber strips with crossbands and face veneer glued on both sides. Fig. 8-7. Generally, lumber-core plywood is five-ply, although some furniture manufacturers use a three-ply variety. Lumber-core plywood is commonly used in furniture, cabinetry, and other pieces that call for dowels, splines, dovetail joints, exposed edges, or butt hinges. Fig. 8-8. Some plywood has a core of particle-board instead of lumber. Fig. 8-9.

BALANCED CONSTRUCTION

Plywood panels tend not to warp, because of their balanced construction. This means that all plies are arranged in pairs, one on either side of the core. For

8-5. This specially constructed plywood has a crossband of asbestos with a face veneer of natural wood. It will comply with the fire laws that are often part of city building codes for commercial structures.

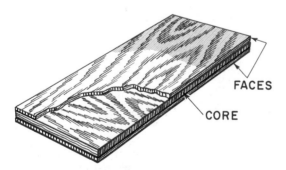

FACES

CORE

3-PLY WITH VENEER CORE

8-6. Three-ply, veneer-core plywood is made in hardwoods and softwoods.

8-7. Here you see the difference between veneer-core and lumber-core plywood. The standard face and back veneer is 1/28" thick for hardwoods. For softwoods it is 1/10" thick, although it can be cut in any thickness from 1/32" to 1/16". Crossband veneers are from 1/24" to 1/10" in thickness and core veneers range from as thin as 1/32" to 7/32".

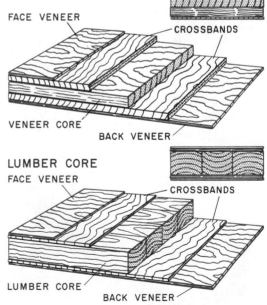

VENEER CORE

FACE VENEER

CROSSBANDS

VENEER CORE

BACK VENEER

LUMBER CORE

FACE VENEER

CROSSBANDS

LUMBER CORE

BACK VENEER

119

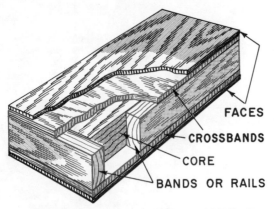

FACES
CROSSBANDS
CORE
BANDS OR RAILS

5-PLY WITH SAWN LUMBER CORE & BANDING OR RAILING

8-8. Smaller pieces of lumber-core plywood are often made with a banding or railing of the same wood as the face veneer. Then machining can be done on the edges.

each ply there is an opposite, similar, and parallel ply. The matched plies should be of the same thickness and have similar properties with regard to shrinkage and density. All plies should also have the same moisture content. However, it is not necessary that the matching plies be of the same kind of wood; in fact, the back ply of many hardwood plywoods is of less expensive wood than the exposed face.

MANUFACTURE OF PLYWOOD

All softwood veneer-core plywood is produced in plants designed specifically for this purpose. Large sheets of lumber-core plywood are also made in plywood

8-9. Plywood made with a particle-board core simplifies production problems and provides a very stable panel.

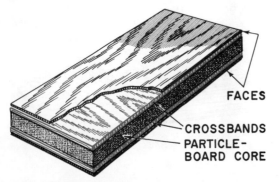

FACES
CROSSBANDS
PARTICLE-
BOARD CORE

5-PLY WITH PARTICLE-BOARD CORE

plants, while smaller sizes, for use in plywood furniture, are sometimes made in furniture plants. Fig. 8-10.

Softwood and hardwood plywoods are made in about the same way. The first step is to cut the log sections, called *peeler blocks* or *flitches,* to a specific length. Figs. 8-11 and 8-12. These sections are then tenderized in a bath of hot water or steam. Temperatures are varied according to the species to obtain veneers with the smoothest possible surface. Veneers are then cut with one of two types of machines.

• A *rotary lathe* is used for most veneer cutting, perhaps 80 to 90 per cent. The log is fastened in the lathe and the lathe spindle rotates the log against a sharp knife which peels off a continuous sheet of veneer, about as paper is unwound from a roll. Fig. 8-13.

• A *veneer slicer* is used for cutting face veneers for such woods as walnut, mahogany, cherry, and oak. The steamed flitch is held securely in a viselike clamp and moved against a razor-sharp knife. Fig. 8-14. This shears off the veneer sheets which are kept in sequence for matching purposes.

Rotary-cut veneer then goes through an automatic clipper that cuts it to the best width and also eliminates most of the defects. Fig. 8-15. Pieces that come from the clipper or directly from a veneer slicer go through driers, huge chambers equipped with heating coils and fans to reduce the wood to the desired moisture content. Fig. 8-16.

While some of the veneer that has been rotary cut is large enough to be used as full-size sheets, most pieces must be edge glued. Fig. 8-17. The narrower veneer sheets are put through an edge jointer and then permanently bonded together at the edges in a tapeless splicer to make sheets of the required width. After this the veneer sheets are repaired as necessary. Fig. 8-18. When panels are to have

120

The Manufacture of Plywood

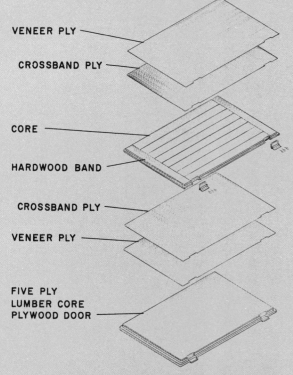

VENEER PLY

CROSSBAND PLY

CORE

HARDWOOD BAND

CROSSBAND PLY

VENEER PLY

FIVE PLY
LUMBER CORE
PLYWOOD DOOR

8-12. Barking is the first step in softwood plywood manufacture. A highspeed gouging wheel rips away the outer surface of the log, down to the solid wood.

8-10. This cabinet door is made of lumber-core plywood. The manufacturer makes the smaller pieces of plywood for specific parts of the furniture and cabinets.

8-13. Giant lathes like this one are used to peel the veneer from the wood. The block is rotated against a keen cutting blade which "shaves" off ribbons of wood. About 2,000 square feet of plywood can be manufactured from one peeler block 50" in diameter and 8' long.

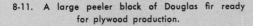

8-11. A large peeler block of Douglas fir ready for plywood production.

8-14. Cutting veneers on a veneer slicer.

8-17. This edge gluer joins varying widths of veneer into a continuous sheet which is then clipped for use in inner plies.

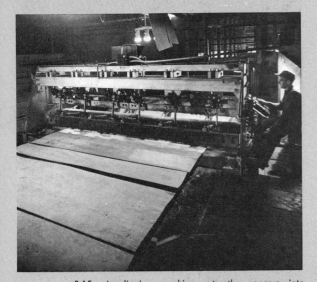

8-15. A clipping machine cuts the veneers into various sizes. The clipper man cuts out the defective portions of veneer and produces the maximum number of full-size sheets.

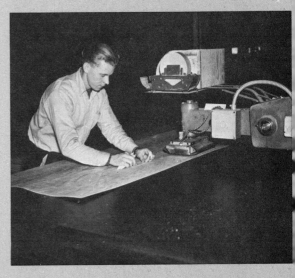

8-18. Repairing veneers. A patch, chosen to fit the opening, is put in place and bonded in a miniature hot press. These repaired veneer sheets are made into plywood.

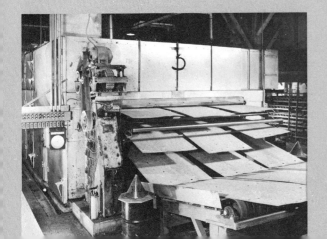

8-16. The veneer travels through these 100-foot long ovens in which the temperature is maintained at about 350 degrees Fahrenheit. During the 6- to 20-minute trip (depending upon the thickness of the veneer), the moisture content is reduced to about 4 per cent.

8-19. Carefully controlled gluing is important in making plywood. The veneer sheets are fed through these large rollers. With glue applied evenly between plies, each sheet of veneer is placed with the grain at right angles to that of the plies above and below. Different types of glues are used for exterior and interior plywoods.

8-20. Gluing up the plywood. Heat, supplied by steam pouring through the press platens, is applied together with great pressure to cure the adhesive. Heat and pressure produce a bond between the plies that is stronger than the wood itself.

a solid lumber core, selected kiln-dried lumber is planed and trimmed so the surfaces and edges are uniform and smooth. Then they are glued edge to edge, forming large sheets.

The veneers and the solid lumber core are now ready for the second gluing operation, in which the plies are bonded together to produce the panel. In assembling panels, the crossband veneers are put through a glue spreader that distributes the adhesive uniformly on both sides. Fig. 8-19. The crossbands are then laid with the grain at right angles to the face, the back, and the core.

As stated earlier, almost all lumber-core plywood has five plies—that is, the core, two crossbands, and face and back veneers—while veneer-core plywood is made in panels of three, five, seven, or nine plies. The assembled wood sandwich is placed in a hot press where the temperature is at least 250 degrees Fahrenheit and the pressure between 150 and 300 pounds per square inch. Fig. 8-20. The controlled heat sets the adhesive, permanently bonding the layers together into a single, strong panel.

After the bonded panel leaves the press it is carefully trimmed to size, and its face and back are sanded. The panel is now ready for inspection, grading, and shipping.

HARDWOOD PLYWOOD GRADING

Plywood of which the face ply is hardwood is called *hardwood plywood*. Of course, in some instances all plies are hardwood. Many species of wood and different kinds of adhesives are used in making the various grades of hardwood plywood.

Grades

Grades designate the quality of the face, back, and interior plies. There are six grades of hardwood plywood:

Premium grade has a face of some

123

specified kind of hardwood, such as walnut or mahogany. The face must be made of tight and smoothly cut veneers which are carefully matched as to color and grain.

• *Good grade* is for a natural finish and is similar to premium; however, the face veneers do not need to be matched as accurately.

• *Sound grade* is used as a base for smooth, painted surfaces. The face is free from open defects, although it may show stains and streaks. The veneer is not matched for grain or color.

• *Utility grade* can have some discoloration, knotholes up to 3/4" in diameter, minor open joints, and small areas of rough grain, but no shake (crack between growth rings) or similar defects.

• *Backing grade* is unselected for grain or color. There may be limited knotholes and splits, as detailed in the grading standards. Small defects are permitted, but none that will impair panel strength.

• *Specialty grade* is used for architectural plywood, matched-grain panels for certain uses, and special veneer selections.

Types of Bonds

Besides the grading system, plywood is also classified according to its adhesive bond, of which there are four types. The *technical fully waterproof bond* will withstand full exposure to water. Type I (exterior) is a *fully waterproof bond* which will withstand exposure to all weather. Type II (interior) is a *water-resistant bond* that will keep its strength through some wetting and drying. This is the most common type for hardwood plywood. Type III (interior) is a *moisture-resistant bond* that will retain its strength when subjected to occasional moisture.

Dimensions

Plywood panels are commonly available in widths from 24" to 48" in 6" intervals, and in lengths from 48" to 96" in 12" intervals. The most common size is 4' x 8'.

Thickness

Veneer-core plywood is available in three, five, seven, and nine plies in the following thicknesses:

3 ply: 1/8", 3/16", 1/4".
5 ply: 5/16", 3/8", 1/2" and 5/8".
7 ply: 5/8" and 3/4".
9 ply: 3/4".

Lumber-core or particle-board-core plywood is available in five plies, 3/4" thick.

Molded Plywood

Many types of hardwood plywood are made in simple and compound curves. Good examples of compound curves are seen in the all-wood chair, Fig. 8-21. Curved and molded plywood is produced either by bending and gluing in one operation or by bending previously glued, flat panels. See Unit 41. Plywood bent and glued in one operation is usually more satisfactory because it holds its shape better.

Appearance of Hardwood Veneers

Frequently the same kind of wood such as walnut or mahogany will appear to have different patterns and figures. This raises the question of how two pieces of veneer from the same species of tree can look so utterly different. In general, the type of figure pattern in fine veneers depends on three things:

• *The wood species.* Rosewood has an entirely different appearance, for example, from walnut or mahogany.

• *The portion of the tree from which it is cut.* Most veneers are cut from the trunk, also called long wood. Other parts of the tree produce veneer that is differ-

ent in appearance. See Unit 42. The
burl develops an unusual and exceptionally fine figure.
• *The method of cutting.* See Unit 42.

SOFTWOOD PLYWOODS

All softwood plywood has veneer-core
construction, with veneer cut by the
rotary method. About 90 percent of plywood is of Douglas fir, with some 30
other species making up the rest. Species
are grouped on the basis of stiffness
(with Group 1 the strongest or stiffest)
as follows:

Group 1: Douglas fir 1; western larch; southern pine
(loblolly, longleaf, shortleaf, slash); tanoak.
Group 2: Port Orford cedar; Douglas fir 2; fir (California red, grand, noble, Pacific silver, white);
western hemlock; lauan (red, white); western white
pine; Sitka spruce.
Group 3: red alder; Alaska yellow cedar; pine
(lodgepole, ponderosa); redwood.
Group 4: cedar (incense, western red); subalpine
fir; sugar pine; western poplar; Englemann spruce.

Standards for this material have been
established by the American Plywood Association. Fig. 8-22. Four basic veneers
are used in the manufacture of softwood
plywood panels. Grade "A" veneer may
contain neatly made repairs but is free
from open defects and gives a suitable
surface for finishing. "B" veneer allows a
solid-type, one-inch knot, plugged, as
well as patches. "C" and "D" veneers allow large, solid knots and certain knotholes. There is also a special grade "N"
for natural finish. For exterior panels, a
waterproof glue (phenolic resin adhesive) is used, and a moisture-resistant
protein glue for the interior type. For
most furniture construction, interior "A-
A" or "A-B" is chosen. (The first letter
indicates the grade of the face veneer,
the second shows the grade of the back.)
These plywoods are available in 3' and
4' widths and 8' lengths. Common thicknesses are 1/4", 5/16", 3/8", 1/2",
5/8", 3/4", and 1".

8-21. This chair shows three types of construction.
The seat and back are molded plywood. The legs,
and the support for the seat and back are of
laminated construction. The cross rails are solid wood.

PLYWOOD PRODUCTS WITH
SPECIAL PROPERTIES

Plywood manufacturers are constantly
improving both the quality and variety
of their products. Many have developed
some special procedure or product of
their own. For instance one manufacturer
has a continuous process for making a
hard-surface panel, called *fiberply,* which
has a tough, smooth surface on both
sides. A new type of hot press, the largest plywood press in the world, is used
for manufacturing this product. A continuous sheet of veneer moves directly
from the log, through driers, into the
press. The plies are heat bonded with dry
glue, and the outside layers are given a
resin-impregnated surface.. This process
eliminates need for a paint undercoating
and reduces checking and grain raising.
Fiberply comes in both interior and exterior grades and has two more plies than
regular plywood—five plies in the 3/8"
thickness, seven plies in the 1/2", 5/8",
and 3/4" thicknesses.

Another material is *prefinished hardwood plywood used for wall panels,*
made with a permanent, factory finish.

Use these symbols when you specify plywood	Description and Most Common Uses	Typical Grade-trademarks	Veneer Grade Face	Veneer Grade Back	Veneer Grade Inner plys	Most Common Thickness (inch)
Interior Type						
N-N, N-A, N-B, N-D INT-DFPA	Natural finish cabinet quality. One or both sides, select all heartwood or all sapwood veneer. For furniture having a natural finish, cabinet doors, built-ins. Use N-D for natural finish paneling. Special order items.	N-N·G-1·INT-DFPA·PS 1-66 / N-A·G-2·INT-DFPA·PS 1-66	N	N,A, B or D	C or D	1/4, 3/4, 1
A-A INT-DFPA	For interior applications where both sides will be on view. Built-ins, cabinets, furniture and partitions. Face is smooth and suitable for painting.	A-A·G-3·INT-DFPA·PS 1-66	A	A	D	1/4, 3/8, 1/2, 5/8, 3/4, 1
A-B INT-DFPA	For uses similar to Interior A-A but where the appearance of one side is less important and two smooth solid surfaces are necessary.	A-B·G-4·INT-DFPA·PS 1-66	A	B	D	1/4, 3/8, 1/2, 5/8, 3/4, 1
A-D INT-DFPA	For interior uses where the appearance of only one side is important. Paneling, built-ins, shelving, partitions.	A-D GROUP 1 INTERIOR	A	D	D	1/4, 3/8, 1/2, 5/8, 3/4, 1
B-B INT-DFPA	Interior utility panel used where two smooth sides are desired. Permits circular plugs. Paintable.	B-B·G-3·INT-DFPA·PS 1-66	B	B	D	1/4, 3/8, 1/2, 5/8, 3/4, 1
B-D INT-DFPA	Interior utility panel for use where one smooth side is required. Good for backing, sides of built-ins.	B-D GROUP 3 INTERIOR	B	D	D	1/4, 3/8, 1/2, 5/8, 3/4, 1
DECORATIVE PANELS	Rough-sawn, brushed, grooved or striated faces. Good for paneling, interior accent walls, built-ins, counter facing.	DECORATIVE·B-D·G-1·INT-DFPA	C or btr.	D	D	5/16, 3/8, 1/2
PLYRON INT-DFPA	Hardboard face on both sides. For counter tops, shelving, cabinet doors, flooring. Hardboard faces may be tempered, untempered, smooth or screened.	PLYRON·INT-DFPA			C & D	1/2, 5/8, 3/4, 1
Exterior Type						
A-A EXT-DFPA	For use in exterior applications where the appearance of both sides is important. Fencing, wind screens, outdoor storage units, cabinet work exposed to the weather.	A-A·G-4·EXT-DFPA·PS 1-66	A	A	C	1/4, 3/8, 1/2, 5/8, 3/4, 1
A-B EXT-DFPA	For use similar to A-A EXT panels but where the appearance of one side is less important.	A-B·G-1·EXT-DFPA·PS 1-66	A	B	C	1/4, 3/8, 1/2, 5/8, 3/4, 1
A-C EXT-DFPA	Exterior use where the appearance of only one side is important. Sidings, soffits, fences, structural uses, privacy screens.	A-C GROUP 2 EXTERIOR	A	C	C	1/4, 3/8, 1/2, 5/8, 3/4, 1
B-B EXT-DFPA	An outdoor utility panel with solid paintable faces.	B-B·G-1·EXT-DFPA·PS 1-66	B	B	C	1/4, 3/8, 1/2, 5/8, 3/4, 1
B-C EXT-DFPA	An outdoor utility panel for farm service and work buildings.	B-C GROUP 3 EXTERIOR	B	C	C	1/4, 3/8, 1/2, 5/8, 3/4, 1

8-22. Softwood plywood grading system.

In manufacture, their surface is given a fine sanding and then a complete finishing so that the panels can be used as they are shipped. Fig. 8-23.

Prefinished plywood planks are available in pieces 16¼″ wide and 6′, 7′, or 8′ long. They can be obtained with tongue-and-groove edges so that they can be used for internal paneling.

Striated plywood has a combed surface that gives it an unusual texture. Fig. 8-24. The surface of *ripplewood plywood* has a grain pattern that is accentuated to produce a three-dimensional appearance. Fig. 8-25. *Plyron* is a composition panel with an interior of plywood and an exterior of hardboard. *Buffed plywood* has a surface with distinct design, obtained by passing the panels between rollers. *Finishield*, used in furniture manufacture, has a thin layer of aluminum foil directly under the outside veneer. This layer imparts beauty and makes the surface resistant to cigarette burns. *Flexwood* is a wood veneer fastened to a special cloth backing which will cover a curved surface. The room shown in Fig. 8-26 has flexwood oak veneer on a curved wall with cabinets and table of rosewood.

WORKING WITH PLYWOOD

Storage

The best method of storing plywood is

8-23. This factory-finished plywood paneling requires only wiping after it is installed.

8-24. Striated plywood has an interesting grain surface.

to lay the sheets flat. If this is not possible, they should be stored on edge and supported. Never lay plywood at an angle as it will warp. This is especially true of thinner panels.

Cutting

When hand sawing, always place the good face of the plywood up and use a saw that has at least 10 points to the inch. Make sure that the panel is supported firmly so it will not sag. Hold the saw at a low angle when cutting and, if possible, place a piece of scrap stock underneath. When using the circular saw, install a sharp combination blade or one with fine teeth. Adjust the blade so that the teeth just clear the top of the stock. Always place the plywood on the table saw with the good side up. However, when cutting with a portable power handsaw, place the good face down.

Selecting Plywood

Never attempt to use interior plywood for exteriors. This is especially important when making furniture and in home construction. Excessive dampness or moisture will cause the plies to separate.

Planing Edges

It is seldom necessary to plane the edges of plywood but, when it must be done, always work from both ends toward the center. This prevents any tear-

127

8-25 Ripplewood plywood.

ing out of the plies at the end of the cut. Use a plane with a sharp blade and take shallow cuts. When using a jointer, adjust it to a very thin cut.

Treating the Edges

There are several ways to finish the edges of plywood. The most common is to use an edge-banding material of the same veneer as the face. In some cases this material has an adhesive on it; all that is required is to peel off the backing paper and apply the banding to the edge. In other cases it is necessary to use contact cement since some edge bands have fabric backing but no adhesive. Also, laminated plastic materials may be applied with contact cement to the edges of tables. Some of the more common edge treatments are shown in Unit 50. If plywood is to be painted, the edge-end grain can be filled with wood putty.

Using Nails and Screws

Nails or screws do not hold well in the edge of plywood. It is important to remember this, especially when attaching hinges. Whenever possible, hinges for plywood doors should be attached to the face rather than to the edge.

When nailing plywood, always choose nails that are the right size in relation to panel thickness. Select as follows: for 3/4″ plywood, 6d casing nails or 6d finishing nails; for 5/8″ plywood,

6d or 8d finishing nails; for 1/2″ plywood, 4d or 6d; for 3/8″ plywood, 3d or 4d; and for 1/4″ plywood, use 3/4″ or 1″ brads. For very careful installations, pre-drill to keep the nails from splitting the edge. The drill should be slightly smaller in diameter than the nail. Space nails about 6″ apart for most work. When nailing thin plywood closer spacing may be necessary to avoid buckling between the joints. Nails and glue together produce a strong joint. Flathead wood screws are needed when nails will not provide adequate holding power. Glue should also be used whenever possible.

The following gives plywood thicknesses and the diameter and length of the *smallest* screws recommended. Use longer screws when the work permits:

3/4″ plywood: No. 8-1½″
5/8″ plywood: No. 8-1¼″
1/2″ plywood: No. 6-1¼″
3/8″ plywood: No. 6-1″
1/4″ plywood: No. 4-¾″

Screws or nails should be countersunk

8-26. Flexwood is ideal for curved walls and cabinets.

128

and the holes filled with wood dough, putty, or plugs. Apply filler until it is slightly higher than the plywood surface and then sand it level after it is dry.

Drilling

If the back side of plywood is going to show, chipped edges can be eliminated by placing a wood block under the back when drilling.

Selecting Corner Joints

When working with plywood, selecting the correct kind of corner joint is important for both strength and appearance. For elementary construction in which the surfaces are to be painted, butt joints can be used. Frame construction with butt joints makes it possible to use thinner plywood. Rabbet joints are simple to make and are excellent for many types of drawers, buffets, chests, or cupboards. The only problem is that the plies are exposed where the faces meet. One method of eliminating this is to cut the rabbet from one piece of the plywood and then cut the entire stock away from the other member, leaving only the face veneer which overlaps the second member. The best joint for plywood corners is the miter joint or some adaptation of it. The more difficult miter joints are the rabbet miter and lock miter.

Protecting the Face Veneer

In working plywood, it is important not to chip off the expensive face veneer, especially in hardwoods. This can happen at an exposed edge or corner. After stock is cut, the face corners can be protected by fastening tape to them during the construction process.

Sanding

Since most good face veneers are only 1/28″ thick, it is very important not to sand the surface too much. Good hardwood plywoods come with a super-fine sanded surface to which a finish can be applied directly. The greatest care in sanding must be taken when plywood is used in combination with solid lumber. It is easy to over-sand plywood surfaces, especially with a portable or stationary belt sander.

Removing Nails

Plywood resists splitting much more than ordinary woods; therefore nails and screws can be fastened close to the edges. However, when removing nails from plywood, pull straight out rather than at an angle. You may splinter the outside ply if you pull or draw out the nails at an angle.

9 Hardboard And Particle Board

Widely used for furniture and cabinets, hardboard and particle board are man-made products of modern wood technology and research. Both combine the best characteristics of wood and adhesives, and reflect modern man's ability to control the size, shape, and working qualities of raw materials.

HARDBOARD

Hardboard is available in boards or panels. Figs. 9-1 and 9-2. As the name implies it is relatively hard.

Manufacture of Hardboard

Hardboard is manufactured from

9-1. The walls of this room are paneled in hardboard of which the top two-thirds is perforated.

refined or partly refined wood fibers. Fig. 9-3. The first step is to chip the wood into thin pieces 5/8″ wide and 1″ long. The chips are then reduced to individual wood fibers either by steam or by a mechanical defibering process. Next, the fibers are further refined through mechanical processes which vary with the method of manufacture. Small amounts of chemicals may be added to improve the resulting board. In a machine called a felter the fibers are interlocked into a continuous mat and compressed by heavy rollers. Lengths of this mat, called *wetlap,* are fed into multiple presses where heat and pressure produce the thin, hard, dry board sheets. After the boards leave the presses, moisture is added in a humidifier to stabilize them to atmospheric conditions. The boards are then trimmed to standard dimensions and wrapped in packages ready for shipment.

130

Types and Sizes of Hardboard

Hardboard is made in three basic types: standard, tempered, and service. *Standard hardboard* is given no additional treatment after manufacture. This board has high strength and good water resistance. It is commonly used in furniture and cabinetwork because it has good sheen characteristics and finishes well. *Tempered hardboard* is standard board to which chemical and heat-treating processes have been applied to improve stiffness, hardness, and finishing properties. *Service hardboard* has somewhat less strength than standard. It is used where low weight is an advantage. It does not have quite as good sheening and finishing characteristics as standard.

Hardboard is manufactured with one or both sides smooth. One side smooth is known as S1S and two sides smooth is S2S. Hardboard is available in thicknesses from 1/16″ to 3/4″, the common thicknesses being 1/8″, 3/16″, and 1/4″. The standard panel size is 4′ x 8′, but it is also available in widths up to 5′ and in lengths to 16′. Fig. 9-4.

Specialty Hardboards

Because hardboard is manufactured, it can be made in shapes, sizes, and sur-

9-2. The backs of most television and hi-fi sets are hardboard.

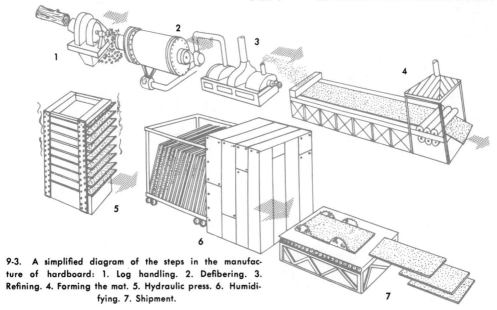

9-3. A simplified diagram of the steps in the manufacture of hardboard: 1. Log handling. 2. Defibering. 3. Refining. 4. Forming the mat. 5. Hydraulic press. 6. Humidifying. 7. Shipment.

faces to meet varying needs of the furniture and cabinetmaking industries. Here are a few of the many kinds available:

• *Perforated hardboard* has very closely spaced holes punched or drilled in the surface. The holes may be round, square, or diagonal and can be fitted with metal hooks, holders, supports, or similar fittings. Fig. 9-5. Such hardboard is in common use not only in homes, but in stores for display and storage.

• *Embossed patterns* are available in simulated leather, wood grain, and basket weave. Fig. 9-6.

9-4. Standard sheets of hardboard.

9-5. A hardboard storage wall suitable for a garage, utility room, or workroom. This hardboard has perforations for pegboard hooks and accessories in two-thirds of the panel, and the bottom third is solid wainscoting.

9-6. A few of the design patterns available in hardboard.

9-7. Wood-grained hardboard makes attractive wall paneling.

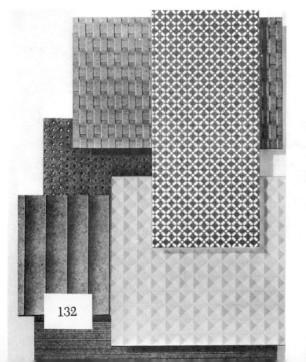

• *Acoustical hardboard* has perforations which improve its properties for controlling sound. It makes an excellent covering for ceilings and walls.

• *Wood-grain hardboard* is printed with wood grain to match the color and texture of oak, walnut, mahogany, and many other woods. Fig. 9-7. It is popular for interior paneling. Many other types of hardboard panels are designed for building construction.

Uses of Hardboard

Hardboard is used not only in wood products like furniture, cabinets, and homes, but also in many basically metal products such as automobiles, refrigerators, and trailers. About 50 per cent of all hardboard is used in building construction for siding, interior paneling, underlaying, kitchen cabinets, and similar purposes. Furniture manufacturers use 20 to 25 per cent for such items as exteriors of television cases, drawer bottoms, and the backs of cases and cabinets. Some furniture manufacturers use hardboard in making their own lumber-core plywood. Strips of solid wood or particle-board are used for the core, then hardboard is applied for the crossbands. Layers of veneer attached to the hardboard complete the panels.

Working with Hardboard

For ordinary interior installations individual sheets of hardboard should stand on edge 24 hours or more, allowing to adjust to the surrounding air. Hardboard that will be subjected to high humidity (for bathrooms, utility rooms, or exterior use), should be "pre-expanded" by long exposure to damp air or by scrubbing water into the back of the panel with a broom. Scrubbed panels should then be stacked back-to-back under a tarpaulin for 24 hours if standard board, 48 hours if tempered.

Sawing

Hardboard may be sawed as any other wood product with hand or power tools. For best results sharp high-speed power saws should be used. For high-production work, saws must be carbide-tipped, of a design recommended by the saw manufacturer.

Machining

Hardboard may be machined the same way as other wood products. Such operations as shaping, routing, and planing give best results if tools are kept sharp. Absence of grain in hardboard allows uniformly fine machining without splintering.

Sanding

The quality of hardboard is such that surface sanding is not normally required. However, sawed edges, machined surfaces, and surface scratches can be dressed up by normal wood-sanding procedures. Also, precision sanding to close tolerance can be done.

Bending

Wide, dry bends may be made by fastening hardboard solidly to curved forms. For smaller-radius bends wet the hardboard, then bend it over heated forms until dry. Tighter bends without rupturing may be made by slow, deliberate bending. The thinner the board, the sharper the curve that can be bent. Also, tempered hardboard will bend tighter than the same thickness of non-tempered varieties.

Drilling

Hardboard may be drilled the same as other wood products. For best results, the face of the piece should be placed upward and a solid backing used to attain clean edges.

Gluing

For gluing hardboard, follow the directions of the glue supplier.

Applying Hardboard Over Studding

If nails may show, good results are obtained by spreading adhesive with a knife or gun on the studs and panels, and securing with a minimum of nails or staples. If no nails can be used, contact cement for plastic laminates is excellent. Follow manufacturer's instructions for proper application.

Fastening

Hardboard may be fastened with any of the common wood fasteners, such as nails, staples, automatic nailers, screws, bolts, adhesives, or rivets.

Nailing Hardboard

Start at the edge adjoining the previous panel and work across the board toward the free edge. Use 3d finishing nails (galvanized preferred) for interiors. As insurance against fiber puffing around nail heads and nail loosening, it is recommended that annular-thread or ring-groove hardboard nails be selected. These nails are designed to be set flush with the work. Allow some freedom of movement between the boards, taking care not to force them tightly together. Space nails 6″ on center. Make joints only where solid support is available. For exteriors, at least a 5d galvanized nail (casing or box), a shake nail, or a hardened siding nail should be chosen.

Staples for Hardboard

For best results staples with narrow crown and divergent points (branching out in different directions) should be used, along with a hammer-type stapler or air gun. Spacing of 4″ or 6″ is recommended. Length of staples should be at least 1/2″ plus the thickness of the board. The power required varies with the thickness and kind of board. For further advice, refer to the staple supplier's directions.

Screws and Bolts For Hardboard

Any thickness of hardboard may be screwed or bolted to a frame or base after drilling holes large enough to accommodate the shank of the screws or bolts. Also, hardboard 1/4″ or 3/8″ thick has excellent screw-holding strength for attaching hinges or other hardware. Drill holes smaller than the screw diameter, and use sheet metal screws.

Hardboard Joints and Edges

Joints and edges may be scored, routed, beveled, grooved, or otherwise treated as use requires. Some hardboards are patterned so that their edges will blend into the overall pattern of the board when butted together. If there are no joints, leave space the thickness of a shingle nail, then apply tape and joint cement as in normal dry-wall construction. This may be painted or otherwise covered. Where joints are exposed, the edge may be beveled or routed. Wood, metal, or plastic battens or inserts may be used to accentuate the joints. Inside corners may be covered with cove molding or may be butted.

Painting Hardboard

Hardboard will take almost any type of finish. Brush, spray, or roller may be used according to the finish required. Interior-wall panels require no special sealer. However, if sealer is to be applied, rubber or vinyl-base white are good choices. Wall paints (oil-base flat) require no special sealer. Water-mix sealers may be used as well as standard oil-base primers. With enamel finishes, apply a pigmented primer-sealer as the

TYPICAL WORKING CHARACTERISTICS OF MANUFACTURED BOARD

| | Thick Panels—¼"—1½" | | Thin Panels—⅛"—⅜" | | |
| | Flake Board 42# cu. ft. | Particle Board 40# cu. ft. | Hardboard | | |
			Standard	Tempered	Specialties
Bending	Fair	Fair	Good	Excellent	Good
Drilling	Excellent	Good	Good	Excellent	Excellent
Hardness	High	Medium	Medium	High	High
Laminating	Excellent	Good	Good	Excellent	Excellent
Nailing	Good	Good	Fair	Good	Good
Painting	Unfilled—Good Filled—Excel.	Unfilled—Fair Filled—Good	Fair	Excellent	Excellent
Punching	Fair	Fair	Fair	Excellent	Good
Routing	Excellent	Good	Fair	Excellent	Good
Sanding	Excellent	Good	Fair	Excellent	Good
Sawing	Excellent	Good	Fair	Excellent	Good
Screw Holding	Excellent	Good	Fair	Good	Good
Shaping	Excellent	Good	Fair	Excellent	Good
Water Resistance	Interior or Exterior	Interior or Exterior	Interior	Exterior	Interior or Exterior

TYPICAL END USES

| | | | Thin Panels—⅛"—⅜" | | |
| | Flake Board 42# cu. ft. | Particle Board 40# cu. ft. | Hardboard | | |
			Standard	Tempered	Specialties
Cabinets	X	X	X	X	X
Core Stock	X	X			X
Counter Tops	X				
Dinettes	X				
Doors	X				X
Furniture Panels	X	X	X	X	X
Paneling (interior)		X			X
Partitions	X			X	X
Shelving	X	X			
Store Fixtures	X		X	X	X
Table Tops	X				

9-8. Comparative working qualities of typical hardboard, particle board, and flake board. This chart shows the recommendations of one manufacturer of these materials.

base coat. Enamel undercoat may be applied and rubber or vinyl emulsions also. Clear finishes require a recommended non-pigmented sealer. Clear varnish or resin sealers should not be used as a first coat. Best results are obtained with transparent filler-sealer, natural paste-wood filler, or clear-drying white vinyl glue. Stain finishes may be obtained with pigmented resin sealers, oil wood stains, colored paste-wood fillers or stain waxes. These are wipe-on finishes. Varnish stains are not recommended. Texture paints or wallpaper may be applied when joints are properly taped and filled. Fig. 9-8.

135

9-9. All exterior parts of this kitchen cabinet are made of particle board.

9-10. Precision-cut shavings are made into flake board.

9-11. This huge hydraulic press can produce 40 million square feet of flake board a year.

PARTICLE BOARD

Particle board is one of the newer composition-type board materials. Fig. 9-9. It is made of wood particles such as chips, splinters, shavings, flakes, even sawdust. Many of the materials used to make particle board were once considered waste at the saw mill. These wood fragments are combined with an adhesive to form a medium-density board. There are about 19 basic kinds of particle board, not merely with different commercial names but of different composition or construction.

Flake board is a high-quality particle board. To make it, flakes are carefully cut with the grain to precise thickness and length, then bonded together with a special adhesive. Fig. 9-10. As a result, flake board has better working qualities than most particle board.

How Particle Board Is Made

Some manufacturers of particle board use only softwoods while others use

9-12. Because of its smooth, grain-free surface, particle board makes a good base for plastic laminated surfaces. Panels are available in a variety of densities, thicknesses, and sizes, and some are treated with fire and insect retardants.

certain hardwoods, especially poplar. Properties of particle board can be changed by varying such things as the kind and shape of chips, kind and amount of adhesive, pressure, and methods of forming. The two basic methods of producing particle board are the *extrusion method* and the *mat-formed, flat-pressed method*. In extrusion, which is the less common method, the board is formed by forcing the wood particles and adhesive through a small opening. (The way you get toothpaste out of a tube is extrusion.)

Most particle board is produced by forming the wood particles and adhesives into a mat, then pressing this in a hot press. Fig. 9-11. There are three basic types of mat-formed particle board. The first one has the same kind and size of shavings throughout and is called *single-layer*. In the second type there are larger shavings in the center of the board and smaller ones at the surface; this is called *multi-layer*. The third type, *variable layer*, has coarser splinters or shavings in the center with a gradual change to finer shavings toward the outside. The last two are much better for the application of plastic laminates or veneers since they are smoother and provide less chance for a splinter to work through to the surface.

Since particle board is a manufactured material, its properties can be varied to suit particular needs. Fig. 9-12. Particle board weighs about 30 to 50 pounds per cubic foot. Varieties used in furniture manufacture have a density of about 30 to 40 pounds per cubic foot; flake board density is slightly higher, about 40 to 50 pounds per cubic foot. Most particle board is used as flat-panel material, although some manufacturers now mold parts to compete with wood laminating.

Particle board is available in thicknesses from 1/4" to 2", in panel widths

9-13. Common uses for particle board and flake board.

137

9-14. Cutting a rabbet on the edge of particle board with a router. Note the smooth, clean cut. Since it has no grain, there is no splintering.

9-15. Two routers with carbide-tipped cutters are set for machining the edges of particle board.

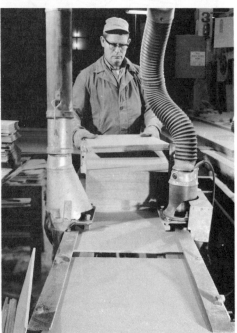

from 2′ to 5′, and in lengths from 4′ to 16′. The more common panel sizes are 1/2″ to 1″ thick and 4′ x 8′ and 5′ x 8′ sheets. Particle board is available from the manufacturer as unfinished sheets or in various stages of finishing with the surfaces and edges filled, colored, and sealed. Particle board and flake board are made by a large number of manufacturers under their own trade names. It is a good idea to check with your lumber supplier concerning the commercial names, characteristics, and the uses of the varieties he sells. There is one that is best for each kind of furniture or cabinet job. Some are well suited for doors, built-ins, and wall surfaces, others are meant to be painted, while still others are best for veneering and applying plastic laminates. Fig. 9-13.

Working With Particle Board

Most of what has been said concerning the methods of working hardboard also applies to particle board. Both are manufactured products without grain. Fig. 9-14. Particle board, however, is not as hard as hardboard. Here are some suggestions:

Sawing and machining. All standard woodworking tools and machines can be used. Because it has no grain, it works with great ease. High production requires the use of carbide-tipped tools. Fig. 9-15.

Joinery. Particle board is often edge banded with solid wood for the tops of tables and cabinets and similar areas. Particle board can be glued directly to solid wood with a butt joint, using a gap-filling urea formaldehyde adhesive. However, it is much better to make some kind of joint such as a spline, tongue-and-groove, dowel, or dovetail. Adding an edge band of solid wood greatly increases the overall strength of the top. It also provides an edge that can be shaped and contoured.

Applying veneers and plastic laminates. With the improved surface qualities of many particle boards, it is not necessary to add crossbands. This permits relatively simple three-ply construction. Veneers and plastic laminates are applied to the core with contact cement. Both the veneer and the particle board should have approximately 6 to 8 per cent moisture content. Wood veneers can be bonded either in a hot or cold press. For small projects and on-the-job construction, it is better to use contact cement when applying veneers and plastic laminates to particle board.

Fastening with nails and screws. The nail-holding power of particle board is affected by the kind of board and the density; its nail-holding power is generally less than solid wood. The best nail to choose is a finishing nail no larger than 4d. The use of annular-thread or cement-coated nails improves holding power. While standard wood screws are satisfactory, it has been found that the same size sheet metal screws have 20 per cent greater holding power in particle board. The pilot hole for all screws should be quite small since there is no cell structure of solid wood to hold the screw in place.

Finishing. Most particle board is used as core stock. Some manufacturers apply a filler and sealer to cover the boards before applying veneer or plastic laminate. Filler and sealer are necessary if the board is to be finished by painting, enameling, or some kind of transparent finish.

10 Millwork Including Molding

Millwork includes all of the machined wood items, such as paneling, doors, window units, mantels (fireplace frames), stairs, shutters, kitchen cabinets, moldings, and trim, that go into homes and commercial buildings. Figs. 10-1 and 10-2.

There are two major groups of millwork: *standard* or *stock* items that are mass produced for wide usage, and *special* millwork that is manufactured by contract following an architect's or designer's plan. Fig. 10-3. The latter group might include special windows and doors, church furniture, and many ma-

10-1. The quality of craftsmanship needed to produce and install windows and other interior mill items is equal to that required for constructing the finest furniture.

139

10-2. Many stock mill items can be seen on the exterior of this attractive home. The finish carpenter must install each one.

10-3. Paneling and shutters are both standard mill items.

chined parts such as railings and certain kinds of paneling for commercial buildings. Fig. 10-4.

Many millwork manufacturers specialize in only one kind of work. For example, one company may make only window units, another only doors. Millwork plants generally have the same type of production equipment found in furniture-manufacturing plants. These companies employ designers, draftsmen, cabinetmakers, and millmen in addition to the semi-skilled workers who operate production equipment and do assembly and finishing. Fig. 10-5. Cabinetmakers and finish carpenters working on a house or commercial building must plan their work carefully so mill items will fit in place. They must also know how to install these items.

10-4(a). The pews and other interior woodwork for this church are special millwork produced especially for this building.

10-4(b). This window with an elliptical head is another special millwork item.

10-5(a). Designers and draftsmen checking a standard window unit.

10-5(b). These semi-skilled woodworkers are assembling a panel door.

10-6(a). Windows are important millwork items.

10-6(b). Common types of windows: (a) Double hung. (b) Horizontal sliding. (c) Casement. (d) Hopper. (e) Awning.

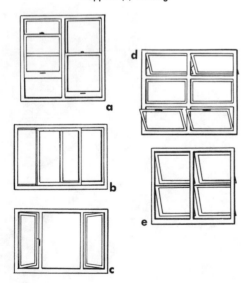

MILLWORK

With their products millwork companies provide drawings and specifications which are useful to the architect, cabinetmaker, and finish carpenter. In the case of windows, for example, the manufacturer will specify the width and height of the opening needed for each glass size. This information is given both for wood buildings and for masonry construction. Following are descriptions of some standard millwork items:

Windows

Window units are made in many common types including double-hung, horizontal-sliding, casement, hopper, fixed, awning, jalousie, and combination. Each is made in many standard sizes and different patterns. The double-hung window, for example, can be purchased with two lights (two pieces of glass) to 24 lights. Installing a window is the responsibility of the all-around or finish carpenter. Detailed installation instructions can be found in any good carpentry book. Fig. 10-6.

Stairs

Stairs require many stock mill items such as treads and risers. Also needed for railings are the balustrade, banister, shoe rail, newel post, and other parts. Fig. 10-7.

Doors

Doors are made in standard thicknesses and in various sizes for all kinds of indoor and outdoor openings. Fig. 10-8. Common designs include panel, flush, folding, French, louver (louvre), sliding, and two-piece. Front entrances can be purchased as complete units with fancy frames, pilasters, and pediments. Fig. 10-9.

Columns

Turned columns, solid and hollow, are

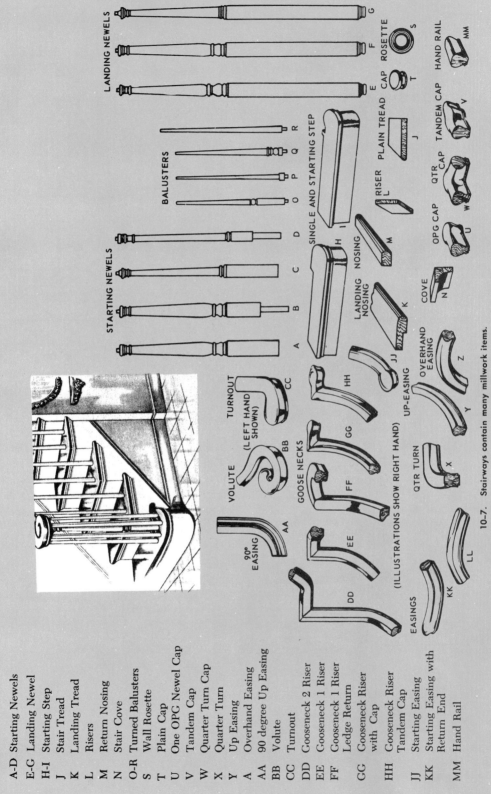

A-D Starting Newels
E-G Landing Newel
H-I Starting Step
J Stair Tread
K Landing Tread
L Risers
M Return Nosing
N Stair Cove
O-R Turned Balusters
S Wall Rosette
T Plain Cap
U One OPG Newel Cap
V Tandem Cap
W Quarter Turn Cap
X Quarter Turn
Y Up Easing
A Overhand Easing
AA 90 degree Up Easing
BB Volute
CC Turnout
DD Gooseneck 2 Riser
EE Gooseneck 1 Riser
FF Gooseneck 1 Riser Ledge Return
GG Gooseneck Riser with Cap
HH Gooseneck Riser Tandem Cap
JJ Starting Easing
KK Starting Easing with Return End
MM Hand Rail

10-7. Stairways contain many millwork items.

143

10-8. An unusual design for a panel door.

10-10. Columns come in many diameters and lengths. These are combined with knotty ponderosa pine paneling to form a room divider, giving the room a Colonial appearance.

10-11. These bathroom cabinets of western pine are mill-made.

10-9. This front entrance shows unusually fine craftsmanship.

This fine collection of classic style furniture illustrates the use of a wide variety of materials. The mahogany solids and veneers used as the basic wood are well complemented by elm burl accents in the drawer fronts. The hardware, including the metal grille, is solid brass and emphasizes the clarity of line. The deep brown marble table top blends in well, as does the cane set into the ends of the davenport. In addition, many fabrics can be used for the upholstered pieces. *Heritage*

The Contemporary furniture in this den blends with many materials used to furnish the room. One wall is plywood while the other is of fiber glass. Solid wood forms the trim and accentuates the vertical lines. The desk is walnut, and the cabinets are plywood with plastic-laminate fronts. Metal, leather, wood, glass, cane, tile, and many other materials were needed to complete the room.

Dunbar

This family room and its furnishings show why a cabinetmaker must be able to work with a wide variety of materials. The V-plank plywood walls have a rich warm color. The finish adds a handsome note to the decor. Often the cabinetmaker must be able not only to install the materials but also to finish them or at least to advise the one who is to do the finishing.   *Sherwin-Williams Co.*

144C

The interior walls of this home with plank-and-beam construction are of solid Philippine mahogany paneling. Of course the raw materials must be of good quality, but the cabinetmaker's skill is equally important to the finished appearance. The drawers and doors are fitted into the walls so they are an integral part of construction. This requires careful cutting and fitting. *Philippine Mahogany Association*

In this family room of Philippine mahogany, a wide range of materials is combined. A metal liner is needed for the planter. The stools are solid wood with leather-upholstered tops and the built-in snack bar is of solid wood with a plastic-laminate counter top. *Philippine Mahogany Association*

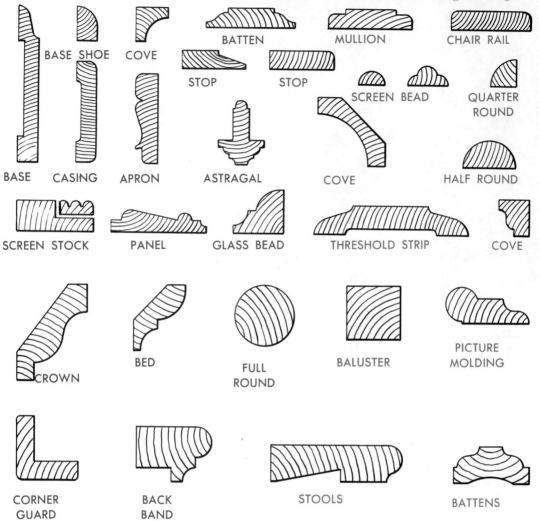

10-12. Standard shapes of moldings.

used for home interiors and exteriors. Fig. 10-10. Solid turnings make decorative room dividers. Hollow columns are installed as porch supports, among other exterior uses.

Cabinets

Storage cabinets for various rooms in a home are usually made by companies that specialize in this type of millwork. Fig. 10-11.

MOLDINGS

Moldings are strips of wood shaped on a molder. See Unit 64. They have a multitude of uses, both decorative and practical. In cabinetwork they help to achieve a finished appearance and in building construction they add decoration to interiors and exteriors. Moldings are also used for picture framing and for enriching furniture design, particularly on such

145

10-13. The design on the lower four drawers was achieved with simple stock moldings and fine hardware.

casework as chests and cabinets. Fig. 10-12. Moldings can be installed horizontally or vertically to serve as drawer or door pulls. They are important on all built-in furniture since they impart a solid finished appearance to cabinets, closets, desks, and shelving. Some of the common molding patterns are shown in Fig. 10-12. Their uses are as follows:

• *Crown moldings* soften sharp lines where two planes meet, usually at the break between wall and ceiling or under exterior eaves.

• *Bed moldings,* are used for the same reason and generally the same places as crown moldings.

• A *cove molding* has a concave face and is used for the same purpose as a bed or crown molding.

• A *casing* is used as trim for doors and windows or as a baseboard where wall and floor meet.

• *Stools* lie flat on the inside of sloping window sills, making a snug joint with the lower sash.

• *Rounds* are used for many purposes.

10-14. Differences in molding and hardware change the entire style of this kitchen-cabinet base. (a) Basic cabinet. (b) French Provincial. (c) Early American or Colonial.

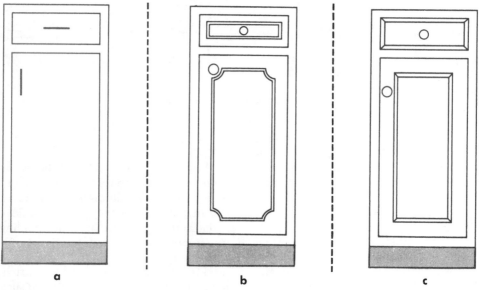

a   b   c

146

Full rounds make curtain rods, banisters, closet poles, and other similar items. *Half rounds* can be used as decorative trim to cover joints. *Quarter rounds* are installed on the inside of corner trim. Rounds can be used as part of a room divider.

• *Balusters* are designed as uprights in railings of all types. These handy squares serve many other purposes also.

• *Battens* are decorative strips placed over breaks in flat surfaces such as the cracks between boards in paneling and siding.

• *Glass beads* are used to hold glass or other materials in frames.

• *Stops* make snug joints and hold window sash in place.

• *Mullions* are decorative trim between windows in a series.

• *Base* and *base shoe* are used where baseboard and floor meet.

• *Corner guards* are designed for interior and exterior "outside" corners. They neatly cover exposed corner construction.

• *Back band* is used in place of corner guards when only one edge is exposed.

- *Picture moldings* are installed where walls meet ceilings; the design allows for picture hanging.

• *Screen stock* is material used for making window and door screen frames.

• *Screen beads* are strips fastened over the edge of a screen to hold it neatly and firmly in place.

Furniture and cabinet manufacturers also make many other kinds of moldings that are machine-shaped and carved for the exterior of furniture. Fig. 10-13. These are nailed, stapled, and/or glued to the exterior of drawers, doors, and edges of casework for decoration. Frequently, moldings can change a simple piece of casework into furniture with a definite style. Sometimes the same basic casework is used for several styles, with only the molding and hardware changed. Fig. 10-14. This technique is popular with kitchen-cabinet manufacturers.

11 Fasteners

Nails, screws, and similar fasteners are chiefly used for two purposes: to hold parts together, and to hold a completed product to a wall, floor, or other part of a building. In furniture construction, metal fasteners are used primarily for holding structural parts and trim. Fig. 11-1. A good example of this is a back panel attached to a case by nails or staples. Screws are used instead of nails in places that require great strength, such as corner blocks in leg-and-rail construction. There is limited use of exposed nails

and screws in furniture. If screws are installed, they are usually covered with a wood plug. Some cabinets are held together with nails alone, or nails and screws, Fig. 11-2, but better-quality ones

11-1. Using a stapling machine to assemble a chair frame.

147

11-2. Nailing is the common method of assembling plywood cabinets.

FINISHING NAILS

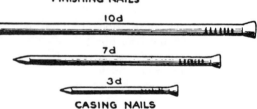

CASING NAILS

11-4. A few common sizes of finishing and casing nails.

have screws only, or screws plus glue. Fig 11-3.

NAILS

Nails for wood construction come in almost endless variety. The right kind of nail must be carefully chosen for each job to avoid splitting the material or distorting the wood fibers, for desired holding power, and for the appearance of the finished work. For interior cabinetwork, general-purpose *casing* or *finishing* nails

11-3. Fastening metal trim to a commercial fixture with screws.

of mild steel are commonly selected. Fig. 11-4. (Nails are also made of aluminum, copper, brass, and other metals.) For most casework a casing nail holds better than a finishing nail. Casing nails are also excellent for window and door frames, cornices, corner boards, and similar construction. Some cabinetmakers prefer them for all interior work. Finishing nails are used largely in cabinetwork trim and in other places where the nail head should not show.

The *penny system* is used to designate the size of a nail in terms of length from head to point. The letter "d" is used as a symbol for penny; thus *two penny* is written *2d*. Lengths range from 2d, which is 1″ long, to 60d, which is 6″ long.

A wire gage system is used to indicate

148

the diameter of a nail. As the gage number goes down, the diameter of the nail goes up. (Note that an opposite gage system is used for wood screws, in which low numbers mean small diameters.) Fig. 11-5 shows length, gage, thickness, and number of nails per pound of casing and finishing nails. Nails are commonly purchased by the pound.

OTHER TYPES OF NAILS AND STAPLES

• *Tacks,* available in lengths from 3/16″ to 1⅛″ and in size numbers from 1 to 24. Fig. 11-6.
• *Escutcheon pins,* small brass (or stainless steel) nails with round heads, available in lengths from 3/16″ to 2″, in gage sizes from 24 to 10, with smooth or annular thread. Fig. 11-7.
• *Wire brads,* small, flathead, mild-steel nails with sharp points, available in length from 1/2″ to 1½″ and in gage sizes from 20 to 14.
• *Staples,* installed with hand-operated tools or with portable or stationary air-operated machines. Fig. 11-8. Staple size is indicated by width and length. Staples must be purchased to match the size of the stapling machine.

NAILING TOOLS

The *claw hammer* is made with a metal head and a wood or metal handle. Hammers are designated by the weight of the head, which varies from 5 to 20 ounces. Most cabinetmakers like to have two hammers, a light one of perhaps 9 or 10 ounces for light work and one of medium weight, 14 to 16 ounces, for heavier work. Fig. 11-9. The *nail set* is a small metal punch with a cupped end. Fig. 11-10. It is used to sink the heads of casing and finishing nails below the wood surface so they can be covered. The *hand-operated stapling tool or gun* is commonly used by the cabinetmaker to install certain types of medium-density or thin panel material such as particle

FINISHING NAILS
FOR FINISHED CARPENTRY, TRIM AND CABINET WORK

SIZE	LENGTH	GAUGE	DIAMETER HEAD GAUGE	APPROX. NO. TO POUND
3d	1¼ inch	No. 15½	12½	850
4d	1½ inch	No. 15	12	575
6d	2 inch	No. 13	10	300
8d	2½ inch	No. 12½	9½	192
10d	3 inch	No. 11½	8½	122

CASING NAILS
FOR INTERIOR TRIM AND CABINET MAKING

SIZE	LENGTH	GAUGE	DIAMETER HEAD GAUGE	APPROX. NO. TO POUND
4d	1½ inch	No. 14	11	450
6d	2 inch	No. 12½	9½	240
8d	2½ inch	No. 11½	8½	145
10d	3 inch	No. 10½	7½	94
16d	3½ inch	No. 10	7	71

Note: The decimal equivalent of common gauge numbers is:

15 = .072	12 = .106	9 = .148	6 = .192
14 = .080	11 = .121	8 = .162	5 = .207
13 = .092	10 = .135	7 = .177	4 = .225

11-5. Comparative sizes of nails. Note that finishing and casing nails of the same pennyweight are made from different-size wire and have different diameters.

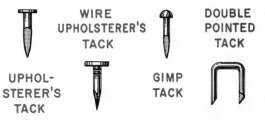

UPHOLSTERER'S TACK

WIRE UPHOLSTERER'S TACK

GIMP TACK

DOUBLE POINTED TACK

11-6. Common tacks.

11-7. Escutcheon pin.

11-8. Installing staples.

149

11-9. The kind of work should determine the weight of hammer to be used.

11-13. In straight nailing, the nails are installed straight or at a slight angle to increase their holding power.

11-10. Nail set.

11-11. Three items necessary for stapling: staples, stapling tool, and mallet.

11-12. Common shapes of ripping bars and chisels.

board. A *mallet* is used to strike the stapler. Fig. 11-11. A *ripping bar* and *chisel* are sometimes needed to remove old cabinetwork and paneling before remodeling. Fig. 11-12.

NAILING TECHNIQUES

Nailing can be done in two ways: *straight nailing* and *toenailing*. Straight nailing is used for most cabinetwork. Fig. 11-13. *Toenailing* is done when joining end grain to face grain. Nails should be driven at an angle of about 30 degrees. Fig. 11-14.

For cabinetwork, the nail heads are driven flush with or slightly below the work surface. In the latter case, first drive the nail until just the head is exposed, then finish driving with a nail set. Fig. 11-15. To nail hardwood, it is a good idea to drill a hole that is slightly smaller than the diameter of the nail shank and about two-thirds its length. Fig. 11-16. In nailing solid lumber, a few staggered nails provide greater strength than more nails in a straight row. Nails for plywood should be selected in terms of thickness of the material, as shown in Fig. 11-17.

150

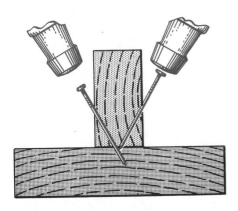

11-14. Toenailing.

11-15. Setting a nail below the surface of the wood.

SCREWS

In furniture building and cabinetmaking screws are used far more than nails for assembly, reinforcing structural parts, and attaching fittings such as hinges, catches, and handles. Screws have much better holding power than nails and also can be removed and replaced without damaging the wood. They are available in a wide variety of types, screw slots, sizes, and finishes. For this reason, it is impossible for a cabinet shop to stock all kinds. Fortunately, most metal items that require screw installations are packaged with the correct screws.

Common screws have flat, oval, or round heads, Fig. 11-18, and are made of mild steel, aluminum, copper, brass, or Monel metal. Roundhead screws of mild steel have a blue finish, flathead screws a bright finish. Ovalhead screws are usually plated with cadmium or chromium since they are used to install hinges, hooks, and other hardware.

Screws are made with either slotted or recessed (Phillips) heads. Fig. 11-19.

11-16. Drilling a small hole before nailing.

11-17. Correct sizes of finishing nails for plywood: For ¾" plywood, use 6d casing or finishing nails; for ⅝", use 6d or 8d finishing nails; for ½", use 4d or 6d finishing nails; for ⅜", use 3d or 4d finishing nails; and for ¼", use ¾" or 1" brads.

151

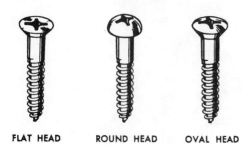

FLAT HEAD   **ROUND HEAD**   **OVAL HEAD**

11-18. Common head shapes of wood screws. Note that all of these have the recessed heads. For an excellent illustration of a slotted-head, see Fig. 11-22.

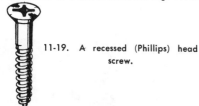

11-19. A recessed (Phillips) head screw.

TYPE "A"

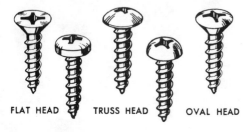

FLAT HEAD   **TRUSS HEAD**   **OVAL HEAD**

PAN HEAD   **ROUND HEAD**

11-20. Common head shapes for Type A sheet-metal screws.

11-21. Installing sheet-metal screws in man-made wood products: a. Drilling the clearance hole. b. Drilling the pilot or anchor hole. c. Countersinking. d. Screw installed. e. Hole for roundhead sheet-metal screw. f. Screw installed.

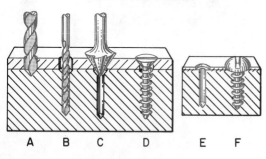

A   B   C   D   E   F

The *recessed head* is used in most production work because it is easier to install and can be drawn up tighter. Such screws require a Phillips-head screwdriver. In buying screws for a small shop it is a good idea to select flathead and roundhead screws in a limited number of lengths and gage sizes, and with only one type of head slot.

Self-tapping sheet-metal screws that are pointed are ideal for joining sheet metal to wood. These are Type A screws. Fig. 11-20. (Type B screws are not pointed and are not used in woodworking.) Type A is made in several head shapes and with either slotted or recessed heads. These differ from wood screws in that they are threaded along their entire length. Sheet metal screws are also recommended for man-made materials such as hardboard and particle board. Fig. 11-21. Another type of wood screw, used primarily for production work, has an off-center slot. Fig. 11-22. No pilot hole is needed with such a screw. (A pilot hole is ordinarily drilled to receive a wood screw, as explained later in this unit.)

Screw Size

Screws come in lengths from 3/16″ to 6″ and in gage sizes from 0 (smallest) to 24 (largest). Fig. 11-23. Note that the higher the number, the greater the diameter of the screw. (You will recall that

11-22. A self-drilling screw with a straight shank.

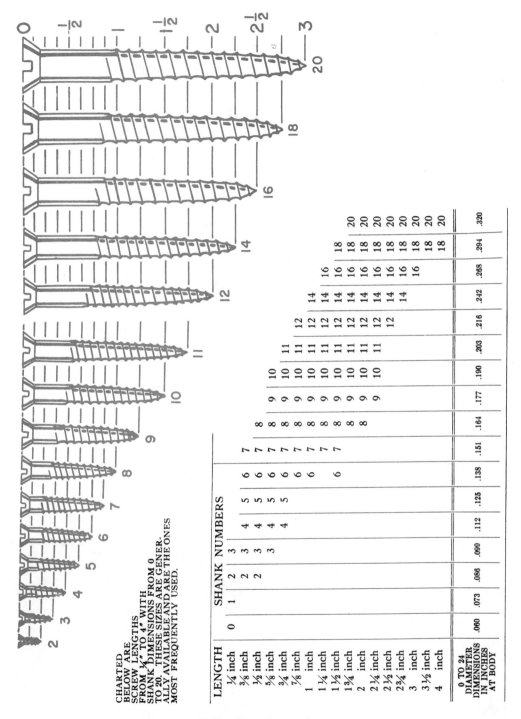

CHARTED
BELOW ARE
SCREW LENGTHS
FROM ¼" TO 4" WITH
SHANK DIMENSIONS FROM 0
TO 20. THESE SIZES ARE GENER-
ALLY AVAILABLE AND ARE THE ONES
MOST FREQUENTLY USED.

SHANK NUMBERS

LENGTH	0	1	2	3	4	5	6	7	8	9	10	11	12	14	16	18	20
¼ inch	0	1	2	3	4	5	6	7									
⅜ inch			2	3	4	5	6	7	8								
½ inch			2	3	4	5	6	7	8	9							
⅝ inch				3	4	5	6	7	8	9	10						
¾ inch					4		6	7	8	9	10	11	12				
⅞ inch							6	7	8	9	10	11	12	14			
1 inch							6	7	8	9	10	11	12	14	16		
1¼ inch								7	8	9	10	11	12	14	16	18	
1½ inch								7	8	9	10	11	12	14	16	18	20
1¾ inch									8	9	10	11	12	14	16	18	20
2 inch							6	7	8	9	10	11	12	14	16	18	20
2¼ inch											10	11	12	14	16	18	20
2½ inch											10	11	12	14	16	18	20
2¾ inch													12	14	16	18	20
3 inch													12	14	16	18	20
3½ inch														14	16	18	20
4 inch															16	18	20
0 TO 24 DIAMETER DIMENSIONS IN INCHES AT BODY	.060	.073	.086	.099	.112	.125	.138	.151	.164	.177	.190	.203	.216	.242	.288	.294	.320

11-23. Chart of screw sizes.

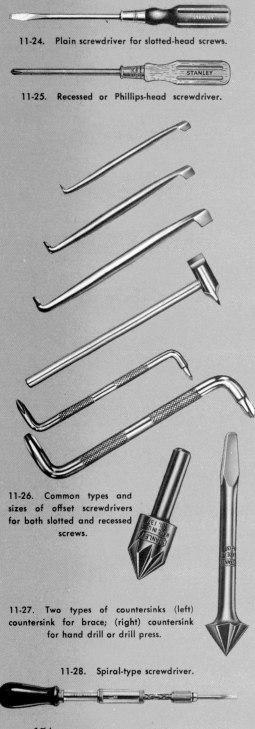

11-24. Plain screwdriver for slotted-head screws.

11-25. Recessed or Phillips-head screwdriver.

11-26. Common types and sizes of offset screwdrivers for both slotted and recessed screws.

11-27. Two types of countersinks (left) countersink for brace; (right) countersink for hand drill or drill press.

11-28. Spiral-type screwdriver.

the wire gage used for *nail* diameters has higher numbers for small diameters.) Each screw length comes in 3 to 10 different gage diameters. The smallest, 0, has a diameter of .060″. The diameter of each succeeding number is .013″ larger. For example, a No. 5 screw is .125″ (.060 + .013 × 5), or 1/8″. Generally, the lower gage numbers are for thinner woods. Screws 4″ and shorter are factory packed by the gross. Those over 4″ come in packages of one-half gross.

KINDS OF SCREWDRIVERS

For slotted head screws a *plain screwdriver* is used. Fig. 11-24. Screwdriver size is designed by the bar length and tip width. The tip should be straight, and the sides nearly parallel, with a slight taper. Several sizes should be available. The blade should just slip into the slot of the head and should be slightly less wide than the diameter of the screw head. A screwdriver that is too small will not provide enough leverage and will mar the slot. One that is too large will damage the wood around the screw. Except when cramped conditions call for a stubby or offset driver, use the longest one possible.

The *Phillips* screwdriver comes in sizes 1 through 4. Fig. 11-25. Use size No. 1

11-29. Using a spiral-type screwdriver to install a hinge screw.

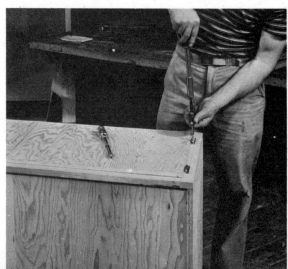

for screws from 0 through 4 gage; No. 2 for gages 5 through 9; No. 3 for gages 10 through 16; and No. 4 for screws 17 gage and larger.

Offset screwdrivers are made for use in close quarters. Fig. 11-26.

An *82-degree countersink* is needed for flathead screws that are to be flush with the surface. There are two types, one for a brace and the other for a hand drill or drill press. Fig. 11-27.

The *spiral-type* screwdriver is sold with four bits, three for plain screws and a No. 2 Phillips bit. Fig. 11-28. This tool provides a quick way of installing screws, but correct-size shank and pilot holes are important. Fig. 11-29.

A *screwdriver bit* in a brace can be used for setting screws. Fig. 11-30.

A *screw-mate drill countersink* is a tool for installing flathead screws. Fig. 11-31. It will do the four necessary things at one time: drill to correct depth, countersink, make the correct shank clearance, and make the correct pilot hole. This tool is stamped with the length and gage number. For example, a 3/4″ × #6 is used for a flathead screw 3/4″ long and No. 6 gage size.

A *screw-mate counterbore* will do all the drill-countersink operations and also drill holes for wood plugs. Fig. 11-32. Use

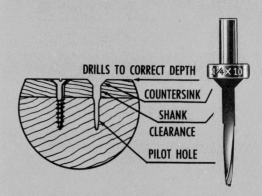

11-31. Screw-mate drill and countersink. The chart shows some common combinations of lengths and gage numbers in which the tool is available.

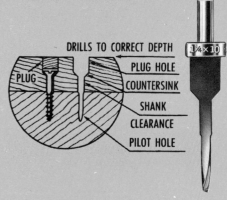

11-32. Screw-mate counterbore.

11-33. Plug cutters are available in different sizes.

11-34. Three methods of covering the heads of screws: a. With plastic wood. b. With a plain wood plug. c. With fancy wood plugs.

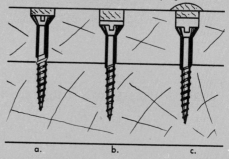

a.   b.   c.

11-30. Screwdriver bit used to install screws.

11-35. A power screwdriver can be operated by air, as the one shown here, or by electricity.

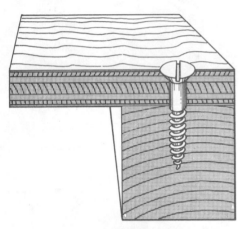

11-36. Make sure the threaded portion goes all the way into the second piece.

a *plug cutter* of the correct size to cut a wood plug for covering the hole. An *auger bit* can be used to counterbore a hole if a screw-mate counterbore is not available. The counterbore hole should be 3/8″ deeper than an ordinary pilot hole. Fig. 11-33. Cover the hole in one of the ways shown in Fig. 11-34.

Screwdriver attachments for portable drills and *power-operated screwdrivers* are used for production work. Fig. 11-35.

INSTALLING SCREWS

Wood screws have two diameters besides that of the head. Therefore two holes must be bored to install such screws: the *shank hole* for the threadless part of the screw, and the *pilot hole* for the threaded portion. Also, if the screw has a flat head it must be countersunk flush with or below the wood surface. When a screw head below the surface is to be concealed by a wood plug, a plug hole must be bored.

Select a screw long enough so that all of the threaded portion—or two-thirds of the screw's length—will go into the second member. Fig. 11-36. Choose a small-diameter screw for thinner woods, a larger diameter for heavier woods. Choose screws of smaller diameters and greater lengths whenever practical. Use enough screws to make the joint as strong as the wood itself.

11-37. Table showing the proper size bit or drill needed for drilling shank holes and pilot holes.

Screw Gage No.	0	1	2	3	4	5	6	7	8	9	10	11	12	14	16	18	20
Shank Hole Hard & Soft wood	1/16	5/64	3/32	7/64	7/64	1/8	9/64	5/32	11/64	3/16	3/16	13/64	7/32	1/4	17/64	19/64	21/64
PILOT HOLE SOFT WOOD	1/64	1/32	1/32	3/64	3/64	1/16	1/16	1/16	5/64	5/64	3/32	3/32	7/64	7/64	9/64	9/64	11/64
PILOT HOLE HARD WOOD	1/32	1/32	3/64	1/16	1/16	5/64	5/64	3/32	3/32	7/64	7/64	1/8	1/8	9/64	5/32	3/16	13/64
Auger Bit Sizes For Plug Hole				3	4	4	4	5	5	6	6	6	7	7	8	9	10

Drill the shank hole to a size *equal* to the diameter of the screw shank; the screw should slip into the hole with a free fit. Fig. 11-37. Next, drill the *pilot hole.* For hardwoods, its diameter should be approximately *10 per cent less* than the root (or smallest) diameter; for softwoods, about 30 per cent less than root diameter and not quite as deep as the threaded portion is long. If flathead screws are used, countersink until the surface diameter equals the largest diameter of the screw head. Fig. 11-38. Install with a screwdriver. Fig. 11-39. *Never hammer the screw into the hole* as this destroys the contact between thread and wood.

If a wood plug is used to cover the head of the screw, it should be cut from the same kind of wood used in the furniture or cabinet piece so the grains will match as much as possible. Plug cutters are available in various sizes. Bore the plug hole 3/8" deep and drive the head of the screw to the bottom of the plug hole. Cut the plug, apply glue to it, and force it into the hole with the grain direction matching the wood itself. After the glue dries, the excess can be trimmed off with a chisel. A piece of dowel rod can be used if the product is to be painted or

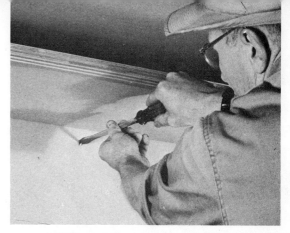

11-39. Installing a wood screw.

11-40. Covering a screw head with crack filler. Apply the filler so it is slightly higher than the wood, then sand level when dry. This method is used primarily for cabinets built on a construction site.

11-41. Choose flathead screws for plywood as follows: for ¾" plywood, No. 8-1½"; ⅝" plywood, No. 8-1¼"; ½" plywood, No. 6-1¼"; ⅜" plywood, No. 6-1"; ¼" plywood, No. 4¾".

11-38. Steps in installing a flathead screw: a. Drill the shank hole. b. Drill the pilot hole. c. Countersink. d. Check the amount of countersink with the screw. e. Screw properly installed.

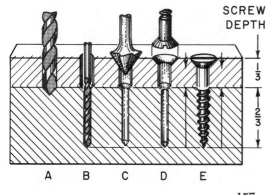

SCREW DEPTH

A   B   C   D   E

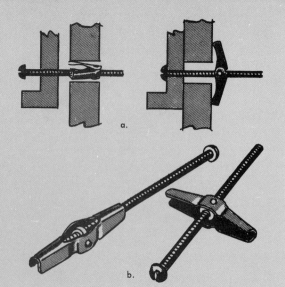

a.

b.

11-42(a). Spring-head toggle bolt. (b). Solid-head toggle bolt.

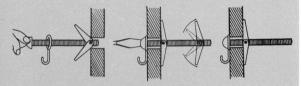

11-43. Installing a toggle bolt.

11-44. Common sizes of hollow-wall anchors. Use a 5/16" drill for 4-S, 4-L, or 4-XL. Use a 7/16" drill for 6-S, 6-L, or 6-XL. Use a 1/2" drill for 8-S, 8-L, or 8-XL.

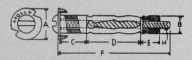

Bolt Series	Head Diam.	Body Diam.	Sleeve Length	Expander Length	Nut Length	Overall Length	Bolt Size	Max. Exp.
	A	B	C	D	E	F	H	
4-S	1/2	1/4	3/8	3/4	1/4	1 1/2	6-32	13/16
4-L	1/2	1/4	7/8	3/4	1/4	1 7/8	6-32	13/16
4-XL	1/2	1/4	1 1/2	3/4	1/4	2 1/2	6-32	13/16
6-S	5/8	3/8	3/8	1 1/8	3/8	2 1/4	10-24	1 1/8
6-L	5/8	3/8	7/8	1 1/8	3/8	2 3/4	10-24	1 1/8
6-XL	5/8	3/8	1 1/2	1 1/8	3/8	3 1/2	10-24	1 1/8
8-S	11/16	7/16	3/8	1 1/8	3/8	2 1/4	1/4-20	1 1/8
8-L	11/16	7/16	7/8	1 1/8	3/8	2 3/4	1/4-20	1 1/8
8-XL	11/16	7/16	1 1/2	1 1/8	3/8	3 1/2	1/4-20	1 1/8

HOW TO SELECT PROPER SIZE

4-S, 4-L, 4-XL are for light objects

6-S, 6-L, 6-XL are for medium objects

8-S, 8-L, 8-XL are for heavy objects

4-S, 6-S, 8-S are for walls 1/8" to 5/8" thick

4-L, 6-L, 8-L are for walls 5/8" to 1 1/4" thick

4-XL, 6-XL, 8-XL are for walls 1 1/4" to 1 3/4" thick

if the plugs are to be part of the design, as in some Colonial furniture. The head of the screw can also be covered with crack filler or wood dough. Fig. 11-40.

Brass screws are always used with oak. If steel screws are used, acid in the oak will make stains. When installing a brass screw, which is relatively soft, be careful not to break it off as it is tightened in place. First lubricate the screw with paraffin. You can also install a steel screw of the same length and diameter first, then replace it with a brass screw.

It is especially important to select screws of the correct gage and length for plywood. Fig. 11-41 shows the correct size of flathead screws for this purpose.

HOLLOW-WALL FASTENING DEVICES

Many devices can be used to fasten cabinets to walls. It is extremely important to select the correct kind. There are two basic types of walls with which the cabinetmaker must deal: *hollow walls* of dry-wall or lath-and-plaster construction found in most wood homes, and *masonry walls* common in basements and commercial buildings. The two fastening de-

11-45(a). Installing a molly screw anchor.
11-45(b). Molly bolt secured.

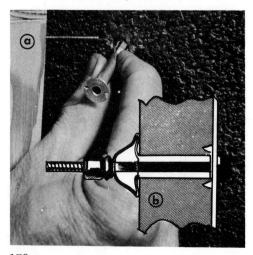

vices most often used for hollow walls are *toggle bolts* and *hollow-wall fasteners* (molly screw anchors).

A toggle bolt is made with either a spring head or a solid head. Fig. 11-42. Such bolts are available in a wide range of sizes from 1/8″ × 2″ to 3/8″ × 6″. Holding power increases with size. A hole must be drilled large enough for the bolt to slip through. Fig. 11-43. At

11-46. This screw anchor is designed especially for fastening brackets, cabinets, and shelving to hollow walls such as plasterboard, wallboard, tile, or plywood. A ¼″ hole must be drilled and a No. 6 through No. 10 sheet-metal screw used. The plug is inserted. After the screw is driven in all the way, a few more turns cause the plug to bulge against the wall, providing a permanent mounting.

11-47. Masonry nails are "fatter" and tougher than ordinary nails. They can be driven into concrete blocks to anchor furring strips of wood or accessories.

11-48. The anchor bolt is excellent for fastening a kitchen cabinet or other heavy object to a masonry wall.

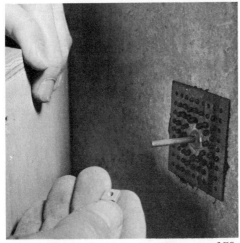

159

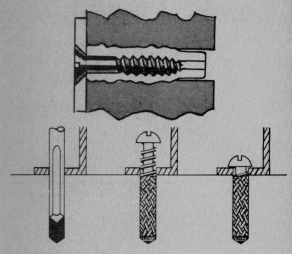

11-49. Installing a rawl plug. Be sure to drill the hole the exact depth of the plug.

11-50. Two kinds of carbide-tipped masonry drills: a. Standard. b. Fast spiral. This kind is faster-cutting, less likely to stall.

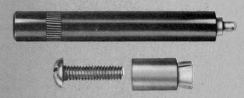

11-51. A lead expansion screw anchor with setting tool. The anchor is inserted in the hole. Then the setting tool is placed over it and given a sharp rap with a hammer to hold it in place. The screw is slipped through the part to be held, and the screw is started in the anchor. As it is tightened, the anchor will expand and grip the wall.

11-52. This plastic plug can be used with any kind of screw or nail. Drill a hole the same diameter as the plug and about ⅛″ deeper than its length. Drive the plug into the hole, then use a screw or nail to hold the part in place.

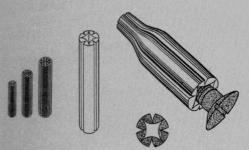

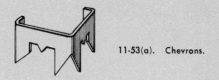

11-53(a). Chevrons.

11-53(b). Clamp nails are flat, with a flanged edge. They can be used on any joint. With a 22-gage circular or band saw, a thin kerf is cut in a miter joint, and the nail is driven in to hold the two parts firmly together.

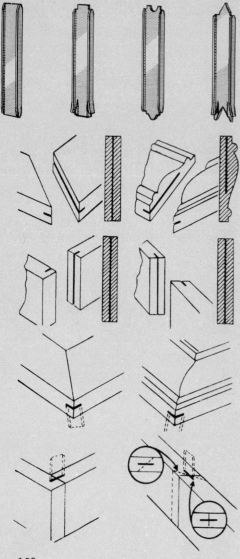

one time there was a problem with toggle bolts. When the screw was removed to replace a fitting, the nut would fall off on the inside of the wall. Nuts are now made with serrated metal along the edge to keep them in place.

Hollow-wall fasteners are available in several lengths and diameters. Fig. 11-44. This type of fastener has several advantages. The anchor shank completely fills the hole, giving a more durable, secure anchoring. Fig. 11-45. The supporting material can be removed and replaced without loss of the anchor. To install, first drill a hole of the correct diameter. Then insert the unit and screw it up tight until the interior sleeve squeezes in place. A fiber washer under the head of the screw protects the screw as it is tightened. When the screw is removed, the item can be fastened in place.

Also available is a *plastic screw anchor* for fastening parts to hollow walls. Fig. 11-46.

Fasteners for Masonry Walls

There are many types of fasteners for attaching cabinets to basement walls or

11-53(c). Corrugated fasteners can be used to hold a joint together.

to buildings of masonry construction. *Masonry nails* of hardened steel with a knurled body are the simplest to use. Fig. 11-47. This nail can be driven through wood into concrete block and other relatively soft concrete. Masonry nails provide a quick way of fastening shelves and similar items to basement walls.

An *anchor bolt* with a perforated plate can also be used on solid masonry walls. The base is attached to the wall with a black mastic or epoxy cement which squeezes through holes in the base. After the adhesive dries, a shelf or similar item can be attached to the wall with relative ease. Fig. 11-48.

The *rawl plug* is made of fiber and is used with wood, sheet-metal, or lag screws. Fig. 11-49. Rawl-plug sizes, which range from No. 3 to No. 20, should match the gage size of the wood screw to be used. For example, a No. 8 rawl plug will accept a No. 7 or No. 8 screw.

There are two ways of boring holes in masonry to install the plug. The quicker way is with a carbide-tipped drill bit in an electric drill. Fig. 11-50. Or you can use a star drill and hammer. To install a rawl plug, first screw the plug onto the wood screw one or two turns, or just enough to hold it; then push the plug into the hole the full depth. Turn the screw into the plug until the shank is about to enter, then withdraw the screw. You are now ready to attach a cabinet or fitting to the plug.

A *lead expansion screw anchor* can be used with a lag or wood screw in masonry construction. Fig. 11-51. A *plastic plug* similar to a rawl plug can be installed in any solid wall. Then nails or screws are fastened into the plug. Fig. 11-52.

MITER-JOINT FASTENERS

Three common types of metal fasteners are used on miter corners. *Chevrons*

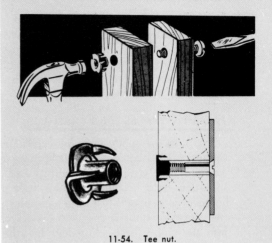

11-54. Tee nut.

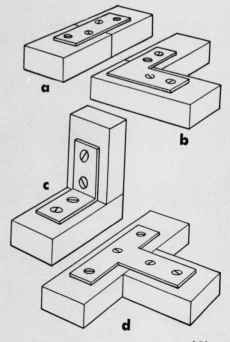

11-55. Hanger screws.

11-56. Repair plates: a. Mending. b. Flat corner. c. Bent corner. d. T plate. In installing a plate, drill for screws slightly off center and away from the break or joint. This insures a tight joint.

161

are designed to draw wood together to make a tight joint. *Clamp nails* are used in place of wood splines. *Corrugated fasteners* or *wiggle nails* are used for holding miter and other joints together. Fig. 11-53(a)-(b)-(c).

OTHER FASTENERS FOR FURNITURE

Tee nuts are made in many types and shapes. Fig. 11-54. The most common has a round base with twisted prongs and a threaded hole in the center. A hole is bored into the wood just large enough for the center portion. Then the nut is driven into the wood for holding legs or other parts. *Hanger screws* have a wood-screw thread on one end and a metal-screw thread on the other. The wood-screw end

is installed in the end of a leg, then the metal-threaded end is fitted into a tee nut. Fig. 11-55.

REPAIR PLATES

Repair and mending plates come in many sizes and shapes and are used primarily for elementary cabinetwork. Fig. 11-56. A *mending plate* can be used in a butt or lap joint. The *flat corner iron* is an excellent device for strengthening the corner of a frame such as a screen door or window. A *bent corner* can be applied to shelves and to inside corners of tables, chairs, and cabinets. It can also be used to hang cabinets and shelves. The *T plate* is used to strengthen the center frame of a rail.

12 Hardware

Since there are so many different kinds and styles of hardware for furniture and cabinetwork, it is impossible to illustrate

12-1. A few kinds of metal hardware used in chair and table construction.

them all. Figs. 12-1 and 12-2. However, there are certain basic facts about hardware which the cabinetmaker must know and be able to apply to various woodworking products.

Hardware is manufactured in many qualities and styles. For example, hinges and pulls can be purchased in Early American, Traditional, Contemporary, French and Italian Provincial, or Spanish styles. Fig. 12-3. Different hardware items are needed for drawers, cases, closets, kitchen cabinets, folding screens, and doors.

The wise cabinetmaker will purchase hardware for a product before building the product. For example, until he knows the kind of drawer guides he will use, he cannot determine their location in the case or cabinet, or provide proper clearances. Hardware stores and building-supply companies handle many of the more

12-2. Square, tubular hardware for tables.

12-4(a). The flush doors on this table have butt hinges.

12-4(b). Butt hinge.

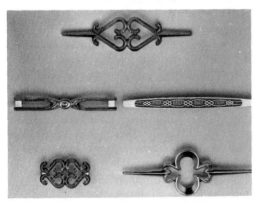

12-3(a). Fancy drawer pulls in Traditional designs.

12-3(b). Drawer pulls for Contemporary furniture.

12-5. H-L surface hinges installed on the lip doors of an Early American buffet.

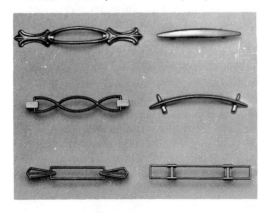

163

12-6. The diamond-shaped metal grille on the doors of this cabinet is strictly ornamental. How many other hardware items do you find in this illustration? Also, note the number of materials shown in addition to the hardware and the furniture wood, including cane, fabric, marble, and glass.

12-7. This Colonial kneehole desk has matching hardware and accessories. In choosing hardware, make sure it fits well with the furniture design.

common hardware pieces. A large number of catalogues are also available for specialized hardware items. For instance, some companies deal exclusively in drawer fixtures while others carry hardware for folding doors only.

In general, hardware requirements are as follows. For *hinge doors* you need pulls, catches, and a lock, besides the hinges. Fig. 12-4. For various doors, the following hinges are required: for a *flush door,* some type of surface hinge; for a *lip door,* a butt, concealed, or semi concealed hinge (Fig. 12-5); for *overlapping doors,* some kind of pivot hinge. *Sliding doors* call for hardware for the slide which may be metal, wood, or plastic. *Rolling doors* require handles and a metal track for rolling the base guides. *Folding doors* must have many special types of hardware including tracks, locks, and ways for moving the door back and forth. *Drop doors* often have a continuous or piano hinge for greater strength, along with some type of lid support, such as a chain or folding hinge, to hold the door open. Some drop doors make use of a special hinge that opens only 45 degrees. *Open-frame doors* require metal grilles. Fig. 12-6.

Hardware for *drawers* includes slides, pulls, and locks. Slides can be shop-made, or there are many of metal or plastic that can be purchased. Fig. 12-7.

Chairs and *tables* must have hardware such as table-top supports, dropleaf hinges, dropleaf supports, and casters. Fig. 12-8.

Cabinet interiors need shelf hardware as does open shelving. Fig. 12-9. A wide variety of metal hardware is made for closets. To name only a few, there are shoe holders, tie racks, holders for trousers, and closet poles. *Kitchen cabinet* fittings also include many different pieces of hardware. There are pieces for holding pots, pans, dishes, garbage pails, and similar items. Fig. 12-10.

164

12-8. Even though these chairs have metal corner blocks, only the casters can be seen.

12-9. Shelves of this built-in rest on metal standards and supports.

12-10. Hardware for this pop-up mixer shelf is typical of many metal items needed in a kitchen.

12-11. Several types of double-action hinges can be installed on a screen to make it fold in either direction.

12-12. Store fixtures require heavy-duty standards and brackets to support shelves and merchandise.

Screens take some type of double action hinge. Fig. 12-11.

The great variety of fixtures used in stores involves an equally great selection of hardware items. One common type of fixture is shown in Fig. 12-12. Its hardboard shelving is supported by metal hardware on a plywood base.

To learn all you can about hardware, follow these suggestions:

• Pay special attention to the most common hardware items. They are discussed throughout this book, wherever basic hardware is specified.

• Become familiar with catalogues that include less common hardware.

• Study the home and commercial hardware sections of Sweet's catalogues in the library.

• Learn how to order hardware as to size, type, style, and design.

• When installing hardware, carefully follow the instructions included in the package.

13   Glass And Mirrors

Glass and glass mirrors are used extensively in furniture, built-ins, and store fixtures. Fig. 13-1. While it is normally not the responsibility of the cabinetmaker to install these items, he must be able to order and handle them.

PRODUCTION OF GLASS

The raw materials of glass consist of about 70 per cent silica, 13 per cent soda ash, and 13 per cent limestone, with the remaining 4 per cent made up of carbon in the form of coal, iron in the form of ferric oxide, and traces of other chemicals.

The making of glass today has become a continuous automated process. First step is mixing the raw materials which are fed into one end of a large tank. Here they are melted at 2,800 degrees Fahrenheit. At the other end of the tank the molten glass flows through forming rolls which shape it into a continuous ribbon. From these rolls the semi-molten ribbon goes through a series of steel rolls where it cools and solidifies into sheet glass or rough plate glass. After the glass has been formed in this manner, it is annealed. For plate glass, the sheets go through a grinding and polishing process. After it is ground, the glass is automatically cut into plates. It then goes to the polishing lines where it is given a beautiful, transparent finish and washed clean. After polishing, plate glass is cut to size, wrapped, and packaged for shipment. For sheet or window glass, the grinding and polishing steps are skipped.

KINDS OF GLASS

There are many different kinds of

13-2. These built-in cabinets for china, stemware, and silver are made of painted Douglas fir and glass. Glass is also used for the shelves.

glass, but the ones of main concern to the cabinetmaker and finish carpenter are those used in furniture and building construction. The common kinds are as follows:

Sheet or *window* glass is characterized by a fine finished surface which is formed or produced as the sheet is drawn from the molten pool. This kind of glass is used for most cabinet doors and windows. Fig. 13-2. It comes in single

13-1. A plate-glass top with beveled edges gives this modern coffee table an appearance of lightness. 24"D x 59"W x 14¾"H.

13-3. The free-standing cases for this pharmacy are made primarily of glass with metal fixtures. Note that both flat and bent glass are used.

13-4. This solid-walnut frame is set with a plate-glass mirror of highest quality. 18"W x 44"H.

strength, which averages .091" in thickness, and double strength, that averages .125" thick. The quality of this glass is rated as AA, the highest; A, which is select quality; and B, which is used in general work. All sheet glass has some inherent wave or distortion which is usually more prominent in one direction than the other. Heavier sheet glass is made in thicknesses of 3/16" and 1/4". Heavier sheet glass, also called *crystal* glass, is sometimes used in furniture and built-ins as a substitute for plate glass. It has the distortion of any window glass.

Plate glass is different from sheet or window glass because of the grinding and polishing mentioned earlier. These produce flat, parallel surfaces with little or no distortion. Standard plate glass is made in common thicknesses of 1/8" and 1/4", and in several grades of quality. The highest quality is completely free from defects. The next best has little or no distortion but is not absolutely perfect. The lowest quality has a little more distortion and is used primarily for windows. Heavy commercial grades of plate glass are made in thicknesses of 5/16" to 3/4".

Glass bent to various shapes is available in both sheet and plate varieties and in many thicknesses. Fig. 13-3. These are used primarily in store and office fixtures. Bent glass is produced by causing flat glass to form in a mold by the action of heat and gravity only. It is not a machined product and is therefore subject to more distortion and wider tolerances than polished plate or window glass.

Other kinds are colored, heat absorbing, and wire glass.

Mirrors are made from highest-quality plate glass. Fig. 13-4. In producing a mirror the glass is first thoroughly cleaned, then given a double coat of silver on one side. A layer of copper is deposited over the silver by electrolysis (an electrochemical process). The copper, in turn, is covered by a pigmented priming coat and, finally, by a special mirror-backing coat.

CUTTING GLASS

Both plate and sheet glass can be cut in the same manner, although more pressure is required for plate glass since it usually is heavier and thicker. Tools needed to make straight cuts include a straightedge, a measuring tape, and an inexpensive glass cutter. Necessary mate-

Steps in Cutting Glass

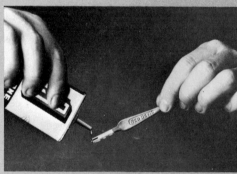

13-5. Lubricate the wheel of the cutter so that it operates freely.

13-6. Wipe the surface of the glass with a cloth, especially along the layout line. The cloth should be dampened with oil, turpentine, or kerosene.

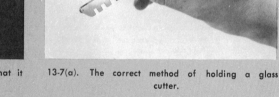

13-7(a). The correct method of holding a glass cutter.

13-7(b). Hold a straightedge on the glass, then draw the cutter along.

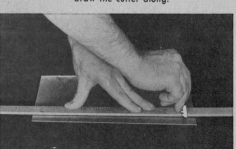

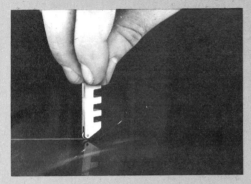

13-8(a). Here you see a sharp, uniform score along the glass.

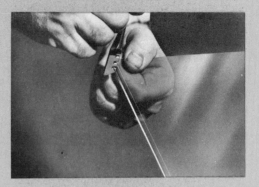

13-10. If a narrow edge must be broken off, apply pressure with one of the cutterhead grooves.

13-8(b). This glass broke unevenly because the scoring pressure was too light.

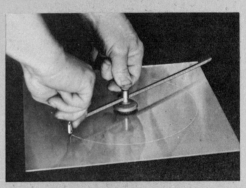

13-11. Try to make a clean, sharp score with one swing of the cutterhead. Don't retrace the entire circle but go over sections that may have been missed.

13-9. Apply quick downward pressure to break the glass. Do this immediately because glass tends to "heal" itself.

13-12. Note that several straight lines have been cut in the waste glass so it can be broken away a portion at a time.

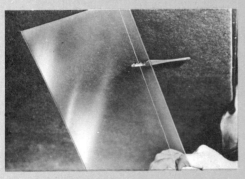

STAPLE TYPE

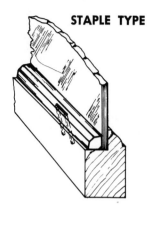

GROOVE TYPE

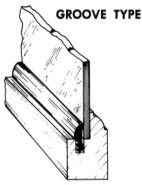

13-13(a). Two kinds of plastic stops or retainers. These can be used for installing glass, grilles, or screens.

13-13(b). Glass or panel-retaining buttons can be used to hold glass firmly in place.

rials include lubricating oil, a rag, and kerosene or turpentine. Make sure the cutting wheel operates freely. Fig. 13-5.

The glass to be cut should be placed on a large bench that has a smooth, even top. If necessary, pad the top with newspapers or an old rug. One simple method of determining where to cut the glass is to draw the full-size pattern on a piece of wrapping paper and place this under the glass.

Wipe the surface of the glass with a rag soaked with oil or turpentine. Wipe along the area to be cut. Fig. 13-6. This will keep the cut edge from chipping.

The secret of successful cutting is to cut a sharp, even groove in the glass.

(This is called *scoring.*) Fig. 13-7. Too-light pressure won't score a line; too-heavy pressure will cause chipping along the groove, resulting in a ragged edge and small cracks. Fig. 13-8. As soon as the score is made, move the glass so that the scored edge is over the edge of the bench; if it is a small piece, raise the glass at an angle. Now snap the waste piece off with a quick downward pull. Fig. 13-9. Another method is to hold the glass at an angle on the bench and tap along the underside of the score with the handle of the cutter. If the waste strip is too narrow to be broken by these methods, use one of the grooves in the cutter head to apply pressure. Fig. 13-10. A pair of

171

pliers with masking tape on the jaws can be used to break off small pieces.

A circle-sweep glass cutter is needed to cut circles from 2″ to 24″ in diameter. To cut out a circle, set the tool to the correct diameter. Hold the center firmly with one hand as you apply pressure, and swing the arm to score the glass. Fig. 13-11. Then use the straight glass cutter to score several lines from the circle to the edge of the glass. In this way the waste glass can be broken away in sections. Fig. 13-12.

INSTALLING GLASS

The cabinetmaker must know how to install glass in cabinets and furniture pieces. (It is usually not his responsibility to replace glass in broken windows.) Glass for interior cabinets does not have to be set in glazing compound as is necessary for exterior windows. Usually the glass is held in place with a wood or plastic stop or a patented glass holder. Fig. 13-13.

PLATE OR CRYSTAL GLASS FOR FURNITURE

If plate or crystal glass is used for furniture, any edge that will be wholly or partly exposed must be ground and polished. Such edges may also be shaped square, round, or at an angle.

You can smooth the edges of cut glass yourself with a stationary belt sander or a portable finishing sander. Use waterproof silicon-carbide paper of a grit number from 80 to 180. Apply soapy water to the edge as a lubricant. Bring the edge and the abrasive into contact and move along slowly. Use plenty of lubricant (water and soap) so that not too much heat is generated. It is usually better to have this done by a glass company.

14 Machine-Made Cane Webbing

Cane is a common decorative feature of furniture, especially chair seats and backs. It is made by cutting bamboo bark into thin strips. A characteristic of fine Chinese cabinetwork is the extensive use of cane webbing as accent and enrichment. In Modern or Contemporary furniture and cabinetwork, cane may be found in many places—on a door enclosure of a hi-fi cabinet, a table shelf, an insert for a screen, or a chair seat or back. In the past, caning was done laboriously by hand by actually weaving the strands into a design. Today machine-made cane is almost universally used for both new construction and re-upholstering.

KINDS OF CANE

Cane weave may be either the tradi-

14-1. The cane back on this Contemporary chair is made with traditional hexagonal weave.

14-2. This chair has a contoured back and gently angled walnut frame. Note that the tightly woven cane is used as an upholstery fabric. It is stretched up and over the top of the chair and down the back, providing a double thickness separated by the width of the frame.

14-3. Woven cane forms the lower shelf of this Contemporary table.

tional hexagonal chair-seat variety or one of the more contemporary basket weaves. Fig. 14-1. Modern weaves include the smaller square and rectangular weaves. Fig. 14-2. The more common weaves of cane are medium, fine, fine-fine, and super-fine mesh. Cane is sold in rolls of common widths from 14″ to 24″, with the price quoted per square foot. The wedge-shaped hickory spline to hold the cane in place and the reed which covers the spline should be purchased with the cane.

INSTALLING CANE

Before cutting the cane, it is important to make a paper pattern, especially if the opening is of irregular shape. Place this pattern over the cane, with the front edge parallel to the design, then cut a piece about 1″ wider in all directions than the size of the pattern.

To install the cane in the frame, it is necessary to cut or rout out a groove about 3/16″ to 1/4″ wide and 1/4″ deep around the opening to be covered, about 3/8″ or 1/4″ from the edge. The groove should be cut so the spline will fit in it

loosely enough so it can be removed without prying. For a shelf, the inner edge of the cane can be undercut slightly so it will be level with the frame. Fig. 14-3.

Cut a dozen or more hardwood taper

14-4. A frame ready for caning. Wedges, as in the upper right-hand corner, hold the cane in place before the hickory spline is installed.

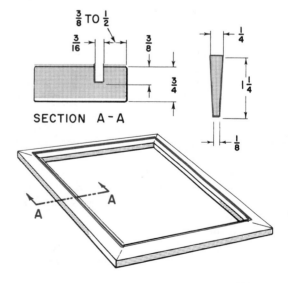

SECTION A-A

173

wedges with the small end slightly less in width than the width of the groove. Fig. 14-4.

Place the cane in a bucket of warm water for about two hours to make it completely pliable. Cane will expand about five per cent.

Then place the cane over the frame so that it overlaps in all directions. Check it for size and to make sure the strands run straight with the groove.

Start driving the wedges at equal distances around the frame to hold the cane tightly in place. It is best to do the part farthest away from you first (usually the back), then the part nearest, and then the two sides.

Now cut the tapered splines to length with a mitered corner to fit the frame. Pour a small amount of white glue into the grooves. Drive the spline into the groove, starting from one corner and working toward the other. Remove the wedges that held the cane in place as you install the spline. After the spline is installed, glue in the reed over it. The extra cane can be cut off with a sharp chisel or trimmed with a sharp knife. Wipe off excess glue with a damp sponge. As the cane dries, it will shrink and become taut.

Sometimes cane is stretched around the frame and held in place by a strip of wood nailed to the edge.

(15) Ordering Lumber And Other Materials

Lumber and other materials are processed, manufactured, and sold according to long-established standards. Fig. 15-1. It is important to know how to order these materials, whether they are for an interior cabinet or a piece of furniture.

SOLID LUMBER

The standard unit of measurement for solid lumber is the *board foot* (Bd. Ft.). It is easy to remember that a board foot is a piece 1″ thick by 1′ square, or 144 cubic inches (1″ x 12″ x 12″). Fig. 15-2. Therefore a board that is 1″ thick, 12″ wide, and 10′ long would contain 10 board feet. Stock that is less than 1″ thick is figured as 1″. Lumber that is thicker than 1″ is figured as its actual thickness. Hardwood lumbers between 1″ and 2″ thick are figured by the nearest 1/4″ thickness. For example, 1¼″ (which is often referred to as 5/4, or five quarter) would be the thickness used in figuring

board feet for lumber delivered as surfaced two sides (S2S). Such lumber actually measures 1¹⁄₁₆″. Fig. 15-3.

The three simple formulas used to figure board feet are:
- Board feet equals thickness in inches times width in feet times length in feet. Bd. Ft. = T (inches) x W (feet) x L (feet). Example: A piece 1″ x 8″ x 12′ contains 8 board feet.

$$\left(\text{Bd. Ft.} = \frac{1}{1} \times \frac{2}{3} \times \frac{12}{1} = 8\right)$$

- Board feet equals thickness in inches times width in inches times length in feet divided by twelve.

$$\text{Bd Ft.} = \frac{\text{T(inches) x W(inches) x L(feet)}}{12}$$

Example: A piece 2″ x 6″ x 10′ contains 10 board feet $\left(\text{Bd. Ft.} = \dfrac{2 \times 6 \times 10}{12} = 10\right)$

- Board feet equals thickness in inches times width in inches times length in

15-1. Lumber stored in a supplier's shed, ready for delivery.

inches divided by 144. Example: A piece 1″ x 12″ x 24″ contains 2 board feet.

$$\text{Bd. Ft.} = \frac{1 \times 12 \times 24}{144} = 2$$

$$\text{Bd. Ft.} = \frac{T \times W \times L \text{ (in inches)}}{144}$$

Lumber is priced at so much per thousand board feet and the Roman numeral *M* is the abbreviation for one thousand. A lumber order of 1,000 board feet at $500 per M would cost $500. At this price, one board foot would cost 50 cents.

When the lumber arrives it is measured, each board at a time, and then totaled to determine whether the amount specified on the invoice is the same as

the amount delivered. (This is explained further at the end of this unit.)

OTHER MATERIALS

Plywood, hardboard, particle board, and other sheet material are sold by the *square foot*. Fig. 15-4. The most common sheet size is 4′ x 8′, or 32 square feet. If the price for a certain thickness of plywood, for example, is 50 cents per square foot, then the standard 4′ x 8′ sheet costs $16. Moldings, trim, dowel rod, and similar materials are sold by the *linear foot* (Lin. Ft.). For example, a 10′ piece of cove molding at 15 cents a foot would cost $1.50.

LUMBER SIZES

Some lumber is purchased just as it comes from the sawmill with the surface rough (rgh). Before it can be used, this lumber must be smoothed by running it through a planer or surfacer. Most lumber is dried, then dimensioned (sur-

15-2. Each of these pieces contains one board foot.

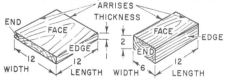

175

COMMON LUMBER ABBREVIATIONS

AD—Air dried
AL—All lengths
ALS—American Lumber Standards
AV—Average
B&B or B&Btr—B and better
BD—Board
BD FT—Board Feet
BDL— Bundle
BEV—Bevel
BM—Board measure
BTR—Better
C/L—Carload
CLG—Ceiling
CLR—Clear
COM—Common
CSG—Casing
CU FT—Cubic Feet
DF—Douglas fir
DIM—Dimension
DKG—Decking
D/S, DS—Drop siding
D&M—Dressed and matched;
    center matched unless
    otherwise specified
D&CM—Dressed and center
    matched
D&SM—Dressed and standard
    matched
E—Edge
EB1S—Edge bead one side
EG—Edge (vertical) grain
FAS—Firsts and seconds
FG—Flat or slash grain
FCTY—Factory lumber
FLG—Flooring
FT—Foot
FT BM or FBM—Feet board
    measure
FT SM—Feet surface measure
GR—Green

H&M—Hit and miss
HDWD—Hardwood
HRT—Heart
HRTWD—Heartwood
IN—Inch or inches
JTD—Jointed
KD—Kiln dried
LBR—Lumber
LGTH—Length
LIN—Lineal
LIN FT—Lineal (or linear)
    foot
M—Thousand
M BM—Thousand (ft.) board
    measure
MC—Moisture content
MLDG—Moulding or molding
MR—Mill run
N—Nosed
OC—On center
OG—Ogee
P—Planed
PC—Piece
QTD—Quartered, when referring
    to hardwoods
RDM—Random
REG—Regular
RGH—Rough
RIP—Ripped
R/L, RL—Random lengths
RND—Round
R/W, RW—Random widths
RWD—Redwood
SAP—Sapwood
SD—Seasoned
SDG—Siding
SEL—Select
SF—Surface foot; that is, an
    area of 1 square foot
SG—Slash grain

SH D—Shipping dry
SM—Surface measure
SQ—Square
SQRS—Squares
STD—Standard
STD M—Standard matched
STK—Stock
STRUCT—Structural
SYMBOLS
    "—Inch or inches
    '—Foot or feet
    x—By, as 4 x 4
    4/4, 5/4, 6/4, etc.—
        thickness expressed
        in fractions of an inch
S&E—Side and edge
S1E—Surfaced one edge
S2E—Surfaced 2 edges
S1S—Surfaced one side
S2S—Surfaced two sides
S4S—Surfaced four sides
S1S&CM—Surfaced one side
    and center matched
S2S&CM—Surfaced two sides
    and center matched
S4S&CS—Surfaced four sides
    and caulking seam
S1S1E—Surfaced one side,
    one edge
S1S2E—Surfaced one side,
    two edges
S2S&SM—Surfaced two sides
    and standard matched
T&G—Tongued and grooved,
    center matched unless
    otherwise specified
VG—Vertical (edge) grain
WDR—Wider
WT—Weight
WTH—Width

15-3. Abbreviations used frequently to order lumber and other materials.

faced) at the mill. The dressed or surfaced (actual) size is smaller than the rough (nominal) size. Lumber sizes are based on the rough, green dimensions. American Lumber Standards for softwoods allow the 2″ x 4″ to measure 1-1/2″ x 3-1/2″ if dried to 19 percent moisture content or less, and 1-9/16″ x 3-9/16″ if the moisture content is over this amount. A 1″ hardwood piece, when surfaced, is reduced to 13/16″, while the dressed 1″ pine becomes 25/32″, or 3/4″. In lumber dimensions, the first figure is always the thickness, the second the width, and the third the length. Fig. 15-5 shows both the rough or nominal thickness and the dressed or surfaced thickness and width for both hardwood and softwood. Softwoods are cut to standard thickness, width and length. Nominal widths are 4″, 6″, 8″, 10″, and 12″. The standard lengths of softwoods

15-4. Sheets of 4' x 8' plywood strapped into large bundles, ready for shipment to lumber dealers.

are from 8' to 20' increasing at intervals of 2'. Hardwood lumber is generally available in standard thicknesses, but because of its high cost it is cut to whatever widths and lengths are most economical and convenient. These are called *random* widths and lengths.

LUMBER GRADING

To know how to order lumber it is necessary to understand something about lumber grading. This is a rather complicated subject and especially difficult for softwoods since uniform standards are not accepted throughout the country. Lumber is divided into two major groups: softwoods and hardwoods. Softwoods are used primarily for paneling and interior cabinetwork. Hardwoods are used for the same purposes and for fine furniture as well. Both hardwoods and softwoods are shipped kiln-dried for use as built-ins, paneling, molding, and trim.

15-5(a). Standard thickness and width of softwoods.

Thickness (Inches)			Width (Inches)		
	Minimum Dressed			Minimum Dressed	
Nominal	Dry	Green	Nominal	Dry	Green
1	3/4	25/32	2	1 1/2	1 9/16
1 1/4	1	1 1/32	3	2 1/2	2 9/16
1 1/2	1 1/4	1 9/32	4	3 1/2	3 9/16
2	1 1/2	1 9/16	5	4 1/2	4 5/8
2 1/2	2	2 1/16	6	5 1/2	5 5/8
3	2 1/2	2 9/16	7	6 1/2	6 5/8
3 1/2	3	3 1/16	8	7 1/4	7 1/2
4	3 1/2	3 9/16	10	9 1/4	9 1/2

Furniture factories usually purchase their rough lumber green or air-dried and then kiln dry it themselves just before use.

Softwood Grading

The National Bureau of Standards of the Department of Commerce has established *American Lumber Standards* for softwood lumber. These standards are intended as guides for the different associations of lumber producers, each of which has its own grading rules and specifications. Most of the major associations, such as the Western Wood Products Association, Redwood Inspection Service, and many others participated in developing these grading rules. One who works with just a few kinds of lumber most of the time should obtain grading rules from the associations involved and become acquainted with them. One of the main ideas of these standards is to divide all softwood lumber for *grading purposes* into two groups:

• Dry lumber, seasoned or dried to a moisture content of 19 percent or less.
• Green lumber, with moisture content in excess of 19 percent.

Complete standards are available from the National Bureau of Standards, Department of Commerce, under Federal Register Volume 34, Number 233.

Softwood lumber is classified according to *use and extent of manufacture* as follows:

Use Classifications. Fig. 15-6.

Yard Lumber. Lumber of those grades, sizes, and patterns which are generally intended for ordinary construction and general building purposes.

Structural lumber. Lumber that is 2 or more inches in nominal thickness and width for use where working stresses are required. (NOTE: See Fig. 15-5 for comparison of nominal sizes with actual or dressed sizes.)

Factory and shop lumber. Lumber

177

Thickness (Widths vary with Grades)

Nominal (Rough)	Surfaced 1 Side (S1S)	Surfaced 2 Sides (S2S)
3/8"	1/4"	3/16"
1/2"	3/8"	5/16"
5/8"	1/2"	7/16"
3/4"	5/8"	9/16"
1"	7/8"	13/16"
1 1/4"	1 1/8"	1 1/16"
1 1/2"	1 3/8"	1 5/16"
2"	1 13/16"	1 3/4"
3"	2 13/16"	2 3/4"
4"	3 13/16"	3 3/4"

15-5(b). Standard thickness of hardwoods.

that is produced or selected primarily for remanufacturing purposes.

Yard lumbers are cut for a wide variety of uses. They are divided into two grade qualities—finish (select) and common grades.

Finish (select) grades are further classified. Grade A is practically clear wood and is used for such items as finish flooring, ceilings, partitions, and siding. Grade B has very few imperfections. It may include small checks or stain marks. Grades C and D have increasingly more imperfections, but are still suitable for a good paint finish.

The common grades of boards are those that are suited for general utility

15-6. GENERAL CLASSIFICATIONS OF SOFTWOOD LUMBER.

Softwood lumber (this classification applies to rough or dressed lumber; sizes given are nominal)

Yard lumber (lumber less than 5 inches thick, intended for general building purposes; grading based on use of the entire piece)

- Finish (less than 3 inches thick and 12 inches and under in width)
  - Grades: A select, B select, C select, D select
- Boards (less than 2 inches thick and 2 inches or over in width). Strips (under 8 inches in width).
  - Grades: No. 1 boards, No. 2 boards, No. 3 boards, No. 4 boards, No. 5 boards
- Dimension (2 inches and under 5 inches thick and 2 or more inches in width).
  - Planks (2 inches and under 4 inches thick and 8 inches and over wide) — No. 1 dimension, No. 2 dimension, No. 3 dimension
  - Scantling (2 inches and under 5 inches thick and under 8 inches wide) — No. 1 dimension, No. 2 dimension, No. 3 dimension
  - Heavy joists (4 inches thick and 8 inches or over wide) — No. 1 dimension, No. 2 dimension, No. 3 dimension

Structural material (lumber 2 inches or over in thickness and width, except joist and plank; grading based on strength and on use of entire piece).

- Joist and plank (2 inches to 4 inches thick and 4 inches and over wide).
- Timbers classified as beams, stringers, posts, caps, sills, girders, purlins, etc., must be 5 or more inches nominally in least dimension.

Factory and shop (grading based on area of piece suitable for cuttings of certain size and quality)

- Factory plank graded for door, sash, and other cuttings 1 inch to 4 inches thick and 5 inches and over wide
  - Factory clears upper grades — Nos. 1 and 2 clear factory, No. 3 clear factory
  - Shop lower grades — No. 1 shop, No. 2 shop, No. 3 shop
- Shop lumber graded for general cut up purposes
  - 1 inch thick (northern and western pine, and Pacific coast woods) — Select shop, Shop
  - All thicknesses (cypress, redwood, and North Carolina pine) — Tank and boat stock, firsts and seconds, selects; No. 1 shop; No. 2 shop, box

and construction purposes. The major differences between the grades are in the number of knots and amount of pitch. These range from Nos. 1 and 2 which can be used without waste to Nos. 3, 4, and 5 which involve a limited amount of waste. (In some grading rules, No. 1 is considered *construction grade;* No. 2, *standard;* No. 3, *utility;* and No. 4, *economy.*)

Manufacturing Classifications

Rough lumber. Lumber which has not been dressed (surfaced) but which has been sawed, edged, and trimmed at least to the extent of showing saw marks on the four longitudinal surfaces of each piece for its overall length.

Dressed (surfaced) lumber. Lumber that has been dressed by a planing machine for smoothness of surface and uniformity of size. Lumber may be dressed on one side (S1S), two sides (S2S), one edge (S1E), two edges (S2E), or a combination of sides and edges (S1S1E, S1S2E, S2S1E, S4S).

Worked lumber. Lumber which, in addition to being dressed, has been matched, shiplapped, or patterned. *Matched lumber* has been worked with a tongue on one edge of each piece and a groove on the opposite edge to provide a close tongue-and-groove joint by fitting two pieces together; when end-matched, the tongue and groove are worked in the ends also. *Shiplapped lumber* has been worked or rabbeted on both edges of each piece to provide a closelapped joint by fitting two pieces together. *Patterned lumber* is shaped to a pattern or to a molded form, in addition to being dressed, matched, or shiplapped, or any combination of these workings.

Hardwood Grading

Grades of hardwood lumber are established by the National Hardwood Lumber Association and are designed primarily for use in the furniture industry. As you can see by studying Fig. 15-7, complete grading standards are rather complicated. However, it is not necessary to understand every detail of this system in order to choose the best grades for certain kinds of products. In all lumber grading, it must be remembered that the pieces are divided into grades on the basis of the number of defects or, to put it another way, the amount of clear cuttings that can be obtained from a piece. See Unit 5. A rather wide difference in quality is found in the same grade since one piece may just barely meet the lowest standard of that grade while another may be almost good enough for the next higher grade. Also, the job of separating lumber into grades is done by human beings; grades are therefore subject to error or wide differences in judgment. Fig. 15-8.

The good woodworker strives to get the maximum amount of clear face cuttings from each piece. Therefore the grade to order depends more on the size of the product to be made than on a wish to fill the lumber racks with large boards. The following is a summary of the grades most commonly purchased:

FAS (firsts and seconds) is the top or premium grade of hardwood. Most FAS lumber must have a minimum width of 6″ and must be 8′ or more in length. The exceptions to this are walnut and butternut that are selected for color if quarter sawed, which must be at least 5″ wide. The average first and seconds grade will produce around 85 to 90 per cent of clear face cuttings. It is important to know that firsts and seconds are graded from the poorer side of the board so that the opposite side is sure to have fewer defects or none at all.

Select grade is good enough for most furniture projects when only one good face is required. The boards must be at

STANDARD HARDWOOD GRADES[1]

Grade and lengths allowed (feet)	Widths allowed	Surface measure of pieces	Amount of each piece that must work into clear-face cuttings	Maximum cuttings allowed	Minimum size of cuttings required
	Inches	Square feet	Percent	Number	
Firsts:[2] 8 to 16 (will admit 30 percent of 8- to 11-foot, ½ of which may be 8- and 9-foot).	6+	4 to 9.........	91⅔	1	4 inches by 5 feet, or 3 inches by 7 feet.
		10 to 14......	91⅔	2	
		15+..........	91⅔	3	
Seconds:[2] 8 to 16 (will admit 30 percent of 8- to 11-foot, ½ of which may be 8- and 9-foot).	6+	4 and 5......	83⅓	1	Do.
		6 and 7......	83⅓	1	
		6 and 7......	91⅔	2	
		8 to 11.......	83⅓	2	
		8 to 11.......	91⅔	3	
		12 to 15......	83⅓	3	
		12 to 15......	91⅔	4	
		16+..........	83⅓	4	
Selects: 6 to 16 (will admit 30 percent of 6- to 11-foot, 1/6 of which may be 6- and 7-foot).	4+	2 and 3......	91⅔	1	Do.
		4+..........	(3)		
No. 1 Common: 4 to 16 (will admit 10 percent of 4- to 7-foot, ½ of which may be 4- and 5-foot).	3+	1............	100	0	4 inches by 2 feet, or 3 inches by 3 feet.
		2............	75	1	
		3 and 4......	66⅔	1	
		3 and 4......	75	2	
		5 to 7.......	66⅔	2	
		5 to 7.......	75	3	
		8 to 10.......	66⅔	3	
		11 to 13......	66⅔	4	
		14+..........	66⅔	5	
No. 2 Common: 4 to 16 (will admit 30 percent of 4- to 7-foot, 1/3 of which may be 4- and 5-foot).	3+	1............	66⅔	1	3 inches by 2 feet.
		2 and 3......	50	1	
		2 and 3......	66⅔	2	
		4 and 5......	50	2	
		4 and 5......	66⅔	3	
		6 and 7......	50	3	
		6 and 7......	66⅔	4	
		8 and 9......	50	4	
		10 and 11....	50	5	
		12 and 13....	50	6	
		14+..........	50	7	

[1] Inspection to be made on the poorer side of the piece, except in Selects.

[2] Firsts and Seconds are combined as 1 grade (FAS). The percentage of Firsts required in the combined grade varies from 20 to 40 percent, depending on the species.

[3] Same as Seconds.

15-7. Standard hardwood grades. In column four, the term "Clear Face Cutting" means that one face of the board is free of defects. The opposite surface must be free from heart pitch, rot, shake, wane, and unsound knots.

15-8. Fresh sawed lumber being graded. This battery of graders marks each board. Quick decisions must be made as to the quality of the piece.

least 4" wide and 6' or more in length. This lumber is also graded from the better side; standards usually require that the better face meet the requirements of firsts and seconds while the poorer side must at least be equal to No. 1 common.

No. 1 common grade is less expensive because it includes narrower and shorter pieces. Note that the minimum sizes of clear face cuttings are 4" wide x 2' long or 3" wide x 3' long. Again, the grading is done from the poorer side of the board. This grade will produce about 66⅔ per cent clear cuttings. It is used for narrow to wide cuttings of medium length for furniture parts.

WRITING LUMBER SPECIFICATIONS

Lumber must be ordered either for a specific product to be built or for general stock to meet a variety of needs. For a specific product, it is relatively simple to determine exactly what and how much

of a certain kind of material is needed. If it is necessary to replenish the lumber racks, the usual practice is to estimate the amount of each kind and grade of lumber based on past experience and usage. In either case it is important that the lumber order be clear, concise, and complete in every detail. This is equally true whether the order is for a few pieces from a local lumber yard or for a large amount from a supplier in some distant city. The following are suggestions for making your written lumber specifications accurate and complete:

1. *Use standard terms in describing the quality.* These should be the terms developed by the governing national associations. For example, in ordering hardwood lumber, always follow the rules of the National Hardwood Lumber Association (NHLA). Not all lumber dealers follow these standards. Therefore it is good practice to specify the following on each order: "NHLA rules to

181

15-9(a). Board measure rule. Note, the head acts as the starting mark.

apply. Measurement and inspection to be in accordance with the rules. Vendor must indicate lumber grade alongside each item appearing on quotation or invoice." For example, if you wish to order the best grade of hardwood, specify FAS (firsts and seconds).

2. *Make your order of hardwood sizes realistic.* Fine cabinet hardwoods are in limited supply. Large logs of woods such as walnut are not readily available. For this reason, these woods are cut in random widths and lengths. Generally, most hardwoods are cut in multiples of 2' lengths (8', 10', 12', etc.) with some pieces in odd lengths. It would be poor practice to ask for all walnut in 12" widths and 16' lengths. The usual practice is to specify random widths and

lengths (RW & L). Remember that the grade specified will limit the minimum sizes included in the delivery.

3. *Always specify rough thickness of the wood, then add such information as S2S (surfaced two sides) if you wish the lumber to be surfaced.* As you know, 1" S2S hardwood measures 13/16". If you wish a different thickness, such as 3/4", then specify as such. For example: 100' 1" FAS white oak S2S to 3/4".

4. *Make your specifications as complete as possible.* This should include:

a. *Quantity.* The number of board feet needed.

b. *Thickness.* The standard thickness in the rough. This can be stated in inches (for example, 1" or 2") or in thickness expressed in fractions of an inch (for example, 4/4, or four quarter, is 1" thick. Other thicknesses are 5/4, 6/4, etc.).

c. *Grade.* As indicated by the national grading rules.

15-9(b). Using a board-measure rule to find the surface measure of a piece. If this board is 8' long, it contains 4 square feet; this would be 4 board feet if it is 1" thick, or 6 board feet if its is 1½" thick. How many square feet are there in the board if it is 10' long? How wide is this board in inches?

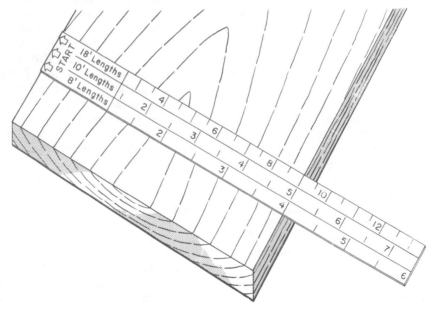

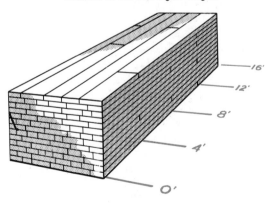

15-10. Essex board-measure table on a framing square.

d. *Species.* Indicate the exact kind of wood, not just the name of a broad group such as oak or pine. Instead, specify white oak or ponderosa pine.

e. *Surfacing.* Specify the kind of surface such as rough (Rgh), surfaced two sides (S2S), or surfaced four sides (S4S).

f. *Condition of seasoning.* Indicate if it is to be air dried (AD) or kiln dried (KD) and to what percentage. The percentage is especially important for kiln-dried lumber.

g. *Widths and lengths.* In softwoods, the specific widths and lengths can be ordered. For hardwoods, unless

15-11. Chalk marks on the floor near the lumber rack simplify the job of determining length. Just slip a board off the pile and place it on the marks. Remember that the measurement is based on the rough thickness. In native hardwoods, the fractional lengths are measured at the next lower foot length. For example, a 10' 6" board would be figured as 10'. In true mahogany, the fractions over 6" are measured as the next higher length.

otherwise specified, you should accept random widths and lengths of lumber for that particular grade as it comes from the sawmill.

A typical order might read:

100′ 1″ FAS Light Red Philippine Mahogany, Rgh, KD to 5% to 8%, RW & L. This order would be interpreted as meaning that you want 100 board feet of nominal 1-inch lumber of light red Philippine mahogany of firsts-and-seconds grade, in the rough, kiln dried to a moisture content from 5 to 8 per cent, in random widths and lengths.

MEASURING THE AMOUNT OF LUMBER

After the lumber has been delivered, you should check to make sure you have received the correct species, grade (this may be difficult), and amount.

Surface or board measure is the way of determining the amount of board feet in a piece or a pile of lumber. Sometimes you will be able to calculate this easily. You know, for example, that for any board 1″ thick and 12″ wide, the number of board feet is the same as the length of the board in feet. If a piece is 1″ thick, 12″ wide, and 8′ long, you know immediately that it contains 8 board feet. For harder problems, use a measuring device called a *board rule,* sometimes called a *lumberman's board stick.* Fig. 15-9. Follow these directions:

1. Determine the length of the board.

2. Place the rule across the width of the board, with the "start" mark exactly even with the left edge of the board.

3. On the rule find the row of figures based on the length of the board.

4. Follow this row to the extreme right edge of the board. The number which appears there indicates board feet.

For instance, suppose a board 1″ thick is 8′ long and 6″ wide. Place the rule across the stock, with the "start" mark lined up with the left edge. Find the

183

TALLY SHEET FORM

FOOTAGE PER BD.	PIECES	TOTAL PIECES	TOTAL FEET

DATE _____

FROM _____

ORDER NO. _____

THICKNESS _____ KIND _____

GRADE _____

FOOTAGE PER BD.	PIECES	TOTAL PIECES	TOTAL FEET
I			
2			
3			
4			
5			
6			
7			
8			
9			
IO			
II			
I2			
ETC.			
TOTAL			

15-12. Simple tally-sheet form. Use a separate one for each thickness of stock. Mark a slanting line through the first four pieces of the same square footage to show a tally of five pieces.

row of figures marked 8′ *Lengths* and follow it across to the right edge of the board where the number 4 appears. Of course you already know that a board this size contains 4 board feet.

The *Essex board-measure table* on the framing or rafter square can also be used to determine board feet quickly. Fig. 15-

10. A board 12″ wide and 1″ thick will contain the number of board feet equal to the number of linear feet in its length. The figure 12, therefore, on the outer edge, represents a board 1″ thick and 12″ wide. To use a simple example, suppose you are checking a board that is 1″ thick, 12″ wide, and 8′ long. Look at the column of figures under the 12 on the square until you reach the figure representing the length of the board in feet; this gives you the answer, 8 board feet.

Let's take another example. Suppose the board is 8″ wide and 14′ long. You again look under the 12 and move your eye down the column until you reach the figure 14 (the length). Then follow along this line to the left until you reach a point directly under the figure 8 (width in inches) on the edge graduations. Here you find 9 to the left of the cross line and 4 to the right of the same line. This tells you there are 9 and 4/12 or (9⅓) board feet in a 1″ thick board. If the board were 2″ thick, the total would be twice this amount. If the board is wider than 12″, the answer will be found to the right of the 12″ mark.

Follow these simple suggestions in measuring the amount of lumber delivered:

1. Use chalk to mark lengths of 4, 8, 12, and 16 feet on the floor. Pile the lumber of one species next to these marks so that the length can be immediately determined. Fig. 15-11.

2. Use a board-measure rule or the Essex board-measure table to determine the *surface measure* in each piece. Surface measure is the *square feet* in the surface of a board of any thickness. Measure lumber as though all pieces were 1″ thick and then add for thickness later.

3. Use several tally-sheet forms, one for each thickness, to keep track of individual pieces as they are measured. Fig. 15-12. Then total the board feet for each

thickness. Now add a per cent for all lumber over 1″. For example, add 1/4, or 25 percent, for 1¼″; add 1/2, or 50 per cent, for 1½″; double the amount or add 100 per cent for 2″ lumber. If only one tally sheet is used for all thicknesses, then it is necessary to convert each thickness to the total board feet after each piece is measured and before it is tallied. For example, if a piece measures 8 square feet and is 1½″

thick, add 50 per cent, make it 12 board feet, and record it as such.

4. If several tally sheets have been used, add them together for the total of each grade. If only one tally sheet has been used, find the total on this one sheet. Then check the total against the order and invoice to see if they agree. The amount should not deviate more than 1 to 2 per cent. If it does, you should check with your supplier.

Reading Prints And Making Sketches

A wood craftsman usually works from a print; that is, a reproduction of a drawing giving dimensions and other information needed to construct an object. Print reading is a basic source of information to the builder. It must be mastered by every craftsman, but especially by the cabinetmaker and the finish carpenter. Fig. 16-1.

Blueprints are very common in the building trades because they do not fade when exposed to direct sunlight as some kinds of prints do. They are made on chemically treated paper which shows the drawing in white against a blue

16-2. Sketch of a furniture piece.

16-1. Every craftsman must be able to read and follow prints.

background. In furniture making and interior cabinetwork, white-background prints are used on which black, blue, or brown lines appear. It is easier to add penciled corrections to these *white prints* than to blueprints.

From prints, a craftsman makes a materials list and layout, and builds his product. He must also decide whether he needs additional information, and frequently must use his own "know how." For instance, a print may give only the overall size of a certain part;

185

SAMPLE	NAME	PENCIL
	Construction	3H or 5H
	Border	H or HB
	Visible or Object	H or 2H
	Hidden or Invisible	H or 2H
	Center Line	H or 2H
	Dimension and Extension	2H or 3H
	Long Break	H or 2H
	Short Break	H or 2H

USE	EXAMPLE

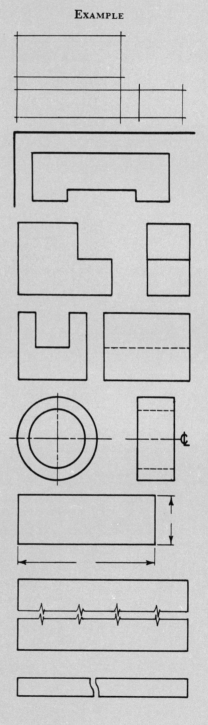

Very light line used to "block in" an object. These lines are made so light that little or no erasing is needed. Serve as base for darkening in the permanent lines.

Heavy, solid line used to frame in the drawing.

A heavy line used to outline the exterior shape of a part. Shows outstanding features.

A medium line used to show edges and contours not visible to the eye.

A light line used as axis of symmetry. Used for center of circle and arcs. Sometimes the symbol ℄ is shown.

Light, thin lines used to show the sizes of the object. Extension lines start about $\frac{1}{16}$" from visible or object line. The dimension line is broken near the center for the dimension.

Light, ruled line with freehand zigzags. To break an object when it is too big for paper.

Wavy line drawn freehand. For same purpose as long break.

TABLE LAMP

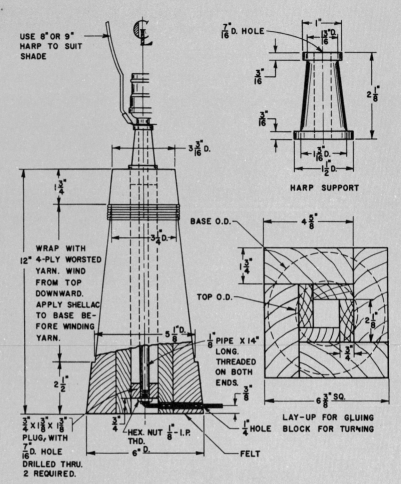

USE 8" OR 9" HARP TO SUIT SHADE

7/16" D. HOLE

1"

13/16" D.

3/16"

2 1/8"

3/16"

13/16" D.

1 1/2" D.

HARP SUPPORT

3 3/16" D.

1 3/4"

3/4" D.

WRAP WITH 12" 4-PLY WORSTED YARN. WIND FROM TOP DOWNWARD. APPLY SHELLAC TO BASE BEFORE WINDING YARN.

BASE O.D.

TOP O.D.

4 5/8"

1 3/4"

2 1/8"

5 1/8" D.

1/8" PIPE X 14" LONG. THREADED ON BOTH ENDS.

3/4"

3/8"

6 3/8" SQ.

2 1/2"

3/4" X 3/8" X 1 3/8" PLUG, WITH 7/16" D. HOLE DRILLED THRU. 2 REQUIRED.

3/4"

HEX. NUT 1/8" - I.P. THD.

6" D.

1/4" HOLE

3/8"

FELT

LAY-UP FOR GLUING BLOCK FOR TURNING

BILL OF MATERIALS
STOCK: White Oak

IMPORTANT: All dimensions listed below are CUTOUT size.

No. of Pieces	Part Name	Thickness	Width	Length
4	Column Stock	3/4"	2 1/8"	12 1/2"
4	Column Stock	1 3/4"	4 5/8"	12 1/2"
1	Harp Support	2"	2"	2 1/2"
2	Plugs	3/4"	1 3/8"	1 3/8"
1	1/8" Std. Pipe			14"
1	1/8" Hex Pipe Nut			
1	Push-Thru Bass Socket			
1	8" or 9" Harp to suit shade			
1	Brass Finial			
1	Lamp Cord—Length to suit			
1	Male Plug			
1	4-Ply Worsted Yarn — Color to suit			
1	Lamp Shade to suit			
1	Felt—6" diameter			

TABLE LAMP

1. Cut all stock to size on circular saw.
2. Glue up center core of column. When dry, true-up on jointer.
3. Glue on outer lamination of column block and glue plugs into ends.
4. Mount column block on lathe and turn design.
5. Mount harp support block on lathe and turn design. Bore 7/16" hole through center.
6. Drill 1/4" cord hole in base of lamp.
7. Finish-sand project and apply modern grey oak finish to harp support and upper and lower portion of column.
8. Mount column on lathe. Wrap center portion with yarn by applying shellac to a small section at a time and turning lathe by hand.
9. Bore 7/16" holes through center of plugs.
10. Assemble lamp and install lamp cord.
11. Glue felt to base of lamp.

16-4. Dimensions must be followed exactly when building this table lamp. The drawing, bill of materials, and plan of procedure are all important.

the craftsman then must use his own judgment about what kind and size of materials to use and what method of joinery to employ.

An architect, designer, or draftsman usually has the responsibility for making the original drawing. However, many cabinetmakers and finish carpenters also have the ability to make a good sketch. Fig. 16-2. Such craftsmen must often take measurements "on the job" and then make sketches. Sometimes these sketches are used to build the product. At other times the sketches are reviewed, refined, and then made into a set of drawings and prints.

ELEMENTS OF DRAWING

A drawing consists of lines, dimensions, symbols, and notes. *Lines* show the shape of a product and include many details of construction. Fig. 16-3. *Dimensions* are numbers that tell the sizes of each part as well as overall sizes. Fig. 16-4. The craftsman must follow these dimensions in making the materials list and the layout. On most furniture and cabinet drawings the dimensions are given in inches, but on architectural drawings they are in feet and inches. *Symbols* are used to represent things that would be impossible to show by drawing—such as materials—or things that would be very hard to draw exactly—doors and windows, electrical circuits, plumbing, and heating. Fig. 16-5. Some drawings also contain *notes* or written information to explain something not otherwise shown. Frequently, *abbreviations* are used for common words in these notes. Fig. 16-6.

SCALE

Drawings must often be reduced from actual size so they will fit on a piece of

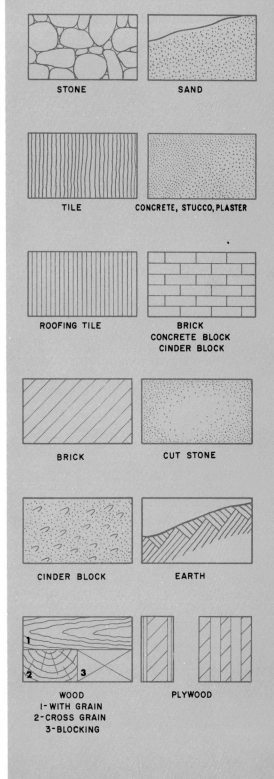

16-5(a). Symbols for materials.

189

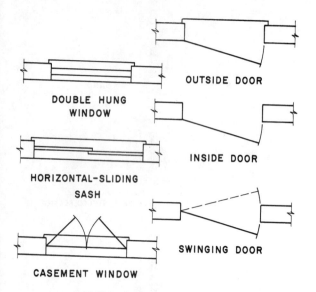

DOUBLE HUNG WINDOW

OUTSIDE DOOR

HORIZONTAL-SLIDING SASH

INSIDE DOOR

CASEMENT WINDOW

SWINGING DOOR

16-5(b). Symbols for doors and windows.

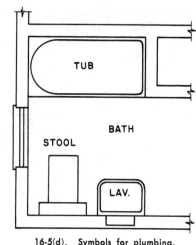

TUB

BATH

STOOL

LAV.

16-5(d). Symbols for plumbing.

16-5(e). Symbols for heating.

16-5(c). Symbols for electrical wiring.

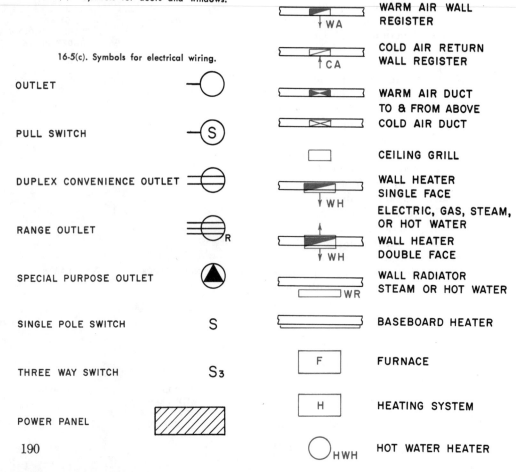

OUTLET			WARM AIR WALL REGISTER
PULL SWITCH		↓ WA	
			COLD AIR RETURN WALL REGISTER
DUPLEX CONVENIENCE OUTLET		↑ CA	
RANGE OUTLET			WARM AIR DUCT TO & FROM ABOVE
SPECIAL PURPOSE OUTLET			COLD AIR DUCT
SINGLE POLE SWITCH	S		CEILING GRILL
THREE WAY SWITCH	S₃		WALL HEATER SINGLE FACE
POWER PANEL		↓ WH	ELECTRIC, GAS, STEAM, OR HOT WATER

WARM AIR WALL REGISTER

COLD AIR RETURN WALL REGISTER

WARM AIR DUCT TO & FROM ABOVE

COLD AIR DUCT

CEILING GRILL

WALL HEATER SINGLE FACE

ELECTRIC, GAS, STEAM, OR HOT WATER

WALL HEATER DOUBLE FACE

WALL RADIATOR STEAM OR HOT WATER

BASEBOARD HEATER

F FURNACE

H HEATING SYSTEM

HWH HOT WATER HEATER

190

AP—Access panel	GL—Grade line
B&C—Bead and cove	GRV—Groove
BT—Bathtub	½RD—Half-round
BASMT—Basement	INSTL—Install
BEV STKG—Bevel	INSUL—Insulation
sticking	INT—Interior
BR—Bed room	KD—Knocked down
BC—Between centers	LAV—Lavatory
B/M—Bill of materials	LIV RM—Living room
BLDG—Building	LOC—Locate
BL—Building line	MATL—Material
BDY—Boundary	MILWK (MLWK)—
BRK—Brick	Millwork
CAB—Cabinet	ML—Material list
CASWK—Casework	MLDG—Molding
CLG—Ceiling	MULL—Mullion
CL—Center line	MUNT—Muntin
C TO C—Center to	NWL—Newel
center	NO. (#)—Number
CS—Cut stone	OA—Over-all
CUP—Cupboard	OC—On center
DSGN—Design	OG—Ogee(sticking)
DET—Detail	OVO—Ovolo
DIN RM—Dining room	PLAS (PL)—Plaster
DVTL—Dovetail	QUAL—Quality
DWL—Dowel	QTY—Quantity
DS—Down spout	RAB (RABT)—Rabbet
DWG—Drawing	RAD—Radiator
DR—Door (or doors)	REQD—Required
DRW (DRWS)—	¼RD—Quarter-round
Drawer(s)	RF—Refrigerator
EL—Elevation	RFG—Roofing
ENT—Entrance	SC—Scale
EST—Estimate	SK—Sink
EXT—Exterior	SB—Standard bead
FAB—Fabricate	S—Stile
FIN—Finish	STKG—Sticking
FL—Floor	SYM—Symbol
FD—Floor drain	T—Truss
FRA—Frame	VARN—Varnish
FDN—Foundation	WD—Windows
FTG—Footing	WC—Water closet
GR—Gas range	

16-6. A few common abbreviations. Others are shown in Fig. 15-3.

paper. Care is taken to make such drawings according to *scale;* that is, exactly in proportion to full size. For example, an architect can represent any size of building on a single piece of paper by drawing it to a certain scale. The scale is not a unit of measurement but represents the ratio between the size of the object as drawn and its actual size. Fig. 16-7. If the drawing is exactly the same size as the object itself, it is called a full-size or full-scale drawing. If it is reduced, as most scale drawings are, it will probably be drawn to one of the following common scales:

6″ equals 1′ (read: six inches equals one foot): half size.
3″ equals 1′: one-fourth size.
1½″ equals 1′: one-eighth size.
1″ equals 1′: one-twelfth size.
3/4″ equals 1′: one-sixteenth size.
1/2″ equals 1′: one twenty-fourth size.
3/8″ equals 1′: one thirty-second size.
1/4″ equals 1′: one forty-eighth size.
3/16″ equals 1′: one sixty-fourth size.
1/8″ equals 1′: one ninety-sixth size.

A scale of 1/4″ equals 1′ is often used for drawing buildings and rooms. Fig. 16-8. Detail drawings, which show how parts of a product are made, are prepared to scales of 3/8″, 1/2″, 3/4″, or 1½″ equals 1′.

KINDS OF DRAWINGS

In woodworking, four basic kinds of drawings are commonly used: the *perspective* drawing, the *cabinet* drawing, the *isometric* drawing, and the *multiview working* drawing. The first three have a picturelike quality and are called *pictorial.*

16-7(a). An architect's scale is used to make a drawing.

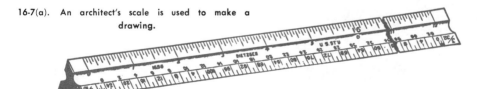

16-7(b). To finish a drawing it is necessary to have a complete set of drafting equipment. The wood box serves as a drawing board.

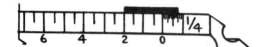

16-8. This shows a measurement of 33", or 2'9". On the scale ¼" equals 1'.

16-9. This is a perspective rendering of a chest.

16-10. A rendering of a bakery showcase.

PICTORIAL DRAWINGS

The pictorial drawing that looks most like a photograph is the *perspective* drawing, sometimes also called a *rendering*. It shows the finished appearance of an object. Fig. 16-9. All house plans include such a drawing. The bakery showcase, Fig. 16-10, is another example of a perspective drawing.

The *cabinet* drawing is used for rectangular objects such as chests, cases, and of course cabinets. It is a simple drawing in which the shape of the front surface is shown in exact scale. The sides and top slant back at an angle of 30 to 60 degrees, but usually 45 degrees. Fig. 16-11. These slanted lines are made just half as long as if they were drawn to scale, giving the drawing a more natural appearance. However, in dimensioning these lines, the actual sizes are always specified.

Isometric means "having equal angles." An *isometric* drawing is constructed around three lines that are exactly 120 degrees apart. Fig. 16-12. One line is drawn vertical and the other two lines are drawn at 30 degrees to the horizontal. All lines parallel to the isometric lines are drawn to scale. For this reason the isometric is best for rectangular objects. All lines not parallel to the isometric lines are called non-isometric and are not true to scale. Non-isometric

16-11. A cabinet drawing of a dining-room chest.

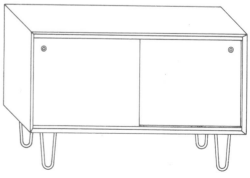

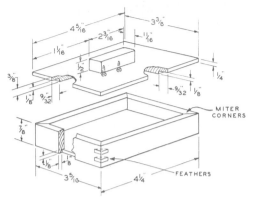

16-12. An isometric drawing of a small accessory.

lines must be drawn by locating the ends of the isometric lines and connecting the points with a straightedge.

MULTIVIEW DRAWINGS

The *multiview* working drawing, also called an *orthographic projection,* is the most common type of drawing in industry. To show the shape and dimensions of a six-sided object, such as a chest, it is usually necessary to draw only three views: front, top, and right side or end. Fig. 16-13. For some objects only

two views are needed. For instance, if the front and top of a chest have the same dimensions, drawings of only the front and right side are necessary. Fig. 16-14.

Because such drawings involve more than one view of an object, you can see why they are called "multiview." "Orthographic" refers basically to straight lines.

The term "projection" also is fairly easy to understand. Assume you have the drawing of the front of a chest, just as you would see it from the front. Directly beside this you want to draw the right end of the chest as it would appear if you stood facing that end. The line which forms the right side of the front view represents the height of the chest. Since the front and the end come together at a corner, the height of the front can be *projected* to form the height of the end. In the same way, the width of the front could be projected to form the width of a top view. If two views are given—for instance, front and side—still more projections to top and bottom views can be made rather simply. It is important to remember that the views of

16-13. A typical three-view drawing (orthographic projection).

TOP

54

FRONT

$1\frac{1}{2}$ $1\frac{1}{2}$

$1\frac{1}{2}$

16

18

RIGHT SIDE
OR
END

$1\frac{1}{2}$ $1\frac{1}{2}$

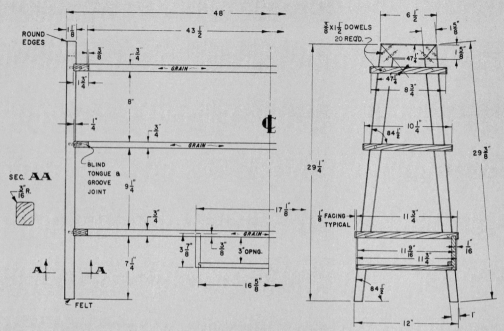

16-14. This room-divider drawing has only two views.

16-15. Section view of a drawer for the divider shown in Fig. 16-14.

16-16. An auxiliary view of a piece of metal hardware.

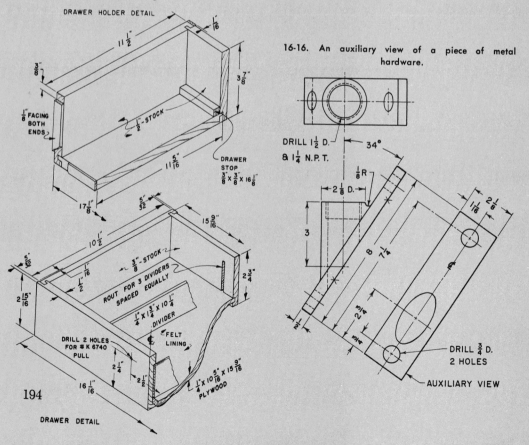

194

16-17(a). Buffet room-divider.

an orthographic projection are shown *all in the same plane,* not at angles to each other.

A *section view* shows the interior of an object as if the surface had been cut away. Fig. 16-15. An *auxiliary view* is needed when there is a slanted surface that does not show in true shape on the front, top, or right-side view. Fig. 16-16.

A complete set of drawings includes not only *detail* drawings but also *assembly* drawings which give information for building the object. Fig. 16-17.

Continued on page 200

16-17(b).   BUFFET ROOM-DIVIDER.

BILL OF MATERIALS
IMPORTANT: All dimensions listed below are FINISHED size.

No. of Pieces	Part Name	Thickness	Width	Length	Material
1	Top	¾″	20¾″	53¾″	Comb Grain White Oak Plywood—S1S
4	Doors	¾″	13⁹⁄₁₆″	23⁷⁄₁₆″	Comb Grain White Oak Plywood—S1S
2	Shelves	¾″	17½″	13½″	Comb Grain White Oak Plywood—S1S
1	Back Panel	¾″	23½″	25¾″	Comb Grain White Oak Plywood—S1S
1	Drawer Front	¾″	5″	25³⁄₁₆″	Comb Grain White Oak Plywood—S1S
2	Drawer Fronts	¾″	6″	25³⁄₁₆″	Comb Grain White Oak Plywood—S1S
1	Drawer Front	¾″	6½″	25³⁄₁₆″	Comb Grain White Oak Plywood—S1S
2	End Panels	¾″	19¼″	25″	Comb Grain White Oak Plywood—S1S
2	Center Dividers	¾″	16¼″	24¼″	Fir Plywood
4	Center Divider Stiles	¾″	2¹⁄₁₆″	25″	Solid White Oak
4	Top and Bottom Frames Front and Back	¾″	2¹³⁄₁₆″	54¾″	Solid White Oak
8	Top and Bottom Frame Cross Pieces	¾″	2¹³⁄₁₆″	13¾″	Hardwood

No. of Pieces	Part Name	Thickness	Width	Length	Material
6	Drawer Frames Front and Back	$\frac{3}{4}$″	2″	$25\frac{3}{4}$″	Hardwood
6	Drawer Frame Ends	$\frac{3}{4}$″	2″	$13\frac{3}{4}$″	Hardwood
2	Drawer Sides	$\frac{3}{8}$″	$4\frac{13}{16}$″	$16\frac{5}{16}$″	Solid Oak
1	Drawer Back	$\frac{3}{8}$″	$4\frac{11}{16}$″	$24\frac{5}{8}$″	Solid Oak
4	Drawer Sides	$\frac{3}{8}$″	$5\frac{3}{16}$″	$16\frac{5}{16}$″	Solid Oak
2	Drawer Backs	$\frac{3}{8}$″	$5\frac{1}{16}$″	$24\frac{5}{8}$″	Solid Oak
2	Drawer Sides	$\frac{3}{8}$″	$5\frac{13}{16}$″	$16\frac{5}{16}$″	Solid Oak
1	Drawer Back	$\frac{3}{8}$″			Solid Oak
4	Tray Sides	$\frac{3}{8}$″	$4\frac{11}{16}$″	$24\frac{5}{8}$″	Solid Oak
4	Tray Fronts and Backs	$\frac{3}{8}$″ $\frac{3}{8}$″	$1\frac{15}{16}$″ $1\frac{15}{16}$″	15″ $12\frac{3}{8}$″	Solid Oak
2	Tray Stops	$\frac{1}{2}$″	$2\frac{1}{2}$″	$13\frac{5}{8}$″	Solid Oak
4	Tray Runners	$\frac{1}{2}$″	$\frac{1}{2}$″	$15\frac{1}{2}$″	Solid Oak
8	Drawer Pulls	$\frac{3}{4}$″	1″	$25\frac{3}{16}$″	Solid Oak
4	Legs	$1\frac{1}{4}$″	$2\frac{1}{2}$″	6″	Solid Oak
2	Rungs	$\frac{3}{4}$″ dia.		$15\frac{3}{4}$″	Solid Oak
2	Rungs	$\frac{3}{4}$″ dia.		$45\frac{3}{4}$″	Solid Oak
2	Top Cleats	1″	$2\frac{1}{2}$″	21″	Solid Oak
8	Top and Bottom Frame Extensions	$\frac{3}{4}$″	$1\frac{3}{16}$″	$13\frac{5}{8}$″	Solid Oak
4	Drawer Bottoms	$\frac{1}{4}$″	$15\frac{5}{8}$″	$24\frac{5}{8}$″	Birch Plywood SIS
3	Dust Bottoms	$\frac{1}{4}$″	$12\frac{15}{16}$″	$22\frac{7}{16}$″	Birch Plywood SIS
1	Dust Bottom	$\frac{1}{4}$″	$12\frac{15}{16}$″	$22\frac{13}{16}$″	Birch Plywood S1S
2	End Compartment Bottoms	$\frac{1}{4}$″	$17\frac{7}{8}$″	$13\frac{5}{8}$″	Birch Plywood S1S
2	Tray Bottoms	$\frac{1}{4}$″	$11\frac{15}{16}$″	$15\frac{1}{16}$″	Birch Plywood S1S
2	Top Supports	$\frac{1}{4}$″	3″	53″	Birch Plywood S1S
2	Top Supports	$\frac{1}{4}$″	3″	$14\frac{3}{4}$″	Birch Plywood S1S
4	Side Edge Facings	$\frac{1}{8}$″	$\frac{3}{4}$″	25″	Solid White Oak
2	Top Edge Facings	$\frac{1}{8}$″	1″	53″	Solid White Oak
4	Shelf Edge Facings	$\frac{1}{8}$″	$\frac{3}{4}$″	$13\frac{1}{2}$″	Solid White Oak
4	Leg Dowels	$\frac{3}{4}$″ dia.		$1\frac{3}{4}$″	Hardwood
8	Shelf Pegs	$\frac{1}{4}$″ dia.		$\frac{7}{8}$″	Dowel
4	Wedges	$0-\frac{1}{8}$″	$\frac{3}{4}$″	$\frac{3}{4}$″	Hardwood
4	Drawer Guides	$\frac{1}{2}$″	$\frac{3}{4}$″	15″	Hardwood
4	Drawer Guides	$\frac{7}{16}$″	$1\frac{1}{2}$″	$15\frac{1}{4}$″	Hardwood
8	Drawer Stops	$\frac{1}{2}$″	$\frac{1}{2}$″	2″	Hardwood
2	Tray Guides	$\frac{3}{8}$″	$2\frac{1}{2}$″	$16\frac{1}{16}$″	Solid Oak
2	Tray Spacing Blocks	$\frac{3}{4}$″	$2\frac{1}{2}$″	2″	Solid Oak
2	Tray Liners	26 ga.	13″	$16\frac{1}{8}$″	Copper
4	pr. 2″ Brass Butt Hinges				
4	No. K6740 Brushed Brass Pulls				
14	No. 10 x $1\frac{1}{2}$″ F.H. Wood Screws				
16	No. 6 x $\frac{3}{4}$″ F.H. Wood Screws				
4	No. 6 x 2″ F.H. Wood Screws				
4	No. 8 x $1\frac{3}{4}$″ F.H. Wood Screws				
4	Adjustable Bullet Catches No. 16 x $1\frac{1}{4}$″ Wire Brads				

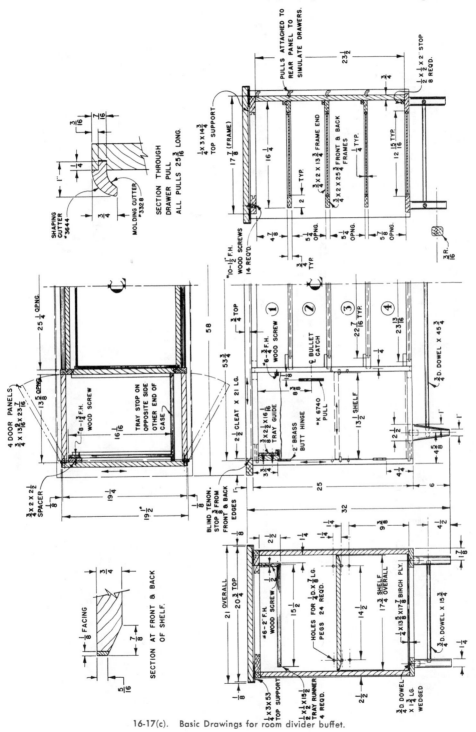

16-17(c).   Basic Drawings for room divider buffet.

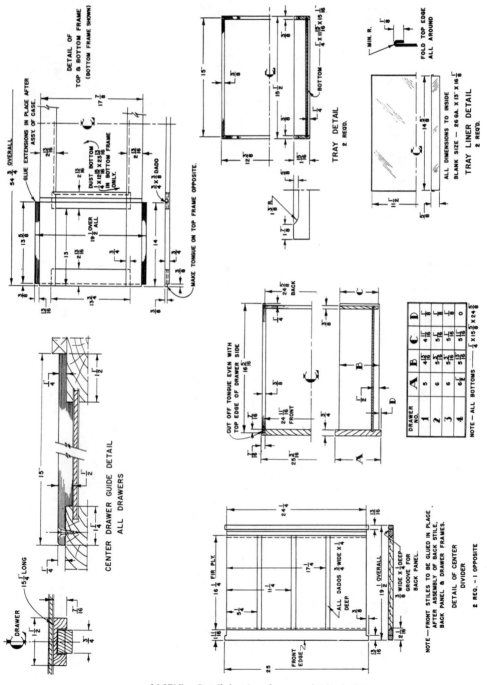

16-17(d).   Detail drawings for room divider buffet.

16-17(e). STEPS IN CONSTRUCTION.

ROOM DIVIDER BUFFET

1. Cut out all frame members, end panels, center dividers and stiles, dust bottoms, and back panel to size on circular saw.

2. Set up dado head to cut 1/4" wide dado. Groove fronts and backs of all frames for tongue and groove joints. Groove all frame members except top frame for dust bottoms. Also groove back panel for imitation drawer pulls.

3. With the same dado, rabbet each end of back panel. Groove edges of center dividers. Cut tongue on stiles and notch ends. Cut tongues on ends of all frame cross pieces.

4. Glue up all frames.

5. Set up dado head to cut 3/8" wide dado. Dado end panels for top and bottom frames. Rabbet ends of top and bottom frames. Groove back stiles for back panel.

6. Change dado head to cut 3/4" wide dado. Dado top and bottom frames for center dividers. Dado center dividers for drawer frames.

7. Drill and countersink screw shank holes in top frame.

8. Bore leg dowel holes in bottom frame.

9. Drill shelf support peg holes in end panels and in center dividers.

10. Glue top and bottom frame assemblies, end panels, and center dividers together.

11. Glue back panel and back stiles into place.

12. Glue drawer frame assemblies and front stiles into place.

13. Cut top and bottom frame extensions and side facing strips to size and glue into place.

14. Cut tray stops and runners to size. Rabbet one end of runners and groove stops. Drill and counterbore stops. Screw stops into place and glue and screw runners into place.

15. Cut legs to size and bore 3/4" holes for rungs and dowels. Cut tapers with circular saw taper jig. Round corners. Cut rungs and dowels to length. Make wedges. Glue rungs into legs. Immediately set case on leg assembly and glue and wedge dowels into place.

16. Check drawer and tray dimensions and cut all pieces to size on circular saw. Note:

Drawers are made narrower in back than in front for smoother operation.

17. Set dado head for 1/4" wide cut and cut tongue and rabbet on ends of all drawer fronts. Dado both ends of drawer sides, and rabbet the ends of tray fronts. Groove all drawer and tray members to receive bottoms. Groove drawer fronts for drawer pulls. Notch drawer backs for drawer guides.

18. Lay out, band saw, and dress down contours of tray fronts and backs.

19. Assemble all drawers and trays with glue and wire brads. On three bottom drawers, trim off tongues on drawer fronts which project above the drawer slides.

20. Make drawer pulls. Cut 8 pieces of stock 3/4" x 1" x 29". Rabbet top edge of each piece on jointer. Shape front contour with No. 3644 cutter on shaper or drill press shaper attachment. Shape bottom contour with No. 3328 moulding cutter on circular saw, shaper or drill. (**For safety,** stop cut about 3" from end). Cut pulls to length on circular saw and glue into place.

21. Make up center drawer guides and drawer stops and install.

22. Cut, fit and glue bottoms in end compartments.

23. Cut and fit doors.

24. Install hinges, pulls and bullet catches in doors.

25. Cut top to size and cut tenon on ends. Trim tenon for blind joint.

26. Cut top end cleats to size. Either cut stop groove or cut groove through and then inlay end grain for blind tenon. Glue top cleats.

27. Cut and glue top support pieces into place.

28. Cut and glue edge facing strips into place.

29. Attach top with F.H. Wood Screws.

30. Cut adjustable shelves to size. Cut and glue facing strips into place. Set saw arbor to 27° and cut chamfer on fronts of shelves.

31. Make and install shelf support pegs.

32. Finish-sand entire project.

33. Apply grey oak finish.

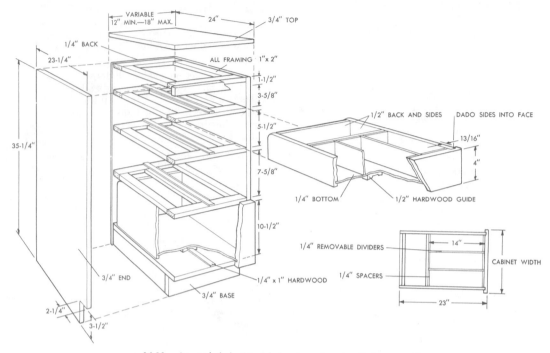

16-18. An exploded pictorial drawing of a utensil drawer cabinet.

Cabinetmakers and finish carpenters must be acquainted with the drawings that are commonly used in the furniture industry, the millroom, and the building industry. Fig. 16-17. A furniture drawing is first made full size with three basic views, namely, the front (or *elevation view*), the top (or *plan view*), and the right-side view. From these, detail drawings to scale are made for each part to be manufactured. The detail drawing, along with the matching route sheet, follows each piece through the factory as it is processed. A full-size engineering drawing or an assembly drawing is used to put the parts together into the finished product. Furniture drawings in popular magazines are often either cabinet or isometric drawings because of their pictorial quality. Cabinet and isometric drawings can be made as *exploded* drawings with the individual

parts separated so the construction can be seen more clearly. Fig. 16-18.

Furniture and cabinet drawings do not always follow the standard drafting practice. Some of the differences include:

• Several types of drawings may be combined. For example, there may be a front view of the object along with a perspective or isometric view of the product.

• In multiview or orthographic-projection drawings, the views are not always in their proper location. For example, the top view may not be directly above the front view as it should be. This is often done to save space on the paper.

• Many drawings do not contain details of construction for joints, drawers, doors, and similar items. Fig. 16-19. The craftsman must then decide on these details which, of course, may be extremely important to the overall design of the product. A finish carpenter who would build the cheapest kind of drawers in a high-quality home would not be considered a reputable craftsman.

• Many drawings contain inch marks on all dimensions. In furniture making and cabinetwork, a craftsman should have a drawing or print of the product, a bill of materials or materials list, and a plan of procedure.

ARCHITECTURAL DRAWINGS

The views of a house are shown in *general* and *detail* drawings. General drawings include the plans and elevations while detail drawings are the sections and small drawings of certain parts of the house. All information as to size must be shown by dimensions written in numbers. The selection of the scale is determined by the size of the house and

ROOM DIVIDER

16-19. This room divider shows how limited is the information found on some kinds of popular woodworking drawings.

COMPONENT PARTS:

1. $\frac{3}{4}'' \times \frac{3}{4}'' \times \frac{1}{8}''$ angle aluminum
2. $\frac{3}{4}''$ plywood
3. Piano hinge for large door
4. Flat-head screws

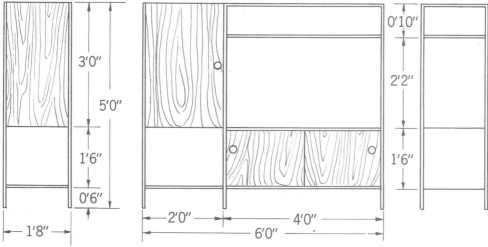

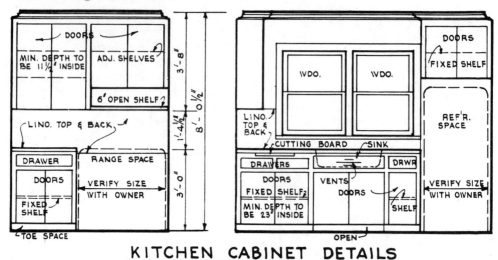

KITCHEN CABINET DETAILS

16-20. Detail drawings of kitchen cabinets.

the size of the drawing paper. General drawings commonly have a scale of 1/4″ equals 1′0″. Less frequently a scale of 1/8″ equals 1′0″ is used. Detail drawings are prepared to scales of 3/8″ equals 1′0″, 1/2″ equals 1′0″, 3/4″ equals 1′0″, or 1½″ equals 1′0″. The draftsman chooses a scale which will be clear and easy to read. A complete set of working drawings consists of the following:

Presentation Drawing or Pictorial Rendering

These are perspective drawings of a house as lifelike as photographs, showing how it will look when completed.

Plans

A plan view is a top view. The several types include:

Site or plot plan. This shows the outline of the lot and the location of the building on it.

Foundation or basement plan. This plan is the top view of the footings or foundation walls showing the exact size and location of foundations.

Building or floor plan. This is a cross-

section view of the house, showing the outside shape of the building, the arrangement, size, and shape of rooms, the types of materials, the thickness of walls and partitions, and the type, size, and location of doors and windows. Since the plan is drawn to a very small scale, symbols are used to indicate fixtures and materials.

Framing plans. These plans show the size, number, location, and spacing of structural members that make up the framework of the house.

Elevations. Elevations are external views of the house made from the front, rear, right side, and left side. They are

16-21. Squared paper for making a sketch.

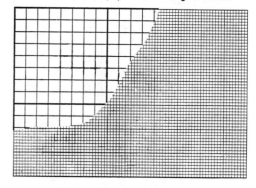

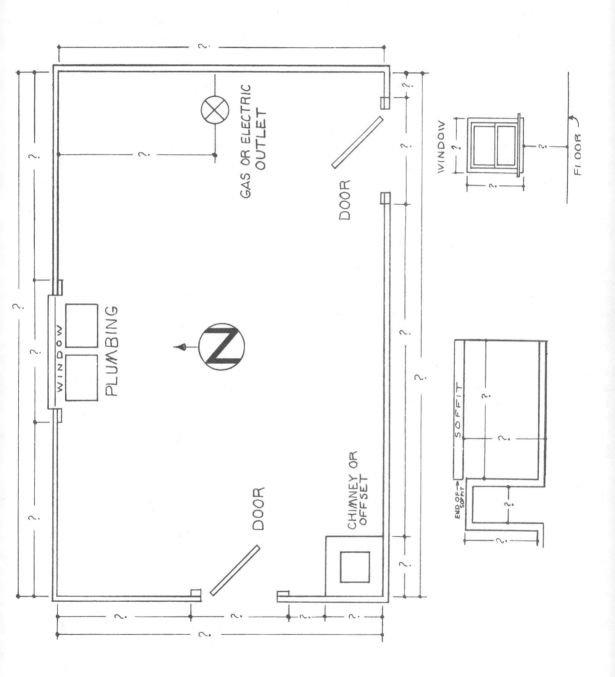

16-22. This kind of sketch must be made before remodeling a kitchen.

picturelike views of the building that show exterior materials, height and width of doors, windows, and other items.

Sectional views. These views, sometimes called sections, show very important information about height. They show how a house would look if it could be cut vertically. Usually they are drawn to a larger scale than the elevations. Typical sections are used to show a cross section of a structural part other than a wall.

Details or detail drawings. These show a specific part of a house that was not made clear on the general plans. Such items as kitchen cabinets, wardrobes, linen closets, and fireplaces are usually drawn to a larger scale than the house plans. Fig. 16-20. Details should be carefully studied along with the general drawings into which the parts fit. Frequently, even these detail drawings do not give all the information needed. For example, kitchen-cabinet details give the overall height, width, and depth, plus dimensions of each cabinet or unit, but omit construction of drawers or doors and interior details. The craftsman must solve these problems himself, based on his knowledge of cabinet construction. He may want to sketch the drawers or cabinet details to help him make a materials list and to guide him in construction.

In home building, a finish carpenter needs a set of prints including all the individual drawings, a detailed materials list or bill of materials, and a complete set of specifications. *Specifications* are written descriptive material that accompanies the plans. They cover all items such as general condition of construction, excavation and grading, masonry, framing, carpentry, sheet-metal lath, plaster, electrical wring, plumbing, heating, painting, and finishing. The specifications also contain such information as standards of workmanship, re-

sponsibilities of the various individuals involved in the construction, time limits, and other matters that could cause disagreement as the building progresses.

MAKING A SKETCH

A *shop sketch* is a simple drawing made with elementary equipment. Actually a sketch can be made with a scratch pad of paper and a pencil. All that is necessary is knowledge of the elements of drawing and how to apply them. The important thing about a sketch—especially in building construction—is accuracy of dimensions. Usual practice is to make measurements on the job, then develop a sketch. For most work, drawing paper is squared or cross-sectioned and lined in squares or dots, eight to the inch. Fig. 16-21. With this paper, it is easier to make the sketch to the correct size, shape, and scale.

To make a sketch, proceed as follows:

1. Decide on the views needed. For example, in planning a new kitchen, a floor-plan sketch is absolutely essential. You may also need several elevation sketches for different sides of the kitchen.

2. Decide on the scale. Some common scales used on squared paper are:
* Full size, with each square representing 1/8″.
* Half size, with each square representing 1/4″.
* Quarter (or one-fourth) size, with each square representing 1/2″.
* Eighth (or one-eighth) size, with each square representing 1″.

3. Take measurements carefully. Fig. 16-22. Show the location and measurement of all windows and doors (including trim) as well as all obstructions such as pipes, radiators, chimneys, offsets, and stairways. Indicate where the doors lead and also show which direction is north. Show the location of plumbing, gas, electrical, and other wall outlets that will affect the design of the new kitchen.

Material Needs, Planning, and Estimating

After a final drawing or print is ready, several additional steps must be taken before construction can begin. You must first make a list called a *bill of materials, materials list,* or *stock bill.* The procedure for making the list is known as *stock billing.* Fig. 17-1. The list includes the following (not always in this order):

a. Number of pieces.

b. Name of part.

c. Finish size in thickness, width, and length.

d. Materials. (This may not be necessary if only one kind of lumber, plywood, or other material is involved.)

e. Rough or cut-out size, also called the *stock-cutting* list. (Sometimes a separate form is used for the stock-cutting list; if this is done, the number of pieces, name of part, and materials information should be repeated.)

It is standard practice to list the pieces in order of thickness, width, and length, but in the furniture industry this is sometimes reversed. Lumber thickness depends on whether the boards are purchased rough or surfaced two sides (S2S). Generally, if the material called for has 3/4" or 13/16" finish thickness, then the rough stock should be 1", or 4/4 (four-quarter). From 1/16" to 1/8" must be allowed for surfacing. For such materials as plywood, hardboard or particle board, the finish cut, and the cut-out or rough thickness are the same. For solid lumber, the width of the cut-out or rough size is usually 1/8" to 1/4" greater; from 1/2" to 1" is normally added to the length.

BILL OF MATERIALS

No. of Pieces	Part Name	Material	Finish Size			Rough Size		
			T	W	L	T	W	L

17-1. Form for a bill of materials, materials list, or stock bill.

LUMBER AND MATERIAL ORDER

No. of Pieces	Dimensions			Kind of Material	Number of: Bd. Ft. Sq. Ft. or Lin. Ft.	Cost per: Bd. Ft. Sq. Ft. or Lin. Ft.	Total Cost
	T	W	L				

17-2. Form for a lumber and materials order.

POINTS TO REMEMBER IN STOCK BILLING

•The *net size* is the actual or *finish size* of the part and is given in thickness, width, and length, usually in that order. Additional length is needed for tenons. When reading a drawing in leg-and-rail construction where only *shoulder length* is shown, you must add the necessary finish length for the tenons.

•Rough or cut-out size is the size that must be cut from the standard piece of lumber. This size allows the amount needed for machining.

•In the lumber order always list plywood, particle board, hardboard, softwood, and hardwood separately.

•Always write sizes in inches and fractions of an inch, not in feet.

MAKING A LUMBER AND MATERIALS ORDER

Lumber and similar materials are purchased in standard sizes. When you know the rough or cut-out sizes, you must next decide which sizes of materials to buy. Fig. 17-2. First, look down the list to find materials of the same kind and thickness. For example, if the list calls for five pieces to be made of the same hardwood, all 1/2″ in thickness, you will want to buy this material in a size that will produce these five pieces with the least amount of waste. Jobs vary greatly, so there are no fixed rules for selecting these sizes. In some cases it is a good idea to make a cutting diagram. Fig. 17-3.

The lumber and material order should

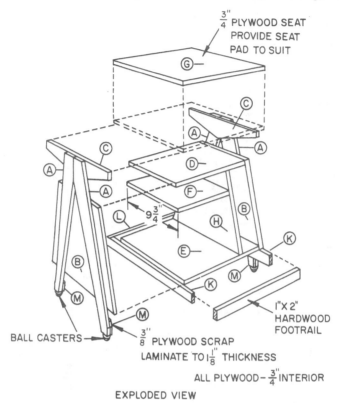

$\frac{3''}{4}$ PLYWOOD SEAT
PROVIDE SEAT
PAD TO SUIT

BALL CASTERS

$\frac{3''}{8}$ PLYWOOD SCRAP
LAMINATE TO $1\frac{1''}{8}$ THICKNESS

1"X 2"
HARDWOOD
FOOTRAIL

ALL PLYWOOD—$\frac{3''}{4}$ INTERIOR

EXPLODED VIEW

FOOTRAILS
BALL CASTERS

17-3(a). Two-view and exploded-view drawing of cleaning stool.

BILL OF MATERIALS
Cleaning Stool

No. of Pieces	Name	Size
4 "A"	Legs	¾ x 2⅞ x 23¾
2 "B"	Sides	¾ x 13⅜ x 16
2 "C"	Seat Supports	¾ x 3 x 15½
1 "D"	Top Shelf	¾ x 8½ x 12½
1 "E"	Bottom Shelf	¾ x 12½ x 16
1 "F"	Center Shelf	¾ x 8⅞ x 9¾
1 "G"	Seat	¾ x 16 x 16
1 "H"	Partition	¾ x 11⅞ x 15½
1 "J"	Footrail (Solid Hardwood Stock)	¾ x 1⅝ x 14
2 "K"	Side Rails	¾ x 1⅝ x 18½
1 "L"	Back Rail	¾ x 1⅝ x 12½
4 "M"	Leg Laminates	⅜ x 2 x 2½
4	Ball Casters	
8	Flat Head Wood Screws	No. 6 x 1¼
	Seat Pad (to suit)	16 x 16

17-3(b). Bill of materials.

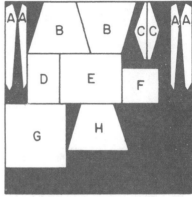

$\frac{3}{4}$" X 48"X 48" D.F. P.A. INTERIOR A-A PANEL

17-3(c). Cutting diagram. Note how all parts can be cut from a 48" x 48" sheet of plywood, with some large scraps left over.

SUPPLIES, FASTENERS AND HARDWARE LIST

Item	Quantity	Size	Unit Cost	Total Cost

17-4. Form for supplies, fasteners, and hardware.

list the number of pieces; sizes in thickness, width, and length; and kind of wood. The list should also mention the number of board, square, or linear feet for each size. You must figure this according to one of the formulas given in Unit 15. You must also determine the cost per board, square, or linear foot. This information can be obtained from any lumber dealer. Then the total cost should also be figured.

In addition to the lumber order, it is wise to make a list of other standard supplies needed such as fittings and finishing materials. Fig. 17-4.

In industry the responsibility for making the drawings, preparing the stock bill, and listing other needed items may be given to one individual or several, depending on the size of the establishment. Fig. 17-5. A man called a *detailer* makes the detail drawings and the stock

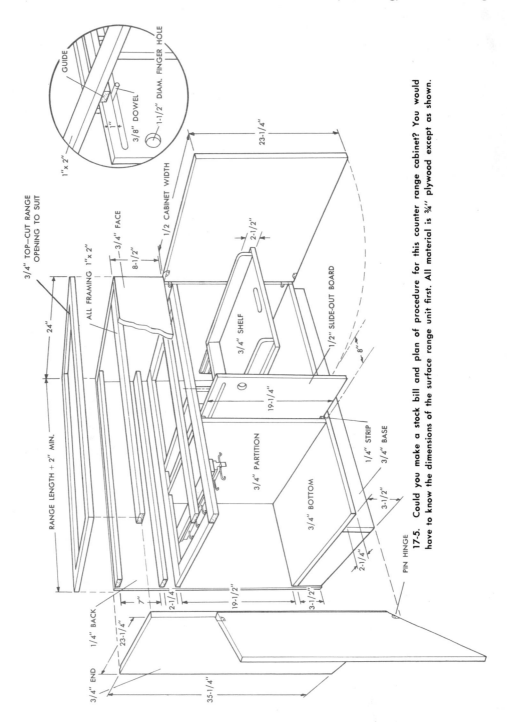

GUIDE

1-1/2" DIAM. FINGER HOLE

3/8" DOWEL

1"

1" x 2"

3/4" TOP-CUT RANGE
OPENING TO SUIT

ALL FRAMING 1" x 2"

3/4" FACE

8-1/2"

1/2 CABINET WIDTH

23-1/4"

2-1/2"

24"

3/4" SHELF

1/2" SLIDE-OUT BOARD

8"

RANGE LENGTH + 2" MIN.

19-1/4"

1/4" STRIP

3/4" BASE

3/4" PARTITION

3-1/2"

3/4" BOTTOM

2-1/4"

PIN HINGE

1/4" BACK

23-1/4"

7"

2-1/4

19-1/2"

3-1/2"

3/4" END

35-1/4"

17-5. Could you make a stock bill and plan of procedure for this counter range cabinet? You would have to know the dimensions of the surface range unit first. All material is ¾" plywood except as shown.

17-6(a). The next four illustrations show plans for this table.

bills. He may also be responsible for making route sheets or rod layouts. (See Unit 18 for rod layouts.) The *stock cutter* is the one who uses the stock bill to select and cut out the material to rough size.

DEVELOPING A PLAN OF PROCEDURE (PROCEDURE LIST)

This plan or list details the steps or operations needed to complete the product. Planning is extremely important when using tools and materials. It helps to avoid costly errors. While the specific steps or operations depend on the kind and complexity of the product, in general they include:

1. Getting out the rough stock.
2. Squaring up the solid stock.
3. Making or cutting (to size) the plywood.
4. Completing the straight parts.
5. Completing the curved and irregular-shaped parts.
6. Making the joints.
7. Sanding the parts.
8. Assembling.
9. Finishing.
10. Installing hardware.

Good plans for a table are shown in Fig. 17-6. In industry, planning for production is done by the design and en-

gineering department. No company would attempt to make wood products without such plans. Most furniture plants have a planning system which uses *route sheets* (actually plans of procedure for each part of the product). A more complete description of their use will be found in Unit 65.

ESTIMATING

It is frequently the responsibility of the self-employed cabinetmaker or finish carpenter to estimate the total cost of producing a piece of furniture or cabinetwork. Larger cabinet shops and fixture manufacturers have full-time employees called *estimators* who specialize in this work. These men make accurate estimates of any job, based on known costs, standard formulas, and expert judgments. Three main factors must be considered, namely, *materials, labor,* and

17-6(b). Boring jig.

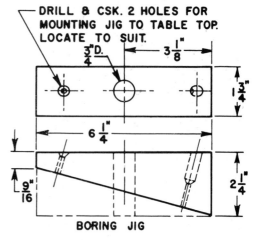

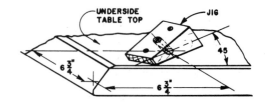

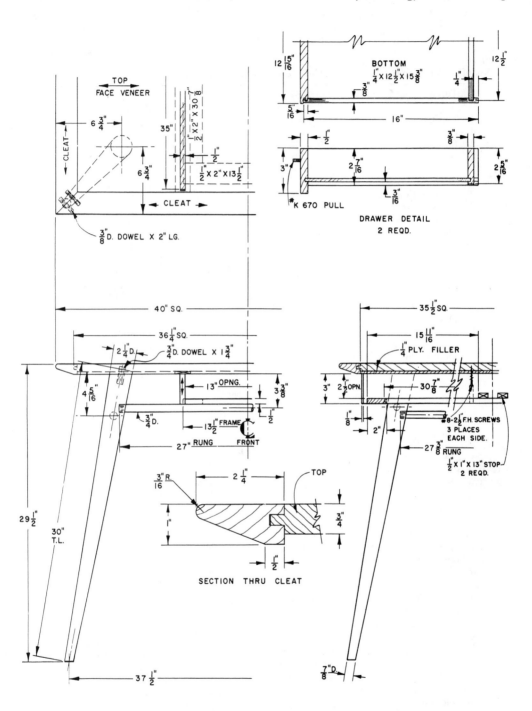

17-6(c). Three-view drawing with details.

TABLE—BILL OF MATERIALS
IMPORTANT: All dimensions listed below are FINISHED size.

Pieces No. of	Part Name	Thickness	Width	Length	Material
1	Top	¾"	36¼"	36¼"	Comb Grain White Oak Plywood
4	Top Cleats	1"	2¼"	40"	White Oak
4	Legs	2¼" dia.		30"	White Oak
2	Rungs	¾" dia.		27"	White Oak
2	Rungs	¾" dia.		27⅜"	White Oak
2	Drawer Case Sides	½"	3"	35"	Comb Grain White Oak Plywood
2	Drawer Frame Fronts	½"	2"	13½"	Hardwood
2	Drawer Frame Sides	½"	2"	30⅞"	Hardwood
2	Drawer Stops	½"	1"	13"	Hardwood
2	Drawer Fronts	½"	3"	12$\frac{15}{16}$"	Comb Grain White Oak Plywood
4	Drawer Sides	⅜"	2$\frac{7}{16}$"	16"	Solid Oak
2	Drawer Backs	⅜"	2$\frac{5}{16}$"	12½"	Solid Oak
2	Drawer Bottoms	¼"	12½"	15⅜"	Birch Plywood
4	Facings	⅛"	½"	3"	White Oak
2	Top Filler Strips	¼"	1½"	35½"	Plywood
4	Dowels	¾" dia.		1¾"	Hardwood
8	Dowels	⅛" dia.		2"	Hardwood
6	No. 8 x 2½" F. H. Wood Screws				
2	Drawer Pulls No. K670				

17-6(d.) Bill of materials.

17-6(e). Plan of procedure.

TABLE

1. Cut all pieces to size on circular saw.
2. Turn legs to shape on wood lathe. Bore dowel hole in top of each leg.
3. Set circular saw arbor to 1¼°, miter gage to 16½°. Cut angle on top of each leg using miter gage on left side of saw. Then put gage on right side of saw and cut bottom of leg to length keeping angle parallel to top.
4. Set drill press table to angle of 16° and bore rung holes. Caution: Be sure angle of top of leg is in right position. Use a jig.
5. Cut tongue on all sides of top panel.
6. Groove top cleats with dado head or molding head on circular saw. Miter corners. Bore dowel holes. Set saw arbor to angle of 22° and cut bevel on cleats. Round edges on drill press or shaper.
7. Assemble top.
8. Make boring jig:
   a. Accurately cut out block 1¾" x 2¼" x 6¼".
   b. Locate and bore ¾" hole through center of block.
   c. Lay out diagonal cutting line. Set miter gage to 69° 50′ and cut out on circular saw.
   d. Locate and drill screw holes for fastening jig to table top. Diagonally-cut face of block should be against drill press table.
   e. Fasten jig into place and bore dowel holes for mounting legs.
9. Glue plywood filler strips into place.
10. Assemble top, legs and rungs.
11. Make up drawer case and fasten into place with flathead wood screws.
12. Make up drawers.
13. Finish-sand entire table and apply modern oak finish.
14. Install drawer pulls.

combined *overhead and profit*. It would be good experience for you to include all of these items in the cost of the product you build. Too often the student considers only the cost of materials.

MATERIALS

The materials estimate must allow for the cost of materials actually used in the product. plus an added amount for waste, spoilage, pieces built or machined wrong, and similar cost-increasing factors. This estimate is usually made in one of two ways. One method is based on actual cost of materials from the supplier. To this total is added a fixed percentage—usually about 35 per cent—for waste and similar items. The other method is simply to use a much higher figure than actual cost per board, square, or linear foot. This higher unit price takes into account such things as waste and spoilage.

LABOR

Labor cost must include not only the actual amount per hour paid to the worker but also such items as social-security tax, pension-fund allotment, and supervisory labor. Usually, total cost per hour ranges from 15 to 25 per cent more than the worker's wages. Even the self-employed worker must not forget about such "hidden" labor costs.

OVERHEAD AND PROFIT

Overhead refers to the more or less fixed costs of running a business. It includes buildings, machines, utilities, and office expenses, among other things. Profit must also be added so there will be a return to the investor, whether he runs his own business or is one of many stockholders. Usually the cost of labor and materials for one year are computed, then a fixed percentage—up to 50 per cent—is added to cover overhead and profit. Even though labor, overhead, and profit are usually not considered in determining the cost of a school-shop project, you will understand industry better if you keep these factors in mind. When figuring the costs of your projects, estimate what an industrial firm would charge for the same products.

18 Making A Layout

The ability to lay out work accurately is one of the distinguishing characteristics of a skilled woodworker. Fig. 18-1. The old adage, "Measure twice and cut once," is good advice since once material is cut there is no way to make it longer. The popular suggestion, "Get a board stretcher," indicates that too often an in-

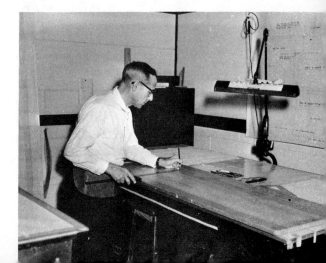

18-1. This skilled furniture designer is preparing to make a "layout on the rod" for the full-size table drawing mounted on the wall.

213

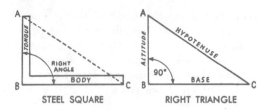

18-2. This right triangle shows the relationship of the three sides.

STEEL SQUARE (CARPENTER'S, FRAMING, OR RAFTER)

For all types of layout, no tool is used more often by the cabinetmaker and finish carpenter than the steel square. (This square is used extensively to determine rafter length. However, this use will not be discussed here because it is a part of rough carpentry and building construction.)

The steel square has two arms which make an angle of 90 degrees (a right angle). As you see in Fig. 18-2, if points **A** and **C** are connected and a straight line drawn, a triangle is formed (ABC), with the angle **B** a right angle and the triangle a right triangle. A right triangle is a figure having three sides: base, altitude, and hypotenuse. The hypotenuse is the longest side and is always opposite the right angle.

The arms of a steel square are called the *body*, or *blade*, and the *tongue*. Fig. 18-3. The body, which is longer and wider, is normally 2" x 24". The tongue is usually 1¼" x 16". The *heel* is the point where the body and the tongue meet on the outer edge. The *face* is the side that is visible when the body is held

correct layout has been made and the stock cut too short.

There are many methods of using drawings (or their equivalent) for making layouts. When working alone, the usual practice is to follow a drawing or sketch and the plan of procedure. The dimensions from the drawing are transferred to the stock, then the cutting, shaping, and assembling are done. Other common methods are the use of *route sheets with accompanying detail drawings of each part* and *layout on the rod*, which is explained later in this unit. Both methods are used in the furniture industry, but route sheets are more common. See Unit 65. The cabinetmaker and finish carpenter, however, have frequent need for the rod.

18-3. Steel square, with tables and scales identified.

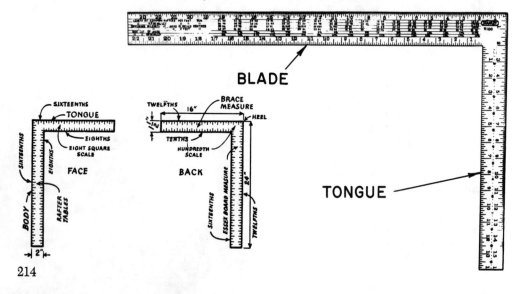

in the left hand and the tongue in the right hand. The *back* is the opposite of the face.

Scales

There are two types of markings on a square: the *scales* and *tables*. The scales are the inch divisions and the graduations in fractions of an inch found on the outer and inner edges of the square. The following scales and graduations are found on the square.

Face of body, outside edge: inches and sixteenths.

Face of body, inside edge: inches and eighths.

Face of tongue, outside edge: inches and sixteenths.

Face of tongue, inside edge: inches and eighths.

Back of body, outside edge: inches and twelfths.

Back of body, inside edge: inches and sixteenths.

Back of tongue, outside edge: inches and twelfths.

Back of tongue, inside edge: inches and tenths.

There is also a hundredth scale located on the back of the tongue in the corner near the brace measure. This scale is one inch divided into one hundred parts. The longer lines represent twenty-five hundredths and the shorter lines five hundredths.

The scales on the square can be used for measurement and layout work that is done on stock. The square can also be used for marking out stock for cutting and for hundreds of other uses.

Tables

Besides the rafter tables, which are found on the face, the square has several other important tables and measures.

The *octagon scale*, or eight-square scale, is found along the center of the tongue face and is used for laying out

lines to cut an eight-square or octagonal piece from a square one. For example, suppose it is necessary to cut an octagon from an 8″ square piece. Through the center of the stock, draw lines AB and CD parallel to the sides and at right angles to each other. Fig. 18-4. With dividers, take as many squares from the scale as there are inches in the width of the stock (8) and lay off this space on both sides of points A, B, C, and D. When these points are connected, as by lines Ab, bc, and cD, you will have a perfect octagon.

The *brace measure* is found along the center of the tongue back and is used to find the exact length of common braces. For example, if the length on both the vertical and horizontal equals 39″, to find the length of a brace you would first find number 39 on the brace meas-

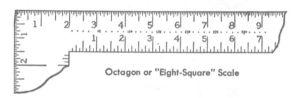

Octagon or "Eight-Square" Scale

18-4(a). Octagon scale on the face of the tongue.

18-4(b). Layout of an octagon on the end of a square piece of material.

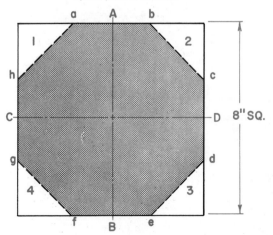

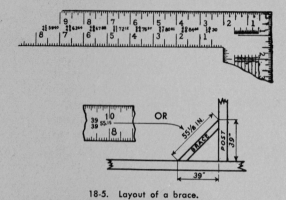

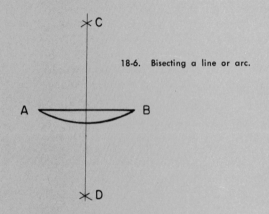

18-5. Layout of a brace.

18-6. Bisecting a line or arc.

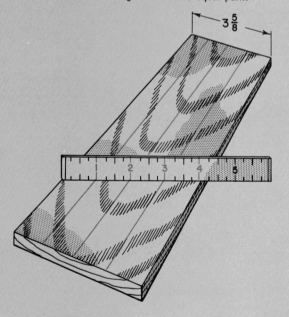

18-7. Dividing a board into equal parts.

ure. Immediately behind it you will find the number 55.1 which is approximately $55\frac{1}{8}''$. Fig. 18-5. For braces in which the vertical and horizontal measurements are different, make use of the rafter tables to find the exact length, since the brace is actually a rafter. (A complete discussion of rafter tables is given in the book *Woodworking for Industry*, by John L. Feirer, Chas. A. Bennett Co., Inc., Peoria, Ill., 1963.)

The *Essex board measure*, which is used to find the board or surface measure of lumber, is discussed in detail in Unit 15.

GEOMETRIC CONSTRUCTION

Many layouts contain geometric shapes. Some of these, such as a circle, square, triangle, or rectangle, are very simple. Many other constructions are used by designers. A few of the more common ones include:

• *Bisecting a line or an arc (dividing it in two equal parts).*

1. To bisect the line or arc *AB*, adjust a compass to a radius greater than one half *AB*.

2. With *A* and *B* as centers, draw arcs that intersect at *C* and *D*.

3. Draw line *CD*. This will divide the line or arc *AB* into two equal parts. Fig. 18-6.

• *Dividing a line into several equal parts.*

This procedure is used frequently with material of odd width. Suppose you want to divide a board $3\frac{5}{8}''$ wide into four equal parts. Hold the rule at an angle across the board with one end of the rule on one edge and the 4″ mark on the other. Fig. 18-7. Mark a point at 1″, 2″, and at 3″. This is the way to do it in drawing. Fig. 18-8.

1. Draw a line of any length, *AB*.

216

2. Draw a line, *AC*, at any acute angle to *AB*.

3. Starting at point *A*, lay off several equal divisions with a dividers, compass, or rule. The number of divisions should equal the number of parts into which you wish to divide line *AB*.

4. Draw a line from the end of *C* to point *B*.

5. Draw lines parallel to *BC* at the division on *AC*. These lines will intersect *AB* and divide it into equal parts.

• *Bisecting an angle.*

1. Draw the given angle *BAC*. Fig. 18-9.

2. Adjust the compass to a radius of about 3/4″.

3. With *A* as the center, strike an arc intersecting *AB* at *D* and *AC* at *E*.

4. Adjust the compass to a radius of more than half *ED*.

5. With *D* and *E* as centers, strike two arcs that intersect at *F*.

6. Draw the line *AF* to divide the angle into equal parts.

• *Drawing an arc at a square corner.*

Many projects have rounded corners to improve the appearance of the object and for utility. In geometry this would be called drawing an arc tangent to lines at 90 degrees. Fig. 18-10.

1. Draw the two lines, *AB* and *AC*, that intersect at *A*.

2. Determine the radius of the arc.

3. Measure in from lines *AC* and *AB* this distance and draw parallel lines to these lines that intersect at *D*.

4. Use *D* as the center and draw the arc.

5. This procedure may be followed in the shop as shown in Fig. 18-11.

• *Drawing an arc tangent to two lines that are not at right angles.* Fig. 18-12. Sometimes an irregular-shaped object has a rounded corner. This can be shown as follows:

217

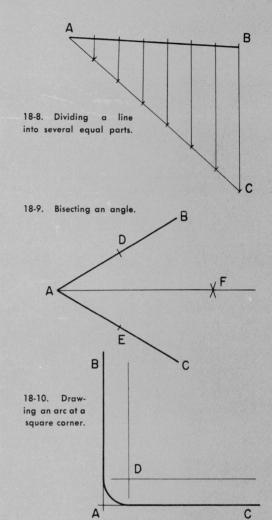

18-8. Dividing a line into several equal parts.

18-9. Bisecting an angle.

18-10. Drawing an arc at a square corner.

18-11. The shop method of drawing an arc at a square corner. Determine the radius of the arc. Mark this distance from the corner on the adjacent side and end. Hold a try square against the edge and end, and draw two lines to locate the center. Use a dividers to draw the arc.

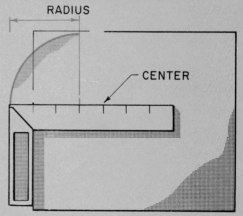

RADIUS

CENTER

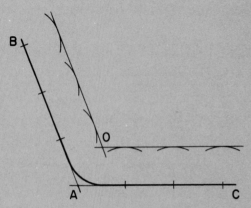

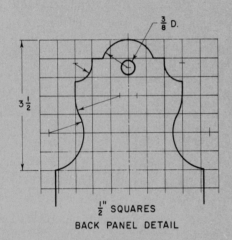

18-12. Drawing an arc tangent to two lines that are not at right angles.

$\frac{3}{8}$ D.

$3\frac{1}{2}$

$\frac{1}{2}$" SQUARES

BACK PANEL DETAIL

18-13. Drawing of the back panel detail showing the tangent arcs.

18-14. Drawing a series of tangent arcs that join.

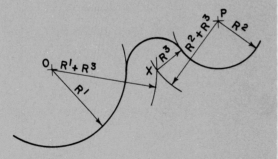

1. Draw two lines to represent the edges of the materials, *AB* and *AC*.

2. Determine the desired radius of the arc.

3. Adjust the compass or dividers to this amount.

4. At several points along both lines, draw small arcs e, f, g, h, etc.

5. Draw straight lines tangent to these arcs until they intersect at *O*.

6. Using *O* as center, strike the arc.

• *Drawing tangent arcs.* Many irregular-shaped objects such as Early American furniture pieces have arcs or circles that are tangent. Fig. 18-13. Arcs or circles are tangent when they touch at only one point but do not intersect. To join a series of arcs, proceed as follows: Fig. 18-14.

1. With *O* as center and *R1* as radius, draw the first arc.

2. With *P* as center and *R2* as radius, draw the second arc.

3. With *O* as center and *R1* plus *R3* as radius, strike a small arc at the approximate center location for the third arc.

4. With *P* as center and with *R2* plus *R3* as radius, strike a second arc that intersects at *X*.

5. With *X* as center and *R3* as radius, strike the last arc.

• *Drawing an arc with a given radius tangent to a straight line and a circle or arc.* Fig. 18-15. The procedure is used often in drawing wood parts. Proceed as follows:

1. Draw line *AB* to the desired length.

2. With *B* as center and with a compass adjusted to radius *R1*, draw arc *CD*.

3. Draw a line (*EF*) the given radius (*R2*) above and parallel to the line *AB*.

4. With *B* as center and with *R1* plus *R2* as radius, strike an arc that intersects the parallel line at *G*.

5. With *G* as center and the compass

218

set at *R2*, draw the arc joining the straight line and the arc or circle.

•*Drawing an octogon.* An octogon has eight equal sides and angles. Fig. 18-16. This shape is often used for wood products such as wastepaper baskets and small tables.

1. Draw a square of the size of the octagon.
2. Draw diagonal lines *AB* and *CD*.
3. Adjust the compass to half the length of one of the diagonal lines.
4. Using points, *A, B, C,* and *D* as centers, strike arcs intersecting the sides.
5. Connect the points where the arcs intersect the square.

•*Drawing a hexagon.* A hexagon has six equal sides and angles. Fig. 18-17. It is another shape we use often in woodworking.

1. Draw a circle with a radius equal to one side of the hexagon.
2. Set the compass equal to the radius of the circle.
3. Start at any point on the circle and draw an arc.
4. Move the point of the compass to this point and strike another arc. Divide the circle into six equal parts.
5. Connect these points.

•*Drawing an ellipse.* An ellipse is a regular curve that has two different diameters. It is a flattened circle. You find this shape often in the tops of tables. Fig. 18-18. Wherever anything round is shown in isometric, draw an ellipse.

1. Draw the major and minor axes at right angles to each other, *AB* and *CD*.
2. Lay out *OE* and *OF*, which are equal to *AB* minus *CD*.
3. Make *OH* and *OG* equal to three fourths of *OE* or *OF*.
4. Draw lines *EK, EL, FH, FG*.
5. Using *E* and *F* as centers and *ED* as radius, strike arcs *IJ* and *KL*.

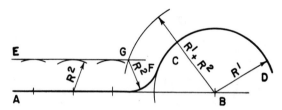

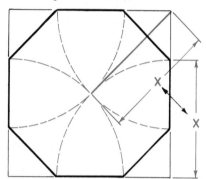

18-15. Drawing an arc with a given radius tangent to a straight line and a circle or arc.

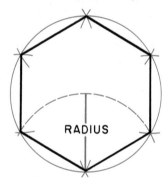

X = ½ DIAGONAL

18-16. Drawing an octagon.

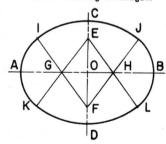

18-17. Drawing a hexagon.

18-18. Drawing an ellipse. This method can be used only if CD is at least two-thirds of AB.

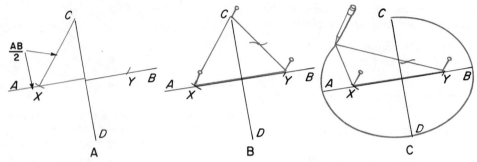

18-19. A shop method of drawing an ellipse.

6. Use *G* and *H* as centers and *GA* as radius. Strike arc *IK* and *JL*.

There is another shop method of drawing the ellipse that is very simple. You will want to use it:

1. Draw the major and minor axes *AB* and *CD*. Fig. 18-19.

2. Set the dividers equal to half the longest diameter (*AB* ÷ 2).

3. Using *C* as center, strike an arc intersecting *AB* at *X* and *Y*.

4. Place a pin at *X, Y,* and *C*. Tie a string around these three pins.

5. Take the pin at *C* away and put a pencil point in its place.

6. Hold the point of the pencil tight against the string. Carefully draw the ellipse.

ENLARGING AND TRANSFERRING AN IRREGULAR DESIGN

Projects found in books and magazines are seldom drawn to full size. If the product contains irregular parts, it is necessary first to enlarge these to full size or scale. Usually the design is drawn on grid squares, with the size of the full-scale squares indicated. For example, in Fig. 18-20, the note tells you that the squares must be 1″ in size for the enlarged drawing.

On a large piece of wrapping paper or cardboard, carefully lay out 1″ squares to equal the number in the smaller drawing. It is a good idea to letter the horizontal lines and number the vertical lines. Using these letters and numbers, locate a position on the original drawing, then transfer this point to its proper place on the full-size pattern. Continue to locate and transfer points until enough are marked for the pattern. Sketch the curves lightly freehand. Then use a French curve to darken the lines and to produce a smooth, evenly curved line.

If the piece is symmetrical (the same on both sides of a center line) you need to lay out only half of the design. Then fold the sheet of paper down the center and cut the full pattern. Place the pattern on the stock and trace around it. If the paper is thin, it may be better not to cut out the pattern but rather to transfer it to the stock by placing carbon paper between the pattern and the stock.

If many parts of the same design are to be made, it is a good idea to make a templet (pattern) of thin plywood or sheet metal from the paper pattern.

LAYOUT ON THE ROD

While a set of drawings or prints is highly desirable for most cabinetwork, it is not absolutely essential, especially for certain simpler millwork and cabinets. Another method makes use of a rod or stick on which the full-size measurements are placed. This is called *lay-*

out on the rod. Sometimes, in finish carpentry, the rod is called a *story pole* (measuring stick) and is used when cutting, installing and checking. The rod or pole is a straight, smooth piece of stock at least 1″ x 2″ or 1″ x 4″, surfaced all four sides. Its length must be slightly greater than the largest dimension of the cabinet or millwork piece.

In the planning and layout room of some furniture and cabinet shops, there are many pieces of wood (rods) with a series of marks on three or four sides. These are usually hanging over the desk or drafting table of the person responsible for making the rod layouts. If an item must be produced again, its dimensions are quickly available on the rod. This layout method is used for the following reasons:

• To provide a full-scale or full-size layout for each part of a cabinet or other structural assembly.

• To provide a quick and easy way of making a stock list or bill of materials.

• To check the material as it is being machined and assembled, to make sure it is the right size.

• To store the information for further use.

Making a Rod Layout for a Base Cabinet

The example for explaining this procedure is a simple base cabinet that

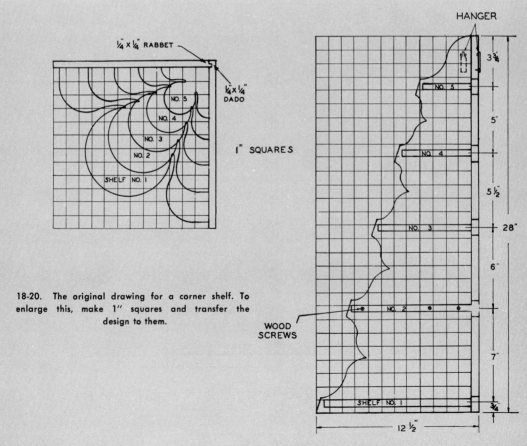

18-20. The original drawing for a corner shelf. To enlarge this, make 1″ squares and transfer the design to them.

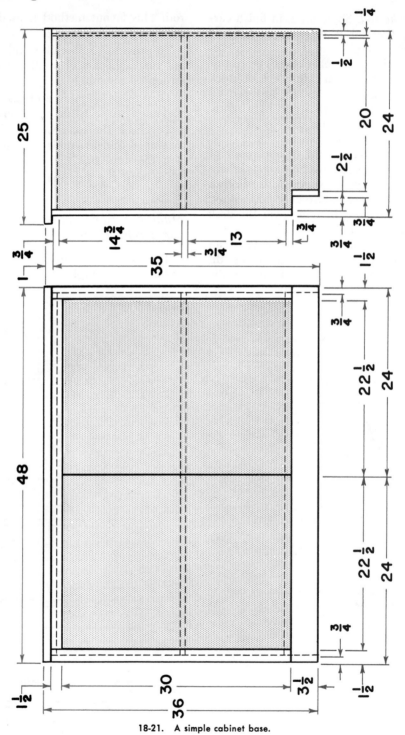

18-21. A simple cabinet base.

might be used for kitchen or other storage. Case size is 24″ x 36″ x 48″, with a 1″ finish top overhang on the front only. To simplify the explanation, all butt joints are used. Fig. 18-21. The case materials consist of the following:

- A 1″ finish top.

- Plywood 3/4″ thick for sides, top, doors, bottom, and shelf.
- Plywood 1/4″ thick for the back.
- Solid stock 3/4″ x 1½″ for face frame and toe board.

Let's proceed to make the rod layout. Fig. 18-22. Note that the edges of the

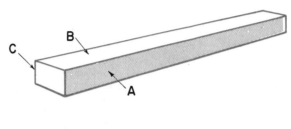

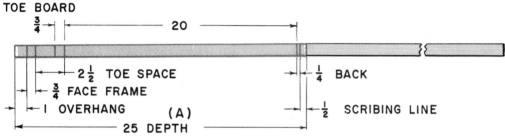

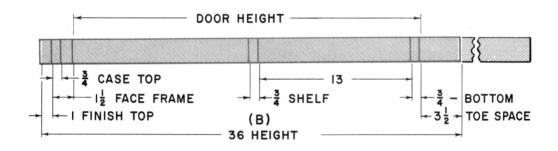

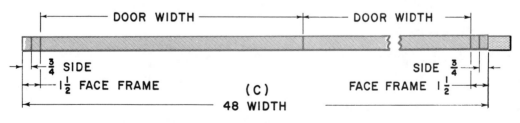

18-22. Rod layout for the cabinet.

rod are marked A and C and the surfaces B and D. Generally, only three sides, namely, A, B, and C, are needed. Side A is used for depth measurements, B for height, and C for width. The fourth side, D, could be used if a matching cabinet were to be made with a different depth, but all other dimensions the same.

1. Place the rod in front of you with the A edge up. Start from one end and mark a line 1″ away from the end to represent the overhang. Mark the next line 3/4″ away from this to represent the face frame. Measure in another 2½″ to represent the toe-space cut. Then measure back 3/4″ to represent the thickness of the toe board. Now measure and mark the overall depth of 25″. From the opposite end, measure in 1/2″ to represent the scribing line. Measure in from the scribing line 1/4″ to represent the thickness of the back.

2. Turn the rod so that side B is up, ready to use for the height layout. Measure in from the end 1″ to represent the finish top. Measure in 3/4″ from this line to represent the case top. Measure from the finish top line 1½″ to represent the face frame. Now measure 36″ and mark a line for the overall height. Measure back 3½″ to represent the toe-space cut. Measure back another 3/4″ for the bottom. Measure up 13″ to represent one face of the shelf, then another 3/4″ for the other face. Note that there is no face frame across the bottom of the cabinet so that the door height is from the face-frame line to the top of the toe-space cut.

3. Turn the rod to side C, ready to use for making the width dimensions. From the end, measure in 3/4″ to represent the thickness of the side. Measure in from the same end 1½″ to represent the face frame. Measure 48″ and mark the overall width. Then measure back 3/4″ from the other end for the thickness of the sides and then 1½″ to represent the width of the face frame. Now divide the 48″ width in the middle. Note then that the door width is the distance from the inside face-frame line to the middle of the rod. Also note that this cabinet is designed with flush doors. If lip doors were used, this would have to be taken into consideration in making the rod layout. Now drill a hole about 2″ in from the end of the rod for hanging it up for storage. If the rod is to be kept for a long time and there is danger that the ends may become damaged, it is a good idea to scribe a line completely around the rod, 1″ in from the end, and use this as the starting line.

SECTION II

QUESTIONS AND DISCUSSION TOPICS

1. Define wood. Is it a simple material to describe? Explain.
2. Name the main parts of a tree.
3. What is the function of the medullary rays?
4. Does hickory or basswood have higher specific gravity?
5. What is specific gravity?
6. What do annual rings indicate?
7. Tell how to determine the age of a tree.
8. Why is springwood often called early wood?
9. Describe the three methods of cutting lumber. Which method is used the least?
10. Hardwoods are not always harder than softwoods. Explain.
11. What is the moisture content of lumber from a freshly cut tree?
12. What is meant by fiber-saturation point?
13. Name the two methods of seasoning lumber.

14. Does lumber shrink equally in all directions when seasoned?
15. Name and describe several common natural defects in lumber.
16. What are manufacturing imperfections in lumber production?
17. Name five kinds of knots.
18. What general term describes all variations from a true or plane surface?
19. Approximately how many kinds of warp are there?
20. Define the two major classifications of woods.
21. Name five popular softwoods.
22. What governmental organization can supply detailed information on any kind of wood?
23. Is Philippine mahogany a true mahogany?
24. Name five furniture woods.
25. Why has walnut always been a popular American furniture wood?
26. What kind of finish did Thomas Chippendale use on mahogany?
27. Why was cherry the common choice for furniture made in the United States during the latter part of the Seventeenth Century?
28. What do maple and birch have in common in regard to their use in furniture?
29. What are the two main kinds of oak?
30. List five exotic woods.
31. Is teak a popular wood for Scandinavian designs? Why?
32. List some advantages of using plywood instead of solid lumber.
33. Name the two major methods of plywood construction.
34. Describe the two common methods of cutting veneer.
35. What kind of core does 3/4″ five-ply hardwood plywood have?
36. What kind of wood is used for most softwood plywood?
37. Describe several wood products and their special properties.
38. Describe hardboard.
39. How is hardboard manufactured?
40. Why can hardboard be available in so many sizes, shapes, and surface treatments?
41. What per cent of the hardboard manufactured is used by furniture makers?
42. What kind of saws should be used on hardboard in high-production work?
43. What is particle board?
44. Describe the difference between particle board and flakeboard.
45. How is particle board manufactured?
46. Name some woods used in making particle board.
47. Describe the similarities and differences in working with hardboard and particle board.
48. What kinds of items are included in millwork?
49. Describe the two major types of millwork.
50. Name five common types of moldings.
51. What are the two major purposes of fasteners?
52. Name three metals from which nails are made.
53. What is the purpose of a nail set?
54. What does *penny* mean as applied to nails?
55. What is the difference between a brad and a finishing nail?
56. Describe the two major methods of nailing.
57. What are the advantages of screws as compared with nails?
58. Describe the advantages of the Phillips head as opposed to the slotted head.
59. Are sheet metal screws used in woodworking? Why?
60. Name three types of screwdrivers.
61. What is the purpose of the shank hole and pilot hole?
62. Describe several hollow-wall fastening devices.
63. What kinds of fasteners can be used in masonry construction?
64. Name half a dozen hardware items.
65. Why is it important to select hardware before construction is completed?
66. What is glass made of?
67. Name the two major kinds of glass used in furniture making and cabinetwork.
68. Describe how to cut glass.
69. How is glass installed in cabinetwork?

70. Why is cane used in furniture construction?
71. Describe the way to install machine-made cane.
72. What is a board foot?
73. How is hardboard sold?
74. Explain the following terms: S2S, FAS, and AD.
75. Why is hardwood grading done primarily for the furniture industry?
76. Why is it difficult to explain the softwood grades?
77. What is the highest quality hardwood lumber?
78. Name the three major classes of softwood lumbers.
79. Explain why it is important to know how to purchase lumber.
80. What four things should be considered in writing lumber specifications?
81. How can the amount of lumber received from a dealer be measured or checked?
82. What is the Essex board measure and how is it used?
83. What is a print?
84. Why must print reading be mastered by the cabinetmaker?
85. What are the four basic elements of a drawing?
86. Describe or define *scale*.
87. What are the three basic kinds of pictorial drawings?
88. Describe the different drawings in a complete set for a home.
89. What is the purpose of a sectional view?
90. How is sketching done?
91. What is included in a bill of materials, materials list, or stock bill?
92. What is a plan of procedure or procedure list?
93. What factors must be included in the overall cost of an item?
94 Why is the steel square an important tool to the cabinetmaker?
95. What is meant by geometric construction?
96. Describe how to make a layout on the rod.

PROBLEMS AND ACTIVITIES

1. Obtain a section of a log and identify the parts by lettering in their names on the trunk itself or by using identification numbers and a code.
2. Using the oven-dry method, determine the moisture content of a piece of wood.
3. Get samples of four or five different woods from a lumber dealer or warehouse and identify them.
4. Describe in detail why maple and birch are the most common selections for Early American furniture.
5. Select one of the exotic woods. Study the geography of the country from which it comes, and the significance of the wood to the economy of that country.
6. Make a model of a plywood manufacturing plant.
7. Compare the working properties of several different particle boards.
8. Study the production of particle board. Gather some chips from the planer and try to make a small piece of particle board.
9. Using wood screws, study the holding power of various woods.
10. Write a report on the use of glass in the furniture industry.
11. Make a full-scale drawing of a furniture piece that you would like to build.
12. Make a rod layout for a cabinet.

Section III

Tools and Machines

Good tools and machines are needed to change raw materials into wood products. Hand- and machine-tool skills are essential for any kind of cabinetmaking. The craftsman must know how to use each tool and machine skillfully, accurately, and safely. He must also know how to care for tools and machines to keep them in good operating condition.

227

Layout, Measuring, And Checking Devices

TOOL	DESCRIPTION	USES
Bench Rule *Fig. 19—1.*	A 12-inch or one foot rule. One side is divided into eighths, the other into sixteenths.	1. To make simple measurements. 2. To adjust dividers. *Caution.* Never use as a straightedge.
Zig-Zag Rule *Fig. 19—2.*	A folding rule of six- or eight-foot length.	1. To measure distances greater than 2′, place the rule flat on the stock. 2. To measure less than 2′, it is better to use the rule on edge. (This instrument is good for inside measurement, since the reading on the brass extension can be added to the length of the rule itself.)

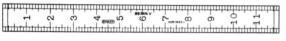

19-1.

19-2.

TOOL	DESCRIPTION	USES
Flexible Tape Rules *Fig. 19—3.*	A flexible tape that slides into a metal case. Comes in lengths of 6′, 8′, 10′, 12′, 50′, and 100′. The steel tape has a hook on the end that adjusts to true zero.	1. To measure irregular as well as regular shapes. 2. To make accurate inside measurements. (Measurement is read by adding 2″ to the reading on the blade.)
Try Square *Fig. 19—4.*	A squaring, measuring, and testing tool with a metal blade and a wood or metal handle.	1. To test a surface for levelness. 2. To check adjacent surfaces for squareness. 3. To make lines across the face or edge of stock.
Combination Square *Fig. 19—5.*	Consists of a blade and handle. The blade slides along in the handle or head. There is a level and a scriber in the handle.	1. To test a level or plumb surface. 2. To check squareness—either inside or outside. 3. To mark and test a 45-degree miter. 4. To gauge-mark a line with a pencil.

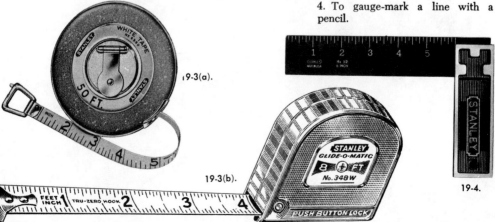

19-3(a).

19-3(b).

19-4.

228

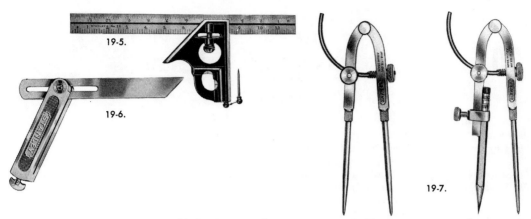

19-5.

19-6.

19-7.

Sliding T Bevel *Fig. 19—6.*	A blade that can be set at any angle to the handle. Set with a framing square or protractor.	1. To measure or transfer an angle between 0 and 180 degrees. 2. To check or test a miter cut.
Dividers *Fig. 19—7.*	A tool with two metal legs. One metal leg can be removed and replaced with a pencil. To set the dividers, hold both points on the measuring lines of the rule.	1. To lay out an arc or circle. 2. To step off measurements. 3. To divide distances along a straight line.
Framing or Rafter Square *Fig. 19—8.*	A large steel square consisting of a blade, or body, and a tongue.	1. To check for squareness. 2. To mark a line across a board. 3. To lay out rafters and stairs.
Carpenter's Level *Fig. 19—9.*	A rectangular metal or wood frame with several level glasses.	To check whether a surface is level or plumb.
Marking Gage *Fig. 19—10.*	A wood or metal tool consisting of a beam, head, and point.	To mark a line parallel to the grain of wood.
Scratch Awl *Fig. 19—11.*	A pointed metal tool with handle.	1. To locate a point of measurement. 2. To scribe a line accurately.
Trammel Points *Fig. 19—12.*	Two metal pointers that can be fastened to a long bar of wood or metal.	1. To lay out distances between two points. 2. To scribe arcs and circles, larger than those made with dividers.
Plumb Bob and Line *Fig. 19—13.*	A metal weight with a pointed end. The opposite end has a hole for attaching the cord.	1. To determine the corners of buildings. 2. To establish a vertical line.

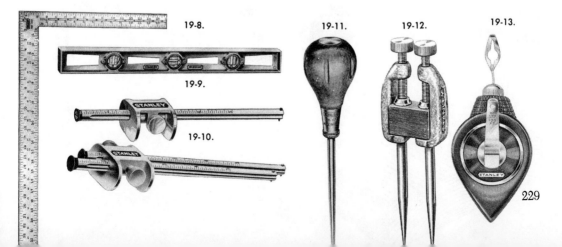

19-8.

19-9.

19-10.

19-11.

19-12.

19-13.

229

Tool	Description	Uses
Back Saw *Fig. 20—1.*	A fine-tooth, crosscut saw with a heavy metal band across the back to strengthen the thin blade.	1. To make fine cuts for joinery. 2. To use in a miter box.
Crosscut Saw *Fig. 20—2.*	A hand saw in lengths from 20″ to 26″ with from 4 to 12 points per inch. A 22″, 10 point saw is a good one for general purpose work.	1. To cut across grain. 2. Can be used to cut with the grain. *Caution:* Never cut into nails or screws. Never twist off strips of waste stock.

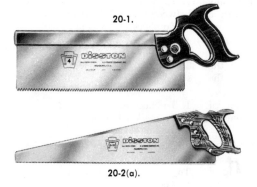

20-1.

20-2(b).

20-2(a).

Tool	Description	Uses
Rip Saw *Fig. 20—3.*	A hand saw in lengths from 20″ to 28″. A 26″, 5½-point saw is good for general use.	To cut with the grain. *Caution:* Support the waste stock. Never allow end of saw to strike the floor.
Compass Saw *Fig. 20—4.*	A 12″ or 14″ taper blade saw.	1. To cut gentle curves. 2. To cut inside curves.
Keyhole Saw *Fig. 20—5.*	A 10″ or 12″ narrow taper saw with fine teeth.	To cut small openings and fine work.

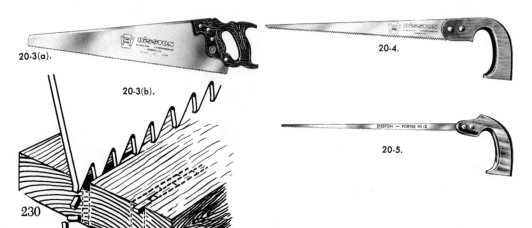

20-3(a).

20-3(b).

20-4.

20-5.

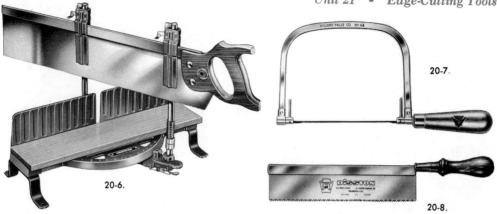

20-7.

20-6.

20-8.

Tool	Description	Uses
Miter Box Saw *Fig. 20–6.*	A longer back saw (24″ to 28″).	Used in a homemade or commercial miter box for cutting miters or square ends.
Coping Saw *Fig. 20–7.*	A U-shaped saw frame permitting 4⅝″ or 6½″ deep cuts. Uses standard 6½″ pin-end blades.	1. To cut curves. 2. To shape the ends of molding for joints. 3. For scroll work.
Dovetail Saw *Fig. 20–8.*	An extremely thin blade with very fine teeth.	For smoothest possible joint cuts.

21 Edge-Cutting Tools

TOOL	DESCRIPTION	USES
Smooth Plane *Fig. 21–1.*	A 7″ to 9″ plane.	1. For general use. 2. For smaller work.
Jack Plane *Fig. 21–2.*	A 14″ or 15″ plane.	1. Ideal for rough surfaces where chip should be coarse. 2. Also used to obtain a smooth, flat surface.
Fore Plane *Fig. 21–3.*	An 18″ plane.	For fine flat finish on longer surfaces and edges.
Jointer Plane *Fig. 21–4.*	A 22″ or 24″ plane.	1. To smooth and flatten edges for making a close-fitting joint. 2. For planing long boards such as the edges of doors.

21-1.

21-2.

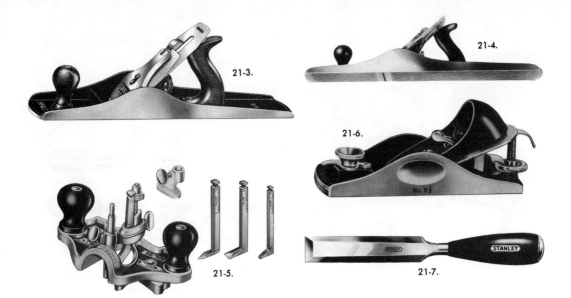

21-3.

21-4.

21-6.

No. 9½

21-5.

21-7.

Router Plane *Fig. 21—5.*	A cutting tool with several cutters.	To surface the bottom of grooves and dadoes.
Block Plane *Fig. 21—6.*	A small plane with a single, low-angle cutter with the bevel up.	1. To plane end grain. 2. For small pieces. 3. For planing the ends of molding, trim, and siding.
Chisels *Fig. 21—7.*	A set usually includes blade widths from ⅛″ to 2″.	To trim and shape wood.
Draw Knife *Fig. 21—8.*	An open-bevelled blade with handles on both ends.	**To remove much material in a short time.**
Surform Tool *Fig. 21—9.*	Available in plane file type. Also round, or block-plane types. A blade with 45-degree cutting teeth.	For all types of cutting and trimming.
Gouges *Fig. 21—10.*	A chisel with a curved blade. Sharpened on the inside or, more commonly, on the outside.	To cut grooves or to shape irregular openings.
Hatchet *Fig. 21—11.*	A cutting tool with a curved edge on one side and a hammer head on the other. Has hammer-length handle.	To trim pieces to fit in building construction. For nailing flooring.

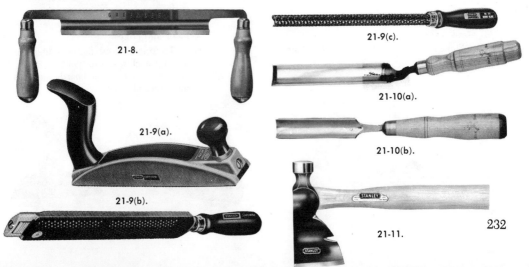

21-8.

21-9(c).

21-9(a).

21-10(a).

21-9(b).

21-10(b).

21-11.

232

21-12.

21-14.

21-13.

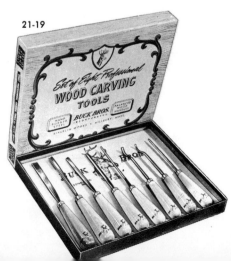

21-15.

Spokeshave *Fig. 21—12.*	A small plane-like tool	To form irregularly shaped objects.
Hand Scraper *Fig. 21—13.*	A blade-like tool.	To scrape the surface of open-grain wood.
Cabinet Scraper *Fig. 21—14.*	A blade in a holder.	To scrape the surface of furniture woods.
Utility Knife *Fig. 21—15.*	An all-purpose knife with retractable blade.	1. To cut and trim wood, veneer, hardboard, and particle board. 2. To make accurate layouts.
Edge-trimming Plane *Fig. 21—16.*	A 6″ edge-cutting plane with a cutter that works on a skew.	To trim or square the edges of boards up to ⅞″ wide for a square or close fit.
Rabbet Plane *Fig. 21—17.*	A small, accurate plane with the sides and bottom ground square to each other.	1. For fine cabinetwork or any job that requires extreme accuracy. 2. Front can be removed to use as chisel to remove glue or uneven places in corners. 3. For trimming a rabbet.
Model-makers Plane *Fig. 21—18.*	A small plane with the bottom curved in both directions.	For planing concave, curved surfaces.
Carving Tools *Fig. 21—19.*	Gouges and chisels of various shapes and sizes. Common types include the skew or flat chisel, parting tool, veiner gouges, and fluters.	1. For making angular and curved cuts. 2. For hand carving designs in furniture. 3. For shaping wood patterns.

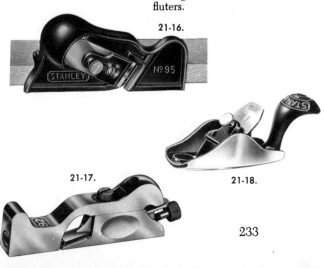

21-16.

21-19

21-17.

21-18.

233

TOOL	DESCRIPTION	USES
Auger Bit *Fig. 22–1.*	May be either single-twist or double-twist bit. Comes in sizes from No. 4 (¼″) to No. 16 (1″).	1. To bore holes ¼″ or larger. 2. Single twist bit is better for boring deep holes.
Dowel Bit *Fig. 22–2.*	A shorter bit with a sharper twist.	To bore holes for making dowel joints.
Expansion Bit *Fig. 22–3.*	A bit that holds cutters of different sizes. Sometimes this tool is called an expansive bit.	1. To bore a hole larger than 1″. 2. One cutter will bore holes in the 1″ to 2″ range. 3. A second cutter will bore holes in the 2″ to 3″ range.
Brace *Fig. 22–4.*	Two common types—the plain for a full swing, and the ratchet for close corners.	To hold and operate bits.
Foerstner Bit *Fig. 22–5.*	A bit with a flat cutting surface on the end.	1. To bore a shallow hole with a flat bottom. 2. To bore a hole in thin stock. 3. To bore a hole in end grain. 4. To enlarge an existing hole.
Bit or Depth Gages *Fig. 22–6.*	Two types—one is a solid clamp, the other a spring type.	To limit the depth of a hole.
Twist Drill *(a)* or Bit Stock Drill *(b)* *Fig. 22–7.*	A fractional-sized set from ¹⁄₆₄″ to ½″ is best.	To drill small holes for nails, screws, etc.

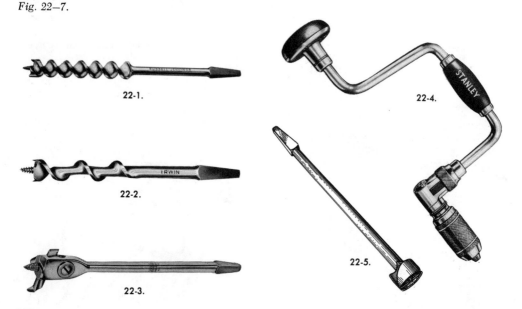

22-1.

22-2.

22-3.

22-4.

22-5.

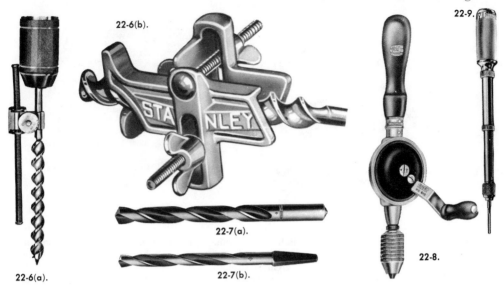

22-6(b).

22-9.

22-7(a).

22-7(b).

22-8.

22-6(a).

Hand Drill *Fig. 22—8.*	A tool with a 3-jaw chuck.	To hold twist-drills for drilling small holes.
Automatic Drill *Fig. 22—9.*	A tool with drill points and handle. Drill point sizes: #1 = $1/16''$; #2 = $5/64''$; #3 = $3/32''$; #4 = $7/64''$; #5 = $1/8''$; #6 = $9/64''$; #7 = $5/32''$; #8 = $11/64''$.	To drill many small holes.

(23) Metalworking Tools*

TOOL	DESCRIPTION	USES
Hacksaw *Fig. 23—1.*	A U-shaped frame with handle. Uses replaceable metal-cutting blades.	To cut all types of metal fasteners, hardware, and metal parts.
Cold Chisel *Fig. 23—2.*	A tool-steel chisel with cutting edge especially hardened and tempered for cutting metal. Angle between bevel surfaces is about 60 degrees.	1. To cut off a rivet or nail. 2. To get a tight or rusted nut started.

23-1.

23-2.

*In cabinetmaking, many metalworking tools are needed to set up and adjust machinery and to work with metal hardware and fasteners.

235

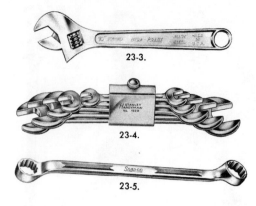

23-3.

23-4.

23-5.

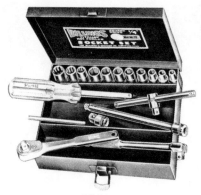

23-6.

Adjustable Wrench *Fig. 23—3.*	An extra-strong, lightweight, thin-jawed tool with one adjustable jaw. Wrench develops greatest strength when hand pressure is applied to the side that has the fixed jaw.	1. To make adjustments on machines, when there is plenty of clearance. 2. To install and replace knives and blades.
Open-end Wrench *Fig. 23—4.*	A non-adjustable wrench with accurately machined openings on either end. Sizes of openings are stamped on the tool. For variety of work, a complete set is needed.	1. To make adjustments on machines where there is plenty of clearance. 2. To install and replace knives and blades.
Box Wrench *Fig. 23—5.*	A metal wrench with two enclosed ends. Heads are offset from 15 to 45 degrees.	To make adjustments where there is limited space for movement.
Socket Wrench Set *Fig. 23—6.*	A series of sockets using a variety of handles.	To assemble and disassemble machinery. Fits many sizes of bolts and nuts.
Vise-grip Wrench *Fig. 23—7.*	An all-purpose tool with double-lever action that locks the jaws on the work.	Used as a substitute for a vise, clamp, pipe wrench, fixed wrench, or adjustable wrench.
Pipe Wrench *Fig. 23—8.*	A tool with hardened, cut teeth on the jaws.	Used on pipes and rods, never on nuts or bolts.
Allen Wrenches *Fig. 23—9.*	Hexagonal steel bars with bent ends.	To tighten and loosen set screws that are often used to hold jointer and planer knives in cutterhead.

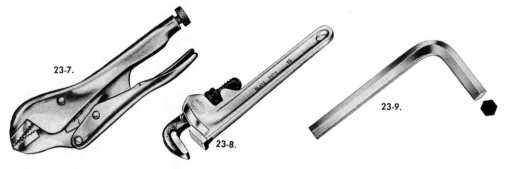

23-7.

23-8.

23-9.

236

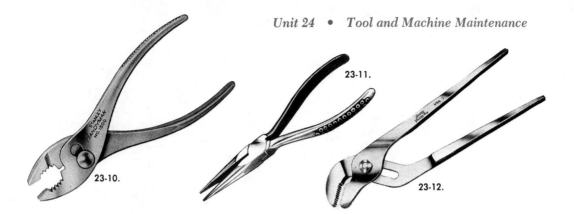

23-11.

23-10.

23-12.

Combination Pliers *Fig. 23–10.*	An all-purpose, slip-joint adjustable pliers.	To hold and turn pieces round. Never used on heads of nuts or bolts.
Long, Flat-nose Pliers *Fig. 23–11.*	Pliers with long, thin, flat nose.	To hold and bend thin wire and metal fittings.
Box-joint Utility Pliers *Fig. 23–12.*	A larger pliers with a slip joint at four positions.	To hold and turn large, round parts.

Tool And Machine Maintenance

The experienced craftsman knows the value of sharp tools. Any time taken off for sharpening tools and adjusting machines will be regained many times over in good workmanship and greater speed.

Most tool and knife sharpening can be done by the person who uses the equipment. In the case of certain types of cutting tools, particularly hand saws and the blades of circular saws and band saws, it is better to have sharpening done by a well equipped professional. Though saw filing and setting can be done by hand, generally this is too time-consuming. Also, some school and cabinet shops are not equipped with saw filing machines and sharpeners.

Grinding should be done when a tool needs a new bevel or when its edge has been nicked. *Honing* alone is enough when the edge is only slightly dull.

EQUIPMENT FOR SHARPENING

Several types of power-driven grinders can be used for sharpening tools. A *standard two-wheel grinder,* Fig. 24-1, should have a motor speed of 1425 or 1725 r.p.m. For general grinding purposes, the motor usually has a speed of 2850 or 3450 r.p.m. However, at the higher speeds care must be taken because tool edges tend to burn very easily.

Silicon-carbide wheels and stones are used primarily for sharpening high carbon tools and for knives. The harder and tougher grains of aluminum-oxide wheels and stones make them ideal for sharpening hard tool steels. Accessories

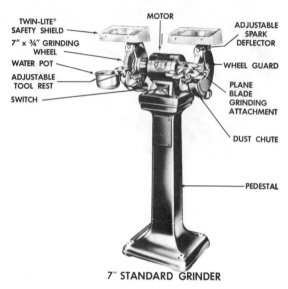

TWIN-LITE® SAFETY SHIELD — MOTOR — ADJUSTABLE SPARK DEFLECTOR — 7" x ¾" GRINDING WHEEL — WATER POT — WHEEL GUARD — ADJUSTABLE TOOL REST — PLANE BLADE GRINDING ATTACHMENT — SWITCH — DUST CHUTE — PEDESTAL

7″ STANDARD GRINDER

24-1. This standard two-wheel grinder is equipped for most types of tool grinding.

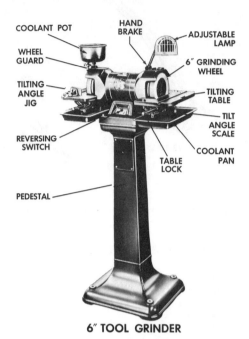

COOLANT POT — HAND BRAKE — ADJUSTABLE LAMP — WHEEL GUARD — 6″ GRINDING WHEEL — TILTING ANGLE JIG — TILTING TABLE — TILT ANGLE SCALE — REVERSING SWITCH — COOLANT PAN — TABLE LOCK — PEDESTAL

6″ TOOL GRINDER

24-3(a). A tool grinder is ideal for many types of grinding. The coolant pot can be placed over either wheel. Note the large pans for catching the coolant when doing wet grinding.

24-2. This plane-blade grinding attachment is ideal for sharpening plane irons, wood chisels, and other single-edge tools. The blade is securely held in place and the attachment adjusted for correct angle. The tool is moved back and forth across the abrasive wheel. Also the tool can be lifted off to inspect the cutting edge or cool it in water.

are available for grinding drills and plane blades on the standard tool grinder. Fig. 24-2.

The *tool grinder* is designed for grinding all types and shapes of edge tools. It is well suited for sharpening single-point tool bits that are either carbide-tipped or of high-speed steel. Fig. 24-3. For grinding carbide-tipped tools, a diamond abrasive wheel designed especially for this purpose is recommended. The tool grinder has a water pot over one abrasive wheel. This keeps the wheel lubricated for wet grinding. It also has tables on both sides that can be tilted 30 degrees in and 45 degrees out to allow for various grinding angles. A *tilting angle jig* that swings 45 degrees to the left and right can also be used for angle cutting. A reversing switch allows either right or left cutting tools to be ground while the wheel turns down towards the cutting edge. This multiple-purpose machine is larger than the standard two-wheel grinder.

Grinding wheels of the correct *size, kind of abrasive,* and *grit,* must be selected. The size of the wheel is determined by the machine on which it is to be used. The thickness and diameter of the wheel and also the arbor-hole size must be specified. The abrasive may be a natural material such as fine white Arkansas stone, or it may be a silicon carbide or aluminum-oxide wheel. See Unit 36. The grit number indicates whether it is coarse, medium, or fine. A 36-grit is a coarse wheel, 60-grit is medium, and 120 is fine. A good selection for a standard two-wheel grinder, for example, would be an aluminum-oxide wheel, 3/4″ x 7″, with 3/4″ arbor hole, either 60-grit or 120-grit. For general-purpose grinding, a 36-grit wheel may be selected.

After considerable use, grinding wheels become clogged with metal and wear down unevenly. They must be cleaned and straightened. While there are several tools for this, the best and simplest is a diamond-pointed wheel dresser. This is a long, thin metal rod with an industrial diamond on one end and a wood handle on the other. The tool is held firmly against the face of the revolving wheel with the rod on the tool rest. Then the face is trued by moving the dresser back and forth across it.

For hand sharpening, there are abrasive stones of all sizes and shapes. Fig.

24-4. Artificial abrasive bench stones. Their advantage is that a combination stone can be made, one side coarse and the other fine.

24-3(b). Using a diamond-pointed wheel dresser. The dresser can be placed in a tool holder as shown here or held freehand with the shaft on the tool rest. Press firmly against the wheel, then move the tool back and forth until the face is straight.

24-4. Again, these may be either natural stones, such as the Arkansas or Washita, but more often they are artificial. If the stone is artificial, half can be coarse and the other half fine. Artificial stones are oil-soaked at the factory for general sharpening of such edge tools as plane irons and chisels. A cutting oil is needed in many sharpening and honing operations for faster work, a finer edge, and to keep the stone free of chips. A good lubricant can be made of equal parts of oil and kerosene. An 8″ taper file and a 10″ mill file are needed to sharpen some tools such as hand saws.

SHARPENING HAND TOOLS

Plane-Iron Blade

Remove the double plane iron from the plane and loosen the screw that holds the cap on the plane iron. Separate the two parts. Look at the cutting edge under a good light to see if there are any nicks or if the bevel is rounded off a good deal. If so, both grinding and honing must be done. If the cutting edge is in good condition, only honing will be necessary.

Hold a try square against the cutting

239

24-5. Checking the cutting edge at a plane blade with a try square.

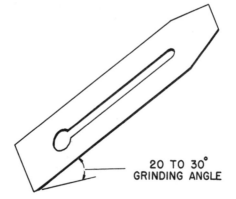

20 TO 30° GRINDING ANGLE

24-7. A plane-iron blade should be ground at an angle of 20 to 30 degrees. The length of the bevel should be about 2 to 2½ times the thickness of the blade. For general-purpose planing, the cutting edge should be straight across.

edge of the plane iron to see if it is square. Fig. 24-5. Grind off the old edge at right angles to the sides until the nicks are removed and the edge is straightened. Move the tool from left to right across the face of the wheel. Dip the tool frequently in water, if using a high-speed grinder. Friction heats the tool and the cutting edge will lose its hardness if it is allowed to get too hot and turn blue. If a grinding attachment is available, fasten the blade to it with the bevel side down. If you don't have a grinding attachment, the blade must be held freehand against the wheel. Fig. 24-6. Use the adjustable tool rest to support the blade. The bevel should be 2 to 2½ times the thickness of the blade to give a 20- to 30-degree angle. Fig. 24-7. Continue to grind the blade until a wire edge (a very thin burr) appears.

Now hone the blade. Apply a few drops of oil or lubricant to the face of an oilstone. Place the blade at a very low angle to the surface, bevel side down. Raise the end slowly until the blade makes an angle of about 30 to 35 degrees with the stone. Fig. 24-8. Note

24-8. Whetting a plane-iron blade by moving it back and forth in a straight line.

24-6. Grinding a plane-iron blade without a guide. With this method, hold the blade at the desired angle to the wheel and move it back and forth as it is being ground. This requires considerable skill to keep the bevel even.

24-9. Another method of honing the edge is to move the tool in a figure-eight pattern.

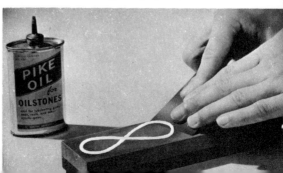

that honing puts a second bevel on the tool. When this honed bevel becomes too long, it is necessary to regrind the tool.

Move the blade back and forth in a straight line or a figure eight. Fig. 24-9. Be sure to hold the blade so the angle will remain the same throughout the stroke. Then turn the blade over and place it flat on the stone. Move it back and forth to remove the burr. Fig. 24-10. Make sure the blade is held perfectly flat. The slightest bevel on the back side will prevent the cap from fitting properly. The chips will get between the cap and the blade, making it impossible to do a good job of planing. Fig. 24-11.

The plane iron can be checked for sharpness in one of several ways. One method is to hold it with the cutting edge down and allow the edge to rest lightly on your thumb nail. As the tool is moved, it tends to "bite" into the nail if it is sharp. If dull, it will slide across easily. Another method is to look closely at the edge. If it is sharp, the edge can't be seen. If it is dull, a thin, white line can be seen. A third method is to cut paper with the plane iron. Fig. 24-12.

Wood Chisel

The chisel is ground and honed in exactly the same way as the plane iron. The angle of the chisel should be from 20 degrees for softwoods to 27 degrees for hardwoods. An angle of about 25 degrees is best for general-purpose work. Notice that plane-iron blades and hand chisels are *hollow-ground;* that is, the major bevel is ground with a slight curve, then a secondary bevel is formed to produce the actual cutting edge.

Auger Bit

Choose a small flat or triangular auger bit file or a small auger-bit stone. Clamp the auger bit in a vise with the cutting end up, or hold the tool over the edge of a bench. File across the inside of the

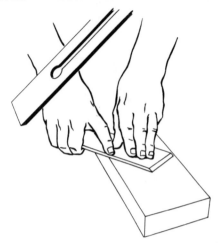

24-10. Removing the burr from the cutting edge by holding the back side of the blade flat on the stone.

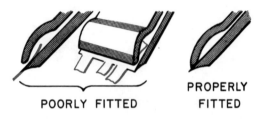

POORLY FITTED   PROPERLY FITTED

24-11. This is what happens if the back of the blade has a bevel on it or if the cap edge is rounded.

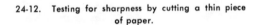

24-12. Testing for sharpness by cutting a thin piece of paper.

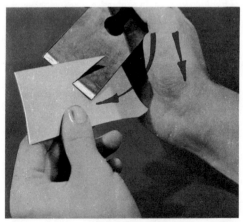

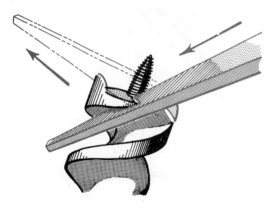

24-13(a). The auger bit must be sharpened at four points. Note that the file is sharpening the cutting edge and the shadow file is sharpening the spur. This must be done equally on both sides.

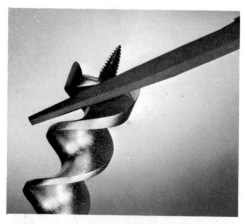

24-13(b). Using a thin abrasive stone to hone the cutting edge. Be careful to retain the original angle of the bevel.

24-14. Honing the cutting edge of a draw knife.

spurs. Fig. 24-13. Never touch the outside spurs as this will change the size of the bit. Also file the lips on the underside or the side toward the shank. Keep the bits in good condition by cleaning off pitch with a solvent.

Draw Knife

If grinding is necessary, the draw knife can be sharpened on a power grinder in the same general manner as a plane iron. The honing can be done in one of two ways. One method is to place a larger stone on the table or bench. Hold the draw knife by its handles at the correct angle to the surface of the stone. Draw it across diagonally so that all parts are equally honed. Fig. 24-14. Another method is to hold the tool with one handle against the top of the bench and the other handle in your hand. Then hold a small oilstone in the other hand and move it back and forth along the bevel at a slightly higher angle to hone a keen edge.

Screwdriver

The screwdriver should be ground with a very light taper on the sides and edges, and the end perfectly flat. Fig. 24-15. A rounded end or sides that are too sharp will cause slipping and burring. The screwdriver can be sharpened on a grinding wheel or with a coarse abrasive stone. Fig. 24-16.

Countersink

Sharpen the faces of the cutting edges. Don't change the shape or angle of the tool by grinding the outside bevel.

Woodturning Tools

The correct shape and grinding angles for each of the woodturning tools is shown in Fig. 24-17. If the tools are to be used for cutting (in contrast to scraping), they must be ground and honed with a flat bevel. Any secondary bevel

242

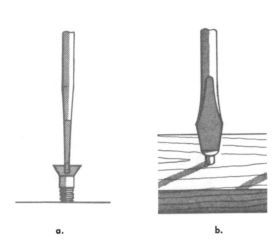

a.   b.

24-15. The tip of a screwdriver should look like this. a. Edge. b. Side.

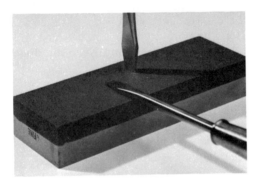

24-16. Sharpening the tip of a screwdriver with a coarse abrasive stone.

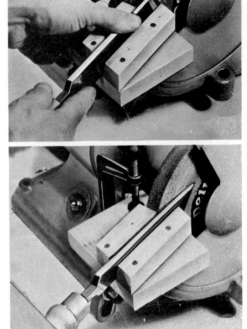

24-18. The bevels on the skew should be ground flat. This simple wood jig will make the work easier.

on the skew, for example, will keep it from cutting. This is not important if the tools are used for scraping. The skew can be ground on the side of a straight or recessed grinding wheel. While the grinding can be done freehand, it is better to use a wood jig, as shown in Fig. 24-18. Hold the chisel against one of the

24-17. The correct shape and grinding angles for wood-turning tools.

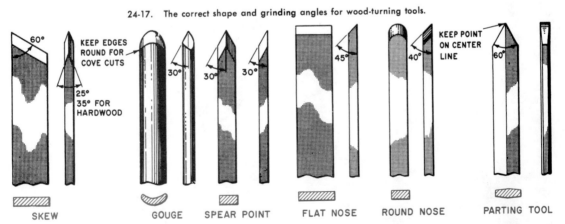

60°

KEEP EDGES ROUND FOR COVE CUTS

25° 35° FOR HARDWOOD

30°   30°   30°

45°   40°

KEEP POINT ON CENTER LINE

60°

SKEW   GOUGE   SPEAR POINT   FLAT NOSE   ROUND NOSE   PARTING TOOL

24-19(a). Hold the skew at exactly the same angle when honing. Don't hone a secondary bevel, especially if the tool is used for cutting.

24-20. Grinding a gouge on a cup wheel.

beveled guide blocks first and then against the other side. When honing the skew, maintain the same angle. Fig. 24-19.

A gouge can be ground in one of several ways. The best method is to use a cup wheel mounted on a wood or metal lathe. The curved interior surface of the wheel helps to shape the cutting edge and less rolling of the tool is required. Fig. 24-20. The gouge can also be shaped by rolling the tool against the face or side of a standard grinding wheel. Fig.

24-21. The honing is done on a gouge slipstone. Hold the stone in one hand and place the convex side of the tool in the concave side of the stone. Fig. 24-22. Hone by pushing the gouge forward and rotating at the same time. Keep the stone flat so that the back edge is not beveled. Fig. 24-23.

Spear-point, flat-nose, and parting tools all require flat-angle grinding and honing that can be done freehand or with a simple jig. The round nose is sharpened in a similar manner to the gouge.

24-21. Grinding a gouge on the face of a flat wheel. In this method, the tool must be rolled to keep the same angle of bevel all around the tool.

24-19(b). A fine wheel can also be used for honing.

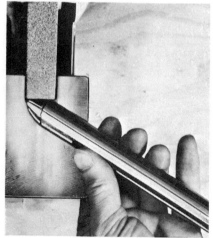

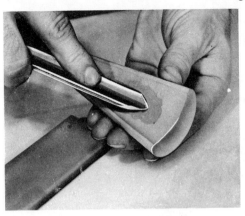

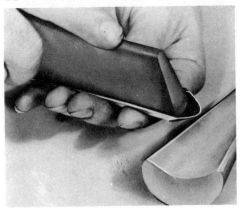

24-22. Honing on outside bevel.

SHARPENING A HAND SAW

Jointing means bringing all the teeth to the same height. This needs to be done only when the teeth are uneven and incorrectly shaped. To joint a saw, place it in a clamp, with the handle to the right. Fig. 24-24. Lay a mill file lengthwise, flat upon the teeth. Pass it lightly back and forth along the length of the blade on the tops of the teeth until the file touches the top of every tooth. Do not allow the file to tip to one side or the other. Fig. 24-27.

Examine the tooth edge of the saw to see if the teeth are uniform in size and shape and if they are properly set. It is not necessary to reset the teeth of a well tempered hand saw every time it needs sharpening. If the teeth are touched up with a file from time to time as the saw is used, the saw will cut better and longer, and sufficient set will remain to enable the saw to clear itself. Study the shape of the teeth. Teeth of saws for crosscutting should be shaped as shown in Fig. 24-25. Teeth of the ripsaw should be shaped like those in Fig. 24-26. A saw cannot give good service unless the teeth are even and uniform in size and properly shaped.

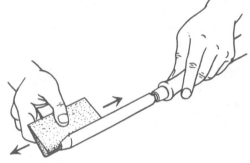

24-23. Honing the inside of a gouge.

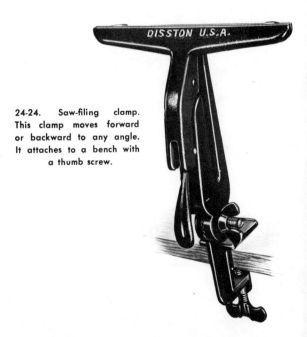

24-24. Saw-filing clamp. This clamp moves forward or backward to any angle. It attaches to a bench with a thumb screw.

245

CROSSCUT HAND SAW

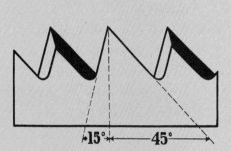

Cross-Cut Saw Teeth

The cross-cut saw is designed for cutting *across the grain* and cuts on the *push stroke*. The front face of cross-cut teeth have an angle of 15 degrees; the back angle is 45 degrees. The beveling of the edges of the teeth of about 24 degrees gives the appearance of a series of *knife-like points* which makes for easy identification of a cross-cut saw.

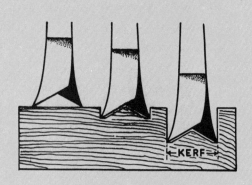

Cross Section of Cross-Cut Teeth

Notice first the "set" of the teeth . . . the bending of the teeth to alternate sides to make the cut or "kerf" wider than the thickness of the saw blade. For even greater clearance, best quality saws are taper ground . . . thinner at the point and back than at butt and teeth. In the above illustrations of the saw cutting into wood, note the knife action, the paring action and the full cut.

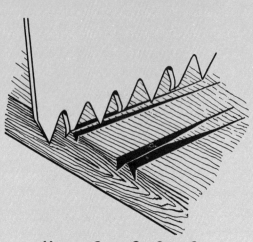

How a Cross-Cut Saw Cuts

The teeth first score the wood like points of two parallel knife blades as the saw is drawn across the grain. Then the edges of the teeth begin paring the groove which is formed and clear the sawdust from the kerf.

TOP VIEW OF CROSS-CUT TEETH

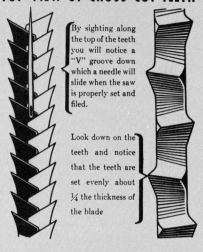

By sighting along the top of the teeth you will notice a "V" groove down which a needle will slide when the saw is properly set and filed.

Look down on the teeth and notice that the teeth are set evenly about $\frac{1}{4}$ the thickness of the blade

24-25. An understanding of the cutting edges of the crosscut hand saw will help in sharpening the tool.

RIP HAND SAW

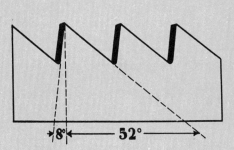

Rip Saw Teeth

The rip saw is designed for cutting *with the grain* and cuts on the *push stroke*. The front face of rip teeth has an angle of 8 degrees; the back angle is 52 degrees. Rip teeth are filed straight across the face and give the appearance of a series of *chisel edges*.

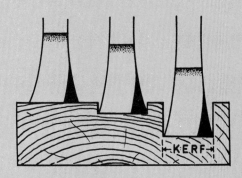

Cross Section of Rip Teeth

Examination of the kerf of a rip saw in action clearly illustrates the chisel-like action with which the rip saw cuts. Observe first how the rip saw cuts into the board. Width of the kerf is determined by the set of the teeth, which are bent alternately to the right and left approximately 1/8 of their thickness.

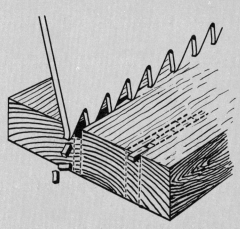

How a Rip Saw Cuts

Rip teeth cut like vertical chisels. First on one side of the set small pieces of wood are cut loose across the grain and pushed out. Then on the other side, the tooth following plows out a similar particle.

TOP VIEW OF RIP SAW TEETH

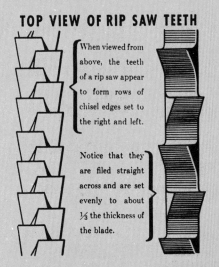

When viewed from above, the teeth of a rip saw appear to form rows of chisel edges set to the right and left.

Notice that they are filed straight across and are set evenly to about 1/8 the thickness of the blade.

24-26. Note how the rip hand saw differs from the crosscut hand saw.

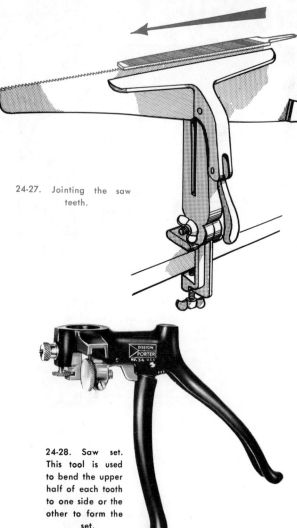

24-27. Jointing the saw teeth.

24-28. Saw set. This tool is used to bend the upper half of each tooth to one side or the other to form the set.

24-29. Correct size files for saw filing.

Jointing teeth—8" or 10" Mill Bastard File

Sharpening Teeth—4½, 5½, 6 points—7" Slim Taper

7, 8 points—6" Slim Taper

9, 10 points—5" or 6" Slim Taper

11, 12, 13, 14, 15 points—4½" Slim Taper

After jointing, all teeth must be filed to the correct shape. The gullets (low parts between the teeth) must be equal in depth. Fronts and backs of the teeth must have proper shape and angle. The teeth must be uniform in size. (Note that merely shaping the teeth does not sharpen them.) Place the file well down in the gullet, then file straight across the saw, at right angles to the blade. If the teeth are unequal in size, press the file against the teeth that have the largest tops until you reach the center of the flat top made by jointing. Then move the file to the next gullet and file until the remainder of the top disappears and the tooth has been brought up to a point.

The purpose of *setting* the teeth of saws (springing over the upper part of each tooth, one to the right and the next to the left) is to make the saw cut a kerf (groove) that is slightly wider than the blade. Fig. 24-28. This prevents friction which would cause the saw to bind and push hard in the cut. Start the setting from the small end (toe) of the saw. Bend to left and right alternately. It is important that the depth of the set go no lower than half the tooth. If deeper, it is likely to spring, crimp, or crack the blade. It could even break out a tooth. Particular care must be taken to keep the set regular. It must be the same width

24-30. First position for filing a hand saw for cross-cutting.

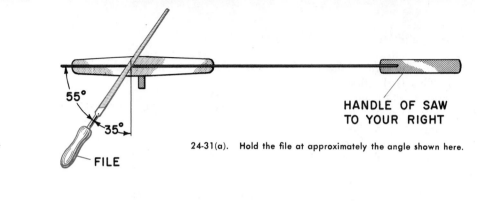

55°

35°

FILE

HANDLE OF SAW
TO YOUR RIGHT

24-31(a). Hold the file at approximately the angle shown here.

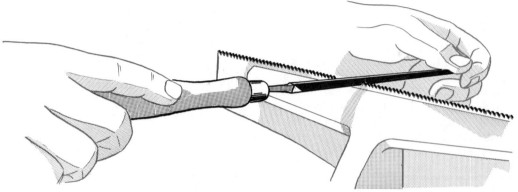

24-31(b). Make sure the file is level as the stroke is made.

from one end of the blade to the other, and the same width on both sides of the blade. Otherwise the saw will not cut true. If not properly set, the saw line and the cut will be "snaky."

Filing a Hand Saw for Crosscutting

Place the saw in a filing clamp *with the handle at the right*. Select the correct size taper file. Fig. 24-29. The bottom of the tooth gullets should be 1/8" above the clamp jaws. If more of the blade projects, the file will chatter or screech. This dulls the file quickly.

Stand at first position, shown in Fig. 24-30. Start at the point. Pick out the first tooth that is set toward you. Place the file in the gullet *to the left of this tooth*. Hold the file directly across the blade. Then swing the file handle *toward the left* to the same angle as the bevel. Keep the file at this angle and level. Be sure the file sets down well into the gullet.

Fig. 24-31. The file should cut on the push stroke. It files the back of the tooth to the left and the front of the tooth to the right at the same time. Skip the next gullet to the right but place the file in the *second* gullet from the one you just filed. Repeat the operation being careful to file at the same angle as before. Continue this way, placing the file in every second gullet until you reach the handle end of the saw.

Study the second position shown in Fig. 24-32. Turn the saw around in the clamp, *with the saw handle to the left*. Take the second position. Place the file

24-32. Second position for filing a crosscut saw.

HANDLE   FILE   CLAMP

CROSS-CUT SAW

STAND HERE→✳

in the gullet *to the right of the first set toward you.* This is the first of the gullets you skipped when filing the other side of the saw. Turn the file handle to the correct angle *toward the right.* Now file until the teeth are sharpened to a point. Continue this, placing the file in every second gullet until you reach the handle of the saw.

Filing Hand Saws for Ripping

With one exception this operation is exactly the same as for crosscut saws. This exception is that *the file is held straight across the saw,* at a right angle to the blade. The teeth should be filed to an angle of 8 degrees at the front and 52 degrees at the back. Check this angle with the protractor head of a combination set.

MACHINE TOOLS

Machines for cutting wood operate at maximum efficiency only when the cutting tools are sharp. Frequently, a little touch up with an oilstone will help if the tool is basically in good condition. However, when a knife or saw has become dull, it is necessary to have it reground. To avoid excessive sharpening costs and delays, the best practice is to buy high-quality cutting tools in the first place. Whenever possible, make use of carbide-tipped tools so that grinding will be needed less frequently.

More important, however, is to use the machines properly. This will prolong the life of cutting edges more than any other single factor. It takes only one board with a nail in it to ruin a set of planer or jointer knives. If power equipment isn't available for sharpening, saws and knives should be sent out periodically to a shop that specializes in this work. While hand methods of sharpening saws are covered in this unit, they are not recommended except for emergencies.

Refitting Narrow Band Saws by Hand

When an automatic filing machine is not available, narrow band saws may be sharpened by hand. Place the saw on a long bench so that its entire length is supported on the same level. Make sure the teeth point to the left. The clamp will hold a section of approximately 50 teeth at one time. The saw is then moved as often as necessary until all the teeth have been sharpened.

However, before filing the teeth it is the usual practice to *joint* the section slightly. This is done by lightly running a mill file over the tops of the teeth to make them uniform in height. Jointing will also assist as a guide in filing, and help keep the saw teeth as much like new as possible.

Choose taper files for sharpening narrow band saws as follows: for saws with 3, 3½, 4, 5, or 6 points—6″ band file; 7, 8, 9, or 10 points—7″ extra slim taper file.

Hold the file in a horizontal position. File each tooth straight across the saw at right angles to the blade, raising the file on the back stroke. Fig. 24-33. If the point of any tooth is not brought up

24-33. A standard band-saw blade has teeth shaped like a ripsaw. The teeth should be filed straight across with a hook from 8 to 15 degrees.

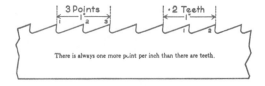

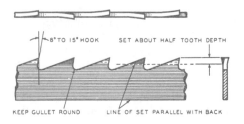

sharp after the stroke of the file, do not immediately file it again. Instead, continue until you have filed the section you are working on. By this method, each section may require two or three repetitions.

Teeth may be set with a pistol-grip saw set, as hand-saw teeth are set. When setting is necessary, it should be done before the teeth are filed. Remember that if the saw is to do only straight-line cutting, best results are obtained with the least set possible. Greater set is necessary when cutting curved lines.

Repairing a Broken Band-Saw Blade

When a band-saw blade breaks, it must be hard soldered or welded into a continuous piece. If only a small section must be removed during repair, the upper wheel can be adjusted to compensate for this. However, if a bent section must be removed, it is necessary to add a piece of the same kind and size. If the blade is to be hard (silver) soldered by brazing, a scarf joint that is one or two teeth long should be filed. Apply brazing flux and a small amount of silver solder. Place the ends together and clamp in position. Turn on the electricity until the joint becomes red hot and the solder melts. Then turn off the electricity and press the handle down firmly to hold the joint together for three or four seconds. Fig. 24-34. Remember that this should be done immediately after the current has been switched off.

Some large band saws have a built-in electric butt welder for repairing blades. This device squares off the ends of the blade and then butt welds them together. Then a small grinding wheel smoothes the sides to the same thickness as the blade itself.

Sharpening Circular-Saw Blades by Hand

As with the band saw, the best meth-

24-34. A brazer for repairing band-saw blades.

od to keeping circular-saw blade sharp is with automatic saw-filing equipment. However, if it is necessary, hand sharpening can be done to a blade that is basically in good condition. Four basic steps must be followed to put a dull blade back in shape: *jointing or rounding*, *gumming*, *setting*, and *filing*. Fig. 24-35(a).

Jointing makes the saw as round as possible so that all teeth are of equal height. Gumming is necessary when the teeth have become shallow after repeated filing, and must be ground deeper. Setting is bending the teeth to the right and left to provide clearance. Filing or grinding sharpens the teeth. This last step is generally the only one that should be attempted by the hand method. In filing, do not reduce the size, shape, or length of the teeth; simply bring them up to a sharp point. Fig. 24-35(b). Have all the teeth the same shape, with gullets of even depth. Filing should be done with the blade held in a blade vise. Use a taper or saw file. Fig. 24-36. Carbide-tipped blades must, of course, be ground with an abrasive wheel.

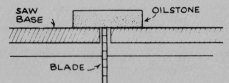

1–JOINTING: REVERSE SAW ON ARBOR RAISE BASE. PLACE STONE IN PLACE AND LOWER BASE UNTIL TEETH STRIKE. DO NOT JOINT ANY MORE THAN IS NECESSARY TO LEVEL TEETH.

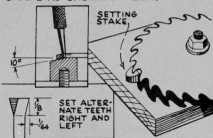

2– GUMMING: MAKE PENCIL MARK TO SHOW BOTTOM OF GULLET (¹¹⁄₃₂″ FROM EDGE OF BLADE). FILE OR GRIND GULLETS TO LINE. FOLLOW SHAPE AS SHOWN IN PLAN.

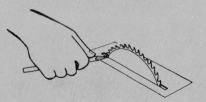

3–SETTING: USE SUITABLE SETTING STAKE OR HAND SET. DO NOT EXCEED AMOUNT OF SET AS SPECIFIED. KEEP SET UNIFORM.

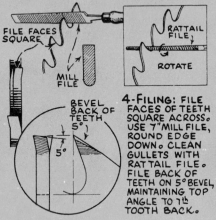

4–FILING: FILE FACES OF TEETH SQUARE ACROSS. USE 7″MILL FILE, ROUND EDGE DOWN. CLEAN GULLETS WITH RATTAIL FILE. FILE BACK OF TEETH ON 5° BEVEL, MAINTAINING TOP ANGLE TO 7⅟₂ TOOTH BACK.

24-35(a).   Steps in sharpening a circular-saw blade.

252

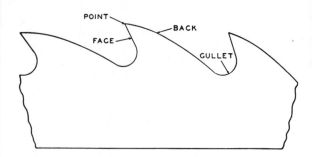

24-35(b).   There are many different shapes of teeth on saw blades. Even saws designed to do the same kind of cutting may have teeth of different shapes. The average cabinetmaker is concerned with these three basic kinds: (A) rip, (B) crosscut, and (C) combination. Also shown are the parts of a tooth.

24-36.   This circular-saw blade vise is made of hardwood. A standard ½″ hexagon nut or a wing nut can be used with the carriage bolt instead of the handle nut shown.

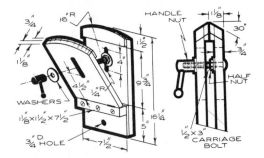

24-37. Complete instructions on how to sharpen saws come with the automatic saw-filing equipment. The same machine can be used for sharpening all types of blades. (a) Sharpening a circular saw blade.

Do not file sharp corners or nicks in the bottom of the gullets. This usually results in cracks in the gullets. Bevel the teeth of cutoff saws on both the face and back edges—more on the face than on the back. File ripsaw teeth straight across to a chisel-like edge. Then give a very slight bevel to the back of the teeth. In filing any saw, take care that the bevel does not run down into the gullets. The bevel on both face and back should be about one-third the length of the teeth.

In filing a flat-ground combination

saw which crosscuts, rips, and miters, follow the same method used in sharpening a crosscut saw. In sharpening a hollow-ground combination saw, also follow this method, but do not set the teeth as the hollow grinding provides ample clearance.

Some combination saws have rakers, or "cleaner" teeth, to remove material left in the cut by the beveled cutting teeth. The points of these rakers should be filed shorter than the points of the beveled teeth—1/64″ shorter for cutting hardwood, 1/32″ for softwood. After filing these raker teeth, square the face of each and bring it to a chisel-like edge by filing on the back of the tooth only.

Saw-filing Equipment

Automatic saw-filing equipment not only provides greater accuracy than can be achieved by hand but also adds mechanical precision to the sharpening. A single machine can be used to sharpen blades for circular, band, and hand saws. Fig. 24-37. The basic principles of sharpening must be followed. Each type of saw tooth (crosscut, rip, or combination) requires a different adjustment of the machine. Also, different attachments must be used to hold and move the various saws.

Automatic saw sharpening is a highly specialized part of the cabinetmaker's trade. Some men, especially those working in the tool rooms of furniture factories or operating their own business,

24-37(b). An attachment has been added to hold a band-saw blade for sharpening.

24-37(c). Another attachment used to sharpen hand saws.

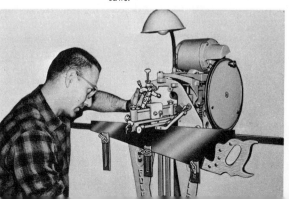

24-38. The knife-grinding attachment in place and ready for use.

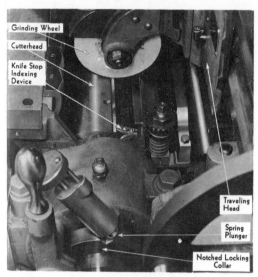

Grinding Wheel

Cutterhead

Knife Stop Indexing Device

Traveling Head

Spring Plunger

Notched Locking Collar

24-39. A close-up view of knife grinding. Note that the knife stop indexing device holds the knife in the correct position.

do saw and knife sharpening on a full-time basis. The skilled all-around cabinetmaker and finish carpenter send their cutting tools to a specialist for sharpening. Even more highly specialized equipment is needed for sharpening carbide-tipped tools.

Grinding and Jointing Planer Blades

Before these blades can be sharpened, the exhaust pipe must be disconnected and the dust hood removed from the surfacer or planer. Modern planers, except for the smallest sizes, are usually equipped with attachments for grinding the knives without removing them from the cutterhead. This equipment consists of a small abrasive wheel with its motor. Fig. 24-38. These devices are attached to a grinding and jointing bar above the cutterhead, and are moved back and forth along the knife edges. Knives are ground one by one while the cutterhead is stationary. Fig. 24-39. The bevel that is ground in this way is not a straight line, but conforms to the circumference of the grinding wheel. Fig. 24-40(a).

Knives on a cutterhead often project unequally and therefore do not cut evenly. With a four-knife cutterhead, for instance, one knife that projects a little too far may wipe out the marks of the other three knives. As stated earlier, the purpose of jointing is to even up the projection of the knives. In jointing, a carrier which holds an abrasive stone is attached to the grinding and jointing bar, and the cutterhead is then set in motion. The stone is lowered until it barely touches a knife edge and is then traversed along that edge. Fig. 24-41(a). This is continued until a fine line, called a *joint* or *land,* appears on the full length of each knife edge. The knives should now project evenly. As they gradually become dull, jointing may have to be repeated several times for sharpening. However, repeated jointing finally causes a pronounced heel. Fig. 24-40(b). The jointed portion of the bevel is part of the cutting circle and therefore has no clearance. The wider it becomes beyond certain limits, the more pounding and rubbing take place, resulting in poor

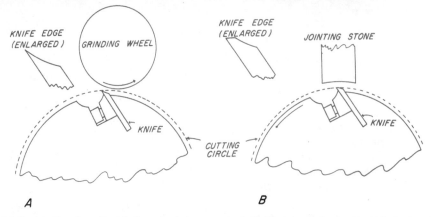

A   **B**

24-40. (a). Note how the grinding wheel sharpens the knife blade to a sharp edge with the bevel in an arc shape. (b). Jointing produces a land or joint (secondary bevel) on the knife. The enlarged edge shows a land that is too wide. When this happens, the knives must be reground.

work. Knives should therefore be reground as soon as the joint reaches a width of about 1/32″.

Most manufacturers supply tools for this, replacing the knives when necessary. One such device is a *knife puller* to remove the knife from the slot after the bolts or set screws in the knife bar or throat piece are loosened. Another device is available for setting all the knives in the cutterhead to the same height. The knife and knife bar are in-

serted in the slot and the set screws lightly tightened with the knife extended a little more than necessary. Put the block in place and strike with a hammer all along the knife. Then tighten the set screws securely. Fig. 24-41(b).

Grinding Jointer Knives

Jointer knives should be ground when:
• The knives are so dull that honing will not put a good cutting edge on them.

24-41(a). Jointing the knives in a cutterhead. The power is on so the cutterhead is revolving at high speed. Great care must be taken when doing this. The stone must just touch each of the blades. The downfeed screw can be moved only a few thousandths of an inch at a time.

24-41(b). Cross section of a cylinder showing the details of a four-knife cutterhead and the method of using the knife puller and knife setting block.

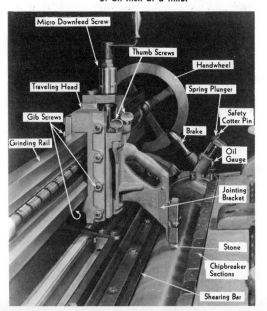

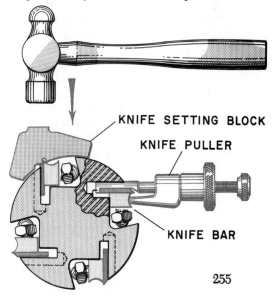

255

• The joint or land becomes too wide (over 1/16″).

• Nicks develop or the knives becomes uneven.

On larger jointers there is a knife-grinding attachment that is a detachable part of the machine. The knives can be ground without removing them from the machine. On smaller machines the knives or the entire cutterhead must be removed to do the grinding. If a surfacer or planer that has a grinding attachment is available, this machine can be used for grinding jointer knives. However, this method should be used only when the planer knives themselves are to be sharpened. Otherwise, resetting the planer knives may cause difficulties. To sharpen, remove one planer knife, place all jointer knives in a line, and grind as a single knife.

Several different machines can be used to grind jointer knives that have been removed from the cutterhead. In each case a wood jig must be constructed to hold the knives. If a two-wheel grinder is to be used, cut a groove at 35 to 36 degrees in the edge of a hardwood piece. Install a wood screw at either end that can hold the knives firmly in place. Dress the grinding wheel. Adjust the tool rest so that the bevel of the knives will be ground at approximately 35 degrees. Clamp a guide block to the tool rest to make sure the grinding is straight along the length of the knife. Fig. 24-42.

Make a single light cut by moving the knife slowly from one side to the other. Check the edge to make sure it is ground to a single bevel. When this is done, grind the other knives. Make sure that each knife is ground the same amount so that all will weigh the same. Otherwise there will be excessive vibration when the cutterhead is revolving at high speeds. After grinding, light honing on the back edge will remove the burr.

If the grinding is to be done on a drill press with a cup wheel, the groove should be cut in one corner of the wood jig. The knife is mounted with the bevel up. Fig. 24-43. The same jig can be used to grind the knives on a circular saw that has an abrasive wheel mounted on the arbor. With this method the bevel is turned toward the edge of the jig. Fig. 24-44.

Changing or Resetting Jointer Knives

Removing and replacing jointer knives must be done with great care. If not, the jointer will not operate smoothly or produce a good surface. Before working on the machine, remember to turn off the power both at the machine and at the master switch. Remove the fence and guard, and move the infeed table as far away as possible so that you can work at the cutterhead freely. To remove the knives, loosen the set screws or bolts that are part of the *knife bar* or *throat piece* (the clamp that holds the knives tightly in the cutterhead). Lift out the knife first and then the throat piece. Turn the head to the next position and repeat this process.

To replace and reset the knives, reverse the process. Insert the throat piece first and then the knife, with the bevel toward the outfeed table. Use a straightedge on the outfeed table as a guide to set all knives to the same height. One of the best methods of doing this is to use a U-shaped or straight magnet as a straightedge. Place a stop block across the front table and then slide the magnet against it. Fig. 24-45. It is a good idea to have an index mark on the magnet. This mark should be in line with the cutting edge of the knife at its highest point. With the knife in the slot and the throat piece loosened, allow the magnet to hold the knife up to the required level. Then tighten one set screw or bolt just enough to hold. Move the magnet to the other end of the knife and repeat.

24-42. Grinding jointer knives on a two-wheel grinder. Note the guide block that is clamped to the tool rest to control the grinding.

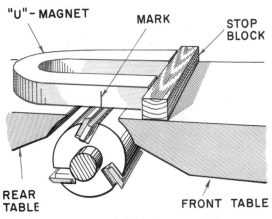

24-45. The magnet will hold the jointer knife at exactly the same height as the rear table. The back of the bevel should clear the cutterhead itself by about 1/16".

Reset the other knives in a similar manner. Make sure you move the magnet from one side to the other so that the knives are the same height along the entire cutterhead.

On some machines the knives can be moved up or down with set screws that are part of the cutterhead itself. With this type of machine a steel bar is used as a positive setting stop. By using screw lifters, raise the knife ends to the correct height and lock them in place. Fig. 24-46. After all knives are in place, tighten the remaining screws or bolts lightly. Then rotate the cutterhead by hand to check the knives. Tighten all screws or bolts again to be sure the knives are held firmly in place. Then recheck with a straightedge to make sure all knives are the same height. Move the infeed table back to the correct position.

24-43. Grinding jointer knives on a drill press. As in Fig. 24-42, a stop block controls the grinding. This one is clamped to the table.

24-44. Grinding jointer knives on a circular saw. The wood jig should be clamped to the miter gage and moved back and forth across the abrasive wheel.

24-46. Adjusting the height of the knives by turning a set screw. Another knife and throat piece are shown ready to be installed in the next position on the cutterhead.

257

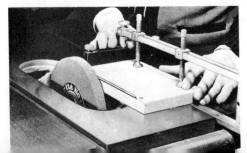

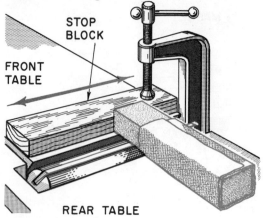

STOP
BLOCK

FRONT
TABLE

REAR TABLE

24-47. Place the stone on the rear table as shown. Remember that the cutterhead is revolving at high speed. KEEP YOUR FINGERS AWAY FROM THE KNIVES AND HOLD THE ABRASIVE STONE FIRMLY. DON'T LET IT SLIP OUT OF YOUR HAND.

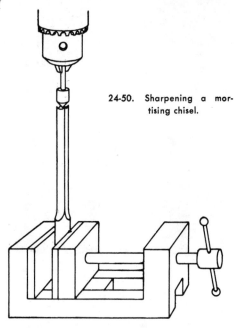

24-50. Sharpening a mortising chisel.

24-48. Honing the face of a shaper cutter.

After the jointer knives have been sharpened and reset, it is wise to joint the knives so they are exactly the same height. Cover all but about one-fourth the length of a large abrasive stone with wax paper. Place the stone on the rear table with the exposed section over the knives. Clamp a wooden stop block to the front table to help guide the stone. Lower the table until the stone barely touches the knives. Fig. 24-47. Turn on the power. When the cutterhead is revolving, move the stone slowly from one side to the other. A true cutting circle will result. Be sure to joint the entire length of the knives. The joint or land (sometimes called the *heel*) should not be wider than 1/32″. After jointing, replace the fence and guard.

Router Bits and Shaper Cutters

In sharpening these tools, it is important not to change the shape of the cutting edge. Therefore most grinding

24-49. The blade faces of a molding head can be honed as shown here.

258

and honing should be done on the face of the tool. To sharpen bits for a portable router you need an accessory for holding the bits. Fasten a small cup-shaped abrasive wheel to the collet of the router to do the grinding.

The face of a shaper bit can be ground on a small grinding wheel. Honing is done as shown in Fig. 24-48. A slipstone can be used to touch up the beveled cutting edge but, remember, take care not to change its shape.

Molding-head Cutter Blades

The individual blades of a molding head can be honed on their front face. Fig. 24-49. The beveled edge can be touched up with a slipstone.

Mortising Chisel

To sharpen a mortising chisel, install a conical-shaped wheel in the chuck of the drill press or lathe. Grind the inside bevel. Then hone the outside, holding the abrasive stone flat against the sides to remove any burr. Fig. 24-50.

Sharpening a Twist Drill

A correctly sharpened twist drill must have a point angle of 59 degrees on either side of the axis. The lips must be the same length, and there must be enough lip clearance (or relief behind the cutting edge) so that the tool can cut into the material. A lip clearance of 8 to 12 degrees is considered right for ordinary work. To grind a drill, hold the shank in one hand and the point between the thumb and forefinger of the other

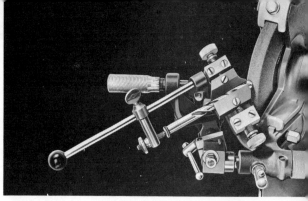

24-52. Grinding a twist drill using a drill grinding attachment.

hand. Hold the drill in a horizontal position at an angle of 59 degrees to the grinding wheel. Grind the cutting edge on the face of the wheel. Then rotate the drill clockwise, at the same time swinging the shank down in an arc of about 20 degrees. Grind a little off both sides. Continue to grind and test the point until the cutting edges are sharp and both are the same length. Fig. 24-51. Usually one or two light twists on both lips will bring the drill to a sharp point.

A drill-grinding attachment is available on some grinders. With this anyone can do an excellent job of sharpening a drill. The grinding is done on the face of the wheel. The drill is clamped in a V groove, and the grinder is turned on. Then an adjustment is made so that the cutting edge of the tool touches the wheel. The handle is rotated to grind one lip. The drill is then reversed in the holder and the other lip is ground. The micrometer setting insures evenly ground lips. Fig. 24-52.

24-51 (a). The correct point angle is 59 degrees on either side of the axis, or an included angle of 118 degrees. (b). Notice the clearance behind the cutting edge. (c). Check the angle and length of the cutting edge with a drill gage.

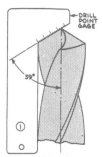

a.

CORRECT POINT ANGLE IS 59°. THIS IS MOST EFFICIENT POINT FOR ALL-AROUND WORK

CLEARANCE

b.

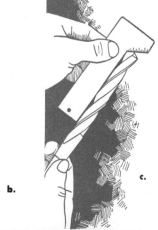

c.

259

The purpose of the planer or surfacer is to smooth stock and to cut it to uniform thickness. *The planer will not correct or straighten warped stock.* The pressure of the infeed roll will momentarily flatten a warped board as it moves under the cutterhead, but the board will resume its warped shape as soon as it leaves the outfeed rolls. Therefore one face of a warped piece should be planed true on the jointer.

Planers are made with either single or

25-1. This planer has a single-surface, wedge-adjusting bed with four rolls. It has a capacity of 40".

25-2. This 30" planer is equipped with a grinding attachment.

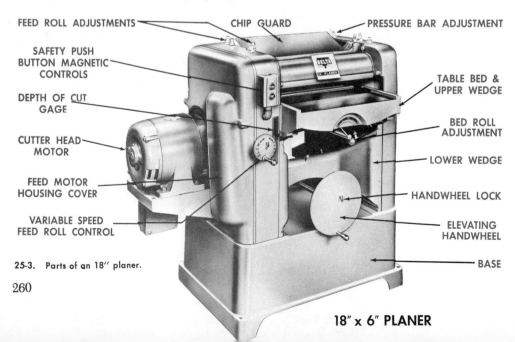

FEED ROLL ADJUSTMENTS

CHIP GUARD

PRESSURE BAR ADJUSTMENT

SAFETY PUSH BUTTON MAGNETIC CONTROLS

TABLE BED & UPPER WEDGE

DEPTH OF CUT GAGE

BED ROLL ADJUSTMENT

CUTTER HEAD MOTOR

LOWER WEDGE

FEED MOTOR HOUSING COVER

HANDWHEEL LOCK

VARIABLE SPEED FEED ROLL CONTROL

ELEVATING HANDWHEEL

BASE

25-3. Parts of an 18" planer.

18" x 6" PLANER

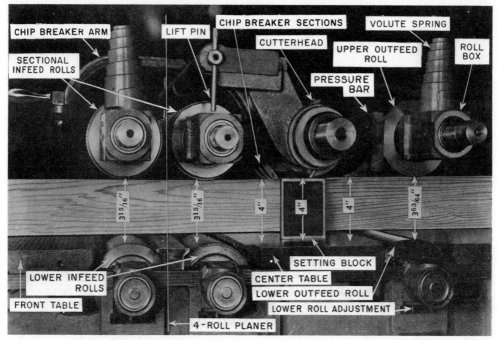

CHIP BREAKER ARM
LIFT PIN
CHIP BREAKER SECTIONS
VOLUTE SPRING
SECTIONAL INFEED ROLLS
CUTTERHEAD
UPPER OUTFEED ROLL
ROLL BOX
PRESSURE BAR

3 15/16"   3 15/16"   4"   4"   4"   3 63/64"

LOWER INFEED ROLLS
SETTING BLOCK
CENTER TABLE
LOWER OUTFEED ROLL
FRONT TABLE
LOWER ROLL ADJUSTMENT
4-ROLL PLANER

25-4(a). Parts of a four-roll planer head. Only larger planers have four infeed rolls.

double surfacing knives. The single planer cuts only the top surface while the double planer cuts both top and bottom at the same time. Fig. 25-1. Most small to medium planers have only one cutting head. See Unit 64.

PARTS AND CONTROLS

The planer is ruggedly built to take the shock and stress of cutting wide lumber surfaces. Fig. 25-2. The size of a planer is determined by the length of the knives, or the widest stock that can

be surfaced. Planers range in size from 12″ to 52″, although the 18″ to 30″ sizes are the most common. Fig. 25-3. The table moves up and down on two screws or by sliding on a wedge-shaped casting. A cross section of the planer head will reveal its major parts. Fig. 25-4.

The upper and lower infeed rolls move the stock into the cutterhead. The *upper infeed roll* is corrugated and usually made in sections. Fig. 25-5. With the sectional infeed roll, several pieces of slightly different thickness can be fed

25-4(b). Parts of a two-roll planer head. Most medium-size planers have two infeed rolls.

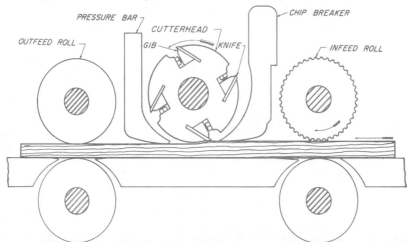

PRESSURE BAR
OUTFEED ROLL
CUTTERHEAD
GIB
KNIFE
CHIP BREAKER
INFEED ROLL

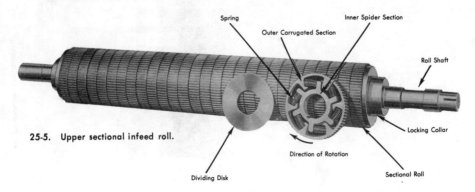

25-5.   Upper sectional infeed roll.

25-6.   Note the advantage of a sectional chip break-er when surfacing two or more pieces of slightly different thickness. If a solid chip breaker is used, there is no pressure on the thinner stock. As a result, the cutterhead tears the grain.

SECTIONAL
CHIP BREAKER

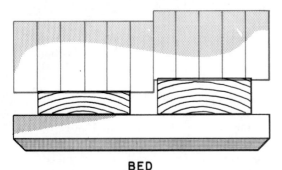

BED

SOLID
CHIP BREAKER

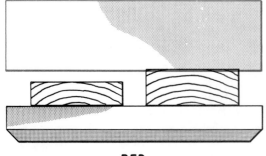

BED

into the machine at the same time. Between the infeed roll and the cutterhead is a *chip breaker* that is also usually made in sections. Fig. 25-6. The edge of the chip breaker is set fairly close to the knives and can be adjusted up and down slightly. This device keeps the stock firmly pressed to the bed and prevents torn grain. If there were no chip breaker, the stock would tend to tear or split off in long slivers.

The *cutterhead* itself is cylindrical. It has three or more knives which smooth the upper surface of the board and cut it to uniform thickness. As the shavings fly off, they are drawn into the exhaust system which is fitted over the top of the planer. Just beyond the cutterhead is the *pressure bar* which holds the stock firmly to the bed after the cut is made. Finally, the board passes between the smooth *upper* and *lower outfeed rolls*. These help to move the stock out of the machine.

The kind and number of controls on a surfacer vary somewhat with its size. There is a switch to turn the power on and off. Fig. 25-7. All machines have an elevating handwheel that moves the bed up and down to control the depth of cut. Fig. 25-8. Additionally, some types have a quick control for changing from rough to finish surfacing. Fig. 25-9. There is usually a feed control that determines

25-7. This push button governs the instant-acting, magnetic controls. When the *off* button is pushed, the motors for both the separate feed drive and the cutterhead are turned off instantly, and the machine stops in seconds.

25-10. The *feed control* changes the rate at which the stock moves through the planer. Usually a fast feed is used for softwoods, slower for hardwoods.

25-8. To adjust for the correct depth of cut, loosen the handwheel *lock* and turn the elevating handwheel up or down. The finish thickness will register on the depth-of-cut gage.

25-9. This *fast bed adjustment* enables the operator to raise or lower the bed from rough to finish surfacing without using the elevating handwheel.

the rate at which the stock moves into the cutters. Fig. 25-10. On some larger machines a speed control is available for changing the r.p.m. of the cutterhead. The two common adjustments, however, are to raise and lower the bed and to adjust the feed. The cutterhead normally operates at a fixed speed of about 3600 r.p.m. The feed rate should be varied with the width of stock, the kind of wood, and the desired quality of the surfaces. Fairly wide, hard pieces of wood should be fed at relatively slow speed, and narrower pieces of softer wood at a higher feed rate.

Operating Procedure

1. It long stock is to be surfaced, it is a good idea to get someone to help at the other end. If no one can help, place a roller (dead man) at the "out" end of the planer to support the stock.

2. Before planing a warped board, true one face on the jointer.

3. If possible, determine the grain direction of each piece and feed *with* the grain. Place the pieces conveniently near the infeed table with the grain in the proper direction.

4. Measure the thickness of the stock and adjust the machine to remove *about* 1/16″ to 1/8″. Generally a piece is surfaced in from one to three cuts. For example, if stock measures 1″ and you

263

25-11. Feeding stock into a planer.

25-12. Surfacing stock that has been glued up.

wish to reduce it to 13/16″, adjust the planer so that the first cut will be 1/8″. Then the second cut should be 1/16″.

5. Turn on the power and allow the planer to come to full speed. To avoid injury from kickback, stand to one side, *never directly behind the stock.* Fig. 25-11. Feed the stock into the infeed rolls and, as soon as it takes hold, remove your hands from the stock. Never let your fingers get under the edges.

6. If the wood starts into the machine slightly crooked, a tap on the edge will straighten it. If the stock sticks, lower the bed immediately and turn off the machine.

7. If large amounts of stock must be removed, always take some off both faces. If this is not done, the board will tend to *cup* because it has slightly more moisture toward the center than it does at the outside. (When a board warps so that its edges are higher than its center, this is called "cup.")

8. When stock has been glued up to make a larger surface, it is impossible to true or face it on the jointer. To do it on the planer, first remove all the glue from the surface. Then adjust the machine to a slow feed and a light cut. Fig. 25-12. Place the best face on the bed of the planer and true one side. Then reverse

the stock, readjust for thickness, and plane.

Squaring Up Legs

A common use for the planer is to square up legs, posts, and other furniture parts. When the stock has been rough cut to size, joint two adjacent sides on the jointer. Mark number 1 on the end grain of the working face and number 2 on the working edge. To square up the stock and reduce it to correct size, adjust the machine to about 1/16″ over finish size. Place the working face against the bed and the working edge to the right, and feed all pieces through the machine. Return all stock to the front of the machine and place it on the bed in the original position. Then turn each piece a quarter turn to the right and repeat the surfacing. Adjust the machine for the second cut and surface the stock to the final size.

Planing Thin Stock

If very thin stock must be planed, it is a good idea to use a backing board. This is true for all stock 3/8″ or less in thickness. Make sure that the backing board is true, smooth, and at least 3/4″ thick.

SURFACER-PLANER

Maintenance

• Make sure the planer knives are sharp. Grind and joint as necessary. (See Unit 24.)
• Check to see that the bed moves up and down easily. If there is too much wear and "play," the *gibs* must be tightened. (A gib is shown in Fig. 25-4.)
• Make sure the feed rolls are clean. If they are coated wth pitch, clean them off with a rag soaked in benzine.
• Adjust the knives, chip breaker, and pressure bar to the manufacturer's specifications.
• Make sure the dust-collection system is not overloaded and is working properly.

Lubrication

• Use S.A.E. No. 40 lubricating oil on the infeed- and outfeed-roll bearings.
• Use S.A.E. No. 10 lubricating oil on the table gibs.

Safety

• Familiarize yourself with the stop switch, elevating handwheel, and brake (if any) so that you can stop the machine quickly.
• Check the wood for defects such as large knots that might cause the board to split under pressure.

• Never surface painted or varnished stock. In fact, used lumber of any kind should not be surfaced.
• Make sure that the board to be surfaced has one true surface.
• The shortest board that should be run through the machine should be 2″ longer than the distance between the infeed and outfeed rolls.
• Always stand to one side of the table, never directly in line with the stock.
• Try to determine grain direction and feed into the machine so that the cutting will be done with the grain.
• As the feed rolls take hold of the stock, allow the machine to do the work. Take your hands off the board.
• If a board gets stuck in the machine, lower the bed and turn off the machine.
• Never stoop down to watch a board being surfaced.
• Be especially careful of your fingers when surfacing a short board. Sometimes the infeed rolls will tip the board up and then down quickly so that the fingers get pinched between the table top and the stock.
• If the stock is long, get someone to help you take the stock off as it leaves the machine.

Place the backing board on the bed and then put the thin stock on it. Adjust for the correct depth of cut, taking into consideration the thickness of the backing board. Then run the two boards together through the surfacer.

Planer Hints

If a clip or snipe appears at the beginning of a board:

• The pressure bar may be set too low.
• The chip breaker may be set too high.
• The upper infeed sectional roll may be set too high.
• The lower infeed roll may be set too high.
• Spring tension may be too light on the pressure bar.

If a clip or snipe appears on the end of lumber:

• The pressure bar may be set too high; it may not be even with the cutting circle.
• The lower outfeed roll may be set too high.
• The upper outfeed roll may be set too low.
• The lumber may not be butted.
• The grain may be running against the knives.

If knives tear out the lumber:

• The feed may be too fast.
• The joint on the knives may be too heavy.
• Moisture content of the stock may be too high.

* The head may be running too slowly.
* The cut may be too heavy.
* The cutting angle may be too large.
* The grain may be running against the knives.

If the knives raise the grain:

* The joint on the blades may be too wide.
* The feed may be too fast.
* The cutting angle may be too large.
* The head may be running too slowly.
* Moisture content of the stock may be too high.
* The cut may be too heavy.

If chip marks appear on the stock:

* The blower system may not be strong enough.
* The feed may be too fast.
* There may be a loose connection in the blower system, resulting in no suction.
* The exhaust pipe may joint at too large an angle to the main blower pipe.

If panels are tapered across the width:

* The center table may not be set parallel with the body of the cylinder.
* The grinding rail may not be set parallel with the body of the cylinder.
* The center table may be worn.

If a washboard finish appears:

* Knives may be dull.
* The feed may be too slow.
* The joint may be too heavy.

If a washboard finish appears:

* The knives may have been driven back into the head.
* The machine may be completely out of adjustment.
* The joint may be too heavy.

If revolving marks show:

* Knives may be ground poorly.
* Knives may need jointing.

If lines appear at right angles to the knife marks:

* Knives may have become checkered or nicked due to overgrinding which has taken the temper out of the steel.
* Chips may have wedged between the roll and the table.
* The pressure bar may be dragging.

If the stock twists in the machine:

* The pressure bar may be cocked.
* The upper outfeed roll may be cocked.
* The upper outfeed roll may have uneven spring tension on it.
* The lower rolls may be cocked.

If the stock sticks or hesitates in the machine:

* The pressure bar may be set too low.
* The lower rolls may be set too low.
* The upper rolls may not be set low enough.
* The cut may be too heavy.

If the machine is noisy and vibrates or pounds:

* The knives may be too dull.
* The machine may not be level.
* The machine may not be on a solid foundation.
* The pulley belt may be jumping.
* The pressure bar may be set too low.

ABRASIVE PLANING

Until quite recently, abrasives in the furniture industry were primarily used for smoothing and finishing operations. All planing was done with knives on a rotating cutterhead. The idea of using abrasives for planing is now developing. This is particularly true for surfacing glued-up stock and some man-made materials such as particle board. Sanding machines that will take an extremely wide abrasive belt have been developed. Glued-up furniture parts can be fed through at higher speed than on the surfacer or planer.

The circular saw, or variety saw as it is sometimes called, is a most versatile machine. Fig. 26-1. It is used more than any other tool in the cabinet shop because a great deal of the basic cutting for construction can be done on it. The saw consists of a heavy frame with a *table* and an *arbor*. The arbor holds the saw and revolves. The shaft in the arbor is connected to the motor by belts and pulleys. Some saws have direct drive from the motor to the arbor.

Usually, the table of the saw remains in a fixed, horizontal position, and the arbor tilts. However, earlier types of saws and some multipurpose machines have a tilting table. A tilted table is awkward for many cuts and can create a hazard.

The size of the saw is determined by the diameter of the blade recommended for use. Sizes range from 8″ bench models to 16″ production machines. Fig. 26-2. Most common for schools and cabinet shops is the 10″ size.

The *rip fence* is a metal guide clamped

26-1. Parts of a 10″ tilting-arbor circular saw.

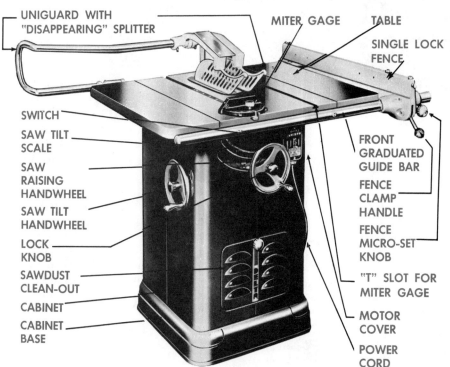

UNIGUARD WITH "DISAPPEARING" SPLITTER

MITER GAGE

TABLE

SINGLE LOCK FENCE

SWITCH

SAW TILT SCALE

SAW RAISING HANDWHEEL

SAW TILT HANDWHEEL

LOCK KNOB

SAWDUST CLEAN-OUT

CABINET

CABINET BASE

FRONT GRADUATED GUIDE BAR

FENCE CLAMP HANDLE

FENCE MICRO-SET KNOB

"T" SLOT FOR MITER GAGE

MOTOR COVER

POWER CORD

10″ TILTING ARBOR SAW

26-2. This heavy-duty tilting-arbor saw can take a 16" to 18" blade. The half table to the left is on rollers so it will move smoothly for crosscut work, instead of having to slide the miter gage. This model features hydraulic saw tilting and elevating for quick, accurate settings.

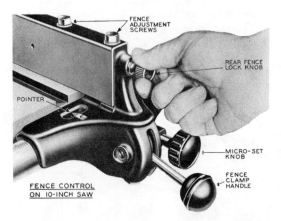

26-3. Fence controls for a 10" circular saw. The fence is a steel guide fastened to the table, parallel with and usually to the right of the blade. The fence clamp handle is released and the fence moved sideways to adjust for width of cut. For final, precise adjustment, the micro-set knob is pushed in and turned. When the exact setting is obtained, the clamp handle is pushed down.

26-4. A miter gage is used for crosscutting. It slides into slots in the table. A stop rod can be fastened to the gage to control length of cut.

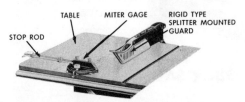

on the table parallel to the saw blade. It is used for all ripping operations. Fig. 26-3. A clamp handle fastens it securely in place after it is adjusted. There is usually a knob for fine adjustments as well. The fence is predrilled with holes so that an auxiliary wood fence can be fastened to it. In many kinds of cutting this is necessary to eliminate danger of the saw blade striking the metal fence. The fence usually is to the right of the saw. It is important that the fence be absolutely parallel to the blade.

The *miter gage* is used for all crosscutting operations. Fig. 26-4. It slides into slots milled in the table top. There is one slot to the left and one to the right of the saw blade. On most saws, the miter gage can be put into either slot, even when the blade is tilted. It is well to check this, however, because there are certain models in which it must be used only on one side when the blade is tilted. A *stop rod* can be clamped to the miter gage to control the length of cut.

COMMON ADJUSTMENTS

The *saw-raising handwheel* raises or lowers the blade. The distance the saw projects above the work is very important. For safety, allow the blade to project only about 1/8" to 1/4" above the stock. A high blade is more dangerous because its greater area of contact with the stock is more likely to cause kickback. However, this does not apply to a hollow-ground blade, which should project well above the stock to keep the edge from overheating. A high blade is actually better mechanically because it cuts with less power and produces a cleaner edge. (Safety measures against kickback are discussed on pages 270 and 271.)

Be sure to loosen the lock nut before making the height adjustment and retighten it afterward. The *tilt handwheel* is used to adjust the blade for angle cutting. It also has a lock nut. A *tilt scale*

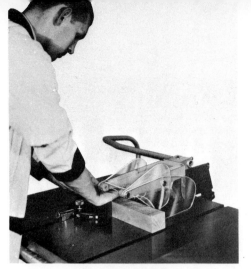

26-5(a). This twin-action plastic guard gives excellent protection throughout the cut. The front shield rises as the work enters, then returns to place as the work moves on to raise the second shield.

with a *pointer* shows the exact angle of the tilt. This should be checked frequently by adjusting the saw to a 45-degree angle and holding a protractor between the blade and the table top. It is also a good idea to check the setting at 90 degrees to make sure the blade is at right angles to the table top. Then check the miter gage with the side of the blade to make sure it is square.

GUARDS AND OTHER PROTECTIVE DEVICES

Several additional protective devices are standard equipment. A *guard* should cover the saw whenever possible. Because protection has always been a problem, many different kinds of guards have been developed. With some guards, certain operations can't be performed. When it is necessary to remove the guard, always use a jig, fixture, or holding device.

The *basket guard,* made of metal or plastic, is the least satisfactory. Fig. 26-4. There are also several types of metal or plastic twin-action guards. Fig. 26-5. The sides of these move independently of one another. Fig. 26-6. Such guards can be used when the blade is at an angle. Another type, all plastic, can be used when performing practically any

26-5(b). Note that the guard can be used with the blade tilted to 45 degrees.

26-6. Sides of this guard operate independently so that one can be lifted up while the other remains in protective position. Short sleeves are safer.

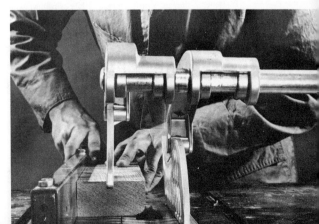

269

CIRCULAR SAW

Maintenance

- Keep all working parts free from sawdust and other substances that might have an abrasive effect on the parts.
- Clean out the sawdust from the base at regular intervals.
- Check the V belts to make sure they are in good condition. Avoid oil, grease, and other substances that would ruin the rubber.
- Keep the belts just snug enough to operate smoothly without slipping.
- Make sure the pulleys are aligned and tight on the shafts. If necessary to align them, use a narrow board with a double bevel on one edge as a guide.
- Make sure all safety devices operate easily, especially the guard.
- Make sure the fence is parallel to the saw blade. This can be checked by aligning the fence with the miter-gage slot. If the fence isn't parallel, check the manufacturer's instructions for correcting it.
- Raise the saw blade to the highest position and check the angle between the table top and the blade. Make sure the combination square is against the blade and between the teeth. If the blade is not perpendicular when set on zero, reset following manufacturer's instructions.
- Keep all machine surfaces, such as the table top, free of rust or corrosion.
- Set the miter gage at the 90-degree position and check with a combination square against the blade to make sure that gage and blade are at right angles. If not, readjust the miter gage. Also check the 45-degree positions right and left to make sure they are accurate.
- Make sure the insert plate is in good condition. Replace it if necessary.

Lubrication

- Clean out all moving parts with a whisk broom or brush, then lubricate with oil or a good grade of ball-bearing grease. Don't over-lubricate since that would just collect dust. Wipe off excess oil or grease, being careful not to get any on the belt.
- Lubricate sliding ways of trunnion brackets with powdered graphite.
- Motor bearings are sealed and require no further lubrication.

standard operation. Fig. 26-7. It is fitted to the side of the table top.

A *splitter*, a piece of metal directly behind the blade, is used to keep the saw kerf open; this prevents the wood from binding on the blade and causing kickback. It is especially important to use the splitter for all ripping operations. Many splitters are equipped with metal fingers or hold-downs that provide added anti-kickback protection.

Commercial Accessories

There are five common accessories available for the circular saw:
- A *dado head,* for cutting wide grooves and dadoes. There are several types but the most common is a set of blades and chippers. Fig. 26-8.

26-7(a). Using a plastic guard while ripping. This transparent guard can be used for all standard cutting operations.

26-7(b). Cutting a dado with the guard in position.

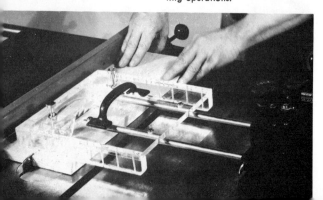

26-8. The most common dado head consists of two blades and several different thicknesses of chippers.

* A *tenoner,* for making tenons and other end-grain cuts. The stock is clamped to it and the device slides along the slot in the table. Fig. 26-9.
* A *clamp attachment* for the miter gage,

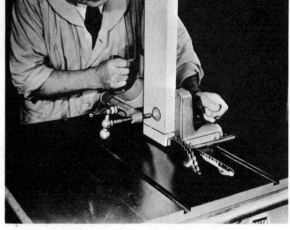

26-9. The commercial tenoner can be used to make all kinds of cuts on end grain. It helps to make accurate cuts and is an excellent safety device since end-grain cuts are dangerous if the stock is not well supported.

CIRCULAR SAW

SAFETY

* Use the saw guard as much as possible. Only a few operations can't be done with the guard in place. This is especially true of flexible guards. If a standard guard can't be used, use other safety devices such as a push stick, feather board, holding jig, fixture, and saw cover.
* Adjust the saw so that it clears the top of the stock by about 1/8" to 1/4". The only exception to this is when using a hollow-ground blade. Then it is better if the blade projects above the stock enough to keep the cutting edge from overheating and burning the teeth.
* Make sure the blade is sharp and properly mounted.
* Make all adjustments with the saw at a "dead" stop. Never try to stop the rotating blade by holding a stick against it.
* Never attempt freehand cuts on the circular saw.
* Always stand to one side, never directly behind the saw blade.
* Make sure the miter gage works freely in the slots and that it will clear both sides of the blade when tilted. On some saws the miter gage can be used on *only one side* when the blade is tilted.
* Hold the work firmly against the miter gage when crosscutting. Keep your fingers away from the line of cut.
* Never reach over the saw to pick up a piece of stock, even with the guard in place. Walk around.

* Never clear scraps away with your fingers. Have a stick at least 2' long for removing them.
* Always fasten a clearance block to the fence when cutting off duplicate parts.
* When ripping long stock, have someone assist you to "tail off" the work. However, never allow the person to pull or tilt the board as it is being ripped. The operator must always be in full charge.
* If a helper is not available, use a roller support to help hold up long stock as it is being ripped.
* When the piece is narrow, use a push stick to complete the cut.
* Before ripping make sure the fence is locked. During the operation use the splitter and anti-kickback fingers as well as the guard.
* Be sure the guard will not strike the saw when the blade is tilted for bevel and angle cuts.
* Allow the saw to come to full speed before starting to cut.
* Turn off the power immediately if the saw doesn't sound right.
* Watch carefully what you are doing. Avoid distractions and never look around while operating the saw.
* When the cutting is complete, turn off the power and stay next to the machine until it comes to a dead stop.
* Always remove special setups and any waste stock, and leave the machine in normal operating condition.

26-10. The clamp attachment holds stock firmly in place for crosscutting. The operator should have short sleeves.

26-11. There are many different designs of molding heads. Matched cutters are needed to fit each type.

26-12. Extension tables can be added to the sides of a saw to aid in cutting large panel stock. Commercial shops do not always follow best safety practices. Short sleeves would be safer.

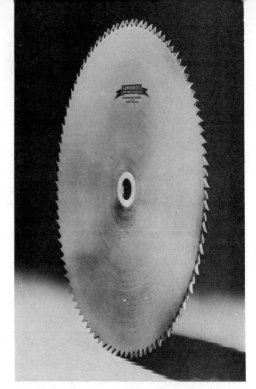

26-13. The cutoff or crosscut blade is for cutting across grain.

26-14. The ripsaw blade is designed for cutting with the grain.

26-15. Two styles of combination saws: a. This has teeth of the most common shape. b. This will do a good job of cutting wood in several directions.

which holds the work securely for accurate miter and cutoff operations. Fig. 26-10.

• A *molding cutterhead,* with many different sets of knives for molding and shaping operations. Fig. 26-11.

• An *extension table,* used when cutting large panel stock. Fig. 26-12.

SELECTING THE SAW BLADES

Some saw blades are designed for special-purpose cutting. The more common ones include:

• The *crosscut* or *cutoff saw,* which has fine crosscut teeth designed primarily for cutting across grain. It is flat-ground, with the teeth set for clearance. Fig. 26-13.

• The *ripsaw,* which has larger teeth and is designed for cutting with the grain on all varieties of woods. Fig. 26-14.

• The *combination saw,* designed for general ripping and crosscut work. It is flat-ground and is good for the faster cutting required for ripping, crosscutting, and mitering. There are several designs. Fig. 26-15. Sometimes the combination saw is hollow-ground to avoid overheating. This makes added clearance possible so that the saw will not tend to overheat. A *planer saw* is a smooth-cutting hollow-ground combination saw. Fig. 26-16. The *plywood combination saw* trims and cuts plywood smoothly, reducing splinters and slivers. Fig. 26-17.

26-16. The planer saw is hollow ground. Such blades are thinner toward the center than near the teeth.

26-17. A plywood saw. This is one of many special-purpose saws. Another is designed specifically for cutting flooring to length, and still others for miter cuts and similar production work.

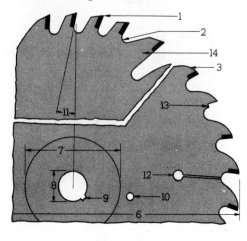

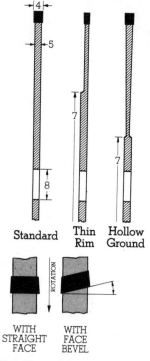

Standard | Thin Rim | Hollow Ground

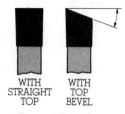

WITH
STRAIGHT
TOP

WITH
TOP
BEVEL

Face of Tooth.

WITH
STRAIGHT
FACE

WITH
FACE
BEVEL

Top View of Tooth

1 Carbide tip	8 Arbor size, also called 'eye' or hole
2 Gullet	9 Key way
3 Shoulder	10 Pin hole
4 Kerf	11 Rake
5 Body thickness, also hub thickness	12 Expansion slot
6 Diameter	13 Tip seat, milled
7 Hub diameter (On Thin Rim and Hollow Ground blades only.)	14 Raker tooth

26-18. **Parts of a carbide saw blade.**

• *Carbide-tipped blades,* extremely useful for high-production work and for cutting hardboard, plastic laminates, and other composition materials. Fig. 26-18. Carbide is the name given to several different alloys of carbon and such metals as tungsten, titanium, and tantalum. It is extremely hard, almost as hard as diamond. It maintains a sharp cutting edge under conditions that would cause other tools to burn. Small carbide tips are brazed on to the blade. Such blades are made in all standard blade designs. Fig. 26-19.

REPLACING A BLADE

A soft metal *insert plate* surrounds the blade. Press the rear of this and lift it out of place. Then select a wrench that exactly fits the arbor nut. Check the direction for loosening the nut before you start. Most arbor shafts have a lefthand

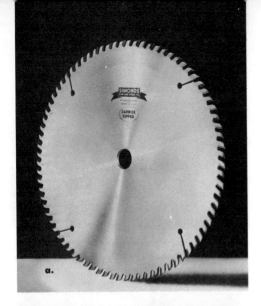

26-19. Common carbide-tipped blades: a. Crosscut. b. Rip. c. Easy cut. This one has only a few teeth and is considered very safe since it practically eliminates kickback. d. Combination.

thread that is loosened by turning it to the right, or clockwise. However, some are just the opposite. Fig. 26-20. Force a piece of softwood against the blade and loosen the nut. Remove the collar and the blade. Slide the new blade over the shaft threads, making sure that the tips point toward the operator and that the manufacturer's name is uppermost. Then replace the arbor washer and the nut. Tighten the nut securely and replace the insert plate. Rotate the blade by hand to make sure it is running free and clear.

26-20. Replacing a blade.

LEFT OR RIGHT

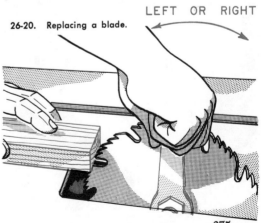

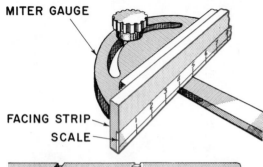

MITER GAUGE

FACING STRIP

SCALE

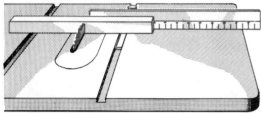

26-21. Note the use of an auxiliary wood fence or facing strip with a rule or scale fitted into it. This is ideal for crosscutting since it is a direct-reading cut-off gage. The rule must be fitted so that its markings begin at the saw line.

26-22(a).* It is good practice to use both hands for crosscutting. One hand should hold the work against the miter gage while the other hand moves the miter gage forward.

276

26-22(b). It is difficult to hold the work and move it with only one hand. There is always danger that it will slip or "creep" into the saw. Sleeves should be rolled up.

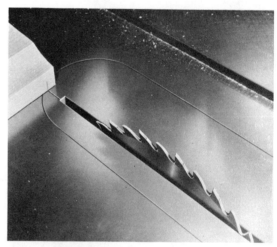

26-23. A scribed line on the table insert, directly in line with the saw blade, makes it easy to line up the cut.

26-24(a). Square crosscutting. The miter gage is set at right angles to the blade. Apply even forward pressure to the stock and gage. Sleeves should be rolled up.

Simple Crosscutting

For all crosscutting operations the miter gage should be used. Frequently an auxiliary fence or facing strip is attached to the miter gage to add support and for making special cuts. An auxiliary fence made of wood can be screwed or bolted to the miter gage; this adds support for all types of work. A scale (rule) can be fitted into the wood fence, and a piece of abrasive cloth can be glued to this fence to help hold the work securely. Fig. 26-21. Normally the miter gage is used in the left slot with the slide in front. The work is then held firmly against the miter gage with the left hand while the right hand pushes the gage along. Fig. 26-22. The usual method is to mark the cutting line across the face or front edge of the stock. Sometimes a fine line is filed in the insert plate directly in line with the saw blade. Fig. 26-23. Then it is easy to align the stock so that it is cut in the proper location. Fig. 26-24. When cutting stock to length, especially for production work, it is often a good idea to use two miter gages. The one on the right side is used to cut the left end square; the one on the left has a stop block attached to the auxiliary fence, for cutting the second end to exact length. The miter gage can also be reversed in the slot for cutting wide stock. Fig. 26-25.

Cutting Duplicate Parts to Identical Lengths

There are several common ways of cutting parts to exact length. These methods are. especially helpful when more than one piece must be cut to the same length.

• One way is to attach a stop block to

*Illustrations marked with asterisk show the guard removed only so details can be seen. *You should use the guard.*

26-24(b). Using a clamp attachment and guard while crosscutting.

26-25.* A wider board can be cut with ease by reversing the miter gage in the slot.

26-26(a).* This method is best when cutting several shorter pieces from a long piece of stock. Note space between the fence and the pieces that have been cut off. This reduces danger of kickback. Short sleeves are safer.

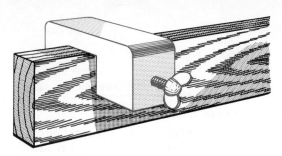

26-26(b).* This method is best when cutting individual pieces to length after the first end has been cut square. Note that both ends can be cut off with one setup. The first end is cut with the stock to the left of the saw and then the stock is cut to length by shifting it over to the right until it strikes the stop block.

26-29(b). A simple wood clamp can be made that will eliminate the need for a block.

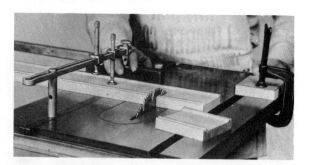

26-27.* This is another good method of cutting shorter pieces to length. The miter-gage clamp is excellent for holding the stock very accurately in the location established by the stop block.

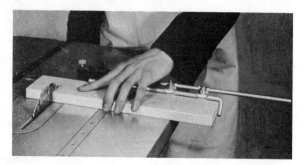

26-28.* Placing the stop rod on the miter gage is a good idea when the pieces are short enough and when only one or two pieces must be cut to length. This is a quick setup. Remember to roll up your sleeves.

26-29(a).* Here a stop block is clamped to the auxiliary fence or facing strip to control the length.

the fence to control the length of cut. Make sure that the block is just in front of the blade itself so that once the cut is made the pieces will be free and clear and will not bind; thus there will be no kickback. *Never attempt to use the fence itself as a stop block.* The block *must not* make contact with the work during the cutting. Fig. 26-26.

• Another way is to clamp a stop block directly to the table top at the front corner, on the side opposite the miter gage. Fig. 26-27.

• A third way is to use a stop rod in the miter gage. The rod can be set to any position so that all pieces are exactly the same length. Fig. 26-28.

• A fourth method is to attach a stop block to the auxiliary fence. Fig. 26-29.

Cutting Flat Miters

Flat miters are diagonal cuts made at an angle to the edge of the work. A 45-degree miter or angle is the most common one for making square or rectangular frames. However, it is often necessary to cut miters at other angles.

The gage can be set and used in either the open or closed position. Fig. 26-30. Closed is usually best because the work is then easier to control. Fig. 26-31. However, unless the stock is held very tightly, it will creep while the cut is being made. This results in a less than perfect fitting angle. This can be corrected by having the saw blade very sharp and feeding the stock slowly.

Several types of jigs can be used for accurate mitering. Fig. 26-32. Either of the jigs shown in Fig. 26-32 or Fig. 26-33

OPEN POSITION   **CLOSED POSITION**

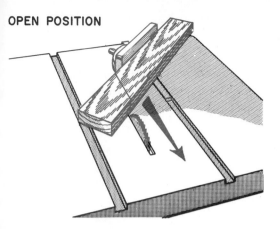
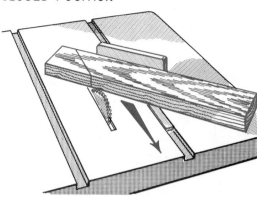

26-30. Gage in open and closed positions. Use the closed position whenever possible for cutting a flat miter.

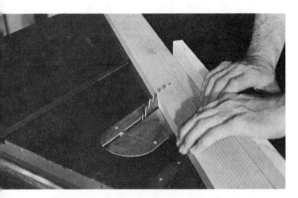

26-31(a).* Cutting a flat miter in the closed position. An auxiliary fence or facing strip helps keep the stock from "creeping." A piece of abrasive paper cemented to the wood fence will provide an added "non-slip" surface.

26-31(b).* What not to do. This opening position for cutting a picture frame is *not good.* It is difficult to hold. *The operator would be much safer without all the jewelry.* The smooth, short miter-gage surface against the *thin* edge of the molding doesn't provide enough holding surface.

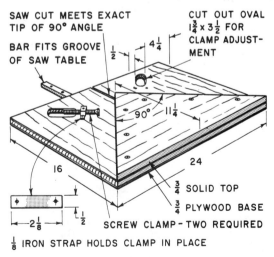

26-32(a). Using a mitering jig to cut a 45-degree corner.

26-32(b). One type of mitering jig, having a plywood base and a solid top.

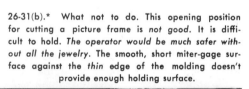

SAW CUT MEETS EXACT TIP OF 90° ANGLE

CUT OUT OVAL $1\frac{3}{4} \times 3\frac{1}{2}$ FOR CLAMP ADJUSTMENT

BAR FITS GROOVE OF SAW TABLE

$\frac{1}{2}$ $4\frac{1}{4}$

90° $11\frac{1}{4}$

16   24

$2\frac{1}{8}$ $\frac{1}{2}$

$\frac{3}{4}$ SOLID TOP

$\frac{3}{4}$ PLYWOOD BASE

SCREW CLAMP—TWO REQUIRED

$\frac{1}{8}$ IRON STRAP HOLDS CLAMP IN PLACE

279

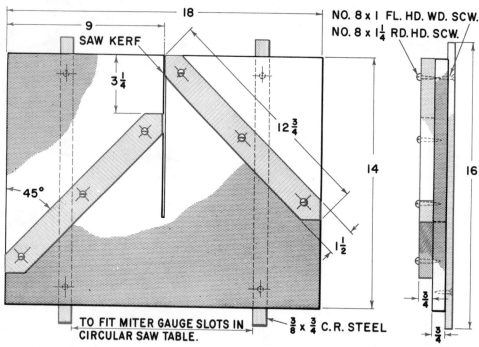

26-33(a). This mitering jig is made from 3/4" plywood, fitted with metal guides that ride in the slots. For precision miter cuts, make the screw holes in the two guide pieces about 1/16" larger than the screw heads to allow for adjustments.

will produce a perfect 45-degree right- and lefthand miter every time. Both types will hold the stock securely.

Cutting a Bevel Across Grain

A bevel or edge miter is made by tilting the blade to the correct angle, usually 45 degrees, and using the miter gage set at right angles. Check the angle of tilt on the tilt gage or, for more accurate work, use a sliding T bevel. Fig. 26-34. Adjust the height of blade for the thickness of stock. Also decide on whether to make the cut from the right or left side of the blade. Before turning on the power, slide the gage along the slot to make sure the blade will not hit the gage. It may be necessary to move the gage to the opposite side. Hold the stock firmly against the gage and make the cut as you would any crosscut.

Cutting Plywood and Other Large Sheet Materials

Because of its size, panel stock is hard to cut. Always adjust the blade so it just clears the top. Place the stock with the good side up. Fig. 26-35. There are several ways of doing the cutting:

• When the cut is started, reverse the miter gage in the groove to guide the stock along as far as possible. Then the gage can be removed and slipped into the regular position to complete the cut. Fig. 26-36.

• Panel stock can be cut with the fence acting as a guide. Fig. 26-37.

• A board with a straight edge can be clamped on the underside of the plywood. Fig. 26-38. This will act as a guide against the edge of the table. This method is especially good if one edge of the plywood is uneven.

No. of Pieces	Name	Size
1	Mounting Board..................	¾ x 14 x 18
2	Guide Strips..................	¾ x 1½ x 12¾
2	Metal Guide Bars (C.R.S.).......	⅜ x ¾ x 16
4	Round Head Wood Screws......	No. 8 x 1¼
4	Flat Head Wood Screws.........	No. 8 x 1

26-33(b). Bill of materials for the mitering jig.

26-33(c). Using the mitering jig. Short sleeves are safer.

26-34.* Cutting a bevel across grain by tilting the saw blade to 45 degrees.

26-35.* Note that the saw just clears the top of the plywood and that the better wood surface is up. If there is any splintering, it will be on the back surface. There are special saw blades for cutting plywood. Remember, in cutting plywood you are cutting both with and across the grain no matter in what direction the cut is made.

26-36.* The miter gage is reversed in the slot and the fence used as a guide when cutting dadoes on a large plywood piece. If cutting *through* the stock, the fence should not be used.

26-37. Wide panel stock can be cut with the fence acting as a guide. An extension table will make it easier to handle the stock. Operator's sleeves should be rolled up more.

26-38(a). A board that has a straight edge can be clamped to the underside of the stock and used as a guide against the edge of the saw table.

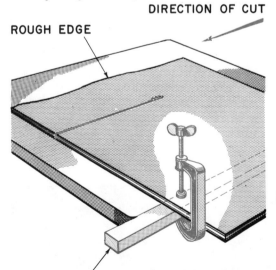

DIRECTION OF CUT

ROUGH EDGE

STRAIGHT EDGE CLAMPED TO STOCK

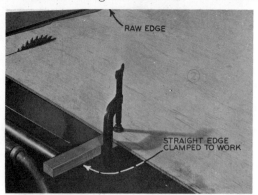

26-38(b).* If there is danger that the surface may be damaged, place a piece of scrap stock over as well as under the panel stock.

TABLE FOR COMPOUND MITER CUTS

Tilt of Work	4-Side Butt		4-Side Miter	
	Blade Tilt	Miter Gauge	Blade Tilt	Miter Gauge
5 degrees	½	85	44¾	85
10 degrees	1½	80¼	44¼	80¼
15 degrees	3¾	75½	43¼	75½
20 degrees	6¼	71¼	41¾	71¼
25 degrees	10	67	40	67
30 degrees	14½	63½	37¾	63½
35 degrees	19½	60¼	35¼	60¼
40 degrees	24½	57¼	32½	57¼
45 degrees	30	54¾	30	54¾
50 degrees	36	52½	27	52½
55 degrees	42	50¾	24	50¾
60 degrees	48	49	21	49

26-39(a). This table of compound angles must be consulted before making a compound miter cut. For example, suppose you wish to cut a four-sided mitered frame with the sides tilted to 20 degrees. Look across the column to the 4-side miter. Note that the tilt of the blade must be 41¾ degrees and that the miter gage must be adjusted to 71¼ degrees.

26-39(b).* Making a compound miter cut, with the blade tilted and the miter gage set at an angle.

Making a Compound Miter Cut

A compound miter cut, sometimes called a hopper or bevel miter, is a combination of a miter and a bevel. To make this cut, adjust the blade to the correct tilt, and the miter gage to the correct angle. Fig. 26-39.

RIPPING OPERATIONS

Ripping is cutting a board lengthwise with the grain. Use either a ripsaw or a combination saw. The fence is normally used as a guide to position and maintain the stock for the correct width of cut. It is usually placed to the right of the blade. In all ripping operations, the stock should make solid contact with the top of the table and the fence so that it will not wobble or get out of line. Before ripping, make sure one edge is straight. The major hazard is kickback. Fig. 26-40. If the kerf that is already formed binds on the saw or closes, the stock is likely to shoot back with great force and injure anyone in its path. Several things can be done to minimize this danger.

• Never stand directly back of the saw or in line with the revolving blade. Always stand behind and to the side of the saw, reaching over with the right hand to push the stock through.

• Use a splitter to keep the kerf open. Fig. 26-41. Often there are anti-kickback fingers attached to the top of the splitter. These bear on the wood and keep it from moving backwards.

• Always make use of a guard when ripping. There are a few ripping operations that can't be done with the guard. If these must be done, use other protective devices.

• Never rip stock with loose or large, unsound knots. If a knot becomes loose just after it is cut in two, it can fly out with terrific force. Always knock out loose knots with a hammer before starting to saw.

282

26-40. This illustration shows many poor practices in ripping. Note that the operator is standing directly behind and in line with the saw blade. In case of kickback, he would be struck in the stomach. The work is *too narrow* for hand feeding and the saw is too high. No splitter is being used, so the long saw kerf may close and bind against the blade.

26-41. The splitter helps to hold the kerf open. A push stick is good for final ripping.

Accessories for Ripping

There are several accessories for ripping. When sawing long lumber, a *roller support* is needed at the outfeed end of the cutting. This device is especially useful if a helper is not available. Fig. 26-42. For ripping narrow stock, a *push stick* or *push block* is needed. There are many types of these. Fig. 26-43. It is good to have several different types and thicknesses ready. In every case, the *thickness* of the push stick should be *less than the distance between the saw and the fence.*

Another device that is extremely useful is a *feather board* or *spring board,* Fig. 26-44. This is a piece of wood cut on one end at an angle of about 45 degrees, with slots cut in the same end to make it somewhat flexible. The feather board, which is used to apply side pressure for ripping, should always be just in front of the saw blade. Fig. 26-45. Side pressure should never be applied to the blade as stock is being cut. A second feather board can be used to hold the stock firmly against the table. Fig. 26-46. Such an arrangement is good for resawing stock.

Many operators like to add an *auxiliary wood fence* to the metal one. While it isn't necessary for straight ripping, it is essential for work that involves the dado or molding head. It is also a good

26-42. Roller support.

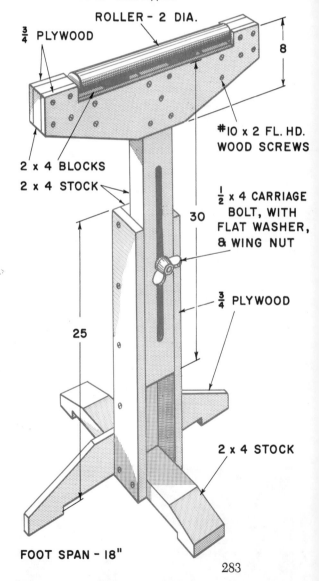

ROLLER - 2 DIA.

¾ PLYWOOD

8

#10 x 2 FL. HD. WOOD SCREWS

2 x 4 BLOCKS

2 x 4 STOCK

½ x 4 CARRIAGE BOLT, WITH FLAT WASHER, & WING NUT

30

¾ PLYWOOD

25

2 x 4 STOCK

FOOT SPAN - 18"

283

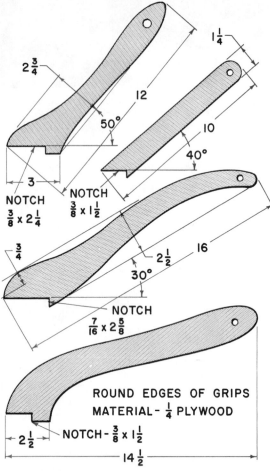

NOTCH $\frac{3}{8}$ x $2\frac{1}{4}$

NOTCH $\frac{3}{8}$ x $1\frac{1}{2}$

NOTCH $\frac{7}{16}$ x $2\frac{5}{8}$

ROUND EDGES OF GRIPS
MATERIAL - $\frac{1}{4}$ PLYWOOD

NOTCH - $\frac{3}{8}$ x $1\frac{1}{2}$

26-43(a). Several different designs of push sticks. Make sure the stick is always thinner than the width of stock to be cut. If the push stick is too wide, it will not clear between the guard and fence. Even more dangerous, if the saw cuts into the end of the stick, it may flip out of your hand, causing your hand to drop into the saw or making the stock kick back.

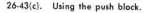

26-43(c). Using the push block.

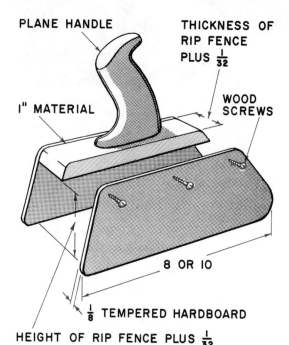

PLANE HANDLE

THICKNESS OF RIP FENCE PLUS $\frac{1}{32}$

1" MATERIAL

WOOD SCREWS

8 OR 10

$\frac{1}{8}$ TEMPERED HARDBOARD

HEIGHT OF RIP FENCE PLUS $\frac{1}{32}$

26-43(b). This push block fits over the fence. It is excellent for cutting thin pieces of panel stock such as hardboard or particle board.

idea when thin stock is being ripped or whenever there is danger that the revolving saw will touch the fence. A piece of wood can be fastened to the inside of the metal fence. However, a wooden fence that fits completely over the metal one, with a recess cut out for the blade, is better. Fig. 26-47.

Ripping Wide Stock

Stock is considered wide when it measures at least 5″ between the blade and the fence. Adjust the blade to the correct height by using the stock as a guide. Fig. 26-48. In the correct setting, the blade extends only slightly above the stock. Although the blade cuts less efficiently this way than if it protrudes 2″ or 3″, this method is safer, and that of course is most important.

The fence may be adjusted for width

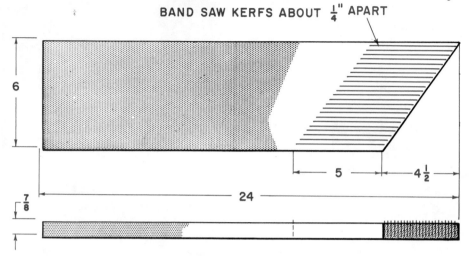

BAND SAW KERFS ABOUT ¼" APART

6

7/8

5

4½

24

USE SOLID LUMBER

26-44. A feather board.

by holding a rule at right angles to it, Fig. 26-49, or by holding a large square against it, and measuring the desired width. A still more simple method is to place the marked stock against the fence and then move the fence until the cutting line is directly back of the saw blade. Fig. 26-50.

Turn on the power. With your left hand, hold the stock against the fence with a slight amount of side pressure and push the stock forward with the thumb of your right hand. Fig. 26-51. Move the stock as fast as the saw will cut. As you near the end of the cut, continue to press forward with the right hand alone (between the blade and the fence); allow the sawed-off stock to fall to the floor or have a helper (tailman) at the rear of the saw remove it. In ripping long stock, it is necessary to have a helper or a roller stand to hold the stock level and against the fence. The helper should never pull the stock.

Ripping Narrow Stock

If stock is less than 5" in width, the hand will not pass safely between the

26-45. Note that the feather board is clamped to the table with a hand screw so that the pressure is just ahead of the saw blade. Apply just enough pressure to hold the stock lightly but firmly against the fence. If side pressure is applied next to the saw, it will cause binding which results in kickback.

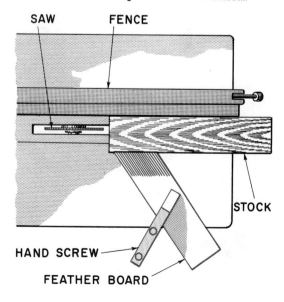

SAW   FENCE

STOCK

HAND SCREW

FEATHER BOARD

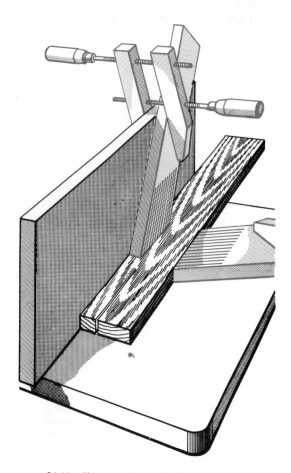

26-47(b).* The auxiliary wood fence is being used here with the molding head. To cut up to the corner of stock, the cutter must be so close to the fence that it would rub on the metal if the extra fence weren't used.

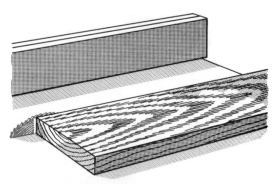

26-48. Adjust the saw blade so it extends about ⅛" to ¼" above the stock.

26-46. This setup is good for ripping long, thin stock. A high auxiliary wood fence should be attached to the metal fence. After the cut is almost complete, stock can be pulled through.

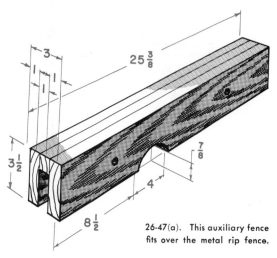

26-47(a). This auxiliary fence fits over the metal rip fence.

saw and the fence. However, there are safe ways to rip narrow stock. Fig. 26-52(a). The best method is to use a push stick. This stick should be thinner than the distance between the blade and the fence so it never comes in contact with the revolving blade. Apply forward pressure with your right hand and use the left hand to hold the stock firmly against the fence as the cut is started. When the end of the stock is over the front of the table, pick up the push stick. Fig. 26-52(b). Continue applying pressure with the push stick to complete the cut and to move the stock beyond the revolving blade. Never reach over the saw itself, even with a guard on it, to pick up the stock.

A second method of ripping narrow stock is to saw slightly more than half the length. Then draw the stock back out of the saw, turn it over end for end, and complete the cut from the other end. Fig. 26-52(c).

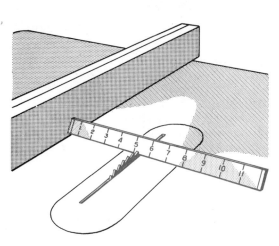

26-49. Using a rule or square to adjust the fence for width of cut.

a.

b.

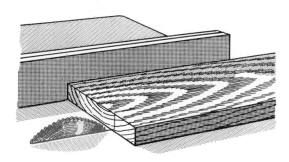

26-50. The line on the end of the stock must be in line with the saw. A light groove in the metal insert will help to line up the cut.

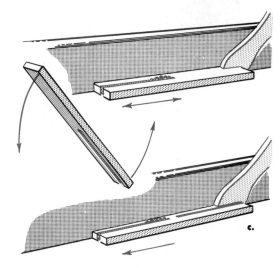

26-51. Ripping stock to width.

c.

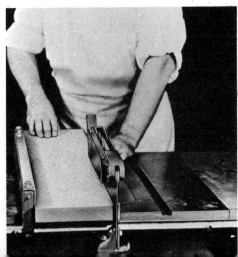

26-52(a). Cutting stock to narrow widths. A push block is used to apply forward pressure. Never run your hand between the revolving blade and the fence.

    (b).   Using a push stick for cutting narrow stock.

    (c).   Another method of ripping narrow stock. Saw halfway through the stock and then move the stock back out of the saw. Turn the stock end for end and complete the cut.

287

26-53.* Cutting a bevel with the grain. Here the blade is set too high.

26-54(a).* Resawing. Raise the saw blade to a little over half the thickness of the stock.

26-54(b). An L-shaped support is clamped to the back of the fence to support a holddown clamp.

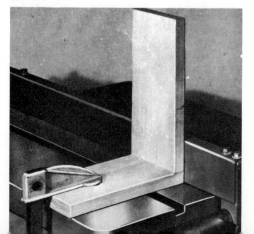

Cutting a Bevel with the Grain

Tilt the blade to the desired angle and adjust for height. On most saws the blade tilts to the right. In such cases the fence should be placed on the right side. (If the blade tilts left, the fence goes on the left side.) Adjust for width and complete the cut as you would for straight ripping. Fig. 26-53.

Resawing

Resawing involves ripping a board to make one or more thin pieces. While this can be done on the circular saw, the band saw is better for it since the blade is narrower and less stock is wasted. Also, a large band saw can make a wider cut to complete the resawing in one step.

The guard on most saws must be removed for resawing. Therefore a setup should be made that will provide plenty of support for the work and protection for the operator. One method is to attach a high auxiliary fence to the metal fence. Then use two feather boards, one to apply pressure from the top and the other to hold the stock against the fence. Adjust the saw to slightly more than half the width of the stock. When resawing hardwood, it is a good idea to make a shallow cut first and then raise the blade so it extends above the stock about 1/4" more than half the stock width. Make a cut from either edge to complete the operation. Another method of resawing is shown in Fig. 26-54. If the cut is still not complete, finish on the band saw.

Ripping Very Thin Stock

Install a hollow-ground blade. Clamp a plywood auxiliary table over the regular table and saw. Turn on the power and raise the blade slowly, cutting through the plywood table. Place the thin stock on the table; hold and feed it with a thick piece. The auxiliary table can be reused.

288

Edge Cutting

It is frequently necessary to make edge ripping cuts—for example, when cutting a raised panel. Whenever such cutting must be done, a wide auxiliary board should be fastened to the metal fence to give plenty of support for the cut. Also, make sure that the metal insert is in good condition so there is no danger that the thin edge may slip into the opening. With both hands hold the stock firmly against the auxiliary fence as the cut is made. Fig. 26-55.

CUTTING WEDGES OR TRIANGULAR PIECES

To cut wedges or triangular pieces, it is necessary to make a wood jig. For example, one should be used for cutting corner blocks. Several sizes and shapes should be available for cutting other common items. Fig. 26-56. A handle can be added to push the jig along. Fig. 26-57. The jig can be made even safer by constructing it in two parts, with a hinge on one end so the jig can actually close over the stock.

Cut the wedge opening in the jig. Place the stock in the notch; adjust the jig while it is held firmly against the rip fence. Cut one wedge, then reverse the stock end for end to cut the second wedge.

26-54(c). Note the setup for completing the second cut. Side pressure is applied to the stock. The work must slide under the parallel clamps and therefore is held firmly to the table. The stock is moved with a push stick.

26-55. This shows edge cutting a bevel on a raised panel.

26-56. This type of jig can be used to cut glue or corner blocks.

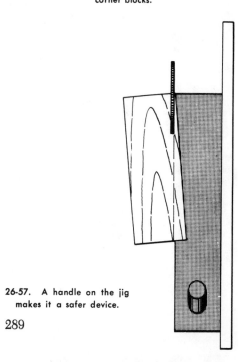

26-57. A handle on the jig makes it a safer device.

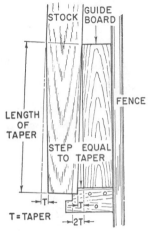

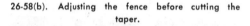

26-58(a).   A fixed jig is easy to make.

26-58(b).   Adjusting the fence before cutting the taper.

26-59.* This type of jig is good for cutting tapered plywood legs.

Taper Cutting with a Fixed Jig

If only one angle of a taper is to be cut, a simple fixed jig is best. The jig consists of a guide board, and a stop block with two notches in it. The distance from the first notch to the end of the guide board must equal the length of taper, and the notches themselves are each equal to the amount of taper on one side of the stock. Fig. 26-58. The jig is placed against the fence and the fence is adjusted so that the jig and the work, laid side by side, just touch the blade. Now place the work against the first notch and make one taper cut. If a four-sided taper is to be cut, saw the adjacent side with the same setting. Then use the next notch to make the taper cuts on the opposite sides. Use a sharp, hollow-ground combination saw blade. Another type of fixed jig can be used when cutting a taper on only one side. Fig. 26-59.

Taper Cutting with an Adjustable Jig

If several different tapers must be cut, it would be wise to make an adjustable tapering jig. Make the jig of two pieces of hardwood about 3/4" x 4" x 34". Join these pieces with a hinge on one end. Fig. 26-60. Add a stop block and slotted adjustment strap. Lay off and make a permanent line 12" from the hinged end. Figure the amount of taper and then adjust the jig to the correct taper per foot.

290

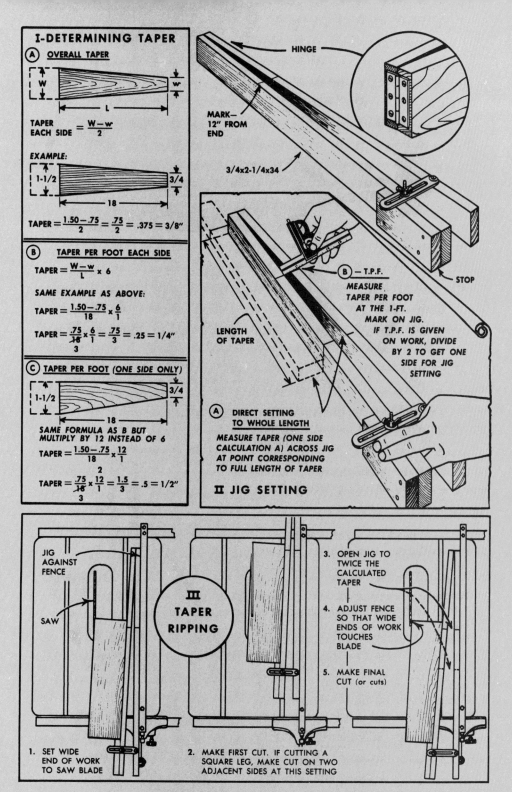

I—DETERMINING TAPER

Ⓐ OVERALL TAPER

$$\text{TAPER EACH SIDE} = \frac{W - w}{2}$$

EXAMPLE:

$$\text{TAPER} = \frac{1.50 - .75}{2} = \frac{.75}{2} = .375 = 3/8''$$

Ⓑ TAPER PER FOOT EACH SIDE

$$\text{TAPER} = \frac{W - w}{L} \times 6$$

SAME EXAMPLE AS ABOVE:

$$\text{TAPER} = \frac{1.50 - .75}{18} \times \frac{6}{1}$$

$$\text{TAPER} = \frac{.75}{\overset{3}{\cancel{18}}} \times \frac{6}{1} = \frac{.75}{3} = .25 = 1/4''$$

Ⓒ TAPER PER FOOT (ONE SIDE ONLY)

SAME FORMULA AS B BUT MULTIPLY BY 12 INSTEAD OF 6

$$\text{TAPER} = \frac{1.50 - .75}{18} \times \frac{12}{1}$$

$$\text{TAPER} = \frac{.75}{\overset{3}{\cancel{18}}} \times \frac{12}{1} = \frac{1.5}{3} = .5 = 1/2''$$

HINGE

MARK 12" FROM END

3/4 x 2-1/4 x 34

STOP

LENGTH OF TAPER

Ⓑ — T.P.F.

MEASURE TAPER PER FOOT AT THE 1-FT. MARK ON JIG. IF T.P.F. IS GIVEN ON WORK, DIVIDE BY 2 TO GET ONE SIDE FOR JIG SETTING

Ⓐ DIRECT SETTING TO WHOLE LENGTH

MEASURE TAPER (ONE SIDE CALCULATION A) ACROSS JIG AT POINT CORRESPONDING TO FULL LENGTH OF TAPER

Ⅱ JIG SETTING

JIG AGAINST FENCE

SAW

Ⅲ TAPER RIPPING

1. SET WIDE END OF WORK TO SAW BLADE

2. MAKE FIRST CUT. IF CUTTING A SQUARE LEG, MAKE CUT ON TWO ADJACENT SIDES AT THIS SETTING

3. OPEN JIG TO TWICE THE CALCULATED TAPER

4. ADJUST FENCE SO THAT WIDE ENDS OF WORK TOUCHES BLADE

5. MAKE FINAL CUT (or cuts)

26-60. Follow these steps in determining the taper, setting the jig, and ripping the taper.

26-61.* Cutting a taper with an adjustable jig.

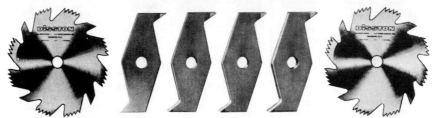

26-62. The typical dado head consists of two outside cutters and several inside chippers.

Another method is to lay out the taper line on the stock. Then place the jig and stock against the fence and open the jig until the layout line is parallel to the fence. Fig. 26-61. Make the first cut. Readjust the jig and make the second cut.

USING THE DADO HEAD

The dado head is a most useful accessory for cutting grooves, dadoes, rabbets, tenons, and lap joints. There are several kinds of dado heads. The most common one consists of two outside cutters, each 1/8″ thick and several inside chippers of different thicknesses. Fig. 26-62. Using various cutters and chippers, it is possible to cut grooves from 1/8″ to 13/16″, increasing by 1/16″. To cut a 7/16″ groove, for example, use two outside cutters of 1/8″ each and two inside chippers, one 1/8″ and one 1/16″. If it is necessary to enlarge the groove slightly, paper washers can be placed between the chippers. To install this kind of dado head, remove the insert plate and the saw blade. Place the inside blade on the

26-63. A dado head attached to the saw arbor ready for use. The insert plate is ready to be replaced.

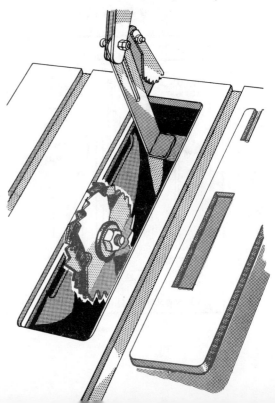

arbor, then the chippers, then the outside blade, the collar, and the nut. When two or more chippers are used, distribute them equally around the saw. Place the two cutting edges of the inside chippers in line with the bottom of the gullets (the spaces between the groups of blade teeth). This is necessary because the inside chippers are swaged (bent) thicker near their cutting edges. This swaged part must be allowed to enter the gullet. If this isn't done, oversized grooves and dadoes will be cut. Fig. 26-63. After the dado-head assembly is attached to the arbor, use the large opening in the insert plate that is designed for this purpose. There are several kinds of one-unit, adjustable dado heads in which the desired width of cut can be obtained by setting a dial. Fig. 26-64.

Cutting Grooves

A *groove* is a slot cut with the grain of the wood. Fig. 26-65. The fence is used as a guide for this operation. Adjust the dado head for height and move the fence

26-64(b). A second type of adjustable one-piece dado head.

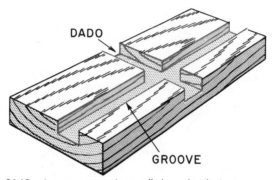

26-65. A groove, sometimes called a *plough*, is a slot cut *with* the grain; a *dado* is a slot cut *across* grain.

26-64(a). A one-piece, quick-set adjustable dado head.

26-66. Cutting grooves with a dado head.

26-67. Cutting a blind dado.

293

to the correct position. It is a good idea to clamp a feather board to the fence directly above the work, in order to hold the stock firmly against the table. The dado head takes a big "bite" out of the wood; therefore there is a strong tendency to kickback. Feed the stock into the dado head, applying side pressure to the fence to keep it in line. Fig. 26-66.

A *blind dado* is one that stops short at one or both ends of the stock. This is made for a blind spline joint. To make this cut, one wood stop must be clamped to an auxiliary wood fence at the beginning of the cut, and another at the end. Fig. 26-67. Turn on the power. Hold one end of the stock against the first stop and lower it into the saw. Push the stock along until it strikes the second stop, then carefully raise the stock. The first stop helps to prevent kickback which takes place most often as the cut is started.

Cutting a Dado

A *dado* is a groove cut at right angles to the edge grain. Remove the fence and use the miter gage with an auxiliary board to support the work. Mark the location of the dado on the edge of the stock and make the cuts. Figs. 26-68. The fence can be used as a stop block and guide to control the location of the dadoes. Fig. 26-69. This is especially useful when cutting matching dadoes for a chest or cabinet. To cut regularly spaced dadoes, the miter gage can be used with

the stop rod as a stop. To position the next dado, the stop rod can fit into the last groove that has been cut.

CUTTING JOINTS

The circular saw can be used for making most joint cuts. For many kinds of joints, two or more methods can be followed. All joint cuts should be made with a standard combination blade, a carbide-tipped combination blade, or a dado head. There are also special purpose saws like the miter saw for joint work. Fig. 26-70. For many joint cuts it is difficult to use a standard guard. However, jigs, fixtures, and protective devices should be used whenever possible. Also, follow all safety rules with great care.

Butt Joints

All basic butt joints can be cut by simple crosscutting operations. A carbide-tipped blade will produce a better surface for gluing. Boring operations should be done on a drill press or boring machine when one is available.

Edge Joints

Edge joints involve ripping. The *plain edge* is a simple ripping operation that can be followed by smoothing the edge on a jointer. However, a carbide saw normally produces a satisfactory edge for gluing. The *rabbet edge* can be cut as described under the next heading. The *spline edge* is cut by using a single saw

26-68.* Cutting a dado with the stock held against the miter gage.

26-69.* Here the fence acts as both guide and stop block to cut several dadoes in a wide board.

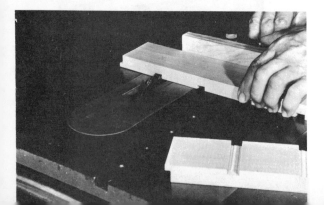

26-70. This miter saw is designed for making accurate angle cuts.

26-71.* Cutting a narrow groove for a spline.

blade to form a groove on the adjoining edges. Two or more passes may be necessary to produce the correct width. Fig. 26-71. A better method is to use a dado head of the correct width. The *tongue* and *groove* is best cut with a dado head. The groove is cut in a single pass with a head of correct thickness. The matching tongue is cut by placing a spacer collar between the blades of the dado head, with a chipper on the outside of each blade to remove waste stock. The *dowel edge* is a plain edge with dowels installed.

Rabbet Joints

An *end rabbet joint* is a crosscutting operation that can be done with a single blade, though using a dado head is far better. If a single blade is used, first mark the width and depth of the rabbet on one edge of the stock. For the first cut, have the end grain against the fence and the face surface against the table. Fig. 26-72. Make the second cut with the end of the stock held against the table and the face against a high fence.

To make this cut with a dado head, always use an auxiliary wood fence so that the dado head can cut into the fence slightly. Then hold the face of the stock against the table, and the edge against the miter gage, to cut the rabbet in one or more passes.

To cut an *edge* rabbet with a single blade, mark the shape of the rabbet on the end grain. Make the first cut with the face against the fence and the edge against the table. Fig. 26-73(a). Make the second cut with the opposite edge against the fence and the edge against the table. Fig. 26-73(b).

The dado head can also be used to cut a *rabbet with or across end grain*. This is ideal for production work since only one setup is needed. Fig. 26-74.

26-72. Making the first cut for an end rabbet.

295

26-73(a).* Making the first cut for an edge rabbet. The operator should roll up his sleeves.

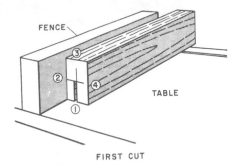

FENCE

TABLE

FIRST CUT

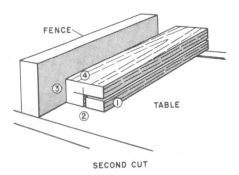

FENCE

TABLE

SECOND CUT

26-73(b). Here are the two cuts for completing a rabbet joint by the safest and best method.

26-74. With a dado head, a single pass will cut a perfect rabbet on all edges. Note the use of the feather board for added protection.

Dado Joints

All standard dadoes are best cut with a dado head, set to exact width. Fig. 26-75. They can also be cut by making several passes with a single blade, then cleaning out the waste with a chisel. The dado can be cut at any angle to the edge. Fig. 26-76.

The *blind* or *stop dado* can be cut by clamping a stop block to the fence or the saw table to control the length of cut. The corner will have to be squared with a chisel. Fig. 26-77. However, it is easier to make this joint on a radial-arm saw. The *corner dado* is cut by holding the stock in a V block against the miter gage. Fig. 26-78. The *full-dovetail dado* is made by first cutting a mortise or slot. Cut a dado to the narrowest width, as indicated on the drawing. Then replace the dado head with a single blade and adjust to an angle of 15 degrees. Make the angle cut on either side to clean out the mortise. (Using a dovetail bit in a router is a more accurate but harder way to make these angle cuts.) The tenon is cut in two steps with a single blade. First cut the kerfs in the faces. Then adjust the blade to a 15-degree angle and make the two shoulder cuts. (Again, a better method is to use the router.) The *half-dovetail dado* is cut the same way except that the angle cuts are made on only one side of the joint.

Lap Joints

All lap joints are best cut with a dado head. To cut the wide dado that is

26-75(a). Cutting dadoes with the edge of the stock held against the miter gage.

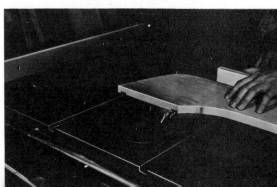

26-75(b).* Note the three-foot rule clamped to the fence as a guide for setting the various cuts. The operator should roll up his sleeves.

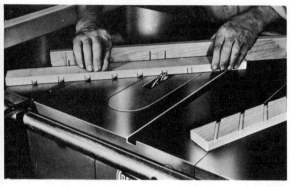

26-76.* Cutting a series of dadoes at an angle. This could be used to make shutters, for example.

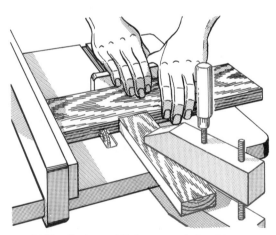

26-77. Cutting a blind or stop dado with a stop block clamped to the table to control the length of cut.

26-78.* Cutting a corner dado with a V block held against the miter gage.

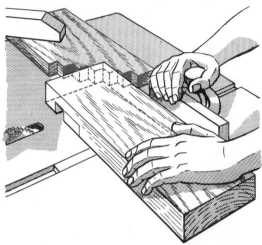

26-79. Using a notched stop block to control the width of cut for a lap joint.

26-80.* Here's another method of cutting a cross-lap joint at an angle. One stop block is attached to the fence to locate one side of the lap, and a second stop block is fitted to the auxiliary fence to locate the other. Start with the stock against the first block, then make several passes until it is firmly against the second. Short sleeves are safer.

26-81.* Cutting a flat miter to length, with one end held against a stop block clamped to the auxiliary wood fence. Short sleeves are safer.

297

needed, clamp a notched stop block to the top of the table, far enough ahead of the saw blade so it won't interfere. Use this stop block as a guide before starting each cut. Fig. 26-79. Several passes will be needed to cut the wide dado (for a cross lap) or wide rabbet (for an end lap). Fig. 26-80. Whenever possible, cut both pieces of stock at the same time to make a single joint.

Miter Joints

All *flat miter joints* are cut by a method similar to that shown in Fig. 26-81. A spline can be added to a flat miter by first making a jig of scrap wood to hold the stock at an angle of 45 degrees. Adjust the height of the blade to equal the depth of the spline cut. Adjust the fence so that the cut will be in the correct position from right to left. Hold the stock firmly against the jig and cut the groove for the spline. Fig. 26-82. If the spline is thicker than the width of the blade, a second pass may be necessary. A special thin blade may be needed if a groove is cut for clamp nails.

There are several methods of cutting the groove for a *spline miter on edge.* Fig. 26-83. The simplest is to tilt the saw blade to an angle of 45 degrees, set the miter gage at 90 degrees, and use the fence as a stop block. Note that an auxiliary wood fence is used so there is no danger that the blade will strike the metal fence. Adjust the height of the blade and cut the groove. Fig. 26-84. To cut a groove for a *blind spline,* it is necessary to cut a recess from the same side of both pieces, about three-fourths the distance across the end grain. Fig. 26-85.

To install a *feather across a miter corner,* make a wood jig to hold the joint at an angle of 45 degrees. Set the blade to the correct height and adjust the fence so that the cut is in the center across the corners. Fig. 26-86. A *miter with rabbet*

26-82. Cutting a groove for a spline for a flat miter joint.

can be cut by following the steps in Fig. 39-71. Lay out and cut the two rabbets, one of which is twice as wide as the other. Then make a miter cut on each piece to complete the joint. A *lock miter* can be cut on a circular saw by first cutting the grooves and then the miter. However, it is much better to cut this joint on a shaper. To cut a *compound miter* or *hopper joint,* adjust the blade and the miter gage to the correct settings. For a *miter with end lap,* the best method is to make the rabbet cuts with a dado head—a square cut on one piece, an angle cut on the other. Then cut the end of one piece at a 45-degree angle.

26-83. A spline is good for holding an edge miter securely in place.

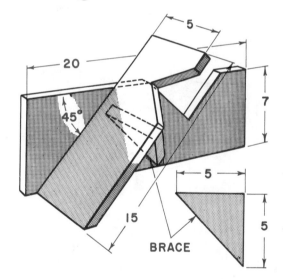

SPLINE

26-84(a). Cutting a groove for a spline. The workpiece is on the table and rides against the fence.

WORKPIECE CUT AT 45°

TABLE   FENCE

SAW BLADE AT 45°

26-84(b). A jig like this makes it possible to cut the groove for the spline with the saw blade at right angles to the table. The jig is held against the miter gage. ➡

20   5

45°   7

15   5   5

BRACE

Mortise-and-Tenon Joints

All enclosed mortises (those with stock on four sides) should be cut with a mortiser, with a mortising attachment on a drill press, or with a router. Fig. 26-87. An open mortise can be cut on a saw by using a dado head of the correct thickness and holding the stock in a homemade or commercial tenoning jig. Fig. 26-88.

Several methods of cutting a tenon are as follows:

• Adjust a dado head to a height equal to the thickness of the stock to be removed on one side of the tenon. Then make one or more passes to cut half the tenon. Reverse the stock and cut the other side. The work is held against the miter gage and a stop block controls the lengths of tenon. Fig. 26-89(a). The stop rod on the miter gage can also be used to control length. Fig. 26-89(b).

26-85. A blind spline is cut about three-fourths of the way across the end, from matching edges on both pieces.

299

26-86. Making a saw kerf across the corner of a frame for installing a key or feather. Note the jig for holding the stock.

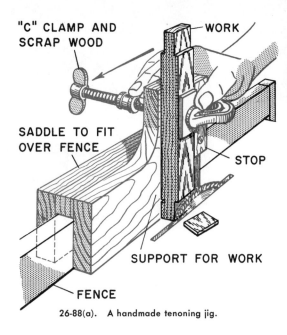

"C" CLAMP AND SCRAP WOOD

WORK

SADDLE TO FIT OVER FENCE

STOP

SUPPORT FOR WORK

FENCE

26-88(a). A handmade tenoning jig.

26-87. Parts of a mortise-and-tenon joint.

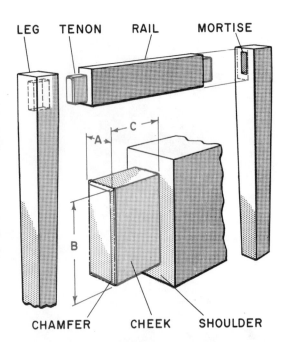

LEG TENON RAIL MORTISE

C

A

B

CHAMFER CHEEK SHOULDER

A - THICKNESS OF TENON
B - WIDTH OF TENON
C - LENGTH OF TENON

26-88(b). A commercial tenoning jig.

26-89(a).* Cutting a stub tenon with the dado head. A stop block is clamped to the auxiliary fence to control the length of the tenon. Short sleeves are safer.

26-89(b).* Using the stop rod on the miter gage to control the length of the tenon being cut with a dado head.

26-90.* Making the shoulder cuts.

• Set the fence so that the distance from the outside of the saw to the fence is equal to the length of the tenon. Adjust the saw height for correct depth of shoulder cut. Use a miter gage. Hold the end of the tenon against the fence and make the two shoulder cuts from each face. Fig. 26-90. Using the same fence setting, adjust the saw height to the correct depth for the shoulder cut. Complete the shoulder cuts from the edges. Now adjust the fence and the height of the saw to make the cheek cuts from each face. Be sure that the waste stock is outside the saw. Use a jig to hold the stock when making these cuts. With the same saw depth, change the fence setting to make the final cheek cuts from each edge of the stock.

• In production work, an excellent method of cutting tenons is with a dado head which has a spacer between the blades, and chippers on the outside to remove the extra stock. A tenoning jig or a special bracket holds the stock. Fig. 26-91.

Miscellaneous Joints

To cut a *box* or *finger joint*, first fasten an auxiliary wood fence on the miter gage. Use a dado head of exactly the same thickness as the width of the fingers and grooves. Adjust the dado head for the correct depth of cut, then cut two dadoes in the auxiliary wood fence with a distance between them equal to the width of the dado. Now mount a guide pin, equal in size to the dado cut, as shown in Fig. 26-92(a). With the auxiliary fence in the same position as for the dado cuts, take the two pieces of stock

26-91(a). Cutting a tenon, using a dado head with a spacer collar. In this setup, a homemade tenoning jig holds the stock.

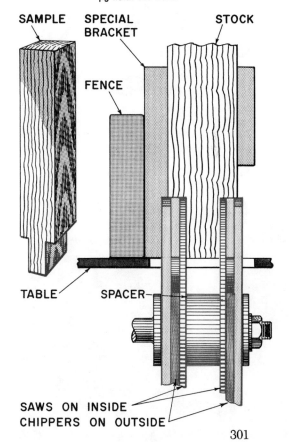

SAMPLE SPECIAL BRACKET STOCK

FENCE

TABLE SPACER

SAWS ON INSIDE
CHIPPERS ON OUTSIDE

301

26-91(b). This is the same setup as in Fig. 26-91(a), except that a commercial tenoning jig is used. Short sleeves are safer.

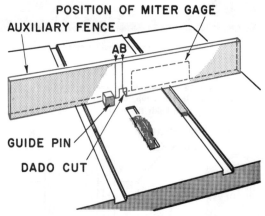

POSITION OF MITER GAGE
AUXILIARY FENCE
AB
GUIDE PIN
DADO CUT

26-92(a). A jig for cutting a box joint. Note the location of the square guide pin. To start the cut, place the edge of one piece in line with line A and the other over line B.

26-92(b). Cutting the box joint. Short sleeves are safer.

which are to be joined, and hold them against the miter gage. One piece should be offset a distance equal to the width of the dado. Cutting both pieces at the same time in this offset position will result in a perfectly fitted joint. After each cut, the two pieces are shifted to the right so they fit over the guide pin. Fig. 26-92(b).

The *lock joint* can be cut on the saw with a dado head, although it is better to cut it on a shaper. If a saw is used, make cuts *a, b, c,* and *e* with a single blade and cut *d* with a dado head. See Fig. 39-86.

A *coped joint* is one which joins two molded pieces, such as window sash or frames. It is a fitted joint in which part of one piece is cut away or shaped to fit over the molded surface of the second piece. The joint is also found in interior trim work where the corners of moldings meet. A coped joint for a corner can be made by cutting one piece square and the other at a 45-degree miter. Then cut on the miter line of the second piece, using a jig saw with the blade at right angles to the back surface.

26-93(a). A handy device for making concave cuts on moldings and picture frames is this cove-setting jig.

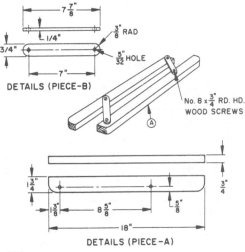

DETAILS (PIECE-B)

No. 8 x $\frac{3}{4}$" RD. HD.
WOOD SCREWS

DETAILS (PIECE-A)

26-93(b). The proper angle of the wood fence is determined by using this set of parallel rules.

CUTTING COVES

A *cove* is a rounded groove that can be made by feeding stock across the saw at a slight angle. It is necessary to take light cuts since there is a considerable amount of side stress against the saw. Coves are especially popular in decorative designs such as Early American Furniture. As a first step, draw a pencil outline on the end grain of each piece. With a dado head, remove as much waste material as possible by making a series of grooving cuts. Now adjust the saw blade to a height equal to the depth of the cove. The proper angle of the temporary fence for cutting the cove is determined by using a jig such as that shown in Fig. 26-93. Open the jig an amount equal to the width of the cove. Place the jig over the saw and turn it until it just touches the front and rear teeth of the blade. This setting deter-

mines the proper angle for the fence. The fence itself is located so that the center line of the work will intersect the center line of the saw blade. Now turn the blade down so it projects about 1/8" to 1/4" above the table; make the first cut. Continue to raise the saw and make cuts until the desired depth is reached. Fig. 26-94.

SAW-CUT MOLDINGS

Attractive saw-cut moldings can be made by cutting a series of kerfs across grain on a piece of stock. The kerfs should be cut to about one half the thickness of the stock. Then reverse the stock and cut another series equally spaced in between the first cuts. The stock then can be ripped to narrow widths. Several procedures for saw-cut moldings are shown in the unit on the radial-arm saw. These can also be carried out on the circular saw. See Fig. 27-69.

MOLDING HEAD

A molding head is used on a circular saw to make many kinds of fancy moldings and joint cuts. Fig. 26-95. There are several types of molding heads, but the best for the circular saw is the cylindrical one in which three blades are securely

26-94. Cutting a cove with a temporary wood fence attached to the table at an angle.

26-95. The cylindrical molding head is the best type for the circular saw.

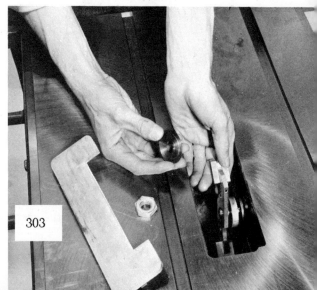

303

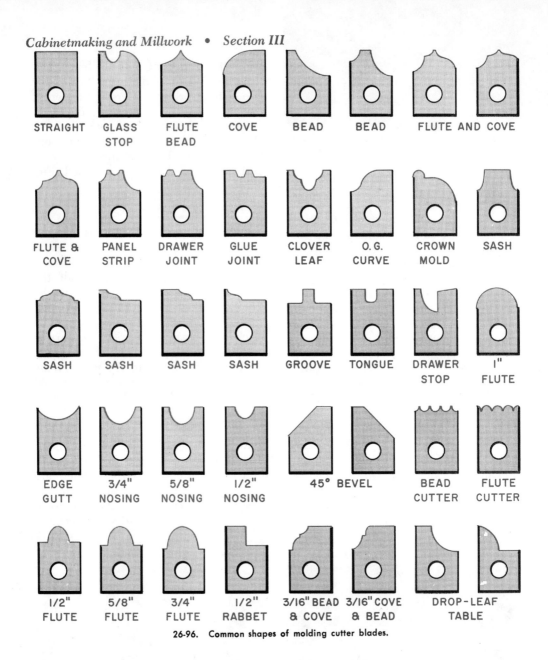

| STRAIGHT | GLASS STOP | FLUTE BEAD | COVE | BEAD | BEAD | FLUTE AND COVE |

| FLUTE & COVE | PANEL STRIP | DRAWER JOINT | GLUE JOINT | CLOVER LEAF | O. G. CURVE | CROWN MOLD | SASH |

| SASH | SASH | SASH | SASH | GROOVE | TONGUE | DRAWER STOP | 1" FLUTE |

| EDGE GUTT | 3/4" NOSING | 5/8" NOSING | 1/2" NOSING | 45° BEVEL | BEAD CUTTER | FLUTE CUTTER |

| 1/2" FLUTE | 5/8" FLUTE | 3/4" FLUTE | 1/2" RABBET | 3/16" BEAD & COVE | 3/16" COVE & BEAD | DROP-LEAF TABLE |

26-96. Common shapes of molding cutter blades.

locked. A wide variety of molding cutter blades can be used. Fig. 26-96. They can be sharpened by rubbing the flat cutting-edge sides on an oilstone. Before using any molding head, attach an auxiliary wood fence to the metal fence. This can be a single piece of wood fastened to one or both sides of the metal fence. Fig. 26-97. To make a molding, first lay out the design on a piece of paper. The design should be identical in size to the end grain of the stock. Then choose the correct set of cutters and lock them firmly in the molding head. Remove the saw blade and attach the molding-cutter saw head. An insert plate with a

26-97. A wood fence should be used for all molding operations.

26-98. Using the molding head to cut a decorative edge on a table top.

wider opening, similar to that for the dado head, is required.

Edge Molding of Straight Stock

Most moldings are cut on the edge or side of large stock. When the cut is made along the side, the operation is much the same as sawing. Fig. 26-98. First use a piece of scrap stock of the same size or thickness as the finished piece to check the operation of the molding head. When the stock must stand on edge, it is good to use a higher wood fence or to provide extra support as shown in Fig. 26-99. If both end grain and edge grain are to be cut, cut end grain first since it may splinter a little. If the stock is held flat on the table, the miter gage can be used to help guide the work.

Molding with the Miter Gage

When molding edge grain or across face grain, the miter gage with an auxiliary wood fence is used to hold the stock. Note that in Fig. 26-100 the auxiliary fence has a metal or wood pin attached to it. Then a guide board with equally spaced slots is attached to the stock. The pin can be located in any position, since the guide board determines the spacing of the cuts. A series of crosscuts forms the molding. The shape of the molding is determined by the shape of the cutters used, by the spacing of the cuts, and by the height of the cutterhead.

26-99. Here's a good way to shape the edge of stock with a molding head. Note the extra piece of stock clamped to the work for support.

26-100. Cutting moldings with the molding head. Note that the molding itself (dark wood) is fastened on top of a guide board (light wood) which has equally spaced cuts or slots. The pin located in the auxiliary fence controls the spacing.

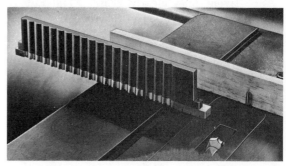

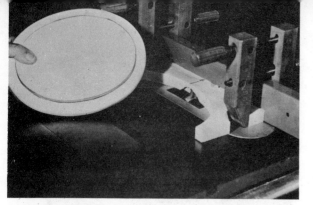

26-101(a). Note the jig used to guide the circular stock.

26-101(b). Press the work into the cutter and rotate it slowly.

Molding on Circular Stock

Circular stock is best shaped by cutting a reverse jig to the same radius as the stock. This jig is clamped or fastened to the fence so that the center line of the work and that of the jig are in line. Push the work gradually into the cutter, then rotate it slowly. Fig. 26-101.

(27) Radial-Arm Saw

The radial-arm saw, or radial saw as it is sometimes called, is an excellent sawing machine. In addition it can be used as a shaper, jointer, drill, boring tool, sander, router, and wood lathe. Fig. 27-1. It is particularly good for fast, convenient, and accurate crosscutting (whereas the circular saw is better for ripping). It is also very useful for making many kinds of joint cuts such as a dado or stop dado. The advantage of this saw is that all cutting is done from the top, making layout lines clearly visible. The saw is never hidden beneath the wood.

The radial-arm saw is almost always used to rough cut lumber to length if a special-purpose cutoff saw is not available. For all types of crosscutting, including straight cutting, cutting miters, bevels, dadoes, and rabbets, the stock is held on the table in a fixed position and the saw is moved in the same direction as its rotation. Fig. 27-2. For ripping operations, the saw is held in a locked position and the stock is moved into the revolving blade. Fig. 27-3.

27-1. The radial-arm saw is made in many sizes. This heavy-duty machine is used in cabinet shops.

306

RADIAL-ARM SAW

MAINTENANCE

• Clean the tracks inside the arm with a cloth dampened with lacquer thinner or carbon tetrachloride. This will remove grease and dirt. Do not lubricate the tracks.
• Make sure the wood table is in good condition. Replace it and the guide fence when they are warped or have too many saw kerfs.
• Check with a square to make sure the saw blade is square with the guide fence and table top when the arm and motor are in the zero position.
• Make sure all clamps and adjustments work easily.

LUBRICATION

• Apply a good grade of lubricating oil to the elevating screw or shaft, miter latch, swivel latch, and bevel lathe.
• Motor bearings are sealed and require no further lubrication.

SAFETY

• When properly used, the radial-arm saw is one of the safest power tools ever made.
• For all crosscutting operations the stock is held against the table and guide fence. This eliminates kickback, a major cause of saw accidents.

• Make sure the blade is sharp and properly mounted. It should be held securely with an arbor collar and nut.
• Keep the safety guard in position when operating the machine.
• Make sure all clamps and locking handles are tight.
• Always return the saw to the rear of the table after completing a cut.
• Shut off the power and wait until the saw comes to a dead stop before making any adjustments.
• Extension tables on the sides of the saw are helpful when working with long stock.
• Never remove stock from the table until the saw has been returned to the rear.
• Use a stick to remove small wood scraps from the table.
• Keep the table clean. Brush off sawdust after the saw has been used.
• Always keep your hands away from the saw's path.
• Use the guard and anti-kickback fingers when ripping.
• When ripping, make sure the blade rotates toward you.
• Also when ripping, feed the stock under the safety guard from the side opposite the anti-kickback fingers. Never stand directly behind or in line with the saw.
• When ripping narrow stock, always use a push stick to complete the cut.

27-2. In crosscutting, the saw blade moves in the same direction it is rotating. The saw's thrust is downward and to the rear, thus holding the stock firmly against the guide fence.

27-3. When ripping stock, always feed it into the rotation of the blade.

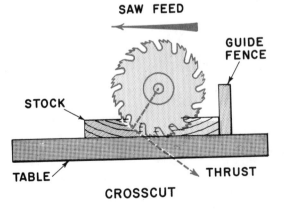

SAW FEED

GUIDE FENCE

STOCK

TABLE

THRUST

CROSSCUT

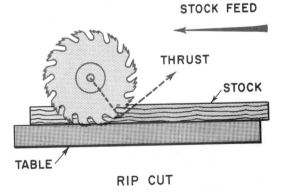

STOCK FEED

THRUST

STOCK

TABLE

RIP CUT

27-4. On this machine the sawing unit moves back and forth directly under the radial arm.

There are several designs of radial-arm saws. On one type, the motor unit containing the saw blade moves back and forth directly under an overarm. Fig. 27-4. On another, an *arm track* that rotates for making certain cuts is fastened to the center of the overarm. Fig. 27-5. The size of the radial-arm saw is determined by the diameter of the blade commonly used and the horsepower rating. A third factor sometimes involved is the length of the overarm or arm track. Machines are available with extra length overarms or tracks for cutting wide stock, particularly panel stock such as plywood, hardboard, or particle board. Common sizes of radial-arm saws are 10", 12", and 14".

ACCESSORIES

Accessories and cutting tools for the radial-arm saw are available in wide variety so this machine can be used for many specialized operations.

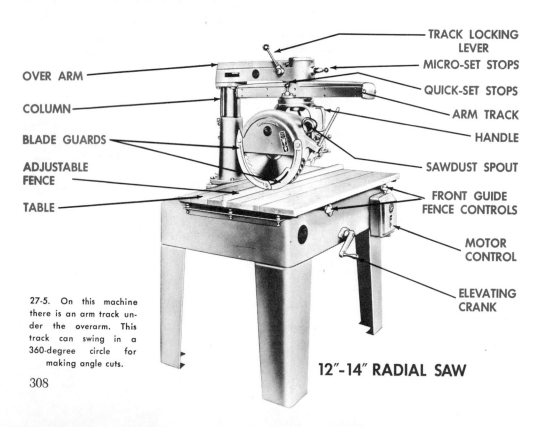

27-5. On this machine there is an arm track under the overarm. This track can swing in a 360-degree circle for making angle cuts.

OVER ARM

COLUMN

BLADE GUARDS

ADJUSTABLE FENCE

TABLE

TRACK LOCKING LEVER

MICRO-SET STOPS

QUICK-SET STOPS

ARM TRACK

HANDLE

SAWDUST SPOUT

FRONT GUIDE FENCE CONTROLS

MOTOR CONTROL

ELEVATING CRANK

12"-14" RADIAL SAW

SAW BLADES

Radial-arm saw blades are similar to those for the circular saw. The basic ones are combination, hollow-ground, rip, and plywood. The combination blade is most commonly used since it can make many kinds of cuts effectively. Blades are made in diameters from 9″ to 18″ to fit saws of different sizes. These saws also use dado heads, similar to those used on the circular saw, for cutting rabbets, dadoes, and other kinds of slots. Many other types of winged and straight cutters can be used, such as the panel raising tool. See Unit 49.

REPLACING A SAW BLADE

Remove the nut that holds the guard in place, then remove the guard assembly. Move the overarm up so the blade will slide off the shaft easily and clear the table top. Lock or hold the shaft and remove the nut and collar from the arbor. Fig. 27-6. Remove and replace the blade, with the teeth pointing in the direction of rotation. Fig. 27-7. Replace the arbor collar and nut, and tighten securely. Then replace the guard. Fig. 27-8.

COMMON ADJUSTMENTS

Three common adjustments are necessary for making setups for all types of sawing. Fig. 27-9. The overarm or track can be rotated in a complete circle, although it is normally moved only 180 degrees. The yoke that holds the motor can be turned 360 degrees. The blade and motor unit in the yoke can be tilted 90 degrees to the right or to the left. The adjustments are made as follows:
• Adjustment for depth of cut is made by turning the elevating crank or handle, located directly above the column or in front of the table. For normal cutting, the saw blade is adjusted so that it is 1/16″ below the table top. Fig. 27-10.
• The angle of cut is adjusted by releasing the miter clamp handle or the

27-6. The arbor can be held with a hex wrench. On some machines it can be locked. Use the correct size wrench to loosen the arbor nut.

27-7. Replacing the saw blade. On many machines an arrow on the motor housing shows the direction of rotation.

27-8. The guard is in place. A wing nut holds it firmly on the motor housing.

309

RADIAL ARM CONTROLS
LEFT SIDE

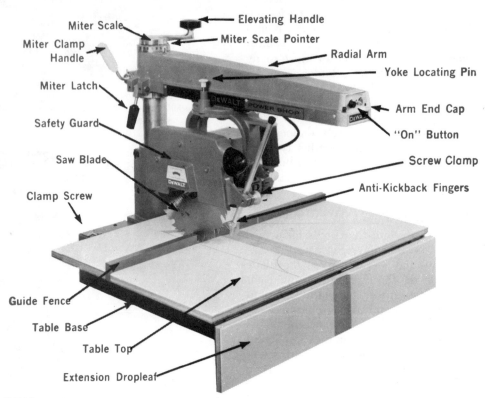

Miter Scale

Miter Clamp Handle

Miter Latch

Safety Guard

Saw Blade

Clamp Screw

Elevating Handle

Miter Scale Pointer

Radial Arm

Yoke Locating Pin

Arm End Cap

"On" Button

Screw Clamp

Anti-Kickback Fingers

Guide Fence

Table Base

Table Top

Extension Dropleaf

27-9(a). Study the names of the parts and controls. You must know them to follow directions for making adjustments and cuts. See Fig. 27-9(b).

track-locking lever and turning the radial arm or track to the correct angle. Most machines have an automatic stop for the 45-degree position both right and left. Fig. 27-11.

•Bevel cuts are made by releasing the bevel clamp handle and tilting the motor and saw unit to right or left to the correct degree. Fig. 27-12.

•For ripping operations, pull up on the yoke locating pin or the quick-set pin, then turn the motor and yoke one-fourth turn for ripping. There are also stops on the radial arm or track for limiting the outward movement of the saw. Fig. 27-13 shows settings being made.

CROSSCUTTING OPERATIONS

Simple Crosscuts

For straight crosscuts make sure that the radial arm or track is at right angles to the fence which is indicated by zero on the miter scale. Adjust the depth of cut so that the teeth of the blade are about 1/16″ below the surface of the wood in the saw kerf. This extra clearance is needed to cut completely through the board. Adjust the guard so it parallels the bottom of the motor. Set the anti-kickback finger about 1/8″ above the surface of the wood to keep your fingers away from the blade. Push the

310

RADIAL ARM CONTROLS
RIGHT SIDE

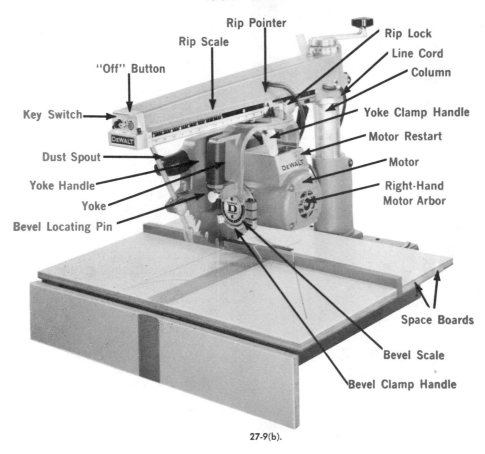

Rip Pointer

Rip Scale

Rip Lock

Line Cord

Column

"Off" Button

Key Switch

Yoke Clamp Handle

Motor Restart

Dust Spout

Motor

Yoke Handle

Right-Hand
Motor Arbor

Yoke

Bevel Locating Pin

Space Boards

Bevel Scale

Bevel Clamp Handle

27-9(b).

27-10. Adjusting the depth of cut. On most machines each full turn of the elevating handle raises or lowers the arm 1/8".

27-11. To adjust for a miter cut, release the arm clamp handle and swing the arm to the angle you want.

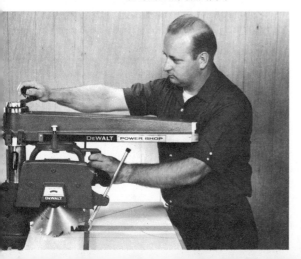

27-12. To tilt the motor, pull out the bevel clamp and locating pin, and move it to the desired angle. The locating pin automatically stops at 0, 45, and 90 degrees.

27-13. Release the yoke clamp and lift the locating pin. Then swing the yoke right or left to the correct position.

27-14. It is easy to crosscut stock with a straight line movement of the saw.

saw all the way back to the column, and mark a line on the stock where the cut is to be made; then slide the work on the table and against the fence until the layout line is in line with the saw blade.

Turn on the power and allow the saw to come to full speed; then hold the stock firmly as you slowly draw the revolving blade into the work. Fig. 27-14. Little or no effort is required since the cutting action tends to feed the blade into the stock. As a matter of fact, never allow the blade to move too quickly through the work. When the cut is complete, return the saw blade behind the fence and turn off the power. In holding the stock for crosscutting, it is possible to use either the right or left hand. Likewise, either hand can pull the saw to do the cutting. Actually, the righthand method, with the longer part of the stock to the left of the blade, is easier. Fig. 27-15.

To cut stock that is thicker than the capacity of the machine, cut through half the thickness, then turn it over and cut from the other side. Fig. 27-16.

Cutting Identical Lengths

When several pieces of the same length are needed, a stop block can be clamped to the table. A rabbet cut at the end of the block will prevent sawdust from catching in the corner and interfering with the accuracy of the cuts. Fig. 27-17. Another method of cutting several pieces to the same length is to clamp or hold them together and cut across all at the same time. Fig. 27-18. To cut a board that is wider than the capacity of the saw, the stop-block arrangement can also be used. Cut from one side as far as possible, then turn the board over; hold it against the stop block again to complete the cut. Fig. 27-19. Extra-length radial arms or tracks are available when a great deal of panel cutting needs to be done. This type is needed by finish carpenters who do interior paneling.

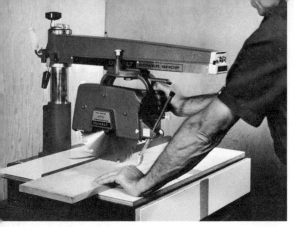

27-15(a). The righthand method of cutting is easier and more comfortable.

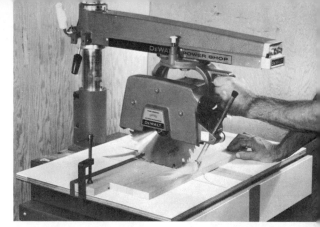

27-17. Clamp a stop block to the table to cut a number of pieces to identical length.

27-15(b). In the lefthand method most of the stock is to the right of the saw. Note the additional free-floating guard. The safety rings are free to adjust automatically for depth and angle of cut.

27-18. Trimming several pieces to the same length at one time.

27-16. To line up the kerf for making the second cut on heavy stock, use the kerf on the table top as a guide. Watches should not be worn.

27-19(a). Hold the stock against a stop block and cut as far as possible on a wide board.

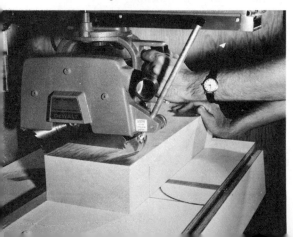

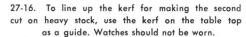

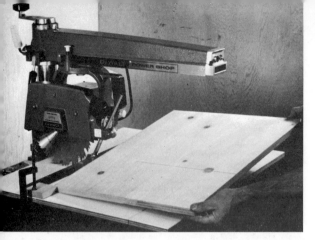

27-19(b). Reverse the board side for side and align the kerf by holding the end against the stop block.

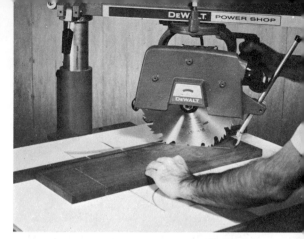

27-21. Hold the stock with your left hand and pull the saw with your right to cut a miter.

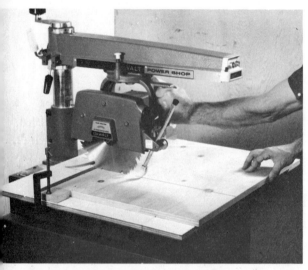

27-19(c). Complete the cut.

27-20. Hold the stock firmly against the guide fence to make a bevel cut.

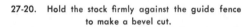

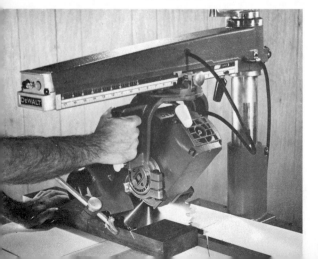

Bevel Cutting

To make a bevel cut, keep the track or radial arm at right angles to the fence, as for straight cutting, but tilt the motor unit to the correct angle. Before making the adjustment, raise the saw so that the blade will clear the table top when you swivel the motor and yoke. Then lower the blade again until it just cuts into the wood table top about 1/16″. If a 45 degree bevel is to be cut, there is a locking pin which will automatically stop at this position. The cutting is done exactly as straight cutting. Fig. 27-20.

Mitering

To cut a miter, the radial arm or the arm track is rotated to the right or left to the correct angle. The cutting itself is done the same as straight crosscutting. To make this adjustment, raise the blade slightly, then release the arm clamp handle or the track-locking lever, and lift the miter latch. Swing the arm or track to the correct angle. For the 45 degree miter there is an automatic stop. After the angle has been set, readjust the blade for correct depth of cut. Adjust the kickback fingers to clear the top of the work. Fig. 27-21. Hold the stock with one hand and pull the saw through with the other. Fig. 27-22. Most miter cuts require a cut on both ends of the stock. This is true in making any kind of frame. Of

314

27-22. After cutting a miter on one edge of stock, readjust the arm or track to the lefthand position to cut a miter on the other edge. Hold the stock with your right hand and pull the saw with your left.

27-23(b). Notice that the beveled edge is held against the table guide board when cutting the second miter. A stop block could be used to control length. The matching pieces would not have to be of identical length when following the method shown here.

course, the arm or track can be moved from one side to the other to make the cut, but there are simpler ways:

Method A. Adjust the arm to the right at 45 degrees, then clamp a straight guide board at right angles to the guide fence. Make sure there is enough space between the extra guide board and the fence for the work to slip in between. Now place the stock against the guide board and also firmly against the fence. Cut one end of the stock. Fig. 27-23(a). Then hold the stock against the regular guide fence and cut the other end. Fig. 27-23(b).

Method B. Another method of cutting both ends is to use a large V block clamped to the table top. The saw is kept in straight crosscutting position. Hold the stock against the left side of the block for cutting one end and against the right side for cutting the other. Fig. 27-24.

27-24(a). Cutting the miter on the first end. Stock is held against the left side of the V block.

27-23(a). Note that the first end is cut with the stock held firmly against the auxiliary guide board. It's a good idea to check with a square to make sure this is at 90 degrees to the table guide board.

27-24(b). Cutting the second end. Stock is held against the right side of the V block. With this method, matching pieces must be of identical length before mitering. Note also that the hands must shift to do the cutting. The right hand is on the saw on the first cut, the left hand on the second cut.

315

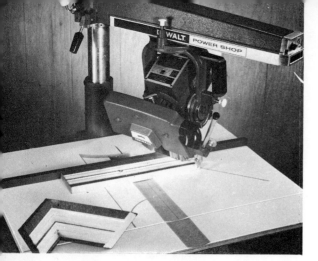

27-25. A shadow-box picture frame has a compound miter cut.

Compound Miter Cuts

The compound miter, sometimes called a hopper or bevel-miter, is a combination of a miter and a bevel. It is used to make a frame or box with sloping sides, and for certain roof framing cuts. Fig. 27-25. To make this cut, the arm or track is adjusted to the correct angle and the motor unit tilted the correct amount. Fig. 27-26. The cutting is done as any crosscutting operation. Fig. 27-27.

RIPPING

For ripping, the radial arm or track must be at right angles to the fence and the saw blade parallel to it. The saw can be adjusted to in-rip or out-rip positions. For the in-rip position, pull the swivel latch and turn the motor and

27-26(a). Chart for adjusting the machine to make compound miter cuts. As an example for using the chart, suppose you need a four-sided picture frame with the sides sloping out at 25 degrees. Follow the circular line marked "square box" and find 25 degrees. Follow the horizontal line across to right or left. It reads 23 degrees. This is your miter setting. Then, from 25 on the curve again, follow the vertical line down and you will find it reads 40. This is the bevel setting.

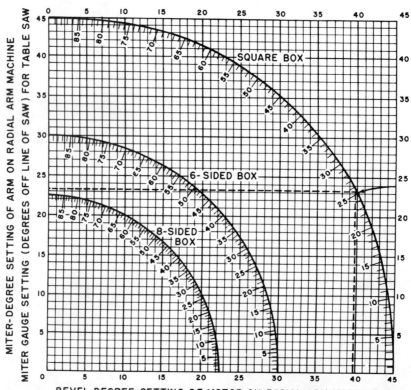

MITER-DEGREE SETTING OF ARM ON RADIAL ARM MACHINE
MITER GAUGE SETTING (DEGREES OFF LINE OF SAW) FOR TABLE SAW

BEVEL DEGREE SETTING OF MOTOR ON RADIAL ARM MACHINE
TABLE OR BLADE SETTING (DEGREES OFF VERTICAL) FOR TABLE SAW

316

The figures in the table below are degrees to nearest quarter-degree, and are for direct setting of track-arm and blade tilt. Taper per inch given in second column applies only to front elevation and only to a 4-side figure.									
Tilt of Work	**Equivalent Taper per Inch**	**4-Side Butt**		**4-Side Miter**		**6-Side Miter**		**8-Side Miter**	
		Blade Tilt	Track-Arm	Blade Tilt	Track-Arm	Blade Tilt	Track-Arm	Blade Tilt	Track-Arm
5°	.087	½	5°	44¾	5°	29¾	2½	22¼	2
10°	.176	1½	9¾	44¼	9¾	29½	5½	22	4
15°	.268	3¾	14½	43¼	14½	29	8¼	21½	6
20°	.364	6¼	18¾	41¾	18¾	28¼	11	21	8
25°	.466	10	23	40	23	27¼	13½	20¼	10
30°	.577	14½	26½	37¾	26½	26	16	19½	11¾
35°	.700	19½	29¾	35¼	29¾	24½	18¼	18¼	13¼
40°	.839	24½	32¾	32½	32¾	22¾	20¼	17	15
45°	1.000	30	35¼	30	35¼	21	22¼	15¾	16¼
50°	1.19	36	37½	27	37½	19	23¾	14¼	17½
55°	1.43	42	39¼	24	39¼	16¾	25¼	12½	18¾
60°	1.73	48	41	21	41	14½	26½	11	19¾

27-26(b). Table of compound angles for use on the radial-arm saw. Note that angles are given for both *butt* and *miter* joints.

yoke one-fourth turn, placing the motor toward the outside and the saw blade toward the column; lock in position. Ripping is then done from the right side of the table. Fig. 27-28.

Move the saw in or out for the correct

27-28. Ripping stock with the blade in the in-rip position. Note the use of a push stick to complete the cut.

27-27. Making the compound miter cut.

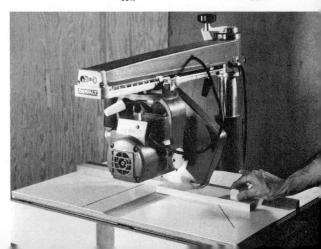

27-29. Fingers of the anti-kickback device should rest firmly on the wood surface.

27-30. Feed the stock from the right side of the machine. Place your left hand about 6" behind the safety guard and use it to hold the stock down and against the guide fence. Feed stock with your right hand. Let the stock slide under your left hand. When the right hand comes up even with the left, that is the time to use a push stick.

27-31. Use a push stick to complete the cut. Push the stock about 2" beyond the saw, then pull the stick directly back.

width of cut, then lock it in position. Now lower the overarm or track until the saw blade just touches the table and is slightly below it. Adjust the guard so that it clears the top of the stock by about 1/8". Set the anti-kickback fingers so that the prongs rest firmly on the wood surface and hold it against the table. Fig. 27-29. The saw must rotate up and toward you. The dust spout on top of the guard should be adjusted to carry the dust away from you.

Turn on the power and allow the saw to come to full speed. Place one edge of the stock against the guide fence; feed the stock steadily and firmly forward to make the cut. Fig. 27-30. As you approach the end of the cut, use a push stick. Fig. 27-31. For extremely wide cuts, the saw can be adjusted to the out-rip position, with the motor toward the column. Fig. 27-32. When the machine is set in this position, the stock must be fed from the left side. Fig. 27-33. Bevel ripping is done by tilting the blade to the correct angle and cutting as for straight ripping. Fig. 27-34.

Cutting Tapers

There are several common methods of cutting a taper on a radial-arm saw. The simplest is to use a step jig exactly like that for the circular saw. Fig. 27-35. The second method is to use an adjustable jig like that used on a circular saw. Fig. 27-36.

The third way involves clamping a piece of narrow stock to the lower edge of the stock, thus making the front edge of the table into a second guide fence. Taper ripping can be done at the correct angle with this method. Just decide the degree of taper, then clamp the lower guide board to the piece to be ripped. Turn the saw to the out-rip position. This allows the blade to be positioned directly over the front edge of the work table. The completed cut will be at the same angle as the guide board.

318

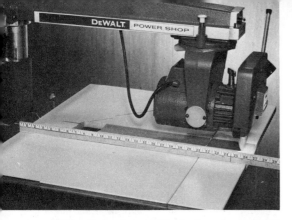

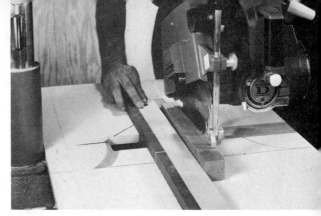

27-32. The maximum width of cut can be made with the saw in the outfeed position. The stock must then be fed from the left side. Note that the guide fence has been moved as far toward the column as possible.

27-35(a). The step or fixed jig is made to cut a specific taper. See Fig. 26-58(a). One end of the stock is placed in the correct notch while the other end rides against the far end of the jig. Place the stock in the first notch, then cut one side of the taper. Turn the stock one quarter turn and use the same notch to make the second cut. Then use the second notch to cut the adjoining tapers.

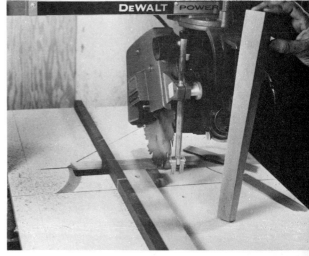

27-33. Ripping a wide panel with the saw in the out-rip position.

27-35(b). The taper is cut on two sides.

27-34. Cutting a bevel with the grain by tilting the motor unit to the correct angle.

27-36. Using an adjusting jig to cut a taper. See Fig. 26-60. Unit 26.

319

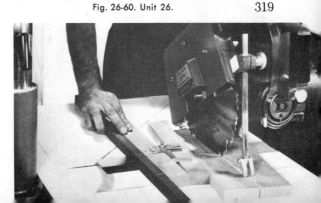

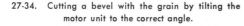

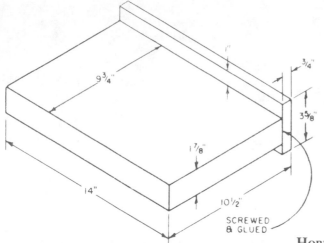

1"

3/4"

9 3/4"

3 5/8"

1 7/8"

14"

10 1/2"

SCREWED & GLUED

27-37. Auxiliary wood table for horizontal cutting. This table is installed in place of the standard guide fence. To do this, release the clamp screws, lift out the guide fence, slide in the auxiliary table, then retighten the clamp screws.

27-38. Cutting across the end of stock, with the work held against the auxiliary table.

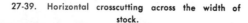

27-39. Horizontal crosscutting across the width of stock.

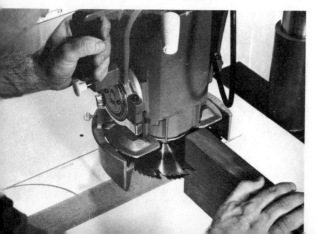

HORIZONTAL CUTTING

In horizontal cutting the motor unit is set to a vertical position so that the saw blade is actually parallel to the table top. Usually an 8″ blade is used with a special guard. An auxiliary wood table is needed for cutting thin stock since the blade can't be lowered more than 1¼″ above the table top. Fig. 27-37.

Horizontal Crosscutting

This is cutting across the end of stock. To position the saw for this, raise the radial arm approximately 3″ above the table top. With the saw in the crosscut position, pull it to the front of the arm. Hold the top of the saw guard in your left hand, then release the bevel clamp handle and bevel latch. Swing the motor into a 90-degree horizontal position and lock the bevel clamp handle by pushing it back. Depth of cut depends upon position of the stock in relation to the saw blade. Fig. 27-38. Turn on the motor and pull the saw through the stock as in crosscutting. Fig. 27-39.

Horizontal Ripping

Horizontal ripping is exactly the same as horizontal crosscutting except that the cut is made on the side of stock instead of on the end. To place the blade in the horizontal rip position, set the saw in

320

the in-rip position and tilt it 90 degrees. Place the stock against a regular or auxiliary table guide fence, depending on the stock's thickness, and locate the height and depth of the cut. Fig. 27-40. A piece of 3/4″ plywood can be used as an auxiliary table.

Using a Dado Head

As mentioned earlier, the same types of dado heads used on the circular saw are also used for radial-arm work. These are used for such operations as cutting grooves, rabbets, dadoes, and tenons, in widths from 1/8″ to 13/16″ in a single cut. The most common type of dado head consists of two outside saws or cutters which are 1/8″ thick, combined with inside chippers of different thicknesses. Teeth on the outside cutters do not have any set. The combinations of chipper thicknesses vary somewhat. Some manufacturers include one 1/16″ chipper and four 1/8″ chippers. Others include one 1/4″ and two 1/8″. The inside chippers are swaged or bent thicker toward the cutting edges to overlap the adjacent cutter or saw. Without this there would not be a clean cut. The bent portion of the chippers must always be placed in the gullets of the outside saws, never against the teeth. Also, the inside cutters should be staggered. For example, if your inside cutters or chippers are to be used, they should be set 45 degrees apart. The chippers must never be used alone, but always in combination with the outside cutters or saws. If the dado or groove is to be wider than the dado head, two or more passes must be made. Three or four paper or cardboard washers can be put between the blades and chippers to control the width exactly. Several other types of dado heads are available that are single, adjustable units. The width of the dado can be set on the unit itself before it is fastened securely to the arbor of the saw. (See Unit 26.)

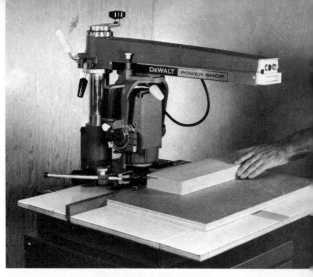

27-40. Horizontal ripping along the edge of stock.

Mounting a Standard Dado Head

A dado head is installed on the shaft or arbor in the same way as a saw blade. For example, if a 1/2″ dado is to be cut, it would be necessary to have two 1/8″ chippers with the two cutters. Place one cutter against the arbor collar, then place the two chippers so that they are 90 degrees apart and fit into the gullets of the cutter. Place the other cutter in the arbor. Fig. 27-41. Then place the arbor collar with the recessed side against the dado head and tighten the arbor nut. If the dado head is more than 1/2″, one of the arbor collars must be eliminated. If a 13/16″ dado must be cut, neither of the arbor collars can be used.

27-41. Mounting the dado head. Note how the chippers are placed an equal distance apart.

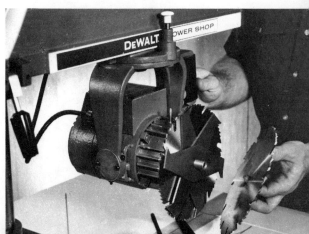

321

27-42. Cutting a plain dado.

Cutting a Plain Dado

A dado is a groove cut across grain. The procedure followed is very similar to crosscutting. Fig. 27-42. Adjust the arm or track at right angles to the fence and lower the blade to the correct height. Radial-arm saws are lowered by turning the elevating crank; on most saws one complete turn lowers the blades 1/8". This feature makes it possible to set the depth of the dado with great accuracy. A piece of scrap stock can be placed under the dado head and the blade lowered until it just touches the surface. Then the piece is removed, and the crank is given the correct number of turns for the desired depth. For example, if a dado is to be 3/8" deep, three complete turns should be made (assuming the usual 1/8" per turn ratio).

In making a chest or cabinet, it is usually necessary to cut several matching dadoes on both of the sides. One method of doing this is with a stop block clamped to the table. In this way a dado can be cut first on one piece, then a matching one cut on the other. Fig. 27-43. If parallel dadoes are needed, a series of marks can be made or a series of stops fastened to the guide fence.

In cutting a dado, always allow the

27-43. Using a stop block to control the position of the dado.

322

27-44(a). For a blind or stop dado, mark the length of the cut on the stock. Then place the stock against the guide fence and fasten a stop clamp to the radial arm to limit the length of cut.

27-44(b). Lower the dado head to the correct depth. Place in the starting position, with stock against the guide fence. Turn on the power and make the cut. If a square cut is needed at the blind end of the dado, it can be made with a hand or mortising chisel.

motor to come to full speed. Then make the cut slowly and smoothly. If extremely deep cuts are required, it is usually best to make them in two steps.

A *blind dado* can be cut by using a stop clamp on the radial arm to control the distance the saw will move. Fig. 27-44. A *corner dado* is often necessary when installing a shelf in a table. This can be made by placing the stock at 45 degrees in a V block that is clamped to the guide fence. Raise or lower the radial arm to the correct depth. Fig. 27-45. An *angle dado* is cut exactly like a plain dado except that the radial arm is set at the desired angle. Fig. 27-46.

With the dado head in the ripping position, many types of grooves can be cut with the grain. In using the dado head for grooving or ploughing, adjust the guard so that the spring clip on the infeed touches the stock. Lock the wing nut and lower the anti-kickback fingers 1/8″ below the surface of the stock. The stock should be held against the fence guide and pushed past the blade. Fig. 27-47. *Feed the wood into the rotation of the blade*. Never feed it from the anti-kickback end of the guard. A V can be cut by tilting the motor to the 45-degree position. Fig. 27-48.

27-46. Cutting dadoes at an angle.

27-47. Using the dado head for grooving (sometimes called ploughing). Note that a push stick is being used to complete the cut.

27-48. Cutting a V groove (bevel ploughing) is done with the radial arm and yoke in the straight ripping position but with the motor tilted 45 degrees. This is a good method of cutting the V block that is often needed as a jig for other machining operations.

27-45. Cutting a corner dado. Note the use of the V block.

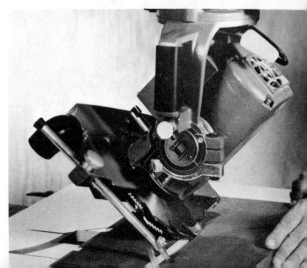

323

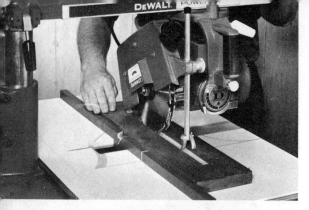

27-49. Cutting a blind groove. Extreme care must be taken, especially when raising and lowering the saw.

27-50(b). Cutting stock to width with a rabbet on the edge.

Blind Grooving

Sometimes it is necessary to cut a groove partway along the center of a board. This can easily be done with the dado head in the rip position. The best method of controlling length of cut is to fasten two stop blocks on the guide fence for the start and stop of the groove. Adjust the motor unit for the correct location of the groove, then raise the dado head. Place the stock underneath the head and against one of the stop blocks at the start position. Fig. 27-49. Then hold the stock firmly and turn on the power. Lower the head to the correct depth of cut. Push the stock along to complete the groove, then raise the dado head and turn off the power.

Cutting and Dadoing

By combining a larger combination-saw blade with a dado head, it is possible to do both cutting and dadoing or cutting and grooving at the same time. This operation would be useful primarily in production work when many pieces of the same kind are needed. With the extra blade on and with the machine in crosscut position, stock can be cut to length with a rabbet across grain; or with the machine in ripping position, stock can be cut to width with a rabbet along the edge. Fig. 27-50. For such operations an 8″ dado head with a 10″ saw blade is commonly used. If thinner stock is to be cut, use an auxiliary wood table to protect the regular table.

27-50(a). Cutting stock to length with a rabbet on the end.

27-51. Raising the special guard to check the setting of the blades.

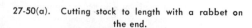

JOINERY

The radial-arm saw is an ideal tool for making many joint cuts. It is particularly useful with the dado head since it allows you to see the cut being made. Also, the length of crosscuts can be easily controlled by putting a stop clamp directly on the arm or track of the machine.

Anytime the dado head is used in a horizontal position, a special tool guard should be substituted for the standard one. After the dado head is installed, place this tool guard on the motor exactly like the standard one. Lock it in place with a wing nut. This guard can be raised high enough to check the position of the cutting tool by loosening the thumb screws on either side of the center nut. Fig. 27-51.

CUTTING JOINTS

With various attachments the radial-arm saw can cut almost all joints used in cabinetmaking. Following are helpful suggestions:
• *Butt joint.* All basic butt joints including a butt joint on edge, a butt joint flat, leg-and-rail joints, corner butt, and middle-rail butt can be cut by simple crosscutting operations. All boring operations for the dowel holes can be done with the boring bit and adapter unit as described in Unit 34.
• *Edge joint.* Most common edge joints involve ripping operations. The *plain edge* is a simple ripping procedure. For a better glue joint, use a carbide-tipped blade. Cuts for the *rabbet edge joint* can be made in two ways. One is to make a simple vertical and horizontal ripping cut on each piece. Fig. 27-52. A 1/4" piece of plywood should be used as an auxiliary table to clear the guide fence when doing this kind of cutting. The other method is to cut the rabbet in each piece with a dado head. Fig. 27-53. A *spline edge* involves cutting a groove along the middle of the edges of two

325

27-52(a). To cut a rabbet along edge grain, first make the layout on the end of the stock. Place the stock on an auxiliary table (a piece of plywood) and against the guide fence. Make the first cut with the saw in the horizontal rip position.

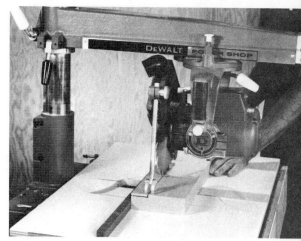

27-52(b). The second cut, which completes the rabbet, is made with the saw in the in-rip position.

27-53. Cutting an L-shaped notch along the end of stock is simple with a dado head and with the motor in a horizontal position.

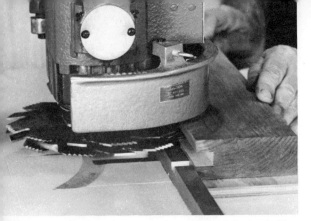

27-54. Cutting a groove with a dado head. Note the plywood placed over the table so the groove just clears the guide fence.

pieces. This is done with the head in a horizontal position and with a dado head of correct width, set to the correct depth. Using the dado head for a wide groove eliminates making several passes that are necessary when grooving with a single saw blade. Fig. 27-54. The *tongue and groove,* commonly used in wood paneling, consists of a tongue, or tenon, on one edge and a groove on the other. The best method of cutting these is to have the saw in a horizontal rip position and to use a dado head to cut all the grooves on one side of each stock piece. The tongue can be cut on the other edge by placing a spacer collar between the saw blades. Cut tongues on all pieces first, then reverse the stock to cut all of the grooves. The *dowel edge joint* is a simple ripping operation. Holes must be

bored for the dowels. The glue joint is cut with the shaper attachment.

• *Rabbet joint.* A simple end rabbet joint is a crosscutting operation that can be done with either a single blade or a dado head. If a single blade is used, vertical and horizontal crosscuts are required. Fig. 27-55. The rabbet can be cut very simply with a dado head in crosscutting position. One or more passes are needed, depending on the rabbet width.

• *Dado joint.* These joints are best cut with a dado head of correct width. However, they can also be cut by making several passes with a single blade, then cleaning out the waste with a chisel. Fig. 27-56. A *simple dado* is a crosscutting operation. The *stop, housed,* or *blind* dado is very easily cut using the dado head and a stop clamp attached to the arm to control the length of the dado. If a square cut is needed at the blind end, this can be done with a wood chisel, with a mortiser, or with a mortising attachment on a drill press. The *dovetail dado* is easy to cut. The mortise or dovetail slot is cut first. Tilt the saw blade to 15 degrees and make two angle cuts as shown in Fig. 27-57(a). Then clean out the mortise. The bottoms of the slots will not be perfect, but this is not essential to a good joint. The tenon or dovetail key is made by first cutting the straight kerfs, then tilting the blade to 15 degrees to complete the key. Fig. 27-57(b).

27-55(a). To make an end rabbet, place the stock flat against the auxiliary table and fence (see Fig. 27-37) and then make the first cut with the saw in horizontal position.

27-55(b). The second cut is a simple crosscut with the blade set for correct depth.

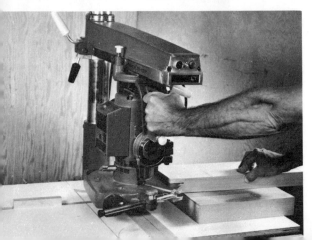

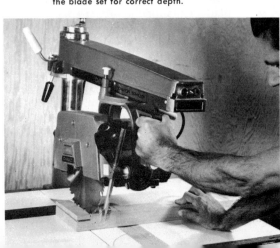

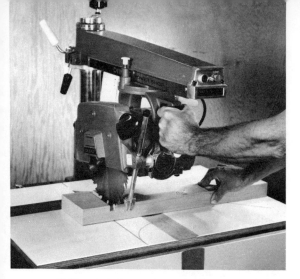

27-56. A dado can be cut with a saw blade by moving the stock slightly after each pass. However, a dado head does this much more quickly and accurately.

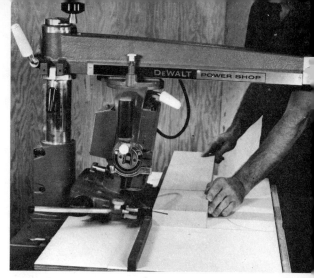

27-57(b). The dovetail cut can also be made with the grain.

27-57(a). This shows the correct method of cutting a dovetail dado across grain. Note the use of the auxiliary table.

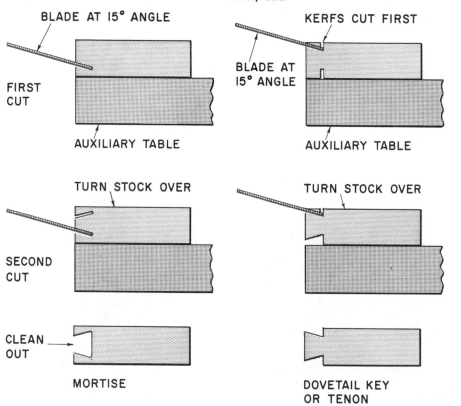

BLADE AT 15° ANGLE

FIRST CUT

AUXILIARY TABLE

KERFS CUT FIRST

BLADE AT 15° ANGLE

AUXILIARY TABLE

TURN STOCK OVER

SECOND CUT

TURN STOCK OVER

CLEAN OUT

MORTISE

DOVETAIL KEY OR TENON

327

27-58(a). Making the cuts for an end-lap joint. The half-lap joint is cut in the same manner except that the pieces are joined end to end.

27-58(b). Cutting a cross-lap joint. The dado is cut the same width as the stock and half as deep as the thickness of the stock.

• *Lap joint.* Lap joints are best cut by using a dado head. Both pieces of stock to form the joint can be cut at one time. Fig. 27-58.

• *Miter joint.* All *flat miter joints* are simple to cut by the methods described in Unit 39. Fig. 27-59. A spline can be added to the flat miter joint by placing the motor in a horizontal crosscutting position with the arm moved right or left 45 degrees. A slot for a key can also

27-59. A simple method of cutting a flat miter is to move the arm or track first to the right at 45 degrees, then left to the same setting to cut the ends.

be cut by adjusting the motor to horizontal crosscutting position with the arm set at zero. Dowel holes can be made with the boring attachment. The *miter with end lap* can easily be made by first cutting one piece to a 45-degree miter, then cutting the rabbet on that piece. The other piece should be cut at a 90-degree angle and then the angle rabbet cut. All *edge miter joints* are made as bevel crosscuts with the motor locked in a 45-degree bevel position. To make the slot for the spline, reverse the stock. Leave the motor in the bevel position but elevate the blade to the correct height, or approximately 3/8". Now the saw blade will not cut completely through. Pull the saw across the bevel cut, leaving a shallow slot. Fig. 27-60. A *blind spline* is very easily cut by using a stop clamp on the radial arm to cut only partway through the beveled edge. A *miter joint with rabbet* can be cut by following the layout shown in Fig. 27-61. The *compound miter joint* is commonly used for frame or open construction such as a shadowbox picture frame or a molding for a cabinet front. The angle of slant or pitch of the sides is important in making this cut. For example, if you wish to make a

328

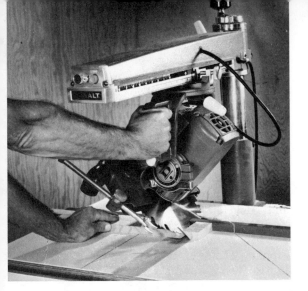

27-60(a). Cut the edge miter by making a bevel crosscut with the motor in the 45-degree position.

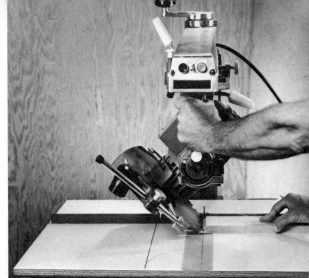

27-60(b). To make the slot for the spline, reverse the stock on the table and, with the motor in the same bevel position, raise it so that the blade will cut only the depth of the slot. The slot width is usually 1/8" or 1/4".

four-sided shadow-box picture frame with the sides sloping at 45 degrees, this means that the pitch is 45. In Fig. 27-26(a), look at the curved line labeled "square box" and find the 45-degree mark. Find the horizontal line that intersects the curved line at 45 and follow it to the left. It reads 35 degrees. This is the miter setting. Then follow the vertical line intersecting at 45 to the top or bottom of the chart. You will find it reads 30 degrees. This is the bevel setting. With the machine set at these two positions, the cut can be made. For six- or eight-sided boxes, use the correct curve and follow the same procedure.

- *Mortise-and-tenon joint.* To make a blind mortise-and-tenon joint, cut the angular opening on a mortiser or with the mortising attachment of a drill press. The mortise can also be cut by using the router attachment. The tenon is cut by placing the motor in a vertical position and a dado head in a horizontal position. A spacer collar is inserted into the dado head so that stock is left to form the tenon. Use an auxiliary table. Place the stock against the fence and mark the stock for the correct tongue or groove depth With the dado head at proper height, pull the motor forward to cut the tenon.

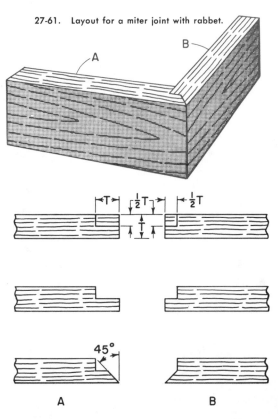

27-61. Layout for a miter joint with rabbet.

329

27-62. Cutting a tenon by using a spacer collar between the dado head blades.

27-63. Cutting a mortise for an open mortise-and-tenon joint. Make sure the length of the tenon is the same as the width of the mortise stock and the depth of the mortise is the same as the width of the tenon stock.

Fig. 27-62. The *bare face tenon* is made with a rabbet cut. For an *open mortise and tenon,* after cutting the tenon reverse the stock and cut the mortise. This is done by cutting a groove the same width as the tenon. Fig. 27-63.

Dovetail joint. This joint is relatively simple to make with a router attachment and a dovetail jig.

1. To make a dovetail jig, refer to Figs. 27-64, 65, and 66. Dado cut the frame support "D," 1/4" deep to receive part E. Use three wood screws and glue to hold these parts together.

2. Dado cut the base, A, 1/4" deep to receive the frame support assembly. Fasten B to base A with four wood screws.

3. Mount the frame support (D and E) into the dado grooves in base A, and glue and nail in place. Riser R can now be nailed in place in front of D.

4. Mount hinge K on the base A with three wood screws. Attach pressure clamp G to hinge K with a countersink bolt 1½" long, a washer, and a winged nut.

5. Drill holes in E to line up with upper slot in G in the position shown in Fig. 27-64.

6. Nail cleats C to base A.

7. With a pair of scissors, cut out a templet that can be traced on thin cardboard from the drawing in Fig. 27-65.

8. Using this as a pattern, carefully trace the exact outline for the dado slots on pressure clamp F.

9. Fasten hinge H to pressure clamp F with three wood screws and to the base A with a 3" bolt, washer, and winged nut.

10. Drill a hole in D to line up with the upper washer slot in F for a 3" bolt, washer, and winged nut.

If you prefer, a simple jig can be made by eliminating the pressure clamps, hinges, and winged nut, substituting pairs of C clamps to hold the drawer front and sides in position.

330

To use a dovetail jig for drawer construction, fasten it to the table top as shown in Fig. 27-66. Turn the motor 180 degrees from the crosscut position. Attach the dovetail router to the arbor. Slide the jig assembly right or left until the router extends exactly 3/8″ deep in *F*, according to the templet lines you have traced. Place a piece of stock 3/4″ x 5¾″ x 10″ behind clamp *G*. It should be tilted evenly against a second piece of stock that is 1/2″ x 5¾″ and as long as needed for the drawer side behind

clamp *F*. These pieces of stock are the front and one side of the drawer. Riser *F* will lift the drawer side 1/4″ for proper offset. Tighten the winged nuts to hold both pieces securely. Lower the arm with the elevating handle until the router is directly in front of the top dovetail slot. Start the motor and push it slowly forward, moving it back and forth to clear the chips. Continue until the shoulder of the router passes through clamp *F*, through the 1/2″ stock, into the 3/4″ stock, and comes to rest against the front edge of clamp *G*. After the first dovetail slot is cut, move the router to the next position, approximately seven turns down, and repeat this operation. Continue until all seven slots have been cut.

MATERIALS LIST FOR DOVETAIL JIG

Base A, 1 pc., 1⅝″ x 9½″ x 13″ long
Guide B, 1 pc., 1″ x 1⅝″ x 9½″ long
Cleats C, 2 pcs., ¼″ x 2″ x 1½″ long
Frame Support D-E, 2 pcs., ¾″ plywood D, 7¼″ x 8″ long. E, 7¼″ x 9″ long
Pressure Clamps F-G, 2 pcs., ¾″ plywood F, 7″ x 8¾″ long. Use full-scale template G, 7″ x 8⅞″ long, two slots 1″ long for bolts
Riser R, 1 pc., ¼″ x ⁷⁄₁₆″ x 8¾″ long
Hinges H-K, 2 butts, 3″ x 3″, slotted 1″ for ¼″ bolts
Bolts, 4 each, ¼″ x 3″ long. 1 only ¼″ x 1½″
Wing Nuts, 5 each, ¼″ with washers
Screws, Nails, Glue, etc., as needed

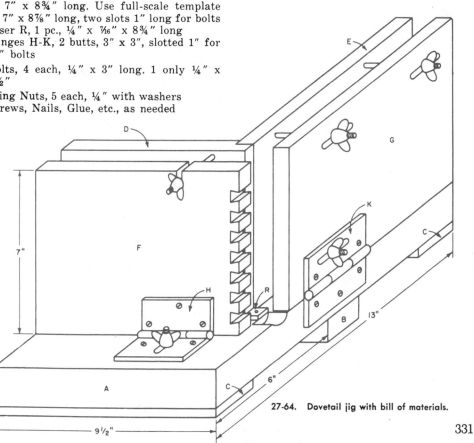

27-64. Dovetail jig with bill of materials.

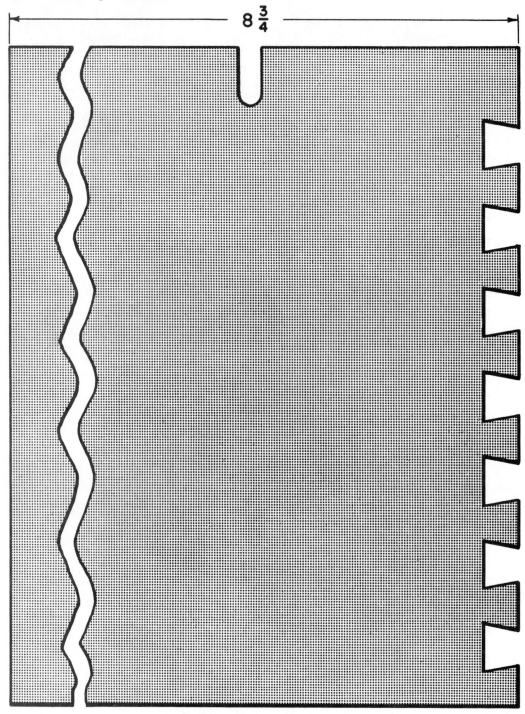

$8\frac{3}{4}$

TEMPLET F FULL SIZE

27-65. Full-size pattern for part F of the jig.

To undercut the back of the drawer side, remove the drawer front from behind *G* and turn the elevating handle to raise the router slightly above the top edge of the drawer side. With the edge of the router extended over the stock about 1/16", set the rip clamp firmly. Now turn the elevating handle slowly downward so that the lip of the router will remove the required undercut from the back edge of the drawer side. Then remove the side from behind *F*. The side and the front should now fit together.

The dovetail jig will cut matching drawer sides and fronts in stock of the following width: 1⅜", 2¼", 3⅛", 4⅞", and 5¾".

• *Finger or box joint.* To make this joint it is necessary to use a saw blade or dado head that will cut a groove of precise width. Fig. 27-67. Place the saw motor in horizontal crosscutting position. Use an auxiliary table to hold the stock the correct distance above the regular table. Also raise one stock piece the width of a groove above the other and clamp them together. Mark the finger joint on the front piece so that the width of the fingers is exactly the same as that of the groove. Lower the saw to the first groove and make the cut; then lower it to the second groove and cut again. Fig. 27-68. Continue until all of the grooves have been cut. If the width of the groove is the same as the thickness of the fingers, they will match exactly and form a box or finger joint.

SPECIAL CUTTING OPERATIONS

Many special cutting operations can also be done on the radial-arm saw with a variety of setups. Following are some of the more common:

Making Saw Moldings

Several types of attractive moldings can be produced by making kerfing cuts in the wood. To do this, have a spacer

27-66. Cutting a dovetail joint.

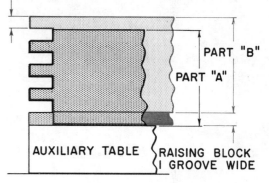

RAISE PART "B" ONE GROOVE WIDTH

PART "B"

PART "A"

AUXILIARY TABLE   RAISING BLOCK 1 GROOVE WIDE

27-67. The matching pieces are clamped or held together against the fence of an auxiliary table. One piece must be exactly a groove above the other. The thickness of the fingers must match the width of the grooves.

27-68. Cutting a finger or box joint.

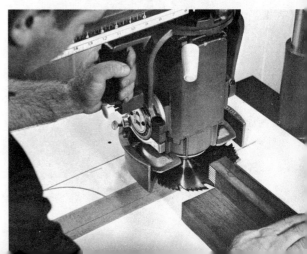

333

27-69(a). Making a series of crosscuts from both sides, about halfway through the thickness of the stock.

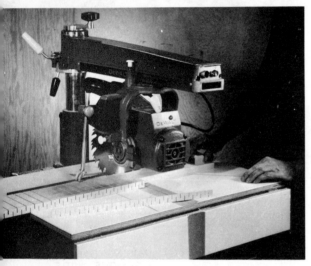

27-69(b). Ripping the stock into thin strips for decorative purposes.

27-70. Cutting a contour surface with a single saw blade. The dado head can also be used for this operation, often with greater success.

334

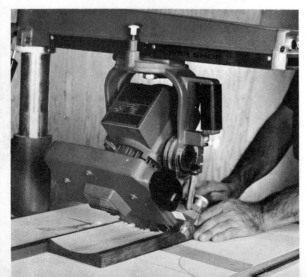

27-71. Saucer cutting. Make sure the saw is lowered a little at a time to make this cut.

mark on a guide fence and make a series of crosscuts along the entire length of the board. Turn the stock over and repeat the operation so that the kerfs on the second side are equally spaced between the first saw kerfs. Fig. 27-69. Then rip the molding into narrow strips. It can be used for many decorative purposes.

Contour Cutting

Cutting coves on a piece of wood for trim is relatively simple with a standard blade on a radial-arm saw. First set the saw at a 45-degree bevel position. Locate the motor so that the lowest part of the blade is on the center line of the stock, and tighten the rip clamp. Now lower the arm or track to about 1/8" below the top of the stock. Feed the stock as you would for ripping. After each cut, lower the arm another 1/8" until the desired depth is cut. The final cut should be very light, to assure a smooth finish. Fig. 27-70. By changing the angle of the motor, various cove cuts can be made. For example, if the motor is set at an angle of 45 degrees and the

27-72. The second cut is being made with the V strip to the right of the saw blade.

yoke turned slightly off center, the radius of the cut will change, giving the cove a different appearance. This kind of sawing is excellent for making certain kinds of picture frames.

Saucer Cutting

A slightly dish-shaped cut is sometimes made in the front of a cabinet door, to add an interesting surface design. This can be done as follows. Remove the guide fence and back table board, and clamp the stock as shown in Fig. 27-71. Raise the column so that the motor can be tilted at a 45-degree bevel position. Locate the blade over the center line of the stock. Tighten the rip clamp. Turn the machine on and lower the motor until it strikes the stock. Hold the anti-kickback rod in your left hand; with your right hand pull out the bevel latch and then swing the blade back and forth in an arc past the stock. Lower the saw blade one half turn of the elevating handle and continue cutting until the proper depth is reached.

Rosette Cutting

A rosette for overlaying on a door can be formed by combining diamond shaped pieces which are made as follows: First bevel rip the stock into V strips. Then set the motor at the 45-degree righthand miter position and the 45-degree bevel position. Make the first cut with the V strips to the left of the blade, then the second with the strips to the right of it. This forms the pieces that are used to make the rosette. Fig. 27-72.

MOLDING OPERATIONS

Many molding and shaping operations are possible on the radial-arm saw. The same kinds of molding heads used on the circular saw can be used on the radial-arm saw. These have knives mounted in a holder. Fig. 27-73. Solid one-piece molding heads can also be used.

27-73(a). This round molding head holds three identical knives by means of socket-head screws. Complete sets of knives for all different types of cuts are available. Since the spindle moves clockwise, all cutters must point in the same direction. In attaching the tool, use one arbor collar, the cutterhead, and the arbor nut.

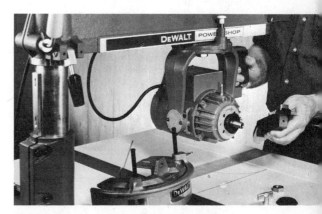

27-73(b). This type holds two knives and is mounted the same as the one in Fig. 27-73(a).

27-73(c). This solid, one-piece cutter is made of tool steel and ground to shape. To install, add both arbor collars, then the cutter, and the nut last. Always place a guard over the molding head.

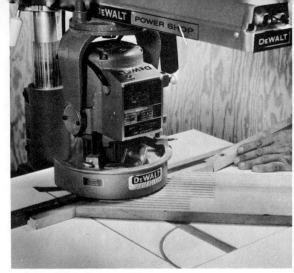

27-74. End shaping. A standard guard is being used, as well as a guide fence made of two pieces of wood with an opening between. To make this mold cut across the end grain, block up the stock and clamp a stop block to the fence. To do the shaping, move the motor forward slowly.

27-76. For cutting the edge of narrow stock, clamp a feather board to the table to hold the stock firmly against the revolving cutter. Also use a push stick to move the stock into and past the cutter.

27-75. A shaper-jointer fence is made in two parts. The outfeed side is adjusted to the same relative position as the outside of the cutterhead. If only part of the edge is to be shaped, use a straightedge to align the infeed and outfeed sides. If the entire edge is to be shaped, the infeed side must be set back an amount equal to the depth of cut.

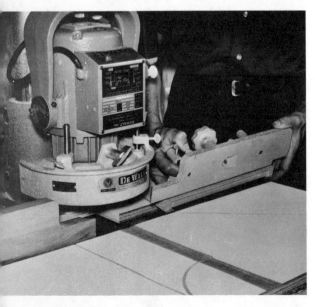

For molding operations it is necessary to install a different kind of fence than is used for sawing. Between the two parts of the fence there must be an opening for the cutter. The standard fence can be replaced by two pieces of wood that are separated at the center to clear the cutters. Fig. 27-74. However, if the complete edge is to be shaped, then it is necessary to have a special shaper-jointer fence. In this way the infeed side of the fence can be adjusted up to its full capacity of 1/2" while the outfeed side remains in a fixed position to support the work after the total edge has been cut. Fig. 27-75.

The proper cutter must be mounted on the motor shaft and a special guard attached. Then the arm is raised or lowered to the correct height. The work must be held firmly against the table and fence. If the complete edge is to be shaped, the infeed fence must be moved back just enough for the outfeed fence to support the machined edge. When extremely deep edges are to be shaped, it is better to make two passes, resetting the fence after the first cut. For making narrow moldings, use a feather board and a push stick. Fig. 27-76.

The band saw is designed primarily for cutting curved or irregular shapes, although it can also do all kinds of straight cutting. Fig. 28-1. This saw gets its name from its narrow steel blade, the ends of which are welded together to form a continuous band. The sawing action of this machine is continuous and, if properly adjusted, the saw will do very true and accurate work. Fig. 28-2.

SIZES AND PARTS

The size of the band saw is indicated by the diameter of the wheels. Typical sizes for the cabinet shop are from 14″ to 36″. Fig. 28-3. The maximum work thickness that can be cut is limited to the distance between the table top and the blade guide in its uppermost position.

The band saw consists of a heavy frame to which are attached two wheels, a table, guides, guards, and a guide post. The lower wheel axle is held in a fixed position and the wheel is rotated by

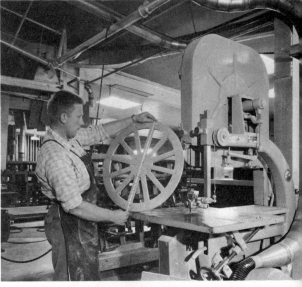

28-2. The outside of this circular pattern can be cut on the band saw. The inside openings must be cut on a jig saw or router. Notice the excellent exhaust system for this heavy-duty band saw.

28-1. The beautiful curved legs of these coffee tables could be cut on the band saw.

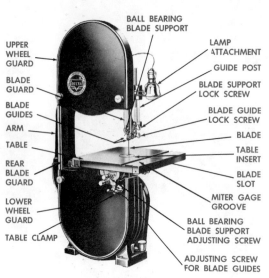

UPPER WHEEL GUARD

BLADE GUARD

BLADE GUIDES

ARM

TABLE

REAR BLADE GUARD

LOWER WHEEL GUARD

TABLE CLAMP

BALL BEARING BLADE SUPPORT

LAMP ATTACHMENT

GUIDE POST

BLADE SUPPORT LOCK SCREW

BLADE GUIDE LOCK SCREW

BLADE

TABLE INSERT

BLADE SLOT

MITER GAGE GROOVE

BALL BEARING BLADE SUPPORT ADJUSTING SCREW

ADJUSTING SCREW FOR BLADE GUIDES

14″ BAND SAW

28-3(a). Parts of a 14″ band saw.

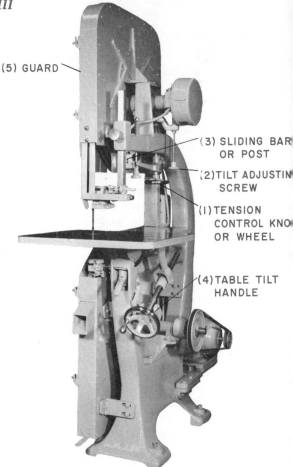

(5) GUARD

(3) SLIDING BAR OR POST

(2) TILT ADJUSTING SCREW

(1) TENSION CONTROL KNOB OR WHEEL

(4) TABLE TILT HANDLE

28-3(b). A heavy-duty 36″ band saw.

28-4. Controls for the band saw.

28-5. Note that the wheels have rubber tires to protect the blade.

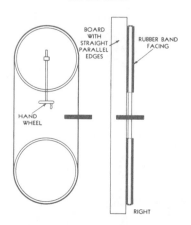

BOARD WITH STRAIGHT PARALLEL EDGES

RUBBER BAND FACING

HAND WHEEL

RIGHT

power delivered from the motor through belts. The upper wheel is free-running, having no power delivered to it. Fig. 28-4. It is adjustable in two ways. The wheel moves up and down to accommodate slightly different lengths of blades. It also can be tilted forward and back to make the blades stay on the wheels. If the upper wheel were clamped in a rigid position, it would cause the blade to break. Therefore there is a tension spring that gives the upper wheel a little play. The tilt adjustment moves the upper wheel forward or back so that the blade will run on the center of the wheel. By tilting the wheel slightly, the saw can be made to run on the front of the wheel rim or farther back. To protect the teeth, a thin rubber tire covers both the upper and lower wheels. Fig. 28-5. Because the blade is a continuous piece of metal, a slot in the table is necessary for replacing it. A larger opening in the center of the table is covered with a table insert or throat plate of soft metal.

On most saws the table can be tilted about 45 degrees to the right and 5 degrees to the left. The saw or blade guides consist of two guide pins (blocks) or small wheels, one above and one below the table. These hold the blade in line. Fig. 28-6. There is also a small ball-bearing guide wheel made of hardened steel, behind the guide pins. This wheel should run free except when cutting is being done. The back of the blade should not quite touch this wheel; the wheel should not turn unless it must absorb pressure against its face. The upper guides are attached to a guide post that can be raised or lowered when cutting different thicknesses of wood. Both the upper and lower wheels and the blade are covered with guards. It is important to keep these guards in place because if the blade breaks it may fly out.

BAND-SAW BLADES

Blades are made in widths from 1/8″

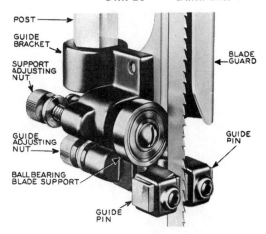

28-6. Guides on a 14″ band saw. On large machines the guide pins or blocks may be replaced with guide wheels for easier action.

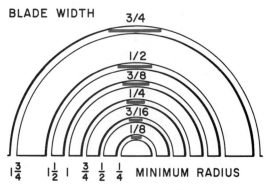

28-7. This chart shows how to select the correct width of blade. For example, a 1/2″ blade cannot cut a circle smaller than 3″ in diameter.

to 1½″. In general, the number of teeth per inch is directly related to blade width—the narrower the blade, the finer the teeth. A narrow blade is needed to cut sharp curves; a wider one is better for larger curves and for resawing. Fig. 28-7. All standard band-saw blades for cutting wood have teeth alternately set in opposite directions.

REPLACING A BLADE

Remove or open the guards that cover the upper and lower wheels. Take out the table insert or throat plate and re-

BAND SAW

MAINTENANCE

• Clean the band saw tires periodically to remove dust, pitch, and gum. Use a rag soaked in benzine.
• Replace the tires when they become worn
• Make sure the belts are in good condition.
• Check the blade for sharpness and to see if it has sufficient set to prevent binding.
• Make sure the guide blocks and rollers are in good condition and properly adjusted.
• Replace the throat plate, if worn.
• Make sure the table tilts easily and that the pointer on the tilt gage is accurate.

LUBRICATION

• Use S.A.E. 20 oil on slide ways of the upper wheel bracket trunnions and adjusting screw.
• Also oil the screw for adjusting table tilt.
• Keep oil and grease away from the band-saw tires as this would soon ruin them.

SAFETY

• Check the stock to make sure it is free of nails before cutting.
• Adjust the sliding bar or post so that the upper guide is about 1/4" above the work. If the guide is too high, the blade will **not** have the proper support.

• Never allow anyone to stand to the right of the saw. If the blade broke, it could fly out in that direction.
• Make sure the saw blade has proper tension and that the teeth are pointing down.
• Avoid backing out of a cut as this could pull the blade off the wheels.
• Never attempt to cut round stock without a holding jig. It will roll out of your hands as the saw starts the cut.
• Hold the stock firmly on the table to do the cutting.
• Never cut a curve of small radius with a wide blade unless you first make relief cuts.
• If you hear a rhythmic click as the wood is being cut, this usually indicates a cracked blade. Stop the machine and inspect.
• If the blade breaks, shut off the power and stay away from the machiné until it comes to a complete stop. Never try to free the blade while the wheels are still turning.
• Never have your fingers or arms in line with the blade.
• Use a helper to handle long stock. Remember that the operator should do all the pushing.
• Keep a well balanced stance as you do the cutting.
• Never try to pick pieces of wood out of the table slot while the saw is operating.

move the pin or set screw at the end of the blade slot. Now release the tension on the upper wheel and remove the blade. Fig. 28-8. If the blade is to be stored, wipe it with an oily rag to prevent rusting. To fold the blade, grip it with the back toward you and the teeth away from you. Place your left hand on the blade with the thumb up and the right hand with the thumb down. Hold the blade firmly. Now rotate the left wrist to turn the thumb down and the right wrist to turn the thumb up. As you twist, the blade will coil into three loops. Fig. 28-9. Tie the blade with a string or fasten it with masking tape.

If a wider blade is to be placed on the band saw, loosen the blade guides,

then release the ball-bearing blade support and move it back. Slip the new blade through the table slot and over the wheels, with the teeth pointing toward the table. Turn the tension handle to apply a small amount of tension to the blade. Now rotate the lower wheel by hand to see if the blade stays in the approximate center of the wheels. As necessary, tilt the upper wheel slightly in one direction or another until the blade stays in the center of the wheel (tracks properly). If the blade does not track properly, it may ride against the guides and ruin them in a hurry. Now tighten the upper wheel until the blade is taut. For a 1/8" to 1/4" blade, the tension is correct when some pressure at the center

28-8. Removing the blade from the band saw.

28-9(b). This blade will be ready for storing after it is fastened with string or masking tape.

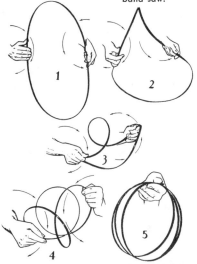

28-9(a). Folding or coiling a blade.

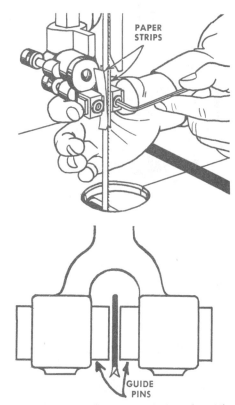

28-10. The strips of paper give just the right clearance between the blade and the pins or blocks.

of the unsupported area will move the blade about 1/8″. Blades should always "give" slightly when pressed. Replace the table insert or throat plate and the alignment pin. Move both the upper and lower ball-bearing blade support wheels until they just clear the back of the blade about 1/64″. Move the blade

guides or wheels forward or back until the front of the guides is just back of the teeth. Now place a heavy piece of paper around the blade and apply pressure to the blade guides or wheels. Fig. 28-10. Tighten them. When the paper is removed, blade clearance will be just right.

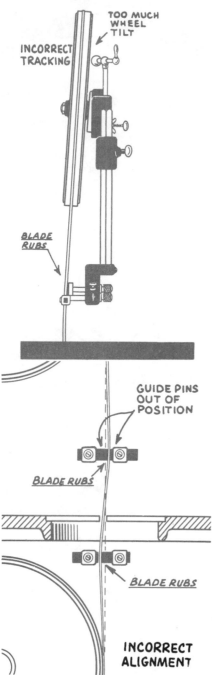

INCORRECT
TRACKING

TOO MUCH
WHEEL
TILT

BLADE
RUBS

GUIDE PINS
OUT OF
POSITION

BLADE RUBS

BLADE RUBS

INCORRECT
ALIGNMENT

28-11. Notice that the guide pins are out of alignment. This will soon break the blade. Too much wheel
tilt will also cause trouble, making the blade ride
too hard against the support wheel.

28-12. This is the correct position when cutting.

It is also important to make sure that
the openings in the upper and lower
guides are in the same plane. A wrong
adjustment, such as that shown in Fig.
28-11, will soon break the blade or ruin
the guides. Before starting to cut, check
to see that the table is perfectly level,
with the pointer on zero position.

BASIC OPERATING TECHNIQUES

The correct cutting position for operators is facing the blade, standing slightly
to the left of it. Fig. 28-12. The key to

28-13. The upper saw guides should just clear the
work to give plenty of support to the blade.

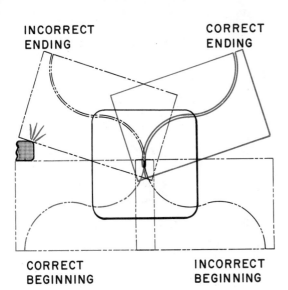

INCORRECT ENDING   CORRECT ENDING

CORRECT BEGINNING   INCORRECT BEGINNING

28-14. Notice that the correct beginning for this cut is with the stock to the left of the blade.

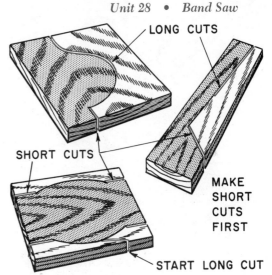

LONG CUTS

SHORT CUTS

MAKE SHORT CUTS FIRST

START LONG CUT

28-15. If you make short cuts first, little backing out is necessary. Note that when the long cut is completed the waste piece will fall away.

successful band-saw work is the operator's skill. You must be able to follow just outside the layout line, allowing extra stock for smoothing the edges later. In cutting, guide the stock with your left hand and apply forward pressure with your right. Move the stock into the blade as rapidly as it will cut. Moving it too slowly will tend to burn the blade. Change the position of the upper guide before each cutting so that it just clears the upper surface of the stock by about 1/4". Fig. 28-13. After turning on the power, do not feed the work into the blade until the machine is operating at full speed.

Watch the feed direction. Before making a cut, think through the path of the cut. Some pieces will swing in such a way as to hit the upper arm. You must have a plan or you will soon find yourself in difficulty and have to backtrack along the cut. Fig. 28-14.

Always make short cuts before long ones. When stock is cut from two sides, cut the short side first so there will be a minimum of backing out. Whenever possible, cut out through waste stock rather

than backing out. It is easier to back out of a short cut than a long one. Fig. 28-15.

Make use of turning holes in the design. These are round or square holes in waste stock, drilled or bored on the drill press or mortising machine to help in the cutting. Fig. 28-16.

Break up short curves. Use a series of relief cuts when it is necessary to cut around a short curve with a fairly wide

28-16. Use the auger bit or mortising chisel to cut starting holes.

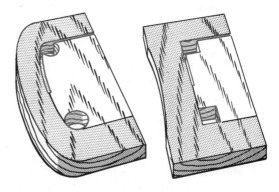

AN AUGER AND MORTISING CHISEL USED TO MAKE TURNING HOLES

343

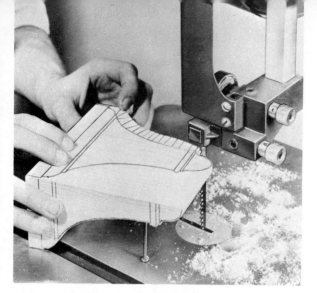

28-17. Relief cuts up to within 1/32" of the layout line eliminate the twisting strain. The waste stock will fall away as the cut is made.

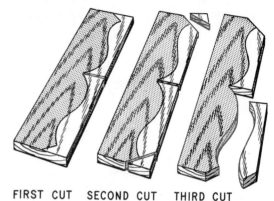

FIRST CUT   SECOND CUT   THIRD CUT

28-18. Combination curves should be broken up into a series of smaller, simple cuts.

blade. Fig. 28-17. Break up complicated curves. Look at each layout and see if a combination of cuts can be made to divide the complicated curve into simpler cuts. Never try to cut a curve of small radius with a wide blade unless you use relief cuts. Fig. 28-18.

On large rectangular openings, cut to one corner, then backtrack slightly before cutting to another corner. Narrow grooves can be cut in the same way except that the ends can be "nibbled" out. Fig. 28-19.

Sometimes beeswax applied to the blade sides will help in cutting hardwood or wood that has a great deal of pitch.

Sometimes the blade tends to run to one side, making it necessary to feed the work at an angle in order to cut a straight line. This condition, called "leading," should be corrected. It is caused by one or more of the following: slight wear on one side of the blade; more set on one side of the teeth than the other; guide too loose or out of line; or too narrow a blade. To correct the first two conditions, hold an abrasive stone lightly against the side on which the blade leads. For the other conditions, readjust the guide blocks or change the blade.

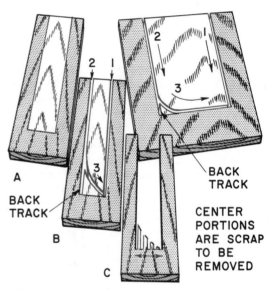

BACK TRACK

BACK TRACK

CENTER PORTIONS ARE SCRAP TO BE REMOVED

28-19(a). Cutting rectangular openings. The numbers indicate the order of cuts. It is necessary to backtrack slightly on cut 2 before the curve is cut to the other corner.

28-19(b). Here's a good example of how the band saw can cut rectangular openings on large pieces.

344

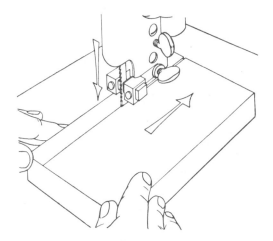

28-20. Straight cutting with the band saw.

28-21. Cutting saw kerfs in the face of stock with the work held against the miter gage. Note the stop block clamped to the table to control the depth of the kerf.

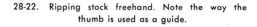

28-22. Ripping stock freehand. Note the way the thumb is used as a guide.

Straight Cutting

While the band saw is designed primarily for cutting curves, circles, and irregular shapes, it has many advantages for straight cutting jobs. It will handle any length of stock and will cut a width equal to the distance from the blade to the arm. The advantages of the band saw over the circular saw are that it will cut thicker material and that the narrow saw kerf results in less waste.

Freehand Cutting

Mark a straight line on the stock. Hold the stock in both hands, at least 2″ away from the saw blade. Guide the stock with the left hand and move it along with the right. Fig. 28-20.

Using a Ripping Fence

A ripping fence can be fastened to either the right or left of the saw blade. Stock can then be fed into the blade, applying slight pressure to the table and against the fence. A straight edge can be clamped to the table to replace the fence.

Cutting with a Miter Gage

A miter gage can be used on the band saw to cut any angle. It can be placed in standard or reverse position. Use the right hand to push the gage and the left hand to hold the stock against the gage. Fig. 28-21.

Cutting Duplicate Parts

A number of identical parts can be cut by clamping a stop block to the table. Hold the stock against the miter gage and the stop block, then move it into the saw to cut it off.

Freehand Ripping

Ripping can be done in a freehand manner by using the thumb of your left hand as a guide and moving the stock along with your right hand. This is most satisfactory for short boards. Fig. 28-22.

345

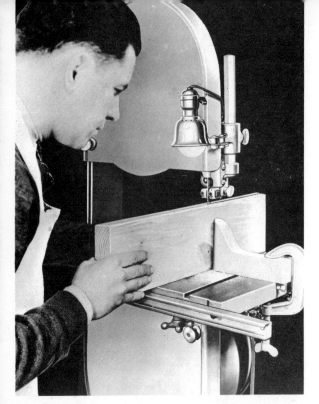

28-23. Resawing stock using a pivot block. Short sleeves are safer.

28-24. Resawing with the metal fence is good if the saw blade has coarse-set teeth and has recently been sharpened and set.

Resawing

Resawing is cutting stock into thinner pieces. The band saw has a distinct advantage for this kind of work since it does not waste as much material as a circular saw. It is sometimes a good idea to cut a shallow kerf in each edge on the circular saw to serve as a guide. The best method for resawing is to clamp a pivot pin to the table as a guide. This is especially good if the saw tends to lead to one side or the other. With the pivot pin, you can shift the board slightly to compensate for this. Fig. 28-23. The ripping fence can also be used as a guide for resawing. Fig. 28-24. In resawing long work, have someone hold the other end of the board or use a roller support.

Bevel Ripping

Tilt the table to an angle of 45 degrees and fasten the fence to it so that it just clears the blade. The clearance between the underside of the fence and the saw table will make it possible to cut bevels up to 45 degrees without the blade hitting the metal fence. Fig. 28-25. A simple V jig can also be used to perform the same operations with the table in a level position. Fig. 28-26.

CUTTING CURVES

Shallow Curves

Most shallow curves can be cut freehand. Cut just outside the layout line so that a small amount of material remains for sanding. Fig. 28-27.

Sharp Curves

A narrow blade is best for cutting sharp curves. Fig. 28-28. If a wide blade is on the machine, a sharp curve can be cut by first making relief cuts to within 1/32" of the layout line. Then, during cutting, the wedges drop off one by one to give added clearance to the blade.

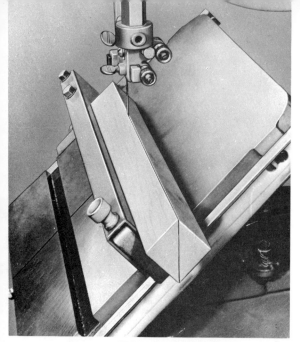

28-25.   Diagonal ripping.

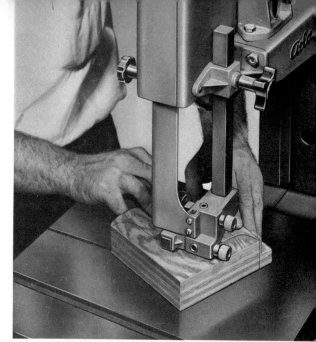

28-28.   Use a narrow blade for cutting sharp curves.

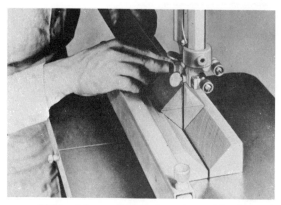

28-26.   A fence and V block can be used for diagonal ripping. This is also a good method of cutting a kerf across the corners to insert the spurs of the live center for wood turning.

28-27.   Roughing out a design on the band saw. Notice that the cut is made just outside the layout line so that some material is left for sanding.

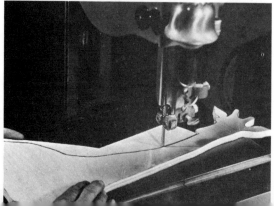

Another method of making sharp cuts is to make several tangent cuts until the final curve is obtained. Rough cut complex curves before finishing the cut. Fig. 28-29.

COMPOUND SAWING

Compound sawing is done in making book ends, bases for lamps, and other decorative shapes cut from two adjoining surfaces of a square or rectangular piece of stock. A simple way to do such cutting is to make a pattern and trace it on two adjoining faces. Then cut the waste stock from two sides of the wood. Fasten this waste stock back in place in the waste

28-29.   Rough cut the curve through the waste stock before completing the final cuts.

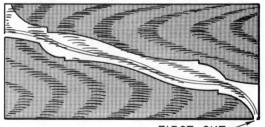

FIRST CUT

347

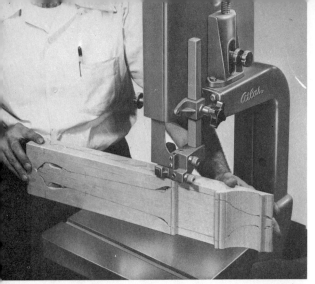

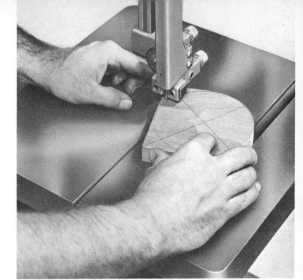

28-30. Compound cutting is necessary to produce this sculptured letter holder. Notice how the saw cuts have been made from one side before the stock is turned on edge to complete the part. A thin nail or pin, placed so it will not be struck by the blade, holds the parts together as the final cut is made.

28-32. Freehand cutting. Great care must be taken in guiding the stock to cut a perfect circle. Turn the stock slowly and evenly so that it cuts just outside the layout line.

CUTTING CIRCLES

The simplest method of cutting a single circular piece is to do it freehand, carefully guiding the stock to follow the layout line. Fig. 28-32.

Using Jigs for Circle Cutting

Several kinds of jigs can be used to cut circles. These are particularly useful in mass production. The commercial circle jig is fastened to the upper saw guide bar. It has an adjustable pivot pin which

portion of the main work. Turn the stock a quarter turn and saw from the other side.

Another method of doing this is to make the first cuts almost to the end of stock so the waste material will stay in place. Fig. 28-30. Then turn the stock over a quarter turn and make the other two cuts. The *cabriole leg* is cut in this manner. Fig. 28-31. Also see Unit 50.

348

28-31. Cutting a cabriole leg. A cut must be made from both sides of stock to form the graceful curve.

28-33. Using an extension guide bar circle jig for cutting a true circle. Short sleeves are safer.

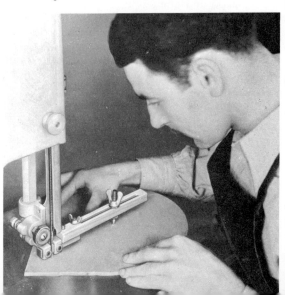

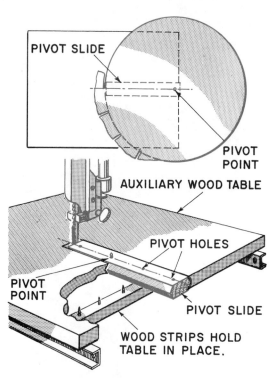

28-34(a). A wood jig for cutting circles.

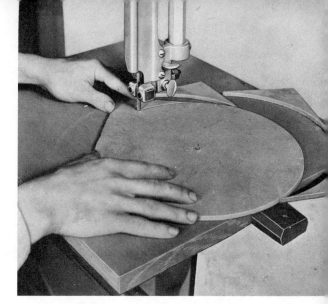

28-34(b). Using a homemade jig for circle cutting.

is set to the correct radius from the cutting edge. Fig. 28-33. It is relatively simple to make a plywood circle jig. Cut a piece of 3/4″ plywood that is slightly wider than the distance from the blade to the table edge. Fasten two cleats to the underside. Cut a groove or a dovetail dado at right angles to the blade, with the center of the groove at the front of the teeth. Cut a small hardwood stick or bar that will slip into the groove and be flush with the table top. Place a sharp pin or screw at the end of the sliding bar. Remember that the pin must be at right angles to the blade and in line with the front of the blade. Fig. 28-34. Adjust the pin to the correct radius and turn the board slowly as the circle is cut.

Cutting Curved Rails or Segments

Pieces or segments of a circle can be cut with a simple jig. Lay out the curve

on thick stock and make the first cut freehand. Then fasten a pivot block or ripping fence to the table a distance from the blade equal to the thickness of the segments you want. Hold the stock against the fence or pin to make this cut.

Curved work can be ripped to equal width in a similar manner with the use of a pivot block. Cut the first edge to the curved shape. Then hold the cut edge against the pivot block to cut the second edge. Fig. 28-35.

28-35. Cutting parallel curves, using a pivot block or pin. Short sleeves are safer.

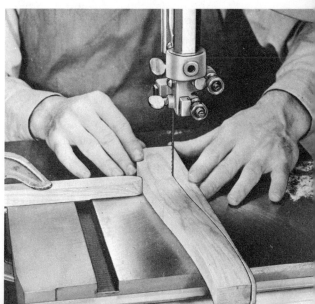

349

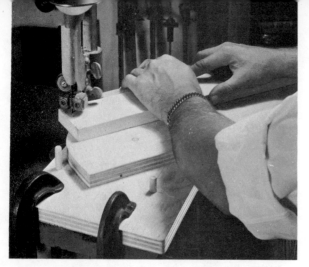

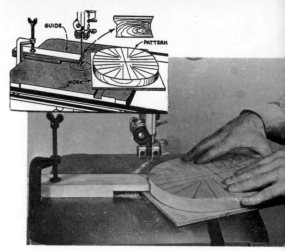

28-36. Cutting a rounded corner, using a jig. Watches should not be worn.

28-37. Sawing with a pattern is an accurate method of cutting duplicate parts.

Cutting Segments of a Circle

Install a temporary wood table and attach an arm to it at right angles to the saw blade. Cut a pattern of the required circle segment. Attach another arm to this. Put two wood screws through the pattern from the underside, with the sharp points exposed. Now fasten the end of the pattern arm to the arm of the table with a single screw located at a point equal to the radius of the arc. Cut the stock, holding it over the pattern. The same technique can be followed for cutting the arc of a circle. Fig. 28-36.

SAWING WITH A PATTERN GUIDE

Another method of cutting duplicate parts is to use a simple wood pattern guide. However, this will work only for cutting broad, shallow curves. The guide arm is clamped to the inner side of the saw table so that the end of the arm is located at the saw blade. A recess is cut on the underside of the arm to permit the passage of waste stock. The end of the arm is curved to match the broadest curve of the pattern. A small slot in the end of the arm permits the recessing of the blade so that the outer side of the blade is flush with the guide arm. The stock is fastened securely to the underside of the wood pattern with sharp

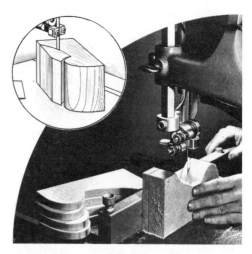

28-38. Cutting duplicate parts by first cutting thicker stock to shape, then resawing to the correct thickness.

28-39. Cutting stock loaded into a box jig.

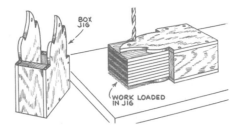

350

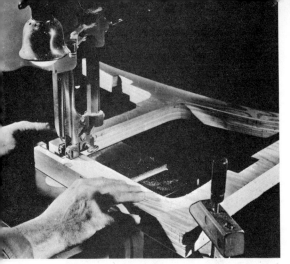

28-40(a). Cutting duplicate parts with the pieces clamped together.

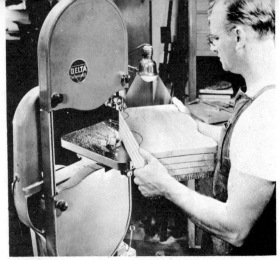

28-40(b). Nail pieces together in the scrap stock when cutting several at a time.

anchor points. To do the cutting, saw through the waste stock to locate the edge of the pattern firmly against the edge of the guide arm. Always keep the pattern squarely against the arm and feed the work around to complete the cut. Fig. 28-37.

MULTIPLE SAWING

There are various methods of cutting several identical pieces. One of the simplest is to cut the shape from thicker stock, then resaw to the thinner pieces. Fig. 28-38. Another method is to make a box into which the identical pieces will fit. On top of the box, nail the pattern to be cut, then follow the pattern to obtain the shape. Fig. 28-39. Still another good method is to clamp or nail the pieces together for cutting. Fig. 28-40.

29 Jig Or Scroll Saw

The jig or scroll saw is used primarily for cutting curved or irregular work. Its main advantage over other curve-cutting saws is that it can be used to make inside cuts without cutting through the stock itself. The machine is particularly useful to modelmakers, for sign and pattern work, and for cutting small parts of wood, metal, and plastic. It has little use in furniture production since most curved and shaped parts are made on the router or shaper.

PARTS AND SIZE

The major parts consist of a work table, cast-iron base, curved removable over-arm, upper and lower chucks, and the driving mechanism. Fig. 29-1. The standard scroll-saw blade is attached to the lower chuck, then passed through the center hole (with the table insert) and connected to the upper chuck at the end of the tension sleeve.

The crank shaft converts the circular motion of the motor pulley to up-and-down motion of the lower chuck. This part of the scroll saw must be precision-balanced to avoid excessive vibration at high speeds. Most jig saws are equipped with a four-step cone pulley on the motor

351

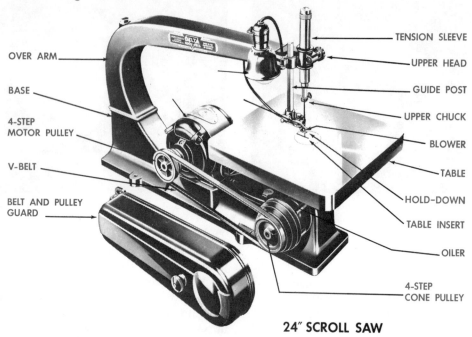

OVER ARM

BASE

4-STEP MOTOR PULLEY

V-BELT

BELT AND PULLEY GUARD

TENSION SLEEVE

UPPER HEAD

GUIDE POST

UPPER CHUCK

BLOWER

TABLE

HOLD-DOWN

TABLE INSERT

OILER

4-STEP CONE PULLEY

24" SCROLL SAW

29-1.   Parts of a 24" jig or scroll saw. This machine will cut to the center of a circle 48" in diameter. It will cut stock up to 2" in thickness.

and saw, with a V belt between them. The usual four speeds are 610, 910, 1255, and 1725 cutting strokes per minute (c.s.m.). However, for jobs that require a wide variety of speeds, a saw with a variable-speed attachment is useful. This attachment is good for light metals, plastic, and delicate inlay work. With the variable-speed attachment and a 1725 r.p.m. motor, speeds from 650 to 1700 c.s.m. can be obtained. In general, high speeds are used for fast, fine work and slow speeds for heavy woods, metal, and other hard materials.

The size of the jig saw is indicated by the distance from the blade to the over-arm measured *horizontally*. The thickness of material that can be cut is also considered in the size of the saw. Fig. 29-2. Jig saws are made in many sizes from

29-2.   This 24" scroll saw cuts stock up to 5" thick. It has only one speed, 1100 cutting strokes per minute.

JIG OR SCROLL SAW

MAINTENANCE

• Make sure the chuck jaws operate freely and that the thumb or set screw is in good condition.
• Make a careful check of the blade guides and hold-down to see that they are adjusted correctly.
• Replace the throat plate, if it is worn.
• See that the belts are in good condition and not too tight.
• Make sure the tilt action of the table is easy.

LUBRICATION

• The crank case should be filled to the correct level with S.A.E. 10, 20, or 30 depending on the manufacturer's recommendation.
• Lubricate the moving parts of the table and adjusting screws with S.A.E. 20.

SAFETY

• Install the blade with the teeth pointing down.
• Adjust for tension by raising the tension sleeve the correct amount.
• Turn the pulley over by hand to be sure the blade operates properly before turning on the power.
• Make sure the blade guide and hold-down are adjusted properly.

---

small bench models to large production machines. The table on the jig saw tilts to permit double-edge cutting, both straight and curved.

BLADE SELECTION

The three main types of blades are the power jig saw blade (also called the fret saw), the saber blade, and the jeweler's piercing blade. In general, the kind of blade as well as the thickness, width, and number of teeth per inch should be determined by the kind of material to be cut and the desired accuracy and smooth-ness of the cut surface. Choose extremely fine-tooth blades for delicate scroll and jewelry work. Thin, fine-tooth blades are needed for sawing thin woods, metal, veneer, plastic, and similar materials. Use medium-tooth blades for sawing wood and metal of medium thickness. Coarse, heavier blades are selected for sawing thick materials. Stiff saber blades, fastened only in the lower chuck, are used for ripping and heavy sawing of large inside curves. The blade selected should have a least three teeth in contact with the stock at all times. Fig. 29-3.

29-3.   Chart for selecting the correct blade.

Material Cut	Thick In.	Width In.	Teeth Per Inch	Blade Full Size	Material Cut	Thick In.	Width In.	Teeth Per Inch	Blade Full Size
Steel • Iron Lead • Copper Aluminum Pewter • Asbestos Paper • Felt	.020 / .020	.070 / .070	32 / 20		Wood Veneer Plus Plastics Celluloid • Hard Rubber Bakelite • Ivory Extremely Thin Materials	.008	.035	20	
Steel • Iron • Lead Copper • Brass Aluminum Pewter • Asbestos Wood	.020 / .020 / .020	.070 / .085 / .110	15 / 15 / 20		Plastics • Celluloid Hard Rubber Bakelite • Ivory Wood	.019 / .019 / .020 / .020	.050 / .055 / .070 / .110	15 / 12 / 7 / 7	
Asbestos • Brake Lining • Mica Steel • Iron • Lead Copper • Brass Aluminum Pewter	.028	.250	20		Wall Board • Pressed Wood Wood • Lead Bone • Felt • Paper Copper • Ivory • Aluminum	.020	.110	15	
Wood Panels and Veneers	.010	.048	18		Hard and Soft Wood	.020 / .028 / .028	.110 / .187 / .250	10 / 10 / 7	
Plastics • Celluloid Hard Rubber Bakelite • Ivory Wood	.010 / .010 / .010	.070 / .055 / .045	14 / 16 / 18		Pearl • Pewter Mica Pressed Wood Sea Shells Jewelry • Metals Hard Leather	.016 / .016 / .020 / .020	.054 / .054 / .070 / .085	30 / 20 / 15 / 12	

29-6. The hold-down can be tilted to match the tilt of the table.

29-7. Feeding the material into the saw from the side, for cutting long work.

29-8. The saber blade is held in the V jaws of the lower chuck and is supported above the table by the blade guide.

29-4. Most blades are held in both upper and lower chucks. Note that the ends of the blade are held between the flat jaws.

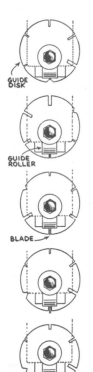

29-5. Different settings of the universal guide can be used to fit different blades. The guide disk can be rotated and the guide roller moved back and forth. The forward edge of the guide disk should be just behind the bottom of the blade teeth.

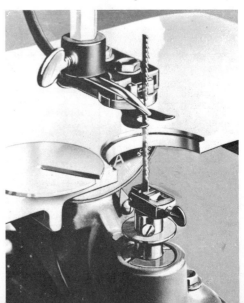

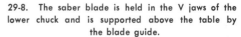

354

Installing a Blade

Since all jig saws are designed to cut on the downstroke, *teeth must point down*. To install the blade, first remove the table insert. Tilt the table to one side so you can easily reach the lower chuck. Slip the blade between the flat jaws of the lower chuck. Tighten securely, making sure the blade is straight. The chuck is usually tightened with a thumb screw. An Allen wrench is needed if there is a set screw. Now loosen the upper tension sleeve and lower it. Fasten the other end of the blade in the flat jaws of the upper chuck. Fig. 29-4. Next raise the tension sleeve to provide the right amount of tension on the blade. Correct tension is difficult to specify, but it should be sufficient to hold the blade straight against the cut, though not enough to cause the blade to break easily.

As part of the guide assembly, most jig saws have a blade guide that prevents the blade from twisting. This guide is a simple slot cut in metal against which the back of the blade rides during cutting. Most jig saws also have a circular universal guide disk which can be readily turned to accommodate blades of varying thickness. Fig. 29-5. If a blade is replaced with one of the same thickness and width, this guide disk does not need to be turned. However, when larger or smaller blades are installed, the disk should be changed to give the blade good support. The guide should be adjusted so that the back of the blade, not the teeth, rides in the guide. On some machines there is a small guide roller or support wheel at the back of the guide. The back of the blade should just touch this roller.

Since there is a tendency for the work to pull away from the table on the upstroke, a *hold-down* is needed. Adjust the hold-down so that it just lightly contacts the top of the stock. On some ma-

29-9. A special guide can be installed below the table to give added support to the saber blade. This guide is essential if there is no support for the blade above the table.

chines the hold-down can be turned to the same angle as the table for making bevel cuts. Fig. 29-6. Replace the table insert and move the table back to a level position. Before turning on the power, rotate the pulley by hand to make sure the blade operates smoothly.

On some jig saws the lower chuck can be rotated 90 degrees and the tension sleeve turned the same amount; with this adjustment the cutting can be done from the side instead of the front of the machine. This is particularly useful for cutting a curve on a long piece. Fig. 29-7.

Saber blades have a sharpened upper end and are fastened only in the lower chuck. They are very good for inside cutting if little or no curvature is involved. Though it isn't necessary for most work, the overarm can be completely removed when using a saber blade to cut an opening in a large surface. The saber blade should be clamped in the V jaws of the lower chuck. To do this, loosen the set screw and turn the lower chuck one quarter turn. Fig. 29-8. A special guide can be fitted below the saw table to give extra support to the saber blade. Fig. 29-9. Of course, the upper guide is also used to support the blade except when the overarm is removed.

External Curve Cutting

Since the major use of the jig saw is to cut curves, it is important to follow these suggestions carefully:

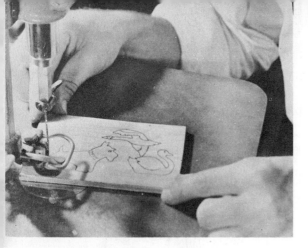

29-10. The scroll saw is ideal for intricate external cutting.

29-12. Cutting a large design on the jig or scroll saw.

The real value of this saw is for accurately cut parts that will require little or no sanding. Before starting the cut, examine the design on the surface to determine how the cutting ought to be done. (For external cutting, much of the waste stock can sometimes be removed first on a band saw.) Hold the stock with the thumb and forefinger of each hand. Fig. 29-10. Apply slight side pressure to get the blade started in the waste stock, then cut up to the layout line. Apply even, slow forward pressure but do not force stock into the blade. Turn the stock slowly when cutting a curve. If you turn too sharply, the blade may break.

Break complicated cuts up into simpler curves. Fig. 29-11. When cutting a curve, always feed straight against the teeth, even when turning a shallow corner. Fig. 29-12. Never apply side pressure against the blade. In a tight spot it

is sometimes good to backtrack slightly and recut up to the line.

INTERNAL CURVE CUTTING

To make an internal cut, drill one or more holes large enough for the blade to start in the waste stock. Fig. 29-13. It is generally a good idea not to drill the holes close to the layout line. To insert the blade into the hole, it is necessary to release the upper chuck and loosen the clamp on the guide post so it can be raised. Then the stock can be slipped over the blade. The other end of the blade is fastened in the upper chuck and the guide post lowered again. Sometimes it is necessary to remove the throat plate, since the blade must be bent slightly to one side as the stock is slipped over it. Now cut from the waste hole up to the layout line at an angle so that you can watch the cutting action and correct the line of cut before it reaches the layout line.

STRAIGHT CUTTING

Straight cutting is usually done on small pieces such as the letters for a raised name plate shown in Fig. 29-14. It is quite difficult to cut a long straight line on the jig saw. Fig. 29-15. However, the saw can be used on thin stock. The best way to do this is to clamp a guide board to the table a short distance from

29-11. Break up a complicated curve into several simpler cuts.

356

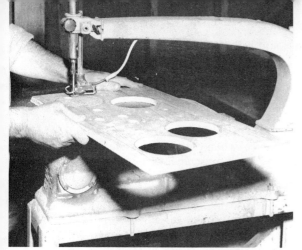

29-13. Cutting large circular openings on the jig saw. If you first drill several holes in the waste stock, you can cut part of the opening from one direction and the rest by turning the stock in the opposite direction.

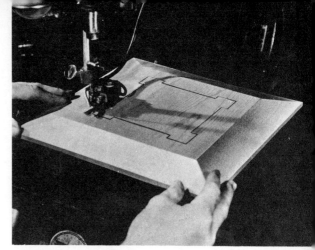

29-15. Cutting an internal opening that has all straight lines. Use as wide a blade as possible for this kind of work.

the blade. Choose the widest blade possible, since this will help eliminate the blade's tendency to stray off the straight line.

There are at least three common ways of cutting a square corner on the jig saw. Never come right up to the corner and attempt to turn 90 degrees since this will twist the blade and usually break it. For an exterior corner, follow one of the methods shown in Fig. 29-16. An interior corner should be cut slightly rounded first; then complete the sharp corner from two directions. To cut a sharp angle, cut to the end along one side, then cut a curve to reach the other side. After most of the waste stock is removed, cut from both sides to the point. Fig. 29-17.

29-14. Cutting letters on the jig saw. Usually it is a better idea to make the external cuts on a band saw and then do the internal cuts on the jig or scroll saw.

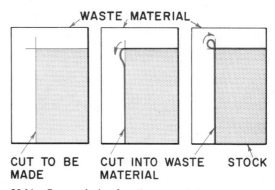

WASTE MATERIAL

CUT TO BE MADE   CUT INTO WASTE MATERIAL   STOCK

29-16. Two methods of cutting an exterior corner. One way is to make a slightly curved cut at the corner, then trim this off with a second cut. Another method is to make a complete circle in the waste stock.

29-17. Cutting a sharp angle. Start from a hole drilled in waste stock. Cut to point B, then make a curve as shown. Follow the layout line from point C to the opposite end, cut another curve, then follow the layout line again until the waste stock drops out. Finally, make the sharp corner by cutting from both B and C to A.

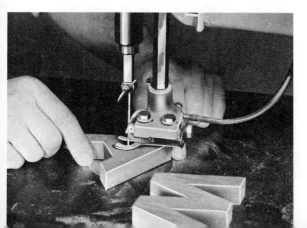

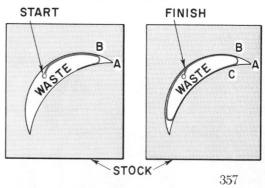

START   FINISH

STOCK

29-18. Cutting the draft on a circular wood pattern.

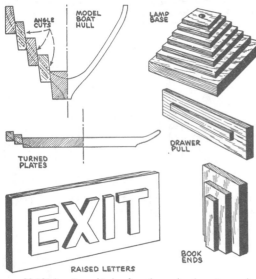

29-19(a). Many kinds of work can be done by angle sawing.

29-19(b). Note that when cut at an angle, the pieces fit together with no visible saw kerf.

BEVEL CUTS OR ANGLE SAWING

The table can be tilted to cut a bevel on straight, circular, or irregular designs. However, when cutting an angle or bevel, the work must always remain on the same side of the blade. For example, in cutting parts for a wood pattern to make a metal casting, a slight bevel (draft) must be cut. If the stock is swung completely around the blade, the bevel will change direction. Fig. 29-18. Other examples are shown in Fig. 29-19.

MAKING IDENTICAL PARTS

If two or more identical parts must be cut, one of the best methods is to make a "sandwich" of the material. Fasten the pieces together with small nails or brads in the waste stock. Fig. 29-20.

CUTTING THIN METAL

It is often difficult to cut thin metal without excessive blade breakage. One method of overcoming this is to clamp the metal between two thin pieces of plywood. A piece of waxed paper included in the sandwich will help lubricate the blade and prevent chipping. Draw the design on the wood and cut as for making identical parts.

MAKING A SIMPLE INLAY

A simple inlay can be made to form a design of two or more kinds of wood. Fasten two pieces of wood together in a pad and nail them with small brads in each corner. Drill a small hole at the inside corner of the design, to start the blade. Now tilt the table about 1 or 2 degrees. Make the necessary cuts, keeping the work on the same side of the blade. Take the pad apart and assemble the design. When pieces with

29-20. Cutting two or more pieces at the same time is a good way of producing duplicate parts.

358

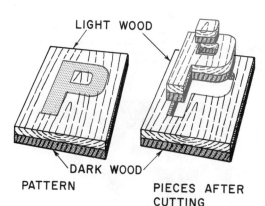

LIGHT WOOD

DARK WOOD

PATTERN

PIECES AFTER
CUTTING

DARK WOOD INLAID
ON LIGHT WOOD

LIGHT WOOD INLAID
ON DARK WOOD

29-21.   Steps in making a simple inlay.

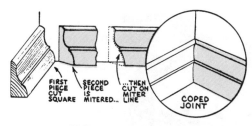

FIRST
PIECE
CUT
SQUARE

SECOND
PIECE
IS
MITERED...

...THEN
CUT ON
MITER
LINE

COPED
JOINT

29-22.   Cutting a coped joint.

beveled edges are fitted together, the saw kerf will not be visible. Fig. 29-21. Sanding the surfaces will tend to bind them even better.

MAKING A COPED JOINT

Cut one piece square at the end, then miter the other piece at 45 degrees. Jig saw the end at 90 degrees, following the contour created on the face by the beveled cut. Fig. 29-22.

MACHINE FILES
With ¼″ shank—Overall length 3¼″
Description

■ Square

▌ Crochet

◀ Half Round

● Round

◀ Triangle

▌ Oblong

29-23(a).   Common shapes of files.

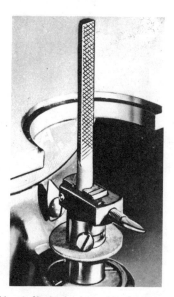

29-23(b).   A file firmly clamped in the V jaws of the lower chuck.

FILING ATTACHMENTS

Small files of different shapes can be used on the jig saw. These are particularly valuable in finishing metal edges for hardware and other special pieces of metal or plastic. The files have either 1/4″ or 1/8″ shanks and come in a wide variety of shapes. The file is held in the V jaws of the lower chuck. The work is usually fed to the tool from the pulley side. Fig. 29-23.

Manufacturers have developed many portable power tools which help the cabinetmaker and finish carpenter. These tools are particularly useful to the woodworker who specializes in building and modernizing homes, stores, and offices. Although portable saws and planes have only limited use in a well equipped cabinet shop which has much stationary equipment, they are ideal for on-the-job construction.

30-2.   Cutting a large sheet of plywood.

PORTABLE POWER SAW

The portable power saw (electric, hand, or cutoff) can be used for many types of cutting, particularly on large panel stock. Fig. 30-1. The size is determined by the diameter of the blade, ranging from 6″ to 10″. The most common size, 7″ or 8″, will easily cut through a 2″ x 4″. Blades are much the same as those for circular and radial-arm saws.

30-1.   Parts of a portable power saw.

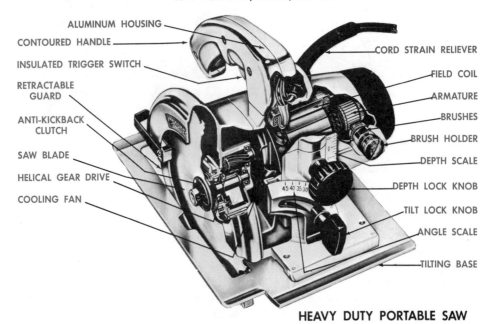

ALUMINUM HOUSING
CONTOURED HANDLE
INSULATED TRIGGER SWITCH
RETRACTABLE GUARD
ANTI-KICKBACK CLUTCH
SAW BLADE
HELICAL GEAR DRIVE
COOLING FAN

CORD STRAIN RELIEVER
FIELD COIL
ARMATURE
BRUSHES
BRUSH HOLDER
DEPTH SCALE
DEPTH LOCK KNOB
TILT LOCK KNOB
ANGLE SCALE
TILTING BASE

HEAVY DUTY PORTABLE SAW

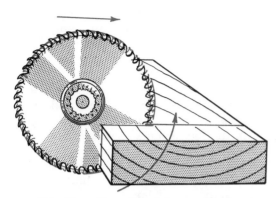

30-3. The cutting action of the portable power saw is exactly opposite that of the circular saw. The portable saw cuts from the bottom up.

A *combination blade,* for both crosscutting and ripping, is most commonly used.

One great advantage of this tool is that sawing can be done on boards that have already been installed. It can, for example, trim off boards that extend beyond the edge of an adjoining surface. When cutting in a horizontal position over sawhorses, always tack an extra strip of stock over the sawhorses to protect them from the blade. Fig. 30-2.

This saw cuts from the bottom up. Therefore, when cutting plywood, *always place the good surface down.* Fig. 30-3. The top of the cut will not be as smooth as the bottom, and there is more tearing of the upper surface.

Crosscutting

Lay out a guide line across the stock. Before you begin, adjust for depth of

cut so that the saw blade will penetrate the lower surface by about 1/8". (The saw will cut quicker and require less power when the blade clears the bottom of the stock by 1/2". However, this is more dangerous and is not recommended except for work fastened in place.) Place the base of the saw on the stock, with the blade in line with the guide line. Fig. 30-4. Turn on the saw and let it run for a few minutes before starting the cut. Guide it into the line gently but firmly, letting the blade and weight of the saw do the cutting. Fig. 30-5. If the saw sticks, pull it back slightly and allow it to come to full speed again before continuing the cut. Although it is not always convenient, use both hands on the saw whenever you can.

The saw can also be used for *bevel cuts.* However, remember to offset your guide line by the distance needed to follow the layout line on the underside. Fig. 30-6. The long side of the bevel must be at the top of the cut since the blade tilts under the saw. Make a practice of cutting just beyond the waste side of your guide line. A miter cut can also be made.

30-4. Starting the saw. Hold it firmly on the work.

30-6. Cutting a bevel. The base must be tilted to the correct angle.

361

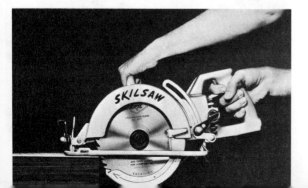

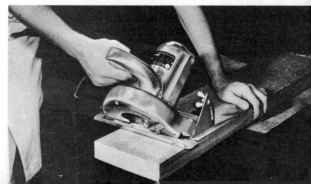

30-7(a). Making a miter cut in a freehand manner.

30-7(b). Making a compound miter cut using a protractor guide.

30-8. Ripping stock with a portable power saw, using a rip guide. Make sure the right edge is true for guiding the saw. Another method is to clamp a long straight edge to the stock as a guide.

This is a crosscut made at an angle. It can be done freehand or with a protractor guide. Fig. 30-7.

Ripping

Ripping can be done freehand in the same way as crosscutting. When making extremely long cuts, it is a good idea to walk the tool along slowly to complete the cut. Another method is to push the tool as far as you can, then hold it firmly in place while you move ahead far enough to make the next cut. To make a really accurate cut in ripping, install a rip guide or fence. This attachment can be fastened to the base. Fig. 30-8. If a rip guide is not available, a board can be clamped on the stock to guide the cutting.

Pocket Cuts

Internal or pocket cuts can be made in a panel. Swing the saw guard out of the way and keep it there. Place the front edge of the base on the work. Start the saw and let it come to full speed. Then slowly lower the blade into the work at the guide line. Fig. 30-9.

PANEL SAW

The panel saw is a portable power saw mounted in a large rack. It is used for

30-9. Starting a pocket cut. Notice that the guard must be held out of the way. Be sure to release the switch and let the blade come to rest before lifting the saw out. Clean out the corners with a hand saw.

PORTABLE SAWS AND PLANES

MAINTENANCE

• Check the sharpness of the blade or knives.
• Check the condition of the belt, if any.
• See that the guards operate easily.
• Check the tool for a broken plug or switch, bad connector, or poor insulation on the core.
• Keep the air passages clear.

LUBRICATION

• Motors on most portable tools have sealed bearings that require no further lubrication.
• Use S.A.E. 20 bearing oil or the best grade of non-detergent motor oil for any places that need oiling. Be sure to clean out the oil holes before adding the oil. Add no more than four or five drops.

SAFETY

• MAKE SURE THE SWITCH IS IN THE "OFF" POSITION BEFORE CONNECTING ANY POWER TOOL TO THE POWER SUPPLY.
• Never run a tool where there is any chance of explosion or fire due to the presence of naphtha, gasoline, benzine, or any other explosive or inflammable substance.
• Never wear loose clothing that might become tangled in the fast-turning parts.
• Keep your fingers away from blades and cutters.
• Turn off the motor immediately after finishing the cut.
• Disconnect the cord plug from the power outlet before making adjustments or replacing a blade or cutter.
• Make sure your hands and feet are dry when using a portable tool.
• Be sure the tool is properly grounded.
• If an extension cord must be used, make sure it is 12-gage wire or heavier for lengths up to 100′ and 10-gage or heavier for lengths up to 150′.

cutting panels of plywood, hardboard, and other sheet materials. To locate the position of the cut, either mark a line across the back of the panel or use the scale that is attached to the base of the rack. Place the panel so the good surface is toward the rack. Turn the saw on and pull it down to do the cutting. Fig. 30-10. A spring tape attached to the saw will help raise it after the cut.

30-10. A panel saw is ideal for cutting large sheets of plywood to smaller sizes.

BAYONET SAW

The bayonet saw (saber, sabre, or hand jig) is most useful for cutting internal and external curves on-the-job. Fig. 30-11. The saw, which operates like a jig saw but has the advantage of being portable, is relatively easy to use. It is particularly useful for internal keyholing or

30-11.   Parts of the bayonet or hand jig saw.

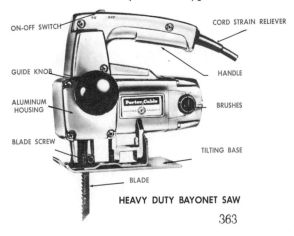

ON-OFF SWITCH

CORD STRAIN RELIEVER

GUIDE KNOB

HANDLE

ALUMINUM HOUSING

BRUSHES

BLADE SCREW

TILTING BASE

BLADE

HEAVY DUTY BAYONET SAW

30-12. This saw has a low speed for cutting aluminum and steel up to 1/4″ thick, and a high speed for cutting wood up to 2½″, plastic, and composition board.

cutting an enclosed opening in a product that has already been assembled. Design varies with the manufacturer, but most of these saws have a tilting base. Fig. 30-12.

The blade, which resembles a saber, is installed with the cutting edges pointing up. The correct kind of blade is shown in Fig. 30-13.

It is most important to hold the saw firmly on the work surface and guide it

30-13. Jig-saw blades for cutting different materials.

METAL CUTTING BLADES—for ferrous metals including mild steel, galvanized sheet; non-ferrous metals including aluminum, brass and copper.

	recommended use	teeth per inch	length
	¼″ to ½″ ferrous; 3⁄16″ to ¾″ non-ferrous.	10	3⅝″
	3⁄16″ to ¼″ ferrous; less than ¼″ non-ferrous.	14	3⅝″
	⅛″ to 3⁄16″ ferrous.	18	3¼″
	Less than ⅛″ ferrous.	32	3¼″

WOOD, PLASTIC AND COMPOSITION CUTTING BLADES—coarse tooth design for fastest cutting in ⅜″ or thicker material.

	blade type—recommended use	teeth per inch	length
	Fast scroll cutting, or "roughing-in" work.	6	4¼″
	Extra wide blade for straight cutting	6	4¼″
	Hollow ground blade for extra-smooth finish	6	4¼″
	Hollow ground, extra-wide blade for smooth finish, straight cutting.	6	4¼″
	Flush cutting blade ¾″ wide, extends to front of jig saw foot, permits cutting up to corners, vertical surfaces.	6	4¼″

WOOD, PLYWOOD, PLASTIC AND COMPOSITION CUTTING BLADES—Fine tooth design for fast smooth finish cutting in ½″ or thinner material.

	blade type—recommended use	teeth per inch	length
	Fast scroll cutting blade hardened for long life in hard compositions (Masonite, etc.) and hard plastics (Formica, etc.)	10	3⅝″
	Hollow ground for smooth finish cutting in plywood, plastics, veneers and hard compositions. Best blade for Formica; other plastic laminates.	10	3⅝″
	Extremely narrow blade for tight, intricate scroll cutting.	10	4¼″

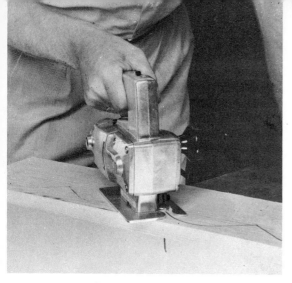

30-14. Cutting a curve. The work must be clamped so that the underside of the layout line is clear.

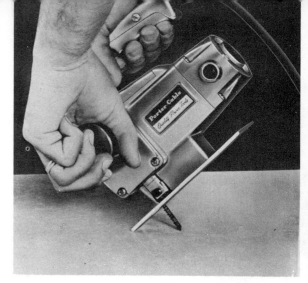

30-16. Starting an inside cut without a clearance hole.

30-15. To cut an opening in this kitchen countertop, a small hole was first drilled in the waste stock. This is typical of this tool's many excellent uses.

30-17. Ripping stock with a bayonet saw, using a guide fence. A long, straight cut can also be made by clamping a straight edge to the stock to use as a guide.

slowly. If these things are not done, the blade will break. Fig. 30-14. To do internal cutting, drill a small hole in the waste stock, then start the saw. Fig. 30-15. It is possible to start an inside cut without drilling a clearance hole. This is called plunge cutting. To do this, rest the saw on the shoe at an angle of about 45 degrees; turn on the power and slowly rock the saw back and forth until the blade cuts through. Fig. 30-16. Move the saw fast enough to keep the blade cutting all the time. Turn corners slowly and not too sharply. Cut curves freehand. Tilt saw base for accurate bevel cutting.

For straight cutting, a guide or fence should be used. Fig. 30-17. This can be a straight piece of wood clamped over the stock, or it may be a metal guide or fence attached to the machine. Circles can be cut freehand or by using the rip guide or fence as a jig. Fig. 30-18.

365

30-18(a). Cutting a circle freehand.

A

B

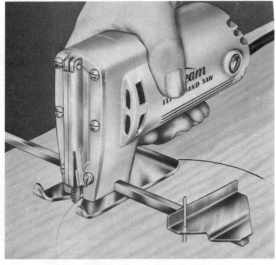

30-18(b). Using the ripping guide to cut a true circle.

C

30-20. Common kinds of saw blades. Choose the blade that will have at least three teeth in contact with the stock at all times. (A). Metal-cutting blades have from 10 to 24 teeth per inch. Choose a high number of teeth for relatively thin and hard materials. (B). Wood-cutting blades have from 3½ to 10 teeth per inch. Choose a blade with few teeth per inch for rough, fast cutting and a blade with relatively more teeth for cutting hardwood, plastic, and hard composition board. (C). A knife blade used for cutting cardboard and leather.

30-19. The reciprocating saw is also known by many other names. It is basically a portable power hack saw or keyhole saw, depending on the kind of blade installed.

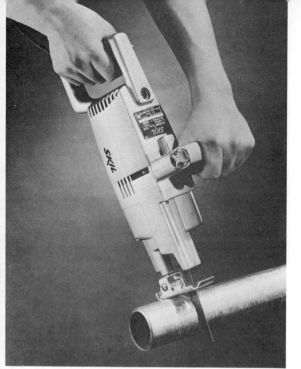

30-21. Metal-cutting blades have fine teeth. Use them at slow speed.

RECIPROCATING SAW

This all-purpose saw operates with back-and-forth movement like a keyhole saw or a hack saw without a frame. Fig. 30-19. Blades are available for cutting wood, plastic, metal, ceramics, and other materials. Fig. 30-20. Most models have a speed adjustment. Use high speeds for fastest cutting in wood, composition board, and plastic; medium speed for plastic laminate; low speeds are best for maximum control in finish wood cutting and for most metal-cutting jobs. Fig. 30-21.

A multi-position foot at the end of the saw can be moved in or out and adjusted to different angles for obtaining variable cutting depths and positions. The saw is held like a drill but cuts like a jig saw. Fig. 30-22. It is extremely useful for finish carpenters, builders, and maintenance men who do building and remodeling work. Fig. 30-23. The saw can start its own hole, but it is better to drill a clearance hole for internal cutting.

30-22. For cutting plastic laminates, use medium speed and a multi-purpose blade with about 8 or 10 teeth per inch.

30-23. For making rough cuts in softwoods, use high speed and a wood-cutting blade with 3½ teeth per inch.

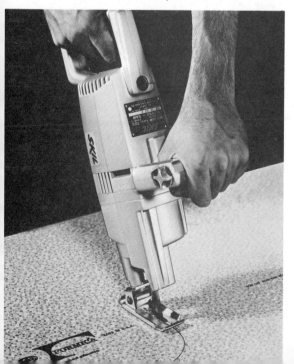

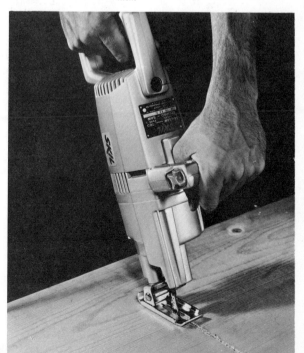

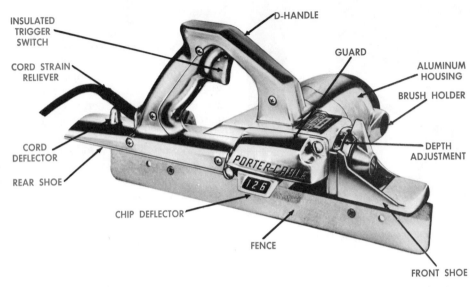

INSULATED TRIGGER SWITCH

D-HANDLE

GUARD

ALUMINUM HOUSING

BRUSH HOLDER

CORD STRAIN RELIEVER

CORD DEFLECTOR

DEPTH ADJUSTMENT

REAR SHOE

CHIP DEFLECTOR

FENCE

FRONT SHOE

16″ PORTABLE PLANE

30-24. Parts of a 16″ portable electric plane.

PORTABLE PLANES

Electric Hand Plane

Also called the portable electric plane, this tool eliminates the difficult and time-consuming hand-planing operation. Fig. 30-24. It is particularly useful for installing large doors and paneling, because it will make a smooth, accurate cut. The actual cutting tool is either a spindle and plane cutter combination or a one-piece plane cutter with a threaded shank. For most jobs the one-piece plane cutter is used.

The cutter must be set at zero before setting for depth of cut. Move the depth-adjustment lever (located at the front of

30-25(a). Using a portable electric plane to surface the edge of a door.

30-25(b). Planing a bevel on the edge of stock.

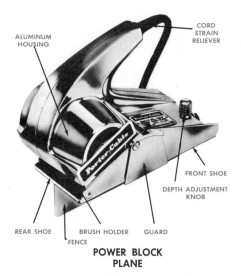

ALUMINUM HOUSING

CORD STRAIN RELIEVER

FRONT SHOE

DEPTH ADJUSTMENT KNOB

REAR SHOE

BRUSH HOLDER

GUARD

FENCE

POWER BLOCK PLANE

30-26. Parts of the power block plane.

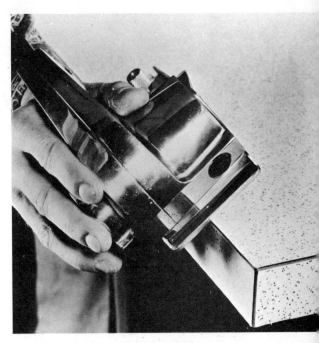

30-27. Beveling the edge of plastic laminate.

the plane) to the zero position and turn the plane over. To the left of the handle and directly behind the motor bracket is a cutter-adjusting lever. Turn this lever toward the rear of the plane and lay a straightedge across the cutter so that it rests on both the front and rear shoes. Turn the cutter by hand until it lifts the straightedge. Then adjust the lever until the tip of the cutting edge just touches the straightedge when it (the straightedge) rests evenly on both shoes. Now the desired depth of cut can be set by rotating the depth-adjustment lever.

To use, place the plane on the work, with the front shoe and fence held firmly against it. Fig. 30-25. Turn on the power. Then apply steady, even pressure as you do the planing. Never overload or push the plane too hard. When working on thick plywood or hardwoods, do not attempt to cut as fast as for softer woods. The plane can also be set for outside bevel cuts from zero to 45 degrees. In planing the edges of plywood, there is danger of breaking out the crossgrain

plies at a corner. The best way to prevent this is to clamp a piece of scrap wood at the end of the plywood before the cut is made. As you near the edge, move the plane very slowly.

Power Block Plane

The power block plane is a small tool with a spiral cutter similar to that of the electric hand plane. Fig. 30-26. It can be used for many procedures such as surface planing, edge planing, making and cleaning up rabbet cuts, planing cupboard doors to size, and beveling the edges of plastic laminates that have been bonded to a wood base. Fig. 30-27. Just under the handle is a knob for adjusting depth of cut. A small fence clamps to the bottom of the plane but can be removed for face planing. This lightweight tool can be controlled with one hand.

The jointer is used primarily for planing the surfaces and edges of stock that have been cut on a saw. Fig. 31-1. It does the same job as the hand plane but operates in an entirely different way. It has a solid steel, circular cutter head into which three or more knife blades are fastened. These knives make a rotating or revolving cut on the wood. The smoothness of the cut depends on the number of knives, the speed of rotation, and the feed.

For most cabinetwork built on the job, lumber is purchased S2S (surfaced on two sides) so that only the edges need to be surfaced. In furniture manufacturing or in shops that have a surfacer, wood is purchased in the rough and must be surfaced on all four sides. With such wood it is important to remove any warp by first cutting *one face flat* on the *jointer*. This is the only sure way to get an accurate, rectangular piece of stock.

31-1. Two jointers in a cabinet shop installed side by side The 8″ jointer is used for surfacing an edge, the 12″ size for truing the face of stock. Watches should not be worn.

While both surfaces can be planed by running the stock through a planer, first with one side up and then the other, this will not remove the warp. Fig. 31-2.

Parts and Sizes

The major parts of a jointer are a heavy base, a front and a rear table, fence, guards, and cutter head. Fig. 31-3. On most jointers, both the front and rear tables can be moved up and down on inclined ways by turning a hand wheel. Fig. 31-4. Some jointers have a fixed rear table and an adjustment for raising or lowering the cutter head. Fig. 31-5. The cutter head has three or more knives mounted in a cylindrical head. The knives revolve at a speed of 3500 to 4500 r.p.m. A fence similar to the one on a circular saw is used to guide the stock. The guard covers the cutter head except for the portion that is actually doing the cutting.

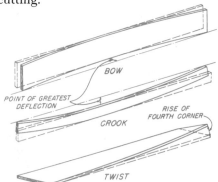

BOW

POINT OF GREATEST DEFLECTION

CROOK

RISE OF FOURTH CORNER

TWIST

31-2. Common kinds of warp that can be removed on the jointer.

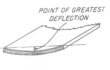

POINT OF GREATEST DEFLECTION

CUP

370

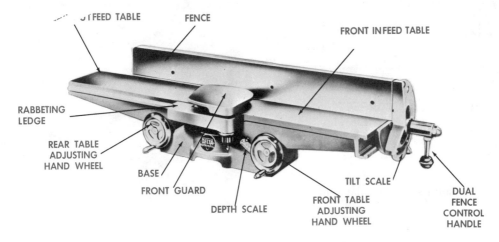

RABBETING
LEDGE

REAR TABLE
ADJUSTING
HAND WHEEL

BASE

FRONT GUARD

DEPTH SCALE

FENCE

FRONT INFEED TABLE

TILT SCALE

FRONT TABLE
ADJUSTING
HAND WHEEL

DUAL
FENCE
CONTROL
HANDLE

6″ JOINTER

31-3.   A 6″ jointer with the parts named.

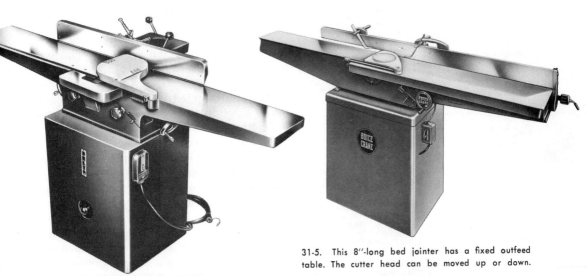

31-4.   This ruggedly constructed 8″ jointer is ideal for school and cabinet shops. It has a rear outfeed table that moves up and down.

31-5.   This 8″-long bed jointer has a fixed outfeed table. The cutter head can be moved up or down.

Adjusting the Rear Table or Cutter Head

Size of the jointer is indicated by the length of the knives or the maximum width of board that can be surfaced. For cabinet or school shops a 6″ or 8″ jointer is a good size. A 10″ or 12″ size is usually found in cabinet and fixture plants.

For accurate cutting, the rear table must be exactly the same height as the knives at their highest point. Fig. 31-6. If the table is too high, it will cut a taper. If too low, it will cut a snipe (a small concave cut at the end of the stock).

Rotate the cutter head until one knife

371

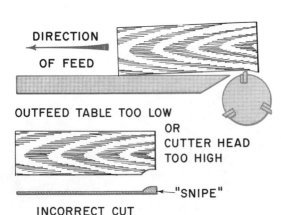

DIRECTION
OF FEED

OUTFEED TABLE AT CORRECT
HEIGHT

CORRECT CUT

DIRECTION
OF FEED

OUTFEED TABLE TOO LOW
OR
CUTTER HEAD
TOO HIGH

←—"SNIPE"

INCORRECT CUT

DIRECTION
OF FEED

OUTFEED TABLE TOO HIGH
OR
CUTTER HEAD
TOO LOW

INCORRECT CUT

31-6. The jointer must be adjusted so the outfeed table is at exactly the same height as the cutter-head knife at its highest point. Otherwise a taper or a snipe will be cut.

372

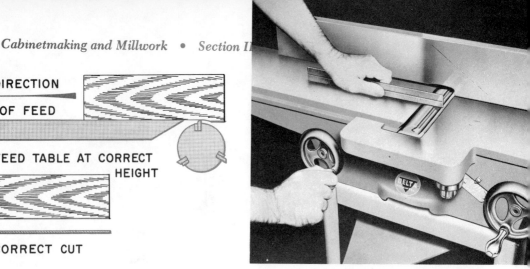

31-7. Adjusting the outfeed table. Raise the table slowly until the straightedge rests evenly on the table and the knife. Always replace the guard after making this adjustment.

is at the top position. If the rear table is adjustable, first release the lock handle on the back of the jointer. Then lower the rear table so that the top is well below the top of the cutting circle. This is done to remove any slack in the screw when the final adjustment is made. Place a straightedge over the rear table and carefully raise the table until it is at exactly the same height as one knife. Fig. 31-7. Check at the middle and at both ends of this knife. Repeat this check for all other knives to make sure they project the same distance.

Once the rear table is adjusted, lock it in position. If the knives are out of alignment or need sharpening, see Unit 24. There is usually no need to change the table adjustment unless the knives need resharpening or you want to do a special cutting job.

On a jointer with a fixed rear table, the cutter head can usually be adjusted up and down with a handle at the front of the jointer, just below the cutter head. Fig. 31-8.

ADJUSTING FOR DEPTH OF CUT

The difference in the height of the two tables determines the depth of cut. A

JOINTER

MAINTENANCE

• Hone jointer knives frequently.
• Grind and reset knives when necessary. See Unit 24.
• Make sure the guard is used and that it operates freely.
• Check the alignment of the tables to make sure they are level and not twisted.
• See that the fence operates properly.
• Adjust the outfeed table or cutter head so that both are the same height (except for special operations).
• Check the pointer on the depth scale on the infeed table to make sure it indicates the correct depth of cut.

LUBRICATION

• Sliding members and table control screws should be oiled with lubricating oil.
• Most jointers have sealed bearings on the cutter head and motor.

SAFETY

• Check the stock carefully before surfacing to make sure it is free of knots and other defects.

• Trying to surface short pieces (less than 12″) is a trap that is sure to lead to injury. Avoid it. Use hand tools for small wood parts. What happens when you attempt to surface short pieces? As the stock starts over the cutter head, the corner is very likely to catch, throwing the wood out of your hand and allowing your fingers to drop into the revolving cutter.
• Use the safety guard at all possible times. (On some jointers the guard can't be used when cutting a rabbet.)
• Check to see that all parts of the machine are locked securely.
• Use a push block when jointing a thin piece or when face planing.
• Hold the board firmly against the fence and the table.
• The maximum depth of cut should be 1/8″.
• Always stand to the left of the machine.
• Never plane the end grain of narrow stock (less than 10″).
• Plane with the grain.
• Keep your fingers away from the revolving cutter head.

special pointer and scale can be used for this adjustment. However, it is a good idea to check for accuracy. One way to do this is to adjust the front of the table to a 1/8″ cut, as shown on the depth scale, then joint the edge for a short distance. Then check to see if this is exactly 1/8″. Never make a cut deeper than 1/8″. The average depth of cut is about 1/16″. Only 1/32″ should be removed for a finish cut.

ADJUSTING THE FENCE

For most operations the fence should be at an exact right angle to the table.

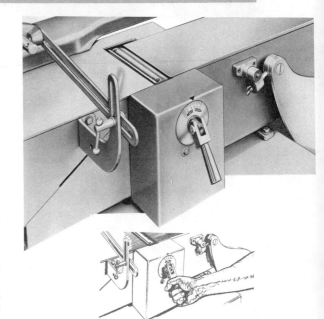

31-8. With the fixed outfeed table, the cutter head can be adjusted up or down a few thousandths of an inch in either direction. With the dial adjustment, as many as five honings are possible without changing the knives.

31-9(a). Loosen the fence control handle to adjust for the angle of cut. The fence can also be moved in and out to distribute the wear on the knives, especially for edge jointing.

31-9(b.) On larger jointers, controls for moving the fence in and out and for tilting the fence are in the center of the fence, behind and just over the rear section of the cutter.

31-10. The proper position for all jointer operations.

Fig. 31-9. There is a tilt scale for making this adjustment but it is a good idea to check with a square. The fence can be tilted in or out to cut a bevel or chamfer. This also can be set with the tilt scale, but again for greater accuracy it is good to check the angle with a sliding T bevel or the protractor head of a combination set. If a great deal of edge jointing is done, move the fence to different positions (in and out) to equalize the wear on the knives.

METHODS OF HOLDING STOCK FOR FEEDING

Stand to the left of the front table with your feet turned slightly towards the machine. Fig. 31-10. There are two common ways of feeding stock across the cutter head. In the first method the hands are kept away from the danger zone above the cutter head at all times. Start the cut by holding the stock with both hands, firmly pressing it against the front table and fence. After a portion of the stock is over the rear table, move the left hand onto that part of the stock. Then, when most of the stock is over the rear table, place the right hand also on that portion of the stock and finish the cut. With this method the hands are never over the danger zone of the cutter head. Fig. 31-11.

The second and more common method is to use the left hand to guide the stock

31-9(c). Use a try square to make sure the fence is set at right angles to the table.

374

START THE CUT

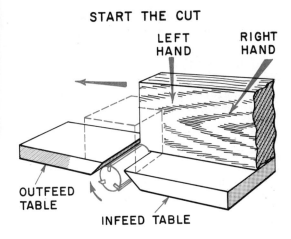

LEFT HAND

RIGHT HAND

OUTFEED TABLE

INFEED TABLE

CONTINUE THE CUT

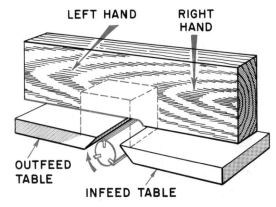

LEFT HAND

RIGHT HAND

OUTFEED TABLE

INFEED TABLE

FINISH THE CUT

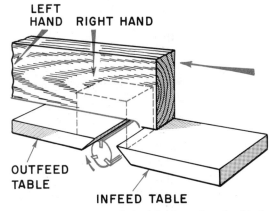

LEFT HAND

RIGHT HAND

OUTFEED TABLE

INFEED TABLE

31-11. Correct method of feeding when the hands are moved as stock passes across the cutter head. The danger area is in red.

375

31-12(a). This is a safe method of using the jointer for edge jointing larger pieces.

and hold it firmly against the table and fence. Use the right hand to move the stock forward. The stock should slide under the left hand for most of the distance, and then it moves along with the right hand to complete the cut. Fig. 31-12(a). Enough side pressure must be applied to keep the stock pressed firmly against the fence.

FACING OR SURFACING

As stated earlier, the only accurate method of producing rectangular shapes is to make sure that one face is cut flat and true. Fig. 31-12(b). Most boards have some type of warp, usually cup or

31-12(b). Starting a surfacing or facing cut.

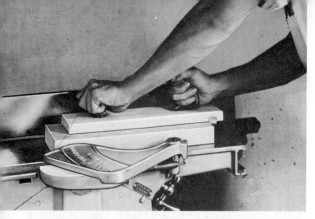

31-13(a). Using a push block to do facing. Note the use of the push block or hold-down. The knob is held in the left hand and the handle in the right.

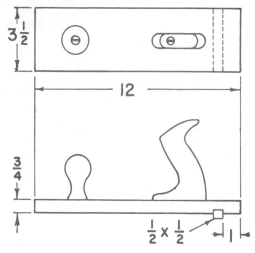

31-13(b). Drawing of a push block. This one has a knob and handle from a hand plane.

31-14. Using a hold-down push block with the right hand. This method is not very convenient or safe, especially for longer pieces.

twist. *Cup* in wood is a dished-out portion from side to side across the board. In *twist* the edges of a board turn or wind so that the four corners of any face are not in the same plane. When a board that has twist is placed on a flat surface, it rocks back and forth on the diagonal corners.

To surface a board that is cupped, place the concave side down and take several light cuts until it is flat. Twist is more difficult to remove. The best method is to mark the high corners and support the work so that stock at only these points is removed. Always use a push block for these operations. Fig. 31-13.

To plane a surface, hold the board firmly on the infeed table with the left hand toward the front of the board and the right hand toward the rear. Move the stock along until the back end is over the front table. Then pick up the push block and use it to move the piece across the cutter head. When surfacing thin stock, it is a good idea to fasten an auxiliary wood fence to the metal one to keep the stock from creeping under the fence. Another method is to use a hold-down push block with a sponge-rubber base in your right hand and move the stock with your left hand until it is over the outfeed table. Then take your hand away and complete the cut, holding the stock with the push block only. Fig. 31-14.

EDGE JOINTING

Edge jointing is the simplest and most common job performed on the jointer. Fig. 31-15. If the board is bowed (if the edges are concave on one side and convex on the other), it is a good idea to cut one edge straight on the saw before cutting it on the jointer. Set the fence at 90 degrees and lower the front table for a cut of about 1/16″. The best surface of the stock should be placed against

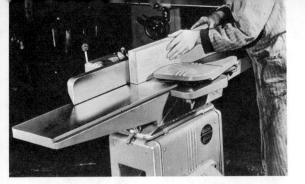

31-15. Edge jointing. Short sleeves are safer.

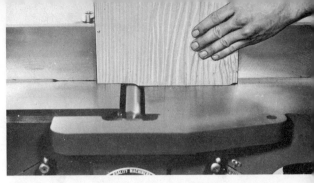

31-16. End jointing. Always make a very light cut to prevent chipping at the end of the cut.

the fence. As the workpiece is pushed over the cutter head, pressure is exerted so that it stays flat on the rear table. The right hand over the front table exerts no downward pressure but simply pushes the workpiece along to the knives. When the workpiece is over the outfeed table, both hands should exert downward and sideward pressure to keep the work in contact with the table and fence.

END JOINTING

Most wood parts for furniture do not require that the end grain be planed. Usually an end that has been sawed is accurate enough. End planing is quite difficult because you are actually cutting off the ends of the wood fibers. Therefore very light cuts should be made. In end jointing there is always a tendency for the wood to split out at the end of the cut. For this reason it is a good idea to make a short, light cut along the end grain for about 1″ and then reverse the board to complete the cut. Fig. 31-16. If the board is quite long, use an auxiliary wood fence for extra support.

SQUARING UP STOCK

If a board must be squared up on all six surfaces, the first step is to surface one face just enough to clean it up. Next, hold the face surface against the fence and joint the end grain. Cut to length (plus 1/16″). Reverse the stock and joint the second end. Then hold the face surface against the fence and joint the first edge. Next cut to width plus

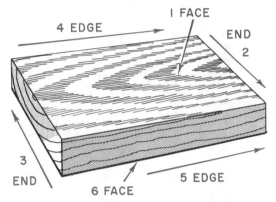

31-17(a). Steps in squaring up stock using a jointer only.

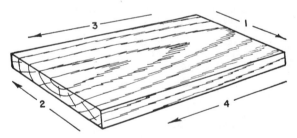

31-17(b). Steps in squaring up stock.

1/16″ and joint the second edge. Now, from the working face, mark the thickness along the edges and ends. If the piece is not uniform in thickness, it will be necessary to take several lighter cuts on the thicker portion before making the final cut. Fig. 31-17(a). Of course, if a surfacer or planer is available, surface to thickness on this machine. If only the edges and ends are to be surfaced, follow the steps shown in Fig. 31-17 (b).

377

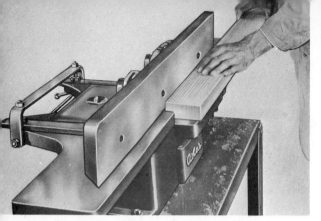

31-18. Cutting a rabbet.

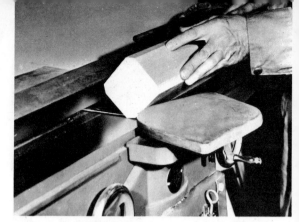

31-20. The fence can be adjusted to cut an octagonal leg.

RABBETING

Remove the guard and adjust the fence to the width of the rabbet. Lower the front table to about one half the depth of the rabbet and make one cut. Then reset the front table to correct depth and complete the rabbet. Cutting a rabbet in two or more passes results in a much cleaner cut. Fig. 31-18.

BEVELING AND CHAMFERING

A bevel is cut by tilting the fence in or out. Generally it is safer to do the cutting with the fence tilted in. Fig. 31-19. The correct angle can be set on the tilt gage. However, it is more accurate to check the fence angle with a sliding T bevel. Make several passes until the bevel is complete.

A chamfer is a sharp edge cut at a slight bevel. The cutting is done the same way as for the bevel except that only a small part of the edge is removed. Since the fence can be tilted both in and out, it is possible to chamfer both edges of a

single face without cutting against the grain. Fig. 31-20.

STOP CHAMFERING

Stop chamfering requires that both the front and rear tables be lowered an equal amount or that the cutter head be raised. Clamp a stop block on the front table so that the stop chamfer will start at the correct spot. Clamp blocks on the front and rear tables so the chamfer will be cut to the right length. Tilt the fence in to the angle you want. Remove the guard, hold one end of the stock against the stop block of the front table, and then carefully lower the stock into the revolving cutter. Push it along until it hits the stop block on the outfeed table. Then raise the rear of the stock to remove it.

CUTTING A LONG TAPER

There are several methods of cutting straight tapers, depending on the length of the stock. Fig. 31-21.

• If the stock is shorter in length than

31-19(a). Cutting a chamfer or bevel with the fence tilted in.

378

31-19(b). Cutting a bevel or chamfer with the fence tilted out.

31-21. Tapered legs like these are found on many chairs and tables.

the front table, lower that table to a depth equal to the taper. The stock is then placed so that the far end of the board rests on the rear table at the start of the taper. From this position the board can be moved forward to cut the taper.

For tapers longer than the front table, divide the taper into two or more parts. Make sure that each section is shorter than the length of the front table. For example, if the taper is 22″ long, divide it into two 11″ sections. If the amount of the taper is 1/4″, adjust the machine for a cut 1/8″ deep. Make the first cut from the halfway point. A stop block can be clamped to the fence to control the start of the cut. Start the second cut at the beginning of the taper. Use a push block to complete the cut. Fig. 31-22.

Cutting a Stop Taper

The stop taper is found on the legs of several Traditional furniture designs. First mark the beginning and end of the tapered area. Draw a line completely around the stock at these two limits. Determine the amount of stock to be removed from the leg at the point where the cut will be deepest. Lower the front table this amount. Remove the guard

31-22(a). Dividing the taper into two or more equal sections.

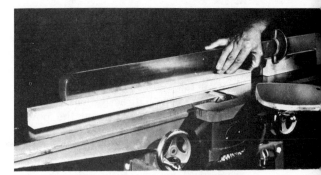

31-22(b). Cutting the first half of a longer taper. Note the stop block clamped to the fence to control start of cut. Use a push block to complete the cut.

31-22(c). Completing the taper cut. When the end of stock is over the front table, use a push block to complete the cut. Don't push the stock across the revolving cutter head with your hand in this position.

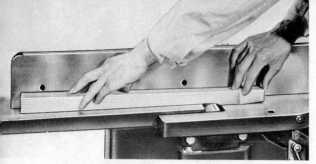

31-23. Cutting a stop taper.

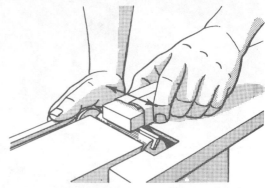

31-25. Honing the knife to keep the cutting edge sharp.

31-24. Cutting a short taper by pulling the stock across the knives.

and move the fence as close to the front of the jointer as you can without making the cut impossible. Lay the leg on the jointer at a slight angle, with the top on the rear table and with the beginning of the tapered area directly over the front edge of this table. Turn on the power. Now carefully lower the leg until it touches the front table. Move the stock along until the other end of the taper is reached. Then carefully raise the end away from the knives. Turn off the power. Stop blocks can be clamped to the fence to control the beginning and end of the cut. Fig. 31-23.

CUTTING A SHORT TAPER

Mark the length of the taper. Draw a line around the stock at this point. Clamp a stop block on the front table so that

the distance from the edge of the rear table to the stop block is equal to the taper. Lower the front table to the depth of cut you want. Cut a small piece of scrap stock. Drive two thin nails or brads through it so that the joints are exposed. Remove the guard. Now stand directly in front of the rear table and hold the end of the stock against the stop block. Lower the stock and then slip the block under the free end of the stock to maintain the correct position. Now pull the stock toward you to cut the taper. The block with the nails or brads will slide along the rear table as the taper is cut. Fig. 31-24.

HONING

Honing at regular intervals will help to maintain a sharp set of knives. To hone the knives, first lock the front table about 1/8″ below the cutting edge of the knives. Cover about two-thirds of the fine side of a large abrasive stone with waxed paper so that it won't scratch the table. Remove the fence and guard. Place the stone on the front table so that the exposed abrasive rests flat on the bevel. Clamp the cutter head in position or hold it from turning by squeezing the belt. Hone the knife by stroking the stone lengthwise with the blade. Make sure you give each knife the same number of strokes. Fig. 31-25. To sharpen and joint the knives, see Unit 24.

The shaper is primarily used for edge cutting on straight and curved pieces, for making decorative edges and moldings, for producing joints, and for grooving, fluting and reeding. While most of its work is done on the edge of stock, the shaper can also be used for face shaping. This relatively simple machine can do a wide variety of operations depending on the kind of cutters available. Fig. 32-1. However, it is a relatively dangerous machine because it must operate at a high speed and its cutters are difficult to guard completely. Shapers are made in many types and sizes and may be either single spindle or double spindle. The double-spindle shaper is used primarily in furniture factories. Most shapers used in cabinet shops are of the single-spindle type.

32-1. The single-spindle shaper is a very simple yet versatile machine. Practically the only limitations on its usefulness are the kinds of cutters available and the resourcefulness of the millman or cabinet-maker using it.

Parts

The shaper consists of a heavy base to which a table is permanently attached. Fig. 32-2. The top of the table has a miter-gage groove and also threaded holes for fastening the fence in place and for installing guide pins. The spindle, located in the center of the table, can be moved up and down to accommodate different thicknesses of cuts at various locations on the edge of the stock. Once it is adjusted to the correct height, the spindle is locked in place.

Many shapers are equipped with a reversing switch which allows the spindle to operate in either direction. In normal use the spindle moves counterclockwise, with the work moving from right to left. However, for many jobs it is better to reverse the work and feed it from left to right with the spindle rotating clockwise. The spindle speed of a shaper is between 5000 and 10,000 r.p.m. The standard spindle is 3/4" in diameter although, on many machines, one with a diameter of

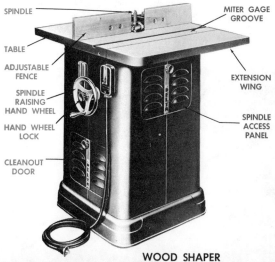

32-2. Parts of a shaper.

SPINDLE

MITER GAGE GROOVE

TABLE

ADJUSTABLE FENCE

SPINDLE RAISING HAND WHEEL

HAND WHEEL LOCK

CLEANOUT DOOR

EXTENSION WING

SPINDLE ACCESS PANEL

WOOD SHAPER

381

32-3. The spindle assembly. Note that a spindle of different diameter or length can be substituted by removing the tie-rod nut at the bottom of the spindle assembly. There are also removable table inserts with three sizes of openings.

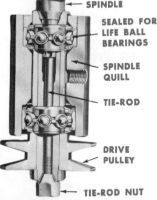

← **SPINDLE**

← **SEALED FOR LIFE BALL BEARINGS**

← **SPINDLE QUILL**

← **TIE-ROD**

← **DRIVE PULLEY**

← **TIE-ROD NUT**

32-6. The tenoner can be used for vertical shaping operations.

1/2″ or 5/16″ can be installed. Fig. 32-3.

The machine comes equipped with a fully adjustable fence. Fig. 32-4. Several accessories are also available to add to the convenience and safety of the machine. Spring hold-downs hold work firmly against the fence and table. A sliding shaper jig is ideal for many horizontal shaping operations such as cutting tenons and grooves. This attachment holds short, narrow pieces tightly and prevents them from slipping. Fig. 32-5. The tenoner can be used for vertical shaping. Fig. 32-6. A safety-ring guard that acts as a hold down can also be used on the machine. Some machines have an exhaust or shaving chute that can be connected to the dust-collection system for clearing away sawdust and chips as the shaping is done. Fig. 32-7.

32-4. The fence is fully adjustable. Both halves move independently. The faces of wood can also be adjusted endwise to make the opening larger or smaller, depending on the diameter of the cutter.

32-5. With the sliding shaper jig, the ends of narrow stock can be shaped with safety.

382

32-7. This chute for shavings will eliminate the hazard and inconvenience of chips clogging the cutter. It also serves as a cutter guard. Note that spring hold-downs will help keep the work firmly on the table.

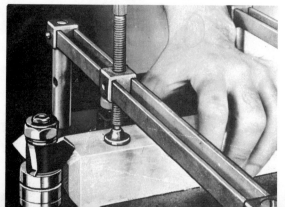

KINDS OF CUTTERS

Four basic kinds of cutters are used on the shaper:

Three-lip cutters are considered safest. These cutters are ground to shape on the back side so that honing the face doesn't change the shape. Fig. 32-8(a). They are made of high-speed tool steel or are carbide tipped, and come in a wide variety of shapes to do many kinds of cutting. The versatility of a shaper is greatly increased by a complete set of these cutters. Fig. 32-8(b). Collars are available for use with them.

32-8(a). A few of the common three-lip shaper cutters.

32-8(b). A complete set of three-lip shaper cutters.

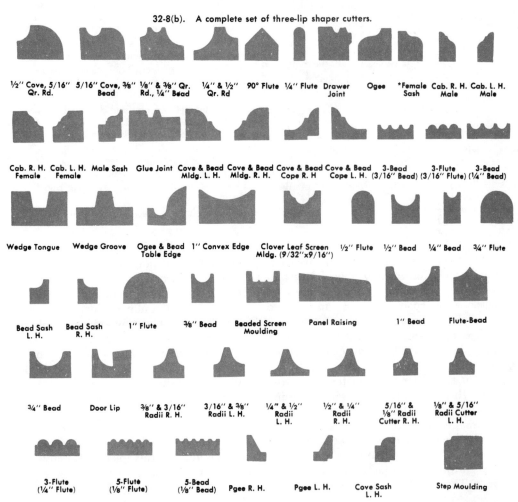

½" Cove, 5/16" Qr. Rd.   5/16" Cove, Bead   ⅜" ⅛" & ⅜" Qr. Rd., ¼" Bead   ¼" & ½" Qr. Rd   90° Flute   ¼" Flute   Drawer Joint   Ogee   *Female Sash   Cab. R. H. Male   Cab. L. H. Male

Cab. R. H. Female   Cab. L. H. Female   Male Sash   Glue Joint   Cove & Bead Mldg. L. H.   Cove & Bead Mldg. R. H.   Cove & Bead Cope R. H   Cove & Bead Cope L. H.   3-Bead (3/16" Bead)   3-Flute (3/16" Flute)   3-Bead (¼" Bead)

Wedge Tongue   Wedge Groove   Ogee & Bead Table Edge   1" Convex Edge   Clover Leaf Screen Mldg. (9/32"x9/16")   ½" Flute   ½" Bead   ¼" Bead   ¾" Flute

Bead Sash L. H.   Bead Sash R. H.   1" Flute   ⅜" Bead   Beaded Screen Moulding   Panel Raising   1" Bead   Flute-Bead

¾" Bead   Door Lip   ⅜" & 3/16" Radii R. H.   3/16" & ⅜" Radii L. H.   ¼" & ½" Radii L. H.   ½" & ¼" Radii R. H.   5/16" & ⅛" Radii Cutter R. H.   ⅛" & 5/16" Radii Cutter L. H.

3-Flute (¼" Flute)   5-Flute (⅛" Flute)   5-Bead (⅛" Bead)   Pgee R. H.   Pgee L. H.   Cove Sash L. H.   Step Moulding

SHAPER

MAINTENANCE

* Keep cutters clean and properly sharpened. Sharpen on the front face only, never on the contour shape.
* Check the belt for condition and tension. Keep the belt just tight enough to prevent it from slipping.
* Clean out the sawdust from the operating mechanism at regular intervals.
* Make sure the fence adjustments operate easily.

LUBRICATION

* Use S.A.E. No. 20 machine oil to lubricate elevating shaft, bevel gears, and column.

SAFETY

* Whenever possible, install the cutter so the bottom of the stock is shaped. In this way the stock will cover most of the cutter and act as a guard.
* Make sure the cutter is locked securely to the spindle.
* Always position the left fence so that it will support the work that has passed the cutters.
* Adjust the spindle for correct height and then lock in position. Rotate the spindle by hand to make sure it clears all guards, fences, etc.

* Check the direction of rotation by snapping the switch on and off; watch as the cutters come to rest. ALWAYS FEED AGAINST THE CUTTING EDGE, THAT IS, FEED THE WORK INTO THE CUTTERS IN THE DIRECTION OPPOSITE TO CUTTER ROTATION. Some shapers have a reversing switch so that the spindle can be rotated either clockwise or counterclockwise.
* Examine the stock carefully before cutting, to make sure it is free of defects. Never cut through a loose knot or stock that is cracked or split.
* Hold the stock down and against the fence with the hands on top of the material, yet out of range of the cutters.
* Use all guards, jigs, and clamping devices whenever possible.
* Always use a depth collar when shaping irregular work. Put a guide pin in the table to start the cutting.
* Do not set spring hold-down clips too tightly against the work. Use just enough tension to hold the work against the fence.
* For contour work, when depth collars and a guide pin are used, the operator must swing the work into the cutters. It is a good idea to keep the stock in motion in the direction of feed.
* Never shape a piece shorter than 10".

Small grooving saws can be used on the shaper for making many kinds of joint cuts. For example, two or more saws with proper spacing collars can be used for making tongue-and-groove joints.

The *three-knife safety cutter head* is very similar to a molding head used on the circular saw or radial-arm saw, except it is smaller in diameter. Fig. 32-4. With this cutter head, the same molding knives used on the saw can be used on the shaper.

The *clamp-type cutter head* with two knives is used in many cabinet shops and furniture manufacturing plants. Fig. 32-9. These are not considered safe for

general use. If not properly adjusted, the knives can work loose and cause a serious accident. Only a highly skilled cabinetmaker or millman, experienced in grinding and in setting knives, should use this cutting tool. Fig. 32-10.

Cutting tools can be selected by name. Sometimes a complicated shape is produced by using two or more cutters. It is good practice to sketch the exact design of the cut on the end of a piece of scrap stock of the same thickness as the piece to be machined. Then check the cutter against this piece to make sure they match. Make a trial cut on a piece of scrap before machining the workpiece.

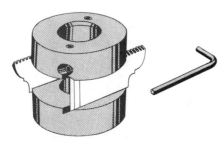

WITH SOLID COLLAR

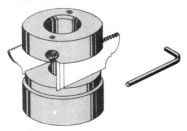

WITH BALL BEARING COLLAR

32-9. These open-face knives with collars may be purchased blank or already ground. They are safe only if set properly.

INSTALLING THE CUTTERS

On some shapers there is a flat portion on the upper end of the spindle which can be held with a wrench to keep the spindle from turning. Other shapers have a pin that slips in place to lock the spindle. If necessary, remove the fence or other setups. Remove the nut collars and cutter. Install the correct kind of cutter. It should usually be installed with the largest diameter towards the table so that most of the cutting is done on the lower side of the work. Fig. 32-11. If the cutting is to be done without a fence, one or more depth collars must be placed above, below, or between the cutters to regulate the depth of cut. Sometimes spacer collars are put between two cutters, as when shaping a rather complicated edge or making moldings. Other spacer collars can be added above the cutter so that the nut will hold the assembly firmly to the spindle shaft. Tighten the assembly before unlocking the spindle.

32-10. The skilled millman can set up two-blade, clamped-type shaper knives for many operations. Straight knives such as these are used for surfacing an edge.

32-11. Note that the cutter is installed so that the rabbet is formed at the lower edge of the stock. This is the safe method of shaping by undercutting.

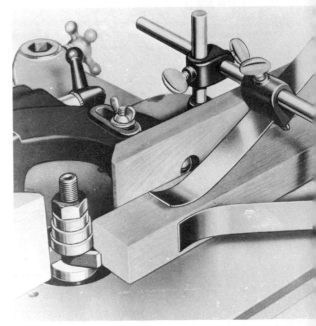

385

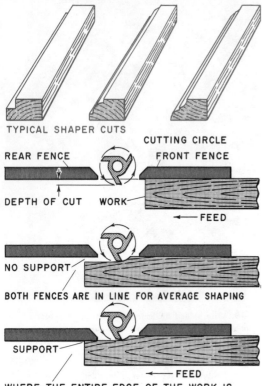

TYPICAL SHAPER CUTS

REAR FENCE · CUTTING CIRCLE · FRONT FENCE

DEPTH OF CUT · WORK

←— FEED

NO SUPPORT

BOTH FENCES ARE IN LINE FOR AVERAGE SHAPING

SUPPORT

←— FEED

WHERE THE ENTIRE EDGE OF THE WORK IS REMOVED, THE REAR FENCE MUST BE ADJUSTED TO FORM A SUPPORT

32-12. The offset of the two fences must be exactly equal to the depth of cut. The rear fence must support the edge after it is shaped.

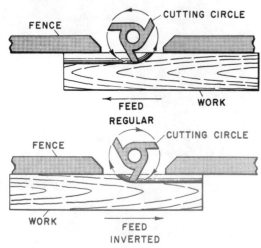

FENCE · CUTTING CIRCLE

FEED · WORK

REGULAR

FENCE · CUTTING CIRCLE

WORK · FEED

INVERTED

DIRECTION OF FEED FOR SHAPING

ADJUSTING THE SHAPER

Place a piece of scrap stock with the design on the end grain on the table top. Loosen the hand-wheel lock and raise the spindle until it matches the design. Then lock the spindle. The two-part adjustable fence can be moved in several ways. The opening between the two faces of the fence can be made wider or narrower. It should never be larger than is required for the cutter. To adjust the opening, loosen the set screws that hold each wood face to the fence, and slide the wood pieces in or out. The entire fence can be adjusted forward and back with the faces in line with one another. It is also possible to move one half of the fence back slightly. This is done when it is necessary to support a cut that has been made, as when cutting the complete edge of stock. Fig. 32-12. The fence should be adjusted parallel to the miter-gage groove by measuring the distance with a ruler at right angles to the slot.

METHODS OF SHAPING

There are four basic methods:
• Shaping with a fence or other guides. This method is used for shaping all straight edges in which the cut edge may be partially or completely machined.
• Shaping with depth collars. This method is used for irregularly shaped material. The depth of cut is controlled by putting depth collars on the spindle.
• Shaping with patterns. When a large number of irregularly shaped pieces are needed, an exact pattern of the desired

32-13. Cutters must rotate so that the *flat side* (not the beveled side) of the cutter hits the workpiece first. Cutters are designed so they will rotate counter-clockwise, with the work fed from right to left. This is called the regular method. However, the cutter should also be mounted to do the majority of the cutting on the lower side of the board. This may necessitate turning the cutter over and reversing the direction of spindle rotation and the feed direction. This is called the inverted method of shaping.

shape is made. The stock is clamped to the pattern, and the unit is held against the shaper cutter.

• Shaping with forms. This method is used primarily for production jobs. Special jigs, fixtures, and other devices are used to hold and guide the work.

Shaping with the Fence Or Other Guides

Select the correct cutter, as explained earlier in this unit. It is frequently necessary to select matching cutters; for example, in making a rule joint for a drop-leaf table.

Mount the cutter so that the major part of the cutting will be done at the bottom edge of the stock. This is not always possible when the complete edge will be machined. Make sure the direction of rotation and feed are correct. Fig. 32-13.

Adjust the fence. If only a partial edge is to be cut, the fence faces should be in line with each other and parallel to the groove in the table top. Fig. 32-14. If the complete edge is to be shaped, half of the fence should support the work before cutting, the other half after cutting.

Whenever possible, cover the spindle with a guard. Turn on the machine and check the cutting action. It is a good idea to run through a piece of scrap stock of the same thickness to check the cut. If the cut is very deep, it is sometimes better to make two passes. Adjust the fence for one light cut and then readjust for the second cut. Fig. 32-15.

For making many kinds of joint cuts when a small-diameter saw is used, a plywood fence can be made for clamping to the table top. The saw can then actually protrude through the fence to do the cutting. This method is very safe.

When face shaping wide or long stock, it is good to use a high wood fence that can be held in place with C clamps. Fig. 32-16. This fence will give added support.

32-14. Both parts of the standard fence must be aligned and parallel to the groove in the table top. Depth of cut is adjusted by moving the entire fence forward or backward.

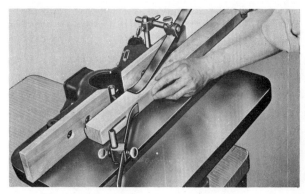

32-15. Shaping the edge of stock using spring hold-downs to help keep the work firmly on the table and against the fence.

32-16. A wood fence with a spindle hole is excellent for face shaping. Adjust the fence so the knives extend the correct distance through the opening. A feather board or spring hold-down can be used to hold the stock against the fence and the table top.

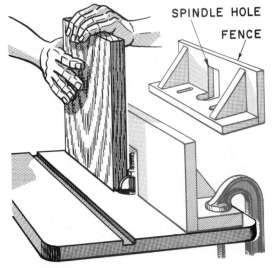

SPINDLE HOLE

FENCE

32-17. Shaping end grain with the work held against a wide board to help steady it as the cut is made.

32-20. Shaping the outer edge of a circular piece using a two-part inside circle fence clamped to the standard fence. Wrist watches should never be worn when doing this work.

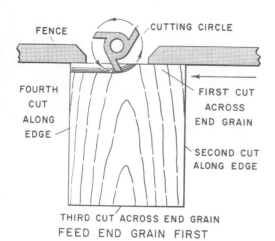

FENCE

CUTTING CIRCLE

FOURTH CUT ALONG EDGE

FIRST CUT ACROSS END GRAIN

SECOND CUT ALONG EDGE

THIRD CUT ACROSS END GRAIN

FEED END GRAIN FIRST

32-18. Always shape one end first. Then make the remaining three cuts.

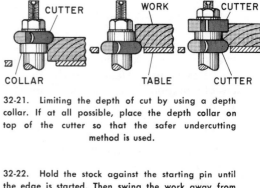

CUTTER

WORK

CUTTER

COLLAR

TABLE

CUTTER

32-21. Limiting the depth of cut by using a depth collar. If at all possible, place the depth collar on top of the cutter so that the safer undercutting method is used.

32-22. Hold the stock against the starting pin until the edge is started. Then swing the work away from the pin and hold it firmly against the depth collar.

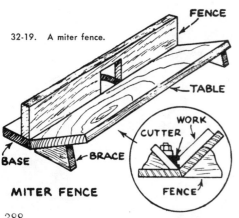

32-19. A miter fence.

FENCE

TABLE

BASE

BRACE

WORK

CUTTER

FENCE

MITER FENCE

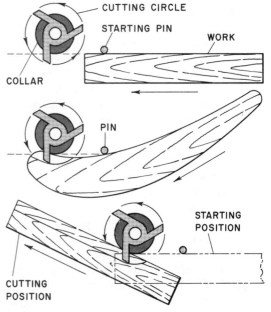

CUTTING CIRCLE

STARTING PIN

WORK

COLLAR

PIN

STARTING POSITION

CUTTING POSITION

When end grain is to be shaped, a miter gage or wide board can be used to help support the work. Fig. 32-17. The stock can also be clamped to the sliding shaper jig before cutting, to keep it from flying out of your hands.

In shaping all edges of stock, there are two methods that can be followed. One is to start on one edge and work completely around in a continuous cut. Depth collars are used in this method. The other is "start-and-stop" cutting, following the plan shown in Fig. 32-18. A miter fence is a useful device. It can be made of plywood. With such a fence, the shaper can cut on a beveled edge or can do molding on an angle cut. Fig. 32-19. Circular fences are useful in shaping the inside and outside edges of circular pieces. For example, for outside cutting on curved pieces, the fence face must have exactly the opposite curvature of the workpiece. Fig. 32-20. A guide with a large V notch cut into it can be used on many different sizes of circular pieces by adjusting its location on the top of the shaper table.

Cutting with Shaper Collars

One of the best methods of shaping an irregular edge is to use a depth collar. The diameter of the depth collar in relation to the diameter of the cutter determines the depth of cut. The collar may be used below, above, or between the cutters. Fig. 32-21. Because the collar rotates with the spindle, it may slightly burn or darken the edge of the workpiece if held too firmly against it. For industrial use, therefore, a ball-bearing collar that rotates freely is used to prevent friction between the collar and the work. When using depth collars, only part of the edge of stock can be machined since it is always necessary to have the other part riding against the collar. This limits the use of collars to some extent. The setup for collar work is about the same as for

32-23. Note that most of the shaping is done on the lower side of the scalloped edge.

fence work except that no fence is used. To support the work at the start of the cut, a guide or starting pin is fastened in the table top. Place the pin in the righthand hole if the cutter is rotating clockwise and in the lefthand hole if it is rotating counterclockwise. When using depth collars it is important that the edge of the stock be smooth and without irregularities. The stock must have the exact shape of the finished piece, and must be held firmly as the cut is started. This is extremely important. Fig. 32-22. Turn on the machine and allow it to come to full speed. Then hold the work against the guide pin and move it into the rotating cutter. When the uncut edge is moved against the knife, it will strike the cutter and bite into the edge. At this time there is a great danger of kickback. As soon as the cut is started, swing the work away from the guide pin and press it against the collar to do the cutting. Fig. 32-23. A starting block, which is a pointed piece of wood, can be used in place of the guide pin. It is clamped to the table top in a convenient position. Fig. 32-24.

32-24. A starting block serves the same purpose as a starting pin. It can be clamped to the table in any convenient position. Here it is used for shaping the inside edge of a circular piece.

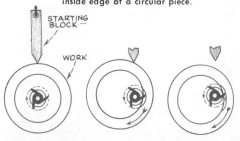

389

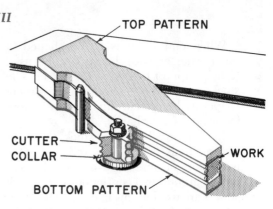

TOP PATTERN

CUTTER
COLLAR
WORK

BOTTOM PATTERN

32-28. Using a double pattern for shaping an edge.

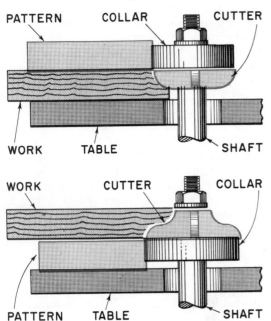

PATTERN

BLANK STOCK

32-25. Attaching blank stock to a pattern.

PATTERN   COLLAR   CUTTER

WORK   TABLE   SHAFT

WORK   CUTTER   COLLAR

PATTERN   TABLE   SHAFT

32-26. The edge of the pattern rides against a collar. The pattern may be either above or below the work.

Shaping with Patterns

Another common method of shaping large numbers of pieces which have irregular design is to use a pattern. The pattern can be made of plywood, hardboard, metal, or plastic. The workpiece is attached to it so that the pattern will follow a guide or collar. Patterns should usually be made of material from 1/2" to 3/4" thick. It is important to cut the pattern accurately and to make sure that the edges are smooth. Then, anchor pins (sharp-pointed nails or screws) must be installed to hold the work on the pattern. Fig. 32-25. The pattern rides against the collar, not the work, making it possible to shape the edge of the stock completely. The work may be either above or below the pattern. Fig. 32-26. Another distinct advantage is that there can be slight variations in the stock since the pattern will cut the entire edge accurately to the same size as the pattern every time. Fig. 32-27. When the complete edge of a piece is to be machined, it is sometimes helpful to use a double pattern, one on top and the other below the workpiece. The work is then sandwiched between the two patterns. The advantage of this method is that it allows the work to be turned over at any time in order to cut with the grain. Fig. 32-28.

32-27. Shaping with a pattern.

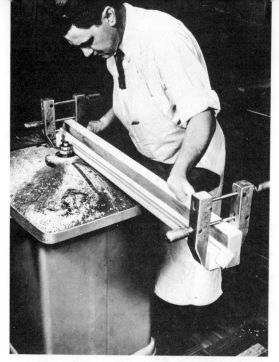

32-29. Shaping the corner of a square leg. The work is held in a fixture, and depth collars are used to control the amount of cut.

32-30(a). Shaping the edges of small pieces in a production shop. Note the fence and holding fixture designed for this purpose.

Shaping with Forms

This means holding the stock securely by means of clamps, wedges, fixtures, jigs or similar devices. Fig. 32-29. In this type of shaping, many special forms are used, primarily for production work. Fig. 32-30(a). They can be used with a special fence, jig or depth collars. Special jigs are needed for certain operations—fluting and reeding, for example, Fig. 32-30(b). See Unit 33. Many of the same jigs and fixtures described for the circular saw can also be used on the shaper.

SHAPING ON THE RADIAL-ARM SAW

Many shaping operations can be done on the radial-arm saw by using a molding head or a three-knife safety cutter head. Fig. 32-31. A two-piece adjustable fence replaces the standard guide fence. This fence is designed so that either the infeed or outfeed side can be independently moved closer to the center of the table or towards the ends. For shaping a complete edge, the infeed side of the

fence must be recessed (moved back) equal to the exact amount of stock being removed. Fig. 32-32. A special guard must be used to cover the cutter.

Straight Shaping

In shaping a molded edge, the pattern is cut on the edge of the stock. Mount the proper cutter on the motor shaft. Place the motor in a vertical position and adjust for correct height. Move the motor unit in or out and lock it in position. Adjust the fence so that the work will be properly supported during cutting. Always feed from the right side into and against the revolving cutters. Hold the work firmly on the table. If the cut is very deep, it may be a good idea to make several passes.

End Shaping

End shaping can be done by holding the work firmly against the standard guide fence and a stop block. Then feed the motor unit slowly forward. Fig. 32-33.

391

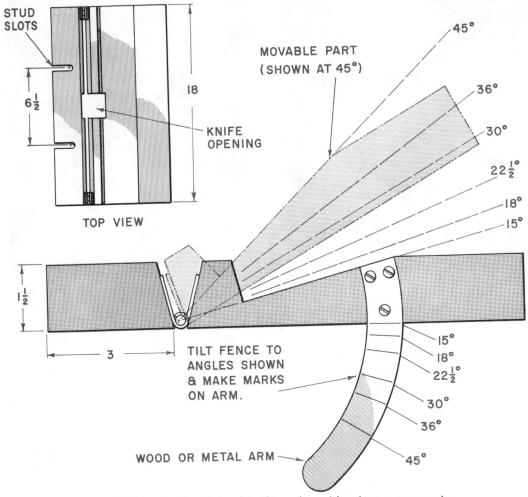

STUD SLOTS

KNIFE OPENING

18

6½

TOP VIEW

MOVABLE PART (SHOWN AT 45°)

45°

36°

30°

22½°

18°

15°

1½

3

TILT FENCE TO ANGLES SHOWN & MAKE MARKS ON ARM.

15°
18°
22½°
30°
36°
45°

WOOD OR METAL ARM

32-30(b). An adjustable bevel jig. This can be used for edge cuts at any angle.

32-31. If only a part of the edge is shaped, the standard guide fence can be used.

32-32. Using the shaper fence and special guard for shaping the complete edge of the stock.

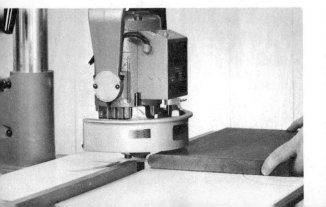

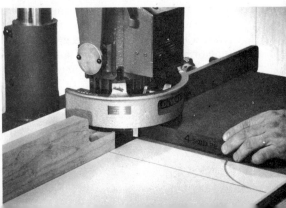

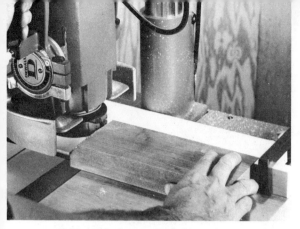

32-33. End shaping by holding the material and moving the cutter.

32-35. Shaping the inside edge of a design on the drill press.

Pattern Shaping

To do shaping with patterns, remove the standard guide fence and make a circular guide ring with the same diameter as the cutting circle of the head. This guide ring must have the inner circle of wood removed so that the motor shaft can project below the surface. Then nail this ring to a scrap piece of 1″ thick wood and use this to replace the standard guide fence. The ring must be directly under the revolving cutter head. Now a pattern can be made to any size and shape. Rub a little paraffin on the edge of the pattern to make it slide easily. Place two or three anchor pins through the pattern to hold the stock firmly in place. Then adjust the collar and pattern

32-34. Shaping with a pattern. Note that the pattern rides against the wood shaper ring mounted to the table just below the cutter.

for the correct depth of cut. The pattern then rests against the shaper ring as the cutting is done. Fig. 32-34.

SHAPING ON THE DRILL PRESS

Shaping can be done on the drill press if the spindle speed is 5000 r.p.m. or higher. It is necessary to replace the chuck with a shaper adapter to hold the cutters. Never attempt to fasten the cutters in a chuck used for drilling. The three-lip cutters used on the shaper can also be used on the drill press. Shaping can be done by using a guide fence or depth collars. Fig. 32-35. The quill must be located in position. Fig. 32-36. Remember to check the setup before turning on the power.

32-36. Using a fence as a guide for shaping on the drill press.

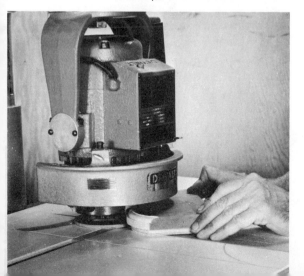

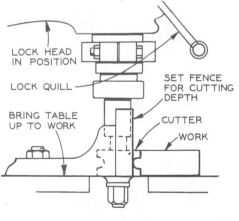

LOCK HEAD IN POSITION

LOCK QUILL

BRING TABLE UP TO WORK

SET FENCE FOR CUTTING DEPTH

CUTTER

WORK

Routers are widely used for shaping the surfaces and edges of stock, and for joinery. With a floor router, the cutting tool is stationary and the work moves. Fig. 33-1. The drill press and radial-arm saw can also be used for routing. With a portable router, the work is held stationary while the tool is moved. Fig. 33-2. The router, an overhead cutting tool, does work that is similar to that done by the shaper. (On the shaper, the cutting tool comes from underneath the table.) The router has the advantage of entering the wood like a drill and then being able to move around to cut a recess in the wood surface. Fig. 33-3.

33-1(a). A floor-type router-shaper. On this machine the work is moved under a revolving cutter.

VIEWS SHOWING FLEXIBILITY OF ROUTER-SHAPER

View shows head-raising mechanism, adjustable stops, tilt indicator, disappearing guide pin assembly and rugged undertable construction.

Routing with small size cutters. Note the safety-type switch and flexible blower cable for chip removal.

Heavy cast fence with adjustable hardwood faces. One face is stationary; the other is adjustable inward and outward so shaping can be done from either direction. Fence measures 27" long x 2½" high.

33-1(b). Adjustments on the floor-type router.

33-2.   Portable router.

PORTABLE ROUTER

The portable router consists of a motor that is adjustable up and down in a base. Fig. 33-4. It operates at high speeds of 20,000 to 28,000 r.p.m. A collet (or split) chuck, attached to the end of the motor, holds the cutting tools. The kind of work that can be done with the router depends on the cutters, fixtures, and attachments used. Fig. 33-5.

33-3.   The keyhole design with shaped edges on these coffee tables was cut on the router.

ROUTER

MAINTENANCE

• Keep all bits sharp. Grinding can be done by hand or with a grinding fixture that attaches to the router. Grind the underside of the lip of the bit.
• Keep the air vents free from sawdust.
• Check the brushes periodically and replace them immediately if worn away.

LUBRICATION

• Ball bearings on the motor shaft are grease-sealed to last the lifetime of the bearings. No further lubrication is required.

SAFETY

• Make sure the router is properly grounded. Most come equipped with a three-wire cord that will fit directly into corresponding grounding receptacles. An adapter for grounding a two-wire receptacle is usually furnished with the tool.
• Turn off the motor when not in use.
• Disconnect the plug from the power circuit when changing bits.
• Hold the portable tool firmly but lightly in your hands.
• Never turn on the power until you are in a working position.
• Make sure the bit is properly installed before turning on the power.
• Never put anything into the ventilating holes of the router.

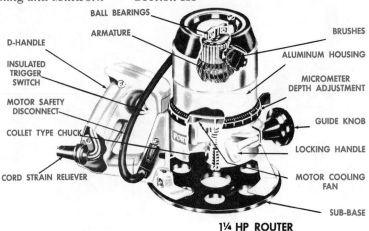

BALL BEARINGS

ARMATURE

D-HANDLE

INSULATED
TRIGGER
SWITCH

MOTOR SAFETY
DISCONNECT

COLLET TYPE CHUCK

CORD STRAIN RELIEVER

BRUSHES

ALUMINUM HOUSING

MICROMETER
DEPTH ADJUSTMENT

GUIDE KNOB

LOCKING HANDLE

MOTOR COOLING
FAN

SUB-BASE

1¼ HP ROUTER

33-4(a). Portable router with parts named.

33-4(b). Exploded view of a router.

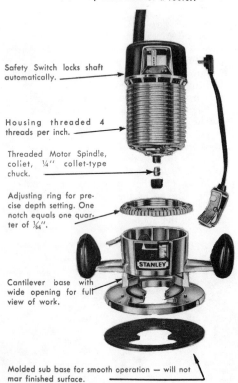

Safety Switch locks shaft automatically.

Housing threaded 4 threads per inch.

Threaded Motor Spindle, collet, ¼'' collet-type chuck.

Adjusting ring for precise depth setting. One notch equals one quarter of ⅟₆₄''.

Cantilever base with wide opening for full view of work.

Molded sub base for smooth operation — will not mar finished surface.

Router Bits

Most router bits are made of selected tool steel. These are adequate for most cutting on hard and soft woods with the portable router. Carbide-tipped bits are normally used in production work and also for trimming the edges of plastic laminates.

Router bits are of two major types. The first and most common is the one-piece bit with a shank built into the cutting head. Some of these bits have a pilot or cylindrical tip built into the lower cutting edge. The shank fits into the collet of the router motor. The other type has a hole threaded completely through the center of the cutting head. When this bit is used with the router, a separate shank or arbor is screwed into the top of the cutting head. Also, if a separate pilot is needed, it is screwed into the bottom of the cutting head. When routing the edge of a board, the pilot controls the horizontal depth of cut by riding along the edge of the work.

Following are some common shapes of cutter bits and their uses: Fig. 33-6.

33-5. Router guide which can be used to control the sidewise movement of the router.

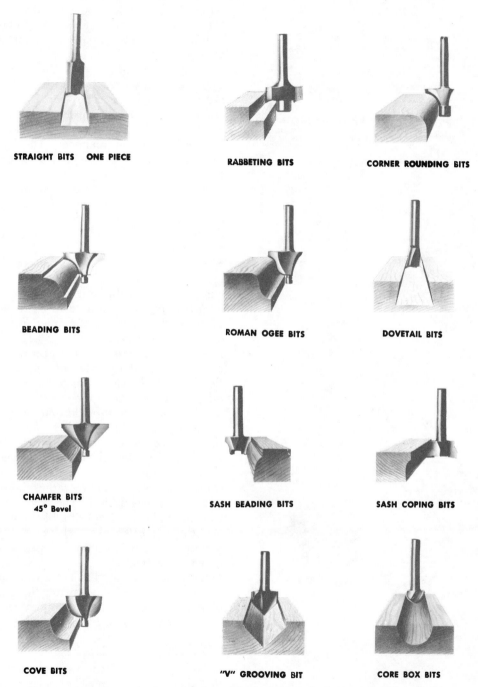

STRAIGHT BITS   ONE PIECE

RABBETING BITS

CORNER ROUNDING BITS

BEADING BITS

ROMAN OGEE BITS

DOVETAIL BITS

CHAMFER BITS
45° Bevel

SASH BEADING BITS

SASH COPING BITS

COVE BITS

"V" GROOVING BIT

CORE BOX BITS

33-6.   Common shapes of router bits. Special shapes for any kind of routing can be ordered.

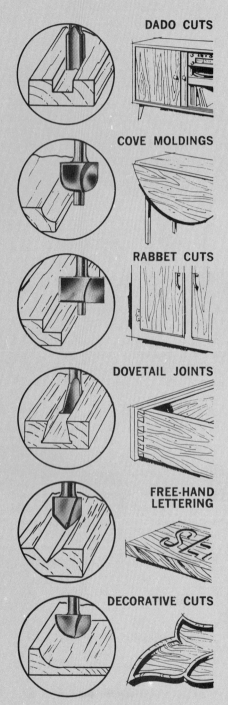

DADO CUTS

COVE MOLDINGS

RABBET CUTS

DOVETAIL JOINTS

FREE-HAND LETTERING

DECORATIVE CUTS

33-7. Common kinds of cuts made with a portable router.

Straight bits are used for general stock removal for cutting grooves, dadoes, inlay work, rabbeting, and background routing. These are available in diameters from 1/8" to 3/4".

Veining or round-end bits are similar to straight bits except that they cut a radius in the wood. They are used for ornamental or decorative figure routing.

Core-box bits are similar to veining bits but larger in diameter. They get their name because of wide use in patternmaking.

Corner-rounding bits are used around the corners of flat surfaces such as tables, desk tops, or cupboard doors.

Chamfer bits cut a 45-degree bevel on the edge of stock.

Sash coping bits are used to cut copings in window-frame rails to match beads cut by a sash beading bit.

Sash beading bits are used to cut beads or decorative edges on the inner surface of a window frame.

Rabbeting bits are used to cut a rabbet or a step cut at the edge of wood.

Beading bits are similar to corner-rounding bits except that they are able to leave a sharp break or decorative bead at each end of the round.

Roman ogee bits cut the decorative edge frequently found on the inside of paneled doors and frames.

Cove bits cut a concave radius in the edge of a warped piece. The cove bit is used for making a dropleaf table joint.

"V" grooving bits make V-shaped cuts to imitate plank construction on panels of plywood or boards.

Dovetail bits are used to cut a dovetail-dado or a straight dovetail on the ends of stock to form a right-angle joint as in drawer construction. Fig. 33-7.

CONTROLLING THE CUTTING

There are five basic ways of controlling the sidewise movement of a portable router:

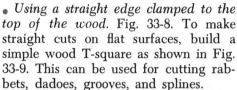

33-8. A piece of lumber with a smooth, straight edge can be used as a guide for making straight cuts on flat surfaces.

33-10. The straight guide is excellent for cutting any kind of groove or slot along the edge or end of stock.

• *Using a straight edge clamped to the top of the wood.* Fig. 33-8. To make straight cuts on flat surfaces, build a simple wood T-square as shown in Fig. 33-9. This can be used for cutting rabbets, dadoes, grooves, and splines.

• *Using a straight or circular guide* (also called edge guide). This is the most practical and inexpensive accessory for the router. It guides the router in a straight line along the edge of a board and is particularly useful in cutting grooves on long pieces. Fig. 33-10. The edge of the guide can be adjusted the correct distance from the cutter so that it will ride along the edge or surface of the stock. Some guides can also be reversed so the machine will make a two-point contact when used on circular work. Fig. 33-11.

• *Using a bit with a pilot end.* Many router bits have a pilot end which limits the depth of cut. When the bit reaches the right amount of sidewise movement, the pilot contacts the stock and prevents a deeper cut. Pilot ends are common on beading, rounding-over, cove, and molding bits. Fig. 33-12.

33-9. A simple T-square device that can be used to guide the router.

33-11. Most router guides can be reversed in order to make cuts that are parallel to curved or circular edges. Watches should not be worn.

33-12. The pilot on the end of the cutter controls the amount of cut. It rides on the edge and does no cutting. Rings could cause an accident.

399

33-13. Using a hardboard templet as a guide in routing out a scroll design.

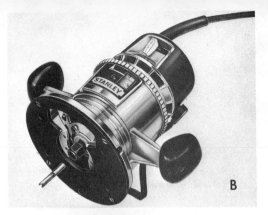

B

33-14. Freehand routing can be done to shape recessed or raised letters. Here, recessed letters are formed by removing the wood to make the letter itself.

C

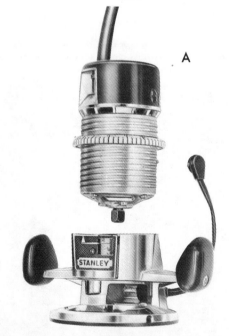

A

D

33-15. Assembling a router: (A) The motor is readily removed from the base by loosening the clamping lever and disconnecting the light wire. (B) Select the correct bit and insert it all the way into the collet chuck. With the safety switch in the locked position, the shaft is held firmly. The chuck can be tightened with only one wrench. Return the motor to the base. (C) Loosen the clamping lever about one quarter of a turn when raising or lowering the motor for exact depth setting. (D) For extremely accurate setting, use the micrometer depth adjustment. Each notch on the depth ring is equal to one quarter of 1/64".

400

• *Using a templet or pattern.* A templet of the correct shape can be made of 1/4″ plywood or hardboard. With small brads attach it to the stock where the work will not show or will be removed if the routing must go completely through the stock. If the cut is to go completely through, clamp scrap wood underneath. Fig. 33-13. Use a straight or a rounding-over bit for corners, as needed. Several commercial templets are also available. The principal ones are for cutting a dovetail and for hinge-butt routing.

• *Freehand routing.* This kind of cutting is done without any guide devices. The quality of the work is determined by the operator's skill. Either the background can be routed out, leaving raised letters, or the letters or pattern can be cut directly into the wood. The pattern is penciled directly on the workpiece. Usually, veining bits are used. It is suggested that the routing be not more than 3/8″ deep. Deeper cuts make it difficult to follow the pattern. For wood carving, some operators use the router to remove much of the background stock before doing the final shaping with a gouge and chisel. Fig. 33-14.

Assembling and Adjusting the Router

Select the correct bit for the kind of work to be done. Fig. 33-15. Remove the motor unit from the base by turning or, if it is a clamp-on type, slip it off. Insert the shank into the chuck to a distance of about 1/2″. Lock the motor so it will not turn, then tighten the nut on the collet to hold it in place. Next, slip the motor into the base and place it over a piece of scrap stock. Move the motor down until the end of the bit touches the work surface.

There are several kinds of routers that are adjusted in different ways. If the motor screws into the base, screw it

in until the router bit is exposed an amount equal to the depth of the cut; if the motor moves up and down by a ratchet arrangement, slip the motor down into the base the correct distance. Lock the base to the motor securely.

Try cutting a scrap piece of the same thickness as the stock. Always make sure that the work is rigidly held in position. Since the cutter rotates clockwise, cutting is more efficient if the router is moved from left to right as you stand facing the work. Fig. 33-16. Also, in working on the inside of a templet, work from left to right. Don't feed the router too slowly for this will make the bit grind the wood.

33-16. The router bit revolves clockwise. Therefore, when cutting straight edges, move the router from left to right. When making circular cuts, move the router in a counterclockwise direction.

DIRECTION OF MOTOR ROTATION (M.R.)

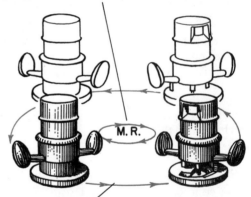

DIRECTION OF FEED

33-17. Cutting a rabbet across grain using a straight bit and a straight guide. The diameter of the bit should be slightly larger than the width of cut you want.

Feeding too fast will produce excessive wear on the bits. For extremely heavy cuts it is sometimes better to take a lighter cut at first, then make a second cut to the correct depth. The sound and feel of the motor will help you decide when to do this.

Cutting a Rabbet

A rabbet is an L-shaped groove along the edge or end of stock. It can be cut either with or across the grain. Use a straight bit and a gage to control the width of the cut. Try the width and depth of the cut on a piece of scrap stock

and, when it is correct, proceed with cutting the rabbet. Figs. 33-17 and 33-18.

Cutting a Dado

While there are many ways of cutting a dado, one of the simplest is with the router. Use a straight cutter of the same diameter as the thickness of the piece to fit into the dado. For example, if you are using 3/4″ material, it is best to use a 3/4″ bit. Fig. 33-19. If a bit this size is not available, use a narrower one and make two or more passes. Fig. 33-20. Either a straightedge or a commercial guide can be used to control the router when cutting. Fig. 33-21. To locate the position of the straightedge, measure from the cutting edge of the bit to the outside edge of the router base. This will give you the distance from the straightedge to the point at which the cut is to be made. A stop dado can also be cut by limiting the distance that the router is moved across the stock.

Cutting a Groove

Grooves are cut in the direction of the grain. An edge guide that is in a straight line and parallel with the edge of the stock is used on the router. Grooves are found on the sides, backs, and fronts of drawers, boxes, and many other boxlike structures. They are also used on the inside edges of frames to make raised or recessed panels for door construction. Fig. 33-22. The simplest method of cutting a groove is to use a commercial guide with a straight cutter bit of correct diameter. Fig. 33-23.

33-18. To cut a rabbet on the inside of an opening such as a picture frame, it is necessary to use the straight router guide with an auxiliary wood block. A triangular wood block that has a 90-degree angle is fastened exactly in the center of the straightedge plate of the router guide. There are two holes in this guide to hold the wood block in place so the rabbet can be cut right up to the corner with only a slight radius. This can be cleaned out by hand, using a chisel.

33-19. A dado is cut by using a bit of the correct diameter and adjusting the router for the desired depth of cut. Notice that the commercial router guide is used to control the position of cut.

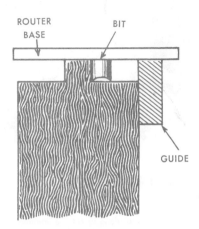

ROUTER BASE — BIT — GUIDE

33-20. When the router bit is not large enough in diameter, two or more passes are necessary to obtain the correct width of cut.

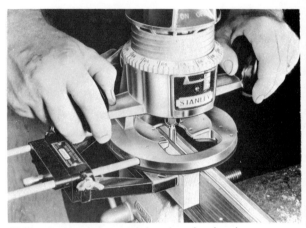

33-22. Cutting a groove in the edge of a board. Note the extra piece of wood about 2" high attached to the commercial guide for added stability.

33-21. Cutting a dado completely across the stock using a straightedge as a guide. To get a clean edge without splitting, it may be a good idea to fasten a piece of scrap wood to the straightedge guide on either edge. Then the router bit must cut through the scrap stock at the beginning and end of the cut.

33-23. A circular groove can be cut by using a trammel point attached to the guide rods of the router guide. The trammel point has a needlelike projection that acts as a center. Circular parts can also be cut by placing the stock over a scrap piece so that the router bit can cut completely through the first piece.

403

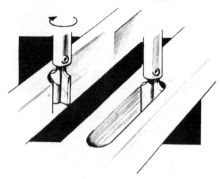

33-24. Notice that the blind mortise has rounded ends. The advantage of the router for cutting mortises is that the bit can be lowered into the stock and then moved along to cut the opening.

Cutting a Blind Mortise and Tenon

The mortise-and-tenon joint is used in frame construction, for doors, fronts of drawers, and for leg-and-rail construction. The blind mortise, when cut with a router, has rounded ends which must be squared off with a hand chisel or else the tenon must be made narrower to cover the opening. Fig. 33-24. Usually the mortise is cut in the exact center of the edge or surface. Use a straight bit and the router guide. When cutting in the edge of stock, it is a good idea to clamp a piece of wood on either side to give the base more support. Fig. 33-25. The tenon can be formed by making rabbet cuts on all four sides. By clamping stock together, several tenons can be cut at the same time.

Spline Joint

The spline joint is used to reinforce the joining edges of two pieces of wood. To cut the groove for this joint, first select a straight bit of the correct width. Normally, splines are made of 1/8″ or 1/4″ plywood or hardboard so a 1/8″ or 1/4″ straight bit can be used. Use a gage to control the location of the groove. In many cases a blind-spline cut is required. Fig. 33-26(a). This is made by dropping the router into the work and moving it along the required distance. Fig. 33-26(b).

33-25. Scrap stock has been clamped to either side of the work so the router is not likely to tilt as the cut is made.

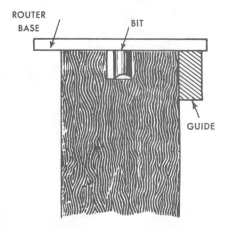

ROUTER BASE

BIT

GUIDE

404

33-26(a). A blind spline has a good appearance. Note that both pieces of material are clamped between scrap pieces. The spline is installed in one part of the miter joint.

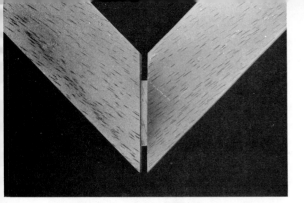

33-26(b). The complete miter joint showing the use of a blind spline.

33-27(a). Cutting the mortise or slot.

Cutting a Dovetail-Dado Joint

The dovetail-dado joint is relatively easy to cut with a router, dovetail bit, and router guide. First cut the slot or mortise portion. Take the board on which the dovetail is to be cut and place it endwise in a vise. Place a scrap piece of wood on either side so that the router base has ample surface on which to ride. Adjust the bit for depth of cut, and position the guide so the cut is exactly centered on the stock. Then cut the slot. Fig. 33-27(a). It is possible to cut a wider dovetail by making two or more passes. However, it is important that the location and width of the dovetail be accurately marked.

To cut the tenon or stub portion of the joint, keep the depth setting the same as for the slot. Adjust the guide so that one cut is made on each side to form the tenon. Fig. 33-27(b). It is essential that the tenon be a few thousandths of an inch narrower than the slot. Before cutting the joint, it is good to make trial cuts on scrap stock of the same thickness.

Cutting a Dovetail Joint

The dovetail joint is used extensively in commercial furniture, especially for fine drawer construction. Furniture factories use large, expensive dovetailing machines. However, the joint can also be cut with a dovetail attachment and a portable router. Both parts of the joint are cut at the same time.

33-27(b). Cutting the tenon or stub. Note that two dovetails are actually cut to form this part.

1. Clamp the dovetail attachment to a bench or table so that the base projects slightly beyond the front. Attach a templet guide tip to the base of the router. Fig. 33-28. Insert a dovetail bit through the templet guide and tighten it in the chuck. Adjust the dovetail bit so that it is exactly 9/32″ below the base. Square up the stock to form the joint. Cut two

33-28. Attach a templet guide to the base of the router.

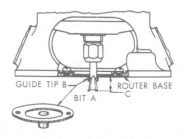

GUIDE TIP B — ROUTER BASE C
BIT A

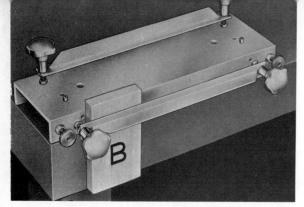

33-29(a). Clamp the side of the drawer in place (Part B).

extra pieces of scrap stock of the same thickness and width to make a trial joint before final cutting. Clamp board B, which will be one side of the drawer or box, with the inner side out against the front of the base, about 1/2″ above the top surface of the base. This is a temporary setting to locate board A. Fig. 33-29(a).

2. Clamp board A, which will be the front or back of the drawer or box, with the inner side up. Make sure that board B is firmly against the locating pin. Then loosen the front clamp slightly and move B until the end grain is flush with the top of A. Fig. 33-29(b).

3. Place the templet over the two pieces and clamp it in place. Make sure the templet rests evenly on the material. Fig. 33-30.

4. Cut a trial dovetail joint, making sure that the guide tip of the router follows the templet prongs. Always hold the router in the same position as it is moved around the templet. Fig. 33-31.

5. Check the dovetail for fit. If it is too loose, lower the bit about 1/64″; if too tight, raise the bit about 1/64″. If the fit is too shallow, set the templet adjusting nuts a little more toward the base; if too deep, set the templet adjusting nuts away from the base. The accuracy of the joint depends on a very fine adjustment which trial cuts will help you make.

6. The left end of the fixture is used for cutting the right front of the drawer and the left-rear corner. The left-front and right-rear corners are cut at the right end of the dovetail.

7. To cut a dovetail on a lip-drawer front that has a rabbet cut on the back surface, the rabbet and the dovetail must be cut separately. Mount the rabbet piece of the drawer front in a horizontal position, firmly against the locating pin. Make a gage block by cutting a groove in a piece of scrap wood to hold the lip end of the drawer front. Use the gage block, as shown in Fig. 33-32, to locate the rabbet surface and align it with the vertical surface of the base of the fixture. When the stock is clamped, remove the gage block and place the templet in position. Cut the dovetail. To cut the side of the drawer, first cut a scrap piece the same thickness as the drawer front. Place this piece on top of the fixture and put the side piece in its correct position, as shown in Fig. 33-32. Then cut the dovetail. The two parts should fit accurately as shown in Fig. 33-33.

33-29(b). Clamp front or back in place (Part A).

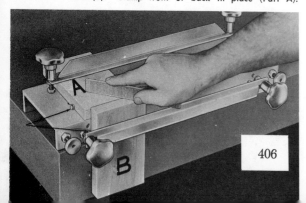

406

33-30. Place the templet over the pieces.

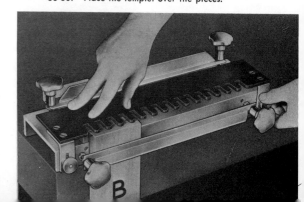

33-31(a). Cut the dovetail with the router.

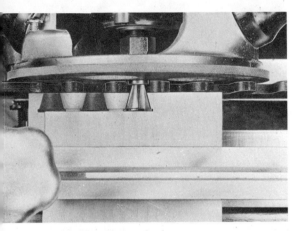

33-31(b). Here you see how the two parts of the joint are cut at the same time.

33-32. Position of the lip end of the drawer for cutting one part of the dovetail.

GAGE BLOCK REMOVED AFTER CLAMP-ING DRAWER FRONT.

ALIGNMENT WITH VERTICAL SURFACE OF BASE

DRAWER FRONT

FIXTURE BASE

LOCATING PIN

33-33. The completed dovetail joint that joins the side to the front of a lip drawer.

Hinge Butt Routing

A special templet is available for hinge butt routing. Because the bits leave a slight curve at the corner of the cut, it is necessary to chisel the corner square for the hinges. Fig. 33-34 shows a metal templet in position on a door. This guides the router so that the hinge mortises are cut to uniform size and depth, easily and quickly.

Decorative Cutting

The router can be used to make all types of decorative cuts in wood. In many cases a templet is needed for curved or irregular-shaped wood. The templet should be made of 1/4" plywood or tempered hardboard. Trace the pattern on the plywood or hardboard.

33-34. Cutting a hinge mortise on a door. If a square corner hinge is used, the corners of the cut must be squared with a chisel. However, many hinges have round corners so they fit directly into the opening. After gains or mortises are cut on the door, the templet guide can be transferred to the door frame for cutting hinge mortises on the jamb.

33-35. A templet traced on a piece of plywood.

33-38. Clamp the finish templet to the work. Place a piece of scrap stock underneath. Make sure the sub-base and templet guide are in place. Use a straight bit that is adjusted to the correct depth. Lower the bit into the waste stock, then guide the router along the edge of the templet. Make sure the templet guide is in contact with the edge of the templet.

33-36. Place the templet over scrap stock. Cut through the waste stock, then cut the stock 1/16" from the layout line. This must be done freehand. Remove the templet, then file and sand up to the layout line.

33-37. A templet guide. Several sizes of these are available.

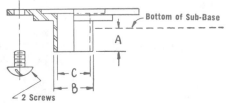

A = Distance Templet Guide tip extends from bottom of base.
B = Outside diameter Templet Guide tip.
C = Inside diameter Templet Guide tip.

Fig. 33-35. Then cut out the templet design on a jig saw or with the router. Fig. 33-36. The templet can then be fastened over the stock. You can use a bit with a smooth edge that will ride against the templet. Or, if a templet guide that fastens to the base of the router is available, use it. This guide rides against the templet. Fig. 33-37. For best results, make the first cut a little distance from the line. Then, on the second pass, cut up to the templet. Fig. 33-38. Decorative work can also be done freehand. Veining and grooving can be done by using the gage to control the location of the cut.

FLOOR-TYPE ROUTER

As stated earlier, on floor-type routers the bit rotates in a fixed position and the

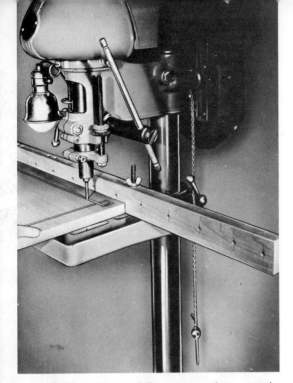

33-39(a). On most drill presses an adapter must be used in place of the chuck when routing. Never attempt to hold a router bit in a drill-press chuck unless you are absolutely sure that the chuck is part of the spindle assembly. Note that the fence is used as a guide.

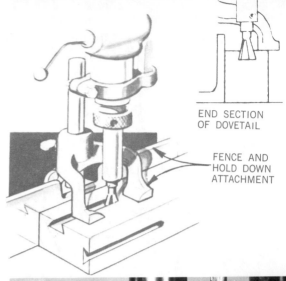

END SECTION OF DOVETAIL

FENCE AND HOLD DOWN ATTACHMENT

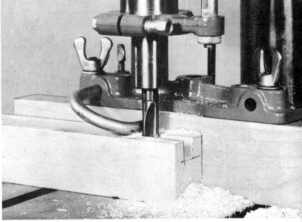

33-39(b). Cutting a dovetail dado. Note the use of the fence and hold-downs.

33-40. Using a guide pin to control the depth of cut.

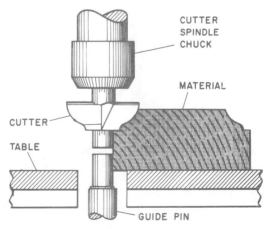

CUTTER SPINDLE CHUCK

MATERIAL

CUTTER

TABLE

GUIDE PIN

work is fed into it. Methods of controlling the cutter and the work are similar to those used with the portable router. Fig. 33-39. However, there are some differences. The main difference is that on these machines the router bit is held in a fixed position and the work moved underneath it.

The five basic methods of floor-type routing can also be used for shaping. They are:

• When the cut doesn't remove stock from the entire edge of the material, a guide pin that extends up from the underside of the table can be used. Straight or circular stock is pressed against this pin to control the depth of cut. Fig. 33-40.

• If the entire edge must be shaped, make a fixture that has the same shape as

409

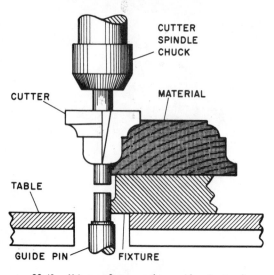

CUTTER SPINDLE CHUCK

CUTTER

MATERIAL

TABLE

GUIDE PIN   FIXTURE

33-41. Using a fixture and a guide pin to shape the entire edge of stock.

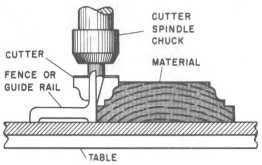

CUTTER SPINDLE CHUCK

CUTTER

FENCE OR GUIDE RAIL

MATERIAL

TABLE

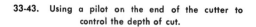

33-42. Using a fence or guide rail to control the depth of cut.

33-43. Using a pilot on the end of the cutter to control the depth of cut.

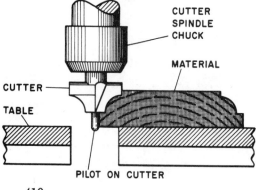

CUTTER SPINDLE CHUCK

MATERIAL

CUTTER

TABLE

PILOT ON CUTTER

410

CUTTER SPINDLE CHUCK

CUTTER   MATERIAL   STOP

GUIDE PIN   FIXTURE   TABLE   BRAD

33-44(a). Using a fixture to do internal routing.

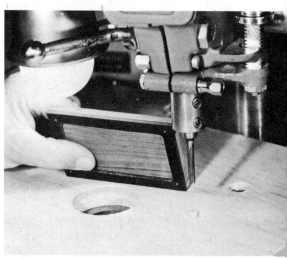

33-44(b). Using a fixture for internal routing. Note the auxiliary wood table. A short dowel pin directly under the router bit acts as a guide pin. Note also that a fixture designed to cut a rectangular recess in the wood is attached to the bottom of the material.

33-44(c). Using a router on a drill press to do internal shaping.

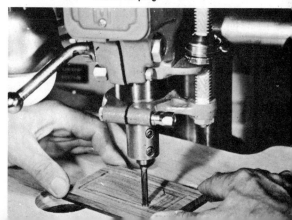

33-45. Using a radial-arm saw for straight routing. Notice that the motor is in a vertical position. Set for the correct location of the cut and lock the rip clamp. Lower the arm to the depth of cut.

33-46. Using a V block as a guide for routing the edge of a round piece of wood. Notice that the block is clamped to the table with a C clamp. The motor can be moved in-or-out and up-or-down to adjust for the correct cut.

the finished part. Put sharp spur points through the fixture to hold the stock in place. Then place the work over the fixture and on the table. The fixture rides against the guide pin so the entire edge of the work can be routed. Fig. 33-41.

• For straight-line, cutting, a fence or guide rail can be used. The stock is held against the fence. The position of the fence in relation to the router bit or cutter determines the amount of material removed. If the total edge is shaped, it is necessary to have a two-part, adjustable fence so half of it can be moved forward to support the work after shaping. The same practice was described with regard to the jointer. Fig. 33-42.

• When only a part of the edge is to be shaped, a router bit with a pilot on the end can be used to control the sidewise movement of the work. However, this is not recommended because the high speeds of floor routers tend to make the pilot burn the edge of the stock as the cut is made. Fig. 33-43.

• For internal routing and flat carving, a pattern is needed. On plywood make a pattern which represents the exact design to be routed. Cut out these areas on a jig saw. Place small pins or spurs

through the pattern to hold the work to be shaped. Use a guide pin in the table. Place the pattern over the guide pin. Then, with the power on, adjust the machine for depth of cut. Press the work firmly against the guide pin to do the routing. Fig. 33-44.

Fixtures for routing should be made of maple, birch, plywood, or hardboard. The edge of the templet must be smooth, since any imperfection will show up on the work itself. Wax the bottom of the fixture so that it slides smoothly over the table.

ROUTING ON THE RADIAL-ARM SAW

The radial-arm saw can be converted into a router by first removing the guard, the arbor nut, the collars, and the saw. Then an adapter to hold the router bits is attached to the right end of the motor or the end opposite that used for sawing. The machine is then used like a floor-type router. In other words, the motor is locked in a fixed position and the work is moved under the revolving cutter. For straight routing, the guide fence can be used. Fig. 33-45. For curved or round

411

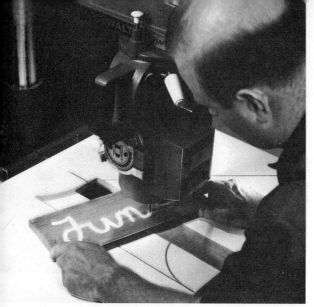

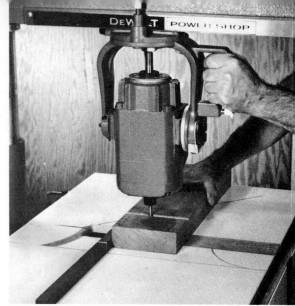

33-47. Carefully follow the layout lines to form the letters. The work will move more easily if placed on a piece of hardboard.

33-48. A dado can be cut by holding the work stationary and then pulling the router bit slowly across to cut the recess.

work, a large wooden guide block is clamped to the table. Fig. 33-46. Freehand routing is done by moving the work under the cutter bit. Fig. 33-47. For cross routing at any angle, the work is held against the guide fence and the bit is moved across the stock as for crosscutting. Fig. 33-48. Several passes may be necessary to get the correct width or depth of cut.

34 Drilling And Boring Machines

Many drilling and boring operations must be performed in cabinetmaking. Sometimes the term "drilling" is used primarily for metalworking and "boring" for woodworking. At other times, "drilling" is used to mean cutting holes that are 1/4" or smaller and "boring" refers to holes that are larger than 1/4".

There are two kinds of drilling and boring operations, namely, *precision boring* and *semi-precision drilling*. Precision boring is necessary in installing dowels. The holes must be in the correct location, accurately spaced, and of the right size and depth. Semi-precision drilling · is done when installing screws and making

openings that require less exacting standards. Drilling and boring are extremely important operations in woodworking since dowels have largely replaced the mortise-and-tenon joint in cabinet and furniture operations.

STATIONARY EQUIPMENT

Three kinds of stationary drilling equipment are commonly used in school and cabinet shops:

Drill Press

Drill presses are of either the bench or floor type. Fig. 34-1. Their size is determined by the distance from the drill

412

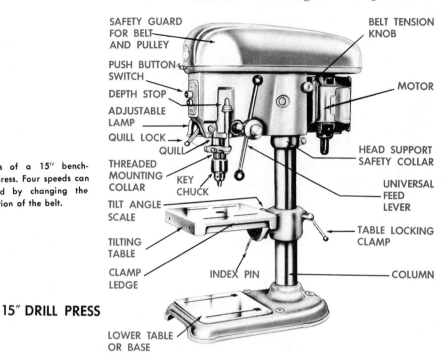

SAFETY GUARD FOR BELT AND PULLEY

PUSH BUTTON SWITCH

DEPTH STOP

ADJUSTABLE LAMP

QUILL LOCK

QUILL

THREADED MOUNTING COLLAR

KEY CHUCK

TILT ANGLE SCALE

TILTING TABLE

CLAMP LEDGE

BELT TENSION KNOB

MOTOR

HEAD SUPPORT SAFETY COLLAR

UNIVERSAL FEED LEVER

TABLE LOCKING CLAMP

INDEX PIN

COLUMN

34-1. Parts of a 15″ bench-type drill press. Four speeds can be obtained by changing the position of the belt.

15″ DRILL PRESS

LOWER TABLE OR BASE

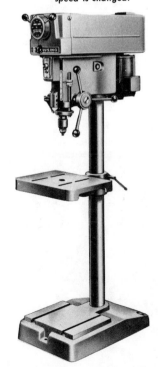

34-2. A floor-type drill press with variable speed pulley. The machine must be operating when the speed is changed.

to the column. For example, a 15″ drill press will bore a hole through the center of a round piece 15″ in diameter. Generally, a key-type chuck is used for holding the cutting tool. The speed is set either by changing a V belt on step pulleys or by the use of a variable-speed pulley arrangement. Fig. 34-2. The variable-speed-pulley drill press is extremely valuable in the wood shop since it provides a wide range of speeds from 500 to 4700 r.p.m. High speeds are necessary for such operations as shaping, routing, and planing. Speeds between 1200 and 3000 r.p.m. are for drilling and boring wood. If the drill press is to be used as a boring machine, it is necessary to attach an auxiliary fence to the table against which the stock can be held.

Universal Drill

The universal drill is a highly versatile tool. Fig. 34-3. It eliminates the necessity of holding work at difficult angles.

413

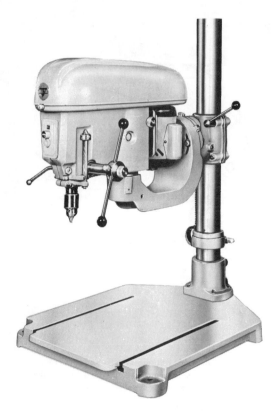

34-3. The head of this drilling machine can be moved in three ways: rotated, tilted, and moved in or out.

34-4. Boring holes at an angle in a stool top. Note that the head is tilted and rotated to the correct location. The stool top is clamped to the table in a horizontal position. All four holes can be bored without moving the work.

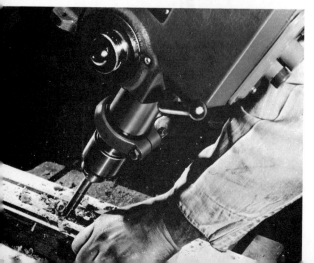

The drill head can be moved and tilted to do many operations. Work can be clamped to the table in a flat position. Because of the double-swivel, the head can be kept at an angle, placing the feed handle within easy reach of one central operating station. It is particularly useful in boring angle holes as for miter joints. Fig. 34-4.

Horizontal Boring Machine

The small horizontal boring machine with one, two, or three spindles is found in many shops. In smaller shops a single-spindle machine is usually used. Larger shops have machines with two or three spindles. Fig. 34-5. Two or three drills or bits are fastened to the drilling heads; distance between the holes is adjusted by moving one or more of the heads. A fence is fastened to the table to hold the stock in place, and an end stop controls the location of holes. The fence can be adjusted to any angle for boring miter-joint holes. A foot pedal usually moves the table or the boring head in and out to do the cutting. The height of the table can also be raised and lowered to take care of different thicknesses of materials and kinds of boring. Boring is particularly useful in producing frames, leg-and-rail construction, and similar joinery. Its advantage is that once the adjustments are made, the holes for stiles and rails or legs and rails can be made with one setting.

PORTABLE EQUIPMENT

Portable electric drills vary in size and horsepower rating. Fig. 34-6. The most common sizes are those that take shanks up to 1/4" or 1/2" diameters. Fig. 34-7. The tool is equipped with a trigger switch. Most have a locking pin that holds the trigger "on" until disengaged. Some large ones have a speed control and can be reversed.

414

34-5. Using a horizontal spindle-boring machine to bore holes in table rails. Three holes, 7/8" center to center, can be bored at the same time with one movement of the machine.

34-7. A heavy-duty 1/2" drill.

34-6. Parts of a 1/4" portable drill.

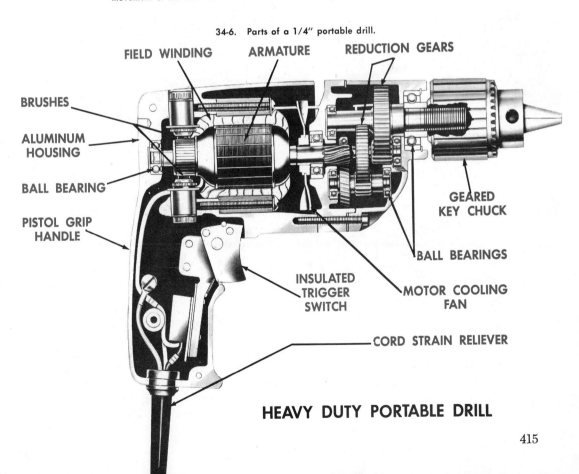

FIELD WINDING   ARMATURE   REDUCTION GEARS

BRUSHES

ALUMINUM
HOUSING

BALL BEARING

PISTOL GRIP
HANDLE

GEARED
KEY CHUCK

BALL BEARINGS

INSULATED
TRIGGER
SWITCH

MOTOR COOLING
FAN

CORD STRAIN RELIEVER

HEAVY DUTY PORTABLE DRILL

34-8. This portable drill has a shockproof housing which eliminates the need of grounding the tool.

34-9. This cordless electric drill has a self-contained battery in the handle. One battery charge from the unit shown at right is enough for drilling up to 300 holes, 1/8" in size.

34-10. Twist drills of several sizes. Note that some have smaller shanks so that holes larger than the portable drill's normal capacity can be drilled.

34-11. Spur machine bit.

DRILLING AND BORING MACHINES

MAINTENANCE

• On machines with step pulleys, check the belt tension. The belt should be just tight enough to prevent it from slipping, no tighter.
• Make sure the correct chuck key is available.
• Check the quill-return spring. It should have light tension.
• Excessive tension prevents sensitive drilling and causes pinion-gear breakage.
• Keep drills and auger bits properly sharpened.
• Keep motor and spindle pulley set screws tight to prevent scoring the motor shaft and spindle.

LUBRICATION

• Cover the outside surface of the quill with powdered graphite.
• Light ball-bearing grease applied to the spindle spline maintains spindle lubrication and eliminates noise.

SAFETY

• Make sure the stock is clamped properly before drilling or boring.
• Never attempt to use a hand auger bit. Use only drills and bits designed for machine use.
• Always position the hole in the center of the table beneath the drill and place a piece of wood beneath the work to keep from drilling holes in the table.
• Use a brush to keep the table free of sawdust.
• Never try to stop the machine by taking hold of the chuck after the power is off.
• On deep cuts, back out often to clean out the hole.

Two types of chucks are available, but most are of the *geared type* that require a special key for opening and closing. The other type, called a *hex key chuck*, requires an Allen wrench to open and close it.

One problem in using a portable drill with a metal housing is the danger of shock, especially when working around damp areas. Many portable drills are now equipped with a heavy-duty, plastic housing to prevent this. Fig. 34-8. Another type of portable drill is battery operated. Fig. 34-9. The battery is built into the drill handle and can be recharged by regular house current. Such a drill will not cause shock anywhere, even in water. It also requires no cord, which is an obvious advantage.

Cutting Tools

Many kinds of cutting tools are used for making holes in wood and also for cutting out circular parts. The two most common are the *twist drill and brad* and the *lip-point bit,* sometimes called the *spur machine bit.* Until recently it was considered undesirable to use the twist drill for accurate dowel boring. However, it has been found by experimentation that the twist drill cutter will do almost as good a job as the spur machine bit. The advantage, of course, is that it is much easier to sharpen the twist drill.

Twist Drills

Carbon-steel twist drills used on wood are available in diameters from 1/32" to 3/4" at intervals of 1/64". High-speed steel drills which may be used on both metal and wood are available in diameters from 1/64" to 1/2" at intervals of 1/64". Fig. 34-10. For general-purpose work, the high-speed steel drill point should have an included angle of 118 degrees. However, if the drills are to be used only for woodworking, an included angle between 60 and 82 degrees is better.

Spur Machine Bits

The spur machine bit has a brad and lip point and is one of the cleanest, fastest-cutting bits for dowel holes. These bits come in standard sizes that are marked in 32nds of an inch. Fig. 34-11.

34-12. Multi-spur bit. This bit will bore plywood without tearing. It will also bore at an angle. It comes in diameters from 1/2" to 3/4", increasing by sixteenths.

DOUBLE SPUR BIT *(FLUTED)*

DOUBLE SPUR BIT *(SOLID CENTER)*

34-13. Power auger bits have straight shanks and brad points.

Multi-Spur Bit

The multi-spur bit is excellent for power cutting of larger holes. Fig. 34-12.

Auger Bit

An auger bit for a power drill should have a straight shank and a brad point. Fig. 34-13. Never try to use a bit with a tang in the power drill. The common auger bits are either made with a solid center or as double spur bits. Common sizes are from No. 4 (1/4") to No. 16 (1").

Speed Bit

These bits, also called flat-power or spade bits, are made in several types and

417

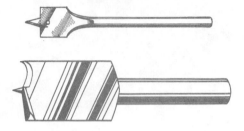

34-14. Speed bits.

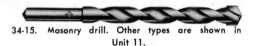

34-15. Masonry drill. Other types are shown in Unit 11.

shapes. Fig. 34-14. Typical sizes are from 1/4″ to 1″, increasing by 1/16″, with 1/4″ shanks. Some are made with changeable cutter heads.

Masonry Bit

The cabinetmaker frequently must install cabinets in a masonry wall and therefore needs a number of masonry drills. Fig. 34-15. These carbide-tipped drills must be used at slow speeds and heavy pressure. Sizes vary. For 1/4″ chucks, the bits range from 1/8″ to 1/2″; for 1/2″ chucks the range is from 1/2″ to 1″.

Rotary Hole Saw

Rotary hole cutters vary as to type, diameter, and depth of cut. They are used to make holes of large diameters in wood, metal, and plastic. Fig. 34-16.

Plug Cutter

In fine cabinet work screw heads are covered with plugs made of the same wood as the cabinet. Two types of plug cutters are shown in Fig. 34-17.

Circle Cutter

Circle cutters are made in a wide variety of styles and sizes to cut holes from 5/8″ to 8″ in diameter. These single-point tools are fastened to the end of a cross bar with a small drill in the center. It is extremely important to clamp the wood securely to the table before any cutting is done. Fig. 34-18.

Foerstner Bit

The Foerstner bit is used for intricate wood cutting. The bit is guided by the edge of the tool, not by the center. This permits boring an arc of a circle in any direction, regardless of grain, to cut oval and curved openings, squared corners, or rounded holes with flat bottoms. It is available in sizes from 1/2″ to 2″. Fig. 34-19.

USING THE DRILL PRESS

General Procedures

1. Select the correct kind of bit or drill and fasten it securely in the chuck.

34-16. Various sizes of hole saws. They are made in diameters from 5/8″ to 3½″. The saws fit on mandrels and have 1/4″ or larger drills at their centers.

418

34-17(a). Plug cutters are available in sizes from 3/8" to 1", increasing by sixteenths. This short, closed type is used only for cutting plugs.

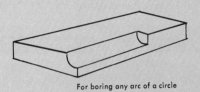

For boring any arc of a circle

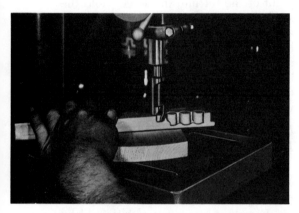

34-17(b). Plug cutters make it easy to cut short plugs or dowel pins. The open plug cutter shown here will make dowels up to 2" long.

For boring at any angle regardless of grain or knots

34-18. Circle cutter. This size cuts circles from 13/16" to 5" in diameter. Larger ones are available. A set screw holds the adjustable high-speed steel bit in the arm. The center pilot hole guide is 1/4".

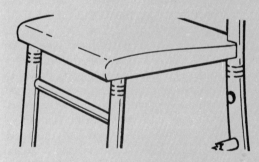

Hole for chair rungs.

Hole for door check

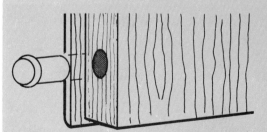

34-19(a). A Foerstner bit.

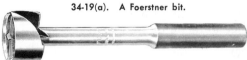

34-19(b). Some common uses for the Foerstner bit.

34-20(a). Countersink bit.

2. Make sure the proper layout has been made and that the position of the hole is well marked.

3. Check to see if the drill or bit is free to go through the table opening in the drill-press table. Also, place an auxiliary piece of scrap wood under the material. This will help prevent splintering when the drill goes through the underside of the work.

4. Adjust the drill press for the correct speed of cutting. The speed should vary with the type of bit, the size, the kind of wood, and the depth of the hole. In general, the smaller the cutting tool and the softer the wood, the higher the speed. Cutting tools up to 3/4" in diameter should operate at speeds from 3000 down to 1800 r.p.m. Bits above this diameter should maintain slower speeds down to 600 r.p.m. Select the approximate speed and then use good judgment when feeding the tool into the material. If the tool smokes, reduce the speed and the feed.

5. Clamp the work securely when necessary, especially when using larger drilling and boring tools, hole cutters, and similar cutting devices. Clamping is

34-20(b). Drilling and countersinking holes for installing screws. The drill is installed in the countersink so that both operations can be done at the same time.

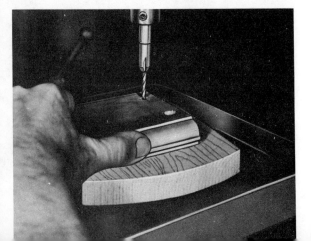

a must if the tool has only one cutting edge, such as a hole cutter.

Drilling Small Holes in Flat Stock

To drill or bore a hole that is 1/4" or smaller in size, use a twist drill. Locate the center of the hole and mark it with a center punch or scratch awl. Place it on the table over a piece of scrap wood. Turn on the power and slowly move the point of the bit into the stock. Hold the stock firmly and apply even pressure to the handle. Fig. 34-20. If the stock is hardwood or the hole is deep, rack up the bit once or twice to remove the chips before finishing the hole. Always bore through the hole and into the scrap wood.

Drilling or Boring Medium-Sized Holes in Flat Stock

Holes from 1/4" to $1\frac{1}{4}$" can be cut with a variety of drilling and boring tools. For example, a twist drill, auger bit, Foerstner bit, or speed bit could be used. Fig. 34-21. In boring a through hole, there are two methods. The simplest is to place a piece of scrap wood under the hole so that the tool will cut through the stock and into the scrap piece. This is necessary to keep the underside from splintering. Fig. 34-22. The second method is to cut until the point of the bit shows through the stock, then drill from the other side. To bore a hole to a specific depth, adjust the depth stop without the power on. Bring the cutting tool down to the side of the work where the depth is marked. Then set the depth stop. Fig. 34-23.

Drilling Large Holes in Flat Stock

Holes larger than $1\frac{1}{4}$" are best cut with a hole saw or a circle cutter. Make sure that the work is firmly clamped, especially when using a hole cutter, since any tool with a single point has a tendency to rotate the work.

420

34-21. Drilling a hole in plywood using a twist drill with a smaller shank.

Boring Deep Holes

On most drill presses the spindle will move only four or five inches; other methods must be found for deeper holes. If the hole is less than twice the quill stroke (the maximum distance the drill will move), one of the following methods can be used:

Clamp a piece of scrap stock to the table. Install a bit of the correct size and bore a small hole. Lower the table to accommodate the stock. To align a hole in the scrap stock with the chuck, it may be necessary to remove the bit and replace it with a long piece of dowel rod. Replace the auger bit and bore the hole to maximum depth. Then cut a short

34-22. Using a Foerstner bit to bore a hole at the edge of stock. Note that a piece of scrap stock is clamped to the work and that another piece of scrap stock is under the work so that the hole can be bored completely through.

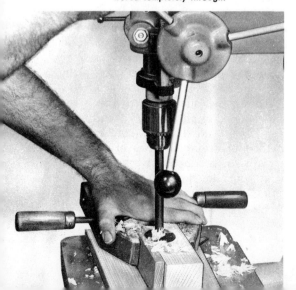

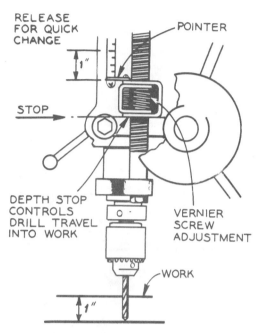

34-23. Use the depth stop to control the depth of a hole. This one is set to drill a hole 1″ into the work.

piece of dowel rod and place it in the hole in the scrap stock. Turn the material to be bored over the dowel rod and then bore from the other side. Fig. 34-24.
• The second method is to turn the table to a vertical position. Fasten an auxiliary fence to the table. The location for the hole must be aligned with the bit. Bore from both ends. If a hole longer than 8″ is to be bored, an extension auger bit can be made by brazing a rod to the shank of the bit; or a commercial bit extension can be used.

Boring Equally Spaced Holes Along a Surface or Edge

To the table clamp a temporary wood fence in which a series of equally spaced holes has been drilled. Adjust the fence with the work held against a dowel rod fastened in one of the holes, the "matching" hole will be correctly drilled. Move

421

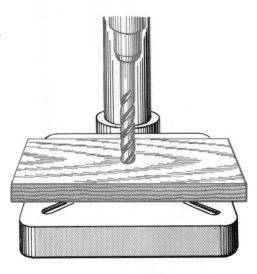

a - BORE HOLE IN SCRAP BLOCK

34-24. Boring a deep hole: (a) Boring a hole in the scrap stock. (b) Aligning the hole. (c) Boring from the second end.

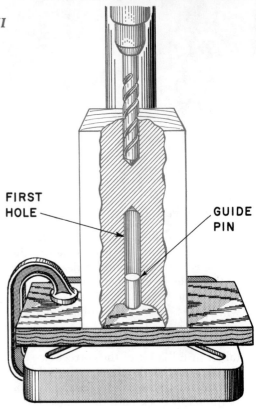

FIRST HOLE

GUIDE PIN

c - BORE SECOND HOLE

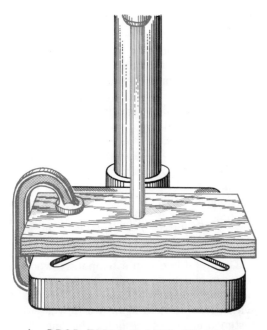

b - DROP TABLE & LINE UP HOLE

the dowel rod to each of the other holes to complete the drilling. Fig. 34-25.

Another method of doing this is to have a stop block clamped to the auxiliary fence. Cut several identical wood pieces equal in length to the distance between the holes. Place these wood pieces against the stop block and then place the end of the work against these blocks. After the first hole has been bored, remove one block, push the work along, and bore the next hole.

Still another method is to use a stop pin clamped to an auxiliary wood fence. Fig. 34-26. And still one more excellent method of boring a series of holes, especially for production work, is to make a large drilling jig into which the material will fit. The guide piece of the jig is made of hardboard. Fig. 34-27.

34-25. Boring equally spaced holes using a fence as a jig.

34-27. Using a drilling jig. Note that the jig and stock are moved from one position to the next to do the drilling.

34-26. Another method of boring holes in series. The stop pin works through a block and is set in the previously drilled hole to locate the next hole. The distance between the first two holes must be accurately marked.

34-28. Using a Foerstner bit to bore a hole in the side of a tapered leg.

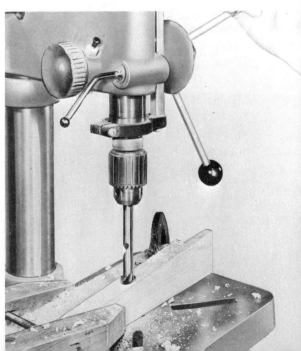

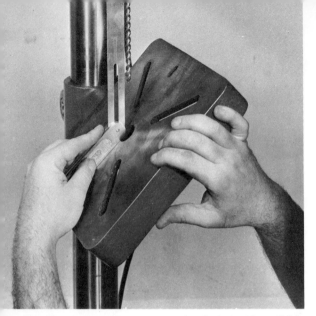

34-29. Tilt settings can be checked with a sliding T bevel.

34-30. Starting an angle hole with a scrap block.

34-31. The table is tilted to bore holes at an angle. Note that the work is clamped securely to the table with a C clamp.

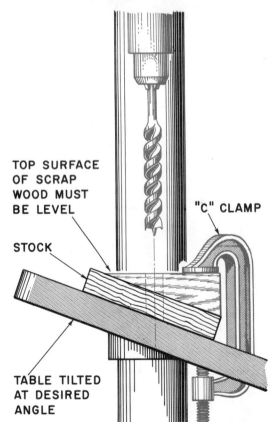

TOP SURFACE OF SCRAP WOOD MUST BE LEVEL

"C" CLAMP

STOCK

TABLE TILTED AT DESIRED ANGLE

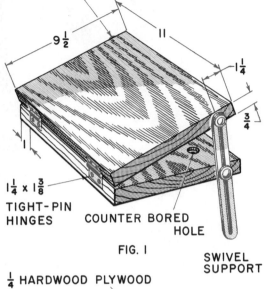

NO. 8 x 1¼ RD. HD. WOOD SCREWS
WITH 3/16 STEEL WASHERS

9½

11

1¼

¾

1

1¼ x 1⅜

TIGHT-PIN
HINGES

COUNTER BORED
HOLE

FIG. I

SWIVEL
SUPPORT

¼ HARDWOOD PLYWOOD

8½

3/16 DIA.

½

3/16 SLOT

⅜

⅜ R

SWIVEL SUPPORT (2 REQ'D.)

FIG. 2

COUNTER BORE FOR ¼" CARRIAGE BOLT

JIG BASE-BOARD

FLAT WASHER
& WING NUT

DRILL PRESS
TABLE

FIG. 3

34-32. Drill-press tilting table.

Boring Holes at an Angle

There are many methods of boring a hole at an angle. The choice depends on the kind of cutting tool and the degree of the angle. In Fig. 34-28, a Foerstner bit is used to cut a hole at a very slight angle. This cutter will start easily, even at an angle. If an auger bit is used, then another method is better. Tilt the table to the correct angle and check with a sliding T bevel or with the protractor head of a combination set. Fig. 34-29. Clamp the work to the table with a wedge-shaped block over it so that the tool can start in a flat surface. Fig. 34-30. If a larger size twist drill is used, the drilling may be done without a guide block. Fig. 34-31.

An excellent device for boring at an angle is an auxiliary wood table, fastened to the table of the drill press. Fig. 34-32. The material to be drilled is then held or clamped to the auxiliary table, which is adjusted to the correct angle. Fig. 34-33.

Boring Holes in Round Work

For small round stock such as dowel, place a V block on the table. Make sure

34-33(a). Drilling a hole on the tilting table at a
low angle.

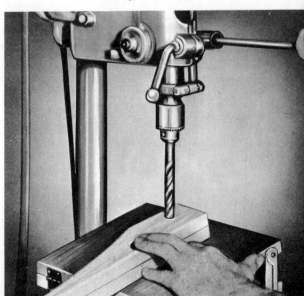

34-33(b). Drilling a hole at a greater angle. Note that the work is clamped to the tilting table with a hand screw to keep it from sliding.

34-34. Drilling holes in dowel rod.

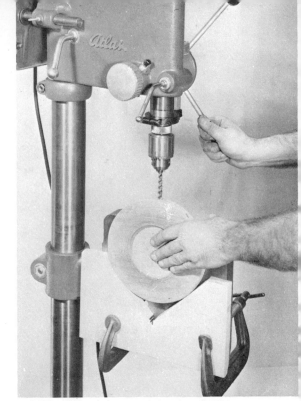

34-35. Boring holes around the edge of a disk.

the center of the V is directly under the center of the drill. Fig. 34-34. To bore holes in the edge of a circular piece, turn the table to a vertical position and clamp a large V block to it. Again, make sure the center of the V is centered under the drill. Fig. 34-35. To drill holes around a circle from one surface, locate and drill two of the holes, leaving the drill in the second hole. Drive a nail through the center of the work to act as a pivot. Place a pin in the first drilled hole. The other holes are then located by using the spacing pin. Fig. 34-36.

Enlarging Smaller Holes and Counterboring

A good method of enlarging a small

34-36. Drilling a series of equally spaced holes around a circle.

PIN

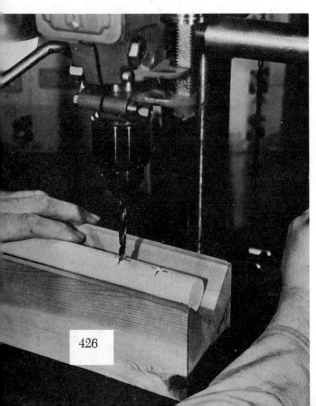

426

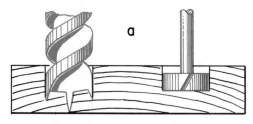

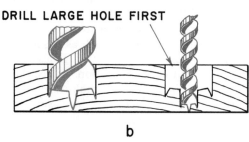

DRILL LARGE HOLE FIRST

34-37. Counterboring: (a) Use a large auger bit or Foerstner bit. (b) Always bore the large hole first and then the small one.

34-38(a). Using a guide board for cutting pocket holes.

hole is with a Foerstner bit. This can be done since the outer cutting edge guides the bit. A second method is to use a large auger bit which has a piece of dowel rod fastened to its point. The rod should be equal in diameter to the hole already bored.

Counterboring is a process of enlarging only part of the outer end of an existing hole. This is often done so that the head of a screw or bolt may be sunk below the surface of the wood and then covered. The best method of doing this is to bore the larger hole first, then the smaller one. Fig. 34-37.

Pocket Holes

The pocket hole is a simple method of attaching rails to tops, or legs to shelves. Use a guide board that is beveled to about 15 degrees, and bore with a machine spur bit. This is actually a counterboring operation, since a larger hole is needed for the head of the screw and a smaller one for its body. Fig. 34-38. Always drill the larger hole first. The same setup can be used for a corner pocket hole except that the work must be supported on edge at the corner.

34-38(b). Examples of pocket holes used in furniture construction.

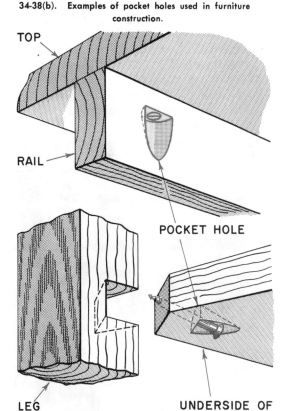

TOP

RAIL

POCKET HOLE

LEG

UNDERSIDE OF LOWER SHELF

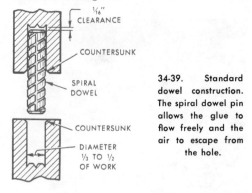

34-39. Standard dowel construction. The spiral dowel pin allows the glue to flow freely and the air to escape from the hole.

Dowel Joints

In the school or cabinet shop that is not equipped with a boring machine, dowel holes are usually cut on the drill press. This is precision boring since the holes must be of correct diameter, depth, and location in order to match holes on the corresponding part of the joint. Methods of marking the dowel-hole location are described in Unit 39. Remember that the dowels should be from one-third to one-half the thickness of the stock, and that the holes must be drilled with at

least 1/16″ clearance at either end. Fig. 34-39.

Edge Butt

Lay out the location of the dowel holes on one stock piece. Mark all pieces with an "X" on the back surface (opposite the face surface). Fasten a fence to the table, using a wood jig such as is shown in Fig. 34-25. In this way all holes can be bored in the same location. Adjust the fence and jig so that the holes are centered. Always place the face surface against the fence so that, if there is any slight variation in thickness, that surface will be even. By using a jig, only one piece needs to be marked. The others will be bored accurately.

Corner Butt

Bore the holes in the edge grain as you would for a butt joint. Then turn the table to vertical position and bore in the end grain. Fig. 34-40. When corner joints are to be rabbeted or grooved, always bore the dowel holes first.

Miter Joint

There are two common methods of boring dowel holes for a miter joint. The first is to tilt the table (or the auxiliary wood table) to an angle of 45 degrees to do the boring. Fig. 34-41. The other method is to turn the table to a vertical position and use an auxiliary wood fence fastened to the table at 45 degrees. Fig. 34-42. A good method of spacing the two holes is shown in Fig. 34-43. A stop block is clamped to the auxiliary fence for the first hole, then a wooden spacer block is used for the second hole. With this method any number of pieces can be bored without an additional setup. Sometimes dowel holes must be installed in the end grain of a piece that is cut at an angle. To do this, adjust the table to this angle so the hole is at right angles to the end grain. Fig. 34-44.

34-40. Drilling holes in the end of a rail for a dowel joint.

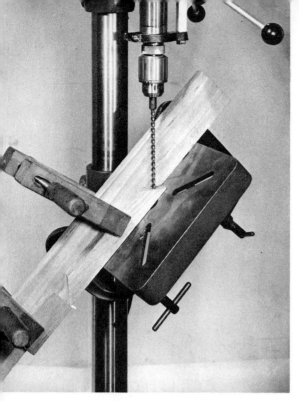

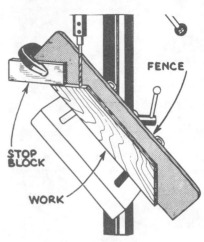

34-41. Drilling dowel holes with the table tilted to the 45-degree position.

34-42. Drilling dowel holes with the table turned to a vertical position.

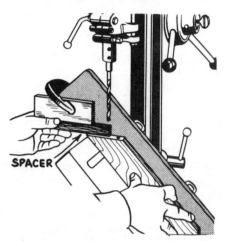

34-43(b). A wood spacer between the stop block and the work locates the position for the second hole.

34-44. Boring a hole in end grain with the table tilted at a slight angle from the vertical position.

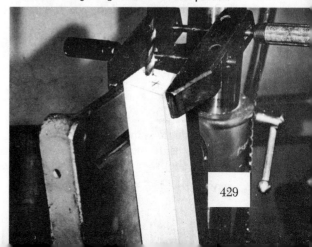

429

34-45. Using a portable drill to install a piece of hardware in a kitchen cabinet.

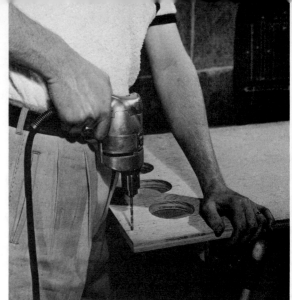

34-46. Drilling clearance holes for wood screws.

USING PORTABLE ELECTRIC DRILLS

The portable electric drill is relatively simple to use. It is commonly employed to drill holes for installing all kinds of metal fasteners and hardware to wood products. Fig. 34-45. Follow these suggestions:

1. Open the chuck far enough to allow the shank to slip in easily. Tighten it securely so that all three jaws hold the bit or drill.

2. Make sure that thin work is backed up with a solid piece of wood.

3. Grasp the control handle firmly and point the drill as you would a pistol. Fig. 34-46. Use your left hand to control the feed as necessary. Turn on the switch and guide the tool into the work. For drilling pilot holes for screws, it may be necessary to use a small block of wood as a depth gage to control the depth of drilling.

USING A SINGLE-SPINDLE BORING MACHINE

The single-spindle horizontal boring machine is found in many school and cabinet shops. Fig. 34-47. It can be used

34-47. A single-spindle boring machine.

430

for boring holes for all types of dowel joints. The machine consists of a heavy base to which is mounted a table and motor unit. The table is raised or lowered by turning a handle just below it and can be locked in position. The hold-down is a hand lever that is adjusted so it will secure the stock. The bit is moved in by depressing the foot lever. To use the boring machine:

1. Mark the location of the dowel across the edge and back surface of the stock. If stop blocks are used to control the pieces, then only one piece needs to be marked.

2. Select the correct-size bit and install it in the machine.

3. Adjust for the correct depth of bore by depressing the foot lever and adjusting the movement-control rod at the back of the stand.

4. Check the bit for elevation by moving the table up or down.

5. Complete the setup for boring. A wood fence can be attached to the table for boring at any angle. For example, if a miter joint with dowels is being made, fasten the guide fence at 45 degrees. Stop blocks can be attached to the fence to locate the holes. Usually at least two holes must be bored in each piece to match corresponding holes in the second piece. Use the lines on the back of the marked pieces for making the setup. Once the setup is made, bore all identical pieces before making any change.

6. Adjust the hold-down so that it will clamp the piece securely to the table. If there is danger of marring the surface, a piece of scrap stock can be placed under the hold-down. However, when boring with the face surface against the table, the clamp can be placed directly on the stock. It is good practice to do all boring with the face surface down. Then, if there is any slight variation in the thickness of the stock, the front surfaces will always be level. Mark all stock with

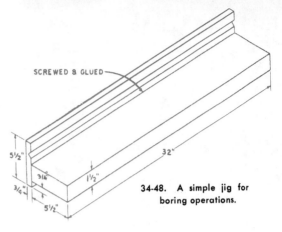

SCREWED & GLUED

5½"

¾"

¾"

1½"

32"

5½"

34-48. A simple jig for boring operations.

an "X" on the back surface so that the pieces will be fed into the machine in the correct way. This mark can also be used for assembly.

7. Check the setup by trying it on a piece of scrap stock. Turn on the power. Then feed the bit slowly into the wood. If the hole is unusually deep, release the bit to clear the hole after part of it is bored. Some boring machines can be converted for mortising by adding a holder for a mortising bit and by changing the fence arrangement.

DRILLING AND BORING ON A RADIAL-ARM SAW

For drilling and boring operations on a radial-arm saw, a simple jig is needed to raise the stock above the table top and to provide a higher guide fence. Fig. 34-48. Place a wedge between the jig and the column for support when boring. A flat board about 6" high can also be employed as a boring jig. To assemble the boring bit and adapter unit, remove the safety guard, the arbor nut, the cutting tool, and the arbor collars from the motor arbor. Place the boring bit in the adapter and tighten it in place with the 1/4" screw located on the motor opposite the arbor end. Insert the Allen wrench into the front of the arbor, holding it securely while using the flat wrench to turn the righthand-threaded adapter on the back of the motor shaft.

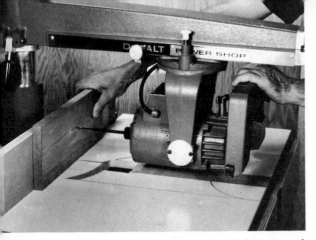

34-49. Face boring. Always use a backing piece of scrap wood to prevent splintering as the bit goes through the wood.

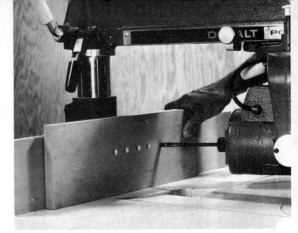

34-51. Boring at an angle after adjusting the arm. The calibrated miter scale on the column will show the exact angle.

For all face-boring operations, be sure to mount the safety guard on the motor to cover the front end of the arbor. First mark the location of the holes on the stock. Then adjust the motor so that the boring tool is in the correct location, with the motor in the out-rip position. The bit will face the column of the machine. Adjust the arm so that the bit touches the stock at the correct location. A stop clamp can also be fastened to control the depth of the boring. If the hole is to be bored all the way through the stock, a piece of scrap wood should be clamped behind it. Fig. 34-49.

Here is a good method for boring a series of equally spaced holes. Bore the first hole in its correct location, entirely through the material and into the back-up piece. Slip a dowel rod into this hole so it enters the back-up. Move both the stock and the back-up the correct distance and bore the second hole. After this point you no longer need to measure the spacing. Remove the dowel rod; move only the stock. When the second hole in the stock is over the first hole in the back-up, insert the dowel rod again, and drill. Continue in this fashion until all the holes are drilled.

Edge boring is done with the material flat on the jig and against the fence. Fig. 34-50.

Angular boring can be done two ways. One method is to position the stock and then move the radial arm right or left so the bit will enter the stock at the correct angle. Fig. 34-51. Another method is to use a V block so that the material tilts toward the column. Fig. 34-52. End boring and miter boring can also be done on a radial arm saw.

432   34-50. Edge boring. Use slow, even pressure.

34-52. Boring at an angle with the work tilted.

A mortiser cuts the rectangular opening for a mortise-and-tenon joint. An upright or vertical hollow-chisel mortiser is used in most shops. Popularly known as, "the machine that bores square holes," it has a square, hollow chisel that clamps to the motor housing. There is a revolving wood bit in the center of the chisel. When the combination of bit and chisel is forced into the wood, the bit bores a hole almost as large as the chisel. The sharp edge of the chisel itself cuts a square opening.

MORTISER

MAINTENANCE

- Check to see that the chisels and bits are properly ground.
- Check the gib adjustments on the head and table to make sure there is no excessive wear.
- Replace the auxiliary wood fence and table as necessary.
- Make sure all screw threads operate freely.

LUBRICATION

- Use S.A.E. No. 20 oil on all adjusting screws.
- Use light grease or No. 20 oil on ways or slides.

SAFETY

- Check the bit clearance at the end of the chisel before starting the machine.
- Make sure the stock is clamped securely whenever possible.
- Make all adjustments with the power off.
- Never apply too much foot pressure when cutting hardwoods.
- Keep your hands away from the revolving bit.
- Clean off the chips with a brush.
- On deep cuts, back out often to clean out the hole.

Because the mortise chisel is of a fixed size, the mortise is always cut first and then the tenon is cut to fit it. In cabinet shops, the tenon is cut on a circular saw, shaper, router or, when available, on the single-end tenoner. Fig. 35-1(a). While the mortise-and-tenon joint is needed for leg-and-rail construction, such as for chairs and tables, it has been replaced in some factories by dowel construction strengthened with corner blocks. The mortise-and-tenon joint is used extensively in framework, especially in sash-and-door manufacturing. However, much framework makes use of the open mortise-and-tenon joint, both parts of which can be cut on a double-end tenoner.

Some sash-and-door manufacturers use a chain-saw mortiser. This has a continuous saw that cuts a square opening with a rounded bottom. Fig. 35-1(b).

PARTS

The mortiser consists of a heavy, cast-iron column, a horizontal table, and a

35-1(a). In some cabinet shops a single-end tenoner (shown here) is used to cut tenons.

35-1(b). The chain-saw mortiser is a faster machine than the hollow-chisel mortiser, and is used to make wide mortises, usually of 1" minimum width.

chisel ram attached to a motor. Fig. 35-2. The table itself can be moved vertically (up and down), transversely (in and out), and longitudinally (back and forth). On some mortisers, the table does not move back and forth; therefore you must move the work. On others the table can be tilted 45 degrees to the right or left. The head is moved up and down on the column by depressing a foot lever. At the lower end is a chuck for holding the bit and the chisel.

Mortising Chisels and Bits

The heart of the hollow-chisel mortiser consists of the hollow chisels and boring bits. Such chisels are available in standard sizes from 1/4" to 1¼", at intervals of 1/16". Common sizes are 1/4", 1/2", and 3/4". The chisel has openings on two sides so that the chips can escape freely. The shank end of the chisel fits into the frame of the motor; the chisel itself does not move. The cutting end of the chisel has a bevel on the inside to make a sheer cut into the wood. Boring bits are made to match the chisels. These are similar to auger bits but without a feed screw. Fig. 35-3. The end of the bit is flared so that its largest diameter is almost equal to the outside of the chisel itself. It is designed in this way so that the bit will remove as much of the material as possible. All the chisel has to do is square up the hole. Fig. 35-4. Because of this flared end, it is extremely important that the cone tip of the bit does not rub against the chisel. If it does. both the end of the chisel and the bit will overheat and lose hardness. There must be from 1/32" to 1" clearance between the end of the bit and the chisel (depending on the size of the chisel and bit).

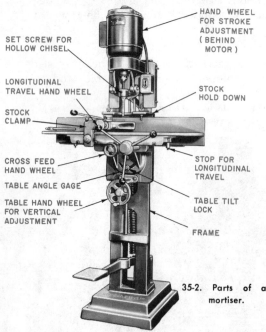

SET SCREW FOR
HOLLOW CHISEL

HAND WHEEL
FOR STROKE
ADJUSTMENT
(BEHIND
MOTOR)

LONGITUDINAL
TRAVEL HAND WHEEL

STOCK
HOLD DOWN

STOCK
CLAMP

CROSS FEED
HAND WHEEL

STOP FOR
LONGITUDINAL
TRAVEL

TABLE ANGLE GAGE

TABLE HAND WHEEL
FOR VERTICAL
ADJUSTMENT

TABLE TILT
LOCK

FRAME

35-2. Parts of a mortiser.

434

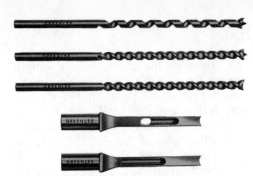

35-3. Mortising chisels and bits.

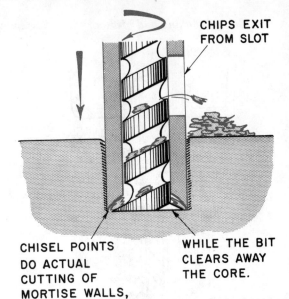

CHIPS EXIT FROM SLOT

CHISEL POINTS DO ACTUAL CUTTING OF MORTISE WALLS,

WHILE THE BIT CLEARS AWAY THE CORE.

35-4. The cutting action of a mortiser.

USING THE MORTISER

Any product which features the mortise-and-tenon joint requires several identical mortises. For example, a simple table with four legs and rails requires eight mortises, two in each leg. When all pieces are identical, it is necessary to lay out the mortises on one leg only.

1. Square up the stock to size and lay out the location for one mortise on each of two sides of one leg. Also mark the depth of the mortise on the end of the leg. Then mark all other legs as shown in Fig. 35-5 (LF means left front and RF means right front). The mortises on the other parts will be in the correct location if all pieces are placed on the table in the same way. When cutting mortises on two sides of a piece, always cut all mortises on one side first. Then reset the machine and cut all the mortises on the second side.

2. Select the correct-size chisel and bit. For example, use a 1/2" bit and chisel for a 1/2" mortise. Also, select the correct-size bushing for the chisel. These split bushings all have the same diameter on the outside, with varying inside dimensions to hold chisels of different sizes.

3. Insert the bushing for the chisel and then install the chisel itself. Place the chisel in the socket, with a slight clearance between its shoulder and the face of the socket. This clearance should be 1/32" for chisels up to 3/4", and 1/16" for larger ones.

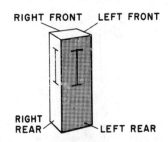

RIGHT FRONT   LEFT FRONT

RIGHT REAR   LEFT REAR

35-5. Right front indicates that the top of the leg is against the right stop when cutting the right-rear mortise. Place the leg against the left stop when cutting the left-rear mortise.

35-6. Use a try square to check the chisel with the fence. Usually the chisel openings are on the right and left so the chips will come out the sides. However, when using the mortising attachment on the drill press, the openings are placed at front and back because of the table fence.

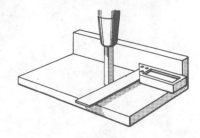

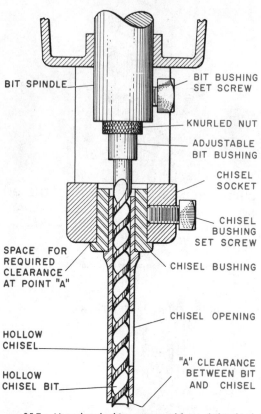

BIT SPINDLE

BIT BUSHING SET SCREW

KNURLED NUT

ADJUSTABLE BIT BUSHING

CHISEL SOCKET

CHISEL BUSHING SET SCREW

SPACE FOR REQUIRED CLEARANCE AT POINT "A"

CHISEL BUSHING

CHISEL OPENING

HOLLOW CHISEL

HOLLOW CHISEL BIT

"A" CLEARANCE BETWEEN BIT AND CHISEL

35-7. Note that the bit must extend beyond the chisel a little to keep it from rubbing the chisel.

35-8. Cutting the mortise.

4. To align the chisel, hold a square against the side of it and also against the fence. Fig. 35-6. Then tighten the set screws that hold the chisel in place. Next, insert the bit until the lips are flush with the cutting edge of the chisel. Fasten the bit securely. Loosen the socket and push the chisel up so that the shoulder rests against the face of the chisel socket. This will give proper clearance for the bit to run free. Fig. 35-7. Another method is to install the chisel so that it is firmly fixed against the shoulder and square with the fence. Then carefully install the bit so there is the correct clearance.

Cutting a Mortise

1. Place the stock on the table with a mark on the end indicating the depth of the mortise. Depress the foot pedal as far as you can. Turn the screw adjustment on the table until the chisel, at the end of its stroke, is in line with the bottom of the mortise. Release the foot pedal.

2. Place the end of the stock under the chisel and move the table in or out until the chisel is directly over the layout. Move the work until the mortising chisel is over the extreme right end of the mortise. Place a stop against the end of the stock so that other identical pieces will be located automatically. Also adjust the stop on the table. Now move the table until the chisel is at the left end of the mortise; adjust the stop. There are two hold-down clamps that can be used to keep the work in place.

3. Move the table back to the starting position, with the chisel at the left end of the mortise. Turn on the machine, depress the pedal, and cut to full depth. Fig. 35-8. Move the table to the right and again cut to full depth. Then move along the layout, skipping a space slightly less

than the size of the chisel after each cut. These alternate strokes are used to equalize pressure by bringing the bit into contact with the stock on four sides when making first passes, and on two sides during final passes. If cutting is done continuously, the bit tends to bend since cutting is done only on three sides. Be sure to center the chisel over the waste stock on the final passes. Fig. 35-9. If a turned leg or a cabriole leg must have mortises, it is necessary to make a holding jig to keep the leg in proper position.

4. Cut all identical mortises before resetting for cuts in different locations. The cutting of matched mortises, as on table legs, requires that the entire setup be reversed before the second mortise of the pair is cut. The righthand stop block should be placed on the left, and vice versa. Check each setup carefully with a sample piece.

MORTISING ATTACHMENT

Attachments are available to convert most drill presses into mortising machines. These devices consist of a fence to guide the work, a hold-down—hold-in that keeps the work against the fence and table, a chisel holder that is clamped to the quill of the drill press, and a bit that is fastened to the chuck. Fig. 35-10.

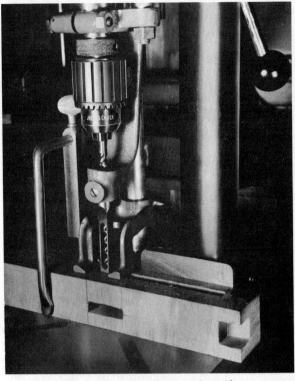

35-10(a). The drill press converts into a mortiser with this attachment. The hold-down—hold-in is adjusted so that the work will just slide along easily.

35-10(b). Setup for the mortising attachment.

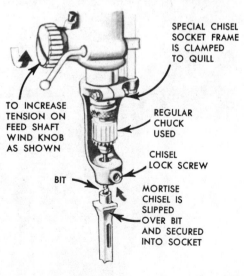

SPECIAL CHISEL SOCKET FRAME IS CLAMPED TO QUILL

TO INCREASE TENSION ON FEED SHAFT WIND KNOB AS SHOWN

REGULAR CHUCK USED

CHISEL LOCK SCREW

BIT

MORTISE CHISEL IS SLIPPED OVER BIT AND SECURED INTO SOCKET

35-9. This is the correct method of making rectangular mortises up to 1/2" in width. Note that cuts are not consecutive. Sometimes, however, consecutive cuts must be made when using a mortising attachment. This is simply because it is often difficult to force the chisel into hardwood when all sides are cutting.

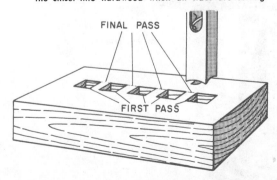

FINAL PASS

FIRST PASS

437

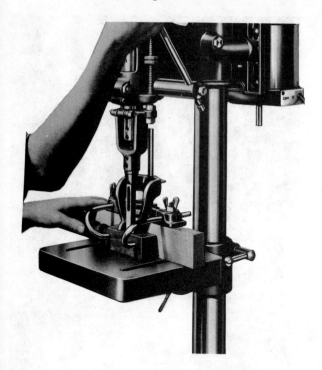

35-11. An adapter can also be used to hold the mortising bit.

In some cases an adapter is used instead of the regular chuck to hold the bit. Fig. 35-11.

To use the mortising attachment, fasten the fence to the table so that it clears the chisel and is in about the final position. This can then be moved in and out to locate the mortise. Now adjust the fence back and forth until it is exactly over the mortise layout. Also fasten the hold-downs to keep the wood firmly on the table. Adjust the drill press to a speed of about 1000 r.p.m. Cut the mortise the same way you would on a mortising machine, as follows:

1. Remove the chuck and the feed-stop bracket from the quill.

2. Replace the feed-stop bracket with the mortise-chisel socket and clamp it in place. Use a depth-stop stud in the chisel

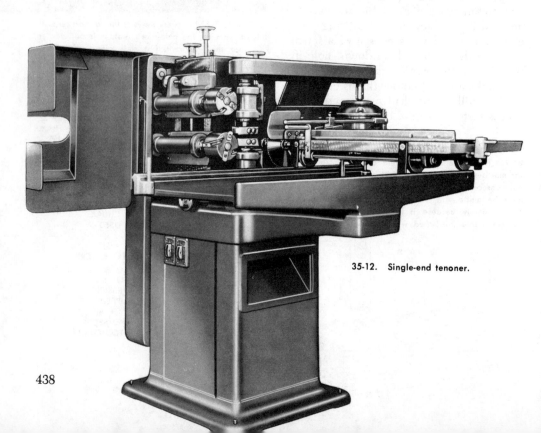

35-12. Single-end tenoner.

socket to keep the quill from turning and to regulate the depth of cut.

3. Replace the drill chuck or install an adapter.

4. Fasten the fence to the table so that it clears the chisel and is in about the final position. It can still be moved in and out to locate the mortise.

5. Install the correct chisel and bit in the socket.

6. Revolve the chuck by hand to see that the bit does not scrape.

7. Adjust the drill press to a speed of about 1000 r.p.m.

8. Cut the mortise. Stop blocks can be clamped to the table top to regulate the length of movement.

SINGLE-END TENONER

Some cabinet and school shops are equipped with a single-end tenoner for cutting tenons and for making other end-shaping cuts. Fig. 35-12. Since this is really a production machine, it should be used only when a reasonably large num-

TENONER

MAINTENANCE

• Check all cutting tools and saws to see that they are properly ground.
• Make sure all adjustments operate freely.
• Check the operation of the table or carriage. See that the movement is free.

LUBRICATION

• Use S.A.E. No. 20 oil on all adjusting screws.
• Use light grease on roller ways.

SAFETY

• Make sure the saw and all cutter heads are mounted properly.
• Check before turning on the power to see that there are no loose knives or blades.
• Keep the guard closed when the machine is operating.
• Clamp stock securely to the table before starting the pass.
• Keep your fingers away from the revolving cutters and saw.

ber of duplicate pieces are needed. Fig. 35-13. It is not, however, the high production machine that a double-end tenoner is. If only a few tenons must be cut, it is much faster to use a circular or radial-arm saw. Like all production equipment, the single-end tenoner requires setup time to install and adjust the knives and saws. Once the setup is made, it is simple to produce the pieces in quantity. The single-end tenoner consists of the following:

• A heavy cast-iron frame mounted on a cast-iron base with heavy sides and guards to cover the cutter heads.
• Two tenon heads that may be adjusted vertically. The top tenon head can also be adjusted horizontally for cutting tenons with offset shoulders. Both heads can be adjusted vertically as a unit to cut tenons of identical thickness on different thicknesses of stock. A separate motor operates the tenon heads and the cutoff saw. Fig. 35-14.

35-13. Samples of the kind of work done on a single-end tenoner.

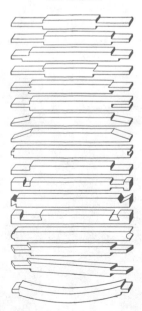

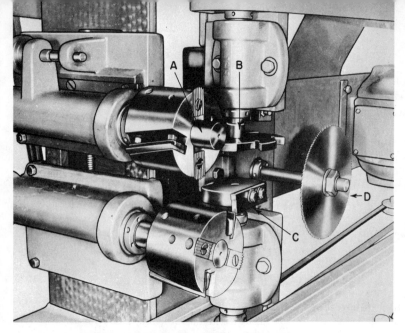

35-14. Closeup of cutter heads: (A.) Tenon heads may be adjusted vertically. Top tenon head may easily be set to cut offset shoulders. (B.) Check-rail slot cutter on upper cope arbor arbor will slot top and bottom stiles. (C.) Cope knives make sash pattern-changes easy. (D.) Cutoff saw.

• Both of the cope heads, which are mounted vertically behind the tenoning heads, may be individually adjusted vertically and horizontally. These are used to make coped shoulders which fit over the molded edges of a door or frame. Fig. 35-15. These cuts are made after the tenons are cut. Since the cope heads are not always used, a separate motor operates them. For example, on a simple tenon with a square shoulder, the cope heads would be removed from the cope spindles. Other types of cutters can be mounted on the spindles to do different shaping operations.

• The cutoff saw is mounted on a horizontal arbor behind the coping heads and is used to cut the tenon to length. This saw arbor can be adjusted both horizontally and vertically. The arbor usually operates off the same motor as the tenon heads.

• The carriage or table is mounted on double rollers and moved back and forth on rails, past the tenon and cope heads and saw. Clamps on the table hold the rails at any desired angle.

As for other production machines, the major skill required in using the single-end tenoner is in making the setup. Once

35-15. End view of cutter heads: (A.) Angle set, high-speed tenon knives. (B.) Various shapes of cutters can be mounted on cope head spindle. (C.) Cutoff saw trims tenon to any length. (D.) Spur cutters cut ahead of tenon knives.

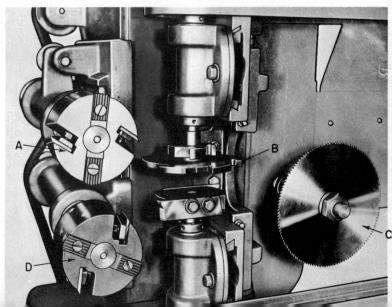

this is done correctly, the machine is relatively simple to use. The power is turned on and the carriage moved to the forward position. The stock to be cut is clamped on the table. The end of the stock first passes between the tenon heads to make the cheek and shoulder cuts on both sides of the piece. If the shoulder must be shaped (coped) to fit over a molded edge, this is then cut by the cope heads. If the tenon is to have a square shoulder these heads are not used.

As the work is moved farther along, the tenon is cut to length by the cutoff saw. All of this is done with one pass. At the end of the table movement, the clamp is released and the stock removed. The table is returned to the forward position, ready for another piece of stock. Once the setup is made, any number of pieces can be cut. After cuts are made in one end, pieces can often be reversed and then the other end can be cut with the same setup.

36 Sanding Machines And Coated Abrasives

Through constant improvement coated abrasives have kept pace with other modern developments in the woodworking industry. When used with the correct sanding machine, they provide an excellent way of cutting, shaping, smoothing, and finishing raw wood. Fig. 36-1. Using a coated abrasive on a power-driven tool is commonly referred to as *machine sanding*.

COATED ABRASIVES

An *abrasive* is any substance rubbed against a surface for the purpose of smoothing it. In woodworking this is commonly done before, between, or after applications of finish coats. Abrasives are also used for machining. Actually, each grain of abrasive is a cutting tool just like a saw or chisel. Some people still refer to coated abrasives as "sandpaper" even though there is no sand whatsoever on them. Coated abrasives consist of three materials: the *abrasive* itself, the *backing* on which it is fastened, and the *adhesive* that fastens the grains to the backing. Fig. 36-2. The backing may be paper, cloth, fiber, or a combination of

these materials. Various types of hide and resin glues are used as adhesives.

The four major abrasives used in the woodworking industry are flint, garnet, aluminum oxide, and silicon carbide. The first two are natural abrasives while the last two are synthetic, or man-made.

Flint

Flint is quartz (silicon dioxide), the material found on common sandpaper used for hand sanding. It is grayish-white or eggshell in color. Flint has only limited use in the woodworking industry because it lacks toughness and durability.

36-1. This beautiful buffet required careful sanding at every stage of production.

441

the 3 basics of modern Coated Abrasives

ADHESIVE BOND

BACKING

Paper, Cloth or Combination

ABRASIVE GRAINS

36-2. Three materials are needed to produce coated abrasives.

SANDING MACHINES

MAINTENANCE

• Make sure the operating controls turn easily.
• Check the belt, disk, or sleeve to make sure the abrasive cloth or paper is not worn. Replace as necessary.
• Make sure the cloth or paper is attached properly. On belt sanders, the arrow on the belt indicates the direction of rotation.
• Maintain proper motor-belt tension.
• Keep the sander clean. When necessary, take it apart and remove all sawdust from operating parts. Make sure air vents are not plugged.

LUBRICATION

• Use S.A.E. No. 20 machine oil for lubricating.
• For the stationary abrasive belt sander, lubricate the idler drum bearing, belt-tension knob screw, and tracking-handle screw.
• For the stationary disk sander, lubricate the spindle bearing when needed.
• Check portable machines for any oil holes. Lubricate, if necessary.

SAFETY

• Use only light pressure—just enough to hold the work against the abrasive.
• Wear goggles when disk sanding.
• Remove sawdust from around the machine to prevent a fire hazard.
• Sand parallel with the grain whenever possible, to obtain a smooth finish.
• Sand only dry wood.
• Use a fixture to hold small pieces of wood when machine sanding.

Garnet

Garnet is another natural material (almandite) that makes a good abrasive both for hand and machine sanding. It is a good deal harder than flint and the grains are narrow wedge shapes. Garnet, which is reddish-brown, is widely used in woodworking, principally for finish sanding.

Aluminum Oxide

Aluminum oxide is much harder than garnet, with a grain shape of wide wedges. It is a product of the electric furnace and is made by purifying bauxite (an ore of aluminum) to a crystal form, then adding small amounts of other materials for toughness. When aluminum oxide comes out of the furnace, it is in large chunk form. If it is to be used for the woodworking trades, the crushing technique is varied to produce a sharper grain than that generally used for metalworking. Aluminum oxide is brown and is considered an excellent abrasive for sanding harder woods.

Silicon Carbide

Silicon carbide, another man-made product of the electric furnace, has grains that are sharp wedge shapes. It is greenish-black and iridescent, and is not only the hardest but the sharpest of the synthetic abrasives. It is the ideal abrasive for fibrous woods, plastic, enamel, and other relatively soft materials. Commonly it is used in the finishing process and is generally considered softer than aluminum oxide.

CRUSHING AND GRADING

All abrasives are crushed and graded by the same method. The crushed particles are separated into grade sizes by passing them through a series of very accurately woven silk cloth screens. The mesh of these screens, or the number of openings per linear inch, ranges from very fine to very coarse. Mesh numbers are used to designate the grade size. For example, particles that pass through a screen with 80 openings per linear inch are called grit size 80. The more openings per inch in the mesh, the finer the grit. Therefore abrasives get finer as the number goes up. The silk-screen method is used for grading up to 220. Finer grits are graded by sedimentation or by air flotation.

An older system based on arbitrary symbols is still used to some extent for garnet paper. For example, garnet marked 30 under the new system is the same as that which is marked 2½ under the old. A mark of 280 in the new system corresponds to 8/0 in the old. Fig. 36-7 gives a complete listing of the two systems.

KINDS OF BACKINGS

Letters after the grit number designate the weight of the backing. Four common kinds of backings are used for coated abrasives:
• A *high-quality paper* made especially for the abrasive industry which comes in four different weights: "A," which is light paper stock, used primarily for light hand-sanding operations; "C," and "D," intermediate papers with more strength and stiffness, commonly known as cabinet papers; and "E," which is strong and durable, used especially for drum or belt sanding. "A" is 40-pound paper. This means that 480 sheets measuring 24" x 36" weigh 40 pounds.
• *Cloth,* which comes in two weights: "J" is lightweight and more flexible, for use in contour work; "X" which is heavier and stronger, best suited for flat work.
• *Fiber,* a very strong, stiff backing, which is made from ragstock paper. Fiber is used primarily for disk and drum sanding.

• Combination type backings. There are two of these, namely, paper and cloth laminated together and fiber and cloth laminated together. The paper-and-cloth combination is used mainly on high-speed drum sanders while the fiber-and-cloth type is used for disk sanders.

ADHESIVES OR BONDS

Several types of bonds or adhesives are used in the manufacture of coated abrasives. These are applied in two layers. The first is called the *bond coat,* the second the *size coat.* Five different types of adhesives or bonds are used:
• Animal hide glue is good for both the bond and the size coat.
• Glue and filler, a hide glue with filler added, produces a bond that is durable and strong. This is used both for the bond and size coats.
• Resin over glue is a combination of pure hide glue for the bond coat and a synthetic resin for the size coat, making an abrasive that is extremely resistant to heat.
• Resin over resin—one layer of synthetic resin is used for the bond and another for the size coat. This is not only heat-resistant but also withstands moisture and humidity.
• Waterproof is a synthetic resin used for the bond and the size coat on a waterproof backing. With this it is possible to use water and other liquids with coated adbrasives.

MANUFACTURING

The general procedure for manufacturing coated abrasives is about as follows. The abrasive-making machine consists of three units, namely, the printer, the adhesive coater, and the abrasive-grain dispenser. Fig. 36-3. First, the backing is started through a press which prints on it the trademark, brand name, manufacturer's name, mineral, grade number, name of the backing, and

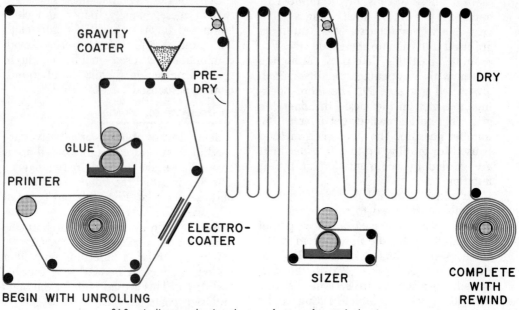

GRAVITY COATER

PRE-DRY

DRY

GLUE

PRINTER

ELECTRO-COATER

SIZER

COMPLETE WITH REWIND

BEGIN WITH UNROLLING

36-3. A diagram showing the manufacture of coated abrasives.

other necessary information. The backing next receives the bond coat of adhesive. The abrasive grains are then applied either by mechanical or electrostatic method. The mechanical method is sometimes called *gravity coating* since the abrasive grains are merely dropped onto the adhesive. In the other method, called *electrocoating*, the grains are made to stand up on end as they are dropped onto the adhesive. Electrocoating has these advantages: the abrasive is longer-lasting because the grains are firmly imbedded in the coating; there is more uniform distribution of the grains; and more grain area is exposed for cutting.

There are two kinds of abrasive-grain coating: *closed coat* and *open coat*. In closed coat, abrasive grains completely cover the adhesive. In open coat, there is space between the grains. Closed coat is used primarily for semi-finish and finish sanding, Fig. 36-4, whereas open coat is best for rough sanding and for removing paint, varnish, or other relatively soft

materials. In the open-coated method, about 50 to 70 per cent of the coated surface is covered with abrasive. Open-coated materials have greater flexibility and resist filling and clogging.

After the abrasive-grain coating, the size coat is applied. The coated abrasive is then dried and cured.

Next, the coated abrasives are made more flexible by controlled bending. The term "flexing" describes the actual controlled break of the bond at 45- or 90-degree angles. Fig. 36-5. The direction and spacing of the breaks are the two most important items to be controlled in the flexing of abrasive-coated cloth.

There are four basic flexing patterns, namely, single, double, triple, and Q-flex. The *single flex* is done along the width of the sandpaper, at 90 degrees to the length, leaving the sandpaper stiff in one direction and flexible in the other. It is used for mold sanding. In *double flex* the sheets are bent lengthwise at two 45-degree angles. The old-time craftsman did this himself, holding one corner of

444

36-4. In *closed coating* (upper right) the abrasive grains completely cover the surface of the backing. The density of the coating makes the sheet last longer. The larger, *open-coated* sheet has about 50 to 70 per cent of the surface covered. This paper is used when chips tend to "load" it, such as in paint or varnish removal. The open spaces allow most of the chips to drop out, affording better cutting action and longer life.

36-5. Types of flexing.

Single Flex

Triple Flex

Double Flex

Q-Flex

445

the sheet in one hand and the diagonally opposite corner in the other hand. He would then draw the back of the sheet over a bench, first in one direction and then the other. Now this is done automatically in the factory. Double-flex paper is needed for sanding fairly intricate contours, such as moldings. The *triple flex* is a combination of single and double flex for sanding sharp or irregular contours. In *Q-flex*, the bending is done in all directions. This gives excellent self-cleaning qualities to the paper and makes it ideal for edge sanding.

The last step in manufacture is to roll the coated abrasives into jumbo-sized rolls for later cutting into various shapes and forms.

FORMS OF COATED ABRASIVES

There are many forms of coated abrasives, but the most common are sheets, rolls, disks, and belts. Fig. 36-6. Of course, abrasive is also used to make

36-6. These are the common forms of coated abrasives. Sometimes the backing is scored with short cuts through the material to make it more flexible.

Mesh or Grit No.	Symbols or 0 Grade		
	Grit No.	0 Grade	Gen. Uses
VERY FINE	400 360 320 280 240 220	10/0 — 9/0 8/0 7/0 6/0	For polishing and finishing after stain, varnish, etc., has been applied.
FINE	180 150 120	5/0 4/0 3/0	For finish sanding just before staining or sealing.
MEDIUM	100 80 60	2/0 1/0 ½	For sanding to remove final rough texture.
COARSE	50 40 36	1 1½ 2	For sanding after very rough texture is removed.
VERY COARSE	30 24 20 16	2½ 3 3½ 4	For very rough, unfinished wood surfaces.

36-7. Table of grit sizes.

abrasive stones, grinding wheels, and similar items. Abrasive is also combined with fiber glass to form a soft abrasive wheel that is extremely useful for wood finishing. Another form is a belt which has a cloth back with a flexible nylon fiber coating impregnated with abrasive grains.

Sheets used for hand sanding and finishing sanders are available in many sizes. The common hand-sheet size is 9″ x 11″. Rolls are used for drum sanding and spindle sanding. Disks are made for both portable and stationary disk sanders. They come in almost every diameter, although the common sizes are 7″ and 9½″. Sander belts come in many widths and lengths to fit the full range of sanders from small portable ones to large industrial equipment.

KINDS OF SANDING

Coated abrasives should be selected in terms of the work to be done. To obtain the same finish on two pieces, one hardwood and the other softwood, choose a slightly coarser grit for the hardwood. Fig. 36-7. For best results it is important that both the kind of abrasive and the grit number be chosen correctly. Fig. 36-8. The relationship between the kind of sanding and the grit size is briefly summarized as follows:

• *Roughing or material removal* is a heavy sanding operation in which the maximum amount of material is removed with a coarse grit abrasive.

• *Blending,* with some material removed and a fairly smooth finish, calls for medium grits. Less material is removed than in roughing, and a better surface is obtained.

• *Fine finishing* is done to remove scratch patterns formed by coarser grits. Fine grits are used.

• *Polishing and rubbing* are burnishing operations which remove or blend the fine scratch patterns left by earlier finishing steps. Extremely fine grits are needed, generally with some kind of lubricant such as oil or water.

When a series of abrasives is to be used, start with one just coarse enough to make the surface level and to eliminate excessive roughness. Then follow with a second, medium grit to improve the surface. Continue with a finer grit until the desired finish is obtained. *Never go from a very coarse to a very fine grit in one step.*

SANDING MACHINES

There is a wide variety of sanding machines designed to do every type of cutting and finishing. In the school and cabinet shop there are seven common pieces of equipment.

Floor-type Belt Sander

The belt sander can be used in vertical, horizontal, or slant positions. Fig. 36-9.

SANDPAPERS FOR WOOD

NAME	GRIT SIZES					AVAILABLE IN	USES
FLINT Paper	Extra Coarse	Coarse	Medium	Fine	Extra Fine	9" x 10" Sheets (See Note)	For hand sanding common woodwork, removing paint, varnish, etc. Also for small miscellaneous jobs.
GARNET Paper	Very Coarse 30-D(2½)	Coarse 50-D(1)	Medium 80-D(0)	Fine 120-C(3/0)	Very Fine 220-A(6/0)	9" x 11" Sheets	Good all-around paper for hand sanding good woodwork, furniture, etc., dry.

NOTE: Flint paper is also available in packs containing an assortment of coarse, medium and fine grits in 4½" x 5" sheets.

SANDPAPERS FOR WOOD AND METAL

	GRIT SIZES					AVAILABLE IN	USES
Paper (Aluminum Oxide)	Very Coarse 30-D(2½)	Coarse 50-D(1)	Medium 80-D(0)	Fine 120-C (3/0)	Very Fine 220-A(6/0)	9" x 11" Sheets	For hand or machine sanding of hardwoods, metals, plastics and other materials.
Cloth (Aluminum Oxide)	Very Coarse 30-X(2½)	Coarse 50-X(1)	Medium 80-X(0)	Fine 120-X (3/0)		Belts for all popular belt sanders. X-weight	Strong cloth-backed belts for sanding wood, metal, plastics and other materials with stationary or portable belt sanders.
Paper-Waterproof (Silicon Carbide)			Very Fine 220-A	Extra Fine 320-A	Super Fine 400-A	9" x 11" Sheets	Best paper for wet sanding by hand or machine, primers and between coats on wood, metal or other materials. Can be used with water, oil or other lubricants.

36-8. Some common abrasive types.

It is set in the desired position by loosening the hand lock and moving the entire unit. The table will tilt 20 degrees toward the belt and 40 degrees away from the belt. A miter gage can also be used on the machine. In the horizontal position, a fence can be attached to guide the work for surface sanding.

To change a belt, first remove the guards. Then release the tension by turning the belt-tension knob. Remove the old belt and slip on a new one. Apply a slight amount of tension, then center the belt on the drums by adjusting the idler pulley with the tracking handle. Next increase the tension and replace the guards. Check the centering adjustment again by moving the belt by hand. Readjust when necessary. If the sander is to be used in a tilted position, the centering should be done after this adjustment.

To do surface sanding, place the machine in a horizontal position. The work can be fed freehand across the belt by applying a very light, firm pressure. However, for more accurate edge sanding, use a fence to guide the work. Fig.

36-9. Parts of a belt sander. This is sometimes called an abrasive-belt finishing machine since it can be used for many kinds of finishing.

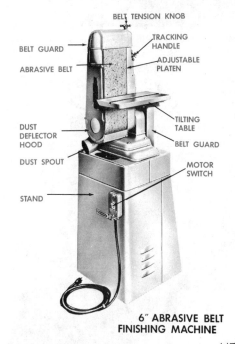

BELT TENSION KNOB
TRACKING HANDLE
BELT GUARD
ABRASIVE BELT
ADJUSTABLE PLATEN
DUST DEFLECTOR HOOD
TILTING TABLE
BELT GUARD
DUST SPOUT
MOTOR SWITCH
STAND

6" ABRASIVE BELT FINISHING MACHINE

36-10. Edge sanding, using the fence as a guide.
Note that this is a combination belt-and-disk sander.

36-11. Freehand sanding the edge of a circular piece.

36-10. Beveling and angle sanding can be done by tilting the fence. For end-grain sanding, the unit should be in a vertical position and the table used as a guide. Fig. 36-11. Bevels and chamfers can also be sanded in this manner by using a miter gage as a guide. Fig. 36-12.

Many types of simple wood jigs can be used for mass production work. To do form sanding, make a wood form that is exactly opposite the shape of the piece to be sanded. Cover the form with a piece of sheet metal. Fasten this to the sanding table so that the belt runs over the form. Fig. 36-13.

Stationary-type Disk Sander

The disk sander is a simple machine that can be used for some types of rough, end-grain sanding and for simple shaping. Fig. 36-14. It has limited use in cabinetmaking, however, because its circular motion causes cross-grain sanding scratches. It is important that the abrasive cloth be firmly fastened to the metal disk. If the disk is worn, the first step is to remove the old cloth. If the abrasive disk is attached with glue, soak it in hot water until loose, then remove with a putty knife. Be sure the disk is dry before mounting the new abrasive. It can be glued to the disk with water glass or a heavy grade of rubber cement. Clamp on a flat piece of wood to prevent wrinkles. If rubber cement or stick cement was used, hold the end of a hardwood stick or screw driver against it and move back and forth to loosen the old adhesive. Fig. 36-15.

To apply the new abrasive, hold the adhesive stick against the metal plate and move it back and forth. Make sure that there is a uniform coat of adhesive on the metal. Fig. 36-16. Then turn off the power and carefully apply the abrasive. Fig. 36-17. Let dry a short time.

36-12. Sanding a bevel or chamfer, using the miter gage and table as guides.

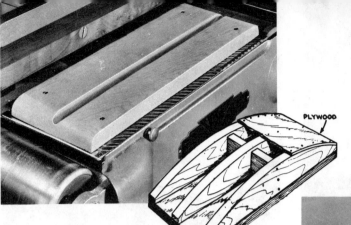

36-13. Form sanding. The form shown in the photograph is used to round the corners of stock. The insert drawing shows a form for sanding a concave, circular part.

PLYWOOD

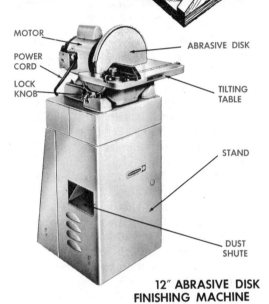

MOTOR

POWER CORD

LOCK KNOB

ABRASIVE DISK

TILTING TABLE

STAND

DUST SHUTE

12" ABRASIVE DISK FINISHING MACHINE

36-14. Parts of a disk sander.

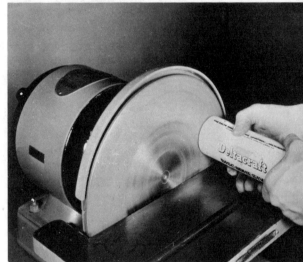

36-16 Applying an adhesive to the metal disk. The adhesive is also applied to the back of the abrasive sheet by laying the sheet on a flat surface and rubbing the adhesive on the back.

36-17. Place the sheet firmly on the metal disk.

36-15. Cleaning off the disk with the end of a screw driver.

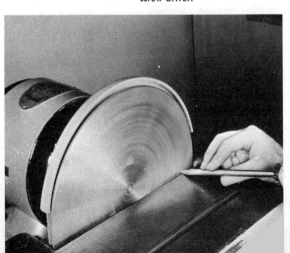

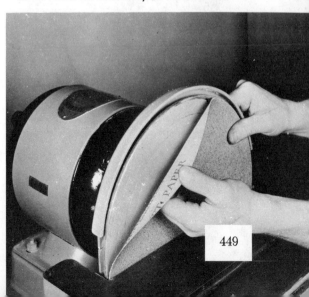

449

36-18(a). This abrasive disk has a pressure-sensitive backing, making it unnecessary to use any glue or adhesive. Just peel the back away from the disk.

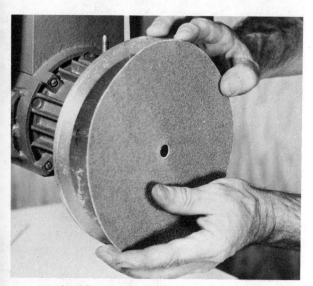

36-18(b). Carefully place the new abrasive on the metal disk and smooth it out. To remove the old disk, just peel it off.

36-20. Sanding a rounded corner.

Abrasive disks can be purchased already cut to exact size and with an adhesive coating on the back. Then all that is necessary is to make sure the metal disk is clean. Strip the cover paper off the abrasive disk, and install. Fig. 36-18. Such disks make it easy to change grades.

A table on the disk sander can be used for end-grain sanding. It can be tilted and used in combination with a miter gage to sand a chamfer or bevel. The disk sander can also sand the edge of a circular piece. Fig. 36-19. Always sand on the "down" side of the disk. Also, move the stock back and forth on this side. Holding it in one position would tend to burn the wood.

Most disk sanding is done freehand. Remember that the edge of the disk is moving much faster than the center, and allow for this. To sand circles or arcs, hold the work firmly on the table and revolve it slowly. Fig. 36-20.

Spindle Sander

This sander is designed primarily for use on edges and irregular curves. It has a revolving, oscillating (moving up and down) spindle on which the abrasive paper or cloth is fastened. Fig. 36-21. The slow up-and-down movement spreads the wear and also prevents the wood from

36-19. Sanding the edge of a large table base. Note that the table is tilted slightly to sand a bevel.

36-21. The spindle sander is constructed like a shaper. It has a cast-iron base and a horizontal table. The spindle projects through the center of the table. The table can be tilted 45 degrees to one side and 15 degrees to the other.

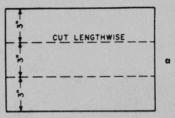

CUT SLEEVES FROM 9" x 11" SHEETS

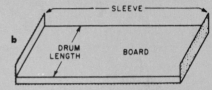

BEND ENDS OF SLEEVES BY USE OF BOARD AS SHOWN. BOARD MUST BE MEASURED ACCURATELY AND CUT SQUARE.

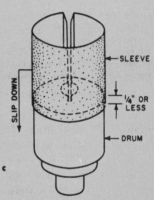

WRAP ABOUT ¼" OF DRUM OR LESS. THEN SLIP ON DOWN OVER DRUM. USE TALCUM POWDER IF NECESSARY TO MAKE SLEEVE SLIP EASILY.

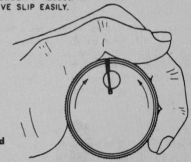

SQUEEZE HARD TO GET SLACK OUT OF SLEEVE AND ENDS DOWN INTO SLOT. THEN INSERT TUBE AND TURN WITH KEY. OVAL TUBE SHOULD FIT SNUGLY. DO NOT FORCE. IF TOO TIGHT PUT IN VISE AND SQUEEZE EDGE IF TOO LOOSE SQUEEZE FLAT SIDE OF TUBE.

36-22. Replacing an abrasive sleeve.

burning. The spindles come in various diameters and are made of metal, wood, soft rubber, or rubber tubing.

To replace the abrasive paper or cloth, remove the worn paper and cut a new one to size. On some sanders, a wedge on one side holds the paper to the spindle. Other spindles are made in two half-segments that can be separated for replacing the paper. Still others have a tube that slips into the drum, with a key that turns to lock it. Fig. 36-22.

Hand-stroke Belt Sander

The hand-stroke belt sander is commonly used for flat-sanding, when it is

36-23. The hand-stroke belt sander has two drums or pulleys with an endless belt around them. One pulley, called the "power stand," is connected to an electric motor. The other pulley is an idler. On this machine the pulley can be moved up or down for sanding different thicknesses of material. Another type has a pulley at a fixed height with the table adjustable up and down. The idler pulley can be moved in or out to adjust for belt tension.

important to produce an even surface with a minimum of raised fibers. It has a long, continuous belt that moves around two drums or pulleys. A movable table rolls back and forth under the belt. Fig. 36-23. The sanding block is held free-hand to the back of the belt to apply pressure for sanding. Fig. 36-24.

36-24. Using the hand-stroke belt sander to sand a wide table top. The operator is using a flat bottom block with round edges. Concave or convex surfaces can be sanded with a sanding block of proper shape. Stroke sanding should be the last machine sanding of the wood before finishing. Therefore it is important to obtain a very smooth surface.

The kind of sanding determines the grade and kind of abrasive belt. Use aluminum oxide for hardwoods and garnet for softwoods. If stock removal is necessary, cloth-backed abrasives having greater resistance to breakage should be chosen. For lighter operations, such as sanding furniture tops, a belt made of paper might be satisfactory. If a piece of hardwood furniture is to be sanded to a very high-quality finish, it may be necessary to use two grades of paper. Sanding on softer hardwoods should be done first with No. 120 grit, then with 180 grit. A sequence of 100 and 150 should be chosen for harder hardwoods. For some woods, such as maple or birch, a single grade of 100 or 120 is satisfactory. For sanding veneers, the final grit should be about 220. The most common problem in stroke sanding is a streaked or non-uniform burnish finish. A worn belt often causes this.

In using the hand-stroke sander, place the pieces on the movable table and do the sanding in one of two ways. In the first method, the sanding block is moved back and forth along the total length of the material. Then the work is moved to a new position and the sanding repeated. The second method is to do the sanding in cross sections. Sand all the

36-25. With an auxiliary metal table clamped to the machine, the hand-stroke belt sander can be used for sanding drawers and other assembled parts. The work is held lightly but firmly against the belt. Notice the stop which keeps the work from moving with the belt.

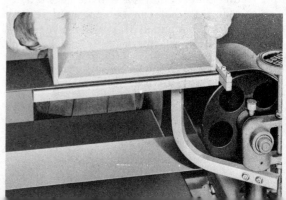

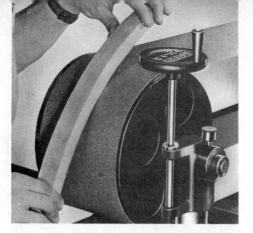

36-26. The hand-stroke belt sander can also be used for open-drum sanding of simple contoured parts, as for a chair or circular table.

36-28. Replacing a belt. The clamp is being closed to apply tension to the belt. Note the large arrow on the underside of the belt to show the direction in which it should move.

way across the end of the material, moving the table a little at a time. Then move the sanding block to a new position and sand slowly across in the other direction. There will be no excessive abrasive line if the cross movement is slow.

With an extra table attached, the top of the belt can be used for sanding assembled parts such as the sides of a drawer. Fig. 36-25. If one end of the sander has no guard, curved parts can be sanded over the drum. Fig. 36-26.

Portable Belt Sander

Portable belt sanders are excellent for sanding assembled cabinetwork and furniture pieces. Fig. 36-27. The size of the machine is determined by the width and length of the belt. The most common are 2″ x 21″, 3″ x 24″, 3″ x 27″, 4″ x 22″, and 4½″ x 26″. The belt should be so installed that the splice runs off the work. An arrow stamped on the back of each belt indicates the direction the belt should run. It is a simple job to replace a belt on most machines. Usually a clamp opens to release the tension on the belt. Fig. 36-28. After a new belt is installed, it can be centered on the pulleys by turning the belt-tracking adjustment. The belt should never rub against the side of the machine. If the belt is a thick, soft one made of nylon impregnated with abrasive, then there must be extra clearance between the pulleys and the housing. Fig. 36-29.

The portable belt sander should be used as follows. Place the cord over your right shoulder out of the way, and hold the machine firmly with both hands. Turn on the power. Lower the sander so that the heel touches the work first. Then move the sander back and forth in a straight line. Sanding is actually done *on the pull stroke*. Fig. 36-30. Never allow the sander to stand still for any length of time as this would cut deep grooves

36-27. Parts of a portable belt sander.

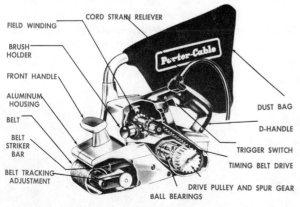

FIELD WINDING

BRUSH HOLDER

FRONT HANDLE

ALUMINUM HOUSING

BELT

BELT STRIKER BAR

BELT TRACKING ADJUSTMENT

CORD STRAIN RELIEVER

DUST BAG

D-HANDLE

TRIGGER SWITCH

TIMING BELT DRIVE

DRIVE PULLEY AND SPUR GEAR

BALL BEARINGS

3″x24″ DUSTLESS BELT SANDER

453

36-29(a). This belt sander is designed to take thick, soft, finishing belts.

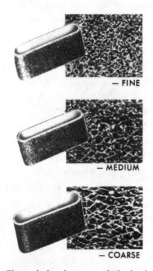

— FINE

— MEDIUM

— COARSE

36-29(b). These belts have a cloth back and a soft, flexible abrasive made by impregnating nylon fibers with abrasive material. Because of the large openings between fibers, there is less loading and clogging. Such belts also run cooler. They can be used with water or oil for wet finishing and polishing.

36-30. The correct method of using a portable sander.

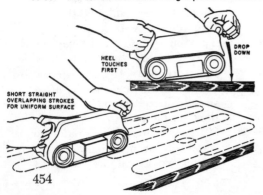

HEEL TOUCHES FIRST

DROP DOWN

SHORT STRAIGHT OVERLAPPING STROKES FOR UNIFORM SURFACE

454

36-31. The belt sander easily removes marks and old finish from a wood surface.

in the wood. Fig. 36-31. It is particularly important to watch this when sanding plywood. Always machine slowly and evenly. Fig. 36-32. Cross sanding is sometimes done first to obtain a level surface. On woods such as fir, with both hard and soft grain, cross sanding should be done as much as possible. To sand the edges of boards, allow the belt to extend beyond the edge a little. Be careful that the sander doesn't tilt. For a panel door, sand the panels before assembly. Then sand the rails and, finally, the stiles. Fig. 36-33.

Finishing Sander

The finishing sander is used primarily for final sanding on the assembled product and for sanding between finishing coats. Fig. 36-34. There are many sizes and styles. All finishing sanders, however, operate with orbital, straight-line, or multi-motion action. Fig. 36-35.

36-32. Sanding flush to a vertical surface.

SAND WITH GRAIN

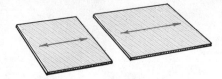

SAND PANELS BEFORE ASSEMBLY

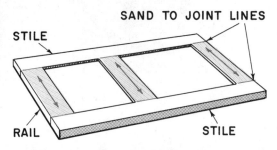

STILE

SAND TO JOINT LINES

RAIL

STILE

SAND RAILS BEFORE STILES

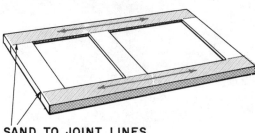

SAND TO JOINT LINES
SAND STILES LAST

36-33. Steps in sanding a panel door.

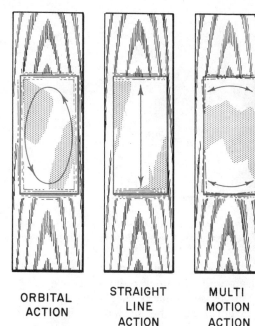

ORBITAL
ACTION

STRAIGHT
LINE
ACTION

MULTI
MOTION
ACTION

36-35. Three kinds of sanding action found in finishing sanders. Orbital and multi-motion action causes some cross-grain scratches. Straight-line action is like hand sanding and results in the best surface.

36-34. Parts of a finishing sander.

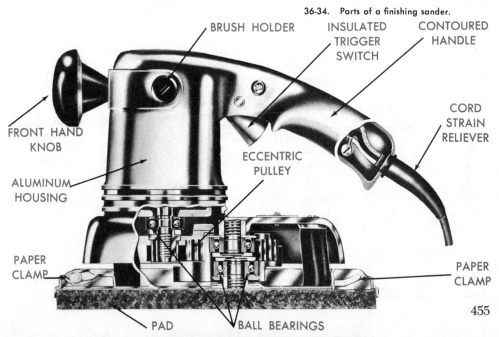

BRUSH HOLDER

INSULATED
TRIGGER
SWITCH

CONTOURED
HANDLE

CORD
STRAIN
RELIEVER

FRONT HAND
KNOB

ALUMINUM
HOUSING

ECCENTRIC
PULLEY

PAPER
CLAMP

PAPER
CLAMP

PAD

BALL BEARINGS

HALF-PAD FINISHING SANDER

455

36-38. Using a finishing sander to smooth a surface before applying a finish.

36-36. A double-action finishing sander. The sander can be switched to either orbital or straight-line action.

Orbital action is best for rapid sanding and fast stock removal. However, it leaves swirl marks that show up under a finish. Straight-line sanding is best for transparent wood finishes such as lacquer or varnish. Some sanders have two kinds of action and can be changed by flicking a switch. Fig. 36-36.

Finishing sanders are relatively easy to use. Clip a sheet of abrasive paper or cloth to the pad. Choose the correct grade for the work to be done. Fig. 36-37. Lower the pad to the surface and move it back and forth slowly. Fig. 36-38.

36-39. This pneumatic (air-driven) pad sander is made with either orbital or straight-line action. The straight-line stroke is used to give a final sanding to white wood (unfinished furniture) just before it goes to the finishing room.

36-37. This shows the kind of abrasive paper or cloth to choose for sanding various materials with the finishing sander.

KIND OF MATERIAL	MATERIAL REMOVAL		MATERIAL REMOVAL WITH FAIR FINISH		FINE FINISH	
	GRIT	SIZE OF GRIT	GRIT	SIZE OF GRIT	GRIT	SIZE OF GRIT
Soft Wood Soft Wallboard	Cabinet Paper (Garnet)	2-1	Cabinet Paper (Garnet)	½-2/0	Finishing Paper (Garnet)	3/0-5/0
Plastics	Cabinet Paper (Aluminum Oxide)	60-100	Wet Paper "C" Weight (Silicon Carbide)	120-220	Wet Paper "A" Weight (Silicon Carbide)	240-600
Hard Wood Hard Compositions Wallboards, Etc.	Cabinet Paper (Aluminum Oxide)	36-50	Cabinet Paper (Aluminum Oxide)	60-100	Finishing Paper (Aluminum Oxide)	120-180
Hard Brittle Minerals and Compositions	Cabinet Paper (Aluminum Oxide)	50-80	Finishing Paper (Aluminum Oxide)	100-180	Wet Paper "A" Weight (Silicon Carbide)	220-320
Hard Tough Minerals and Compositions	Metalworking Cloth (Aluminum Oxide)		Metalworking Cloth (Aluminum Oxide)	80-120	Finishing Paper (Aluminum Oxide)	150-320
Paints, Varnishes	Cabinet Paper (Opencoat Garnet)	2½-1½			Wet Paper "A" Weight (Silicon Carbide)	240-400

456

36-40. This multi-speed rotary sander has a 6" disk. It operates at 1600, 2700, or 3800 r.p.m.

36-41. Installing the disk sander on the motor spindle.

Some school and cabinet shops have *air-operated*, orbital, or reciprocating sanders. Fig. 36-39. These are similar to the finishing sander but are more powerful and therefore more efficient. These sanders are highly effective for final sanding before applying a finish and also between finishing coats.

Rotary-action Portable Sanders

This sander is good for fast, rough sanding, but it has little use in cabinetmaking since, like the disk sander, it sands cross-grain. Fig. 36-40. If this tool is used to remove an old finish, hold it so that about the outer third of the sanding sheet is on the surface. Never try to use the entire abrasive surface at one time, as this will cause the sander to bounce and gouge the wood.

RADIAL-ARM SAW AS A SANDER

The radial-arm saw can be quickly converted to a disk, spindle, or small drum sander to perform many power-sanding operations. To use the machine as a disk sander, first remove the safety guard, arbor nut, cutting tool, and the arbor collars from the motor shaft. Then replace one arbor collar and the disk plate on the shaft. Tighten this counterclockwise with your hand. Fig. 36-41. Sanding can be done by moving the work against the disk which rotates in a fixed position.

36-42. Sanding a circle. Use a jig as shown and place the stock on the center pin of the sliding strip. Set the motor to the proper height and lock it in place, directly in front of the jig. Turn on the machine and slowly rotate the stock clockwise on the center pin. After the first sanding, move it slightly closer to the disk and repeat until a smooth circle is obtained.

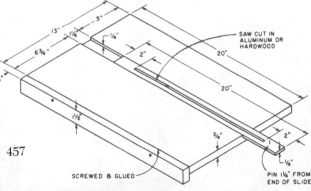

457

36-43. Bevel sanding. Place the radial arm in the crosscut position with the motor at the desired angle. Place the stock on an auxiliary table. Pull the disk across the beveled end of the board.

36-45(b). Freehand sanding. Place the motor in the vertical position and center the drum over the shaper slot in the table. Tighten the rip clamp and lower the arm so the entire edge can be sanded. Move the work past the drum from left to right.

36-44. Surface sanding. Place the motor in a vertical position; move it along until the disk is directly over the path of the stock. Lock the unit in place, then push the board from right to left along the fence.

Fig. 36-42. Another method is to fasten the work securely, then move the disk across the work as you would for sawing. Fig. 36-43. For surface sanding, the disk can be used vertically, like a disk sander, or horizontally. Fig. 36-44.

The disk can be removed and replaced with either a 1″ or 2½″ drum sander. Fig. 36-45(a). Unlike a spindle sander, the drum doesn't move up and down as it rotates; however, the drum sander is used for many edge sanding operations, similar to the spindle sander. Fig. 36-45(b) and (c). When the drum is in the horizontal position, an auxiliary table may be needed to raise the work slightly. Fig. 36-46.

BAND SAW AS A SANDER

The band saw can be used as a thin

36-45(a). Mounting the drum sander. Remove the sanding disk, then place the drum sander on the rear end (opposite the spindle end) of the motor shaft. Turn the disk by hand until it is tight.

458

36-45(c). Internal sanding can be done like freehand sanding. Keep the stock moving so it doesn't overheat and scorch the wood.

36-46. Surface sanding narrow boards. Place the shaft in a horizontal position. Use the table top and the fence as guides. Place the stock tight against the fence. Lower the radial arm until the abrasive touches the stock. Remove the stock and turn on the power. Then feed the work against the rotation of the drum.

belt sander by first removing the saw and the guide. Then a narrow, endless belt is used instead of the saw blade. A support is needed just above the table so that slight pressure can be applied to the belt. A support of wood or metal can be clamped to the table just back of the belt. Fig. 36-47.

DRILL PRESS AS A SANDER

A wide variety of sanding jobs can be done on the drill press by using sanding disks and drums. For spindle and drum sanding, replace the chuck with a sanding drum attachment. Lock the quill and adjust the machine to a speed of about 1800 r.p.m. The work can be held against the drum freehand, or it can rest on an auxiliary wood table. Figs. 36-48 and 36-49.

36-47. Sanding the edge of an irregular shape on the band saw.

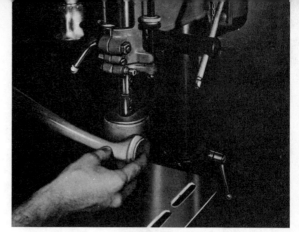

36-48. Sanding a table leg by holding it against the revolving drum.

JIG SAW WITH SANDING ATTACHMENT

The sanding attachment for the jig saw is designed to finish concave, convex, or flat surfaces. It replaces the blade in the lower chuck of the jig saw. Before attaching it, remove the table insert. A knurled knob expands the body of the attachment, thus holding the abrasive paper securely in place. Fig. 36-50. Sleeves are changed simply by loosening the knob. Sanding should be done at slow speed—the finer the abrasive, the slower the speed.

HAND SANDING

Even though most sanding can be done with machines, there are places a machine can't reach. This is true even in high-production furniture factories, where skilled cabinetmakers must do such sanding by hand.

These are the basic rules for hand sanding:

36-49. Resting a design on a piece of wood to raise it so the entire edge can be sanded at the same time. 459

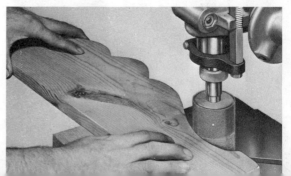

36-50. Sanding attachment on a jig or scroll saw.

36-52. Even in mass-production furniture plants, some hand sanding must be done after the product is assembled and before it is finished. This is especially true of ornate styles such as French Provincial.

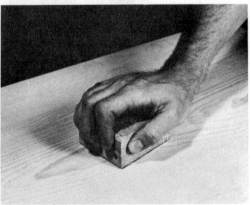

36-51(a). A simple block of wood can be used as a sanding block.

36-51(b). A much better sanding job can be done if a little time is spent setting up the pieces conveniently. Here a sheet of sandpaper is held in a commercial holder.

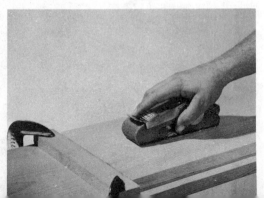

- Select the correct kind and grade of abrasive for the job to be done. Garnet paper is generally used for hand sanding.
- Make sure all cutting operations are completed before sanding. Except for abrasive machining (see Unit 25), sanding is designed to smooth and finish the surface after cutting and shaping have been done with other tools.
- For flat surfaces and edges, use a sanding block so the surfaces will be square. Fig. 36-51. There is a tendency in sanding to round all edges and surfaces. Never ruin the accuracy of your work with poor sanding.
- Always sand with the grain of the wood. Apply just enough pressure to make the abrasive cut the surface.
- Clean off the abrasive paper or cloth frequently with a brush.
- Never attempt to sand off glue or pencil marks.
- Many curved and irregular surfaces which must be hand sanded are quite smooth and require only a light sanding with finer grades of paper. Fig. 36-52.
- Break all edges slightly to prevent splintering. Round the corners just enough to give them a smooth "feel" when you run your hand across them.

The hand wood lathe combines the skill of hand-tool work with the power of a machine. Fig. 37-1. Some woodworkers use a hand lathe for recreational purposes. In production work, its value is limited. The primary occupational value of this machine is for the model maker, the patternmaker, and those who restore and rebuild antique furniture. A few cabinetmakers who are employed by furniture manufacturers must hand turn original patterns that are used to set the knives for the automatic lathe.

The automatic lathe used in industry is a high-production machine that will do all types of turning and many other special kinds of cutting for furniture parts. Fig. 37-2.

PARTS AND SIZES

37-1. This cherry occasional table has parts that were expertly turned on the hand lathe.

Lathe size is designated by the largest diameter that can be turned, by the bed

37-2(a). Turned parts for Early American and Colonial furniture are produced on an automatic lathe.

461

WOOD LATHE

MAINTENANCE

• Keep all lathe tools properly ground.
• Check the condition of the lathe centers. Grind or replace as necessary.
• Keep headstock and tailstock spindles wiped clean of sawdust and dirt.
• Make sure all adjustments on the tool rest and tailstock operate freely.
• Always remove the live center to drive it into the stock with a mallet.

LUBRICATION

• On variable-speed lathes, use S.A.E. No. 20 oil on counter shaft, bracket screw, variable-speed drive screw, dovetail ways, variable-speed pulley shaft, and tailstock quill adjusting screw.
• On belt-driven lathes, use S.A.E. No. 20 oil on beds, ways, tailstock, quill, and adjusting screws.
• Motors usually have sealed bearings that require no lubrication.

SAFETY

• Never wear loose clothing or a tie.
• Wear goggles or a face shield.
• Check the wood to make sure it has no defects that would cause it to break when turning.
• Check all glue joints before mounting the stock. A weak joint may come apart when revolving at high speeds. Make sure glued-up stock is completely dry before turning.
• Fasten stock securely between centers. Make sure the tailstock is locked before turning on the power.
• Adjust the tool rest as close to the stock as possible. Then revolve the stock by hand to make sure it clears the rest.
• Always stop the lathe before making any adjustments such as changing the position of the tool rest.
• Run all stock at the slowest speed until it is rounded.
• For stock over 6″ in diameter, maintain slower speed; from 3″ to 6″, medium speed; under 3″, faster speeds.
• Hold turning tools firmly in both hands.
• Keep the tool rest as close to the work as possible. At intervals, stop the lathe and re-adjust.
• Make sure the stock is firmly fastened to the faceplate before turning.
• Remove the tool rest when sanding or polishing. If you don't, your fingers may get caught between the tool rest and the stock.

37-2(b). This automatic lathe is turning the posts for beds like that shown in Fig. 37-2(a). The operator has only to fill the hopper with pieces of stock. The lathe automatically centers each piece. Then a series of shaper-like knives, revolving at high speed, moves toward the work which is turning at slow speed. After the piece is turned, it drops into a container to be removed later by the same operator. Once the setup is made, one operator can take care of several machines.

length, the distance between centers, and the overall length. A typical diameter is 12″, with an overall length of 57″. *Swing* is twice the distance from line center to the bed. A gap-bed lathe may have a swing over the bed of 12″ and a swing over the gap of 15½″, with 4″ thick stock. Fig. 37-3. This feature makes it possible to do larger faceplate turning on the inside of the lathe.

A lathe may be belt-driven (using step pulleys), it may have a variable-speed pulley, or it may have a direct-drive motor. The speed ranges depend on this drive arrangement. For example, the gap-bed lathe in Fig. 37-3 has a variable-speed control drive which allows it to turn at any speed from 340 r.p.m., for turning rough wood, up to 3200 r.p.m. A

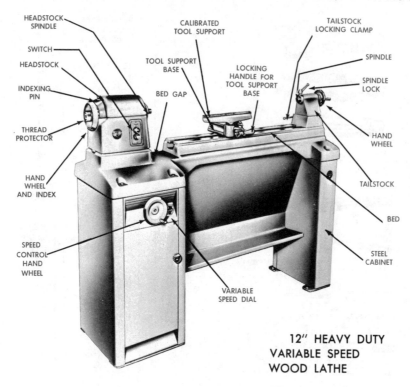

HEADSTOCK
SPINDLE

CALIBRATED
TOOL SUPPORT

TAILSTOCK
LOCKING CLAMP

SWITCH

HEADSTOCK

TOOL SUPPORT
BASE

SPINDLE

LOCKING
HANDLE FOR
TOOL SUPPORT
BASE

SPINDLE
LOCK

INDEXING
PIN

BED GAP

THREAD
PROTECTOR

HAND
WHEEL

HAND
WHEEL
AND INDEX

TAILSTOCK

SPEED
CONTROL
HAND
WHEEL

BED

VARIABLE
SPEED DIAL

STEEL
CABINET

12″ HEAVY DUTY
VARIABLE SPEED
WOOD LATHE

37-3. Parts of a gap-bed lathe.

37-4. Parts of a 12″ standard wood-turning lathe:
(1) pulley guard, (2) headstock, (3) headstock
spindle, (4) index pin, (5) bed, (6) tool-rest base,
(7) tool rest, (8) tool-rest base clamp, (9) tool-rest
clamp, (10) tailstock base, (11) tailstock, (12) tailstock
spindle, (13) tailstock spindle clamp, (14) tailstock-
spindle feed handle, (15) tailstock clamp handle,
(16) set-over adjusting screw, (17) headstock wrench,
(18) small tool rest, (19) spur center, (20) cup center,
(21) wrench, (22) small faceplate, and (23) belt.

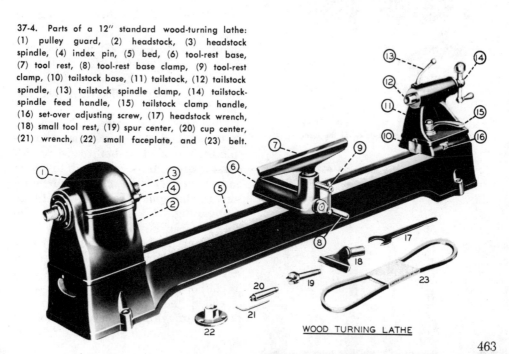

WOOD TURNING LATHE

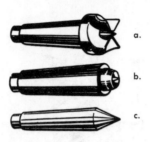

37-5. Kinds of centers: (a) Spur or drive. (b) Cup. (c) Cone.

37-6. Common accessories for the lathe.

37-7(a). A set of turning tools. The flat nose is not commonly used except for faceplate scraping and is not included.

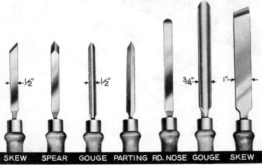

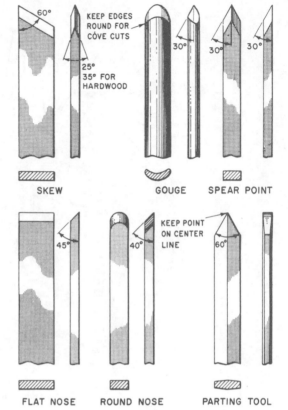

37-7(b). The correct shape of cutting edges of turning tools.

standard lathe equipped with four-step pulleys has speeds of 915, 1380, 2150, and 3260 r.p.m. Fig. 37-4. On some lathes, speeds up to 3600 r.p.m. are possible.

The headstock is permanently mounted on the left end of the bed. It has a hollow spindle, threaded on both ends, so that a faceplate can be attached to either end. A *spur or drive center* can be inserted in the spindle for turning between centers. Fig. 37-5. The tailstock is movable and can be located at many positions along the belt. It also has a hollow spindle in which the *cup center* is inserted. Sometimes a *cone center* is used instead of a cup center. In either case it is called the *dead center* because it doesn't turn with the stock. The tool rest

464

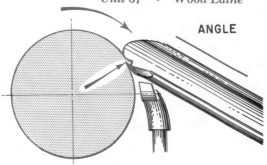

ANGLE

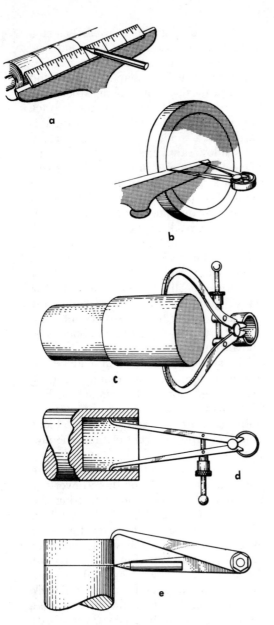

37-9. The *cutting method* is faster and results in a smoother surface than does scraping. However, it requires much greater skill and more practice.

consists of a base that clamps to the bed, and the tool rest itself that clamps to this base.

Many accessories can be used on the lathe, not only for turning but also for buffing, grinding, horizontal boring, disk sanding, and drum sanding. Fig. 37-6.

TOOLS

The six common types of tools for wood turning are: *gouges* for rough cutting stock to round shape, *skews* for smooth cuts to finish a surface, *parting tools* to cut a recess or groove, *spearpoint* or *diamond tools* to finish the inside of recesses or corners, *flat tools* for scraping a straight surface, and *roundnose tools* for scraping concave recesses and circular grooves. Fig. 37-7. Measuring tools include a rule, dividers, outside caliper, inside caliper, and hermaphrodite caliper. Fig. 37-8.

KINDS OF TURNING

There are two basic methods of turning, namely, cutting and scraping. Cutting tools include the gouge, skew, and parting tool, while the scraping tools are the flat nose, round nose, and spear point. All of the cutting tools can be used for scraping operations also. In the cutting method, the outer skin of the wood is pierced and a shaving is peeled off. Fig. 37-9. In scraping, the tool is forced into

37-8. Common measuring tools. (a) The *rule* is needed for making measurements for spindle and faceplate turning and for setting dividers and calipers. (b) The *dividers* is used for drawing circles and stepping off measurements. (c) The *outside caliper* is needed for checking the outside diameter of turned work. (d) The *inside caliper* is used for making measurements on the inside diameter. (e) The *hermaphrodite caliper* is used for laying out distances from the end of stock and for locating the centers for turning.

465

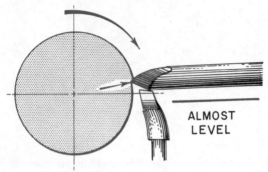

37-10. The *scraping method* is easier to do and is accurate but the rougher surface that results requires more sanding. All faceplate turning is done by scraping.

the wood so that particles are scraped away. Fig. 37-10. When only a limited amount of turning is to be done, the scraping method is completely satisfactory.

SPINDLE TURNING

Turning with the stock held between the live (or moving) center and the dead (or stationary) center is called spindle turning.

Turning a Plain Cylinder

A plain cylinder is turned with the work held between the live and dead

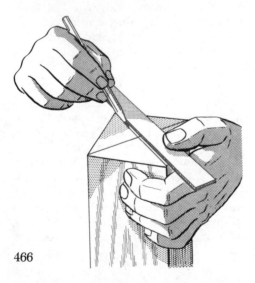

centers, and a gouge is used. Select a piece of wood of the right kind and size. If the stock is more than 3″ square, first cut it to octagonal shape on the band saw. Locate the center of the stock. Fig. 37-11. Mark the center with a prick punch or scratch awl. If the wood is hard, drill a small hole at the center and cut shallow saw kerfs across the corners. Place a spur center in position and strike it with a mallet to seat it firmly. It is a good idea to mark the end of the work so that, if you take it out of the lathe, it can be put back in the same position.

Place the work between centers and turn the tailstock handle until the cup center seats firmly on the wood. Release the pressure slightly and apply a little oil or graphite. Fig. 37-12. Adjust the tool rest to clear the stock by about 1/8″, with the top of the tool rest about 1/8″ above center.

The speed of the lathe should be adjusted in terms of the diameter, using faster speeds for smaller diameters. Fig. 37-13. Always start turning at low speed until the wood becomes a cylinder. Plant your feet firmly in front of the lathe and stand erect.

There are two methods of holding the tool. One is to place the thumb over the tool and the fingers under it, using the forefinger as a guide against the rest. Fig. 37-14. The second is to place the hand over the tool, with the wrist bent and against the tool rest. Fig. 37-15. To cut the cylinder to size, begin about one third of the way in from the tailstock and twist the gouge to the right so that a shearing cut can be taken. Cut towards the tailstock. Fig. 37-16. After each cut, begin about 2″ closer to the live center.

37-11. Draw lines across the corners to locate the center of square stock. To locate the center of an irregularly shaped piece, use a hermaphrodite caliper adjusted to slightly less than half the thickness. Then mark from each of four sides until the center can be located.

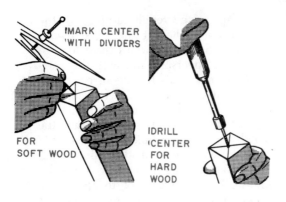

MARK CENTER WITH DIVIDERS

FOR SOFT WOOD

DRILL CENTER FOR HARD WOOD

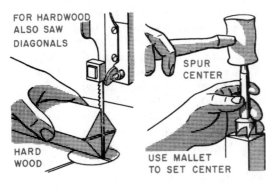

FOR HARDWOOD ALSO SAW DIAGONALS

HARD WOOD

SPUR CENTER

USE MALLET TO SET CENTER

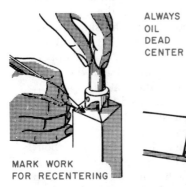

ALWAYS OIL DEAD CENTER

MARK WORK FOR RECENTERING

37-12. Preparing the stock for spindle turning.

37-14. The first method of holding a gouge: the thumb is placed over the tool and the fingers under it. Note that the forefinger is used as a guide against the rest.

37-15. The second method of holding a gouge: the hand is placed over the gouge with the wrist bent and against the tool rest. This is not as comfortable as the first method.

37-13. Speeds for wood turning.

DIA. OF STOCK	ROUGHING TO SIZE	GENERAL CUTTING	FINISHING
Under 2 In. Diameter	900 to 1300 R.P.M.	2400 to 2800	3000 to 4000
2 In. to 4 In. Diameter	600 to 1000 R.P.M.	1800 to 2400	2400 to 3000
4 In. to 6 In. Diameter	600 to 800 R.P.M.	1200 to 1800	1800 to 2400
6 In. to 8 In. Diameter	400 to 600 R.P.M.	800 to 1200	1200 to 1800
8 In. to 10 In. Diameter	300 to 400 R.P.M.	600 to 800	900 to 1200
Over 10 In. Diameter	200 to 300 R.P.M.	300 to 600	600 to 900

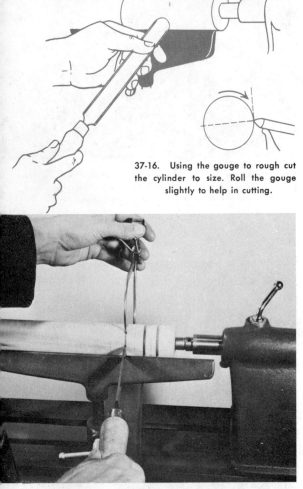

37-16. Using the gouge to rough cut the cylinder to size. Roll the gouge slightly to help in cutting.

37-17. Making sizing cuts with a parting tool. Hold the tool in one hand and the caliper in the other. When all of the grooves are cut away along the cylinder, you know the piece will have the same diameter throughout. Short sleeves are safer.

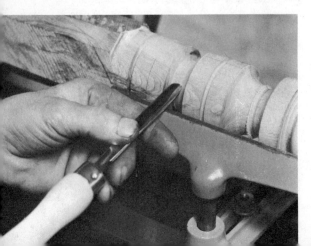

To complete the rough turning, tip the cutting tool to the left and work toward the live center. Now adjust the caliper to about 1/8″ oversize and, with the parting tool, make cuts to the correct diameter about every inch or two. The parting tool is held with the narrow edge against the rest and is forced into the wood; at the same time the diameter is checked with the outside caliper. Fig. 37-17. When using the caliper on revolving stock, be careful not to apply any pressure as this may cause the caliper to spring over the stock, resulting in an accident. Now, continue to rough turn to size with the gouge. The cylinder can also be turned to size by using the gouge as a scraping tool. With this method the point of the gouge is held at right angles to the work, with the tool in a level position. Force the point into the wood and then move it slowly from side to side. Fig. 37-18. It is important to remove the tool occasionally so the point will not overheat and burn.

Finish turning on a cylinder is done with a skew. Use either the cutting or scraping method. Place the skew on its side with a cutting edge slightly above and beyond the cylinder. (The uppermost point is called the *toe* and the lower point the *heel*.) Start at a point 2″ or 3″ from the end. Hold the side of the tool firmly against the tool rest. Slowly draw the skew back until the cutting edge is over the cylinder at a point about halfway between the heel and toe. Be careful not to catch the toe of the tool in the revolving cylinder. Tip the skew slightly until the cutting edge can be forced into the wood. Fig. 37-19. Then push the tool along toward the tailstock, taking a shearing cut. Fig. 37-20. Reverse the direction and cut toward the headstock.

37-18. Hold the gouge straight for scraping.

37-19. Two methods of holding the skew for cutting a cylinder to size: (a) The overhand method provides firm support for heavy cuts. (b) The underhand method gives better control for light cuts.

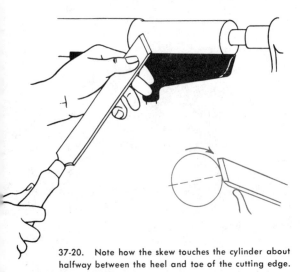

37-20. Note how the skew touches the cylinder about halfway between the heel and toe of the cutting edge.

37-21. Using the skew as a scraping tool. Hold the full cutting edge against the work and press lightly. Remove only a little material at a time.

A simpler way of doing this is to scrape it to size. You can use either a square-nose (flat) tool or a larger skew. Maintain a high speed. Hold the cutting edge parallel to the cylinder and force it into the work until the scraping begins. Then move it from side to side. Fig. 37-21. Always start the scraping some distance from the end to prevent the tool from catching and splitting the wood. Check with an outside caliper until the finished size is reached.

A block plane can also be used to smooth a cylinder to finish size. Adjust the plane to take a fine shaving. Hold it at an angle of about 45 degrees to the axis of the work. Use a tool rest to support the plane. Start at the center and move it to one end as you would any other cutting tool. Then reverse the tool and cut in other direction. Fig. 37-22.

37-22. Using a block plane to smooth a cylinder to finish size.

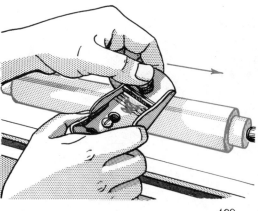

469

37-23. Marking stock to length with a pencil.

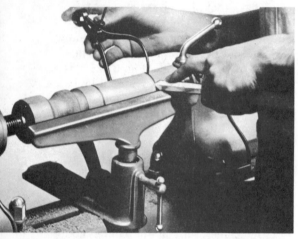

37-24(a). Using a parting tool to reduce the diameter of the end of the cylinder.

37-24(b). The tool is slowly pushed into the work, its point slightly above the center. As the tool advances into the work and the diameter is reduced, the handle should be raised slightly until the correct diameter is reached.

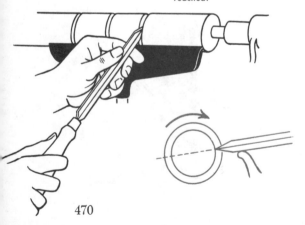

470

INCORRECT   CORRECT

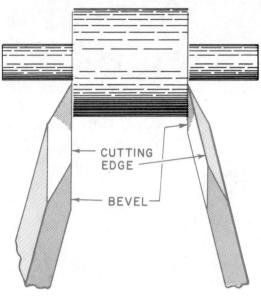

CUTTING EDGE

BEVEL

37-25. To cut to length, the toe of the skew is used to remove thin shavings from the side. Hold the skew so that its bottom edge is nearly parallel to the shoulder. Turn the cutting edge away at the top so that only the toe itself does the cutting. Start with the handle low, then raise it slowly to do the cutting.

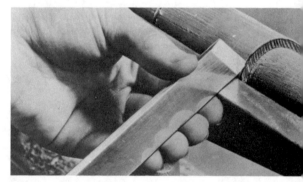

37-26(a). Using the toe of the skew to make the vertical cut.

37-26(b). Using the skew to make the horizontal cut for a shoulder. The heel of the skew must do most of the cutting.

37-27. Forming a shoulder by the scraping method. A skew or a flat-nose tool can be used to do the scraping.

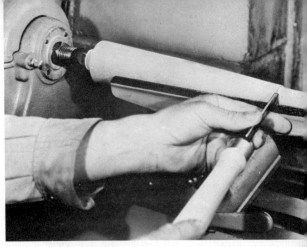

37-28. Using a parting tool to mark a diameter for taper turning.

37-29. Finishing a taper with the skew. Always cut from the large to the small diameter.

To square off the ends, first mark the proper length with a pencil. Fig. 37-23. The ends may be squared by first scraping with a parting tool and then cutting with a skew. Force a parting tool into the revolving cylinder about 1/8" beyond the measured length. Always make the groove slightly wider than the width of the tool so the cutting edge will not burn. As the tool is advanced into the wood, raise the handle slowly to keep producing the scraping action. Fig. 37-24. Reduce the stock at this point to a diameter of about 3/8".

Now locate the toe of the skew in line with the point at which the finish cut must be made. The ground edge of the skew must be parallel with the cut to be made. Tip the heel of the skew slightly to the right or left, away from the cut. Force the toe of the skew into the wood, holding it against the shoulder. Remove a shaving about 1/32" deep with each cut. Fig. 37-25. As the cut becomes deeper, provide clearance for the tool by turning the handle away from the cut, then making some taper cuts to form a half V.

Cutting a shoulder is similar to squaring off an end. Use a parting tool to cut a groove, reducing the diameter at this point to slightly more than the smaller diameter. Then, with a small gouge, remove most of the stock from the smaller diameter. Cut the vertical part of the shoulder with the toe of the skew. Fig. 37-26(a). Cut the horizontal part of the shoulder, using the heel of the skew in a manner similar to finish turning. Fig. 37-26(b). A shoulder can be formed or the end squared by the scraping method. Fig. 37-27.

Taper Cuts

Rough turn to the largest diameter. Then use a parting tool to mark the smallest and several intermediate diameters. Fig. 37-28. Rough cut the taper with a gouge by either cutting or scraping. Then finish turn the taper with a skew. Fig. 37-29.

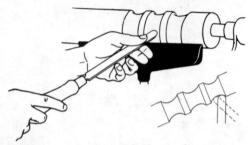

37-30. Cutting a cove with a round-nose chisel. The correct movement of the tool is shown at the lower right.

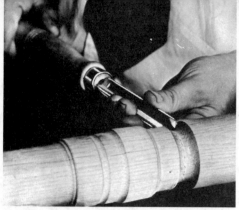

37-31. Finish the cove in two cuts, one for each side.

37-32. Procedure for finishing a cove cut. Hold the gouge with the handle high and the tool almost on edge. The blade should be held between the thumb and forefinger. Then roll the tool to complete the cut to the bottom.

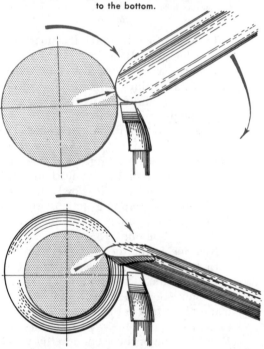

Cutting Coves

Mark the center and ends of each cove and adjust the caliper to the smallest diameter. To use the scraping method, force a round-nose tool into the center of the cove. Swing the tool from side to side, using the tool rest as a fulcrum point. Fig. 37-30. Continue to measure the center with a caliper until depth is reached.

Coves are scraped to rough shape with a small gouge. Hold the gouge in a vertical position and keep the handle high enough so the cutting edge is pointed at a line on center. Begin the cut near the center of the cove. Work toward the finished layout line. Fig. 37-31. In making the cut, roll the gouge to follow the correct shape. Fig. 37-32.

Cutting V's

To scrape a V, use a diamond- or spear-point tool held flat. Force it into the wood.

To cut a V, mark its edges and center. Hold a skew on edge with the heel down, then force it into the stock at the center of the V. Use a slight pump-handle action. Work from one side of the V, cutting with the heel of the skew. Continue to force the tool into the center of the cut and cut one side of the V to correct depth. Then cut the opposite side in a similar manner. Fig. 37-33.

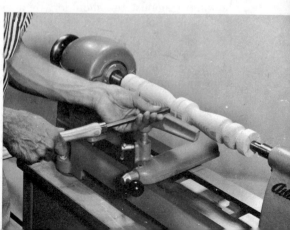

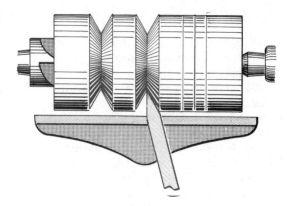

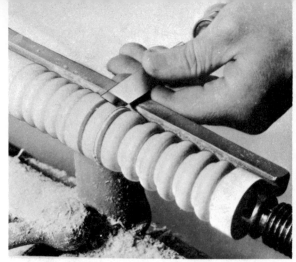

37-35. Cutting beads, using the heel to do most of the cutting.

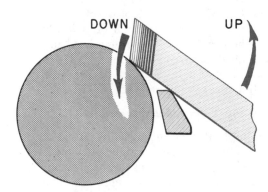

37-33. Cutting V's with a skew. The skew is rotated down into the stock, using the rest as a pivot. Cutting should be done by the heel.

37-34. Marking the ends of the beads with the toe of the skew. Make a deep vertical cut in preparation for cutting the beads.

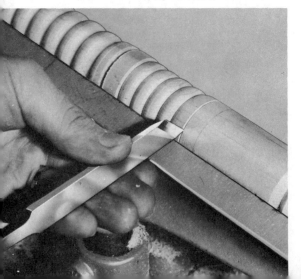

37-36. Correct steps in cutting beads separated by sizing cuts: (a) Use a parting tool to cut to depth between the beads. (b) Place the skew at right angles with the workpiece, flat against the surface and near the top of the bead. (c) The heel should start the cutting at the top of the bead. Then draw the skew back, slowly raising the handle and turning the blade. (d) As the cutting is done, roll the tool into the groove. The tool must turn 90 degrees in forming the bead.

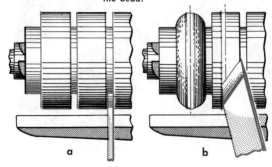

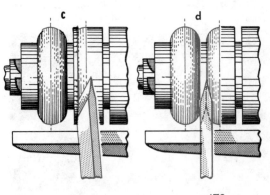

473

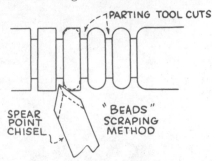

37-37. Shaping a bead by scraping. Push the spear-point tool straight into the groove and rotate it horizontally to form the bead. The tool must be pulled back slightly as it is rotated so that the point will not cut into the next bead.

Bead Cuts

Bead cuts are rather difficult and will require some practice. Mark the position of the beads with a line indicating the ends and center of each one. Begin the cut as you would for a V, using the toe of the skew to start it. Fig. 37-34. Then hold the skew on its side, with the heel doing most of the cutting. Start quite high on the cylinder, in the center of the bead, and turn the tool in the same arc as the bead. At the same time draw it backward and move it to a vertical position. Fig. 37-35. If the tool is not turned as the cut is made, the heel will dig into the next bead. If separated by sizing cuts, beads are easier to form. Fig. 37-36. They can also be formed by scraping with a spear-point tool. Fig. 37-37.

Turning Complicated Designs

Complicated designs usually consist of a combination of straight turnings, tapers, V's, beads, coves, and long concave or convex surfaces. Fig. 37-38. The first step is to draw a full-size pattern of the part that can be used for taking off measurements. To get a piece of material large enough for the parts you will sometimes have to glue up pieces to form a laminated structure. When this is necessary, make sure the pieces match and that you have a good glue joint. Then mount the stock in the lathe and

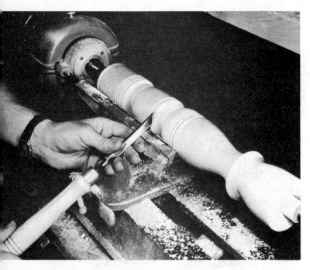

37-38. Turning a complicated leg for a table.

37-39. Carefully measure all diameters as the turning proceeds.

37-40(a). Smoothing the surface of a cylinder with abrasive paper.

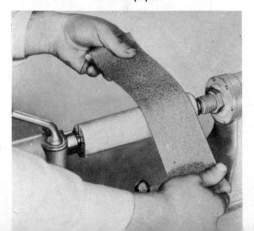

rough turn to its maximum size. Use a pencil or pattern to mark important locations on the cylinder. With a parting tool turn the important diameters at various positions along the cylinder. Use the gouge, skew, and other tools to turn the various parts of the design. Measure the diameters frequently with a caliper. Fig. 37-39.

If more than one complicated design is needed, it is best to follow some method of duplicating the parts accurately as described in the next paragraph. When the design is completed, smooth the surface by sanding. Turnings should be sanded with the machine operating at one of the slower speeds, but not the slowest. For flat cylinders use a sheet of abrasive paper. Fig. 37-40(a). For complicated designs use narrow strips of abrasive paper from grades 2/0 to 4/0, depending on the roughness of the surface. Fig. 37-40(b).

Turning Duplicate Parts

Turning identical pieces requires great care and accuracy. There are several ways to make the job simpler. One is to make a thin cardboard or wood pattern, exact and full-size, representing a half section of the turning in reverse. This pattern or templet can then be held against the turning from time to time to check the design.

Another method is to use a templet and diameter board. This method is effective when many turnings of the same design are needed. Turn one piece to the exact shape, then mount it on a board. Place the board behind the lathe on hinges so it can be moved next to the turnings for comparison. Fig. 37-41. Then cut a diameter board. This is a thin board with semi-circular cuts along the edge. These cuts correspond to important diameters along the turning and can be held against the turning instead of using a caliper. Fig. 37-42.

37-40(b). Using a thin strip of abrasive paper to sand a complicated design.

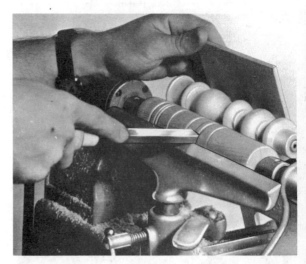

37-41. Checking the location of major diameters with the original turning. Wrist watches should not be worn in a woodshop.

37-42. Using a diameter board to check the diameter at important locations.

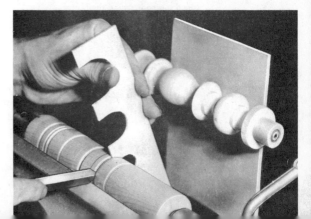

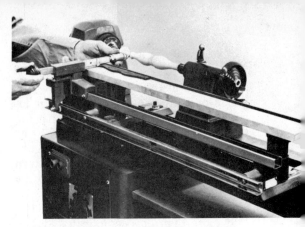

37-44(b). The wood-turning duplicator in operation.

37-43(a). This attachment for hand wood lathes makes wood turning easy. Note the pattern guide (a thin piece of steel) that rides along the edge of the pattern to duplicate the design. Only one cutting tool is needed.

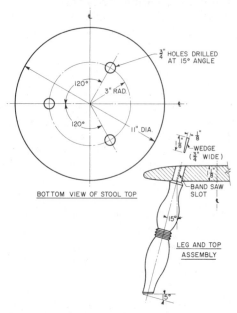

BOTTOM VIEW OF STOOL TOP

¾" HOLES DRILLED AT 15° ANGLE

120°

3" RAD.

120°

11" DIA.

WEDGE (¾" WIDE)

BAND SAW SLOT

LEG AND TOP ASSEMBLY

15°

5°

37-43(b). This is another style of lathe duplicator. Here a turned piece is used as a pattern, along with a metal lathe tool bit and holder.

37-45(a). Steps in using a wood-turning duplicator. The leg of this stool is the part to be turned. Remaining pictures in this series show the operation.

37-45(b).

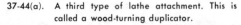

37-44(a). A third type of lathe attachment. This is called a wood-turning duplicator.

If you have tried to turn a complicated design on the lathe, you know that it takes great patience and skill to turn four identical parts—for example, a set of legs for a table. However, with a lathe duplicator or wood-turning duplicator, it is easy to form any number of identical parts automatically. There are several models of duplicators and all are made to fit any model of lathe. Fig. 37-43(a). With this attachment, the tool holder and tool rest are removed and the duplicator fitted between the headstock and tailstock. Fig. 37-43(b). The carriage that holds the cutter moves in two directions: back and forth, and in and out. A pattern guide or templet attached to the carriage rides along the pattern (or a turned piece) and guides the cutting edge to assure duplicating accuracy. The pattern templet or a turned piece is clamped to a holder. Regular turning tools are not used. Instead, use a cutter such as a pointed metal lathe bit that is thin enough to reproduce an intricate design. Another type of wood-turning duplicator is shown in Fig. 37-44.

Wood-turning Duplicator

The following instructions explain the setup and operating procedure for using a wood-turning duplicator. The steps shown are for turning the legs of a small three-legged stool. Fig. 37-45(a).

1. Select the wood (a hardwood such as maple is best). Apply three coats of resin sealer. Rub after each coat with steel wool, then wax.

2. There are several ways of producing the templet. One is to turn one leg to the correct shape. Then a thin section of the very center of the turning is cut on the band saw. Another method is to make a full-size drawing of the templet on heavy paper. Then paste the drawing

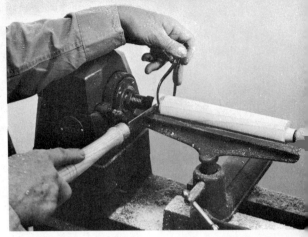

37-45(c).

on hardboard and cut it out on the jig saw. Fig. 37-45(b). A third method is to sandwich a piece of 1/8" hardboard between two pieces of wood. The pieces should be 3/4" longer than the part to be made, so the sandwich can be held together at the ends with wood screws. Then turn the piece freehand. Disassemble the sandwich, and the templet is ready. Be sure the contours have smooth, unbroken lines. Drill two small holes in the templet to attach it to the duplicator.

3. Prepare the three pieces for the legs. The drive center should be driven into the workpiece with a soft hammer or a block of wood. *Never* pound the drive center with a steel hammer. On hard woods, diagonal saw cuts should be made to receive the live center.

4. Turn each piece round to the largest diameter. On only one of the pieces turn a shoulder on each end, estimating the diameter very accurately with the parting tool and caliper as shown in Fig. 37-45(c). The diameter should be the same at each end of the templet. This is very important because you will set the templet from these diameters.

5. Place the two clamps (A) on the lathe bed as shown in Fig. 37-45(d).

6. Place the duplicator on the lathe bed, attaching it to the two clamps, as

477

37-45(d).

A

A

37-45(h).

A

B C D

37-45(e).

37-45(f).

A

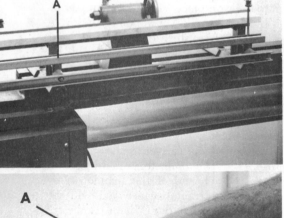

A

37-45(g).

shown in Fig. 37-45(e). When using the duplicator on 11″ lathes, the four 1″ riser blocks located between the horizontal and vertical brackets are removed.

7. Attach the guide rail (A), Fig. 37-45(f), to the duplicator. The long end of the guide rail should be toward the headstock end as shown.

8. Slide the cutting head (A), Fig. 37-45(g), on the rails as shown.

9. With the duplicator assembled on the lathe bed in about the right position, bring the tool bit (A), Fig. 37-45(h), near the point of one of the centers. The tool bit should be about 1/16″ above the point of the center. To adjust the tool bit higher or lower, loosen nut (B) and the set screw (D), and revolve eccentric (C) until the tool bit is about 1/16″ above center. The tool bit can be moved in or out or turned to the correct position. Tighten set screw (D) and nut (B).

10. Place the turning (with the shoulders) between centers and adjust the duplicator by moving it in or out so the tool holder overhangs just the minimum amount when the tool bit touches the turning at the largest diameter. Fig. 37-45(i). Adjust the duplicator parallel to the lathe bed, and tighten the clamp nuts.

11. Bring the tool bit up to one end of the turning. Fig. 37-45(j). At the same time place the templet (A) so that the end of the templet touches the corre-

478

37-45(k).

sponding end of the stylus (B) when the tool bit touches the locating point on the workpiece. Hold the templet in place with a small C clamp.

12. Bring the tool bit up to the opposite end and move the templet, if necessary, so it touches the stylus when the tool bit touches the locating point on the workpiece. Fig. 37-45(k).

13. Double check the position of the templet. When it is lined up properly, fasten it in place with two wood screws.

14. With the tool bit clear of the turning, turn on the lathe. Work the tool holder freehand, Fig. 37-45(l), or use the "fine feed" by turning the knurled feed knob (A).

15. Do not attempt to take too big a cut but feed the cutting tool gently until you get the feel of the work. The cutting is a scraping action. When turning softer woods, a very light cut should be taken to obtain best possible results.

16. If the turning has very sharp shoulders or grooves, you will not be able to duplicate them exactly because the end of the cutting tool is ground to a small radius. Merely place the turning between centers as usual and, with the spearpoint tool or small skew, clean up the corners as shown in Fig. 37-45(m).

17. Make the stool top and drill the three holes by following the dimensions shown in Fig. 37-45(a). Assemble the legs in the stool top.

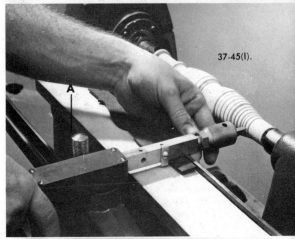

37-45(l).

37-45(m).

479

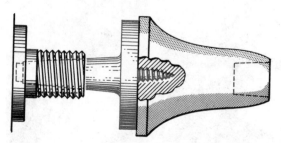

37-49. Using a screw center for holding small turnings.

FACEPLATE TURNING

Bowls, trays, and many other small circular objects are turned on a faceplate. Fig. 37-46. To do the turning, the wood is fastened to a faceplate and shaped by scraping. Faceplates commonly used are the *screw center*, for small objects—no larger than 4″ in diameter—and the *standard faceplate*, that has screw holes for fastening the wood in place. Fig. 37-47. For turning extremely small decorative pieces, it may be necessary to make a special holding chuck. Fig. 37-48. If a screw center is used, only a single hole is drilled in the wood to mount the stock. Fig. 37-49.

The first step in faceplate turning is to determine the size and kind of material needed. To make a larger bowl or tray it is often necessary to glue up the stock. For a square object, carefully mount the wood on the faceplate. Fig. 37-50. If the object is to be circular, cut the stock on a band saw to a disc shape, about 1/4″ larger than the finished diameter and about 1/8″ thick. It may be desirable to

37-46. Bowls and trays are typical of the accessories turned on a faceplate.

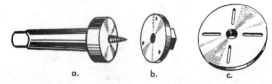

37-47. Common holding devices for faceplate turning: (a) Screw center. (b) Small 3″ diameter faceplate with three screw holes. (c) Larger 6″ diameter faceplate with special thread that fits both the right- and lefthand threaded spindles to allow it to be used on either end of the headstock spindle.

37-48. Using a wood chuck on a screw center to hold a small object for turning.

37-50. Sometimes it is necessary to turn the center of a square object such as this small tray.

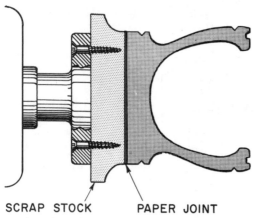

SCRAP STOCK   **PAPER JOINT**

37-51(a). Scrap stock is glued to the turning with a piece of paper between for easy separation.

37-52. Adjust the tool rest so that it clears the work by about 1/8".

37-51(b). Notice that the lighter piece of scrap stock is made small enough so that both the front and sides of the tray can be turned easily.

37-51(c). A very small turning can also be mounted on a piece of scrap stock. The faceplate should be of a smaller size.

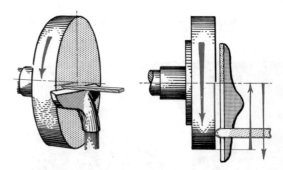

37-53. Keep the cutting tool on the side nearest you. Never try to cut across the entire diameter.

37-54(a). Convex curves can be shaped by scraping with a flat-nose or small skew. Sharp corners are formed with a spearpoint tool or skew.

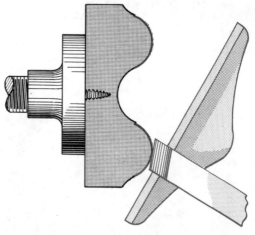

481

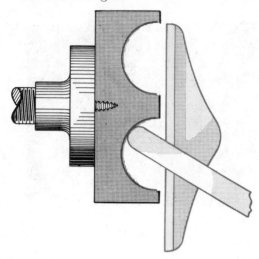

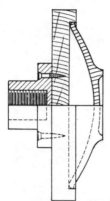

37-56. This is a typical recessed wood chuck.

37-54(b). Concave curves are shaped with a round-nose tool.

37-57(a). Using a recessed wood chuck to complete the turning on the front of a shallow tray.

37-57(b). Sometimes it is necessary to do some final shaping on the face surface. If the chuck is deep enough, and if the outside diameter is not changed, either side will fit into the recessed chuck for turning.

37-55(a). Shaping the inside of a bowl with a round-nose tool.

37-55(b). Shaping the edge of a base using a spear-point tool.

treat the wood to prevent splits, checks, or warping. See Unit 38.

If screw holes on the back of the turning are objectionable, cut a piece of scrap stock at least 1″ thick and about the same size as the base of the bowl. Glue the two pieces together with a piece of wrapping paper between so they will separate easily afterwards. Fig. 37-51. Then locate the center of the scrap stock and place the faceplate over it. Mark the hole locations and fasten the faceplate to it with screws about 3/4″ long. They should be just long enough to go through the scrap stock without marring the bottom of the bowl stock.

Remove the live center and fasten the work to the spindle. For extremely large bowls and trays, the faceplate must be attached to the outside end of the spindle. This may require a special stand to hold the tool rest. Another method is to move a second lathe near the outside of the first lathe so that the rest can be used on the end of the bed of the second lathe as the turning is done on the first one. At this point it is often good to make a thin templet of the interior and exterior shapes to use as a guide.

Adjust the tool rest across the edge of the stock and set the lathe to a slow speed. Fig. 37-52. Use a flat round-nose or spear-point tool to true and dress the outside of the disk. Then adjust the tool rest across the face of the disk, and trim the face. Start at the center and take scraping cuts toward the outside. Never attempt to cut across the entire diameter since, once you pass the center, the tool will move up and away from the tool holder. Fig. 37-53.

Now you are ready to shape the inside of the bowl. Use various turning tools to remove as much waste material as necessary. Fig. 37-54. Remove stock to within 1/8″ of the finished size. Use the templet to check the progress of the interior design. On some bowls and trays it is also possible to turn the outside or edge

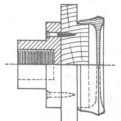

37-58. A spindle chuck for holding work.

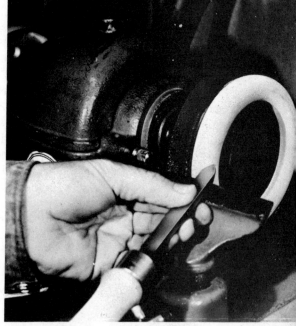

37-59. Turning a ring held on a spindle chuck. The spindle chuck is dark wood, the ring is light.

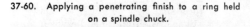

37-60. Applying a penetrating finish to a ring held on a spindle chuck.

483

to finished shape with the same setup. Fig. 37-55.

Some faceplate jobs require that both sides of the object be turned. To do this, first turn the front or top and edge of the bowl or tray. When the front is completed, do all the sanding necessary. Then apply mineral oil or other finish. Separate the scrap stock from the finished piece by driving a sharp chisel between them. Then make a holding chuck. The two common kinds are the recessed and the spindle. The *recessed* chuck is made with a depression in it to hold the face or back of a bowl or tray. Fig. 37-56. The recess cut in the scrap stock should be just large enough in diameter so that the object will go in with a press fit. Fig. 37-57. If the recess is slightly oversize, a piece of paper can be placed between the bowl and the chuck to hold it secure.

On a *spindle* chuck the object to be turned fits over the chuck as, for example, a ring design. Figs. 37-58 and 37-59.

FINISHING

There are several ways of applying a finish to a turning. A simple method is to apply paste wax to a cloth and hold it on the revolving stock so that it is completely covered. Then, in about ten minutes, run the lathe at a slow speed and polish the surface with a dry cloth. A second coat of wax can be applied as needed. To apply a French oil finish, fold a piece of fine cotton or linen cloth into a pad. Then apply about one teaspoon of white shellac to the pad and add several drops of boiled linseed oil. Hold the pad over the work, moving it from one side to the other. Apply even pressure. Add shellac and oil as needed to keep the pad moist. Apply several coats until you get a mirror like finish.

Another method is to apply several coats of penetrating finish with a cloth. Fig. 37-60. Sometimes mineral oil is used for bowls that are to hold food. Vegetable oils are not a good choice since they may become rancid.

SECTION III

QUESTIONS AND DISCUSSION TOPICS

1. Name several kinds of common rules.
2. What are four uses for the combination square?
3. Why are flexible tapes useful measuring tools?
4. What is the difference between a crosscut saw and a ripsaw? Describe their teeth.
5. Name the hand saws that are used for cutting irregular curves.
6. What is the difference between a back saw and a dovetail saw?
7. Why are planes made in different lengths?
8. Arrange the following planes in order of length: (a) fore, (b) jack, (c) jointer, (d) smooth.
9. What kind of plane is used to clean out the bottoms of grooves and dadoes?
10. How are chisels and gouges similar? How are they different?
11. When would you use a drawknife and when a spokeshave?
12. Name three special-purpose planes.
13. How are chisels and gouges related to carving tools?
14. How does a bit differ from a drill?
15. Name the tool used for operating bits. For operating drills.
16. Describe several uses for the Foerstner bit and the two devices that are used to limit the depth of a hole.
17. Why are metalworking tools needed in a wood shop?
18. Name four kinds of wrenches that are

of specific size to fit certain bolts or nuts.

19. Should a pipe wrench be used on bolts and nuts? Explain.
20. Name several common kinds of pliers.
21. Name two types of tool grinders.
22. Tell how to sharpen a plane-iron blade.
23. What is the correct angle for grinding a parting tool?
24. What is the purpose of jointing the teeth of a hand saw?
25. Why must saw teeth be set?
26. What is the difference between grinding and jointing planer knives?
27. What is the difference between single and double planers?
28. Will a planer correct or straighten warped stock? Explain.
29. Tell how to square up legs on a planer.
30. Tell why the circular or variety saw is so important in cabinetmaking.
31. List four maintenance checks that should be made for a circular saw.
32. List six safety suggestions that should be followed when using a circular saw.
33. Describe four accessories that are available for the circular saw.
34. Name several common types of circular saw blades.
35. Describe four methods of cutting stock to identical length.
36. Is cutting a flat miter a crosscutting or a ripping operation? Explain.
37. What is the major hazard in ripping stock?
38. Describe three accessories for ripping that contribute to safety.
39. When should a push stick be used in ripping stock?
40. Describe two methods of cutting a taper.
41. Name three kinds of dado heads.
42. Describe the way a dado joint is cut on the circular saw.
43. Can both the mortise and the tenon be cut on the circular saw? Explain.
44. What is a finger or box joint? How does it compare with the dovetail joint?
45. What is a molding head and what is it used for?
46. How can molding be done on circular work?
47. How does the radial-arm saw differ from the circular saw?
48. In using a radial-arm saw, what operation requires that the stock be moved into the revolving saw blade?
49. Describe the way mitering is done on the radial-arm saw.
50. Does the work or the saw move for crosscutting operations? Explain.
51. How does horizontal cutting differ from vertical cutting on the radial-arm saw?
52. Explain how to make a lap joint on the radial-arm saw.
53. Describe several of the special cutting operations that can be done on the radial-arm saw.
54. What is the primary purpose of a band saw?
55. Explain how to replace a band-saw blade.
56. Can the band saw be used for straight cutting? Explain.
57. Describe how to use a jig for circle cutting on the band saw.
58. Is the jig saw an important production machine? Explain.
59. Describe three kinds of portable saws.
60. When is an electric plane a valuable tool for the cabinetmaker?
61. How is the size of a jointer indicated?
62. Is the outfeed table of all jointers adjustable? Explain.
63. Describe how to square up stock on a jointer.
64. Explain how to cut a long taper on a jointer.
65. Why is a portable router a valuable machine?
66. Explain the five methods of controlling depth of cut with a router.
67. Describe how to cut a dovetail joint with a router and attachment.
68. Explain how to use the drill press for a router.
69. Describe how the radial-arm saw can be used as a router.
70. Why is the shaper a dangerous machine?
71. Name three methods of controlling the depth of cut when shaping.
72. What is the safest kind of cutter to use on a shaper?

73. Explain how to shape with a pattern.
74. Can the radial-arm saw be used as a shaper? Explain.
75. What is the difference between drilling and boring?
76. Can boring be done on a drill press?
77. List and explain the uses of several kinds of boring tools.
78. Describe the way a deep hole is drilled on a drill press.
79. Explain how to drill or bore a hole at an angle.
80. Tell how to use a horizontal-spindle boring machine.
81. Tell how the radial-arm saw can be used as a boring tool.
82. What is the purpose of a mortiser?
83. Is the tenoner available in most smaller cabinet shops? Explain.
84. When a tenoner is not available, what machine can be used to cut tenons?
85. Is the mortise-and-tenon joint as important as it was 25 years ago? Explain.
86. Is sandpaper used for sanding operations? Explain.
87. Describe the common man-made abrasives.
88. Name some common stationary sanding machines.
89. Describe three kinds of portable sanders.
90. Can sanding be done on the following machines: radial-arm saw, drill press, band saw, jig saw? Explain.

91. Is the hand wood lathe a valuable production machine? Explain.
92. Describe the two methods of turning.
93. What is the difference between cutting and scraping in wood turning?
94. Describe the use of a duplicator attachment for the wood lathe.
95. What kind of turning is done by using a faceplate?

PROBLEMS AND ACTIVITIES

1. Trace the history of one hand tool from earliest times to its present design.
2. Trace the history and development of a stationary power tool.
3. Develop a model of the cutting head of a planer or surfacer.
4. Design and make a tool holder for a hand tool, portable power tool, or an accessory for a stationary power tool.
5. Compare the relative safety of the radial-arm saw and the circular saw.
6. Write a complete set of specifications for ordering a power tool for your own shop.
7. Compare the advantages and disadvantages of blades and knives tipped with high-speed steel or carbide.
8. Trace the history of abrasives.
9. Compare the relative values of the planer and surfacer in contrast to the high-speed sander for surfacing rough edges to finish thickness.

Section IV
Construction

Doors, drawers, shelves, frames, and cases, all assembled with nails, screws, adhesives, and hardware—these are some basic ingredients of cabinetmaking. When you've learned about these essentials, you can apply that knowledge to any building job or wood product.

Basic Construction Problems

38-1. The skilled woodworker understands tools and materials.

It is important to understand the construction problems involved in using different kinds of lumber and processed materials. The wood technician must thoroughly understand the sometimes complex relationships between materials and machines. He must also cope with the problems and difficulties that result when various species of wood are machined under different conditions. Fig. 38-1.

KINDS OF CONSTRUCTION

The three common ways to make a large surface for cabinets or furniture are (1) by gluing up solid stock, (2) by using plywood or other large sheet material, and (3) by building a frame and

38-2(a). Here you see the three basic methods of large surface construction and how they react to moisture content changes resulting in warpage, expansion, and contraction.

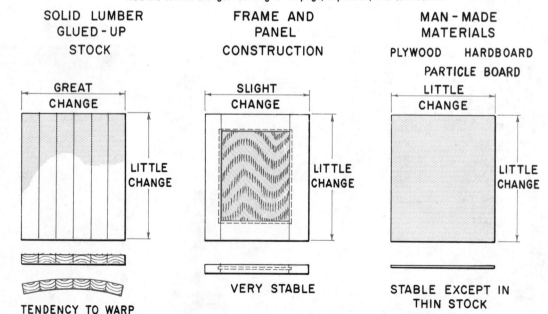

SOLID LUMBER GLUED-UP STOCK	FRAME AND PANEL CONSTRUCTION	MAN-MADE MATERIALS PLYWOOD HARDBOARD PARTICLE BOARD
GREAT CHANGE / LITTLE CHANGE	SLIGHT CHANGE / LITTLE CHANGE	LITTLE CHANGE / LITTLE CHANGE
TENDENCY TO WARP	VERY STABLE	STABLE EXCEPT IN THIN STOCK

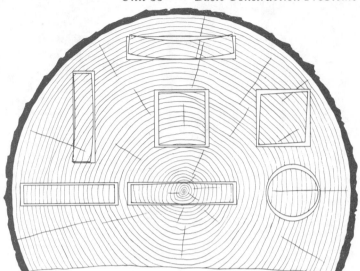

38-2(b). This shows the way a board will change in shape, depending on where it comes from in the log. Because distortion is greatest in wide pieces of solid wood, it is recommended that plywood or particle board be used for wide surfaces.

panel. Fig. 38-2. The furniture industry uses solid lumber for structural parts, and lumber-core plywood or frame and panel for large surfaces. Fig. 38-3(a). In building construction, cabinets and built-ins are usually made of veneer-core plywood or particle board, with some use of solid stock for trim. Fig. 38-3(b). Frequently, school and small cabinet shops use only solid lumber. Fig. 38-3(c).

If solid, glued-up stock is used for larger surfaces, problems of warpage and expansion-contraction must be solved. In gluing up a large surface of solid stock, the standard procedure is to rip the material into narrower widths of 4″ to 6″ and then to glue them up with the growth rings running in opposite directions. This reduces warping but will not completely eliminate the problem. Grooving or slotting the underside of a table top to relieve tension also helps somewhat.

38-3(a). This cherry end table makes use of solid lumber for the legs and other structural parts while the top and shelves are lumber-core plywood. Why are both kinds of materials used?

38-3(b). This planter table is constructed entirely of veneer-core plywood. All the parts can be cut from one 4′ x 8′ sheet.

38-3(c). This Contemporary dining-room table and matching chairs are of solid birch construction, including the table top. Check the methods of attaching table tops described in Unit 50 and indicate which ones you could use for this kind of construction.

38-5. The top of this conference table is made of lumber-core plywood. Veneer gives it the appearance of solid glued-up stock with banded ends.

The second problem, expansion and contraction due to change in humidity, is even more difficult. A wide glued-up surface is constantly changing in size as the moisture content in the air varies. As a matter of fact, a solid, glued-up table top may vary as much as 3/4″ in width. Such a table top should be fastened to the base so that this movement will not cause the wood to buckle or crack.

Sometimes a beginner will attempt to glue a band of solid stock to the end of a solid, glued-up table top. This is extremely poor practice since wood changes in size much more across the grain (width) than with the grain (length). Much change in humidity is likely to break the glue joint between the band and the end grain. Fig. 38-4.

You may wonder why lumber-core plywood does not cause the same kind of difficulties as solid lumber when it is

38-4. Note what will happen if bands of solid stock are glued to the ends of a large glued-up solid stock surface.

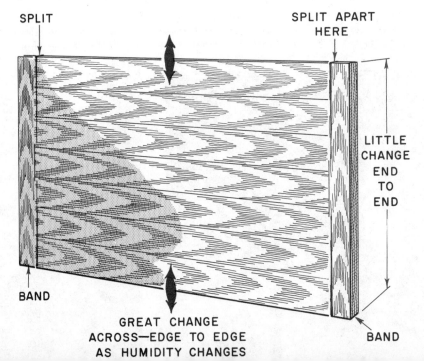

SPLIT

SPLIT APART HERE

LITTLE CHANGE END TO END

BAND

GREAT CHANGE ACROSS—EDGE TO EDGE AS HUMIDITY CHANGES

BAND

490

38-6(a). Stripping the paper off the back of band veneer that has the adhesive already on it.

used for a large surface. While lumber-core plywood has a core of solid strips of lumber glued edge to edge, the faces are covered both with crossbands and a face and back veneer. Also, the edges are usually banded. As a result, there is little chance for moisture to be absorbed by the core itself. Fig. 38-5.

Frame-and-panel construction is commonly used because of its dimensional stability. If plywood is used as the panel center, there is little problem from either warpage or expansion and contraction. However, if solid wood covers the center of the frame, the groove which holds the panel must be deep enough to allow for change in size. Also, a great deal of stain must be put on the edges of the frame, so that when the panel does contract, white wood will not show.

In any solid wood construction, the wood must be free to move without breaking a joint. For example, if the sides of a chest are made of glued-up stock, then the frames should be a little narrower than usual and *should not* be glued into the dadoes. Rather, they should be assembled with screws so that there will be some freedom of movement.

Edge Banding of Plywood And Particle Board

A major drawback of plywood, particle board, and other man-made materials is that the edges are unattractive. Therefore, in all better-quality construction, some type of edge band must be attached to all exposed edges. There are many ways of treating the edges. Most common in simple casework and on-the-job construction is covering the edges with a thin veneer or plastic laminate. For most table and counter tops, the edge is built up in thickness by adding a strip of material directly under the top. Then the veneer or plastic laminate is applied. Veneer in various wood species to match the table or counter top is

38-6(b). Gluing thin veneer to the edge of plywood with contact cement. Allow the cement to dry at least 15 minutes before doing step 4.

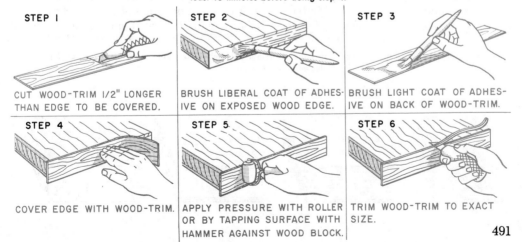

STEP 1	STEP 2	STEP 3
CUT WOOD-TRIM 1/2" LONGER THAN EDGE TO BE COVERED.	BRUSH LIBERAL COAT OF ADHESIVE ON EXPOSED WOOD EDGE.	BRUSH LIGHT COAT OF ADHESIVE ON BACK OF WOOD-TRIM.

STEP 4	STEP 5	STEP 6
COVER EDGE WITH WOOD-TRIM.	APPLY PRESSURE WITH ROLLER OR BY TAPPING SURFACE WITH HAMMER AGAINST WOOD BLOCK.	TRIM WOOD-TRIM TO EXACT SIZE.

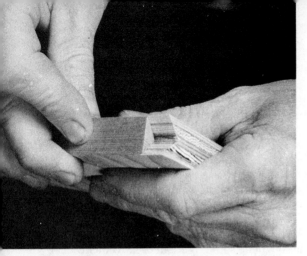

38-7(a). Using a V-shaped piece of solid material to cover the edge of plywood.

available in edge-banding rolls. If this material has an adhesive on it, simply peel off the backing paper and apply to the edges. Fig. 38-6(a). Otherwise use contact cement. Fig. 38-6(b).

Another common method of edge banding both plywood and particle board is to cut a V groove in the edge of the top, then fit a V-shaped piece of solid stock into it. Fig. 38-7(a).

In the best-quality construction, a band of solid wood is attached to the man-made material, using a tongue-and-groove joint. The band must be of the same wood as the exterior veneer of the plywood, or the exterior veneer must cover the band to the outside edges. Fig. 38-7(b). Other methods of banding the edges are shown in Unit 50. Only lower-quality cabinetwork features painted edges. When paint or an opaque finish

is applied, the holes must be filled and the edges machine sanded.

Solid or Laminated Leg-and-Post Construction

Legs, posts and many other structural parts are usually made of either one-piece solid lumber or laminated materials. The advantage of one-piece material is that there is no chance for a glued joint to show or for breakage at the glue line. Solid lumber also tends to eliminate the wide variations in color from one strip of wood to another, which is often a problem with laminated material. However, laminating does make better use of the material available and is essential in producing many curved parts. See Unit 41.

Humidity Control

It is extremely important to make sure that kiln-dried lumber is chosen for all cabinetmaking. This lumber should always have less than 10 per cent moisture content, preferably in the 7 to 8 per cent range. It is best if the lumber is slightly overdried to about 5 or 6 per cent, then stored where the temperature and humidity are correct to bring it up to 7 or 8 per cent.

Even if the lumber has been properly kiln-dried, there can still be moisture problems. A piece of wood will take on or give off moisture until it reaches a balance with the surrounding air. The

38-7(b). Two other common methods of edge banding. Remember to apply pressure when gluing this edge band in place.

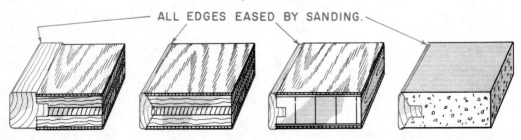

ALL EDGES EASED BY SANDING.

amount of moisture in a piece of wood when it reaches a balance with the air at a certain temperature and humidity is called the *equilibrium moisture content,* or EMC. This is the moisture content at which the wood neither gains nor loses moisture from the surrounding air. However, as the humidity changes, the moisture content of the wood will change.

Air can hold only a certain amount of moisture, and this amount varies as the temperature changes. *Relative humidity* expresses the percentage of this maximum which is actually being held by the air. For example, at 75 degrees Fahrenheit, air can hold five times as much moisture as it can at 32 degrees. Consider a sample of air at 32 degrees and 100 per cent relative humidity. If the sample is heated to 75 degrees, and the moisture content does not change, the relative humidity will drop to 20 per cent, that is, one-fifth of 100.

The woodworker constantly faces this humidity problem. In cold weather, the outside air can hold little moisture. As the air enters the shop and is heated, its relative humidity becomes only a fraction of what it was outside. This is why wood in a home or shop tends to dry out excessively in the winter months; wood becomes checked or warped and very difficult to machine. Therefore it is desirable to increase the moisture in the air during the winter months and to reduce it in the summer. In the winter, the relative humidity inside many large furniture manufacturing plants is raised and held at the correct point by equipment. Fig. 38-8. The school or small cabinet shop can apply some limited moisture-control methods, such as a pan of

38-8. This humidity control apparatus is found in most furniture factories, especially in the machining and white-wood storage areas.

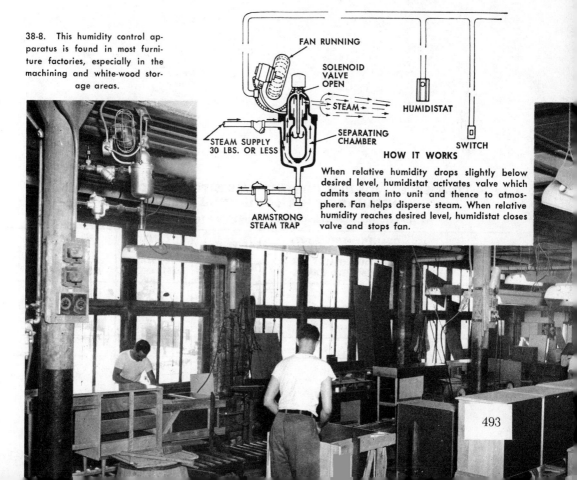

FAN RUNNING

SOLENOID VALVE OPEN

STEAM

HUMIDISTAT

SEPARATING CHAMBER

SWITCH

STEAM SUPPLY 30 LBS. OR LESS

ARMSTRONG STEAM TRAP

HOW IT WORKS

When relative humidity drops slightly below desired level, humidistat activates valve which admits steam into unit and thence to atmosphere. Fan helps disperse steam. When relative humidity reaches desired level, humidistat closes valve and stops fan.

water on the radiator or a small humidifier in the warm air ducts during winter. In the case of steam heat, a valve may be opened to release moisture in the air.

SELECTION AND TREATMENT OF WOODS

The following points should be con-

sidered when selecting and preparing lumber and treating finished products:

Have the wood at a uniform and proper moisture content before it is put through woodworking machines or applied in use. If the wood is too wet, it will swell. If too dry, it will shrink. This response to changes in atmospheric hu-

38-9. Recommended moisture content averages for interior finishing of woodwork in various parts of the United States. Note the difference between the dry deserts and the wet coastal areas. Of course, humidity varies a great deal from one season of the year to another.

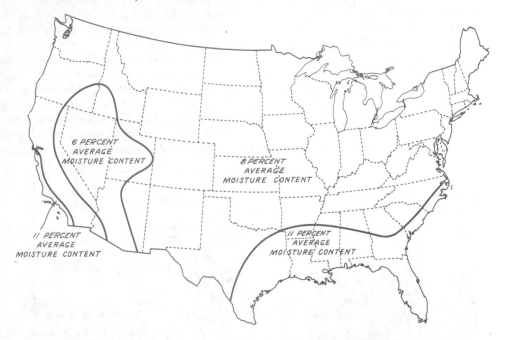

RECOMMENDED MOISTURE CONTENT VALUES FOR WOODWORK AT TIME OF INSTALLATION FOR CONTINENTAL UNITED STATES

In percentages of oven-dry weight. Modified from "Wood Handbook."

SERVICE CONDITION	QUANTITY—ENTIRE LOTS ARE SATISFACTORY IF INDIVIDUAL PIECES ARE IN PRESCRIBED RANGE	DRY SOUTH-WESTERN STATES	DAMP SOUTHERN COASTAL STATES	REMAINDER OF THE UNITED STATES
INTERIOR WOOD FINISH	Average	6	11	7
	Range permitted in individual pieces	4-9	8-13	5-10
EXTERIOR TRIM	Average	9	12	12
	Range permitted in individual pieces	7-12	9-14	9-14

midity is more rapid when the wood is cut into smaller pieces.

If shrinkage across the face of the article is likely to cause a serious problem, use edge- or vertical-grained softwood and quarter-sawed hardwood.

If the product is to be exposed to humidity, the moisture content of the lumber at the time of construction should correspond with the atmospheric conditions in which the finished article will be placed. Fig. 38-9. Protective coatings on manufactured articles are helpful because they prevent great differences in moisture distribution, especially between the wood surface and the interior.

As much as possible, protect the wood against extremes of atmospheric humidity during and after manufacture.

DETERMINING MOISTURE CONTENT OF LUMBER

There are two basic ways of determining how much moisture lumber contains. The more scientific method, called *oven drying*, employs laboratory techniques. In this method, samples of the wood are cut from a green board and baked in an oven at 214-221 degrees F. until they stop losing their moisture. The percentage of moisture content equals weight when cut minus oven-dried weight, divided by oven-dried weight, times 100. Written as an equation, this formula is:

Pct. moisture content =

$$\frac{\text{weight when cut} - \text{oven-dried weight}}{\text{oven-dried weight}}$$

$$\times \, 100.$$

In schools and cabinet shops a moisture meter is used. There are two types. One is supplied with needles that pierce the wood and measure the electrical resistance of current flow through the wood. Fig. 38-10. The other type measures the relationship between moisture content and a constant setting. This type can be recognized by the metal plate or

38-10. Using a moisture meter. It is good practice to test the end grain since the surface of the lumber may be drier than the center. Cut off the end of the board and insert the needles in the center of the end grain. Never check moisture content on foggy days or during periods of extremely high humidity.

shoe which is applied to the lumber surface. These moisture meters are accurate to within plus or minus one per cent of the true figure.

PEG-TREATED WOODS

A chemical treatment that gives solid woods a high degree of dimensional stability has been developed by the Forest Products Laboratory. This process reduces shrinking and swelling to less than that of most plastics. It practically eliminates splits, checks, and other seasonal defects. For best results, the chemical must be applied to the green wood from the saw or after machining to rough size. Fig. 38-11. PEG refers to the chemical called polyethylene glycol, developed by the Dow Chemical Company. The PEG treatment consists of soaking wood in a 30 per cent (by weight) water solution of polyethylene glycol-1000 for six weeks

38-11. Rough turning a bowl from a solid block of green wood. Later treatment with PEG will prevent checking, splitting, and warping.

at a temperature of about 70 degrees F. or above. Treating time can be reduced about two weeks by increasing the temperature of the treating solution to 140 to 160 degrees F. and by increasing the concentration of the solution to 50 per cent. Before the treatment can be done, it is necessary to have a container of wood lined with plastic to make it waterproof, and large enough to hold the lumber. After soaking, the wood can be air dried or seasoned under cover for two or three months, depending upon the drying conditions, or it can be kiln dried in about seven days.

The polyethylene-glycol treatment gives dimensional stability to wood because the chemical diffuses into and lodges in the fine structure of the fiber walls. This prevents the cell walls from shrinking as the wood dries. This process is common for treating many small wooden items such as sports equipment (gun handles, golf-club heads, tennis racquets) and decorative and accessory

products. It has great potential for all wood usage. Because of the nature of the chemical, only a polyurethane resin-base finish can be used. Such a finish forms a protective coating over the chemical.

The polyethylene-glycol treatment should be applied to green wood, fresh from the cutting saw. It is not recommended for lumber that has been exposed to drying conditions for even a few days and, certainly, the process should not be used for air-dried or kiln-dried lumber. A great advantage of the PEG treatment is that much shaping and carving can be done while the wood is green, before it is soaked in the solution. After the wood is treated and dried there are almost no splits, checks, or defects.

WORKING WITH HARDWOODS°

To build furniture successfully, you need to know not only how to set up and operate the machines, but also a great deal about the wood you are using. Wood, in general, is relatively easy to cut, shape, and fasten together, but it varies greatly from one species to another. The more you know about the behavior of wood when it is sawed, planed, shaped, turned, and sanded, the better you will be able to work with it. Since most furniture is made of hardwoods, these will be considered.

CHARACTERISTICS THAT AFFECT MACHINING

Many factors affect the machining properties of wood, making some species better for furniture and fine cabinetmaking than others. Some of the most important include specific gravity, rings per inch, cross grain, shrinkage, and warp. Fig. 38-12.

°All tests described in this unit were performed at the Forest Products Laboratory, Madison, Wisconsin.

Specific Gravity

Specific gravity is a measure of the relative density of materials. It is expressed as a ratio of the weight of a substance to the weight of an equal volume of water at 4 degrees Centigrade. Different species of wood vary in their average specific gravities largely because of differences in the relative proportion of wood substance and air space. Of course, different pieces of the same kind of wood will also vary considerably in specific gravity. In general, heavier woods give a smoother finish and machine better than lighter pieces. On the other hand, heavy woods are relatively hard to work by hand, require more power, dull tools quickly, and tend to split. Fig. 38-13.

Hardness can be measured numerically. When this is done, a relationship is seen between hardness and specific gravity. As specific gravity increases, hardness increases $2\frac{1}{4}$ times faster. This hardness is one reason the heavier woods are chosen for the exposed parts of lumber-core plywood and structural parts, and lighter woods for the core of plywood.

Rings Per Inch

The number of annual rings per inch of trunk radius may affect the appearance, workability, and other properties of wood. Pieces of wood that are to be used together should be fairly similar in appearance. Sometimes this means searching through a pile of lumber for pieces that match. Diffuse-porous woods like the maples are less affected by this problem than are ring-porous woods such as oak and elm. The fastest growing species (cottonwood) has about three times as many rings per inch as the slowest (birch). When ring-porous woods are used for fine furniture, slow to medium growth wood should be selected because it machines better.

Cross Grain

Cross grain causes many difficulties in machining. While almost all woods have some cross grain, certain species have more than others. The three kinds of cross grain are *diagonal, spiral,* and *interlocking* or *interlocked.* Diagonal grain is usually the result of sawing the board in a particular way. Spiral grain is caused when fibers run around the trunk of the tree in a spiral rather than in a vertical fashion. Interlocked grain, caused by fiber ends that slope in opposite directions, causes perhaps the greatest amount of difficulty in machining. For example, in steam bending, woods with the highest percentage of breakage are those that have the most interlocked grain. When planing such a board the knives must revolve against the grain in certain portions of the board and this often causes chipping. Also, the woods in which interlocked grain is most common are the ones that twist most when drying. Twist is the most pronounced form of warp.

Shrinkage

As you know, wood swells or shrinks as it takes on or loses moisture. Comparative freedom from shrinking and swelling is very important in furniture construction. Before starting to construct a piece, be absolutely certain that the wood has been dried properly to the correct moisture content, that is, less than 10 per cent. Remember that shrinkage averages about twice as much across a piece of wood as it does at right angles to the wood. Therefore quarter-sawed hardwood shrinks about half as much in width as does flat-grained.

Although changes in the dimensions of lumber cannot be avoided entirely, some woods do hold shape better than others. As a general rule, the heavier and harder species shrink more than the lighter

38-12.—Characteristics of Hardwoods that Affect Machining.

| Kind of wood | Specific gravity average | Rings per inch average | Cross grain | | Shrinkage (tangential) in moisture content reduction | | Warp (per 7-inch widths)— twist |
			Slope—spiral grain	Inter-locked—pieces	Green to 6 percent	12 to 6 percent	
		Number	*Percent*	*Percent*			*Inch*
Ash	0.50	13	5.6	0	5.7	2.1	0.107
Basswood	.35	16	4.3	0	7.2	1.4	.168
Beech	.55	15	6.9	0	8.9	2.8	.303
Birch	.58	21	5.5	0	7.5	2.2	....
Cottonwood	.38	8	4.3	24	6.7	2.0	.224
Elm, American	.48	14	4.9	19	7.5	2.4	.281
Hickory	.61	15	3.1	0	7.9	2.7	.193
Mahogany	.46	....	6.2	10	3.4	1.3	....
Maple, sugar	.57	17	7.9	0	7.8	2.3	....
Maple, soft	.45	12	6.5	0	6.1	2.1	.246
Oak, red	.55	10	4.4	0	9.0	2.5	.119
Oak, white	.56	17	5.3	0	8.8	2.4	.113
Pecan	.58	14	4.3	0	6.6	2.2	.187
Sweetgum	.46	15	8.2	48	8.4	2.4	.465
Walnut, black	.51	9	5.7	0	6.7	1.7	....
Willow	.34	9	7.7	0	6.2	1.8	.123
Yellow-poplar	.41	12	5.2	0	6.2	1.9	.218

and softer ones. You can see this if you compare the shrinkage of oak with that of basswood. Since no hardwood with more than 12 per cent moisture should ever be used, and since most furniture manufacturers use lumber at approximately 6 per cent, the change in dimensions from 12 to 6 per cent moisture content is most important in selecting woods. On Fig. 38-12, note that mahogany changes the least (1.3 per cent) while beech changes the most (2.8 per cent).

38-13. What are the characteristics of this piece of birch? Is it a relatively hard wood? Why is it popular for Early American furniture?

Warp

Warp has previously been defined as the variation from the true or plane surface. While all woods will warp to some extent, proper drying can keep this problem at a minimum. Warp includes bow, cup, crook, and twist. Cup and twist are the most serious. Cup is defined as a curve across the width of the piece. Twist is the turning or winding of the piece so that the four corners are no longer in the same plane.

Cup is so common a problem that it should be compensated for when gluing up for wide surfaces. This is why the pieces for a table top or other large surface are cut into narrower boards, usually not over 4″ to 6″ in width. The amount of cup in any piece determines the amount of waste in planing and jointing.

Twist is an even more serious problem. Comparison shows that twist is often two or three times greater than cup for the

38-14.—Machining and Related Properties of Hardwoods.

Kind of wood	Planing—perfect pieces	Shaping—good to excellent pieces	Turning—fair to excellent pieces	Boring—good to excellent pieces	Mortising—fair to excellent pieces	Sanding—good to excellent pieces	Steam bending—unbroken pieces	Nail splitting—pieces free from complete splits	Screw splitting—pieces free from complete splits
	Percent	*Percent*	*Percent*	*Percent*	*Percent*	*Percent*	*Percent*	*Percent*	*Percent*
Ash	75	55	79	94	58	75	67	65	71
Basswood	64	10	68	76	51	17	2	79	68
Beech	83	24	90	99	92	49	75	42	58
Birch[1]	63	57	80	97	97	34	72	32	48
Blackgum	48	32	75	82	24	21	42	65	63
Buckeye	..	6	58	75	18	..	9	..	..
Cherry, black	80	80	88	100	100	..	..	..	..
Chestnut	74	28	87	91	70	64	56	66	60
Cottonwood	21	3	70	70	52	19	44	82	78
Elm, soft	33	13	65	94	75	66	74	80	74
Hackberry	74	10	77	99	72	..	94	63	63
Hickory	76	20	84	100	98	80	76	35	63
Mahogany	80	68	89	100	100	..	41	68	78
Maple, bigleaf	52	56	80	100	80	..	..	..	..
Maple, hard	54	72	82	99	95	38	57	27	52
Maple, soft	41	25	76	80	34	37	59	58	61
Oak, red	91	28	84	99	95	81	86	66	78
Oak, white[2]	87	35	85	95	99	83	91	69	74
Pecan	88	40	89	100	98	..	78	47	69
Sweetgum	51	28	86	92	58	23	67	69	69
Sycamore	22	12	85	98	96	21	29	79	74
Tupelo	55	52	79	62	33	34	46	64	63
Walnut, black	62	34	91	100	98	..	78	50	59
Willow	52	5	58	71	24	24	73	89	62
Yellow-poplar	70	13	81	87	63	19	58	77	67

[1] Includes yellow, sweet, and all other commercial birches except white or paper birch.
[2] Includes chestnut oak and other commercial white oaks.

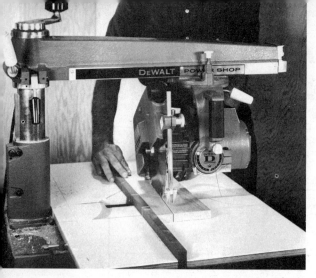

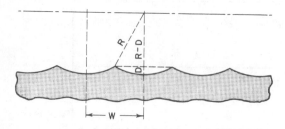

38-15. What kind of saw blade would be used for this ripping operation?

38-16. Knife marks: R—radius of cutting circle. W—distance between knife marks. D—wave height.

38-17. When the planer is operating properly it is difficult to see the knife marks. (a) Good-quality surface on flat-grained redwood. (b) Satisfactory surface on vertical-grained redwood.

same wood. However, woods that have the most twist also tend to have the most cup. Note, for example, that sweetgum (red gum) has over four and one half times as much twist defect as ash.

Machining Properties

How hardwoods react when they are planed, shaped, turned, and sanded is very important to the furniture and cabinet builder. Fig. 38-14. Unless a wood can be fairly easily machined to produce a smooth surface it is not suitable for furniture and fixtures, even though it may have many other good characteristics.

SAWING

The first step in machining any wood is usually to cut out the stock. This is commonly done with a radial-arm saw or a circular saw. Most saws operate at a speed of about 3450 revolutions per minute (r.p.m.). A crosscut or combination saw blade is a good choice for sawing to length. For ripping and resawing, a rip saw should be used. Fig. 38-15. For finish sawing and trimming, the blade should be hollow-ground or carbide-tipped. The rate of feed should be about 70 to 100 feet per minute. When hand feeding lumber, feed as rapidly as the saw will cut without burning the wood or slowing down.

PLANING

Planing is done on both a planer (surfacer) and jointer. All hardwoods that go into furniture construction must be surfaced on a planer and/or jointer. You must learn to judge when the machine is producing a good surface.

All machine-planed surfaces consist of a series of wave marks that are really knife marks made on the lumber as it is fed under or over the revolving cutter head. Fig. 38-16. These marks are at right angles to the edge of the stock. The

500

number of knife marks per inch is determined by four things: the diameter of the cutting head, the number of knives on the cutter head, the speed (the number of revolutions per minute of the cutting head), and the feed. On most medium- and small-size planers the only factor that can be controlled is the feed.

Best planing results are obtained when knives are of equal diameter and sharpness. Fig. 38-17. In other words, each knife must be ground correctly along its length to the same uniform diameter, so that each knife strikes the wood and does an equal amount of cutting.

Most modern planers are equipped with an attachment for grinding the knives without removing them from the cutter head. This consists of a small abrasive wheel on a motor that moves along a bar across the cutter head. Knives can be ground one by one while the cutter head is stationary. The bevel that is ground is not a straight line but a curve that conforms to the circumference of the grinding wheel. However, even after careful grinding, all knives do not always project equally. It is therefore very important to joint the knives to make them cut equally and produce a smooth surface. Fig. 38-18. In jointing, a carrier that holds an abrasive stone is attached to the grinding and jointing bar and the cutter head is set in motion. The stone is lowered until it barely touches a knife edge and then moves across the length of the knife. This will produce a short joint, or *land*, on the full length of each knife. See Unit 24. In general, the feed should be adjusted so that on dry lumber there are about 10 to 12 knife marks per inch. On extremely cross-grained or curly-grained wood, it is better to have 15 or more knife marks per inch.

Some common lumber defects are the result of planing or surfacing. These include:

Raised grain is a roughened surface

38-18. (a). These wide marks resulted when one knife was too high. Only that one knife made a cut on each revolution. (b). After grinding, all the knives began to cut, leaving four knife marks per revolution. Note the improved quality of the surface.

38-19. Different degrees of raised grain on soft elm. Woods that develop the least raised grain include ash, birch, hickory, and maple.

38-20. Different degrees of fuzzy grain in willow.

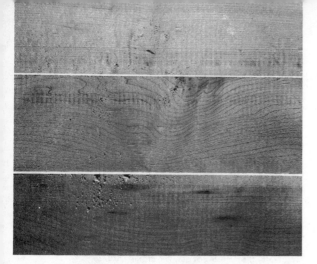

38-21. Various degrees of chipped grain in hard maple. Woods such as birch, maple, and hickory tend to have more chipped grain. Jointing or surfacing *with the grain* tends to eliminate the problem.. Also, be sure the chip breaker is working properly.

38-22. Different degrees of chip marks in yellow poplar. If you are not certain whether the defect is chip marks or chipped grain, test by placing a few drops of water on each defect and wait a few minutes. Chipped grain (which is actually broken-out particles) will not change. Chip marks (which are dents) will swell as they absorb water.

38-23. A machine burn.

condition in which an annual ring is raised above the general surface but not torn loose. Fig. 38-19. The most common causes of raised grain are dull knives, too much joint on knives, and excessive moisture content. It can also be caused by too low head speed, too high feed, or cutting too light.

Fuzzy grain consists of small particles of fibers that are not cut cleanly. Fig. 38-20. In most cases fuzzy grain is due to an unusual wood condition. It can be kept to a minimum by keeping the knives sharp and making sure that the moisture content of the wood is well below 12 per cent.

Chipped grain is a surface on which small particles have broken out below the line of cut. Fig. 38-21. Chipped grain is most often the result of machining cross-grain lumber against the grain or having the feed speed too high. The most important step in preventing chipped grain is making sure there are enough knife marks—16 to 20—per inch. This is done by adjusting the cutting feed.

Chip marks are shallow dents in the wood surface caused by shavings that are not taken out by the exhaust system. Fig. 38-22. The chips drop back onto the wood surface and are crushed under the outfeed rolls. Chip marks generally can be prevented if the blower system is

38-24. Shaping the edge of stock.

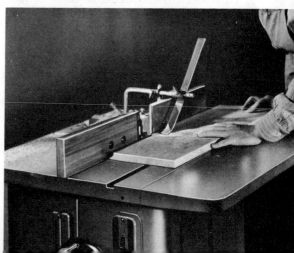

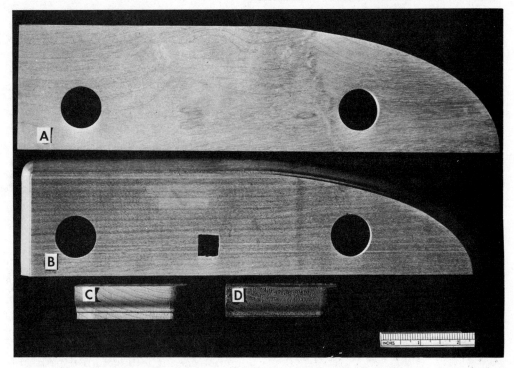

38-25. Samples of shaping operations: A. The blank (rough stock). B. The finished sample. C. End-grain cut on maple. D. End-grain cut on red alder. As might be expected, best shaping results were obtained with the grain, and poorer work resulted when the cut was made across end grain. At right angles to the grain, surface roughness was the most serious defect.

working properly, with not too much air leakage. Sometimes feeding too fast will cause chip marks.

Machine burns are black marks across the wood surface, caused when lumber sticks in the machine. Fig. 38-23. This often happens when too light a cut is taken and the infeed and outfeed rolls do not keep the lumber moving. Knife marks are much more common than roller burns.

To summarize, the major factors in good planing are to make sure that the moisture content is below 12 per cent, that the cutter head is sharp, that the blades are of equal length, and that the feed is adjusted for at least 10 but preferably 12 to 20 cuts per inch. The quality of the planed surface is also affected

by the depth of cut. Forest Products Laboratory conducted a series of tests in which cuts were made at four depths—1/32″, 1/16″, 3/32″, and 1/8″. Although a heavy cut may be satisfactory for removing stock, the tests showed that the shallowest cut is far better for producing a very smooth surface.

SHAPING

Shaping can be done for straight-line cuts such as in making moldings. Fig. 38-24. However, it is more commonly done to form the edge of a curved or irregularly shaped part such as a table top. Important factors in good shaping include the kind of wood, the moisture content, the arrangement of the pores, and the specific gravity. Fig. 38-25.

503

38-26. These test samples were cut on a hand wood lathe but with a milled-to-pattern knife using the back-knife principle. The method of cutting the samples is similar to that used on the lathe duplicator described in Unit 37. The samples range in quality from No. 1 which represents perfect turning to No. 5 which is a reject. Differences in the wood resulted in the variation in quality.

38-27. Difference in smoothness of bored holes. No. 1 shows a smooth-bored hole in pecan. No. 2 is a rough-bored hole in willow. Holes bored in dry wood increase in size as the moisture content increases. For good dowel construction the wood and the dowel must be at the same moisture content when gluing is done. Plastic dowel pins eliminate part of the problem.

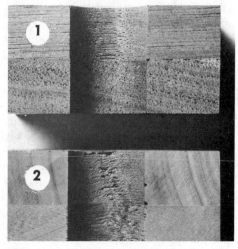

Another major factor that affects the quality of work is the peripheral (outside cutter) speed. Higher peripheral speeds generally produce better surfaces. This speed is determined both by the revolutions per minute of the shaper and the diameter of the cutting tool. With a shaper revolving at 3600 r.p.m., peripheral speed will vary from as little as 470 feet per minute for a 1/2″ router cutter to 9400 feet per minute for a 10″ saw. The best woods for shaping are cherry and the hard maples; the poorest is cottonwood.

WOOD TURNING

Wood turning is important in producing tool and implement handles, certain furniture parts, toys, and sporting goods. There is a definite relationship between specific gravity and turning quality. Fig. 38-26. The poorest turning woods are the lightest ones. The best turned parts are made from walnut, beech, oak, mahogany, pecan, and cherry. Moisture content should be from 6 to 12 per cent.

BORING

Boring is done extensively in furniture construction when using dowels, spindles, and rungs, or when installing screws. Fig. 38-27. A smoothly cut, accurately sized hole is especially important for a good dowel joint. Woods of higher specific gravity require more power and are more difficult to bore than the softer woods. In general, however, best results are obtained on heavy woods. The medium to heavy species produce 90 per cent or more of good to excellent holes, based on smoothness of cut. The same bit, when used in different woods, can produce both oversized and undersized holes. These differences in the way woods react to boring explain why some woods split more than others when doweled.

MORTISING

The mortise-and-tenon joint is not as common as it was in the past but is still used extensively in furniture and cabinet construction. Fig. 38-28. In general, specific gravity is the principal factor in high-quality mortise cutting. Heavier woods produce mortises that are smoother and of more uniform size than do lighter woods. Good results are obtained in cherry, mahogany, oak, hickory, and pecan.

SANDING

Sanding is one of the most important steps in the completion of furniture. Although sometimes done for surfacing and for making slight corrections in the fitting of parts, sanding is usually done to produce a smooth surface for a fine finish and to smooth the finish itself.

A series of sanding tests was conducted with wood at 6 per cent moisture content, using both the drum sander and the belt sander. The grit used was garnet of 2/0 coarseness. Results were checked for fuzz-free and scratch-free surfaces. In general, the harder woods sanded better. Also, coarse-textured woods showed less scratching than fine-textured woods, and hard species fuzzed less than soft ones. Fig. 38-29.

COMPATIBILITY OF GRAIN AND COLOR

In building products of wood it is highly desirable to use individual pieces that are in harmony with one another. This is true for both solid wood and plywood. Harmony of grain is determined by the position in the log from which the boards are sawed. Color compatibility depends largely on the growing conditions under which the tree developed. Since both grain and color harmony are difficult to obtain, the best method is to

38-28. Contrast in smoothness of cut in mortising different woods: 1, 2 and 5 maple; 3, 4 and 6 red oak; 1 and 3 show side-grain surfaces, 2 and 4 end-grain surfaces. Note that the cuts in side grain or those parallel to the grain are much smoother than the cuts across grain. Soft maple is one of the poorest woods for mortising.

38-29. Scratching tendencies of three different sizes of grit on hard maple. Note that the 3/0 grit, or 120, produces a surface on which the scratches are not visible to the eye. On fine-textured wood you may have to use an abrasive two grit sizes finer than you would use on oak to produce the same quality surface.

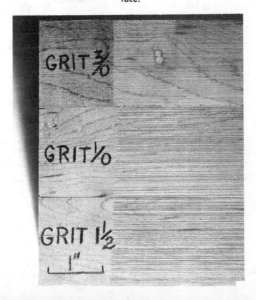

505

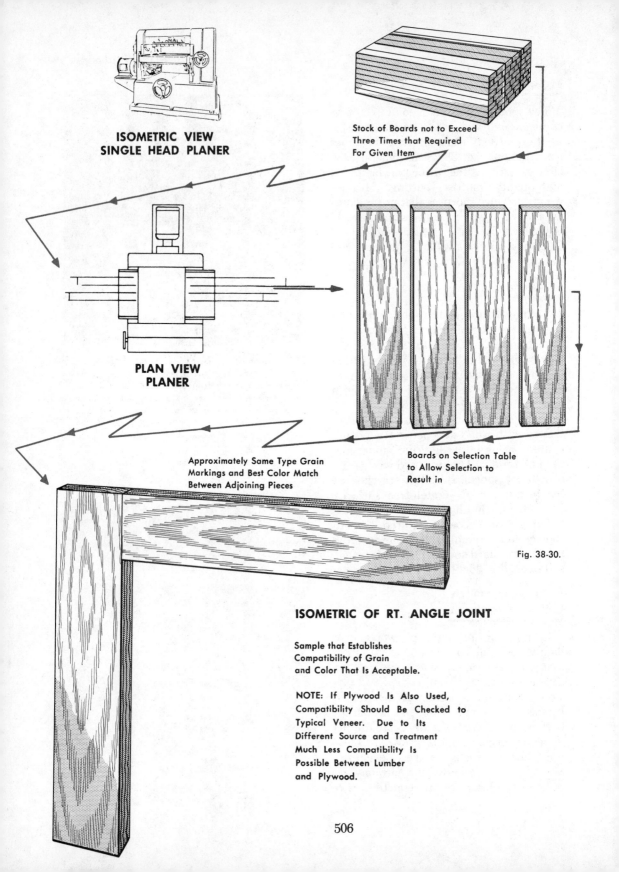

**ISOMETRIC VIEW
SINGLE HEAD PLANER**

Stock of Boards not to Exceed
Three Times that Required
For Given Item

**PLAN VIEW
PLANER**

Approximately Same Type Grain
Markings and Best Color Match
Between Adjoining Pieces

Boards on Selection Table
to Allow Selection to
Result in

Fig. 38-30.

ISOMETRIC OF RT. ANGLE JOINT

Sample that Establishes
Compatibility of Grain
and Color That Is Acceptable.

NOTE: If Plywood Is Also Used,
Compatibility Should Be Checked to
Typical Veneer. Due to Its
Different Source and Treatment
Much Less Compatibility Is
Possible Between Lumber
and Plywood.

506

surface at least three times as much lumber as is needed for a particular product. This provides a good supply of boards for matching. Often the total stock of lumber can be used to make three items, each of which will have above average compatibility of grain and color. Fig. 38-30.

39 Cabinetmaking Joints

The skilled cabinetmaker must have a thorough knowledge of joinery. Fig. 39-1. He must know how to select the correct kind of joint for a particular product and how to lay out, cut, fit, and assemble the joint. The term "joint" is used to describe the close securing or fastening together of two or more smooth, even surfaces. The construction quality of any cabinetwork or furniture largely depends on the quality of the joints. Fig. 39-2.

Although there are over 100 kinds of joints in cabinetmaking and furniture construction, they can be grouped into several basic types. You may know other names for some of the joints in this unit, but the terms used here are commonly accepted. The joint to select for each kind of construction depends to some extent on the need for strength, the desired appearance, and the equipment available. Simple joints can be made by hand or with basic machines. More complicated ones, like the dovetail, require special equipment.

It is generally best to choose the simplest joints that will do the job satisfactorily. Often the selection of a joint is determined by the cost factor and the amount of material involved. Instead of the mortise-and-tenon joint, many furniture and cabinet manufacturers use dowels and corner blocks to reinforce butt joints where the rails and legs of tables and chairs are joined. Using dowels with a butt joint saves time and materials and is, therefore, less costly. Strength tests have revealed that this simpler construction is equally as strong as the mortise and tenon.

ELEMENTS OF JOINERY

Follow these basic principles in all joinery:
• Make all measurements from a com-

39-1(a). Although you can't see it in a finished product, interior joinery must be sound. In this casework the base is fitted into the sides with a rabbet joint and into the back rails with a dado joint. The back is fitted into grooves in the top and bottom back rails.

507

39-1(b). Quality joinery is important in all furniture and cabinet construction. Sometimes the joints are exposed such as the finger or box joints on the corner of the trays in this buffet. *(John Stuart, Inc.)*

mon starting point. This will eliminate the possibility of error.

• Use the *superimposing method* of laying out a joint as often as you can. In this method, one piece is placed over another to do the marking. A good example of this is laying out the width of a rabbet or dado. Fig. 39-3.

• Mark all duplicate parts at the same time. Often this can be done by clamping the pieces together and then marking across them. Fig. 39-4. Whenever possible, cutting should be done in duplicate.

• Whenever a joint is made of two pieces of solid wood, make sure that there is room for the fitted part of the joint to ex-

pand. For example, if a solid shelf is fitted into a plywood case, the shelf should be slightly narrower than the side of the case so that it can shrink and swell without harming the case. Also, the shelf should be fastened with screws rather than glue so that the parts can move.

• Undercut joints wherever a close fit is not required. A good joint requires a close fit for most surfaces. For example, the cheek of a tenon must fit the sides of the mortise snugly. However, the end of a tenon can be undercut so there is space for glue.

• As mentioned earlier, use the simplest joint that will serve the purpose. The quality of the product should dictate the

39-2. Architectural woodwork such as that shown in this elegant family room also requires fine joinery. The walls are hemlock and the casework is fine walnut.

kind of joinery. Design of the product also has an effect on the kind of joint to select. Fig. 39-5.

• Keep the parts of the joint in correct proportion so that there will not be a weak link in the chain. There is no point, for example, in making a mortise-and-tenon joint if the tenon is so small that it will break under a reasonable load.

• Use only quality wood, kiln dried, for all parts of the product.

• *Remember,* quality in cabinetmaking means many things: workmanship, wood selection, type of construction, and, most important, the *kind of joint.* A piece of furniture is no stronger than its weakest joint. The U.S. Army has this to say in detailing its furniture specifications: "In order to be strong and durable, furniture shall be securely framed and braced throughout, and mortised, tenoned or doweled in the most skilled and workmanlike manner. Parts subject to stress shall be strengthened with glue blocks and screws."

FASTENING AND STRENGTHENING JOINTS

Most joints are permanently fastened together with glue and sometimes screws. Quality joints are always glued under pressure. Nails and staples are rarely used for exposed surfaces in quality construction. Furniture and cabinet manufacturers do use staples and nails to fasten structural parts together. For example, they are used to fasten glue blocks, drawer guides, and other hidden parts. Exposed nails are used in on-the-job construction of cabinets and built-ins. The following are common methods of strengthening joints:

Dowels

A dowel is a pin or peg of wood, plastic, or metal that fits into two matching holes. Joints which use such pins are

39-3. Marking the width of the rabbet by super-imposing. This insures accuracy.

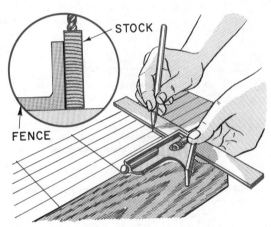

39-4. Marking the location of dowels for edge joints. Note that all pieces are being marked at the same time. The insert drawing shows a fence installed on the drill press so that all holes will be centered.

39-5. Box or finger joints fasten the arms and legs of this Danish chair. Such joints become part of the design of the chair.

509

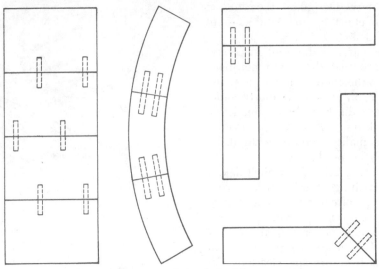

39-6. Common uses of dowels for joint construction.

39-7(a). A dowel pin with spiral grooves.

39-7(b). A dowel pointer cuts a small chamfer on the ends of dowels so they will enter the holes more easily.

39-8. Using dowel centers to locate the matching holes for an edge dowel joint.

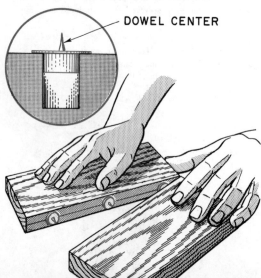

DOWEL CENTER

called *dowel joints.* Fig. 39-6. Dowel rod is made of birch, hickory, or maple in diameters of 1/8″ to 1″ and in lengths of 3′. Small dowel pins of wood or plastic are made with spiral grooves and pointed ends. Fig. 39-7. The grooves help the glue to flow more freely and allow the air to escape from the bottom of the holes. It is important to keep the moisture content of wood dowels to 5 per cent or less. Actually, a very dry dowel with less than 5 per cent moisture is best. If the moisture content is too high, the dowel will later dry out, reduce in diameter, and cause joint failure. When a dry dowel covered with glue is driven into a hole of correct diameter, it will absorb moisture, swell in diameter, and tighten up. Always store wood dowel in a dry place, next to a heater if possible.

The diameter of the dowel should not be less than one-third or more than one-half the thickness of the wood. The length of the dowel should be 1/8″ to 1/4″ shorter than the combined depth of the two holes. When using dowels, always use two or more.

510

¼" DIAMETER HOLE   90° Angle

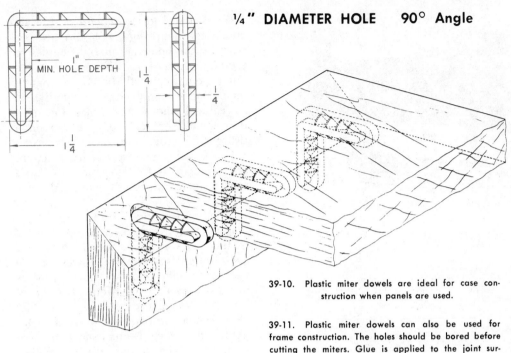

1"
MIN. HOLE DEPTH

39-10. Plastic miter dowels are ideal for case construction when panels are used.

39-11. Plastic miter dowels can also be used for frame construction. The holes should be bored before cutting the miters. Glue is applied to the joint surfaces and the dowel holes.

1"
MIN. HOLE DEPTH

⅜" DIAMETER HOLE   90° Angle

39-9. Marking dowel locations with a metal pattern and scratch awl. This method is especially good when the rails are set back from the leg.

SCRATCH
AWL

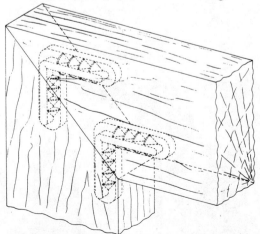

39-12. This wall-hanging telephone stand of teak and oak makes use of dowel rod for the lower shelf.

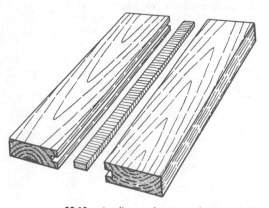

39-13. A spline used to strengthen an edge joint.

39-14. A blind spline helps make a strong, neat miter joint.

Good dowel joints depend on the accuracy of hole alignment and also on whether the holes are at right angles to the face surfaces. In other words, if the holes are not correctly bored, the matching surfaces cannot be properly aligned. In cabinet shops, the holes for most dowel work are drilled or bored on a drill press or small horizontal boring machine. Usually some sort of jig or fixture is used to hold the stock to make sure that all matching holes are aligned properly.

If only a few joints are to be made, it may be faster and easier to use a hand method. One common way is to lay out the location for the dowel holes on one part of the joint and then bore the holes using a doweling jig. Metal *dowel centers* are then placed in these holes. Fig. 39-8. When the two pieces are held together, the dowel centers show the hole location in the second piece. Another good method for boring matching holes for legs and rails is to use a small metal templet with corners cut out. When used on both the leg and the rail, the templet will insure matching holes. Fig. 39-9.

Plastic dowels are also made in right-angle shapes for strengthening miter joints. Fig. 39-10. With these dowels the holes can be bored at right angles to the face surfaces instead of at right angles to the cut surfaces. Fig. 39-11.

Dowel rod is also used for small turned parts on many accessories. Fig. 39-12.

Splines

A spline is a thin piece of wood, plywood, hardboard, or metal that is inserted in a groove (kerf or slot) between two parts of a joint. It is most common in miter joints. Fig. 39-13. The groove or slot must be cut in both parts of the joint. Then the thin spline is inserted in these grooves to help hold the parts in alignment and to strengthen the joint. A

512

39-15. A cross-grain lemon spline makes a strong corner for trim. Note that any correction of irregularities must be carried at least 5" from the outside corner of the miter.

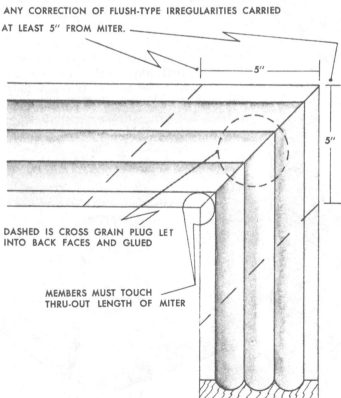

DASHED IS TYPICAL
CROSS-GRAIN LEMON
SPLINE

MEMBERS MUST TOUCH
THRU-OUT LENGTH OF MITER

ANY CORRECTION OF FLUSH-TYPE IRREGULARITIES CARRIED
AT LEAST 5" FROM MITER.

DASHED IS CROSS GRAIN PLUG LET
INTO BACK FACES AND GLUED

MEMBERS MUST TOUCH
THRU-OUT LENGTH OF MITER

39-16. A large hole is bored partway through the joint from the back side. Then a cross-grain plug is glued in place to strengthen the miter.

513

39-17(a). Clamp nails.

39-17(b). Clamp nails can be used to join miters. On wider trim stock that exceeds 3″, nails must be driven from both ends.

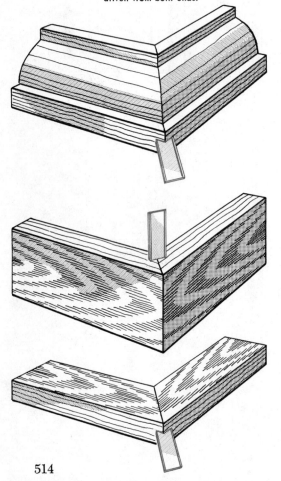

good groove or slot should be about 1/8″ wide and 1/4″ deep. On a flat miter, the spline is centered between the face surfaces. On an edge miter the groove should be closer to the inside corner.

When joining solid woods, the spline should also be of solid wood, with grain direction at right angles to the edge. In other words, the grain direction of the spline should be the same as that of the joint. For plywood construction, 1/8″ three-ply birch plywood or hardboard makes a good spline.

The slot, kerf, or groove for the spline can be cut with a saw blade or dado head on a circular or radial-arm saw. Most splines are made the full length of the joint. Sometimes, however, a blind spline is used. Fig. 39-14. Another kind of blind spline is lemon shaped. Fig. 39-15. Sometimes a wood plug is used as a spline and is let into the back face of a miter joint to strengthen it. Fig. 39-16. Clamp nails are commonly used instead of wood splines for less expensive construction. The clamp nail is flanged slightly on both edges so that it acts as a wedge to hold the two parts firmly together. The groove or kerf for clamp nails must be cut with an extra-thin, 22-gage circular-saw blade to a depth from 7/32″ to 3/8″, according to the width of the fastener. See Unit 11. Clamp nails

39-18. A key is another good device for locking two parts of a joint together.

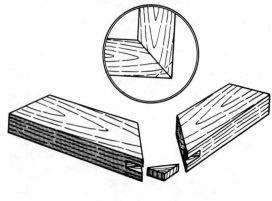

for miter corners should be set below the surface of the wood to allow for filling. Fig. 39-17.

Key

A key is a small piece of wood inserted in a joint to hold it firmly together. Fig. 39-18. The key is sometimes called a *feather*. It is often placed across the corners of miter joints.

Glue Blocks

Glue blocks (sometimes called rub blocks) are small triangular or square pieces of wood used to strengthen and support two adjoining surfaces. Fig. 39-19. If you examine the inside of a quality chest or cabinet, you will find many glue blocks installed for strength.

Corner Blocks

A corner block, which is larger than a glue block and triangular in shape, is used for added strength at the corners of frames or where legs and rails join. Fig. 39-20. As made in the cabinet shop it is

39-19(b). In quality construction, glue blocks are used to give added strength to the unit.

39-20. A simple corner block is often installed with dowel construction to give proper bracing for maximum strength.

39-21. The dovetail corner block adds rigidity to corner construction.

39-19(a). Glue blocks can be square or triangular. They are used to strengthen adjoining surfaces.

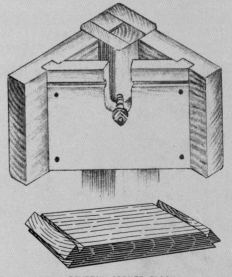

DOVETAIL CORNER BLOCK

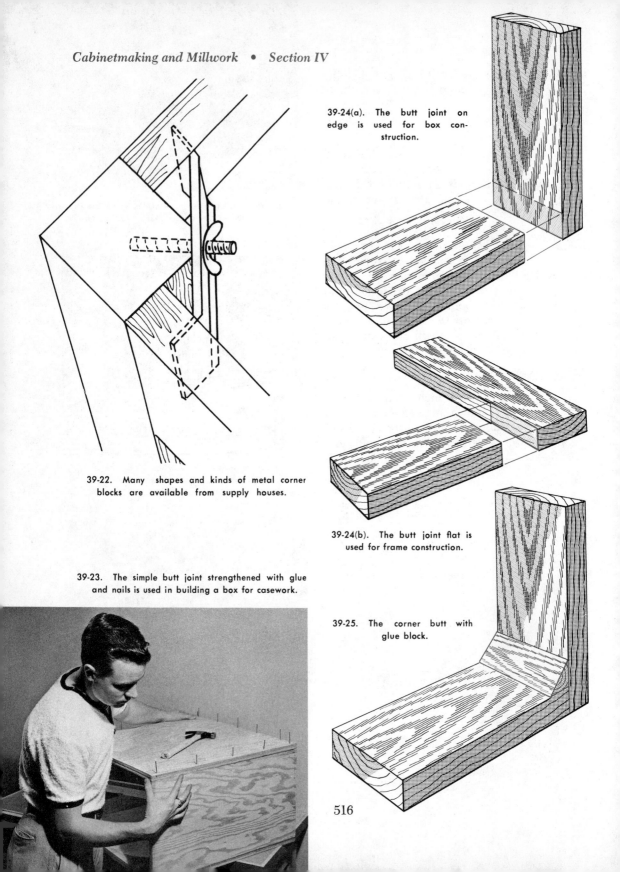

39-24(a). The butt joint on edge is used for box construction.

39-22. Many shapes and kinds of metal corner blocks are available from supply houses.

39-24(b). The butt joint flat is used for frame construction.

39-23. The simple butt joint strengthened with glue and nails is used in building a box for casework.

39-25. The corner butt with glue block.

516

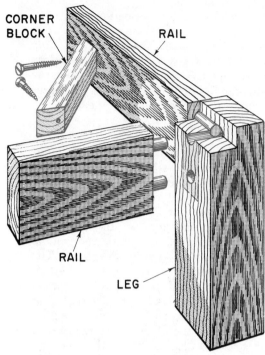

CORNER BLOCK

RAIL

RAIL

LEG

39-26(a). The butt joint with dowels is given added strength by means of a corner block. Glue and wood screws hold the parts permanently together.

39-26(b). The rails and legs of this fine coffee table are constructed with butt joints strengthened with dowels and corner blocks.

a simple, triangular piece of wood cut to fit into the corner. It is fastened in place with glue and screws. Many furniture manufacturers install corner blocks that have dovetail-dado joints. Fig. 39-21. There are also many kinds of patented metal corner blocks. Fig. 39-22.

KINDS OF JOINTS

The following are the more common joints used in cabinetmaking. Basically, these same joints are used in all wood construction:

Butt Joints

On the butt joint, sometimes called the plain joint, the square end of one piece or member fits against the flat surface or edge of the second member. Fig. 39-23. Without reinforcement the butt joint is very weak, since end grain is poor for joining. However, with dowels it becomes a high-quality joint. The simplest *butt joint* is one fastened on edge or as a *flat butt joint*. Fig. 39-24. The corner of the joint is often reinforced with a glue block. Fig. 39-25. The *butt joint strengthened with dowels* is used to join the ends of rails (aprons) to the edges of legs for leg-and-rail construction. Fig. 39-26. The *corner butt with dowels* is used for some types of case

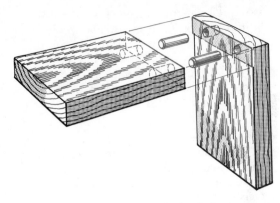

39-27. The corner butt with dowels is sometimes found in case construction.

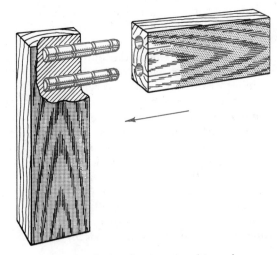

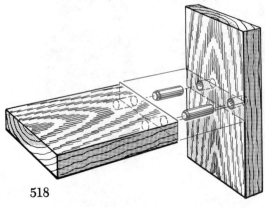

39-28. Usually two dowels are used in each corner of a butt-frame joint.

39-29(a). The middle-rail butt with dowels.

518

and box construction. Fig. 39-27. A *frame butt with dowels* is an end-to-edge joint that is often made for a web or skeleton frame. Fig. 39-28. The *middle-rail butt with dowels* is an end-to-face or edge-to-surface joint commonly used when installing dividers in furniture and casework. Fig. 39-29.

Edge Joints

Edge joints are used primarily to build up larger surfaces for such things as the tops of tables and desks, the core of plywood, and for interior paneling and door construction. Fig. 39-30. These joints are made with the grain of the two parts running parallel, but with the annual rings facing in opposite directions. The simplest edge joint is called the *butt or plain edge*. Fig. 39-31. It is cut with a carbide-tipped blade on a circular or radial-arm saw. The edges don't require surfacing. If the blade is a standard one, it is a good idea to surface the edges on the jointer. When the edges are carefully cut or surfaced and glued under pressure, the joint will be as strong as the wood itself.

39-29(b). Middle-rail butt joints with dowels are used to install the horizontal dividers in this combination dressing table and chest.

39-30. Tongue-and-groove vertical paneling of white pine is applied to the interior of this dining room.

A *dowel edge* strengthens the adjoining edges. It is important to locate and drill matching holes accurately. The outside ones should be about 3″ or 4″ from the edges and the rest should be about 1″ to 18″ apart. Fig. 39-32. This is best done on a drill press or a horizontal boring machine.

The *spline edge* is another joint for adding strength. With a dado or molding head, a groove with a width of 1/8″, 3/16″, or 1/4″, is cut along each of the adjoining edges. Then a spline of solid wood, plywood, or hardboard is fitted into the grooves. Note that if solid wood is used, the grain should run at right angles to the length. Fig. 39-33.

The *tongue and groove* is used for paneling, flooring, and other interior construction. Fig. 39-34. This is usually mill-produced and purchased as a stock mill item. Usually a small V is formed at the exposed surface for better appearance. The tongue and groove can be cut with matching sets of cutters or blades with the dado head or molding head of a cir-

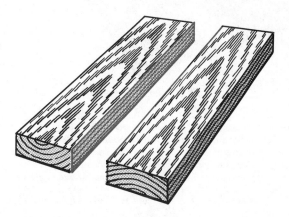

39-31. Plain or butt edge

39-32. Dowel edge.

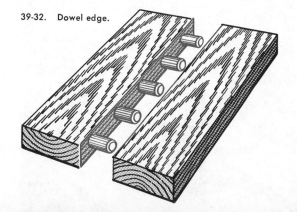

519

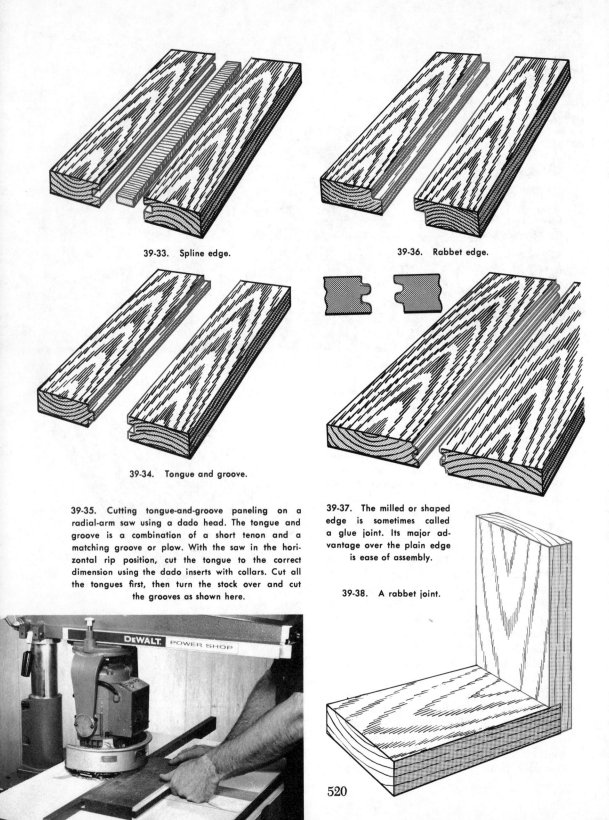

39-33. Spline edge.

39-36. Rabbet edge.

39-34. Tongue and groove.

39-35. Cutting tongue-and-groove paneling on a radial-arm saw using a dado head. The tongue and groove is a combination of a short tenon and a matching groove or plow. With the saw in the horizontal rip position, cut the tongue to the correct dimension using the dado inserts with collars. Cut all the tongues first, then turn the stock over and cut the grooves as shown here.

39-37. The milled or shaped edge is sometimes called a glue joint. Its major advantage over the plain edge is ease of assembly.

39-38. A rabbet joint.

cular or radial-arm saw or on a shaper. Fig. 39-35.

The *rabbet edge* is made by cutting two rabbets, one on each edge but from the opposite surfaces. Fig. 39-36. This is best done with a dado head on a circular or radial-arm saw.

The *milled or shaped edge* is used in cabinet shops primarily to speed assembly and to add surface for gluing. Fig. 39-37. It doesn't greatly increase the strength of the joint. It is best cut with a molding head on a saw or with a cutter on a shaper or router.

Rabbet Joints

The rabbet joint is found in simple box-and-case construction. A rabbet is an L-shaped groove cut across the edge or end of one piece. The joint is made by fitting the other piece into it. Fig. 39-38. Width of the rabbet should equal the thickness of the material, and its depth should be one-half to two-thirds the thickness. Fig. 39-39. The rabbet joint conceals one end grain and also reduces the twisting tendency of a joint. Fig. 39-40. Backs of most cases, cabinets, bookcases, and chests are joined with the end grain facing the back. Fig. 39-41. For this joint, called a *back-panel rabbet joint,* the rabbet is cut to a depth equal to the thickness of the back panel. Fig. 39-42. However, for casework that is to be hung

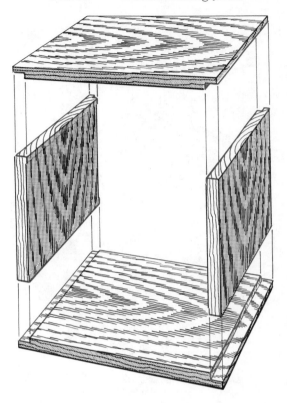

39-40. Applying a rabbet joint to simple case or box construction.

39-41. A small storage table. The backs of cabinets and cases such as this one are often installed with rabbet joints.

39-39. The correct shape for a strong rabbet joint.

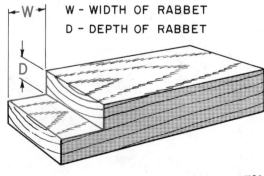

W – WIDTH OF RABBET
D – DEPTH OF RABBET

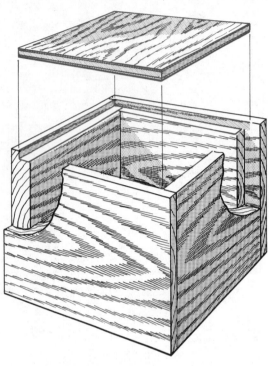

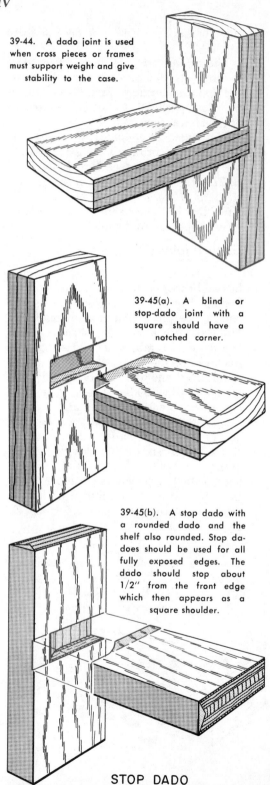

39-44. A dado joint is used when cross pieces or frames must support weight and give stability to the case.

39-42. A back panel fitted into a case or box with a rabbet joint.

39-43. The shelves of this buffet are joined to the sides by means of dado joints.

39-45(a). A blind or stop-dado joint with a square should have a notched corner.

39-45(b). A stop dado with a rounded dado and the shelf also rounded. Stop dadoes should be used for all fully exposed edges. The dado should stop about 1/2″ from the front edge which then appears as a square shoulder.

STOP DADO

on a wall, the rabbet is cut to a depth from 1/2″ to 1″, so there will be material to trim off to fit the back of the cabinet against the wall.

There are many simple ways of cutting a rabbet joint on circular and radial-arm saws, jointers, shapers, and routers. Perhaps the easiest method is on a circular or radial-arm saw, either by making two cuts or by cutting the rabbet in one pass with a dado head. The rabbet joint is usually fastened with glue and nails or screws.

Dado Joints

Dado joints are found in cabinets, bookcases, chests, or wherever a joint is needed to provide a supporting ledge. Fig. 39-43. The dado is a groove cut across grain. In the *simple dado joint,* the butt end of the second piece fits into this groove. Fig. 39-44. The major objection to the simple dado is that, unless a face-plate trim is added to the front of the case, it has an unattractive appearance.

39-46(a). The lower shelf of a table can be installed with a corner dado.

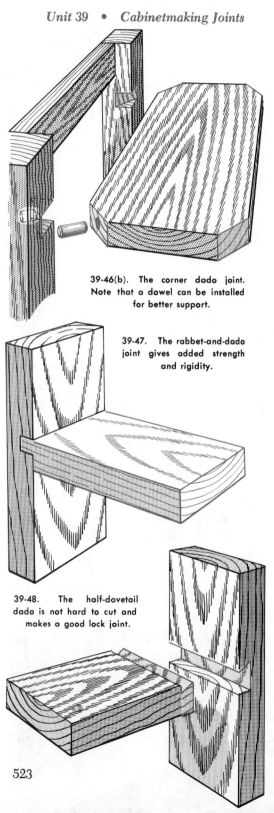

39-46(b). The corner dado joint. Note that a dowel can be installed for better support.

39-47. The rabbet-and-dado joint gives added strength and rigidity.

39-48. The half-dovetail dado is not hard to cut and makes a good lock joint.

523

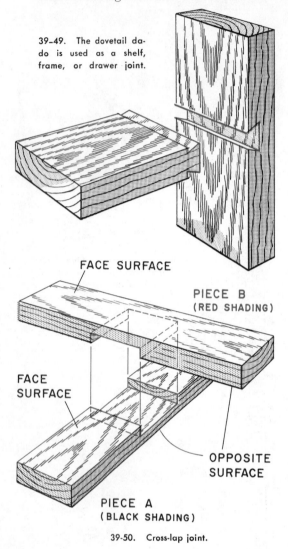

39-49. The dovetail dado is used as a shelf, frame, or drawer joint.

FACE SURFACE

PIECE B
(RED SHADING)

FACE
SURFACE

OPPOSITE
SURFACE

PIECE A
(BLACK SHADING)

39-50. Cross-lap joint.

39-51.* Cutting a cross-lap joint at an angle of 45 degrees. This is used as a cross support for an outdoor table.

For better appearance, a *stop or blind dado* is best. Fig. 39-45. In this joint, a dado is cut partway across the first piece; then a corner is notched out of the second piece so the two pieces fit together. However, when this joint is cut with a dado head, a rounded surface forms at the end of the cut. This must either be cleaned out with a hand chisel or the notch must be cut to fit into the full depth of the dado.

In the *corner dado joint* a rectangular groove is cut across the edge of one member, and a corner is cut off the second member to fit into the groove. Fig. 39-46. A dowel may be added. This joint is sometimes used for installing a lower shelf on a table.

The *rabbet and dado,* sometimes called the *dado and tenon,* or *dado box corner,* is a combination of a dado on one piece and a rabbet on the other. Fig. 39-47. The rabbet cut forms a tenon that fits into the dado. It is used as a back corner joint in good drawer construction since it holds the two pieces square. The joint is cut with a dado head on a saw.

The *half-dovetail dado joint* is an excellent locking joint that will carry a great deal of weight. Fig. 39-48.

The *full-dovetail dado joint,* sometimes called a *housed dovetail or through dovetail,* is excellent for any type of construction in which a lock joint is required. Fig. 39-49. All dovetail-dado joints can be cut with the router or on a circular or radial-arm saw.

Lap Joints

This is a large group of joints in which one member laps over the other. The *cross lap* joins two pieces with flush faces. Fig. 39-50. The pieces may cross at any angle. Fig. 39-51. The joint is made by cutting dadoes of equal width and depth on the two pieces so that the face surfaces are flush when assembled.

The *edge cross lap* is very similar to it

524

39-52(a). An edge-lap joint is used on the cross stretchers of this coffee table.

39–52(b). Edge cross lap.

39-53. Middle or T lap.

and is commonly used in making egg-crate or grid designs. Fig. 39-52.

In the *middle lap or T lap,* the end of one member joins the middle of the other. Fig. 39-53. In this joint a dado is cut on one piece and a rabbet on the other.

The *dovetail lap* is similar to the middle lap except that it is a lock-type joint. Fig. 39-54.

The *end lap* is made by cutting a rabbet at the ends of both pieces, which usually join at right angles. This joint is used in constructing simple frames. Fig. 39-55. Most lap joints are cut with a dado head on a circular or radial-arm saw. Fig. 39-56.

Miter Joints

A miter joint is an angle joint that hides

525

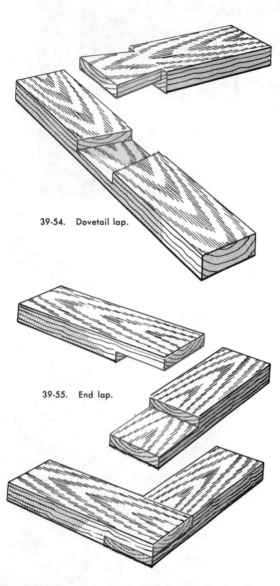

39-54.   Dovetail lap.

39-55.   End lap.

39-56.   Cutting a series of grooves for cross-lap joints.

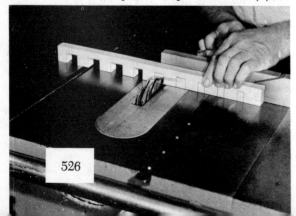

39-57.   A miter joint is used in frame construction.

39-58(a).   The exposed miter joint on this table leg and rail is a design feature.

39-58(b).   The miter joints on the frames of this table must be cut at odd angles to form the six sides.

the end grain of both pieces. Fig. 39-57. Miter joints are commonly used for frame and case construction and are usually cut to form right-angle joints. Fig. 39-58. The joint is relatively weak unless strengthened with a spline, key, feather, or dowel.

A simple miter can be *flat* or *on edge*. Fig. 39-59. Both types can be strengthened as mentioned above. Fig. 39-60 to 39-64. Usually two or more dowels are placed at each corner.

If a spline is used, it can run either the full length of the groove or only partway across it. The latter is called a *blind-spline* (splined) *miter*. Fig. 39-65. The spline on an edge miter should be placed closer to the inner corner for strength.

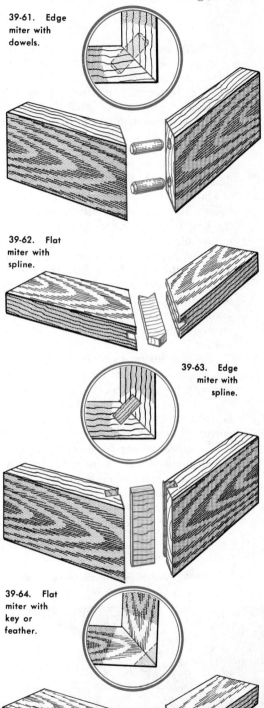

39-61. Edge miter with dowels.

39-62. Flat miter with spline.

39-63. Edge miter with spline.

39-64. Flat miter with key or feather.

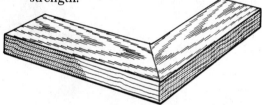

39-59(a). A flat miter can be held together with nails, corrugated fasteners, or screws.

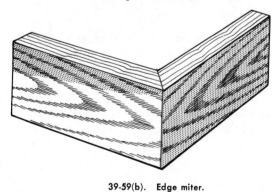

39-59(b). Edge miter.

39-60. Flat miter with dowels.

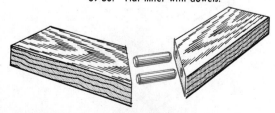

527

Polygon miters are those cut at angles of more or less than 45 degrees to form three- to ten-sided objects. Fig. 39-66. The correct setting for cutting the angles is shown in Fig. 39-67.

The *compound miter or hopper joint* is used to make shadow-box picture frames, tapered containers, and similar work. Fig. 39-68. The cut is a combination miter-and-bevel cut. Fig. 39-69.

The *miter-with-rabbet joint* (sometimes called the *offset miter*) combines the best features of both the rabbet and miter joints. It is especially good for plywood casework and corner joints for paneling since it helps to hold the corner square and also provides plenty of gluing surface. Fig. 39-70. The layout for this joint is shown in Fig. 39-71. Cut the joint on a radial-arm or circular saw or on a shaper.

The *lock miter* is excellent because it combines the appearance of a miter corner with the strength of a dado. Fig. 39-72. The best method of cutting this joint is with a matching pair of lock-miter cutters on a shaper or router.

The *miter-with-end-lap joint* combines the strength of a lap joint with the neat appearance of a miter joint. Note that the end grain shows only from one side of the frame. This joint is used in frame construction for cabinet doors. Fig. 39-73.

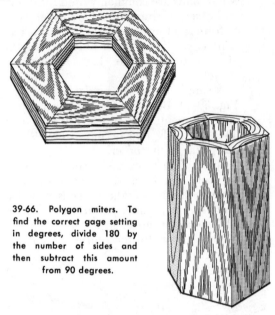

39-66. Polygon miters. To find the correct gage setting in degrees, divide 180 by the number of sides and then subtract this amount from 90 degrees.

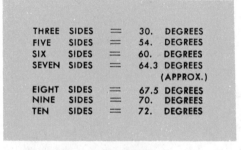

THREE	SIDES	=	30.	DEGREES
FIVE	SIDES	=	54.	DEGREES
SIX	SIDES	=	60.	DEGREES
SEVEN	SIDES	=	64.3	DEGREES
				(APPROX.)
EIGHT	SIDES	=	67.5	DEGREES
NINE	SIDES	=	70.	DEGREES
TEN	SIDES	=	72.	DEGREES

39-67. Correct angles for common polygons.

39-68. A tapered box formed by making compound miter cuts.

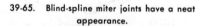

39-65. Blind-spline miter joints have a neat appearance.

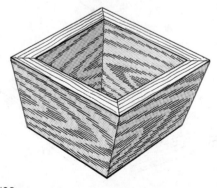

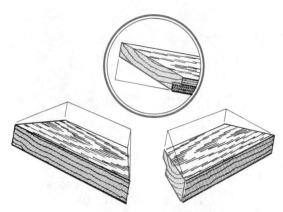

39-69. Compound miter or hopper joint. See Figs. 26-39 and 27-26 for correct saw settings.

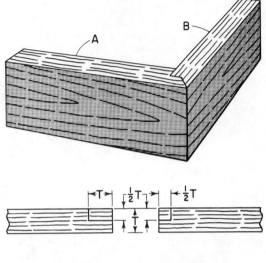

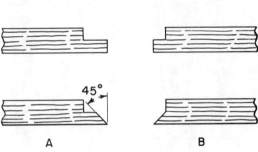

A   B

39-71. Layout for cutting a miter-with-rabbet joint. Part A is cut at a 45-degree angle and then the dado head is used to cut the rabbet. Part B can be cut in two steps, first with a rabbet cut and then with an angle cut; or it can be cut entirely by making two saw cuts.

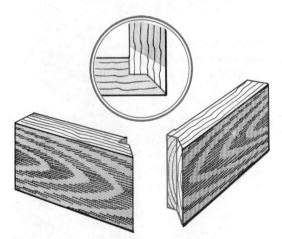

39-70. Miter with rabbet or offset miter.

Mortise-and-Tenon Joints

There are many kinds of mortise-and-tenon joints in frame construction, leg-and-rail construction, and many other types of assembly. The *blind or simple mortise and tenon* is used in leg-and-rail construction. Fig. 39-74. In making this joint it is necessary to decide if the mortise will have square corners or rounded ends. For square corners the cut is made on a mortiser or mortising attachment. Fig. 39-75. Rounded ends are cut on a router. The mortise should be at least 5/16″ from the outside face and

39-72. Lock miter.

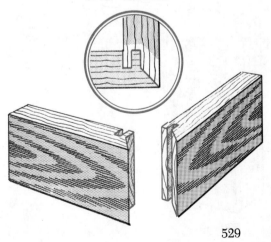

529

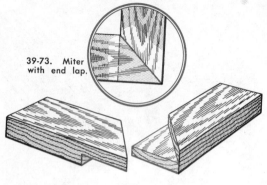

39-73. Miter with end lap.

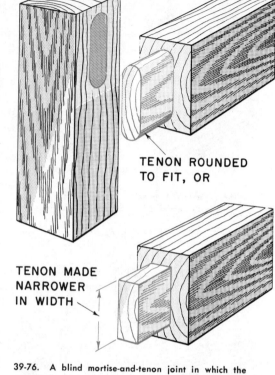

TENON ROUNDED TO FIT, OR

TENON MADE NARROWER IN WIDTH

39-76. A blind mortise-and-tenon joint in which the mortise is cut on a router. The router is a simpler machine for mortise cutting.

39-74. Some manufacturers of Early American furniture use the mortise-and-tenon joint for leg-and-rail construction.

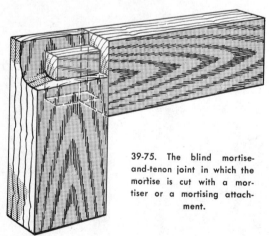

39-75. The blind mortise-and-tenon joint in which the mortise is cut with a mortiser or a mortising attachment.

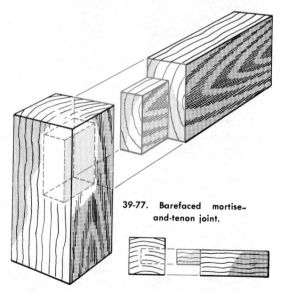

39-77. Barefaced mortise-and-tenon joint.

at least 1/8" deeper than the tenon for clearance. The tenon should be about one half the thickness of the stock.

For a simple or a barefaced joint, the tenon should be about 1/2" to 3/4" narrower than the total width. If a router-cut mortise is used, then the tenon must be rounded on the sides to fit or it must be cut narrow enough to fit into the straight part of the mortise. Fig. 39-76. The stock must always be wide enough to cover the ends of the mortise. The tenon is cut on a saw, shaper, or tenoner. A simple base for a table requires eight mortise-and-tenon joints. The barefaced mortise-and-tenon joint is used with leg-and-rail construction where the surfaces must be flush. The tenon has only one cheek. Fig. 39-77.

The *haunched mortise-and-tenon joint* is used in frame construction for added strength. Fig. 39-78. The tenon is made the same thickness as the groove or plow in the frame. The mortise is cut deeper than the depth of the groove. The haunch is then cut out from the tenon.

The *concealed haunched mortise-and-tenon joint* is quite similar to the haunched joint except that the groove for the haunch is cut at an angle and the tenon is cut to match. Fig. 39-79.

The *open mortise-and-tenon joint* is most commonly used in simple frame construction where an exposed tenon end is not objectionable. Fig. 39-80. The advantage of this joint is that both mortise and tenon can be cut with a dado head on the circular or radial-arm saw. The *stub mortise-and-tenon joint* is sometimes used in frame construction and is made with a short tenon that fits into the groove of the frame. Fig. 39-81.

Dovetail Joints

The dovetail joint is found in the finest grades of drawer construction and decorative boxes. Most common are the *lap or multiple dovetail* and the *stopped-lap*

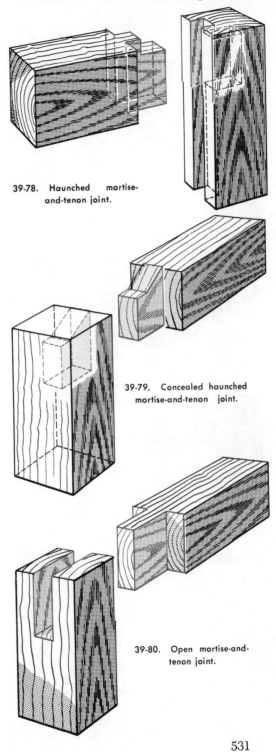

39-78. Haunched mortise-and-tenon joint.

39-79. Concealed haunched mortise-and-tenon joint.

39-80. Open mortise-and-tenon joint.

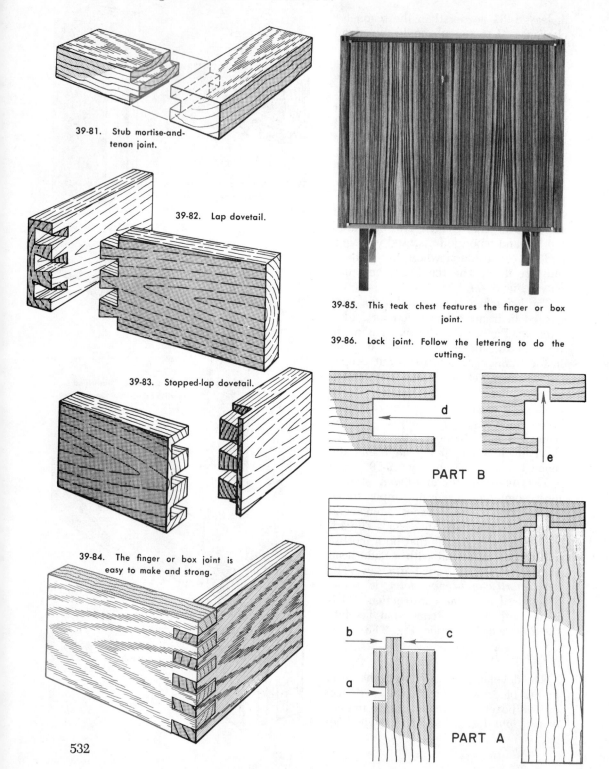

39-81. Stub mortise-and-tenon joint.

39-82. Lap dovetail.

39-83. Stopped-lap dovetail.

39-84. The finger or box joint is easy to make and strong.

39-85. This teak chest features the finger or box joint.

39-86. Lock joint. Follow the lettering to do the cutting.

PART B

PART A

dovetail. Figs. 39-82 and 39-83. This is a difficult joint to make unless the proper equipment is available. In small cabinet and school shops, the joint can be cut with a dovetail attachment on a portable router or with a fixture on the radial-arm saw. In large shops and factories, a dovetailer machine is used which is designed especially for production work.

Other Joints

The *box or finger joint* is a simplified form of dovetail joint. It is made by cutting matching notches and fingers in the two pieces to be joined. Fig. 39-84. This joint can easily be cut on the circular or radial-arm saw without special equipment. It is found in many Scandinavian designs for both structural and appearance purposes. Fig. 39-85.

The *lock joint* is found in drawer and box construction. This extremely solid joint can be made on the circular or radial-arm saw with a dado head. The correct cutting method is shown in Fig. 39-86. There must be a slight clearance between the parts so the two pieces can slide together.

---

40   Gluing And Clamping

Gluing and clamping are important cabinetmaking processes at several stages of construction. Fig. 40-1. In the early stages it is necessary to glue up stock to form wide surfaces or large areas for legs, rails, or posts. Later, subassemblies must be glued together. Final assembly of a piece of furniture or cabinetwork again calls for gluing. Fig. 40-1.

There are also many special gluing operations involved in wood lamination, veneering, and installing plastic laminates. Particle board and plywood are good examples of how wood and adhesives can be combined to produce materials that are, in many respects, superior to wood alone. Since there are a great many kinds of adhesives and glues,

40-1. The graceful furnishings shown here depend on modern gluing techniques for much of their beauty and soundness of construction.

533

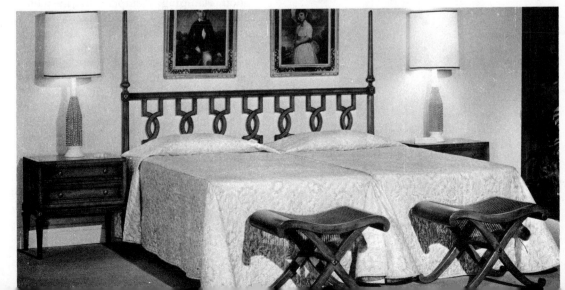

it is important to know how to select and use the right one for each particular job.

PROBLEMS IN GLUING

An *adhesive* is a substance capable of holding other materials together by surface attraction. Glues, cements, pastes, and mucilage are common forms. The use of all adhesives is sometimes loosely called "gluing." The kind of adhesive to select for a particular job depends on many factors.

Nature of Wood

Wood, you recall, is porous, and each kind of wood has different properties. For these reasons, wood is not easy to glue. Further differences arise from the way the pieces are to be fastened together. Gluing edge to edge is simplest. Gluing face to face is more difficult, and gluing end grain is particularly complicated because the many cut-off ends of hollow fibers absorb so much adhesive. Even when end grain is glued to the edge or face of wood, extra adhesive is needed because of this absorption. Fig. 40-2.

40-2. An enlarged view of a tiny piece of wood, showing the tubular structure. Can you see why it is more difficult to glue end grain than edge or face grain?

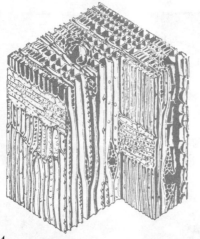

Moisture Content of Wood

The amount of moisture in wood affects both the rate at which glue dries and the strength of the finished joint. If wood has too much moisture before it is glued, a weak joint results. If wood takes on too much moisture during gluing, it first swells and then shrinks. This can set up stresses along the glue line which could result in failure of either the wood or the glue.

Fit of Joints

A joint that fits well is important for most gluing. Some adhesives have better gap-filling properties than others. Therefore, if the joint is not accurately made, an adhesive with good gap-filling properties should be selected.

Assembling and Curing

Several factors affect the assembly of parts and the curing. Some adhesives must be mixed immediately before assembly. Others come ready mixed. Some must be heated, and spread while hot. Others will spoil if not used rapidly. Still others remain usable for long periods. The amount of pressure needed to hold parts together after gluing is variable. Some adhesives, such as contact cement, require no clamping while others require good clamping. Temperature at which gluing is done is also a factor; many glues must be applied at 70 degrees or above. The rate at which glues dry also varies greatly. Certain synthetic glues can be dried instantly using high-frequency gluing equipment. Still another factor is the quality of the machined surfaces to be glued. A smooth, unsanded surface is usually required. The use of carbide-tipped blades will eliminate the need for jointing wood before bonding.

Glues should be applied in a clean, dust-free area. Apply just enough adhesive to hold and no more.

KINDS OF ADHESIVES

Only a few of the great variety of adhesives available will be described here. These can all be purchased under trade names that are widely advertised. The description on the label indicates the kind of glue and the procedure for mixing and applying it, which should be followed carefully. This is especially true for such adhesives as contact cement, of which there are a great many kinds, each involving different chemical formulas. Fig. 40-3.

Animal Glue

Animal (hide) glue, made from hooves, bones, and hides of animals, is one of the oldest glues of the cabinetmaker. In liquid form it is excellent for all types of interior furniture. Also it is available in a flake form which requires careful mixing and heating and is therefore not commonly used except in certain kinds of fine furniture manufacturing. Animal or hide glue is one of the best gap-filling adhesives and is a good choice when joints are not perfect. This glue gives best results with wood that has a moisture content from 4 to 6 per cent.

Casein Glue

Casein glue is made from milk curd and is purchased in powder form. It must be mixed with cold water to the consistency of heavy cream. It is extremely important that the glue be neither lumpy nor too thin. Though not 100 per cent waterproof like resin glues, casein glue will withstand considerable moisture. This glue will bond at any temperature above freezing but the warmer the better. This is a great advantage when gluing out-of-doors in cool weather. This glue has fair gap-filling properties and is best when moisture content is from 5 to 15 per cent.

There are two difficulties: Casein glue has an abrasive effect on cutting tools and therefore must sometimes be avoided. Also, it stains some woods, making it necessary to bleach the area around the glue joint before finishing.

Polyvinyl or White Liquid Glue

This is one of the handiest and most common glues for simple cabinetwork. It is available in almost any hardware or supply store in the familiar plastic squeeze bottle. This glue is always ready for use, non-staining, economical, and odorless. It gives a colorless glue line and cures rapidly at room temperature. It does not cure by chemical action, as some glues do, but sets by losing water to the wood and air. This glue is moderate in cost and has good strength and gap-filling properties. Its disadvantages are that it has relatively poor resistance to moisture and tends to soften at high temperature.

Plastic Resin Glue

This glue comes in powdered form and must be mixed with water to the consistency of heavy cream. Major uses are for furniture veneering and cabinetmaking. It sets hard, produces a very strong water-resistant bond, is non-staining and easy to use.

Aliphatic Resin Glue

This cream-colored, ready-mixed glue has an extremely high-strength bond. As a matter of fact, it produces a joint that is stronger than wood itself. It also has high resistance to heat and solvents and is easy to sand. The major weakness of this glue is that it lacks moisture resistance and therefore is satisfactory only for interior work.

Resorcinol Resin Glue

This bonding material is thermosetting (sets with heat) and is made by mixing

Kind	Animal (Liquid Hide) Glue	Powdered Casein	Polyvinyl White Liquid Resin Glue	Plastic Powdered Resin

CHARACTERISTICS

Especially good for:	First choice for furniture work and wherever a tough, lasting wood-to-wood bond is needed. A favorite for cabinetwork and general wood gluing.	Will do most woodworking jobs and is especially desirable with oily woods: teak, lemon, yew.	A fine all-around household glue for mending and furniture making and repair. Excellent for model work, paper, leather, and small assemblies.	Use it for woodworking and general gluing where considerable moisture resistance is wanted.
Disadvantages:	Because it is not waterproof, do not use it for outdoor furniture or for boat building.	Not moisture resistant enough for outdoor furniture. Will stain acid woods such as redwood. Must be mixed for each use.	Not sufficiently moisture-resistant for exposure to weather. Not so strong and lasting as liquid hide glue for fine furniture work. Softens under heat and solvents.	Do not use with oily woods or with joints that are not closely fitted and tightly clamped. Must be mixed for each use.
Advantages:	Very strong because it is rawhide-tough and does not become brittle. It is easy to use, light in color, resists heat and mold. It has good filling qualities, so gives strength even in poorly fitted joints.	Strong, fairly water-resistant, works in cool locations, fills poor joints well.	Always ready to use at any temperature. Non-staining, clean and white. Quick-setting qualities recommend it for work where good clamping is not possible.	Very strong, although brittle if joint fits poorly. Light-colored almost waterproof.
Source:	From animal hides and bones.	From milk curd.	From chemicals.	From chemicals.

USE

Room Temperature	Sets best above 70°. Can be used in colder room if glue is warmer.	Any temperature above freezing. But the warmer the better.	Any temperature above 60°. But the warmer the better.	Must be 70° or warmer. Will set faster at 90°.
Preparation	Ready to use.	Stir together equal parts by volume glue and water. Wait 10 minutes and stir again.	Ready to use.	Mix 2 parts powder with 1/2 to 1 part water.
Apply	Apply thin coat on both surfaces; let get tacky before joining.	Apply thin coat to both surfaces. Use within 8 hours after mixing.	Spread on and clamp at once.	Apply thin coat to both surfaces. Use within 4 hours after mixing.
70° Clamping Time	Hardwood: 2 hrs.	2 hrs.	1 hr.	16 hrs.
	Softwood: 3 hrs.	3 hrs.	1½ hrs.	16 hrs.

Aliphatic Resin	Resorcinol	Contact Cement	Epoxy Cement	Urea Resin

CHARACTERISTICS

Aliphatic Resin	Resorcinol	Contact Cement	Epoxy Cement	Urea Resin
Good for furniture and case goods assembly. Also, edge and face gluing. Same as poly-vinyl but with better results.	This is the glue for any work that may be exposed to soaking: outdoor furniture, boats, wooden sinks.	For bonding ve-neer, plastic laminates, leather, plastic, or canvas to wood.	Will bond wood to metal or other dis-similar materials. Use in combination with wood, tile, metal, glass, etc. Will not shrink or swell dur-ing hardening. Water-proof, oil proof, and non-inflammable.	Edge gluing with high frequency and steam heated pressing. Inte-rior and limited exte-rior use.
Lacks moisture resist-ance. Tends towards separation of glue and thinner during storage.	Not good for work that must be done at temperatures below 70°. Because of dark color and mixing, not often used unless wa-ter-proof quality is needed.	Parts can't be shifted once contact is made. Dangerous without proper ventilation.	Not good for fastening wood to wood in large products. (Must be used in well-ventilated room. Avoid getting into eyes.)	Poor gap-filling prop-erties. Limited pot life. Requires careful mixing and handling. Moisture content of wood must be from 7 to 10 per cent.
Compared to poly-vinyl it resists heat better, sands better, spreads easier, and is less affected by lac-quers. Not easily rub-bed off.	Very strong, as well as waterproof. It works better with poor joints than many glues do.	Adheres immediately on contact. No clamp-ing. Test for dryness by pressing wrapping paper to surface. If paper doesn't stick, surfaces are dry and ready for bonding.	Can be painted, sand-ed, filled, drilled, or machined. Can fill large holes.	Highly moisture re-sistant. Ideal for high frequency bond-ing. Dries white or nearly colorless.
From chemicals.	From chemicals.	Synthetic rubber (neo-prene, nitrile, or poly-sulfide).	From chemicals.	From chemicals. A thermosetting resin.

USE

Aliphatic Resin	Resorcinol	Contact Cement	Epoxy Cement	Urea Resin
Any temperature above 45°.	Must be 70° or warm-er. Will set faster at 90°.	70° or warmer.	Any temperature.	70° or warmer.
Stir before using. Ready for use.	Mix 3 parts powder to 4 parts liquid cat-alyst.	Ready to use.	Resin and hardener mixed in amounts stated on container.	Resin and catalyst must be carefully mixed.
Spread on and clamp.	Apply thin coat to both surfaces. Use within 8 hours after mixing.	Brush on liberal coat. Dry for 30 minutes. Apply second coat.	Apply with stick or brush.	Apply with roller.
1 hr.	16 hrs.	No clamping. Bonds instantly.	No clamping. Drys faster with heat.	A few seconds with high frequency heat.
1½ hrs.	16 hrs.			

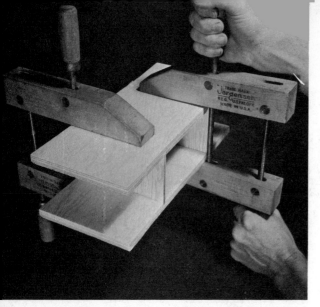

40-4. Using hand screws to hold plywood parts together.

No.	5/0	4/0	3/0	2/0	0
Length, jaws	4"	5"	6"	7"	8"
Jaw opening	2"	2½"	3"	3½"	4½"
No.	1	2	3	4	5
Length, jaws	10"	12"	14"	16"	18"
Jaw opening	6"	8½"	10"	12"	14"

40-5. Common sizes of hand screws.

40-6. Opening or closing a hand screw.

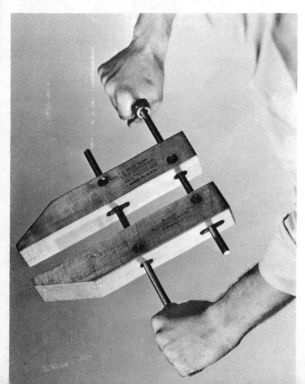

liquid resin with a powder catalyst. It comes in a can divided into two compartments and must be mixed as needed. This glue is excellent for exterior use because it is completely waterproof. The major disadvantage is that it creates a dark glue line.

Contact Cement

Contact cement is a ready-mixed rubber or butane material available in liquid form. It can be used for applying plastic laminates or veneers to wood or plywood. This cement requires no pressure or clamps. A disadvantage is its relatively low resistance to heat, cold, and solvents. Many commercial types of contact cement are available. When using one, it is important to follow the manufacturer's directions.

Epoxy Resin

This is generally a two-part adhesive that will produce a strong, waterproof bond when used on wood, plastics, ceramics and practically any other material. It has good gap-filling properties and can be used on non-porous surfaces. Many furniture designs call for fastening a wide variety of materials such as ceramic tile to a table top or metal to wood; for such work, epoxy resin is ideal.

Urea Resin

Urea resin has been found the best adhesive to use with electronic gluing equipment. This glue is a thermosetting resin of synthetic origin. Since so many combinations of the adhesive are possible, a glue manufacturer should be contacted to determine the exact content for any application other than those given on the container.

CLAMPING DEVICES

The following are the more common clamping devices. In the furniture in-

538

dustry many mechanical, hydraulic, and air-operated clamping devices are used in addition.

Hand Screws or Wooden Parallel Clamps

The best holding device for wood, plastic, and many other materials, these clamps can be used on finished surfaces without any protective wood strips or cauls. Fig. 40-4. They are made in sizes from 5/0, which has a jaw length of 4" and a maximum opening between jaws of 2", to size 7, with a length of 24" and a maximum opening between jaws of 17". Fig. 40-5. When using hand screws, the center spindle is held in the left hand and the outside spindle in the right hand. Then the hand screw can be opened or closed by twisting the handles in opposite directions.

Rough adjustment of the hand screw is done rapidly by swinging it. Hold the handles firmly with the arms extended. By moving your wrists only, the jaws can be revolved around the spindle. Fig. 40-6. When the jaws are open about the right amount, place the end spindle in the upper position with the middle spindle as close to the stock as possible. Adjust the spindles so that the jaws will be parallel when the hand screw grips the stock. Turn the end spindle clockwise to close the ends of the jaws on the work. All final pressure should be applied by turning the end spindle only, using the middle spindle as a fulcrum.

Hand screws can be used not only when gluing stock face to face but also for many other clamping jobs. Fig. 40-7 shows a use in furniture repair. The hand screw can also be used as a picture-frame clamp by making a simple jig such as that shown in Fig. 40-8.

Steel Bar Clamps

Steel bar clamps or cabinet clamps are used primarily for edge-to-edge gluing,

for clamping up large surfaces, and for assembling furniture. Common lengths are from 2' to 10'. One end is adjusted by a friction clutch or catch while the other end has a screw for applying pressure. Fig. 40-9. When using bar clamps, the screw should be turned out completely; then the friction clutch or catch is moved until the clamp is slightly wider than the total width of the stock to be clamped. Fig. 40-10. When using bar clamps on finished stock, as in assembling furniture, the surface of the wood must be protected. Place pieces of scrap stock between the jaws and the wood.

40-7. Using one large and two small hand screws in furniture repair.

40-8(a). A picture-frame clamp that consists of two halves exactly alike and a single hand screw.

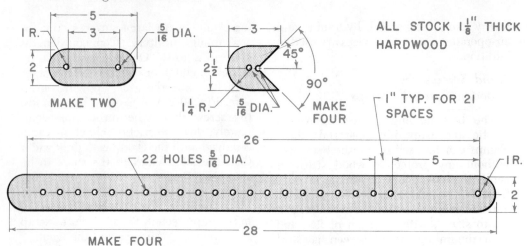

ALL STOCK 1⅛" THICK
HARDWOOD

MAKE TWO

MAKE FOUR

1" TYP. FOR 21 SPACES

26

22 HOLES 5/16 DIA.

5

MAKE FOUR

28

40-8(b). Details for making the parts for a picture-frame clamp. Use a hardwood such as maple. The parts of the clamp are held together with 5/16" bolts. The notched blocks which hold the corners of the frame should be relieved by drilling holes in them.

40-9(a). Using steel bar clamps for edge-to-edge gluing. Notice that the clamps are reversed to equalize the pressure.

40-9(b). The friction clutch can be moved in or out into any clamping position. The screw pressure must be removed before the clutch will move.

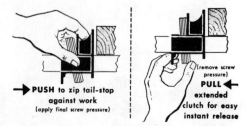

PUSH to zip tail-stop against work
(apply final screw pressure)

PULL
extended clutch for easy instant release
(remove screw pressure)

Wood Bar Cabinet Clamps

These are similar to steel bar clamps except that the bar itself is of wood rather than metal. Fig. 40-11. This kind of clamp is used for the finest cabinetwork, upholstery, and antique repair work. The major advantage is that the wood bar is less likely to injure a finished surface. Fig. 40-12.

Spring Clamps

Spring clamps are used for many kinds of clamping. They operate like overgrown clothespins. Fig. 40-13. They are particularly good when light pressure is all that is needed or when the clamp must be applied and removed quickly. Some have rubber-covered jaws to protect the work. There is a heavy-duty type that has pivoting jaws made of stainless steel with double rows of serrated teeth along the pressure edge. Such jaws can hold parts at any angle so that miter joints and other odd-shaped pieces can be clamped together easily. Fig. 40-14.

C or Carriage Clamps

C or carriage clamps are made in a

40-10. Bar clamps and speed clamps are used in edge-to-edge gluing. Wood blocks placed across the grain keep the surface level.

40-13. Using spring clamps to hold the molding in place on a window screen.

40-11. Wood bar cabinet clamps eliminate the danger of marring the surface.

40-14. Using heavy spring clamps with pivoting stainless steel jaws. Along the pressure edge these jaws have serrated teeth that grip the two surfaces. Notice how the clamps are used for gluing cabinet sides.

40-12. Using wood bar clamps to glue up a finished product. Note the wood blocks (cauls) placed under the metal jaws to protect the wood surface.

40-15(a). C clamps can be used to hold stock face to face and for many other purposes.

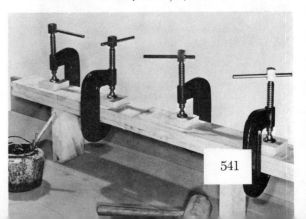

40-15(b). C clamps are also used to hold jigs, fixtures and stop blocks to machines and for clamping irregular-shaped parts together. The 6" to 10" sizes are best for general work.

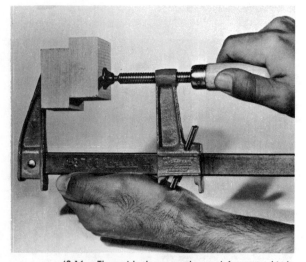

40-16. The quick clamp can be used for many kinds of small clamping operations in place of a C clamp.

40-17. Using an edge-clamp fixture to hold a piece of molding on the edge of a table top.

542

wide variety of sizes and shapes and are commonly used when gluing stock face to face. Fig. 40-15. They vary in maximum-opening size from 2" to 12". Some C clamps are made with an extra-deep throat which gives maximum working clearance. When clamping a finished surface with C clamps, always use cauls to protect the surface.

Quick clamps do the work of heavy C clamps. Actually a short bar clamp, it can be adjusted instantly by sliding the head along the bar. Fig. 40-16. An *edge-clamp fixture* works with a quick clamp to help in solving a common and difficult problem: gluing strips of wood to the edges of plywood or solid wood. The quick clamp grasps the work and the edge clamp applies pressure to the edge material. Fig. 40-17.

Band Clamps

Band clamps are made with a metal clamp and a band of steel or canvas. They are used primarily for clamping round or irregular-shaped sections such as furniture frames. Steel bands are best for round objects while canvas bands are better for odd shapes. Fig. 40-18.

Hinged Clamps

These clamps fasten to the underside of a bench and are easily swung out of the way when not in use. Fig. 40-19. They can be used for many types of gluing and clamping operations.

40-18(a). Band clamps can be used for gluing round or irregularly shaped sections such as a chair frame.

Clamp fixtures can be purchased for use with 1/2" or 3/4" metal pipe to make clamps of any needed length. Fig. 40-20. A *miter-and-corner clamp* is ideal for assembling frames. Once the two parts are clamped together, the corner can be trued up with a back saw if it doesn't fit perfectly. Since the corner is open, any kind of metal fastener can be installed easily. Fig. 40-21.

GLUING PROCEDURE

Make sure the wood is at correct moisture content and that all pieces are as dry as they should be. If the moisture content is too high, the glue that penetrates the cell cavities will be thinned, resulting in a very weak joint. On the other hand, if moisture content is too low, the wood will absorb glue too rapidly. All gluing should be done when the wood is at a moisture content below 10 per cent. However, some woods glue better at even lower moisture content. Any glue that contains water will raise the moisture content of the wood surrounding the joint, and this causes a raised glue line. If boards are surfaced before the moisture content of the glue line equals that of the remainder of the wood, the glue joint will sink after the surfacing, resulting in what is called a

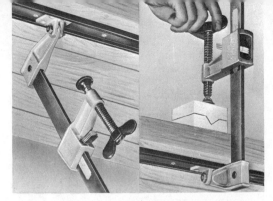

40-19(a). Hinged clamps hang free under the bench and out of the way. The work is placed on the bench top and the clamp swings over it. Then push the sliding head against the work and apply final pressure by turning the screw.

40-19(b). These clamps can be used for all types of face gluing. Here, scrap stock is being glued to the back of disks in preparation for faceplate turning.

40-18(b). Some common uses of band clamps.

40-20. Single- or double-bar pipe clamps can be made by putting clamp fixtures on ordinary black pipe. The double-bar design exerts equal pressure on both sides of the work, preventing any tendency to buckle. This is a fine clamping tool for thin-edge gluing.

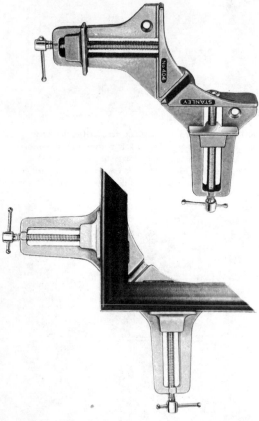

40-21. This miter-and-corner clamp is good for gluing up frames.

40-22. This is what will happen if a glued-up panel is surfaced while there is a raised glue line.

JOINT EXPANDED BY MOISTURE IN GLUE.

WOOD SURFACED BEFORE WOOD IS DRY.

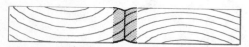

SUNKEN WOOD JOINT WHEN DRY.

sunken joint. Fig. 40-22. This is especially noticeable on large, finished surfaces.

Some adhesives work well only with carefully fitted joints while others have better gap-filling properties. *Follow the manufacturer's directions.* Make sure that you use the proper proportions for all mixing and that all lumps have been removed. Also, mix glue only as needed so that each batch is fresh.

Make a trial assembly, making sure that all surfaces are clean and dry and that joints are well fitted. Do this by dry clamping all pieces together. Fig. 40-23. Also, make sure that you have the necessary cauls. Fig. 40-24. Mark the pieces that are to be glued for correct assembly. In edge gluing several pieces together it is a good idea to draw a large X across the face of the pieces when they are dry-clamped. Use carpenter's crayon or a heavy pencil. Then, when actually gluing up the stock, it is easy to fit the parts in correct order again. Make sure that there are enough clamps and that they are adjusted correctly.

Bar clamps should be spaced 10″ to 15″ apart. They should be alternated, one above and the next below. On extremely wide surfaces it is a good idea to put cleats or cauls across the ends to prevent buckling, with waxed paper underneath to keep them from sticking. Clamp in place with hand screws or C clamps. Never glue parts that should be free to

40-23. Dry clamp the parts to make sure they fit.

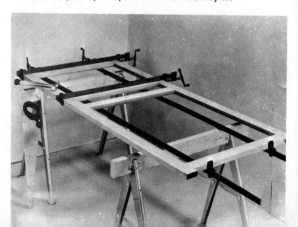

move. For example, a drawer bottom should always be assembled without glue.

Edge Gluing

In edge gluing, follow these suggestions:

• The grain of all pieces should run in the same direction. Then, after gluing up, the completed piece will not be difficult to surface. Fig. 40-25.
• Alternate the pieces so that the growth rings run in opposite directions. This helps to prevent cupping.
• Try to match the pieces to form an interesting grain pattern.
• Pieces to be glued should be no wider than 4″ to 6″.

Spreading Glue

The common methods of applying glue are with a brush, stick, paddle, or squeeze bottle. Fig. 40-26. A hand- or power-operated glue roller can also be used. Fig. 40-27. Glues can be applied either to one surface, called *single spreading*, or to both surfaces, called *double spreading*. Glue from a squeeze bottle should be applied in a zig-zag line. Then the two parts should be pressed together and moved back and forth to produce an even spread.

Generally, tiny beads of glue will appear along a good glue joint at regular intervals of 2″ to 3″. A starved glue joint may result from using too little glue

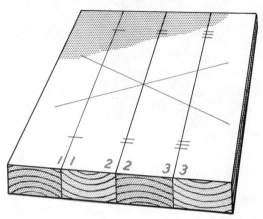

40-25. Note the correct arrangement of the pieces before gluing up. The large "X" and other markings will make assembly easy.

40-26(a). Hot glue is usually applied with a brush. Hot animal glue is still used in certain furniture manufacturing.

40-26(b). When gluing end grain, apply a thin coat to it first. Then apply a second coat to the end grain and one coat to the other surface. This is done because end grain absorbs more glue.

40-24. To prevent marring, put cauls (protective pieces of wood) between the clamps and the stock.

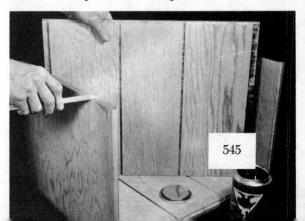

545

40-27(a). A hand glue spreader has a plastic chamber for holding the glue. A knurled steel roller in the bottom of the chamber dispenses the glue to the rubber roller.

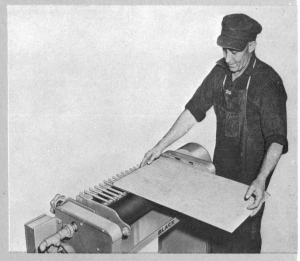

40-27(b). A power-operated, roll-type glue spreader is used in many cabinet shops.

40-28. Assemble the parts immediately after gluing.

or too much pressure. It is a good idea to allow the glue to become tacky by letting it set a short time before assembling the parts. Never apply so much glue that squeeze-out is a problem. For example, the mortise-and-tenon joint should not have glue visible around the tenon where it fits against the mortise section.

Applying the Correct Pressure

After gluing, assemble the parts. Some glues, such as hot animal glue, require that this be done very rapidly. With other glues, such as white liquid glue, the assembly time can be longer. Fig. 40-28. At normal room temperature, it is important that the glue is still fluid when the pressure is applied.

Applying excessive pressure after assembly will cause a "starved" joint, that is, one that is weak because too much glue has been squeezed out. However, there is usually more danger of applying too little pressure than of applying too much. In edge gluing, the clamps should be alternated, one from one side and one from the other, about every 10″ to 15″. When pressure is correctly applied, a slight amount of glue should be visible along the glue line. This should be allowed to dry, then scraped away. In edge gluing it is frequently necessary to apply a moderate amount of pressure and then to line up the pieces by striking one or more with a wood mallet before continuing to tighten the clamps. It is important that correct pressure be allowed to remain on the joint until the pieces are firmly bonded and the glue is dry.

Curing Time

The rate at which glues dry varies greatly with the type of glue and the room temperature. However, with many of the chemical glues, heat is applied to speed the cure. The higher the tempera-

546

40-29(a). A portable electronic gluer or welder consists of a high-frequency electric generator, an electronic hand gun, the conductors to the hand gun, and the various styles of electrodes.

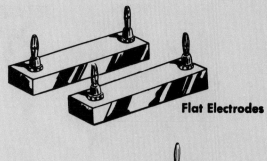

Flat Electrodes

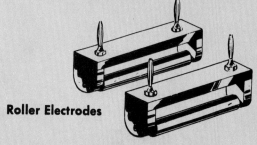

Roller Electrodes

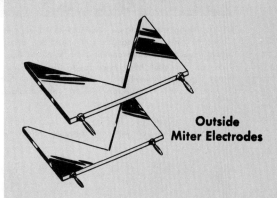

Outside Miter Electrodes

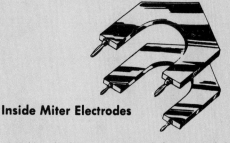

Inside Miter Electrodes

40-29(b). The four common sets of electrodes include flat electrodes that are used for edge gluing; roller electrodes for paneling, banding, moldings, and other edges; outside miter electrodes for any square or miter corner; inside miter electrodes for gluing inside corners.

ture, the faster the cure. The most common methods of applying heat are by contact heat with a hot platen and by a high-frequency electrical field.

High-Frequency Gluing Equipment

It has been found that a wet glue joint is a good conductor of electricity. When the joint is placed in an electrical field of high frequency, alternating current passes along the glue line and generates heat. This heat dries the glue in a matter of seconds. Animal and casein glues are not suitable for this. It is necessary to use one of the thermosetting resin glues. The urea-resin glues are used for over 90 per cent of all high-frequency gluing.

A portable high-frequency electronic gluer or welder is quite easy to use. Fig. 40-29. It comes equipped with a hand gun designed for applying the electricity. The trigger switch turns the electricity on and off. Fig. 40-30. Different woods, different glues, the amount of glue, and the thickness of the material create a change of load in the hand gun. A tuning knob on the hand gun can be turned to allow for this change of load.

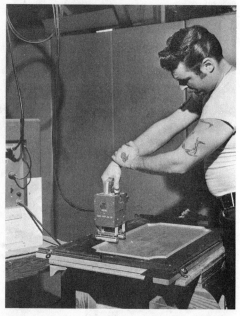

40-30. Using the electronic welder with roller electrodes to fasten moldings to kitchen-cabinet doors. Apply glue to the edge and place it over the door. Then apply enough hand pressure to bring the joint firmly together. Otherwise, the glue will be cured but a weak joint will result. Apply pressure and roll along the molding.

40-31. Hold the gun with firm pressure across the joint.

A knob on the hand gun must be adjusted so the panel meter on the electronic welder will always read in the medium-to-high range.

To edge glue, apply glue to one or both edges of the wood and use bar clamps as you would for other gluing. Then apply the flat electrodes across the glue line and pull the trigger switch. Move the tuning knob to the maximum heat. Keep the hand gun in place until the glue dries enough to stop boiling. Fig. 40-31. This usually takes from two to five seconds for softwoods and a little longer for hardwoods. In edge gluing, weld about every 8″ and near the ends. Release the bar clamps, and the board is ready to be processed. The glued-up stock has sufficient strength to be worked immediately. The full strength of the bond develops in 8 to 24 hours, depending on the adhesive used.

There are electrodes specially designed for gluing inside and outside corners of casework. Fig. 40-32. Also there are roller electrodes for gluing a plastic-laminate edge. Fig. 40-33. Remember, always place the electrodes across the glue line on all joints where the glue line is exposed.

ASSEMBLING CABINETS AND FURNITURE

Before assembling cabinets and furniture, it must be decided whether the product can be assembled all at one time or whether it is necessary to glue up subassemblies. Generally, tables and chairs consisting of legs and rails are glued up in two steps. The legs and rails on either end are glued up first, then the entire product is assembled. After the dust panels are assembled, most casework is glued up in one step except for the application of molding and edging. Follow these general steps:

1. Have the correct number of clamps adjusted to the right openings.

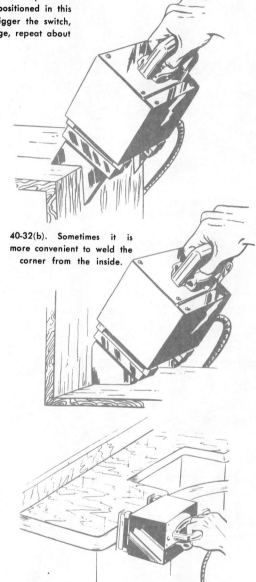

40-32(a). The miter electrodes are cut square so that the joint to be welded can be positioned in this square. Apply hand-gun pressure, trigger the switch, and weld the corner. On a long edge, repeat about every 8".

2. Have enough cauls ready so they can be placed under the clamps to protect the finished surfaces. A mallet is needed for striking the parts to make sure they fit together firmly. A straightedge and square are needed for checking the assembly.

3. Mix the right amount and kind of glue to proper consistency.

4. Apply glue to the joints. Generally, both parts of the joint should be covered. However, in mortise-and-tenon construction, it is better to apply most of the glue to the mortise since the glue will scrape off the tenon as it is pushed in place. Never apply so much glue that it will squeeze out where it is difficult to remove, as around a leg or rail.

5. After the parts are assembled and clamped, make these three checks:

a. With a square, make sure that the parts are at right angles to one another. Fig. 40-34.

b. Use a straightedge to make sure the pieces are all in one plane and are not warped. Fig. 40-35.

c. Place a stick across the corners to make sure that the diagonal distance is the same. Fig. 40-36.

6. Allow the glue to dry thoroughly before removing clamps. The clamps can be removed immediately after high-frequency gluing.

7. Prepare the surfaces for finishing. Remove excess glue with a sharp chisel. Sand the joints thoroughly; bleach if necessary.

GLUING PROBLEMS

If the correct kind of glue has been

40-32(b). Sometimes it is more convenient to weld the corner from the inside.

40-33. Using the roller electrodes to apply self-edging. This would be done to apply plastic laminate to the edge of a counter top. Apply glue evenly to both surfaces. Press the roller electrodes in the small gap position and across the edging strip, and apply pressure. Start at one end and slide or walk the gun along the edge, keeping an even, flat pressure. If the strip is added after the plastic-laminate top, place masking tape along the top edge to insure easy removal of excess glue that may boil out.

40-34. Checking the product for squareness.

40-35. Checking for levelness.

40-36. Checking the length across corners to make sure the distances from corner to corner are equal.

used and the joint properly made, it should be stronger than the wood itself. A test glue joint can be checked by placing a blunt chisel at the glue line and striking it with a hammer. A good joint will not split along the glue joint.

A weak glue joint may have many causes such as poor fit, inadequate pressure, too short a pressure time, or a fuzzy glue line. Other conditions that may cause a weak joint are: a *starved joint* or one with too little glue; a *chilled joint* in which the glue became jelly before or immediately after applying pressure; or a *dried joint* in which the glue dried without bonding. Another problem that sometimes develops is discoloration due to iron in the glue. This particularly affects such woods as oak, walnut, cedar, maple, redwood, and cherry.

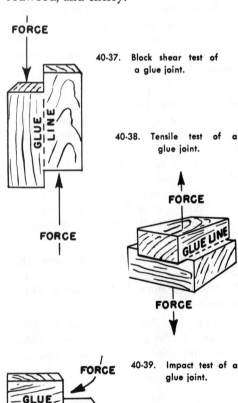

40-37. Block shear test of a glue joint.

40-38. Tensile test of a glue joint.

40-39. Impact test of a glue joint.

550

Testing the Glue Joint

In industry there are three common methods for testing wood adhesives. The *block shear test* is one in which sample hardwood blocks are glued together under ideal conditions. Then a compression force is applied to the end of the block to determine at what point the parts will break. A high-quality glue may run as high as 3000 to 4000 pounds per square inch, or a total shear strength of 9000 to 12,000 pounds for a block 3″ square in area. Fig. 40-37. The *tensile test* is used to determine when the glue blocks will fail under tension. Fig. 40-38. The *impact test* determines the impact strength of wood adhesives when force is applied. Fig. 40-39. This is an important test for gluing since bowling pins, chairs, and many other glued products are often subject to severe impact rather than static loads.

41 Bending And Laminating

Many styles of furniture and cabinetwork require curved parts such as a drawer front, the rail of a table, or the jamb or head for a window. Fig. 41-1. Bent-wood and molded-plywood chairs are an example of extreme bends in furniture. Fig. 41-2. Frequently the corner of a paneled wall or counter is curved. All of these require some method of *bending*.

Often combined with bending is *laminating*, that is, the process of building

41-1. The curved parts of these dining chairs are made of solid wood cut to shape. The curved rails or aprons of the table are of laminated construction.

551

41-2. This large swivel chair has a laminated frame of walnut with cushion and arms shaped to fit the body for utmost comfort.

41-3. This chair is a combination of molded plywood on seat and back, with laminated legs and brace.

up the thickness or width of material by gluing several thinner pieces together, all with the grain *running in the same direction*. Fig. 41-3. Making *molded plywood* is very similar except that the layers are *at right angles to each other*. (Laminating is also done without bending for many straight parts.)

Following are common methods of producing curved parts for furniture pieces.

• *Cutting from solid stock*. The simplest way is to cut the curved part from solid stock on the band saw. Figs. 41-4 and 41-5. However, this is satisfactory only for cutting a relatively limited number of pieces that have slight curvatures. On a sharp curve there is so much short grain at the end that the piece is very weak.

• *Brick or segment method*. Circular parts can be built up of rows of solid wood pieces called segments or bricks. Fig. 41-6. The joints are staggered so that there is no weakness. Since all of the pieces are fairly short, there is no extensive end grain on the surface. The pieces are cut to shape, fitted together, then glued into one piece. In constructing a curved piece of segments or bricks, always make sure that there are at least three layers to equalize the stresses. After the pieces are glued together and shaped, the segmented structure is often covered with a face and back veneer.

• *Cross kerfing solid lumber or plywood*. In this method a series of short kerfs is cut to within 1/16″ of the outside surface so the material will be more flexible for bending. Fig. 41-7. These deep cuts are made side-by-side in the surface that will form the back of the circular part.

To determine the correct spacing for the saw kerfs, first decide on the radius of the curve or circle to be formed. Measure this distance (the radius) from the end of the stock and make a saw kerf at this point. Fasten the stock to the

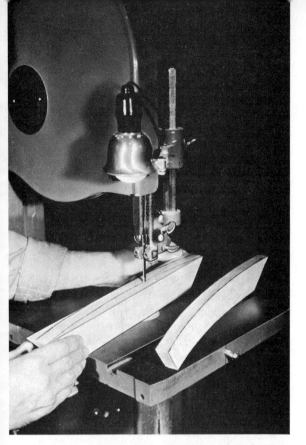

41-4. Cutting curved rails from solid stock on a band saw.

41-5. The curved stretchers (lower rails) of this nest table were cut from solid lumber.

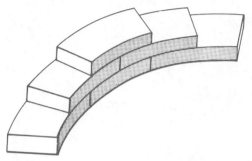

41-6. The brick or segment method of making curved parts uses solid stock that has been cut to shape on the band saw. The width is built up using several pieces of material, with the end joints staggered. The pieces should be glued together with a water-resistant adhesive.

41-7. Cross kerfing is a practical method of bending wood. This method can be used to round off the corners of paneled walls, to shape rails or aprons, and for similar jobs. The kerfed side forms the back or underside of the bend.

41-8. The correct method of determining the distance between saw kerfs. The distance between the kerfs determines the flexibility of the material.

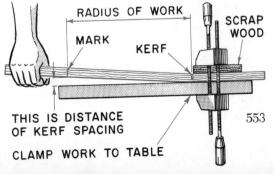

RADIUS OF WORK

MARK

SCRAP WOOD

KERF

THIS IS DISTANCE OF KERF SPACING

CLAMP WORK TO TABLE

553

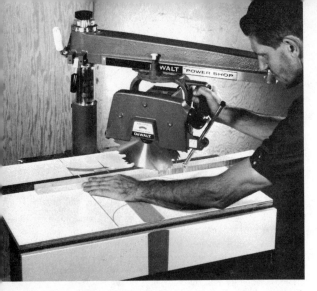

41-9. Cutting equally spaced kerfs at an angle in preparation for bending a spiral curve.

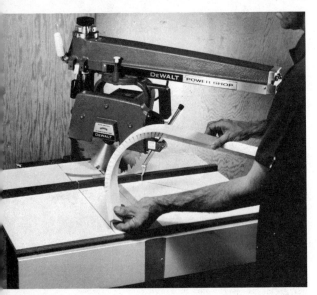

41-10. Notice how the wood can be twisted as it is bent.

41-11. Apply adhesive to the veneer and slip it into the saw kerfs.

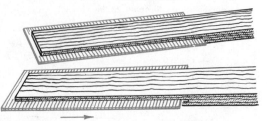

table top with a clamp; then raise the end of the stock until the kerf closes. Fig. 41-8. The distance the end of the stock is raised above the table is the distance needed between kerfs. (Note that in Fig. 41-8, a mark indicates one end of the radius; therefore the height is measured at that mark, not at the end of the stock.)

After the first kerf, mark the space for the second kerf and make the cut. Before moving the stock, mark a pencil line on the guide fence of the radial-arm saw. Make the remaining cuts by locating each new saw kerf at the guide mark.

A spiral curve can be produced by cutting kerfs at an angle. Fig. 41-9. When the cuts are complete, the stock is bent slowly until the right curve is obtained. Fig. 41-10. Soaking the wood in warm water will help the bending. Compound curves can be formed in this way by kerfing both sides of the stock. The exposed surface can be covered with veneer.

• *Kerfing parallel to the face.* Sometimes a piece is needed that is straight for most of its length but curved at the end. The easiest method of producing this kind of bend is to make a series of saw kerfs from the end grain, parallel to the face surface. Usually at least two or three kerfs should be made. Then cut sheets of 1/8″ veneer slightly wider and longer than the kerfs. Apply a good grade of waterproof glue to both surfaces and slip the veneer in place. Fig. 41-11. Fasten the end in a form and use clamps to hold it to shape. Fig. 41-12. Allow the piece to remain in the form until the glue is thoroughly dry. Then trim the extra veneer away from the sides and ends. If extremely thick material is to be bent, it may be necessary to steam the ends to make the wood more plastic before the veneer is inserted.

• *Bending solid wood to a form.* Solid wood can be bent to shape by first soft-

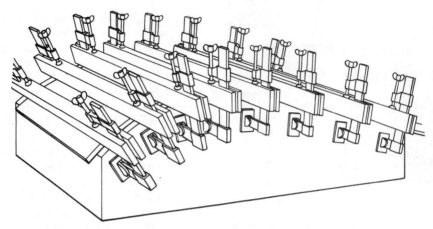

41-12. The end of the material can be clamped in a form or mold like this until dry.

ening (plasticizing) the wood with steam or hot water, then placing it in a form until it dries out. Fig. 41-13. Certain chemicals can also be used to make solid wood pliable.

As a piece of wood is bent, it is stretched on the outer (convex) side and compressed on the inner (concave) side; the convex side is longer than the concave side. For this reason the wood must first be softened with moisture and then heated before it is bent. In general, the moisture content for bending should be between 12 and 20 per cent, although it can be as high as 30 per cent. The higher moisture content is necessary for sharper bends. When bending solid wood, remember that the face or exterior surface cannot be stretched more than 1 to 2 per cent while the back surface can be compressed as much as 20 per cent.

The following woods, arranged in order of bending quality, are commonly used by the furniture industry for bent

41-13(a). In industry, solid wood is usually plasticized or softened with steam heat.

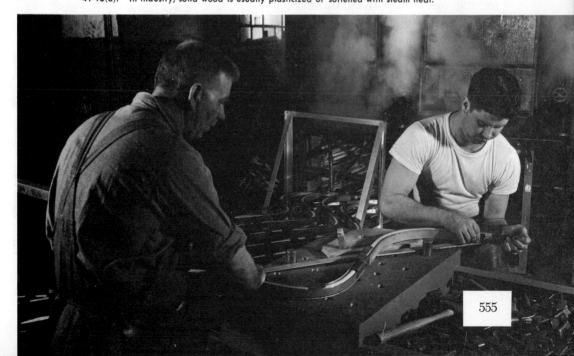

555

41-13(b). This hot-plate press is used to bend furniture parts. It consists of hollow metal forms or platens heated by steam. The stock is placed between the forms which are brought against the stock by hydraulic pressure. The bent pieces are held to shape and dried between the heated plates.

parts: white oak, red oak, pecan, walnut, elm, hickory, ash, beech, birch, maple, mahogany and sweet gum.

To produce bent parts from solid wood, it is necessary to have a method of soaking or steaming and also a form or mold in which to clamp the wood until it is dry. If the shop is in a steam-heated building, it may be possible to run the steam by a hose into a retort for softening the wood. Fig. 41-14. However, in most situations it is simpler to soak the wood in boiling water. This requires a metal container such as an old hot-water

tank, a large milk tank, or a large-diameter pipe with a welded bottom. Fig. 41-15. The top of the container should be partly covered with a rubber tube or a metal cover with small holes. Heat should be applied until the water boils. The material to be bent is placed in the boiling water. Usually an hour of soaking is needed for each inch of thickness, although more time may be required.

The form or mold for bending can be made of either wood or metal. Generally, for a simple drawer front, a mold cut from a piece of hardwood is satisfactory. Fig. 41-16. In bending over a mold, a piece of sheet metal, preferably stainless steel, should be placed over the exterior of the stock and the clamps tightened a little at a time as the material is forced around the mold. Fig. 41-17. Allow the material to dry thoroughly before removing it from the mold.

41-15. Using hot water to soften wood. An old hot-water heater or a large metal pipe with one closed end can be used. Place some kind of burner under the closed end to heat the water. Place a rubber sleeve over the other end to keep the steam in; this will also act as a safety valve.

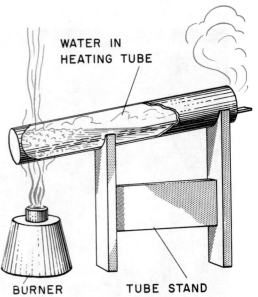

WATER IN HEATING TUBE

BURNER TUBE STAND

41-14. A method of softening wood with hot steam. An old hot-water tank acts as a retort (a container for steam). The steam comes from the heating plant.

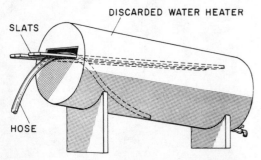

DISCARDED WATER HEATER

SLATS

HOSE

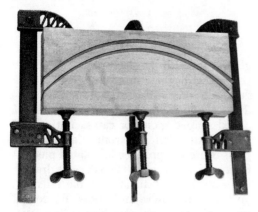

41-16. A simple wood form or mold such as this can be used to bend small pieces, as for a wood drawer front.

41-17. Clamping the softened wood to a form with a metal strap over it. The bent pieces are clamped to the form and then allowed to dry.

41-18. This attractive log holder is made of laminated materials. Two molds are needed.

41-19(a). Loading an electronic laminating press with veneers to produce such pieces as curved drawer fronts, rails, chair arms, table aprons, end panels, and doors.

41-19(b). The upper half of the mold is lowered with hydraulic pressure; at the same time the electronic gluing unit is turned on. The pieces are immediately bonded together in the correct shape. The upper half of the mold is then used.

41-19(c). Removing the dry laminated piece. Note that the mold is built of plywood with a metal lining.

557

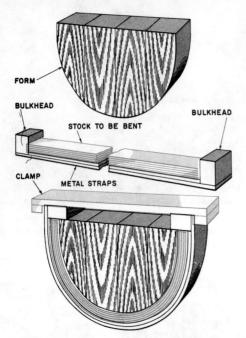

FORM

BULKHEAD

STOCK TO BE BENT

BULKHEAD

CLAMP

METAL STRAPS

41-20. One type of mold that can be used for producing curved or semi-circular parts.

41-21. This mold is used to produce the rough blanks for a salad server. Note that the hardwood forms are reinforced by installing several dowels.

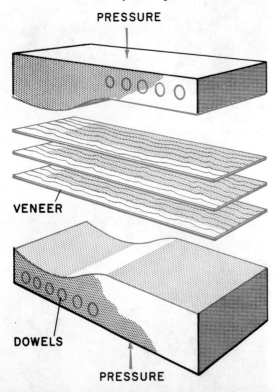

PRESSURE

VENEER

DOWELS

PRESSURE

PROCEDURE FOR LAMINATING AND BENDING

Curved laminated parts are made by gluing together several pieces of thin veneer with the grain running in the same direction. Fig. 41-18. These are then clamped in a form (sometimes called shaped molds or cauls) until dry. In industry, an electronic laminating press is used to produce laminated pieces for such furniture parts as curved drawer fronts, rails, chair arms, table rails or aprons, end panels, and doors. By combining the pressure of a hydraulic press with the instant curing of high-frequency gluing, the parts can be produced in large volume in a very short time. Fig. 41-19. The manufacturer must have a different form for each shape that is required. In a small cabinet or school shop, laminating and bending call for the following equipment:

• *A form or mold of the correct shape.* The mold can be made of glued-up plywood or thick, solid stock such as birch or maple. Fig. 41-20. The form can be cut to shape on the band saw. It is a good idea to line the form with rubber (cut from an innertube) or cork to make the pressure more even. Fig. 41-21. Forms can also be built of metal. Apply a sealer finish like shellac to wood forms. For production jobs, a special form or mold with built-in V-bolt clamps can be constructed. An adjustable form that can be used for many different shapes is shown in Fig. 41-22. This, however, is satisfactory for only rather narrow parts. First lay out the curvature of the piece on 3/4" plywood. The same pieces of plywood can be used for several different shapes merely by changing the location of the wood clamps. Then fasten metal pins or nails on the curved lines at intervals of 4" or 5". Make a series of wood clamps similar to those shown in Fig. 41-23. Place the clamps over the metal pins so each drops into a guide

558

hole. After the veneers are glued and assembled, C clamps can be put between the wood clamps for more even pressure.

• *Veneer stock of the same or contrasting woods to build up the piece to thickness.* The standard thickness of commercial veneer is 1/28", although veneer can be purchased in thicknesses of 1/20" and 1/16" also. Thin stock can be cut on the band saw and then surfaced on a planer, although this is a rather difficult job that involves a great deal of waste material. Some of the better woods for furniture and accessory laminating are hardwoods such as birch, maple, walnut, mahogany, cherry, and teak. The thickness is usually built up with an odd number of plies—for example, three, five, or seven. However, many furniture manufacturers prefer four layers of veneer for curved laminations. Fig. 41-24. This makes it possible to use two good-quality veneers for the face and back surfaces and two less-expensive layers for the inside. Sometimes woods of contrasting

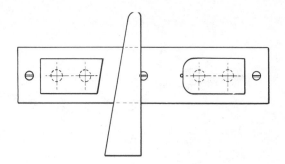

DRILL $\frac{1}{16}$ GUIDE HOLE

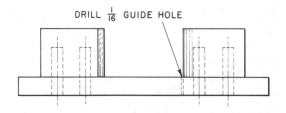

WEDGE CLAMP

41-23.   Homemade wood clamps to hold the materials.

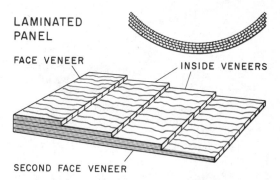

LAMINATED PANEL

FACE VENEER

INSIDE VENEERS

SECOND FACE VENEER

41-24.   Four-ply laminated panels for curved furniture parts.

41-25.   A small veneer press can be used to form curved panels. A two-part form or mold is necessary.

41-22.   A form or mold for laminating simple curved materials.

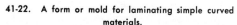

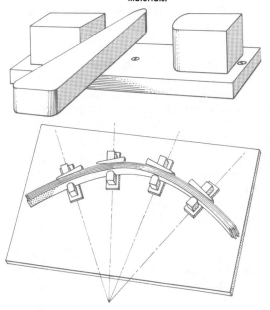

ROUGH LAMINATED PANEL

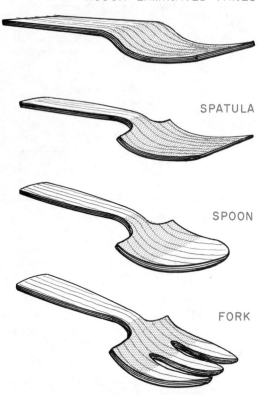

SPATULA

SPOON

FORK

41-26. This serving set is typical of the many laminated products that can be made.

colors are used to form the parts of accessories.

• *An adhesive to bind the materials together permanently.* The best adhesive is one of the synthetic-resin glues such as urea-resin (plastic resin) or polyvinyl (white) glue. In commercial fabrication of laminated beams, casein glue is the most commonly used adhesive.

• *Clamping devices to hold the veneers together.* Any of the standard clamps for gluing can be used to apply the needed pressure. An old metal wheel can be used as the form and a band clamp as the pressure device for forming circular shapes. Fig. 40-18(b). A veneer press can also be used to apply needed pressure to the form. Fig. 41-25.

Steps in Laminating and Bending

1. Cut several pieces of veneer slightly larger than the finished size of the part. Usually the pieces should be about 1/2" wider and about 1" to 2" longer than the completed part to allow for the bond and for slippage.

2. Clamp the pieces together without glue to check the assembly and to make sure enough clamping devices are available. As the pieces are removed, stack them in the exact order in which they must be glued.

3. Apply glue with a brush or roller to both sides of the inside pieces and one side of the outside pieces. Stack the pieces together after each is glued so that you can place the whole stack in the form at the same time. Stacking will keep the glue from setting too rapidly before pressure is applied.

4. Place a piece of wax paper or thin plastic in the lower part of the form, then the stack of veneers, and finally another sheet of wax paper or plastic. Several thicknesses of old newspaper can be placed above and below the stack. It is very important to keep the glue off the form and the rubber or cork liner.

5. Apply pressure by tightening each clamp a little at a time so the pieces will bend slowly all along the form. When the final tightening is done, apply pressure first at the points of greater curvature and then toward the open ends.

6. Allow the part to dry thoroughly, then remove it from the form. Usually the paper or plastic will have stuck to the edges of the rough laminate. These should first be removed.

7. Trace the final shape on the rough laminate, using a templet. Fig. 41-26. Cut to shape on a band saw and round the edges. Then sand the entire piece.

Veneering is one of the oldest wood-working arts, one that has been practiced for centuries. Fig. 42-1. Through modern techniques, veneers are available in standard-sized panels. Such panels are produced in plywood plants and are used for most paneling, built-ins, kitchen cabinets, and on-the-job construction. See Unit 8.

However, standard panels are not well suited for every purpose. For instance, furniture manufacturers often make their own plywood to the specific sizes they need, or when banded plywood is required. (Banded plywood is lumber core plywood with a band or frame of solid stock of the same species as the face veneer.) Some custom and architectural woodworking plants also make their own plywood, especially when case-work and interiors call for an exotic wood

such as rosewood or limba. Fancy veneers are purchased from an importer who specializes in these fine, expensive woods. Fig. 42-2.

At times you will want to produce your own flat or curved veneer panels. For example, when building a table of expensive wood such as teak, you may want to make the top of inexpensive core stock such as fir plywood or particle board, then cover it with the teak veneer. Fig. 42-3. Another time to do this would be when you need a curved part with a special matching in the veneer surface. Fig. 42-4.

The veneering process requires careful workmanship but it is not too complicated if a few precautions are taken. Large furniture-manufacturing plants have a veneering department with ex-

42-1. The handsome design of this occasional table incorporates rich, fine, imported Javanese veneers and English yew wood inlay. W—23", D—29", H—22".

42-2. Veneers in storage ready for shipment to furniture plants and for other uses. Note the way the thin veneers curl slightly.

561

42-3.   This bench-table has a base of oak and a teak top. W—71″, D—20″, H—16″.

tensive equipment such as a tapeless veneer splicer, edge-gluing devices, and veneer driers.

Method of Cutting

Veneer is a thin layer or sheet of wood that is sliced or cut from a log or part of a log called a *flitch*. Fig. 42-5. The way in which veneers are cut greatly affects their final appearance. Fig. 42-6. There are five principal ways of slicing or cut-

42-4(a).   An interesting Danish design, this desk with curved, sliding top is a Contemporary version of the roll-top desk. Note the interesting diamond pattern in the matched veneers.

42-4(b).   The top slides back and the writing leaf pulls out.

42-5. Quarter slicing red-gum veneer. The flitch moves up and down in a vertical plane against the knife. Workmen at left catch and stack the strips. The pieces from one flitch are bonded together and shipped as a unit so that the user can get a good match of grain surfaces.

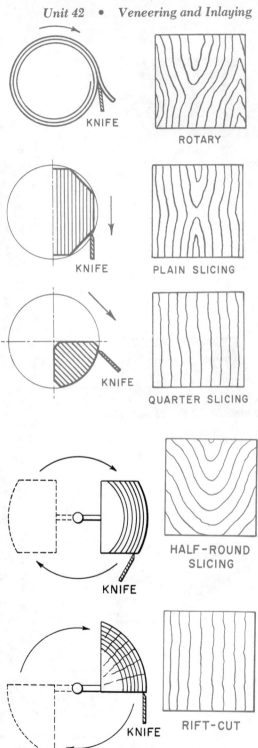

ting veneers. The first three are the most common in plywood production.

Rotary

The log is mounted centrally in a lathe and turned against a razor-sharp blade; the veneer is cut off much as a roll of paper would unwind. Since this cut follows the log's annual growth rings, a bold grain marking is produced. Almost all softwood plywood is produced in this manner. Rotary-cut veneer results in very wide sheeting. In hardwood, the length of rotary-cut veneer is usually not more than 8'.

Flat or Plain Slicing

Half the log or flitch is mounted with the heart side flat against the guide plate of the slicer. The slicing is done parallel to the center of the log. This produces a most interesting grain pattern, like that of plain-sawed lumber.

42-6. The cutting method is an important factor in producing veneers of different appearances. Veneers cut from two logs of the same species, even if their colors are similar, will not look alike if they are cut differently.

563

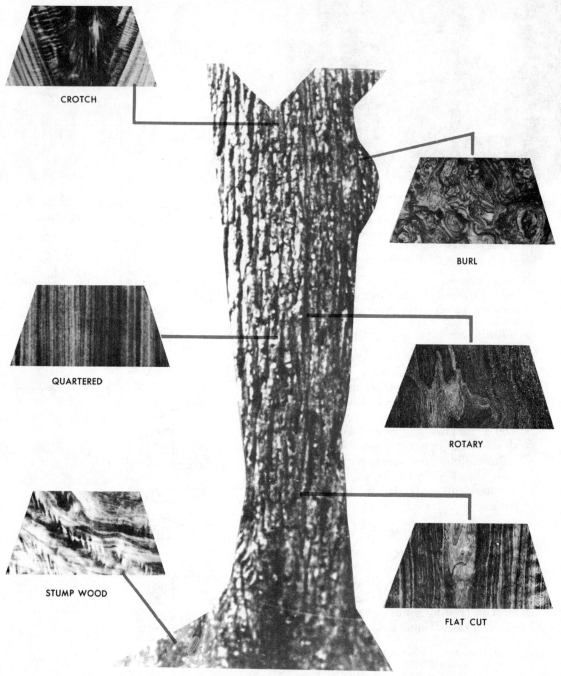

42-7. Sections of the tree from which various veneer patterns are obtained. Some species produce several figure types. Crotch. Quartered. Flat Cut. Stump Wood. Burl. Rotary.

Quarter Slicing

One-fourth of the log (flitch) is mounted on a guide plate so that the growth rings of the log strike the knives at approximately right angles. This produces a series of stripes or straight lines in some woods and varied figures in others.

Half-Round Slicing

This is a type of rotary cutting in which the log segments or flitches are mounted off-center in the lathe. The result is a cut slightly across the growth rings. This is done most often for cutting veneers from red oak.

Rift Cut

The rift cut is done to various kinds of oak. Oak has medullary ray cells which radiate out from the center of the log like the curved spokes of a wheel. The rift-grain effect is obtained by cutting perpendicular to these rays, either on a lathe or a slicer. Most veneer is sliced off the log with a sharp knife. Some veneer is cut with a saw, but since this technique is rather wasteful, it is usually limited to the red and white oaks.

KINDS OF VENEERS

All standard veneers are cut 1/28″ thick although in a few cases veneers are available in 1/16″ thickness. Veneer imported from many foreign countries is 1/60″ thick. These are so thin that it is very easy to damage or sand through them. Extra-fancy veneers are produced from certain unusual parts of the tree. Fig. 42-7. These include the following:

Burl

Burls are large, wartlike, deformed growths on the trunk of a tree. Usually these are caused by an injury to the tree just under the bark which makes the cells divide and grow excessively. Additional growth follows the contour of the original deformity, producing little swirls or knots. The twisted, thickened wood fibers have a very beautiful peacock-tail pattern.

Butt or Stump Wood

Butts are obtained from the base or stump of the tree where wood fibers are compressed and tend to wrinkle or twist. This produces an unusual figure in

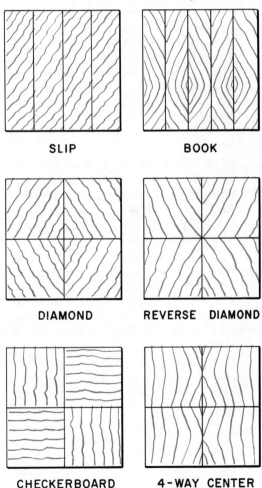

42-8. Common kinds of matching.

SLIP   BOOK

DIAMOND   REVERSE DIAMOND

CHECKERBOARD   4-WAY CENTER
                 AND BUTT

the wood. Butt or stump-wood figures usually have a wavy, rippled marking.

Crotch

A crotch is the part of a tree just under a fork where a main branch joins the trunk. Here the fibers are twisted creating various figures and grains that are very beautiful. The front and back of the crotch have distinctive figures that gradually fade into a swirling pattern. Veneers from these portions are known as *swirls*.

MATCHING VENEERS

A veneer surface of any size is made by gluing together two or more pieces of veneer. Because veneers are thin, sheets that are joined must have similar grain or figure marks. By utilizing this duplication of pattern, all sorts of designs are possible. Fig. 42-8. The following are the most common methods of matching veneers:

• *Slip match*. In slip matching, veneer sheets are joined side by side to make them look as if the pattern is repeated. All types of veneer may be used, but this kind of matching is most common with quarter-sliced veneers.

• *Book match*. All types of veneers are used. Adjacent pieces of veneer from the flitch are fastened side by side. Every other sheet is turned over, just as are the leaves of a book. The back of one veneer joins the front of the next. Fig. 42-9.

• *Diamond match*. This is made up of four pieces of veneer that are cut diagonally from the same piece of material. They are fitted together to form a diamond pattern. Veneers with striped grains are particularly attractive in diamond match.

• *Reverse diamond*. The pieces are fitted exactly opposite the way they are in a diamond match.

• *Checkerboard match*. Each piece is turned one quarter turn to give a checkerboard effect.

• *Four-way center and butt*. This match is usually applied to butt, crotch, or stump veneers since it effectively shows the beauty of the surfaces. Four pieces are joined side to side and end to end.

• *Other matches*. Some other common matching patterns are *vertical-butt-and-horizontal-bookleaf match, random match,* and *herringbone match.* Fig. 42-10. For the tops of tables and other furniture pieces, special matching effects are obtained by combining veneers from different species. Fig. 42-11.

TOOLS AND MATERIALS FOR VENEERING

The tools and materials that are necessary depend on the veneering to be done.

42-9. Here is an example of book match featuring two pieces of American walnut.

Usually, however, only a few simple hand tools are needed. These include a fine saw or slicing shears, a knife, veneer pins (plastic-headed pins with very hard, sharp steel points), veneer or masking tape, white glue, contact cement, and a ruler or straightedge. Small brads can be used in place of veneer pins. A veneer press is needed for making lumber-core plywood.

CUTTING VENEERS

Veneer that has been sliced from a log or flitch must be cut into smaller pieces. There are several common ways to do this. A veneer saw will do an excellent job but, if veneering is done only occasionally, a dovetail saw is satisfactory. Fig. 42-12. The best method for

42-10. Other kinds of matching. (a). Vertical-butt-and-horizontal-bookleaf match is used when the height of the flitch is not enough to produce a panel of the desired height. The match may be vertical as well as horizontal. (b). In random match the veneers are joined with the intention of creating a casual, unmatched effect. Veneers from several logs may be used. (c). The pattern in herringbone match is formed by lines intersecting at acute angles.

42-11. Beautiful veneer matching produces a special effect in this table top.

42-12. Dovetail saw for cutting veneers.

42-13. A sharp knife with a guide is excellent for cutting veneers.

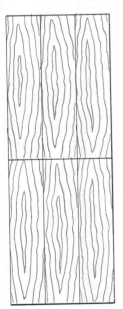

b

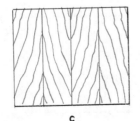

a

c

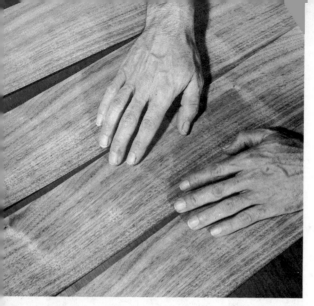

cutting veneer is to clamp a guide board over the line at which the veneer is to be cut and then saw with a dovetail or veneer saw. A sharp veneer knife can also be used. Fig. 42-13. Veneers can also be cut successfully on a metal squaring shears or with a hand sheet-metal shears.

APPLYING FINE VENEER TO A PANEL CORE

The simplest method of making a fancy

42-14. Select face veneers for matching grain, using as many pieces as needed to make up the faces of the panel.

42-15. Layout of pieces for a diamond match.

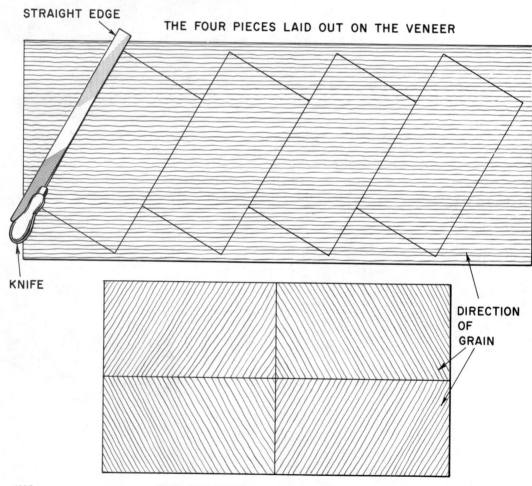

STRAIGHT EDGE

THE FOUR PIECES LAID OUT ON THE VENEER

KNIFE

DIRECTION OF GRAIN

THE FORMING OF THE DIAMOND MATCH

veneer is to use fir plywood, particle board, or hardboard as the core. Fir plywood is best since it has smooth, even, sanded surfaces. It is important, of course, to select plywood that has good face veneer on both surfaces. Particle board can also be used but, unless a cross band is applied, a sliver of the particle board may force its way through the face veneer. Hardboard is also a satisfactory material for core stock. Many commercial veneer panels have a core of particle board, cross bands of hardboard, and face and back veneers of wood.

To produce veneer plywood, follow these steps:

1. Determine the total thickness of stock needed. Since veneers are only 1/28″ thick, for most work the core will make up nearly the total thickness of the material required. Veneer is sold by the square foot so it is important to pick a fancy veneer for a face surface and less expensive veneer (preferably of the same species) for the back. It is essential that the veneer layer for the back surface have the same thickness as that applied to the face, for balanced construction and to prevent warping.

2. Match the face veneers, using as many pieces as needed. Fig. 42-14. Remember always to allow extra material for trimming after it is applied. The most common methods are random match, slip match, or book match. However, if diamond match is needed, the pieces must be cut from a veneer of striped grain. The best way to do this is to lay out rectangular pieces with a steel square. Four will be needed. Fig. 42-15. It is a good idea to make the pattern full-size on a piece of paper and then to cut one piece of material from the veneer. Next, turn the sheet over and cut the second piece. Reverse the material again for the third, and again for the fourth.

3. Clamp the adjoining pieces of veneer between two hardwood boards with

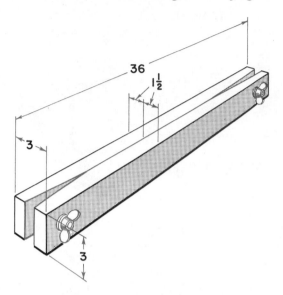

42-16. Fixture for holding veneer for planing.

the edges just protruding, and plane the edges true. Fig. 42-16. The planing can be done with a hand plane or on a jointer. Fig. 42-17. Another method of making a veneer joint is to overlap one sheet of veneer with the adjoining piece by about 1″. Then clamp a straightedge along the middle of the overlap. Fig. 42-18. With a very sharp knife or chisel, cut along the straightedge, making sure that both thicknesses are cut at the same time. *Never make more than one cut.* Remove the straightedge and take away

42-17. Planing can be done with a hand plane or on a jointer. If a jointer is used, clamp the book between two pieces of scrap lumber and pass over the jointer. Repeat this step on the other side of the book.

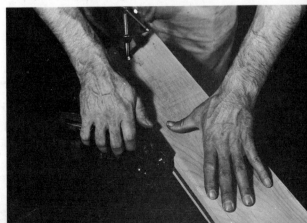

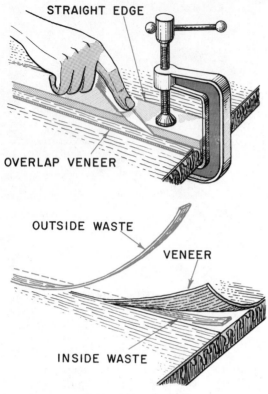

STRAIGHT EDGE

OVERLAP VENEER

OUTSIDE WASTE

VENEER

INSIDE WASTE

42-18. Cutting a veneer joint.

process for each joint necessary to produce the face and back veneers.

5. Turn the sheet over on the bench. Open the joints and apply a good grade of white glue to the edges of the adjoining pieces. Fig. 42-20. Wipe off any excess glue and straighten out the veneer sheet. Then tape the back sides of the joint together. Fig. 42-21. Do this for all pieces. Now allow the total sheet to dry overnight. Remember that you must also have the same size sheet of less expensive veneer for the back surface.

6. After the glue is dry, remove the tape from the back or poor side of the veneer, keeping the other tape in place.

7. Cut the core material, usually fir plywood, to the size you want. Use contact cement to fasten the veneer in place. This adhesive can be applied with a brush, roller, or spreader. Two coats must be applied to the core material and one to the veneer. Allow both to dry at least 15 minutes. Dull spots that appear after drying indicate that additional cement must be applied. After the cement is dry, there should be a high gloss over the entire surface. Test for dryness by tamping a piece of brown wrapping paper on the cemented surface. When the paper won't stick, the cement is ready. Remember that when two surfaces covered with contact cement touch, there is an immediate bond and the materials cannot be moved again.

8. Place the veneer carefully over the core stock. Keep in mind that the face and back veneers must be applied at right angles to the face ply of the core. Otherwise there is a tendency for cracks to develop. After the veneer is in place over the core stock, remove the tape. Use a veneer roller on the surfaces, both with and across grain, to make sure the veneer is fastened securely to the core stock. Fig. 42-22. After face veneer has been applied, reverse the stock and follow same procedure to apply back veneer.

both pieces of waste veneer. The edges should then fit accurately without planing. Repeat for each of the adjoining pieces of veneer. Before taping the veneers together, place the two pieces on a cutting board with the edges together to make sure the joint is very tight. Veneer pins or brads are pressed into both pieces about an inch away from the joint, at the extreme edges, to hold them in place. Slant the veneer pins towards the joint to hold the edges firmly together.

4. Use gummed veneer tape or masking tape to join the pieces temporarily on the face side. Fig. 42-19. Remove the veneer pins and reverse the sheet to check for any cracks. If there are any imperfections, take the joint apart and replane it until it is perfect. Repeat this

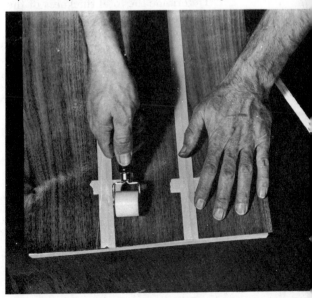

42-19. Fasten the pieces together with masking tape. Turn the sheet over and inspect the joints. Any cracks showing at this time will appear in the finished panel. Therefore it is important to get a perfect joint.

42-20. It is advisable to edge glue the sections together, making one complete sheet of veneer. Turn the panel over and fold back the sections. Apply white glue to the edge. Lay the panel flat and wipe off any excess glue. Then tape this side also with masking tape.

42-21. Taping at this point will keep the glued edge secure until thoroughly dried. Then remove the tape from the back side.

42-22. Place the veneer on the core stock and roll firmly both with the grain and across it. Remove the masking tape and roll each side again. Allow the panel to dry 24 hours before further handling.

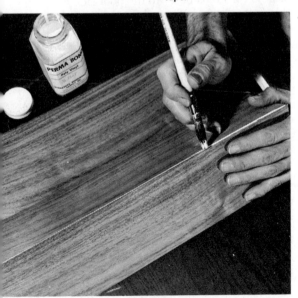

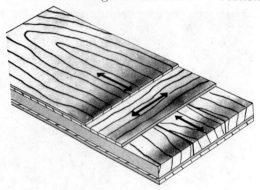

Lumber Core Construction
(5 ply panel)
1. face veneer   3. lumber core
2. crossband   4. crossband
5. face or back veneer

42-23. Lumber-core plywood is made of narrow, solid wood strips (arranged to equalize stress) which are edge glued together. The core is covered on both sides with crossbands and a face and back veneer.

MAKING LUMBER-CORE PLYWOOD

Lumber-core plywood is built of a core of solid, glued-up stock, with cross bands on either side and veneer on face and back. Fig. 42-23.

Make lumber-core plywood as follows:

1. Determine the total thickness of the finished panel. Standard American veneer is 1/28″ thick and crossbanding stock is available in thicknesses of 1/20″, 1/10″, and 1/8″. If, for example, you use two thicknesses of 1/28″ veneer and two thicknesses of 1/10″ crossband stock and you wish to produce a 3/4″ panel, the core must be approximately 17/32″ thick.

2. Select, match, and join the face and back veneers, as previously described.

3. Construct the core. Saw pieces of softwood lumber, such as poplar or basswood, into pieces 2″ to 4″ wide and slightly longer than needed for the furniture piece. Reverse every other board so that the heart side is up for half the boards and down for the other half. This will help reduce the tendency to warp.

If the edges of a piece are to be machined, such as the edge of a table top, it will be necessary to band a piece of solid wood of the same material as the face veneer to the edges and ends of the core. For example, if the face veneer is mahogany, then a band of mahogany should be added to the sides and ends of the core stock. The more common commercial method is to build a frame of the solid material and fit the plywood into it. See Unit 50. After the core stock has been glued up, plane both surfaces to thickness. Glue the core material together and, after it is dry, surface to thickness.

4. Cut the crossbanding material slightly larger than the overall size of the core. Whenever possible, the crossbanding material should have no joints.

5. Prepare the veneer press for the gluing operation. Fig. 42-24. Place a thick piece of plywood at the base of the veneer and then place a piece of waxed paper over this. Also have a second piece of waxed paper and heavy plywood for the top of the sandwich.

6. Assemble and glue the lumber-core plywood. Apply a good grade of any type of glue (white is best) to the poor side of the face veneer. Place the veneer with the tape side down in the bottom of the veneer press and over the waxed paper. Now apply glue to both sides of the first piece of crossbanding material and

42-24. This shop-made veneer press can be used to construct small veneer panels.

put this in place with the grain running at right angles to the face veneer. Do the same for the core stock and the second piece of crossbanding material. Then apply glue to the inner surface of the back veneer. When arranging the materials, remember that alternate layers of veneers, crossbands, and core should have the grain running at right angles to each other. Veneer pins or brads can be placed in the waste stock to keep the pieces from slipping. Now cover the sandwich with another piece of heavy waxed paper and then a plywood pressure pad. Apply even pressure with the veneer press and allow to dry overnight. In assembling the sandwich, it is important to work as quickly as possible so that the veneers will not absorb too much moisture from the glue. Since veneers are thin, they tend to expand very rapidly from any moisture that is applied.

7. Lumber-core plywood can also be manufactured (or laid up) by the following process: First, glue the crossbands to the core. After this sandwich is dried in the press, remove and check to make sure there are no loose areas in the crossbands. If there are, cut with a sharp knife and force glue under such areas. Put back into the press and allow to dry. Next glue the face and back veneers over the crossbands. Replace in the press and allow to dry.

8. After the unit has dried thoroughly, trim and sand the edges.

MARQUETRY AND BUILT-UP PATTERNS

Marquetry is a decoration such as fitting pieces of different veneer together to form a picture or design. Sometimes a cabinetmaker will cut and fit the pieces to form such a design. However, if many small pieces are needed, it is more common to purchase the materials already cut.

A rather simple form of marquetry can

42-25. This clock face is made of several different colors of veneer stock.

be done by combining several different-colored veneers to form a design such as the face of the clock in Fig. 42-25. It is first necessary to make a full-size pattern of the design on paper. Then a templet, preferably of metal, should be cut for each different part. Place this templet over the veneer and cut around the edge with a small sharp knife. Use the same templet to cut the opening in the background veneer. This is a very exacting job and must be done with great care. It is important that the templet does not move when the inner and outer shapes are being cut. After all the pieces are cut, place the fitted parts on a flat surface. Apply tape to the face surface to hold all the parts in place. Use contact cement to fasten the design permanently to a core stock.

INLAYING

Inlay is a process whereby strips of rare woods are set into the surface of solid wood or other veneers. With a

573

router it is a relatively simple job. First select the inlay banding (material) to determine the width of groove needed. Usually the banding is 1/20" thick. Put a lefthand spiral bit in the router; this cuts clean and doesn't leave any fuzz on the top of the cut. Adjust the depth of cut to slightly less than the thickness of the inlay. Use a straight guide to control the location of the groove. Fig. 42-26. Make one pass to cut a groove equal in width to the banding. After the groove is machined, it has rounded corners. These have to be squared up with a small chisel. When the groove is cut, miter the corners of the inlay strip and then make a trial assembly to be sure the pieces fit. Remove the inlay and apply a small amount of white glue to the groove. Replace the inlay and cover with wax paper. Clamp a strip of wood over the top until the inlay is dry. Fig. 42-27.

You can purchase rare-wood block inlays of contrasting or blending colors for mounting in the tops of tables, buffets, fancy boxes, and similar items. Block inlays are usually made to a thickness of 1/20". To apply, first mark the location on the table top or other wood product,

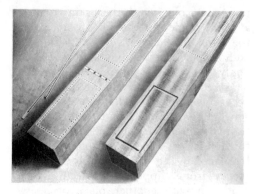

42-27. Here you see two table legs with inlays. The one to the right has the groove cut and ready for the multi-colored inlay banding. The one to the left has the banding glued in place.

42-28. An artistic inlay. The opening into which the inlay will go is already routed out. The bit and knife for cutting the opening are also shown.

42-29. A templet and ring guide for cutting an inlay and routing out a recess.

42-26. Using a router with a guide to cut the groove for the inlay.

then cut around the design with a sharp knife. Use a router with a straight bit. Adjust for a depth of cut slightly less than the thickness of the inlay. Use a guide to remove as much of the material as possible where the inlay is to go. Then remove the rest of the wood within this area by freehand routing or with a chisel. Fig. 42-28. Inlays come with paper on one side. Apply glue to the opposite side and insert in the recess. Clamp until the glue is dry and then sand off the paper.

A special recess and insert guide with ring is available so that the same templet can be used to cut the inlay and rout out the recess. The ring controls depth of cut. First, from 1/8″ hardboard make a templet of the same shape as the inlay. Fasten the templet in position over the material into which the inlay is to fit. Rout out the recess with the ring attached to the guide. Then remove the ring and cut out the inlay, using the same templet. Fig. 42-29.

43 Plastic Laminates

Because high-pressure plastic laminates are widely used in furniture, cabinets and interiors, the cabinetmaker or finish carpenter should thoroughly understand them and their use. Plastic laminates are known by such common trade names as Textolite, Formica, Micarta, and Panelyte. Fig. 43-1.

High-pressure plastic laminates are surfacing materials that combine beautiful colors and designs with exceptional durability. These materials are composed of the following: layers of craft paper impregnated with specially formulated phenolic resins covered by a melamine resin; a pattern sheet saturated with plastic and topped by a protective wear sheet; and, finally, a coat of additional melamine resins. Fig. 43-2. These built-up materials are placed in a large hydraulic press between stainless-steel plates and subjected to extremely high heat and pressure to form a hard-surface sheet. Plastic laminates are popular for cabinet and table tops, walls, and built-ins because they resist wear, burns, stains, and soil. Fig. 43-3. Soap and water will clean them.

Plastic laminates are available in several different surface finishes such as gloss, satin, textured or brushed, and furniture. The textured or brushed finish is an excellent wall covering because it is non-glare. In addition to plain colors and designs, plastic laminates are sometimes made to imitate wood grain. Fig. 43-4. Textured and furniture finishes in wood-grain patterns look and feel like

43-1. Plastic laminates are popular for surfacing kitchen cabinets because they are attractive, have excellent wearing qualities, and are easy to keep clean.

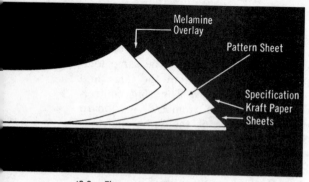

43-2. The composition of high-pressure, decorative plastic laminate. The material is stain-and-heat-resistant, colorfast, and moisture-resistant.

43-4. This attractive accessory table, made of rosewood, has a removable plastic-laminate top.

natural woods or veneers, yet have the same excellent wear resistance as conventional satin-finish laminates. Fig. 43-5.

GRADES OF LAMINATES

General-purpose or standard grade is 1/16" thick. It is used for a wide variety of interior surface applications such as table, kitchen counter, or desk tops, vanities, walls, fixtures, case goods, and furniture. It can be applied to both vertical and horizontal surfaces where good appearance, durability, and resistance to

43-3. All exposed surfaces of this dormitory furniture are covered with plastic laminate. The result is a room that is easy to keep clean and one that will remain attractive for many years.

stain and heat are necessary. Fig. 43-6. The standard grade can be used for edging. It will bend to a 9″ radius without heating and to a 2½″ radius when heated.

The *postforming grade* is approximately 1/20″ thick and is designed to permit heating and forming into short radii for applications around doors and sill ledges, rolled or covered counter tops, and on small-radius table tops.

The *vertical grade* is about 1/32″ thick and is designed only for vertical surface application as on cabinet fronts and the vertical sides of fixtures and furniture. This same grade is cut into narrower bands 1⅝″ wide and called *edge banding or trim*. Fig. 43-7. It can be curved to a 3″ radius at room temperature; by heating it to about 325 to 360 degrees F., it can be bent to a 3/4″ radius.

Backer sheets of about 1/32″, 1/20″, or 1/16″ thickness are placed on the underside or back of free-standing tables for dimensional stability. These are low-cost materials which will provide balanced construction when core material is used. Backer sheets are not needed if the underside of the top is well fastened to the base. For example, no backer sheet is needed for a standard coffee table or a kitchen cabinet. Backer sheets should be used when a top has an unsupported area of more than four square feet.

Flame-retardant grade, 1/16″ thick, is especially designed for wall paneling, doors, and other vertical surfaces which require such protective treatment, as in hotels or dormitories.

Sheet Sizes

Widths commonly available are 24″, 30″, 36″, 48″, and 60″. Most manufacturers add 1/4″ to the width so that two 12″ widths can be cut from a 24″ width. The most common lengths are 60″, 72″, 84″, 96″, 120″, and 144″. Since plastic

43-5. This desk of walnut has a plastic-laminate top of natural walnut design. The two materials match so beautifully that it is difficult to tell them apart.

43-6. General-purpose or standard grade laminate is most commonly used.

43-7. Edge banding or trim is convenient to use, especially for curved edges.

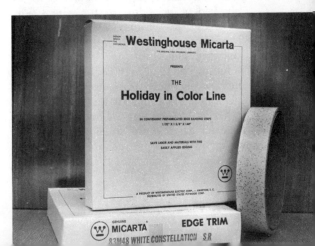

43-8. Here you see the edge of plastic laminate being trimmed off after it has been attached to a core.

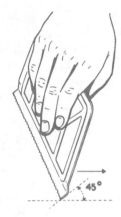

43-9. Hold the metal spreader teeth at 90 degrees to the horizontal when applying contact cement to a soft, low-density, or uneven material such as fir or Philippine mahogany plywood. Hold the teeth at 45 degrees when applying cement to hard, high-density, smooth surfaces such as hardboard.

laminates are relatively expensive, it is important to keep these sizes in mind when designing tables and cabinets. For example, it would be poor design to specify a 19″ width since only one piece could be cut from a 36″ width. Plastic laminates are sold by the square foot with the 1/16″ standard grade as the base.

CORE MATERIALS

Since plastic laminates are quite thin and brittle, they must be fastened or attached to a core. The most common core materials are plywood, particle board, or hardboard. Plywood should be not less than 3/4″ thick, 5-ply lumber core or 7-ply veneer core for all horizontal surfaces. Fig. 43-8. Lumber-core and veneer-core plywood for wall and other vertical surfaces should be not less than 1/2″ thick and have at least 5 plies. Normally, interior plywood can be used, but if plastic laminate is to be used in bathrooms or other humid places, it is better to choose exterior grade. Some manufacturers recommend Philippine mahogany plywood because it is smoother than fir plywood.

Plastic laminates can also be bonded to particle board or flakeboard that is 1/2″ or 3/4″ thick. Hardboard at least 3/16″ thick can also be used, but not tempered hardboard. In furniture and architectural woodworking plants, high-pressure plastic laminates are bonded to a core of 3/4″ particle board or closed-grain hardwood veneer-core plywood. A water-resistant glue is used and the materials are clamped in a laminating cold press until dry.

ADHESIVES

Many kinds of adhesives can be used to bond plastic laminates to core materials. However, casein, polyvinyl, resin and other slow-setting glues can be used only when the materials are clamped together under pressure long enough to cure the adhesive. Fig. 43-9. For this reason, contact cement or adhesive is used for most on-the-job applications. Since there are a great many kinds of contact adhesives, it is important to follow the manufacturer's recommendations for each one.

Adhesive is applied to the surface by

578

brushing, rolling, or with a notched spreader. Fig. 43-10. The brushing method is usually best for edge gluing while the roller is best for vertical surfaces. A solvent should be available for cleaning off excess cement. There are two basic types of solvents for this. One is a flammable mixture that must be kept away from heat and open flame. The other has water as a solvent.

CLAMPING AND PRESSURE FOR BONDING

For all adhesives except the contact type it is necessary to apply even pressure to the plastic laminate until the adhesive is dry. If, for example, you wish to fasten a piece of plastic laminate to a core for a table top, place a pressure pad of plywood over the laminate and apply clamps or weights such as sand bags until the adhesive is dry, Fig. 43-11. However, for most on-the-job construction, a contact cement should be used.

METHODS OF CUTTING

One of the first steps is to cut the plastic laminate sheets to a smaller size. Since the material is hard, thin, and rather brittle, it is important to support it as it is cut. The layout line can be marked with a grease pencil. While standard woodworking and metalworking tools can be used, they become dull rather rapidly. For this reason, carbide-tipped cutting tools are recommended. Some final trimming is usually necessary so it is suggested that the rough-cut pieces be about 1/2″ wider and longer than the piece to which they will be glued.

Here are the ways plastic laminate can be cut:

If little or no equipment is available, the sheets can be cut to smaller sizes by scoring the face with a file ground to a sharp point or with an ice pick or an awl. Fig. 43-12. By cutting back and

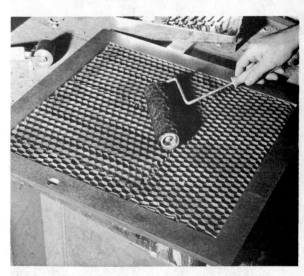

43-10. Applying contact cement with a roller to a honeycomb core. Cabinet doors are often made in this way. The rails and stiles are hardwood and the center is filled with impregnated paper honeycomb. Then the surfaces and edges are covered with plastic laminate.

43-11. Many glues, including resin adhesives, require that the plastic laminate be clamped to the core stock or held in place with weights until dry. Before using clamps, a piece of plywood should be placed over the laminate to distribute the pressure equally over the surface so bubbles will not form between the laminate and the core.

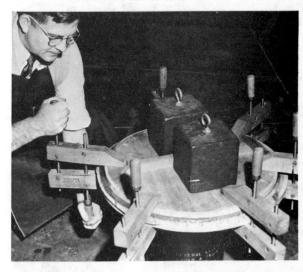

43-12. A sheet can be cut into smaller pieces by scoring the face with a sharp-pointed tool. Cut back and forth in the scored groove until the plastic is almost cut in two.

43-13. Place a straight edge over the scored line and apply pressure as you pull up on the sheet to break it.

43-14. Cutting plastic laminate with a hand saw.

forth in a scored groove, the plastic can be cut almost in two and then broken the rest of the way. This method is good for scoring to a templet or cutting irregular shapes. Always break upward with the face up. Fig. 43-13.

• A crosscut hand saw with 12 points can be used provided the angle of cut is kept very low, almost flat against the sheet. Fig. 43-14. The finish side should be up.

• A metal hacksaw with a blade that has 32 teeth per inch can be used for short cuts where the frame will not interfere.

• Several different portable power tools can be used including the cutoff saw and the hand jig saw. With both of these tools, the decorative side should be down as this will confine any chipping to the back surface of the material. Fig. 43-15. To cut plastic laminate to size, it is a good idea to clamp it to a bench top, using a piece of wood as a straight-edge guide for cutting. Fig. 43-16.

• A portable router can also be used to cut sheets to size. Fig. 43-17. This machine is used also to trim the edge of plastic laminate after it is installed. Fig. 43-18.

• A circular saw can be used. The best blade is one that is hollow-ground or carbide-tipped. Cutting should be done with the finish side up. Keep the saw cutting into the surface at a very sharp angle, as close to straight up and down as possible. Fig. 43-19. This means that great care must be taken, especially when the saw guard must be removed to accommodate a large sheet of material.

• The band saw can be used to cut plastic laminate with the decorative side up. The band saw with a buttress-type tooth is normally used only when cutting plastic laminates that have already been bonded to the core material. Fig. 43-20.

DRILLING AND BORING

For hand work, a brace and bit with

43-15. Cutting plastic laminate with a cut-off saw. Note the straight edge clamped over the material to guide the saw.

43-18. The router is also used to trim the edge of the material after it is applied.

43-16. Cutting with a hand jig saw. This is a very practical power tool for the on-the-job fabricator since it can also be used to make the cutout for a sink or other opening.

43-17. The router can be used to cut sheets to size if no other power tool is available. The small-diameter, straight carbide cutter bit should be used. Never attempt to use a regular cutter bit since the speed of the router and the amount of the material to be cut will dull the standard bit too quickly for practical use.

43-19. Cutting plastic laminate on the circular saw. Note that the blade must be set very high. Otherwise the blade will overheat and also dull very quickly. However, such a blade setting makes the operation dangerous. Great caution must be exercised. The standard basket guard doesn't function well for this but the guards described in Unit 26 are very satisfactory.

43-20. Using the band saw to cut plastic laminate already bonded to a core material. While a blade with standard teeth can be used, the buttress tooth is better because the teeth stay cleaner.

581

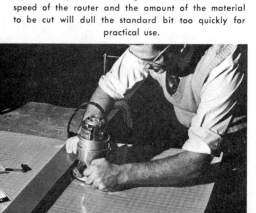

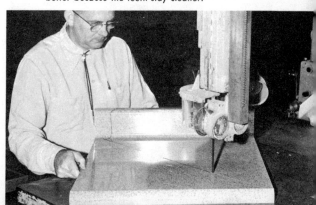

43-21. Using a standard auger bit and brace to bore holes in a plastic-laminate counter top.

43-22(b). When the adhesive is dry, carefully align the strip of material and place it on the edge. Remember that the material can't be moved after it makes contact. Use the roller to make sure the edge is firmly attached.

regular boring bits or a bit-stock drill can be used. Fig. 43-21. A standard metal twist drill is also good. For production work, carbide-tipped drills are best. All material to be drilled should be backed with wood to prevent break-out at the bottom of the hole.

EDGE TREATMENT AND BANDING

There are many kinds of edge treatment for a plastic-laminate top. Fig. 43-22(a). The laminate should be applied to the top and trimmed before adding any edges except the self edge or edge banding type. For example, for a metal

edge with a T molding, the plastic laminate is applied, then a slot is cut in the edge of the core to receive the molding. If an auxiliary wood fence is not used in cutting the slot, strips of masking tape should be applied to the saw fence to protect the polished surface of the laminate. For self edge or edge banding, the best practice is to apply the edge *before* applying the top surface whenever possible. If the table top or counter top has rounded corners, the postforming grade should be used. A plastic-laminate top has a more pleasing appearance if the edge is built up by adding a strip of

43-22(a). Common edge treatments that can be used with plastic laminates. The most popular is the edge-banding treatment.

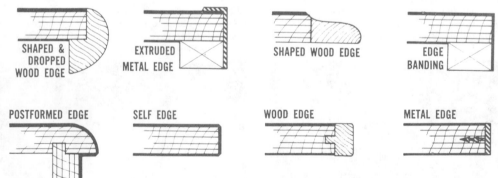

SHAPED & DROPPED WOOD EDGE

EXTRUDED METAL EDGE

SHAPED WOOD EDGE

EDGE BANDING

POSTFORMED EDGE

SELF EDGE

WOOD EDGE

METAL EDGE

582

43-22(c). Applying plastic laminate on a counter top with a built-up edge (edge banding).

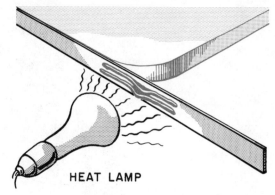

HEAT LAMP

43-23. Apply heat until the crayon melts.

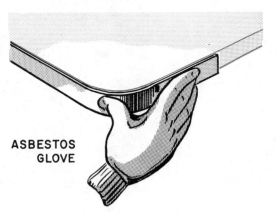

ASBESTOS GLOVE

43-24. Then curve the strip manually around the corner as shown.

43-25. A small wood block used as a guide for the saw in removing excess strip material at the butt joint.

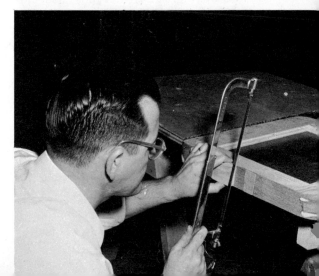

wood or plywood of equal thickness directly under and flush with the front edge.

After the edge is smooth, apply one or more coats of contact adhesive to it and one coat to the back of the edge strip. Allow the adhesive to set until it is dry to the touch but still a little soft. Another test of dryness is to tamp a small piece of brown paper on the cemented surfaces. When the paper will not stick, the adhesive is ready for bonding. Now carefully align the strip and bring it in contact with the edge. *Warning: Once the two surfaces touch, there is an immediate bond. No further positioning is possible.* Roll the strip to make sure it is firmly in place. Fig. 43-22(b) and (c).

On rounded corners that have a small radius, the strip must be heated to a temperature of about 300 degrees F. The best way to do this is with a heat lamp. With special crayon or marking material draw two short lines on the material where the curve is to be, then apply heat from the lamp. When the lines melt, the strip is ready to be bent. Fig. 43-23. Put on heat-resistant gloves. Wrap the strip around the corner by pulling it manually. Fig. 43-24. Then roll it until a good bond is obtained.

583

43-26. Routers equipped for trimming the edges. The router at left has a straight bit for trimming at right angles to the surface. The one on the right has a beveling bit and a guide for trimming the edge with a bevel cut.

The butt joint between the ends of two strips is made by cutting away the excess with a hacksaw and then rolling the joint. Fig. 43-25. After the edge banding is dry, trim the excess away until it is flush with the top to be surfaced. A router with a straight bit is the best tool for doing this. Fig. 43-26. Remember: Don't bevel the upper edge of the banding. Any variation in this edge will cause a poor glue line. Fig. 43-27. The bottom edge can be trimmed with a bevel cut. When applying the top, be sure to cover the top of the edging with adhesive, as well as the rest of the core.

In edge banding a table or counter, a good policy is to cover all front-to-back

43-27. Trimming the excess material. Keep this edge smooth and free from nicks or bevel.

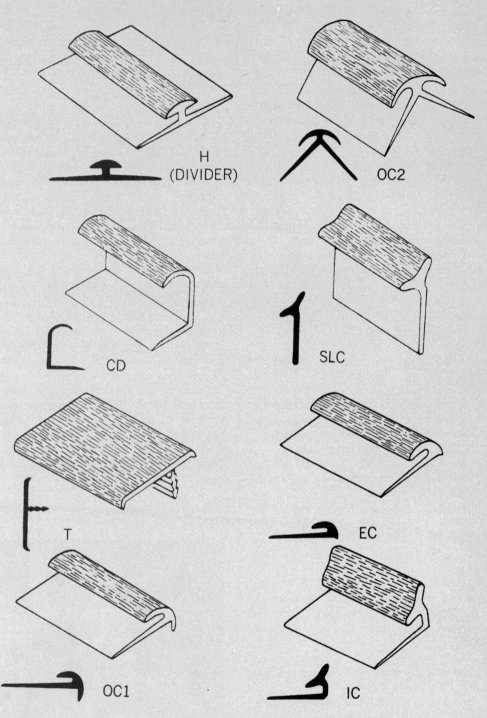

H
(DIVIDER)

OC2

CD

SLC

T

EC

OC1

IC

43-28. Aluminum or stainless-steel moldings for counters and wall installations.

vertical surfaces first, then cover all side-to-side vertical surfaces, and finally cover all horizontal surfaces.

METAL MOLDINGS

Aluminum or stainless-steel extruded moldings can be used with plastic laminates for table and counter tops and all other installations. Fig. 43-28. These moldings give any job a finished appearance; permanently bonded to the exposed surface they have veneer that perfectly matches the plastic laminate being used.

The common table and counter-top moldings include the following:

T molding for table and counter tops in widths from 3/4″ to 1½″. This is a drive-in, T-type molding that requires a saw kerf for installing. It can be bent around a 4″ minimum radius.

Straight leg cove (SLC), a molding for joining a counter top with a back-splash or the wall. It is installed by nailing the molding to the back of the counter.

Clamp down (CD), used for non-drip edges. The molding is snapped on the counter edge and nailed underneath.

Common wall moldings include:

Inside corner (IC), used by sliding the first panel into place and then positioning the molding before nailing.

Divider (H), used by placing the divider molding on the panel before putting it in position. Nail the exposed end of the divider and then insert the next panel.

Outside corner (OC1 and OC2) used by placing the molding in position and then inserting the panel and nailing the exposed edge. Insert the adjoining corner panel.

End cap (EC), used for wainscoting. First nail the molding to the plumb line and then insert the panel.

Moldings should be nailed every 8″ to 12″ with flat-head wire nails. In order-

ing the molding it is necessary to specify the shape, size of opening (usually 1/16″ for plastic laminates), and the pattern.

APPLYING LAMINATE TO A TABLE TOP

Plastic laminates can be applied to a table top with simple hand tools found in any school or cabinet shop. Tools and materials needed include a 2″ bristle brush, small hand roller, block plane, flat mill file, hammer, two pieces of heavy wrapping paper (each piece slightly larger than half the top to be installed), a block of soft wood, contact cement and abrasive cloth. Steps in applying the material are as follows:

1. Cut the plastic laminate to size, about 1/8″ to 1/4″ larger in both directions than the top.

2. Make sure the plywood or core material is smooth and has no imperfection in its surface. Fill any holes in the surface and then sand the surface smooth. Fig. 43-29.

3. Decide on the kind of edge treatment you want. The most common treatment is to build up the edge (edge banding) with an extra piece of plywood along the underside of the table. Then install a band of plastic laminate before applying the top.

43-29. When necessary, sand the surface to make sure it is smooth.

4. Apply a heavy coat of contact cement to the table top and the back side of the plastic laminate. Make sure, after the cement dries about 15 minutes, that there is a glossy film over the entire surface. If dull spots appear, it means that additional contact cement must be applied. If a second coat is needed on the core material, make sure the first coat is dry before applying the second.

5. Check to see that the adhesive is dry. This can be done by lightly pressing a piece of wrapping paper on the surface. When the paper will not stick, the cement is ready for bonding.

6. Remember that a permanent bond is formed the moment the two surfaces touch. This can scarcely be repeated too often. Place the two pieces of wrapping paper lightly on top of the core material. Place the plastic laminate over these papers. Now move the laminate until it is aligned correctly. Gently slip one piece of paper from under the plastic laminate. The two adhesive surfaces will bond immediately. Take care not to jar the work as the paper is removed. When the first half is in contact, carefully remove the second half.

7. Roll the surface from the center to the outside edges with a small roller. Fig. 43-30. Work towards the edges in all directions. A piece of soft wood can be used in place of the roller; place this over the plastic laminate and tap it with a hammer, covering the entire surface so that there is a complete bond.

8. Remove the excess plastic laminate with a hand plane. Then file the edges smooth. If the edge has already been applied, file at an angle of 20 to 30 degrees. Use long downward strokes. If the edge is not already installed, file it flush with the core materials so that a good joint can be made when the edging is applied. If a router or laminate trimmer is available, this can be used to trim the edge and bevel it at the same time. Figs. 43-31 and 43-32.

43-30. Rolling the surface after the plastic laminate has been applied.

43-31. Using a plastic-laminate trimmer to remove the excess material and to bevel the edge. This is a simple one-step job if the tool is properly set.

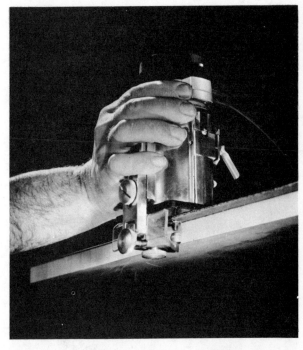

587

43-32. With a standard router it is usually necessary to trim the excess material away first with a straight router bit. Then a bevel bit is used to finish off the edge at an angle.

43-33. Plastic laminates have been applied to the vertical and horizontal surfaces of this kitchen cabinet. The cabinets themselves are made of vertical-grained Douglas fir.

9. Clean the adhesive from the surface by scraping with a scrap piece of plastic laminate. Use soap and water or alcohol to clean the surface and bring back its original surface luster.

APPLYING LAMINATE TO COUNTER TOPS

One of the most common uses of plastic laminates is for counter tops, as in kitchens and bathrooms. Fig. 43-33. The procedure for such installations is as follows:

1. Make sure that the wood counter top is in good condition. If it is old, remove all paint, varnish, cement and dirt. Sand until clean, bare wood is exposed. Fill all holes with plastic wood. Sand again.

2. Cut the plastic laminate by one of the methods shown in Figs. 43-12 to 43-20.

3. Fit the plastic laminate to the top of the wood surface as accurately as possible before any adhesive is applied. If a seam or butt joint is required near a sink, try to locate it at the center of the sink. This makes fitting easier.

4. If a self edge or edge banding is used, apply this first. If a metal edge is used, apply this after the top is in place.

5. Apply the contact adhesive. Follow the manufacturer's instructions as to application, use, and drying. To test for dryness, press a small piece of brown paper on the cement surface; when the paper will not stick the cement is ready. Again, remember the bond is immediate and permanent. Therefore, to align the plastic laminate properly, place several pieces of heavy brown wrapping paper between the surface and the laminate. Overlap them for easy removal. Center the laminate and move the first piece of paper a few inches at a time, pressing the laminate by hand as you go. Remove the remainder of the paper. Roll the laminate using a two-inch roller, work-

588

ing from the center towards the edges to finish the bonding operation. For places that are hard to reach, use a piece of scrap wood and tap with a hammer to assure a complete bond.

6. Trim the edges. Trim off any excess overhang or rough edge with a portable electric router or trimmer, or with a flat cabinet rasp. Carefully file with downward strokes at an angle.

7. If a backsplash is needed, it can be applied in two ways. Fig. 43-34(a). Usually a wood core is used for the backsplash. This should be fastened to the wall with screws or other metal fasteners. Cut a piece of plastic laminate to fit the front of this. The vertical piece can butt against the horizontal or a piece of metal cove molding can be nailed to the backsplash and fitted snugly to the counter top. Then apply the adhesive and fasten the plastic laminate in place.

8. Fit the sink. Set the frame or rim (usually the Hudee or Ardee is best) in position and secure it in place according to the instructions supplied on the rim. Fig. 43-34(b). For a good watertight seal, apply caulking compound before fastening the sink in place. Remove the excess adhesive with the cleaner recommended for the adhesive you are using.

APPLYING LAMINATE TO KITCHEN-CABINET FRONTS

Plastic laminates can be installed on either new or old kitchen-cabinet fronts to improve their appearance and utility. If the kitchen is being remodeled, remove all doors, drawers, and hardware. Sand the backs and faces of the doors and drawers and also the rails, stiles, and end panels. Fig. 43-35. Make sure the surfaces are free from oil, grease, water and, if possible, most of the paint or varnish. For new construction, a honeycomb-core door is the simplest to make and is light in weight. Fig. 43-36. If an existing lip door is to be used, cover both

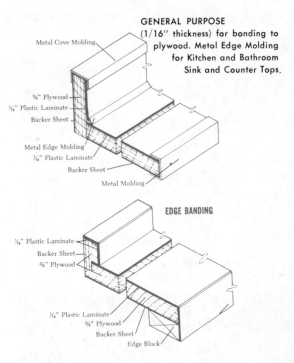

GENERAL PURPOSE (1/16″ thickness) for bonding to plywood. Metal Edge Molding for Kitchen and Bathroom Sink and Counter Tops.

Metal Cove Molding
¾″ Plywood
¹⁄₁₆″ Plastic Laminate
Backer Sheet
Metal Edge Molding
¹⁄₁₆″ Plastic Laminate
Backer Sheet
Metal Molding

EDGE BANDING

¹⁄₁₆″ Plastic Laminate
Backer Sheet
¾″ Plywood
¹⁄₁₆″ Plastic Laminate
¾″ Plywood
Backer Sheet
Edge Block

43-34(a). Two common methods of installing plastic laminate to counter tops. Note, in the top drawing, that the backsplash is fitted into the metal cove molding that was nailed to the vertical surface. Metal edge molding is used both on the front of the counter edge and on the top of the backsplash. In the lower drawing the edge banding is attached first, then the counter top, then the backsplash and, finally, the top edge of the backsplash.

43-34(b). Set the Hudee or Ardee frame or rim in position and fasten in place following the instructions furnished by the manufacturer.

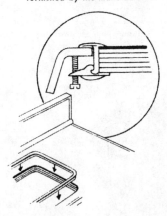

Laminating Kitchen-Cabinet Fronts

43-35(a). Sand the faces of the rails, stiles and panels on the cabinets.

43-35(b). If the old doors are to be used, sand the backs and faces.

43-36. If new doors are to be used on the cabinets, it is best to choose a lightweight honeycomb core covered with plastic laminate. Blocks of wood the same thickness as the rails must be inserted in the honeycomb at all points where handles, knobs, locks or other hardware is to be fastened.

43-37(a). Applying the plastic laminate to the old doors. Laminate for the fronts of doors must be of the same thickness as that for the backs to keep the doors from warping. A less expensive sheet can be applied to the back side. For better appearance, however, it is best to have the front match the back.

43-37(b). Roll firmly and heavily over the entire surface of the plastic laminate to make sure there is a good bond.

43-38(a). Trimming the edges with a router. The setup on the router and the depth of cut are important.

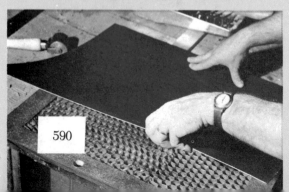

43-38(b). Notice how the plastic laminate comes just to the start of the radius of the curve on the lip.

43-39. Carefully cut and fit· the end panels so that all wood surfaces are covered.

43-40. Notice how the rail pieces are cut to receive the stile strips. Careful fitting before installation will result in a good, tight joint and neat appearance.

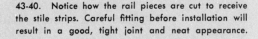

43-41. Fastening the stile strips in place. Notice how one end is carefully fitted before the entire piece is allowed to touch the stile itself. Remember, once the adhesive surfaces touch, the material can't be moved. It's not like working with other glues. Roll the strip to make sure there is a complete bond. Trim the rail and stile strips flush with the wood with a straight panel bit in the router.

43-42. Here you see the completed cabinets. These should match the doors and drawers. Cabinets are sometimes covered with wood-grain plastic laminate, and counter tops with a plain color or pattern.

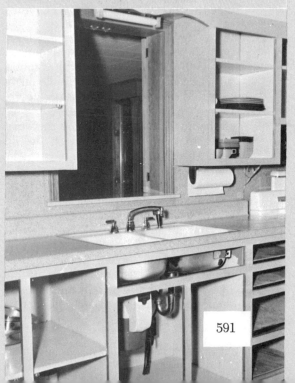

591

43-43. Installing plastic-laminate wall panels in a bathroom. The panels are usually fabricated in a cabinet shop so that the finish carpenter is responsible only for installation. Here the panels are being fastened to firring strips with mastic adhesive. Other methods are described in Unit 69.

the back and front with plastic laminate. Fig. 43-37. Trim the edges with a router bit set deep enough to trim the laminate back to the edge of the radius on the lip. Fig. 43-38. Then clean excess adhesive off the surfaces. Sand and finish the wood edges that are still exposed on the lip door with an enamel of matching shade. Don't try to cover the rounded front edge of the door with plastic laminate.

Now apply plastic laminate to all exposed surfaces of the cabinet itself. First cut and fit all end panels and cement them in place. Fig. 43-39. Then trim these end panels before fitting the face pieces on the rails and stiles. Cut the pieces for the faces of rails and stiles so their grain (if wood-grained plastic

592

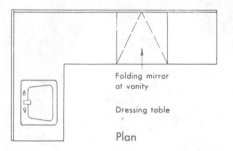

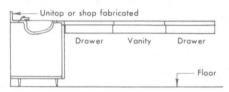

Folding mirror at vanity

Dressing table

Plan

Unitop or shop fabricated

Drawer   Vanity   Drawer

Floor

43-44. Typical bathroom plan for a conventional on-the-job installation of plastic-laminate counter tops.

laminate is used) follows that of natural wood. The grain of the stiles, for example, should be vertical and that of the rails horizontal. Carefully cut the pieces for the rails and stiles. Fig. 43-40. First fasten the rail pieces and then the stile pieces. Fig. 43-41. Then trim the facing flush with the wood. If the trimming can't be done with a router, complete this work with a file. Always file on the push stroke and lift the file away on the return stroke. This will give a good clean edge without chipping. The counter top and backsplash can be covered either before or after the cabinets. The last step is to replace the doors and drawers. Fig. 43-42.

OTHER USES FOR PLASTIC LAMINATES IN THE HOME

Plastic laminates have many other uses in the home. Some homes have plastic-laminate walls in bathrooms, dens, or recreation rooms. Fig. 43-43. The tops of counters in bathrooms, workrooms, and utility rooms are also commonly covered with plastic laminates. Fig. 43-44.

Although a room must be functional, it need not appear unattractive. Plastic laminates can add beauty as well as ease of maintenance to any built-in unit such as this bathroom sink. Such a counter top will give many years of hard service without fading, chipping, or peeling. *Formica*

Plastic laminates add both beauty and utility to this kitchen. The cabinet exteriors are plain white while the counter and desk units have a teakwood pattern. The red is an effective accent. *Formica*

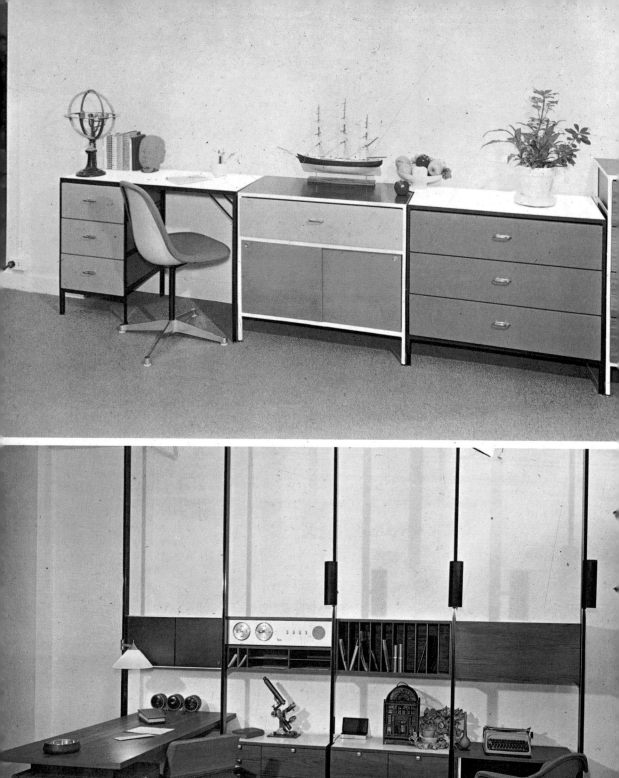

Plastic laminate or high pressure laminated plastic comes in a wide variety of colors and can be used for many applications, as in these four illustrations. Shown at the top of the opposite page are modular cabinets, covered with various colors of plastic laminates on tops and fronts. The illustration below it shows an attractive study. At the top of this page is a handsome table for a den, and below is a dressing-table unit. *Micarta*

This combination studio and kitchen has an exposed beam ceiling with a translucent roof area which admits natural light. The wood-grain plastic laminate is highlighted with hardware, lighting fixtures and accessories of Early American design. The plain yellow counter tops have a molded edge. This kind of counter top must be fabricated in a plant and then installed by the cabinetmaker.

Formica

Frame-And-Panel Construction

Frame-and-panel construction is widely used in cabinetmaking for doors and windows, sides and fronts of cabinets, and for interior casework. Fig. 44-1. While man-made materials such as plywood and particle board have become increasingly popular for built-ins and on-the-job cabinets, the frame and panel is still a favorite construction method in millrooms and furniture-manufacturing plants. The following are its distinct advantages:

• The unit has good dimensional stability and will change little in width or height with changes in humidity.

• The unit does not warp. (A large area of glued-up solid stock will warp and,

to a more limited extent, so will plywood and other man-made materials.)

• The unit adds design qualities to furniture. Fig. 44-2. A frame-and-panel door on a fine piece of furniture is much more interesting than a simple flat surface. It can also be made in any style from the simple rectangles of Contemporary furniture to the graceful curves of Traditional. Fig. 44-3.

• By using frame construction, glass or a metal grille can be set into the opening instead of a wood panel. Fig. 44-4.

INTERIOR CABINET PARTS

An *open or skeleton frame* (sometimes called a web frame) consists of two

44-1(a). Frame-and-panel construction is used for all kinds of doors from the cupboard doors on this Early American buffet to the large interior and exterior ones used in building construction. The doors shown here have a panel that is bevel raised on one side.

44-1(b). Panel doors like these are often called stile-and-rail doors. The panels are bevel raised on two sides. Joints between the stiles, rails and mullions must be mortised and tenoned or doweled. (Curtis Companies Inc.)

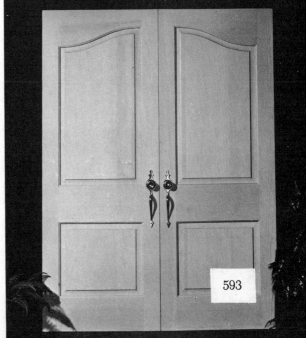

593

44-2. Frame-and-panel construction was used for the doors, drawer fronts, and sides of this tall handsome chest. The panels are straight, or plane. Note the half-tulip outline on the inside stiles of the doors and on the rails of the drawer fronts.

44-3. Note the arch-shaped stiles on the doors of this record cabinet. W—30″, D—30″, H—19″.

44-4. This stately cabinet has frame-and-panel doors. The upper section is inset with brass grillwork for display of art objects. The sides are also of frame-and-panel construction.

44-5(a). The simplest method of making a web or skeleton frame is to install two dowels at each joint.

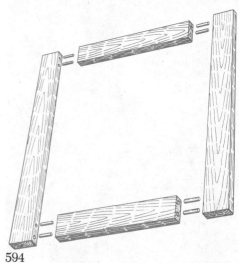

44-5(b). All frames must be glued under pressure to assure a solid unit.

44-6. The common joints used in making dust panels. A groove (plow) is cut around the inside edges of the rails and stiles to receive the panel of plywood or hardboard.

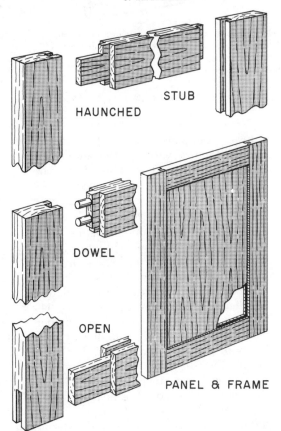

HAUNCHED

STUB

DOWEL

OPEN

PANEL & FRAME

vertical members called *stiles* and two horizontal members called *rails*. Fig. 44-5. The parts usually are joined with dowels, a haunched mortise-and-tenon joint, or a stub-tenon joint. Fig. 44-6. These frames are installed on the interior of a chest, desk, or cabinet to add stability to the unit and to provide horizontal support for the drawers. Fig. 44-7. While an open frame is adequate for many uses, better-quality furniture makes use of a *dust panel* which is a simple frame with a center of plywood or hardboard. Such a panel is installed in chests to keep the dust from seeping down from one drawer to the next. For this kind of construction a groove must be cut around the inside edges of the rails and stiles to receive the panel which usually is 1/4" hardboard or plywood.

44-7. Frames are used in cabinets to strengthen the unit and also to serve as drawer supports.

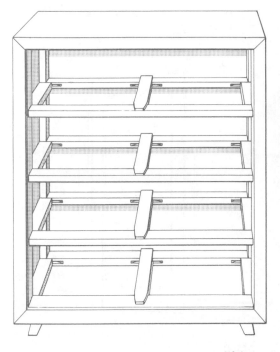

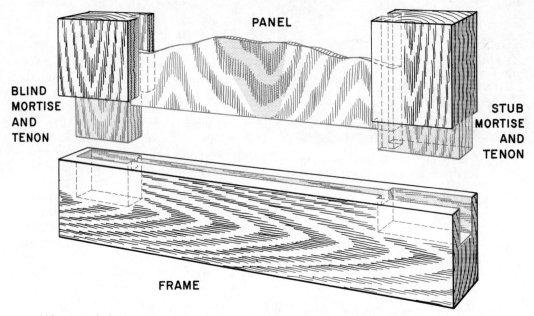

PANEL

BLIND
MORTISE
AND
TENON

STUB
MORTISE
AND
TENON

FRAME

44-8. A simple frame-and-panel door can be made with stiles and rails that have a square inside edge and a flat panel. The stiles and rails can be joined with a blind mortise-and-tenon or a stub mortise-and-tenon joint. Better-quality frames can be made with a haunched mortise-and-tenon joint, or dowels can be added to the stub mortise-and-tenon joint.

44-9. Parts of a door.

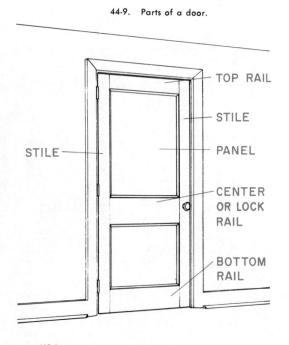

STILE

TOP RAIL

STILE

PANEL

CENTER
OR LOCK
RAIL

BOTTOM
RAIL

Exterior Furniture Parts and Architectural Woodwork

Frame-and-panel surfaces for exterior furniture parts vary greatly in design and construction. Fig. 44-8. Some of these differences are as follows:

Frame

The frame is usually made of solid wood and requires four or more pieces: two pieces for the vertical stiles and two pieces for the horizontal rails. If an intermediate horizontal divider is used, this is called a *cross rail* or *lock rail*. Fig. 44-9. An intermediate vertical divider called a *cross stile* or *mullion* may also be used. For most furniture and cabinet doors, the thickness of the frame is 11/16″ surfaced stock (3/4″ minimum thickness is allowed). For heavier doors, 1⅛″, or 1⅜″, or 1¾″ surfaced material is used. For interior and exterior

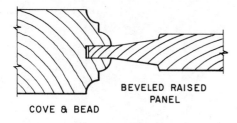

COVE & BEAD

BEVELED RAISED PANEL

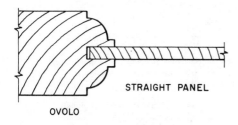

OVOLO

STRAIGHT PANEL

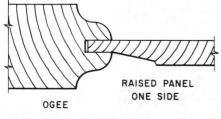

OGEE

RAISED PANEL ONE SIDE

44-10. Standard molded stickings are the ovolo, the bead and cove, and the ogee.

door frames, glued-up, low-density stock covered with 1/8" veneer is sometimes used.

Sticking

Sticking is the term used to describe the shape of the inside edge of the frame. The sticking may be square or molded. Some of the standard molded stickings are the *ovolo*, the *bead and cove*, and the *ogee*. Fig. 44-10. A panel groove or plow is cut around the inside edge to receive the panel. Usually the groove is cut to a depth of 3/8". However, if a solid wood panel is used, the groove should be 3/8" deep in the rails and 1" deep in the stiles. The extra depth in the stiles takes care of the cross-grain expansion of the solid panel. However, solid panels are usually limited to not more than 10", which means that they are installed only on small cupboard doors for furniture and cabinets.

Corner Joints

Many kinds of corner joints can be used. The normal practice in good construction is to use either a haunched mortise-and-tenon joint or a dowel joint

44-11. The two common methods of stile-and-rail construction when square sticking is used and there is a square coped shoulder on the tenon.

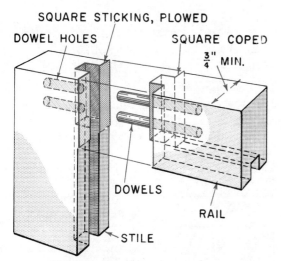

SQUARE STICKING, PLOWED

DOWEL HOLES

SQUARE COPED

$\frac{3}{4}$" MIN.

DOWELS

RAIL

STILE

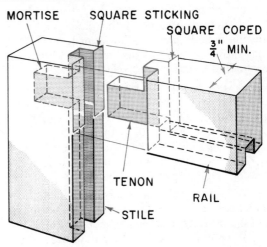

MORTISE   SQUARE STICKING

SQUARE COPED

$\frac{3}{4}$" MIN.

TENON

RAIL

STILE

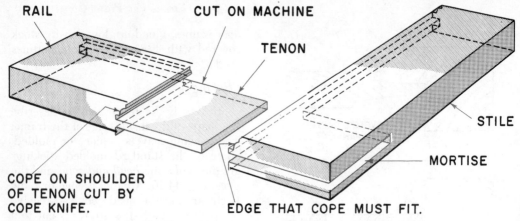

RAIL

CUT ON MACHINE

TENON

STILE

MORTISE

COPE ON SHOULDER
OF TENON CUT BY
COPE KNIFE.

EDGE THAT COPE MUST FIT.

44-12. Stile-and-panel work with a molded edge. The edge on the stiles is cut on a shaper, sticker, or molding machine. The cope on the shoulder of the tenon is cut on a shaper or tenoner.

with a stub tenon for all work that has square sticking on the inside edge. Fig. 44-11. Stiles and rails that have molded edges have a mortise-and-tenon joint with the tenon shoulder coped to fit the molded edge of the stile. Fig. 44-12.

Panel

The panel can be made of either plywood (which is the usual practice) or solid glued-up stock. There are many kinds of panel surfaces including the following (Fig. 44-13):

● The *flush panel* is often used for the sides of furniture cases and cabinets. A groove or plow is cut in the frame and a rabbet is cut around the panel so that the outside surface is flush, or level. This construction makes use of a square edge on the frame.

● The *elevated or raised panel* is sometimes used for furniture doors. A groove is cut in the frame and the edges of the panel are cut to fit so that the panel is elevated above the frame itself. The edges of the panel are usually rounded for better appearance.

● The *straight or plane panel* is the simplest, especially when used with a square-edge frame. (Note that Fig. 44-13 shows an ovolo rather than a square edge.)

598

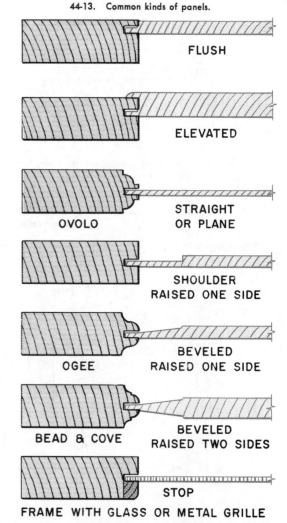

44-13. Common kinds of panels.

FLUSH

ELEVATED

OVOLO   STRAIGHT OR PLANE

SHOULDER RAISED ONE SIDE

OGEE   BEVELED RAISED ONE SIDE

BEAD & COVE   BEVELED RAISED TWO SIDES

STOP

FRAME WITH GLASS OR METAL GRILLE

44-14(a). This TV hostess server has panel doors that are bevel raised on one side.

44-14(b). Notice that the backs of the panels are flat and so is the sticking on the back.

• The *shoulder raised-one-side panel* adds a design characteristic that is especially attractive on Modern or Contemporary furniture.

• The *beveled raised-one-side panel* is the most common one for furniture doors. The interior of the door has a flat panel appearance while its exterior shows a raised panel. Fig. 44-14. In the cabinet shop the raised panel is cut on a circular saw, radial-arm saw, or shaper. If veneer-core plywood panels are used, the plies are exposed on the beveled surfaces. These show up very distinctly when a finish is applied. Therefore furniture and cabinet manufacturers construct lumber-core plywood panels so that the plies won't show. This is done in various ways. If three-ply construction is used, extra-heavy veneers are chosen for the face and back so they can be cut at an angle without exposing the core. Fig. 44-15. For five-ply construction, the crossbands are made of thick, good-quality wood and the face and back veneers are of very thin material. Then the cutting is

44-14(c). A typical door with panel raised on one side.

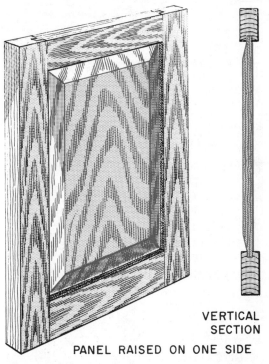

VERTICAL SECTION

PANEL RAISED ON ONE SIDE

599

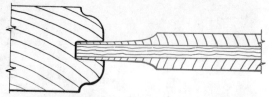

44-15. Notice how the three-ply panel is made with the face veneer thick enough to allow for the raise.

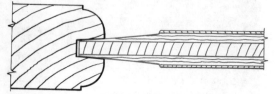

44-16. This five-ply panel has a thick crossband so the bevel is cut in this.

44-17. This raised panel is made with a mitered rim of solid stock that is grooved into and glued to the edge of the plywood. Notice also the use of molding with a square sticking to give it the appearance of a molded sticking.

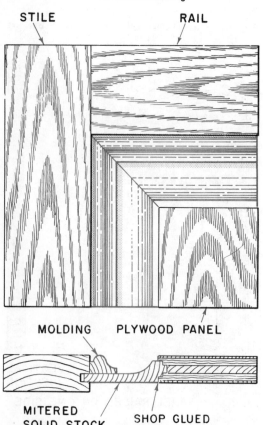

STILE   RAIL

MOLDING   PLYWOOD PANEL

MITERED SOLID STOCK   SHOP GLUED

done through the crossbands as shown in Fig. 44-16. Note that the face veneer starts at the upper edge of the raised panel. Still another method is to cut a mitered rim around the plywood panel that is grooved and glued into the edge of the plywood. Fig. 44-17. The bevel is actually cut in the solid wood rim. This rim can be reinforced with splines, dowels, or clamp nails.

• The *beveled raised-two-sides panel* is used primarily in larger doors where the door is normally seen from both sides.

• A *frame for a glass or metal grill* is made by cutting a rabbet around the inside edge. Fig. 44-18. The glass or grille is usually held in place with a *wood stop* nailed or stapled to the frame. There are also patented metal or plastic holders that can be used. See Unit 13.

CUTTING THE MOLDED EDGES (STICKING)

Simple frame-and-panel construction has square-edge stiles and rails with grooves for the panels. The panel groove can be cut with a dado head on a circular or radial-arm saw or with cutters on a shaper or router. On quality furniture and cabinets, the inside edges of the stiles and rails have a molded edge. In a small shop these decorative edges are cut to shape on a shaper or router. Furniture and cabinet manufacturers use a molding machine (sticker) and tenoner for these operations. When molded sticking is used in frame-and-panel construction, it is necessary to have a matched set of *sticking* and *coping* cutters for the thickness of the frame stock being used. Fig. 44-19. The set of sticking cutters is fastened to the spindle of the shaper, and the inside edges of the stiles and rails are cut to shape. Fig. 44-20. Then a set of coping cutters is fastened to the spindle of the shaper and the ends of the rails (rail shoulders) are coped to fit over the molding on the stiles. Fig. 44-21. If there is a

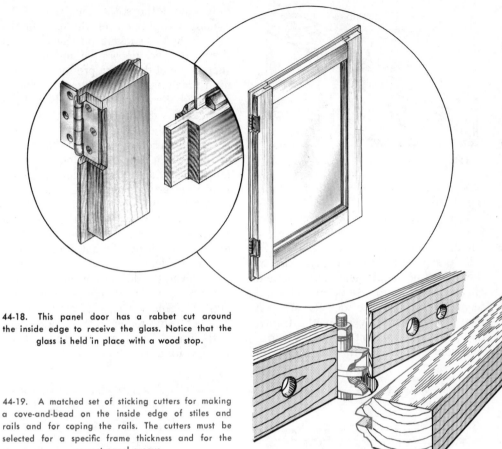

44-18. This panel door has a rabbet cut around the inside edge to receive the glass. Notice that the glass is held 'in place with a wood stop.

44-19. A matched set of sticking cutters for making a cove-and-bead on the inside edge of stiles and rails and for coping the rails. The cutters must be selected for a specific frame thickness and for the correct panel groove.

COVE & BEAD DOOR COPING

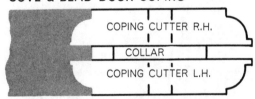

COPING CUTTER R.H.

COLLAR

COPING CUTTER L.H.

COVE & BEAD DOOR STICKING

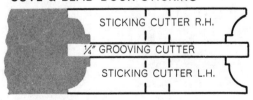

STICKING CUTTER R.H.

¼" GROOVING CUTTER

STICKING CUTTER L.H.

44-20. Setup for cutting sticking on a shaper.

44-21. Setup for cope cutting on the ends of the rails.

SLIDING JIG

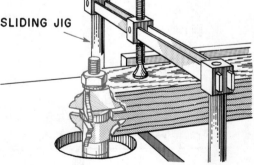

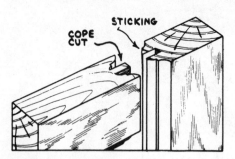

44-22. The completed joint ready for the panel.

miter joint at the corners, only the sticking cutters are needed.

You will remember that a coped joint is one between two molded pieces in which the end grain of one piece (the rail) is shaped to fit the molded edge of the stile. Fig. 44-22. The usual method of assembly is to use a mortise and tenon or one or two dowels at each joint. If you carefully study the frame-and-panel construction of quality furniture, you will see that the rails appear to

butt against the stiles. This is done by making a coping cut on the ends of the rails to fit the sticking on the edges of the stiles. Very decorative and unusual-shaped panel doors are produced in furniture factories on the automatic shaper and double-end tenoning machine. Simpler designs can be made in the school or cabinet shop. Fig. 44-23.

Cutting decorative edges on the inside of frames is a time-consuming operation unless it is done on a production basis. It is necessary to have the correct set of coping and sticking cutters for the thickness of frame stock being used. Also, a great deal of setup time is required. For this reason it is usually not done for only one or two doors.

However, the decorative effect of sticking can be achieved by applying moldings to the door. One way of doing this is to cut a stub tenon on the inside edges of the frame. The tenon should be of the same width as the thickness of the panel.

44-23. A simple French Provincial frame and panel can be made with standard power tools. The rails are cut on the band saw and the groove is cut on the shaper. The raised panel can also be cut on the shaper.

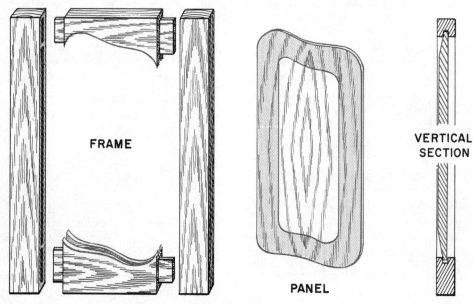

FRAME

PANEL

VERTICAL SECTION

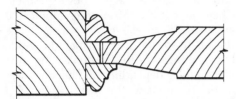

44-24. Decorative molding installed on either side of the frame to hold the panel in place.

Fig. 44-24. Then decorative molding is nailed to both edges to hold the panel in place. Another way is to use square sticking on the stiles and rails and then nail or staple the molding in the corner between the edge and the panel. Fig. 44-25. When moldings are applied to the frames or surfaces of flush panels, they should be spot glued to the frames, not to the panels, before they are nailed or stapled.

Cutting a Raised Panel

There are three common ways of cutting a raised panel: with the circular saw, the radial-arm saw, and the shaper. In furniture plants an automatic shaper or tenoner sometimes is used.

On the Circular Saw

Tilt the saw blade to 15 degrees from the vertical. On most saws this will be 75 degrees. Adjust the fence to within 3/16″ of the saw blade at the table. The blade must tilt away from the fence. Raise the blade to about 1½″ above the table. When you are certain the saw is set properly, place the panel on edge with the back surface against the fence and make a cut on each of the four edges. See Fig. 26-55.

On the Radial-Arm Saw

To cut a raised panel on a radial-arm saw, the machine must be set up for bevel ripping. Use an 8″-diameter blade in place of the standard 10″ one. The 10″-blade may strike the column base. Place the saw in the outward position

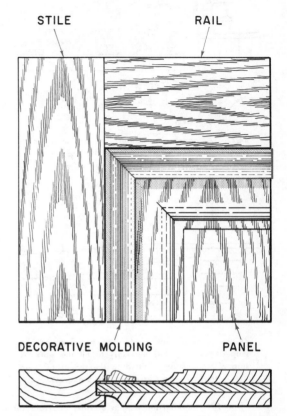

STILE   RAIL

DECORATIVE MOLDING   PANEL

44-25. Decorative molding installed in the corner along the edge of the frame.

44-26. Cutting a raised panel on the radial-arm saw.

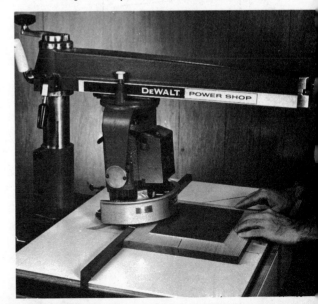

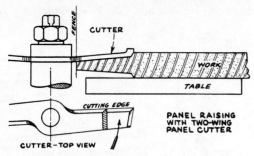

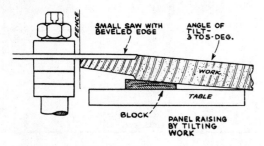

CUTTER

FENCE

WORK

TABLE

CUTTING EDGE

CUTTER—TOP VIEW

PANEL RAISING
WITH TWO-WING
PANEL CUTTER

44-27. A panel-raiser cutter can be used on a shaper. This two-wing cutter can be used with the work held flat against the table.

SMALL SAW WITH BEVELED EDGE

ANGLE OF TILT—3 TO 5 DEG.

FENCE

WORK

TABLE

BLOCK

PANEL RAISING BY TILTING WORK

44-28. A small saw blade can be used on the shaper. However, it is necessary to tilt the work. A strip of wood must be fitted to the shaper table so that the work tilts about 3 to 5 degrees.

and tilt it to a 90-degree bevel position. Then raise it 5 to 10 degrees (indicated as 80 to 85 on the bevel scale). Place the blade so that it overhangs the guide fence, either on the stationary or auxiliary table, depending on the thickness of the material or the width of cut. To do this, move the saw the correct distance from the column and lock it in position with the rip clamp. Before turning on the machine make sure that the blade moves freely. Then place the stock on the table with the back against the table top and the edge against the fence. Feed from right to left. Remember to cut the end grain first and then the edge grain. Fig. 44-26.

On the Shaper

It is necessary to have a panel-raiser cutter mounted on the spindle so that the cutting is done on the upper surface of the panel. The tool can be used to cut a bevel-raised panel on one or two sides. Fig. 44-27. It is ground with proper clear-

44-29. Marking the lengths of stiles and rails for a flush door. Remember to allow additional length on the rails for the joints.

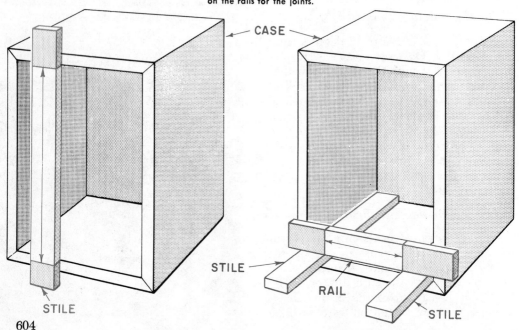

CASE

CASE

STILE

STILE

STILE

RAIL

STILE

44-30. Fitting panel doors. Notice that the frames and rails have molding sticking and that a haunched mortise-and-tenon joint is used. Hardboard panels are installed in the frames.

44-31. Installing flat panels in a stile-and-rail door. Notice that dowels are used to hold the stiles and rails together.

ance to make clean cuts with no feather. A small saw can also be used for cutting a raised panel. Fig. 44-28. The disadvantage of the saw is that the work must be tilted. Usually one or more cuts must be made to produce the beveled edge. Generally one or more heavy roughing cuts followed by a light finishing cut will produce the best surface.

MAKING A FRAME AND PANEL

1. Determine the overall size of the frame. For example, you must decide whether a door is to be the flush, lip, or overlapping type. Then cut the stiles to length. Cut the rails to the correct length, making sure to provide for the correct joint. Fig. 44-29.

2. Square up the stock.

3. If the frame is to have a square inside edge, lay out and cut a groove on all edges into which the panel is to fit. The groove should be as deep as or slightly deeper than it is wide. Usually a groove that is 1/4" wide is cut 3/8" deep. If the inside edge is to have molded sticking, both the groove and molded edge are cut on the shaper at the same time. Then another set of matching

cutters must be used on the shaper to do the coping on the ends of the rails to match the sticking and to form the tenon. Fig. 44-30.

4. Lay out and cut the panel to the correct size. If necessary, cut the raised panel on one or both sides. The panel should be slightly less in overall dimensions than the distances to the bottom of the frame grooves. The edges of the panel should be about 3/16" thick to fit a 1/4" groove. If the panel has an irregular shape, first cut to outside size on a band saw and then cut the raised panel. Fig. 44-31.

5. Join the rails to the stiles. In making a stub mortise and tenon, the thickness of the tenon is the same as the width of the groove, and the length of the tenon is the same as the depth of the groove. In making a haunched mortise-and-tenon joint, the thickness of the mortise should be the same as the width of the groove. The mortise should be started far enough away from the ends of the stiles to prevent breaking out. The width and depth of the mortise should be about two-thirds the width of the rail. The length of the tenon should be equal to the depth of the mortise plus the depth of the groove. Cut

605

a notch in the tenon so that the long part will fit into the mortise opening and the short part into the groove. If a molded edge is used, install one or two dowels at each joint. The diameter of the dowels should be equal to half the thickness of the frame.

6. Make a dry assembly of the panel in the frame to see that all parts fit. Then take the unit apart. Give the panel a final sanding. Wax the edges of the panel. Then apply glue to the frame joints, *never to the groove or panel*. Clamp securely and allow the unit to dry thoroughly. Then remove any excess glue and sand the frame.

45 Cabinet And Furniture Doors

Doors for furniture and cabinets must be both functional and attractive. Usually designed to close off open shelves or trays, doors also should add interest to the exterior design. Glass, a metal grille, or mesh is often used when silverware and china are to be displayed. Fig. 45-1. Doors are made from many materials and are hung (fitted into an opening) in various ways.

Doors can be divided into two major groups, depending primarily on their size and use. Smaller doors for furniture and casework including built-ins are called *cupboard* or *case* doors. Fig. 45-2. Larger doors for homes and commercial buildings are designated as *exterior* or *interior* doors of a particular type, such as panel, solid, flush, hollow-core, louver, or French. Fig. 45-3. In this unit, stress is

45-1. The doors in the base of this credenza are different from those in the upper section. Notice the use of both glass and metal grillwork in the upper doors.

45-2. The small doors on this lamp table are typical case or cupboard doors. They are of frame-and-panel construction with routed panel inserts. Note the pin hinges at each corner.

606

placed on the construction and installation of cupboard or case doors since these are usually produced as part of the total product. On the other hand, most interior or exterior doors are purchased as standard millwork items. The cabinetmaker or finish carpenter is responsible only for hanging these doors. A few larger cabinet and architectural woodworking plants produce exterior and interior doors of unusual shapes and designs as special millwork items.

MATERIAL FOR FURNITURE AND CASE DOORS

• *Solid, glued-up stock* is used primarily for small furniture doors made in school and cabinet shops. These doors have the disadvantage of being subject to warpage, expansion, and contraction.

• For built-ins and interior cabinets, doors of *tongue-and-groove paneling* can be constructed to any width and length. Fig. 45-4. Lay the pieces to be fabricated flat on the floor, with the tongues fitted snugly into the grooves. Cut a piece of 1" x 2" material for cross pieces at least 2" narrower than the width. Center this on the paneling for the door. Nail or

45-3. This interior Dutch door is a standard millwork item that can be ordered by thickness, width, and height to fit any standard frame opening.

screw the cross pieces to the paneling at both the upper and lower ends. Now cut a piece of 1" x 2" stock to fit diagonally between the two pieces already nailed in place. Install screws to hold the pieces permanently. After the door has been fabricated, trim off the exposed tongue and groove with a saw or plane.

• For most built-ins and kitchen cabinets constructed on the job, *veneer-core ply-*

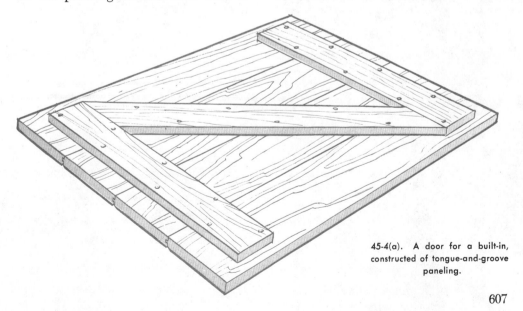

45-4(a). A door for a built-in, constructed of tongue-and-groove paneling.

607

45-4(b). Doors for this built-in are made from hemlock panel (tongue and groove) boards held by Z-shaped bracing. All hardware is concealed and the doors are equipped with spring latches that open by finger pressure.

45-5. The rolling doors for this tall storage cabinet are made of 3/4" veneer-core plywood.

45-6(a). This Contemporary chest has a door made of fine lumber-core plywood. Notice the continuous hinge (piano hinge) installed along the left edge. Instead of a handle, the door has a touch latch.

45-6(b). With a touch latch, no exterior hardware is needed to open the door. Just push to open and close.

45-6(c). Five-ply lumber-core construction of a lip door.

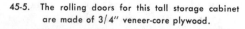

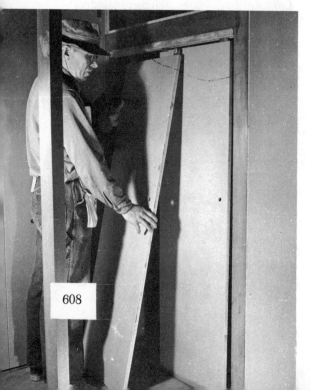

45-7. The doors of these laundry-room cabinets are constructed of particle board.

45-8. The sliding doors over the sink are made of wood-grained hardboard to match the fir cabinets and fir-paneled walls.

wood is used for the doors because it is easy to cut and fit. Fig. 45-5. Generally no attempt is made to cover the exposed edges except by painting or finishing. It is important to select the correct hinges for veneer-core plywood. They must be the kind that screw into the back surface of the door—not into the edge—since the edges of veneer-core plywood have poor holding power.

Many furniture factories make their own *lumber-core plywood* doors. Fig. 45-6. This makes it possible to edge band the doors with the same hardwood lumber as the face veneer. A decorative edge can be machined on the door.

Particle board is frequently used as a base for doors made of plastic laminate. When cupboard doors are made of this, a backing grade of laminate should be added for balanced construction. For storage cabinets, painted particle board doors are excellent. Fig. 45-7.

Hardboard is often used for small sliding doors for cabinets and built-ins. Fig. 45-8. Perforated hardboard is a good choice when ventilation is needed.

45-9. The doors of this Early American hutch cabinet are of frame-and-panel construction. The upper doors have butt hinges while the lower ones have surface "H" hinges. Note that the cabinet has flush doors rather than the lip doors usually found on this style of furniture.

609

45-10(a). The upper section of this buffet has all-glass doors. Note the "handle" ground into the glass for easy opening. The lower doors are covered with leather for interesting contrast to the wood. From this interesting combination of materials you can see that a cabinetmaker must know more than how to work with wood.

45-10(b). A metal or plastic track must be used. This track is made of "slippery plastic" to make the glass slide easily. It also has a built-in "feather" in the top track to keep the glass from rattling. This track is installed in a 3/4" groove and will accept glass from 3/16" to 1/4" thick.

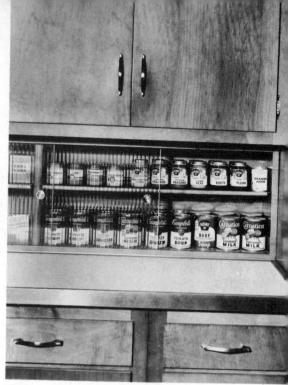

45-10(c). Sliding glass doors installed in a kitchen-cabinet unit between the wall and the base units.

45-11. Cutout showing a honeycomb door covered with plastic laminate. This makes an ideal, light cabinet door. A simple wood frame is the basic support of the door.

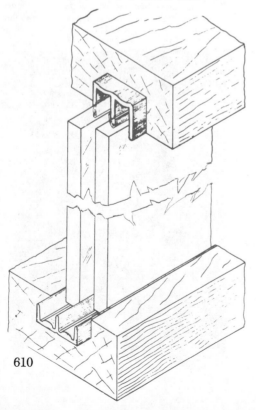

• *Frame-and-panel* doors are commonly found on fine furniture and high-quality kitchen cabinets. Fig. 45-9. Frame-and-panel doors are built as described in Unit 44. Sometimes a frame with glass, a metal grille, or mesh is installed, especially on china cabinets. A door of glass set in a wood frame is called a *glazed* door.

• *All glass* is often installed in the upper part of china cabinets. Fig. 45-10. Glass requires a special metal or plastic track.

• *Honeycomb-core* doors, very light in weight, are made by building a frame of solid wood and then using a honeycomb filler made of kraft paper and plastic. Fig. 45-11. The surfaces are covered with veneer or plastic laminate. In building these doors it is important to remember that there must be solid wood wherever the hinges or locks are to fit.

• *Flexible or tambour* doors are made of vertical pieces of wood fitted together

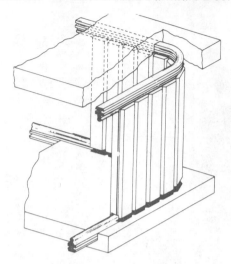

45-12(b). This kind of track is needed for a tambour door. While the door can be made to slide along a wood groove, it will slide more easily if a plastic track is installed. The track follows the slot or groove routed into the cabinet. A single track at the bottom works well, but a double track, one above and one below, is still better.

45-12(a). A flexible or tambour door covers two-thirds of this handsome teak sideboard.

45-13(a). The wood folding or accordion door is popular for cabinets, interior doors, and many special purposes.

with a flexible wood or plastic joint. They may also be constructed of vertical slats mounted on a heavy canvas back. Fig. 45-12(a). They are made to slide in a track around a corner so that the full width of the cabinet is exposed when the doors are open. They have the advantages of sliding doors without the disad-

vantages. Fig. 45-12(b). They operate like an old-fashioned roll-top desk.

• *Folding or accordion* doors are made of vertical sections of wood that fold against one another into a compact unit. Fig. 45-13(a). The sections of a wood folding door are usually fitted together with plastic hinges. Fig. 45-13(b).

Hanging Doors

Flush Door in Frame

The flush door fits into the face or plate frame of a case or carcass so that all surfaces are level. Fig. 45-14. For many furniture pieces the flush door must fit into a four-sided frame or face plate. To get an accurate fit, special care is required. For most kitchen-cabinet installation, the flush door is fitted into a frame or face plate on only three sides, with the lower part of the door just covering the lower shelf. Remember that the flush door is always made about 1/16″ thinner than the frame to allow for slight clearance behind the door.

For a pair of flush doors in a frame, one of several methods can be followed to prevent a crack from appearing between the doors. Fig. 45-15. These are:
• Cut a small chamfer on each door at

45-13(b). Plastic Hinges that mount in a slot or over the edge of a door are usually used with a wood folding door.

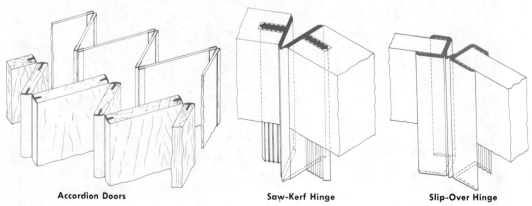

Accordion Doors   Saw-Kerf Hinge   Slip-Over Hinge

45-14. This buffet has flush doors with butt hinges.

45-15. Common methods of treating the edge of a double door.

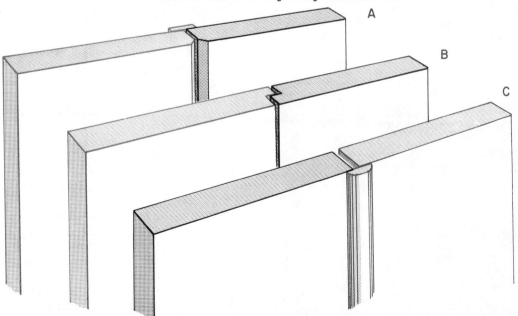

A

B

C

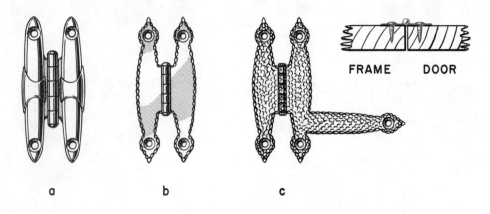

45-16(a). Common surface hinges: (a) Modern, (b) "H", and (c) "HL".

the point where they meet so there appears to be a V groove at the center. Then put a wood or metal stop behind the doors.

• Cut a rabbet on the front of the lefthand door and on the back of the righthand door. The right door will overlap the left one when it is closed. Remember that extra width is needed for the rabbets.

• Add a raised edge or molding for the righthand door.

• Cut a rounded edge on the left door

45-16(b). Surface hinges are quickly mounted since they require no gain. They add an ornamental touch.

and a matching concave recess on the righthand door. Then both doors will open at the same time.

Hinges for Flush Doors

While many types of hinges can be used for flush doors, the most common are the butt, pivot, or decorative surface hinge. To install, follow this procedure:

• Determine the size and number of hinges. For doors up to 3' high and 2' wide, two hinges are enough. Larger doors should have three hinges. Use 2" hinges for smaller doors and 2½" or 3" hinges for larger ones.

• With a square, check the frame of the opening. If the opening is slightly out of square, the door must be carefully trimmed to fit. Also decide in what direction the door will swing. In some cases, hinges may be placed on either side. However, on kitchen cabinets and built-ins, the door is usually hinged so that it will swing against the wall. If the doors are to fit into a four-sided opening, measure the inside height of the door at several points. Cut off the top and bottom of the door so that it will slip into the frame. Plane the top and bottom edges. If there is no lower rail, measure the vertical distance in the opening to the

614

45-17. Butt hinge.

bottom of the shelf so that the door will just cover the lower shelf.

• Measure the width of the door at several places and transfer these measurements to the door. The opening edge needs to be under beveled a little so that the door will swing out easily. Generally, a frame door should have about 1/16" clearance all around if it is to be painted. Less clearance (about .10") is necessary on a fine piece of furniture. Place the door in the frame opening and check it carefully.

• If decorative surface hinges are to be used, fit them first to the door and then install one screw each in the frame. Fig. 45-16. Try the door. If it works properly, install the other screws. Make sure the knuckles of the two hinges are in line. If not, make the necessary adjustments.

• Install the butt hinges. Fig. 45-17. With the door wedged in place, measure up from the bottom and down from the top, and mark a line on the door and the frame to indicate the top and bottom of the two hinges. Remove the door from the opening. With the try square, continue the line across the edge of the frame and the door to indicate the position of the hinge. Place the hinge over the edge of the door. Determine how far the hinge is to extend beyond the door. Draw a line to indicate the depth of the hinge. Do this on both the door and frame. Measure the thickness of the hinge from one side to the center of the knuckle. Mark a line on the door and frame to indicate this depth. Cut the

gain by hand or with a router. Fig. 45-18. Place the hinge in the door edge. Drill the pilot holes for the screws and attach the hinge. Hold the door against the frame and mark the position of one hole on either hinge. Drill a pilot hole. Insert one screw in each hinge. Now check to see if the door opens properly. If the door stands away too much from the frame side, it may be necessary to do more trimming. This should be done towards the front edge of the frame. If the door binds on the hinge side, cut a little piece of cardboard to go under the hinge. When the door opens properly, install the other screws.

45-18. A gain cut in the door and the frame or face plate to receive the butt hinge.

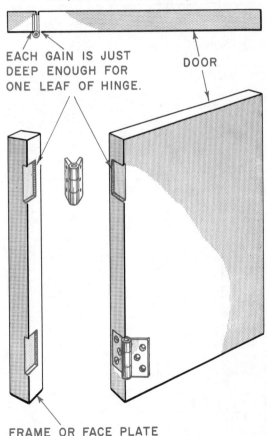

EACH GAIN IS JUST DEEP ENOUGH FOR ONE LEAF OF HINGE.

DOOR

FRAME OR FACE PLATE

• This simplified method of installing butt hinges is commonly used for good furniture. Cut a recess (shallow dado) across the entire edge of the door. The depth of the recess should equal the thickness of the barrel or knuckle. Then one leaf of the hinge is attached to the door and the other leaf to the face plate. The leaf on the case side is actually surface mounted. Fig. 45-19.

• Use a concealed loose-pin hinge for doors of veneer-core plywood. The concealed loose-pin hinge looks like an ordinary butt hinge when the door is closed, since only the barrel shows. However, the hinge is made so that the screws

FRAME   DOOR

45-20(a). A concealed wrap-around hinge with a loose pin for 3/4″ doors.

45-19. A deeper recess (shallow dado) is cut in the door. Both leaves fit into this recess.

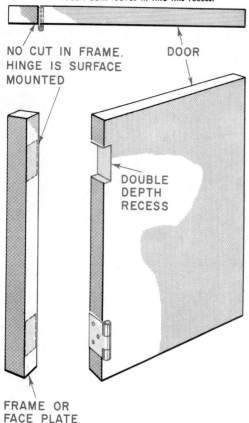

NO CUT IN FRAME.
HINGE IS SURFACE
MOUNTED

DOOR

DOUBLE
DEPTH
RECESS

FRAME OR
FACE PLATE

616

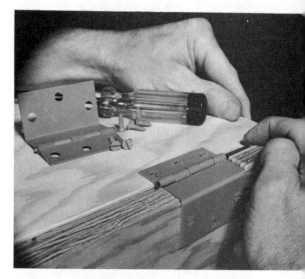

45-20(b). Installing a concealed wrap-around hinge in a plywood case. Note that the short leaf is surface-mounted and that a recess with a depth equal to the diameter of the barrel is cut in the door.

45-21(a). A lip door covers part of the opening of the frame. Note the semi-concealed hinge for lip doors.

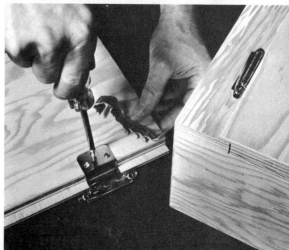

45-21(b). **Lip doors on kitchen cabinets.**

45-22(a). This beautiful china cabinet top and cupboard base have lip doors with surface hinges designed for offset or lip doors.

go into the back face of the plywood instead of the edge grain. Fig. 45-20. It is necessary to cut a recess into the door equal to the thickness of the barrel. The alternative method is to cut the recess in the frame slightly deeper than twice the thickness of the two leaves.

Lip Door

The lip door is easier to fit because it covers part of the face frame or plate; therefore no crack shows. A rabbet is cut around three or four edges (three if there is no frame at the bottom) so that part of the door fits inside the frame and the rest covers the frame. The outer edge of the door is usually rounded on simpler kitchen cabinets or built-ins. Fig. 45-21. When a lip door is installed on fine furniture, a decorative edge is cut on the exposed surface. Fig. 45-22. A simple lip door can be made in two stages. The rabbet is cut on a circular saw, jointer, or router, then the front edge is rounded

617

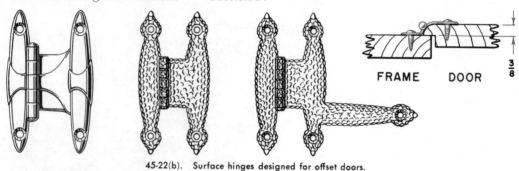

FRAME DOOR

3/8

45-22(b).   Surface hinges designed for offset doors.

45-23.   Shaper cutter for lip doors.

618   45-24(a).   This stereo hi-fi cabinet has overlay doors.

with a router. The complete edge can be cut in one operation, using the correct cutter on a shaper. Fig. 45-23.

Decide on the kind of hinges. A lip door is usually fitted with semi-concealed hinges, although other types can be used. Semi-concealed hinges are made in many styles and finishes to match Modern, Traditional, or Early American furniture. It is important to buy the hinges before the door is cut, to be sure that the correct size rabbet is cut. There are hinges for different thicknesses of doors. The depth of the rabbet cut determines the hinge dimension. Butt hinges are also used on commercial furniture but should not be selected if the door is made of veneer-core plywood.

45-24(b).   With pin hinges the doors swing all the way back against the sides.

If a lip door is to cover all four edges of the frame, measure the width of the opening and add twice the amount of the lip or overhang to the width. Also, measure the height of the opening. If the lip is to be only the upper edge, add an amount equal to the lip. If it is to be on both upper and lower edges, add twice the amount of the lip. Cut a rabbet equal to half the amount of the lip around all four sides of the door, or only around three sides if the fourth will not have a lip. Round off the front edge of the door on all sides. Check the door in the opening. Install the hinges on the door itself and then fasten them to the frame.

Doors without Frames or Overlay

Many modern cabinets and cases are designed so that the doors cover two, three, or four edges of the case or carcass. The doors may cover only the sides, with the top and bottom of the case protruding. The edges may be flush with the face surface of the door or the door may cover all four sides of the case. Fig. 45-24. With this construction, pin and pivot hinges are used. The pivot hinges are particularly useful for plywood and particle-board doors. Fig. 45-25. Only the pin or pivot shows from the front when the door is closed. These units come in pairs for small doors; for larger doors they are in sets of three, called a pair and a half. A slight angular cut must be made at the top and bottom of the door to receive the hinge. When the door is closed, all you can see of the hinge is a small ball or knuckle at each corner. If the door is fairly high, a third hinge of slightly different design is installed in the center of the door.

Rolling Doors

A track for rollers is mounted above a rolling door. Fig. 45-26. The bottom of the door is kept from moving in and out

45-25. Pivot hinges are very similar to pin hinges except that there is a large metal surface for mounting. Pivot hinges are mounted directly on the cabinet side and on the back of the door. A small angle cut must be made at the top and bottom of the door as shown in the enlarged view. Sometimes a middle hinge is also installed.

45-26. This is the kind of hardware needed to mount rolling doors. The insert shows how the bottom of the door is held in a vertical position.

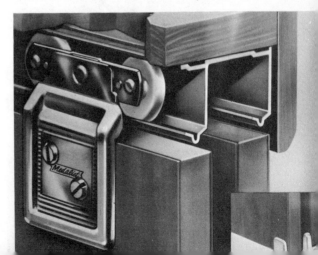

619

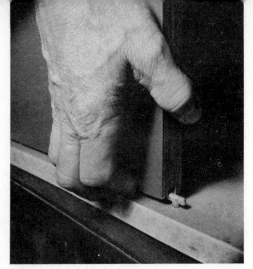

45-27. Another way to hold the lower edge of a door in position.

45-28. Rolling and sliding doors are equipped with finger cups. A small handle, round or rectangular, can be mounted when clearance between the doors is adequate or when the doors don't have to pass one another.

45-29. This attractive Contemporary sideboard has two sliding doors with round finger cups. Note the perfect book match on the doors.

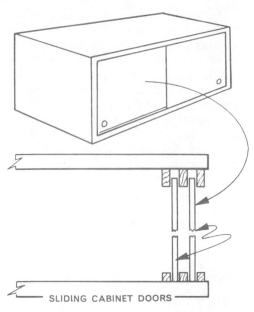

SLIDING CABINET DOORS

45-30(a). The simplest track for sliding doors is three pieces of wood mounted as shown here.

by a plastic guide. One type of guide encloses the lower edge; another rides in a groove cut in the lower edge. Fig. 45-27. These doors are usually equipped with finger cups. Fig. 45-28.

Sliding Doors

Sliding doors are useful when space is limited or when a hinged door would take up too much room. Fig. 45-29. Sliding doors are also used for safety when the doors are all glass. The major disadvantage of a sliding door is that only one-half of the cabinet interior is accessible at a time. Sliding doors are made of hardboard, plywood, or glass. There are several ways of installing them and it is important to determine the method to follow before starting to cut and fit them. The simplest shop construction consists of a square piece of stock and two pieces of quarter round mill stock which form the track on the inside of the case. Fig. 45-30. Rectangular pieces can be used in place of the quarter round. The second

620

45-30(b). The exterior appearance is better when quarter round is used for the front section of the door slide.

45-31(a). Grooves cut into the case for the sliding doors. Note that the top grooves are deeper than the bottom ones so the doors can be removed when necessary.

45-31(b). Installing hardboard doors in a case. A bored hole serves as a finger cup.

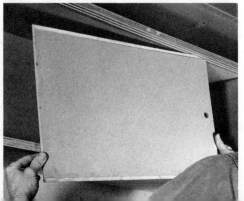

45-31(c). Sliding doors in an overhead cabinet.

45-32(a). Double sliding-door track for mounting in a 3/4" groove at top and bottom of a case. This can be used with either glass or panel doors.

method is to cut two grooves in the top and two in the bottom near the front edge of the case for each door. Then a rabbet is cut on the back of the front door and the front of the back door. This allows the doors to meet with only a little gap between, and also increases the effective depth of the cabinet. For doors of 3/8" plywood, rabbet half the thickness. Always seal the edges and backs of the doors with the same material as the front so the doors will not warp. To make the doors removable, cut the bottom grooves 3/16" deep and the top grooves 3/8" deep. After the doors are finished, they can be inserted by slipping them into the excess space in the top grooves. Fig. 45-31. Then they are dropped into the bottom grooves.

The best method of mounting sliding doors is with some kind of plastic or metal track. Fig. 45-32. One kind of metal track has ball bearings on which glass doors can roll to open and close.

621

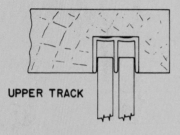

UPPER TRACK

GLASS OR PANEL
3/16 TO 1/4 THICK

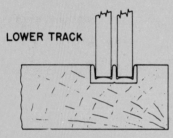

LOWER TRACK

45-32(b). This is the way the track is mounted in the case.

45-32(c). A simpler type of track for double sliding doors that can be used with plywood or other man-made materials. A groove or kerf is cut in the top and bottom of the doors. The track is mounted directly in the base without any machining.

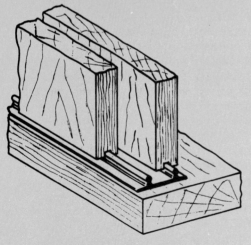

45-33. This planning desk consists of a lip door that drops down to form a writing desk. There are three semi-concealed hinges across the bottom of the lip door and stay-and-support hinges on either side to hold the door open at 90 degrees.

45-34. Installing a continuous or piano hinge for a drop door.

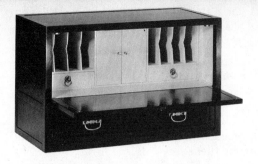

45-35. This small drop-lid or fall-front desk unit has special hinges on either side that open only 90 degrees to hold the door in a horizontal position.

45-36. Two sizes of magnetic catches: (a) Single. (b) Double.

a.

b.

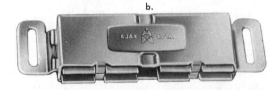

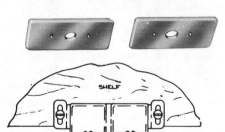

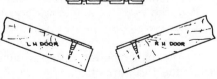

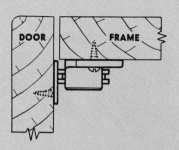

FLUSH OVERLAY DOOR

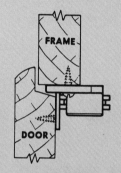

LIP DOOR

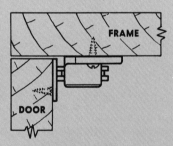

FLUSH DOOR

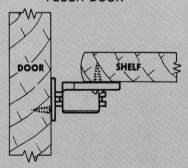

UNDERSHELF

45-37. Common methods of mounting magnetic catches in casework.

623

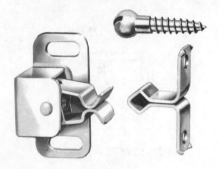

45-38(a). Friction catch.

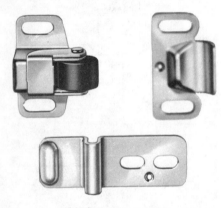

45-38(b). Roller catch

45-39. The drawer pulls of this commode table are located at the exact center of each door for perfect formal balance.

Glass doors should be at least 1/4″ thick and should have ground and polished edges with finger cups ground into the glass. Other sliding doors should be equipped with finger cups or handles for opening them.

Drop Doors

Drop doors can serve as writing surfaces for desks or cabinets. These doors may be either flush or lip. The hardware includes: hinges, some type of desk lid support to hold the door open at 90 degrees, catches, and handles or pulls. Fig. 45-33. A continuous or piano hinge can be put on a drop door. Then, to hold it in position for writing, a folding stay and lid support or a metal chain stay can be installed. Fig. 45-34. For small drop doors, special hinges are available that open only 90 degrees. Fig. 45-35.

CATCHES

There are many kinds of catches for holding doors in position. Most popular is the magnetic catch. Fig. 45-36. This is made to fit various positions inside a case. Fig. 45-37. The metal plate is attached, usually to the door, and the magnetic catch is attached to the inside of the case. These are commonly found on fine furniture cabinets and, when the doors are not too large, on kitchen cabinets. Two other common catches are shown in Fig. 45-38.

PULLS AND KNOBS

Door and drawer pulls and knobs are made in a wide variety of sizes, styles, and designs. On a door such hardware is usually located quite close to the opening edge and at a convenient position. However, knobs and pulls are sometimes fitted to the exact center of a door, for design reasons. Fig. 45-39. Examples of this hardware are shown in Fig. 45-40. The design of the pulls and knobs should match the furniture style.

45-40(a).   **Common styles of knobs.**

45-40(b).   **Common styles of pulls.**

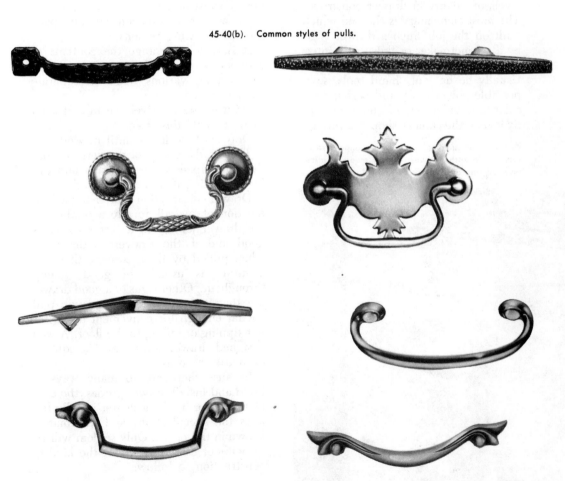

Drawers And Drawer Guides

Drawers cause some of the hardest problems in furniture construction. Because of the frequent pushing and pulling they receive, drawers must be soundly built. Still, within the limits of good workmanship there is a wide range of quality, from simple cigar-box construction to the finest dovetail joint of production furniture. Fig. 46-1.

Generally speaking, there are three levels of quality in drawer construction. The most elementary is the one which is built on the job. Such a drawer is built by a cabinetmaker or finish carpenter as he builds a kitchen cabinet or built-in. Usually he has only hand tools, several portable power tools, and perhaps a circular or radial-arm saw. The second quality level is the cabinet-shop drawer, made by a cabinetmaker who has fairly extensive equipment such as saws, routers, and shapers. Top-quality drawers are made in fine-furniture factories in which the most modern production equipment, including a dovetailer, is available. More detail about these three quality levels is given later in this unit.

Remember, saying that a drawer is of lower quality does not mean that it is poorly constructed.

Drawers make excellent storage space for the following reasons:
• It is easy to arrange the contents of a drawer since dividers can be installed for keeping various items in separate compartments.
• Drawers are relatively clean and keep their contents dust free.
• Drawers hide items until needed.

The disadvantages of drawers are that they are expensive to construct and can be frustrating if improperly made.

Drawer construction is often a good indication of overall furniture quality. If the drawer joinery in a certain piece is good and if the drawers slide easily when pulled by their corners, then the furniture is usually of good quality throughout. Other signs of a good drawer are that it does not stick and will pull out far enough for convenient use without tipping or falling to the floor. A well designed drawer must stay "in square" even after hard use.

Because there are so many ways to build and install drawer guides, the cabinetmaker or finish carpenter usually follows the specifications and information shown in the prints. Only seldom will he be without directions about the kind of construction to follow.

46-1(a). The quality of drawers ranges from the very simple kitchen-cabinet drawer made of softwood plywood with simple joints and nailed assembly to . . .

626

46-1(b). . . . these fine drawers in which the fronts are made of frame-and-panel construction with all parts of finest hardwood, all multiple dovetail construction, and the finest drawer guides.

46-1(c). This quality drawer is made with dovetail joints at both front and back, and is finished on the inside.

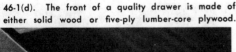

46-1(d). The front of a quality drawer is made of either solid wood or five-ply lumber-core plywood.

46-1(e). The bottom of a quality drawer fits into a groove on both sides, front, and back.

TYPES OF DRAWERS

There are three basic types of drawers:

- The *flush drawer*. The front of this drawer fits flush with the face plate or frame of the cabinet or chest. It is the most difficult to make since careful clearances are necessary. Fig. 46-2.
- The *lip drawer*. The front of a lip drawer covers part of the face plate or frame on three or four sides. On such drawers a rabbet is cut around three or

46-2. This Contemporary china cabinet has flush drawers, which require very careful fitting.

four sides of the drawer front so that part of the drawer front actually fits over the face of the frame. Fig. 46-3.

• The *overlap or overlay drawer*. On this drawer, the sides of the front overlap or cover only the sides of the cabinet. Fig. 46-4.

PARTS OF A DRAWER

All drawers consist of five basic parts, namely, one front, two sides, one back, and one bottom. Fig. 46-5. Before constructing a drawer you must know what is required for each of these parts since design and quality vary greatly. Fig. 46-6.

Front

Drawer fronts normally are made of either solid stock or of lumber-core plywood and are usually not less than 3/4" nor more than 1⅛" thick. Some fancy drawer fronts are made of lumber-core plywood with an overlay of solid wood so that the surface can be carved for decoration. Sometimes the drawer front is

46-3. This Early American double desk with pull-out shelf has four lip drawers to hold writing equipment.

46-4. This teak chest has an overlap or overlay drawer front with a recessed back spacer which provides finger space for opening the drawers. This construction eliminates the need for hardwood pulls and makes possible the clean horizontal lines of the chest. A dovetail-dado joint (sometimes called a *through dovetail*) joins the sides to the front.

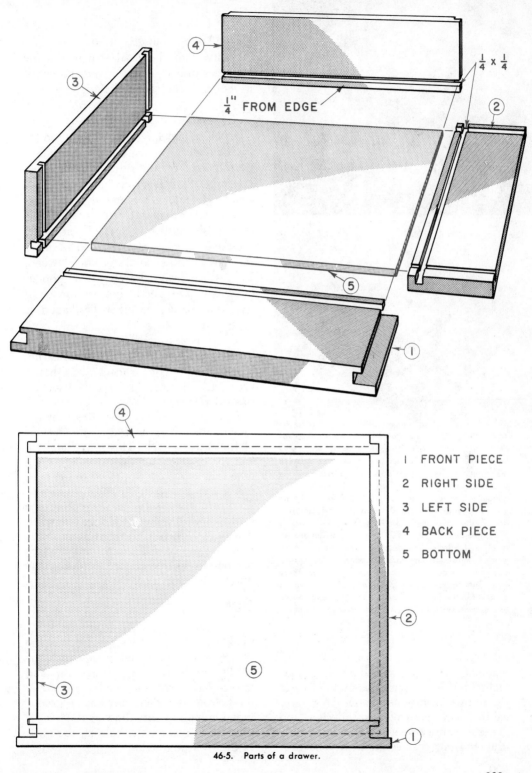

$\frac{1}{4} \times \frac{1}{4}$

$\frac{1}{4}''$ FROM EDGE

1 FRONT PIECE
2 RIGHT SIDE
3 LEFT SIDE
4 BACK PIECE
5 BOTTOM

46-5. Parts of a drawer.

46-6. Compare the quality of these two drawers: (a) This simple all-plywood drawer is made with only hand tools. There is a simple rabbet joint between the front and sides and a butt joint between the sides and back. The parts are nailed together. The bottom is nailed to the sides and the back since no groove is provided. (b) By contrast, this furniture drawer illustrates the finest in construction. There is a multiple-dovetail joint at all four corners. The drawer is of all-hardwood construction except the bottom which is hardwood plywood. Top edges of the drawer sides are rounded on a stop shaper or router. There is a slight recess cut on either end of the front. A groove for the bottom is cut around the lower inside of the front, sides, and back. The drawer is assembled with glue under pressure.

made of plywood to which molding is attached for design purposes. In most cases the drawer front must match the case or cabinet as to kind of wood, design, and general appearance. Sometimes the drawer front is covered with veneer or

plastic laminate to give it an appearance of unity with the total structure. Fine furniture drawer fronts are sometimes of frame-and-panel construction.

Sides

A pair of matching sides is required for each drawer. One-half inch material is usually used for the sides. It can be less expensive than the front. For extremely small drawers, 3/8" material is satisfactory. Thicker material, often 3/4", is better if a side guide is to be used (for which a groove is cut in each side). The material may be either solid stock or plywood. For less expensive drawers, pine, poplar, or willow are good choices; for quality, oak, maple, or other hardwood is preferred.

Sides of less expensive drawers are usually rectangular. In quality construction, the upper edge is machined (shaper rounded) and there is a relieved section toward the center.

Drawer sides are sometimes made much longer than the interior dimensions of the drawer itself. This is particularly true of drawers for an extremely deep case. The ends, which extend to the rear, can act as a stop in closing the drawer. They are also useful in preventing the drawer from tipping or falling out when it is pulled open to the maximum. Most drawer sides have a groove cut towards the bottom on the inside, to receive the drawer bottom.

Back

The back is usually made of 1/2"-thick material of the same kind as the drawer sides. The joint varies with the quality of the drawer. In medium- and lower-quality drawers, the back sits over the bottom and, therefore, has no groove in it. On high-quality drawers the back is grooved to receive the bottom, the same as the front and sides.

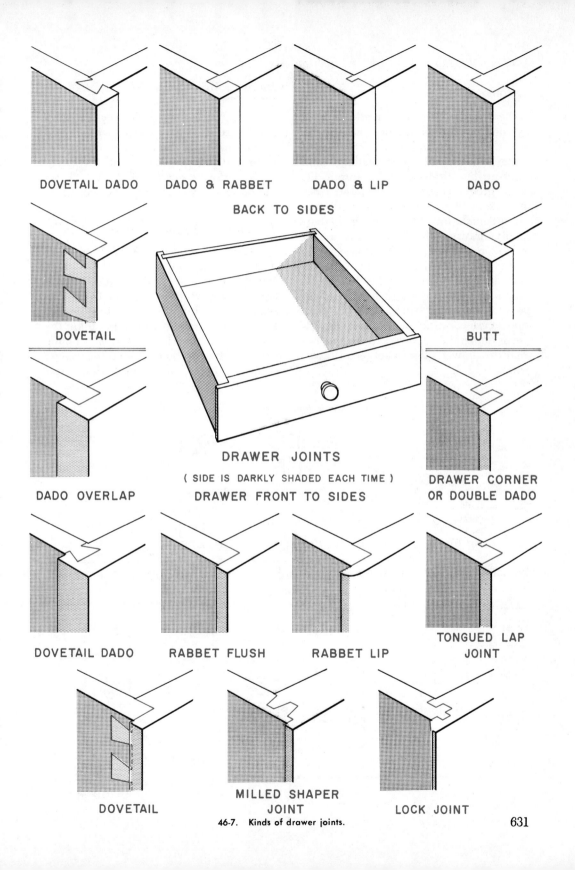

DOVETAIL DADO DADO & RABBET DADO & LIP DADO

BACK TO SIDES

DOVETAIL

BUTT

DADO OVERLAP

DRAWER JOINTS

(SIDE IS DARKLY SHADED EACH TIME)

DRAWER FRONT TO SIDES

DRAWER CORNER
OR DOUBLE DADO

DOVETAIL DADO RABBET FLUSH RABBET LIP TONGUED LAP JOINT

DOVETAIL MILLED SHAPER JOINT LOCK JOINT

46-7. Kinds of drawer joints.

631

Bottom

The bottom normally is made of 1/4″ plywood or hardboard since these materials do not expand or contract with changes in humidity. For medium- and lower-quality drawers, the bottom fits into a groove cut in the sides and front and is sometimes nailed or stapled from the underside into the back. On higher-quality drawers, the bottom fits into a groove on all four sides. For very simple on-the-job construction, when power tools are not available, the bottom is sometimes nailed directly to the lower parts of the front, sides, and back. In simple case construction, the drawer bottom is sometimes allowed to extend beyond the drawer sides to act as a drawer guide.

DRAWER JOINERY

Joints for fastening drawer parts together are chosen primarily with regard to the quality of the drawers, the equipment and time available, and the quantity of drawers needed. Fig. 46-7 shows the basic joints used in drawer construction.

Joining the Front to the Sides

The *rabbet joint* can be used for either a flush or lip drawer. For both of these the depth of the rabbet should equal two-thirds the thickness of the front. The width of a rabbet for flush drawers should be about 1/16″ more than the thickness of the sides; in this way the exposed edge of the rabbet on the drawer front can be tapered slightly for better

46-8(a). Steps in making a drawer corner joint.

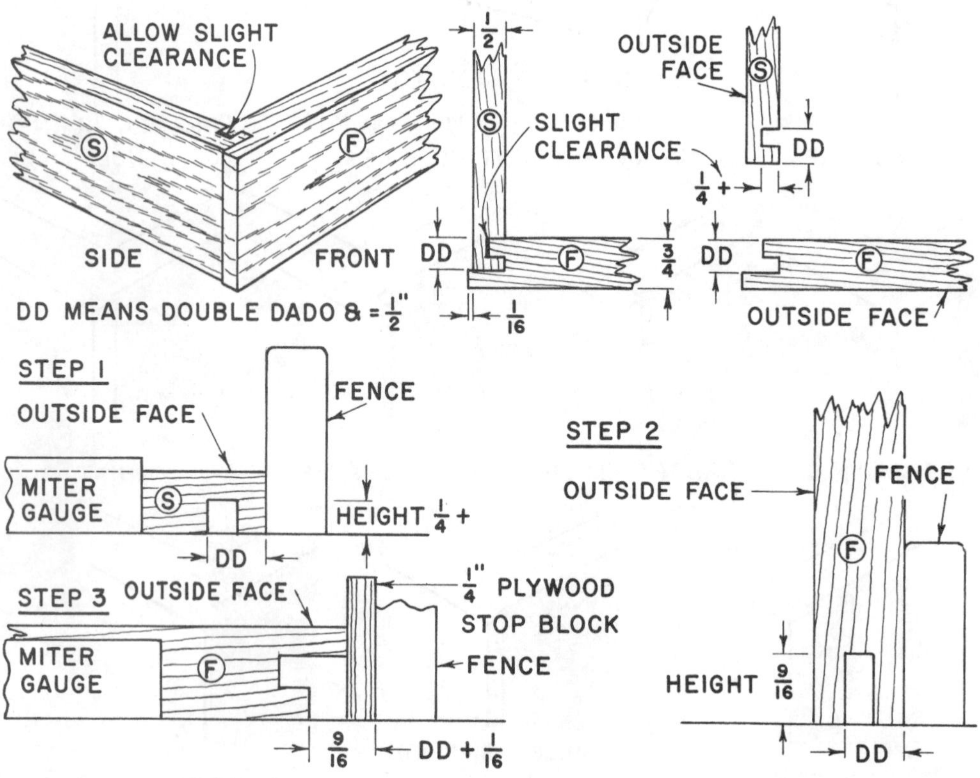

46-8(e). Joint assembled.

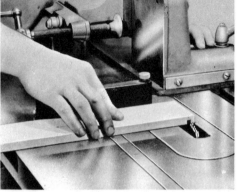

46-8(b). Cutting the dado in the sides.

46-8(c). Cutting the dado in the front.

46-8(d). Joint ready except for cutting off the tenon.

clearance. For lip drawers the width of the rabbet must be equal to the amount of the lip, plus the thickness of the drawer sides, plus 1/16".

The *drawer-corner joint* is often used to fasten sides to front because it is strong and easy to make on the circular saw. Fig. 46-8(a) to (e) shows this joint made with a 3/4" drawer front and 1/2" sides. A clearance of 1/16" is allowed for the front to extend beyond the sides. The steps in making this joint are as follows:

1. Use a dado head that is 1/4" wide. Adjust the dado head to a height of slightly more than 1/4". Set the ripping fence to a distance of twice the width of the dado head measured from the left edge of the blade (double dado), or 1/2". Cut dadoes on the inside face of the sides at the front end.

2. Set the height of the dado head to an amount equal to the thickness of the sides plus 1/16" (for front overlap), or 9/16". With the inside face of the front held against the fence, cut a dado across both ends of the front.

3. Set the dado head to a height of slightly more than 1/2". Adjust the fence to a distance of 9/16" from the left edge of the dado head. Use a piece of 1/4" plywood for a stop block. Place the inside face against the table and trim off 5/16" from the inside tenon of the drawer front. The joint should slide together easily.

This joint can also be used for box construction when all parts are of equal thickness. Fig. 46-8(f).

The *tongued-lap joint* is similar to the drawer-corner joint except that the di-

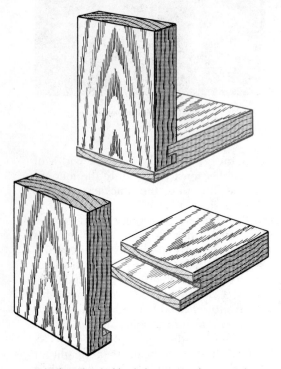

46-8(f). The double dado joint is also a good one for box construction.

5. Adjust spindle height so that the lip of the drawer just passes over the top of the cutter.

6. Adjust the stop for depth of cut in the ends of the drawer front.

7. Cut the drawer front and stack.

To cut the joint on a radial-arm saw, use a glue-joint cutter. It is symmetrical and cuts both parts of the front-to-side joint. Fig. 46-10. The front of the drawer is cut first with a depth of cut equal to the thickness of stock used for the sides. It is possible to cut to within 1/8" of the front surface. The side of the drawer is cut with the work flat on the table. Make test cuts on scrap stock to see that the joint fits perfectly.

The *multiple dovetail joint* is found on all high-quality furniture. Fig. 46-11. Furniture manufacturers use a special-purpose machine called a dovetailer to

mensions are different. It has a better appearance.

The *milled shaper joint* is excellent when cutters are available for the shaper or the radial-arm saw. This matched joint is made on the shaper as follows:

1. Adjust the spindle, Fig. 46-9(a), so that the distance "*D*" to the table top is exactly the same length as edge "*C*." This is very important; otherwise the joint will not fit.

2. Adjust the tenoning jig so that the smallest diameter of the cutter, edge "*C*," Fig. 46-9(a), is exactly in line with the drawer's inside face. The cutter must not cut into it, just tangent to it. Fig. 46-9(b).

3. Cut drawer sides as required and stack.

4. Assemble the cutter on the stub spindle of the shaper.

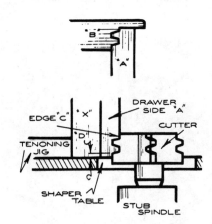

46-9(a). Cutting the side of the drawer for the joint.

46-9(b). Cutting the front of the drawer for the joint.

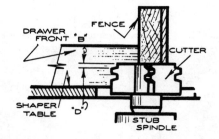

make this joint. In the cabinet shop, a dovetailing attachment can be used with the portable router or radial-arm saw to cut the joint. See Units 27 and 33.

The *lock joint* can be cut on a shaper or circular saw using a dado head.

Two joints commonly used when drawer fronts are to extend beyond and cover the sides of the case are the *plain dado joint* and the *dovetail-dado joint*. The dado is found only on lower-quality construction because it requires that the front be nailed or screwed to the sides. Fig. 46-12. Otherwise there is a tendency for the parts to pull apart. The dovetail-dado or through-dovetail joint is excellent for this kind of construction since it is a good lock-type joint. Fig. 46-13(a). The dovetail-dado joint can be produced with the circular saw or router or with a combination of these machines.

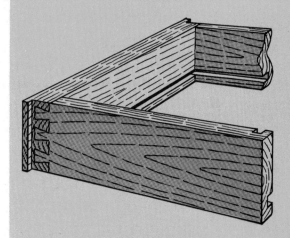

46-11. The multiple dovetail joint is found in the finest drawer construction.

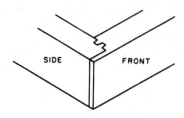

46-10(a). Dovetail-dado joint.

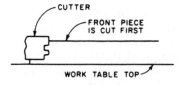

CUTTER

FRONT PIECE IS CUT FIRST

WORK TABLE TOP

46-10(b). Cutting the front.

46-10(c). Cutting the sides.

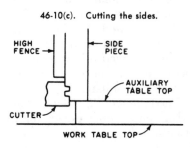

HIGH FENCE

SIDE PIECE

AUXILIARY TABLE TOP

CUTTER

WORK TABLE TOP

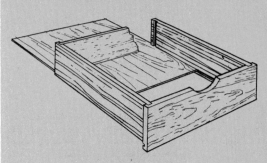

46-12. Basic steps in constructing a simple drawer with overlap or overlay front. Dado depth should not exceed half the thickness of the front.

46-13(a). Dovetail-dado joint on a drawer.

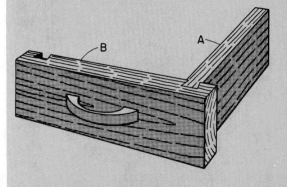

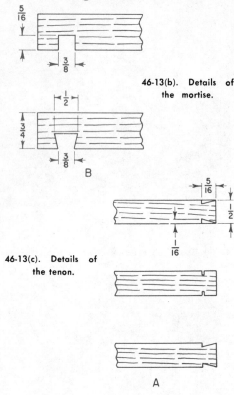

46-13(b). Details of the mortise.

B

46-13(c). Details of the tenon.

A

46-14(a). This beautiful night stand has flush drawers with exposed dust panels. With this construction, the front edge of the frame must be of the same wood as the exterior of the cabinet.

A well proportioned dovetail-dado joint is one in which the front is made of 3/4" stock and the sides of 1/2". Always cut the mortise first. Follow these steps for cutting the joint on a circular saw.

1. Cut the mortise [Piece *B* of Fig. 46-13(a)]. Cut a dado 3/8" wide and 5/16" deep. Fig. 46-13(b). Replace the dado head with a cross-cut blade. Adjust the blade to an angle of 15 degrees and make the angle cut on either side to clear out the mortise. A blade with the teeth ground off at 15 degrees can be used for this. Place the ripping fence first to the right and then to the left to do the cutting.

2. Cut the tenon [Piece *A* of Fig. 46-13(a)]. Set the blade to a height of 1/16", with 5/16" between the fence and the left side of the blade. Make the two shoulder cuts. Adjust the blade to an angle of 15 degrees and set it at a distance of 1/2" to the left of the fence. Fig. 46-13(c). Hold one face against the fence and make the first cut; then reverse the stock and make the second.

Joining the Back to the Sides

There are six basic joints for fastening the back to the sides:

1. The *butt joint,* the simplest, is found on some on-the-job construction. It is usually made in combination with a rabbet joint on the front of the drawer. The length of the back piece should be slightly less than the distance to the rabbet on the front of the drawer. This way there is a slight taper to drawer side.

2. The *dado joint* is much better for this purpose. With this joint the dado should be located not less than 1/2" from the back end of the sides.

3. The *dado-and-rabbet joint* is slightly better still, because it tends to hold the drawer "in square."

4. The *dado-and-lip joint* is similar to the dado and rabbet except for the dimensions.

636

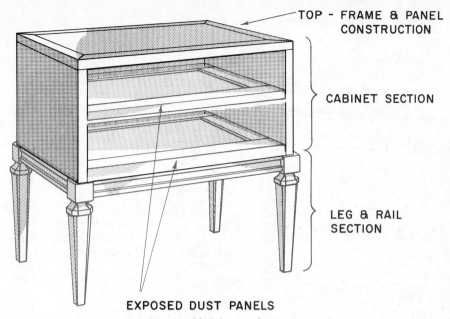

TOP - FRAME & PANEL
CONSTRUCTION

CABINET SECTION

LEG & RAIL
SECTION

EXPOSED DUST PANELS

46-14(b). Simplified drawing showing construction.

5. The *dovetail-dado joint* is made on good-quality drawers.

6. The *dovetail joint* is found in best furniture construction.

Cutting the Bottom

The bottom is installed in the drawer in a groove cut on the inside of the front and both sides. The back rests on the drawer bottom. This is not true of high-quality work. For this, a groove is cut in the back also so that the bottom fits into the front, back, and sides of the drawer. The 1/4″ dado attachment should be used to cut the groove to a depth of at least 5/16″. There should be 1/16″ clearance for the drawer bottom in the groove. The location of the drawer bottom in relation to the lower edge of the sides and front is determined by the drawer guides used. With a side guide, the bottom can be lower than if a center guide is installed.

KINDS OF DRAWER SUPPORTS

Most furniture and better-quality cabinets have a web (skeleton) frame or dust panel to support the drawer and drawer guide. In the finest furniture the dust panel may be either exposed or invisible, depending on the furniture design. Figs. 46-14 and 15. However, in much construction of kitchen cabinets, particularly the plywood box (non-frame), there are no horizontal supports or web frames in the drawer section. Fig. 46-16. The drawers operate on metal guides and plastic rollers and bearings.

46-15(a). This sleek chest of drawers has invisible dust panels.

637

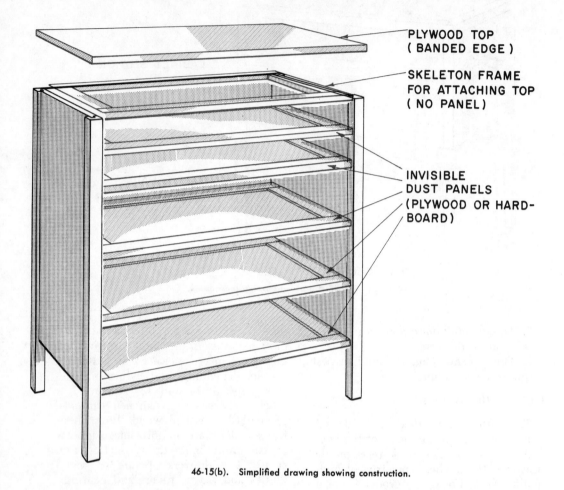

PLYWOOD TOP
(BANDED EDGE)

SKELETON FRAME
FOR ATTACHING TOP
(NO PANEL)

INVISIBLE
DUST PANELS
(PLYWOOD OR HARD-
BOARD)

46-15(b). Simplified drawing showing construction.

46-16. With this metal and plastic hardware, no interior frames or other supports are needed to hold the drawer in place and provide a guide. This greatly speeds up construction.

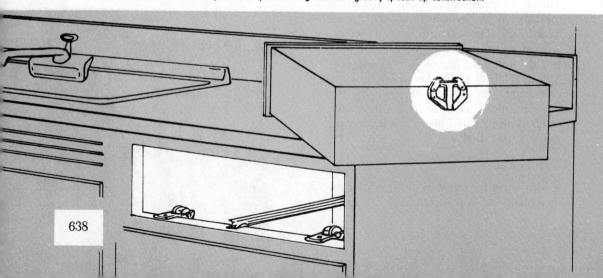

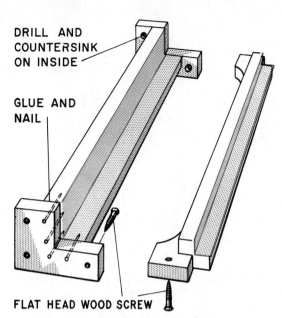

**GLUE AND
NAIL**

FLAT HEAD WOOD SCREW

46-17. A simple drawer guide that can be used on tables and desks. A pair of these is needed for each drawer. This kind works well when fitting a drawer between rails.

Unit 46 • *Drawers and Drawer Guides*

This greatly lowers the cost of construction because of reduced labor. All that is needed is the front opening for the drawer and a vertical strip at the center back to which the back mounting can be nailed or stapled.

Drawer Guides

Drawer guides are needed to keep the drawer in line and to make opening and closing easier. Usually the drawer guides are all wood, made either on the job or in the cabinet shop. However, there is increasing use of commercial guides made of metal, metal and plastic, or metal, plastic and wood. Such guides should be purchased before the drawer is constructed because it is important to know how much clearance to allow. The following are the basic kinds of drawer guides.

46-18(a). This drawing illustrates two drawer guides. The one on the right combines simple pieces with a rabbet cut. It is necessary to use a *kicker* with this to keep the drawer from tipping. The one on the left has a single center wood guide with a plastic slide attached to the drawer.

**ONE CENTER GUIDE
NO DRAWER KICKER**

DRAWER KICKER ABOVE DRAWER

DRAWER GUIDES AT LOWER CORNERS

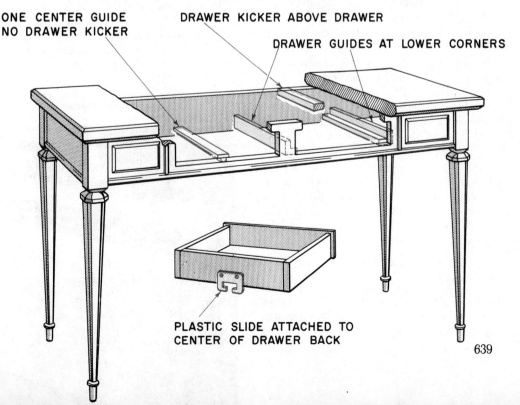

**PLASTIC SLIDE ATTACHED TO
CENTER OF DRAWER BACK**

46-18(b). This striking table-desk has two drawers fitted between the front and back rails or aprons.

46-19(a). A plastic roller eliminates friction between wood parts.

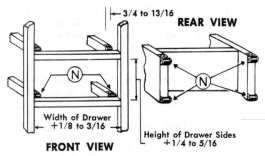

46-19(b). Rollers can be installed in many ways. One method is shown here.

46-20. The thick drawer side is better when using side guides and runners.

Runner for Drawer Sides

The simplest guide is one in which the sides of the drawer fit into the corner formed by the frame and sides or frame and wood side guides of the cabinet. Sometimes an extra piece with a rabbet cut out of it, is fastened between the front and back of a table or desk. Fig. 46-17. This type requires a *kicker*, a piece mounted above the sides of the drawer to keep it from tipping when it is pulled out of the case. Fig. 46-18. The operation of this drawer can be improved by placing nylon-headed tacks on the frame under the drawer sides or by installing small fiber or plastic rollers in the face frame and on the drawer. Fig. 46-19.

Side Guides and Runners

These are commonly used in case and cabinet construction. Fig. 46-20. There are two methods of making this kind of drawer guide. The simplest is to cut

640

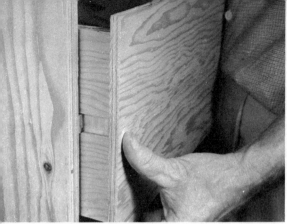

46-21. Side guide and runner with the groove cut in the drawer sides.

46-22. Side guide and runner with the groove cut in the side of the case.

grooves (plows) on or slightly above center along the outer face of the drawer side. Then a strip or cleat of hardwood is fastened to the inside of the case on which the drawer slides. Fig. 46-21. This procedure can be reversed and a groove or dado cut in the case. Then a cleat or guide is fastened to the side of the drawer. Fig. 46-22.

Center Guide and Runner

The best-quality drawer construction features center guides and runners. This kind of guide can be made in many ways. The most common method is to cut a groove in a piece of stock to serve as a runner. This is fastened to the drawer

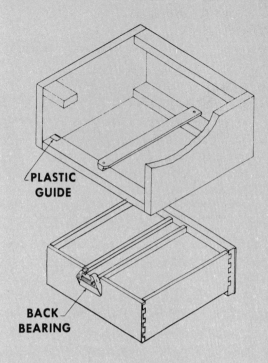

PLASTIC GUIDE

BACK BEARING

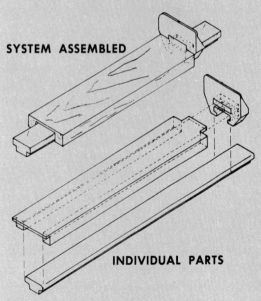

SYSTEM ASSEMBLED

INDIVIDUAL PARTS

46-23(a). Center guide and runner of wood. The plastic bearing fastened to the back of the drawer isn't necessary, but it greatly improves drawer action. The plastic guide also help the drawer to slide more easily.

641

46-23(b). The drawer operates quietly and smoothly on three plastic guides. There is no wood-to-wood contact with these guides. The center guide of hardwood keeps the drawer from pulling to either side.

46-24. Center guides installed in a chest.

46-25. All commercial guides are supplied with complete instructions for installation.

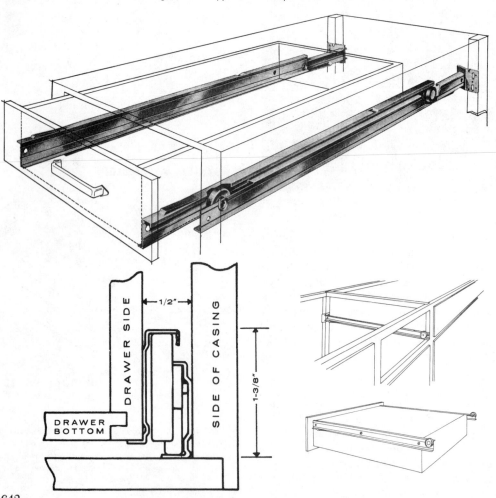

DRAWER SIDE

1/2"

SIDE OF CASING

DRAWER BOTTOM

1-3/8"

642

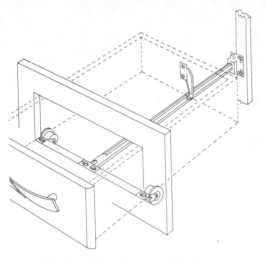

46-26(a). Typical bottom drawer slide hardware correctly installed. Notice that only a vertical piece of wood is needed at the center back of the case to support the mounting bracket.

a. FRONT CENTER BRACKET
Self aligning spurs hold in place during installation.

b. FRONT ROLLER BRACK-ET. Note the deep counter-sink and the reinforcing rib for extra strength.

c. DRAWER ROLLER ARM. V-shaped roller and reinforcing rib for extra strength.

d. STEEL MOUNTING BRACKET. Steel — locks rail — no rattle — exceptional adjusting features.

e. PLASTIC MOUNTING BRACKET. Plastic — can staple, nail or screw on from inside or outside of cabinet.

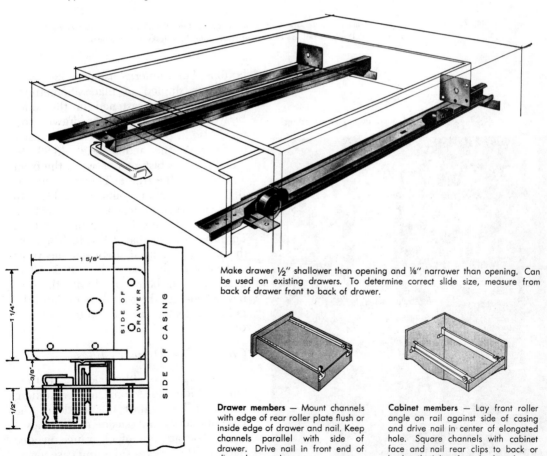

Make drawer ½" shallower than opening and ⅛" narrower than opening. Can be used on existing drawers. To determine correct slide size, measure from back of drawer front to back of drawer.

1 5/8" · 1 1/4" · 3/8" · 1/2"

SIDE OF DRAWER · SIDE OF CASING

End View

Drawer members — Mount channels with edge of rear roller plate flush or inside edge of drawer and nail. Keep channels parallel with side of drawer. Drive nail in front end of channel on angle.

Cabinet members — Lay front roller angle on rail against side of casing and drive nail in center of elongated hole. Square channels with cabinet face and nail rear clips to back or back rail. Adjust front for free drawer movement, then nail securely.

46-26(b). Typical under-drawer slides with instructions for installing.

46-27. Drawer slides for commercial use are usually designed so that the drawer will pull completely out of the case. It allows full use of drawer space built into desks and cabinets.

46-28. Hardware of good quality is important.

bottom. The runner is usually glued and nailed or stapled in place. Sometimes glue blocks are fastened in the sides between the runner and the drawer bottom. Also, a plastic bearing can be used to improve the action. Fig. 46-23. A wood guide is fastened between the front and back of the frame. The front end of the guide is often rounded slightly. In chest construction, for example, this type of guide is fastened by cutting a rabbet on either end so that it fits flush against the dust panel itself, between the front and back of the frame. Fig. 46-24. The procedure can be reversed with the runner fastened to the case or chest, and the guide fastened to the bottom of the drawer.

Commercial Drawer Slides

These can be either side or bottom guides. Side slides come as a matching pair that fits against the inside of the case and along the outside of the drawer sides. The amount of clearance needed between the drawer sides and case varies

644

46-29. These all-wood handles blend with the drawer design.

with the size and kind of slides. Therefore it is important to buy the slides before building the drawers. Fig. 46-25. A single bottom drawer slide may be placed along the center of the bottom, or a pair may be installed, one towards each side. Fig. 46-26. Some side guides will allow the drawer to be pulled out well beyond the front of the case or cabinet. Fig. 46-27.

DRAWER OPENING DEVICES

There are many devices for opening a drawer. Usually some kind of metal or plastic hardware is attached to the exterior of the drawer front. Fig. 46-28. In selecting this hardware it is important that it match the furniture style. Fig. 46-29. Sometimes the drawer pulls are made of matching wood. Many styles of drawers are made without hardware. A recess is cut under or above the front so that it is easy to pull out. Fig. 46-30. In other cases an opening is cut out at the center of the top edge. Fig. 46-31.

46-30. This shows how space can be provided for drawer pulls so there is no need for exposed hardware.

46-31. The opening in the lower drawer is used for pulling out the upper drawer.

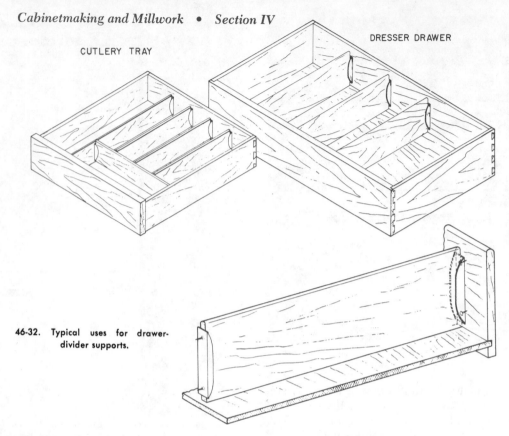

CUTLERY TRAY

DRESSER DRAWER

46-32. Typical uses for drawer-divider supports.

DRAWER DIVIDERS

For greater convenience, a drawer is frequently divided into sections. There are several ways of doing this. One is to cut dadoes in the sides or between the front and back so that dividers will slip into place. Fig. 46-6(b). There are many small plastic and metal channels or drawer-divider supports that can be nailed inside the sides or inside the front and back in which 1/4" stock will fit. Fig. 46-32. If the drawer is to be divided into four parts, an edge-lap joint can be used on the drawer dividers. Sometimes a small tray is installed inside a drawer. Fig. 46-33. This is actually a small box that fits the drawer from side to side but is shorter from front to back. Usually extra strips for the tray to slide on are fastened inside the drawer sides.

PLANNING FOR DRAWER CONSTRUCTION

Before starting to design and build a drawer, several things must be considered. These are as follows:

The drawer guide. Is it to be a side or center guide and runner? Will it be shop-made or commercial?

The drawer front. Will the drawer fit flush into the frame, will it be a lip drawer, or will it be an overlap or overlay drawer?

The joinery. The kind of joints will affect the dimensions of the parts.

The web frame or dust panel. This is extremely important in chest construction. Some chests are made with the front of the web frame or dust panel exposed. In such instances the same wood is used as for the front of the chest frame. Others

have a skeleton or web frame that is set back from the chest and is covered by the drawers. Sometimes the drawer front covers the next lower frame; in other cases the drawer front covers the next higher frame.

• *The dimensions of the parts.* All the above points must be considered when measuring for these dimensions.

CONSTRUCTING A DRAWER

1. Determine the size of the drawer parts. Measure the opening for height, width, and depth (or run). Fig. 46-34. If it is a flush drawer that will be painted later, there must be about 1/16″ clearance all the way around the drawer front on the top and sides. In other words, a dime should slip into the crack easily. For higher-quality drawers the fit should be much closer.

2. Select the material for the drawer (size and kind) and rough cut it.

3. Lay out the drawer front and try it in the opening. For a lip drawer a rabbet must be cut before checking it.

4. Cut the joints that will fasten the sides to the front. Also cut a groove on the inside of the drawer front and sides at least 1/4″ up from the bottom, into which the drawer bottom will fit.

5. If it will be a flush drawer front, bevel or recess the ends slightly (about 1/16″). Sometimes the top edge is also beveled slightly.

46-33. This tall narrow chest has a top drawer beautifully lined with red velvet. The compartmented jewelry liner has another sliding jewelry drawer on top.

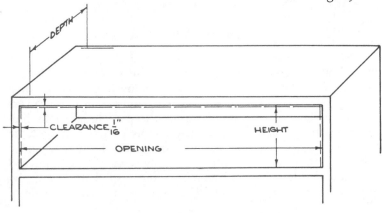

46-34. Measuring the size of the drawer opening.

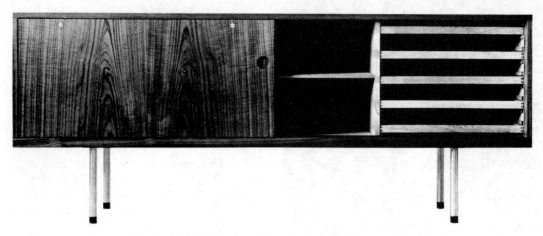

46-35. This buffet has five pull-out trays behind the sliding doors.

6. Cut the joints to join the back to the sides. The overall length of the back should be such that, when the drawer is assembled, the completed drawer is slightly narrower in back than in front. If the back of the drawer is to fit over the bottom, then it must be equal in height to the distance from the top of the bottom groove to the top of the sides. If the bottom is to fit into a groove in the back, then the back must have the same dimensions as the sides and must have a groove in it to receive the bottom.

7. Assemble the drawer. For less expensive drawer construction, glue, nails, or screws are used. For medium- or high-quality drawer construction, only glue is used. If the bottom slips under the back, assemble the sides to the front and the back to the sides. Then wax the edges of the bottom and slide it into place. Never apply glue to the drawer bottom itself. It can be nailed to the back with No. 3 box nails.

For finer drawer construction, assemble the front to the sides, then wax the edges of the bottom and slip it in place. Next install the back. Install glue blocks between the bottom and sides of the drawer on the underside. For a cen-

ter guide, glue and nail or staple the runner to the bottom, making sure that it is square with the front. For commercial slides follow the manufacturer's directions.

8. For a flush drawer it may be necessary to install drawer stops. These are small blocks of wood that are fastened to the back of the drawer guides so that the drawer will not push in too far. Drawer stops are not necessary for a lip or overlap drawer front.

QUALITY OF DRAWER CONSTRUCTION

There are three general qualities of drawer construction, as follows:

On-the-Job Construction

The least expensive and simplest is on-the-job drawer construction, done by the cabinetmaker or finish carpenter when he builds kitchen units or installs drawers in built-ins on the site. He is usually limited to hand tools only or, at best, he has a circular or radial-arm saw and a jointer. The drawer may be all plywood or a combination of solid stock and plywood. The drawers are usually made of

3/4″ stock for the front and 1/2″ to 3/4″ stock for the sides. This can be purchased with a groove already cut to receive the drawer bottom. Usual construction consists of a rabbet joint on the front and sides and a butt or dado joint on the sides and back. In most cases the bottom fits into a groove in the sides and front although, in some cases, the bottom may be nailed directly to the sides, front, and back. If it is an overlap drawer front, then a simple dado joins the front to the sides. A kicker will be needed over the sides of the drawer. Fig. 46-18(a).

Cabinet-Shop Drawer Construction

A cabinet shop has need for all the standard machine tools; therefore drawers constructed in such a shop can be of much better quality than those built on a construction site. Cabinet-shop built drawers should have some type of lock joint between the sides and front, and either a dado and rabbet or a dado and lip between the sides and the back. This will keep the drawer "in square" and will prevent the drawer front from being pulled away from the sides. If an overlap drawer front is used, a dovetail dado should be cut.

Furniture-Production Construction

The finest quality drawers are made in factories where furniture parts are mass produced. The very finest drawers always have multiple dovetail joints both front and back. The ends and top of the drawer front are machined to a slight bevel. The upper edges of the drawer sides are machined to a slight recess to provide extra clearance and the edges are rounded. The drawer bottom always fits into all four sides of the drawer and glue blocks are installed on the under-

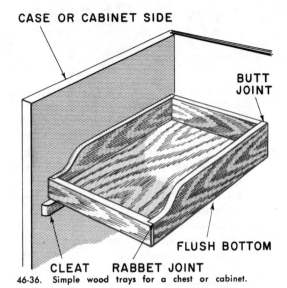

CASE OR CABINET SIDE

BUTT JOINT

FLUSH BOTTOM

CLEAT   RABBET JOINT

46-36.   Simple wood trays for a chest or cabinet.

side of the drawer for better and stronger construction. There is always some kind of center guide, with the back of the drawer notched at the bottom to receive the runner of the guide.

TRAYS

Trays are drawers that are fitted to the inside of a case or cabinet. Usually they are hidden from sight by doors. Fig. 46-35. Trays might be found, for example, in a bedroom cabinet for storing clothing. They are used extensively in store and restaurant fixtures. For home furniture, it is quite simple to build the tray and the drawer slide. Fig. 46-36. In commercial fixtures, heavy and more durable construction is needed for a tray. Such trays operate on heavy-duty slides that are mounted on the sides. These slides allow the tray to extend beyond the case and provide automatic stops for both the out and in positions.

A most important factor in designing a storage unit, whether it is a bookcase, kitchen cabinet, room divider, desk, cupboard, or closet, is the interior arrangement. Fig. 47-1. Every possible convenience should be provided. Size and arrangement of shelves must be well planned. Fig. 47-2. A bookcase that is not wide and deep enough is useless. Kitchen cabinets with fixed shelves that are spaced too far apart or too high for the housewife's reach are equally poor. Interiors should be planned to eliminate waste space.

DESIGNING THE SHELVING

Three things must be considered:
• Material. Shelves can be made of solid wood, plywood, glass, or one of the man-made materials. Fig. 47-3. In built-ins of better quality, shelves are made of particle board or plywood with a band of solid wood glued to the front edges. The shelf material should be thick enough to keep from bending under weight. Shelving that is not supported for a length exceeding 42″ must be at least 1″ thick. Glass shelves are frequently found in china and display cabinets.

• Stationary or adjustable construction. Decide which type serves your purpose best. Most adjustable shelving requires some kind of metal or plastic hardware.

• Depth and spacing. Shelf depth should be determined by the overall dimensions of the cabinet. Fig. 47-4. Standard book shelves are usually at least 8″ deep while those for oversize books are a minimum

47-1. This built-in sideboard which separates the dining room from the hallway was designed for convenience. Storage features are a china cupboard with adjustable shelves; drawers for flat silver, hollow ware, and linens; fixed display shelves; and a serving counter. The divider sideboard is built of western red cedar with tongue-and-groove panels for end and back and edge-glued stock for the door and drawer fronts.

47-2. This china cabinet has one fixed and two adjustable shelves with glass doors to display glassware and china.

47-3. This open china cabinet has fixed shelves of plywood banded with solid wood.

of 10". Upper kitchen cabinets should be 12" to 14" deep and lower cabinets 24". Spacing between stationary shelves is particularly important. In bookcases, upper shelves should be no less than 9½" apart and the lower shelving should have a spacing of not less than 12½". Correct spacing for kitchen-cabinet shelving is discussed in detail in Unit 53. If the upper half of a china cabinet has wood shelves, cut a shallow groove at a distance of 1½" to 2" from the back edge for displaying dishes on edge.

STATIONARY OR FIXED SHELVING

The common methods for installing stationary or fixed shelving in cabinets and furniture are:

• A *butt joint reinforced with quarter rounds, wood cleats, or metal shelf*

47-4. This wall assembly is made up of modular units; that is, standard-size units that fit together to form large assemblies. The base units are: W-39½", D-14", and H-26". The top units are: W-39½", D-9". The two shelves are: H-22". The three shelves are H-34". The five shelves on both sides are: H-56". Note that the combination of the two and three shelves makes a height of 56". What are the advantages and disadvantages of this storage arrangement?

651

47-5. Metal shelf brackets and wood cleats (battens) are two simple ways of installing fixed shelving.

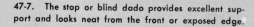

47-6. A series of dadoes cut in the uprights is a good way of installing fixed shelves.

47-7. The stop or blind dado provides excellent support and looks neat from the front or exposed edge.

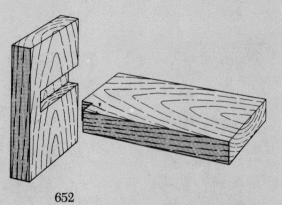

brackets. Fig. 47-5. The cleats or quarter rounds can be screwed or nailed into the sides and the shelves. If a molding strip or face plate is attached to the front of the case, the cleats will not show. On an extremely long shelf where there is danger of bowing in the center, a cleat or batten can be fastened along the back of the shelf for added support. Another method of handling long shelving is to fasten an upright support about midway between the sides.

• *Shelves fastened to the sides with a dado joint.* This provides great rigidity to the case and also helps to hold the shelves in place. Fig. 47-6. The disadvantage of the plain dado is that the exposed edge is not attractive. However, this is not important if a face-plate molding is put around the case. A better arrangement is a stop-dado joint which has a neat appearance at the front edge. Fig. 47-7. A lock joint such as a dovetail-dado or a half dovetail-dado is also a good choice.

ADJUSTABLE SHELVING

The trend in most furniture and cabinetwork is to install adjustable shelving

47-8(a). This storage wall, designed as a room divider, has many interesting features. Grooved plywood supports the shelves. The support shelves and small storage units can slide into the grooves at varying heights.

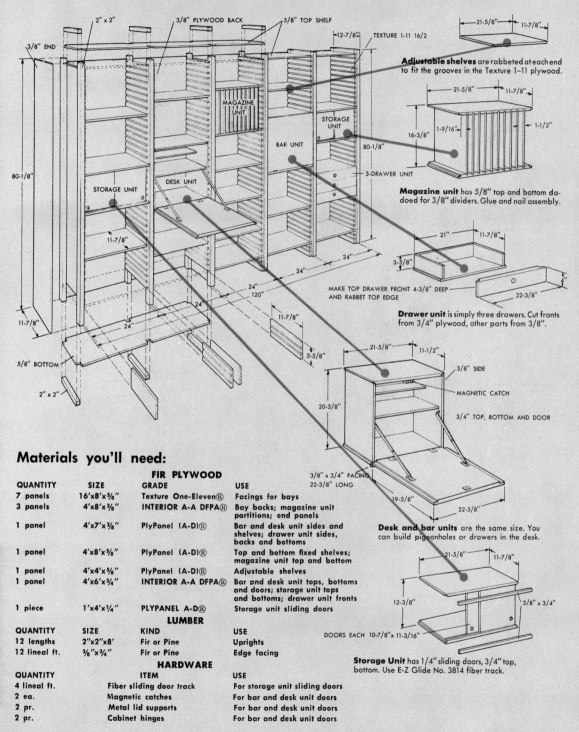

Adjustable shelves are rabbeted at each end to fit the grooves in the Texture 1–11 plywood.

Magazine unit has 5/8" top and bottom dadoed for 3/8" dividers. Glue and nail assembly.

MAKE TOP DRAWER FRONT 4-3/8" DEEP AND RABBET TOP EDGE

Drawer unit is simply three drawers. Cut fronts from 3/4" plywood, other parts from 3/8".

Desk and bar units are the same size. You can build pigeonholes or drawers in the desk.

DOORS EACH 10-7/8" x 11-3/16"

Storage Unit has 1/4" sliding doors, 3/4" top, bottom. Use E-Z Glide No. 3814 fiber track.

Materials you'll need:

FIR PLYWOOD

QUANTITY	SIZE	GRADE	USE
7 panels	16'x8'x⅝"	Texture One-Eleven®	Facings for bays
3 panels	4'x8'x⅜"	INTERIOR A-A DFPA®	Bay backs; magazine unit partitions; end panels
1 panel	4'x7'x⅜"	PlyPanel (A-D)®	Bar and desk unit sides and shelves; drawer unit sides, backs and bottoms
1 panel	4'x8'x⅝"	PlyPanel (A-D)®	Top and bottom fixed shelves; magazine unit top and bottom
1 panel	4'x4'x⅝"	PlyPanel (A-D)®	Adjustable shelves
1 panel	4'x6'x¾"	INTERIOR A-A DFPA®	Bar and desk unit tops, bottoms and doors; storage unit tops and bottoms; drawer unit fronts
1 piece	1'x4'x¼"	PLYPANEL A-D®	Storage unit sliding doors

LUMBER

QUANTITY	SIZE	KIND	USE
12 lengths	2"x2"x8'	Fir or Pine	Uprights
12 lineal ft.	⅜"x¾"	Fir or Pine	Edge facing

HARDWARE

QUANTITY	ITEM	USE
4 lineal ft.	Fiber sliding door track	For storage unit sliding doors
2 ea.	Magnetic catches	For bar and desk unit doors
2 pr.	Metal lid supports	For bar and desk unit doors
2 pr.	Cabinet hinges	For bar and desk unit doors

47-8(b). Drawing and list of materials for the storage wall.

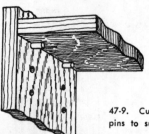

47-9. Cut short wood dowel pins to support the shelves.

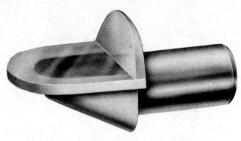

47-12(a). A smooth-shank plastic pin.

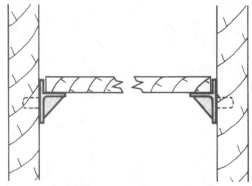

47-12(b). Another shape of plastic pin.

47-10. These metal shelf pins require blind holes 1/4" in diameter and 5/8" deep. Enough holes should be drilled to allow for moving the shelves freely.

47-13. A fluted plastic pin.

47-11. A detail drawing of the pin is usually included in the package so the diameter and depth of hole can be easily determined.

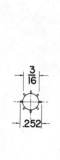 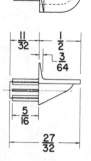 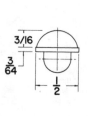 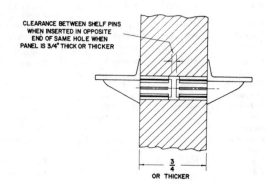

$\frac{1}{4}$" HOLE DIA.

CLEARANCE BETWEEN SHELF PINS WHEN INSERTED IN OPPOSITE END OF SAME HOLE WHEN PANEL IS 3/4" THICK OR THICKER

47-14. An unusual and versatile curio cabinet in classic styling. The cabinet is made of cherry with the interior painted in yellow ochre. Note the holes for adjusting the top and bottom shelves.

since it will take care of changing conditions and increase efficiency. In designing adjustable shelving, it is important to consider the items that will be stored on the shelves. This also affects the placement of the hardware and the drilling of holes in the sides. The following are common ways of handling adjustable shelving.

• Cut slightly oversize dadoes in the sides, spaced equally apart. Fig. 47-8. Cut a rabbet (tenon) on the ends of the shelves. The shelves can then be slipped in wherever needed. The equally spaced dadoes in the sides are also a clever design feature.

• Bore holes for dowel pins. Drill a parallel series of equally spaced holes on either side of the vertical supports. Simple wood dowel pins can be installed in these holes to support the shelves. Fig. 47-9. Make sure that the holes are fairly close to the front and back edges of the sides so the shelf will not wobble or tilt.

• Use plastic or metal shelf pins. A double row of equally spaced, 1/4″ holes should be drilled on the inside surface of the cabinet or case sides. Fig. 47-10. The holes should be drilled about 1″ to 2″ from the front and back edges to a depth slightly more than the length of the pin shank. Fig. 47-11. Four pins fit into the holes at each shelf location. Plastic pins will not scratch glass or wood finish and will not rust, corrode, or tarnish. Fig. 47-12. They are made in several different shapes with either smooth

47-15(a). Some common uses for metal hardware.

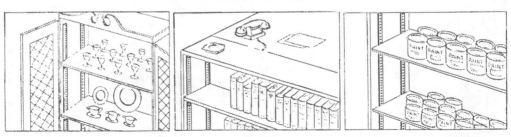

For China Cabinet   **For Bookcase**   **For All Types of Shelving**

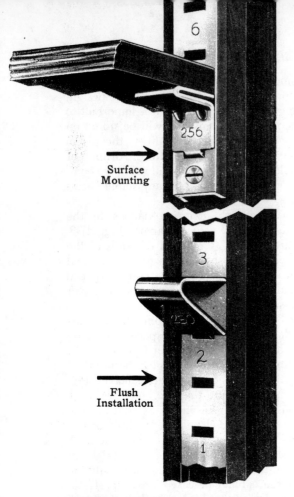

47-15(b). Most shelf standards can be either surface mounted or flush mounted. The flush mounting is neater since the shelves can be cut the full width of the cabinet. If the standards are surface mounted, then the shelves must be shortened slightly or notched.

Surface
Mounting

Flush
Installation

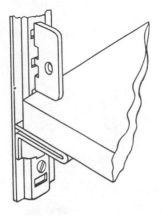

47-16. The hold-down clips are installed against the top of the shelves. The support clips are installed below to help prevent the wood shelf from warping.

47-17. This breakfront has metal standards and supports for adjustable shelving. The shelves are glass and require that the supports have rubber cushions.

47-18(a). Shelf standards and brackets used as a room divider.

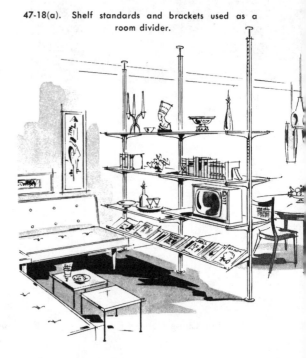

47-18(b). Adjustable shelf standards are available in lengths from 18″ to 114″ in black, chrome, and brass finishes.

or fluted shanks. The fluted shank is flexible enough to adjust automatically to holes that are slightly over- or under-size. Fig. 47-13. This neat arrangement is found on much high-quality furniture. Fig. 47-14.

• Install adjustable shelf standards and supports for side mounting. This hardware consists of perforated metal strips that can be flush or surface-mounted along either side of a cabinet or case. Fig. 47-15. For flush mounting, two parallel vertical grooves must be cut on the insides of the case or cabinet. When the standards are flush mounted, the shelves can be cut the full width of the cabinet interior. The standards are attached with threaded nails or drive screws. Support clips can be located at any position along the standards. Hold-down clips are also available to keep shelves from tipping. Fig. 47-16. While only one standard need be put on each side of the case, the usual practice is to use a pair. Any material can be used for the shelf itself. For glass, supports with rubber cushions are available. Fig. 47-17.

• Install adjustable shelf standards and brackets for back wall mounting. Metal hardware that consists of slotted metal standards and brackets can be fastened against any wall to serve as flexible, open shelving. Fig. 47-18. Both the standards and brackets are made in light- and heavy-duty weights. The brackets are made in sizes (for width of shelves) from 4″ to 20″, in 2″ intervals. Fig. 47-19. The shelving can be glass, wood, or any of the man-made materials.

• Another way to mount shelves is to cut two pieces of 1″ x 4″ stock and drill a series of 1¾″ holes at equal distance in the two pieces. Then saw the two pieces in half and mount a pair on each side of the cabinet. Now cut 1″ x 2″ stock with rounded ends to fit between the two uprights. The shelves should be notched at all four corners to fit and rest on the 1″ x 2″ shelves. Fig. 47-20.

47-19. Shelf standards and brackets used for the open shelving in a modern kitchen.

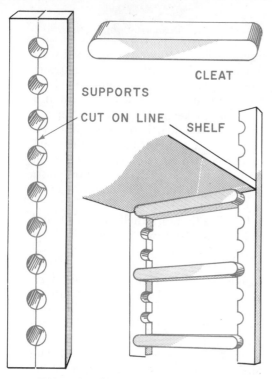

47-20. Adjustable shelving of all-wood construction.

CLEAT

SUPPORTS

CUT ON LINE

SHELF

Use other commercial shelf holders. Many kinds of commercial shelf holders are used by furniture manufacturers and cabinetmakers. One has a spring-wire clip that fits into two small holes on each side of the case. A small groove is cut partway along the end grain on both ends of each shelf. The shelf then slips over the spring clip so that the front appears to have a butt joint. The small holes on the cabinet interior are hardly noticeable.

Closet Shelving and Fixtures

Closet shelving is usually made of 3/4″ particle board or plywood and supported on the ends with wood battens fastened to the walls. The front or exposed edge should be banded with solid strips of wood. Many types of metal closet fixtures are available for storing all kinds of clothing conveniently. Fig. 47-21.

47-21. Well fitted closets like these are neat and convenient.

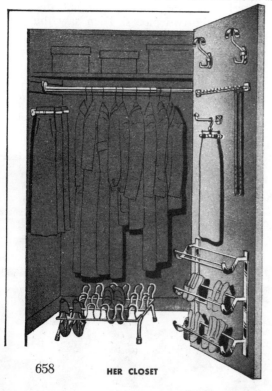

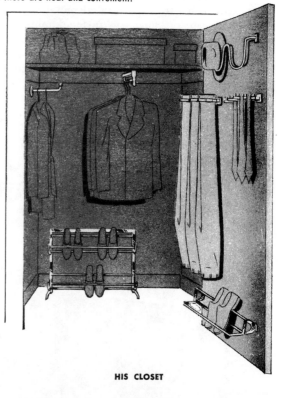

HER CLOSET

HIS CLOSET

Legs and posts are an essential structural part of all tables and chairs and many chests, desks, beds, and other furniture pieces. Legs are also a major design feature which provides one of the quickest ways of identifying a furniture style. Fig. 48-1. Legs and posts can be shop produced of solid lumber or laminated materials, or they can be purchased. The trend, even among furniture manufacturers, is to purchase the legs from companies that specialize in their manufacture. Leg kits can be purchased

48-1. These tables are similar in size and function but not in appearance. Leg shape is the major design feature of each table. (a) The square, tapered leg on an Italian Provincial table. (b) The square, straight leg on a Contemporary table. (c) The turned leg on an Early American table. (d) The graceful cabriole leg on a French Provincial table.

a.

c.

659

b.

d.

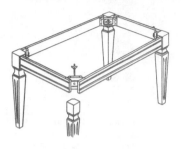

ITALIAN PROVINCIAL

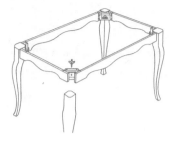

FRENCH PROVINCIAL

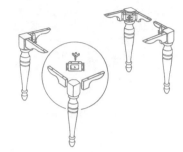

EARLY AMERICAN

DUTCH COLONIAL

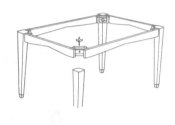

SQUARE LEG CONTEMPORARY

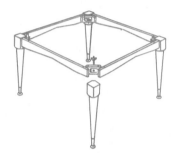

ROUND LEG CONTEMPORARY

48-2. Common kinds of leg sets for small tables.

48-3. These metal legs are all 7″ in height. They illustrate the variety of styles that can be purchased. They are available in finishes of satin or polished brass, chrome, pewter, copper, old English, and antique.

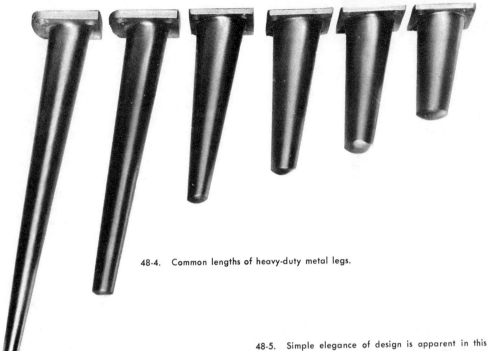

48-4. Common lengths of heavy-duty metal legs.

48-5. Simple elegance of design is apparent in this lamp table with square, straight legs. The brass hardware which forms the corner framing design has a gold-wash finish.

to match any furniture style. Fig. 48-2. They are made in wood, metal, and plastic in various styles, finishes and lengths. Figs. 48-3 and 48-4.

COMMON LEG SHAPES

Common shapes of legs for cabinet construction include the following:

Square, Straight Legs

The square, straight leg is the simplest to make and is commonly found on Contemporary furniture. Fig. 48-5. The leg is made of either solid or laminated stock, by the method described in Unit 25.

Square, Tapered Legs

The square, tapered leg is made in several designs. Legs with tapers on only the two inside surfaces are also popular for many Contemporary pieces. The inside taper gives a feeling of lightness to the total design. Fig. 48-6. Square legs tapered on all four sides are found on

661

48-6. This Contemporary footstool has square legs tapered on the two inside surfaces. This makes the legs appear to be at a slight angle.

many Traditional and Provincial furniture pieces. The Italian Provincial leg, for example, has a taper on four sides with a graceful recess or molding just below the rail or apron. Fig. 48-7. Reeding or fluting often is a part of the design.

To make a tapered leg, first square up the legs on which the taper is to be cut. Lay the four legs side by side and mark the position at which the taper is to start. Then square a line around all four sides of each leg. Next determine the amount of stock to be removed at the foot of the taper. Set a gage to this amount and mark a line across the lower end of the leg on the two opposite sides, if all four

48-7. This Italian Provincial desk has the graceful tapered legs characteristic of this furniture style.

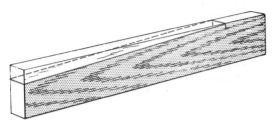

48-8(a). Laying out a taper.

FIRST TAPER MARKED

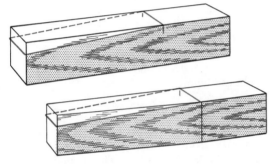

FIRST TAPER CUT, SECOND TAPER MARKED

48-8(b). When the taper is to be cut on two adjoining surfaces, one side should be laid out and cut before the second layout is made.

Record Cabinets, Hi-Fi & End Tables

Card & Dinette Tables

Snack Tables

Coffee Tables

Benches

48-10. Common uses for tapered legs of metal, wood, or plastic.

48-9. The round tapered leg on a Contemporary drum table. These legs would be easy to turn with a woodturning duplicator.

48-11(a). A nest of tables with simple turned legs.

663

48-11(b). This tea wagon has fairly ornate turned legs and wheel spindles.

sides are to be tapered, or on one side, if only two sides are to be tapered. Draw a line along each side to indicate where the taper is to be cut. Fig. 48-8.

Cut the taper with a radial-arm or circular saw. Plane the tapered surface smooth and true. After the one or two sides have been cut, do the other one or two the same way.

Round, Tapered Legs

The round, tapered leg is also found on much Contemporary furniture. Fig. 48-9. It is often a commercial product that may be made of wood, plastic, or metal. Fig. 48-10. The legs usually have brass ferrules with a self-leveling base and come with metal brackets for attaching them.

Turned Legs and Posts

Turned legs and posts made on a lathe can vary from relatively simple to very ornate shapes. Fig. 48-11. The turned leg

48-12. The turnings on these ladder-back chairs are classic in design.

48-13(a). Closeup of knives on the cutter head of an automatic lathe. For a complete description of the turning operation of this machine, see Unit 64. (Copyright by Wisconsin Knife Works, Inc.)

is a combination of many shapes. The *concave* curve is called a *cove* and the *convex* curve a *bead*. There are also many combinations of these curves. Short, straight lines called *fillets* separate different parts of the turned leg. Tapered surfaces may be short or long. All of these elements may be combined with a short section of a square leg. Some of the designs, such as the Windsor chair

48-13(b). Samples of wood turnings done on an automatic lathe.

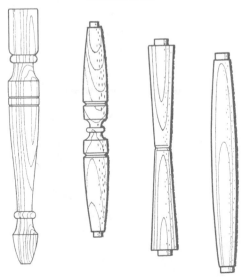

leg, the Sheraton-style table pedestal, and the Duncan Phyfe pedestal, have become classic. Fig. 48-12. The turned leg or post is characteristic of Early American and Colonial furniture and also of many Traditional pieces. In industry most of these legs and posts are turned on an automatic lathe. Fig. 48-13. If two or more identical turned legs are needed for a custom-made chair or table, the best method is to use some kind of templet or, better still, a woodturning duplicator on a hand wood lathe. See Unit 37.

A compression joint is used in some manufacturing plants for all installation of turned legs and rungs in Early American furniture. Fig. 48-14. The end of the spindle is turned a few thousandths of an inch larger than the hole size. Then the dowels or ends of the spindles are slightly reduced in diameter by running the wood through rollers which actually compress the wood fibers. The wood remains compressed as long as it doesn't take on moisture. After glue is applied and the dowel or end inserted in the hole, the moisture in the glue causes the wood to expand back to its original size, making an extremely strong bond. Fig. 48-15.

Cabriole Legs

The cabriole leg is characteristic of Eighteenth-Century Traditional furniture. Although it was originated by French designers who liked its "S" shape, it is still found on much of today's Traditional furniture as well as French Provincial. Fig. 48-16. The word "cabriole" (cab-ree-ol) is thought to come from Capri, Italy.

These legs can be varied in style. For instance, English designers emphasize the knee while the French center attention on the graceful foot and ankle. This leg is made with a square top if it is to be attached to a rectangular or square table or chair. It is made with a cat-faced top if it is to be used on a circular or

665

48-14. Compression spindles and rung joints were used to assemble parts of this rocker.

48-15. The compression spindle makes a very permanent joint for turned parts.

48-16. The cabriole leg is shaped in a double curve with the upper section swelling outward.

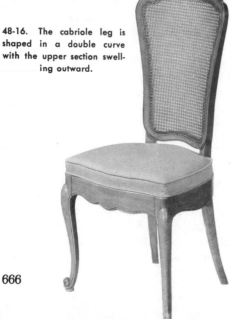

oval chair. (A cat face has a large rabbet cut out of the top of the leg to fit against the rail.)

At first glance, the cabriole leg would appear quite difficult to produce in the cabinet shop. This is not so, however, if an accurate pattern is made and certain steps followed.

The best way to make the cabriole leg is first to develop an accurate pattern on a heavy piece of cardboard. Then select a piece of stock thick enough for the leg design. If the leg has a rather pronounced "S", it may be necessary to glue up pieces to provide the added stock needed at only these places. In this case it is important to match the grain at the protruding sections. When the stock is ready, trace the design on the two adjoining surfaces. Fig. 48-17. On the band saw make two cuts to form one side of the profile. Fig. 48-18. Save these pieces of waste stock and nail them back on in such a way that they will not interfere with the cutting and also will not be a part of the finished leg. Then cut from the other layout line to complete leg.

A second method of doing the cutting is to make the first two cuts almost up to the end of the stock, leaving about 1/4" of unfinished cut. This will support the waste stock when it is turned over to make the second two cuts. Then the waste material is cut off by hand.

After the leg is rough cut to size, it must be smoothed and sanded.

REEDING AND FLUTING

Reeding and fluting are decorative cuts on legs and posts. *Reeding* is a series of equally spaced convex (curved out) divisions on a leg or post. Fig. 48-24. *Fluting* is exactly the reverse of reeding, namely, a series of equally spaced concave (curved in) divisions. Fig. 48-19. Both processes are done in the same general way except that a differently shaped cutting tool is used.

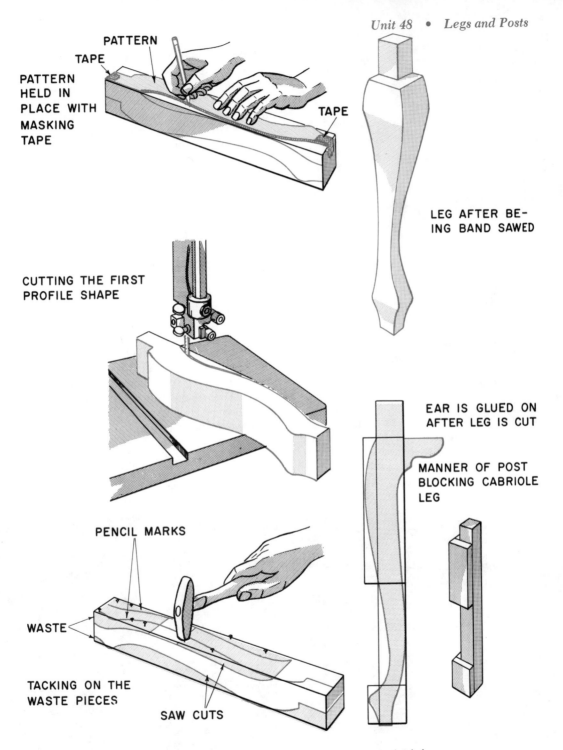

PATTERN

TAPE

PATTERN
HELD IN
PLACE WITH
MASKING
TAPE

TAPE

LEG AFTER BE-
ING BAND SAWED

CUTTING THE FIRST
PROFILE SHAPE

EAR IS GLUED ON
AFTER LEG IS CUT

MANNER OF POST
BLOCKING CABRIOLE
LEG

PENCIL MARKS

WASTE

TACKING ON THE
WASTE PIECES

SAW CUTS

48-17.   Steps to follow in laying out and cutting a cabriole leg.

48-18. Cutting the graceful curve to form one side of a cabriole leg.

If the reeding or fluting is done on a turned leg, it is necessary to have a fluting jig or wood lathe to hold the leg and to divide the circumference into an equal number of parts. The fluting jig is really a small lathe in which the work is held; the cutting is done on a shaper, drill press, or portable router. A drawing of the fluting jig is shown in Fig. 48-20. This jig has an indexing head with 24 holes which allows 4, 6, 8, 12, or 24 divisions around a leg. Note that the indexing head is held in place with a nail.

Stops are used to control the length of the cut. These may be pieces clamped to the straight edge, as shown in Fig. 48-21, or pins located in the jig and on a temporary wood table.

If the jig is to be used on the shaper, a form board with the same contour as the leg is fastened to the base of the jig. The form then rides along a depth collar the same as for other shaping operations. Fig. 48-22. Fig. 48-21 shows the flutes being cut on a tapered leg in which case the form is a simple, straight, tapered piece of wood.

48-19(a). This table is a good example of close fluting.

48-19(b). This mahogany end table has widely "spaced" fluting to enhance the design.

668

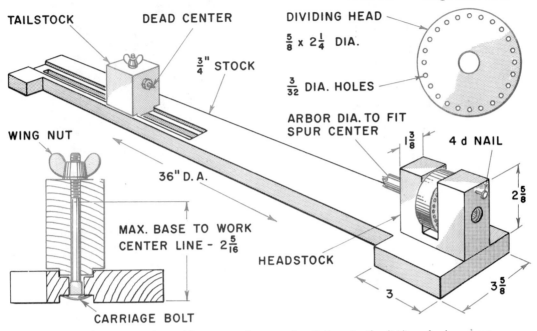

TAILSTOCK

DEAD CENTER

DIVIDING HEAD
$\frac{5}{8} \times 2\frac{1}{4}$ DIA.

$\frac{3}{4}"$ STOCK

$\frac{3}{32}$ DIA. HOLES

ARBOR DIA. TO FIT
SPUR CENTER

$1\frac{3}{8}$

4 d NAIL

WING NUT

36" D. A.

MAX. BASE TO WORK
CENTER LINE - $2\frac{5}{16}$

HEADSTOCK

$2\frac{5}{8}$

3

$3\frac{5}{8}$

CARRIAGE BOLT

48-20. This fluting jig can be used for many cutting operations that require the dividing of a leg or post into equal parts.

If the cutting is to be done on a drill press, a depth collar is placed just below the shaping cutter. Fig. 48-23. A ball-bearing collar is best for this work so that it will turn easily and not burn the wood as may happen with a solid depth collar.

Another method of doing the reeding and fluting is on the wood lathe using a portable router. Fig. 48-24. Most lathes are equipped with an indexing head. The tool holder must be removed from the lathe bed and a plywood base fastened in place. The number and spacing of the cuts around the turning can be arranged

with the indexing head. The portable router is used in an attachment which consists of a motor holder mounted to a wood sub-base. This sub-base slides along the plywood base attached to the bed of the lathe. There are two methods for controlling the depth of cut. A depth collar can be held directly against the work so that it follows the contour. The second method is to fasten a form board to the plywood on the lathe bed at the correct location. Then the rounded end of the wood router base rides against the form board. A fluting jig attached to a bench top can also be used with a router.

48-21. Cutting flutes on a shaper. Note the stops used to control the length of cut.

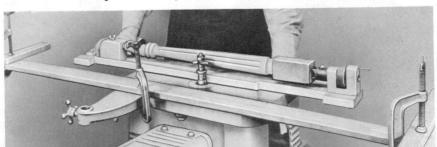

669

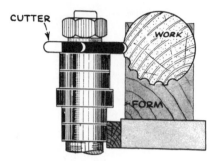

CUTTER
WORK
FORM

48-22. This shows how the flutes are cut with the form board at the base of the jig following the depth collar.

48-25. Italian Provincial chest and mirror which feature an overlay of fretwork on the top drawer fronts, fluted posts, and square, tapered legs. This kind of fluting can be done on a shaper or radial-arm saw.

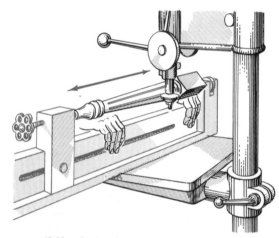

48-23. Cutting flutes on a drill press. An auxiliary wood table fastened to the table is a good idea. Then two nails in this fence and two more in the base of the jig will control the length of cut.

48-24. Cutting reeds on a tapered leg with a portable router.

48-26. Cutting V-shaped flutes on the radial-arm saw. This method can be followed for square legs and posts and other flat surfaces.

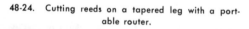

Reeding and Fluting on Square Legs and Flat Surfaces

If reeding or fluting is to be done on a square leg or post, the work should be held in the fluting jig and the cutting done on the shaper or router. Mark the location of the flutes or reeds on one surface of the leg. Adjust the cutting tool to the correct position for one groove on one side of the leg. Then make this and the matching cuts on all four sides. Readjust the cutter to the next location and make the next four cuts. Fluting that consists of a series of parallel V grooves on a flat surface can also be done on the radial-arm saw using a dado head. Fig. 48-25. Turn the motor to the bevel-ripping position. Adjust for correct position and depth of cut. The rip scale on the radial arm makes it possible to position the grooves an equal distance apart. Fig. 48-26. Finish cuts can be applied to the front of posts or stiles to simulate pillars or columns.

JOINING TRIPOD TABLE LEGS

The tripod or stem-leg assembly has three legs which are joined to a central pedestal. Fig. 48-27(a). This construction is common in certain Traditional, Duncan Phyfe, and Early American furniture. Fig. 48-27(b). The legs should be cut with the grain direction approximately in line with the angle of the leg from the foot to the place where it joins the pedestal. A major problem is to join the three legs accurately so they are equally spaced around the bottom. Fig. 48-28. The three common joints are the dowel, blind mortise-and-tenon, and the dovetail-dado. The best method of constructing the joints is to hold the pedestal with the fluting jig. Then the leg can easily be divided into three equal parts, 120 degrees apart. If dowels are used, the holes should first be located and drilled in the pedestal. Notice that the

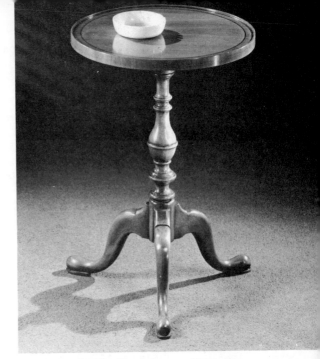

48-27(a). This small table of cherry and birch shows the use of a pedestal stem with three legs.

48-27(b). An example of excellent workmanship by a woodworking student. It is a walnut tilt-top table with a turned stem and three gracefully shaped legs.

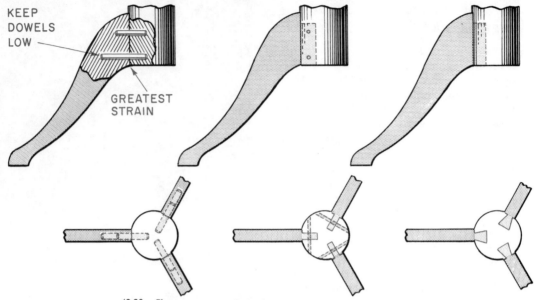

KEEP
DOWELS
LOW

GREATEST
STRAIN

48-28. Three common methods of joining a leg to a pedestal.

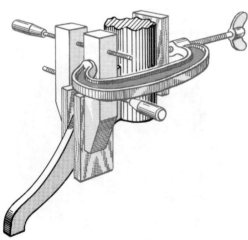

48-29. Clamping a leg to a pedestal while the glue dries.

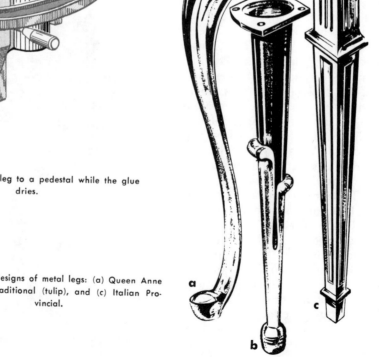

48-30. Three designs of metal legs: (a) Queen Anne cabriole, (b) Traditional (tulip), and (c) Italian Provincial.

672

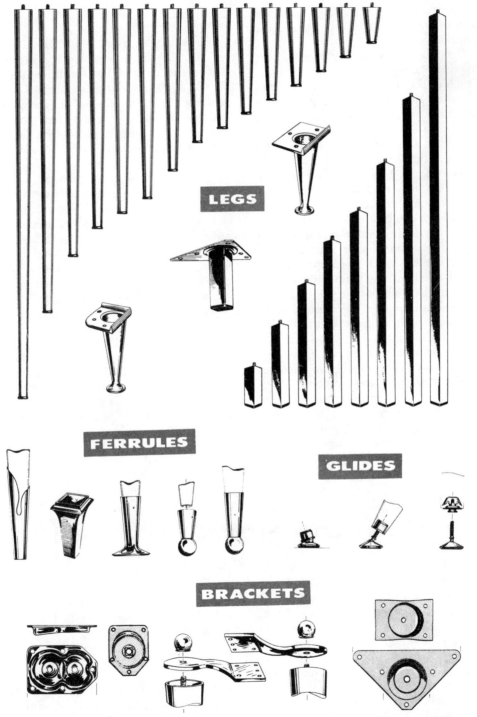

LEGS

FERRULES

GLIDES

BRACKETS

48-31. A few examples of commercial legs, brackets, ferrules, and glides. Many others are available.

dowels should be kept low since the greatest strain is near the bottom of the pedestal.

When the holes in the pedestal are drilled, use dowel pins to locate the holes in each of the three legs. After the holes in the legs have been drilled, it is necessary either to shape the upper end of each leg to fit the curve of the pedestal or to cut a flat surface on the pedestal at each of the three leg positions. This is necessary for a tight joint between the parts. If a mortise-and-tenon or dovetail-dado joint is used, the mortise or dovetail slot can best be cut with a portable router and a cutter of the correct shape. The tenon or tongue on each leg can be cut by hand or on the circular saw. If a flat surface is not provided at each joint location on the pedestal, then the cheek cuts on each leg must be made at an angle of 20 degrees so that the leg will fit tightly around the pedestal leg. After the joints have been cut, apply glue to the joining surfaces and clamp the legs in place. One of the best methods of applying the necessary clamping pressure is to fasten a hand screw to the leg, parallel to the pedestal, and then to fasten another clamp from the hand screw to the pedestal. Fig. 48-29.

COMMERCIAL LEGS

For most construction of tables and chests, it is best to purchase commercial legs in the style of the furniture piece. Fig. 48-30. Most turned wood legs and posts are mass produced on an automatic lathe. Once the knives are ground and set for a particular design, large numbers can be turned out in a very short time. Cabriole legs are produced in quantity on a profile shaper. However, even with the most modern production techniques, some skilled hand carving and sanding are often necessary. Most table legs come with bracket attachments so the legs can be attached in either vertical or slightly slanted position. The brass ferrules have a self-leveling base. Fig. 48-31. For chests, beds, and other pieces of furniture that may be subject to a great deal of weight or side movement, it is better to attach a leg that has a flange permanently mounted to the leg itself. The important items to specify in ordering furniture legs include: correct size (length), shape, material, finish, and method of attaching.

Legs are available in matched sets of wood, metal, and plastic with many different finishes.

49 Leg-And-Rail Construction

Most tables and chairs and the stands for many chests and cabinets feature leg-and-rail construction (sometimes called *frame construction*). Fig. 49-1. The simple table base consists of four legs and four rails (aprons) with the rails normally joined to the legs just under the table top. Fig. 49-2. Sometimes lower rails, called stretchers, are added for extra strength. In construction of small tables, a drawer is often added directly under the top or under a lower shelf, or a shelf-and-drawer are installed between the table legs.

KINDS OF LEG-AND-RAIL JOINERY

The traditional method of joining a leg to a rail is with a blind mortise-and-tenon joint. Fig. 49-3. With this method the

49-1(a). These nest tables of cherry are good examples of leg-and-rail construction.

49-1(b). The base of this chest unit is of leg-and-rail construction.

mortises are cut from the two interior, adjoining surfaces of the legs so that the mortises meet. Then the tenons are cut and mitered at the end to make maximum use of the mortise opening. There must be slight clearance between the ends of the tenons so they will not bind. Fig. 49-4.

Another mortise-and-tenon joint that may be used is the open mortise with a stub tenon. The advantage of this construction is that the mortise can be cut on a circular saw and the tenon can be cut on the same saw or with a router or shaper. Fig. 49-5. An adaptation of this joint is the open mortise and tenon with edge-lap rails. Fig. 49-6.

Still another possible construction is the dovetail-dado joint. Fig. 49-7. This is a good lock joint that can be used with a metal corner brace for simple furniture that can be "knocked down" for storage or shipping.

Not many years ago it would have been considered poor construction if legs

49-2. Each of these tables consists of four legs, four rails or aprons, and a top.

49-3. This hand-crafted table has legs and rails assembled with blind mortise-and-tenon joints.

49-4. The mortises are cut from the adjoining surfaces so that they meet. The tenon is mitered on the end for a glue pocket and to keep the tenon from binding and causing a crack between the shoulder of the tenon and the face of the leg.

49-5. This open mortise with a stub tenon is satisfactory only for light construction.

49-6. An open mortise and-tenon joint with edge-lap rails.

MORTISES JOIN

RAIL FITS OPEN MORTISE

TENONS HAVE CLEARANCE AT ENDS

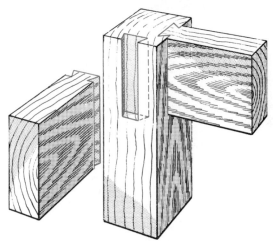

49-7. Dovetail-dado joint for legs and rails.

49-8(a). This coffee table has dowel construction in legs and rails. W-30", D-30", H-16".

and rails were not fastened together with mortise-and-tenon joints. Today, however, many manufacturers of fine furniture no longer use this joint for leg-and-rail construction. Instead, a butt joint strengthened with two or three dowels is common. A strong wood corner block installed with screws, or a metal corner block, is used for strength. The whole unit is held together with a good adhesive. Fig. 49-8.

There are several good reasons for the change. First, with improved adhesives and good corner blocks, the dowel corner is just as strong as the mortise-and-tenon corner. Second, the dowel corner is much quicker and less expensive to produce. This can easily be seen if we compare the time required to make a layout and cut a mortise and tenon with the time required to cut a butt joint and install two or three dowels. The difference in labor costs is tremendous. Third, reinforced dowel leg-and-rail construction saves material since the extra length needed for tenons is eliminated. Finally, leg-and-rail construction in which the leg

49-8(b). This exploded view shows leg-and-rail construction (table frame) using dowels and corner blocks. Note how much simpler this is than mortise-and-tenon.

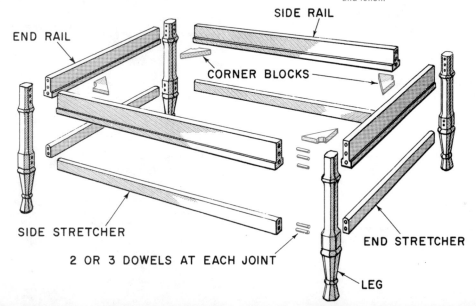

END RAIL

SIDE RAIL

CORNER BLOCKS

SIDE STRETCHER

END STRETCHER

LEG

2 OR 3 DOWELS AT EACH JOINT

677

49-9. A drawer front replaces one of the rails in this lamp table. A study of its construction would reveal a web frame just below the drawer.

and rail are not at right angles to each other makes construction extremely difficult with the mortise-and-tenon joint. In contrast, with dowels the problem is far simpler. It is for these reasons that many vertical or horizontal spindle boring machines are used in furniture plants today.

The important point in doweled leg-and-rail construction is to make sure that the holes are spaced accurately and that they are bored at a right angle to the edge of the leg and in the grain of the rail.

INSTALLING A DRAWER

On many smaller tables made by leg-and-rail construction, a drawer is installed directly under the top as an added storage convenience. Fig. 49-9. This requires a modification of the rail construction. Sometimes the front of the drawer completely replaces one of the rails. Then an interior web frame, with an exposed front edge of the same ma-

49-10. A single dowel at each corner holds this shelf in place.

49-11. This occasional chair features the same basic construction methods found on most tables.

678

Party Chair
19W 18D 40H
Seat Height 16½"

Captain's Chair
Seat Height 17"

Side Chair
Wood Seat, Catkin back

Arm Chair
Wood Seat, Catkin back

Arm Chair
Rosewood Inlay

Side Chair
Rosewood Inlay

49-12.   After studying this unit, do you see why wooden chairs such as these are so complicated to make?

terial as the drawer front and rails, is installed. This frame supports the drawer and also is used to install the drawer guides. For smaller drawers, an opening is cut in one of the rails into which the drawer fits. Then some type of drawer guide is fitted between the two rails.

INSTALLING THE LOWER SHELF

If a lower shelf is to be installed in a table, one of several methods can be followed. The simplest way is to fit the shelf between the legs and then to install a dowel at each corner. Fig. 49-10. Another method especially successful on square, straight, and tapered legs is to cut a corner dado on the legs and then cut off the corners of the shelf to fit into this corner dado.

CHAIR CONSTRUCTION

Most wood chairs are made with leg-and-rail construction. Fig. 49-11. Chair

49-13.   The basic frame design of this chair is extremely simple.

679

49-14(a). Dining-room chair.

construction is the most difficult job in furniture work for several reasons. Rarely is any part at a right angle to the next. The front of the chair is wider than the back. The back legs are arched or angular. The distance across the top of the back legs is greater than the distance across the bottom. The wood seat is shaped or contoured. The back rungs or cross supports are frequently made in a slight arc shape for comfort. Because of these difficult construction problems, most chairs are manufactured in furniture factories rather than in cabinet shops. Fig. 49-12. Such factories have the necessary equipment for shaping the seats, legs, and rails, for bending and laminating the parts, and for doing the necessary upholstery. Only very simple chair designs should be attempted in the school or cabinet shop. Fig. 49-13. In Fig. 49-14 you will find directions for constructing a simple dining-room chair that requires no production equipment.

49-14(b)—Bill of Materials

IMPORTANT: All dimensions listed below, except for length of dowel, are FINISHED size.

No. of Pieces	Part Name	Thickness	Width	Length	Material
2	Back Posts	1⅛"	*3 9/16"	32⅛"	White Oak
2	Front Legs	1⅛"	2 3/16"	16⅝"	White Oak
2	Side Rails	¾"	2⅜"	18"	White Oak
1	Front Rail	¾"	1 9/16"	18½"	White Oak
1	Back Rail	1"	2 5/16"	14"	White Oak
1	Top Rail	1"	1 3/16"	13⅛"	White Oak
1	Front Rung	¾" dia.		17⅜"	Wh. Oak Dowel
2	Side Rungs	¾" dia.		16½"	Wh. Oak Dowel
1	Back Rung	¾" dia.		14⅞"	Wh. Oak Dowel
4	Back Spindles	½" dia.		16⅞"	Wh. Oak Dowel
2	Corner Blocks	1"	2¼"	5 7/16"	Hardwood
2	Corner Blocks	1"	2¾"	5⅞"	Hardwood
1	Seat Panel	½"	16⅝"	18⅜"	Fir Plywood
14	Dowels	⅜" dia.		1½"	Hardwood
6	No. 10 x 1¼" F.H. Wood Screws				
4	No. 10 x 1½" F.H. Wood Screws				
4	No. 8 x ¾" F.H. Wood Screws				
	Foam Rubber				
	Upholstery Material				

**Two posts can be cut from a standard 6" wide board.*

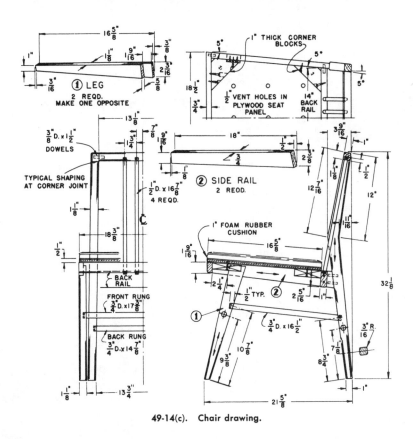

49-14(c). Chair drawing.

49-14(d)—Chair—Plan of Procedure.

1. Lay out back posts (two posts can be cut from standard 6″ board) and cut out on band saw. Dress front edges on jointer and back edges with hand plane and sandpaper.
2. Cut all remaining pieces to size on circular saw.
3. Taper front legs and side rails on circular saw with the aid of a taper jig.
4. Cut necessary angles on ends of front legs, and on all rails, on a circular saw.
5. Cut end lap joint on front legs.
6. Cut angle on top and bottom edge of front rail.
7. Locate and bore all dowel holes.
8. Carefully lay out limits of corner shaping on all pieces and shape on drill press with 3/16″ radius rounding-over router bit. In-

side corners can best be shaped with hand router after project is assembled.
9. Sand all pieces smooth.
10. Assemble chair in following order: Join front legs and side rails with glue and F. H. wood screws. Add side rungs and back posts to these sub-assemblies. Assemble back spindles, back rail and top rail. Join back assembly, front and back rungs, and front rail to side assemblies.
11. Lay out, cut out and drill corner blocks. Glue and screw into place.
12. Complete shaping of corners and finish sand entire project.
13. Apply oak finish.
14. Cut out plywood seat panel. Bore 1/2″ vent holes.
15. Upholster seat and install.

681

The tops for most tables, cabinets, desks, and many chests are made as a removable part that is installed after the other construction is completed. Fig. 50-1. There are many different methods of constructing such tops. The method to choose is determined to a large degree by the kind of part, the quality of construction, and the design. Some methods of construction are suitable for cabinets built on the job while others require equipment usually found only in cabinet shops or furniture factories.

KINDS OF TABLE AND CABINET TOPS

Softwood Plywood

The simplest way to build a table or cabinet top is first to choose plywood of an adequate thickness, usually 3/4". The major problem in using plywood is that the exposed edges must be treated. Fig. 50-2.

Core Stock Covered With Plastic Laminate

The most popular top construction for cabinets and built-ins is core stock of plywood or particle board covered with plastic laminate. This is discussed in Unit 43.

50-1(b). The table top is constructed separately from the base and then the two are assembled.

50-1(a). The base and the top of most casework are also constructed as two separate units and then the top is attached after the base is installed.

682

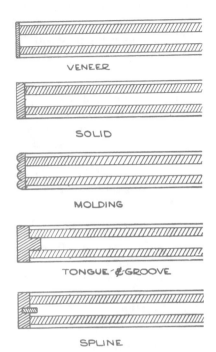

VENEER

SOLID

MOLDING

TONGUE-&-GROOVE

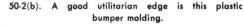

SPLINE

50-2(a). Common methods of treating the edges of plywood.

50-2(b). A good utilitarian edge is this plastic bumper molding.

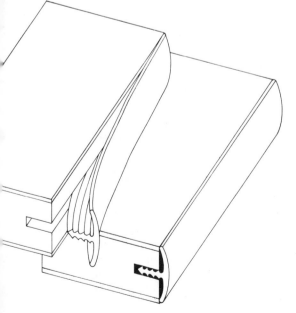

Hardwood Plywood

Many fine tables and cabinets are made of veneer-core or lumber-core hardwood plywood. For veneer-core plywood, the simplest edge treatment is to add another thickness of material along the underside and then to apply a thin veneer to cover the edge grain. Fig. 50-3. In furniture production, the manufacturer usually makes his own tops of lumber-core plywood and includes edge banding of the same hardwood as the surface veneer. Then many kinds of edge moldings can be cut. Other methods of treating the edges are shown in Fig. 50-4.

Plywood Center with a Band or Frame

Many small- to medium-size furniture pieces have tops that consist of a hardwood plywood center with a wide band of solid wood. This can easily be done in school and cabinet shops. The band may have mitered or other corner construction. Fig. 50-5. A good example is the finger joint, Fig. 50-6, which gives the appearance of a butt joint on the face surface. This band or frame construction has several distinct advantages. It will not warp and there is little or no expansion and contraction. Because there is a solid wood band, any kind of edge treatment is possible. The band is joined to the plywood with dowels, a spline, or a tongue-and-groove joint. Fig. 50-7.

50-3. This table top is quite simple to make. The top has a built-up edge and then is edge banded with thin veneer.

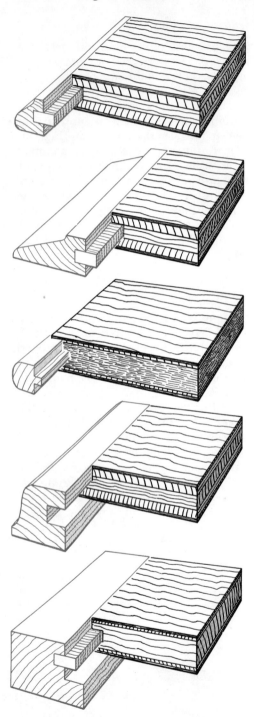

Usually a slight saw kerf is cut where the solid wood joins the plywood. In this way, the solid wood does not have to match the plywood exactly.

In some cases, fir plywood is used for the center and covered with a plastic laminate. When this is done, the band should be 1/16″ thicker than the plywood to allow for the thickness of the plastic laminate. A good example of this is the table leaf shown in Fig. 50-6. The black plastic-laminate center has a band of teak. For an unusual table top made of an exotic wood or a matching pattern, softwood plywood or particle board can be used for core stock and then covered with a fancy veneer. Also, the back of the sheet material is covered, but with an inexpensive veneer, to maintain balanced construction.

Solid Glued-up Stock

Solid glued-up lumber is sometimes used for hand-crafted furniture products made in small cabinet shops and in schools. The two major problems of working with solid glued-up lumber for wide surfaces are warpage and the change in size caused by expansion and contraction. Wide boards tend to cup as the wood takes on moisture or dries out. Therefore when gluing large surfaces together it is a good idea to cut the pieces into small strips not over 4″ to 6″ wide. Then alternate the pieces so that the heart side is up on every other board. This tends to minimize warpage. Another help is to cut small router grooves across grain on the underside of the top before the top is fastened to the legs and rails. The biggest problem is the expansion and contraction of a large solid surface. Since lumber expands more across than with grain, it is important that the top be fastened to the base in such a way that it can move without buckling or cracking the joints.

50-4. Edge treatments with hardwood plywood.

50-5.   Most small tables have tops which consist of a plywood center with a wide edge band or frame of solid wood. Notice that this top has mitered corners.

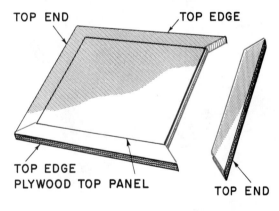

TOP END   TOP EDGE

TOP EDGE
PLYWOOD TOP PANEL

TOP END

50-6.   This teak table has many interesting design features. Note that the table top is of banded construction with a finger joint at each corner. The edge is square. There is a single drop-leaf. Notice also the single center stretcher used to hold the end stretchers together. (John Stuart, Inc.) W-59″, D-21″ and H-18″ with leaf down.

50-7.   The band illustrated here is joined to the plywood center by a tongue-and-groove joint which can be cut in one of two ways.

CUT TONGUE ON
PLYWOOD PANEL.

CUT GROOVE IN
BAND.

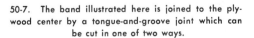

CUT GROOVE IN
PLYWOOD PANEL.

CUT TONGUE ON
BAND.

685

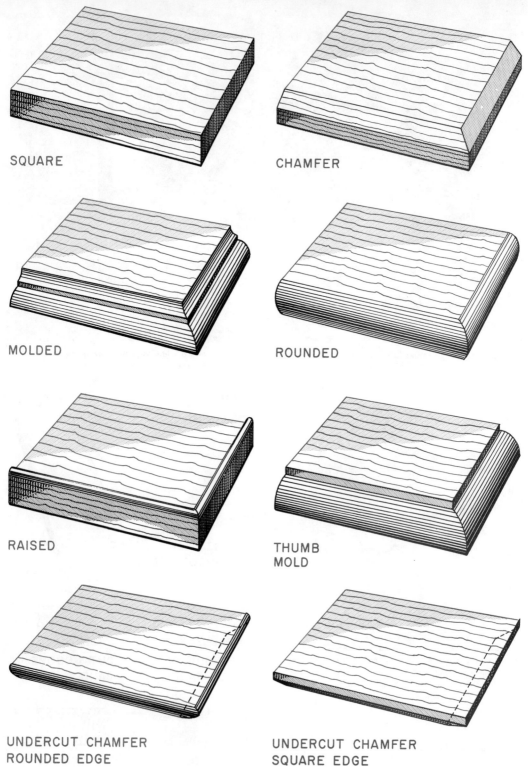

SQUARE

CHAMFER

MOLDED

ROUNDED

RAISED

THUMB
MOLD

UNDERCUT CHAMFER
ROUNDED EDGE

UNDERCUT CHAMFER
SQUARE EDGE

50-8. Some typical edges for table tops.

50-9(a). Cutting a chamfer edge with a radial-arm saw.

50-9(b). Cutting an edge molding on a table top with a portable router.

EDGE TREATMENT

The edge treatment for tables, chests, desks, and cabinets depends on whether plywood or solid wood is used, and on the furniture style. Fig. 50-8. Simple edge treatments such as the square edge are used on many Modern or Contemporary pieces. Fig. 50-9. Danish Modern often has an undercut chamfer edge with the outer edge flat or rounded to give the top a feeling of lightness. Simpler Early American and Colonial designs have rounded edges. Other furniture styles feature a wide variety of molded edges. The illustrations in this book will give you some idea of the wide variety of edge designs that are possible. Most of the more intricate edge designs must be cut on a shaper or router in the school or cabinet shop. Furniture factories have routers, shapers, or double-end tenoners for cutting edge moldings.

DROP-LEAF TABLES

To design a table with drop leaves, you must decide on the kind of joint, the

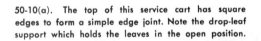

50-10(a). The top of this service cart has square edges to form a simple edge joint. Note the drop-leaf support which holds the leaves in the open position.

687

50-10(b). A rule or drop-leaf joint on a harvest table of Colonial design.

50-11. This hinge-and-leaf support, sometimes called a flap table hinge, increases the beauty of Contemporary furniture by eliminating the unsightly gap formed by butt hinges. It provides a flush, clean-cut appearance. When installing the hinge, fasten the small leaf to the table top. This hinge is designed for 3/4" tops only.

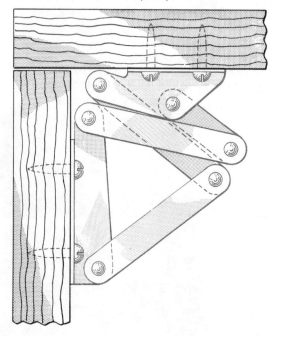

place where the leaves will attach, and the method of supporting the leaves. The common joints are the simple edge joint and the rule or drop-leaf joint. Fig. 50-10. If a simple or plane joint with square edges is chosen for the table top and leaf, several different kinds of hinges can be used. The simplest are two or three *butt hinges* or *a piano hinge* installed between the top and the leaf. When closed, the leaves drop down but extend beyond the top. Some kind of drop-leaf support is needed. Another hinge that can be used is a *flap or drop-leaf table hinge*. This combines the function of both the hinge and the support. When it is closed, the leaf drops below and in line with the edge of the top. Fig. 50-11. The rule joint is best for certain styles of furniture since it is neater in appearance and is characteristic of Traditional furniture. This joint has a cove molding on the leaf that slides over the "thumbnail" molding on the top. The rule joint can be cut on a shaper or router or with the molding head on a circular or radial-arm saw. It is extremely important to lay out the joint carefully and to select the correct kind of cutters. *It is always wise to cut a test joint on two scrap pieces of wood of the same thickness as the finished table top, and to mount the hinges to make sure that adjustments are correct.* To lay out a rule joint proceed as follows:

1. Measure half the thickness of the knuckle of the hinge, and gage a line (X) from the underside on both the table top and the drop leaves. The center of both the concave and convex cuts lies in this gage line. Fig. 50-12.

2. Set a marking gage to a distance that is 1/8" less than the thickness of the table and draw a line (Y). Set dividers equal to the distance between these two lines (A) and scribe an arc on the table top from the outer edge to a point on the upper gage line.

3. Draw a vertical line from the center of the arc to the top of the table to complete the layout.

4. Using the same setting, scribe another arc on the drop leaves. Frequently the radius is 1/32″ larger on the drop leaves to provide clearance between the two moving wood parts.

5. Now select a cove bit that will fit the convex curve and cut both edges of the center section.

6. Select a cutter that is the reverse of the concave cutter for the leaves. A matched set of rule-joint cutters or bits can be used for tops 3/4″ thick. If the edge is to be cut on a shaper, the required cutter is mounted on a spindle and the height of the cutter adjusted to the layout lines. The cut on the leaves requires only that the cutter be reversed, with the spindle height and pin setting exactly the same.

7. After the cuts have been made, turn the table and leaves upside down and place them flat on a bench.

8. Hinges for rule joints must have one long and one short leaf. Fig. 50-13. These are called *back flaps*. It is necessary to cut a shallow groove so that the knuckle fits into the wood with the center of the knuckle exactly on the center of the radius used for cutting the joint. Rout out this groove with a core box bit using the router guide against the edge of the table. A hinge with a slightly bent leaf is available. It does not require a hinge gain.

9. The short leaf is fastened to the top. The longer half of the hinge must reach across the joint with the screws set in the drop-leaf. The center pin must be in line with the center of the radius used to lay out the joint. If it is impossible to obtain the correct drop-leaf hinges, ordinary hasp hinges can be used.

Supporting the Leaves

There are several common ways of

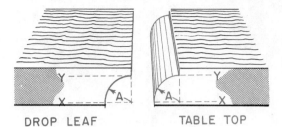

DROP LEAF   TABLE TOP

50-12(a). Layout of a rule joint.

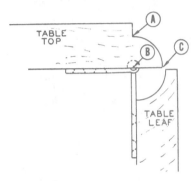

TABLE TOP

A
B   C

TABLE LEAF

50-12(b). Notice that the distance from A to B and from B to C must be the same. Point B is the center of the hinge barrel.

50-13. Table-leaf hinge.

supporting the leaves in the various positions. Fig. 50-14. The most common is to use a table-leaf support. These come in several common sizes including 6″, 8″, and 10″. They should be mounted between the rail or apron and the drop leaf as shown in Fig. 50-15. A second common method, used especially in Early American and Colonial furniture, is to use a wood wing that swings out to support a leaf. In this construction, a wing is cut and then a wood or metal dowel

50-14. This dining table has a rule joint between the top and the leaves. The birch table top is banded in walnut. A pair of table-leaf supports is installed on either side to keep the leaves in an open position.

50-16. This butterfly drop-leaf end table has two wood wings that turn on dowel pins to support the leaves.

pin is fastened permanently into it. A hole is then bored into the rail and stretcher into which the wing fits. Fig. 50-16. This method can also be used on tables of Modern or Contemporary style. A third common method is to use a sliding support of wood that fits through the rail and under the center section of the table.

DINING TABLE TOPS WITH REMOVABLE LEAVES

Many table tops that do not have drop leaves are made in two halves. The table is cut across the middle. Then heavy hardwood or metal extension-table slides are installed under the top so that the two table halves can be pulled apart to add leaves. Fig. 50-17. There is another way of doing this when there are drop

50-15. Directions for mounting a table-leaf support.

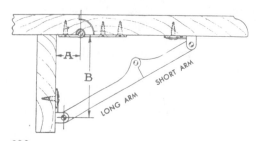

Dimension A (inches)	Dimension B (inches)		
	6" Size	8" Size	10" Size
½	3½	3½	5
1	3¼	3³⁄₁₆	4¹¹⁄₁₆
1½	2¹³⁄₁₆	2⅞	4⁷⁄₁₆
2	2½	2½	4
2½	2⅛	2⅛	3⁹⁄₁₆

690

50-17(a). This Contemporary extension table of metal and wood illustrates the use of hardwood table slides.

50-17(b). The table open.

50-17(c). The table extended.

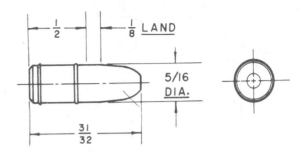

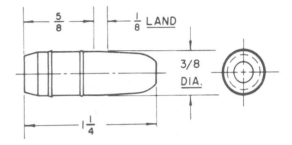

50-18. Plastic or wood table pins are used to align the leaves of an extension table. They are available in several diameters.

50-19. This extension table has leaves of unusual design, and a "floating top" which conceals the leaves tucked beneath it. They are easily pulled free and fit naturally in place.

50-17(d). Solid wood table slides.

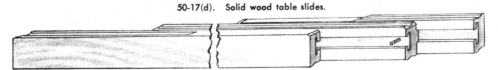

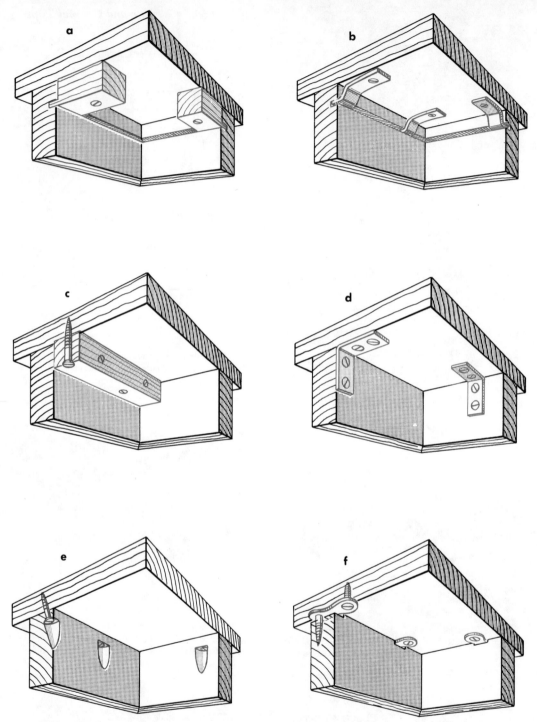

50-20. Common methods of fastening the tops of furniture: (a) Rabbeted blocks or wood buttons. (b) Metal table-top fasteners. (c) Wood screws through web or skeleton frame. (d) Angle irons. (e) Wood screws through pocket holes in the rails. (f) Desk-top clips.

leaves. The rails under the table are cut in half and hardwood slides installed so that the folding leaves can be raised and then slid out, allowing for the addition of extra leaves. Several table-leaf pins of wood or plastic are installed along the opening edge of one half of the table top and on each extra leaf. Fig. 50-18. These pins keep the leaves in line when the table is extended. Many other commercial fittings can be used for increasing the size of a table, for locking the sections of a table top together, and for guiding the leaves so they will be perfectly even. There are also several unusual methods of supporting extension leaves. Fig. 50-19.

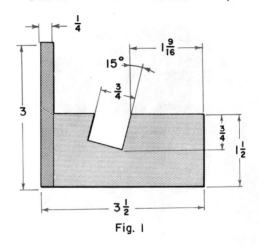

Fig. I

FASTENING TOPS TO FURNITURE

There are many common ways of fastening a table top to a cabinet or rails (apron) and legs. The most important point to remember is this: If the top is made of solid lumber, there must be some provision for it to expand and contract without buckling or cracking a joint. For this reason, only methods (a) and (b) shown in Fig. 50-20 should be followed, if the top is of solid lumber. Metal table-top fasteners or clips are the best. A groove is cut around the rail and the fasteners are installed at about 12" intervals. Method (a) has a rabbeted block and requires a slightly wider groove cut in the rail. The blocks or wood buttons are screwed to the top. They can be made with square ends, as shown, or with an arc projection that enables the buttons to be turned and the top removed without unscrewing the buttons. Methods (c) to (f), shown in Fig. 50-20, can be followed wherever sheet material such as plywood or particle board has been used or when a banded top is to be fastened in place. The jig for boring the pocket holes at an angle in the rail for method (d) is shown in Fig. 50-21.

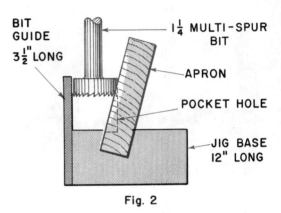

Fig. 2

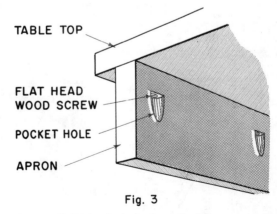

Fig. 3

50-21(a). Jig for boring pocket holes.

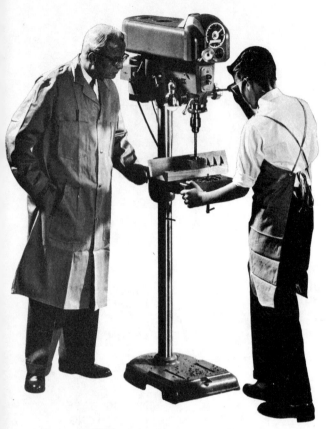

50-21(b). Using the jig on a drill press for boring the pocket holes.

FASTENING TOPS TO CASEWORK

Methods for fastening tops to casework vary with the quality of construction. As a rule, the best construction for casework is the same as that for furniture construction. Usually a web or skeleton frame or false top is installed at the top edge of the case. Then the top is fastened from below with metal fasteners or clips, glue blocks, or wood screws. On built-ins and cabinets of lesser quality, the top is often fastened directly to the case sides from the outside with nails or screws. Then the heads are covered with plastic wood or other wood filler. The surface may then be painted or covered with plastic laminate. Fig. 50-22.

DROP-LEAF TABLE

Many of the procedures required to build a table top, to install it on the base, and to support the table leaves are also needed to build the dining table shown in Fig. 50-23. A study of the plans will show the application of these basic steps.

50-22. Common methods of fastening the top to a case body. Tops should be fastened to sub or web frames with concealed clips, screws, glue blocks, or similar hidden fastenings.

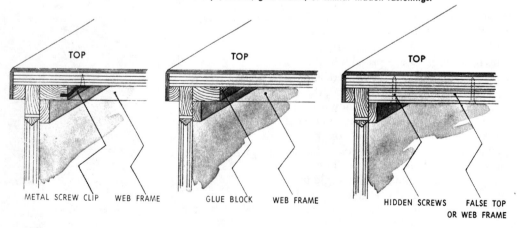

TOP   TOP   TOP

METAL SCREW CLIP   WEB FRAME   GLUE BLOCK   WEB FRAME   HIDDEN SCREWS   FALSE TOP OR WEB FRAME

50-23(a)—DRAWING FOR THE DROP-LEAF TABLE.

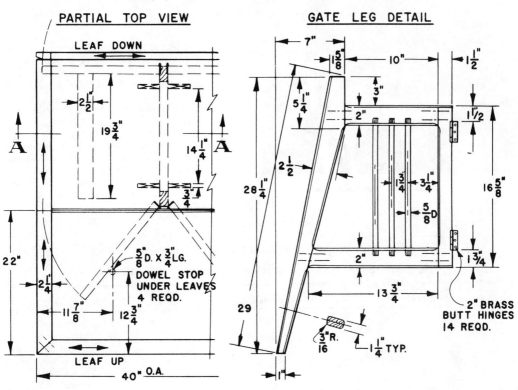

PARTIAL TOP VIEW

LEAF DOWN

A A

2 1/2"

19 3/4"

14 1/4"

3/4"

5/8 D. X 3/4 LG.
DOWEL STOP
UNDER LEAVES
4 REQD.

22"

2 1/4"

11 7/8"

12 3/4"

LEAF UP

40" O.A.

GATE LEG DETAIL

7"

1 5/8"

10"

1 1/2"

3"

5 1/4"

2"

1"/2

2 1/2"

1 3/4"

3/4"

5/8 D

16 5/8"

28 1/4"

2"

1 3/4"

29

13 3/4"

2" BRASS
BUTT HINGES
14 REQD.

3/16"R.

1 1/4" TYP.

1"

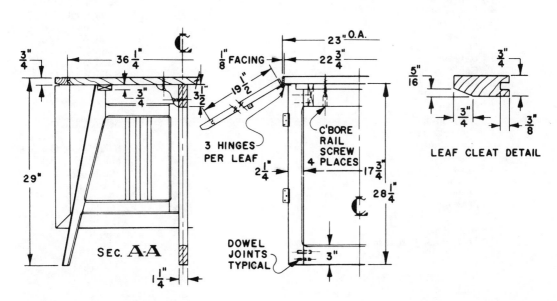

3/4"

36 1/4"

C

1/8" FACING

23" O.A.

22 3/4"

3/4"

3/4"

3/4"

5/16"

3/8"

LEAF CLEAT DETAIL

19 1/2"

3 HINGES
PER LEAF

C'BORE
RAIL
SCREW
4 PLACES

29"

2 1/4"

17 3/4"

28 1/4"

SEC. AA

1 1/4"

DOWEL
JOINTS
TYPICAL

3"

C

50-23(b). Drop-leaf table.

50-23(d)—PLAN OF PROCEDURE FOR THE DROP-LEAF TABLE.

1. Cut all center frame and gate members to size on circular saw.
2. Taper legs with taper jig on circular saw.
3. Cut angles on one end of bottom rail of gates.
4. Locate and bore dowel holes in all members.
5. Drill and counterbore screw shank holes in top rail of center frame.
6. Glue up center frame and gates.
7. Round corners of all frame members on shaper or drill press, or, use a file and sandpaper. Sand all pieces smooth.
8. Cut gains in all frames and install hinges.
9. Lay out brackets and cut out on bandsaw

50-23(c)—BILL OF MATERIALS FOR THE DROP-LEAF TABLE.

IMPORTANT: All dimensions listed below are FINISHED size.

No. of Pieces	Part Name	Thickness	Width	Length	Material
1	Top	¾"	22¾"	36¼"	Comb Grain White Oak Plywood S1S
2	Leaves	¾"	19½"	36¼"	Comb Grain White Oak Plywood S1S
2	Top Cleats	¾"	2¼"	23"	Solid White Oak
4	Leaf—End Cleats	¾"	2¼"	22"	Solid White Oak
2	Leaf—Side Cleats	¾"	2¼"	40"	Solid White Oak
4	Legs	1¼"	2½"	29"	Solid White Oak
4	Gate Top Rails	1¼"	2"	10"	Solid White Oak
4	Gate Bottom Rails	1¼"	2"	13¾"	Solid White Oak
4	Gate Side Rails	1¼"	1½"	16⅝"	Solid White Oak
2	Center Frame Side Rails	1¼"	2¼"	28¼"	Solid White Oak
1	Center Frame Bottom Rail	1¼"	3½"	17¾"	Solid White Oak
1	Center Frame Top Rail	1¼"	3½"	17¾"	Solid White Oak
4	Edge Facings	⅛"	¾"	35½"	Solid White Oak
4	Brackets	1¼"	3½"	3½"	Hardwood
2	Top Battens	¾"	2½"	19¾"	Hardwood
40	Dowels	½" dia.		1½"	Hardwood
12	Dowels	½" dia.		13¾"	Hardwood
8	Dowels	⅜" dia.		1½"	Hardwood
4	Gate Stops	⅝" dia.		¾"	Dowel
7	Pr. 2" Brass Butt Hinges with Screws				
4	No. 10 x 2¼" F.H. Wood Screws				
8	No. 10 x 1¼" F.H. Wood Screws				
8	No. 8 x 1¼" F.H. Wood Screws				
6	Glides				

or jig saw. Cut top battens to size on circular saw. Drill and countersink screw shank holes. Drill anchor holes in top rail of center frame.

10. Cut top and leaves to size on circular saw.
11. Cut tenons on ends of top and three sides of leaves. Trim tenons for blind tongue and groove joints.
12. Groove all cleats. Stop groove ½″ from ends for blind joints, or groove thru and inlay end grain piece for blind.
13. Miter leaf cleats and bore dowel holes.
14. Glue cleats onto top and leaves. Glue facing strips into place.
15. Locate and bore 5/8″ diameter holes 1/2″ deep and glue stops onto underside of leaves.
16. Locate and drill screw anchor holes in top. Attach battens to top with glue and No. 8 x 1¼″ F. H. wood screws.
17. Cut gains in top and leaves for hinges. Install hinges.
18. Fasten top to frame with No. 10 x 2¼″ F. H. wood screws thru top rail and No. 10 x 1¼″ F. H. wood screws thru brackets.
19. Finish sand entire project.
20. Apply oak finish.

(51) Basic Casework

Basic casework consists of a box turned on its end or edge and then fitted with dividers, shelves, frames, face plates, and drawers or doors to make the enclosure for a particular kind of storage. Such construction is used for kitchen cabinets, cases, counters, desks, and similar items. Basic casework varies in quality from the most elementary box construction of softwood plywood with butt-joint corners and painted surfaces to premium cabinets of hardwood plywood with lock-miter-corner joints, web frames for rigidity, and a fine transparent finish. Fig. 51-1(a) and (b). The materials, machining techniques, and joinery are less complicated than those employed for fine furniture cabinetwork described in the next unit. Fig. 51-1(c).

MATERIALS

Most casework is constructed of softwood or hardwood veneer-core plywood, particle board covered with plastic laminate, or solid and glued-up lumber.

51-1(a). This casework of fir plywood was made by the simplest construction methods and finished by painting.

51-1(b). This handsome desk and cabinet of hemlock illustrate a finer quality of casework.

51-1(c). Many characteristics of quality workmanship are represented in this kitchen-cabinet unit. The base plate or frame is joined at the corners with stub mortise-and-tenon joints. The bottom is reinforced with corner blocks and bottom support strip. These reinforcements are permanently secured with glue and screws.

51-2. Some casework is built by making a frame and then covering it with plywood or hardboard.

51-3. A dado joint produces neat dividers and shelves.

When using such lumber it is necessary to allow for parts to swell or shrink. For example, if a web or skeleton frame is fitted into glued-up lumber, the frame must be fastened so that the width of the case can change without bowing or cracking when the humidity changes. The average movement due to humidity change is about plus or minus 1/8″ per 12″ of width. Skeleton frames must therefore always be slightly narrower than the sides and fastened with screws (not glue). Slightly elongated screw holes should be used in the frame itself. For certain kinds of cabinets, a light framework is built and then covered with thin plywood or hardboard. Fig. 51-2.

INTERIOR CONSTRUCTION

The interior construction in lower- to moderate-quality casework consists of solid wood or vertical dividers and horizontal shelves of plywood. These dividers and shelves can be fitted into the case with a simple butt joint, a better dado joint, or the finest rabbet-and-dado or dovetail-dado joint. Fig. 51-3. In best-quality casework skeleton or web frames support the drawers. Fig. 51-4. These frames are set into the sides with a through or plain dado, a stop dado, or a dovetail dado. If a stop dado is used, it must end about 1/2″ from the front edge of the case. Stop dadoes are not necessary if the front edge is to be covered with a faceplate or frame.

BASE OR LEGS

The base of casework can be constructed in several ways. On many cabinets (particularly kitchen cabinets), the sides are notched at the front bottom edge so that there is a recess about 4″ high and 3″ deep. A solid bottom fits into a dado joint just above this notch. Usually the face frame or plate fits around three sides of the case and the door cov-

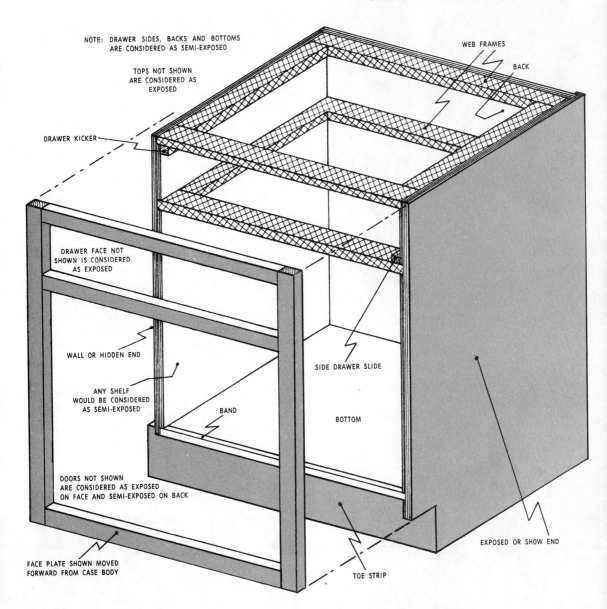

NOTE: DRAWER SIDES, BACKS AND BOTTOMS ARE CONSIDERED AS SEMI-EXPOSED

TOPS NOT SHOWN ARE CONSIDERED AS EXPOSED

WEB FRAMES

BACK

DRAWER KICKER

DRAWER FACE NOT SHOWN IS CONSIDERED AS EXPOSED

WALL OR HIDDEN END

ANY SHELF WOULD BE CONSIDERED AS SEMI-EXPOSED

BAND

SIDE DRAWER SLIDE

BOTTOM

DOORS NOT SHOWN ARE CONSIDERED AS EXPOSED ON FACE AND SEMI-EXPOSED ON BACK

FACE PLATE SHOWN MOVED FORWARD FROM CASE BODY

TOE STRIP

EXPOSED OR SHOW END

Isometric of Case Illustrating the Defined Exposure of Case Parts

Legend: Exposed Surfaces are Shown Shaded.

Semi-Exposed Surfaces are Shown Plain.

Hidden Surfaces are Shown Cross Hatched. (Also Includes any Concealed Blocking.)

51-4(a). Parts of high-quality casework. The exposed parts include all surfaces visible when doors and drawers are closed. The semi-exposed parts include those pieces behind opaque doors such as shelves, dividers, interior faces of ends, case backs, drawer sides, backs and bottoms, and the back face of doors. The concealed parts include sleepers (front-to-back base supports), web frames, dust panels, and other parts not usually seen after installation of the casework.

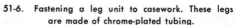

51-4(b). This manufactured kitchen-cabinet casework piece has paneled sides instead of plywood for the basic enclosure.

ers this bottom. Fig. 51-5. There is no frame at all across this bottom edge. The opening below the bottom is set back from the case front and covered with a *toe strip* that is rabbeted on either end to fasten over the case sides. Heavy wood pieces called *sleepers* are placed on edge from front to back under the case to give extra support. For some casework an extra base frame (sometimes called a plinth) is built to provide toe clearance on two, three, or four sides. A *plinth* is the lowest square or rectangular shape of a cabinet or furniture piece. This base or plinth is fastened to the case with glue blocks and cleat strips. There are also many types of shop-made or commercial legs that can be attached to casework. Fig. 51-6.

51-5. Notice that this casework consists of two distinct units. The lower base unit with a toe space has a frame around only three sides so that the doors cover the edge of the bottom. The upper casework has a frame around all four sides, with sliding glass doors fitted into it.

51-6. Fastening a leg unit to casework. These legs are made of chrome-plated tubing.

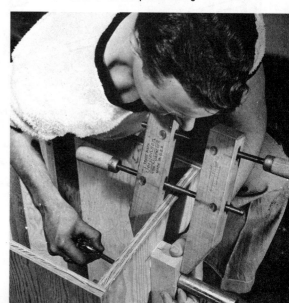

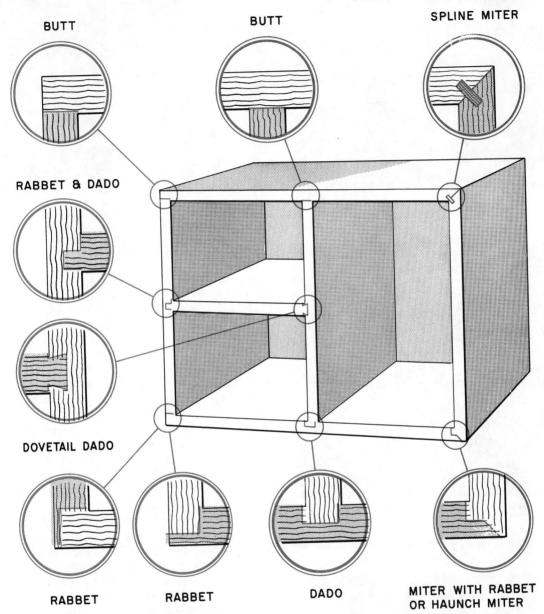

BUTT

BUTT

SPLINE MITER

RABBET & DADO

DOVETAIL DADO

RABBET

RABBET

DADO

MITER WITH RABBET OR HAUNCH MITER

51-7. The most common joints made in casework are shown here with the exception of the block miter.

CONSTRUCTION OF CORNERS AND BACKS

Many types of joints can be used for exterior corner construction. Fig. 51-7. The simplest is the butt joint, but the rabbet joint is found on slightly better con-struction. Fig. 51-8. The finest corner joints, especially for plywood, are the spline miter, the miter with rabbet (off-set miter), and the lock miter. The lock miter is usually made only when the cabinet shop has shaper equipment and

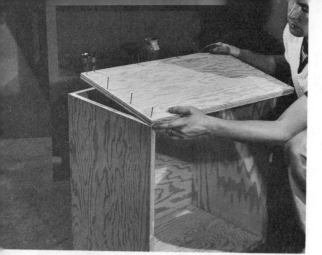

51-8(a). A butt-joint box nailed together is the simplest case.

51-9. The case on the right has a rabbet just deep enough to take the back panel. The one on the left has a deeper rabbet so that the remaining lip can be trimmed off as necessary to get a good fit between the casework and the wall.

51-8(b). A well fitted rabbet joint is better for most work.

51-8(c). Gluing and clamping a simple case. Note the protective strips under the clamps.

cutters. If the case is to have a back, a rabbet should be cut around the inside of its back edges. This cut usually should be just deep enough to take the plywood or hardboard panel. If the unit is to fit against a wall, the rabbet should be cut as deep as 1/2" to 3/4" so that the remaining lip can be trimmed to get a good fit against the wall. Fig. 51-9. If an extra top is to be applied to the casework, the top of the box itself may be either a web or skeleton frame or a false top (solid plywood or some other solid material over which another top is fitted).

INSTALLING DRAWERS AND DOORS

Drawers are installed in casework following any of the procedures described in Unit 46. For the very simplest box construction, dadoes can be cut in the sides. Then the bottom of the drawer can be built to extend beyond the sides to act as the drawer guide. Fig. 51-10. A better method for softwood-plywood cases is to install a side guide and runner. Fig. 51-11(a). Fasten cleats to the inside of the case to serve as the guides. Fig. 51-11(b) and (c). The finest casework has a web or skeleton frame to support the drawer with the guide fas-

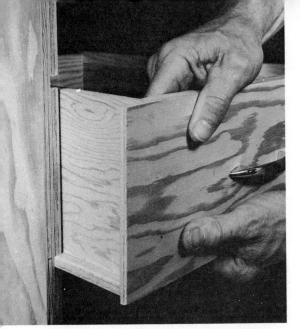

51-10. This inexpensive drawer is made by fastening the bottom to the sides with nails. The extended bottom serves as a guide in the dado runner.

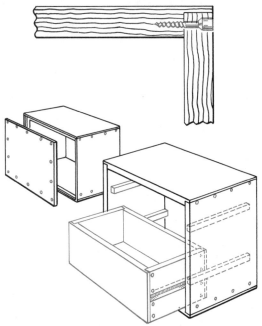

51-11(a). A medium-quality case has side guides and runners. The corners are assembled with glue and screws.

51-11(b). Installing a hardwood cleat in a case to act as a drawer guide.

tened to this frame. Dust panels are not normally installed in basic casework but are included in fine furniture cabinetwork.

Any kind of door described in Unit 45 can be used. Doors for the finest casework should be made of lumber-core plywood or particle board covered with veneer or plastic laminate. On casework of lower quality, veneer-core plywood can be used. The thickness of material limits the size of the flush doors that can be used. The following standards should be followed for best-quality construction: For 3/4″ material, the doors should not be wider than 26″ nor higher than 28″; for 1″ to 1¼″ doors, the maximum size can be 36″ wide and 66″ high; small sliding doors not exceeding 6 square feet in area can be made of 1/4″ tempered hardboard.

FACEPLATE AND TRIM

Only the lowest-quality casework of plywood or particle board has exposed edges filled and painted. On medium-quality casework the shelves, dividers, and edges have bands of veneer or solid

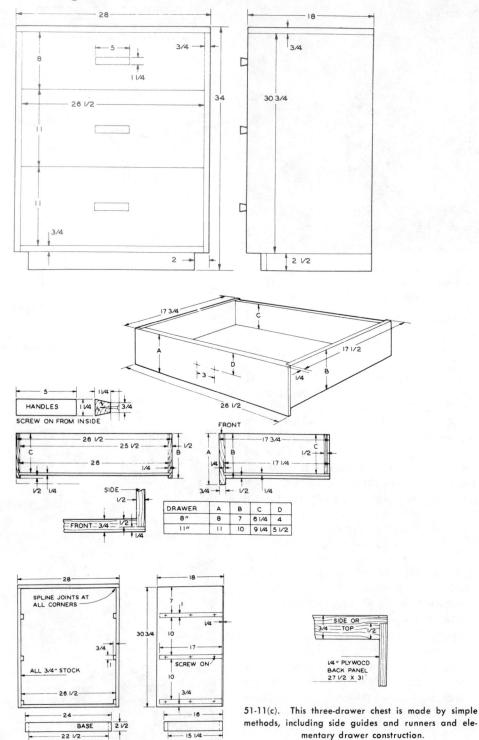

DRAWER	A	B	C	D
8"	8	7	6 1/4	4
11"	11	10	9 1/4	5 1/2

51-11(c). This three-drawer chest is made by simple methods, including side guides and runners and elementary drawer construction.

51-12. Attaching solid wood trim to the exposed edge of a plywood case.

51-13. Assembling a simple boxlike case with glue and nails.

wood glued and nailed in place. Fig. 51-12. In finest-quality casework all edges are banded with material that has been glued in place under pressure. The front of best-quality casework has a faceplate or frame (sometimes called rails). This frame is joined at the corner with a stub mortise-and-tenon, dowel, or haunched mortise-and-tenon joint. The frame or faceplate is then fastened to the case with nails alone or nails and glue. On the very best-quality casework built in the shop, the frame is fastened to the case with glue under pressure. Only a few nails or staples may be used to position the frame. Sometimes the exposed end of highest-quality casework is joined to the face frame with a spline-miter or a lock-miter joint.

ASSEMBLY

Simplest casework is assembled with nails and glue. Fig. 51-13. On better-quality pieces the fastening is done with glue and screws. Finest-quality casework is assembled with glue only, using pressure clamps until the unit is dry.

FINISH

The exterior of casework (those surfaces that can be seen when all doors and drawers are closed) should be carefully sanded before finishing. For a painted or opaque finish, the sanding can be done by machine with medium-grade, 60-grit (1/2) sandpaper. For a fine, transparent finish, both machine and hand sanding must be done on exposed surfaces; final sanding requires 100- or 120-grit sandpaper. All cross scratches must be avoided when a transparent finish is to be applied. Apply the finish to the casework as described in Section V.

Since most of the simple casework is constructed of softwood plywood, a painted or opaque finish is usually applied. Some casework may be constructed from prefinished plywood.

51-14(a). Fishing-tackle cabinet.

PARTS SCHEDULE

Code	No. Req'd	Size	Part Identification
A	2	17"x84"	Side
B	1	11¾"x22½"	Drawer Shelf
C	3	12½"x22½"	Shelf
D	2	4½"x11¼"	Drawer Front
E	1	24"x80½"	Door
F	1	17"x23¼"	Top
G	2	3¼"x77¼"	Door Side Frame
H	3	3"x20½"	Door Shelf
I	1	3¼"x20½"	Door Top Frame
J	1	3½"x22½"	Base
K	1	23¼"x80⅛"	Back
L	2	3"x11"	Drawer Back
M	4	3¾"x12⅛"	Drawer Side
N	2	10¾"x12⅛"	Drawer Bottom
P	1	7"x20½"	Door Shelf Facia
Q	2	2"x20½"	Door Shelf Facia
U	1	4¾"x10"	Dowel Board
V	1	12½"x22"	Standard
W	2	11¾"x12½"	Shelf
X	1	16¾"x22½"	Bottom Shelf

1 Door Bolt; 4 Pin Hinges; 2 ½" Diam.–8¾" Long Hardwood Dowels; 1 Pc. ¼"x20½"x55" Cork Backing; 1 Metal Clothes Hanger. Miscellaneous—4d and 6d Finish Nails and Glue; Clips as required.

51-14(b). Parts schedule or bill of materials.

EXAMPLES OF SIMPLE CASEWORK

The construction of the following two cabinet units illustrates simple casework materials, methods, and techniques that can be used with limited hand and power tools.

Fishing Tackle Cabinet

The plywood cabinet for fishing tackle (Fig. 51-14(a)) is made as follows:

1. Lay out the cabinet parts on three panels of softwood plywood as shown in the cutting diagram. Fig. 51-14(b) and (c).

2. Saw out the parts and true up the edges of the plywood. Rabbet one end of each side panel for the top.

3. On the floor, assemble the cabinet, back side down, with glue and finishing nails. Square all corners. When the top, bottom, and back are completed, build the shelves and drawers as shown in the drawing.

4. Draw the door-framing strips on the door panels, allowing 1" clearance all around. Then add the shelves and facings. These facings should be flush with the frame.

5. Lay the cabinet on the floor, with the back down. Install the doors with four pin hinges. Smooth all the joints and slightly round all the corners.

6. After filling nail holes and exposed plywood edges with wood filler, smooth up the entire unit with fine sandpaper.

7. Prime the cabinet with enamel undercoat, sand lightly, and then give it at least two coats of top-grade, semi-gloss enamel.

8. Install the door bolt and cheek cork lining in the door to finish the job. Fig. 51-14(c).

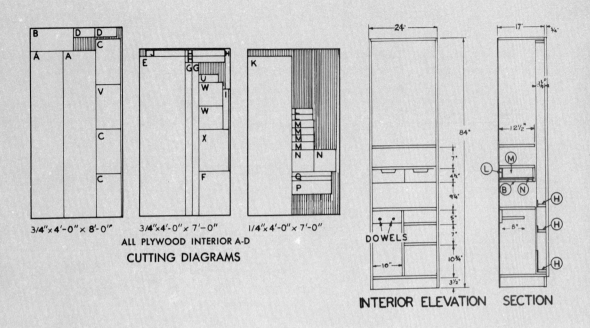

$3/4'' \times 4'-0'' \times 8'-0''$ $3/4'' \times 4'-0'' \times 7'-0''$ $1/4'' \times 4'-0'' \times 7'-0''$

ALL PLYWOOD INTERIOR A-D

CUTTING DIAGRAMS

INTERIOR ELEVATION   **SECTION**

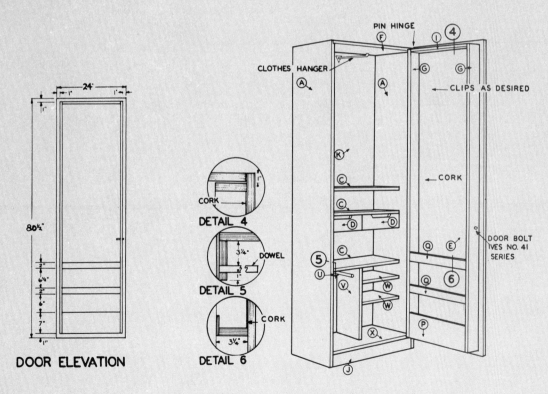

DOOR ELEVATION

DETAIL 4

DETAIL 5

DETAIL 6

51-14(c).   Drawing of cabinet.

707

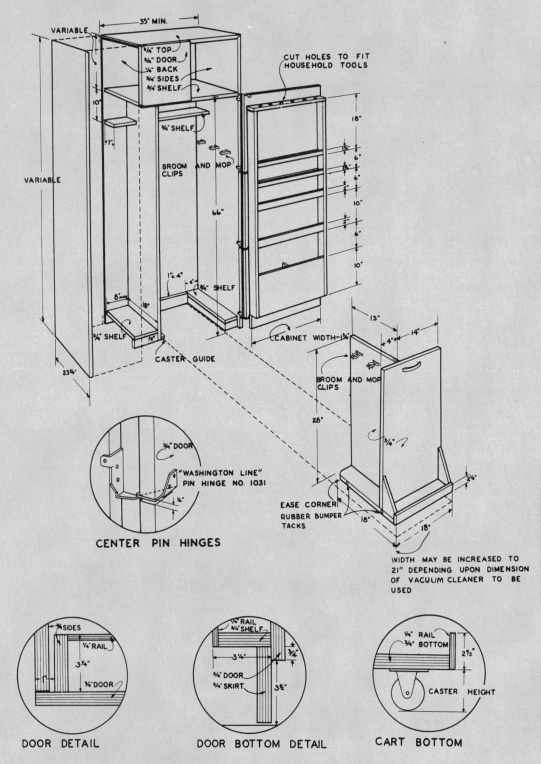

VARIABLE

35" MIN.

¾" TOP
¾" DOOR
¼" BACK
¾" SIDES
¾" SHELF

CUT HOLES TO FIT
HOUSEHOLD TOOLS

10"

¾" SHELF

7"

18"

6"

6"

VARIABLE

BROOM AND MOP
CLIPS

66"

10"

2"

6"

10"

1"x 4"

4"

¾" SHELF

8" MIN.

18"

¾" SHELF

½"

CABINET WIDTH-1¾"

13"

4"

14"

CASTER GUIDE

23¾"

BROOM AND MOP
CLIPS

¾"

¾" DOOR

28"

"WASHINGTON LINE"
PIN HINGE NO. 1031

¼"

2½"

CENTER PIN HINGES

EASE CORNER
RUBBER BUMPER
TACKS

18"

18"

WIDTH MAY BE INCREASED TO
21" DEPENDING UPON DIMENSION
OF VACUUM CLEANER TO BE
USED

¾" SIDES

¼" RAIL

3¼"

1"

¼" DOOR

¼" RAIL
¾" SHELF

¾"

3¼"

¾" DOOR

¾" SKIRT

3½"

¼" RAIL

¾" BOTTOM

2½"

CASTER HEIGHT

DOOR DETAIL

DOOR BOTTOM DETAIL

CART BOTTOM

51-15.   This utility cabinet is another illustration of simple casework made of plywood.

Hobby and Work Center

This casework piece is made of solid Idaho white pine, with hardboard used only for drawer bottoms. The idea is to design this cabinet to fit a particular-size work space or wall. Fig. 51-16(a). Designing and building a unit like this will provide experience in handling simple cabinet construction.

1. Make a drawing showing the exact dimensions of the cabinet. It can be varied in size. Make a bill of materials for all stock. Cut out the white pine stock.

2. The bottom of the cabinet consists of a case with doors and drawers. This part should be built with rabbet joints at the corners and with web or skeleton frames to serve as drawer supports which hold this part of the cabinet together. Fig. 51-16(b). Since solid lumber is used, the frames should not be glued to

51-16(a). The dimensions of this hobby center can be adapted to individual needs and the amount of space available. It is made of solid or glued-up Idaho white pine.

51-16(b). Web or skeleton frames being fastened with screws to the side of the hobby center. Note that the other pieces for the cabinet have been cut to size and are stacked in the background.

51-16(c). Assembling the top-center section of the hobby center by installing wood screws.

709

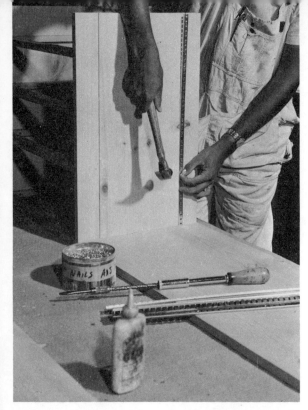

51-16(d). Installing adjustable shelf standards in the lower section of the hobby cabinet by nailing them into the grooves. Notice that the web or skeleton frames in the drawer section provide trouble-free movement of the drawers.

51-17(a). Snack bar and stools.

the sides but rather installed with wood screws. It is not necessary to dado the frames into the sides.

3. The top-center divider shelves behind the shutter doors are assembled with dado joints. The width of the dadoes is cut equal to the thickness of the shelves with a dado attachment on a circular saw. The parts are assembled with wood screws. Fig. 51-16(c).

4. Adjustable shelf standards are installed by nailing them into grooves cut into the vertical pieces. After the casework is completed, it is fastened to the wall with flathead wood screws. Fig. 51-16(d).

5. Doors and drawers should be fitted to the casework last.

Snack Bar and Stools

This basic casework is made of solid wood, plywood and hardboard. Complete directions are shown in Fig. 51-17.

PLAN OF PROCEDURE FOR THE SNACK BAR

1. Saw out front, back, and two ends of base. Miter the two front corners and assemble with glue blocks, glued and screwed in place.
2. The bottom shelf (top of base) consists of four rails and a plywood panel. Cut four rails with mitered corners and dado to receive panel, see Base Detail. Shape the outside edge of the front and end rails. Assemble with dowels and glue.
3. Cut the knotty pine paneling to length, mitering the two front corners. Each end is notched 3/4" x 2½" at back to fit the bar top.
4. Make three top rails with mitered corners and lower edges formed on the shaper. Make top back rail and fasten to the two back end panels with screws.
5. Tack front and side panels to top rail. Screw lower panel cleats to bottom edge of panels. The two front mitered corners should be glued.
6. Fasten upper bar to base with screws through lower panel cleats into the bottom shelf rails.
7. Cut the two long pilasters for the back; dowel to bar sides and top back rail.

710

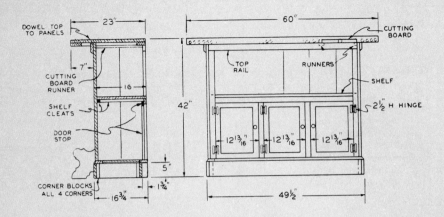

DOWEL TOP TO PANELS

23"

CUTTING BOARD RUNNER

7"

16

SHELF CLEATS

DOOR STOP

42"

CORNER BLOCKS ALL 4 CORNERS

16¾"

1¾"

5"

60"

CUTTING BOARD

TOP RAIL

RUNNERS

SHELF

2½" H HINGE

12¹³⁄₁₆" 12¹³⁄₁₆" 12¹³⁄₁₆"

49½"

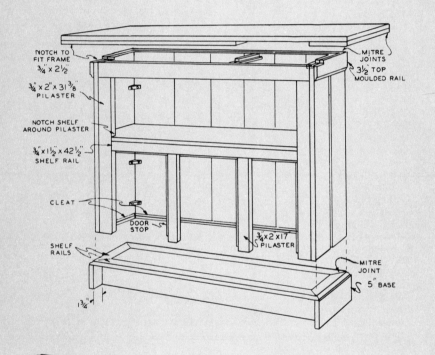

NOTCH TO FIT FRAME
¾" x 2½"

¾" x 2" x 31⅜" PILASTER

NOTCH SHELF AROUND PILASTER

¾" x 1½" x 42½" SHELF RAIL

CLEAT

DOOR STOP

SHELF RAILS

1¾"

MITRE JOINTS

3½" TOP MOULDED RAIL

¾" x 2 x 17 PILASTER

MITRE JOINT

5" BASE

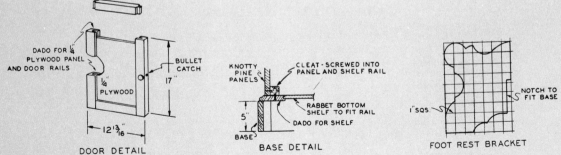

DADO FOR ¼" PLYWOOD PANEL AND DOOR RAILS

¼" PLYWOOD

BULLET CATCH

17"

12¹³⁄₁₆"

DOOR DETAIL

KNOTTY PINE PANELS

CLEAT-SCREWED INTO PANEL AND SHELF RAIL

RABBET BOTTOM SHELF TO FIT RAIL

DADO FOR SHELF

5"

BASE

BASE DETAIL

1" SQS.

NOTCH TO FIT BASE

FOOT REST BRACKET

51-17(b). Drawing for snack bar.

711

51-17(c)—BILL OF MATERIALS FOR SNACK BAR

IMPORTANT: All dimensions listed below, except for length of dowel, are FINISHED size.

No. of Pieces	Part Name	Thickness	Width	Length	Wood
1	Base Frame Front	¾″	5″	49½″	Pine
1	Base Frame Back	¾″	5″	48″	Pine
2	Base Frame Ends	¾″	5″	16¾″	Pine
2	Lower Shelf Rails	¾″	2½″	49⅜″	Pine
2	Lower Shelf Rails	¾″	2½″	16⅝″	Pine
1	Bottom Shelf Panel	¼″	12″	44¾″	Plywood
12	Knotty Pine Paneling	¾″	8″	35½″	Pine
2	Top Rail Ends	¾″	3½″	16¾″	Pine
1	Top Front Rail	¾″	3½″	49½″	Pine
1	Top Back Rail	¾″	3⅜″	46½″	Pine
2	Lower Panel Cleats	¾″	1″	14½″	Pine
1	Lower Panel Cleat	¾″	1″	48″	Pine
2	Long Pilasters	¾″	2″	31⅜″	Pine
1	Top Shelf Rail	¾″	1½″	42½″	Pine
2	Short Pilasters	¾″	2″	17″	Pine
2	Top Shelf Cleats	¾″	1″	14½″	Pine
1	Top Shelf Cleat	¾″	1″	46½″	Pine
1	Top Shelf	¾″	15¼″	46½″	Fir Plywood
1	Bar Top	¾″	23″	60″	Fir Plywood
2	Bar Top Rails	¾″	2½″	23″	Pine
2	Bar Top Rails	¾″	2½″	60″	Pine
1	Cutting Board	¾″	11″	14″	Plywood
2	Cutting Board Runners	¾″	1½″	14½″	Pine
2	Cutting Board Guides	¾″	¾″	14½″	Pine
6	Top and Bottom Door Rails	¾″	1¾″	9¹³⁄₁₆″	Pine
6	Door Side Rails	¾″	1¾″	17″	Pine
3	Door Panels	¼″	9¹³⁄₁₆″	14″	Plywood
2	Foot Rest Brackets	¾″	7″	9″	Plywood
1	Foot Rest	1¾″	Round	44″	Pine
1	Dowel	1¼″		36″	Hardwood
6	Corner Blocks	¾″	1″	3″	Hardwood

Covering material, tacks, etc.

51-17(d)—BILL OF MATERIALS FOR STOOL

IMPORTANT: All dimensions listed below, except for length of dowel, are FINISHED size.

No. of Pieces	Part Name	Thickness	Width	Length	Wood
1	Top	¾″	13″	13″	5 Ply Fir
4	Legs	¾″	6¾″	27¾″	Knotty Pine
2	Top Rails	¾″	2½″	12″	Knotty Pine
2	Foot Rails	¾″	1¾″	11″	Knotty Pine
2	Cleats	¾″	2″	8¾″	Knotty Pine
1	Dowel	⁵⁄₁₆″		36″	

No. 3 Ornamental Tacks

Upholstering and Covering Material

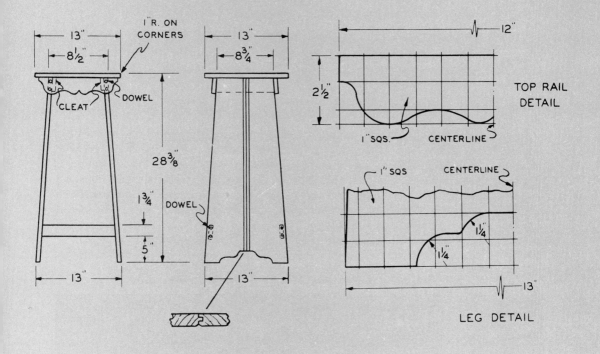

51-17(e). Drawing for stool.

8. Cut top shelf rail and short pilasters and dowel in place.
9. Fasten top shelf cleats in place with screws.
10. Saw out top shelf, notch rear corners to fit around pilasters and fasten in place with screws into the shelf cleats.
11. Cut the bar top to size. Make rails for frame on underside of top. Miter the corners and nail in place.
12. Fasten on the bar top with flathead screws, countersunk flush with the surface. Dowels may be used instead.
13. Make runners and guides for the cutting board and fasten in place.
14. Make doors as shown with tongue-and-groove joints, and dado for 1/4" plywood panels.
15. Attach door stops to the edges of the door openings opposite hinges and install doors.
16. Lay out foot rest bracket on paper, trace on stock and cut out with jig saw. Attach with screws from inside of bar.
17. Install foot rail with heavy wood screws through each foot rest bracket.
18. Cover bar top with plastic or other suitable material. Fold material over edge and tack to underside of top with ordinary tacks. Then put ornamental tacks around the edges.
19. Apply an Antique Pine finish.

Plan of Procedure for the Stool

1. Cut out the stock for the top, and round the corners to a 1" radius.
2. Make each leg by gluing together two pieces of knotty pine, using a tongue-and-groove joint chamfered on the outside edge.
3. Lay out leg scroll on paper, trace on legs and cut out with jig or band saw.
4. Glue and screw a cleat to the inside top of each leg.
5. Lay out top rail design, trace on stock and cut out.
6. Dowel and glue top rails to legs.
7. Cut foot rails to fit, dowel and glue in place.
8. Screw top to legs.
9. Lay kapok or upholsterer's moss to a depth of about 2½". Tack tapestry, plastic or other covering along bottom of one side of top. Pull covering tightly over the kapok and tack to the bottom of opposite side. Repeat on remaining sides. Pleat and tack the corners. Decorate edges with ornamental upholsterer's tacks.
10. Apply Antique Pine finish.

713

52 Fine Furniture Cabinetwork

Fine furniture cabinetwork includes chests, desks, china and other storage cabinets, radio and hi-fi cabinets, and similar furniture pieces. Fig. 52-1. Most fine furniture cabinets include drawer and door construction, shelves, and other internal cabinet details. It is difficult to describe in specific detail the construction of such pieces since each cabinet shop or furniture factory has its own distinct methods. Fig. 52-2. It is true, however, that there is a wide range of quality both in materials and construction. The experienced cabinetmaker recognizes this immediately when he studies the interior construction, doors, and drawers of a cabinet.

Many methods of construction are

52-1. This striking chest illustrates many characteristics of fine cabinetwork.

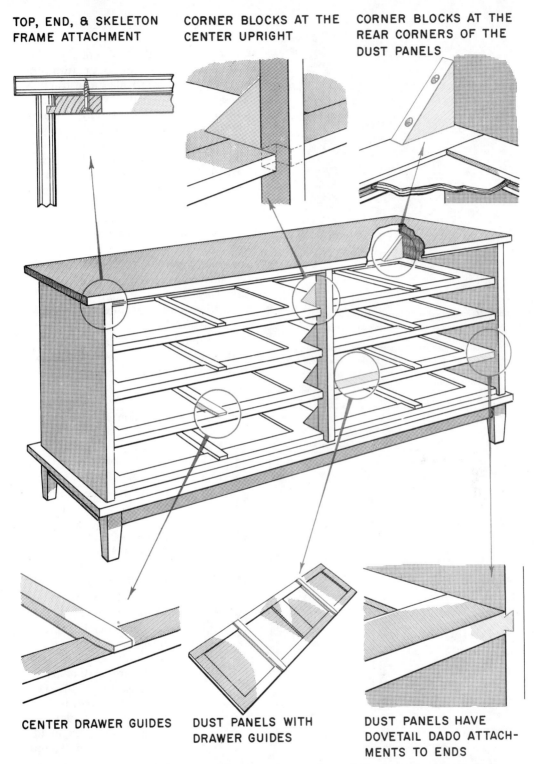

TOP, END, & SKELETON FRAME ATTACHMENT

CORNER BLOCKS AT THE CENTER UPRIGHT

CORNER BLOCKS AT THE REAR CORNERS OF THE DUST PANELS

CENTER DRAWER GUIDES

DUST PANELS WITH DRAWER GUIDES

DUST PANELS HAVE DOVETAIL DADO ATTACHMENTS TO ENDS

52-2. This drawing shows the structural features and construction methods of one manufacturer. Study the details of this well made case.

52-3(a). This Contemporary refreshment bar has a plastic-laminate top and rosewood-veneer exterior. The finest methods of construction are represented.

52-3(b). This drawing suggests very simple construction techniques for the carcass of the refreshment bar. More complicated joinery techniques were used in the unit shown in Fig. 52-3(a).

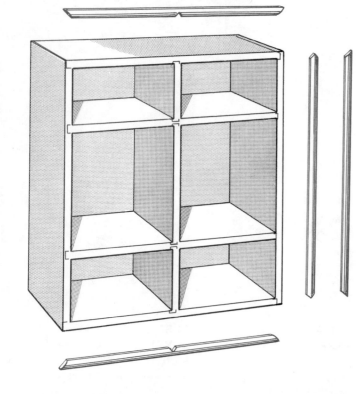

shown in this and other units of this book. Sometimes a piece of furniture shown with a particular construction method was not made by that precise method. The illustration only suggests how the product *could be* built. Fig. 52-3.

Basic casework and fine furniture cabinetwork have much in common. Both require the construction of a box or carcass that is fitted with shelves, drawers, or doors. Fine furniture cabinetwork differs from basic casework in the following ways:

• A greater variety of fine woods and plywoods is used in furniture cabinetwork. These include not only the fine native hardwoods but also exotic imported woods. Fig. 52-4.

• Many different materials, including wood, glass, ceramics, metal, cane, and fabric, are part of fine furniture cabinetwork.

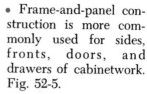

• Frame-and-panel construction is more commonly used for sides, fronts, doors, and drawers of cabinetwork. Fig. 52-5.

• Greater use is made of solid wood for legs, posts, rails, and other exposed structural parts. Legs and posts are frequently an integral part of a fine piece of furniture cabinetwork. Fig. 52-6.

• Fancy, machined surfaces, including turned and carved legs and posts, are part of many designs. Fig. 52-7. The exposed surfaces including doors and drawers often have fancy moldings, inlays, overlay, and carving.

716

52-4. This spacious but small-scaled desk has post and tapered legs with sculptured detailing. Butternut veneer accented with fine hardware in antique gold completes the rich appearance. The fronts of the top drawers are made of *violin burl*, the same rare wood used for centuries for the finest violins.

52-7. To construct an elegant French Provincial chest like this one, the furniture maker must have such equipment as the multiple-spindle carving machine and automatic shaper.

52-8. This library unit is made of selected domestic hardwoods. The chest has two doors fitted with magnetic catches and antiqued brass pulls. The hutch top has two glass doors. Notice the molded edges of the door frames and the arched top. Machines such as the molder, profile shaper, and double-end tenoner are needed for this complicated machining.

52-5. Most parts of this commode are of frame-and-panel construction.

52-6. Note that the legs of this storage lamp table are made as a part of the sides. The beautiful sculptured surfaces on the door fronts are another feature of fine cabinetmaking.

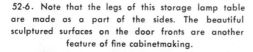

52-9. This handsome desk of walnut and pecan has a stainproof finish that will remain attractive for years.

52-10. This bedside table features original hardware made of solid milled brass with antique finish. Note the carved tulip legs and Gothic relief on the front. The table is solid pecan with veneer of koa wood.

718

52-11. The case of this storage cabinet is made of lumber-core plywood with sharp right-angle corners.

• More complicated joinery is possible, since furniture plants have many specialized pieces of equipment such as the dovetailer, profile shaper, and double-end tenoner. Fig. 52-8.

• Fine furniture finishes of a transparent type are typical. Fig. 52-9.

• Fancy hardware, many pieces of which are designed specifically for a certain style of cabinetwork, is used to enhance the beauty of furniture. Fig. 52-10.

• Plastic laminates of matching wood-grain are usually used only for the tops of tables, chests, or cabinets and rarely for the total exposed surfaces.

• Tables, chairs, beds, and other open-frame units are not considered cabinetwork even though much of the construction is the same.

TYPES OF CABINET CORNER CONSTRUCTION

Many fine pieces of cabinetwork have fine hardwood plywood for the casework, with the sides, top, and bottom joined at the corners with a lock-miter joint (or other joint of equal quality) to form a sharp right angle. Fig. 52-11. Other cabinets are constructed so that the sides overlap at top and bottom. Fig. 52-12. On this construction, the top and bottom may fit into the sides with some kind of dado joint or with dowel construction. Other fine cabinets have exactly the reverse arrangement with the top and bottom overlapping the sides.

52-12. This sideboard has the sides overlapping the top and bottom. The base is of leg-and-rail construction.

52-13(a). A high chest in which the top and bottom overlap the sides.

Fig. 52-13. With such overlapping it is sometimes common to use a web or skeleton frame to complete the inner rectangular box; then the exposed top and bottom are fitted to the frame.

TYPICAL CHESTS

The typical chest of drawers consists of a case which is divided and held together by dust panels. Such panels may be either invisible or exposed, with the front of the frame made of the same wood as the exterior of the chest. Drawers are usually fitted into the case with center guides and runners. Drawer fronts may be flush, lip, or overlay (overlap). Fig. 52-14.

LARGER CABINET PIECES

Larger pieces of furniture, particularly cases, chests, china cabinets, and buf-

52-13(b). This drawing *suggests* the materials and construction that could be applied to any chest of this type.

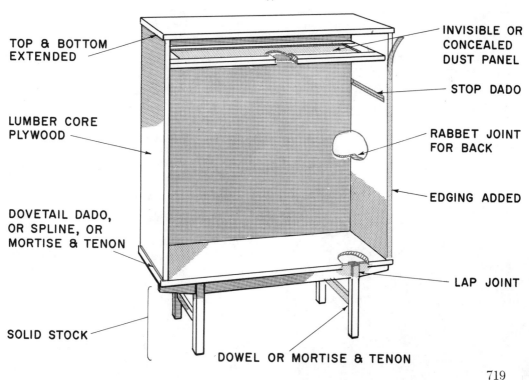

TOP & BOTTOM EXTENDED

INVISIBLE OR CONCEALED DUST PANEL

STOP DADO

LUMBER CORE PLYWOOD

RABBET JOINT FOR BACK

EDGING ADDED

DOVETAIL DADO, OR SPLINE, OR MORTISE & TENON

LAP JOINT

SOLID STOCK

DOWEL OR MORTISE & TENON

52-14(a). A unit with flush drawers. Notice that the legs are a structural part of the sides (ends).

52-14(b). Lip drawers are usually found on Early American pieces such as this double dresser.

52-14(c). This eight-drawer walnut chest has a natural oil finish. The base has a sculptured detail that continues upwards, outlining the sides of the chest.

fets, consist of two, three or four separate and distinct structural parts that are constructed separately and then fastened together with cleats, glue blocks, corner blocks, and screws. Fig. 52-15. These structural parts include the following:

Base Unit

The base unit, which is the lowest part of cabinetwork, may be one of the following:

• *Legs* attached directly to the lower casework or carcass. These may be shop-made or commercial in Contemporary, Early American, Traditional, or Provincial style to match the cabinetwork. Fig. 52-16.

• *Leg-and-rail construction,* similar to the bottom of a table or chair. Fig. 52-12.

720

52-15(a). This large buffet is constructed of several units with a plinth base.

52-16. Straight, square commercial legs are attached to this handsome office cabinet.

52-15(b). This simplified drawing shows how a large buffet or china cabinet could consist of four distinct structural parts.

52-17(a). This stereo hi-fi cabinet has a plinth base.

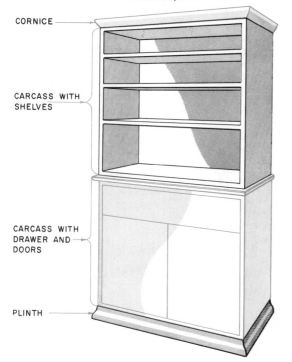

CORNICE

CARCASS WITH SHELVES

CARCASS WITH DRAWER AND DOORS

PLINTH

LOCATION OF COMPONENTS

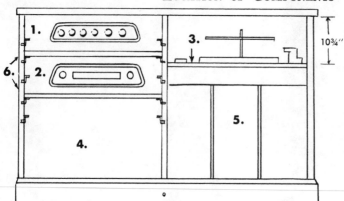

(1) Amplifier compartment

(2) Tuner compartment

(3) Changer mounting panel

(4) Area for storage, power amplifier, or tape deck

(5) Record storage with removable dividers

(6) Adjustable shelves for tuner and amplifier

52-17(b). Location of components in the stereo hi-fi cabinet.

A *plinth* or an *enclosed base*. Fig. 52-17. The plinth should be from 2″ to 4″ high, depending on the size of the furniture piece. Sometimes the front is set back a few inches from the lower case to protect against shoe marks. Fig. 52-18. Some plinths are recessed on all sides. There are many ways to make a plinth but the common one is to build a simple, hollow, rectangular frame. Usually a spline-miter-corner joint is used and a corner block added for greater strength. Fig. 52-19. The plinth is usually attached to the lower casework or cabinet, with cleats on all four interior surfaces.

Lower Case or Cabinet Unit

This case or cabinet usually consists of a carcass fitted with doors, drawers, shelves, or other interior details.

Upper Case or Cabinet Unit

This case or cabinet usually consists of shelves, doors, and sometimes one or more drawers. Glass doors, in wood frames or of the sliding type, are often installed.

Cornice

The uppermost part of the unit is called the *cornice*. This may be anything

52-18. A recessed plinth has been built on this wood-and-plastic-laminate filing cabinet. A recessed plinth is standard on pieces of this kind.

52-19. Typical plinth construction. Many other kinds of corner joints could be used.

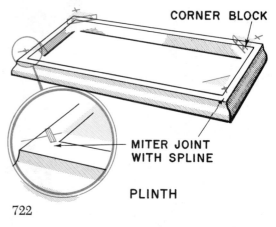

CORNER BLOCK

MITER JOINT WITH SPLINE

PLINTH

from a simple molding to an extremely complicated rectangular unit consisting of several highly decorated parts.

Server and China Top

The pieces shown in Fig. 52-20 are typical of fine furniture cabinetwork that can be built in a school or small cabinet shop. The base unit is of leg-and-rail construction, and the lower case is a chest of drawers; the upper case is a china cabinet with one drawer and sliding glass doors.

While this chest is of modern design with a bleached oak finish, the styling could be changed by making certain modifications. For example, to give it a traditional styling, cherry or walnut could be selected for the wood. Then cabriole legs could be used on the base unit. The front of the drawers could be simplified and traditional decorative hardware added. Decorative molding could also be used on the drawer fronts and the top of the china cabinet.

PLAN OF PROCEDURE FOR
BUILDING SERVER SECTION

1. Cut side panels and all frame members to size on circular saw.
2. Cut tongue-and-groove joints in frame members. Dado the edges for dust bottoms on a circular saw.
3. Glue and assemble all frames.
4. Set up dado head for 3/8" x 3/8" cut and stop-dado sides for top and bottom frames. Rabbet ends of these frames with same dado setting.
5. Change dado head for 3/4" x 3/8" cut, and cut stop-dadoes in side pieces for drawer frames.
6. Rabbet back edge of sides for back panel, using a jointer or circular saw.
7. Rabbet inside surface of sides for 1/8" x 1 9/16" facing and glue facing into place. Trim facing for top and bottom stop-dadoes.
8. Drill and countersink screw shank holes in top frame.
9. Bore 3/4" dowel holes thru bottom frame for legs.
10. Glue and assemble sides and frames.
11. Cut legs to size and bore 3/4" holes for rungs and dowels. Cut tapers with circular

52-20(a). Server with china top.

saw taper jig. Round corners. Cut rungs and dowels to length. Make wedges. Glue rungs into legs. Set case on leg assembly. Glue and wedge dowels into place.

12. Check drawer dimensions and cut all pieces to size on circular saw. (Note: Back of drawer is made narrower than front for smooth operation. Also, note that drawer fronts on top three drawers project below drawer sides. This prevents drawer sides from sliding on drawer pulls when drawers are opened and closed.)
13. Set up dado head and cut tongue and rabbet on ends of all drawer fronts. Dado both ends of drawer sides. Groove all drawer members to receive bottoms. Groove drawer fronts for drawer pulls. Notch drawer backs for drawer guides.
14. Assemble all drawers with glue and wire brads. On three bottom drawers trim off the tongue on drawer fronts that project above the drawer sides.
15. Make drawer pulls. Cut 4 pieces of stock 3/4" x 1" x 37". Rabbet top edge of each piece on jointer. Shape front contour with cutter on shaper or drill press shaper attachment. Shape bottom contour with
(Continued on page 726)

723

DRAWER NO.	A	B	C	D
1	5	$4\frac{13}{16}$	$4\frac{11}{16}$	$\frac{1}{8}$
2	6	$5\frac{3}{16}$	$5\frac{1}{16}$	$\frac{1}{8}$
3	6	$5\frac{3}{16}$	$5\frac{1}{16}$	$\frac{1}{8}$
4	$6\frac{1}{2}$	$5\frac{13}{16}$	$5\frac{11}{16}$	0

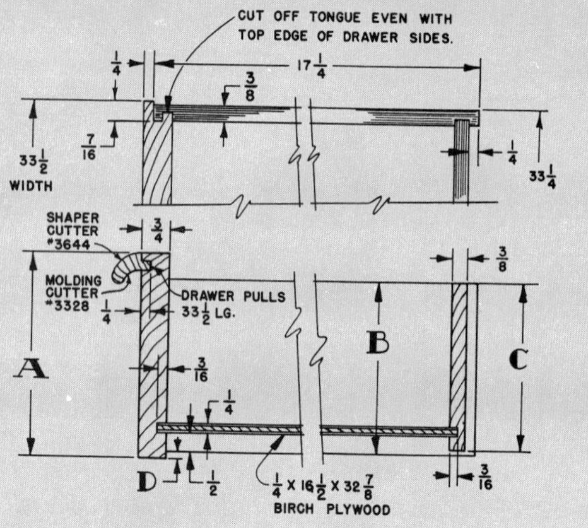

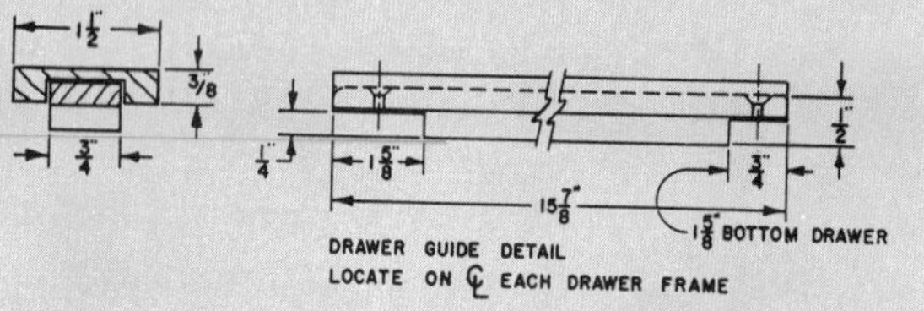

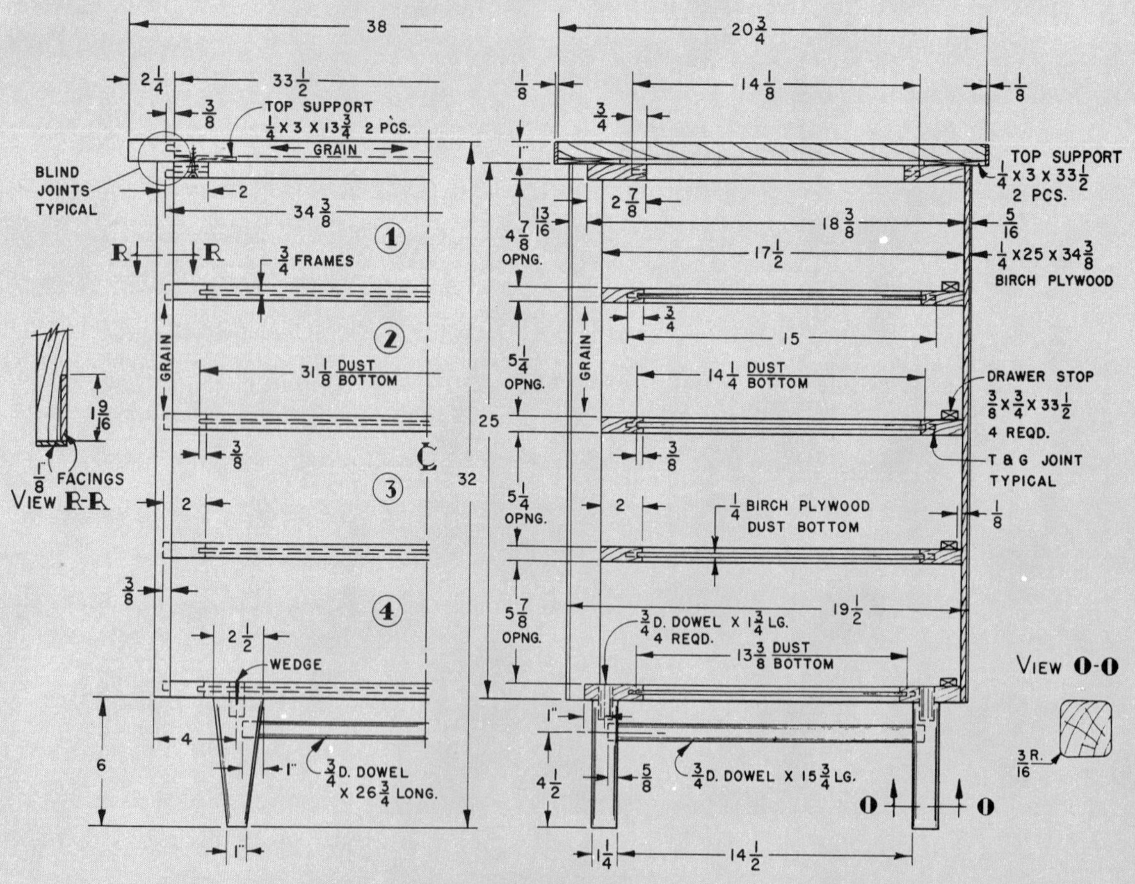

52-20(b). Drawing of the server.

52-20(c)—BILL OF MATERIALS FOR THE SERVER

IMPORTANT: All dimensions listed below are FINISHED size.

No. of Pieces	Part Name	Thickness	Width	Length	Material
1	Top	¾″	20¾″	34¼″	Comb Grain White Oak Plywood S1S
2	Ends	¾″	19⅜″	25″	Comb Grain White Oak Plywood S1S
1	Drawer Front	¾″	5″	33½″	Comb Grain White Oak Plywood S1S
2	Drawer Fronts	¾″	6″	33½″	Comb Grain White Oak Plywood S1S
1	Drawer Front	¾″	6½″	33½″	Comb Grain White Oak Plywood SIS
2	Top and Bottom Frames—Front	¾″	2⅞″	34⅜″	Solid White Oak
2	Top and Bottom Frames—Backs	¾″	2⅞″	34⅜″	Hardwood
4	Top and Bottom Frames—Ends	¾″	2″	14⅛″	Hardwood
6	Drawer Frames	¾″	2″	34⅜″	Hardwood
6	Drawer Frames	¾″	2″	15″	Hardwood
2	Drawer Sides	⅜″	4¹³⁄₁₆″	17¼″	Solid Oak
4	Drawer Sides	⅜″	5³⁄₁₆″	17¼″	Solid Oak
2	Drawer Sides	⅜″	5¹³⁄₁₆″	17¼″	Solid Oak
1	Drawer Back	⅜″	4¹¹⁄₁₆″	32⅞″	Solid Oak
2	Drawer Backs	⅜″	5¹⁄₁₆″	32⅞″	Solid Oak
1	Drawer Back	⅜″	5¹¹⁄₁₆″	32⅞″	Solid Oak
4	Drawer Bottoms	¼″	16½″	32⅞″	Birch Plywood S1S
1	Dust Bottom	¼″	13⅜″	31⅛″	Birch Plywood S1S
3	Dust Bottoms	¼″	14¼″	31⅛″	Birch Plywood S1S
2	Top End Cleats	1″	2¼″	21″	Solid White Oak
4	Legs	1¼″	2½″	6″	Solid White Oak
2	Rungs	¾″ dia.		26¾″	White Oak Dowel
2	Rungs	¾″ dia.		15¾″	White Oak Dowel
4	Dowels	¾″ dia.		1¾″	Hardwood
4	Drawer Pulls	¾″	1″	33½″	Solid White Oak
2	Top Facings	⅛″	1″	33½″	Solid White Oak
2	Side Facings	⅛″	¾″	25″	Solid White Oak
2	Side Surface Facings	⅛″	1⁹⁄₁₆″	25″	Solid White Oak
2	Top Supports	¼″	3″	33½″	Birch Plywood
2	Top Supports	¼″	3″	13¾″	Birch Plywood
1	Back Panel	¼″	25″	34⅜″	Birch Plywood
4	Drawer Guides	½″	¾″	15⅞″	Hardwood
4	Drawer Slides	⅜″	1½″	15⅞″	Hardwood
4	Wedges	0″-⅛″	¾″	¾″	Hardwood
4	Drawer Stops	⅜″	¾″	33½″	Hardwood
10	No. 10 x 1½″ F. H. Wood Screws				
	No. 16 x 1¼″ Wire Brads				
6	No. 6 x ¾″ F. H. Wood Screws				

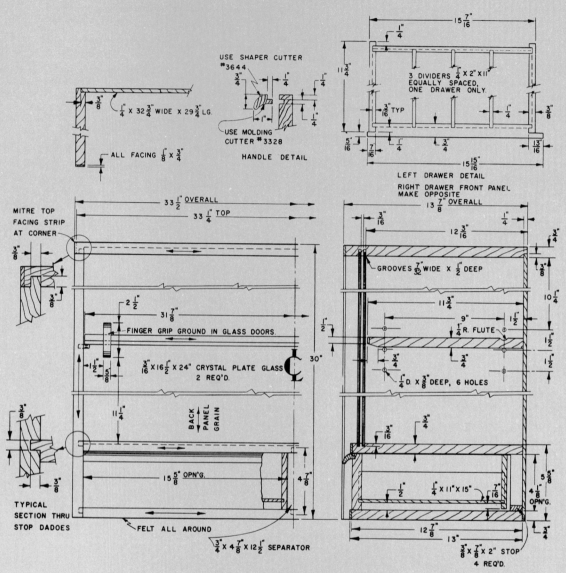

52-20(d). Drawing of the china top.

Procedure for Building Server Section *(Continued from page 723)*

(Continued from page 723)

moulding cutter on circular saw. (For safety, stop cut about 3″ from end.) Cut pulls to length on circular saw and glue into place.

16. Make up center drawer guides, and drawer stops, and install.

17. Cut, fit and nail back panel into place.

18. Cut top end cleats to size. Either cut stop groove or cut groove thru and then inlay end grain for blind tenon.

19. Cut top to size and cut tenon on ends on circular saw. Trim tenons off for blind tenon.

20. Glue cleats in place.

21. Cut and glue top supports in place.

22. Cut all edge facing strips to size and glue in place.

23. Attach top with F.H. wood screws.

24. Finish sand entire project.

25. Apply oak finish.

52-20(e) — Bill of Materials for the China Top

IMPORTANT: All dimensions listed below are FINISHED size.

No. of Pieces	Part Name	Thickness	Width	Length	Material
2	Sides	3/4″	13¾″	29⅝″	Comb Grain White Oak Plywood—S2S
1	Top	3/4″	13¾″	33¼″	Comb Grain White Oak Plywood—S2S
1	Adjustable Shelf	3/4″	11⅝″	31⅞″	Comb Grain White Oak Plywood—S2S
1	Bottom Shelf	3/4″	12⅞″	32¾″	Comb Grain White Oak Plywood—S1S
1	Bottom	3/4″	12⅞″	32¾″	Fir Plywood—S2S
1	Back Panel	1/4″	32¾″	29⅝″	Comb Grain White Oak Plywood—S1S
2	Drawer Fronts	3/4″	4 1/16″	15 15/16″	Comb Grain White Oak Plywood—S1S
4	Drawer Sides	3/8″	4 1/16″	11¾″	Solid Oak
2	Drawer Backs	3/8″	4″	15 1/16″	Solid Oak
3	Drawer Dividers	1/4″	2″	11″	Solid Oak
2	Drawer Pulls	3/4″	1″	15 15/16″	Solid Oak
1	Facing—Top	1/8″	3/4″	33½″	Solid Oak
2	Facings—Top	1/8″	3/4″	13⅞″	Solid Oak
2	Facings—Sides	1/8″	3/4″	29¼″	Solid Oak
2	Facings—Bottom	1/8″	3/4″	32″	Solid Oak
1	Facing—Shelf	1/8″	3/4″	31⅞″	Solid Oak
2	Drawer Bottoms	1/4″	11″	15 1/16″	Birch Plywood—S1S
4	Drawer Stops	3/8″	7/8″	2″	Hardwood
1	Drawer Separator	3/4″	12½″	4⅞″	Fir Plywood—S2S
4	Shelf Sup. Pegs	1/4″ dia.		7/8″	Dowel
2	Sliding Doors	3/16″	16½″	24″	Crystal Plate Glass
1	Felt		13⅞″	33½″	
	No. 16 x 1¼″ Wire Nails				

Plan of Procedure for Building China Top

1. Cut all case members to size on circular saw.
2. With 3/8″ wide dado head on circular saw cut stop dadoes in sides to receive bottom and bottom shelf. Also cut dado on ends of top. Cut stop dadoes in case bottom and bottom shelf for drawer separator. With the 3/8″ dado setting, cut rabbets on top edges of sides and ends of case bottom, bottom shelf, and also the drawer separator.
3. Set up dado head to make 7/32″ wide cut. Groove top and bottom shelf for glass doors.
4. On a jointer cut rabbets on back edge of top and on sides pieces, for recessing back panel.
5. Drill 1/4″ holes 1/2″ deep in sides for shelf support pins.
6. Smooth pieces with sandpaper.
7. Assemble case with clamps and check for squareness.
8. Assemble case with glue.
9. Cut adjustable shelf to size on circular saw. Groove shelf with flute cutter.
10. Cut facing strips and glue in place.
11. Check drawer dimensions and cut all pieces to size on circular saw.
12. Set up dado head and cut necessary dadoes and grooves in drawer parts.

13. Set up 1/4" router on drill press and rout front and back of one drawer for drawer dividers.
14. Assemble drawers with glue and wire brads.
15. Make drawer pulls. Cut one piece of stock 3/4" x 1" x 36". Rabbet top edge on jointer. Shape front contour with cutter on shaper or drill press shaper attachment. Shape bottom contour with moulding cutter on circular saw. (For safety, stop cuts approximately 3" from end.) Cut pulls to length on circular saw.
16. Glue drawer pulls in place.
17. Set saw arbor to proper angle and cut 1/4" x 3/4" chamfer on front of adjustable shelf.
18. Cut and fit back panel, but do not install.
19. Finish sand entire project.
20. Apply oak finish.
21. Make four shelf support pins from 1/4" dowel.
22. Install back panel with No. 18 x 1" wire nails.
23. Cement felt to entire bottom of cabinet.
24. Have sliding glass doors made at your glass dealer's.

53   Kitchen Cabinets

Kitchen cabinets constitute one of the major areas of cabinetmaking. The chief purpose of kitchen cabinetry is to provide functional storage and work convenience. Fig. 53-1. It is for this reason that cabinets must be carefully planned and well built. Functional kitchen cabinets must be adaptable to changing conditions. They must be built to take care of all different kinds of appliances. The interiors must be suitable for storing various sizes and shapes of dishes, silverware, packaged and canned goods, and hundreds of other items. Fig. 53-2. All

53-1(a). An adaptable, functional, energy-saving kitchen is essential to the well designed home.

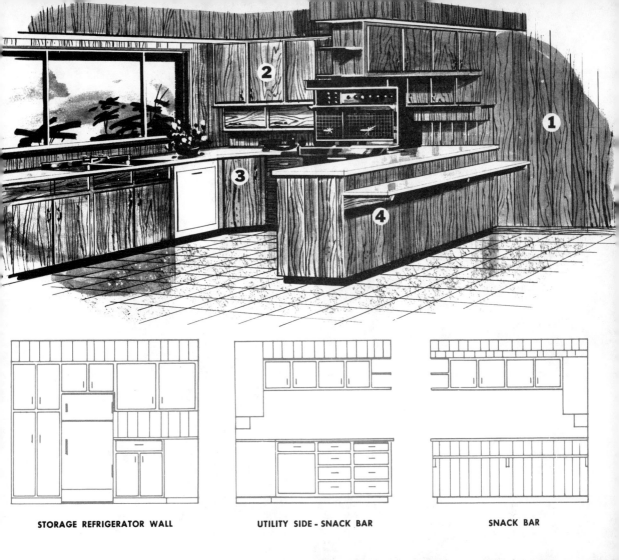

STORAGE REFRIGERATOR WALL

UTILITY SIDE · SNACK BAR

SNACK BAR

53-1(b). This kitchen includes many excellent features: new valance lighting, set-in lazy Susan, built-in snack bar and hardwood paneling that resists cooking grease, stains and fingermarks. The materials used include: 1. Hardwood wall panels with V grooves. 2. Cabinets of hardwood plywood with particle board cores. 3. Hardboard drawer bottoms and cabinet backs. 4. Fir plywood drawer and cabinet sides, shelving, and counter tops.

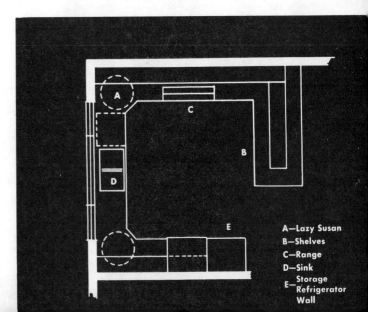

A—Lazy Susan
B—Shelves
C—Range
D—Sink
E—Storage Refrigerator Wall

53-2(a). Adjustable shelves are very useful in a kitchen cabinet.

53-2(b). This swing-away shelf unit is another example of convenience in a kitchen. It brings utensils out where they are easy to reach. It is also easy to clean.

53-3. This finish carpenter is fitting a lip door to a cabinet.

53-4. Inspecting a base cabinet unit as it moves along the assembly line.

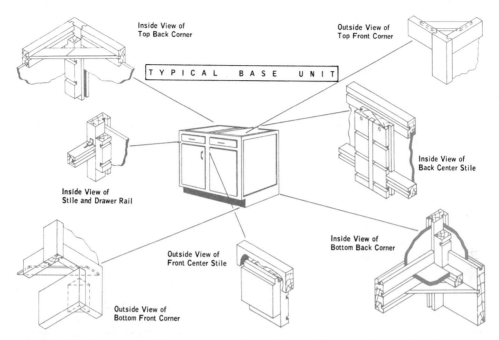

Inside View of
Top Back Corner

Outside View of
Top Front Corner

TYPICAL BASE UNIT

Inside View of
Back Center Stile

Inside View of
Stile and Drawer Rail

Outside View of
Front Center Stile

Inside View of
Bottom Back Corner

Outside View of
Bottom Front Corner

53-5(a). This shows the typical base construction of one kitchen-cabinet manufacturer. All units are constructed of kiln-dried hardwood and hardwood plywood. All joints are mortised and tenoned. Stiles and rails for frame-and-panel construction are of maple. All corners are reinforced with glue blocks driven into the grooves of the adjacent rails. Plywood bottoms are recessed into the back rails, and the fronts are supported so the top surfaces are flush with the front rails (faceplates). The plywood back panel is fitted into grooves on all sides. Toe space is 3″ deep and 4″ high.

cabinetmakers and finish carpenters need to have a thorough understanding of every aspect of kitchen planning and cabinetry.

METHODS OF PRODUCING KITCHEN CABINETRY

There are three basic ways in which kitchen cabinets are produced. Many are built on the construction site by a craftsman. Fig. 53-3. He builds them piece by piece from the detail elevations and floor plans supplied by the architect. The design of the home, whether it is Contemporary, Early American, or Traditional, may influence to some extent the design of the cabinets. In general, however, their construction is relatively simple, and the assembly is with glue and nails. Primar-

ily, cabinetmakers use softwood or hardwood plywood, with solid wood for facings and perhaps for drawer fronts and sides. Usually the cabinets have either flush or lip doors and drawers. Such on-the-job construction is on the decline because shop- or factory-built units are usually of better quality and often less expensive.

The second method is to purchase mill-made kitchen cabinets in a knocked down condition. The craftsman then assembles the parts and installs the cabinets. These usually have medium-quality joinery with perhaps a lock joint on the drawers. Most parts are nailed or stapled together. Fig. 53-4.

The third basic method is to purchase kitchen cabinets that are mass produced

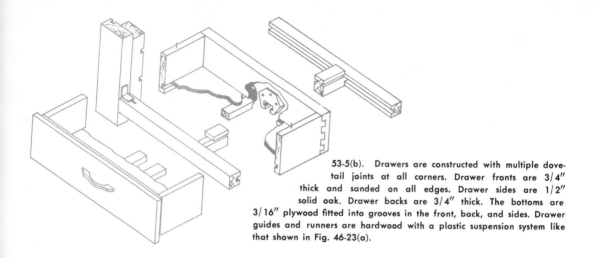

53-5(b). Drawers are constructed with multiple dovetail joints at all corners. Drawer fronts are 3/4" thick and sanded on all edges. Drawer sides are 1/2" solid oak. Drawer backs are 3/4" thick. The bottoms are 3/16" plywood fitted into grooves in the front, back, and sides. Drawer guides and runners are hardwood with a plastic suspension system like that shown in Fig. 46-23(a).

in shops and factories. The quality of such cabinets varies widely. The least expensive are only slightly better than those built on the job, but the best are of a quality equal to the finest furniture. Highest-grade kitchen cabinets have exactly the same standards of construction, materials, and workmanship as do top-quality furniture cabinets or chests of drawers. The use of production equipment makes it possible for manufactured kitchen cabinets to have such features as all lumber-core-plywood construction, complicated joinery such as multiple dovetail joints on fronts and backs of drawers, commercial drawer guides, and the finest finishes. Fig. 53-5. Such kitchen cabinets come in a wide range of designs similar to those found in other fine furniture. Fig. 53-6 (a) and (b). Some manufacturers use the same basic cabinets for all designs, adding moldings, trim, hardware, and finish to achieve styling. Fig. 53-7.

53-6(a). A bright kitchen of Early American design.

53-6(b).   The cabinet trim and hardware give this kitchen its Traditional appearance.

53-7(a).   The same basic unit can be changed by adding wood molding and different hardware:
(a) Basic. (b) Traditional molding. (c) Colonial molding.

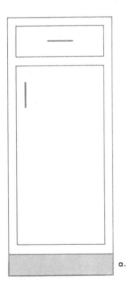

a.

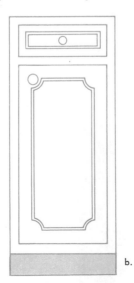

b.

c.

53-7(b). Another way of changing the appearance of cabinets is to use variously shaped machined blocks of wood as an added decoration. These are glued to the fronts of doors and drawers.

53-8(a). Standard base unit.

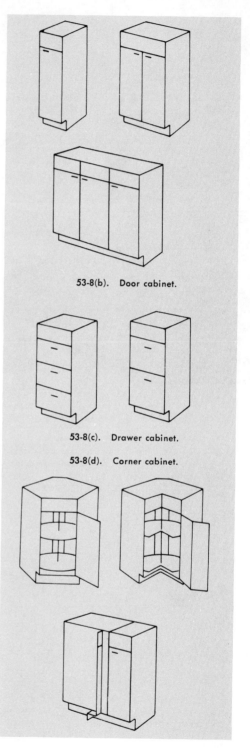

53-8(b). Door cabinet.

53-8(c). Drawer cabinet.

53-8(d). Corner cabinet.

53-9(a). Standard wall cabinet.

KINDS OF CABINETS

Four basic kinds of cabinets are used in the completed kitchen: base unit, wall unit, tall unit, and special-purpose unit. The base cabinet is the basic storage section of every kitchen. Fig. 53-8. It is designed with drawers, doors, shelves, and

pull outs for a wide variety of storage. It performs more functions than the wall unit or any special-purpose unit, and is used for both storage and work surface. Pots and pans, serving dishes, food staples, and cleaning supplies are usually kept in it. The drawers hold silverware, utensils, and linen. The top of the base cabinet, which is usually covered with plastic laminate, is used for food preparation and for at least a part of the after-meal clean-up. A good base unit must be extremely sturdy, with no sticking doors or drawers, loose hardware, or sagging doors. The base unit should always be designed with a recessed toe board.

Wall units are hung above the counter top, usually for storage of dinnerware, glassware, and serving dishes. Fig. 53-9. Certain food staples are also stored there. The well designed wall unit has flexible shelving to accommodate materials that

53-9(b). Wall cabinets. (a) Standard. (b) Over-appliance. (c) Combination. (d) Corner.

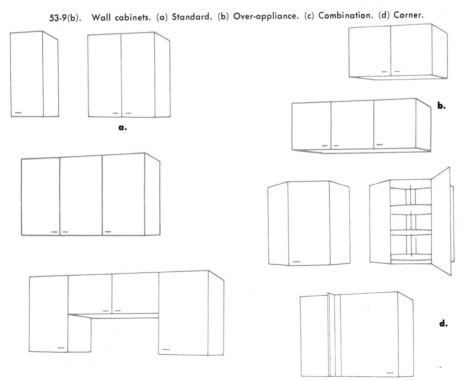

a.

b.

c.

d.

53-10(a). Tall cabinet unit for oven.

53-10(b). For storage.

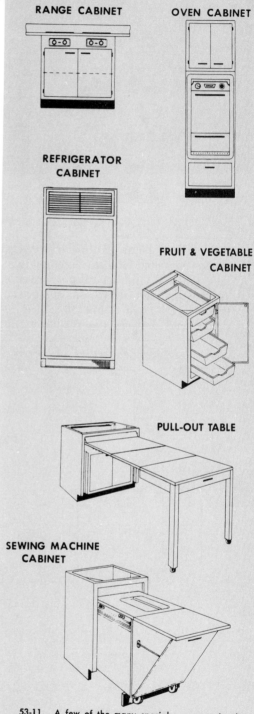

RANGE CABINET

OVEN CABINET

REFRIGERATOR CABINET

FRUIT & VEGETABLE CABINET

PULL-OUT TABLE

SEWING MACHINE CABINET

53-11. A few of the many special-purpose units that are available.

vary widely in size and shape. Fixed shelving is not flexible enough for most wall units. Plates, cups, and saucers frequently take more than their share of overhead space in the ordinary cupboard.

Tall units are designed for many purposes. The basic storage unit usually has shelves for dishes, linens, packaged goods, and cleaning supplies. Some tall units also have cabinet drawers at top or bottom. Fig. 53-10.

In addition to these three basic cabinets there are many special designs such as the desk unit, sink cabinet, stove-and-oven cabinet, and pull-out table. Fig. 53-11. Various doors are available. Fig. 53-12.

PLANNING THE KITCHEN LAYOUT AND CABINETS

It is usually the responsibility of the architect to plan the kitchen layout and to design the general appearance of the kitchen cabinets for a new home. The specifications will indicate whether the cabinets are to be built on the home site or purchased as manufactured units and then installed. The responsibility of the finish carpenter or cabinetmaker is much greater if the kitchen cabinets are to be built on the site since even the detail elevation of the kitchen cabinets does not indicate specific construction details for the cabinet interiors. Results can be poor if the cabinetmaker does not know what is needed for an efficient kitchen. The finish carpenter or cabinetmaker has even greater responsibility when it comes to remodeling a kitchen. Frequently no architect is involved and the craftsman himself must measure the kitchen carefully and make the new layout for it. He must decide whether the cabinets should be built on the job, purchased knocked down, or purchased already assembled.

To plan a new kitchen, first make a careful layout of the existing area, as follows: Measure the kitchen carefully, taking the measurements 36″ from the floor. This is the line of the counter tops which must fit snugly to the wall. Draw the old kitchen layout to scale on 1/4″ squared paper. Fig. 53-13. Start from any corner and continue around the entire room using the sample layout at right as guide. Be sure to show location and measurements of windows and doors (including trim), as well as obstructions such as pipes, radiators, chimneys, flues, and stairways. Indicate where doors lead. Show the location of plumbing. If the new kitchen is to be enlarged to include a second room, such as pantry or breakfast nook, show this area on the floor plan. Indicate any partitions, windows, or other features that can be eliminated

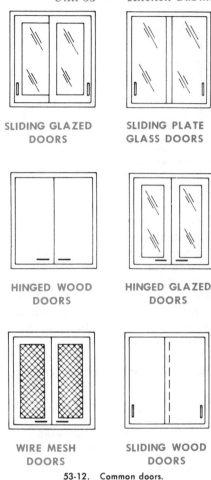

SLIDING GLAZED DOORS

SLIDING PLATE GLASS DOORS

HINGED WOOD DOORS

HINGED GLAZED DOORS

WIRE MESH DOORS

SLIDING WOOD DOORS

53-12. Common doors.

53-13. Sample of the measurements needed when planning a kitchen.

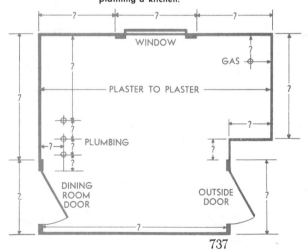

737

windows

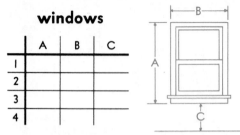

	A	B	C
1			
2			
3			
4			

53-14. Measure all windows and doors and record the information about them. For the doors, measure the height and width and make another list like this one.

or moved. Show all present appliances and built-ins that will continue to be in use. Number the windows and doors shown on the floor plan and give their dimensions. Fig. 53-14. *Measurements must be correct to 1/8".* To check the accuracy of individual measurements, measure the total length of each wall, plaster to plaster.

Once the layout is complete, standard units from a particular line of manufac-

turer's cabinets can be fitted into the available space. Several arrangements can be suggested. If cabinets are to be built in, a detail floor plan and elevations should be drawn.

KITCHEN ARRANGEMENTS

Although the ways to arrange a kitchen may seem countless, there are three basic arrangements from which most kitchens are adapted. The advantages and disadvantages of each arrangement, as well as the space available, largely determine the choice of plan.

The *parallel-wall, two-wall,* or *pullman* kitchen is frequently found in small homes in which the eating area is not included in the kitchen. Fig. 53-15. At least 4'6" to 5'4" is needed between the facing equipment for two people to work and pass by each other. The doors are located in such a way that a major traffic lane does not go through the working area. Whenever possible, the refrigerator

53-15. A typical arrangement of units in a parallel-wall kitchen. Many other arrangements are possible.

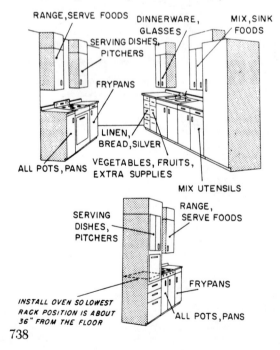

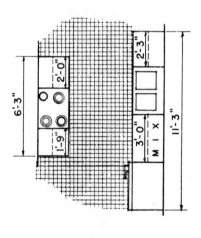

IF YOU CHOOSE A WALL OVEN AND SURFACE COOKING UNIT, MAKE THESE CHANGES.

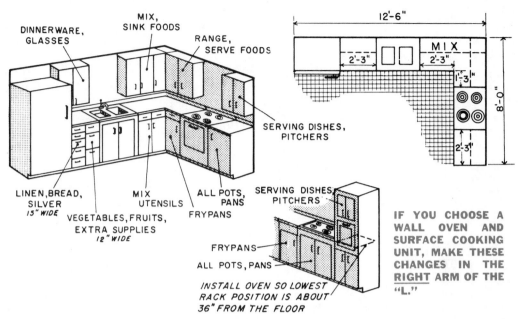

DINNERWARE, GLASSES

MIX, SINK FOODS

RANGE, SERVE FOODS

12'-6"

2'-3"   MIX   2'-3"

8'-0"

2'-3"

SERVING DISHES, PITCHERS

LINEN, BREAD, SILVER
15" WIDE

MIX UTENSILS

VEGETABLES, FRUITS, EXTRA SUPPLIES
12" WIDE

ALL POTS, PANS
FRYPANS

SERVING DISHES, PITCHERS

FRYPANS

ALL POTS, PANS

IF YOU CHOOSE A WALL OVEN AND SURFACE COOKING UNIT, MAKE THESE CHANGES IN THE RIGHT ARM OF THE "L."

INSTALL OVEN SO LOWEST RACK POSITION IS ABOUT 36" FROM THE FLOOR

53-16(a). The L-shaped kitchen makes possible many arrangements of individual cabinet units.

and oven are situated so they do not open across a doorway.

A second popular design is the *L-shaped kitchen.* This can be designed with eating facilities in the kitchen. Fig. 53-16. The width of each work area is based on the recommended counter widths and the cabinet space needed above and below the counter.

The third basic arrangement is the *U-shaped kitchen.* Fig. 53-17. In this arrangement, again, at least 4'6" to 5'4" is needed between facing counters and equipment. Either the sink or the stove can be located in the center of the U.

In designing all three types of kitchens, specific clearances and counter widths must be taken into consideration. It must be remembered that counter areas between equipment can often serve two purposes. For instance, a counter mixing center next to a sink can also be used for stacking dishes. These are the standards that should be followed:

• When the mixing center extends into

the corner, the arm of the counter next to the sink should provide 24" to 36" of flat surface.

• When the cabinet is between two pieces of equipment, provide 36" to 42" for the mixing surface.

• Provide 12" to 24" on both sides of the surface cooking area.

• Provide 18" to 36" of counter to the left and 24" to 36" to the right of

53-16(b). Typical layout for an L-shaped kitchen.

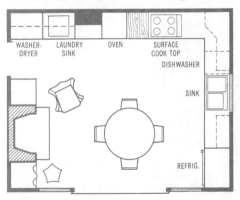

WASHER-DRYER   LAUNDRY SINK   OVEN   SURFACE COOK TOP

DISHWASHER

SINK

REFRIG.

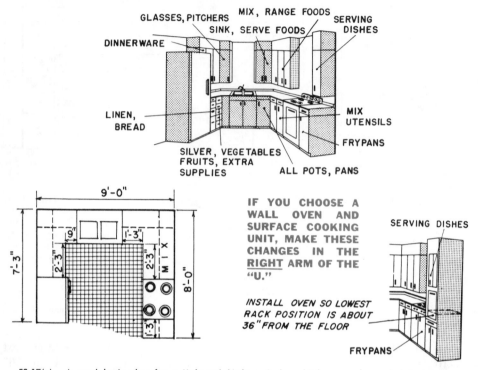

IF YOU CHOOSE A WALL OVEN AND SURFACE COOKING UNIT, MAKE THESE CHANGES IN THE <u>RIGHT</u> ARM OF THE "U."

INSTALL OVEN SO LOWEST RACK POSITION IS ABOUT 36" FROM THE FLOOR

53-17(a). A good basic plan for a U-shaped kitchen. Such a kitchen can be varied in many ways.

53-17(b). This U-shaped kitchen has a cooking island in the center.

the sink. If there is a dishwasher, allow 24″ for it, either to the left or right of the sink.

Provide at least 16″ of clearance between the latch side of the refrigerator and the turn of the counter. Provide counter space near the refrigerator for foods taken from it.

Provide at least 14″ of clearance between the center of the sink bowl and the turn of the counter for standing.

Provide at least 14″ of clearance between the center of the front unit or burner and the turn of the counter for standing.

Provide at least 16″ of clearance between the center of the front unit or burner and a wall or high equipment unit, and between the center front of a wall oven and the adjoining wall.

Shelf Spacing and Drawer Depth

Wall cabinets are usually built from 12″ to 14″ deep, although 12″ is considered standard. If the clearance between

53-17(c). Another example of the U-shaped kitchen. This one has a separate breakfast area.

53-18. Shelf spacing for wall cabinets.

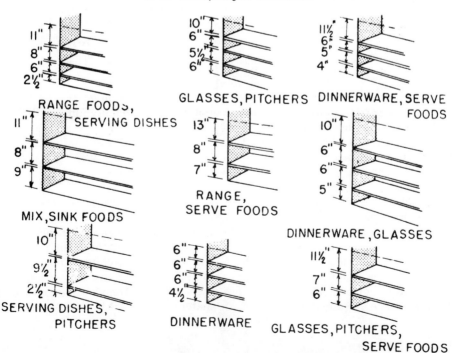

RANGE FOODS, SERVING DISHES

GLASSES, PITCHERS

DINNERWARE, SERVE FOODS

MIX, SINK FOODS

RANGE, SERVE FOODS

DINNERWARE, GLASSES

SERVING DISHES, PITCHERS

DINNERWARE

GLASSES, PITCHERS, SERVE FOODS

741

Mix foods
3 canisters (flour, sugar, meal)
1 each, cake flour, cornstarch, raisins, salt, cocoa, soda, dessert mix, vinegar, sirup, shortening, baking powder
2 sugars
3 flavorings
5 spices

Range foods
1 coffee, 1 tea
2 uncooked cereals
1 each, macaroni, rice, spaghetti

Sink foods
1 dried fruit
2 dried beans/peas
6 canned foods

Ready-to-serve foods
1 cereal
2 cookies/crackers
4 spreads/relishes

Dinnerware (**service for 8**)
1 stack each, dinner plates, salad plates, saucers, sauce dishes
2 stacks soup bowls
4 stacks cups

Glasses, pitchers, etc.
8 juice, 8 water glasses
1 large, 1 small pitcher
2 relish dishes
1 creamer and sugar
4 refrigerator dishes

Serving dishes
4 bowls
2 platters

Silver
Service for 8

Mix utensils
1 each, flour sifter, pint measure, cup measure, baking dish, biscuit pan, piepan, muffin pan
2 cakepans
3 mixing bowls

Pots, pans, frypans
1 each, double boiler, coffeepot, 2-quart saucepan, 1-quart saucepan, 4-quart saucepot, colander, 10½-inch frypan, 9-inch frypan
2 3-quart saucepans

Kitchen linens
16 hand and dish towels
6 dishcloths
4 pot holders
4 aprons
1 box paper napkins
1 tablecloth

Bread
2 loaves

Vegetables and fruit
10 lb. potatoes
3 lb. each, vegetables, fruits

53-19. There should be space in kitchen cabinets to store these items conveniently. This is a minimum list.

the counter top and the cabinets is not more than 15", persons of average height should be able to reach the top shelf. It is recommended that all shelves be adjustable to the heights shown in Fig. 53-18. These heights are the most efficient for storing part of the items listed in Fig. 53-19. Base cabinets should be 36" high and have toe space 4" high. In some custom-designed kitchen cabinets this height may be varied an inch or two in either direction, depending on the height of the homemaker. The shelf spacing and drawer depths shown in Fig. 53-20 will accommodate some of the items listed in

Fig. 53-19. Remember, shelves that slide out increase the usability of base cabinets.

INSTALLING MILL OR FACTORY-BUILT CABINETS

Most kitchen cabinets are built in a mill cabinet shop or in kitchen-cabinet manufacturing plants, and then installed by a skilled carpenter following plans supplied by an architect or kitchen planning specialist. Since many kitchen cabinets are of extremely fine construction, materials, and finish, the carpenter must

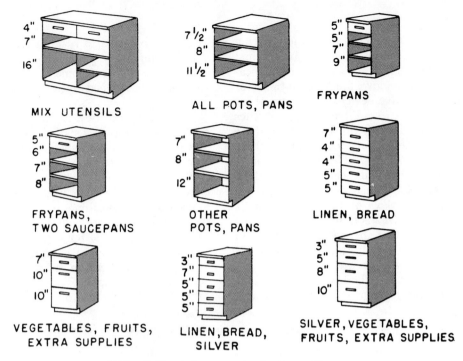

MIX UTENSILS

4"
7"
16"

ALL POTS, PANS

7 1/2"
8"
11 1/2"

FRYPANS

5"
5"
7"
9"

FRYPANS,
TWO SAUCEPANS

5"
6"
7"
8"

OTHER
POTS, PANS

7"
8"
12"

LINEN, BREAD

7"
4"
4"
5"
5"

VEGETABLES, FRUITS,
EXTRA SUPPLIES

7"
10"
10"

LINEN, BREAD,
SILVER

3"
7"
5"
5"
5"

SILVER, VEGETABLES,
FRUITS, EXTRA SUPPLIES

3"
5"
8"
10"

53-20. Shelf and drawer spacing for base cabinets.

53-21. Two standard base cabinets can fit so that the face frames almost meet. Then a filler strip can be added.

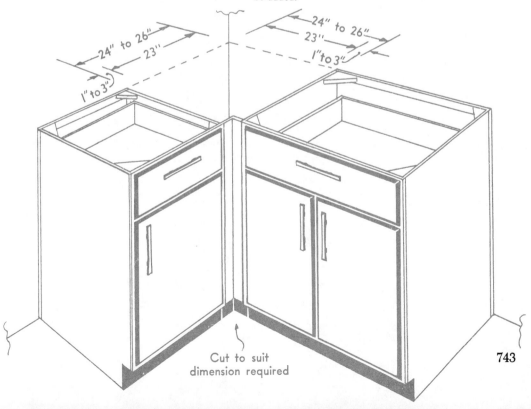

24" to 26"
23"
1" to 3"

24" to 26"
23"
1" to 3"

Cut to suit
dimension required

743

be very careful not to harm them during installation. To install base cabinets, first place the cabinet in its approximate location. Then remove the skids, braces, or other protective devices. Make sure there is no quarter round, baseboard, or other protrusion behind the cabinet. If there are any defects in the cabinet, these should be repaired before installation.

Always fit corner cabinets first since a corner is a special problem. There are three basic ways of handling a corner installation. One is to have two standard cabinets so that there is blank space in the corner. Usually a filler strip is cut to fit the space between. Fig. 53-21.

The second method is to use a rectangular cabinet designed for corner storage.

Though a bit hard to reach, such space is usable for many purposes. Fig. 53-22. On such installations some kind of filler strip must be placed between the cabinets.

The third and best solution to the corner problem is to install a corner cabinet that is fitted with shelves or with a lazy Susan that revolves. Fig. 53-23.

Move all cabinets, one at a time, as close to the wall as possible. Use a level to make sure each cabinet is plumb (vertical) and level (horizontal). Commercial cabinets provide for a good wall fit in two ways. The most common way is to have the back set in from the sides and the bottom open. Then either the cabinet ends or the bottom can be

53-22. A rectangular cabinet designed so that corner space can be used. This is called a blind-island base.

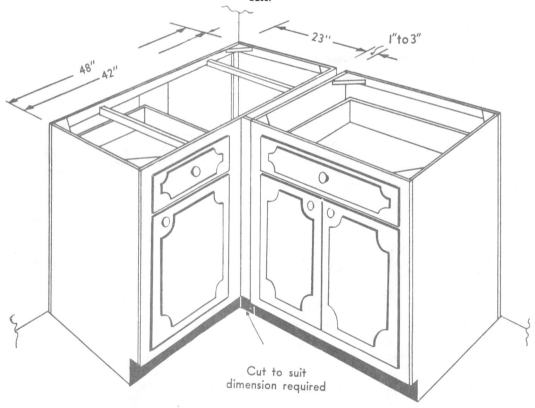

48"
42"
23"
1" to 3"

Cut to suit dimension required

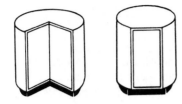

53-23. Base corner units for revolving shelves.

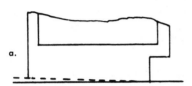

53-24. Measuring and trimming the bottom of the cabinet. a. The broken line shows the mark made by the dividers when the cabinet was level. b. Trimming off the base to fit a floor that slopes toward the center of the room.

trimmed off. A floor or wall can be uneven in two ways. Usually a floor slopes away from the wall. In this case, open a pair of dividers to the widest space between the bottom of the cabinet and the floor, and scribe a line along the bottom edge of the base. Then trim the base ends with a saw. Fig. 53-24. If the floor is level and the wall slopes away, the backsplash (part of the top) will be away from the wall. This can be corrected with wooden strips of proper thickness placed on the wall from the bottom of the wall cabinet to below the splash line. These strips can be covered with plywood or hardboard. Fig. 53-25.

A second method of fitting cabinets is first to place them as close as possible to the wall and block them up so they are plumb and level. Then cut the spacer strips that come with the cabinets to fit between the cabinets and the wall.

Once the base cabinets are properly fitted, they are fastened to the wall with wood screws through the back frames or nailing strips and into the studs. Screws must always go into the studs so the cabinet will be solidly attached. Cabinets should be bolted together side to side just back of the front facing or faceplate.

While some cabinets come with counter tops already covered with plastic laminate, this is usually not a part of the cabinetry. The usual practice is to fit the 3/4" plywood or particle board on the cabinet tops with the proper backsplash. Then plastic laminate is installed as described in Unit 43.

To install wall cabinets, first build a simple brace or support of scrap material on which the cabinets can rest while they are being installed. Place the cabinets in position, starting with the corner ones. Check to make sure they are plumb and level. If the wall is uneven and out of plumb, place wood shims behind the cabinets. Fig. 53-26. Then fasten the cabinets to the wall with long wood screws or toggle bolts which should go through the back rail. Screws must be fastened into the wall studs.

Quarter round or trim can be put on the exposed corners between the cabinets and the wall. Fig. 53-27. This is always necessary when much shimming was done.

BUILDING KITCHEN CABINETS
ON THE JOB

The most difficult job for the finish carpenter or cabinetmaker is to build cabinets on the job since this requires a thorough knowledge of cabinetmaking and also the ability to read and carry out the house plans prepared by the architect. Fig. 53-28. The first step is to check the plans and specifications for the location of all appliances such as the stove, refrigerator, and dishwasher. The rough plumbing and electrical outlets are al-

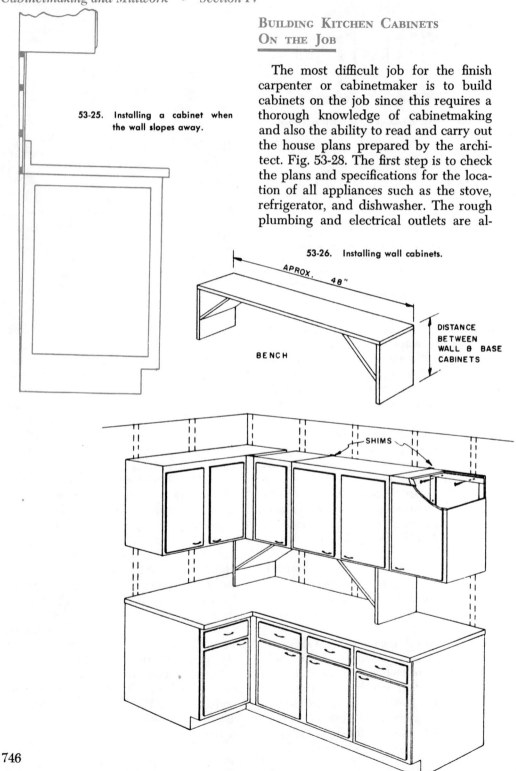

53-25. Installing a cabinet when the wall slopes away.

53-26. Installing wall cabinets.

APROX. 48"

BENCH

DISTANCE BETWEEN WALL & BASE CABINETS

SHIMS

53-27. Final result of cabinet installation is an appearance of unity.

ready in and these must be considered also for the location of sinks and appliances. Carefully check the cabinet measurements and mark these on the walls. Also check the walls and floor to make sure they are plumb and level.

The height of the wall cabinet will depend on its location: whether it is over the sink or range or above the base cabinets, and whether or not there is a drop ceiling. In most kitchen construction a drop ceiling over the cabinets is roughed in so that the cabinets do not have to go all the way up to the ceiling. Fig. 53-29. Usually the upper shelves are unused if they are too high. If there is no drop ceiling, it is better to have two sets of cabinets: small ones towards the ceiling for dead storage and larger ones below for more useful storage.

53-28. These handsome kitchen cabinets were built on the job by a true craftsman. The wood is knotty pine. Notice the feeling of unity that comes from the matching materials.

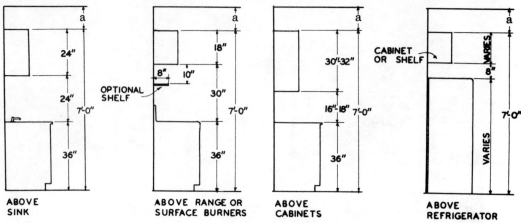

NOTE: Dimension "a" above wall cabinets varies with ceiling height. Space above wall cabinets may be furred down, left open or utilized for additional cabinets as "dead" storage space.

53-29.   Standard dimension for kitchen cabinets.

The cabinetmaker has a choice of two methods of building on-the-job cabinets. The first and most common is to build the cabinets *piece by piece as built-ins.* This is usually much simpler since no backs are required. The cabinets are built against a plastered or finished dry wall. Also, the interior construction can be kept very simple by using center drawer guides of metal. The other choice is to build the cabinets as *separate units* (like factory-built cabinets) and then fit them in place.

The cabinetmaker also has a choice of two kinds of cabinet construction. The *frame* makes use of solid wood framing material (about 1″ x 1½″) that is covered with thin plywood and other panel stock. Fig. 53-30. The second is the *non-frame* (box) or all-panel construction which makes use of plywood, hardboard, and particle board as both the exterior of the case and the structural support. Fig. 53-31. The only solid wood used in this second method is for drawer guides and runners and face framing (or face-plate).

All base cabinets are built with a toe strip. This can be done in one of two ways. A *base frame* (plinth) can be built on which the cabinet rests. The more common method is to have the cabinet sides (sometimes called jams) go completely to the floor. Then these sides are notched out at the bottom front to provide toe space. The toe strip is fitted against the cabinet ends.

For a flush or lip door and drawer, the front of the cabinet should have a face frame or plate attached to it. This is usually made of solid wood 1″ thick and 1½″ to 2¾″ wide. On non-frame cabinets with overlap doors and drawers, the face frame is not needed. The top of all base cabinets generally extends 1″ to 1½″ beyond the top of the case.

SAMPLE KITCHEN CABINETS

The following are some of the kitchen cabinets that can be built with hand and machine tools. They are typical of on-the-job construction. All of these cabinets are built with non-frame (box) construction.

Mobile Mixing Center (Fig. 53-32.)

Begin by assembling the basic plywood

748

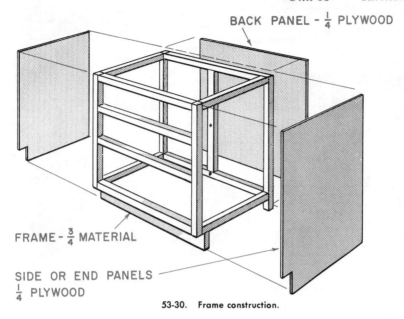

BACK PANEL - $\frac{1}{4}$ PLYWOOD

FRAME - $\frac{3}{4}$ MATERIAL

SIDE OR END PANELS
$\frac{1}{4}$ PLYWOOD

53-30.   Frame construction.

53-31.   Non-frame or box construction.

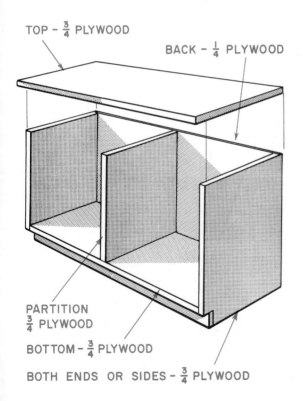

TOP - $\frac{3}{4}$ PLYWOOD

BACK - $\frac{1}{4}$ PLYWOOD

PARTITION
$\frac{3}{4}$ PLYWOOD

BOTTOM - $\frac{3}{4}$ PLYWOOD

BOTH ENDS OR SIDES - $\frac{3}{4}$ PLYWOOD

box as shown in the basic construction detail. Be sure to cut the grooves for dividers (I) and (J) in bottom piece (C) before assembly. Note that the bottom (C) is set up 3/4″ from the bottom of side pieces (B). Set the back piece (D) in 3/8″ x 3/8″ rabbets in pieces (B) and (C) as shown. Nail in divider (E) and shelf (F). Be sure to cut grooves in shelf (F) before fastening in. Put in dividers (I) and (J) and nail on spacers (G) and (H). These spacers compensate for the thickness of the facing to allow the drawers to clear. Nail on the facing as shown. Note that the top of the bottom facing piece is flush with the top of piece (C). Assemble the top piece (A) and its frame, then nail it on. Note that the top overlaps the basic cabinet by 1″ all around. Apply plastic laminate to the top and edges.

Hang doors (K) with flush door hinges. Apply pulls and catches at convenient locations. Screw casters to the underside of the unit as shown. Build the canister rack from scrap 3/8″ plywood. This is simply a small plywood box

53-32(a). Mobile mixing center. (Courtesy of Better Homes and Gardens)

53-32(b)—Materials List for Mobile Mixing Center

(All pieces plywood unless otherwise specified.)

A	—	26 x 50 x ¾	1 pc.
B	—	23¼ x 33 x ¾	2 pcs.
C	—	23¼ x 46½ x ¾	1 pc.
D	—	32⅝ x 47¼ x ⅜	1 pc.
E	—	22⅞ x 31½ x ¾	1 pc.
F	—	22⅞ x 20 x ¾	1 pc.
G	—	3¾ x 22⅞ x ¾	2 pcs.
H	—	8 x 22⅞ x ¾	2 pcs.
I	—	8 x 22⅞ x ⅜	2 pcs.
J	—	12½ x 22⅞ x ⅛ hardboard	2 pcs.
K	—	21¾ x 30 x ¾	2 pcs.

Drawer 1

L	—	2¼ x 21⅝ x ¾	1 pc.
M	—	2¼ x 19¾ x ½	2 pcs.
N	—	2¼ x 19¼ x ½	2 pcs.
O	—	20½ x 19 x ⅛ hardboard	1 pc.

Drawer 2

L	—	2¾ x 21⅝ x ¾	1 pc.
M	—	2¾ x 19¾ x ½	2 pcs.

N	—	2¾ x 19¼ x ½	2 pcs.
O	—	20½ x 19 x ⅛ hardboard	1 pc.

Drawer 3

L	—	6 x 21⅝ x ¾	1 pc.
M	—	6 x 19¾ x ½	2 pcs.
N	—	6 x 19¼ x ½	2 pcs.
O	—	20½ x 19 x ⅛ hardboard	1 pc.

Facing—1½ x ¾ pine—approx.
Frame for top—2 x ¾ pine—approx.
Cutting board—as shown on drawing
Pull-out plastic drawers
Wire Lid rack
Flush door hinges
Metal drawer slides
Casters
Knob
Catches
Door pulls
Plastic laminate for top—to fit

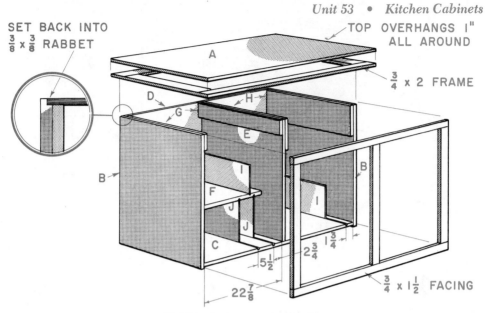

SET BACK INTO
$\frac{3}{8}$ x $\frac{3}{8}$ RABBET

TOP OVERHANGS 1"
ALL AROUND

$\frac{3}{4}$ x 2 FRAME

$22\frac{7}{8}$

$5\frac{1}{2}$

$2\frac{3}{4}$

$1\frac{3}{4}$

$\frac{3}{4}$ x $1\frac{1}{2}$ FACING

53-32(c). Basic construction details.

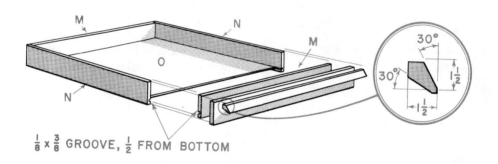

$\frac{1}{8}$ x $\frac{3}{8}$ GROOVE, $\frac{1}{2}$ FROM BOTTOM

30°

30°

$1\frac{1}{2}$

$1\frac{1}{2}$

53-32(d). Drawer detail.

53-32(e). Cutting-board detail.

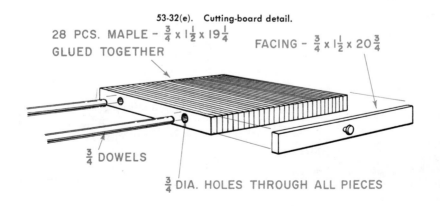

28 PCS. MAPLE – $\frac{3}{4}$ x $1\frac{1}{2}$ x $19\frac{1}{4}$
GLUED TOGETHER

FACING – $\frac{3}{4}$ x $1\frac{1}{2}$ x $20\frac{3}{4}$

$\frac{3}{4}$ DOWELS

$\frac{3}{4}$ DIA. HOLES THROUGH ALL PIECES

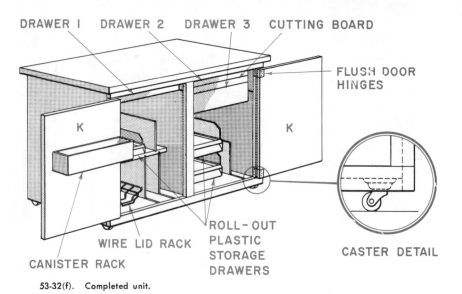

DRAWER 1   DRAWER 2   DRAWER 3   CUTTING BOARD

FLUSH DOOR HINGES

K

K

WIRE LID RACK

CANISTER RACK

ROLL-OUT PLASTIC STORAGE DRAWERS

CASTER DETAIL

53-32(f). Completed unit.

53-33(a). Overhead storage units. (Courtesy of Better Homes and Gardens)

which you fasten to the door. Be sure to make it short enough to clear as you open and close the door. Build the drawers as shown. They are simple plywood boxes with hardboard bottoms. You install them with metal drawer slides. They have been dimensioned for 1/2″ clearance on each side for the slides. Apply the fronts (L) after the basic drawers have been installed to make fitting easier. Make the cutting board as shown from strips of maple glued together with waterproof glue. Cut to exact width (20¾″) and apply drawer slides to the sides. The plastic storage drawers are commercial units which you simply buy and install according to directions. Set all nail heads, fill over them, and sand the whole unit as necessary. Finish it with one coat of enamel undercoat, plus two coats of semi-gloss enamel, sanding between coats.

Overhead Storage Unit (Fig. 53-33.)

This unit is simply a large plywood box, with sliding doors on the front, which provides storage space in kitchens with high ceilings. Since it must be built to fit existing space, no exact dimensions or materials list can be given. However, you should plan to make the shelves no

This Early American kitchen is well planned for efficiency and ease of maintenance. A U-shaped kitchen, it has the cooking unit in the round island which also serves as a snack bar. Note that the upper cabinets do not have hardware. The doors can be opened simply by a touch of the hand.
National Lumber Manufacturers Association.

The walls of this simple kitchen are paneled with a lovely honey-tone oak. Notice the overhang on one side of the base cabinet, which allows the cabinet to serve as a dining area or snack bar.
Georgia Pacific

This snack bar is built of knotty incense cedar. The kitchen is L-shaped and was built on the job by a skilled cabinetmaker. Solid wood was used in all of the construction. *Western Wood Products Association*

752B

Here is a truly elegant kitchen. The design, with its graceful paneled door and drawer fronts, is Traditional in flavor. It has a satiny white, baked-on lacquer finish, accented with softly muted gold. The kitchen is L-shaped, which is one of the most practical plans. An island in this plan includes the sink, dishwasher and snack bar. *I-XL Furniture Co.*

752C

No longer just a place to prepare meals, a spacious and beautiful modern kitchen has become a center for family activities in many homes: When wood cabinets dominate the room, as shown here, you can give them added interest with well-planned use of color. Lilac tones are used in this kitchen, with turquoise on the chairs and insides of the wall cupboards. Touches of bright red heighten the effect. *Sherwin-Williams Co.*

752D

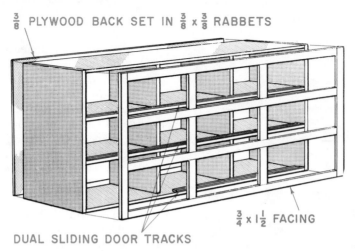

$\frac{3}{8}$ PLYWOOD BACK SET IN $\frac{3}{8}$ x $\frac{3}{8}$ RABBETS

DUAL SLIDING DOOR TRACKS

$\frac{3}{4}$ x $1\frac{1}{2}$ FACING

53-33(b). Overhead storage detail.

deeper than 18″, and the bottom of the cabinet should be about 6′8″ from the floor. You build the basic box as shown, then fasten it in place with screws through the back, sides, and top into the wall studs and ceiling beams. Install the aluminum dual sliding door track and fit in the 1/4″ hardboard sliding doors. Now nail on the 1½″ x 3/4″ facing. Notice that the vertical facing pieces are

toenailed to the horizontal facing only. The sliding doors bypass each other behind these facing pieces.

Oven and Storage Unit (Fig. 53-34.)

Built-in ovens are practical and easy to install even in kitchens not designed for them. Space is also provided for bulky utensils often awkward to store. Carefully measure the space for the cabinet.

53-34(a). Cabinets for this food preparation center consist of three separate units.
(Courtesy American Plywood Association)

753

Determine the final dimensions according to the kitchen and the particular oven unit you are to install. Cut all structural parts to size. For a natural finish, cut matching doors and faces from the same panel so the grain pattern will be uniform. Sand all edges and check all parts for proper fit before assembly. Assemble the cabinet face down on the floor. Attach the ends and back to the bottom, top, and shelves with glue and finishing nails. Stand in place on the base and level up if necessary to compensate for an uneven floor. Fit and install the face panels and doors. Make certain all door edges are carefully primed and finish both faces of the doors with an equal number of coats. Install the shelf supports and pan dividers after finishing.

Range Counter Cabinet (Fig. 53-35.)

Determine the exact final dimension to suit the range unit and the space the cabinet will occupy. Cut all structural parts and framing members to size. Sand

53-34(b). Storage section of the unit shown at the left in Fig. 53-34(a).

53-34(c). Basic construction of cabinet housing the oven and storage compartments.

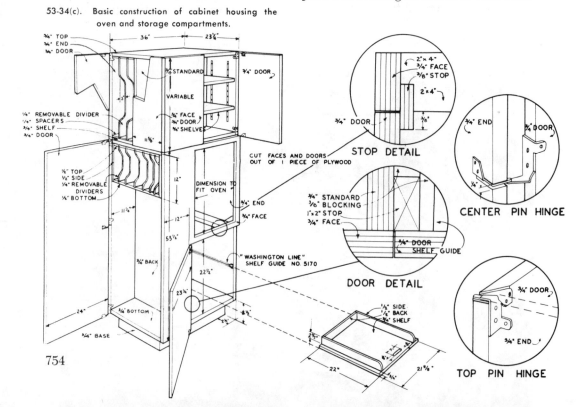

754

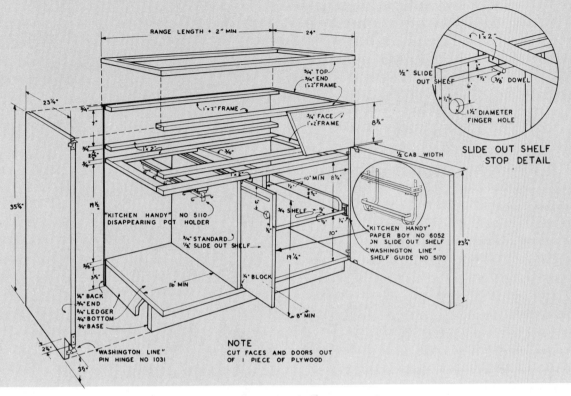

53-35. Construction of range counter unit.

Labels in figure:
- RANGE LENGTH + 2" MIN
- 24"
- 23¼"
- ¾" TOP
- ¾" END
- 1×2" FRAME
- 1×2" FRAME
- ¾" FACE
- 1×2" FRAME
- 8½"
- 1×2"
- ¾"
- ½" SLIDE OUT SHELF
- 1×2"
- ½" 3⁄8" DOWEL
- 6"
- ½"
- 1½" DIAMETER FINGER HOLE

SLIDE OUT SHELF STOP DETAIL

- 35¼"
- 11½"
- "KITCHEN HANDY" NO 5110 DISAPPEARING POT HOLDER
- ½ CAB WIDTH
- 10" MIN 8¾"
- ¾" SHELF
- ¾" STANDARD
- ½" SLIDE OUT SHELF
- 10"
- 19¼"
- "KITCHEN HANDY" PAPER BOY NO 6052 ON SLIDE OUT SHELF
- "WASHINGTON LINE" SHELF GUIDE NO 5170
- 23¼"
- ¼" BACK
- ¾" END
- ¾" LEDGER
- ¾" BOTTOM
- ¾" BASE
- 16" MIN
- ¼" BLOCK
- 8" MIN
- 2¼"
- "WASHINGTON LINE" PIN HINGE NO 1031
- 3½"

NOTE
CUT FACES AND DOORS OUT OF 1 PIECE OF PLYWOOD

the edges and check for correct fit. Assemble by attaching the base and ledge to the bottom shelf. Then install the ends, back, intermediate standards and frame. Join with glue and nails. Install the face panel and countertop. Hang the doors and do the finishing. Fit sliding shelves in place after finishing. Attach accessories.

Range Utensil Drawers (Fig. 53-36.)

Variable dimensions on this plan make it easy to fit nearly any space with the drawer cabinets. Cut all structural parts and framing members to size, sand edges, and fit in place. Start the assembly by attaching the bottom shelf to the base and ledge strips, then assemble ends, back and frames. Use glue and finishing nails. Level the cabinet as required. Cut draw-

er parts, sand edges, fit into openings, and assemble with glue and nails. The facing strip and all drawer fronts should be cut from one panel if the wood grain pattern is to match. Attach the top, applying plastic laminate.

Sliding Spice Rack (Fig. 53-37.)

This sliding spice rack and tuckaway shelf puts space to maximum use and provides for tall bottles as well as small cans and boxes. It can easily be added to the shelves in an existing cabinet or built into a new overhead cabinet. Its size is determined by the dimensions of the cabinet. Cut all parts to size. Sand the edges and check for proper fit. All joints should be glued and nailed. Fasten the tuckaway shelf to the cabinet shelves and back with finishing nails. Also use

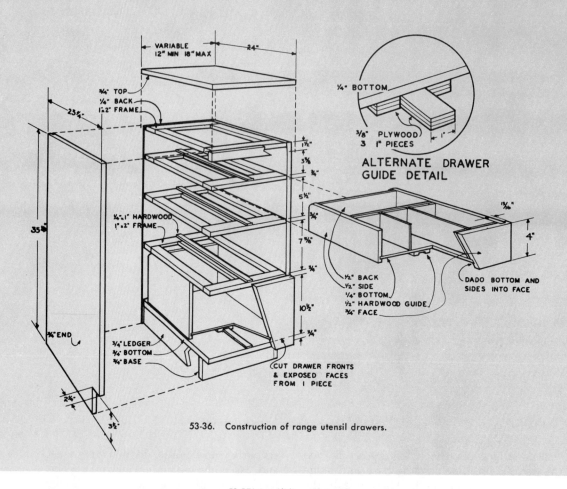

VARIABLE
12" MIN 18" MAX

24"

¾" TOP
¼" BACK
1½2" FRAME

25½"

35½"

¼"ᴬ,1" HARDWOOD
1"ᴬ2" FRAME

¾"END

¾" LEDGER
¾" BOTTOM
¾" BASE

2¾"

3½"

1½"
3⅜"
¾"
5½"
¾"
7⅝"
¾"
10½"
¾"

¼" BOTTOM

⅜" PLYWOOD
3 1" PIECES

ALTERNATE DRAWER GUIDE DETAIL

¾"

¾"

½" BACK
½" SIDE
¼" BOTTOM
½" HARDWOOD GUIDE
¾" FACE

1³⁄₁₆"

4"

DADO BOTTOM AND
SIDES INTO FACE

CUT DRAWER FRONTS
& EXPOSED FACES
FROM 1 PIECE

53-36.   Construction of range utensil drawers.

53-37(a).   Sliding spice rack.

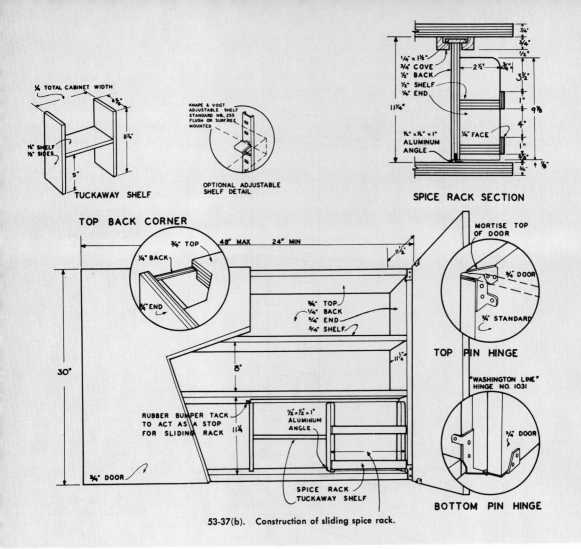

53-37(b). Construction of sliding spice rack.

finishing nails and glue to assemble the sliding spice rack. Install track and hang doors on cabinet. Finish as recommended. Be very careful to prime edges of doors and finish both faces alike.

Tall Storage Unit (Fig. 53-38.)

Canned goods can be orderly and easy to find when you build storage shelves like these. Cabinet height is variable, so the piece may even be built for use above a base cabinet. Decide on the dimensions, then cut sides, top, bottom, back, and shelves to size. Sand all edges and check for fit. You can assemble this cabinet in place or flat on the floor. If you put it together on the floor, be sure the diagonal of the sides does not exceed the ceiling height. Glue and nail all joints with finishing nails. After nailing the bottom shelf to its base, fasten the sides, top, back, and upper shelf in place. Slide or tip the cabinet into position and level the base if necessary. For matching grain pattern, cut all doors from a single panel. Sand the edges, fit and hang the doors. All door edges should be well primed and both faces should have the same number of finishing coats. Finish the complete unit, including movable shelves, and install shelf supports.

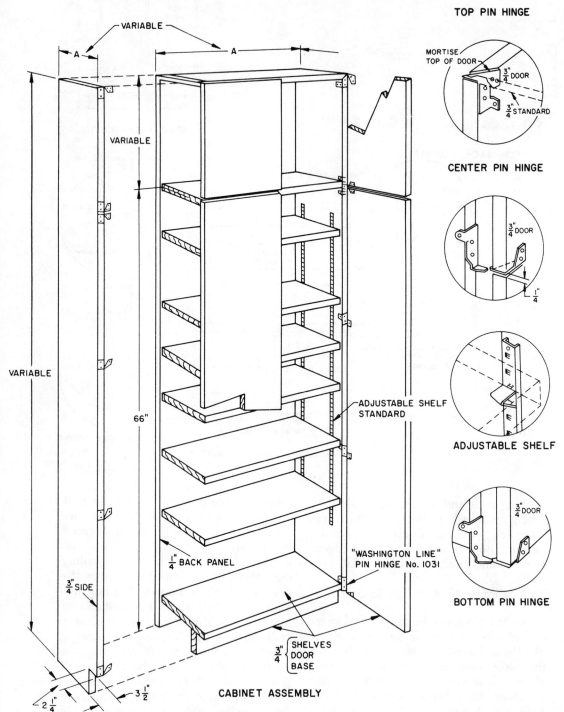

TOP PIN HINGE

MORTISE
TOP OF DOOR
$\frac{3}{4}$" DOOR
$\frac{3}{4}$" STANDARD

CENTER PIN HINGE

$\frac{3}{4}$" DOOR
$\frac{1}{4}$"

ADJUSTABLE SHELF

BOTTOM PIN HINGE

$\frac{3}{4}$" DOOR

VARIABLE

A

VARIABLE

VARIABLE

66"

VARIABLE

ADJUSTABLE SHELF
STANDARD

$\frac{1}{4}$" BACK PANEL

"WASHINGTON LINE"
PIN HINGE No. 1031

$\frac{3}{4}$" SIDE

$2\frac{1}{4}$"

$3\frac{1}{2}$"

$\frac{3}{4}$" { SHELVES
DOOR
BASE

CABINET ASSEMBLY

53-38. Construction of the tall storage unit. Fig. 53-2(a) shows such a unit in use.

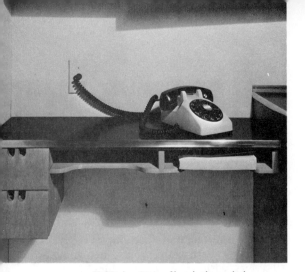

53-39(a).   Recipe-file telephone desk.

Recipe-File Telephone Desk
(Fig. 53-39.)

Today's modern kitchen needs an "office" area for efficiency. Little space is needed as this plan shows. This attractive desk can be tucked into any convenient corner, between two base cabinets, or suspended from a dinette wall. Cut parts for the two recipe drawers. Sand the edges, fit in place and assemble. Attach 3/4" top, apply surfacing material, and band edges at front and sides as required for location where the desk will be installed. Finish the entire unit and fasten to the wall studs or between cabinets.

53-39(b).   Construction of recipe-file telephone desk.

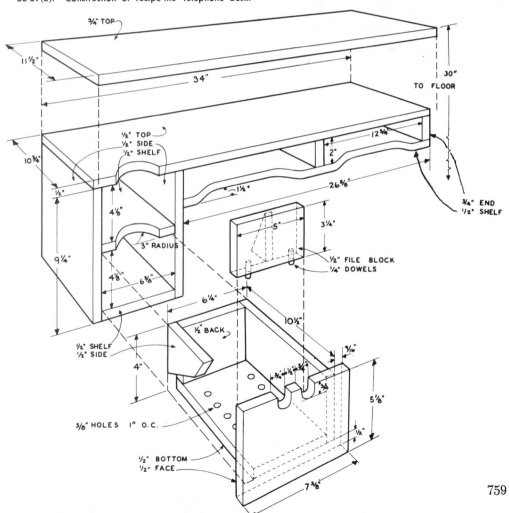

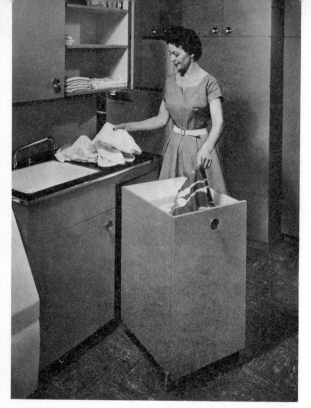

53-40(a). Using the laundry cart.

Laundry Cart and Sink Cabinet
(Fig. 53-40.)

This handy cart is divided into separate compartments for white and colored clothes. When empty, it fits out of the way under the sink counter. You can decide on the dimensions to suit the space and the sink to be installed. Cut all structural panels and frames to size. For any sink cabinet, use only fir plywood made with waterproof glue. Make all joints with glue and finishing nails. Sand all edges and check for fit. Then fasten the bottom shelf to the base and ledger strips. Attach ends, back, face, and framing members next. Then attach the top. Apply counter surfacing material, band the edges, and install the sink. Move the unit into place, leveling the base if the floor is uneven. Cut, fit, and hang the door. Sand and prime all

53-40(b). Construction of the laundry cart-sink cabinet.

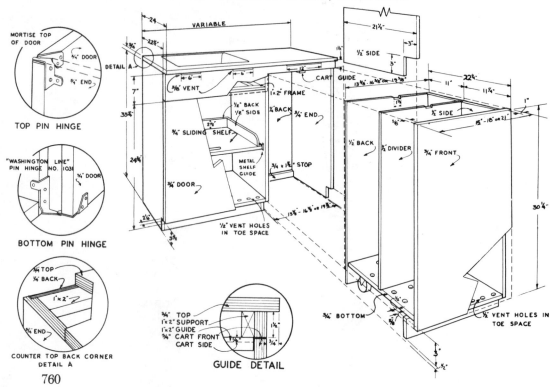

door edges thoroughly. Finish both inner and outer door faces alike. Cut the parts for the laundry cart. Sand the edges and check how it fits in place. Dado the side panels, or form slots with 1/2″ wood

strips for removable 1/2″ divider. Glue and nail bottom to toe piece. Apply sides and ends. Attach casters. Cut the sliding shelf to size. Assemble and install the shelf after finishing the cabinet and cart.

54   Paneling

There are many kinds of paneling that may be installed by the finish carpenter or cabinetmaker. Fig. 54-1. Frequently an entire wall from floor to ceiling is covered with paneling. In other rooms, only the lower third or so is paneled, and the area above is painted or papered, the upper edge being finished off with a

molding called *wainscoting*. Paneling is frequently done just before or after built-ins are constructed.

KINDS OF PANELING

• Solid wood paneling is made of many kinds of softwoods and hardwoods with tongue-and-groove joints for assembling

54-1. This redwood paneling is designed for interiors that must be acoustically excellent without sacrifice of decorative values.

54-2. An attractive interior featuring a plank-and-beam ceiling with paneled walls of southern pine.

54-3(b). This room has knotty ponderosa pine paneling with fancy, machined edges.

54-4. An attractive office with vertical pine paneling.

the boards. Fig. 54-2. Paneling comes in random widths of 4″, 6″, 8″, 10″, and 12″. There is usually a V joint where the two boards meet, although some types of paneling have much more decorative edge patterns. Fig. 54-3. Finish grades of lumber can also be used for paneling. The attractive interior in Fig. 54-4 features *board-on-board* installation.

• Plywood, a most satisfactory paneling material, is available in many different hardwood face veneers and designs. The

54-3(a). Patterns of solid wood paneling.

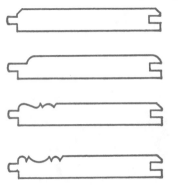

762

54-5. A dramatic effect results from using black, recessed inserts to separate the walnut plywood panels. Built-ins, faced in the same veneers, complete the theme.

54-6(a). This old-fashioned office was remodeled by installing wall paneling of plywood.

54-6(b). Notice the grooves of random width cut in the plywood paneling to give the impression of solid wood paneling. This treatment completely changes the old office into a modern one.

standard size is 4' x 8', which simplifies installation and shortens the time required. Fig. 54-5. The face veneer may be plain or it may be cut with equally spaced or random-width grooves. The latter gives the appearance of solid wood paneling. Fig. 54-6. Other plywood has face veneer strips of various woods, for contrast. Many kinds of plywood paneling come with a factory finish which eliminates the problem of finishing after installation. Extreme care must be taken during installation not to mar these surfaces.

• For commercial installation, paneling with a face of plastic laminate in wood designs is very popular.

• Hardboard paneling is made in various surface textures and wood-grain designs.

INSTALLING SOLID WOOD PANELING

Preparing the Wall

It is important to check the condition of the wall before installing paneling in either new or old construction. If vertical paneling is to be put over any kind of masonry surface, it is absolutely necessary first to apply furring (or nailing) strips horizontally around the room. Such strips should range in size from 1" x 2" to 1" x 8" (see *Application*, page 766) and they should be spaced 16" or more

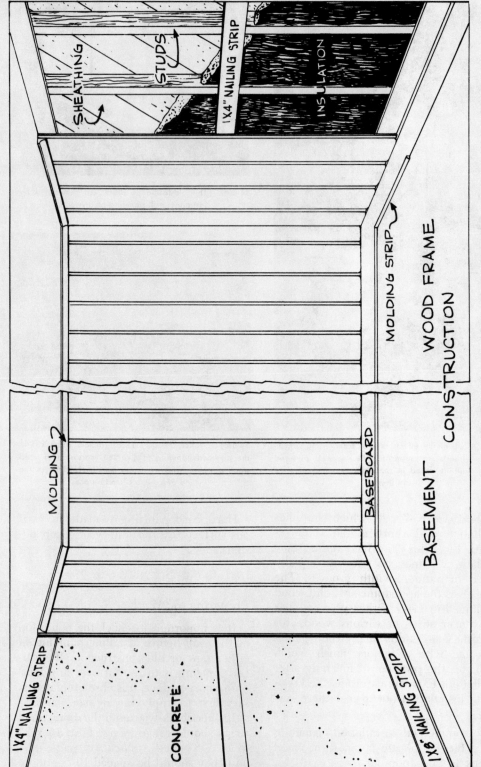

54-7. Furring or nailing strips should be installed for either vertical or horizontal solid wood paneling over a masonry wall. Notice that there are only three furring strips.

SHEATHING

STUDS

1X4" NAILING STRIP

INSULATION

MOLDING STRIP

WOOD FRAME CONSTRUCTION

MOLDING

BASEBOARD

BASEMENT CONSTRUCTION

1X4" NAILING STRIP

CONCRETE

1X6" NAILING STRIP

NAILING TO FURRING STRIPS ATTACHED TO STUDS
(Preferred Application)

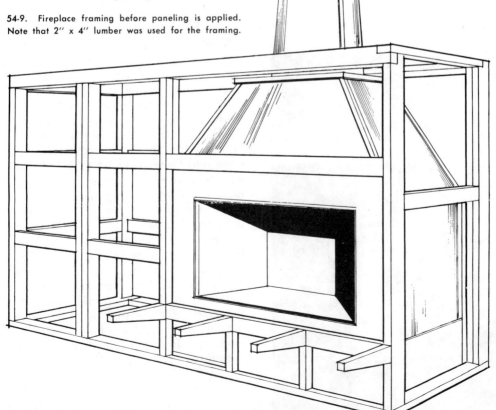

STUD

1" x 2" Furring Strips over studs spaced on 16" centers. 1" x 3" Furring Strips over studs spaced greater than 16" but less than 24" centers.

54-8. For thinner material, such as 1/4" plywood, more furring strips are needed to make the wall more solid. Arrows indicate that furring strips at the top and bottom of the wall are necessary to support the paneling.

54-9. Fireplace framing before paneling is applied. Note that 2" x 4" lumber was used for the framing.

apart. With heavy solid wood paneling, only three strips (top, middle, and bottom) are needed. Fig. 54-7. For thinner materials more and narrower strips are needed. Fig. 54-8.

On masonry walls, these furring strips must be installed with masonry nails or some other kind of masonry wall fastener. If the paneling is to be applied to a wood frame, it can be attached directly to the studs, but the preferred installation is to use furring strips also. All wiring and insulation must be completed before the furring strips are installed. When attaching furring strips to a plastered wall, use steel or resin-coated nails. Check to make sure the furring strips are straight and true. When necessary, place wood shims behind the strips to true them up. In remodeling, as in new construction, it may be necessary to rough in a fireplace or unused doorway before applying the paneling. Fig. 54-9.

54-10. Red cedar paneling installed horizontally on a single dining room wall.

54-11. Paneling resting on the baseboard for a smooth appearance.

54-12. Checking the paneling with a level.

Application

Solid wood paneling can be installed in a vertical, horizontal, or angular pattern. Fig. 54-10. If such paneling is to go from floor to ceiling, it is best to apply furring strips horizontally across the studs. The top and bottom furring strips should be at the extreme top and bottom of the wall. Then face nailing can be done into these strips because the nails will be covered by a baseboard at the bottom and by molding at the top. Another method of handling the baseboard is to install a wide, 1" x 8" baseboard furring strip. Then nail a 1" x 6" baseboard to it as shown in Fig. 54-11. This leaves 2" as a nailing surface at the bottom of the paneling. Paneling is then installed with the bottom end resting on the baseboard. The surface of the paneling and baseboard are flush. With this method, only edge nailing is done at the bottom.

766

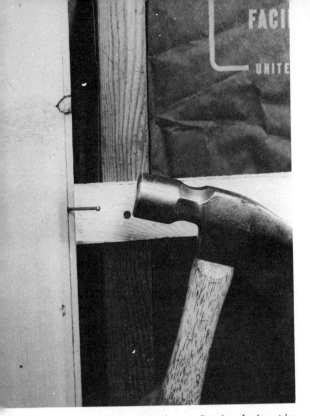

54-13. Blind nailing the paneling into furring strips.

54-14. Fitting a piece of paneling in place.

54-15. Installing the baseboard.

Start the paneling by making sure the first piece is vertical. Check with a level to be certain it is plumb. Fig. 54-12. Blind nail the paneling to the furring strip with 5d finishing nails. Install the nails at an angle through the tongue of each panel, into the thicker part of the paneling and then into the furring strip. Fig. 54-13. Countersink the nails with a nail set. When the groove of the next panel is slipped over the tongue, the nails are hidden. Make sure each piece of paneling is set firmly against the next. Use a block of paneling as a buffer for hammering in each piece. This will guarantee a snug fit. Fig. 54-14. At floor level most paneled walls have a baseboard which is mitered at the corners. The nails can be countersunk and the holes filled before the paneling is finished. Fig. 54-15. For a neater appearance at the baseboard, carefully gouge up a sliver of the

767

54-16. Gouging out a sliver before nailing the baseboard in place.

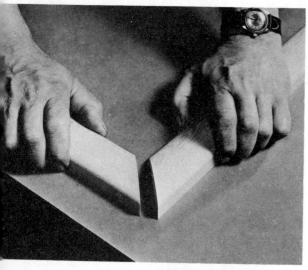

54-17. Checking the corner fit of trim.

54-18. Tracing the cut for a V joint between moldings.

surface of the molding. Then bury the finishing nails under this sliver. Fig. 54-16.

For trim around doors and windows, cut a neat miter joint. Fig. 54-17. If one piece of trim must meet another at right angles, cut the first piece of a right-angle corner and then trace the cut out on the molding of the second piece. Cut along the guide lines and then trim the V until the first molding fits. Fig. 54-18.

When the paneling is not to extend the full height of the wall, there is an installation method that requires no nails. A rabbet cut is made in the back of the baseboard, equal to the thickness of the panel. This provides two sides of the groove, and the wall or furring strip gives a third side. Then fit and nail the baseboard in place. Cut all the panels to exact length and fit these in the groove. Then cut a rabbet in the back side of the wainscoting and install this to hold the upper edge of the paneling in place.

INSTALLING PLYWOOD PANELS

Plywood panels are easy to install. The methods and procedures outlined below are suggested for simple installations.

Preparing the Wall

Check the wall to see if it is plumb. There should be no loose plaster or other irregularities. Panels may be applied directly to an old wall but it is generally better to install furring strips. If insulation is to be installed in an outside wall, this should be done before the furring strips are applied. A common method is to apply furring horizontally about the room with vertical members let in on 16″ centers or where the panel joints are. Generally, horizontal members are spaced 2′ apart, although this may be varied if there is to be a chair rail (30″ to 36″ from the floor). If the wall appears to be hollow in spots, insert shingles or wooden shims so the furring

768

54-19. Installing large panel stock over furring strips. Notice that both vertical and horizontal furring strips are used to give the wall plenty of solid backing.

54-20. Installing quarter round at the outside corner of plywood paneling.

strip is straight and true. Use cut steel or resin-coated nails for attaching the furring to plaster walls.

Laying Out the Job

Plan the way the panels will be placed around the room so that there is a pleasing pattern in color and grain. Lay the panels against the wall for this. For most interiors it is practical to start paneling from one corner and then work around the room. If there is a fireplace or picture window, start the paneling on either side or at the center of it. If all panels are of the same width and there are windows or doors in several places about the room, start at the center of one wall and work both to the left and right around the room. Don't be too concerned about the natural color variations in the panels; this actually enhances the appearance of the room as long as pattern arrangement is pleasing.

Application

Although there are several ways that paneling can be joined, the simple V joint is generally preferred. If a flush butt joint is required, the panel should be grooved to receive a spline so the surface of the panel will be aligned. Panels may be fastened by small finishing nails or brads which are later countersunk and filled with matching plastic wood. Heavier nails may be used at the base and top where they will be covered later. A combination of small brads and spot gluing is also a good method. When nailing, be sure to start along one edge of the panel and work across the width to avoid bulges.

Some manufacturers make panels that are grooved or splined on the edges. Others make special wood-covered metal moldings that hold panels in place. See Unit 66. Several types of splines, raised panels, or recessed panels are also available. Fig. 54-19.

In an inside corner the panels are usually joined with a simple butt joint and then covered with a cove or quarter round. For outside corners (a wall that forms a right angle into the room), panels should be cut to fit flush to the edge of furring strips or the wall studding. This will permit installation of a quarter round of the same thickness as the panels to hide the joint and provide a smooth, rounded edge. Fig. 54-20. An alternate method is to use a mitered joint; special care must be taken to get a perfect fit. Special moldings for many different uses are available in almost every kind of wood.

All nails should be below the surface, but the nail holes should not be filled until after the first coat of sealer or shellac has been applied to the paneling. After installation, the paneling, edges, and moldings should be lightly sanded and then wiped clean before the finish is applied.

55 Built-Ins, Including Room Dividers

There are two major ways of building and installing the many cabinets and other interior units needed for a home or office. Fig. 55-1. One is to purchase factory- or cabinet-shop casework that is built according to an architect's plans and specifications. Such pieces are then brought to the site and installed. The second method is to build the cabinets on the job, adding one piece of material to another in its permanent location. These are called built-ins. Fig. 55-2.

There are several important differences between a piece of casework built in the shop and a completely built-in cabinet piece that fits into a house. With mill- or shop-built cabinets, the work is done with the square. Each part is checked to make sure it is square with the other pieces. Also, production equipment is available, so complicated joinery is possible. Sometimes, mill-built cabinets also are made of panel construction, and this is rarely used for built-ins.

For the built-in, a good deal of the preliminary work is done with a level. The reason for this is that no wall or floor is exactly plumb (vertical) or level (horizontal). The built-in must be made to fit these irregular surfaces. Generally, the architectural plans give the overall dimensions that are necessary for the built-ins as well as a front elevation detail that shows the general appearance

55-1. In some modern homes, much of the furniture and storage is in the form of built-ins which are integral parts of the house.

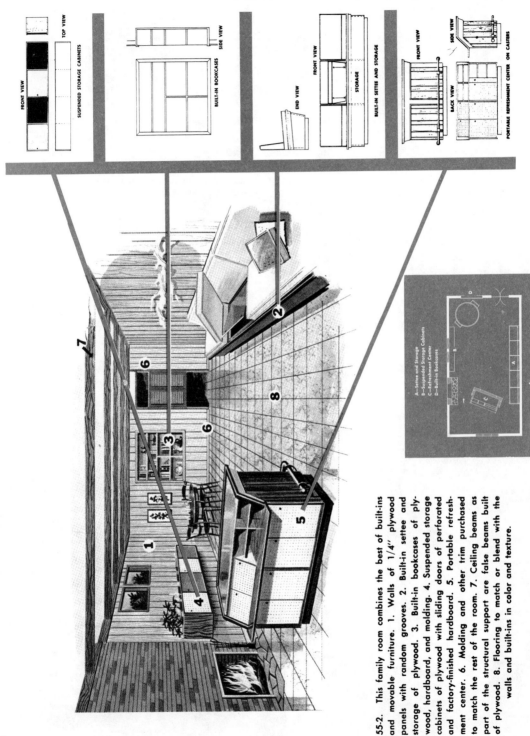

FRONT VIEW

TOP VIEW

SUSPENDED STORAGE CABINETS

SIDE VIEW

BUILT-IN BOOKCASES

FRONT VIEW

END VIEW

STORAGE

BUILT-IN SETTEE AND STORAGE

SIDE VIEW

FRONT VIEW

BACK VIEW

PORTABLE REFRESHMENT CENTER ON CASTERS

A—Settee and Storage
B—Suspended Storage Cabinets
C—Refreshment Center
D—Built-in Bookcases

55-2. This family room combines the best of built-ins and movable furniture. 1. Walls of 1/4" plywood panels with random grooves. 2. Built-in settee and storage of plywood. 3. Built-in bookcases of plywood, hardboard, and molding. 4. Suspended storage cabinets of plywood with sliding doors of perforated and factory-finished hardboard. 5. Portable refreshment center. 6. Molding and other trim purchased to match the rest of the room. 7. Ceiling beams as part of the structural support are false beams built of plywood. 8. Flooring to match or blend with the walls and built-ins in color and texture.

771

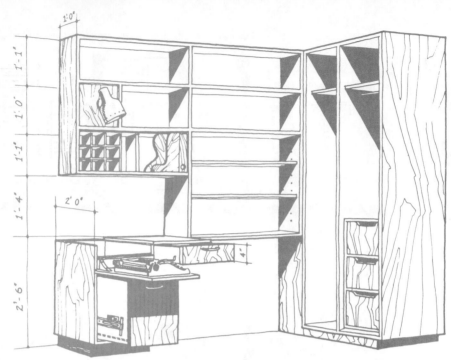

55-3. A drawing with more dimensions would be needed to prepare the materials list and build this unit.

55-4. The shadow box around the fireplace and the built-in bookcase are combined with horizontal wall paneling in this living room.

772

and dimensions. However, it is the responsibility of the cabinetmaker or finish carpenter to apply his knowledge of cabinetmaking in determining the dimensions for such items as drawer or door parts, interior construction, and other measurements not given on the prints. Built-ins often must be planned for such equipment as a sink, a sewing machine, or a hi-fi set. Sometimes only a sketch with a very few dimensions is available. In this case, a more complete drawing and a materials list must be made by the cabinetmaker. Fig. 55-3.

KINDS OF BUILT-INS

Built-ins are used in every part of a home. Their popularity continues to grow, largely because the demand for more storage space and greater efficiency is ever increasing. Built-ins can provide

necessary drawers and closet space as well as special storage for hobbies and other activities. A custom-built appearance is one advantage of built-ins; they also make many movable pieces of furniture unnecessary, which simplifies housecleaning and eliminates many dust-catching areas. Built-ins in every room of the home are illustrated in this unit.

Living Room

Many homes have built-in units around the fireplace, which include shelving. Fig. 55-4. There may be a built-in book cabinet with areas for hi-fi equipment, television, and hobby or entertainment items. The living room may be set off from the front hallway or other parts of the house by a built-in divider wall. Fig. 55-5.

55-5. This curved wall divider of western red cedar separates the living room from the entrance hall. It is designed for many uses. The tall section at the left is a closet that opens from the entrance side. A music system is housed in the opposite end, with shelving for record storage.

Bedroom

More and more bedroom plans illustrate built-ins for nearly all furniture—beds, dressing tables, storage drawers, desks, counters, and other. Fig. 55-6. Some homes have no movable furniture except chairs. Fig. 55-7.

Kitchen

While most kitchen cabinets are factory- or mill-built and then installed, some carpenters and cabinetmakers like to build their own. This is necessary if the house has an unusual design. Sometimes, standard mill-built cabinets just cannot be used. Fig. 55-8. The walls of the kitchen may be at an angle or curved so that the cabinets must be built on the job in order to fit.

Playroom and Family Room

In playrooms and family rooms, built-ins are usually designed to hold items for recreation and housework. Sewing, ironing, photography, tennis, table

55-6. This bedroom-playroom of western pine has many details. The built-in bed establishes the dominant theme, but the drawers below and the scalloped detail over the bed give the room warmth and distinction.

55-7. Except for the bed and the chair, all the "furniture" in this bedroom-playroom is built in. The study desk, drawers, and open shelves are constructed of Douglas fir that is cut and fit to utilize every inch of wall space.

55-8. The built-in features of this Early American kitchen and breakfast room show the use of plywood, solid wood, and paneling.

games—equipment for all these and many other activities is often stored in built-ins. Separate storage may be provided for each activity. A cedar chest for out-of-season clothing is another built-in commonly found in such rooms.

Bathroom

Probably no other room of the home except the kitchen makes as much use of built-ins as does the present-day bathroom. At one time this was not possible; use of lumber products in the bathroom was limited because of the moisture problem. Today, however, the synthetic sealers and super paints make it possible to build cabinets under the sink, in the walls, even around the bathtub, without fear that they will buckle or that the finish will come off. Fig. 55-9.

55-9. This vanity wall divider in a bathroom is made of Douglas fir. With its many drawers and cupboards, it provides plenty of space for linens, household supplies, and other storage.

775

55-10. The major horizontal members of this desk-and-storage unit consist of the cabinet bottom and top and two full-length shelves. Since this unit fits into a recessed area, these pieces may have to vary in length just a little to fit the opening. The vertical members and the short shelves are fastened together with dadoes. These joints must be cut before fastening in the major horizontal members. Then the vertical members can be fitted into the dadoes. Trim, doors, and desk unit can then be added. Western pine is the wood chosen since it is easy to work and will take any paint or finish.

55-11(a). Good designing is important in a small bedroom. A desk and wall-hung shelves of Douglas fir built against one wall free the floor area and provide a counter that will later become a study table.

GENERAL PROCEDURE FOR CONSTRUCTING BUILT-INS

Since every built-in is different, it is impossible to give specific directions for completion. However, the first step should be to check the space available along the wall and floor with the architectural plans. Make sure there is enough space for the built-in you are going to make. Check the wall with a level to see if it is exactly perpendicular. Check the floor to see if it is out-of-level and, if so, how much. Check the corners to see how much out-of-square they are. All of these must be taken into consideration in cutting pieces that will fit. Also check and mark the wall studs and floor joists where major parts of the built-in can be permanently attached with nails or screws. Check the sizes of any equipment to be included, such as a refrigerator, washing machine, ironer, television set, speaker, or tuner. Verify all the dimensions that are necessary to fit the built-in into the area.

A materials list must be made and the necessary lumber, plywood, and other materials ordered and delivered before work can go ahead. Usually the major vertical pieces must be adjusted to the overall ceiling height and the major horizontal pieces adjusted to the distance from side to side. Fig. 55-10. Cut and install the major horizontal and vertical pieces and shim them up as necessary so they are plumb and level. Then fit the intermediate pieces in between these major units. After this, the necessary face frame can be installed and the necessary interior work done for shelves, drawer guides, dividers, and other parts. The final step is usually to build the doors and drawers for the built-in and fit them in place.

Fig. 55-11 shows a typical dressing table and desk for a child's bedroom. Check the plan and recess to find the

776

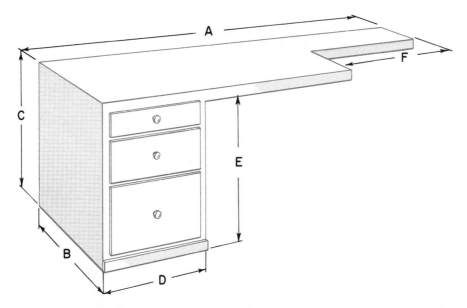

55-11(b). Check the exact dimensions from the plans and then measure the actual space available. A is the distance between the left and right wall of the recess. B will be determined by the depth of the recess. C is very important since the person who will use the desk may want this much lower than the standard 30" usually specified for a desk. The height might need to be a compromise between present and future needs. D could vary in size depending on the space needed between the bed and the drawers for a chair. E is important especially on a lower counter so there will be adequate leg room. F should be about equal to the width of a bed pillow.

major dimensions for A, B, C, D, E, and F. Prepare the major vertical and horizontal members of the dressing table-desk combination. Cut to size and install the drawer ends. Install the necessary wall cleats to which the top will be attached. Cut the top to shape and install it. Fit the frames or dividers for drawers. Cut and install the face-frame baseboard and the trim on the unit. Build the drawers and install them. The upper shelf is relatively simple since it is a rectangular storage unit. Vertical wall members are installed first. The long horizontal shelves are fastened above and below. The vertical dividers are added, and finally the face frame.

BUILDING A STORAGE WALL

A storage wall is very practical. Fig. 55-12. Study the drawings carefully and then construct. See details on next three pages:

55-12(a). Storage wall. Note that this photograph shows the reverse arrangement of the right- and lefthand unit shown in the drawing. Either arrangement is practical.

777

CHILD'S STORAGE WALL

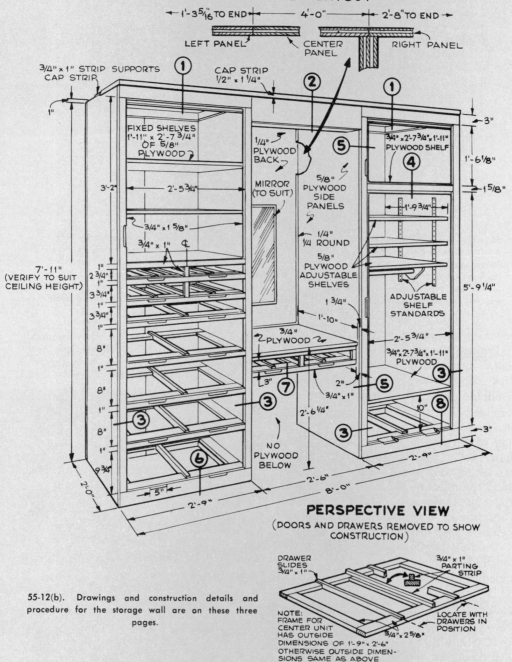

BACK PANEL LAYOUT

← 1'-3 5/16" TO END → ← 4'-0" → ← 2'-8" TO END →

LEFT PANEL

CENTER PANEL

RIGHT PANEL

3/4" x 1" STRIP SUPPORTS CAP STRIP

CAP STRIP 1/2" x 1 1/4"

1"

① ② ①

FIXED SHELVES 1'-11" x 2'-7 3/4" OF 5/8" PLYWOOD

1/4" PLYWOOD BACK

3/4" x 2'-7 3/4" x 1'-11" PLYWOOD SHELF

3"

3'-2"

2'-5 3/4"

MIRROR (TO SUIT)

⑤

④

1'-6 1/8"

1 5/8"

5/8" PLYWOOD SIDE PANELS

1'-9 3/4"

3/4" x 1 5/8"

3/4" x 1" ¢

1/4 ROUND

5/8" PLYWOOD ADJUSTABLE SHELVES

7'-11" (VERIFY TO SUIT CEILING HEIGHT)

1"
2 3/4"
1"
3 3/4"
1"
3 3/4"
1"

1 3/4"

1'-10"

ADJUSTABLE SHELF STANDARDS

5'-9 1/4"

8"

3/4" PLYWOOD

2'-5 3/4"

8"

3/4" x 2'-7 3/4" x 1'-11" PLYWOOD

1"

③

⑦

②

3"

2"

3/4" x 1"

⑤

③

8"

1"

③

2'-6 1/4"

⑧

10"

③

3"

9 3/4"

⑥

NO PLYWOOD BELOW

2'-6"

2'-9"

3"

2'-0"

5"

2'-9"

8'-0"

PERSPECTIVE VIEW
(DOORS AND DRAWERS REMOVED TO SHOW CONSTRUCTION)

55-12(b). Drawings and construction details and procedure for the storage wall are on these three pages.

DRAWER SLIDES 3/4" x 1"

3/4" x 1" PARTING STRIP

NOTE: FRAME FOR CENTER UNIT HAS OUTSIDE DIMENSIONS OF 1'-9" x 2'-6" OTHERWISE OUTSIDE DIMENSIONS SAME AS ABOVE

3/4" x 2 5/8"

LOCATE WITH DRAWERS IN POSITION

HORIZONTAL FRAME FOR DRAWER PAIRS

CONSTRUCTION DETAILS

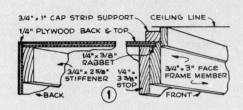

3/4" x 1" CAP STRIP SUPPORT — CEILING LINE
1/4" PLYWOOD BACK & TOP
1/4" x 3/8" RABBET
3/4" x 2 5/8" STIFFENER
BACK
3/4" x 3" FACE FRAME MEMBER
1/4" x 3/8" STOP
FRONT
①

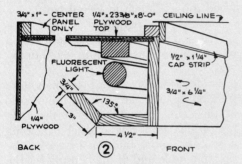

3/4" x 1" – CENTER PANEL ONLY
1/4" x 23 3/8" x 8'-0" PLYWOOD TOP — CEILING LINE
FLUORESCENT LIGHT
1/2" x 1 1/4" CAP STRIP
3/4" x 6 1/4"
3/4"
135°
1/4" PLYWOOD
3"
4 1/2"
BACK
②
FRONT

LOWER ADJUSTABLE SHELF OF 5/8" PLYWOOD
CENTER BRACKET ON SHELF
3/4"   2"
3 1/2"
SECURE WITH SCREWS
1"
NAIL THROUGH BRACKET AND POLE
4"

CLOTHES POLE DETAIL

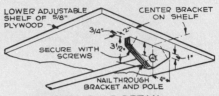

1/4"
1/2" PLYWOOD BACK
3/4"
1/4"
1/2" PLYWOOD SIDE
3/4" PLYWOOD FRONT

CORNERS AT TOP OF DRAWERS

3/4"
FRONT (SIDE SIMILAR)
1/4"
1/2"   1/2"
1/4"
BACK
1/2"

CORNERS AT BOTTOM OF DRAWERS

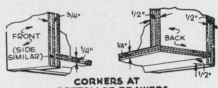

1/2" DRAWER SIDE
NOTE: DRAWER GUIDE CENTERED ON BOTTOM
1/4"
1 5/8"
DRAWER BOTTOM
DRAWER FRONT
3/4"
1/4"

DRAWER GUIDE

5/8" PLYWOOD UNIT SIDES
3/4" x 1 5/8" UPRIGHT FACE FRAME
1/4" PLYWOOD BACK
3/4" PLYWOOD SHELF
1/4"
3/4" x 1 5/8" FACE FRAME
3/4" x 2" STOP
LEFT ③ RIGHT
BACK ④ FRONT

1'-10"
DRAWERS IN LEFT UNIT
1'-9"
1'-6"
DRAWERS IN CENTER UNIT
DRAWER IN RIGHT UNIT

FRONT TO BACK DRAWER DIMENSIONS

TYPICAL DRAWER DETAILS

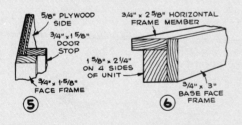

5/8" PLYWOOD SIDE
3/4" x 2 5/8" HORIZONTAL FRAME MEMBER
3/4" x 1 5/8" DOOR STOP
1 5/8" x 2 1/4" ON 4 SIDES OF UNIT
3/4" x 1 5/8" FACE FRAME
3/4" x 3" BASE FACE FRAME
⑤ ⑥

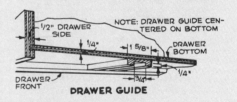

2'-7 3/4"
1'-11"
DRAWER SLIDE 3/4" x 1"
3/4" x 2 5/8"
SLIDE
FACE PIECE ON LEFT & CENTER UNITS ONLY

HORIZONTAL FRAME FOR WIDEST DRAWER

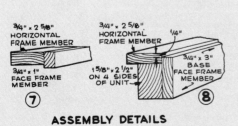

3/4" x 2 5/8" HORIZONTAL FRAME MEMBER
3/4" x 2 5/8" HORIZONTAL FRAME MEMBER
1/4"
3/4" x 1" FACE FRAME MEMBER
1 5/8" x 2 1/2" ON 4 SIDES OF UNIT
3/4" x 3" BASE FACE FRAME MEMBER
⑦ ⑧

ASSEMBLY DETAILS

779

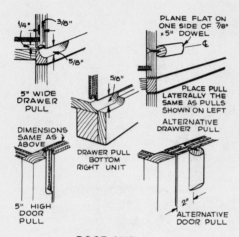

1/4" 3/8"

5/8"

5" WIDE
DRAWER
PULL

PLANE FLAT ON
ONE SIDE OF 7/8"
x 5" DOWEL

5/6"

PLACE PULL
LATERALLY THE
SAME AS PULLS
SHOWN ON LEFT

ALTERNATIVE
DRAWER PULL

DIMENSIONS
SAME AS
ABOVE

DRAWER PULL
BOTTOM
RIGHT UNIT

5" HIGH
DOOR
PULL

2"

ALTERNATIVE
DOOR PULL

DOOR AND DRAWER PULLS

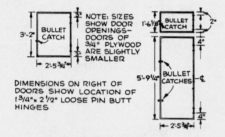

3'-2"

BULLET
CATCH

2'-5 3/4"

NOTE: SIZES
SHOW DOOR
OPENINGS—
DOORS OF
3/4" PLYWOOD
ARE SLIGHTLY
SMALLER

1'-6 1/8"

BULLET
CATCH

2"

4"

5'-9 1/4"

BULLET
CATCHES

2'-5 3/4"

4"

DIMENSIONS ON RIGHT OF
DOORS SHOW LOCATION OF
1 3/4" x 2 1/2" LOOSE PIN BUTT
HINGES

DOOR SIZES—LOCATION OF HINGES AND CATCHES

1. Cut the center back panel to size. Nail it in place on the wall, making sure the vertical edges are plumb.

2. Set up the sides and back on the lefthand unit, building in the base framing as shown in Detail No. 6. Working from base to top, assemble and fit the drawer framing and drawers, then the fixed plywood shelves. Install the front facing. Note that the top edge of the top facing is rabbeted for the 1/4" plywood top as shown in Detail No. 1.

3. Erect the righthand cabinet in a similar manner. Back up the front facing with door stops as shown in detail drawings.

4. Move the two end cabinets into position against the wall on either side of the center panel. Slide in the 1/4" top, which is a single panel extending across the entire built-in. Frame in the dressing table and fit the housing for the overhead fluorescent lamp. A narrow cap strip nailed to the cabinet facing will conceal the ceiling joint.

5. Fit and sand the doors. Door and drawer pull details are shown.

6. Sand all joints and fill nail holes with wood filler. Then smooth sand the entire unit. Apply a finish.

CONSTRUCTION TIPS

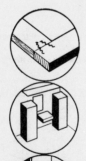

JOIN HORIZONTAL
(DRAWER) FRAMES
WITH CORRUGATED
FASTENERS. CHECK
FOR SQUARENESS

TO AVOID SPLITTING
DRILL NAIL HOLES TO
PART DEPTH WITH
PUSH DRILL OR CUT-OFF
NAIL IN POWER DRILL

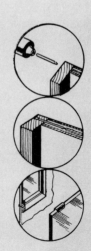

ASSEMBLE UNITS SEP-
ARATELY. FASTEN CENTER
BACK PANEL TO WALL
THEN MOVE OTHER
UNITS INTO POSITION

USE GLUE AS MUCH AS
POSSIBLE FOR RIGIDITY.
SECURE WITH 4d OR 6d
FINISHING NAILS AS
NEEDED. SET AND PUTTY

TO ASSEMBLE UNITS
SECURE SIDE PIECES
IN POSITION, THEN BUILD
FROM BOTTOM UP, USING
DRAWERS AND BLOCKS TO SPACE

FASTEN FRAMED MIRROR
FROM BACK. HANG
UNFRAMED MIRROR
WITH STANDARD UN-
FRAMED MIRROR CLIPS

ROOM DIVIDERS

Room dividers are built-ins that are used to separate two parts of a room. They are popular for living rooms in homes that do not have a separate entrance hallway. These dividers are semi-walls of either closed or open construction. The solid screen is usually built partway to the ceiling with standard lumber and paneling. Fig. 55-13. The open room dividers may be built on the job, or commercial architectural grillwork can be installed for part or all of the divider wall. Figs. 55-14 and 55-15. Frequently, storage units are combined with room dividers for greater utility.

55-14(a). This redwood grillwork is used as a room divider.

55-13. This entrance hall is formed by room dividers built at the edge of the living room and family room. The dividers are 1″ x 4″ tongue-and-groove paneling set in a box frame of 2″ x 6″ members. The wood is west-coast hemlock finished in clear flat varnish.

55-14(b). This room divider is easy to build and has the general appearance of the one shown in Fig. 55-14(a). A 2″ x 4″ is nailed to the floor and the ceiling. Then 1″ x 4″ pieces with blocking between are installed to give an open look.

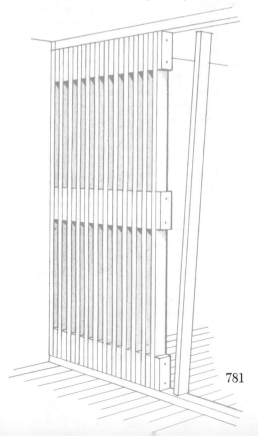

781

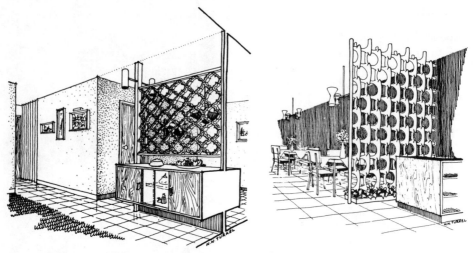

55-15. Sculptured grillwork can be purchased for use as a room divider with or without storage units. Designs range from simple decorative forms to Contemporary shapes.

SECTION IV

QUESTIONS AND DISCUSSION TOPICS

1. What are the three basic types of construction for large surfaces or areas? List the advantages and disadvantages of each.
2. Discuss a major problem that arises when plywood, particle board, and other materials are used in cabinet construction.
3. Define "equilibrium moisture content".
4. What is relative humidity and how does it affect woodworking production?
5. Describe two methods of determining the moisture content of lumber.
6. What is the P.E.G. treatment and what is its use?
7. How are hardness and specific gravity of wood related?
8. Do fast-growing trees have more annual rings per inch than slow-growing trees? Tell about the three kinds of cross grain and how they affect the machining of wood.
9. Does quarter-sawed hardwood shrink more or less than flat-grained material of the same species?
10. Define warp.
11. Describe the different kinds of warp.
12. How do you decide when a surface is properly planed?
13. Name some common defects that may result when lumber is planed or surfaced.
14. What are some of the best woods for shaping an edge?
15. Is there any relationship between specific gravity and the turning qualities of wood?
16. How does specific gravity affect boring and mortising?
17. On what types of woods can the best sanding results be achieved?
18. Describe joinery. Name some basic principles involved in all joinery.
19. Describe four methods of strengthening a joint.
20. Discuss the basic use of butt joints.
21. Tell where the rabbet joint is most commonly used in case construction.
22. Name the kind of dado joint that must be made if the joint should not show at the front edge.
23. What are four kinds of lap joints?

24. Describe several methods of strengthening a miter joint.
25. Is the mortise-and-tenon joint increasing in importance in cabinetmaking? Explain.
26. What is the purpose of a dovetail joint?
27. How does a finger joint compare with a dovetail joint?
28. Describe several good lock joints for drawer construction.
29. Is there any difference between the terms "glue" and "adhesives"?
30. Describe three common problems in gluing.
31. Name five types of glues that can be used for woods.
32. List four kinds of clamps used in cabinetmaking.
33. Name the clamps that can be used on a surface without protective blocks.
34. Describe the operation of portable high-frequency gluing equipment.
35. Name three common methods for testing a glue joint.
36. Is veneering a relatively new process?
37. What is veneer?
38. Describe the common methods of cutting veneer.
39. Name some of the unusual parts of a tree from which veneer is cut.
40. Name the common methods of matching veneer.
41. Tell how to apply a fine veneer to a core of plywood.
42. What are plastic laminates?
43. Name four common grades of plastic laminates.
44. What are the correct cutting tools for high-production work with plastic laminates?
45. What kind of adhesive is used for on-the-job installation of plastic laminates?
46. Describe the ways of treating edges for plastic laminates.
47. List the steps for applying plastic laminates to a table top.
48. Discuss the use of plastic laminates in kitchen construction.
49. Describe five methods of producing curved wood parts. What machines are needed for each method?

50. Explain the difference between wood lamination and molded plywood.
51. Why is wood lamination an important process in furniture construction and cabinetmaking?
52. Describe the simplest type of frame-and-panel construction and tell where it is used.
53. Name the five basic parts of simple frame-and-panel construction.
54. Describe the various types of panels that can be used in frame-and-panel construction.
55. What is sticking? When is it used in frame-and-panel construction?
56. Describe several types of cabinet doors.
57. What are the three methods of fitting a door to a case?
58. Describe the common types of door hinges.
59. Explain how to hang a door flush with the face of a frame.
60. Why are drawers the most difficult construction problem in cabinetmaking?
61. Name the basic types of drawer fronts.
62. Explain the various joints that can be used for assembling a drawer.
63. What is the best joint to use in drawer construction?
64. What is the difference between a drawer and a tray?
65. Describe the various levels of quality in drawer construction.
66. What three factors must be considered in designing shelves for cabinets?
67. Name several methods of constructing adjustable shelving.
68. What types of metal hardware are needed for adjustable shelving?
69. Can the design of furniture be determined by the appearance of the leg? Discuss.
70. Tell how to cut a tapered leg.
71. What is a cabriole leg? On what furniture styles is it found?
72. What is the difference between reeding and fluting?
73. Explain how to attach the legs for a tripod table.
74. Discuss the use of commercial legs in furniture construction.

75. Describe the various joints that can be used in leg-and-rail construction.
76. Explain some of the production problems in chair construction.
77. Describe five types of table-top construction.
78. List several methods of supporting a dropleaf.
79 What is a rule joint and how is it constructed?
80. What methods should be followed for attaching a table top if the top is made of glued-up solid wood? Explain.
81. Describe four methods for attaching table tops made of plywood.
82. Describe some of the most common corner joints used in basic casework.
83. Describe how to install a back in a piece of casework.
84. What kind of corner joint should be used for a faceplate or for casework?
85. How does fine furniture cabinetwork differ from basic casework? Discuss.
86. What are the four parts sometimes needed for a large piece of cabinetwork such as a china cabinet?
87. Why are kitchen cabinets the most important part of cabinetmaking?
88. Describe three ways of producing kitchen cabinets.
89. Tell how to plan a kitchen layout.
90. Describe the method of installing a base cabinet that has been made in a factory.
91. How do you install factory-made wall cabinets?
92. Describe the two basic methods of building on-the-job cabinets.
93. Describe the two ways in which kitchen-cabinets are commonly constructed on-the-job.
94. Name several kinds of paneling.
95. Tell how to install solid wood paneling.
96. Explain how to install plywood paneling.
97. What is the difference between built-ins and casework built in a shop?
98. Describe several kinds of built-ins.
99. Explain the general steps in installing a built-in cabinet.
100. Describe several methods of building room dividers.

PROBLEMS AND ACTIVITIES

1. Design an experimental joint of *all-wood construction* that is different from any shown in this book.
2. Design a joint, making use of some plastic or metal reinforcement. Test the strength of this joint.
3. Design an assembly method for cabinets that does not make use of adhesives, nails, or screws.
4. Develop plans for an item to be mass-produced, including the drawings, jigs, fixtures, route sheets, and work stations.
5. Compare the strength of various common corner joints.
6. Compare the machining qualities of two common cabinet woods.
7. Study the holding power of some common adhesives.
8. Study the use of plastic laminates in commercial construction and compare their advantages and disadvantages with those of solid wood or plywood.
9. Develop a form or mold for laminating a wood product.
10. Visit some houses being built and inspect the kitchen-cabinet construction.

The beauty and warmth of wood and the skills of the cabinetmaker's art were combined to produce this handsome all-wood home. Floors, ceilings, and walls all lend beauty and durability to the surroundings. Construction of this quality requires a highly skilled cabinetmaker or carpenter, since the final result must show all the characteristics of fine workmanship including good fit with no marred surfaces. *National Lumber Manufacturers Assn.*

The interior of this living room is paneled in pre-finished walnut V-plank plywood. On one wall the panels were placed horizontally to give the impression of greater width. Similar panels were then placed vertically to act as a room divider. The divider was attached to the backs of two storage cabinets, one for the dining-room side and the other on the living-room side. The cabinets are made of ¾" walnut plywood with plastic-laminate tops. *United States Plywood*

The walls of this living room are paneled with pre-finished pecan plywood of V-plank design, grooved vertically in random-plank style. Edges are beveled and trimmed for perfect joints. The cabinetmaker who installs this paneling in four-foot widths must be extremely careful in fitting the parts not to damage the surfaces. The beamed ceiling is of solid pecan. *United States Plywood*

784C

This practical and useful built-in wall of storage cabinets and bookcases is a structural part of the home. The wood is California redwood with a reddish finish to accentuate the grain and to combine harmoniously with the brick exterior wall. *California Redwood Assn.*

This handsome living room is also paneled in solid redwood. However, a brownish stain was used to give the wood a more formal appearance. The floor-to-ceiling bookcases, another example of the fine art of cabinetmaking, would be a welcome addition to any home. *California Redwood Assn.*

Quality wood products deserve a "fine" finish. Spraying is one of the most important techniques. However, many hand skills and plenty of "elbow grease" are also needed to achieve the desired appearance.

Section V — Finishing

Before actually finishing a product, it is essential that all of the pre-finishing operations be completed. Fig. 56-1. These include removing any exterior surface glue, repairing imperfections, and final sanding. For some finishes, bleaching must also be done. Remember that any imperfections or scratches left after the final sanding will be greatly intensified when the final finish is applied.

REMOVING EXCESS GLUE

It is important in assembling products to apply the right amount of glue. If too much is applied, some will have to be removed, which is a problem. Also, your fingers should not be covered with glue or oil during assembly, since these materials will seal wood pores and prevent stains and other finishing materials from going on the wood evenly. When the product is ready for finishing, check it carefully for excess glue on the surface, particularly around the joints. Remove any such glue with a sharp chisel. Glue spilled on the surface should be removed by scraping; never attempt to sand it off since this forces the glue into the wood, causing an imperfection. Make sure every bit of glue is removed since glue will not take stain.

REPAIRING WOOD SURFACES

In the process of building any wood product there is always the chance of small damage. There are four common ways to repair a wood surface.

56-2. Swelling a dent in wood with a damp cloth and a hot iron. Don't wet the wood too much, especially when working with plywood.

56-1. A beautiful finish cannot be achieved unless the surface first is properly prepared.

56-3(a). An electric furnace with a pair of burn-in knives.

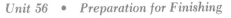

56-5. Picking up the material with the knife.

• It is possible to raise a shallow dent with a wet cloth and a hot iron. Place the cloth over the dent and the iron over the cloth. Fig. 56-2. This will usually raise the grain enough so that it can be sanded to an even surface.

• A good way to fill small cracks is by the burn-in method. Fig. 56-3. Shellac or lacquer sticks are used. These are hard pieces of material that become soft when heated. They come in many different colors such as light oak, dark oak, light and dark walnut, and mahogany of various colors. In industry the furniture patcher must have a complete set of these materials for repairing damaged furniture. When heated, the patching material will blend with the wood surface, just like paint, to match any color.

Clean out the crack or hole carefully, making sure that it is completely dirt free. Heat one or two knives, either with a special electric furnace or over an alcohol torch. Fig. 56-3. An electric knife can also be used. Fig. 56-4. Pick up the patching material on the tip of the hot knife. Fig. 56-5. Roll the knife over and drop the material into the opening. Fig. 56-6. While it is still in a semi-liquid condition, pull the burn-in material into the

56-3(b). An ordinary knife and a can of inflammable alcohol can also be used.

56-4. In a complete kit for repairing furniture, an electric knife is furnished to apply the burn-in sticks.

56-6. Roll the knife over and drop the material into the defect on the back stroke.

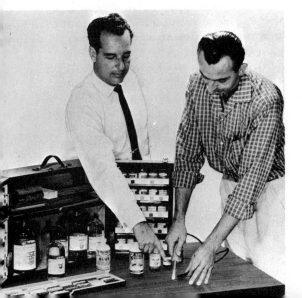

787

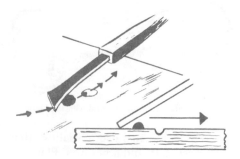

56-7. Now pull the knife forward over the defect. Never allow the hot knife to come to a stop.

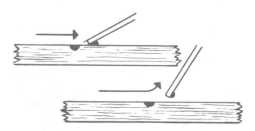

56-8. Pick up the excess material with the end of the knife. Notice how the knife is brought up to a vertical position at the end of the stroke.

depression with the return stroke. Fig. 56-7. Never stop the motion, or the hot knife may mar the wood surface. Continue the movement to wipe the excess into a thin film and lift it away with the knife. Fig. 56-8. This method requires considerable practice and should not be done the first time on the product itself. It should be practiced on scrap stock.

• A third method of filling cracks and holes is to use a filler material such as wood dough, putty, or plastic wood. Plastic wood comes in many different colors including natural, light mahogany, oak, walnut, maple, and many others. Wood dough is a synthetic wood that comes in many colors. In using both plastic wood and wood dough, make sure that the color is correct before applying. Then add enough material to make a slight hump on the surface. Allow it to dry, then sand off smooth and level.

• A good way to cover nail or screw holes is with wood pegs or plugs. For small nail holes, pegs of the same wood as the product can be made from 1/32″ stock. Point the end in a pencil sharpener. Apply glue to the point and insert in the hole. Then cut off and sand smooth. Wood plugs for screw holes can be cut with a plug cutter, or fancy wood plugs can be purchased. These are glued in the counterbored holes.

BLEACHING

Bleaching is a process of lightening a wood surface by applying a solution. While the trend in furniture finishing is away from the bleached appearance, this step is still necessary for many of the honey-toned, colored finishes. As a matter of fact, in the furniture industry, bleaching is often a necessity, especially in applying medium-tone finishes to such woods as walnut, mahogany, and pecan. Bleaching removes color by oxidation.

Kinds of Bleaches

The simplest kind of bleach is made by mixing oxalic-acid crystals in hot water. This relatively mild solution is satisfactory only for small furniture pieces. The most common commercial bleach consists of two solutions. Solution No. 1 is normally a caustic soda (bleach activator) while solution No. 2 is hydrogen peroxide in a concentrated form with approximately 35 per cent peroxide. This commercial bleach is a powerful oxidizing agent that removes wood colors by oxidizing them into colorless forms. While these two solutions can be applied one after the other, usually they are mixed together and applied at the same time. Fig. 56-9. The strongest bleach is obtained when equal parts of both solutions are used. A weaker bleach can be made by using twice as much of No. 2 as No. 1 and then adding a small amount of water.

A bleach leaves a thin residue that must be washed off and then sanded before the finishing can proceed. A major disadvantage of bleaching is that moisture content is added to the wood when the residue is washed off. It is absolutely necessary that the wood be properly dried before proceeding with the finishing; usually a piece must dry overnight at 70 degrees if heating ovens are not available.

Another problem that can develop, particularly when applying bleach to solid glued-up stock, is that the water applied to the face surface during bleaching will cause the wood to cup. Therefore, when washing off the bleached surface, it is often a good idea to apply plain water to the opposite face also so that the moisture content of the wood will be equalized.

Safety

Wood bleaches are powerful substances that can injure the person applying them. They are also inflammable due to their high oxygen content. (Oxygen is one of the two gases used in welding torches.) Follow these safety suggestions:

• Wear eye goggles or a face mask, rubber gloves, and a rubber apron.

• Mix the bleach in a glass, ceramic, or stainless-steel container.

• Do the bleaching in conditions of good ventilation and away from any open flame or spark.

• If bleach comes in contact with the skin, wash it off immediately with soap and water.

• Apply bleach with a rope brush or cellulose sponge. Never use rags.

• Never allow mixed bleach to stand around for any length of time. Always clean out the container and mix a fresh batch when needed.

789

56-9. There are several kinds of bleaches. Always follow the manufacturer's directions for mixing and applying.

56-10. Applying a commercial bleach with a synthetic rubber sponge.

56-11. Hardware must be removed before the finishing is done.

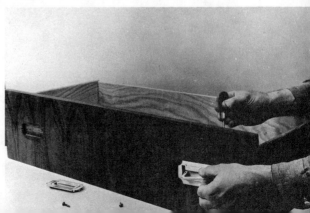

56-12. All final sanding should be done with a portable machine or by hand with closed-coat abrasives (sandpapers that have the complete surface covered with abrasive grains).

Application

In industry, bleach is usually applied by spraying it on the wood surface. However, for most school and cabinet shops, a rope brush or sponge is satisfactory. Fig. 56-10. The following is the correct procedure:

1. Mix the bleach to the correct proportion.

2. Apply the bleach, working from the top down.

3. Allow the bleach to remain about 30 minutes. If necessary, apply a second coat.

4. Wash down the bleach with a 50-50 solution of clear water and white vinegar, using a sponge to wipe it off.

5. Allow the surface to dry at least 12 hours at 70 degrees F. Make sure there is good air circulation around it.

6. Carefully sand the bleached surface with 6/0 garnet paper and wipe it clean before finishing.

56-13. Three major types of final sanding. From left to right: portable belt sanding, hand sanding, and oscillating sanding.

56-14(a). Hand sanding a table top.

56-14(b). Using a strip of sandpaper on a crevice that is hard to get at with a machine.

REMOVING HARDWARE

The preliminary fitting of hardware is usually done while the product is in the white-wood (unfinished) stage of construction. Holes and openings are drilled for handles, catches, locks, or other hardware. Most of these items, except certain hinges, are removed before final sanding and finishing. Fig. 56-11.

FINAL SANDING OF CASEWORK AND BUILT-INS

The final sanding of casework and built-ins depends on the kind of finish to be applied and the quality of construction. If paint or some other opaque finish is used, final sanding with 1 or 1/2 garnet paper is satisfactory. However, if a transparent finish is to be applied, the surfaces should be given a final sanding with 2/0 garnet paper. Fig. 56-12. Care should be taken so that there are no cross scratches, especially where there is a solid wood frame around a plywood center.

56-15. Sanding recommendations for the cabinet room.

CABINET ROOM			
Type of Operation	Type Mineral and Technical Grades	Product Form (Rolls, Discs, etc.)	Special Remarks Concerning Usage
Drawer Sanding	40-X (1½) or 50-X (1) or 60-X (½) GARNET Cloth	Drawer Sanding Belts	Sanding dovetails—on lip type machine. Usually Oak sides most severe test for belt joint.
Portable Belt Sander	80-X (0) or 100-X (2/0) ALUMINUM OXIDE Cloth	Belts	Portable belt machine — take sander to assembled case to flush — square backs, tops of drawer fronts — general touch-up fitting.
Hand Sanding	100-C (2/0) or 120-C (3/0) or 150-C (4/0) GARNET Cabinet Paper	Sheets	Breaking edges using sheets and felt blocks touch-up.
Vibrator Sanding or (Oscillating) Finishing Sander	120-A (3/0) or 150-A (4/0) GARNET Finishing Paper	Sheets	Final inspection station—white wood sanding. Tops — final touch-up before top coat.

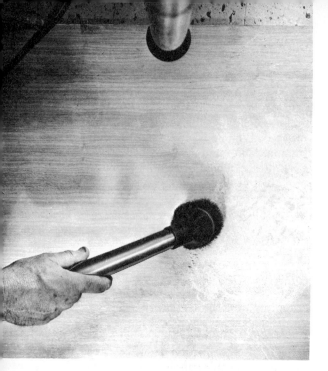

56-16(a). Using a vacuum cleaner to remove fine dust from the surface to be finished.

56-16(b). Brushing out the dust from a carving before finishing.

FINAL SANDING OF FURNITURE

Final sanding is usually done in the cabinet-assembly room before the product is ready for finishing. Fig. 56-13. Exterior surfaces are sanded with portable belt and finishing sanders. Sides and fronts of drawers are sanded as they are fitted into the case or cabinet. Hand sanding must also be done. Fig. 56-14.

There is no complete agreement among finishers as to what constitutes suitable sanding before finishing. The final sanding recommendation of a leading abrasives manufacturer is shown in Fig. 56-15. Other finishers recommend that the final sanding be done with garnet paper at least as fine as 6/0 for dense woods like oak or maple and 7/0 for low-density woods.

Some finishers recommend that, before final sanding, a glue size be applied to the exterior surface to hold the wood fibers firmly in place during finishing. This glue size is made by mixing one-fourth pound of liquid animal glue to one gallon of warm water. This is applied with a brush and allowed to dry thoroughly. Then the final sanding is done. This procedure is particularly recommended for the fibrous woods. However, care must be taken in the final sanding since, if too much of the size is left on the surface, it will interfere with the finishing process. On the other hand, if too much sanding is done, all of the size will be sanded away.

Generally the surface should be hand sanded with 5/0 to 7/0 garnet paper. Remember that sanding must always be done with the grain. Care must also be exercised when sanding 1/28" veneer surfaces with a portable sander so that the surface is not sanded too thin. After final sanding, all dust must be removed. This can be done first with a brush or vacuum cleaner. Fig. 56-16. Then wipe the surface with a *tack rag*, that is, a piece of cheesecloth or cotton rag moistened with thinned varnish or similar liquid. Such a rag will pick up small particles of dust from a wood surface.

792

The kind of finish is determined to a large degree by the equipment available. Some finishes can be applied with a rag, brush or roller. Fig. 57-1. In industry, however, most are applied by spraying with either lacquer or some synthetic finish. Fig. 57-2.

There are many different kinds of spraying equipment. Stationary spraying equipment used in a cabinet shop or well equipped school workshop consists of the following:

* An *air compressor* takes the air at atmospheric pressure and delivers it at a higher pressure through pipe and hose, to operate a spray gun. Fig. 57-3. The high air pressure provides a means of atomizing the finishing material into a fine spray. The capacity of a compressor is determined by the cubic feet of air delivered per minute (cfm). Compressors with a high cfm force more air through the hose to the spray gun.

* A *metal pipe* or an *air hose* connects the compressor to the transformer.

57-1. Some finishes for simple projects can be applied with a brush.

57-2. Most industrial finishes, however, are applied by spraying as in this furniture factory. Furniture pieces move along on a conveyer belt as the spraying is done.

57-3(a). This compressor and storage tank is the stationary type, commonly found in school and industrial shops.

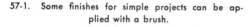
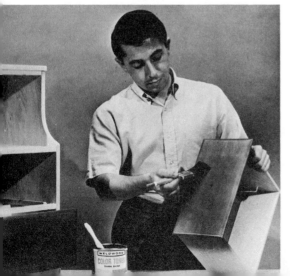

793

One Way Valve

Air

57-3(b). This portable compressor and tank can be used at any common electrical outlet. The tank assures constant pressure at the spray nozzle. All large compressors have a piston action that compresses air in a cylinder. The air then enters a pulsation chamber where the strokes are smoothed into a steady flow before traveling through the hose to the gun.

• An *air transformer* removes all of the oil, dirt, and moisture from the compressed air. Fig. 57-4. It also filters and regulates the air. A gage on the transformer indicates the air pressure by pounds. There are at least two outlets on the transformer, one for the spray-gun hose and another for other air tools. The air regulator, which is part of the transformer, maintains the correct air pressure with a minimum of change.

• A *hose* carries the air from the transformer to the spray gun. In some types of machines hoses also carry the paint or

57-4. For small shops this spray equipment is needed for most finishing. It includes an air transformer and regulator, a flexible hose, a spray gun with suction cups, and an air-dusting gun.

57-5(a). This equipment is needed for larger capacity spraying. It consists of (top row) an air transformer, a spray gun, and a pressure feed tank; (bottom row) an air hose for compressor to transformer, a fluid hose for tank to gun, and an air hose for compressor to gun. The air hoses are red and covered with rubber.

57-5(b). Typical heavy-duty portable spraying equipment including: portable air compressor (1), hose to convey air from compressor to material tanks (2), pressure feed tank (3), hose to convey air to the spray gun (4), hose to convey finishing material to the gun (5), pressure feed spray gun (6), air controlling device, such as an air adjusting valve attached to the spray gun (7), or an extra air regulator and gage installed at the tank (8).

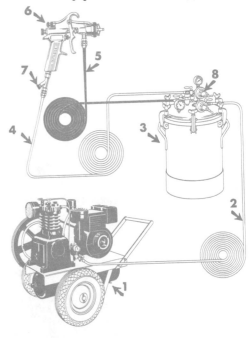

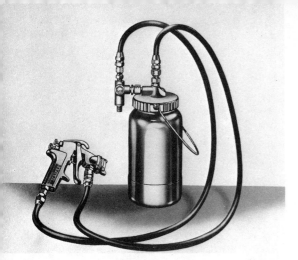

57-5(c). Smaller portable pressure feed tanks can also be used.

finishing material from the paint or fluid container to the gun. Some systems have pressure feed tanks that hold the finishing fluid. Fig. 57-5. Air pressure forces the fluid up from the container to the gun. Fig. 57-6.

- A *spray gun* is the heart of a good system. The finishing material is fed through the gun either by means of a suction cup attached directly to the gun, or by a hose from the pressure feed tank. A *suction-* or *siphon-fed* gun, on which a container is directly mounted, uses a stream of compressed air to create a vacuum. Fig. 57-7. This allows the atmospheric pressure to force the material from the attached container to the spray head. The *pressure-fed* gun has an air cap that does not necessarily cause a vacuum. The air

57-6. In a pressure feed system, air forces the paint or finishing material into the gun and then breaks up or atomizes the fluid into a fine mist.

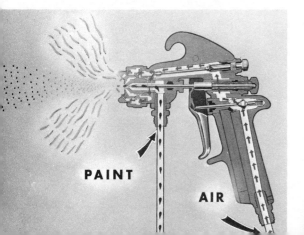

57-7. With a suction or siphon feed gun, the compressed air passes over the fluid tube inside the nozzle, creating a vacuum which draws the finishing material up from the container. A suction feed gun always has an air hole in the paint container cover. This type is recommended for finer atomization where an extra-fine finish is required.

57-8. With a pressure feed gun the compressed air in the container forces the material through the fluid hose to the nozzle. Pressure feed guns are usually used for fastest spraying and heavier materials.

795

INTERNAL   EXTERNAL

57-9. Spray guns have two types of nozzles, internal mix and external mix. The external mix can be used with either pressure or suction feed guns and is better for fast-drying material such as lacquer. The internal mix is best for heavy-bodied paints and can be used only with a pressure-type feed gun.

is forced through the gun by air pressure from the tank or cup. Fig. 57-8. In both pressure-fed and suction-fed guns the mixing of the air and fluid usually takes place outside the gun. This is called *external mix*. This is the only type suitable for lacquer and other fast-drying materials. In an *internal-mix* spray gun, the mixing takes place inside the cap. Fig. 57-9.

57-10. The bleeder gun has air flowing from the nozzle all the time, but material flows only when the trigger is pulled. This gun must be used only with a compressor that runs all the time. The non-bleeder gun has a trigger that controls the flow of both air and finishing material. Non-bleeder guns are used only with air storage-tank spraying outfits.

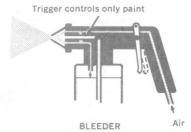

Trigger controls only paint

BLEEDER   Air

Trigger controls air and paint

NON-BLEEDER   Air

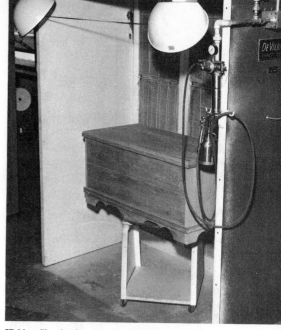

57-11. The dry booth is simpler to install and is most common in school shops. The booth is used when it isn't necessary to prevent overspray from being discharged to the outside.

57-12. The air-water spray booth reduces fire hazard and is used where the exhausted air must be clean as it leaves the stack. A touchup gun is being used on a night cabinet which is on a revolving table.

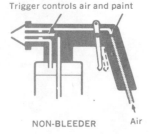

Spray guns may also be classified in two ways according to air control. In the *bleeder-type* gun there is no air valve, so a certain amount of air is constantly going through the gun. The *non-bleeder-type* is more common. It does have a valve which shuts off the air when the trigger is released. Fig. 57-10.

• Spraying should be done in a *spray booth* whenever this is at all possible. There are two common types: *dry* and *water-wash*. The dry one is mainly used for smaller shops where quick-drying material like lacquer is used and spraying is not done continuously. Fig. 57-11. In the dry booth, the contaminated air is drawn through baffles and expelled. The booth may be anything from a small bench type to a large floor model. The water-wash booth makes use of a curtain of water to trap the overspray and to cool the air as it is drawn through to the outside. Fig. 57-12. When spraying is done in a booth, a respirator is not required.

• A *respirator* or *mask* is worn over the nose and mouth to prevent inhaling finishing materials. This is needed if spraying is done outside a booth. The organic vapor mask that covers only the nose and mouth is the most common. Fig. 57-13. It comes with replaceable cartridges which remove the organic vapors.

PORTABLE SPRAYING

The simplest spraying equipment consists of a small portable compressor, a length of air hose, and a suction-fed spray gun. Fig. 57-14. Most compressors are of the piston type in which the air is drawn through an intake valve, compressed, and then expelled through the exhaust valve to the air line to provide the air pressure. Only the very simplest portable units have a diaphragm compressor in which the pressure is developed by the reciprocating action of a

57-13. Make sure a respirator or mask is worn whenever spraying is done outside a booth.

57-14. The main parts of a spraying outfit are the compressor, hose, and gun. Spraying outfits come in a wide range of sizes and for many different purposes.

flexible disk. Fig. 57-15. Red is the standard color for air hoses that connect the compressor to the spray gun on portable or low-pressure units; however, some units have black and orange, braid-covered hose. The spray gun of a portable unit is usually of the bleeder type, with external mix and suction feed. Such guns are designed for use on small air-compressor outfits that do not have an air-valve control. They can be used inside in a spray booth. When there is no spray booth, the spraying must be done out of doors on a very quiet day. It is necessary for the operator to wear a respirator.

USING A SPRAY GUN IN A BOOTH

Connect the air hose leading from the transformer to the air inlet of the spray gun. If a small portable unit is being used, lacquer is usually thinned half and half with lacquer thinner. Fig. 57-16. For spray outfits that have greater air pressure, lacquer can be used just as it comes from the can. Some lacquer may have to be strained through fine cheese-

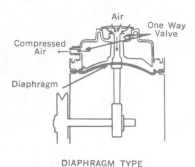

DIAPHRAGM TYPE

57-15. The diaphragm-type compressor compresses air by the flexing of a plastic diaphragm.

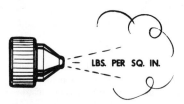

LBS. PER SQ. IN.

57-16. Larger spray outfits deliver more pounds-per-square-inch (psi) at the nozzle of the spray gun. A unit with a higher psi rating can spray thicker materials with less thinning required.

57-17. Always mix finishing materials to manufacturer's instructions. When necessary, strain the fluid into the container.

cloth or fine window screening to remove any impurities, but normally this is not needed. Fig. 57-17.

There are two common adjustments on the suction-feed spray gun. The *fluid adjustment screw* controls the amount of fluid flow. Fig. 57-18. Flow can also be controlled by limiting the amount the trigger is pulled. The *spreader-adjustment valve* changes the spray pattern. The patterns may be round, flat, or fan-shaped. Fig. 57-19. When a transformer and pressure-feed tank are used, start the fluid pressure at 15 pounds and the air pressure at 75 pounds. This should be changed as necessary until the best spray is obtained. First test the action of the gun. If the spray patterns seem starved for material, open the fluid adjusting screw. If necessary, thin the material. If the spray is too fast, reduce the flow by turning in the screw or lowering the air pressure. If the spray is too fine, reduce the pressure, making sure the fluid adjustment is wide open. If the spray is too coarse, increase the air pressure or reduce the amount of fluid flow.

Following are some common difficulties that must be corrected if the spraying is jerky or fluttering:

• The container is at too sharp an angle. Straighten it.
• There isn't enough fluid in the container.
• Dirt or other impurity is in the fluid passageway.
• The fluid tip is damaged.
• There is a crack in the fluid tube. When this happens on a suction-feed gun, it is usually because the material is too thick. It must be thinned. It may also be caused by a clogged air vent in the cup lid.

Spraying Techniques

The only way to learn to spray correctly is to get plenty of practice. The following are some helpful suggestions:

798

57-18. The fluid-adjusting screw can be set to control the fluid flow.

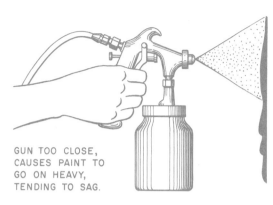

GUN TOO CLOSE, CAUSES PAINT TO GO ON HEAVY, TENDING TO SAG.

GUN TOO FAR AWAY, CAUSES EXCESSIVE DUSTING, AND A SANDY FINISH.

57-19. Patterns can be changed by adjusting the spread-adjustment valve.

57-20(b). Keep the gun the correct distance away from the surface.

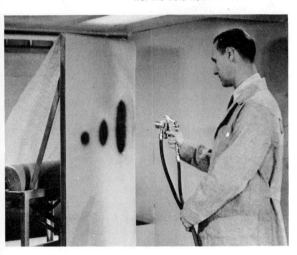

57-20(a). Move the gun in a straight line, never in an arcing motion.

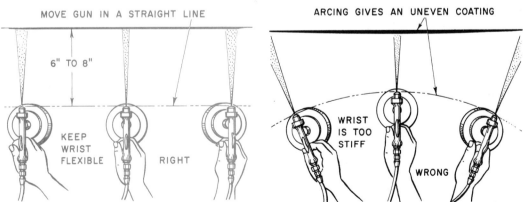

MOVE GUN IN A STRAIGHT LINE

6" TO 8"

KEEP WRIST FLEXIBLE   RIGHT

ARCING GIVES AN UNEVEN COATING

WRIST IS TOO STIFF

WRONG

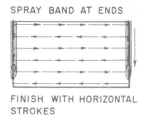

SPRAY BAND AT ENDS

FINISH WITH HORIZONTAL
STROKES

OVERLAP STROKES
ONE-HALF

FIRST STROKE IS AIMED AT EDGE OF PANEL

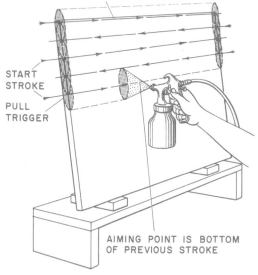

START
STROKE

PULL
TRIGGER

AIMING POINT IS BOTTOM
OF PREVIOUS STROKE

LONG PANEL CAN BE SPRAYED WITH UP & DOWN
STROKES

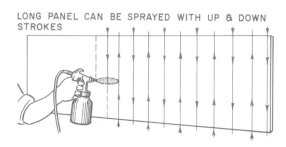

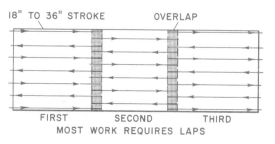

18" TO 36" STROKE   OVERLAP

FIRST   SECOND   THIRD
MOST WORK REQUIRES LAPS

1. Hold the gun about 6" to 8" from the surface being sprayed. This distance can be determined by following the technique shown in Fig. 57-20.

2. Move your arm, not your wrist, when spraying. Keep the gun at right angles to the surface at all points along the stroke.

3. The ends of the stroke should be feathered out by triggering the gun. Fig. 57-21. To trigger correctly, begin the stroke before pulling the trigger and release it before ending the stroke. Never move the gun in an arc since this will make the spray uneven.

4. Spray corners by holding the gun so that these surfaces will be sprayed equally and at the same time.

5. Overlap strokes about 50 per cent as the gun is moved back and forth across the surface. This will eliminate the need for double or cross coats.

6. When spraying curved surfaces, hold the gun at the normal distance but use a curved stroke. Fig. 57-22.

COMMON SPRAYING PROBLEMS

• "Orange peel" is a common defect that occurs when using lacquer and other synthetic materials in furniture finishing. It is so called because the surface has the appearance and texture of an orange peel. Common causes are improper thinning, pressure that is too high or too low, holding the gun too far away from the surface or too close, not having the material mixed thoroughly, or spraying a surface that has not been properly prepared.

• Streaks are caused by tipping the gun up or down or by dirt in the air cap.

57-21. **Banding.** Vertical bands sprayed at the ends of a panel prevent wasted spray from the horizontal strokes. Long work is sprayed in sections of convenient length, each section overlapping the previous one by 4". When spraying a panel, use alternate right and left strokes, releasing the trigger at the end of each stroke. The spray should overlap one half the previous stroke vertically.

- Runs and sags are caused by applying too much material or tilting the gun when spraying. Runs can also result when the spraying material is thinned too much. Sags are usually due to applying too much finishing material.
- Mist or fog is caused by having the material too thin or the air pressure too high.
- Starving the spray gun means that insufficient air or fluid reaches the gun itself. This is often due to dirt in the hoses.

CLEANING A SUCTION-FEED GUN

1. Loosen the air cap two or three turns and remove the fluid container. Hold a cloth over the air cap and pull the trigger. This will force the fluid that remains in the gun back into the container. Fig. 57-23.

2. Empty the container and clean it thoroughly with lacquer thinner.

3. Fill the container about one half full of lacquer thinner and reassemble the gun. Spray the thinner to flush out the fluid passages.

4. Remove the air cap and clean it Soak it in the thinner to remove all traces of the finishing material. Then brush or scrape until it is perfectly clean. Fig. 57-24.

5. Clean out any clogged holes with a tooth pick or match stick. Never use a sharp wire or nail. Wipe off the gun with a solvent-soaked rag and reassemble so it is ready for the next use.

FINISHING SUPPLIES

The following supplies are needed for the various finishing processes:
- *Turpentine*, made from the resin of pine trees, is used as a solvent for paint and enamel.
- *Linseed oil*, made from flaxseed, is used in paints, fillers, and stains.
- *Alcohol*, a colorless liquid made from wood drippings or chemicals, is used as a thinner and solvent for shellac. The

57-22. When spraying a curved surface such as the back of this chair, the operator must follow the curve of the surface.

57-23. Cleaning out the gun.

57-24. Brushing off the air cap with thinner.

57-25. Steel wool is frequently used to remove small blemishes.

57-26. A wide, thick varnish brush is ideal for applying finishing materials to large surfaces.

57-27. Three common kinds of brushes.

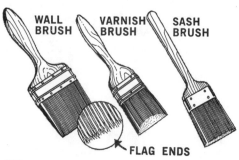

WALL BRUSH VARNISH BRUSH SASH BRUSH

FLAG ENDS

U. S. government has established a standard alcohol mix called Formula Special No. 1 denatured alcohol, which contains ethyl alcohol and wood alcohol.

• *Benzene,* used as a solvent and a cleaning fluid, is made from coal tar.

• *Mineral spirits* is a pure distillation of petroleum that will do everything that turpentine will do. It can be used as a thinner or solvent.

• *Waxes* can be either liquid or paste. Both types are made from a base of beeswax, paraffin, carnauba wax and turpentine. Wax provides a water-resistant surface that can be renewed often.

• *Steel wool* is made of thin metal shavings. It comes in pads or rolls and can be purchased in grades from 000, very fine, to 3, coarse. Fig. 57-25.

• *Pumice* is a white-colored powder made from lava. It is available in several grades. The most common grades for wood finishing are FF and FFF. It is combined with water or oil to rub down the finish.

• *Rottenstone* is a reddish-brown or grayish-black iron oxide that comes from shale. Much finer than pumice, it is used with water or oil to produce a smoother finish after the surface has been rubbed with pumice.

• *Rubbing oil* should be either petroleum or paraffin oil. If oil refined from petroleum is used, be sure it is a thin grade.

• *Abrasive papers* needed are garnet or aluminum oxide finishing papers in grades No. 4/0 (150) and No. 6/0 (220). No. 4/0 (150) is used for sanding after staining, after applying the first coat of shellac, and before applying the filler coat. No. 6/0 (220) is used for final smoothing after shellac coats or other finish. These may be used dry or with oil.

• *Waterproof (wet-or-dry) abrasive papers* in grades from 240 to 400 grit are used with water for hand sanding between lacquer coats or for rubbing enamel or lacquer.

• A *tack rag* is a piece of cheesecloth or cotton rag moistened with thinned varnish. It is used to pick up tiny particles of dust from the wood surface before applying finish.

BRUSHES

Many kinds and sizes of brushes can be used to apply finishing materials. Most are made with Chinese or Russian boar or nylon bristles. Fig. 57-26. Nylon bristles are most common for varnish and enamel. Bristle length determines the flexibility of the brush and its quality. When the ends of the bristles are bent over, they should spring back in place without any loose ends. In a good-quality brush the bristles should be set in rubber and there should be enough of them to give a full feeling when they are squeezed between the fingers. On animal-hair brushes the bristle ends should be split for better performance. Fig. 57-27.

A *varnish* or *enamel brush* is sturdy. It is used for applying heavier paints, as well as varnish and enamel. It has a chisel edge. Nylon-bristle brushes 2″ to 4″ wide and 3/8″ to 11/16″ thick are best for most surfaces.

A *wall brush* is more flexible than a varnish brush and it has longer bristles. It is usually 4″ to 5″ wide with a straight-cut edge for use with sweeping strokes on large, flat surfaces.

A *utility brush* is a small brush for painting trim of window frames. It should be about 1″ to 1½″ wide.

Sash brushes are used for fine work in painting around windows and doors. These brushes have long handles and oval, round, or flat-bristle heads. They come in various bristle lengths, either straight-cut or chisel-cut.

To break in a brush, soak it in a solvent up to the metal cap for about one hour. Fig. 57-28. Then wrap the brush in a heavy piece of paper for some time before using it. After a brush has been

57-28. Soaking a brush in solvent.

used, keep it suspended in a solvent of the proper type, according to these rules:
• Varnish and enamel brushes in a solution of half turpentine and half varnish.
• Paint and stain brushes in one part turpentine and two parts linseed oil.
• Shellac brushes in alcohol.
• Lacquer brushes in lacquer thinner.

To clean a brush, proceed as follows: slosh the brush in solvent to remove excess paint. Press out any excess solvent with a piece of smooth wood. Use a comb to remove paint imbedded in the bristles. Finish cleaning by pulling the brush against the palm of your hand, first in the solvent and then inside an empty can. Wipe the bristles dry with a clean cloth. Use a commercial cleaning solvent mixed in water, or a good grade of detergent to wash the brush thoroughly. Wipe dry and comb straight. Wrap the bristles in brown paper. Store brushes in a box or drawer, or hang them up.

Good Use of Brushes

The following are some general suggestions for using brushes:
• Revolve a new brush rapidly by the handle to dislodge loose bristles. Remember that all new brushes have them.

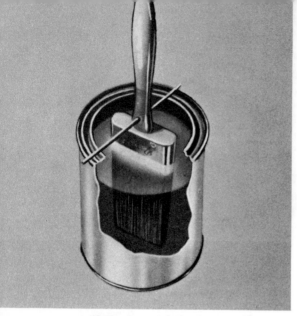

• Dip the brush into the finishing material about one third the bristle length. Tap the excess against the side of the can. Never scrape against the rim of the can, because this loosens the bristles.

• When using a brush, always hold it at a slight angle to the work surface.
• Never paint with the side of the brush. This is one of the main causes of "fingering."
• Never use a wide brush to paint small, round surfaces such as dowel rods. Your brush will "fishtail."
• Never let the brush stand on its bristle end. Its own weight bends and curls the bristles. Fig. 57-29. This would make painting difficult.

ROLLERS

Roller coaters can be used for some painting of large, flat surfaces and for applying some oil finishes. They cannot be used for finishes that dry rapidly. The simple-type roller is dipped into the paint. A self-feeding type is sometimes used by commercial painters. Various roller covers are available which make it possible to achieve different textures.

 # Finishing Procedures

Good design and a fine finish are two important characteristics of good-quality furniture. A fine finish, one which truly enhances the beauty and utility of the furniture piece, can be difficult and time-consuming to achieve. This is largely because wood is a variable material, with light and dark areas, natural colors and dyes, and soft and hard spots.

Today the furniture finisher has a choice of many materials. He can use not only standard spray finishes, such as varnish, synthetics, and lacquer, but also commercial finishes that can be applied with rag or brush. Fig. 58-1.

Several steps or procedures may be necessary to obtain a final finish. However, the steps are not the same for every kind of finish. As a matter of fact, some good finishes can be obtained through processes involving just three, two, or even one step.

The finishing process to choose depends partly on the type of wood and the appearance wanted. Also it is important to consider what finishing facilities and equipment are available. If the shop is equipped with a spray booth and good drying facilities, then a lacquer finish may be applied. Otherwise a simple finish that can be applied with a rag or brush is better.

58-1(a). This Contemporary lamp table has a standard surface finish. Ten separate and distinct finishing procedures were followed to complete its fine finish.

A Standard Finishing System

The following are the basic steps necessary for a fine wood finish. Covering capacities and drying times are shown in Fig. 58-2.

Bleaching

Bleaching removes color from wood. It is necessary for very light and for medium-light or honey-colored finishes. Many of the natural and darker finishes require

no bleaching. Bleaching is also done when the natural color of the wood is to be changed. For example, when finishing mahogany, it may be desirable to achieve a light honey color rather than red. This can be done by bleaching the red from the mahogany, then staining to the desired tone.

Pre-Staining

This is sometimes called *sap staining* because it is necessary when starting with natural woods in which color variation is great. A good example of this is walnut in which the sapwood is very light and the heartwood is quite dark. Sap staining is also done when different kinds of wood such as gum and mahogany are combined in the same product and a uniform color is desired for the final finish.

Staining and Coloring

Staining adds color to the wood and emphasizes the grain. It is also done to change the tone or shade of a wood surface. Many different kinds of stains or toners can be used.

58-1(b). In contrast, this hi-fi cabinet was given a finish that was completed in a simple three-step process called a penetrating "oil-rubbed" finish.

COVERING CAPACITIES*

Material	Sq. Ft. Per Gal.
Bleaching Solutions	250-300
Lacquer	200-300
Lacquer Sealer	250-300
Liquid Filler	250-300
Water Stain	350-400
Oil Stain	300-350
Pigment Oil Stain	350-400
Non-Grain Raising Stain	275-325
Paint	400-500
Spirit Stain	250-300
Shellac	300-350
Rubbing Varnish	450-500
Flat Varnish	300-350
Liquid Wax	600-700

*General average — will vary considerably, depending on thickness of coat, application to porous or non-porous surface, etc.

58-2(a). Covering capacities of common finishing materials. The general average will vary considerably, depending on such things as thickness of coat and application to porous or non-porous surfaces.

DRYING TIMES†

Material	Touch	Recoat
Lacquer	1-10 min.	1½-3 hrs.
Lacquer Sealer	1-10 min.	30-45 min.
Paste Wood Filler	. . .	24-48 hrs.
Water Stain	1 hr.	12 hrs.
Oil Stain	1 hr.	24 hrs.
Spirit Stain	Zero	10 min.
Shading Stain	Zero	Zero
Non-Grain Raising Stain	15 min.	3 hrs.
NGR Stain (Quick Dry)	2 min.	15 min.
Pigment Oil Stain	1 hr.	12 hrs.
Pigment Oil Stain (Q.D.)	1 hr.	3 hrs.
Shellac	15 min.	2 hrs.
Shellac (Wash Coat)	2 min.	30 min.
Varnish	1½ hrs.	18-24 hrs.
Varnish (Q.D. Synthetic)	½ hr.	4 hrs.

†Average Time. Different products will vary.

(Courtesy of Practical Builder)

58-2(b). Average drying times for finishing materials. Different products vary somewhat from these figures.

Wash Coating

Wash coating is done to keep the stain from bleeding into the filler and to provide a hard surface for applying the filler. The wash coating is a very thin coating of shellac or lacquer sealer that leaves the pores open so that filler can be added. A good sealer for many stains is a wash coat of white shellac that is a mixture of seven parts alcohol to one part of four-pound-cut shellac. Lacquer sealers are frequently used for wash coating when the final finish is to be spray lacquer.

Filling

Fillers add color and close the pores of wood. Closed-grained woods with very small pores, such as pine, cherry, poplar, fir, and cedar, require no filler. Others such as birch, gum, and maple may take a liquid filler. Open-grained woods, particularly oak, mahogany, and walnut, require a paste filler. With these woods, the filler is sometimes eliminated to give the wood an open-pore appearance. For blond finishes, the filler can be white lead, white zinc, or a natural paste with a light color in oil.

Sealing or Wash Coating

A sealer or wash coat is applied over the stain and/or the filler to prevent the color from bleeding into the finish. A good sealer for most finishes is a shellac wash coat. If a lacquer finish is to be applied, a lacquer sealer can be used in place of the wash coat of shellac.

Glazing

Glazing is the application of a coat of thin, transparent finishing material over filler or sealer to give a highlighted, shaded, or antique effect. This is used most frequently in the finer finishes. To antique by glazing, thoroughly wipe off the glaze from the flat surfaces and edges that should appear worn, and leave the glaze in the recessed areas.

Topcoats

A varnish, synthetic, or lacquer finish can be applied as topcoat after all coloring and filling have been completed.

Rubbing, Polishing, and Cleaning

After the topcoat is on, the surface is rubbed, polished, and waxed to a high sheen.

FINISHING OPEN-GRAINED WOOD

The following are the usual steps in producing a fine finish on mahogany, walnut, oak, and other open-grained woods. For a lighter or honey-toned finish, it is necessary to bleach the wood before starting the finishing process. For medium to darker finishes, this procedure should be followed:

1. Apply a thin glue size mixed in water, and allow to dry. Then sand well with 3/0 garnet paper. Clean the surface thoroughly with a tack rag.

2. Apply water stain and allow it to dry thoroughly. Sand lightly with 3/0 garnet paper.

3. Apply a wash coat of shellac or lacquer sealer. Allow it to dry three to four hours. Then sand the surface with 5/0 garnet paper.

4. Apply a colored filler with a brush. Rub across grain with a circular motion, forcing the filler into the pores. Then wipe across grain with burlap to remove excess filler. Next wipe along the grain with a fine cloth, using a light stroke to even up the surface. Allow it to dry overnight.

5. Apply a sealer coat of shellac or lacquer, allow to dry, and sand with 6/0 or 7/0 garnet sandpaper.

6. A glaze can be applied over the sealer to give a highlighted, shaded, or antique effect. This step is not necessary for Contemporary or Modern finishes.

7. Apply three coats of lacquer with sufficient drying time between each coat. Sand lightly.

8. Rub to a light sheen with pumice stone and water or paraffin oil.

9. Rub with a good paste wax and polish.

COMMERCIAL SYNTHETIC FINISHES

Many commercial finishes can be used in the shop with little difficulty. Most of

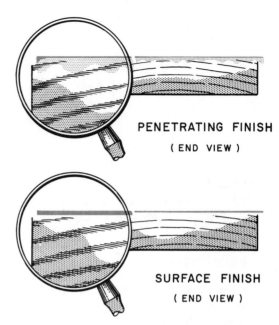

PENETRATING FINISH
(END VIEW)

SURFACE FINISH
(END VIEW)

58-3. Here you see the difference between a penetrating finish and a surface finish. Most simplified finishes are penetrating while standard finishes are of the surface type.

these sink into the wood. Fig. 58-3. Such finishes do away with the dust problem that is so bothersome when using varnish. Penetrating and wipe-on finishes are synthetic chemical materials.

Sealacell

This three-step process involves three different materials, each of which can be applied with a rag or cloth. The materials include the following:

• *Sealacell*, a moisture-repellent, penetrating wood sealer, is applied over the raw wood. (Ground-in-oil pigments can be mixed with the Sealacell to serve as a stain). Stain and filler can be applied in one step by mixing paste filler in the Sealacell and then adding ground-in-oil pigment to get the right color. Apply very liberally with a cloth, as the depth of penetration depends on the amount applied. Let dry overnight. Buff lightly with fine steel wool.

• *Varno wax* is a blend of gums and waxes. To apply, make a small cloth pad

807

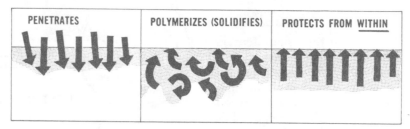

| PENETRATES | POLYMERIZES (SOLIDIFIES) | PROTECTS FROM WITHIN |

58-4. A chemical action takes place when the material is applied.

about 1″ x 2″. Coat with wax and rub with a circular motion first, then wipe out with the grain. Buff lightly with 3/0 steel wool.

• *Royal Finish* is the final coat. It is applied in the same manner as the Varno wax. Two or more applications of Royal Finish increase the depth of luster. A soft egg-shell finish can be obtained by buffing with fine steel wool.

Minwax

Minwax is a penetrating wood seal and wax that is applied directly to raw wood. Two coats will complete the job. The natural beauty of the wood is preserved because this finish penetrates and seals, leaving the finish in the wood with very little on the surface. Minwax is available in natural or light oak, pine, dark walnut, Colonial maple, and red mahogany. It dries rapidly, and more than one coat can be applied in one day. Although it isn't necessary to rub between coats, it is a good idea to use 4/0 steel wool to obtain a very fine finish.

Deft

Deft is a semi-gloss, clear, interior wood finish. It is easy to use, requires no thinning, will not show brush marks, and will not darken. This material seals, primes, finishes the wood, and dries in 30 minutes. Three coats are recommended. The first coat seals the wood, the second adds depth, and the third results in a mirror-smooth, fine furniture finish. The third coat can be sanded with 6/0 wet-dry sandpaper or rubbed mirror-smooth with pumice and rottenstone. All three coats can be applied in a few hours. Deft can also be applied from an aerosol spray can.

Watco Natural Wood or Danish Oil Finish

These are super-penetrating oil finishes consisting of oils and resins which are used for all natural wood furniture and interiors. They seal, prime, finish, and preserve wood in a single application. After penetrating the wood surface they actually combine with it chemically. Fig. 58-4. Ideal for fast, simple finishes, these products result in that flat, natural appearance so popular for Danish Modern furniture. The finish is particularly recommended for walnut, teak, and rosewood. Fig. 58-5. The process is relatively simple:

1. Finish sand the wood surface with 6/0 garnet paper. Make sure the surface

58-5. This walnut phonograph cabinet has a natural oil finish.

58-6. Notice that the oil is applied very generously to the surface.

58-7. Rubbing the oiled surface with abrasive paper.

is clean and dry. If necessary, stain and fill the wood surface, using oil-paste fillers mixed with the oil-finishing material. A ready-mix wood stain can also be applied under the oil finish.

2. Apply the wood oil liberally, flooding and saturating the surface. This can be done with a brush or by spraying. Fig. 58-6. Keep the surface wet for 15 to 30 minutes to assure penetration and saturation.

3. While the surface is wet, scuff-sand with 6/0 wet-dry, silicon-carbide paper, keeping it well lubricated with the oil. One or two minutes of wet sanding is usually enough. Fig. 58-7.

4. Remove all surplus oil with a soft, lint-free cloth. Fig. 58-8. Allow to dry about 12 hours, or overnight.

5. Wipe lightly with an oil-dampened rag. Wipe dry and buff with a soft cloth. If desired, a liquid carnauba satin wax may be applied and buffed to a soft luster.

One major advantage of these finishes is that they can easily be repaired. Fig. 58-9.

Synthetic Sealer Finishes

Many different companies make a penetrating sealer finish that can be used for

58-8. Cleaning off the excess with a rag.

58-9. A fire accident on this oil-treated walnut desk could be repaired easily by rubbing with light steel wool, followed by the application of an oil finish.

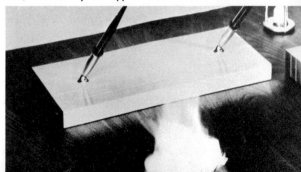

58-10. Select the color and tone, and then add the necessary tinting color to the base.

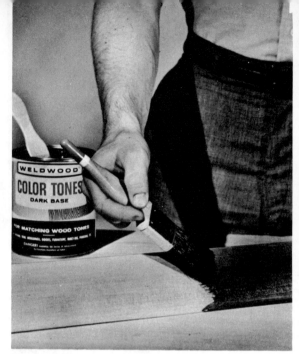

58-11. Applying the finish with a brush. Allow time for penetration.

the entire finishing system. These materials are used only on new or unfinished wood or wood from which the old finish has been completely removed. The sealer finish can be applied with a lint-free cloth or a brush. The final finish gives a "close-to-the-grain" appearance. The sealers are often made in two basic types: a light and a dark. The color is achieved by adding a tube or package of tinting color. Fig. 58-10. The sealer is then applied with a brush or cloth. Fig. 58-11. Allow a short time for penetration, less than 20 minutes for most woods. If the penetration does not appear uniform before wiping, apply a second coat after the first one dries. Then wipe off the excess with a clean cloth. Fig. 58-12. As the protective topcoat, the same sealer or a clear finish is usually used without the color. When thoroughly dry, a rich polish can be obtained by buffing with extra-fine steel wool. Wax may be applied.

SIMPLIFIED SHOP FINISHES

There are several fine finishes that do not require special equipment or many commercial materials. Two of these are shellac and natural oil. The shellac finish is not a good choice if the wood is to be exposed to moisture, because shellac turns cloudy in dampness.

Shellac Finish

White shellac is a clear finish that adds no tone at all. It is particularly good for light, closed-grained woods such as pine, birch, and maple.

1. Go over the surface for final sanding with 5/0 garnet paper.

2. Mix an equal amount of four-pound-cut shellac and alcohol in a glass or porcelain container.

3. Apply the shellac evenly with a good-quality 1½" to 2" brush.

4. Allow to dry four hours, and smooth evenly with 4/0 steel wool.

5. Apply three or four thin coats, rubbing down between coats.

6. After the final coat, rub down with 4/0 steel wool and apply paste wax. The time needed for shellac to dry depends to some degree on weather conditions.

58-12. Wipe off the excess with a clean cloth.

Oil Finish

Contemporary furniture of walnut or teak is frequently given an oil or oil-varnish finish to emphasize the beauty of the grain and to preserve the wood. This finish is especially attractive when several coats are applied and rubbed thoroughly. The finish grows slightly darker and richer with time, and additional coats of the same oil can be applied as needed, usually once a year.

1. Use a mixture of two parts boiled linseed oil and one part turpentine *or* equal parts of spar varnish, boiled linseed oil and turpentine.

2. Place the container with the mixture in boiling water for 10 to 15 minutes to thin the oil properly.

3. Apply the finish by saturating a cloth with the oil and rubbing the entire surface until a uniform color is obtained.

4. Rub small sections of the surface for 10 to 25 minutes at a time. Wipe off the excess with a lint-free cloth.

5. Allow 24 hours between coats. A week to a month later, additional coats can be applied.

59 Staining

Stains provide a rich undertone and bring out the beauty of the grain. Fig. 59-1. It is the first step in the standard finishing process, provided the wood is not bleached.

Staining is extremely important to color harmony of furniture. Changing the kind and color of stain will make the same wood appear entirely different. For example, dark-red stain has been widely used in Traditional mahogany furniture. Many people even today think of mahogany as a dark-colored wood. Actually, much Contemporary mahogany furniture is light, honey-toned brown.

Stains can also be used to make a less

811

59-1(a). This Early American step table is made of genuine cherry throughout. The natural color of the wood varies from light straw to amber with a grayish cast. Stain gives this table the uniform golden-brown color so commonly associated with cherry.

expensive wood look like a costly one. Gum, for example, is often stained to imitate mahogany. Stains are important in equalizing the color of a wood surface, as in sap staining. Fig. 59-2.

SAP STAINING

When there is wide variation in wood color, especially between sapwood and heartwood, sap staining should precede regular staining. Use either an alcohol-base sap stain or a water-soluble stain. Apply to the light areas, either by brushing or spraying. By continuing to apply the stain, the light areas can be made as dark as the rest of the wood. Then standard staining procedures can be followed.

INGREDIENTS IN STAINS

Stain consists of two materials: *coloring* and *vehicle*. The coloring matter is soluble color (dye) or pigment color. *Soluble colors or dyes* actually go into the solution; when they are applied to the wood, they penetrate the pores and dye the wood surface. Some are made from natural substances such as certain plant and animal extracts. The great majority, however, are modern industrial chemicals obtained from coal-tar. Many of these dyes are very similar to fabric dyes used in the textile industry.

Pigment colors are finely ground color particles that disperse in the vehicle but do not dissolve. When pigment colors are used as stain, the particles of color remain on the wood surface, giving it a uniform appearance. Pigment colors may also be made from natural materials or have a chemical base. The natural color pigments include iron oxide, yellow oxide, burnt sienna, raw sienna, burnt umber, raw umber, ochre organic pigment, titanium oxide, zinc sulfate, cadmium sulfate yellow, cadmium sulfate orange, lead-chromate yellow, and orange chromate.

KINDS OF STAINS

Water Stains

Water stains are natural and acid dyes that are mixed in water. The water soluble powder is purchased and then mixed in hot water. From one to eight ounces of powder per gallon of water is used, depending on the color wanted. Generally, the mixture is about four ounces of powder per gallon. Water stains are available in common colors such as brown mahogany, mahogany, orange, green, yellow, golden oak, fumed oak, and red mahogany. Water stains have several important advantages:

• The stain is absorbed by the wood and therefore shows a greater contrast in figure than is possible with other kinds of stains.

• Water stains are easily applied with a brush and do not require extensive production equipment.

812

59-1(b). The base of this table is cherry, but it has been stained to give it a fruitwood appearance.

• Water stains are cheaper than most other stains because they are purchased as dry powder and mixed in water.

• Water stains do not bleach when exposed to light as much as pigment oil stains will.

• Water stains can be darkened by applying a second or third coat if the first is not suitable.

• Water stains dry quickly.

Some disadvantages are: Water stains swell the wood fibers and raise the grain. If several coats must be applied, water stains may have an adverse effect on glue joints.

Applying Water Stains

Mix a small amount of powder in a gallon of boiling water, then test the stain on a piece of scrap wood of the same kind as the product. The color of water stains will appear somewhat darker on larger surfaces than on the small test piece. Therefore it is a good idea to apply a slightly lighter coat than seems necessary. Before applying the water stain, sponge the surface lightly with water. Fig. 59-3. It may help to add just a little hide glue to the water to hold the surface fibers in place. This should dry four to five hours and then be sanded with 5/0 sandpaper. Fig. 59-4. Always sponge end grain with water before applying the stain to keep it from absorbing too much stain and darkening too much. Apply the stain evenly with a

59-2. Differences in color and other irregularities that can be eliminated with stains. (a) Pith flecks in basswood are narrow streaks resembling pith. (b) Streaks of different degree in oak.

59-3. Sponging the surface in preparation for water staining.

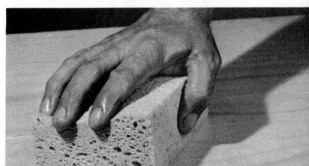

813

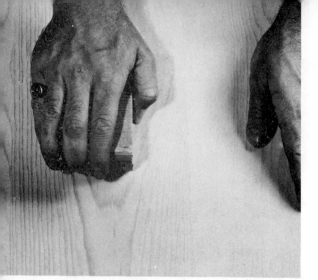

59-4. Sanding the surface after sponging.

COMMON COLORS IN OIL (TINTING COLORS)

Lt. Yellow	Raw Umber	Orange	Dark Green
Medium Yellow	Burnt Umber	Light Green	Blue
Raw Sienna	Ochre	Medium Green	Toluidine Red
Burnt Sienna			Deep Red
White		Lamp Black	Chrome Orange

59-5(a). Common tinting colors that can be used to make oil stains or to change the color of the stain.

59-5(b). Sample colors that can be shop-made for finishing.

USING COLORS IN OIL FOR FINISHING

White	Use zinc oxide ground in oil
Golden Oak	Use white zinc tinted with yellow ochre and raw sienna
Light Brown	Use Vandyke brown
Medium Oak	Use raw sienna and burnt sienna
Dark Brown	Use Vandyke brown and drop black
Walnut	Use half Vandyke brown and half burnt umber
Black	Use drop black

brush or sponge, then wipe it off with a rag or sponge. Allow the stain to dry overnight and then sand lightly. Water stains are not used in industrial finishing except for sap staining.

OIL STAINS

There are two common kinds of oil stain: *pigment* and *penetrating*.

Pigment-oil stains are made by adding pigment color to boiled linseed oil and turpentine. Fig. 59-5. Such stains are usually purchased ready-mixed in a wide variety of colors. These stains are often used in finishing furniture in school shops. Advantages of pigment-oil stains are: They are available ready-mixed, are easy to apply, do not raise the grain, and can be mixed with wood filler to make a combination stain and filler. Disadvantages: They are more expensive than water stains, do not penetrate deeply and therefore sand off easily, and they are slow to dry. Pigment-oil stains are best used on wood with small pores such as birch, gum, beech, and maple. They are also good when the surface has an uneven color.

Applying Pigment-Oil Stains

Sand the surface smooth and wipe free of any dust. Always wipe the surface with a tack rag before applying the stain. Make sure the stain is of the right color and is well stirred so there is an even distribution of pigment. Fig. 59-6. Then brush on an even coat of linseed oil to keep the end grain from absorbing too much of the color. Apply the stain with a soft clean brush. Fig. 59-7. Dip the brush in the stain about one-third its length. After the stain has been applied, allow it to dry for a few minutes. Then use a soft, lint-free rag to wipe the stain to "blend" or even up the color and pick up any excess. Wipe with the grain. If the wood varies greatly in color between sapwood and heartwood, wipe the

59-6. (a). If possible, select stain color from a chart. Then test the color on a separate piece of matching wood or on an inconspicuous part of the furniture piece. Stain colors can be adjusted by mixing one with another or by adding a tube of tinting color. (b). If stains have been mixed or if tinting color has been added, it is especially important to mix the stain thoroughly before applying.

darker areas more quickly and allow the stain to remain on the lighter areas for a longer time. The longer the pigment-oil stain remains on the wood without wiping, the more it darkens the surface. After the stain has been applied, allow it to dry overnight before proceeding with the remaining finishing steps.

Penetrating-oil stains are made by mixing soluble dyes in oil. While these stains can be purchased as dry material and then mixed in oil, they are more commonly used in ready-mixed form. Pentrating-oil stains are relatively easy to apply and do not show streaks. They can also be mixed with wood filler to make a combination stain-filler.

Penetrating-oil stains are not commonly used with lacquer finish because they tend to bleed through the sealer; also, they fade in sunlight.

Spirit stains are made by dissolving soluble dyes in alcohol. They dry very rapidly but do not penetrate deeply into the wood. Because of their fast-drying action, the second coat needed to produce the darker shades can be applied almost immediately. A difficulty is that spirit stains tend to bleed.

Non-Grain-Raising Stains (NGR)

Non-grain-raising stains, made by mixing color dyes in a solution of glycol and alcohol, have all the advantages of

59-7. Brushing on stain. Apply even pressure, working with the grain of the wood. Avoid skips or pile-up of stain along the edges.

water stains without the disadvantages. They are so named because they tend not to raise wood grain. They can be purchased in ready-mixed colors or as a concentrated base color that can be mixed to different shades. These stains have bright, transparent colors and are excellent in sunlight since they do not fade. Another advantage is that they are non-bleeding, especially when lacquer or varnish is used as the top coat. Because it is necessary to apply these stains by spraying, they are used primarily in industrial finishing.

SEALER STAINS

Sealer stains, commonly called commercial stains, are really synthetic sealers that can be used both as stains and sealers. They give a "close to the grain" appearance that is partly penetrating and partly surface in nature. Color can be added by mixing in tinting colors from a tube.

Transparent Lacquer Toners

Made from dyes and lacquer, these give a combined staining and sealing effect. However, their staining properties are not especially good. They are sometimes used over another stain or a filler to add color.

To start, mix enough stain for the entire job. Test for color on scrap wood of the kind to be stained. It is better to apply two light coats of stain than one heavy one. It is much easier to darken the wood than it is to lighten it.

Wash Coat

Wash coating (sealing) is done to keep stain from bleeding, to provide a hard surface for applying filler, and to improve the toughness of the finish. Good sealer for many stains is a wash coat of shellac. This is a mixture of seven parts alcohol to one part of four-pound-cut shellac. In furniture production in which lacquer is used as the final finish, *lacquer sealers* are used.

A wash coat must be applied very thin so it doesn't completely fill the pores and prevent the use of fillers. If shellac is used, brush on a light coat and allow it to dry about one hour. If lacquer sealer is sprayed on, it will dry in about one-half hour. Then sand lightly with 6/0 or 7/0 sandpaper. Wipe clean. The surface is then ready for filling.

Filling

Wood fillers are used in the finishing process for two purposes. Fig. 60-1. They fill and level the pores of the wood and add color to the final finish. Fig. 60-2. The filler may be about the same color as the stain; or a lighter filler can be used with a darker stain to achieve a two-toned effect. Fig. 60-3. While application of the filler may seem simple, it can ruin the complete finish if done incorrectly.

KINDS OF FILLERS

Woods with large pores, such as walnut, mahogany, oak, chestnut, hickory, and ash, require a paste filler. These fillers consist of about 75 per cent pigment and 25 per cent liquid. The pigment is primarily ground silica and color; the liquid is usually oil. Paste fillers can be purchased in the natural color and then tinted by adding stains or such pigment

The appearance of fine furniture can be changed by the application of different finishes. This Early American or Colonial furniture has a handsome, dark, English-tavern finish that blends with the motifs of the past. The darker finish also contrasts well with the bright red, white, and blue background of the walls, fireplace, trim, and floor. The curio cabinet has a lighted interior and a back panel covered with felt that is a perfect background for a collection of old glass or pewter. Color and accents are the keynote of this room.   Drexel

Color is used to make this bedroom as bright and gay as the morning sunshine. The furniture is made of pecan in both veneers and solids. The dressing table doubles as a desk. To reveal its warmth and natural beauty, the wood is finished in a light brown. Wall colors, accents, and wood finishes get along well together. *Drexel*

This gaily decorated kitchen-playroom displays bright reds, white, and green in a circus theme. Plastic laminates make the room more colorful and more practical. This room is a good example of why the cabinetmaker must understand color, not only in the form of finishes but also in colored materials such as plastic laminates. *Formica*

816C

The beautiful red oak kitchen cabinets in this home of plank-and-beam construction were built on the job. Finishing was done after construction. The red oak plywood on the drawer and door fronts is sequence matched. This means that the veneers are from the same part of one log. Construction and finish are the highlights of this divider wall.   Georgia-Pacific

60-1. A paste filler was one step in producing the fine finish on this round mahogany table.

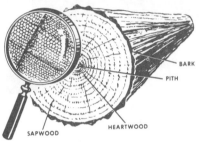

60-2(a). Many hardwoods contain large vessels and are very porous. When this lumber is surfaced, the tubular cells are ruptured, leaving tiny troughs that run lengthwise.

60-2(b). Unfilled pores make a filler necessary for certain hardwoods. This sample is red oak.

60-3. A pickled finish is one in which the wood filler contrasts sharply with the basic finish of the wood. For example, an ebony-stained wood might be filled with white paste filler. Can you see the results of pickling in this frame?

colors as burnt sienna or raw umber. White and off-white fillers are usually made from titanium oxide mixed with oil and resin. A liquid filler may be used on birch, maple, gum, or cherry. Fig. 60-4. Liquid fillers can be purchased from commercial sources or made by thinning paste filler with turpentine. While no filler is needed for closed-grained woods such as poplar, fir, pine, and basswood, it is a good idea to apply a sealer.

APPLYING PASTE FILLERS

Add turpentine, benzene, or naphtha to paste filler until it has the consistency of heavy cream. Mix oil color with a little turpentine and then add this to the filler until you get the color you want. Test on a sample piece that has been stained.

817

60-4. Semi-porous woods like the maple in this bedroom furniture have vessels so small that they may require only liquid filler or no filler at all.

60-5(a). Applying filler with a brush. Brush first with the grain.

60-5(b). Brush across grain, over the first filler coat. Rub into the pores.

Apply the filler with a stiff brush, rubbing it into the pores. Fig. 60-5. Brush both across and with the grain. In industry, the filler is sprayed on and then brushed into the grain. Rub the filler in with the palm of the hand or with a piece of burlap or a heavy rag. Fig. 60-6. Always add extra filler to end grain.

In applying filler, the idea is to work the paste well into the pores. After it has dried about 30 minutes (until the gloss disappears), rub across the grain with burlap or coarse cloth to remove most of the excess filler. Then, with a fine cloth, wipe very lightly with the grain to make sure the filler is evenly applied. Fig. 60-7. Remember that the filler must be packed firmly into the pores. Otherwise it may come loose after the topcoat has been applied and ruin the finish. However, do not rub too hard as this would remove some of the filler from the pores. To obtain the best results, the cleaning must be done while the excess is still soft. To remove extra filler from sharp corners, use a sharpened wood stick covered with a rag. This job must be carefully done so there is no residue to become hard and dry. Such residue would have to be removed with a rag moistened with turpentine.

APPLYING LIQUID FILLERS

Liquid fillers are sometimes used on woods such as birch, beech, cherry, and redwood. If the filler is made from paste, add turpentine until it is very thin. Apply with a brush and follow the same general process as for a paste filler.

FILLING DEFECTS

Several common defects can occur when filler is not applied properly, rubbed in well, and the excess removed. *Pinholing* occurs when air is tamped into an improperly filled pore. After the topcoat has been applied, a bubble of air will show on the surface. *Flow-out* re-

819

60-6. Rubbing filler into the pores with a heavy cloth.

60-7. Wiping off excess filler with a clean cloth.

sults when a good wash coat has not been applied between the stain and the filler coats. The filler appears to squeeze out of the pores. *Graying* is a condition that often develops after filler has dried for several hours. The surface appears to have a grayish cast. This is usually because the binder has been absorbed by the wood or because the wrong kind of filler has been used. *Bleeding* results when a good sealer coat is not applied over the filler or when the filler is not properly dry before sealing. It is caused by a mixing of the filler and the sealer.

APPLYING A SEALER

Before the top or finish coats are applied, it is necessary to seal the surface to form a barrier coat over the filler and to provide a good foundation for the topcoats. Even when woods have not been stained and filled (sometimes this is the case with plywood), it is important to have a good sealer on the surface. There are three common kinds of sealers: shellac, lacquer, and synthetic resin. White shellac is an excellent sealer but is not commonly used when lacquer is the finish coat. Shellac sealer is made by mixing one part of four-pound-cut white shellac with seven parts of alcohol. Shellac sealer is applied with a brush. A lacquer sanding sealer is made especially to be sprayed on as an undercoat for a lacquer finish. A penetrating resin sealer is a ready-mixed material commonly used on closed-grained and small-pore woods or on plywood to seal the surface and prevent the wood from absorbing moisture. There are also glazing sealers applied over the filler and before glaze is put on the surface. After a sealer is applied, it should be sanded lightly and then wiped with a tack rag.

⑥① Distressing, Glazing, And Other Overtone Treatments

There are several overtone treatments that add interest to the finish on a furniture piece or give it an antique appearance. Most of these are done after the filler and sealer are applied and before the final topcoats.

DISTRESSING

French and Italian Provincial furniture is given a distressed treatment to imitate the appearance of age and wear. Fig. 61-1. This can be done either mechanically or with a finishing material. In mechanical distressing, coral rock, a chain, a hammer, and many other items can be used to put small gouges, scratches, and dents in the wood surface.

Fig. 61-2. These are frequently filled with black glaze or dark stain to imitate wear marks on a genuine antique.

61-1. The legs and rails of this Italian Provincial dining table of walnut and cherry have been given a distressed finish.

61-2. The furniture finisher uses chain, coral rock, and other sharp instruments to produce small scratches, dents, and similar defects. This is done to imitate the wear marks found in the original furniture.

Many types of finishing materials such as heavy wax crayons, black paint, or dark stains can be applied or brushed on to add this worn look.

GLAZING

After the filler or sealer is applied, glazing is done to give a furniture piece a highlighted, shaded, or antique appearance. Fig. 61-3. Glaze can also be applied over a painted or enameled surface. Traditionally, antique glaze was applied over white or ivory enamel. However, the trend is toward a base color coupled with a tinted glaze. There are many commercial glazing materials; some are already colored, while others must be tinted with lamp black or other pigments. A simple antique glaze can be made in the shop by mixing a tablespoon of burnt umber in one-half pint of pure turpentine, then adding one teaspoon of drop black.

Glazing Over a Stain and Filler

The traditional method of glazing furniture that has a transparent finish is to use a light color for the stain and filler. Next a darker glaze is added, then wiped off except around the edges and in the corners so that they appear to be worn. A thin glaze coat is sometimes applied over the entire piece to even up the color.

Glazing Over a Painted Or Enameled Surface

Glazing over a painted or enameled surface gives an antique finish that is two toned, blended, or shaded. It is achieved by applying a tinted glazing liquid over an enameled base. This finish can be applied to either new or old furniture. The procedure is as follows:

1. Apply an undercoat of either "flat" paint or enamel of the color you want. Two coats are needed for new wood, while one may be enough for a surface already finished. Apply the undercoat generously, but make sure there are no drips or sags. Always brush with the grain. Allow the undercoat to dry thoroughly, at least 24 hours.

2. Mix the glaze thoroughly and tint

61-3. This bench-chest illustrates the use of glazing over an undercoat of paint. The colors range from rich terra cotta to light apricot on the raised and smooth surfaces. The full beauty of carved panels can be fully achieved by glazing.

821

if necessary. The glaze has a gelatin-like consistency; it will not drip, sag or run. Brush a thin coat of glaze on the entire surface, making sure indentations and low places are coated. If the furniture piece is large, it is better to apply the glaze in sections and then wipe it off. Allow the glazed surface to "set up" (become slightly tacky). This may take as much as 15 minutes.

3. Wipe off the glazing liquid in several places. Then use a cheesecloth to blend unwiped areas into the wiped ones. Wipe lightly at first then more heavily in those places where more highlights are wanted (usually the high points of carvings or the center of door panels). Wipe in long, straight lines in the direction of the grain. Paper towels, rags, burlap, and similar materials can be used. Each texture contributes a slightly different effect. Every effort should be made to create the illusion of excessive wear by blending, that is, having one coat of finish show through another.

4. After the glaze is completely dry (allow at least 24 hours) additional highlighting can be done mechanically. Fine sandpaper (No. 280) can be used to highlight certain areas, such as the centers of panels. Always leave a heavy glaze near the edges by gently "feathering" the edges of highlight so there won't be an abrupt or obvious line between the highlighting and shading. Steel wool can also be used to highlight rounded or carved surfaces. For a heavy, durable finish, a topcoat must be applied over the glazed surface.

OTHER TREATMENTS

Shading is done by adding a darker stain, sealer, or glaze around the edges and in corners. *Spattering* is a method of adding a speckled texture to the surface by flipping a glaze or other finishing material off the end of a stiff brush. This process also imparts an antique appearance. When applying this, bend the bristles with your fingers or a stick to get the spring action that throws the spray. To avoid blobs of finishing material, do not overload the brush. To be effective, spattering must not be overdone. Good *imitation worm holes*, to give the impression of antique furniture, can be made by spattering.

Protective Coatings

The last step in producing a wood finish is called the *topcoat*. Fig. 62-1. The three common topcoatings are lacquer, varnish, and synthetics. Chemical synthetics are constantly being developed and are slowly replacing lacquer for jobs that require a very tough surface. Since cold-spraying lacquers are the most practical for school and small cabinet shops, these will be covered in greatest detail.

After the topcoats are dry, they are usually rubbed, polished, and cleaned, then waxed and polished again.

LACQUER

Production of Lacquer

Lacquer is commonly defined as any finishing material that dries quickly by evaporation to form a protective film on a wood surface. In industry, approximately 80 per cent of all lacquers are of the nitrocellulose type. Cellulose, you will recall, is one of the four basic chemicals obtained from wood. However, most of the cellulose used in making lacquers comes from cotton. Cellulose must be made soluble by various acid treatments. The resulting substance, nitrocellulose, will dissolve in various chemical solvents. When lacquer is sprayed on a surface, the solvents evaporate, leaving a thin film of nitrocellulose and other additives.

By itself, nitrocellulose is rather hard and tough but not very elastic. For this reason, other things are added, such as plasticizers, resins, and oil. Plasticizers increase the elasticity of nitrocellulose. Resins and oils give more body.

Many kinds of lacquers are produced by using different additives and solvents. Lacquer should be carefully selected by studying the description supplied by the manufacturer. Lacquer should be used just as it comes from the container. The only thing that may be added is lacquer thinner *made by the same manufacturer*. Don't mix lacquers or use a different brand of thinner.

The most common lacquer topcoat for the school or cabinet shop is a cold-spraying variety made with 20 to 30 per cent solids. It is water-white and semi-gloss. Clear lacquers that have more than about 25 per cent solids tend not to spray easily. If the lacquer contains too many solids and is sprayed cold, it may not atomize (break up into fine particles) properly, resulting in orange-peel defect. The best spraying lacquer is one that contains a proper balance of solids for good coverage and liquids for free flow-out.

Advantages and Disadvantages

Some common advantages of lacquer finishes are:

• Lacquers are fast-drying; therefore several coats can be applied in a short time. It is not necessary to have special drying equipment.

• A lacquer coating is thin and clear. This is well suited to Contemporary American and current European styles that require a close-to-the-wood appearance. Fig. 62-2.

• Damage in lacquer finishes is easy to repair.

• Lacquer finishes have good durability. They are relatively high in resistance to damage by water, beverages, and food.

• They do not get soft and tacky when exposed to extreme temperatures.

• They are easy to rub, polish, and wax.

62-1. While good materials, attractive design, and quality workmanship are important, they are not enough. A fine product, such as this desk, must be given a good protective finish.

62-2. This walnut and teak end table with fancy parquetry top has a lacquer finish.

Some common disadvantages of lacquer finishes are:
• Lacquers are not highly resistant to such substances as nail polish and perfume.
• Excessive moisture (such as in a bathroom) may cause the lacquer to peel off the wood. Also, white water spots may develop.
• Lacquers dry so rapidly that it is very difficult to apply them with a brush.
• Lacquers are not as tough as some of the newer synthetic finishes.

Kinds of Lacquers

Since lacquers are made from such a wide variety of formulas, it is important to be very specific when ordering the kind needed for each furniture finish. Some lacquers are primarily for use on metals while others are for wood only. Never apply a metal lacquer over wood since it may check badly. Also, some lacquers are meant for brushing, others for spraying.

Wood spraying lacquers are sold in a variety of sheens ranging from full gloss to flat. The three usually kept in stock are gloss, semi-gloss, and flat. However, the final sheen of a lacquer coat can be changed greatly by the amount of rubbing and polishing done after application. There is a lacquer wood sealer made especially for applying a sealer coat over filler before spraying on the lacquer. Most lacquers are clear, although there are also colored lacquers.

Applying a Spray Lacquer Finish

Spraying is the most common industrial method of applying a lacquer finish. It is best to do this in a spray booth. Spraying can be done out of doors on a calm day; however, a mask must be worn. For more thorough discussion of spraying equipment, see Unit 57.

Spraying a Project

1. Clean the surface first with a tack rag.
2. Check the spray gun to make sure it is clean.
3. Use enough lacquer to make the spray container about half full. If the spraying equipment is of small capacity and low pressure, the lacquer must be thinned with about 50 per cent lacquer thinner. With larger capacity equipment, the lacquer can be used just as it comes from the container.
4. Try the spray gun on a piece of scrap stock. It should spray with a fine, even mist. Hold the gun about 6″ to 8″ from the work and move back and forth with straight, uniform strokes. Fig. 62-3. Always keep the gun perpendicular to the surface. Start the stroke off the work and pull the trigger when the gun is just opposite the edge. Release the trigger at the other end. Spray on four or five coats of thin lacquer. Sand lightly between coats. Usually the first coats are gloss or bright and the last coats are made dull or semi-gloss by rubbing. After you have finished spraying, clean all equipment with lacquer thinner.

Applying a Clear, Brushing Lacquer Finish

Apply the stain and filler coats the same as you would shellac and varnish

824

finishes. It is better to use a water stain than an oil stain because it won't bleed so much. Apply a thin coat of shellac as a sealer before using the lacquer.

Open a can of clear, brushing lacquer and stir it well. Lacquer usually does not have to be thinned; if it does, use a commercial lacquer thinner. Select a brush with soft bristles such as a camel's-hair brush. Dip it about one-third of the way into the lacquer, but do not wipe it on the side of the container. Load the brush heavily. Apply with long, rapid strokes. Lap the sides of each stroke. Do not attempt to brush the lacquer in as you would paint or varnish. Remember that lacquer dries very quickly and gives a smooth, tough surface. Allow the lacquer to dry about two hours. Then go over the surface lightly with No. 6/0 sandpaper.

Apply second and third coats in the same way. After the third coat is dry, rub and polish the surface.

VARNISH

Varnish was at one time the mainstay of furniture finishing. However, varnishes have been largely replaced by lacquer because they are slow-drying and their color retention is not good. They are still used to some extent in school and small cabinet shops. Their slow drying makes it extremely important to apply them in a very clean, dust-free place. Oleoresinous varnishes are made from vegetable drying oils such as linseed or tung oils combined with resins. *Oleoresinous* means a combination of oil and resin. The original resins used in these varnishes were natural, but today most of them are synthetic. The great advantage of varnish is that it is relatively low in cost. It contains from 45 to 50 per cent solids and can be reduced with an inexpensive thinner. Varnishes are easy to apply and have good coverage. When dry, they are tough and quite durable. They are high in water resistance and

excellent for exterior uses. However, because of the slow drying characteristic they have been largely discontinued in furniture production.

Applying Varnish

Varnishing should be done in a well ventilated room and at a temperature of 65 degrees F. or more. Always use a good-quality, clean brush. Stir the varnish before using, but do not shake it. Brush varnish on evenly and liberally, stroking across the grain first. Follow immediately with light strokes *with the grain* and always in the same direction. Fig. 62-4. Finish a small area at a time and proceed quickly before the edges have a chance to set. Brush from the drier area into the wet area. Do not try to touch up spots that may be partially dry. On wood that has been stained, filled and coated, or previously varnished, apply one or two coats of selected varnish without thinning. On new or unfinished wood, thin the first coat of varnish with mineral spirits or turpentine, one

62-3. Spraying is the best method of applying a good finish.

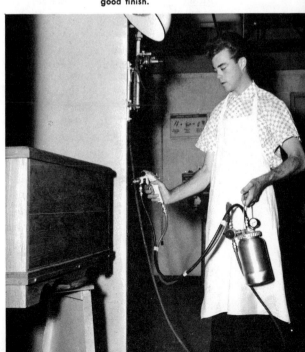

825

62-4. Brush the varnish both across and with the grain to even the surface.

pint spirits or turpentine to one gallon of varnish. The second coat should not be thinned. Allow each coat to harden thoroughly, normally from six to eight hours. Sand lightly with very fine sandpaper before recoating.

SYNTHETICS

In a sense, almost all finishing materials can be considered synthetics, since they are made in whole or in part from manufactured chemicals. However, the term *synthetic* is especially applied to some of the newer finishes, such as epoxies, polyurethanes, and polyesters. Most of these are used in large production plants for specialized purposes.

You may have noticed that some of these finishes have the same names as adhesives mentioned in Unit 40. As a matter of fact, these basic chemical substances (which are really a part of the plastics industry) are used as adhesives, finishes, structural materials, and for still other purposes. For example, various forms of epoxy are used for adhesives, furniture-protective coatings, production tools in furniture manufacture, and plastic laminate construction.

As you can see, plastics and woodworking are closely related. Not only do we combine many plastics with wood in making furniture and cabinets, but also we use plastics in the construction processes for gluing, laminating, and finishing.

RUBBING, POLISHING, AND CLEANING

After topcoats are dry, the surface should be rubbed, polished, and cleaned to provide a sheen and additional protective coating. The time between the application of the last topcoat and these final operations depends on the finishing materials used. If a lacquer finish is applied, the final rubbing and polishing can be done almost immediately, although it is best to allow the lacquer to dry from one to four hours. If the surface has been varnished, at least a week should be allowed for it to dry thoroughly.

Equipment needed for rubbing, polishing, and cleaning includes wet-dry abrasive paper, pumice, rottenstone, and waxes. See Unit 57. Abrasive manufacturers make various commercial rubbing and polishing compounds for these operations. They also make many different cleaners and polishes for final work.

Rubbing is done to smooth the surface and to remove irregularities that may have developed during finishing. It is

826

62-5. Polishing with a two-pad rubbing machine. The back-and-forth movement of the pads is supplied by air pressure. Note the lubricant in the trough at the end of the desk.

done with abrasive paper and lubricant. The lubricant is important because it keeps the paper from filling up with material rubbed off the surface.

Polishing is a burnishing action that removes or blends together fine scratch patterns. Polishing requires extremely fine abrasives such as pumice or rottenstone and some kind of lubricant such as oil or water. A felt pad is attached to a machine or to a wood block to do the polishing. Fig. 62-5.

Cleaning removes from the surface all foreign matter that resulted from rubbing and polishing. This is usually done with a detergent-moistened cloth. Cleaning is usually followed by waxing and/or polishing. Many waxes and polishes contain water-repellent silicones which provide excellent protection for a fine finish. They give a clean, dry surface, when wiped with a dry, lint-free cloth.

COMMERCIAL FINISHING METHODS

Sanding Topcoats

Topcoats are sanded to remove "orange peel" and any foreign matter from a surface before producing a satin or luster finish. Fig. 62-6. It is common practice to do this sanding with wet-dry sandpaper, a straight-line or reciprocating sander, and lubricant or rubbing oil. It can also be done with an air-operated, reciprocating machine or by hand. Whether the rubbing operations should be done with only a single grade of abrasive paper or a sequence of grades depends on such factors as the hardness of the surface, the speed with which the operation must be completed, and the desired quality of finish. If several grades

62-6. Sanding the topcoats with air-operated sanders.

827

62-7. Final cleaning before applying wax or polish is important to assure a fine finish.

62-8. Rubbing down a surface by hand with pumice and water, using a felt pad.

of paper are to be used, grade 280 should be used first, then use progressively finer papers including grades 300, 400, and 500. Grades 360 to 500 should be used for the final rubbing.

Dull Satin Finish

To obtain a dull satin finish, first rub by hand with grade 360 to 400 wet-dry sandpaper. Then apply a good coat of furniture cleaner and polish.

Period Satin Finish

To produce a satin finish for period-type furniture, first rub with grade 360 to 400 wet-dry sandpaper. Follow this by polishing with a slurry (mixture) of pumice and oil. As a final step, apply a furniture cleaner and polish or wax.

High-Sheen Satin

To obtain a high-sheen satin, rub with grade 500 wet-dry sandpaper. Follow by polishing with a slurry of rubbing oil and fine pumice (FF or FFF) and then rottenstone and rubbing oil.

Deep Luster Finish

To obtain a deep luster finish, do the

828

final rubbing with grade 500 wet-dry sandpaper. Then use a deep pile buffer to remove all scratches and bring the surface to a mirrorlike finish. Clean with lamb's wool. As the final step, polish with furniture cleaner. Fig. 62-7.

Shop Methods

Here are two other simple methods of rubbing, polishing, and cleaning a surface after topcoats have been applied.
• Make a paste consisting of FFF pumice and rubbing oil or water. Rub with the grain, applying medium pressure. Fig. 62-8. A felt pad is best for this. Continue to rub until the surface is very smooth. Then wipe the surface clean with a dry cloth. Make another paste or slurry of powdered rottenstone and rubbing oil, and repeat the rubbing process. Wipe dry with a cloth and then apply a wax coat.
• Rub the surface with water and grade 400 wet-dry sandpaper, sanding with the grain and applying medium pressure. Then wipe the surface clean. Rub the surface with a commercial polishing compound or with rottenstone or oil mixture. Finally, apply paste or liquid furniture wax.

Interior finishing is usually a much larger project, and one that takes more time than finishing a piece of furniture. Figs. 63-1 and 63-2. Some finishes for paneling are factory-applied. Fig. 63-3. However, most lumber and plywood come as raw wood and must be finished after installation. To do this work effectively it is necessary to know not only the kinds of finishes and how to apply them, but also the various materials commonly used for interiors, and the possible color arrangements. This unit is properly part of cabinetmaking because built-ins must be finished. The cabinetmaker and finish carpenter need to know how to do this work.

FINISHING SOLID WOOD PANELING AND INTERIORS

While some paint and enamel are used for interiors, most finishes are transparent or semi-transparent. Their beauty depends on starting with a perfectly prepared surface. The first step is to fill nail holes, cracks, and gouges with plastic wood or spackle. Allow to dry hard and then sand smooth with medium-fine sandpaper. Dust and then sand again with very fine sandpaper until the surface is smooth. Dust carefully. A vacuum cleaner is a good tool for removing fine dust. Wipe the sanded wood with a tack cloth to remove all of sanding dust.

63-1. A commercial oil finish was used on the paneling and wood interiors of this office.

63-2. This wall is board and batten, redwood-textured with an interior natural sealer finish.

63-3. These walls of cherry plywood have a polymerized finish that was applied at the factory. The only "finishing" required is to wipe off the dust which accumulated during construction. Of course, it takes the skill of a cabinetmaker to install the paneling so that the pre-finished surface isn't full of nicks and scratches. A rough carpenter wouldn't be expected to do this job.

The next step is to add color by stain, thinned paint, or pigment color in solvent. When the colored material has dried, a sealer coat should be added. Most softwoods for paneling do not require a filler, but if the paneling is open-grained wood like mahogany, oak, or walnut, the pores need to be filled and a sealer again applied. After the sealer coat, sand with 6/0 sandpaper. Apply two or more coats of varnish, lacquer, or synthetic finish. Sand between coats and then rub down with 3/0 steel wool after the last coat.

Because the basic wood colors will vary with different kinds of wood, it is a good idea to make a color test first. Use scraps of the same wood as is to be finished. Fig. 63-4. Some trial and error may be necessary.

Following are some methods which the Western Wood Products Association recommends for achieving color effects on paneling.

830

• *Red*—Mix red color in oil with thinner. Apply liberally with a brush. Wipe off with a soft rag. Apply clear finish or wax.

• *Gold for rough-sawn paneling*—Stain dark brown. Then spray at a low angle with gold gilt paint. A light coat of lacquer may be sprayed on to hold the gilt.

• *Gold for smooth paneling*—Brush gold paint directly onto the paneling. Wipe off immediately with a soft rag, leaving golden particles in the wood grain. Apply clear finish or wax.

• *Green*—Mix equal parts of chrome green and chrome yellow in oil with mineral thinner. Brush on wood, then wipe off. Apply clear finish or wax.

• *Dark green*—Mix two parts black paint with one part deep blue. Add two table-spoons of chrome yellow per quart. Brush on the panels, then wipe off immediately. Apply clear finish or wax.

• *Black*—Brush black paint directly on the wood. Allow it to stand a few minutes, then wipe with a soft cloth. Apply clear finish or wax.

• *Maroon*—Mix two parts red paint with one part deep blue. Apply directly to panels and wipe off immediately. Apply clear finish or wax.

• *Yellow*—Mix chrome yellow in mineral thinner to stainlike consistency. Apply liberally with a brush, then immediately wipe with soft cloth. Apply clear finish or wax.

• *Yellow for rough-sawn paneling*—Apply thick layer of yellow paint, then scrape off while still wet. Liberal application assures solid coverage with pigment, yet the knot-and-grain figuration will show through. Do not apply a surface finish.

• *Salmon*—Mix one part red color in oil to 16 parts white undercoat paint. Brush on liberally and wipe off with a soft cloth. Let dry, then apply clear finish or wax.

63-4. Color testing the finish that will be applied to a solid panel wall.

63-5. Apply this penetrating finish freely with a lamb's-wool applicator, lint-free cloth, or brush. Allow it a short time to penetrate, usually less than 20 minutes on most woods. Wipe off the excess with a soft cloth before it has a chance to set. If penetration doesn't appear uniform before wiping, apply a second coat after the first coat dries. When thoroughly dry, a rich luster can be obtained by buffing with extra-fine steel wool. Wax the surface if you wish.

63-6. A synthetic sanding sealer makes an excellent clear natural finish for closed-grained woods. Apply liberally in an even coat. When thoroughly dry, in two to three hours, sand lightly with very fine sandpaper. Then add two or three more coats, sanding between them as in a complete finishing process.

- *Brown*—Mix one part of black oil paint with two parts of gold gilt paint. Brush on paneling liberally, then immediately wipe off. Let dry, then apply clear finish or wax.
- *Copper*—Mix three parts red, three parts blue, and one part white. Brush onto paneling liberally, then wipe off with soft cloth. Apply clear finish or wax.
- *Blue*—Mix Prussian blue with paint thinner until it is of stainlike consistency. Brush on liberally, then wipe off. Let dry a few minutes, then rub lightly with 4/0 steel wool to bring out the grain. Apply clear finish or wax.

Finishing Hardwood Plywood

Procedures for furniture finishing can also be used for all hardwood plywood interiors. If the plywood is open-grained

wood such as oak, walnut, or mahogany, the surface must be filled for a perfectly smooth finish. For a Traditional finish, the wood is stained or left natural, then filled. Finally, lacquer or a low-gloss varnish is applied for a rich, hand-rubbed appearance. For Modern or Contemporary interiors, especially with furniture that has a commercial oil finish, a penetrating product can be applied. Fig. 63-5. For closed-grained woods such as maple, birch, and beech, no filler is needed. For a natural finish on these woods, three coats of a sanding sealer should be applied. Fig. 63-6. Whatever finishing system is used for interiors, it should first be pre-tested by completely finishing a small piece of plywood. It is often difficult to visualize the final appearance if only stain or the first coat is applied.

Finishing Softwood Plywood

The following are some suggested finishes for softwood plywood:

Paint or Enamel

Any standard woodwork finish is easy to apply if the manufacturer's directions are followed closely. For durability on surfaces that must be cleaned frequently, use washable enamels. After sanding, brush on flat paint, enamel undercoat, or resin sealer. Paint may be thinned slightly to improve brushability. Fill surface blemishes with spackling compound or putty when the first coat is dry. Sand lightly and dust clean. Apply a second coat. For a high-gloss enamel finish, mix equal parts of flat undercoat and high-gloss enamel. Tint the undercoat to about the same shade as the finish coat. Sand lightly when it is dry and dust the surface clean. Apply a final coat of high-gloss enamel just as it comes from the can.

A two-step finish, without the second undercoat, also may be applied.

Color Toning

Color toning requires companion stains and non-penetrating sealers. These have the advantage of requiring only one step for application of stain and sealer. It is necessary to tint a small amount of sealer with stain until the right color (tone) is obtained on a sample. Then mix enough stain and sealer to do the entire job, and apply by brush or spray. After drying and light sanding, a coat of clear finish is added to give the surface luster and durability.

Clear or Colored Lacquer

Lacquer can be sprayed, brushed, or wiped on. Use the type made for the job you are doing. Sand lightly or rub with steel wool between coats.

Light Stain-Glaze

A natural finish which mellows a contrasting wood-grain pattern with effective warm colors is always popular. When using any finish that retains the natural grain pattern, carefully select the plywood for its pattern and appearance. Four steps are recommended:

1. Whiten the panel. Use pigmented resin sealer or thin interior white undercoat with turpentine or thinner in a half-and-half proportion. After 10 to 15 minutes, or before it becomes tacky, dry brush or wipe with a dry cloth to permit the grain to show. Sand lightly with fine sandpaper when dry.

2. Seal the wood. Apply thinned white shellac or clear resin sealer. Sand lightly with fine sandpaper when dry. Omit the seal coat for greater color penetration in the next step.

3. Add color. There is almost no limit to the colors and shades you can get. Use a tinted interior undercoat, thinned enamel, pigmented resin sealer, or color in oil. With care, light stains may also be used. Apply thinly and wipe or dry brush to the proper depth of color. Sand lightly with fine sandpaper when dry.

4. Apply one coat of flat varnish or brushing lacquer to provide a wearing surface. For additional richness, rub with fine steel wool when dry.

SECTION V

QUESTIONS AND DISCUSSION TOPICS

1. Describe several methods of repairing a dent or crack.
2. What is the purpose of bleaching wood?
3. Is bleaching done only for blonde finishes?
4. What are some of the problems in bleaching wood?
5. List the steps in sanding white wood.
6. Name the parts of a spraying unit.
7. What is the purpose of an air transformer?
8. Spray guns can differ in construction and operation in three ways. Explain these.
9. Describe two kinds of spray booths.
10. What are some of the common spraying techniques?
11. Describe four spraying problems.
12. List the steps in applying a standard finish.
13. Describe some of the special synthetic finishes.
14. Name two simple shop finishes.
15. What is the purpose of staining?
16. Why is sap staining sometimes necessary?
17. Describe the materials that go into stain.
18. Discuss the advantages of water stains.
19. Describe the two types of oil stains.
20. Is non-grain-raising stain commonly used in small shops? Explain.
21. What types of wood require a paste filler?
22. What is the basic difference in cellular structure between most hardwoods and softwoods?

23. Describe some of the common problems in applying a filler.
24. What is a glaze and why is it used?
25. Discuss the methods of producing a distressed finish.
26. Name the three common kinds of finishing topcoats.
27. What is lacquer and how is it made?
28. What are the advantages and disadvantages of lacquer?
29. Tell how to apply a spray lacquer finish.
30. Why are varnishes difficult to use?
31. What is the difference between rubbing and polishing? Explain some of the materials used for rubbing and polishing.
32. Name some of the common interior finishes.
33. Do both softwood and hardwood plywood take the same kind of finish? Explain.

PROBLEMS AND ACTIVITIES

1. Cut test panels from one kind of wood and apply several different finishes. Compare the results.
2. Study the use of chemicals for bleaches on wood and write a report.
3. Compare the advantages and disadvantages of varnish and lacquer when used for topcoating.
4. Investigate the chemical composition of a finishing material used by one of the large furniture manufacturers.
5. Study the procedure for producing prefinished paneling in home construction.

Large, complicated equipment is essential to the wood industry. A machine such as this one almost resembles a giant octopus, with many arms to hold, move, cut and shape the materials. While these powerful machines have many automatic controls, they still require the services of millmen who know how to sharpen the tools and make the setups.

Section VI
Industrial Production

Heavy production equipment is a must in the modern woodworking industry. This includes furniture manufacturers, millwork plants, fixture producers, architectural woodworking plants, and producers of such items as musical instruments, sports equipment, and educational materials, among many others. Fig. 64-1. This heavy equipment is described in this unit.

Of course, not all woodworking manufacturers have the same amount, size, or variety of equipment. The millwork manufacturer, for example, may have no need for carving, dovetailing, laminating, and veneering equipment which the furniture manufacturer has to have. Some woodworking machines used in industry are very much like those in the school or cabinet shop except that they are larger and have automatic feed and power con-trols. Others are designed specifically for high production. Certain machines operate on a principle entirely different from that of any machine used in smaller shops.

The machines described here are grouped according to the departments in which they are commonly used. The specific plant layout, however, would depend on the kind of products produced.

CUTTING ROOM OR ROUGH MILL

In the cutting room or rough mill, pieces are cut to specific thickness, width, and length. Natural defects and those caused by drying are removed here. It is the responsibility of the rough mill to produce basic, unmachined pieces for wood products. The machines needed for this work are:

64-1(a). This woodworking plant is planned for the production of small wood drafting equipment.

64-1(b). Part of a furniture-manufacturing plant. This will give you an idea of how large some of these plants are.

• The *automatic cutoff saw*. Stock is cut to rough lengths with this machine. It is similar to a radial-arm saw in that the saw is mounted above the work. The hydraulic foot control moves the saw to cut off the stock. Fig. 64-2.

• *Straight-line ripping saw*. This is a power-fed saw which cuts stock to width. The undercut-type ripsaw is similar to a circular saw except for the power feed. The overcut design has saws mounted above. An endless chain moves in the table under the saw to feed the stock through the machine. Fig. 64-3.

• *Facer*. The facer does the same job as a hand jointer. It is used in the rough mill to produce one surface that is flat and true. In other words, it removes the warp from one face. Fig. 64-4.

• *Band resaw*. This is a large band saw with an attachment for cutting thick stock to thinner pieces. Fig. 64-5.

64-2. The power stroke of this straight-line cutoff saw is started when the floor pedal is depressed. A pneumatic cylinder (fluid power) moves the ram (arm) out so the saw can cut. When the ram reaches a certain set distance, it returns to the starting position.

64-3. This high-speed production machine rips heavy stock with smooth precision. Exposed joints can be glued direct from the saw. This machine is of overcut design with the saw blade mounted above the table. It has a single chain with one-piece, jam-proof blocks under the saw that move the stock.

64-4. A facer is a high-production jointer with chain-operated power feed. Pressure rolls mounted above the knives move the stock across the cutter head to flatten one face.

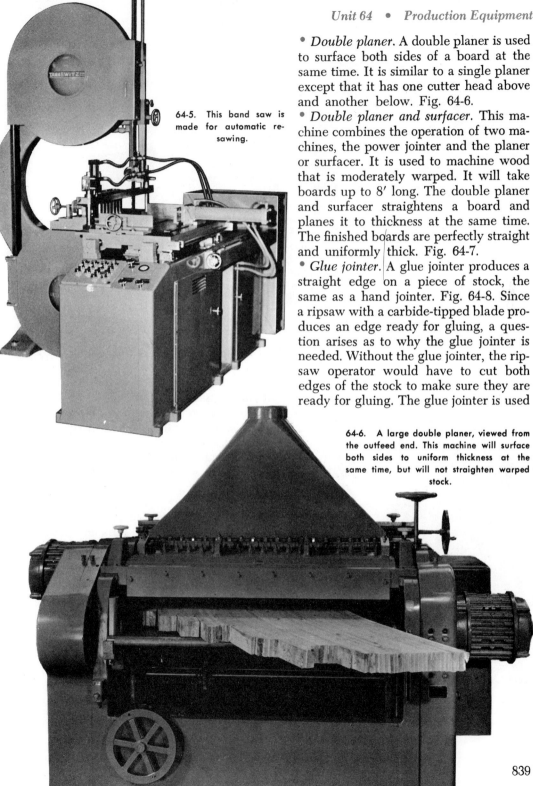

64-5. This band saw is made for automatic resawing.

• *Double planer.* A double planer is used to surface both sides of a board at the same time. It is similar to a single planer except that it has one cutter head above and another below. Fig. 64-6.

• *Double planer and surfacer.* This machine combines the operation of two machines, the power jointer and the planer or surfacer. It is used to machine wood that is moderately warped. It will take boards up to 8′ long. The double planer and surfacer straightens a board and planes it to thickness at the same time. The finished boards are perfectly straight and uniformly thick. Fig. 64-7.

• *Glue jointer.* A glue jointer produces a straight edge on a piece of stock, the same as a hand jointer. Fig. 64-8. Since a ripsaw with a carbide-tipped blade produces an edge ready for gluing, a question arises as to why the glue jointer is needed. Without the glue jointer, the ripsaw operator would have to cut both edges of the stock to make sure they are ready for gluing. The glue jointer is used

64-6. A large double planer, viewed from the outfeed end. This machine will surface both sides to uniform thickness at the same time, but will not straighten warped stock.

64-7. This single machine does the work of both planer and jointer or facer.

64-8. Edge jointer.

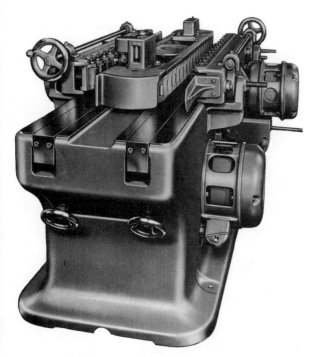

in the rough mill after the cutoff saw, facer, and planer. It is used to true up one edge of stock so that the operator at the ripsaw can use this edge for cutting the stock to uniform width.

In the rough mill, two kinds of ripping are done. Certain items—for example, the rails of a table—must be cut to specific width. The second kind of ripping is done primarily in making core stock for lumber-core veneer. If a table top or other part is too wide to be made from one piece, stock is cut to random widths and then glued up.

GLUING EQUIPMENT

Gluing and clamping are done at two stages of construction. In the early stages, it is necessary to glue up stock (a) edge to edge to form wide surfaces or (b) face to face to form large areas for legs, rails, or posts. Gluing and clamping are also necessary to make plywood and laminated parts. Later, after machining and sanding are completed, individual parts must be glued and clamped into sub-assemblies and these in turn glued and clamped to make the completed product.

Equipment for the early stages of gluing large surfaces may be part of the rough mill. Gluing is also a major part of the veneering and laminating department. Assembling the gluing equipment is part of the cabinet-room activity. To glue up wide surfaces for furniture parts or for the core of lumber-core plywood, these machines are used:

Glue Spreaders

Glue can be applied with a single open-roller spreader (Fig. 40-27), with a double-roller spreader (Fig. 64-16), by spraying (Fig. 64-9), or with a continuous open-roller spreader that is part of the gluing and clamping equipment.

Glue Reel Clamping Equipment

With this equipment a conveyor-type glue applicator delivers boards with glue applied to the edges. Fig. 64-10. The

64-9.   Applying glue by spraying.

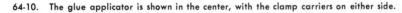

64-10.   The glue applicator is shown in the center, with the clamp carriers on either side.

841

64-11. The glue applicator is to the right, just above the layup table. Edge-glued pieces are placed on the layup table. They go through the machine and come out at the bottom completely glued and ready for further machining.

pieces are assembled to form the complete panel, and held tight by push-button, air-operated clamps. The panels are revolved, usually drying in one revolution, and are then removed.

Continuous Edge Gluers

These are high-production machines used to apply glue, clamp stock together as it moves along, and dry the glue. When the panels come out of these gluers they are ready for further machining. On some machines, the panels come out the same end at which they were laid up so that one man can handle the entire operation. Fig. 64-11. On others the panels move along an enclosed trough and come out the other end where a second workman unloads them. Fig. 64-12.

High-Frequency Batch Press

This machine instantaneously dries glued stock by high-frequency electricity. The pieces arrive at the batch press on a conveyor that edge glues them. They are loaded onto the layup table and clamped up. Fig. 64-13. Then the panels

move into an electrical field where the glue is instantly cured. Finally they move out and are unloaded.

This discussion has covered only a few pieces of specialized, high-production equipment. There are many others. The fundamental principles of gluing and clamping are the same as those covered in Unit 40.

Veneering, Laminating, and Bending Department

This department produces lumber-core plywood for furniture parts and also the curved parts made by bending and laminating. Remember, lumber-core plywood for furniture usually has five plies, although some manufacturers use the three-ply variety. The core of the plywood consists of narrow strips glued together. If the edge is to be shaped, a band of the same wood as the face veneer is glued to the edge. Crossbands are added at right angles to the core, and then the face and back veneers are added. Common equipment for veneering includes:

842

64-12(a). This is the infeed end of a steam-heated, continuous-feed, edge-gluing machine. Notice the conveyor with glue applicator that brings the pieces to the operators, ready to be loaded.

64-12(b). The outfeed end of the machine, where panels come out glued and ready for further machining.

64-13. Laying up a core on the table of a high-frequency gluing machine.

Edge-gluing equipment, similar to that described above.

Veneer driers. Most furniture manufacturers buy cut veneers in flitches already dried, but it is sometimes necessary to dry the veneers again to a specific moisture content. This is done in ovens where the veneers pass between heated rollers or plates.

Veneer clippers and jointers. These machines cut the veneer to correct size for making crossbanding materials and face and back veneers. In large plants a veneer jointer is used with a glue spreading attachment. This cuts the veneers, making them ready for joining, and applies the glue. Fig. 64-14.

Tapeless veneer splicer. While some plants still employ machines that tape pieces together, most plants now have tapeless splicers. With these machines the glued edges of the veneer pass through a splicer that applies edge and top pressure. Fig. 64-15. Electrically heated strips at the top and bottom of the glue line cure the glue. Paper tapes are not used in this method; consequently there is no chance that paper will be "buried" in the plywood during construction, as occasionally happens when tape is used.

64-14. View of the traveling head veneer jointer showing the exhaust piping and the header mounted on the machine as well as the glue-spreading attachment.

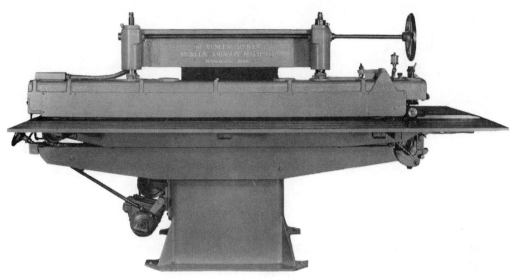

64-15(a). Veneer splicer.

64-15(b). Feeding veneer sheets into the splicer.

64-16. Feeding veneers into a glue spreader.

• *Veneer glue spreader.* This machine applies glue to both sides of the crossbands for plywood construction. The spreader has two grooved, rubber covered rolls. It also has a metal "doctor" roll which carries the glue to the rubber rolls. Fig. 64-16.

• *Hot veneer press.* These large presses apply heat, either by steam or high frequency electricity, to bond the various layers of plywood together. Fig. 64-17.

• *Cold veneer batch press.* A cold press is sometimes used to bond layers together. This is a long process since the glue must cure without heat. Fig. 64-18.

Equipment similar to that just described is needed to form *curved plywood and laminated* parts for furniture. The major difference is that special forms are required. Fig. 64-19. The production of these parts is about as follows: The necessary form is placed in a press, usually one that cures with high frequency current. The veneer sheets are run through the veneer glue spreaders. Every other sheet is coated with glue on both sides. At this stage the glue is cold. The assembled layers are placed in the press.

846

64-18. Cold batch presses. The plywood is clamped together by means of hydraulic power (fluid power).

64-19(a). The 14-foot panels for these church pews were a big, special-order job.

64-19(b). This large plywood form had to be built to produce the molded plywood seats for the pews.

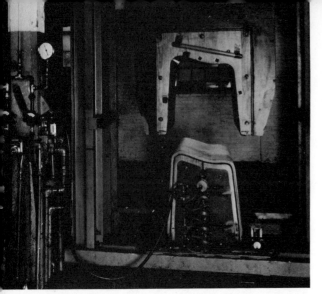

64-20. Molding press for making laminated chair arms. See also Fig. 41-19.

64-21. This rim-type bending machine will bend a chair part through an arc of 180 degrees.

Fig. 64-20. The operator closes the press and switches on the current to cure the glue. After sufficient curing time has been allowed, the finished panel is removed from the press.

If *solid wood must be bent*, two other pieces of equipment are needed. One is a retort, a steam oven to soften or plasticize the lumber. The second is a bending machine. This may be a rim-type bending device for chair parts or a flat press for shallow bends. Fig. 64-21.

MACHINING DEPARTMENT

Machines of many types, sizes, and models are used by wood manufacturers to cut, shape, form, and join wood parts. Some of the machines in the following paragraphs may be found in the rough mill department and others in the cabinet shop. These machines would not necessarily be arranged in a plant layout in the order given here.

The *hand jointer, variety saw, and band saw* used in industry are the same machines described earlier in this book except that they are usually much larger, with greater capacity. Fig. 64-22.

A *molder*, sometimes called a *"sticker"*, has four cutter heads that rotate at high speed to make all types of cuts on straight stock. It is similar to a shaper in its operation except that there are heads on four sides. All moldings, regardless of shape, can be made on this machine. As with most production equipment, the main problem is the setup. The knives must be ground and fitted into the heads. Fig. 64-23.

64-22. A combination rip and cutoff saw that does the same kinds of cutting as a variety or circular saw.

848

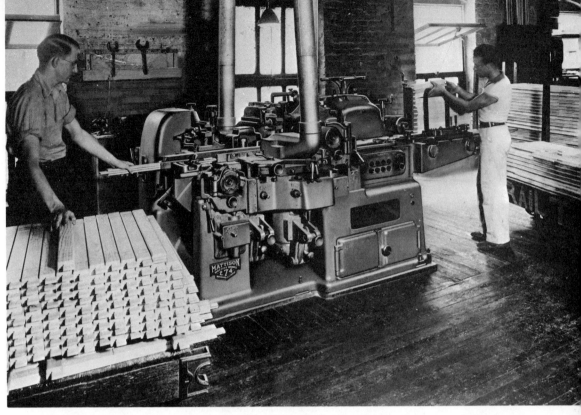

64-23. This high-speed molder produces identical moldings. It can be adjusted to cut many shapes. Here you see pieces being loaded in a hopper that automatically feeds them into the machine one at a time. The man at the outfeed end is loading the finished pieces onto a dolly.

The *tenoner* is a machine for shaping and joinery. Fig. 64-24. Originally designed for cutting tenons, it is made either as a single- or double-end machine. See Unit 35. The double-end tenoner is actually two machines joined together. Fig. 64-25(a). One machine is fixed while the other can be moved in or out for stock of different widths. The stock rides on a continuous chain as it moves through the cutter heads. Fig. 64-25(b). As the stock moves into the machine, adjustable cutoff saws trim it to correct length. Next the stock contacts the top and bottom tenon heads. These can be set to shape the upper and lower ends, as may be necessary to cut a tenon. For simple end tenons, the cutting is completed and the stock moves out the other side. For special shapes, cutters are mounted on the vertical cope spindles.

64-24. A matched double-joint tenon such as this can be cut on the ends of stock with a double-end tenoner.

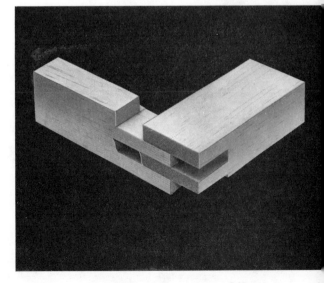

64-25(a). This double-end tenoner is really two machines in one. It is one of the most valuable production machines in woodworking.

64-25(b). A double-end tenoner in use. (Curtis Companies)

64-26. Using the coping heads on the tenoner to make cuts on end grain.

Fig. 64-26. These spindles can be moved up and down to locate the cut correctly.

For many types of end cuts both the tenon heads and the cope heads are used. This is actually a three-step process: cutting to length, tenoning, and coping. Fig. 64-27. In addition, automatic lathe-type cutter heads can be used on the dado arbor between the operating ends. Then the wood surface is machined either as

64-27. Cuts and joints that can be made on a double-end tenoner.

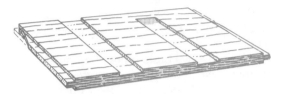

CASE OR CABINET WORK

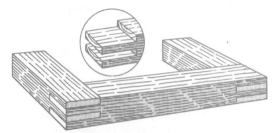

DOUBLE JOINT TENON

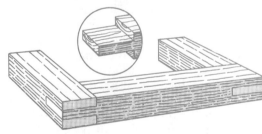

SINGLE JOINT TENON

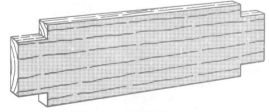

FOUR CORNER NOTCH

UPPER SASH CHECK RAILS

LOWER SASH CHECK RAILS

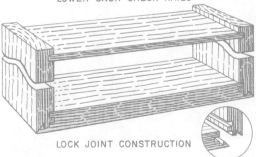

LOCK JOINT CONSTRUCTION

851

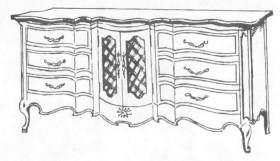

64-28(a). Many Early American and French Provincial cabinets have solid-hardwood serpentine fronts and drawers.

64-28(b). Lathe-type cutter heads on the arbor of a double-end tenoner are used to cut these designs. (Copyright Wisconsin Knife Works, Inc.)

64-28(c). Shaping the ends and surfaces of furniture parts on the double-end tenoner. (Copyright Wisconsin Knife Works, Inc.)

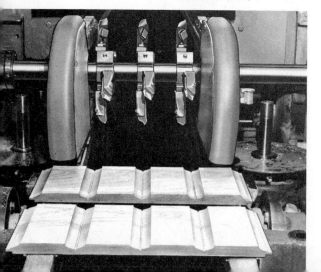

a separate operation or at the same time as the end cutting and shaping are done. Fig. 64-28.

Two types of *shapers* are used in industry, the hand-operated and the automatic. Manually operated shapers are identical to those described in Unit 32, except that they are larger and most have two spindles that rotate in opposite directions. Fig. 64-29. A double-spindle shaper is used so that the operator can shift from one spindle to the other as the grain direction of the stock changes. This makes it possible to cut with the grain at all times, resulting in a much smoother cut.

There are two basic types of automatic shapers, each of which operates on a different mechanical principle. Either one is capable of forming the graceful curves and radii so important in shaping wood parts, particularly legs and arms of chairs and tables. One such shaper has a sprocket-and-chain drive. Fig. 64-30. This one is much like the hand-operated shaper, but with power feed. It does the same work as the hand-operated model does when shaping with forms or patterns. The outside edge of the pattern has a sprocket on it that engages the teeth of the sprocket wheel. The underside of the pattern has a groove running all around it; the groove, which has the same shape as the outside of the form, fits over a pressure roller that protrudes from the top of the table. The work is placed on top of the pattern with the groove of the form over the pressure roller. Fig. 64-31. A spring-action hold-down keeps the work firmly on the pattern. The pressure roller then moves in and out to keep the sprocket in contact with the sprocket wheel as the edge of the work is shaped. This machine is also made as a double-spindle shaper with each spindle operating independently of the other. In this way two shapes can be cut, one on one spindle and a different one on the other.

64-29. Double-spindle shaper.

64-30. The Whitney automatic single-spindle shaper: (a) Base. (b) Table. (c) Pressure roller. (d) Sprocket drive. (e) Spindle. (f) Hold-down.

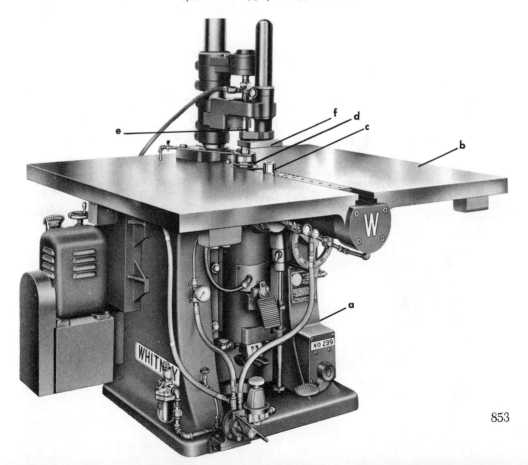

64-31. The operator has placed the form or pattern with the workpiece on it over the pressure roller. Then the hold-down will be fastened to hold the work on the pattern. Around the bottom of the form you see a sprocket chain, similar to the kind on a bicycle. Air pressure (fluid power) is applied to hold the chain against the sprocket drive. This arrangement moves the sandwich around as the edge is shaped.

Fig. 64-32. One operator can load and unload this machine.

The second type of automatic shaper operates in an entirely different way. It also makes use of a wooden form or pattern that cuts to the shape of the completed part. Fig. 64-33. The form or pattern is solidly clamped to a large, circular, slotted table that revolves. The work is held onto the form with air clamps. The cutters are mounted above the table (as on a router) on an arm that swings. Just below the cutter is a guide collar that rides on the edge of the form. This collar is held against the form by air pressure so that, as the table turns, the arm swings in and out to follow the form. Fig. 64-34. This machine can also be used to do inside cutting. Fig. 64-35.

The *contour profiler or profile shaper* does the job of two machines. It replaces both the band saw and shaper by cutting

64-32.   A double-spindle automatic shaper.

854

and shaping either straight-line or contour work at very high speeds. The various types of this machine all operate on the same basic principles. A wood pattern is made to the correct shape. This is placed on the table of the machine, and the pieces to be shaped are stacked on top of the pattern. The sandwich is held firmly to the table with air clamps. The table moves back and forth in a straight line. A floating cutter head moves in and out at right angles to the table travel, following the form. Some machines have a cutter head on only one side; if both edges must be shaped, it is a two-step process. Fig. 64-36. Others have a cutter head on each side so that both edges can be shaped at the same time. Fig. 64-37. The advantages of this machine are many. For example, curved edges on rails or stretchers do not have to be marked out, cut on the band saw, or trimmed on a hand shaper. This machine makes cutting and shaping a single

64-34. The operator is clamping workpieces to the form, using air clamps. This is an eight-station pattern. The ends of eight pieces are shaped in one complete revolution of the table.

operation, and the edge of stock is cut so smooth that it rarely needs sanding. A contour-profiler attachment can be added to a hand shaper. However, with this device the workpiece, not the cutter head, moves in and out.

The high-speed *router* used in industry is one of the most versatile woodworking machines. It can do a wide variety of cutting and shaping. Fig. 64-38. The router is actually a shaper with the cutting tool above the table. A review of Unit 33 will illustrate the versatility of

64-35. Inside shaping can also be done on an automatic shaper. This is a major advantage of such machines.

64-33. Another type of automatic shaper.

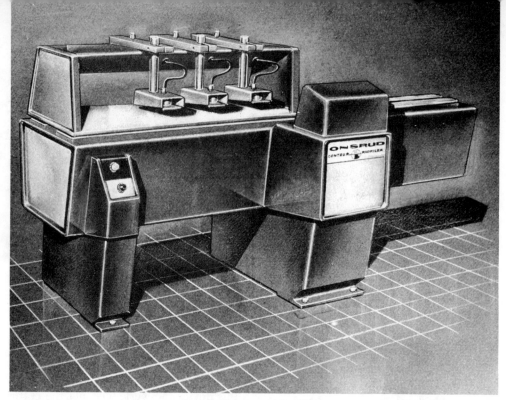

64-36(a). Contour profiler.

this machine. The router can do the same work as the shaper as well as doing pierced work (inside cutting), because the cutter is above the table. It also can be used as a carving machine and a mortiser. One type of router that is extremely valuable to industry has a *floating spindle*. Fig. 64-39. With this machine, the cutter not only rotates at high speed but can move up and down by hydraulic action to follow a pattern. It can be used for serpentine parts, drawer fronts, table and cabinet rails, and other parts requiring decorative routing. Some routers still employ mechanical linkage to raise and lower the head on a floating-head router.

64-36(b). Schematic plan view of a contour profiler. Note that this machine has one cutter head.

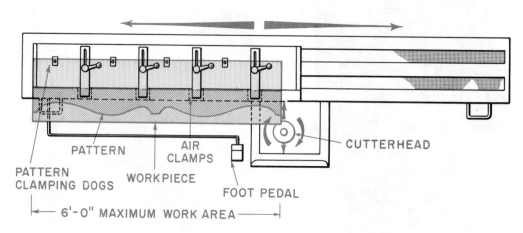

PATTERN

AIR CLAMPS

PATTERN CLAMPING DOGS

WORKPIECE

FOOT PEDAL

CUTTERHEAD

← 6'-0" MAXIMUM WORK AREA →

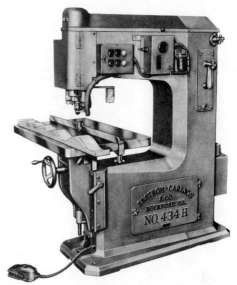

64-39(a). Hydraulic-activated spindle router for routing, fluting, veining, and heading serpentine parts.

64-37. A profile shaper with a cutter head on either side of the table.

The *single-spindle, vertical* and *chainsaw mortisers* described in Unit 35 are also used in industry. For high production, a multiple-spindle machine, constructed with either vertical or horizontal spindles, is used to cut a series of mortises at the same time. Fig. 64-40. Mortisers are not as widely used in industry as many other machines.

64-38. Floor-type router used in industry.

64-39(b). The head of a floating spindle router.

64-40. Multiple-spindle horizontal mortiser.

64-41(a). Multiple-spindle, hydraulic-feed, horizontal borer.

64-41(b). Using a multiple-spindle vertical boring machine to bore many holes at the same time. (Curtis Companies)

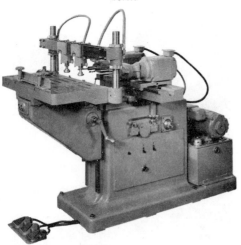

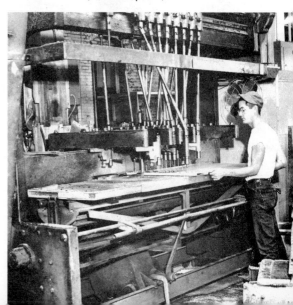

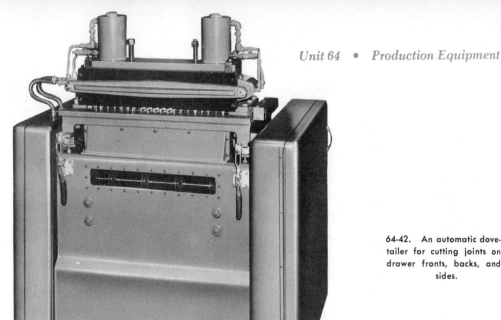

64-42. An automatic dove-tailer for cutting joints on drawer fronts, backs, and sides.

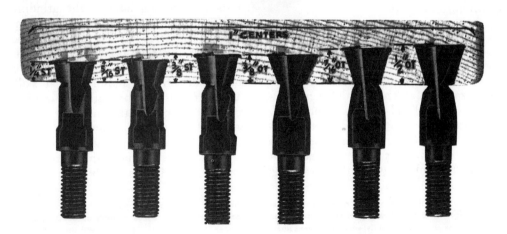

Boring Machines

The drill press and the small horizontal boring machine described in Unit 34 are sometimes used in industry. However, for most production work, a multiple-spindle machine, either vertical or horizontal, is more common. With such a machine each spindle can be moved and located at a specific position, and as many or as few holes as necessary can be bored at one time. Fig. 64-41. These holes may have the same or different diameters. Each spindle is driven by a telescoping shaft with a universal joint at either end.

Dovetailer

The dovetailer or automatic dovetail machine is specially designed for cutting dovetails for corner joints on drawers and other box structures. Fig. 64-42. The

859

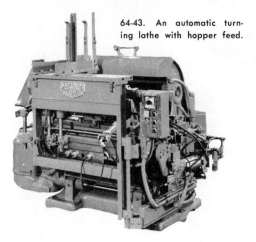

64-43. An automatic turning lathe with hopper feed.

machine has a series of carbide cutters which cut half the dovetail in one pass. The machine is set in one position for cutting drawer sides and in another for drawer fronts or backs.

Automatic Turning And Shaping Lathe

The automatic turning lathe is one of the most important pieces of equipment in woodworking production. Fig. 64-43. It operates on an entirely different principle from the hand wood lathe on which the cutting is done by holding a single-edge tool against revolving stock. The automatic lathe has a cutter head that extends the full length of the stock. Fig.

64-44. This head is made up of a variety of knives that are ground to shape and clamped in place to cut the part to the desired shape. The cutter head rotates at a high speed, the stock at low speed. The stock is mounted between centers and then moved against the knives so that the final shape of the part is achieved in one operation. The automatic turning lathe will turn not only geometric shapes but irregular ones also. By the use of dies or cams that move the work in and out, odd-shaped parts can be produced. Fig. 64-45. For example, the front of a French Provincial door or drawer can be shaped even though the final part is almost square or rectangular. Some models are designed so that the stock is fed one piece at a time, but most machines have an automatic hopper feed. Fig. 64-46.

The great skill involved in using the automatic turning lathe is the grinding and fitting of the knives. Once the machine is properly set and adjusted, the actual turning is a routine operation. Setting up a lathe cutter-head assembly is a difficult job that requires great skill. A pattern must first be made by turning a sample on a hand lathe and then cutting it in half on the band saw. The pattern can also be laid out full size on a wooden templet which will fit in the knife marking machine. The assembly of the knives

64-44. Note that a series of paired knives is needed. The cutting must be done with a shearing action; therefore an extremely sharp angle is used. The cutter head operates at speeds as high as 3600 r.p.m. The stock spindle speed is very low, somewhere from three to 30 r.p.m. (Copyright Wisconsin Knife Works, Inc.)

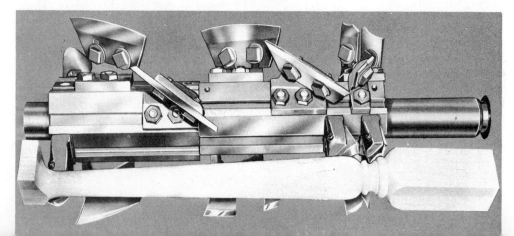

64-45. Octagon turning is done with standard heads and a special die which can be made by the setup man. Squares, ovals, hexagons and other shapes can also be cut with these special dies. (Copyright Wisconsin Knife Works, Inc.)

must be started with the short knives at the largest part of the turning. Each pair of knives and knife holders must be perfectly balanced. Most knives come already shaped and sharpened, ready for assembly. Blank knives can be used and sharpened to the correct shape with an aluminum-oxide wheel.

Special-Purpose Saws

There are many kinds of special purpose saws for crosscutting and ripping solid wood and for cutting and trimming panel stock to size. Fig. 64-47. The *double-cutoff saw* is very similar to the double-end tenoner in appearance and in the operations it can perform. It can be used to trim the edges and ends of panels to exact width and length. Both ends or edges are accurately cut to the exact dimensions in a single pass through

64-46. A set of heavy-duty knives is used to turn these bowling pins. This is a hand-feed operation in which the operator inserts the blank, turns the pin, and then removes it. (Copyright Wisconsin Knife Works, Inc.) See Fig. 37-2(b) for a hopper-feed setup.

861

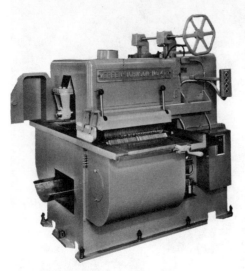

64-47(a). A chain-feed, straight-line, multiple-gang rip saw.

the machine. It can also be used for certain joinery cuts. Fig. 64-47(c). These saws may be used either in the rough mill or in the machine room.

CARVING DEPARTMENT

This department does the intricate carving so common to Traditional, French Provincial, and Italian Provincial furniture. Three common kinds of machines are used in the carving department. The *single-spindle carver* consists of a spindle mounted horizontally on a frame or base. Fig. 64-48. Various carving cutters can be fitted at the end of these spindles. The operator holds the workpiece against the cutter freehand. Here great skill is required since it is really a hand operation with the aid of power. The *multiple-spindle carving machine* is used in high production. This machine has a long bed in which 10 to 30 pieces to be carved can be mounted over the same number of spindles, each of which has a cutting tool. Fig. 64-49. At one end of the machine a duplicate of the part or a pattern is fastened to the bed. A sharp tracer point follows this pattern. As the operator moves the tracer point on the pattern or the original piece, all of the other spindles move in unison. The third kind of carving machine is the *hand, air-operated router*. On this machine, various-shaped cutter bits or sanding discs can be mounted. Fig. 64-50. For good work, much skill is required of the operator.

SANDING DEPARTMENT

Sanding is most important at every stage of production. Abrasives are used for machining, sanding, and finishing.

64-47(b). A gang-type trimmer saw.

64-47(c).   Infeed of a double cutoff saw. Notice the chain feed engaging the door panel to be trimmed.

64-49.   A multiple-spindle carving machine. The operator is moving the sharp tracer point along the pattern. All of the other cutting tools work in unison and carve the legs.

64-48.   A single-spindle carving machine.

64-50. This air-operated portable tool can be used for both carving and sanding of intricate shapes and designs.

The following are some of the machines normally used in the sanding rooms of high-production plants only. (See Unit 36 for machines used in smaller shops.)

Drum Sanders

Multiple-drum sanders used in larger plants are generally of the endless belt-type and may have two, three or four oscillating drums equipped with pressure controls. These machines do the initial white-wood sanding as soon as stock comes from the planer or veneer press. Such sanding removes roughness from the surface of stock and, in the process, brings the wood to correct dimensions. Fig. 64-51.

Stroke Sanders

In addition to the hand-block type of stroke sander found in smaller shops, the woodworking industry makes use of two others, the *lever-arm (hand-stroke) or*

64-51. A multiple-drum sander for use on flat surfaces. The stock is placed on a continuous belt and carried under the revolving drums. Each drum can be raised or lowered individually so the complete sanding job can be done with one pass through the machine.

64-52. A hand-stroke or lever-arm sander used for the final flat sanding of wide surfaces such as table tops.

semi-automatic sander and the *automatic or power sander.* In the lever-arm or semi-automatic type, the sanding pad or shoe is mounted on a horizontal track with limited vertical action. Fig. 64-52. The operator controls pressure and pad movement with a hand lever. The automatic or power type has a lever controlled sanding shoe that moves back and forth and is operated by fluid power. Stroke sanding improves the surface finish left by a drum sander. In plants where a finishing material is applied to the product, stroke sanding is normally the last white-wood machine sanding operation. Stroke sanding must produce a very smooth surface with a minimum of raised fiber.

Wide-Belt Sanders

Wide-belt refers to any sanding machine that takes a belt 12″ or wider. Such sanders have a straight-through feeding device similar to a multiple-drum sander. The three basic types of wide-belt sanders, classed according to arrangement of the rolls, are shown in Fig. 64-53. The wide-belt sander can replace the planer or the drum sander in some operations. An important feature of this machine is the rapid feed. Sanders are made for either single- or double-side sanding and have one or more sanding heads per side.

Edge Sanders

Edge sanders use belts that run in a vertical plane and have a horizontal table (sometimes one on each side) on which the stock rests during sanding. The table

64-53. Wide belt sanders are used for such operations as reducing particle board to the correct dimension and at the same time smoothing the surfaces. This operation used to be performed on a planer or surfacer. A typical machine for wide belt sanding is shown in Fig. 1-20.

THREE BASIC TYPES OF WIDE BELT SANDERS

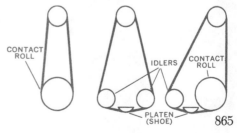

865

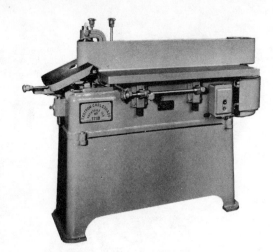

64-54. Edge sander.

64-55. Notice that a shaped hardwood block is held against the back of the abrasive belt to sand these moldings.

can be adjusted vertically to obtain full use of the abrasive belt. Fig. 64-54. Some types oscillate (move up and down) as they rotate to make full use of the belt.

Molding Sanders

Molding sanding includes a wide range of operations, from sanding the simple curvatures found on interior trim to the intricately shaped edges of furniture tops. For this work, the sanding belt runs around two pulleys. A sanding block of the desired shape, either held by hand or mechanically supported, is pressed against the back of the abrasive belt to do the sanding. Fig. 64-55.

Pneumatic Drum Sanders

The pneumatic drum is an air-inflated contact roll which is fitted with an abrasive belt of the same length as the circumference of the drum. When inflated, the drum expands, holding the belt in place. It is used for sanding mildly contoured areas or for breaking shaped edges. Fig. 64-56.

Open-Drum Sanders

The open-drum sander consists of a steel cylinder about 18″ in diameter and 2′ long. The drum is covered with a cushioning material—a piece of carpeting or something similar. The abrasive is held by a clamp in a slot across the face of the drum. The open-drum sander is usually used for sanding simple contour parts such as those used in the manufacture of chairs. Fig. 64-57.

Backstand Sanders

Equipment for backstand sanding consists of a contact roll (either hard or soft) mounted on a driving spindle, a long abrasive belt, and an adjustable

64-56. A pneumatic drum will conform to the contour of a piece, producing a finish very similar to one produced by hand sanding.

866

64-57. Open-drum sanding on the back posts of chairs.

64-58. Backstand sanding, using a pneumatic drum and the contact wheel.

roller called a *backstand idler*. A backstand sander uses abrasives much more economically than does an open-drum sander. The long belt cuts faster and wears longer. Fig. 64-58.

Vertical-Belt Variety Sanders

These sanders consist of a heavy base and an overarm. There are three pulleys below the table and two above, over which the narrow belt operates. The belt is supported by a metal plate in back of it. The advantage of this machine is that it can sand sharp, inside corners such as those formed by the lip of a drawer front. Fig. 64-59.

Scroll Sanders

On these machines a narrow belt runs over the center of the table and through a small metal support. This makes it possible to do all kinds of inside sanding such as grille work. Fig. 64-60.

Pearson Sanders

This sander is designed for use on concave surfaces of irregular-shaped moldings. The machine is a kind of single-spindle sander which can be set

64-59. Vertical-belt variety sander. Notice how this machine can sand the dovetail joint on a lip drawer.

867

64-60.   Using a scroll sander on the inside edges of grill work.

64-61.   A Pearson sander used on moldings.

at any angle. The machine can be used with or without an overhead backstand idler. Fig. 64-61.

New Kind of Abrasive

The development of a new abrasive material is changing the kinds and uses of sanding and finishing equipment. The new material, which consists of abrasive grains distributed throughout non-woven nylon, can be made into sheets, belts, discs, and wheels. As the material wears away, the abrasive action remains the same since the abrasive grains are evenly dispersed throughout. It is used not only in sanding but also for many finishing operations. Since the material itself is soft, it is better for contour surfaces than any of the standard sanding products. Fig. 64-62.

ASSEMBLY DEPARTMENT

Much of the assembly equipment used in industry is the same as that found in school and cabinet shops. However, there are certain additional pieces of equipment for gluing, clamping, nailing, and stapling that are larger and power operated (either electric or pneumatic). Fig. 64-63. Included are the following:

Glue-Mixing Equipment

To prepare cold glues in quantity, only a motorized mixer is necessary. Fig. 64-64. Hot glues require a mixer with a heater that is connected to steam, electricity, or gas.

Glue Spreaders

Glue spreaders have a motor-driven roll that picks up the glue from a storage tank. The edge or surface of the wood is moved against the roll to spread the glue. Fig. 64-65. A *dowel gluer and driver* is a machine that coats the inside of dowel holes with glue and drives the dowels into them. Fig. 64-66.

64-62(a). This is a wheel of non-woven nylon with abrasive grains throughout.

64-64. A cold glue mixer of the type used in a furniture factory.

64-65. A roll-type glue spreader in use.

64-62(b). Using a soft abrasive roll to put a satin finish on a veneer surface.

64-63. Using a glue gun to assemble furniture parts. The glue is fed through a rubber hose from a central supply. A valve on the gun controls the glue flow.

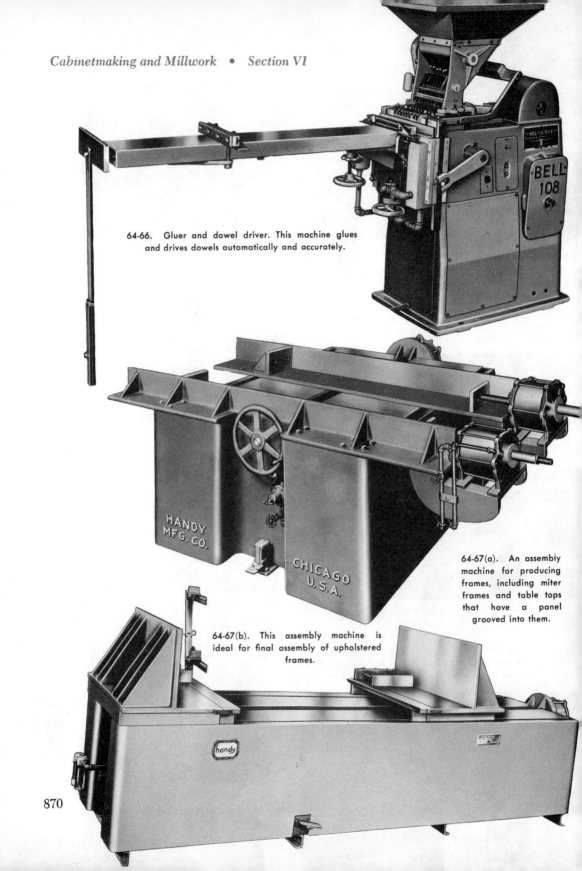

64-66. Gluer and dowel driver. This machine glues and drives dowels automatically and accurately.

64-67(a). An assembly machine for producing frames, including miter frames and table tops that have a panel grooved into them.

64-67(b). This assembly machine is ideal for final assembly of upholstered frames.

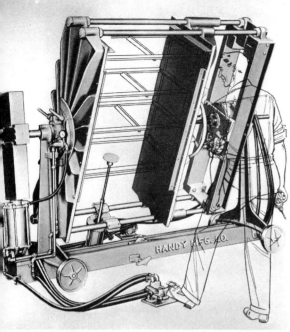

64-68(a). Using a large, power-revolving, air-case clamp.

64-68(b). Using a mechanically revolving assembly machine.

Clamping Equipment

There are many different power operated-clamps. The *assembly machine* for flat sub-assemblies is ideal for frame work. One side is stationary and the other moves in or out by air pressure. Fig. 64-67. This can be used in combination with a portable electric gluer so that the assembly can be clamped and the glue cured in a very few seconds. *Large case clamps* are used for final assembly of casework including cabinets, desks, and chests. Fig. 64-68. There are also many specialized power-operated clamps for assembling drawers, chairs, and other products.

Nailing and Stapling Equipment

A floor-type automatic nailing machine makes screw-nails from continuous threaded wire and drives them at speeds up to three nails per second. If used with glue, the automatic nailer presses the stock together to squeeze glue to a uniform coating, and the nail provides a permanent assembly. Since the nail is easily countersunk below the wood surface, it can be used for many assembly operations in cabinetwork and furniture construction. Fig. 64-69. The nailing stroke is controlled by a foot pedal. A

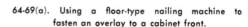

64-69(a). Using a floor-type nailing machine to fasten an overlay to a cabinet front.

871

Dinette chair backs.

Molding.

Decorative application.

Banded table top.

Cleated hardboard.

Bed rail slat bearer.

64-69(b). Common nailing applications for cabinet and furniture work.

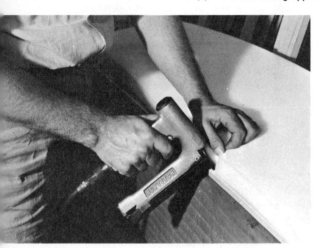

64-70(a). Using a portable power nailer to attach foam rubber to a base.

64-70(c). A picture-frame-corner nailing machine assembles frames as precisely as would a skilled craftsman.

64-70(b). A picture-frame-corner nailing machine that is a combination of a jig and two portable nailing machines.

second kind of machine is the *portable nailer.* Fig. 64-70. This machine, which operates by pneumatic pressure, installs specially designed nails, staples, or pins. As with all power production tools, a great deal of time is saved. Electrical or air-operated screwdrivers are also used in industry.

SPRAYING DEPARTMENT

In addition to the conventional cold spraying done in school and cabinet shops, there are several other important

872

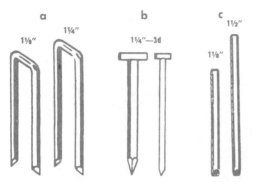

64-70(d). The portable pneumatic nailer will drive all three of these fasteners: (a) Staples. (b) Nails. (c) Pins.

64-71. Conventional cold spraying.

methods of finishing. Many furniture factories, of course, have cold-spraying equipment, making use of pressure-feed tanks to hold the finishing materials. Fig. 64-71.

Hot Spray

A modification of the cold spray is the addition of a finishing material heater. We know that heat reduces the viscosity (stickiness) of a solution without reducing the solid content. Most finishing materials are relatively stiff and slow-flowing when cold. As the temperature rises, they become thin and free-flowing and can be sprayed with lower air pressure. Such spraying puts on more material because less bounces back. Most of the heated finishing material that leaves the spray gun reaches the surface, cutting down the cost. The heater unit may be operated by electricity or hot water. The only basic difference between the conventional cold-spray and hot-spray methods is the use of this heating equipment. Fig. 64-72.

64-72. Hot-spraying equipment in operation in a furniture plant. The heaters are suspended from above on the right and left.

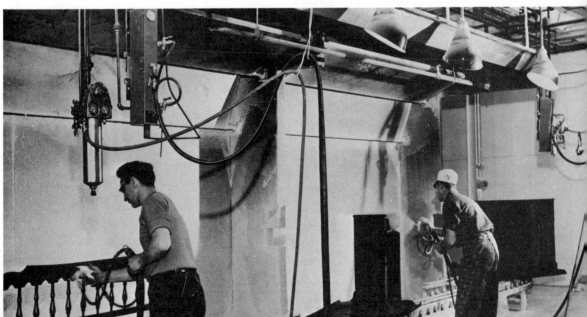

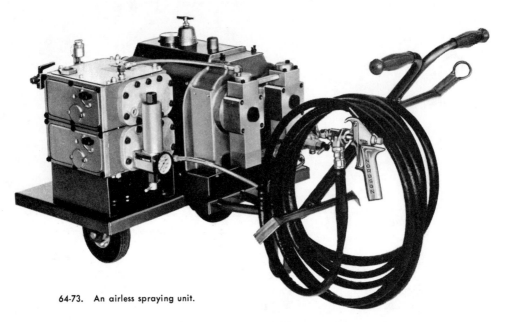

64-73. An airless spraying unit.

Airless Spray

Airless spray works on an entirely different principle. Fig. 64-73. The finishing material is atomized (broken up into a fine spray) by forcing it at high pressure through accurately designed openings in the spray gun. As the finishing material passes through the small openings and into the atmosphere, it not only moves very fast but also expands rapidly. This causes the stream of material to atomize. Because no air is used in this method, the insides of cabinets, drawers, and other small, enclosed spaces can be coated with a minimum of fog and rebound. Fig. 64-74. Airless spray can be used either with or without a heating unit.

Often it is done to the interior of a product which had its exterior sprayed conventionally.

Dipping

Another method of coating furniture parts or a completed piece is to dip it in a tank. A conveyor belt carries the item into the tank and out again.

Rolling

Another common coating method is to roll on the finishing material. This is frequently done when wood-grain printing is applied to hardboard or less expensive wood. See Unit 9 for further discussion of this.

64-74. Using an airless spraying unit to finish the inside of wooden kitchen cabinets in a trailer kitchen.

65 Woodworking Manufacturing

Many manufacturing industries require wood as the basic raw material for their products. The largest is the furniture industry. Fig. 65-1. Others include manufacturers of kitchen-cabinets, architectural woodwork, sports equipment, musical instruments, educational equipment, and fixtures. Such firms vary widely in size and the diversity of their products. Some of the largest companies utilize highly automated equipment to produce identical products in large numbers. Smaller furniture manufacturers may be much less automated, producing relatively small quantities or runs. For example, a small company may produce only 50 to 100 of a particular style table or desk. Perhaps not more than five or six types of products will be manufactured in the plant at one time. Once a run is completed, it is usually stored in the warehouse in white-wood condition (unfinished), then given final sanding and finishing as there is a demand. This is necessary since the same furniture piece may be finished in one of several ways. A large manufacturer of kitchen cabinets, on the other hand, would have a standard production line, producing the same items continuously. The following are three typical kinds of woodworking manufacturers.

FURNITURE MANUFACTURING

Wood remains the dominant material in furniture manufacturing even though such others as glass, metal, cane, and ceramics are used also. Therefore, furniture manufacturing is primarily a series of woodworking operations. While the

65-1. Every piece of furniture in this showroom was manufactured from the same raw material—wood. Each style and design involves many different operations or steps.

65-2. Stacking lumber in open sheds where it will air dry. Over a year is required between the purchase of the green lumber and the sale of furniture. Great care must be given to the lumber so that it can be made into fine furniture with minimum waste.

65-3. After air drying, the lumber is moved into these drying kilns where the moisture content is further reduced to make it ready for working.

65-4. Kiln control room. Here you see the controls which carefully measure and regulate the temperature and humidity of the air which circulates gently and evenly through kilns. When the lumber is removed from the kiln it is stored in a heat- and moisture-controlled room until it has time to adjust to the conditions in the factory.

series must vary with the style and kind of furniture, the general procedure is always about as follows:

Conditioning the Raw Material

Lumber used by the average manufacturer is hardwood which comes to the factory in random widths and lengths and in rough condition. The wood may be either green or air-dried. After arriving at the factory site, it is stored in open sheds to air dry for several months. Fig. 65-2. Then it is moved from the outside sheds into kilns. Here the moisture is reduced to approximately four to nine per cent before the lumber is processed further. Fig. 65-3. Normally, the furniture manufacturer will reduce the moisture content to three to five per cent and then allow it to return to seven or nine per cent. This helps relieve some of the stresses in the wood. Fig. 65-4.

Design and Engineering Department

Some furniture designers are regularly employed by a manufacturer. Others free-lance; that is, they have no employer but try to sell their designs to various firms. The normal practice in either case is for the designer to make sketches and a scale drawing of each piece, adding such enlarged details as seem necessary. Management then approves particular designs for manufacture. As each design is approved, the factory draftsman or designer makes full-size working drawings and details giving necessary mechanical information. Once these final drawings are approved, they are given to the experimental or model shop where cabinet-makers produce a model of the piece. These highly skilled men use hand and machine tools such as those used in a school or cabinet shop. This sample or model is set up "loose" (not glued) so that designers and engineers can study it to check out possible errors in draw-

876

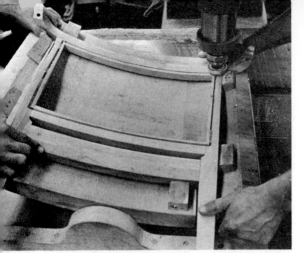

65-5. This fixture is designed to hold the curved back of a chair as a groove is machined around the opening on a router. Many types of fixtures and jigs are needed, especially for furniture that has curved or unusual-shaped parts.

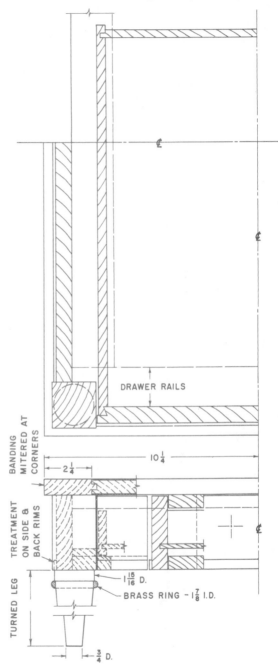

DRAWER RAILS

BANDING MITERED AT CORNERS

TREATMENT ON SIDE & BACK RIMS

TURNED LEG

$10\frac{1}{4}$

$2\frac{1}{4}$

$1\frac{15}{16}$ D.

BRASS RING – $1\frac{7}{8}$ I.D.

$\frac{3}{4}$ D.

65-6(b). This engineering working drawing would be made *full size*. A drawing for a large chest, for example, might be six or seven feet long and five or six feet wide.

ings or design. (This step may sometimes be omitted if the furniture piece is very similar to one previously produced or is only slightly different in size.) The same cabinetmakers who produce the model are also responsible for building jigs and fixtures for production. Fig. 65-5.

Once the design and engineering department have approved the model, it is necessary to "tool up" for production. The first step is to produce the detailed drawings and route sheets for each of the parts to be manufactured. Fig. 65-6.

65-6(a). To produce this lamp table in a typical industrial plant, the steps shown in the next four illustrations would be followed.

877

Job No.   Stock No. 5567

Date   LAMP TABLE

| NO. SQUARE FEET | QUANTITY | MATERIAL | ROUGH | | ROUGH THICK-NESS | NAME OF PIECES | NET | | NET THICK-NESS | ITEM NO. |
			LENGTH	WIDTH			LENGTH	WIDTH		
	1	African Mahogany Plywood	Net 22½	Net 16	3/4	Top	22½	16	3/4	1
	1	Oak Plywood	Net 15	Net 17½	3/16	Drawer Bottom	15	17½	3/16	2
	1	Mahogany	Net 16 7/16	Net 3 11/16	4/4	Drawer Front	15 7/16	3 7/16	13/16	3
	2	Mahogany	Net 28	Net 2 3/4	4/4	Top Side Bands	27	2½	13/16	4
	2	Mahogany	Net 21 ½	Net 2 3/4	4/4	Top End Bands	20 ½	2½	13/16	5
	2	Mahogany	Net 23	Net 3 3/4	4/4	Side Rims	22	3½	13/16	6
	1	Mahogany	Net 16½	Net 3 3/4	4/4	Back Rim	15 ½	3½	13/16	7
	2	Gum	Net 18 7/8	Net 2	4/4	Drawer Rails	17 7/8	1 3/4	5/8	8
	2	Gum	Net 18	Net 2	5/4	Drawer Guides	17	1 3/4	1	9
	1	Gum	Net 17	Net 7/8	4/4	Drawer Tilter	17	5/8	3/4	10
	2	Oak	Net 18 5/8	Net 2 7/16	5/8	Drawer Sides	17 5/8	2 3/16	3/8	11
	1	Oak	Net 16 3/8	Net 2 3/8	5/8	Drawer Back	15 3/8	2 1/8	3/8	12
	4	Mahogany	Net 24 1/4	Net 2 3/8	2 pcs. 5/4	Legs Turn	23 1/4	2 1/8	2 1/8	13
	1	Pull 3/4" Screws Brushed Brass								
	4	Brass Sockets Satin Brass Finish								
	4	Brass Rings Satin Brass Finish								
	6	Screws 1 1/4" #8 F.H.B.								
	2	Screws 1" #7 F.H.B.								
	4	1/2" Glides								

65-6(c). **This stock list of parts for the table is like the bill of materials you would make for any piece of furniture to be built.**

SPECIFICATION AND STANDARD COST SHEET

SKETCH							

Patt. Name __Lamp__   Patt. No. __5567-9__

Part Name __Top Side Bands__   Part No. __4__

No. Used Per Unit __2__   Material __Mahogany__

RIP MATCH		LENGTH	WIDTH	THICK	GRADE	FOOTAGE
21	ROUGH	28	2 3/4	4/4		GROSS
NO. OF PLY		MAKES	FINAL PIECES			
BET. SHO.		LENGTH	WIDTH	THICK	GRADE	NET
	FINISH	27 Miter	2 1/2 Moulder	13/16		

Oper. No.	Mach. No.	Rate	Set-up	OPERATION AND INSTRUCTIONS	Unit Equiv.	No. of Men	Total Oper. Time	Total Set-up Time
1	1	9.5	–	Cut off	2	2		
3	10	5.	2	Rough plane	2	2		
7	5	10.	–	Rip defects and gauge rip 75%	1	2		
5	5	5.	–	Rip match (7 in 1) 25%	1	2		
12	16	16.	–	Edge glue	1	2		
11	6	9.	–	Rip glued panels	1	2		
2	9	5.	Face plane		2	2		
20	13	8.1	28	Moulder to pattern	2	2		
41A	25	18.	8	Miter 1 end	2	1		
41B	25	18.	8	Miter 1 end	2	1		
32	21	24.	23	Bore for dowels (1H2E)	2	1		
69	–	15.	–	Inspect and patch	2	1		

65-6(d). This process route sheet is needed for the production line. Thirteen of these are required, one for each part and each with different instructions.

Some manufacturers still use the rod method of layout and planning. See Unit 18. In mass production, the individual worker on the production line is concerned only with a single part. It is necessary only for him to follow the detail drawing and the route or process sheet for that particular part. In making the set of process or route sheets and detail drawings, the experimental model and the full-sized engineering drawings are used. Fig. 65-7. From this set of papers, a stock list of the needed parts is prepared. This stock list is similar to a bill of materials. It indicates the quantity of pieces needed. An extra quantity

65-6(e). This detail drawing goes in the space marked "sketch" at the upper left on the process route sheet.

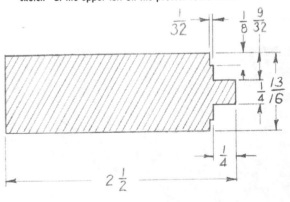

65-7. An engineer and a designer checking each part of a "loose" chair frame against the stock list and individual process route sheets to make sure that all information is accurate and complete.

65-8(a). The manufacturer of a chair like this would have to decide whether it was less expensive to make all the parts himself or buy them fully machined.

65-8(b). These fully machined chair parts can be purchased in any quantity.

(sometimes called an overrun) is always produced to make up for any rejects. For example, if 1000 tables, each with four identical rails, are to be produced, 4000 rails plus four to seven per cent extra (160 to 280) will be produced. The route sheet, detail drawing of the part, and the lumber are kept together throughout the entire manufacturing process. Each furniture factory utilizes its own form of route or process sheet, some of which include other information such as the time needed to produce the item, the cost per item, and the materials cost.

At this point in the production schedule, management must decide whether all the pieces are to be manufactured in their own plant or whether part or all of them will be purchased from a hardwood-dimension plant. Fig. 65-8. Hardwood-dimension manufacturers specialize in producing individual parts rather than a completed, assembled product. Usually located near an excellent source of raw materials, these manufacturers will produce anything from drawer sides to the total parts needed for a chest or cabinet. Furniture manufacturers usually find it more economical to purchase the more standardized parts of furniture, such as the frames for dust panels, the sides and backs of doors and drawers, and similar parts. Fig. 65-9. All parts not purchased from a hardwood-dimension plant must be completely processed by the furniture manufacturer. Some manufacturers also purchase molded plywood and curved laminated parts rather than making their own.

Cutting Room or Rough Mill

When the rough lumber is dried to the correct moisture content, it is moved into the cutting room or rough mill. Here the lumber is cut to rough lengths with large cutoff saws, faced on one surface, and planed to thickness. Fig. 65-10. The stock is then rough cut to width on single or

65-12. "Laying up" lumber-core plywood parts for furniture. Notice that this is five-ply material. The assemblies are then placed in the hot press which is seen in the background. Here the glue is cured under accurately controlled heat and pressure.

gang ripsaws. Fig. 65-11. This section of the plant may also be responsible for edge gluing stock for core work or for large panels.

Veneering and Laminating Department

The veneer room is responsible for "laying up" the lumber-core plywood, that is, putting the pieces together. Fig. 65-12. This department also produces fancy veneer surfaces for table tops and chest fronts. Fig. 65-13.

65-10. Rough cutting stock to dimensional length.

65-11. Stock has been cut to correct size and shape and is now ready for further processing.

65-13. Fancy veneer matching such as the elm burl inlay on this table top is the work of a highly skilled cabinetmaker.

65-14(a). Transferring a full-size veneer design to the material.

65-15(c). Boring holes in rectangular parts using a multiple-spindle horizontal boring machine.

65-14(b). A large, assembled veneer design taped and ready for "laying up" into a completed table top.

65-15(a). Machining rectangular drawer fronts on the double-end tenoner.

65-15(d). Setup for cutting dovetail joints on drawer parts.

65-15(b). Shaping rectangular parts on the molder.

65-16(a). Closeup of an automatic lathe producing a spindle part.

65-16(b). Machining parts on a floor-type router.

In this work, a highly skilled craftsman lays out the design on a piece of paper and transfers it to the veneer pieces. Then he cuts the pieces to size and shape, and tapes them together by hand. Fig. 65-14. The laminating department produces molded plywood and laminated parts.

Machining Department

The machine room or machining department is responsible for mass producing solid parts needed for furniture and for cutting all of the joints. A wide variety of machines is used for making the straight parts including the double-end tenoner, molder, boring machine, and dovetailer. Fig. 65-15. Other machines are needed to produce such irregularly shaped parts as curved and carved legs, arms, drawer fronts, and table-top edges. Some of the more common machines for these operations are the automatic lathe, the automatic shaper, multiple-spindle carver, and router. Fig. 65-16. Even with all this automatic equipment, there is still need in furniture manufacturing for craftsmen who can do accurate work with hand tools. Fig. 65-17.

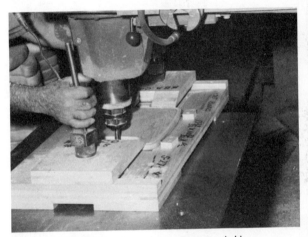

65-16(c). Closeup of a jig used on a router to hold the part and also to guide it for the shaping operation.

65-17. The final carving on this cabriole leg must be done by hand with gouges and chisels. Machines have never completely replaced the hand-tool skills.

883

65-18(a). Sanding a table top on a hand-stroke belt sander.

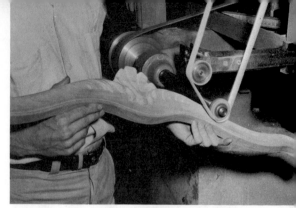

65-18(d). Sanding a carving with a narrow-belt spindle sander.

65-18(b). Sanding drawer fronts on a drum sander.

65-18(c). Finish sanding the back for a captain's chair with an abrasive belt running over a pneumatic drum.

Sanding Room or Area

Here all parts are sanded before assembly. This includes work done on drum, stroke, edge, and mold sanders, and many other abrasive machines. Fig. 65-18.

Cabinet Room

Once all of the parts have been manufactured and the joints cut, the pieces come to the cabinet room either on dollies or on a conveyor system, ready for assembly. Fig. 65-19. Here many different operations are necessary. The first step is to inspect each part for defects. Assembly itself includes such steps as gluing, clamping, nailing, and stapling. Fig. 65-20. The craftsman may need to do a little hand shaping and fitting to assemble the parts and to fit the drawers and doors into the chests and cabinets. Basic hand tools and small portable tools like a hand drill, router, and sander are needed for this work. In this department the assembled piece is made ready for finishing. Final machine and hand sanding must be done. Fig. 65-21. The cabinet room is also responsible for adding the hardware including such items as hinges, locks, and pulls. Unfinished pieces are called white wood, regardless of the wood used. The finishing is not necessarily done immediately. Instead, white-wood products may be stored under conditions of controlled humidity and heat until there is a demand for them.

65-19. Furniture parts in various stages of assembly.

65-20(a). Assembling and fitting parts of a case.

65-20(b). Clamping the assembly in a case clamp.

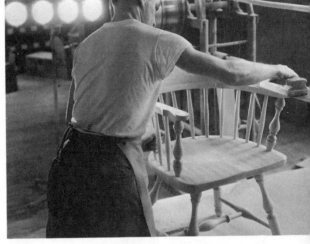

65-21(a). Finish sanding chairs. Horizontal beams from the lights in the background help show up surface irregularities.

65-21(b). The final hand sanding of a chest of drawers.

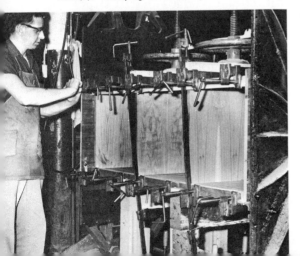

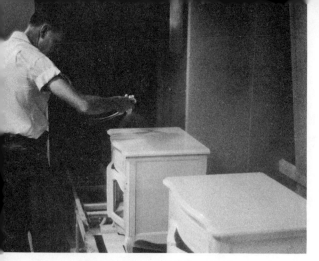

65-22(a). Applying a lacquer finish to small chests.

65-22(b). Rubbing down the finish on dining tables.

65-23(a). Using a large power sewing machine to do upholstering.

Finishing Room

The finishing room of a large furniture manufacturer contains many items needed for applying a good finish. Included are automatic spraying equipment, drying trucks, and automatic rubbing and polishing equipment. Fig. 65-22.

Exposed pieces of hardware may have been fitted before the product comes to the finishing room. Such hardware is removed, then the finish is applied, usually about as follows:

1. *Stain.* Gives the wood a background coloring.

2. *Wash coat.* Seals the stain, making it possible to smooth the surface.

3. *Hand sanding.* Makes the surface smooth and ready for finishing.

4. *Filler.* Is rubbed on the surface with and across the grain, filling pores to provide a firm base for the following steps. Prevents bleeding.

5. *Hand stain.* Makes the base coloring uniform.

6. *Overshade.* Brings out highlights in the wood figure.

7. *Sealer.* Fills and evens out the pores, making the surface smooth.

8. *Hand sanding.* Further smooths the surface, making it ready for glaze.

9. *Glaze.* Brings out highlights of the wood and blends coloring.

10. *Lacquer.* Provides a protective coat. Prepares surface for next steps.

11. *Machine sanding.* Makes surface smooth for the second coat of lacquer.

12. *Lacquer.* Insures a clear, firm coating to hold finish.

13. *Hand sanding.* Done with steel wool. Drawer interiors are waxed.

14. *Machine rubbing.* Done on tops, ends, and fronts.

15. *Hand rubbing.* Cleans and smooths surfaces not reached by machine.

16. *Rubbing compound.* Smooths over

886

65-23(b). Using a pneumatic stapler to install base springs on a chair.

65-24(a). Hand painting the decorations on a French Provincial chest.

all scratches and rough surfaces caused by preceding operations.

17. *Wax.* Used without an oil base. Put on by hand and rubbed.

18. *Hand polishing.* Rubbed with dry, clean, soft cloth for lasting luster.

Upholstery Area

Upholstery is done in a department especially set up for that purpose. Some upholstery processes have been mechanized and a few automated, but a great deal of the work is still done by hand, with the craftsman's skill being highly important. Fig. 65-23.

Trimming Room

All-wood furniture and upholstered pieces are brought to the trimming rooms where any necessary hand decorating, including gold leafing, is added. Fig. 65-24. The hardware that had been fitted and then removed for finishing is replaced. Fig. 65-25. Any scratches, checks,

65-24(b). A hi-fi cabinet in antique white with hand-painted decorations.

65-23(c). Upholstering is one of the highly skilled crafts in furniture manufacturing. This craftsman had at least six years of training and experience to qualify him as a journeyman upholsterer.

65-25. Replacing the hardware on a desk.   887

65-26. Final inspection of a desk before it is placed in a carton for shipping.

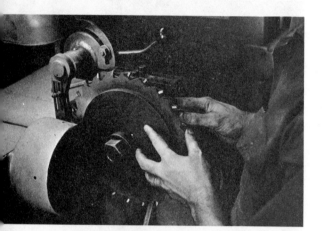

65-27. Making the "setup" for grinding a carbide-tipped circular saw. Safety goggles or glasses must be worn during the actual grinding.

or imperfections are also repaired before final inspection. The furniture piece is then placed in a carton or wood crate ready for shipment. Fig. 65-26.

Tool Room

Tool room workers are responsible for keeping the cutting edges of tools in top-notch condition. Not only are they concerned with blades for such equipment as ripsaws, variety saws, and band saws, but also with the cutter tools used on shapers, routers, molding machines, and double-end tenoners. They may also be responsible for shaping and grinding the knives on automatic lathes, if these knives are not preground. Perhaps the tool room does not sound as impressive as some other departments, but actually its importance is great, and the men who work there must be highly skilled. Fig. 65-27.

KITCHEN-CABINET MANUFACTURING

Kitchen-cabinet manufacturing is another of the large areas of woodworking. Fig. 65-28. It is much simpler than furniture manufacturing since only a few basic pieces of casework are needed, and fancy turning, carving, and upholstery are unnecessary. This type of manufacturing can be highly automated because of the slight variation in design. Design

65-28. Manufactured kitchen cabinets are quality-controlled all the way from forest to finish.

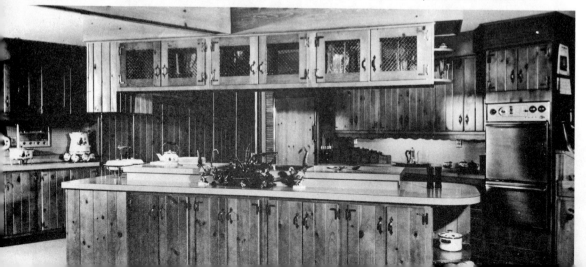

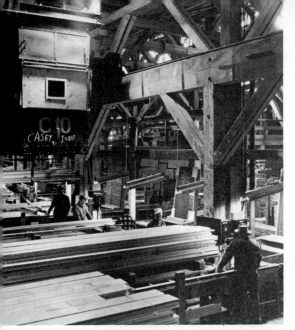

65-29. This cutting department has consolidated cutting lines. An overhead crane places the lumber between the cutoff saws, convenient to the operators.

changes on fronts of doors and drawers are often accomplished simply by adding molding.

In kitchen-cabinet manufacture, the rough mill or cutting department cuts all individual pieces to correct rough size. Fig. 65-29. The pieces are then moved by conveyor belts to the machining department, where the necessary shaping and joinery are done. These procedures involve the use of the double-end tenoner or double molder, cutoff saw, and boring machine. Fig. 65-30. Since all of these parts and units are flat, they can be sanded with machines such as the continuous belt sander and the edge sander. Fig. 65-31. After sanding, they are moved to the assembly department where sub-assemblies are made. Then

65-30(a). A double-cutoff saw trims both edges simultaneously.

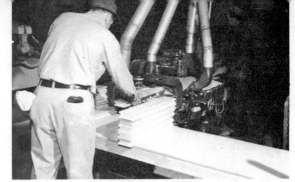

65-30(b). The molder shapes the edges of panel parts.

65-30(c). The boring machine drills holes at the correct locations.

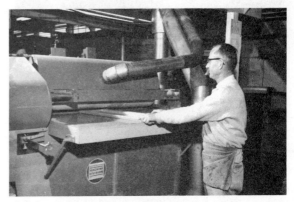

65-31(a). Face frames for cabinets are fed into a continuous belt sander.

65-31(b). The edges and ends of doors and drawers are sanded on an edge sander.

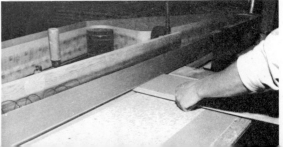

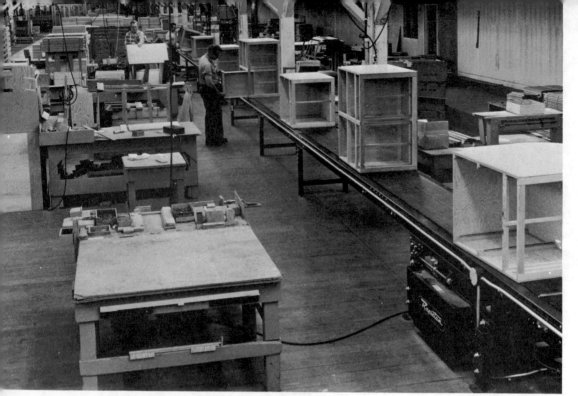

65-32. This assembly department uses a conveyor system. The cabinets progress through several assembly stations.

65-33. Pneumatic guns are used to staple the face frame to the basic cabinet box.

65-34. Fitting the doors and drawers.

the complete cabinet is assembled. Fig. 65-32. Doors and drawers are also manufactured as sub-assemblies, then fitted to the cases. The parts of the cabinet are assembled with glue and pneumatic staplers. Fig. 65-33. Doors and drawers are then hung and fitted. Fig. 65-34. Sometimes the hinges are removed and the doors, drawers, and cases finished separately. A finish is then applied to the cabinets. Fig. 65-35. The cabinets are inspected and then packed into cartons. Fig. 65-36.

Many manufacturers produce their kitchen cabinets (of the same design) in two ways: (1) completed and ready for installation, and (2) "knocked-down" for assembly by the purchaser. Fig. 65-37.

ENGINEERING AND DRAFTING EQUIPMENT MANUFACTURING

A plant that produces drafting boards, T-squares, and scales is typical of specialized wood product manufacturers.

890

65-35(a). In finishing, a sealer is first applied. The cabinets are sanded inside and out.

65-36(b). Packaging the completed cabinets. Note that they are assembled, ready for installation.

65-37. Packaging "knocked-down" cabinet units. They are transported by conveyor from the assembly line to the storage area.

65-35(b). Several coats of hot lacquer are applied with an airless spray.

65-36(a). Inspecting the completed cabinets.

891

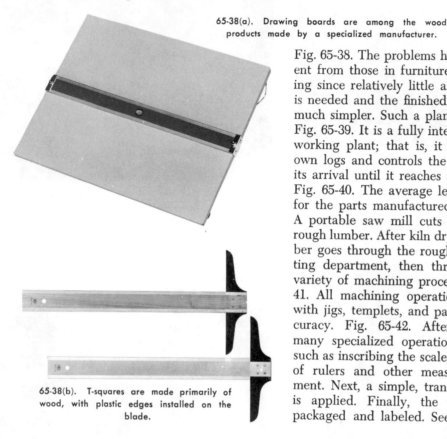

65-38(a). Drawing boards are among the wood products made by a specialized manufacturer.

65-38(b). T-squares are made primarily of wood, with plastic edges installed on the blade.

Fig. 65-38. The problems here are different from those in furniture manufacturing since relatively little assembly work is needed and the finished products are much simpler. Such a plant is shown in Fig. 65-39. It is a fully integrated woodworking plant; that is, it purchases its own logs and controls the lumber from its arrival until it reaches the customer. Fig. 65-40. The average length of stock for the parts manufactured is only 21″. A portable saw mill cuts the logs into rough lumber. After kiln drying, the lumber goes through the rough mill or cutting department, then through a wide variety of machining processes. Fig. 65-41. All machining operations are done with jigs, templets, and patterns for accuracy. Fig. 65-42. After machining, many specialized operations are done, such as inscribing the scales on the faces of rulers and other measuring equipment. Next, a simple, transparent finish is applied. Finally, the products are packaged and labeled. See page 894.

65-39(a). Aerial view of a manufacturing plant.

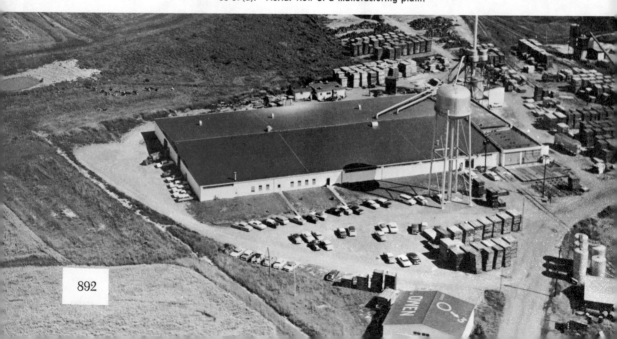

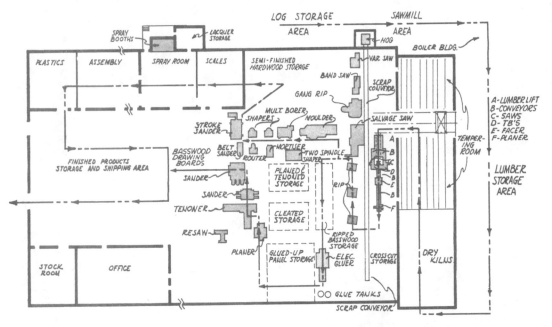

65-39(b). This layout shows the principal manufacturing operations in order as wood moves through the plant.

65-40(a). Raw material for the drawing boards, T-squares, and countless other small products.

65-40(c). This rough-cut lumber is air dried in the open to 20 per cent moisture content before it is brought into the dry kilns.

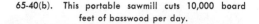

65-40(b). This portable sawmill cuts 10,000 board feet of basswood per day.

65-41(a). This multiple ripsaw cuts stock accurately, smoothly, and with a small kerf.

65-41(b). This electronic gluer produces glued panels for drawing boards and converts rejected materials into veneer cores.

65-42(a). Shaping the heads of T-squares with a pattern and an air-operated clamp.

65-42(b). Shaping the inside openings of large wood blackboard triangles on a router. Note that a jig and clamp are used to hold and guide the workpieces as the internal cutting is done.

65-41(c). Trimming drawing boards to size on a double-cutoff saw.

65-41(d). Sanding the drawing boards on a drum sander.

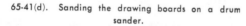

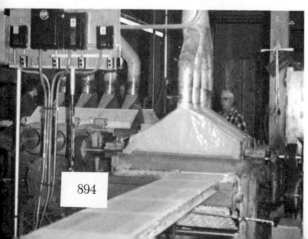

66 Store, Office, and Institutional Fixtures

Display cases, shelves, counters, and similar furnishings are commonly called fixtures. Such pieces are manufactured in plants that specialize in this kind of production. While these plants have many construction problems and procedures similar to those of furniture manufacturers, their work is quite different since fixtures include not only wood but also extensive use of glass, metal, and upholstery materials. Fig. 66-1. Also, many fixtures must be fitted or built around reflector lighting, metal containers, and refrigeration units which must have plumbing or gas connections. Fig. 66-2.

Fixtures are usually specified and purchased under a sub-contract that is separate from the contract for the building. They vary greatly with the kind of store, office, or financial institution. Food and drug stores often have high and low wall shelving, long center gondolas, and check-out stands. Food stores must also have a wide variety of vegetable stands, cooling units, and refrigerator bins. Fixtures for financial institutions are designed primarily for handling money and for related paper work. These fixtures must also provide a counter between tellers and customers.

66-1. This bakery-shop fixture is similar in construction to other casework except that all the exterior is covered with plastic laminate.

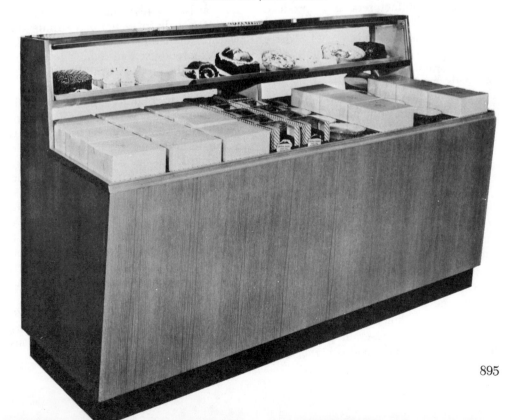

895

66-2. Fluorescent lighting units are built into most store cases.

Fixture manufacturers also produce the custom-designed furniture needed for commercial establishments. These manufacturers make standard units that can be fitted together for a variety of needs, and also customized fixtures designed and built specifically for one installation. Some cabinetmakers are employed in fixture plants, while others specialize in installing fixtures.

MATERIALS

Fixtures for such public places as offices and stores must be designed for extremely hard wear, with a minimum of maintenance and upkeep. Therefore there is an extensive use of plastic laminates for walls, cases, and the tops of desks, tables, and seating units. In designing the interior of a bank or large office, a logical choice for walls and cabinets would be wood-grain plastic laminate, even though the cost is higher than

for hardwood plywood. While plastic-laminate walls may not have quite the warmth of natural wood, they can take much more abuse and require less maintenance and repair. Another material extensively used for display purposes is perforated hardboard. Fig. 66-3. While the traditional, perforated hardboard (with round holes) can be used, there is a greater demand for heavier, primed hardboard that has square- or diamond-shaped openings. A variety of metal fittings is available to use with perforated hardboard for displaying many kinds of merchandise. Glass is also used extensively for store and office fixtures. Fig. 66-4. Not only is glass used in the cases themselves but also for shelving and doors, especially for displaying jewelry and other luxury items. Many cases also have curved glass. There is extensive use of metal hardware since stores require many kinds of fittings to accommodate various merchandise.

896

66-3. The backs of these jewelry cases are perforated hardboard. Many kinds of hooks and holders can be used for display.

66-4(a). Glass is used extensively for commercial casework, especially for jewelry and gift shops. The edge of the glass is usually covered with a stainless-steel channel, although sometimes the glass butts edge to edge. A special cement is needed to fit the glass into the channel.

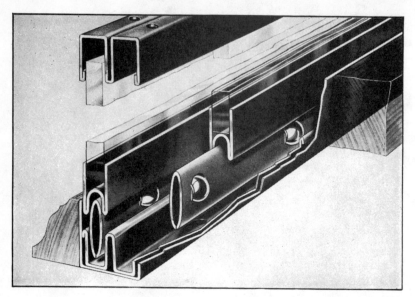

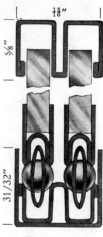

End View.

66-4(b). Ball-bearing track for sliding glass doors.

Durability is extremely important in fixture work. Drawers are built extra-strong, with heavy duty metal guides. Fig. 66-5. Chain stores are often standardized so that each store in the chain can use the same type of units, but most other stores require custom installation of fixtures. There is a trend toward the use of modular wall cases, show cases, and other display units. All of these are standard-width items, usually in widths of four, six, or eight feet that can be placed one next to the other to fill up whatever wall length is available. Fig. 66-6(a) and (b). Walls not covered with cases are usually paneled with perforated hardboard display surfaces.

WALL CASES

Wood wall cases have the same basic parts that a large china cabinet might

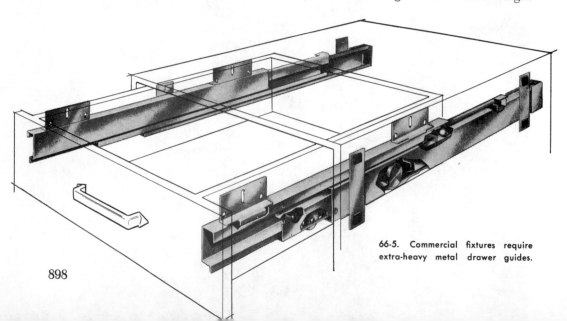

66-5. Commercial fixtures require extra-heavy metal drawer guides.

898

66-6(a). These units for card display and storage are made in standard widths so that as many as possible can be fitted along a wall. Note that most of the wall area above the cases is covered with perforated hardboard. Furring strips must be attached to the wall to allow a little clearance for hooks between the hardboard and the wall.

have, including: a *plinth or base* which is a frame with sleeper to support the total unit, and a *lower unit* consisting of sides, top, bottom, and back. Many cases are fitted with a *lower unit* containing shelves, drawers, and doors, an *upper unit* also with shelves or doors and draw-

ers, and a *cornice* around the top. Some wall cases may have only two or three of these units. Fig. 66-7. The general construction of wall cases varies greatly. Fig. 66-8. In some construction the sides extend beyond the top by approximately 1/2". The back is usually rabbeted.

66-6(b). A fastener like this can be installed between the cases to hold them firmly together. This is especially important if the units are not permanently attached to the wall.

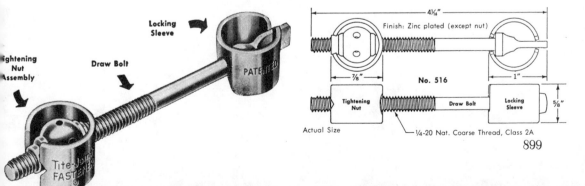

66-7. These wall cases consist of three units: the base, the lower casework, and the upper casework. Note that the lower case units, used primarily for storage, have either drawers or sliding doors. The upper case units also vary in design. Some have drawers, other vertical divider shelves, and still others horizontal glass shelves.

66-8(a). These jewelry wall cases feature open shelving.

900

66-8(b). Several different wall cases are shown here. The lower ones at left have sliding doors. Those directly ahead have drawers and vertical shelving.

66-9(a). Display cases for the candy section of a department store. Note that the cases stand on metal legs. Lower sections are enclosed shelving of wood and plastic laminate. Upper parts are made of glass and metal.

66-9(b). The display cases in this bakery have simple wood bases, but most of the upper parts are made of glass and metal.

66-10. Note that the counter in this dress shop has a front overhang so that customers can be seated when shopping.

While the shelving is sometimes fixed, more often adjustable shelving is necessary. This requires that the sides be grooved vertically to receive the adjustable shelving strips, or else the shelving must have back supports. The face frame or plate for wall cases consists of two vertical stiles and two or more horizontal rails. Doors usually are of frame-and-panel or flush construction, of either the hinged or sliding type. The base or the plinth is usually 3½" high and sits back approximately 2½" from the front base to provide toe space. The toe-space strip hides the sleepers. Drawers for wall cases are extra-heavy with lock-joint construction (usually dovetail) between the front and sides and also between the sides and back. The drawers are usually fitted with extra-heavy extension metal guides so that all merchandise can be seen easily when a drawer is pulled completely out of the case. The cornice is usually fitted to the case after the other units have been installed.

Show or Display Cases

Show or display cases vary greatly in design, depending on their use. Fig. 66-9. Many consist of two major parts: the lower section which is enclosed and used primarily for storage, and the upper section, often made of glass for display purposes. Normally, 1/4″ plate glass with ground edges is used for the top. Metal molding is commonly used to join the glass at the corners. These cases also have fluorescent lighting. The lower section is usually made of plywood or core stock faced with plastic laminate. Display cabinets may stand on legs or on a base (plinth) that is recessed.

Counters

Counters are usually enclosed on three sides and open in the back. The height of the counter depends on its use. Some counters, used primarily in selling clothes, are designed with a front overhang so the customer can be seated. Fig. 66-10. The counter top can be of solid plastic laminate or, for display, glass.

Central Shelving and Gondolas

Many types of stores, including drug stores, department stores, and super markets, make use of long central shelving, sometimes called gondolas. Fig. 66-11. These units are made in a number of ways. Some are basically open wood cases with adjustable shelving to handle various merchandise. Fig. 66-12. Still others are a combination of shelving and slide-out trays and are made of wood, metal, and plastic laminates. Fig. 66-13. The simplest gondolas, used in many large chain drug stores and food markets, consist of a heavy wood frame base topped with metal display standards and accessories. These units can be easily changed from one use to another. Fig. 66-14. Dividers and often the shelves are made of perforated hardboard.

66-11. This gondola for a jewelry store is really a special display fixture of wood, plastic laminate, metal, and glass. The base unit is covered with frosted glass over lighting fixtures.

66-12. The open shelving in this drug store is a basic wood unit with adjustable wood shelves. One section has sliding glass doors.

903

66-13. The central shelving in this men's clothing store is a combination of many materials.

66-14(a). A cabinetmaker can construct floor displays and gondolas by first building a wood base and then adding metal display standards and accessories.

66-14(b). Metal display stand used in constructing gondola units.

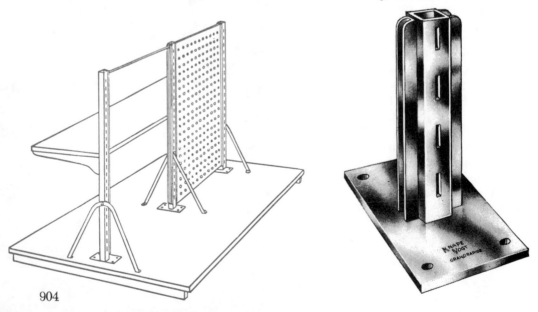

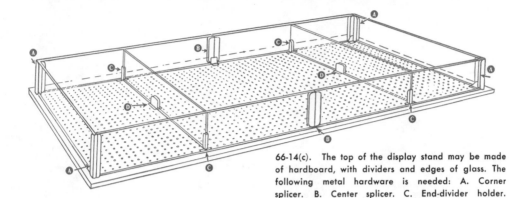

66-14(c). The top of the display stand may be made of hardboard, with dividers and edges of glass. The following metal hardware is needed: A. Corner splicer. B. Center splicer. C. End-divider holder. D. Divider holder.

FIXTURES FOR DINING ESTABLISHMENTS

Establishments that serve food and beverages must have fixtures of two types, some for preparing and storing foods and others for serving. Some of the common units include counters, stools, tables, chairs, booths, bus stations, and cashier stands. Fixtures for food businesses resemble home furniture more than most fixtures do.

OFFICE AND BANK FIXTURES

Fixtures for offices and banks include partitions, walls, railings, and counters. Fig. 66-15. Partitions are frequently made of wood and glass. Often they are six to seven feet high to allow open space between partition and ceiling. Fig. 66-15(c). Offices and banks use a great deal of custom-designed furniture, such as desks, tables, and seating facilities. Fig. 66-15(d). Such units are similar to home furnishings except that they are built more sturdily.

HEALTH, RESEARCH, AND OTHER INSTITUTIONAL FIXTURES

Hospital pharmacies and research laboratories are typical of the health facilities which require specialized counters, cabinets, and other fixtures. Fig. 66-16(a). Some companies make only this type of equipment. Others specialize in fixtures for libraries and schools. Music

rooms, art rooms, shops, laboratories for science and home economics, all need particular kinds of fixtures. Companies that make these may be primarily woodworking or metalworking manufacturers.

66-15(a). All exposed parts on the counters and desks of this savings and loan office are made of plastic laminates.

66-15(b). The low counters and dividers in this executive office suite are functional and attractive.

905

66-15(c). Wood and glass walls six feet high effectively divide the large room into cubicles, each one an individual office.

66-15(d). The semicircular design of this reception area made it necessary that all furnishings be custom-made for proper fit.

66-16(a). The storage and wall cabinets of this hospital pharmacy are made primarily of wood with plastic-laminate tops.

If the casework is made of wood, it is very similar in construction to high-quality kitchen cabinets made in production plants. Figs. 66-16(b) and (c).

INSTALLING PLASTIC-LAMINATE PANELING

For commercial and institutional applications, plastic-laminate paneling is the most satisfactory wall covering. This paneling can be used for new or remodeled walls. There are several systems for joining the panels together. Most common are the metal-molding, wood molding, and spline systems. Described and illustrated here is the spline system. A groove and rabbet are cut in both edges of the panels so that splines will fit between them. With a narrow spline, the panels edge-butt together. With a wider spline it is possible to place insert strips of plastic laminate between panels to harmonize with or to accent the panel colors. Basic installation steps are as follows:

66-16(a). The storage and wall cabinets of this hospital pharmacy are made primarily of wood with plastic-laminate tops.

66-16(b). Elementary-school furniture.

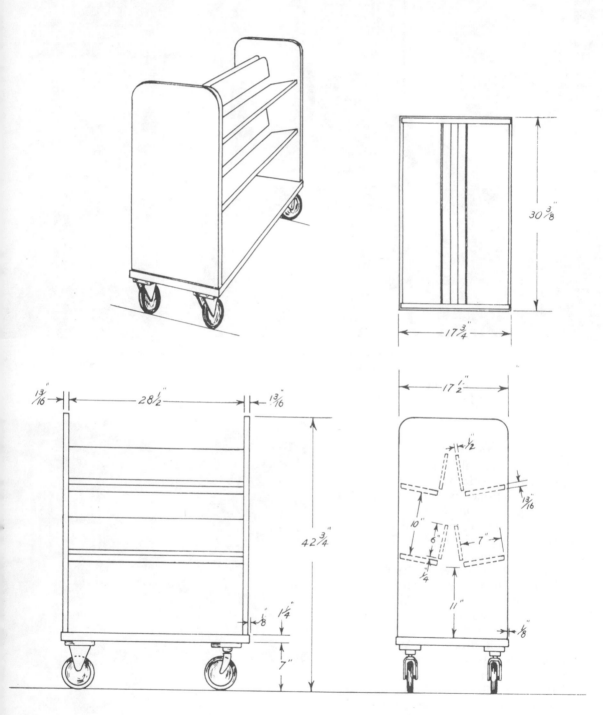

66-16(c). A typical piece of library equipment.

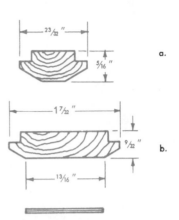

66-19(a). The narrow spline will give an edge-butt joint. With the wider spline, a piece of plastic laminate of different color can be fitted between the panels.

1. Apply furring strips horizontally, 16″ on center. Rabbet the inside corner edge of the first panel 3/16″ to provide a method of fastening and for inserting the panel on the opposite wall. Fig. 66-17.

66-17. Install furring strips to walls of masonry and wood.

66-18. Make sure that the edge of the panel is plumb (vertical).

66-19(b). Driving a nail through the spline.

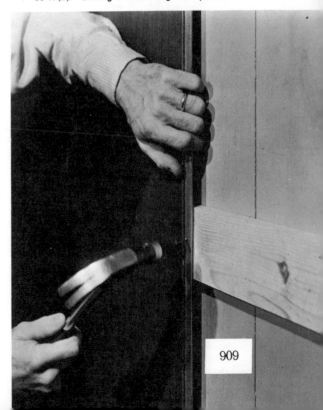

909

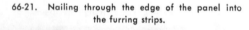
66-20.   Fitting the next panel onto the spline.

66-22.   Installing the corner molding.

66-21.   Nailing through the edge of the panel into
the furring strips.

66-23.   Installing the ceiling molding.

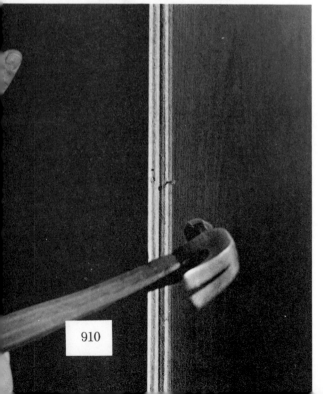

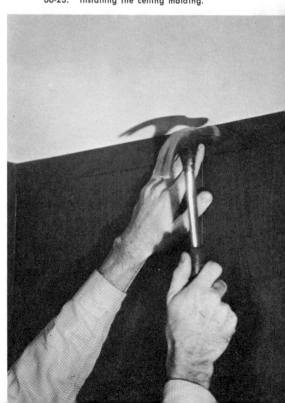

2. Start paneling at an inside corner. Plumb and fit the first panel accurately, using another panel on the opposite wall to obtain the correct position of two corner panels. Fig. 66-18. Then nail the first panel into the furring strips through the rabbet.

3. Insert the spline into the right edge of the first panel. Nail this to the furring strips with 3d coated nails. Fig. 66-19.

4. Slide the second panel into position over the spline and continue to install the splines and panels. Fig. 66-20.

5. Rabbet the edges of the corner panels so that the corner molding will fit in place. Then nail into furring as shown. Fig. 66-21.

6. Install outside corner molding evenly into the rabbeted edges. Nail through the pre-drilled holes. Fig. 66-22. Set and fill with matching plastic wood.

7. Position the ceiling molding at the top of the panel, and nail through the face with 3d coated finishing nails. Fig. 66-23. Set and fill. Fig. 66-24.

Other systems for installing wall panels and doors of plastic laminate are shown in Fig. 66-25.

INSTALLING FIXTURES

Some companies specialize in the design of commercial establishments so that they will be as attractive and efficient as possible. Frequently the interior design is completed at the same time the building is planned. The specifications and prints are sent to the fixture manufacturer to use in building the fixtures. When the building is already constructed, it is necessary to make the interior measurements and plan the layout inside the existing shell. This kind of layout is made in a manner similar to that for kitchen cabinets. An accurate scale layout of the space must be made, noting all such items as entrances, exits, windows, recesses, and stairways. If gas and

66-24. The completed wall.

electrical outlets or plumbing must be installed or changed, these should be noted. Then paper templets or standard fixtures can be used to make the layout. If custom fixtures are to be built, these must be designed and engineering drawings made. In addition to the fixture order, a stock bill or bill of materials must be made for all paneling, molding, and other standard items.

Fixtures are installed in much the same way as kitchen cabinets except that most of the walls and floors will be of masonry construction. Usually the installer has a portable gun or other unit for fastening furring and other wood parts to the walls by means of explosives. For simpler installations, any of the fasteners described in Unit 11 can be used. Usually the wall cabinets and cases are installed first and then the paneling is fastened in place. Finally the counters, show cases, and central shelving are installed.

Wall panels—ceiling and base details

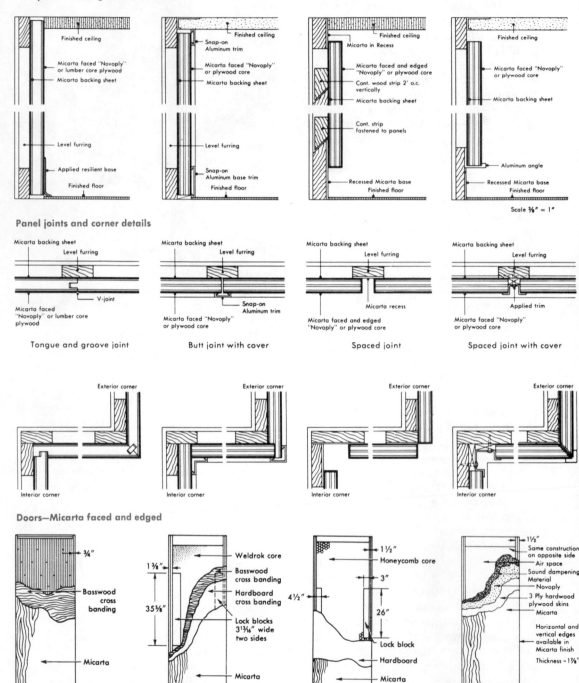

Finished ceiling

Micarta faced "Novoply"
or lumber core plywood

Micarta backing sheet

Level furring

Applied resilient base

Finished floor

Finished ceiling

Snap-on
Aluminum trim

Micarta faced "Novoply"
or plywood core

Micarta backing sheet

Level furring

Snap-on
Aluminum base trim

Finished floor

Finished ceiling

Micarta in Recess

Micarta faced and edged
"Novoply" or plywood core

Cont. wood strip 2' o.c.
vertically

Micarta backing sheet

Cont. strip
fastened to panels

Recessed Micarta base
Finished floor

Finished ceiling

Micarta faced "Novoply"
or plywood core

Micarta backing sheet

Aluminum angle

Recessed Micarta base
Finished floor

Scale ⅜" = 1"

Panel joints and corner details

Micarta backing sheet

Level furring

V-joint

Micarta faced
"Novoply" or lumber core
plywood

Tongue and groove joint

Micarta backing sheet

Level furring

Snap-on
Aluminum trim

Micarta faced "Novoply"
or plywood core

Butt joint with cover

Micarta backing sheet

Level furring

Micarta recess

Micarta faced and edged
"Novoply" or plywood core

Spaced joint

Micarta backing sheet

Level furring

Applied trim

Micarta faced "Novoply"
or plywood core

Spaced joint with cover

Exterior corner

Interior corner

Exterior corner

Interior corner

Exterior corner

Interior corner

Exterior corner

Interior corner

Doors—Micarta faced and edged

¾"

Basswood
cross
banding

Micarta

**Staved lumber
core construction**

1⅜"

35⅝"

Weldrok core

Basswood
cross banding

Hardboard
cross banding

Lock blocks
3¹³⁄₁₆" wide
two sides

Micarta

Stay-Strate® construction

1½"

Honeycomb core

3"

4½"

26"

Lock block

Hardboard

Micarta

**Hollow core
construction**

1½"

Same construction
on opposite side
Air space
Sound dampening
Material
Novoply
3 Ply hardwood
plywood skins
Micarta

Horizontal and
vertical edges
available in
Micarta finish

Thickness – 1⅞"

**Acoustical core
construction**

66-25.   Other systems for installing plastic-laminate walls and doors.

912

Dormitory rooms must be both functional and attractive. For this reason plastic laminates are used extensively in such rooms. The wide variety of colors and wood-grain patterns makes it possible to change the appearance of the rooms. Note the many built-in items, including the beds, the storage units for the wardrobe, and the desk units. An interesting feature is the built-in drawing board. The board can be lowered to make the desk level or raised for drawing.   *Formica*

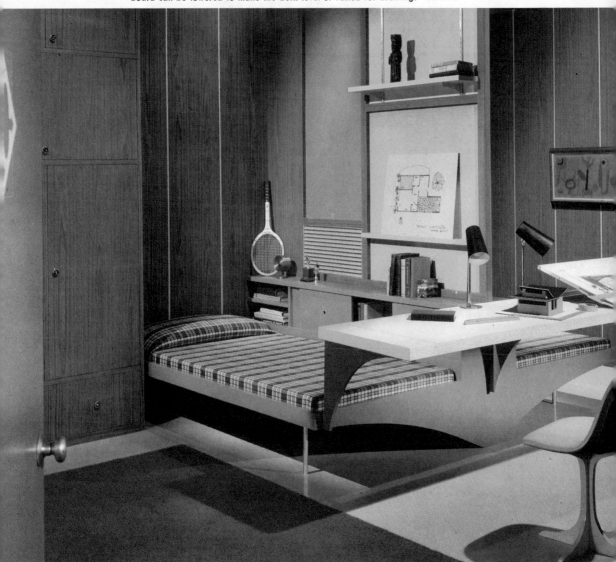

The extremely hard, non-absorbent surfaces of plastic laminates perform a double duty in this most unusual restaurant. One obvious attribute is their color, which greatly adds to customer appeal. Also, normal maintenance and food-service sanitation are simplified because even harsh detergents cannot harm the laminated surfaces. After years of service, these fixtures will retain an appearance of newness. *Formica*

Fixtures like this clothing-store counter unit are constructed of many different materials. This one has a basic construction of plywood, covered with plastic laminate. It has legs of metal and a plate-glass top. It would be an asset to any clothing shop. *Micarta*

Plastic laminates are used for the walls and counter tops of this restaurant. Commercial fixtures must be built to take hard wear and still remain attractive. *Textolite*

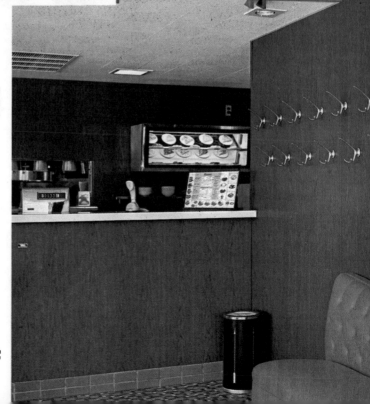

912C

Furniture for schools and institutions can be made very attractive through combining such materials as wood, metal, and plastic laminates. Tough plastic laminates are usually mounted on closed-grain plywood. Other materials such as particle board, or honeycomb material can also be used to vary the colors and textures. *Micarta*

SECTION VI

Questions and Discussion Topics

1. Do all woodworking manufacturers need the same equipment? Explain.
2. What is the basic purpose of a cutting room or rough mill?
3. Describe some common machines used in a cutting room or rough mill.
4. What kind of machine can do both surfacing and planing?
5. Describe production gluing equipment.
6. What is a tapeless veneer splicer and what advantage does it have over one using tape?
7. What kinds of presses are used for making veneer?
8. Are a molder and sticker the same machine?
9. Explain why a double-end tenoner is such an important production machine.
10. Describe some common machining that can be done on a double-end tenoner.
11. Describe two types of automatic shapers.
12. What work can best be done on a contour profiler?
13. How does a router compare with a shaper in its method of operation?
14. Describe two types of boring machines.
15. Why is the automatic turning and shaping lathe important in production?
16. Describe the setup for an automatic lathe.
17. Name three kinds of carving equipment.
18. Describe three machines used for flat sanding.
19. Name some of the special sanders used for edge work.
20. How does assembly equipment used in industry differ from that used in a small cabinet shop?
21. What nailing and stapling equipment is used in cabinetmaking?
22. What is the difference between hot and cold spray?
23. What is airless spraying?
24. Discuss some of the differences between producing furniture and kitchen cabinets.
25. What is a route sheet; what is its use?
26. List similarities and differences between furniture manufacture and automobile manufacture.
27. What department is responsible for getting the assembled furniture ready for finishing?
28. Is furniture always finished immediately after it is assembled? Explain.
29. Is kitchen-cabinet manufacturing simpler or more complex than furniture manufacturing?
30. What advantage in mass production does the kitchen-cabinet manufacturer have over the furniture manufacturer?
31. Are plant layouts for furniture manufacture usually very similar?
32. What is a store fixture?
33. How does store-fixture manufacturing differ from other woodworking manufacturing?
34. Describe the general construction of wall cases.
35. Is there much standardization of construction in fixture manufacturing?
36. Describe show and display cases.
37. What are counters and what are their major purposes?
38. What is a gondola and what kinds of stores feature them?
39. Tell how to install plastic-laminate paneling.

Problems and Activities

1. Compare the operation and use of a large piece of production equipment with a similar type used in your shop.
2. Visit a wood-product manufacturing plant and study the plant layout and production methods.
3. Make a careful study of fixtures in a new store, office, or bank in your city.
4. Study the way a large furniture-manufacturing plant is managed. Choose a company in which the stock is publicly held, and get a copy of the annual report to stockholders.
5. Compare the woodworking and metalworking manufacturing industries as to their use of production equipment and mass-production techniques.

913

INDEX

A

Abbreviations
    for describing lumber, 176
    used in drawing, 189
    used in print reading and sketching, 191
Abrasive(s)
    choosing for various materials (table), 456
    coated, 441-460
    common types (table), 447
    in non-woven nylon, 868, 869
    paper, 802
    planing, 266
    stones, 239, 258
Accessory table, illustrated, 576
Accidents, treatment of, 63
    (Also see *Safety*)
Accordion doors, 612
Acoustical hardboard, 133
Activities (See *Problems and activities, Projects*)
Adams Brothers, 20, 33, 34, 104
Adapter, mortising, 438
Adhesives
    for abrasives, 441-444, 448, 449
    for laminating wood, 560
    for plastic laminates, 578, 579
    general discussion, 534-538, 543-551
    (Also see *Glue, Gluing*)
Adjustments
    for radial-arm saw, 309, 310
    for router, 401, 402
    for shaper, 386
Air compressor, 793
Air drying, 73, 74, 876
Airless spraying, 874, 891
Air transformer, 794
Alcohol, 801, 802
Aliphatic resin glue, 535, 537
Allen wrenches, 236
Aluminum-oxide paper, 441, 442, 447, 452
Aluminum-oxide wheel, 237, 239, 250
American basswood, 89, 90
American beech, 89, 90
American elm, 93-95
American Lumber Standards, 177
American Plywood Association, 125
Anchor bolts, 159, 161
Anchors, hollow-wall (table), 158
Angle, bisecting, 217
Angle dado, 323
Angle sanding, 448
Angle sawing, 358
Angles, compound, for use on radial-arm saw
    (table), 317
Angular boring, 429, 432
Animal hide glue, 443, 535, 536
Annual growth rings, 68-70, 497, 498
Anti-kickback finger, 310, 318, 323
Apothecary chest, illustrated, 31
Aprons (rails), 674
Arbor, tilting, on circular saw, 267
    (Also see specific names of cutting machines)
Arc
    bisecting, 216
    drawing, 217-219
Architect, 24, 28
Architect's scale, 191
Architectural drawings, 201-204
Arm chair, illustrated, 679
Arm track, 308-310
Ash (wood), 87, 88
Assembly drawings, 195, 200
Assembly machine, 870, 871
Auger bit
    boring deep holes, 421
    counterboring, 156
    enlarging small holes, 427
    general discussion, 234, 417, 425
    sharpening, 241, 242
Automatic cutoff saw, 837
Automatic drill, 235
Automatic lathe, 461, 462, 883
Automatic sander, 865
Automatic turning and shaping lathe, 860, 861
Auxiliary table
    circular saw, 288
    plywood, 228
    radial-arm saw, 320, 321, 324

Auxiliary view, 194, 195
Auxiliary wood fence
    circular saw, 268, 277, 283, 284, 286, 288
    for boring operations, 428
Average furniture sizes (table), 42
Awl, scatch, 229
Awning window, 142

B

Back band, 145, 147
Backs (casework), constructing, 701, 702
Backer sheets (used with laminates), 577
Backing board, 264, 265
Backing, for abrasives, 441, 443-445
Back-panel rabbet joint, 521, 522
Back saw, 230
Backstand sanders, 866, 867
Balance (in design), 51, 52
Ball-bearing collar, 385, 389
Balsa wood, 56
Balusters, 143, 145, 147
Bamboo, split, illustrated, 48E
Band clamps, 542, 543
Band construction, table tops, 683-685
Banded plywood, 561
Banding, edge, plastic laminates, 577, 582-586
    illustrated, 48B
Band resaw, 837, 838
Band saw
    coiling blade, 340, 341
    external cutting, 356, 357
    general discussion, 337-351
    refitting by hand, 250, 251, 253
    repairing broken blade, 251
    resawing, 288
    sanding on, 458, 459
    used in industry, 848
Band veneer, 491
Bank fixtures, 895, 905, 906
    (Also see *Commercial fixtures*)
Bar clamps, 539-541, 543, 544
Barefaced mortise-and-tenon joint, 330, 530, 531
Bark of tree, 66, 68
Bark pocket (lumber defect), 77
Base cabinet, making a rod layout for, 221-224
Base, for casework, 698, 700
Base kitchen cabinet, 734, 735, 742-745
Basement plans, 202
Base molding, 145, 147
Base (plinth), 899
Base shoe, 145, 147
Base unit, of cabinetwork, 720-722
Basket guard, 269
Basswood, 89, 90
Bast, 66, 68
Batch press, high-frequency, 842, 844
Bathroom built-ins, 775
Battens, 145, 147, 652
Battery-operated portable drill, 416, 417
Bayonet saw, 363-366
Beads
    cutting, 473, 474
    definition, 665
    glass and screen, 145, 147
Bead and cove sticking, 597, 598
Beading bit, 397, 398
Bed moldings, 145, 146
Bedroom furniture, illustrated, 36, 48, 48B, 48D-
    48F, 718, 816B, 904A
    built-ins, 774, 776
Bedside table, illustrated, 718
Beech, 89, 90
Beeswax, 344
Belt abrasives, 445, 446, 454
Belt sander
    floor-type, 446-448
    hand-stroke, 451-453, 884
    portable, 453, 454
    vertical-belt variety, 867
    wide, 865
Bench-chest, illustrated, 821
Bench rule, 228
Bench-table, illustrated, 562
Bending
    general discussion, 551-560

914

Bending (*continued*)
  hardboard, 133
  in production work, 842-848
Bent corner plate, 161, 162
Benzene, 802
Bevel
  cuts, 358
  cutting across grain, 280, 281
  cutting on jointer, 374, 378
  cutting on portable saw, 361
  cutting on radial-arm saw, 310, 312, 314, 319
  cutting with grain, 288
  jig, adjustable, 392
  miter cut (See *Compound miter*)
  panel, raised, 598-600
  ploughing, 323
  ripping, on band saw, 346, 347
  sanding, 448, 450, 458
  sliding T, 229
  with plane, 369
Bill of materials, 205, 208
  (Also see *Projects*)
Birch, 90, 91, 108-110, 498
Bits
  auger, 234, 241, 242, 417, 425
  beading, 397, 398
  core box, 397, 398
  corner rounding, 397, 398
  countersink, 420
  cove, 397, 398
  dowel, 234
  expansion, 234
  Foerstner, 234, 418, 419, 427
  gage, 234, 235
  masonry, 418
  mortising, 434-436
  multi-spur, 417
  proper size for shank and pilot holes (table), 156
  router, 258, 259, 396-398
  sash beading and coping, 397, 398
  speed, 417, 418
  spur machine, 417, 427
  stock drill, 234, 235
  straight, 397, 398
  veining, 398
  "V" grooving, 398
Black cherry, 91, 92
Black knot (lumber defect), 79
Black walnut, 99, 100, 102
Blades
  band saw, 251, 337-342, 346
  carbide-tipped, 274, 275, 294, 325, 500
  circular saw, 267, 272-275, 290, 304
  crosscut, 272, 273, 500
  jig or scroll saw, 353-355, 364
  molding-head cutter, 259
  planer, grinding and jointing, 254, 255
  portable power saw, 360, 361
  radial-arm saw, 309
  reciprocating saw, 366
  selecting the correct (table), 353
Bleaching wood, 788-790, 805
Bleeder spray gun, 796, 797
Bleeding (filling defect), 820
Blending, 446
Blind dado, 293-297, 322, 326, 524, 652
Blind groove, 324
Blind mortise-and-tenon
  cutting on router, 404
  joint, 529, 530, 674-676
Blind spline joint, 294
Blind spline miter, 298, 299, 512, 514, 527, 528
Block plane, 232, 469
Block shear test, 550, 551
Blueprint, 185
  (Also see *Drawings, Plans, Prints*)
Board and batten paneling, illustrated, 830
Board, backing, 264, 265
Board feet, 174, 175
Board, manufactured, typical working characteristics
  (table), 135
Board measure rule, 182-184
Board-on-board installation of paneling, 762
Bolts
  anchor, 159, 161
  hardboard, 134
Bond coat for abrasives, 443
Bonding plywood, 124
  (Also see *Adhesives, Glue, Gluing*)
Book matched veneer, 565, 566, 620
Booth, spray, 796-798
Boring
  angular, 429, 432
  in basic construction, 504

Boring (*continued*)
  machines, 412-432, 858, 859, 889
  plastic laminates, 580, 582
Bow (lumber defect), 79, 80
Box construction (kitchen cabinets), 748-761
Box jig, 350, 351
Box joint
  general discussion, 301, 302, 333, 533
  illustrated, 508, 509, 532
  utility pliers, 237
Box wrench, 236
Brace, 234
Brace measure, 215, 216
Brackets, 652, 656, 657, 673, 674
Brad-point bit, 417
Brads, wire, 149
Branch knot (lumber defect), 77
Brazing, 251
Breakfronts, illustrated, 105, 656
Brick method of making curved parts, 552, 553
Brushes, 802-804
Buffed plywood, 127
Buffets, illustrated, 163, 441, 508, 522, 593,
  610, 613, 648, 721
  room-divider (project), 194-199
Building materials, 189, 205-213
  (Also see specific materials)
Built-ins
  general discussion, 770-782
  illustrated, 117, 144D, 167, 592A, 608,
  784D, 904A
    hardware, illustrated, 165
    sideboard, illustrated, 650
Built-up patterns, 573
Bumper molding, plastic, 683
Burl
  general discussion, 564, 565
  illustrated, 48F, 114, 144A, 717, 881
Burn-in method for repairing wood surfaces, 787, 788
Bushings, 435
Butt edge joint, 518, 519
Butterfly drop-leaf end table, illustrated, 690
Butternut veneer, illustrated, 717
Butt hinge, 615, 616, 688; illustrated, 163
Butt joints, 294, 325, 516-518, 636, 701
Butt wood, 565, 566

C

Cabinet
  base, making a rod layout for, 221-224
  china, illustrated, 38, 50, 617, 628, 651
  clamps (See *Steel bar clamps*)
  doors, 606-625
  drawings, 191, 192, 200, 202, 203
  fishing tackle (project), 706-708
  hardware, 164, 165
  interiors, 650-658
  portable, Colonial, illustrated, 106
  scraper, 233
  tops, 682-697
Cabinets
  assembling, 548, 549
  bathroom, illustrated, 144
  carcass, 716, 721, 722
  kitchen, 728-761
    applying laminate to fronts, 589-592
    manufacturing, 888-890
  modular, illustrated, 592B
  storage, 145, 146
Cabinetmaking
  definition and background information, 16-28
  joints, 507-533
Cabinetwork, fine furniture, 714-728
Cabriole leg, 33, 39, 48H, 348, 437, 665-668, 883
California Redwood Association, 177
Calipers, 465, 466
Cambium, 66, 68
Cane, illustrated, 29, 48E, 144A, 144B, 164
  webbing, 172-174
Captain's chair, illustrated, 679
Carbide-tipped tools
  bits, 396
  cutters, 383
  drills, 159
  grinding, 238, 251, 888
  saw blades, 274, 275
Carcass (of cabinets), 716, 721, 722
Carpenter's level, 229
Carpenter's square (See *Steel square*)
Carpentry, 18
Carriage clamps (See *C clamps*)
Carving machines, 862-864

Carving tools, 233
Case clamps, 871
Case doors, 606, 607
Casein glue, 535, 536
Casement window, 142
Casework, 697-713
Casing molding, 145, 146
Casing nails, 147, 148
Catches, 623, 624
Cauls, 544, 545, 558
C clamp, 387, 411, 424, 540-542
Ceiling, exposed beam, illustrated, 592D, 784C
Cell structure of wood, 69
Center guide, 641-644
Centers, wood lathe, 464
Central shelving, 903, 904
Chain-saw mortiser, 433, 434
Chair(s)
    arm, illustrated, 679
    Captain's, illustrated, 679
    construction, 678-681
    Danish, 509
    dining-room (project), 630, 681
    ladder-back, illustrated, 664
    molded plywood and laminated legs, 552
    swivel, illustrated, 552
    Windsor, 30, 31, 48A
Chalkboard drawing instruments, illustrated, 22
Chamfer, 300, 686
    bit, 397, 398
    cutting on jointer, 374, 378
    sanding, 448
    stop, 378
Charts
    compound miter adjustments, 316
    forest regions of the United States, 81
Check (lumber defect), 76, 77
Checkerboard matched veneer, 565, 566
Checking devices, 228, 229
Cheek (mortise-and-tenon joint), 300, 301
Cherry, 91, 92, 105-107
Chest
    apothecary, illustrated, 31
    Contemporary, illustrated, 608
    dining-room, 192
    drawer, cedar, Early American, illustrated, 30
    French Provincial, illustrated, 37, 714, 717,
      719, 720
    movable, illustrated, 19
    perspective rendering of, 192
    six-drawer, illustrated, 109
    teak, illustrated, 113, 532, 628
Chest-on-chest, illustrated, 32
Chevrons, 160-162
Chilled glue joint, 550
China cabinet, illustrated, 38, 50, 617, 628, 651
Chip breaker, 261, 262
Chip marks, 502, 503
Chipped grain, 502
Chippendale, Thomas, 20, 30, 33, 104
Chippers, 270, 271, 321
Chisel
    cold, 235
    general discussion, 150, 232
    mortising, 259, 434, 435
    wood, sharpening, 241
Chuck
    collet, 395, 396
    geared, 416
    jig or scroll saw, 351, 352, 354, 359
Chute (shaving), 382
Circle cutter, 418, 419
Circle jigs, 348-351
Circles, cutting
    with band saw, 348, 349
    with portable saw, 365, 366
Circle-sweep glass cutter, 170, 172
Circular saw
    blade vise, 252
    cutting a raised panel on, 603
    general discussion, 267-306
    sharpening blades, 251-253
Circular stock, molding on, 306
Clamp attachment, for circular saw, 271-273
Clamp down molding, 585, 586
Clamp fixtures, 542, 543
Clamping, 533-551, 579, 871, 885
Clamp nails, 160, 162, 514, 515
Clamps
    band, 542, 543
    bar, 539-541, 543, 544
    case, 871
    spring, 540, 541
    steel bar, 539-541

Clamps (continued)
    stop, 322, 323, 325
Clamp-type cutter head, 384
Claw hammer, 149
"Cleaner" teeth (See Rakers)
Cleaning, 826-828
Clearance hole, 365, 367
Cleats, wood, 652, 658
Clock
    French Provincial, illustrated, 107
    inlay, illustrated, 573
Closed coat, abrasives, 444, 445
Closets, 658
    (Also see Built-ins)
Cloth, for abrasives, 443, 447, 456
Clothing (See Safety, general rules)
Coated abrasives, 441-460
Coating, abrasive grain, 444
Coatings, protective, 822-828
Coffee tables, illustrated, 34, 39, 53, 167, 395
Cold chisel, 235
Cold spraying, 872, 873
    lacquers, 822, 823
Collars, 383-391
Collet chuck, 395, 396
Colonial furniture, 29-32, 48A, 55, 106, 109, 110,
    461, 592D, 688, 752A, 816A
Color(s)
    effects, achieving on paneling, 830-832
    harmony in woods, 505-507
    in design, 47, 49
    of wood, 70
    tinting, in oil (table), 814
    toning, 833
    using in oil for finishing (table), 814
Coloring
    stains, 812
    wood, 805
Color wheel, 47
Columns, 142, 144, 145
Comb grain (See Rift-sawed lumber)
Combination blade, 361, 500
Combination saw, 252, 253, 273
Combination square, 228, 229
Combination window, 142
Commercial drawer slides, 642-645
Commercial legs, 673, 674
Commercial fixtures
    hardware, 166
    illustrated, 18, 168, 169, 904B, 904C
    rendering of, 192
    (Also see Institutional fixtures, Office
      fixtures, Store fixtures)
Commode table, illustrated, 624, 717
Compass saw, 230
Compound miter
    adjustments (chart), 316
    cuts, 282, 298, 316, 328, 362
    joint, 528, 529
Compound sawing, band saw, 347, 348
Compression joint, 665, 666
Compressor, air, for spray finishing, 793, 797, 798
Concealed haunched mortise-and-tenon joint, 531
Concealed wrap-around hinge, 616
Cone-bearing trees (See Conifers)
Cone center of lathe, 464
Conference table, illustrated, 490
Conifers, 72, 82-88
Construction
    band, table tops, 683-685
    basic problems, 488-507
    built-ins, 776, 777
    frame-and-panel, 593-606
    geometric, 216-220
    kitchen cabinets, on the job, 746-749
    of furniture, 44, 45
Construction-grade lumber, 179
Contact cement, 534, 537, 538
Contemporary
    chest, illustrated, 608
    china cabinet, illustrated, 628
    footstool, illustrated, 662
    furniture, 29, 35-37, 48D, 48E, 55, 110, 115, 116,
      144B
      wood used in, 102, 103
    refreshment bar, illustrated, 716
    sideboard, illustrated, 620
    table, illustrated, 659, 660
Continuous edge gluers, 842, 843
Contour cutting, 334, 335
Contour profiler, 854-857
Coped joint, 302, 359
Cope heads, 440
Coping saw, 231

Core box bit, 397, 398
Core materials, plastic laminates, 578
Core stock, 682
Corner blocks, 289, 515-517
Corner butt joint, 428, 516-518
Corner dado, 296, 323, 523, 524
Corner guards, 145, 147
Corner joints, 129, 597, 598
Corner kitchen cabinets, 734, 735, 743-745
Corner pocket hole, 427
Corner rounding bit, 397, 398
Corners
　constructing, 701, 702
　cutting square, 357
Cornice, 721-723, 899
Corrugated fasteners, 160, 162
Costs, estimating, 211-213
Cottonwood, 91, 92
Counterbore, screw-mate, 155
Counterboring, 427
Countersink, 154, 155
　sharpening, 242
Countersink bit, 420
Counter(s), 902, 903
　applying laminate to tops, 588, 589
　top moldings, 585, 586
Cove, 665
　bit, 397, 398
　cutting, 302, 303, 472
　molding, 145, 146, 398
Covering capacities of common finishing materials
　(table), 806
Credenza, illustrated, 606
Crook (lumber defect), 79, 80
Crossbands, 118, 119, 123, 133
Crosscut
　blade, 272, 273, 500
　hand saw, 245, 246, 248-250, 253
　saw, 230
Crosscutting
　horizontal, radial-arm saw, 320, 325, 326
　on a circular saw, 276-282
　on a portable saw, 361, 362
　on a radial-arm saw, 306-316, 326, 334
　square, 276
Cross grain, 497, 498
　lemon spline, 513, 514
　plug, 513, 514
Cross kerfing, 552, 553
Cross lap joint, 297, 328, 524, 526
Cross rail, 596
Cross sanding, 454
Cross stile, 596
Crotch, 102, 108, 564, 566
Crown, 66, 67
Crown moldings, 145, 146
Crystal glass, 168
Cube table, illustrated, 48E
Cup (warp), 79, 80, 264, 376, 498
Cupboard doors, 606, 607
Cup center of lathe, 464
Curing glue, 546-549
Curio cabinet, illustrated, 655, 816A
Curved furniture parts, cutting, 552, 553
Curves, cutting
　on band saw, 339, 343, 344, 346, 347
　on jig saw, 355-357
　with portable saw, 365
Custom furniture plants, 21
Cutoff blade, 272, 273
Cutoff saw
　automatic, 837
　tenoner, 439-441
Cut-out size, 206
Cutters
　head, 254, 255, 262, 370-373
　plane, 368, 369
　router, 394, 397, 409
　shaper, 383-385
Cutting
　bevels, 280, 288
　compound miter cut, 282
　contour, 334, 335
　coves, 302, 303
　curves, on a jig saw, 355-357
　dado, 293, 294
　duplicate parts to identical lengths, 277, 278
　edge, 289
　flat miters, 278-281
　glass, 169-172
　grooves, 293, 294
　horizontal, radial-arm saw, 320, 321, 325
　identical lengths, radial-arm saw, 312, 313
　joints, 294-302

Cutting (*continued*)
　large sheet materials, 280, 281
　lumber, 71, 72
　metal, 358
　molding, 333-335
　on a band saw, 342-351
　on a router, 398-408
　on a wood lathe, 465
　plastic laminates, 579-581
　plywood, 127, 280, 281
　raised panel, 603-605
　rosette, 334, 335
　saucer, 334, 335
　sticking, 600-603
　straight, 356, 357
　taper, 290-292
　tools for drills, 417, 418
　triangular pieces, 289
　veneer, 562, 563, 565, 567, 568
　wedges, 289
　(Also see *Sawing*)
Cutting diagram, 206, 208
Cutting room, 836-840, 880, 881

D

Dado
　and-lip joint, 636
　and-rabbet joint, 636
　and-tenon joint (See *Rabbet-and-dado joint*)
　angle, 323
　blind, 293-296, 322, 323
　box corner joint (See *Rabbet-and-dado joint*)
　corner, 323
　cutting on a circular saw, 270, 293, 294
　cutting on a router, 398, 402, 403, 412
　head, 270, 271, 283, 292-294, 321-324
　joints, 296, 297, 326, 522-524, 701
　plain, 322, 323
Danish chair, illustrated, 509
Danish oil finish, 808, 809
Dead center of lathe, 464
Decay (lumber defect), 77
Deciduous trees, 72, 82, 88-101
Decorative cutting, on a router, 398, 407, 408
Deep luster finish, 828
Defects
　filling, 819, 820
　in lumber, 76-80
Deft, 808
Den furniture, illustrated, 144B, 592B
Density (of wood), 70, 71, 76
Depth
　collar, 385, 386, 388, 389, 391
　gage, 234, 235
　of cut on a jointer, 372, 373
　of cut on a radial-arm saw, 309-311, 322
　stop, 421
Design
　elements of, 45-50
　enlarging and transferring an irregular, 220
　fundamentals of, 41-44
　furniture, 24, 29-40, 48A-48H, 144A-144C
　interior, 24, 26, 144D, 592A-592D, 752A-752D,
　　784A-784D, 816A-816D, 904A-904D
　principles of, 50-53
Designing furniture and cabinets, 41-57, 876-880
Desks, illustrated
　Colonial, 31, 32, 164, 628
　French-styled, 38
　Italian Provincial, 38, 662
　miscellaneous, 622, 623, 717, 718
　plastic-laminate top, 577
　Scandinavian, 36, 562
Detail drawings, 191, 195, 198, 200
　architectural, 201, 202, 204
Detailer, 208, 210
D-handles, 88
Diameter board, 475
Diamond matched veneer, 565, 566, 568
Diamond tool, 464, 465
Dimension lumber, 176
Dimensions, defined, 189
Dining room chairs (project), 680, 681
Dining room furniture, illustrated, 29, 34, 41,
　42, 490, 816A
Dining tables, 690-693
Dipping (finishing), 874
Discussion topics (See *Questions and discussion topics*)
Disk
　abrasives, 445, 446
　sander, 448-450, 457

Display cases, 901-903
    (Also see *Commercial fixtures*)
Distressed finish, 39, 107, 820-822
Dividers (tools), 229, 465
Divider(s)
    drawer, 646
    molding, 585, 586
    room, 781, 782
    wall, illustrated, 784B, 816D
Doors, 141-143, 606-626, 702, 703
    hardware, 163-165, 624, 625
    kitchen cabinet, 736, 737
    sliding glass, 898
    symbols for, 190
Dormitory furniture, illustrated, 576, 904A
Dote (lumber defect), 77
Double-cutoff saw, 861-863, 889, 894
Double dresser, Early American, illustrated, 720
Double-end tenoner, 433, 439, 849-852, 882
Double-hung window, 142
Double-joint tenon, 849
Double planer and surfacer, 261, 839, 840
Double-spindle shaper, 852-854
Double spreading of glue, 545
Douglas fir, 82, 83, 125
Dovetail
    bit, 397, 398
    corner block, 515, 517
    dado joint, 296, 326, 405, 409, 524, 635-637, 701
    jig, 330-333
    joint, 330-333, 405-407, 531-533, 637
    lap joint, 525, 526
    saw, 231, 567
Dovetailer, 859, 860, 882
Dowel(s), 509-512, 527
    bit, 234
    edge joint, 265, 326, 519
    gluer and driver, 868, 870
    joints, 428, 595, 597, 598
    miter, 511
    pins, 654, 655
Draft, 358
Drafting equipment, illustrated, 192
    manufacturing, 890, 892-894
Drawer-corner joint, 633, 634
Drawer(s)
    and guides, 626-649, 702, 703, 898
    cedar chest, illustrated, 30
    hardware, 162-164
    installing, 678, 679
    pulls, 624, 625
    slides, 642-645
    spacing, 741-743
    (Also see specific types of drawers such as
        Lip drawers, Flush drawers, etc.)
Drawing boards, 891-893
Drawing(s)
    arcs, 217-219
    assembly, 195, 200
    detail, 191, 195, 198, 200
    Golden mean rectangle, 50
    elements of, 189
    ellipse, 219, 220
    hexagon, 219
    instruments, chalk-board, 22
    octagon, 219
    room divider buffet, 197, 198
    working drawings, making from a sketch or picture,
        56, 57
    (Also see specific types of dawings such as
        Isometric, Multiview, Working, etc.)
Draw knife, 232, 242
Dress, 58, 60
    (Also see *Safety*)
Dresser wheel, diamond pointed, 239
Dressing table, illustrated, 518, 592C, 816B
Dried glue joint, 550
Drills, 156, 234, 235, 259
Drilling
    hardboard, 133
    jig, 422, 423
    machines, 412-432
    plastic laminates, 580, 582
    plywood, 129
Drill press, 409-413, 418, 420-429
    for mortising, 435, 437-439
    sanding on, 459
    shaping on, 393
    tilting table, 425
Drive center of lathe, 464
Drop doors, 624-626
    hardware, 164
Drop-leaf table, 687-690, 694-697
    hinge, 688
    project, 694-697

Drum sanding, 864, 866
Drum table, illustrated, 34
Dry clamping, 544
Drying
    lumber, 73-75, 492
    times for finishing materials (chart), 806
Dry spray booth, 796, 797
Dry-wall fasteners, 158-160
Dull satin finish, 828
Duplicate parts
    cutting, 350, 351, 358
    turning, 475-479
Duplicator attachment, lathe, 477-479
Dust-collection system, illustrated, 61
Dust panel, 595, 636, 637, 703
Dutch Colonial leg sets, illustrated, 660
Dutch door, illustrated, 607

E

Early American
    double desk, illustrated, 628
    hutch cabinet, illustrated, 609
    kitchen, illustrated, 732, 775
    miscellaneous furniture, 29-32, 48A, 55, 461,
        592D, 752D, 816A
    step table, illustrated, 812
    table, illustrated, 659, 660
Early wood (See *Springwood*)
Ebony, 116
Economy grade lumber, 179
Edge banding, 128
    plastic laminates, 577, 582-586
Edge boring, 432
Edge butt joint, 423, 428
Edge-clamp fixture, 542
Edge cross lap joint, 524, 525
Edge cutting, 289
Edge gluing, 545, 842, 843
Edge-grained lumber, 71, 72, 75, 76
Edge jointing, 374, 376, 377, 839, 840
Edge joints, 294, 295, 325, 326, 518-521
Edge miter joint, 298, 328, 527
    (Also see *Bevel*)
Edge molding, of straight stock, 305
Edge rabbet joint, 294-296, 325
Edge sanding, 447, 448, 450, 454, 865, 866, 889
Edge treatment
    plastic laminates, 582-586
    table tops, 683, 684, 686, 687
Edge-trimming plane, 233
Edging hardboard, 134
Electrical wiring (symbols for), 190
Electric knife, 787
Electric portable plane, 368, 369
Electrocoating, 444
Electronic gluing machine, 547-549
Electronic laminating press, 557, 558
Electronic welder, 547-549
Elevated panel, 598
Elevating handwheel, 262, 263
Elevation (front) view, 200, 202, 204
Ellipse, drawing, 219, 220
Elm burl, illustrated, 48F, 114, 144A
Embossed hardboard, 131, 132
Emphasis (in design), 53
Enamel, 803, 832
Encased knot, 79
Enclosed base (See *Plinth*)
Enclosed mortise, 299
End banding, 491, 492
End boring, 432
End cap molding, 585, 586
End-grain sanding, 448, 450
End jointing, 377
End lap joint, 298, 328, 525, 526
End rabbet joint, 295, 326
End shaping 391, 393
End tables, illustrated, 489, 824
Engineer, wood products, 24, 27
Enlarging and transferring an irregular design, 220
Epoxies, 826
Epoxy resin, 537, 538
Equilibrium moisture content (EMC), 493
Escutcheon pins, 149
Essex board-measure table, 183, 184, 216
Estimating material needs and costs, 205-213
Exhaust system, illustrated, 337
Exotic woods, 112-116
Expansion bit, 234
Exploded drawings, 200
Exposed beam ceiling, illustrated, 592D, 784C
Exposed joints, 508, 509, 526

Extension table, 691
  for circular saw, 272, 273
External mix, 796
Exterior doors, 606, 607
Exterior furniture parts, 596-600
Extrusion, method of manufacturing particle board, 137
Eye protection, illustrated, 60
  (Also see *Safety*)

F

Face boring, 432
Faceplate, 703, 705
Faceplate turning, 466, 480-484
Facer, 837, 838
Facing, 375, 376
Facing strip, 276, 277
Factory and shop lumber, 177, 178
Family room, illustrated, 144C, 144D
  built-ins, 771, 774, 775
  (Also see *Den furniture*)
FAS (lumber grade), 179, 180
Fastening devices, 147-162
  for furniture tops, 692-694
  for hardboard and particle board, 134, 139
  for hollow and masonry walls, 158-161
  for joints, 161, 162, 509-517
Feather, across a miter corner, 298, 300
  (Also see *Key*)
Feather board, 283, 285
Feed control, 262, 263
Feeding stock (jointer), 374, 375
Fence, 267, 268, 283, 284, 373, 374, 386-389
  ripping, 345, 346
Ferrules, 673, 674
Fiber, for abrasives, 443
Fiber glass wall, illustrated, 144B
Fiberply, 125
Fiber-saturation point, 75
Figure (of wood), 70
Files, 248, 250
Filing, 241, 242, 245, 248-252
  on a jig saw, 359
Filing cabinet, illustrated, 722
Fillers, 788
Fillets, 665
Filling, 806, 816-820
Fine finishing (abrasive), 446
Finger cups, 620, 621, 624
Finger joint, 301, 333, 508, 509, 532, 533
Finish
  carpentry, 17, 18, 23
  distressed, 39, 107, 820-822
  grade of lumber, 178, 179
  sanding, 884, 885
  sawing, 500
  size of lumber, 206
  turning, 468, 469
Finishes (See specific woods, especially *Birch, Cherry, Fruitwood, Maple, Oak*)
Finishield, 127
Finishing
  casework, 705
  equipment and supplies, 793-804
  furniture, 886, 887
  interior, 829-833
  kitchen cabinets, 890, 891
  materials, tables concerning, 806, 814
  nails, 147, 148
  particle board, 139
  plywood edges, 128
  preparation for, 786-792
  procedures, 804-811
  sander, 454-457
  turnings, 484
Fir, 82, 83
Fire control, 62, 63
Fireplace framing, 765
Firsts and seconds (lumber grade), 179, 180
Fishing tackle cabinet (project), 706-708
Fixed jig, 290
  radial-arm saw, 318, 319
Fixed shelving, 651, 652
Fixed window, 142
Fixture manufacturers, 21
Fixtures (See *Commercial fixtures, Institutional fixtures, Office fixtures, Store fixtures*)
Flake board, 136-138
Flame-retardant grade plastic laminates, 577
Flap table hinge, 688
Flat butt joint, 516, 517
Flat corner plate, 161, 162
Flathead screws, 151, 152, 155-157

Flat miter, 278-280
  joint, 297, 298, 328, 357
Flat-nose, long pliers, 237
Flat-nose tool, 464, 465
  sharpening, 243, 244
Flat-power bit (See *Speed bit*)
Flat sanding, 451
Flat-sawed or flat-grained lumber, 71, 76
Flat slicing, 563, 564
Flat stock, drilling holes in, 420
Flexible doors, 611, 612
Flexible tape rule, 228
Flexing, abrasives, 444, 445
Flexwood, 127, 128
Flint paper, 441, 447
Flitch, 120, 562
Floating spindle (router), 856, 857
Floors
  parquet, 110
  plans, 202
Floor-type router, 394, 408-411
Fluorescent lighting, 896
Flower-petal legs, 101
Flow-out (filling defect), 819, 820
Fluid adjustment screw, 798, 799
Flush door, 612-617
  hardware, 163, 164
Flush drawer, 627, 628; illustrated, 720
Flush panel, 598
Fluted plastic pin, 654, 657
Fluting, 666, 668-671
Foerstner bit, 234, 418, 419, 427
Folding, band-saw blade, 340, 341
Folding doors, 612
  hardware, 164
Footstool, Contemporary, illustrated, 662
Fore plane, 231, 232
Forester, 24, 27
Forest Products Laboratory, 495
Forest regions of the United States (chart), 81
Formal balance, 51, 52
Formica, 575
Form sanding, 448, 449
Forms, for laminating and bending, 555-559
Form shaping, 387, 391
Foundation plans, 202
Frame, 596, 597
  panel for glass or metal grille, 598, 600
Frame and panel construction, 488, 491, 593-606, 716, 717
Frame-and-panel doors, 609, 611
Frame butt joint, 518
Frame construction
  kitchen cabinets, 748, 749
  table tops, 683-685
  (Also see *Leg-and-rail construction*)
Framing plans, 202
Framing square, 184, 229
  (Also see *Steel square*)
Freehand
  cutting and ripping, band saw, 345, 348
  routing, 400, 401, 412
  sanding, 448, 450, 458
Free water, 75
French oil finish, 484
French Provincial
  chest, illustrated, 717
  frame and panel, illustrated, 602
  miscellaneous furniture, 37-39, 48H, 820
  table, illustrated, 659, 660
Fret saw, 353
Fretwork, illustrated, 33, 670
Fruitwood finish, 48H, 106, 107
Full-dovetail dado joint (See *Dovetail dado joint*)
Function (in design), 41, 43
Fundamentals of good design, 41-44
Furniture
  assembling, 548, 549
  cabinetwork, 714-728
  construction, 44, 45
  design, 24, 29-40, 48A-48H, 144A-144C
  designing, 41-57, 876-880
  doors, 606-625
  dormitory, illustrated, 576, 904A
  glass used in, 167, 172
  hardware, 162-165
  institutional, illustrated, 904D
  manufacturing, 875-881
  plants, custom, 21
  school, 904D
  sizes, average, (table), 42
  woods used in, 101-116
  (Also see *Joinery, Laminating, Commercial fixtures,* and various styles of furniture)

Furring strips, 763-765, 768, 769, 909
Fuzzy grain, 501, 502

G

Gage
    bit, 234, 235
    depth, 234, 235
    marking, 229
    system for measuring diameter of nails, 148, 149
    (Also see specific gages such as *Miter,* etc.)
Gap-bed lathe, 462, 463
Garnet paper, 442, 447
Geared chuck, 416
General drawings (architectural), 201
Geometric construction, 216-220
George Washington desk and tier tables, illustrated, 31
Glass, 166-172, 610, 611, 896, 897
    beads, 145, 147
Glazed door, 611
Glazing, 806, 820-822, 833
Glides, 673
Glues, 535-537
    (Also see *Abrasives* and specific names of glues)
Glue applicators, 841, 842
Glue blocks, 515
Glued-up stock, 488-490, 607, 684
Glue mixing equipment, 868, 869
Glue reel clamping equipment, 841
Glue, removing excess, 786
Glue size, 792
Glue spreaders, 841, 846, 868-870
Gluing
    equipment, 840-842
    general discussion, 533-551
    hardboard, 134
    high-frequency gluing equipment, 547-549
    plywood, 125
Goggles, 62
    (Also see *Safety*)
Golden Age of furniture design, 20
Golden mean rectangle, 50
Gold leafing, 887
Gondolas, 903, 904
Gouges, 232, 464, 465
    sharpening, 243-245
Grades of laminates, 576, 577
Grading
    abrasives, 442, 443
    lumber, 177-181
    softwood plywood (table), 126
Grain, 70, 505-507
    (Also see specific woods)
Gravity coating, 444
Graying (filling defect), 820
Grille, metal, illustrated, 164
Grinder, standard two-wheel, 237, 238
Grinding, 237-244, 251, 254-259
Grit sizes for abrasives, 443, 446, 447, 452; (table), 446
Grooves, 323, 324, 326
    cutting, 293, 294, 402, 403
    spline, 298, 299
Grooving saws, 384
Growth rings (See *Annual growth rings*)
Guards, 269, 270
Guide
    arm, 350, 351
    band saw, 338, 339, 342
    drawer, 626-649, 702, 703, 898
    fence, 362, 365
    jig saw, 352, 354, 355
    pattern, 350. 351
    pins, 341, 342, 409-411
    shaping with, 386-389
    templet, 405-408
Gullets, 248-250
Gumming, 251, 252

H

Hacksaw, 235
Half-dovetail dado, 296, 523, 524
Half-round slicing, 563, 565
Hammer, claw, 149
Hand sanding, 459, 460
Hand screws, 538, 539
Hand-stroke sander, 864, 865, 884
Hand tools
    drill, 235
    jig (See *Bayonet saw*)
    gun, 547, 548

Hand tools (*continued*)
    jointer, 848
    lathe, 461, 462
    plane, electric, 368, 369
    safety, 60, 61
    saw, sharpening, 245, 248-250, 253
    scraper, 233
Hanger screws, 161, 162
Hanging doors, 612-624
Hardboard
    bending, 133
    general discussion, 129-139, 609
    paneling, 763
    perforated, 896-898
    shelving, illustrated, 166
Hardness (of wood), 71
Hardware, 162-166, 791
    (Also see *Hinges, Knobs, Pulls*)
Hardwood dimension plants, 22, 880
Hardwoods
    characteristics that affect machining (table), 498
    cutting methods, 71, 72
    defined, 72
    diffuse porous, 70
    grades, 179-181
    machining and related properties (table), 499
    plywood, 123-125, 683, 684, 832
    ring porous, 69, 70
    semi-ring porous, 70
    specific varieties, 88-112
    standard thicknesses (table), 178
    working with, 496-500
Harmony (in design), 52, 53
Harvest table, illustrated, 32, 688
Hatchet, 232
Haunched mortise-and-tenon joint, 531, 595, 597
Haunch rabbet joint, 701
Health fixtures, 905, 907
Heart pith, 77
Heartwood, 66-70, 76
Heating, symbols for, 190
Heel, 258
Hepplewhite, George, 20, 30, 33, 34, 104
Hermaphrodite caliper, 465, 466
Herringbone matched veneer, 566, 567
Hexagon, drawing, 219
Hex key chuck, 416
Hickory, 94, 95
Hi-fi cabinet, illustrated, 35, 805
High-frequency batch press, 842, 844
High-frequency gluing equipment, 547-549
High-pressure plastic laminate, 575, 576
High-sheen satin, 828
Hinge butt routing, 407
Hinged clamps, 542, 543
Hinge doors, hardware, 164, 165
Hinges
    for doors, 612-619, 622
    for tables, 688, 689
    double action, 165, 166
Hobby center, 709, 710
Hold-down, 354, 355, 409, 431, 437
Hold-down clips, 656, 657
Hold-down push block, 376
Hollow-chisel mortiser, 434
Hollow grinding, defined, 241
Hollow-ground blades, illustrated, 273, 274
Hollow-wall fasteners, 158-160
Honeycomb-core doors, 610, 611
Honing, 237, 240-245, 258, 259, 380
    (Also see *Sharpening*)
Hopper cut (See *Compound miter*)
Hopper joint, 298, 528, 529
Hopper window, 142
Horizontal boring machine, 414, 415
Horizontal-sliding window 142
Hot-plate press, 556
Hot spray, 873
Hot veneer press, 846
Housed dado (See *Blind dado, Stop dado*)
Housed dovetail joint (See *Dovetail dado joint*)
Humidity, 490-495
    (Also see *Moisture content*)
Hutch cabinet, Early American, illustrated, 32, 49, 609

I

Identical parts (See *Duplicate parts*)
Impact test, 550, 551
Industrial production, 835-912
Infeed rolls, 261, 262
Informal balance, 51, 52
Inlay, 40, 102, 106, 115, 116, 358, 359;
    illustrated, 48B, 881

Inlaying, 561-575
Inner bark, 66, 68
Inside calipers, 465
Inside corner molding, 585, 586
Installing kitchen cabinets, 742-745
Institutional fixtures, 895-912
   (Also see *Commercial fixtures*)
Institutional furniture, illustrated, 904D
Intergrown knot (lumber defect), 79
Interior cabinet parts, 593-595
Interior construction, casework, 698, 699
Interior designers, 24, 26
Interior doors, 606, 607
Interior finishing, 829-833
Interlocked cross grain, 497, 498
Internal mix, 796
Internal routing, 410, 411
Internal sanding, 458
Inverted method (shaping), 386
Isometric drawings, 191-193, 200
Italian Provincial
   desk, illustrated, 662
   furniture, 38-40, 48F, 820
   table, illustrated, 659, 660

J

Jack plane, 231
Jalousie window, 142
Jeweler's piercing blade, 353
Jig, 289-291, 299, 306
   adjustable, 290, 292, 392
   boring, 431, 693
   box, 350, 351
   circle, 348-351
   dovetail, 330-333
   doweling, 512
   drilling, 422, 423
   fixed, 290
   fluting, 669
   mitering, 278-281
   radial-arm saw, 318, 319
   sliding, shaper, 382
   tenoning, 299-301
Jig saw, 351-359, 459
   blades (table), 364
Jobs (See *Occupations*)
Joinery, 507-533
   cuts for, on radial-arm saw, 325-333
   hardboard, 134
   particle board, 138
   (Also see *Adhesives, Fastening devices*, specific
      kinds of joints)
Jointer, 260, 264, 370-380
   edge, 839, 840
   hand, 848
   knives, 255-258
   plane, 231, 232
   veneer, 844
Jointing (teeth of a saw), 245, 248, 250-258

K

Kerf, 270, 283, 552-554
Kerfing, 552-555
Key (in joinery), 300, 514, 515
Keyhole saw, 230
Kickback, 270, 271, 282, 283
   (Also see *Safety*)
Kicker, 639, 640
Kiln drying, 73-75, 492, 876
Kitchen
   arrangements, 738-742, 752A-752C
   built-ins, 774, 775
   cabinets, 728-761
      applying laminate to fronts, 589-592
      drawings, 202, 203
      hardware, 164, 165
      illustrated, 15, 18, 592A, 592D, 752A-752D,
         775, 816C, 816D
      manufacturing, 888-890
      plywood, illustrated, 118
      production of, 21
Kitchen-playroom, illustrated, 816C
Kneehole desk, Colonial, illustrated, 164
Knife, electric, 787
Knife marks, 501
Knives, 232, 242, 254-258
Knobs for doors, 624, 625
Knots, 77-79, 282
Korina (See *Limba*)

L

Labor, estimating cost of, 211, 213
Lacquer, 816, 822-825, 833
Ladder-back chair, illustrated, 664
Laminated plastic, 103, 575-592; illustrated, 48D, 48E,
   144B, 144D, 592A-592D, 784B, 816C, 912A-D
   (Also see *Plastic Laminates*)
Laminating wood, 551-560, 842-848, 881-883
Lamp table
   Contemporary, illustrated, 35, 36, 103, 805
   French Provincial, illustrated, 38
   miscellaneous, illustrated, 523, 606, 661, 717
   project, 188
   storage, illustrated, 53
Land (fine line), 254
Lap dovetail joint, 531, 532
Lap joints, 296-298, 328, 524, 526
Larch, 82, 83
"Larch-fir," 83
Latches, 608
Lath-and-plaster, wall fasteners, 158-160
Lathe
   automatic, 860, 861, 883
   general discussion, 461-484
   rotary, 120
   wood, 504
Lattice work, illustrated, 33
Layout, 213-224, 228, 229
Lead expansion screw anchor, 159, 161
Leading, 344
Leafing, gold, 887
Leaves (of tables), 687-691, 693
Leg-and-post construction, 492
Leg-and-rail construction, 674-681, 718, 720;
   illustrated, 530
Legs, 659-674, 720, 721
   cabriole, 33, 665-668
   commercial, 673, 674
   flower-petal, 101
   for casework, 698, 700
   sets, illustrated, 660
   squaring up, 264
Level, carpenter's, 229
Lever-arm sander, 864, 865
Library cabinet, illustrated, 717
Library equipment, illustrated, 908
Light-stain glaze, 833
Limba, 115, 116
Line(s)
   bisecting, 216
   in design, 45
   kinds of, illustrated, 186, 187, 189
Linear feet, 175
Linseed oil, 801
Lip doors, 616-619
   hardware, 163, 164
Lip drawers, 627, 628; illustrated, 720
Lip-point bit (See *Spur machine bit*)
Liquid fillers, 817, 819
Living room
   built-ins, 772, 773
   furniture, illustrated, 39, 48A, 48E, 48G, 144A,
      784B-784D
Lock joint, 302, 532, 533, 635
Lock miter joint, 298, 528, 529, 701
Lock rail, 596
Log holder, illustrated, 557
Long taper, 378, 379
Loose knot (lumber defect), 79
L-shaped kitchen, 739; illustrated, 752B, 752C
Lubrication (See *Maintenance*)
Lumber
   abbreviations (table), 176
   actual dimensions, 176
   allowance for surfacing, 205
   cutting methods, 71, 72
   defects, 76-80
   drying, 73-75, 492
   estimating, 205-213
   grading, 177-181
   kiln-dried, 492
   kinds of, 80-101
   measuring, 183-185
   ordering, 174-185, 205-210
   properties of, 70, 71, 76
   seasoning, 72-75
   shrinkage, 74-76, 497, 498
   sizes, 175-177
   specifications, 181-183
   specific gravity of, 67
   Standards, American, 177
   strength of, 67
   tally sheet, 184, 185

Lumber-core plywood, 118, 119, 491, 572, 573, 683, 684
Lumberman's board stick, 182-184

M

Machine(s), 227-484
    maintenance, 237-259
    sanding, 441-460
    tools, 250-259
    (Also see specific types of machines)
Machine burn, 80, 502, 503
Machining
    equipment, 848-862
    hardboard, 133
    hardwood, 800
    particle board, 138
Magnetic catch, 623, 624
Mahogany (authentic or true), 94, 95, 103-105
Mahogany, Philippine, 95-97
Maintenance
    band saw, 340
    circular saw, 270
    drilling and boring machines, 416
    jig or scroll saw, 353
    jointer, 373, 380
    mortiser, 433
    portable saws and planes, 363
    radial-arm saw, 307
    router, 395
    sanding machines, 442
    shaper, 384
    surfacer-planer, 265
    tenoner, 439
    wood lathe, 462
Mallet, 150
Manufactured board, typical working characteristics of (table), 135
Manufacture of plywood, illustrated, 121-123
Manufacturing (See Woodworking plants)
Manufacturing abrasives, 443-445
Maple, 96, 97, 108-110
Marble table top, illustrated, 144A
Marking gage, 229
Marquetry, 573
Mask, 797
Masonry
    bit, 418
    drills, nails, and fasteners, 159-161
Massed pitch, 79
Mass (in design), 47
Matching veneers, 565-569
Materials, estimating cost of, 211, 213
Materials (in design), 43, 44
Materials
    building, 189, 205-213
    used in casework, 697, 698
Materials list (See Bill of materials)
Measure, brace, 215, 216
Measuring devices, 228, 229, 465
Measuring lumber, 183-185
Mediterranean furniture, 40, 48G
Medullary ray cells (See Rays)
Mending plate, 161, 162
Metal
    cutting, 358, 364, 366, 367
    hardware, 655-657
    legs, 660, 661, 672
    shelf pins, 654, 655
Micarta, 575
Middle lap joint, 525
Middle-rail butt joint, 518
Milled edge joint, 520, 521
Milled shaper joint, 634, 635
Millman, 23
Millwork, general information, 20, 21, 139-147
    (Also see specific types)
Mineral spirits, 802
Minwax, 808
Mirrors, 166-172
Miter
    adjustments, compound (chart), 316
    and-corner clamp, 543, 544
    boring holes for, 428, 429, 432
    box saw, 231
    cutting on circular saw, 297, 298
    cutting on portable saw, 361, 362
    cutting on radial-arm saw, 309-311, 314-316, 328, 329
    dowels, 511
    fasteners, 161, 162
    fence, 388, 389
    flat, 278-280
    gage, 268, 277-279, 345

Miter (continued)
    joints, general discussion, 525-530
    with end lap joint, 298, 328, 528, 530
    with rabbet, 298, 328, 528, 701
Mitering jig, 278-281
Modelmaker, 24, 25
Modelmaker's plane, 233
Modern furniture, 35, 37, 48C, 55, 110, 115, 116
    (Also see Contemporary furniture)
Modular cabinets, illustrated, 592B
Moisture content
    of dowels, 510
    of wood, 72-75, 488-498, 876
    related to gluing, 534
    (Also see Air drying, Kiln drying, Seasoning)
Moisture meter, 495
Molded edge, 686, 687
Molded plywood, 124, 125, 552
Molder, 848, 849, 882, 889
Moldings
    blades for cutting, 259, 304
    cutting on circular saw, 272, 273, 302-306
    cutting on radial-arm saw, 333-336
    decorative, 334, 335
    metal for walls and counters, 585, 586
    on circular stock, 306
    saw cut, 303, 333, 334
    types of, 145-147, 585, 586
    using miter gage when cutting, 305
Molding press, 848
Molding sanders, 866
Molds, for bending, 555-559
Molly screw anchors, 158-160
Monel metal, 151
Mortise-and-tenon joint
    barefaced, 530, 531
    blind, 329
        cutting on router, 404
    cutting on mortiser, 433, 435
    general discussion, 299-301, 505, 529-531
    in leg-and-rail construction, 674-676
    open, 330
Mortiser, 433-441, 857, 858
Mortising
    attachment and adapter, 437-439
    chisel, 259
    general discussion, 505
Mouldings (See Moldings)
Mullions, 145, 147, 596
Multi-motion action sanding, 455
Multiple dovetail joint, 634, 635
    (Also see Lap dovetail joint)
Multiple sawing, 350, 351
Multiple-spindle boring machine, 858, 859, 882
Multiple-spindle carving machine, 862, 863
Multiple-spindle mortiser, 857, 858
Multi-spur bit, 417
Multiview drawings, 191, 193-195, 200
Myrtle, 115

N

Nailing
    hardboard, 134
    particle board, 139
    plywood, 128, 129, 151
    removing nails, 129
    techniques, 148, 150, 151, 871-873
    tools and equipment, 149, 150, 871-873
Nailing strips (See Furring strips)
Nail sizes (table), 149
National Hardwood Lumber Association (NHLA), 179, 181, 182
Nest table, illustrated, 533, 663
Net size (finish size), 206
Night stand, illustrated, 636
    Early American, 55
Nitrocellulose, 823
Nominal dimensions of lumber, 176
Non-bleeder spray gun, 797
Non-grain-raising stains (NGR), 815, 816
Notes, in drawing, 189
Not-firm knot (lumber defect), 79

O

Oak, 96-99, 110-112
    screws for, 158
Occasional table, illustrated, 561
Occupations related to cabinetmaking, 23-26
Octagon
    drawing an, 219
    scale, 215

Office cabinet, illustrated, 721
Office fixtures, 895-912
Offset miter joint, 701
    (Also see *Miter-with-rabbet joint*)
Offset screwdriver, 154, 155
Ogee sticking, 597, 598
Oil finish, 811
Oil stains, 814, 815
Oleoresinous varnish, 825
Open coat abrasives, 444,445
Open-drum sander, 866, 867
Open-end wrench, 236
Open frame, 593-595
Open frame doors, hardware, 164
Open-grained wood, finishing, 807
Open mortise
    cutting on circular saw, 299
    cutting on radial-arm saw, 330
    general discussion, 531
    in leg-and-rail construction, 675, 676
"Orange peel," finishing defect, 800
Orbital-action sanding, 455, 456
Ordering lumber and other materials, 174-185, 205-210
Oriental furniture, 36, 37, 113
Orthographic projection, 193-195, 200
Outer bark, 66, 68
Outfeed rolls, 261, 262
Outfeed table, 371-373
Outside calipers, 465
Outside corner molding, 585, 586
Out-rip position, radial-arm saw, 318, 319
Ovalhead screws, 151, 152
Oven drying to determine moisture content of lumber, 495
    (Also see *Kiln drying*)
Overhead, estimating cost of, 213
Overlap (or overlay) doors, 164, 618, 623
Overlap (or overlay) drawer, 628
Overtone treatment, 820-822
Ovolo sticking, 597, 598
Oxidation, 70

P

Paint, 829-833
    (Also see *Finishing, Spraying*)
Painting hardboard, 134, 135
Paldao, 115
Panel-and-frame construction, 593-606
Panel door, 454, 455
    (Also see *Millwork*)
Paneling
    board and batten, illustrated, 830
    general discussion, 761-769
    hardboard, 132, 133
    oak, illustrated, 111
    Philippine mahogany, illustrated, 144D
    plastic laminate, installing, 907, 909-912
    solid wood, finishing, 829-832
Panel raising tool, 309
Panel saw, 362, 363
Panel stock, cutting, 280-282
Panelyte, 575
Paper, for abrasives, 443, 447, 456
Parquet floors, 110
Particle board, 129-139, 491, 492, 609
Parting tool, 464, 465
    sharpening, 243, 244
Party chair, illustrated, 679
Paste fillers, 816-819
Pattern guide, illustrated, 476, 477
Pattern, guide, sawing, 350, 351
Patternmaker, 23, 25
Patterns, shaping with, 388, 390, 393
Pearson sanders, 867, 868
Pecan, 98, 99, 101
Peck (lumber defect), 77
Peeler blocks, 120
PEG (See *Polyethylene glycol*)
Pegs, wood, 788
Penetrating finish, 807, 815
Penny (nail sizes), 148
Perforated hardboard, 130-132, 896-898
Period satin finish, 828
Perspective drawings, 191, 192, 202
Persian walnut, 102
Phenolic resin glues, 125
Philippine mahogany, 95-97
    paneling, illustrated, 144D
Phillips head screws, 151, 152
Phillips screwdriver, 154, 155
Phloem, 66, 68
Phonograph cabinet, illustrated, 808

Phyfe, Duncan, 20, 33-35
Piano hinge, 608, 622, 688
Pictorial drawings, 191-193, 200
Picture-frame clamp, 539, 540
Picture moldings, 145, 147
Pigment-oil stains, 812, 814, 815
Pilot-end router bit, 399, 410, 411
Pilot hole, 152, 155-157
Pine, 83-86, 101
Pin, fluted plastic, 654, 657
Pinholing (filling defect), 819
Pin knot (lumber defect), 79
Pin, shelf supports, 654, 655
Pin wormhole (lumber defect), 77, 78
Pipe wrench, 236
Pistol-grip saw set, 251
Pitch and pitch pocket (lumber defects), 79
Pith, 67, 68
Pivot block, 346, 349
Pivot hinge, 619
Pivot pin, 346, 348, 349
Plain dado, 322, 323, 635
Plain edge joint, 294, 325
Plain joint (See *Butt joint*)
Plain-sawed lumber, 71, 76
Plain screwdriver, 154
Plain slicing, 563
Plane-iron blade, sharpening, 238-241
Plane panel, 598
Planer blades, grinding and jointing, 254, 255
Planers, 260-266, 273, 839, 840
Planes, 231-233, 360-369, 469
Planing
    abrasive, 266
    general discussion, 500-503
    on jointer, 370-376
    plywood edges, 127, 128
    thin stock, 264, 265
    veneer, 569
Plank-and-beam ceiling, illustrated, 762
Planning, in building, 205-213
Plan of procedure, 210, 212
    (Also see *Projects*)
Planter table, illustrated, 489
Plan (top) view, 200, 202, 204
Plastic bumper molding, 683
Plastic dowels, 511, 512
Plasticizing (wood), 554, 555
Plastic laminates
    applying to particle board, 139
    general discussion, 575-592, 896
    illustrated, 48D, 48E, 144B, 144D, 592A-592D,
        784B, 816C, 904A-904D
    paneling, installing, 907, 909-912
    wall paneling, 763
    (Also see *Laminated plastic*)
Plastic plugs, 159, 161
Plastic resin glue, 535, 536
Plastic screw anchor, 160
Plastic shelf pins, 654, 655
Plastic wood, 788
Plate glass, 168, 169
Playroom, built-ins, 774, 775
Pliers, 237
Plinth, 700, 899
    base and recessed, 721, 722
Plot plans, 202
Plough (See *Groove*)
Plugs, 155-157, 159, 161
    cutter, 156, 418, 419
Plumb bob and line, 229
Plumbing fixtures, symbols for, 190
Plunge cutting, 365
Plyron, 127
Plywood
    banded, 561
    buffed, 127
    cutting, 273, 280, 281, 309
    edge banding, 491, 492
    finishing, 832, 833
    general discussion, 116-129
    grading system, softwood (table), 126
    lumber-core, 118, 119, 489-491, 572, 573
    manufacture of, 121-123
    paneling, 762, 763, 768, 769
    screws, 157
    softwood, 125, 126, 682, 832
    veneer-core, 118, 119, 125, 607, 609; illustrated,
        489
    V-plank, 144C, 784B, 784C
    wall, illustrated, 144B
Pneumatic drum sander, 866, 884
Pneumatic pad sander, 456
Pneumatic staple gun, 890

Pocket cuts, 362
Pocket hole, 427, 692-694
Pole, story, 221
Polishing, 446, 826-828
Polyester, 826
Polyethylene glycol (PEG), 76, 495, 496
Polygon miter, 528
Polymerized finish, 830
Polyurethane, 826
Polyvinyl glue, 535, 536
Ponderosa pine, 43, 84
Poplar, 100, 101
Pores in wood, 69
Portable drilling equipment, 414-417, 430
Portable nailer, 872
Portable planes, 360-369
Portable power tools, safety with, 61
Portable router, 394-396, 398-408
Portable sanders, 453-457
Portable saws, 360-369
Portable sprayers, 793-795, 797
Posts and legs, 659-674
Power jig saw blade, 353
Power sander, 865
Precision boring, 412
Prefinished materials, 125, 127
Pressure, applying after gluing, 546
Pressure bar, 261, 262
Pressure-fed spray gun, 795, 796
Pressure, for bonding, 579
Pre-staining, 805
Primary colors, 47
Primavera, 116
Principles of design, 50-53
Prints, 185-204
    (Also see *Drawings, Plans, Working drawings*)
Problems and activities, 64, 226, 486, 784, 834, 913
Procedure list (See *Plan of procedure*)
Production equipment, 836-874
Production furniture plants, 21
Profile shaper, 854-857
Profit, estimating, 213
Projects
    buffet room-divider, 194-199
    dining-room chair, 680, 681
    drop-leaf table, 694-697
    fishing tackle cabinet, 706-708
    server with china top, 723-728
    snack bar and stools, 710-713
    table, 210-212
    table lamp, 188
Properties of lumber, 70, 71, 76
Proportion (in design), 50, 51
Protective coatings, 822-828
Protoplasm, 69
Pulls, drawer, 624, 625, 645
Pumice. 802
Push block, 283, 284, 287, 376
Push stick, 283, 284, 286, 287, 336

Q

Quarter-sawed lumber, 71, 72, 76
Quarter slicing, 563-565
Queen Anne cabriole leg, illustrated, 672
Questions and discussion topics, 63, 64, 224-226, 484-486, 782-784, 833, 834, 913
Quick clamps, 542
Quill stroke, 421

R

Rabbet, 324-326
    cutting on jointer, 378
    cutting on router, 402
Rabbet-and-dado joint, 523, 524, 701
Rabbet edge joint, 325, 520, 521
Rabbeting bit, 397, 398
Rabbet joints, 295, 296, 325, 326, 520-523, 632, 633
Rabbet plane, 233
Radial-arm saw
    compound angles for use on (table), 317
    cutting a raised panel on, 603, 604
    drilling and boring on, 431, 432
    general discussion, 306-336
    parts, illustrated, 308
    routing on, 411, 412
    sanding on, 457, 458
    shaping on, 391-393
Rafter tables, 216
Rafter square, 184, 229
    (Also see *Steel square*)
Rails, 349, 593-598, 600-605

Raised edge, 686
Raised grain, 501, 502
Raised panel, 598
Rakers, 253
Random matched veneer, 566, 567
Random widths (of lumber), 177
Rawl plug, 159, 161
Rays, 67, 68, 71, 72, 76
Recessed chuck, 482, 484
Recessed (Phillips) head screws, 151, 152
Recessed plinth, 722
Reciprocating saw, 366, 367
Record cabinet, illustrated, 594
Red knot (lumber defect), 79
Red oak, 97-99, 111
Redwood, 86, 87
Reeding, 666, 668-671
Refreshment bar, Contemporary, illustrated, 716
Relief cuts, 343, 344
Removable leaves, 690-693
Rendering, 192
Repairing wood surfaces, 786-788
Resawing, 288, 500
    on band saw, 339, 346, 350
Resin, 443
    synthetic, 820
    urea, 537, 538
    (Also see *Glue*)
Resorcinol resin glue, 535, 537
Respirator, 797
Restaurant fixtures, 905
    (Also see *Commercial fixtures*)
Reverse diamond matched veneer, 565, 566
Rhythm (in design), 52, 53
Rift cutting, 563, 565
Rift-sawed lumber, 72
Rim-type bending machine, 848
Rings, growth, 68-70, 497, 498
Rip guide, 362
Ripping
    bar, 150
    fence, 345, 346
    hand rip saw, 230, 247, 250
    horizontal, radial-arm saw, 320, 321
    narrow stock, 285-287
    on band saw, 345-347
    on circular saw, 270-273, 282-289, 291
    on portable saw, 362
    on radial-arm saw, 306-312, 316-319
    saw, straight-line, 837, 838
Ripplewood plywood, 127, 128
Rock elm, 92, 93
Rod, layout on the, 214, 220-224
Roll abrasives, 445, 446
Roller check (lumber defect), 80
Roller coaters, 804, 874
Roller support, 283
Rolling doors, 608, 619, 620
    hardware for, 164
Roman ogee bit, 397, 398
Room dividers, 194-199, 781, 782
Roots, 66, 67
Rosewood, 114-116, 576
Rot (lumber defect), 77
Rotary
    cutting, 563, 564
    hole saw, 418
    lathe, 120
    sander, 457
Rottenstone, 802
Rough cutting, 347
Roughing, 446
Rough mill, 880, 881
    equipment, 836-840
Rough size, 206
Rough turning, 468
Rounded edge (for table top), 686
Round-end bit, 398
Roundhead screws, 151, 152
Round-nose tool, 464, 465
    sharpening, 243, 244
Rounds (molding), 145-147
Router
    for cutting inlays, 574, 575
    general discussion, 394-412
    hand, air-operated, 862
    high speed, 855-857
    plane, 232
Route sheets, 210, 214
Royal Finish, 808
Rubbing, 446, 826-828
    oil, 802
Rub blocks (See *Glue blocks*)
Rule joint, 688, 689

Rules
    bench, tape, zig-zag, 228
    board measure, 182-184
    lathe, 465
Runner, 640, 641, 644

S

Saber blade (jig saw), 353-355
Saber saw (See *Bayonet saw*)
Safety
    band saw, 340
    circular saw, 268-271, 276, 278
    drilling and boring machines, 416, 432
    general rules, 57-63, 294
    hand tools, 60, 61
    jig or scroll saw, 353
    jointer, 373, 374
    mortiser, 433
    portable electric drills, 416, 430
    portable power tools, 61
    portable saws and planes, 363
    radial-arm saw, 307
    ripping operations, 282, 284, 286, 287
    router, 394, 395
    sanding machines, 442
    shaper, 382, 384, 387
    surfacer-planer, 265
    tenoner, 439
    when bleaching wood, 789
    wood lathe, 462, 468
    woodworking machines, 61
Sanding
    final, before finishing, 790-792
    general discussion, 441-460
    hardboard, 133
    production sanders, 862-868, 884
    veneers, 129
    (Also see *Abrasives*)
Sap, 66, 70
Sap staining, 812
Sapwood, 66-68, 70, 76
Sash beading bit, 397, 398
Sash brush, 802, 803
Sash coping bit, 397, 398
Satin finish, 828
Satinwood, 113
Saw(s)
    back, 230
    band, 250, 251, 253
    blades, 252
    circular, 251-253
    compass, 230
    coping, 231
    crosscut, 230, 245, 246, 248-250
    dovetail, 231
    filing, 245-250
    grooving, 384
    hand, sharpening, 245, 248-250, 253
    jig or scroll, 351-359
    keyhole, 230
    mill, portable, 892, 893
    miter box, 231
    portable, 360-369
    radial-arm, 306-336
    rip, 230, 245, 247, 250
    set, illustrated, 248
Saw-cut moldings, 303, 333, 334
Saw-filing clamp, 245
Saw-filing equipment, 250, 251, 253, 254
Saw-raising handwheel, 267, 268
Sawing
    angle, 358
    compound, band saw, 347, 348
    in basic construction, 500
    hardboard, 133
    multiple, band saw, 350, 351
    particle board, 138
    safety, 269-271, 307, 340
Scale (of drawings), 189, 202, 204
Scale (rule) for crosscutting, 276, 277
Scale, octagon and steel square, 215
Scale, tilt, on circular saw, 267, 268
Scandinavian furniture, 36, 37, 110, 113
School fixtures, 907; illustrated, 904D
Scientists in forest-products industry, 24
Scoring (in cutting glass), 171
Scraping, 465, 466, 474
    cabinet and hand, 233
Scratch awl, 229
Screen(s), 165, 166
    beads and stock, 145, 147
Screw(s)
    center (on lathe), 480

Screw(s) (*continued*)
    for hardboard and particle board, 134, 139
    for plywood, 128, 129
    general discussion, 147-162
    sizes (tables), 153, 538
Screwdrivers, 152, 154-156
    sharpening, 242, 243
Screw-mate counterbore and drill countersink, 155
Scroll sanders. 867, 868
Scroll saw, 351-359, 460
Sealacell, 807
Sealing (wood finishing), 806-811, 816, 820
Seasoning lumber, 72-75
    (Also see *Air drying, Kiln drying*)
Secondary colors, 47
Sectional views, 194, 195, 204
Segment
    cutting, 349, 350
    method of making curved parts, 552, 553
Select grade of lumber, 178-181
Self-drilling screw, illustrated, 152
Semi-precision drilling, 412
Server with china top (project), 723-728
Service cart, drop-leaf, illustrated, 687
Service hardboard, 130
Setting (teeth of saws), 248-252
Shading, 822
Shake (lumber defect), 77
Shank hole, 156, 157
Shape (in design), 46, 47, 53
Shaped edge joint, 520, 521
Shaped molds, 558
Shaper, 381-393, 604, 605, 852-857
Shaper-jointer fence, 336
Shapes of legs for cabinet construction, 661-666
Shaping in basic construction, 502-504
Sharpening
    auger bit, 241, 242
    band saw, 250, 251, 253
    circular-saw blades, 251-253
    countersink, 242
    draw knife, 242
    hand saw, 245, 248-250
    knife, 254, 255
    plane-iron blade, 238-241
    router bits, 258, 259
    screwdriver, 242
    shaper cutters, 258, 259
    wood chisel, 241
    woodturning tools, 242-244
Shaving chute, 382
Sheet abrasives, 445, 446
Sheet glass, 167, 168
Sheet-metal screws, 152
Shellac, 810, 820
Shelves, 650-658. 678, 679
    hardware, illustrated, 166
    in commercial fixtures, 902-904
    kitchen, 741-743
    standards, 656, 657
Sheraton, Thomas, 20, 30, 33, 34, 104
Shims, 745, 746
Shop sketch, 204
Shortleaf pine, 84, 85
Short taper, 380
Shoulder
    cut, 471
    length, 206
    mortise-and-tenon joint, 300, 301
    raised-one-side panel, 598, 599
Show cases, 901-903
    (Also see *Commercial fixtures*)
Shrinkage of wood, 74-76, 497, 498
Shutters, illustrated, 140
Sideboard, illustrated, 52, 54, 718
    built-in, 650
    Contemporary, 117, 620
Side chair, illustrated, 679
Side guides (drawer), 640, 641
Silicon carbide
    paper, 441, 442, 447
    wheels, 237, 239
Simple dado joint, 522, 523
Simple mortise-and-tenon joint, 530, 531
Single-end tenoner, 433, 438-441
Single-head planer, illustrated, 506
Single planer, 261
Single-spindle boring machine, 430, 431
Single-spindle carver, 862, 863
Single-spindle shaper, 852, 853
Single spreading, 535
Siphon-fed spray gun, 795
Site plans, 202
Sitka spruce, 87, 88

Size coat for abrasives, 443, 444
Skeleton frame, 593-595
Sketches, 185-204
    (Also see *Drawings, Plans, Working drawings*)
Skew, 464, 465
    sharpening, 243, 244
Skip (lumber defect), 80
Sleepers (in casework), 700
Sliding doors, 609, 610, 620-622, 624, 648
    glass, 898
    hardware for, 164
Sliding shaper jig, 382
Sliding support, 690
Sliding T bevel, 229, 280, 374, 378, 424, 425
Slip matched veneer, 565, 566
Slipstone, 259
Small grooving saws, 384
Smooth plane, 231
Snack bar, illustrated, 752A, 752B
    and stools (project), 710-713
Snipe, 371, 372
Soaking wood, for bending, 556
Socket wrench set, 236
Softwood
    cutting methods, 71, 72
    grades, 177-179
    lumber, general classifications (table), **178**
    plywood, 125, 126, 682, 832
    special types discussed, 82-88
    standard-thickness and width (table), 177
Solid wood paneling, 761-768
    finishing, 829-832
Soluble colors or dyes (stains), 812
Sound knot (lumber defect), 79
Southern Cypress Manufacturers Association, 177
Southern Pine Association, 177
Spacer collar, 329, 330, 384, 385
Spade bit (See *Speed bit*)
Spanish furniture, 40, 48G, 111
Spattering, 822
Spear-point tool, 464, 465
    sharpening, 243, 244
Special millwork, 139, 141
Special-purpose kitchen cabinets, 736
Specifications, lumber, 181-183
Specific gravity, 67, 497, 498
Speed bit, 417, 418
Spike knot (lumber defect), 78, 79
Spindle chuck, 483, 484
Spindle router, 856, 857
Spindle sander, 450, 451, 459
    narrow belt, 884
Spindle shaper, 381, 382, 852, 853
Spindle turning, 466-476
Spiral cross grain, 497, 498
Spiral curve, producing, 554
Spiral-type screwdriver, 154, 155
Spirit stains, 815
Splicer, veneer, 844, 845
Spline, 512-515, 526, 527
    blind, 298, 299, 328
    joint, cutting on router, 404, 405
    miter joint, 701
Spline edge joint, 294, 295, 325, 326, 519, 520
Split bamboo, illustrated, 48E
Split bushings, 435
Splitter, 270, 282-285
Spokeshave, 233
Spray finishing
    general discussion, 793-801
    lacquers, 822-824
    production, 872-874
Spreader-adjustment valve, 798, 799
Spreading glue, 545, 546
Spring board, 283, 285
Spring clamps, 540, 541
Springwood, 68-70
Spruce, 87, 88
Spur center of lathe, 464
Spur machine bits, 417, 427
Square
    combination, 228, 229
    crosscutting, 276
    edge, 686
    framing or rafter, 184, 229
    try, 228, 374, 435
Squaring up legs, 264
Squaring up stock, 377
Stain (lumber defect), 77, 78
Staining, 805, 811-816
Stairs, 142, 143
Standard faceplate, 480
Standard grade lumber, 179
Standard grade plastic laminate, 576, 577
Standard hardboard, 130, 131, 133

Standard millwork, 139-141
Standards, American Lumber, 177
Standard two-wheel grinder, 237, 238
Stapler, pneumatic gun, 890
Stapling, 147, 149, 150
    hardboard, 134
    production equipment, 871, 872
Starting pin and block, 388, 389
Starved glue joint, 545, 546, 550
Stationary drilling equipment, 412-414
Stationary shelving, 651, 652
Stationary spraying equipment, 793-797
Steaming, 556, 557
Steel bar clamps, 539-541
Steel square, 214
Steel wool, 802
Stem-legs (See *Tripod table legs*)
Step jig, radial-arm saw, 318, 319
Step table, Early American, illustrated, 812
Stereo hi-fi cabinet, illustrated, 618, 721, 722
Sticker, 73
    (Also see *Molder*)
Sticking, 597, 598
    cutting, 600-603
Stile-and-rail doors, illustrated, 593
Stiles, 593-598, 600-605
Stock bill (See *Bill of materials*)
Stock billing, 205, 206
Stock cutter, 210
Stock-cutting list, 205
Stock millwork, 139-141
Stock, squaring up, 377
Stools (molding), 145, 146
Stop block, 277, 278, 345, 428, 429
Stop chamfer, 378
Stop clamp, 322, 323, 325
Stop dado, 296, 297, 326
    joint, 522, 524, 652
Stopped-lap dovetail joint, 531-533
Stop rod, 268
Stops, 145, 147
Stop taper, 379, 380
Storage cabinet, illustrated, 718
Storage table, illustrated, 521
Storage wall, 652, 653, 777-780
Store fixtures, 166, 895-912
    (Also see *Commercial fixtures*)
Storing plywood, 127
Story pole, 221
Straight bit, 397, 398
Straight cutting
    on band saw, 345
    on jig saw, 356, 357
Straightedge, 399, 402, 403
Straight leg cove molding, 585, 586
Straight-line action sanding, 455, 456
Straight-line ripping saw, 837, 838
Straight nailing, 150
Straight panel, 598
Straight shaping, 391
Strength of wood, 67
Strengthening joints, 509-517
Stretchers, 674
Striated plywood, 127
Stroke sander, 864, 865
Structural lumber, 177, 178
Stub mortise-and-tenon joint, 531, 532
Stub-tenon joint, 300, 595, 598
Study, illustrated, 592B
Stump, 102, 108
Stump wood, 564-566
Styles of furniture, 29-40
    (Also see specific types such as *Early American, Italian Provincial*, etc.)
Suction-fed spray gun, 795, 798, 801
Sugar maple, 96, 97, 108
Sugar pine, 85, 86
Summerwood, 68, 70
Sunken joint, 543, 544
Superimposing (method of laying out joints), 508, 509
Supports, drawer, 637-639
Surface
    finish, 807
    measure, 184
    repairing wood, 786-788
    sanding, 447, 458, 459
Surfacer, 260-266
Surfacing, 375, 376
    allowance for, 205
    (Also see *Jointer, Planing*)
Surform tool, 232
Sweetgum, 98, 99
Swing (of lathe), 462
Swivel chair, illustrated, 552

Symbols
for electrical wiring, 190
for heating, 190
in drawing, 186, 187, 189, 190
Synthetic finishes, 807, 808
Synthetic protective coatings, 826
Synthetic resin glue, 443
Synthetic resin sealer, 820
Synthetic sealer finishes, 809-811, 820

T

Table, auxiliary wood, 228, 320-324, 410, 425
Table, extension, for circular saw, 272, 273
Tables (charts)
abbreviations in print reading and sketch making, common, 191
abrasives, choosing for various materials, 456
abrasive types, common, 447
adhesives, common, 536, 537
angles for common polygons, correct, 528
blade, selecting the correct, 353
colors in oil for finishing, using, 814
compound angles for use on the radial-arm saw, 317
compound miter cuts, 282
end uses, typical, 135
finishing materials
covering capacities of common, 806
drying times for average, 806
furniture sizes, average, 42
grit sizes (abrasives), 446
hand screws, common sizes, 538
hardwood grades, standard, 180
hardwood, machining and related properties, 499
hardwoods, characteristics that affect machining, 498
hardwoods, standard thickness of, 178
hollow-wall anchors, common sizes of, 158
jig-saw blades, 364
lines, kinds of and their uses, 186, 187
lumber abbreviations, common, 176
moisture content values for woodwork, 494
nail sizes, 149
pilot holes, proper size bit or drill needed for drilling, 156
screw sizes, 153
shank holes, proper size bit or drill needed for drilling, 156
softwood lumber, general classifications of, 178
softwood plywood grading system, 126
softwoods, standard thickness and width of, 177
tinting colors in oil, common, 814
wood turning, speeds for, 467
working characteristics of manufactured board, typical, 135
Tables (furniture)
accessory, illustrated, 576
butterfly drop-leaf, end, illustrated, 690
coffee, illustrated, 489
design cut on router, 395
free form, illustrated, 34
Italian Provincial, illustrated, 39
commode, illustrated, 624
conference, illustrated, 490
cube, illustrated, 48E
drop-leaf, 694-697
Early American, illustrated, 109
project, 687-690
drum, illustrated, 34
Early American, illustrated, 45, 109, 688, 812
harvest, 32
Colonial, illustrated, 688
lamp, illustrated, 523, 606, 717
bedside, illustrated, 718
Contemporary, illustrated, 35, 36, 805
French Provincial, illustrated, 38
project, 188
miscellaneous, illustrated, 659, 661, 668, 671
nest, illustrated, 533, 663
occasional, illustrated, 561
octagonal, illustrated, 46
planter, illustrated, 489
project, 210-212, 687-690
step, Early American, illustrated, 812
storage, illustrated, 521
trestle harvest, illustrated, 32
Table-leaf pins, 691, 693
Table-leaf supports, 689, 690
Table, of a saw, 267
(Also see specific tools such as *Band saw, Circular saw, Jointer*, etc.)
Tables, on a steel square, 215, 216
Tables, rafter, 216

Table tops, 682-697
applying laminate to, 586-588
moldings, 585, 586
Tack rag, 792, 803
Tacks, 149
Tall kitchen cabinets, 736
Tambour doors, 611, 612
Taper, 378-380
Taper cuts, 471
Taper cutting, 290-292
on radial-arm saw, 318, 319
Teacher, industrial education, 24, 26
Teak, 103, 110, 112-114
chest, illustrated, 532, 628
Tea wagon, illustrated, 664
Technologist, 24, 27
Tee nuts, 161, 162
Teeth, saw, 245-253
Telephone stand, wall-hanging, illustrated, 512
Tempered hardboard, 130, 133
Templet (pattern), 400, 401, 405-408
(Also see *Guide*)
Tenon, 299-301, 326
bare face, 330
Tenoner, 271, 382, 433-441, 849-852
Tenoning jig, 299-301
Tensile test, 550, 551
Textolite, 575
Texture
in design, 48-50
of wood, 70
Thin stock, ripping, 288
Three-knife safety cutter head, 383, 384
Three-lip shaper cutters, 383, 393
Throat piece, 256, 257
Through dovetail joint (See *Dovetail-dado joint*)
Thumb mold edge, 686
Tier end table, illustrated, 50
Tight knot (lumber defect), 79
Tilt gage, 280, 378
Tilt handwheel, 267, 268
Tilting angle jig, 238, 239
Tilting table, drill press, 425
Tilt scale, 267, 268, 371, 374
Tinting colors in oil, common (table), 814
T lap joint, 525
T molding, 585, 586
Toenailing, 150, 151
Toe strip, 699, 700, 748
Toggle bolts, 158-160
Tone (in design), 48-50
Tongue-and-groove joint, 295, 326, 384, 519-521
Tongue-and-groove paneling, 607, 608
Tongued-lap joint, 633, 634
Toning, color, 833
Tool grinder, 238
Tools
hand, described and illustrated, 228-237
in furniture manufacturing plants, 888
maintenance, 237-259
Topcoats, 806, 822, 827
(Also see *Finishing*)
Tops, table and cabinet, 682-697
Torn grain (lumber defect), 80
Touch latch, 608
T plate, 161, 162
Track, for doors, 610, 611, 619-622
Traditional
furniture, 30, 33-35, 48B, 55, 105, 752C
kitchen, illustrated, 733
tulip leg, illustrated, 672
Trammel points, 229, 403
Transferring and enlarging an irregular design, 220
Transformer, air, 794
Transitional furniture, 36, 37
Transparent lacquer toners, 816
Transpiration, 67
Trays, 649
Tree, 66-80
(Also see *Hardwood, Lumber, Softwood, Wood*)
Tree trunk, cross section, illustrated, 68
Trestle harvest table, illustrated, 32
Trim, 703, 705
plastic laminates, 577
(Also see *Molding*)
Tripod table legs, 671, 672, 674
Trunk of tree, 66-68
Try square, 228, 374, 435
T-squares, 891-893
Tulip legs, illustrated, 672, 718
Turned legs and posts, 663-665
Turning
finishing, 484
holes, 343

Turning (*continued*)
    methods, 461-484
    tools, 464, 465
    (Also see *Lathe*)
Turpentine, 801
Twist (warp), 79, 80, 498, 500
    surfacing to remove, 376
Twist drill, 234, 235, 259
    and brad, 417, 421
Two-wheel grinder, standard, 237, 238
Typical working characteristics of manufatured
    board (table), 135

U

Universal drill, 413, 414
Universal guide, 354
Unsound knot (lumber defect), 79
Upholstery, 886, 887
Urea resin, 537, 538
U-shaped kitchen, 739-741; illustrated, 752A
Utility brush, 803
Utility grade lumber, 179
Utility knife, 233

V

Variety saw, 267-306, 848
Varnish, 825, 826
    brush, 802, 803
Varno wax, 807, 808
V block
    for drilling, 425, 426, 432
    for ripping on band saw, 346, 347
    for routing, 411
"V," cutting, 472, 473
Veining bit, 398
Veneer
    applying to particle board, 139
    band, 491
    in manufacture of wood products, 881-883
    knife, 567, 568
    mahogany, 105
    presses, 846, 847
    production equipment for veneering, 842-848
    slicer, 120; illustrated, 122
    veneering and inlaying, 561-575
    walnut, 102, 103
Veneer-core plywood, 118, 119, 607, 609, 683;
    illustrated, 489
Vertical-butt-and-horizontal-bookleaf matched
    veneer, 566, 567
Vertical-belt sanders, 867
Vertical grade plastic laminate, 577
Vertical-grained lumber, 71, 72, 75, 76
V groove, 323
"V" grooving bit, 397, 398
Violin burl, 717
Vise, circular-saw blade, 252
Vise-grip wrench, 236
V jig (block), 346, 347
V-plank plywood, walls, illustrated, 144C, 784B,
    784C

W

Wainscoting, 761
Wall brush, 802, 803
Wall moldings, 585, 586
Walls
    cases, 898-902
    kitchen cabinets, 735, 736, 741-746
    paneling, 132, 133, 140
    storage, assembly, illustrated, 651-653
Walnut, 99-103
Wane, 79, 80
Warp, 79, 80, 260, 375, 376, 498, 500
Wash coating, 806, 816
Watco natural wood finish, 808, 809
Water in wood (See *Moisture content*)
Waterproof abrasive paper, 802
Water stains, 812-814
Water-wash spray booth, 796, 797
Waxes, 802

Web frame, 593-595
Western larch, 82, 83
Western white pine, 85, 86
Western Wood Products Association, 177, 830
Wetlap, 130
Wheel dresser, diamond-pointed, 239
White ash, 87, 88
White liquid glue, 535, 536
"White mahogany" (See *Primavera*)
White oak, 96, 97, 111
White prints, 185
White wood (unfinished), 875, 884
White shellac, 810, 820
Wide-belt sander, 865
Wide stock, ripping, 284-287
Wiggle nails (See *Corrugated fasteners*)
Windows
    general discussion, 139-142
    glass, 167, 168
    symbols for, 190
Windsor chair, 30, 31, 48A
Wing, wood, 689, 690
Wire brads, 149
Wood
    bending, 551-560
    bleaching, 788-790
    cell structure, 69
    clamps, bar cabinet, 540, 541
    color, 505-507
    composition of, 66
    cutting methods, 71, 72
    defects in, 76-80
    dough, 788
    exotics, 112-116
    finishing, 786-833
    grain, 505-507
    identifying, 80
    kinds of, 80-101
    moisture content, 488, 490, 492-495, 497, 498,
        534
    nature of, 534
    parts of a tree, 66, 67
    seasoning, 72-75
    shrinkage, 74-76, 497, 498
    specific gravity of, 67
    strength of, 67
    surface, repairing, 786-788
    tubular structure of, 534
    turning, 461-484, 504
    wing, 689, 690
Wood chisel, sharpening, 241
Wooden parallel clamps (See *Hand screws*)
Wood-grain hardboard, 132, 133
Wood lathe, 461-484, 504
Wood spacer block, 428, 429
Wood spraying lacquers, 824
Wood stop, 600
Wood-turning duplicator, 476, 477
Woodturning tools, sharpening, 242-244
Woodworking
    machines, safety in, 61
    manufacturing, 875-894
    occupations in, 23-26
    plants, types of, 21-23
    (Also see specific woodworking machines and
        operations)
Working drawing
    defined, 193
    making from a sketch or picture, 56, 57
    (Also see *Projects*)
Wormholes (lumber defect), 77, 78; imitation, 822
Wrap-around hinge, concealed, 616
Wrenches, 236

X-Y-Z

Yard lumber, 177, 178
Yellow birch, 90, 91, 108
Yellow-poplar, 100, 101
Yew, 116
Yoke, 309, 311
Zebrawood, 115
Zig-zag rule, 228
Z-shaped bracing, 608